S0-BMU-317

BIBLIOGRAPHY OF ENGLISH-LANGUAGE WORKS
ON THE BÁBÍ AND BAHÁ'Í FAITHS
1844–1985

BIBLIOGRAPHY OF ENGLISH-LANGUAGE WORKS ON THE BÁBÍ AND BAHÁ'Í FAITHS 1844–1985

by

William P. Collins

GEORGE RONALD
OXFORD

George Ronald Publisher
46 High Street, Kidlington, Oxford OX5 2DN

British Library Cataloguing in Publication Data

Collins, William P. *1950–*
    Bibliography of English language works on the Babi and
    Baha'i faiths 1844–1985.
    1. Babism. Bibliographies   2. Bahaism. Bibliographies
    I. Title
    016.29792

ISBN 0–85398–315–1

Typeset in Plantin by Photoprint, Torquay, Devon
Printed in the United Kingdom by The Alden Press

CONTENTS

To my teachers

Pauline Atherton Cochrane
Marta Dosa
Antje Lemke
Bernard Ziemski

and to that great Teacher Who teaches us all

Foreword

Great movements of the racial soul come at first 'like a thief in the night', and then suddenly are discovered to be powerful and world-wide. Religious emotion – stripped of all corruptions and freed from its last priestly entanglements – may presently blow through life again like a great wind, bursting the doors and flinging open the shutters of the individual life, and making many things possible and easy that in these present days of exhaustion seem almost too difficult to desire.
H.G. WELLS, *The Outline of History* (London 1920)

FOUR times in the century and a half since its birth in 1844 has the Bahá'í Faith aroused widespread interest in the English-speaking world.

The first was during the early decades of its existence, when the heroic career of the Báb and his martyred followers became the talk of educated society in Europe, and Edward Granville Browne of Cambridge University made its rise the subject of his intense study.

The second was marked by the travels of 'Abdu'l-Bahá, the eldest son and successor of Bahá'u'lláh, to Europe and America in the years 1911–1913 following his release from imprisonment as a result of the Young Turk revolution of 1908. Broken in health from a lifetime of imprisonment and exile, approaching the seventieth year of his life, 'Abdu'l-Bahá undertook a series of journeys to France, Switzerland, the United States, Canada, the United Kingdom, Germany, Austria and Hungary. The significance of this period is stressed by Shoghi Effendi in his history of the first century of the Bahá'í Faith:

It was in the course of these epoch-making journeys and before large and representative audiences, at times exceeding a thousand people, that 'Abdu'l-Bahá expounded, with brilliant simplicity, with persuasiveness and force, and for the first time in His ministry, those basic and distinguishing principles of His Father's Faith, which together with the laws and ordinances revealed in the Kitáb-i-Aqdas constitute the bed-rock of God's latest Revelation to mankind. The independent search after truth, unfettered by superstition or tradition; the oneness of the entire human race, the pivotal principle and fundamental doctrine of the Faith; the basic unity of all religions; the condemnation of all forms of prejudice, whether religious, racial, class or national; the harmony which must exist between religion and science; the equality of men and women, the two wings on which the bird of human kind is able to soar; the introduction of compulsory education; the adoption of a universal auxiliary language; the abolition of the extremes of wealth and poverty; the institution of a world tribunal for the adjudication of disputes between nations; the exaltation of work, performed in the spirit of service, to the rank of worship; the glorification of justice as the ruling principle in human society, and of religion as a bulwark for the protection of all peoples and nations; and the establishment of a permanent and universal peace as the supreme goal of all mankind – these stand out as the essential elements of that Divine polity which He proclaimed to leaders of public thought as well as to the masses at large in the course of these missionary journeys. The exposition of these vitalizing truths of the Faith of Bahá'u'lláh, which He characterized as the *'spirit of the age'*, He supplemented with grave and reiterated warnings of an impending conflagration which, if the statesmen of the world should fail to avert, would set ablaze the entire continent of Europe. He, moreover, predicted, in the course of these travels, the radical changes which would take place in that continent, foreshadowed the movement of the decentralization of political power which would inevitably be set in motion, alluded to the troubles that would overtake Turkey, anticipated the persecution of the Jews on the European continent, and categorically asserted that the *banner of the unity of mankind would be hoisted, that the tabernacle of universal peace would be raised and the world become another world*.

With the outbreak of the First World War and during the tensions which followed it, the upsurge of interest aroused by the travels of 'Abdu'l-Bahá was submerged by an ocean of suffering and conflicting passions. The small Bahá'í community lapsed into almost total obscurity, continuing nevertheless its quiet growth and its spread from country to country.

In 1955, however, an outbreak of renewed persecution in Iran aroused the concern of the governments of the West, and only their protestations and the intervention of the United Nations were able to curb the attacks of fanatical opponents upon the Faith in the land of its birth. For the third time the Bahá'í Faith was drawn to the attention of the world at large.

The fourth time was likewise opened by persecution, unleashed on this occasion by the Islamic Revolution in Iran in 1979. By then, however, the Bahá'í Faith had spread to almost every country in the world and its members, organized as the Bahá'í International Community, had long played a recognized role in fostering international collaboration as an International Non-Governmental Organization accredited with consultative status to ECOSOC and UNICEF. Although, during these years, over 200 Bahá'ís have been killed, all Bahá'í Holy Places in Iran have been sequestered, and the followers of the Faith still suffer grave deprivations of human rights, the international stature of the Faith and the protests of world public opinion have preserved the Bahá'í community in Iran from the extirpation that its opponents there so ardently desired.

Having had their attention drawn to the Bahá'í Faith by the persecutions, increasing numbers of people have been attracted to its teachings. Thus, from 1979 until the present day (1990), public knowledge of the Bahá'í Faith and its tenets has steadily increased as has the number of its followers, reaching some five million with a worldwide diffusion that, according to the 1988 *Britannica Book of the Year*, is second only to that of Christendom.

A religion whose cardinal teaching is the unity of mankind, which fosters the individual investigation of truth and maintains the principle of harmony between religion and science, and which has demonstrated its ability to build a worldwide community bridging all differences of creed, nationality, class and sex is clearly of immediate interest at a time when the goal of world peace seems tantalizingly close and yet is threatened by a multitude of dangers.

Bahá'ís regard religion as the central driving force of human evolution. They look upon the different world religions as stages in a progressive, worldwide process of the divinely-instituted education of the human race. This process raises individuals from ignorance to knowledge and replaces suspicion and enmity with understanding and concord. It imparts to human society a series of impulses that carry forward an ever-advancing civilization. Writing in March 1941, Shoghi Effendi, the Guardian of the Bahá'í Faith, outlined the Bahá'í understanding of the present stage of human history:

> What we witness at the present time, during 'this gravest crisis in the history of civilization', recalling such times in which 'religions have perished and are born', is the adolescent stage in the slow and painful evolution of humanity, preparatory to the attainment of the stage of manhood, the stage of maturity, the promise of which is embedded in the teachings, and enshrined in the prophecies of Bahá'u'lláh. The

tumult of this age of transition is characteristic of the impetuosity and irrational instincts of youth, its follies, its prodigality, its pride, its self-assurance, its rebelliousness, and contempt of discipline.

The ages of its infancy and childhood are past, never again to return, while the Great Age, the consummation of all ages, which must signalize the coming of age of the entire human race, is yet to come. The convulsions of this transitional and most turbulent period in the annals of humanity are the essential prerequisites, and herald the inevitable approach, of that Age of Ages, 'the time of the end', in which the folly and tumult of strife that has, since the dawn of history, blackened the annals of mankind, will have been finally transmuted into the wisdom and the tranquillity of an undisturbed, a universal, and lasting peace, in which the discord and separation of the children of men will have given way to the worldwide reconciliation, and the complete unification of the divers elements that constitute human society.

This will indeed be the fitting climax of that process of integration which, starting with the family, the smallest unit in the scale of human organization, must, after having called successively into being the tribe, the city-state, and the nation, continue to operate until it culminates in the unification of the whole world, the final object and the crowning glory of human evolution on this planet. It is this stage which humanity, willingly or unwillingly, is resistlessly approaching. It is for this stage that this vast, this fiery ordeal which humanity is experiencing is mysteriously paving the way. It is with this stage that the fortunes and the purpose of the Faith of Bahá'u'lláh are indissolubly linked.

So great will be the difference between the peaceful future and the turmoil of mankind's past that this period has been longed for in all earlier religions, and is described in Christianity as the time of the coming of the Kingdom of God on earth.

The magnitude of this vision, the implications of the claim of Bahá'u'lláh to be the harbinger of such a climacteric in human development, the details of His teachings and the nature of the Bahá'í community are all open to study in the literature listed in this bibliography, as the Bahá'í community itself is available for investigation.

Bahá'ís are drawn from all strata of society, but the majority – like the majority of human beings – are peasant farmers of the Third World. The spirit of devotion which religion inspires, and which binds Bahá'ís of all backgrounds strongly together, is expressed not only in activities to diffuse the Bahá'í teachings but also in the practical development of society. Much effort is devoted to projects of social and economic development. In these the greatest attention is paid to the ideas and wishes of the people directly affected, whether they are Bahá'ís or not, fostering grass-roots efforts rather than externally imposed plans. An essential concomitant of unity in the Bahá'í view is appreciation of diversity. Oneness of mankind and world citizenship are the fundamental concepts, but they are inextricably linked with care for minorities and the fostering of those many differences of tradition and culture that enrich the warp and woof of world society.

The Bahá'í community has no clergy. It is governed by elected councils at local, national and international levels and conducts its affairs through consultation both within these councils and between them and the mass of the faithful. As a matter of conscience, Bahá'ís are loyal citizens, obedient to the government of every country in which they reside. They regard conflict and contention as destructive of human well-being and rely confidently on the power of united, constructive effort in obedience to the laws of God to overcome the evils and deficiencies that are the source of such tragedy in the present world.

Each Bahá'í sees himself (or herself) in pursuit of a twofold quest: the spiritual development of his own soul in preparation for a fuller life beyond the death of the body; and the advancement of human society through service to his fellow human beings. Each quest reinforces the other. Increase in knowledge and improvement of the individual character act as leaven in the lump of society; while it is in the pursuit of one's trade or profession, in the care of one's family, and in service to one's community, as well as in prayer, meditation and worship of God that one best develops the qualities of one's inner reality.

For those who seek a better understanding of the phenomenon of the Bahá'í Faith and of reactions to it, this bibliography provides an invaluable guide to the mass of material now available in the English language.

Ian Semple
Haifa, Israel
August 1990

Introduction[1]

The Publication and Dissemination of Literature in English on the Bábí and Bahá'í Faiths

I testify that no sooner had the First Word proceeded, through the potency of Thy will and purpose, out of His mouth . . . than the whole creation was revolutionized, and all that are in the heavens and all that are on earth were stirred to the depths. Through that Word the realities of all created things were shaken, were divided, separated, scattered, combined and reunited, disclosing, in both the contingent world and the heavenly kingdom, entities of a new creation . . .[2]

FOR Bahá'ís, the descent of the eternal Word of God, and its expression in a perfect being and a revelation, are the central facts of each religious dispensation. Moses and the Torah, Krishna and the Gītā, Zoroaster and the Avesta, Jesus and the Gospels, Muḥammad and the Qur'án, are the dual manifestations of God's timeless utterance. One is the living mouthpiece of the divine will; the other a perspicuous book speaking beyond the time of the divine Manifestations' living witness to mankind. In our own time the Creator has vouchsafed to the world a fresh measure of His Word through two messengers for this era of human history – the Báb and Bahá'u'lláh – and through the scriptures revealed by their pens.

Bahá'u'lláh has also created an agency designed to ensure the protection, preservation and interpretation of the Bahá'í religion's scriptural foundations. The strong and binding Covenant ordained by Bahá'u'lláh established 'Abdu'l-Bahá as the interpreter and perfect exemplar of Bahá'í teachings. 'Abdu'l-Bahá appointed Shoghi Effendi as Guardian of the Cause of God to succeed him. The continued development of the Bahá'í community, and its ability to move forward with the changed circumstances of society, are assured by Bahá'u'lláh through the powers granted to the Universal House of Justice to legislate on all matters not dealt with in the Bahá'í sacred texts.

The Bahá'í religion has been founded upon nearly forty-six years of revelation by the Báb and Bahá'u'lláh, sixty-five years of interpretation from 'Abdu'l-Bahá and Shoghi Effendi, and has received to this time more than two and a half decades of legislation and elucidation by the Universal House of Justice. Bahá'ís believe that the will of God for this age has been stated. Bahá'í publication is dedicated to the goals of bringing to mankind the story of a new revelation and the education and upliftment of the entire human race.

---

1. Based on an essay of the same title in *The Bahá'í World* v. XVII 1976–1979, pp. 546–553 and an article entitled 'Bahá'í Faith, Literature of,' *Shorter Bahá'í Encyclopedia*, to be published by the Bahá'í Publishing Trust, Wilmette, Illinois.
2. Bahá'u'lláh. *Prayers and Meditations by Bahá'u'lláh* (Wilmette, Ill.: Bahá'í Publishing Trust, 1969), p. 295.

Classification of Bahá'í Literature

The Bahá'í Faith is a religion of text, of 'the Word', as evidenced by the community's strong emphasis on the existence and authentication of the originals of its sacred scriptures and interpretation, as well as on the production and dissemination of publications. Bahá'í literature consists of several types and categories:

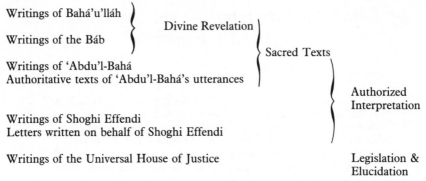

Writings of Bahá'u'lláh

Writings of the Báb

Writings of 'Abdu'l-Bahá
Authoritative texts of 'Abdu'l-Bahá's utterances

Divine Revelation

Sacred Texts

Writings of Shoghi Effendi
Letters written on behalf of Shoghi Effendi

Authorized Interpretation

Writings of the Universal House of Justice

Legislation & Elucidation

Pilgrims' notes and reported utterances of Bahá'u'lláh, the Báb, 'Abdu'l-Bahá and Shoghi Effendi

Compilations

Other works
  Introductory/Apologetic
  Scholarly/Historical/Biographical
  Literary/Inspirational
  Children's Literature
  Periodicals
  Reference Works

Among the many works relating to the Bahá'í Faith one may categorize separately:

Oppositional works
  By non-Bahá'í opponents of the Faith
  By Covenant-breakers

1. Sacred Writings

The holy texts of the Bahá'í Faith are the original documents in the handwritings of Bahá'u'lláh, the Báb and 'Abdu'l-Bahá; those written by the hand of their amanuenses at their dictation; reliable transcripts from well-known and trusted scribes; and, for 'Abdu'l-Bahá, authoritative transcripts of his utterances. These documents are in Arabic and Persian, with a small portion of 'Abdu'l-Bahá's writings in Turkish.

From a literary point of view, the sacred texts include the following categories:

- Tablets, letters, epistles which fall within an established tradition of Eastern epistolary writing
- Commentaries, usually on Qur'ánic texts
- Doctrinal treatises
- Histories by 'Abdu'l-Bahá
- Talks given by 'Abdu'l-Bahá for which authorized transcriptions exist. .

As previously noted, the possession of originals of these texts, either in the handwriting of the author, by the hand of amanuenses acting on the direction of one of the Central Figures, or in the hand of a reliable scribe, endows a text with authority as a part of Bahá'í canonical scripture. In addition, the texts have a rank based upon the status of the author, in the order Bahá'u'lláh, the Báb, 'Abdu'l-Bahá. However, for purposes of doctrinal value, the works of Bahá'u'lláh and 'Abdu'l-Bahá are of greater importance, while those of the Báb form a type of 'Old Testament', especially insofar as laws of personal status and laws of state are concerned.

Lists of the major works of the Central Figures of the Bahá'í Faith may be consulted in the latest volume of *The Bahá'í World*.

2. Interpretation

The Bahá'í religion contains provision for interpretation of the revelation through authorized interpreters – 'Abdu'l-Bahá and a succession of Guardians. 'Abdu'l-Bahá's unique station as the Perfect Exemplar of Bahá'í life places his interpretative texts in the category of sacred writings. Shoghi Effendi, the first Guardian (who died without a successor), carried on a voluminous correspondence in which he analyzed and expounded the implications of Bahá'u'lláh's revelation and interpreted its specific provisions. This correspondence, originals of which are in English and Persian, includes:

- Letters in his handwriting
- Letters written on his behalf by his secretaries
- Cables

The interpretations of Shoghi Effendi, though of lesser rank than the sacred texts, are normative for the Bahá'í community. No individual's understanding of the Bahá'í scriptures has any particular authority; Shoghi Effendi's interpretation is as binding as the sacred text itself and is the filter for approaching the meaning of the sacred text.

Shoghi Effendi's style in English and Persian is quite distinctive. His English matured at Oxford University, where it attained an elevated and complex style based upon Victorian standards and upon the writing of historians such as Edward Gibbon, whose beauty of expression Shoghi Effendi greatly admired.

Shoghi Effendi wrote only one book, *God Passes By*, his one-volume history of the first century of the Bahá'í era. All the other major published works are either long single letters (as in the case of *The Advent of Divine Justice* and *The Promised Day Is Come*) or collections of letters (such as *The World Order of Bahá'u'lláh: Selected Letters* and *Citadel of Faith*). Shoghi Effendi's works have not generally been as widely translated into other languages as have those of Bahá'u'lláh and 'Abdu'l-Bahá.

3. Legislation/Elucidation

The Universal House of Justice is charged, among other duties, with legislating on all questions not revealed in the sacred texts or dealt with in authorized interpretations and with elucidating questions that are obscure. The rulings of the Universal House of Justice can be modified or abrogated by itself according to the exigencies of the time, as they do not form a part of the scriptural canon. This category includes letters and cables/telexes in English and Persian. Its communications are most widely available in Bahá'í periodicals, excerpted in compilations and in pamphlets. Two compilations in English have been published as well as compilations in German and Persian. Individual letters usually appear first in Bahá'í periodicals. The first major address to the non-Bahá'í world from the Universal House of Justice appeared in 1985 under the title *The Promise of World Peace* and has been published in over 50 languages.

4. Pilgrims' notes, reported utterances of Bahá'u'lláh, the Báb and 'Abdu'l-Bahá

Reports by pilgims, including reported sayings of the Central Figures and Shoghi Effendi, have no binding authority over the community and are not stressed or given official recognition. Pilgrims' reports that have been published are almost exclusively those that relate to 'Abdu'l-Bahá and were originally published early in this century when very little literature was available on Bahá'í teachings.

5. Compilations

The Bahá'í Faith as a religious community has developed a strong tradition of 'compilation' – bringing together relevant texts, interpretation and legislation on specific themes. The Bahá'í World Centre now takes the lead in providing such compilations to the Bahá'í community, having issued compilations on such topics as Bahá'í institutions, funds and contributions, music, education, teaching, consultation, family life, divorce, women, and peace. These have been published in English and in most other major western languages. Other compilations have been independently produced by major Bahá'í publishers. This 'compilational' tradition stems from a long-standing literary practice in the Muslim world and in the codification of religious laws and teachings in major world faiths.

6. Other Bahá'í Literature

The vast majority of expository works are in the English language, with significant amounts in Persian and major European languages. Their standards of writing and thought vary considerably, as do method and quality of publication and breadth of distribution.

The authority of such works is generally secondary to that of sacred literature, interpretation and legislation. But within this category, rigor of scholarship, literary style or methodology will raise some works to prominence. A special case in this category is Nabíl's *The Dawn-Breakers*, which was excerpted, translated, edited and annotated by Shoghi Effendi. Though a secondary source and neither a work of scripture nor interpretation, the association of Bahá'u'lláh and the Guardian with this volume has endowed it with a special status in the community in comparison with other histories.

a. *Introductory/Apologetic Literature*
A number of Bahá'í authors have given a systematic exposition of the history and fundamental precepts of the Bahá'í revelation in English. The most outstanding of these is John E. Esslemont whose *Bahá'u'lláh and the New Era* was first published in 1923 in England and is now available in over 60 languages in its fourth revised edition. Its enduring value as the major introductory Bahá'í textbook and its place in the vanguard of Bahá'í literature is attested by Shoghi Effendi in his message at the time of Dr Esslemont's death: 'His book, however – an abiding monument to his pure intention – will, alone, inspire generations yet unborn to tread the path of truth and service as steadfastly and unostentatiously as was trodden by its beloved author.'[3]

3. Shoghi Effendi. *Bahá'í Administration* (Wilmette, Ill.: Bahá'í Publishing Trust, 1968), p. 97.

Expounders of Bahá'u'lláh's teachings to the Christian world have included early western believers such as Thornton Chase, Nathan Ward FitzGerald, Arthur Pillsbury Dodge, Elizabeth Herrick and particularly George Townshend who wrote the introductions to *God Passes By* and *The Dawn-Breakers*, and who was the author of three major titles relating the Bahá'í Faith to Christianity. Recent writers on Christian themes include William Sears, Ruth Moffett, Robert Riggs and Huschmand Sabet.

A number of other texts have gone through several editions: John Ferraby's *All Things Made New*, Rúḥíyyih Rabbani's *Prescription for Living*, Hushmand Fathea'zam's *The New Garden*, Howard Colby Ives's *Portals to Freedom*, David Hofman's *The Renewal of Civilization*, and Gloria Faizi's *The Bahá'í Faith: An Introduction*. Introductory books continue to be written – for example, William Hatcher and J. Douglas Martin's *The Bahá'í Faith: The Emerging Global Religion* (1985) as well as a number published more recently which fall outside the scope of this Bibliography.

b. *Scholarly/Historical/Biographical*

Since the appearance of Mírzá Abu'l-Faḍl's *Hujaju'l- Beheyyeh: The Behai Proofs* in 1902, scholarly books by Bahá'ís have appeared at irregular intervals. The primary scholar outside the Bahá'í community has undoubtedly been E.G. Browne, whose many essays, translations and edited works on the Bábí and Bahá'í Faiths are still some of the most thorough work on the subject. Other non-Bahá'í scholars such as Joseph Arthur Comte de Gobineau, Louis Alphonse Daniel (A.-L.-M.) Nicolas, Jean-Albert-Bernard Dorn, Victor Rosen and Aleksandr Kazem Bek added significantly to early studies of the religion in French, German and Russian. Shoghi Effendi's own contributions to Bahá'í historical scholarship are extremely important. As noted above, the only actual book the Guardian wrote was *God Passes By*, a lengthy spiritual-historical essay on the Bahá'í Faith's first century, while he edited, translated and supplemented with notes the first part of Nabíl's narrative *The Dawn-Breakers*, one of the most important and meticulously-recorded sources on the time of the Báb. The last decade or so has seen the publication of the results of scholarly research both by Bahá'ís and by a few non-Bahá'ís. The Bahá'í Publishing Trust of the United States, the British publisher George Ronald, and Kalimát Press in California have been major sources of this type of material. Particularly noteworthy was the prodigious output of H.M. Balyuzi, whose works on the Central Figures of the Faith, on the orientalist E.G. Browne and on eminent Bahá'ís during the time of Bahá'u'lláh have provided a wealth of historical material in the area of Bahá'í history and biography. Adib Taherzadeh's four-volume series *The Revelation of Bahá'u'lláh* (1974–1988), though written on a more popular level, nevertheless brings an impressive amount of scholarship to bear on the historical context of the writings of Bahá'u'lláh. Moojan Momen published the findings of his research into government and official sources from 1844 on in *The Bábí and Bahá'í Religions* (1981).

Among journals, *World Order* (1966–) has been a steady contributor to the flow of scholarly articles and studies on many aspects of the Bahá'í Faith, relating 'contemporary life and contemporary religious teachings and philosophy', and from time to time opening up exciting debate, as in the case of Juan Ricardo Cole's study of Bahá'u'lláh's 'Lawḥ-i-Ḥikmat'. The *Bahá'í Studies Bulletin*, circulated in photocopied form under the editorial direction of Stephen Lambden since 1982, was an attempt to make available scholarly work of intellectuals in the Bahá'í community on serious historical, textual and methodological issues. Linked with the *Bulletin* were a series of Bahá'í Studies Conferences in Lancaster, England, and seminars on scholarly methodology held in Cambridge, England. Contributors to these gatherings included Denis MacEoin (a member of the Bahá'í Faith until 1980), Moojan Momen and Peter Smith.

One of the goals set in the Five Year Plan of the Bahá'í community (1974–1979), was to 'cultivate opportunities for courses on the Faith in Canadian institutions of higher learning'. This goal led to the establishment of the Canadian Association for Studies on the Bahá'í Faith. This association changed from a specifically Canadian body in 1980 when it became the Association for Bahá'í Studies. Since its founding, the Association has produced fourteen in its monographic series called *Bahá'í Studies*, as well as issues of *Bahá'í Studies Notebook*, and has held regular Bahá'í Studies Conferences in North America. There are sister associations in Australia, West Africa, Europe (French, German, English and Spanish), India, Colombia, Chile and Brazil.

There have been several translations into English of scholarly Bahá'í works originally published in other languages. *The Heavens Are Cleft Asunder* by Huschmand Sabet reached into theological circles in Germany under its original title *Der Gespaltene Himmel* where it provoked debate over the significance of Bahá'u'lláh's claims for the Christian church. Udo Schaefer wrote a number of essays on the Bahá'í Faith and Islam and on refutations of orthodox Christian criticisms of the Bahá'í Faith, which were translated and published as *The Light Shineth in Darkness*. This volume was named by *Choice* as one of the outstanding academic books of 1978. The 1980s saw a resurgence of interest in the works of the foremost Bahá'í scholar Mírzá Abu'l-Faḍl of Gulpaygán with a new edition of *The Bahá'í Proofs* and a new translation of *ad-Durar al-Bahiyyah* by Juan Ricardo Cole under the title *Miracles and Metaphors* (1981).

With the opening of many collections of the Bahá'í National Archives in Wilmette, Illinois, the Bahá'í Publishing Trust of the United States began to receive scholarly biographies based on primary sources, such as that by Gayle Morrison on Louis G. Gregory. The Bahá'í Publishing Trust has also embarked on two major projects: the publication of a three-volume history of the Bahá'í Faith in America by Robert Stockman, and the production of a Bahá'í encyclopaedic dictionary.

c. *Literary/Inspirational*

The dramatic potential of Bábí and Bahá'í history was early recognized in the West. The legendary actress Sarah Bernhardt was reported to have requested plays on the Báb and Ṭáhirih, though there is no record of any result from her interest. A Russian poet, Izabella Grinevskaya, wrote plays on the Báb and Bahá'u'lláh in Russian which were performed in Leningrad in the opening years of this century. The only serious published play on Bahá'í history by a Bahá'í was Laura Clifford Barney's *God's Heroes* in 1910.

Several non-Bahá'ís have used Bahá'í characters in their novels: E.S. Stevens in her novel *The Mountain of God* (1911) and Clara Edge in *Tahirih* (1964). Another interesting use of Bahá'í themes, though not always positive, has been in science fiction, such as Philip K. Dick's *Eye in the Sky*. Novels by Bahá'ís with Bahá'í themes have begun to appear more frequently only in the last decade.

Poetry with Bahá'í content has been included as a regular feature in *The Bahá'í World*. Howard Colby Ives's *The Song Celestial*, as well as some poetry of Horace Holley's and George Townshend's, treated Bahá'í themes. More recently, Roger White has published several collections of poetry. Robert Hayden is now being recognized as one of the major American poets of the twentieth century. Many of his poems make specific reference to the Bahá'í Faith.

d. *Children's Literature*

In recent Bahá'í teaching and development plans, goals have been set for the production of children's literature. Almost no children's literature was produced until the decade of the 1950s, when such items as Janet Lindstrom's *The Kingdoms of God*, David Hofman's *God and His Messengers* and Zoe Meyer's *Children's Stories from the Dawn-Breakers* appeared. Many countries have produced children's prayerbooks in English to introduce young Bahá'ís to the sacred texts of their Faith. Colouring books, puzzles and games have been developed. The Bahá'í Publishing Trust of the United States established the imprint of Bellwood Press in order to develop and publish Bahá'í books for children, while other Bahá'í publishers have added new titles to their lists each year. Bahá'í children's literature still suffers from limited audience and less glossy production than that of more commercial firms, requiring as it does significant financial investment for materials from which Bahá'í publishers rarely recover their costs at the present time.

e. *Periodicals*

The first Bahá'í periodical in English was *The Bahai Bulletin* published in New York City from 1908 to 1909. It was followed by an international organ, *Star of the West*, issued in Chicago from 1910 to 1935. In its presentation of first-hand reports about people and events connected with the early development of the faith, it is an unparalleled source of historical information. Other important early Bahá'í journals include *Herald of the South*, published in Australia and New Zealand in several series, beginning in 1926 and recently revived; *The Dawn* published in Burma, 1923–1929; *World Order*, the successor to *Star of the West*, published in 1935–1949; and *World Order*, 1966 to date. The vast majority of other Bahá'í periodicals are limited-distribution productions, many of them in mimeographed format on poor paper. Nearly every one of the 149 National Spiritual Assemblies produces its own national periodical, as well as several newsletters published by national committees. A recent development is the launching of several special-interest periodicals for Bahá'í ham radio operators, mothers, single Bahá'ís and medical professionals, signifying a diversification of the community and the growing cooperation of Bahá'ís within specific areas of expertise.

f. *Reference Works*

No discussion of Bahá'í publishing would be complete without mention of the multi-volume survey of the activities of the international Bahá'í community, *The Bahá'í World: An International Record*. Now in its eighteenth volume, and spanning over half a century, it is a source book for information on current activities, growth and development of the Bahá'í administrative order, biographies of deceased Bahá'ís, poetry and articles.

The 1980s have seen the development of a number of concordances and indexes to Bahá'í sacred texts. James Heggie's *An Index of Quotations from the Bahá'í Writings* and a series of concordances to works of Bahá'u'lláh produced for Kalimát Press by Lee and Miriam Nelson using computer technology, are the beginnings of the establishment of better access to the contents of Bahá'í holy writings.

g. *Oppositional Works*

Most anti-Bahá'í literature in the first Bahá'í century has been religious polemic by Christian and Muslim opponents. The success of Bahá'í teaching in the early stages of its introduction into several countries inspired a number of locally-produced tracts against it by denominations such as the Lutherans, United Church of Canada, Methodists, Seventh-Day Adventists, Southern Baptists, Anglicans and Roman Catholics, as well as independent evangelical churches and groups such as the Inter-Varsity Christian Fellowship. The major Christian opponents who have dedicated themselves fully to the task of attacking the Bahá'í Faith have been few in number – Samuel Graham Wilson and William McElwee Miller of the Presbyterian Church, J.R. Richards of the Anglican Church and Robert P. Richardson – all active in missions. Presbyterianism and Anglicanism made very few converts in the Iranian mission field. The Bahá'ís, however, continued to grow in numbers in that country. An early Christian sympathy with the Bahá'í Faith as a possible way-station between Islam and Christianity was replaced by a growing awareness that the seriousness of Bahá'í commitment was itself a dangerous competition. These men in particular became obsessed with exposing the Bahá'í Faith's alleged errors to their Christian compatriots in the West. Their attacks focused on a supposed doctrinal inferiority to Christianity in the areas of sin and salvation, alleged immoral action on the part of Bahá'í founders, accusations of Bahá'í distortion of their history and Bahá'í misuse of Christian scriptures. A new challenge to the Bahá'í Faith is now gathering momentum from Christian fundamentalism which sees any movement toward world order as a plot of the devil.

Apart from a very few relatively short works in English, Islamic attacks have been in Arabic and Persian. Fundamentalist arguments from the Qur'án are linked to political arguments of alleged Bahá'í connection with Zionism and the intelligence services of Britain, Russia and America.

Criticisms of the Bahá'í Faith, in English, on political grounds by parties and special-interest groups have not been numerous, though racist and extremist attacks have occurred.

Works by Covenant-breakers (see Section XII) form a very small portion of published materials on the Bahá'í religion and have been much overemphasized by bibliographers and writers whose purpose is not solely scholarly.[4] The material is of interest in underscoring the central problems seen by these writers as being of enough importance to warrant risking their spiritual status as believers. Bahá'ís are not forbidden to read Covenant-breaker publications but they are warned of the dangers of doing so without being well-grounded in the overall teachings of the Bahá'í Faith or without having knowledge of the background and the motivations behind the campaign of any excommunicant group.

Translation

The most important languages to be considered with regard to the question of translation are Arabic, Persian and English, the first two being languages of revelation and the latter two being the languages of interpretation.

Bahá'í publications and translations now exist in more than 800 languages. Of these, many are represented only by a single prayer or a few passages. The prime language for first translation of sacred writings is English and then from English into other languages (except for Turkish, Arabic and Urdu which are translated directly from the original Persian and Arabic). Any translations of sacred texts into English that are to be used as source text for translation into other languages must generally be authorized by the Universal House of Justice, which safeguards the authenticity and correctness of the

---

4. An outline of the Bahá'í doctrine of the covenant, and a description of the main Covenant-breaker groups, are included in the introduction to section XII. Joel Bjorling, Vernon Johnson, and William McElwee Miller make much of these publications but a bias in favour of Christianity's truth claims on the part of at least two of these authors has led them to consider Covenant-breaker activities as illustrative of the falsehood of Bahá'í beliefs.

texts. Such authorization requires a translation in elevated English style and faithfulness to the original.

Early translators of Bahá'í sacred writings into English were Ali-Kuli Khan, Ameen Ullah Fareed and Ahmad Esphahani (Ahmad Sohrab). The standard, however, was ultimately set by Shoghi Effendi from the early days of his guardianship with his superb translations of *Kalimát-i-Maknúnih* (*The Hidden Words*), *Kitáb-i-Íqán*, (*The Book of Certitude*), *Lawḥ-i-Ibn-i-Dhi'b* (*Epistle to the Son of the Wolf*) and the two compilations entitled *Gleanings from the Writings of Bahá'u'lláh* and *Prayers and Meditations by Bahá'u'lláh*. At present, all authorized English translations are made or reviewed at the Bahá'í World Centre where a committee either performs the translation work itself or reviews work of such translators as Marzieh Gail and Habib Taherzadeh.

Among early translators into major European languages, the most important were Hippolyte Dreyfus (an accomplished scholar of Persian) into French, Wilhelm Herrigel into German and Leonora Stirling Armstrong into Spanish and Portuguese. Translation into other languages is done under the auspices of National Spiritual Assemblies and Bahá'í Publishing Trusts based upon an assessment of literature needs for particular national and linguistic communities. The International Teaching Centre has been assigned the duty of examining literature needs and recommending goals for translation and publication.

Publication and Distribution

1. Policies

Guidelines for Bahá'í writers and publishers are set down in a 'Memorandum on Bahá'í Publishing' issued by the Universal House of Justice on 28 March 1971. These guidelines include:

a. *Review of works by Bahá'ís about their religion*
At this time, all works by Bahá'ís dealing with the Bahá'í Faith must be approved before publication, whether by a Bahá'í or non-Bahá'í publisher. The competent authority is either a Local Spiritual Assembly in the case of purely local material, or a National Spiritual Assembly; works by Hands of the Cause of God may be reviewed in Haifa. Approval implies no obligation on a Bahá'í publisher to publish a manuscript. This measure is a temporary one which Shoghi Effendi says 'will be definitely abolished'.[5] Its purpose is to ensure a dignified and accurate presentation of the Bahá'í Faith and to protect it from misrepresentation at a time when it is as yet largely unknown, though emerging from the obscurity of its immediate past.

b. *Sale and promotion of Bahá'í literature*
Bahá'í publications reviewed and published in one country may be sold, offered for sale or promoted anywhere in the world, although National Spiritual Assemblies, Bahá'í Publishing Trusts or Bahá'í Publishing Committees cannot be required to stock, promote, advertise, or sell specific publications. Believers may not be prevented from purchasing Bahá'í books reviewed and published in other countries.

c. *Deposit of Bahá'í publications with the Bahá'í World Centre*
The International Bahá'í Library has established a general set of depository requirements for Bahá'í publishers, carrying on a practice set by Shoghi Effendi and continued by the Universal House of Justice.

5. *World Order of Bahá'u'lláh* 2nd rev. ed. (Wilmette, Ill.: Bahá'í Publishing Trust, 1974), p. 9.

2. History of Bahá'í Publishing

During the early decades of the Bábí and the Bahá'í Faiths, sacred texts and commentaries were disseminated in manuscript form. Late in the 19th century some of these texts were lithographed in Bombay – the *Kitáb-i-Aqdas*, *Kitáb-i-Íqán* and *Kalimát-i-Maknúnih* among others. Bahá'í publication was always restricted by religious and judicial opposition in Iran, forcing the believers to reproduce literature by means of cyclostyle and offset.

English translations first appeared in 1891 through the instrumentality of the Cambridge orientalist E.G. Browne who made a special study of Bábí history and texts and himself translated and edited such works as *A Traveller's Narrative* by 'Abdu'l-Bahá and the *Táríkh-i-Jadíd* by Mírzá Ḥusayn of Hamadan.

Dr Ibrahim Kheiralla, a Syrian Christian convert to the Bahá'í Faith, was the second Bahá'í to reach the United States, settling there in 1892, and the first to begin a systematic teaching of Bahá'í tenets. The first publication in the United States attempting to expound Bahá'í principles was Kheiralla's *Za-ti-et Al-lah: The Identity and Personality of God* (Chicago: Grant's Printery, 1896), later enlarged into a book entitled *Bab-ed-Din: the Door of True Religion . . . Revelation from the East* (Chicago: Charles H. Kerr & Co., 1897). Although of interest as the first introductory books by a Bahá'í in English, Kheiralla's works were far from being authoritative statements of Bahá'í beliefs.

Centres of English language Bahá'í publishing first appeared in the major American cities of New York (the Behai Board of Counsel) and Chicago (Behais Supply and Publishing Board) in 1900. The latter soon became known as the Bahai Publishing Society and served for over two decades as the most prolific publisher of English language Bahá'í literature. By the end of this century's first decade, the Bahá'ís had available, though in inadequate translations, the *Kalimát-i-Maknúnih* (*The Hidden Words*), *Suratu'l-Ḥaykal*, *Kitáb-i-Íqán* (under the titles *The Book of Assurance* and *The Book of Ighan*), and *Tablets of Baha'o'llah*.

It was through prayers and letters received from 'Abdu'l-Bahá that early western believers received their deepest education in the verities of their religion. The few early believers exchanged typewritten copies of communications received from 'Abdu'l-Bahá, which in many instances were then published as small pamphlets during the century's first decade.

The visits of pilgrims to 'Abdu'l-Bahá, beginning with the first contingent of western Bahá'í pilgrims to visit 'Akká in 1898, resulted in a number of important publications, including the memoirs of May Maxwell, Thornton Chase, Helen S. Goodall and Ella S. Cooper, and Julia Grundy. Up until the death of 'Abdu'l-Bahá in 1921 a steady stream of pilgrims from the Occident was able to meet him. Some of these pilgrims later shared their experiences and impressions of 'the Master', as well as records of his words to them, in published accounts. The most significant of such notes, collected by Laura Clifford Barney and known under the English title of *Some Answered Questions*, were recorded in Persian with the assistance of 'Abdu'l-Bahá's secretaries, reviewed, corrected and approved by him, thus entering the canon of authentic Bahá'í scripture. *Some Answered Questions* was published in 1908 in London and Philadelphia in English, in Paris in French, and at the same time in Persian under the title *Mufávaḍát*. 'Abdu'l-Bahá's journey to Europe and North America in 1911–13 resulted in a number of compilations of his talks and accounts of his activities.

Shoghi Effendi, the Guardian of the Bahá'í Faith from 1921 to 1957, was a master of the English language with which he sought to interpret to the West the basic truths and social programme of the Bahá'í movement. In a succession of cogent letters, he expanded the vision of the believers and clearly defined for them the nature of their responsibilities under 'Abdu'l-Bahá's divine plan. Shoghi Effendi's early letters to the western Bahá'ís awakened them to the newly-emerging administrative institutions of their Faith. In 1928 a collection of the Guardian's letters was published in the United States under the title *Bahá'í Administration*. The series of letters penned between 1929 and 1936, first published separately and then collectively under the title of *The World Order of Bahá'u'lláh*, are a treatise on the processes shaping the Bahá'í community, a mandate for the role of the American believers in raising Bahá'u'lláh's 'world commonwealth' and a sketch of the Bahá'í vision of a future golden age for mankind. *The Advent of Divine Justice* (1939) and *The Promised Day Is Come* (1941) define the spiritual prerequisites for the American Bahá'í community in the prosecution of its tasks, and place global upheavals and conflicts in the context of the process of integration seen in the Bahá'í community. Numerous compilations of the Guardian's letters have been made under other titles, mostly of letters to a single country or administrative institution.

During the period of his Guardianship Shoghi Effendi supported Bahá'í publishing through letters of guidance and encouragement as well as through his own translation activities and the founding of publishing trusts and committees. The first publishing trust was founded in the United Kingdom in 1937, followed by the transformation of the United States Bahá'í Publishing Committee into a trust in 1955. As the religion has spread worldwide, official publishing houses, committees and independent Bahá'í publishers have increased in number. The publishing arm of the Bahá'í World Centre has been established since 1963 and some 26 Bahá'í Publishing Trusts have been created covering every continent. Official publication, however, goes beyond these institutions to include nearly every national Bahá'í body, many of their committees and other official agencies such as the Association for Bahá'í Studies. Several independent publishing firms specializing in Bahá'í materials have emerged, particularly George Ronald in England (1947), Kalimát Press in California (1979) and New Era/Oneworld in England (1985); while in other languages there are Horizonte Verlag (German) and Tacor International (French).

3. Issues and Future Prospects

In its messages to the Bahá'í world announcing overall goals of the Six Year Plan (1986–1992), the Universal House of Justice called for a vast and widespread increase in the publication and dissemination of Bahá'í literature and the founding of local Bahá'í libraries. Already the growing number of publishers and publications has raised a number of issues.

First, not every believer is able to, or wishes to, have a complete library of all Bahá'í publications in his language. Where this may once have been possible, it is now not feasible economically and logistically for any but those with sufficient funds and dedication to the bibliophile's task.

Second, there is an obvious need to help the Bahá'í reader to make the best choices based upon his interests and needs. This requires more timely and knowledgeable book review mechanisms, which will make it possible for readers to winnow out poorly-written or unuseful material from their selection.

Third, the system of administrative review of publications by Bahá'ís on the religion will probably undergo some change as a response to the need to streamline the process of approval and publication. Administrative review and approval will not disappear within the immediately foreseeable future, but will very likely become simpler and less time-consuming under the pressure exerted by a voracious Bahá'í reading audience.

Fourth is the question of peer review. In the 1970s and 1980s the question was raised whether academic works prepared under the methodologies current in Western academic disciplines can be adequately reviewed for publication by those without scholarly training. Although questions of dignity and accuracy of presentation are not necessarily dependent on such training, some countries, such as the United Kingdom, have already introduced a system for peer review for certain kinds of academic works.

Fifth is the important issue of tolerance for the diversity of ideas. In a religion where creative thought is encouraged and indeed required as Bahá'ís strive to come to a better understanding of the teachings of their Faith and attempt to relate them to current issues, and given the cultural and educational diversity of the Bahá'í community, tensions can arise between innovative and traditional thinking, between scholarly and popular study. Greater diversity and a larger Bahá'í community are lessening the perceived importance of most individual contributions to the literature, but the need for openmindedness on the one hand and responsibility on the other will continue to challenge the present generation of Bahá'í readers and writers.

Sixth, the inability of every individual to own a complete Bahá'í library will force the creation of not only local, but regional, national and specialized Bahá'í libraries as well. Such a development will require the training of professional librarians and library technicians, as well as a considerable outlay of Bahá'í funds for purchase of literature.

Seventh is the difficulty of bibliographic control and the dissemination of information about the abundance of literature. The International Bahá'í Library is, at time of writing, the single library institution dedicated to collecting all Bahá'í materials and seems destined for a time to be the only holder of a reasonably complete collection, though such a task is rendered difficult by uneven publishing practices, failure to deposit publications with the Library, and lack of connection between many Bahá'í publishers and their national bibliographic agencies.

Eighth, cooperation among Bahá'í publishers, whether official or independent, will become an absolute economic necessity. In a still relatively small and limited market, competition among the current publishers can lead to losses. A number of Bahá'í publishers' conferences have been held and more are being planned to enhance cooperation and sharing of information.

Ninth is the monitoring of literature needs, which falls under the aegis of the International Teaching Centre. Consistency in reporting of publishing achievements and the statistical mechanisms for obtaining a view of gaps in the corpus of Bahá'í literature are only now being created.

The present trends clearly point to a growth in the number of private Bahá'í publishing houses, specialization in publishing for specific audiences, wider diversity of materials, and ultimately to the streamlining of the review procedures for publications.

Preface

Genealogy and Purpose

Of all the literature about the Bahá'í Faith ever published, more than 60% of the titles are in English. Such a large proportion of Bahá'í publications in a single language would seem to warrant the establishment of bibliographic control over the corpus of literature in that tongue. A number of preliminary attempts have been made to compile a bibliographic record of Bahá'í literature and published references to the Bahá'í Faith in English. Of particular interest, although incomplete and sometimes inaccurate, are the entries in the 'Bahá'í Bibliography' section in successive volumes of *The Bahá'í World* from Vol. I, 1925–26 (called *The Bahá'í Year Book*) through Vol. XVI, 1973–6. Vol. XVII, 1976–9, included valuable contributions by Robert Cadwalader and Maureen Thur which were far more adequate than the previous entries in this section. Other individual collectors and bibliographers, including Alan Coupe, Ray O. Ball and Payam Afsharian, have compiled lists of their own. The latter in particular has given some helpful leads from the materials in his own personal library. More recently, Joel Bjorling compiled *The Baha'i Faith: A Historical Bibliography* (New York: Garland Publishing, 1985). While of some interest, his claim to having produced a 'comprehensive' and 'exhaustive' bibliography of Bahá'í works in English must be dismissed. Except in the case of works by Covenant-breakers, he has consulted only the most obvious major works which are easily available, thoroughly bypassing the enormous amount of Bahá'í literature in English published around the world. The care taken with Covenant-breaker works, and the emphasis placed upon these groups, swells out of all proportion their actual numbers, influence or importance to Bahá'í history. Bjorling's work, moreover, misses some of the most basic works that must be included in a bibliography, such as Elder and Miller's translation of Bahá'u'lláh's Most Holy Book which they title *Al-Kitab al-Aqdas* (London, 1960); routinely lists titles incorrectly and even includes one item [Bjorling 892] that has nothing to do with the Bahá'í religion at all.[1]

Academic research on the Bahá'í Faith is increasing and some doctoral dissertations have attempted to redress the balance in terms of bibliographic control. One of the finest bibliographic essays is included in Abbas Amanat's *The Early Years of the Babi Movement: Background and Development* (unpublished PhD thesis, University of Oxford, 1981); Peter Smith's *A Sociological Study of the Babi and Baha'i Religions* (unpublished PhD thesis, University of Lancaster, 1982) includes a short bibliographical essay and a lengthy bibliography; and additional helpful information on Covenant-breaker literature is included in Vernon Elvin Johnson's *An Historical Analysis of Critical Transformations in the Evolution of the Baha'i World Faith* (unpublished PhD thesis, Baylor University, 1974). Many of the other academic dissertations show a lack of familiarity with the range and extent of Bahá'í literature in English. It is therefore clear that any bibliographical work on the Bábí and Bahá'í Faiths should bear in mind the needs of the researcher and academic.

---

1. For this reason, a number of items included in Bjorling, but not seen by the compiler, have been included in this volume with a note that they are from Bjorling's bibliography.

As the Bahá'í Faith becomes better known, particularly through media coverage of the persecution of the Bahá'ís in Iran and other countries, and as Bahá'í doctrine and culture become recognized as legitimate subjects of scholarly study, librarians will be called upon to provide ever more comprehensive and authoritative collections of material about the religion. This compiler, himself a librarian, has endeavoured to include helps which will make this a reference work of significant value in the selection and identification of Bahá'í materials.

Bahá'í bibliophiles will become more interested in Bahá'í publishing history and will attempt to create personal libraries reflecting their own interests. Therefore notes and helps of a type designed to assist the book collector have been included.

Scope

This bibliography attempts to list all known published English-language pamphlets, books and journal articles which are about the Bábí and Bahá'í Faiths or which contain reference to them, for the period 1844 up to the end of 1985. It cannot claim to be definitive but the compiler can say with reasonable confidence that this bibliography is as comprehensive a listing of English-language publications on the Bábí and Bahá'í religions as is possible to create for the years covered.

For the purpose of this bibliography, a publication means any item duplicated by means of printing, offset, mimeograph, cyclostyle or other methods for distribution to a large number of people.

The bibliographer has specifically chosen at this stage to *exclude*:

Advertisements
Analytics for articles in Bahá'í journals or in collections of essays
Audio-visual materials
Conference and convention portfolios (containers of various loose materials)
Correspondence courses
Greeting cards
Kits
Local Bahá'í periodicals
Maps
Newspaper articles
Official documents (government and parliamentary records; resolutions of official bodies)[2]
Posters and broadsides
Programs of local meetings and non-permanent summer schools
Publishers' catalogues
Puzzles, buttons, pens and other ephemera
Teaching cards

While the above categories are legitimate candidates for bibliographic listing, the inclusion of these would have prolonged the task of compilation unduly. They will, it is hoped, be covered in future volumes.

Theses and dissertations for academic degrees in all languages are already fully covered in a section of the reference work *The Bahá'í World* beginning with volume XVIII, 1979–1983. English-language theses only are covered in section XIII of this bibliography.

The decision of what to include was also complicated by the fact that a local mimeographed production in the United States would very likely be ephemeral under current circumstances whereas such an item would be significant

---

2. The bibliographer has included a handful of major official documents which either deal exclusively with the Bahá'ís or have some significance by being commonly known and frequently cited.

for some of the emerging national Bahá'í communities in Africa and Asia. The bibliographer has decided to err on the liberal side and to include material that might otherwise be considered of minor interest. In the case of books and articles containing reference to the Faith (sections X, XI), no judgement was made as to the significance of the reference for the item to warrant inclusion; introductory remarks to these sections help to set a context and a few annotations have been included for clarification.

Arrangement and Conventions

The bibliography is divided into a number of sections: I. Writings of Bahá'u'lláh; II. Writings of the Báb; III. Writings of 'Abdu'l-Bahá; IV. Works compiled from the writings of Bahá'u'lláh, the Báb and 'Abdu'l-Bahá (including items with quotations from Shoghi Effendi and the Universal House of Justice); V. Writings of Shoghi Effendi; VI. Works and Messages by the Universal House of Justice; VII. Works on the Bábí and Bahá'í Faiths; VIII. Braille materials; IX. Bahá'í periodicals; X. Works containing reference to the Bahá'í Faith; XI. Articles (from non-Bahá'í journals); XII. Works of Covenant-breakers; XIII. Theses.

Entries in parts I–VI and IX are arranged alphabetically by title. Entries in parts VII–VIII and X–XIII are arranged alphabetically by author's last name where one is known or specifically mentioned in the publication (names beginning Mc and Mac are alphabetized as though spelled Mac). If no author is known, or the work owes its existence to an editor or compiler, the item is entered alphabetically under title, ignoring initial articles. Each entry follows bibliographic format adapted from the major American style manuals (University of Chicago's *A Manual of Style* and the Modern Language Association's *MLA Style Sheet*), using familiar abbreviations: n.p. means 'no place of publication' and n.d. signifies 'no date'. The Latin *idem.* means identical or the same, referring to repetition of the same bibliographic information as in the immediately previous item. Information enclosed in square brackets [] is information which is known or surmised, but which is not actually shown on the publication. The abbreviation 'ca.' before a date signifies *circa*, meaning around the date, e.g. ca.1980 means 'about 1980'. The letter c before a date indicates a copyright date which may not necessarily be the date of publication, e.g. c1980 means 'copyright 1980'.

Each separate entry in the bibliography has been assigned a number in sequence, so that no two items have the same number. A number of items, discovered as the manuscript was being prepared for publication, appear with an appended alphabetical extension, e.g. 4.195a. It is hoped that, in the future, additions and addenda to this bibliography will be published. Those future continuations will carry on the numbering, in sequence, from the last numbers in each section of this instalment. It will thus be possible to make standard reference to each item in the bibliography by number. The numbers are arranged in such a way that it is possible to tell from which section of the bibliography any item comes. Thus, item 7.135 is item number 135 from section VII. Corrections of errors will also be made by reference to the number in the bibliography. This volume and all future volumes will show clearly on the spine the primary time period covered, although later volumes will also include categories not covered in this first instalment dating from previous years, as well as any earlier publications of which the bibliographer was unaware while this volume was being compiled. Ultimately it is to be hoped that there will appear bibliographies of publications on the Bahá'í Faith in other languages, with a view to establishing, in time, complete coverage of all publications on the religion.

A separate entry is included for: each title; each edition of a specific title; each printing where the publisher or place of publication has changed; or where a printing shows itself to be an entirely new bibliographic item because of significant variation in paging. If a number of unchanged reprintings have been done, and none of the above indications for separate entry apply, the dates of the reprintings are all listed under the single entry. Where a succeeding printing shows only a small variation in paging, the variant is included in the same entry as the previous printing(s) with a note of the paging difference. Notes are also added about other physical variations such as two sizes or different covers in a single printing. A reference '*See* ——' has been added to some entries in order to relate items which are selections from another text, or which are differently titled editions of the same work. Book reviews which appeared outside of Bahá'í journals, and which mentioned the Bahá'í Faith, are listed in a paragraph with the entry of the particular item being reviewed. Reviews of books that are not directly related to the Bahá'í Faith are included only when the review itself mentions the Faith. Where no paging is shown, the bibliographer has been unable to examine the item, but is reasonably sure of its existence. Pagination is given according to the library conventions whereby separate roman and arabic numeral paging is noted, using only the last numbered page, unless significant unnumbered pages warrant inclusion in the collation.

Titles and publishers are recorded exactly as spelled on the actual publications themselves, and with or without diacriticals as the case may be, for the purposes of strict bibliographic accuracy. This is particularly obvious in the case of the spelling of Bahá'í (which may also appear as Baha'i, Bahai, etc.), Bahá'u'lláh (Baha'u'llah, Bahaullah, Baha Ullah, Baha Allah), and 'Abdu'l-Bahá (Abdul-Baha, 'Abdu'l-Baha, Abdul Baha, Abd al-Baha, Abd Ul-Baha), where diacritical marks are often not present in the title or publishing information.

Annotations are included for most items of significance. The bibliographer has tried to give a sense of the content, importance and special features of major publications. The compiler makes no claim, however, that the annotations are exhaustive or academically critical.

Library of Congress card numbers are appended to the bibliographic entries for those Bahá'í items that have been catalogued by that library. An appendix listing standard abbreviations for major works in English is also provided. Three indexes have been compiled to provide comprehensive access to the items listed by name, title and subject.

The overwhelming majority of items listed here are held in the International Bahá'í Library. A large number of references in section X were verified at the Library of Congress, a number of smaller libraries and from the libraries of private collectors. Where it has not been possible to verify completely the existence of an item, it has been decided not to include it until further information becomes available.

The compiler has attempted to record bibliographic details with strict accuracy. Nevertheless, errors and omissions will inevitably be found in a work of this type. The compiler and the publisher are eager to be informed of all corrections, with appropriate documentary evidence, to be included in future editions and supplements.

I wish to thank the Universal House of Justice for the inestimable privilege of being called to serve as the Director of the International Bahá'í Library, providing me as it has with so many opportunities for professional and spiritual growth, and the only real opportunity available at this time to compile such a bibliography. To Betty J. Fisher of the U.S. Bahá'í Publishing Trust for her early encouragement and guidance, and to reviewers Patrice Holliday and E. Christian Filstrup who offered helpful suggestions, I owe my heartfelt thanks.

To Payam Afsharian for the many entries in section X that were previously unknown to me, my grateful appreciation. I owe a special debt of gratitude to Wendi Momen and May Ballerio for their assiduous labours, under a gruelling timetable, to bring my work to fruition on the printed page. The staff of the International Bahá'í Library, who over the years have borne the varying circumstances and trials of service to the Faith with equanimity and good grace, deserve special recognition for the support they extended to me as their Director and colleague. A particular note of thanks to Ian Semple, member of the Universal House of Justice, for his constant encouragement and for taking time from a busy schedule to write the Foreword to this book. Most of all, to my wife Rachel, and to my children, who endured my many hours absent from home, a constant flow of paper through our apartment, and my nagging frustrations with the slowness of the work, I express my undying love: without you, there would have been no will to finish.

I
The Writings of Bahá'u'lláh

BAHÁ'U'LLÁH was born Mírzá Ḥusayn-'Alí in Ṭihrán in 1817 of a noble family. He became a follower of the Báb in the 1840s and soon was established as one of the outstanding exponents of the Bábí Cause. During the persecutions of the Báb's followers in the 1850s Bahá'u'lláh was imprisoned in Ṭihrán and there became conscious of his mission as the one foretold by the Báb – the Promised One of all religions. After Bahá'u'lláh's declaration of his mission in 1863 while in exile in Baghdád, and his subsequent public proclamation in 1868 from his banishment in Adrianople, the vast majority of Bábís accepted Bahá'u'lláh as the promised Manifestation of God and became known as Bahá'ís. Bahá'u'lláh suffered further exile to Ottoman Palestine where he was in confinement or under house arrest for the last twenty-four years of his earthly life. He died in 1892. Bahá'u'lláh's writings, penned in Arabic and Persian, are regarded as sacred scriptures by Bahá'ís, with the same weight as has the Bible for Christians and the Qur'án for Muslims. Most of Bahá'u'lláh's works were written in the form of long letters to believers although a few were written as individual expositions. Much of the published material is in the form of compilations, selections and extracts. Shoghi Effendi's translations of Bahá'u'lláh's works are regarded as authoritative by Bahá'ís.

1.1. *The Bahá'í Faith: Selections from the Writings of Bahá'u'lláh.* introduction by Shoghi Effendi. Banjul: National Spiritual Assembly of the Bahá'ís of the Gambia, 1980. 46 p.

1.2. *A Bahai Prayer for Unity; Shared with the People of the Solomon Islands on Their Achieving Independence.* Honiara: National Spiritual Assembly of the Bahais of the Solomon Islands, 1978. 4 p. Text in English and six Pacific languages.

1.3. *Baha 'U'llah's Hidden Words.* trans. Ameen U. Fareed. San Diego, Calif.: J.E. Gazvini, 1931. 59 p. LC card 31–23683 rev.
   See 1.29, 1.49–1.73, 1.143.

1.4. *Baha'u'llah's Letter to a Physician.* Mokelumne Hill, Calif.: Health Research, n.d. [197–?] 1 p.

1.5. *Bahá'u'lláh's Long Healing Prayer and Qad Iḥtaraqa'l-Mukhliṣún, the 'Fire Tablet'.* [Kingston]: National Spiritual Assembly of the Bahá'ís of Jamaica, n.d. [1979 or 1980]. [20]p.

See 1.30–1.34, 1.47–1.48, 1.91, 1.107–1.108, 1.129, 4.133.

1.6. *Behai Principles, Prayers, Supplications, Directions, and Communes.* n.p., n.d. [190–?] Collection of prayers of Bahá'u'lláh compiled by Behaists, followers of I.G. Kheiralla.

1.7. *Blessed Is the Spot.* il. Anna Stevenson. Wilmette, Ill.: Bahá'í Publishing Trust, 1958. 32 p. LC card 58–8815.
   Well-known prayer of Bahá'u'lláh illustrated for children.

1.8. *Blessed Is the Spot.* il. Mark Fennessy. n.p. [Wilmette, Ill.]: National Teaching Committee, n.d. [197–?] 16 leaves.

1.9. *Blessed Is the Spot = Bendito Sea el Punto: Prayer by Bahá'u'lláh.* n.p. [Panama: National Spiritual Assembly of the Bahá'ís of Panama], n.d. [1967?] [16] leaves. Dittoed.

1.10. *The Book of Assurance (The Book of Ighan).* trans. Ali Kuli Khan, assisted by Howard MacNutt. New York: Brentano's Publishers for the Baha'i Publishing Committee, n.d. [1924] vi, 190 p.
   See 1.12–1.14, 1.77–1.85.

1.11. *idem.* New York: Bahá'í Publishing Committee, 1929 (New York: J.J. Little and Ives). vi, 190 p.

1.12. *The Book of Ighan.* trans. Ali Kuli Khan, assisted by Howard MacNutt. New York: George V. Blackburne Co., 1904. viii, 190 p. LC card 4–35753.
   The earliest translation of this important scriptural work. Superseded by the translation of Shoghi Effendi.
   See 1.10–1.11, 1.77–1.85.

1.13. *idem.* 2nd ed. Chicago: Bahai Publishing Society, 1907. viii, 190 p.

1.14. *idem.* 3rd ed. Chicago: Bahai Publishing Society, 1915, vi, 190 p.

1.15. *The Book of the Covenant, Kitab-el-Ahd Revealed by the Blessed Perfection.* New York: Board of Counsel, n.d. [1901?]. 4 p.
   See 1.76.

1.16. *A Compilation of Passages from the Writings of Bahá'u'lláh.* comp. Universal House of Justice. New Delhi: Bahá'í Publishing Trust, 1980. 94 p.

1.17. *idem.* [Manila]: Bahá'í Publishing Trust of the Philippines, 1980, 59 p.

1.18. *A Compilation of Published Extracts from the Kitáb-i-Aqdas.* n.p. [Wilmette, Ill.]: National Spiritual Assembly of the Bahá'ís of the United States, 1973. 10 p.
   See 1.27–1.28, 1.75, 6.54.

1.19. *The Dawn of World Civilization.* Wilmette, Ill.: Bahá'í Publishing Committee, 1945, 1945. 8 p.
   Two variants, one stated to be 'published in tribute to the purposes of the World Security Conference, San Francisco, April 25, 1945'.

1.20. *Die drei tägliche Gebet.* In arabisch geoffenbart von Bahá'u'lláh; Deutsch nach der Englischen Übersetzung. Langenhain: Nationale Geistige Rat der Bahá'í in Deutschland, 1973. 46 p. Cover title: *Das tägliche Gebet.* Text in Arabic, English and German.
   Multi-language edition of the three Obligatory prayers, 'revealed in Arabic by Bahá'u'lláh; translated into German from the English'.

1.21. *A Drop from the Ocean: Words of Bahá'u'lláh.* selected by G. Faizi. New Delhi: Bahá'í Centre, n.d. [1975?]. 28 p.

1.22. *The Earth Is God's.* n.p. [London]: National Spiritual Assembly of the Bahá'ís of the British Isles, n.d. [1954?] 4 p.
   Excerpts from the writings of Bahá'u'lláh, presented by Shoghi Effendi in *The Advent of Divine Justice.*
   See 1.74, 1.96–1.98.

1.23. *idem.* London: Bahá'í Publishing Trust, 1947. 4 p.

1.24. *Epistle to the Son of the Wolf.* trans. Julie Chanler. New York: Bahá'í Publishing Committee, 1928. vi, 140 p.
   Bahá'u'lláh's last major work, translated from the French of Hippolyte Dreyfus by Julie Chanler. Superseded by Shoghi Effendi's translation. See 1.25–1.26.

1.25. *Epistle to the Son of the Wolf.* trans. Shoghi Effendi. Wilmette, Ill.: Bahá'í Publishing Committee, 1941, 1953. xix, 193 p. LC cards 41–9492, 53–18798.
   Shoghi Effendi's rendering into English of 'the last outstanding Tablet revealed by the Pen of Bahá'u'lláh', written to a Muslim clergyman of Iṣfáhán whose father had sent two Bahá'ís to their martyrdom. Bahá'u'lláh argues the validity of his cause and quotes from his previous works. The authoritative translation for Bahá'ís.
   See 1.24.

1.26. *idem.* Wilmette, Ill.: Bahá'í Publishing

Trust, 1962, 1969, 1970, 1971, 1976, 1979. xix, 193 p.

1.27. *Excerpts from the Kitáb-i-Aqdas Already Published in Authorized Bahá'í Publications.* n.p., n.d. [196–]. 17 p.
   See 1.18, 1.28, 1.75, 6.54.

1.28. *Extracts from the Kitáb-i-Aqdas, the Most Holy Book of the Revelation of Bahá'u'lláh.* trans. Shoghi Effendi Rabbani. n.p. [Las Vegas, N.M.?: National Bureau of the Orthodox Bahá'í Faith of the United States and Canada], n.d. [197–?] 31 leaves. LC card 76–353450.
   See 1.18, 1.27, 1.75, 6.54.

1.29. *Fapi Thin Nib Mith ni Yoloy Bahá'u'lláh = The Hidden Words of Bahá'u'lláh.* Ponape: National Spiritual Assembly of the Bahá'ís of the Caroline Islands, 1980. 17 leaves. Text in English and Yapese.
   See 1.3, 1.49–1.73, 1.143.

1.30. *The Fire Tablet.* Thornhill, Ont.: Bahá'í Canada Publications, n.d. [1980] 8 p.
   See 1.5, 1.31–1.34, 1.107–1.108, 1.129, 4.133.

1.31. *idem.* Managua: National Spiritual Assembly of the Bahá'ís of Nicaragua, n.d. [1981] 6 p.

1.32. *Fire Tablet, Long Healing Prayer.* Auckland: National Spiritual Assembly of the Bahá'ís of New Zealand, 1980. 6, 6 p.
   See 1.5, 1.30–1.31, 1.33–1.34, 1.91, 1.107–1.108, 1.129, 4.133.

1.33. *The 'Fire Tablet' and the Long Healing Prayer.* n.p. [Manila: National Spiritual Assembly of the Bahá'ís of the Philippines], n.d. [1980?] 6 p.

1.34. *The Fire Tablet. Qad-Iḥtaraqa'l-Mukhlisun. Long Healing Prayer.* n.p. [Singapore: National Spiritual Assembly of Singapore], n.d. [1980]. 6 p.
   See 1.5, 1.30–1.33, 1.48, 1.91, 1.107–1.108, 1.128, 4.133.

1.35. *First National Bahá'í Convention of Dominica Souvenir.* Roseau: [National Spiritual Assembly of the Bahá'ís of Dominica], n.d. [1983] (Roseau: Tropical Printers Ltd.). [5] p.

1.36. *From Suratul-Heykle, the Book of the Temple.* trans. Habib Katibah assisted by L.K. Saleeby. n.p., n.d. [190–?] [4] p.
   See 1.122.

1.37. *Gleanings from the Writings of Bahá'u'lláh.* comp. and trans. Shoghi Effendi. New York: Bahá'í Publishing Committee, 1935. 353 p. LC card 36–25279 rev.
   Shoghi Effendi's own translation and compilation of selections from the writings of

Bahá'u'lláh which has become a standard scriptural volume for all Bahá'ís.

1.38. *idem.* New York: Bahá'í Publishing Commitee, 1939. 360 p.

1.39. *idem.* Wilmette, Ill.: Bahá'í Publishing Committee, 1943, 1946, 1948, 1951. xii, 346, [20] p. LC card 52–24896.

1.40. *idem.* rev. ed. Wilmette, Ill.: Bahá'í Publishing Committee, 1952. xvi, 346, [20] p.

1.41. *idem.* rev. ed. Wilmette, Ill.: Bahá'í Publishing Trust, 1956, 1963, 1969, 1971. xvi, 346, [20] p.

1.42. *idem.* 2nd rev. ed. Wilmette, Ill.: Bahá'í Publishing Trust, 1976, 1982. xvi, 346, [20] p. LC card 76–45364.
Review:
Bush, Richard C. *New Review of Books and Religion* (New York), v. 2 no. 9 (May 1978).

1.43. *idem.* 2nd rev. ed. Pocket-size ed. Wilmette, Ill.: Bahá'í Publishing Trust, 1983, 1984. xvi, 346, [20] p.

1.44. *idem.* London: Bahá'í Publishing Trust, 1949. 350 p.

1.45. *idem.* rev. ed. London: Bahá'í Publishing Trust, 1978. 350 p.

1.46. *idem.* 1st Indian ed. New Delhi: Bahá'í Publishing Trust, 1973. xvi, 346, [20] p.

1.47. *Healing Prayer.* trans. Dr Ali Kuli Khan and Mrs Marzieh Gail. Ada County, Idaho: The Spiritual Assembly of the Bahá'ís of Ada County (1956 printing). 10 p.
See 1.5, 1.48, 1.91, 1.108.

1.48. *The Healing Prayer.* n.p. [Hofheim-Langenhain]: Bahá'í-Verlag, n.d. [1981], n.d. [1983] 12, 10 p. English and Arabic text.
See 1.5, 1.47, 1.91, 1.108.

1.49. *The Hidden Words.* n.p. [United States], n.d. [1900] 15 p.
See 1.3, 1.29, 1.143.

1.50. *The Hidden Words.* (Persian section only). Chicago: Behais Supply and Publishing Board, n.d. [1900?] 15 p.

1.51. *The Hidden Words from the Arabic.* London: Kenneth Mackenzie, 1915. 12 p.

1.52. *Hidden Words from the Persian, Revealed by the Blessed Perfection.* New York: The Board of Counsel, n.d. [190–] 15 p.

1.53. *Hidden Words from the Supreme Pen of Baha'u'llah.* Cairo, Egypt: Cairo Bahai Assembly, 1921 (Cairo: Oriental Advertising Co.). 62, 47 p. Original with English translation.

1.54. *The Hidden Words of Bahá'u'lláh.* trans. Shoghi Effendi. London: Bahá'í Assembly, 1923. 90 p. Cover title: *Hidden Words, Words of Wisdom, Prayers.*
Translation by Shoghi Effendi which was superseded by his later translation done 'with the assistance of some English friends'. *See* 1.57.

1.55. *idem.* New York: Baha'i Publishing Committee, 1924. 62 p.

1.56. *idem.* New York: Baha'i Publishing Committee, 1925. 53 p.

1.57. *The Hidden Words of Bahá'u'lláh.* trans. Shoghi Effendi with the assistance of some English friends. London: National Spiritual Assembly of the Bahá'ís of Great Britain and Northern Ireland, 1929. 55 p.
Referred to by Shoghi Effendi as 'that marvellous collection of gem-like utterances', this volume of Bahá'í scripture contains over 150 profound epigrammatic sayings. The Guardian ranked it as 'of unsurpassed pre-eminence among the doctrinal and ethical writings' of Bahá'u'lláh. The translation by Shoghi Effendi, with the assistance of some English friends (among whom were George Townshend, John Esslemont and Ethel Rosenberg), is the standard authoritative version.

1.58. *idem.* New York: Bahá'í Publishing Committee, 1932. 56 p.; 1939, 1940. 52 p.

1.59. *idem.* London: National Spiritual Assembly of the Bahá'ís of the British Isles, 1932. 56 p. LC card 36–21902 rev.

1.60. *idem.* Wilmette, Ill.: Bahá'í Publishing Committee, 1943. 52 p.; 1952, 1954. ix, 52 p. LC card 54–7328.

1.61. *idem.* Manchester, U.K.: Bahá'í Publishing Trust, 1944. LC card 45–14396.

1.61a. *idem.* Manchester, U.K.: Bahá'í Publishing Trust, 1949 (Dorchester: The Dorset Press). 53 p.

1.62. *idem.* London: Bahá'í Publishing Trust, 1966, 1975 (Welwyn Garden City: Broadwater Press). 52 p.

1.63. *idem.* rev. ed. Wilmette, Ill.: Bahá'í Publishing Trust, 1954, 1963, 1966, 1970, 1971, 1975. ix, 52 p. LC card 54–7328; 1979, 1982, 1985. 52 p. (type re-set).

1.64. *idem.* New Delhi: Bahá'í Publishing Trust, 1957. 52 p.

1.65. *idem.* New Delhi: Bahá'í Publishing Trust, 1964, 1973 (New Delhi: Deluxe Printery). [4], xi, [116] p.

1.66. *idem.* n.p. [Georgetown: National Spiritual

Assembly of the Bahá'ís of Guyana], n.d. [1982] 7 p.

1.67. *idem.* Ṭihrán: Mu'asassiy-i-Millíy-i-Maṭbú'at-i-Amrí, 120 B.E. [1963–64], 128 B.E. [1971–72] 79, 55 p.

Offset of London 1929 ed. published with original texts in Arabic and Persian.

1.68. *The Hidden Words of Bahá'u'lláh = (Kalimát-i-Maknúnih).* [translated from the original Persian and Arabic by Shoghi Effendi; calligraphic design by Mishqín-Qalam] Hofheim-Langenhain: Bahá'í-Verlag, c1983. [144] p.

1.69. *The Hidden Words of Bahá'u'lláh = (Yīn Yán Jīng).* [3rd retranslated ed.] [Tái Nán Shì]: Bahá'í Publishing Trust of the National Spiritual Assembly of the Bahá'ís of Taiwan, 1984. [164] p.

Decorative edition in English and Chinese.

1.70. *Hidden Words, Words of Wisdom, and Communes from the Supreme Pen of Baha'u'llah.* Chicago: Bahai Publishing Society, 1905. 93 p.

This edition includes two pages at the end in which 'Abdu'l-Bahá answers questions about *The Hidden Words.*

1.70a. *Hidden Words, Words of Wisdom, and Communes from the Supreme Pen of Baha'u'llah.* trans. Mirza Ameen 'Ullah Fareed. Chicago: Bahai Publishing Society, title page 1905 [i.e. 1906], n.d. [between 1906 and 1910], 1914. 94 p.

This edition includes three pages at the end in which 'Abdu'l-Bahá answers questions about *The Hidden Words.*

1.71. *idem.* East Sheen, Eng.: Unity Press; Printed for the London Bahais, 1911. 44 p.

1.72. *idem.* 2nd ed. Rangoon: Bahai Publishing Society, 1914. 94 p.

1.73. *Hidden Words, Words of Wisdom and Communes from the Supreme Pen of Baha'u'llah; The Seven Valleys.* Chicago: Bahai Publishing Society, n.d. [between 1906 and 1910] 94, 56 p.

Two works bound together, the first work has no mention of translator (Fareed), the second was translated by Ishteal Ibn Kalantar (Ali Kuli Khan).

1.74. *Immortal Passages: Dynamic and Typical Examples of Bahá'u'lláh's Sublime Utterance Cited by Shoghi Effendi in The Advent of Divine Justice, December 25, 1938.* n.p. [Haifa: Hooper Dunbar], n.d. [1981]. 28 p.

See 1.22–1.23, 1.96–1.98.

1.75. *al-Kitab al-Aqdas, or the Most Holy Book.* trans. Earl E. Elder and William McE. Miller.

London: Royal Asiatic Society, sold by Luzac & Co., 1961. 74 p. LC card 61–18801.

The first published full translation of Bahá'u'lláh's Most Holy Book, the repository of the laws and ordinances of the Bahá'í Dispensation. This version is an unpoetic, dry rendering of Bahá'u'lláh's major work by two Protestant missionaries whose purpose is largely polemical. The authoritative translations by Shoghi Effendi of a large number of passages from this volume, wherein he captures the beauty of Bahá'u'lláh's words, is included in item 6.54.

Reviews:
Teinonen, Seppo A. *The Muslim World* (Hartford, Conn.), v. 54, no. 4 (Oct. 1964), pp. 310–11.

See 1.18, 1.27–1.28, 6.54.

1.76. *Kitab-El-Ah'd, Book of the Covenant, the Will and Testament of Baha'o'llah.* Chicago: Bahai Publishing Society, 1913. [3] p.

Bahá'u'lláh's will in which he appointed 'Abdu'l-Bahá as his successor. The current authorized translation is included in 1.134.

See 1.15.

1.77. *The Kitáb-i-Íqán, the Book of Certitude.* trans. Shoghi Effendi. New York: Bahá'í Publishing Committee, 1931, 1937. 283 p. LC cards 32–16947 rev., 40–10147 rev.

The volume of Bahá'í scripture that ranks second only to the *Kitáb-i-Aqdas* in importance. Bahá'u'lláh quotes and explains a number of passages of the Bible and Qur'án and elucidates the meanings of many of the symbols used in previous religions. Shoghi Effendi's translation is authoritative for Bahá'ís.

See 1.10–1.13.

1.78. *idem.* Wilmette, Ill.: Bahá'í Publishing Committee, 1943. 261 p.

1.79. *idem.* 2nd ed. Wilmette, Ill.: Bahá'í Publishing Committee, 1950, 1954. xxii, 276 p. LC card 51–22838.

1.80. *idem.* 2nd ed. Wilmette, Ill.: Bahá'í Publishing Trust, 1960, 1970. xxii, 276 p.

There are two versions of the dust jacket of the 1960 printing: the first states erroneously that the *Íqán* was revealed in 1858, while the latter gives the correct date of 1862.

1.81. *idem.* 2nd ed. Wilmette, Ill.: Bahá'í Publishing Trust, 1974, 1981. 274 p.

Introduction eliminated and glossary corrected.

1.82. *idem.* 2nd ed. Pocket-size ed. Wilmette, Ill.: Bahá'í Publishing Trust, 1983, 1985. 274 p.

Definite article removed from title; now reads *Kitáb-i-Íqán.*

1.83. *idem.* London: Bahá'í Publishing Trust, 1946. 167 p.

1.84. *idem.* 2nd ed. London: Bahá'í Publishing Trust, 1961. 167 p.

1.85. *idem.* 3rd ed. London: Bahá'í Publishing Trust, 1982. 167 p.
Published in hardcover and lightweight formats.

1.86. *Lawh-El-Akdas: The Holy Tablet Revealed by the Blessed Perfection at Bagdad.* n.p., n.d. [190–?] 4 p.
Also known as the Tablet to the Christians. Authorized translation is now included in 1.134.

1.87. *Lawh-El-Akdas: The Holy Tablet Revealed by the Blessed Perfection (Baha Ullah) at Baghdad.* Stuttgart, Germany: Dr Edwin Fisher, Sitzburgstrasse, 1907. 4 p.

1.88. *Lawh-El-Akdas: The Holy Tablet Revealed by the Blessed Perfection (Baha'o'llah) at Bagdad.* Chicago: Bahai Publishing Society, 1913. 4 p.

1.89. *Lawh-El-Akdas: The Holy Tablet Revealed by the Blessed Perfection (Beha'u'llah).* Chicago: Chicago Beha'i Center, 1932. 10 p.
Version published by Behaists, followers of I.G. Kheiralla.

1.90. *Laws of the New Age: Tablet of Ṭarázát.* New Delhi: National Spiritual Assembly of the Bahá'ís of India, n.d. [196–?] [18] p.
One of the Tablets supplementary to the *Kitáb-i-Aqdas*, the authorized translation of which is included in 1.134.

1.91. *Long Healing Prayer.* London: Bahá'í Publishing Trust, 1980. [12] p.
See 1.5, 1.47–1.48, 1.108.

1.91a. *Marriage.* n.p. [Freetown: National Spiritual Assembly of the Bahá'ís of Sierra Leone], n.d. [1985] 2 p.

1.92. *The Mission of Bahá'u'lláh.* Wilmette, Ill.: Bahá'í Publishing Trust, 1952 (two variants: one has white cover with black lettering, second has orange cover with lettering in orange and black), 1971. 15 p.
Passages selected from *Gleanings from the Writings of Bahá'u'lláh.*

1.93. *Naw-Rúz Tablet.* n.p. [London: National Spiritual Assembly of the Bahá'ís of the United Kingdom], n.d. [1985] [4] p.

1.94. *O Queen in London!.* n.p. [London: National Spiritual Assembly of the Bahá'ís of the United Kingdom], n.d. [1979?] [4] p.
Tablet of Bahá'u'lláh to Queen Victoria.

1.95. *idem.* n.p. [London: National Spiritual Assembly of the Bahá'ís of the United Kingdom], n.d. [1981?] [8] p. (4 pages form a cover).

1.96. *The Power of His Utterance.* New Delhi: Bahá'í Publishing Trust, n.d. [1978] 14 p.
Passages from writings of Bahá'u'lláh quoted by Shoghi Effendi in *The Advent of Divine Justice.*
See 1.22–1.23, 1.74, 1.98.

1.97. *idem.* [London]: National Spiritual Assembly of the Bahá'ís of the United Kingdom, 140 B.E. [1983] 14 p.

1.98. *The Power of Utterance.* Port-of-Spain: National Spiritual Assembly of the Bahá'ís of Trinidad and Tobago, 1980.
Passages from writings of Bahá'u'lláh quoted by Shoghi Effendi in *The Advent of Divine Justice.* 12 p.
See 1.22–1.23, 1.74, 1.96–1.97.

1.99. *Praise and Thanksgiving.* n.p., n.d. [195–?] [4] p.
Passages from section 184 in *Prayers and Meditations by Bahá'u'lláh.*

1.100. *Prayers and Meditations by Bahá'u'lláh.* comp. and trans. Shoghi Effendi. New York: Bahá'í Publishing Committee, 1938. 347 p. LC card 38–10000 rev.
Shoghi Effendi's own compilation and translation of important prayers and meditations by Bahá'u'lláh, now a standard volume of scripture for Bahá'ís.

1.101. *idem.* 3rd ed. Wilmette, Ill.: Bahá'í Publishing Committee, 1954. 347 p. LC card 53–10767.

1.102. *idem.* Wilmette, Ill.: Bahá'í Publishing Trust, 1962, 1969, 1974, 1979. 347 p.

1.103. *idem.* 1st British ed. London: Bahá'í Publishing Trust, 1957. 263 p.

1.104. *idem.* rev. ed. London: Bahá'í Publishing Trust, 1978. 263 p.

1.105. *Proclamation of Bahá'u'lláh Centenary, October 1867–1967: Excerpts from His Message to the Kings, Rulers & Religious Leaders of the World.* Sydney, N.S.W.: National Spiritual Assembly of the Bahá'ís of Australia, 1967. 11 p.

1.106. *The Proclamation of Bahá'u'lláh to the Kings and Leaders of the World.* Haifa: Bahá'í World Centre, 1967, 1972, 1978. xiv, 127 p. LC card 72–237435.
A number of passages and Tablets compiled at the Bahá'í World Centre and published on the 100th anniversary of Bahá'u'lláh's proclamation of his mission to the crowned heads and religious leaders of his day and to mankind in general.

1.107. *Qad-Iḥtaraqa'l-Mukhliṣún. The Fire Tablet.* London: Bahá'í Publishing Trust, 1980. 10 p.
  See 1.5, 1.30–1.34, 1.108, 1.128–1.129, 4.133.

1.108. *Qad-iḥtaraqa'l-mukhliṣún. The Fire Tablet. Long Healing Prayer.* n.p. [Enskede: National Spiritual Assembly of the Bahá'ís of Sweden], n.d. [1980]. 3, 3 p.
  See 1.5, 1.30–1.34, 1.47–1.48, 1.91, 1.108, 1.128–1.129, 4.133.

1.109. *Selected Writings of Bahá'u'lláh.* Wilmette, Ill.: Bahá'í Publishing Committee, 1942. 43 p. LC card 45–1691.
  91 passages from 1.25, 1.37, 1.57, 1.77, 1.100, 5.1 and 5.149, arranged by theme.

1.110. *idem.* Wilmette, Ill.: Bahá'í Publishing Trust, 1967, 1975. 40 p.

1.111. *idem.* 1st cloth ed. Wilmette, Ill.: Bahá'í Publishing Trust, 1979. xiii, 128 p. LC card 79–15136.

1.112. *Seven Valleys.* trans. Julie Chanler from the French version of Hippolyte Dreyfus. New York: New History Foundation, 1933. 37 p.

1.113. *The Seven Valleys.* trans. Ali Kuli Khan. Chicago: Bahai Publishing Society, 1906, n.d. [between 1906 and 1914?], 1914. 55 p.

1.114. *The Seven Valleys and the Four Valleys.* trans. Ali Quli Khan. New York: Bahá'í Publishing Committee, 1936, 1937. 60 p. LC card 36–20412 rev.

1.115. *The Seven Valleys and the Four Valleys.* trans. Ali Kuli Khan and Marzieh Gail. rev. ed. Wilmette, Ill.: Bahá'í Publishing Committee, 1945, 1948. LC card 75–295121. [4], 62 p.; 1952, 1954. xviii, 62 p. LC card 53–12275.
  The Seven Valleys was written in response to questions from a Persian student of Sufi philosophy. It catalogues the seven stages of the soul's journey toward God. *The Four Valleys*, revealed subsequently to another questioner, elucidates further mystical concepts.

1.116. *idem.* Wilmette, Ill.: Bahá'í Publishing Trust, 1957, 1963, 1967, 1968, 1971, 1975. xviii, 62 p. LC card 76–356964.

1.117. *idem.* 3rd rev. ed. Wilmette, Ill.: Bahá'í Publishing Trust, 1978, 1984. xiii, 65 p. LC card 77–23326.

1.118. *Short Obligatory Prayer.* Johannesburg: National Spiritual Assembly of the Bahá'ís of South and West Africa, 1984, 2 p. card.

1.119. *Some Utterances of Bahá'u'lláh.* London: Bahai Library, n.d. [between 1910 and 1930]. viii p.

1.120. *The Source of Spiritual Qualities.* New York: Bahá'í Publishing Committee, n.d. [1924?]. 4 p.

1.121. *The Sun of Truth Is the Word of God: Passages from the Writings of Bahá'u'lláh.* [Victoria]: National Teaching Committee of the National Spiritual Assembly of the Bahá'ís of the Cameroon, n.d. [1981] 13 p.

1.122. *Surat'ul-Hykl: Sura of the Temple.* Chicago: Behais Supply and Publishing Board, 1900. 63 p.
  The only full English translation of a Tablet in which Bahá'u'lláh discusses his own station as God's 'temple'.
  See 1.36.

1.123. *The Tablet of Aḥmad.* n.p. [Port-of-Spain: National Spiritual Assembly of the Bahá'ís of Trinidad and Tobago], n.d. [1980] 4 p.

1.124. *The Tablet of Aḥmad.* Hofheim-Langenhain: Bahá'í-Verlag, n.d. [1982?] [8], 6 p.

1.125. *Tablet of Ishrakat (Effulgences), Preceded by the Tablet on the Most Great Infallibility.* trans. Ali-Kuli Khan. Chicago: Bahai Publishing Society, 1908. 45 p. LC card 19–9815 rev.

1.126. *Tablet of Tarazat, Tablet of the World, Words of Paradise, Tablet of Tajalleyat, The Glad Tidings, Revealed by Baha'u'llah at Acca.* trans. Ali Kuli Khan. Chicago: Bahai Publishing Society, 1906, 1913. 92 p. LC card 19–9816 rev.
  A few Tablets revealed subsequent to the *Kitáb-i-Aqdas. See* 1.135.

1.127. *The Tablet of the Branch.* n.p., n.d. [190–?] 7 p.
  Tablet in which Bahá'u'lláh extols his son, 'Abdu'l-Bahá, and foreshadows his appointment of 'Abdu'l-Bahá as Centre of the Covenant.

1.128. *The Tablet of the Holy Mariner = Lawḥ-i-Mallḥu'l-Quds. Fire Tablet = Lawḥ-i-Qad Iḥtaraqa'l-Mukhliṣún.* Hofheim-Langenhain: Bahá'í-Verlag, 1985. [84] p.
  See 1.5, 1.30–1.34, 1.107–1.108, 4.133.

1.129. *The Tablet of the Holy Mariner. The Tablet of Fire.* n.p. [Germany: Sa'íd Mu'tamid], n.d. [1980]. 80 p.
  See 1.5, 1.30–1.34, 1.107–1.108, 4.133.

1.130. *The Tablet of the World, 'the Great Message': From the Supreme Pen Beha'u'llah, Revealed at Acca, Syria.* Chicago: Chicago Behai Center, 1931. 20 p.
  Version translated and published by Behaists, followers of I.G. Kheiralla.

1.131. *Tablet of Wisdom Revealed by Bahá'u'lláh.* n.p., n.d. [191–?]. 15 leaves.

Tablet supplementary to the *Kitáb-i-Aqdas*, which deals with the interrelationship of philosophy and religion. Authorized translation in 1.134.

1.132. *Tablet to Pope Pius IX.* [Toronto, Ont.]: National Spiritual Assembly of the Bahá'ís of Canada, 1958. [2] p.

1.133. *Tablets of Baha'o'llah Revealed at Acca, Syria: Tablet of Tarazat, Tablet of the World, Words of Paradise, Tablet of Tajalleyat, the Glad Tidings, The Tablet of Ishrekat, Preceded by the Tablet on the Most Great Infallibility.* trans. Ali Kuli Khan. Chicago: Bahai Publishing Society, 1917. 137 p. LC card 40–10148.

Several Tablets revealed subsequently to the *Kitáb-i-Aqdas*. See annotation for 1.134.

1.134. *Tablets of Bahá'u'lláh Revealed After the Kitáb-i-Aqdas.* comp. the Research Department of the Universal House of Justice. trans. Habib Taherzadeh. Haifa: Bahá'í World Centre, 1978. vi, 276 p.

Sixteen important Tablets revealed by Bahá'u'lláh after the fundamental laws of his dispensation were announced in the *Kitáb-i-Aqdas*, and supplementary to that book, are collected here. Several had been translated into English on the instructions of 'Abdu'l-Bahá and published in 1917 (*see* 1.133). It became clear, after the appearance of Shoghi Effendi's incomparable translations, that these early renderings could be improved upon. Therefore, the Universal House of Justice commissioned this volume containing new authorized translations. No index, several misattributions of recipients.

1.135. *idem.* Lightweight ed. Haifa: Bahá'í World Centre, 1982. vi, 298 p.

Corrected, with excellent index.

1.136. *Tajalli.* New Delhi: National Spiritual Assembly of the Bahá'ís of India, n.d. [196–]. 15 p.

One of the Tablets supplementary to the *Kitáb-i-Aqdas*. Authoritative translation included in 1.134.

1.137. *Three Obligatory Daily Prayers.* trans. Shoghi Effendi. New York: Bahá'í Publishing Committee, 1937, 1940. 14 p.

1.138. *Three Spiritual Truths for a World Civilization.* Wilmette, Ill.: Bahá'í Publishing Committee, n.d. [193–?] 8 p.

1.139. *Three Tablets of Baha'o'llah, Revealed at Adrianople, Acca, and Bagdad: Tablet of the Branch, Kitab-el-Ah'd, Lawh-el-Akdas.* trans. Ali Kuli Khan. Chicago: Bahai Publishing Society, 1918. pp. 141–67.

Two Tablets relating to 'Abdu'l-Bahá and one addressed to Christians.

See 1.15, 1.76, 1.87, 1.127.

1.140. *Tokens from the Writings of Bahá'u'lláh.* comp. Jay and Constance Conrader. Wilmette, Ill.: Bahá'í Publishing Trust, 1973, 1975. 80 p. LC card 73–78441.

A selection of Bahá'u'lláh's writings, with accompanying photographs of natural scenes.

1.141. *Words of Bahá'u'lláh.* n.p., n.d. [before 1940?]. [2] p.

1.142. *Words of Wisdom.* San Francisco, Calif.: Paul Elder & Company, n.d. [1910?] 6 p.

1.143. *Words of Wisdom, and Selections from Hidden Words of Bahá'u'lláh.* n.p. [Kuala Lumpur: Bahá'í Publishing Trust Committee of the Spiritual Assembly of the Bahá'ís of Malaysia], n.d. [1983?] 11 p.

See 1.3, 1.29, 1.49–1.73.

II
The Writings of the Báb

THE BÁB was born Siyyid 'Alí Muhammad in 1819 into a merchant class family of Shíráz, Iran. As a youth he was known for his piety and devotion. In 1844 he claimed to be the bearer of a new revelation, specifically fulfilling a number of promises of Islam, particularly of the Shí'í branch of Islam. During his meteoric career the Báb gained a substantial following and attracted the attention of clergy and state. The challenge of the Bábí Faith to Shí'í orthodoxy (which claimed that no Manifestation of God could possibly appear after Muhammad) led to clashes with the entrenched reactionary elements of Iranian society. A number of upheavals involving the Báb's supporters and the army, together with the rapid spread of the religion, made the clergy and state determined to stamp out the new movement. The Báb himself was martyred in 1850, and within a few years the top ranks of the movement had been all but destroyed. Only a handful from among the leadership of the community survived.

The Báb revealed a number of major works, in Arabic and Persian, which Bahá'ís regard as sacred scripture, though second in rank to the works of Bahá'u'lláh. His major theme was the imminent appearance of 'Him Whom God Shall Make Manifest', the Manifestation of God who would fulfil the promises of all the revealed religions of the past. Bahá'ís regard Bahá'u'lláh as having fulfilled this promise.

2.1. *The Báb's Address to the Letters of the Living.* New York: Bahá'í Publishing Committee, n.d. [193–] 5 leaves.

Address recorded by Nabíl in *The Dawn-Breakers* in which the Báb charges his first 18 disciples to spread his message.

2.2. *idem.* Wilmette, Ill.: Bahá'í Publishing Committee, 1949. 5 leaves.

2.3. *idem.* Wilmette, Ill.: Bahá'í Publishing Committee, 1953. 4 p.

2.4. *idem.* Wilmette, Ill.: Bahá'í Publishing Trust, n.d. [196–?] 6 p.

2.5. *A Compilation of Passages from the Writings of the Báb.* comp. Universal House of Justice. New Delhi: Bahá'í Publishing Trust, 1980. 56 p.

2.6. *idem.* [Manila]: Bahá'í Publishing Trust of the Philippines, 1980. 35, 2 p.

2.6a. *O My Beloved Friends! You are the bearers of the name of God in this Day.* n.p. [United States], n.d. [197–] [1] leaf.

2.7. *Selections from the Writings of the Báb.* comp. Research Department of the Universal House of Justice. trans. Habib Taherzadeh. Haifa: Bahá'í World Centre, 1976, 1978. vii, 223 p. LC card 79–670141.

Review:
Bush, Richard C. *New Review of Books and Religion* (New York), v. 2 no. 9 (May 1978).

The first compiled volume of authorized translations of writings of the Báb. Without index.

2.8. *idem.* Lightweight ed. Haifa: Bahá'í World Centre, 1982. vii, 235 p.

Corrected, with an excellent index.

2.9. *Some Prayers of the Báb.* [London]: Bahá'í Education Committee of the National Spiritual Assembly of the Bahá'ís of the United Kingdom, n.d. [1981?] [4] p.

III
The Writings of 'Abdu'l-Bahá

'ABDU'L-BAHÁ (1844–1921), the son of Bahá'u'lláh, shared his father's exiles and imprisonment. He was given a complete grounding in the verities of the Bahá'í Faith by his father and was named its head in Bahá'u'lláh's Will. 'Abdu'l-Bahá has a station unique in religious history in that he is not only the interpreter of the Bahá'í teachings, but also their perfect exemplar. While he is not a Manifestation of God, 'Abdu'l-Bahá cannot be regarded merely as another human being. His writings are regarded as holy writ, standing next in rank to the works of Bahá'u'lláh and the Báb.

Most of 'Abdu'l-Bahá's works were in the form of letters or 'Tablets' to believers in Persian, Arabic and Turkish, although there is also extensive record of his talks and other verbal reports. Bahá'ís regard 'Abdu'l-Bahá's written works as having most authenticity, followed by records of his talks for which reliable Persian transcriptions are held, and finally other reports of his words such as those remembered by pilgrims.

3.1. *'Abdu'l-Bahá in Canada.* comp. National Spiritual Assembly of the Bahá'ís of Canada. [Toronto, Ont.]: National Spiritual Assembly of the Bahá'ís of Canada, 1962. 64 p.

Includes his addresses in Montreal, letters addressed to Canada, and newspaper reports of his Canadian sojourn.

3.2. *'Abdu'l-Bahá in Edinburgh.* comp. National Spiritual Assembly of the Bahá'ís of the British Isles. London: National Spiritual Assembly of the Bahá'ís of the British Isles, 1963. 19 p.

Includes 'Abdu'l-Bahá's address in Edinburgh, excerpts taken from *The Chosen Highway* describing his visit there, and an exchange of letters in a Scottish newspaper regarding the wisdom of allowing 'Abdu'l-Bahá to use public forums in Scotland.

3.3. *Abdul-Baha in London.* [comp. Eric Hammond]. London: Longmans Green & Co., 1912. xiv, 134 p.

Public addresses delivered by 'Abdu'l-Bahá in London, plus a number of notes of conversations. While the absence of original Persian texts for most of these reports makes it impossible to verify 'Abdu'l-Bahá's words, this volume gives a sample of the range of 'Abdu'l-Bahá's discourse and the interest of the British in the Bahá'í Faith.

3.4. *idem.* East Sheen, Surrey: The Unity Press, 1912. xiv, 134 p. LC card 18–12995 rev.

3.5. *idem.* Chicago: Bahai Publishing Society, 1921. xiv, 134 p.

3.6. *'Abdu'l-Bahá in London.* London: Bahá'í Publishing Trust, 1982. 127 p.
Same as 3.3 with new typography.

3.7. *Abdul Baha in New York, the City of the Covenant, April–December 1912.* New York: Bahai Assembly, 1922. 79 p.
Compiled talks given by 'Abdu'l-Bahá in New York City.

3.8. *idem.* 2nd ed. New York: Bahá'í Publishing Committee, 1931. x, 77 p.

3.9. *Abdul Baha on Divine Philosophy.* comp. Isabel Fraser Chamberlain. Boston: The Tudor Press, 1916. 161 p. LC card 18–12993 rev.
A collection of wisdom attributed to 'Abdu'l-Bahá. Sources are not indicated for most of the items and some of the quotations are questionable, thus lessening the value of this compilation. It does, nevertheless, give a sense of how early Western Bahá'ís were introduced to the teachings of their faith.

3.10. *idem.* Boston: The Tudor Press, c1917, c1918. 184 p.

3.11. *idem.* Boston: The Tudor Press, c1918. 189 p. LC card 18–12992 rev.

3.12. *idem.* comp. Soraya Chamberlain. New York: Bahá'í Publishing Committee, c1918 [i.e. 1928?] 189 p.

3.12a. *Abdul Baha's Words to His Loved Ones in London, in Regard to the War Raging in Tripoli Between Italy and Turkey.* London: Unity Press, n.d. [191–?] 4 p.

3.13. *Address by Abdul-Baha delivered at New York City, July 5, 1912.* New York; Washington; Chicago: Bahai Assembly, n.d. [1912?] 8 p.

3.14. *Address by Abdul-Baha at the Bowery Mission, 227 Bowery, New York City, Friday Evening, April 19th, 1912.* New York: Andrew Hutchinson, n.d. [1913?] 5 p.

3.15. *Address of Abdul Baha on the International Language, Esperanto, Delivered in Edinburgh.* Schaller, Iowa: United States Esperanto Association n.d. [after 1913] [4] p.

3.16. *America's Spiritual Mission.* [trans. Ahmad Sohrab]. New York: Bahá'í Publishing Committee, 1936. 54 p.
First edition of *Tablets of the Divine Plan.*
See 3.154–3.156, 7.2432.

3.17. *idem.* Wilmette, Ill.: Bahá'í Publishing Committee, 1948. 54 p.

3.18. *Appendix to London 1908 Edition, Some Answered Questions, Collected and Translated from the Persian by Laura Clifford Barney: Subject, Strikes.* Chicago: Bahai Publishing Society, 1918. pp. 313–318.
See 3.117–3.129.

3.18a. *Baha Pleads for Nations League: Leader of Cult Founded on Brotherhood of Man Writes from Syria to Ex-Governor Sulzer.* trans. Dr Zia M. Bagdadi. n.p. [United States], 1919. [1] p. Reprinted from: *New York World* (Oct. 6, 1919).

3.19. *A Bahá'í Child's Illustrated Prayerbook.* arranged by the Child Education Committee; il. Mervyn Jones. Sydney, N.S.W.: National Spiritual Assembly of the Bahá'ís of Australia and New Zealand, 1952. 8 leaves.

3.20. *Bahá'í Faith, the Circle of Unity.* [Auckland]: National Spiritual Assembly of the Bahá'ís of New Zealand, 1969. [2] p.

3.21. *The Bahá'í Peace Program.* New York: Bahá'í Publishing Committee, 1930. 48 p. LC card 30–11396 rev.

3.22. *Bahá'í Peace Programme: Addresses Given by 'Abdu'l-Bahá in Paris in 1912.* Karachi: National Spiritual Assembly of the Bahá'ís of Pakistan, n.d. [after 1965] 36 p.

3.23. *Blessed Is He Who Is Charitable . . .* n.p., n.d. [193–?] 1 p.

3.24. *Christians, Jews and Muhammadans.* New York: Bahá'í Publishing Committee, 1939. 7 p. (Bahá'í Reprint; no.2).

3.25. *idem.* Wilmette, Ill.: Bahá'í Publishing Committee, 1940, 1945. 7 p. (Bahá'í Reprint; no.2).

3.26. *Christ's Promise Fulfilled.* Wilmette, Ill.: Bahá'í Publishing Committee, 1954. 76 p.
Excerpts from *Some Answered Questions.*
See 3.130.

3.27. *idem.* Wilmette, Ill.: Bahá'ı Publishing Trust, 1959, 1963, 1970, 1973, 1975, 1977, 1978, 1980, 1981. 76 p.

3.28. *The Commands of Our Blessed Master Abdul-Baha, as Revealed in Tablets and Instructions for the Beloved in America.* Rangoon, Burma: Bahai Assembly, n.d. [191–?] [4] p.

3.29. *Commune Revealed by 'Abdu'l-Bahá, Feb-* ruary 3, 1917: *From Tablet to the Believers of God and the Maidservants of the Merciful of the Southern States.* n.p., n.d. [193–?] 1 p.

3.30. *idem.* trans. March 27, 1919, Ahmad Sohrab. Washington, D.C., 1919. [3] p.

3.31. *Commune Revealed February 8, 1917: From Tablet to the Believers and the Maid-servants of God in the Central States.* trans. Ahmad Sohrab. n.p., n.d. [1919?] 3 p.

3.32. *A Compilation of Passages from the Words of 'Abdu'l-Bahá.* [Manila]: Bahai Publishing Trust of the Philippines, 1980. 38 p.

3.33. *idem.* New Delhi: Bahá'í Publishing Trust, 1980. 58 p.

3.34. *A Compilation of Tablets and Words Pertaining to the Center of the Covenant of God on Violation.* comp. Mrs H. Emogene Hoagg. n.p., n.d. [191–] 26 leaves.

3.35. *Compilation of Utterances from the Pen of Abdul Baha Regarding His Station.* n.p., Nov. 29, 1906. 19 p.

3.36. *Conversation, February 26, 1899, at Acca: Answers in Reply to Various Questions.* n.p., 1899 [possibly 1900?] [3] p.

3.37. *Definition of Love by Abdul Baha.* New York, Dec. 7, 1902.

3.38. *Ditemana tse di Tswang mo Mekwalong ya seBahá'í ka ga Tekatekano ya Banna le Basadi = Selections from the Baha'i Writings on the Equality of Men and Women.* Ganorone [i.e. Gaborone]: Spiritual Assembly of the Baha'is of Botswana, 1975. 14 p. Tswana and English text.

3.39. *The Divine Art of Living.* comp. Mary M. Rabb. Chicago: Bahai News Service, 1924. [188] p. in various pagings.
Bound set of issues of *Star of the West*, v.7 no.16 (Dec. 31, 1916) – v.8 no.13 (Nov. 4, 1917) which contained the Rabb compilation. Bound in leather.

3.40. *The Divine Art of Living.* comp. Mary M. Rabb. New York: Brentano's, 1926. xv, 191 p. LC card 26–9783 rev.

3.41. *Divine Pearls from the Tablets of Abdul Baha.* Montclair, N.J.: Mission Press, n.d. [possibly between 1909 and 1916]. 14 p.

3.42. *idem.* Montclair, N.J.: Mission Press, n.d. [possibly 1916] 33 p.

3.43. *Excerpts from Mysterious Forces of Civilization, Written by an Eminent Bahai Philosopher in 1875: Excerpts from A Traveler's Narrative Written to Illustrate the Episode of the Bab.* n.p., n.d. [191–?] 7 p.

3.44. *Excerpts from the Will and Testament of 'Abdu'l-Bahá.* comp and ed. National Spiritual Assembly of the Bahá'ís of the British Isles. Manchester, U.K.: Bahá'í Publishing Trust, 1950. 27 p. Cover title: *The Will and Testament of 'Abdu'l-Bahá.*
 See 3.45, 3.113, 3.199–3.204.

3.45. *Excerpts from the Will & Testament of Abdu'l Baha.* Delhi: National Spiritual Assembly of the Bahais of India & Burma, n.d. [195–?] (New Delhi: Bahai Publishing Committee). 13 p.
 See 3.44, 3.113, 3.199–3.204.

3.46. *Exhortation: Words of the Master Abdul-Baha Abbas.* n.p. [Washington, D.C.?: Remey?], n.d. [191–?] [3] p.

3.47. *Faith for Every Man.* London: Bahá'í Publishing Trust, 1972. 80 p.

3.48. *Farewell Message.* n.p. [United States]: Curtis D. Kelsey, n.d. [193–?] [4] p.

3.49. *Foundations of World Unity.* comp. Horace Holley. New York: World Unity Publishing Corp., 1927. 112 p.
 Selections from public addresses delivered by 'Abdu'l-Bahá during his journey through Europe and America in 1911–13.

3.50. *idem.* New York: Bahá'í Publishing Committee, 1936. 112 p.

3.51. *idem.* Wilmette, Ill.: Bahá'í Publishing Committee, 1945. 178 p.

3.52. *idem.* Wilmette, Ill.: Bahá'í Publishing Trust, 1955, 1968, 1971, 1979. 112 p. LC card 68–5946.

3.53. *From Abdul Baha to a Lady Who Visited Acre in Feb., 1906.* Edinburgh: T & A Constable, 1907. 7 p.
 See 3.54.

3.54. *From Abdul Baha to A Lady Who Visited Acre in February, 1906.* trans. Monever Khanum. London: The Unity Press, 1907. 5 p.
 See 3.53.

3.55. *From the Divine Art of Living.* n.p., n.d. [193– or 194–?] [6] p.

3.56. *He Is a True Baha'i* . . . n.p., n.d. [195–?] [4] p. Quotation is said to be from 'Tablet of East and West'.

3.57. *He Is God.* n.p. [Chicago? : Bahai Publishing Society?], n.d. [191–?] 3 p.

3.58. *He Is God: O Lord My God! O Thou Helper of the Feeble* . . . n.p. [Mona Vale, N.S.W.: National Spiritual Assembly of the Bahá'ís of Australia], n.d. [1983] 1 p.
 Prayer for the martyrs and their relatives.

3.59. *He Is God! O Ye Children of the Kingdom!* n.p., n.d. [191–?] [4] p.
 Greatest Name on cover; Naw-Rúz Tablet and talk given at Ramleh, with photograph of 'Abdu'l-Bahá.

3.60. *He Is the All-Glorious!* calligraphy by J. Randall Dighton. n.p. [United States: Dighton], n.d. [197–] 1 p.
 Tablet of Visitation executed in a calligraphic design in the shape of 'Abdu'l-Bahá's face.

3.61. *A Heavenly Feast: Some Utterances of Abdul-Baha to Two American Pilgrims, in Acca, Syria, February 1909.* interpreter Dr Ameen U. Fareed (taken verbatim stenographically by M. H.). n.p. [United States], 1910 [see note at foot of title page] 36 p.
 Talks to Charles and Mariam Haney.

3.62. *The Image of God: Address Delivered at the Fourth Annual Conference of the National Association for the Advancement of Colored People, Chicago, April 30, 1912.* New York: Bahá'í Publishing Committee, 1939. 4 p. (Bahá'í Reprint; no. 1).

3.63. *idem.* Wilmette, Ill.: Bahá'í Publishing Committee, 1940, 1943. 4 p. (Bahá'í Reprint; no. 1).

3.64. *In Commemoration of the Declaration of His Holiness the Bab, 1844–1920: Tablet Revealed by Abdul Baha.* Washington, D.C., 1920. [4] p.

3.65. *In the Name of the Lord! O Lord My God and My Haven in My Distress.* n.p., n.d. [before 1950?] 2 p.

3.66. *Industrial Justice.* New York: Bahá'í Publishing Committee, 1940. 7 p. (Bahá'í Reprint; no. 3).

3.67. *idem.* Wilmette, Ill.: Bahá'í Publishing Committee, 1941, 1946. 7 p. (Bahá'í Reprint; no. 3).

3.68. *Letter and Tablet from Abdul Baha to the Central Organization for a Durable Peace, The Hague.* Chicago: Bahai Publishing Society, 1920. 15 p.
 'Abdu'l-Bahá's letter on the prerequisites for establishing permanent peace.
 See 3.145, 3.180.

3.69. *Letter from Abdul-Baha Abbas to the Friends in Persia.* trans. Ameen 'Ullah Fareed. Chicago: Bahai Publishing Society, Jan 21, 1906. 9 p.

3.70. *A Letter from St Jean d'Acre.* East Sheen, Eng.: Unity Press, 1906. [1], 5, [1] p.

3.70a. *idem.* n.p. [London]: T. and A. Constable, 1906. [1], 7, [1] p.

3.71. *Letter from the Master.* n.p., n.d. [1900?] [4] p.

3.72. *Letter of 'Love' from ABDUL-BAHA ABBAS to the 'Beloved' in America. Received by Mr George E. Witte at New York, December 7, 1902.* Chicago: Bahai Publishing Society, 1902, 3 p.

3.73. *Letters of Abdul Baha to the Children: Presented by Roshan on His First Birthday, December 29, 1909.* n.p. [Washington, D.C.?: Aseyeh Allen?], 1909. 16 p.

3.74. *Mashriqu'l-Adhkar: Quotations from Tablets and Talks of 'Abdu'l-Baha.* n.p., n.d. [192–?] [3] p.

3.75. *Memorials of the Faithful.* trans. Marzieh Gail. Wilmette, Ill.: Bahá'í Publishing Trust, 1971, 1975. xii, 208 p. LC card 77–157797.
   Brief biographical/hagiographical sketches of early followers of Bahá'u'lláh.
   Review:
   Theology Digest, v.20 no.4 (Winter 1972), p. 349.

3.76. *Messages from Abdul Baha to the Honolulu Bahais.* Honolulu, Hawaii: Advance Press, 1924. 14 p.

3.77. *idem.* Honolulu: National Spiritual Assembly of the Bahá'ís of the Hawaiian Islands, n.d. [196–], n.d. [197–] 14 p.
   Two variants: one is 15 cm., the other 13 cm., possibly published in the 1960s and the 1970s respectively.

3.78. *The Most Great Peace.* London: Bahá'í Publishing Trust, n.d. [1985] [4] p.

3.79. *The Mysterious Forces of Civilization.* trans. Johanna Dawud. London: Cope & Fenwick, 1910. 242 p.
   See 3.107.

3.80. *idem.* Chicago: Bahai Publishing Society, 1910, 1918. 131 p. LC card 19–71 rev.

3.81. *The Mystery of God.* comp. Mrs Iran F. Muhajer. New Delhi: Bahá'í Publishing Trust, 1971. 203 p.
   Released in commemoration of the 50th anniversary of 'Abdu'l-Bahá's passing. Quotations by and about 'Abdu'l-Bahá are taken from several sources. The major feature is the rich assortment of photographs of 'Abdu'l-Bahá.

3.82. *idem.* rev. ed. London: Bahá'í Publishing Trust, 1979. 327 p.
   Improved binding and printing, and further enrichment of the photographs, which are valuable despite frequent misidentifications.

3.83. *New Year's Greeting.* n.p. [Tokyo: Agnes Baldwin Alexander], n.d. [192–?] [4] p. Text in English and Japanese.

3.84. *O Pure Friends of God.* n.p. [New York or Chicago?], n.d. [1907?] [4] p.

3.85. *On Industrial Justice: A Basis of World Economy.* Wilmette, Ill.: Bahá'í Public Relations, 1946. [3] p.

3.86. *Paris Talks: Addresses Given by 'Abdu'l-Bahá in Paris in 1911–1912.* 9th ed. London: Bahá'í Publishing Trust, 1951. 184 p.
   Talks given by 'Abdu'l-Bahá during his sojourn in Paris from October to December 1911. As with other collections of talks by 'Abdu'l-Bahá, the topics covered are many and diverse.
   See 3.166–3.172, 3.205–3.206.

3.87. *idem.* 10th ed. London: Bahá'í Publishing Trust, 1961. 184 p.

3.88. *idem.* 11th ed. London: Bahá'í Publishing Trust, 1969, 1971, 1972, 1979. 184 p.

3.89. *idem.* 1st Indian ed. New Delhi: Bahá'í Publishing Trust, 1971. 184 p.

3.90. *Portion of a Tablet Explaining the Inscription upon the Ring-Stone.* n.p., n.d. [after 1913] 5 leaves.
   Dittoed compilation of Tablets regarding the Greatest Name and the ringstone symbol. Includes an essay by Thornton Chase entitled 'Greatest Name'.

3.91. *Portion of 'Letter of Love'.* n.p. [United States], n.d. [191–?] 4 p.

3.92. *Prayer for America.* n.p. [Wilmette, Ill.: National Spiritual Assembly of the Bahá'ís of the United States], n.d. [196–] [4] p.

3.93. *A Prayer for Canada. The Twelve Basic Bahá'í Principles.* Thornhill, Ont.: Bahá'í National Office, n.d. [197–?] [2] p.

3.94. *A Prayer for the Confirmation of the American Government.* n.p. [United States], n.d. [191–?] 1 p.

3.95. *Prayer, He Is God!.* n.p. [Washington, D.C.?], n.d. [1905?] 18 p.

3.96. *Prayers and Tablets, Abdul-Baha Abbas.* n.p., 1906. 16 p.

3.97. *The Principle of Religious Unity: For the Promotion of the Oneness of Mankind.* Wilmette, Ill.: Bahá'í Public Relations, 1946. [7] p.

3.98. *The Promulgation of Universal Peace.* [comp. Howard MacNutt]. Vol. I, Chicago: Bahá'í Publishing Committee, 1922; [New York]: Bahá'í Publishing Committee, 1922 [i.e. 1925]. vii, [29], 232, xiii p. Vol. II, New York: Bahá'í Publishing Committee, 1925. pp. 233–467, x p. LC card 31–18173 rev.
   Talks given by 'Abdu'l-Bahá during his travels

in North America in 1912. 'Abdu'l-Bahá tailored his talks to the capacities and backgrounds of his audiences, here providing a thorough review of Bahá'í belief and philosophy.

3.99. *idem.* [New York]: Bahá'í Publishing Committee, 1922 [i.e. 1939]. 2 v. in 1 (vii, 1–232, xiii, 233–467, x p.).

3.100. *idem.* Wilmette, Ill.: Bahá'í Publishing Committee, 1943. 2 v. in 1 (vii, 1–232, xiii, 233–467, x p.).

3.101. *idem.* 2nd ed. Wilmette, Ill.: Bahá'í Publishing Trust, 1982. xx, 513 p. LC card 81–21689.

3.102. *The Reality of Man.* comp. Horace Holley. New York [intro.]: Publishing Committee of the National Spiritual Assembly of the Bahá'ís of the United States and Canada, 1931. viii, 51 p.

3.103. *The Reality of Religion: Words of Abdul Baha.* New York: Bahá'í Publishing Committee, n.d. [1924?] 4 p.

3.104. *Religious and Political Peace.* by Abdul Baha Abbas. *The New Thought and the New Age.* by Ellis B. Guild. New York: Roger Bros., 1912. 13 p.

3.105. *Revealed by the Master.* n.p., n.d. [191–?] 1 p.
Text begins: 'O ye real friends who long for the beauty of God!'

3.106. *Sacred Tablet to Miss Fanny Knobloch, Washington, D.C.* n.p., n.d. [1920?] 3 p.

3.107. *The Secret of Divine Civilization.* trans. Marzieh Gail. Wilmette, Ill.: Bahá'í Publishing Trust, 1957. xi, 116 p. LC card 56–12427.
Earlier issued as *The Mysterious Forces of Civilization* by another translator, this was 'Abdu'l-Bahá's message to the government, clergy and people of Iran on the requirements of true civilization. It applies as well to the present as mankind's traditional political and social philosophies have shown themselves incapable of renewing human civilization.
See 3.79–3.80.

3.108. *idem.* 2nd ed. Wilmette, Ill.: Bahá'í Publishing Trust, 1970. xi, 126 p. LC card 73–14895.
Review:
Theology Digest, v.20, no.4 (Winter 1972), p. 349.

3.109. *idem.* 2nd ed. Wilmette, Ill.: Bahá'í Publishing Trust, 1975. ix, 126 p.
Identified on verso of title page as second printing of 2nd ed., but introduction has been shortened.

3.110. *idem.* 3rd ed. Wilmette, Ill.: Bahá'í Publishing Trust, 1979, 1983. ix, 126 p.
Indicates on verso of title page that 1975

printing was actually the 3rd ed. of which these are the second and third printings.

3.111. *Selected Writings of 'Abdu'l-Bahá.* Wilmette, Ill.: Bahá'í Publishing Committee, 1942. 44 p. LC card 45–13012.

3.112. *idem.* [Suva]: National Spiritual Assembly of the Bahá'ís of the Fiji Islands, n.d. [197–] 20 p.

3.113. *Selections from the Will and Testament of 'Abdu'l-Bahá.* Wilmette, Ill.: Bahá'í Publishing Committee, 1948. 20 p.
This is the 1948 printing of items 3.199 and 3.201. The title has been changed to reflect the fact that the publication was not the full text of the Will and Testament.
See also 3.44, 3.199–3.204.

3.114. *Selections from the Writings of 'Abdu'l-Bahá.* comp. Research Dept. of the Universal House of Justice; trans. by a Committee at the Bahá'í World Centre and Marzieh Gail. Haifa: Bahá'í World Centre, 1978. vi, 325 p. LC card 79–670256.
Not since the publication of *Tablets of Abdul Baha Abbas* (1909–16) had any large compilation in English of 'Abdu'l-Bahá's correspondence been made. Many of the letters in that earlier work have here been re-translated, in addition to the inclusion of previously untranslated ones. No index.

3.115. *idem.* Lightweight ed. Haifa: Bahá'í World Centre, 1982. vi, 345 p.
Corrected, with an excellent index.

3.116. *Soldiers of the World! Strike!.* [Attributed to 'Abdu'l-Bahá by Ahmad Sohrab]. New York: New History Society, n.d. [193–] [4] p.

3.117. *Some Answered Questions.* comp. Laura Clifford Barney. London: Kegan, Paul, Trench, Trübner & Co., 1908. xiv, 344 p. LC card 33–28644 rev.
Laura Clifford Barney, the translator and compiler, visited 'Abdu'l-Bahá in the Holy Land between 1904 and 1906, putting to him a variety of questions on Christian, philosophical and doctrinal subjects. The answers, which 'Abdu'l-Bahá says were given in 'my tired moments', make one of the unique volumes of scripture in the corpus of the world's religious literature.

3.118. *idem.* Philadelphia: J.B. Lippincott Company; London: K. Paul, Trench, Trübner & Co., 1908. xiv, 344 p. LC card 9–4927 rev.

3.119. *idem.* 2nd ed. Chicago: Bahai Publishing Society, 1918. xiv, 350 p. LC card 19–1045 rev.

3.120. *idem.* 3rd ed. New York: Bahá'í Publishing Committee, 1930. xiv, 350 p.

3.121. *idem.* 4th ed. New York: Bahá'í Publishing Committee, 1937. xiv, 350 p. LC card 40–10145 rev.

3.122. *idem.* 5th ed. Wilmette, Ill.: Bahá'í Publishing Committee, 1943. xiv, 350 p.

3.123. *idem.* 6th ed. Wilmette, Ill.: Bahá'í Publishing Trust, 1947. xiv, 350 p.

3.124. *idem.* 7th ed. Wilmette, Ill.: Bahá'í Publishing Trust, 1954. xxv, 350 p. LC card 53–10766.

3.125. *idem.* 1964 ed. Wilmette, Ill.: Bahá'í Publishing Trust, 1964, 1968, 1970, 1971. xxi, 350 p. LC card 64–55340.

3.126. *idem.* [1981 ed.] Wilmette, Ill.: Bahá'í Publishing Trust, 1981, 1982. xviii, 324 p. LC card 81–2467.
Some passages quoted from Bahá'u'lláh have been changed to authorized translations in this ed. Added clarifying notes.

3.127. *idem.* [1981 ed.] Pocket-size ed. Wilmette, Ill.: Bahá'í Publishing Trust, 1984, 1985. xviii, 324 p.

3.128. *idem.* London: Bahá'í Publishing Trust, n.d. [196–] xiii, 292 p.

3.129. *idem.* New Delhi: Bahá'í Publishing Trust, 1973. xxi, 350 p.

3.130. *Some Christian Subjects.* London: Bahá'í Publishing Trust, 1946. 72 p.
Excerpts from *Some Answered Questions.*
See 3.26.

3.131. *Some Prayers of 'Abdu'l-Bahá.* [London]: Bahá'í Education Committee of the National Spiritual Assembly of the Bahá'ís of the United Kingdom, n.d. [1981] [4] p.

3.132. *Some Vital Bahäi Principles Compiled from the Words of Abdul-Baha.* Washington, D.C., n.d. [190–?] 8 p.

3.133. *idem.* Chicago: Bahai Publishing Society, n.d. [191–?] and n.d. [1920?] 8 p.

3.133a. *Soul, Spirit and Mind.* Oconomowoc, Wis.: National Committee on Bahá'í Questionnaires, n.d. [193–?] [1] leaf.

3.134. *The Spirit of World Unity: From the Addresses and Tablets of 'Abdu'l-Bahá.* New York: Bahá'í Publishing Committee, 1926. 22 p.

3.135. *The Spiritual Opportunity of the Bahá'ís of the United States and Canada.* New York: Bahá'í Publishing Committee, 1926. 19 p.

3.136. *Supplication: To the Believers of God and the Maid-Servants of the Merciful, Portland, Oregon.* Portland, Ore., n.d. [191–?] 1 p.

3.137. *Table Talks at Acca by Abdul Baha Abbas.* as expressed by Mirza Moneer and Mirza Nured-Din, interpreters; notes taken stenographically, transcribed and revised by Arthur S. Agnew. Chicago: Bahai Publishing Society, 1907. 23 p.

3.138. *Table Talks by Abdul Baha Taken Down in Persian by Mirza Hadi at Acca, Feb. 1907. Notes Taken by Corinne True.* trans. A.U. Fareed. Chicago: Bahai Publishing Society, 1907. 32 p. Cover title: *Notes Taken at Acca.*

3.139. *Table Talks with Abdel-Baha-Abbas Regarding Reincarnation, Mystery of Self-Sacrifice and Other Subjects.* n.p., n.d. [1900?] [14] p.

3.140. *A Tablet Concerning the Building of the Mashrak-el-Azkar, To the Friends and Maidservants of the Merciful in America.* n.p., n.d. [1908?] 7 p.

3.141. *Tablet Revealed to Louise Hopkins, John Alexander Hopkins, Elinore Hiscock* [et. al.]. n.p. [Washington, D.C.?: Remey?], n.d. [1906?] [2] leaves.

3.142. *Tablet Through the Mediation of His Honor Mirza Assad'ullah to the House of Justice, Chicago.* n.p., n.d. [1902?] [4] p.

3.143. *Tablet to the Beloved of God in America.* trans. Ali Kuli Khan. Cambridge, Mass., 1906.

3.144. *Tablet to the Beloved of God of the Occident.* trans. Ahmad Esphahani [Sohrab]. n.p., 1906. 16 p.

3.145. *Tablet to the Hague.* London: Bahá'í Publishing Trust, n.d. [195– or 196–] 12 p.
Abdu'l-Bahá's letter on the prerequisites for establishing permanent peace.
See 3.68, 3.180.

3.146. *Tablet, Translation: To the Bahais of God and the Maid-Servants of the Merciful, Upon Them Be Baha-ollah El Abha.* trans. Lotfullah S. Hakim. London, 1914. [4] p. Includes, pp. [2]–[4], translation of Tablet entitled *The Voice of Universal Peace.*
See 3.198.

3.147. *Tablets Containing General Instructions.* trans. M.A.E. [Mirza Ahmad Esphahani Sohrab]. Washington, D.C.: Bahai Assembly, 1907. 19 p.

3.148. *Tablets Containing Instructions.* trans. Mirza Ahmad Esphahani [Sohrab] and Ali Kuli Khan. Washington, D.C., 1906. 12 p.

3.149. *Tablets from Abdul Baha to E.E. Wrestling Brewster.* Washington, D.C., 1907. [8] p.

3.150. *Tablets from Abdul Baha Abbas to Some American Believers in the Year 1900: The Truth*

Concerning A. Reincarnation, B. Vicarious Atonement, C. The Trinity, D. Real Christianity. New York: Board of Counsel, 1901. 14 p.

3.151. *Tablets of Abdul Baha Abbas.* [comp. Albert R. Windust]. Chicago: Bahai Publishing Society, Vol. I, 1909, 1912, 1919. viii, 238 p.; Vol. II, 1915, 1919. pp. 239–484; Vol. III, 1916, 1919. pp. 485–730. 3 v. (730 p.). LC card 19–5505 rev.

Letters by 'Abdu'l-Bahá to institutions and individual Bahá'ís in the United States and Canada, covering a wide range of topics. These unofficial translations have, in part, been superseded by item 3.115.

3.152. *idem.* New York: Bahá'í Publishing Committee, Vol. I, 1930; Vol. II, 1940; Vol. III, 1930. 3 v. (730 p.).

Indexes included but are quite inadequate.

3.153. *Tablets of Abdul Baha Received by the Persian American Educational Society and the Orient-Occident Unity.* trans. Mirza Ahmad Sohrab. Washington, D.C.: Persian American Educational Society, 1914. 8 p.

3.153a. *Tablets of 'Abdu'l-Bahá to Dr. Clement Woolson.* n.p. [United States?], n.d. [194–?] 3, 5, [1] leaves.

Privately produced collection, probably by the Woolson family.

3.154. *The Tablets of the Divine Plan.* 2nd ed. Wilmette, Ill.: Bahá'í Publishing Trust, 1959. 54 p.

Written during the first World War, these Tablets invest the Bahá'ís of the United States and Canada with an international mission to plant the Bahá'í Faith in all the countries of the globe. These directives for spreading the Bahá'í Faith are the charter for the international teaching plans launched by Shoghi Effendi and the Universal House of Justice.

See 3.16, 7.2432.

3.155. *idem.* 3rd ed. Wilmette, Ill.: Bahá'í Publishing Trust, 1962, 1965, 1969, 1971, 1974, 1975, 1976. 54 p.

3.156. *idem.* rev. ed. Wilmette, Ill.: Bahá'í Publishing Trust, 1977, 1980. xii, 107 p. LC card 76–10624.

3.157. *Tablets Revealed by Abdul Baha Abbas to the East and the West.* trans. Ahmad Esphahani [Sohrab]. Washington: Bahai Assembly of Washington, D.C., 1908. 35 p.

3.158. *Tablets Revealed by Abdul-Baha in Reference to the Erection of the Mashrek-el-Azkar (The Bahai Temple of Worship).* n.p., n.d. [after 1906] [4] p.

3.159. *Tablets Revealed by the Master Abdul Beha*

Abbas to the House of Justice at Chicago, to the Ladies' Assembly of Teaching, to Mirza Assad-'Ullah and to Other Individuals, also One to the Believers in Persia. Chicago: Press of the Hollister Bros., 1901. 16 p.

3.160. *Tablets to Japan.* [comp. Agnes Alexander]. New York: Bahá'í Publishing Committee, 1928. 15 p.

3.161. *A Talk Given by Abdul-Baha, from Notes Taken by L.A.C.B.* [Laura Clifford Barney]. Chicago: Bahai Publishing Society, n.d. [191–?] 4 p.

3.162. *Talk Given by the Master at the Home of Mrs Thornburgh-Cropper. September 13, 1911.* n.p.: Printed in Memory of the Wedding of Ursula Newman and Mehdi Samandari, 1951. 4 p.

3.163. *A Talk Given by the Master in Acca.* from notes taken by L.A.C.B. Rangoon, Burma, n.d. [191–?] (Rangoon: St Joseph's Press). [2] p.

3.164. *A Talk Given by the Master in Acca.* n.p., n.d. [192–?]. [2] p.

3.165. *idem.* n.p.: Howard Pr., n.d. [before 1940?] 3 p.

3.166. *Talks by Abdul Baha Given In Paris.* East Sheen, Surrey: The Unity Press, 1912. 176 p.

Review: The Moslem World (Hartford, Conn.), v.6 no.1 (Jan. 1916), p.105.

See 3.86–3.89, 3.205–3.206.

3.167. *idem.* Chicago: Bahai Publishing Society, 1912.

3.168. *idem.* 2nd ed. London: G. Bell & Sons, Ltd., 1915. 171 p. LC card 18–12994 rev.

3.169. *idem.* 3rd ed. London: G. Bell and Sons, 1916 (London: Norwich: London and Norwich Press). 171 p.

3.170. *idem.* 4th ed. London: G. Bell & Sons, Ltd., 1920. 171 p.

3.171. *idem.* 5th ed. London: G. Bell & Sons, Ltd., 1923. 171 p.

3.172. *idem.* supplementary historical note and introduction, [by Helen Pilkington Bishop] 5th ed. London: [G. Bell and Sons], 1936. xii, 171, viii p.

3.173. *This Radiant Age.* New Delhi: Bahá'í Publishing Trust, n.d. [196–?] 41 p.

Excerpts from 'Abdu'l-Bahá's talks in America.

3.174. *Through His Honor Mirza Ahmad Esphahani and Mr. Chas. T. Jones, to the Board of Counsel, New York City.* n.p. [Washington, D.C.?], n.d. [1907?] [3] p.

3.175. *To Aga Ahmad Yazdi (Upon Him Be the Glory of Abha).* n.p. [Washington, D.C.?: Remey?], n.d. [190–?] 1 p.

3.176. *To Live the Life.* n.p. [Malaysia?], n.d. [197–?] [4] p.
Back cover shows 'Ganesh 1594G.'

3.176a. *idem.* n.p. [Seoul, Korea?], n.d. [197–?] [4] p.

3.177. *To the Bahais in Persia, India, Turkey and Other Parts of the East.* trans. Mirza Ahmad Sohrab. Chicago, n.d. [1909?] 3 p.

3.178. *To the Beloved of God in General in America (Upon Them Be Baha Ullah).* n.p., n.d. [1906?] [8] p.

3.179. *To the Chicago Assembly: To the Kenosha Assembly.* Chicago: Hollister Bros., n.d. [190–?] 14 p.

3.180. *Translation of Abdul-Baha's Letter to the Central Organization for a Durable Peace at the Hague.* n.p., n.d. [1920 or 1921] 24 p.
'Abdu'l-Bahá's letter on the prerequisites for the establishment of permanent peace.
See 3.68, 3.145.

3.181. *A Traveller's Narrative Written to Illustrate the Episode of the Bab.* trans. Edward Granville Browne. Cambridge: Cambridge University Press, 1891. The 1891 ed. is in two volumes, the first of which is the Persian text (211 p.), the second the English translation and notes (liii, 447 p.). LC card 40–679.
A copy of this work, with no indication of authorship, was given to E.G. Browne, who published the Persian and his English translation, accompanied by a lengthy introduction and copious notes. It is an attempt to place early Bábí-Bahá'í history in the context of orthodox Bahá'í understanding in the 1880s.
Reviews:
Asiatic Quarterly Review (London), v.3 no.6 (1892), pp. 502–503.
Athenaeum (London), v.99 no.3370 (May 28, 1892), pp. 690–691.
The Calcutta Review, no.189 (July 1892), p. xxxvi.
'The Episode of the Bab,' *The Spectator* (London), v.68 (Apr. 23, 1892), pp. 560–561.
Nation (New York), v.54 no.1403 (May 18, 1892), p. 380.
Vambery, Arminius. *The Academy* (Syracuse, N.Y.), no. 1036 (Mar. 12, 1892), pp. 245–6.

3.182. *idem.* New York: Bahá'í Publishing Committee, 1930. liii, 447 p. LC card 40–15241.

3.183. *idem.* Amsterdam: Philo Press, 1975. liii, 447, 211 p. LC card 75–31695.

3.184. *idem.* New and corrected ed. Wilmette,

Ill.: Bahá'í Publishing Trust, 1980. v, 110 p. LC card 79–19025.
Browne's translation without the introduction and footnotes.

3.185. *True Belief.* n.p., n.d. [191–?] 4 p.

3.186. *idem.* n.p. [United States?]: Press of Geo. E. Howard, [191–?] [4] p.

3.187. *idem.* Chicago: Bahai Publishing Society, n.d. [191–?] [4] p.

3.188. *idem.* Rangoon, Burma, n.d. [191–?] (Rangoon: St Joseph's Press). [4] p.

3.189. *The True Gardener, a Talk Given By Abdul Baha.* comp. L.A.C.B. [Laura Clifford Barney]. Rangoon, Burma: Rangoon Standard Press, 1903.

3.190. *idem.* London: The Unity Press, n.d.

3.191. *idem.* n.p. [Washington, D.C.], n.d. [191–?] 7 p.

3.192. *idem.* from notes by L.A.C.B. [Laura Clifford Barney]. n.p. [United States?], n.d. [191–?] [8] p.

3.193. *Unity of Conscience, the Basis of Universal Peace.* Geneva: Bahá'í International Bureau, 1948. 37 p.
Excerpts from *Tablet to the Hague.* Text in English and French.

3.194. *Utterances of Abdul Beha Abbas to Two Young Men, American Pilgrims to Acre, 1901.* New York: Board of Counsel, 1901. 24 p.

3.195. *A Visiting Tablet Revealed for the Maidservant of God, Mrs. Amalie Knobloch, Who Has Ascended to the Kingdom of the Almighty.* n.p., n.d. [1910?] 3 p.

3.196. *idem.* n.p. [Washington, D.C.?], n.d. [1910?] 1 sheet (pp. 39–40).

3.197. *Visiting Tablets for Our Recent Martyrs Who Suffered in Persia in 1901, with Some Tablets and Prayers for the American Behais.* New York: Behais Board of Counsel, 1902. 32 p.

3.198. *The Voice of Universal Peace.* trans. by Mirza Ahmad Sohrab. n.p., n.d. [1914?] [4] p.
See 3.146.

3.199. *The Will and Testament of 'Abdu'l-Bahá.* New York: Bahá'í Publishing Committee, 1935, 1940. 20 p.
One of the charters of the World Order of Bahá'u'lláh in which the institution of the Guardianship is created and qualifications for succession clearly defined; the method of election of the Universal House of Justice is set out; the Secondary or National Spiritual Assembly

is instituted; and other details of the Bahá'í administrative order are set forth.
See 3.44–3.45, 3.113.

3.200. *idem.* Wilmette, Ill.: National Spiritual Assembly of the Bahá'ís of the United States and Canada, 1942. 17 leaves.

3.201. *idem.* Wilmette, Ill.: Bahá'í Publishing Committee, 1944. 20 p. LC card 45–14775.
See 3.113.

3.202. *idem.* Wilmette, Ill.: National Spiritual Assembly of the Bahá'ís of the United States, c1944. 26 p.

3.203. *idem.* Wilmette, Ill.: Bahá'í Publishing Committee, 1944, c1944 [before 1954] 26 p.
See 3.113.

3.204. *idem.* Wilmette, Ill.: Bahá'í Publishing Trust, c1944 [after 1954], 1968, 1971. 26 p.

3.205. *The Wisdom of Abdul Baha.* New York City: Bahá'í Publishing Committee, 1924 (Paulton, Somerset, Eng.: Purnell and Sons). 171 p.
See 3.86–3.89, 3.166–3.172.

3.206. *idem.* Wilmette, Ill.: Bahá'í Publishing Committee, n.d.

3.207. *Wisdom Talks of Abdul-Baha (Abbas Effendi) at Chicago, Illinois, April 30th to May 5th, 1912.* Chicago: Publishing Committee, 1912 (Chicago: Press of Bahai News Service). 22 p.

3.208. *Woman's Great Station in the Bahai Dispensation.* n.p., [1913]. 3 p.

3.209. *Words of Abdul Baha.* n.p., n.d. [191–?] 1 p.

3.210. *Words of Abdul Baha.* n.p., n.d. [before 1940?] 3 p.

3.211. *Words of Abdul-Baha Concerning the Mashrak-el-Azkar.* n.p., n.d. [191–?] 1 p.

3.212. *Words of Abdul-Baha in Tablets Recently Received Concerning the Laying of the Foundation of the Mashrekol-Azkar in America.* n.p., n.d. [1918?] [2] p.

3.213. *World Order Through World Faith.* Wilmette, Ill.: Bahá'í Publishing Committee, 1946. 32 p. LC card 46–8547.

IV
Works Compiled from the Writings of Bahá'u'lláh, the Báb and 'Abdu'l-Bahá

(including items with quotations from Shoghi Effendi and the Universal House of Justice)

A STRONG tradition of compiling relevant Bahá'í texts on a given subject has existed since the beginning of the Bahá'í Faith. The material included in this section ranges from general compilations to those on very specific topics, with quotations from the central figures of the Bahá'í Faith, the Guardian, the Universal House of Justice, and also from other relevant Bahá'í and non-Bahá'í sources where compilers have felt that the subject warranted their inclusion. The tracing of the original sources for many of the quotations in such compilations is often a serious problem; readers should be cautioned about the lack of authenticity for many of the quotations used in some compilations, and the importance of verifying the original source of any quotation before citing it. The primary sources for authentic and well-documented compilations are the Bahá'í World Centre and the major Bahá'í Publishing Trusts.

4.1. *Alláh'u'abhá!: A Selection of Baha'i Prayers.* comp. Kate Ball. San Diego, Calif.: Local Spiritual Assembly of the Bahá'ís of San Diego, 1980. 24 p.

4.2. *America's God-Given Mission: A Compilation for Round-Table Study.* Wilmette, Ill.: Bahá'í Publishing Committee, 1952. 49 p.

4.3. *Arise to Serve: A Compilation.* New Delhi: Bahá'í Publishing Trust, 1971. 122 p.
Includes compilations on the Local Spiritual Assembly and Bahá'í funds and contributions.

4.4. *Assurance of Immortality: Excerpts from the Words of Bahá'u'lláh and 'Abdu'l-Bahá.* New York: Bahá'í Publishing Committee, 1939. [2] p.

4.5. *idem.* Wilmette, Ill.: Bahá'í Publishing Committee, 1942. 4 p.

4.6. *Bahá'í Answers: A Compilation.* comp. Olivia Kelsey. Independence, Mo.: Lambert Moon Printers and Publishers, 1947. 258 p. LC card 47–27307.
Quotations from Bahá'í scripture grouped under a series of questions that might be asked by a student of the Bahá'í Faith.

4.7. *idem.* rev. 2nd ed. Independence, Mo.: Lambert Moon Printers and Publishers, c1947. 258 p.

4.8. *Bahá'í Code of Conduct: Selections from the Sacred Writings: Guidance Two, Proclamation.* 2nd ed. Kuala Lumpur: National Bahá'í Information Service, 1967. 40 p.

4.9. *Bahá'í Consultation.* comp. Universal House of Justice. [Auckland] National Spiritual Assembly of the Bahá'ís of New Zealand, 1978. 13 p.
See 4.10, 4.104–4.105, 4.141, 4.267.

4.10. *Bahá'í Consultation: The Lamp of Guidance.* comp. Universal House of Justice. Mona Vale, N.S.W.: Bahá'í Publications Australia, 1978. 20 p.
See 4.9, 4.104–4.105, 4.141, 4.267.

4.11. *Bahá'í Daybook: Passages for Deepening and Meditation.* Wilmette, Ill.: Bahá'í Publishing Trust, 1985, 1985. x, 374 p.
Selection of daily meditations from the Bahá'í writings, the Bible and the Qur'án, with explanations of difficult words and concepts.

4.12. *Bahá'í Education: A Compilation.* Wilmette, Ill.: Bahá'í Publishing Trust, 1977, 1978. xi, 77 p.
See 4.99–4.100.

4.13. *idem.* n.p. [Thornhill, Ont.]: Bahá'í Community of Canada, c1977. xi, 77 p.

4.14. *idem.* 1st Indian ed. New Delhi: Bahá'í Publishing Trust, 1984. xii, 129 p.

4.15. *Bahá'i Family Life.* Umtata: National

Spiritual Assembly of the Bahá'ís of Transkei, 1984. 15 leaves.

4.16. *Bahá'í Family Life: A Compilation.* comp. Mary K. Radpour. n.p., n.d. [196–?] 38, [3] p.

4.17. *Bahá'í Institutions: A Compilation.* New Delhi: Bahá'í Publishing Trust, 1973. 140 p.

4.18. *Bahá'í Marriage and Family Life: Selections from the Writings of the Bahá'í Faith.* Thornhill, Ont.: Bahá'í Canada Publications, 1983. 82 p.

4.19. *Bahá'í Meetings, the Nineteen Day Feast.* comp. the Universal House of Justice. Wilmette, Ill.: Bahá'í Publishing Trust, 1976, 1980. iii, 33 p.
   See 4.181, 4.250.

4.20. *The Bahai Message: From the Creative Words of Baha'o'llah and Abdul Baha.* Chicago: Bahai Publishing Society, 1920. 20 p.

4.21. *The Bahai Movement and Esperanto.* Schaller, Iowa: United States Esperanto Association, n.d. [after 1913] (New York: Hanover Press). [4] p.

4.22. *A Baha'i Perspective on Peace and Disarmament: A Compilation from the Baha'i Writings.* n.p. [Thornhill, Ont.: National Spiritual Assembly of the Bahá'ís of Canada], n.d. (1983?) 30 p.

4.23. *Bahá'í Prayers.* New York: Bahá'í Publishing Committee, 1927, 1929, 1929 [1936 with newer translations] 16 p.[1]

4.24. *Bahá'í Prayers.* New York: Bahá'í Publishing Committee, 1933. 34 p.; 1935, 1938. 40 p.

4.25. *Bahá'í Prayers.* Wilmette, Ill.: Bahá'í Publishing Committee, 1941, 1942, 1944, 1945, 1947. 72 p. LC card 41–22308.

4.26. *idem.* Wilmette, Ill.: Bahá'í Publishing Committee, 1949, 1952. 121 p.

4.27. *idem.* Wilmette, Ill.: Bahá'í Publishing Committee, 1954. 189 p. LC card 54–10901.
   The standard United States prayerbook for almost 30 years, comprising prayers of Bahá'u'lláh and 'Abdu'l-Bahá, with two prayers of the Báb. Divided into two sections of general and occasional prayers.

4.28. *idem.* Wilmette, Ill.: Bahá'í Publishing Trust, 1957, 1962, 1967, 1969, 1970, 1973, 1975, 1978, 1981. 189 p.

4.29. *idem.* [New, expanded and rev. ed.] Wilmette, Ill.: Bahá'í Publishing Trust, 1982, 1982 [i.e. 1983] ix, 276 p. LC card 82–11502.

The most recent standard United States prayerbook, rearranged, corrected, and with considerably more prayers by the Báb. Includes a first line index which is not arranged alphabetically by first line. Comes in soft cover, hard cover and deluxe bindings. Printing of 1983 has *Bahá'í Prayers* on the spine.

4.30. *Bahá'í Prayers.* 1985 ed. Wilmette, Ill.: Bahá'í Publishing Trust, 1985. ix, 277 p.
   Two more prayers added and first line index rearranged alphabetically.

4.31. *Bahá'í Prayers.* Wilmette, Ill.: Bahá'í Publishing Committee, 1954. 112 p.
   White prayerbook containing only the first section of what is included in 4.27.

4.32. *idem.* Wilmette, Ill.: Bahá'í Publishing Trust, 1962, 1967, 1970, 1974, 1978, 1979. 112 p.
   White prayerbook containing only the first section of what is included in 4.28.

4.33. *Bahá'í Prayers.* Mona Vale, N.S.W.: Bahá'í Publications Australia, 1982. xvi, 141 p.

4.34. *Bahai Prayers.* n.p. [Canada?], n.d. [196–?] 16 p.

4.35. *Bahá'í Prayers.* n.p. [Canada?], n.d. [1972?] [2] p. Mimeograph.

4.36. *Bahá'í Prayers.* Baker Lake, N.W.T.: Baker Lake Bahá'í Group, 1964, 13 p.

4.37. *Bahá'í Prayers.* Suva, Fiji: Bahá'í Publishing Trust, 1978. 18 p.

4.37a. *idem.* rev. [ed.] Suva, Fiji: Bahá'í Publishing Trust, 1985. [1], 16 p.

4.38. *Bahá'í Prayers.* Tallahassee, Fl.: Local Spiritual Assembly of the Bahá'ís of Tallahassee, n.d. [1970 or 1971] [8] p.

4.39. *Bahá'í Prayers.* n.p. [Kuala Lumpur]: Bahá'í Publishing Trust, 1970. 62 p.

4.40. *Baha'i Prayers.* Lagos, Nigeria: Baha'i Publishing Trust, 1984. xvi, 109 p.

4.41. *Bahá'í Prayers.* Manila: National Spiritual Assembly of the Bahá'ís of the Philippines, 1976. 23 p.

4.42. *Baha'i Prayers.* n.p. [Port-of-Spain]: National Spiritual Assembly of the Bahá'ís of Trinidad and Tobago, n.d. [1976]. 16 p.

4.43. *Bahá'í Prayers.* London: Bahá'í National Spiritual Assembly, 1927. 16 p.

4.44. *Bahá'í Prayers.* Lusaka: National Spiritual Assembly of the Bahá'ís of Zambia, 1979. 13 p.

4.45. *Bahá'í Prayers: A Selection.* London: Bahá'í Publishing Trust, n.d. [1939] 110 p.

---

1. A large number of compilations under the title *Bahá'í Prayers* have been published. Note the annotations for those that follow.

The standard British Bahá'í prayerbook. Selection of prayers is different from the American prayerbook and contains many older translations which have since been corrected.

4.46. *idem.* rev. ed. London: Bahá'í Publishing Trust, 1951. 107, 62 p.

4.47. *idem.* new ed. London: Bahá'í Publishing Trust, 1967. 107, 58 p.

4.48. *idem.* rev. ed. London: Bahá'í Publishing Trust, 1975. 108, 58 p.

4.49. *Bahá'í Prayers: A Selection.* London: Bahá'í Publishing Trust, 1945. 95 p.
Contains only the first section of 4.45–4.48.

4.50. *idem.* rev. ed. London: Bahá'í Publishing Trust, 1951. 107 p.
Contains only the first section of 4.45–4.48.

4.51. *idem.* rev. ed. London: Bahá'í Publishing Trust, 1975. 108 p.
Contains only the first section of 4.45–4.48.

4.52. *Bahá'í Prayers: A Selection.* rev. ed. New Delhi: Bahá'í Publishing Trust, 1970, 1976. 107, 58 p.
See 4.47.

4.53. *Bahá'í Prayers: A Selection for All Occasions.* [Kuala Lumpur]: Bahá'í Publishing Trust Committee, Spiritual Assembly of the Bahá'ís of Malaysia, 1981. [2], 78 p.

4.54. *Bahá'í Prayers: An Introductory Selection.* [Kuala Lumpur]: Bahá'í Publishing Trust, Malaysia, 1973.

4.55. *Bahá'í Prayers and Tablets for Children.* Lusaka: National Spiritual Assembly of the Bahá'ís of Zambia, n.d. [1979?] 40 p.

4.56. *Bahá'í Prayers and Tablets for the Young.* Wilmette, Ill.: Bahá'í Publishing Trust, 1978. 30 p. LC card 77–2228.

4.57. *Bahá'í Prayers for Children.* Karachi: Pakistan: Bahá'í Publishing Trust, n.d. [1976?], n.d. [1980?] 33 p.

4.58. *Bahá'í Prayers for Children.* n.p., n.d. [1929 or later] (Prayers from 1929 prayerbook).

4.59. *Bahá'í Prayers for Children.* Wilmette, Ill.: Bahá'í Publishing Trust, 1956. 53 p. LC card 55–13990.

4.60. *Baha'i Prayers for Children.* [Kuala Lumpur]: Baha'i Publishing Trust of Malaysia, n.d. [1984?] 37 p.

4.61. *Bahá'í Prayers for Children = Sala za KiBaha'i kwa Watoto.* Nairobi: Bahá'í Publishing Trust, 1983 (Nairobi: Acme Press). 11, 10 p. English and Swahili text.

4.62. *Bahá'í Prayers for Special Occasions.* rev. ed. London: Bahá'í Publishing Trust, 1951. 62 p.

4.63. *Bahá'í Quotations on Education.* comp. National Child Education Committee. Honolulu: National Spiritual Assembly of the Bahá'ís of the Hawaiian Islands, 1971. 47 p.

4.64. *idem.* Honolulu: National Spiritual Assembly of the Bahá'ís of the Hawaiian Islands, 1974. 72 p.

4.65. *Bahá'í Readings: Selections from the Writings of the Báb, Bahá'u'lláh and 'Abdu'l-Bahá for Daily Meditation.* Thornhill, Ont.: Bahá'í Canada Publications, 1984. 390 p.

4.66. *idem.* 2nd ed. Thornhill, Ont.: Bahá'í Canada Publications, January 1985. 390 p.

4.67. *Bahá'í References on Education.* ed. Advisory Committee on Education. Wilmette: Bahá'í Publishing Trust, 1966, 1970. 102 p. (Bahá'í Teacher's Handbook; v. 1).

4.68. *The Bahá'í Revelation.* London: Bahá'í Publishing Trust, 1955. xi, 339.
A compilation of writings of Bahá'u'lláh and 'Abdu'l-Bahá from numerous sources. One of the few places where the 'Tablet to Dr Forel' is published.

4.69. *idem.* rev. ed. London: Bahá'í Publishing Trust, 1970. xi, 339 p.

4.70. *Bahá'í Sacred Writings: Prayers & Selections from the Revelation of Bahá'u'lláh, Prophet-Founder of the Bahá'í Faith.* n.p. [Kingston, Jamaica: National Spiritual Assembly of the Bahá'ís of Jamaica], n.d. [1985] [2] p. Words of Bahá'u'lláh and 'Abdu'l-Bahá.

4.71. *Bahai Scriptures.* comp. Horace Holley. New York: Brentano's, 1923. xii, 576 p. LC card 23–10801 rev.
The first general book-length compilation of writings of Bahá'u'lláh and 'Abdu'l-Bahá. Many passages are early and unauthoritative translations. Superseded by *Bahá'í World Faith.*

4.72. *idem.* 2nd ed. New York: Bahá'í Publishing Committee, 1928. xii, 576 p. LC card 28–28973 rev.

4.73. *Bahá'í Teachers.* London: Bahá'í Education Committee of the National Spiritual Assembly of the United Kingdom, n.d. [1980?] [4] p.

4.74. *Bahá'í Teachings on Economics: A Compilation.* prepared by Bahá'í Teaching Committee from material gathered by Committee on Economics, 1933–34. New York: Bahá'í Publishing Committee, 1934. 15 leaves.
Two variants, one having large lettering on

cover with double underlining; the second has '10¢ per copy net'.

4.75. *Bahá'í World Faith*. Wilmette, Ill.: Bahá'í Publishing Committee, 1943. 465 p. LC card 42–12770.

Intended to 'offer the student of religion a compilation of Bahá'í Sacred Writings which, in one convenient volume, discloses their universal range of themes . . .' The volume was intended to replace the earlier compilation *Bahai Scriptures*. Many of the translations in this volume have since been superseded by more authoritative versions.

4.76. *idem*. Wilmette, Ill.: Bahá'í Publishing Committee, 1943. 465 p.

Bound in red leather and inscribed in gold '1844–1944' as a special centennial souvenir of only 500 copies.

4.77. *idem*. 2nd ed. Wilmette, Ill.: Bahá'í Publishing Trust, 1956, 1966, 1969, 1971, 1976. vi, 465 p. LC card 56–8259.

4.78. *Bahá'í Writings: Prayers Revealed by Bahá'u'lláh and 'Abdu'l-Bahá, also excerpts from Bahá'í Writings*. Wilmette, Ill.: Bahá'í Publishing Committee, 1942, 1947. 56 p. LC card 42–50046.

4.79. *Bahá'í Writings on Music*. [London]: Bahá'í Publishing Trust, n.d. [1973?] 11 p. (Bahá'í Publishing Trust Compilation Series; no. 4).

See 4.95–4.96.

4.80. *idem*. [Karachi]: National Youth Committee of the Baha'is of Pakistan, 141 B. [1985] 11 p.

4.81. *Bahá'u'lláh's Message*. New Delhi: Bahá'í Publishing Trust, 1967. 24 p.

4.82. *Book of Prayers*. n.p., n.d. [190–?] 96 p.

4.83. *idem*. n.p., n.d. [191–?] (Newark: Brant & Borden). 107 p.

4.84. *idem*. n.p., n.d. [191–?] 107 p.

Hard cover variant, no printer listed.

4.85. *idem*. n.p., n.d. [191–?] 107 p.

Title on cover, printed on bible paper.

4.86. *The Chalice of Immortality*. comp. Hushidar Motlagh. New Delhi: Bahá'í Publishing Trust, 1978. xv, 118 p.

Compilation of Bahá'í sacred texts on the subject of life after death.

4.87. *Children's Teaching: A Compilation of Quotes Pertaining to the Education of Children*. Thornhill, Ont.: Bahá'í National Office [i.e. National Spiritual Assembly of the Bahá'ís of Canada], n.d. [ca. 1970].

4.88. *A Child's Prayer Book*. Wilmette, Ill.: Bahá'í Publishing Committee, 1942, 1943. 15 leaves.

4.89. *Communion With God*. Wilmette, Ill.: Bahá'í Publishing Committee, 1943, 1945, 1947. 22 p.; 1950, 1951, 1953. 23 p.

An often-reprinted pocket compilation of prayers.

4.90. *idem*. Wilmette, Ill.: Bahá'í Publishing Trust, 1960, 1963, 1966, 1969, 1976, Aug. 1976, 1978, 1979, 1982. 24 p.

4.91. *idem*. Monrovia: National Spiritual Assembly of the Bahá'ís of Liberia, 1971. 31 p.

4.92. *A Compilation, Extracts from the Baha'i Teachings Discouraging Divorce*. n.p. [Lagos, Nigeria: Bahá'í Publishing Trust], n.d. [1984] 15 p. Cover title: *Extracts from the Bahá'í Teachings Discouraging Divorce*.

See 4.103, 4.119.

4.93. *idem*. [Auckland]: National Spiritual Assembly of the Bahá'ís of New Zealand, 1980. 14 p.

4.94. *A Compilation of Baha'i Writings for Deepening: Prayer and Meditation, Baha'i Consultation, the Hidden Words, the Baha'i Community*. Kenya, 1973. 53 p.

4.95. *A Compilation of Bahá'í Writings on Music*. comp. Research Department of the Universal House of Justice. 2nd ed. Oakham; London: Bahá'í Publishing Trust, 1983. v, 13 p. (Bahá'í Publishing Trust Compilation Series; no.4). Cover title: *Bahá'í Writings on Music*.

See 4.79–4.80, 4.96.

4.96. *Compilation of Extracts from the Baha'i Writings on Music*. n.p. [Johannesburg: National Spiritual Assembly of the Bahá'ís of South and West Africa], 1972. 6 leaves.

See 4.79–4.80, 4.95.

4.97. *Compilation of the Holy Utterances of Baha'o'llah and Abdul Baha Concerning the Most Great Peace, War and Duty of the Bahais Toward Their Government*. Chicago: Authorized by the 10th Annual Convention of the Bahais of America, 1918. 200 p.

4.98. *idem*. 2nd ed. Boston: The Tudor Press, 1918. 200 p. LC card 19–13018 rev.

4.99. *A Compilation on Bahá'í Education*. comp. Research Department of the Universal House of Justice. Haifa: Bahá'í World Centre, 1976. 83 p.

See 4.12.

4.100. *idem*. London: Bahá'í Publishing Trust, 1976. vi, 83 p. (Bahá'í Publishing Trust Compilation Series; no. 7).

4.101. *A Compilation on the Importance of Deepen-*

ing Our Understanding and Knowledge of the Faith. comp. Research Department of the Universal House of Justice. Oakham; London: Bahá'í Publishing Trust, 1983. iv, 44 p. (Bahá'í Publishing Trust Compilation Series; no. 15). Cover title: *Deepening.*
   See 4.147–4.149, 4.197–4.198.

4.102. *A Compilation on the Importance of Prayer, Meditation and the Devotional Attitude.* comp. Research Department of the Universal House of Justice. London: Bahá'í Publishing Trust, 1981. 20 p. (Bahá'í Publishing Trust Compilation Series; no. 11). Cover title: *The Importance of Prayer, Meditation and the Devotional Attitude.*
   See 4.150–4.152, 4.208, 4.269–4.270.

4.103. *Concord.* [Kingston]: National Spiritual Assembly of the Bahá'ís of Jamaica, 1980. 13 p.
   See 4.92–4.93, 4.119.

4.104. *Consultation: A Compilation.* comp. Research Department of the Universal House of Justice. Wilmette, Ill.: Bahá'í Publishing Trust, 1980. 23 p.
   See 4.9–4.10, 4.141, 4.267.

4.105. *Consultation: A Compilation = Filifiliga Faatasi: Tuufaatasia.* [Apia: National Spiritual Assembly of the Bahá'ís of Samoa, 1978?] 5 leaves. English and Samoan text.

4.106. *The Covenant of Bahá'u'lláh: A Compilation.* Manchester: Bahá'í Publishing Trust, 1950. xxi, 155 p. LC card 51–27787.
   A compilation from the Bahá'í writings, with some passages from the Bible and the Qur'án, on the subject of God's Great Covenant and the Covenant of Bahá'u'lláh with his followers. Arranged thematically under three broad categories: Expectancy, Fulfilment and Denial.

4.107. *idem.* London: Bahá'í Publishing Trust, 1963. xxiv, 154 p.

4.108. *The Dawn of World Civilization.* n.p. [Wilmette, Ill.]: World Order Magazine, 1945. 8 p.

4.109. *idem.* Wilmette, Ill.: Bahá'í Publishing Committee, 1945. 8 p.

4.110. *Death, the Messenger of Joy.* comp. Madeleine [sic] Hellaby. London: Bahá'í Publishing Trust, 1980. 9, 34 p.

4.111. *Deepening the Spiritual Life.* [Santurce]: Puerto Rico Bahá'í Teaching Committee, 1976. 41 p.

4.112. *Distinctive Characteristics of a Bahá'í Life: A Compilation.* n.p.: Continental Board of Counsellors in Southern Africa, 1974. 25 p.

4.113. *Dithapelo tsa Bana ba Baha'i = Baha'i Children's Prayer Book.* Gaborone: National

Spiritual Assembly of the Bahá'ís of Botswana, 1975. 35 p. English and Tswana text.

4.114. *The Divine Art of Living.* comp. Mabel Hyde Paine. Wilmette, Ill.: Bahá'í Publishing Committee, 1944, 1946, 1949, 1953. 132 p. LC card 44–9844.
   A selection from the Writings of Bahá'u'lláh and 'Abdu'l-Bahá that 'treat of outstanding qualities which characterize holy living . . .' The title was borrowed from a previous compilation by Mary M. Rabb that appeared in *Star of the West. See* 3.39.

4.115. *idem.* Wilmette, Ill.: Bahá'í Publishing Trust, 1956. 132 p.

4.116. *idem.* rev. ed. Wilmette, Ill.: Bahá'í Publishing Trust, 1956, 1960, 1965, 1970, 1972, 1973, 1974. 130 p. LC card 73–305486.

4.117. *idem.* 4th rev. ed. Wilmette, Ill.: Bahá'í Publishing Trust, 1979. 130 p.

4.118. *Divine Wisdom: Brief Excerpts from the Writings of Bahá'u'lláh and 'Abdu'l-Bahá.* London: Bahá'í Publishing Trust, 1946. ix, 63 p.

4.119. *Divorce: A Compilation Dealing with the Bahá'í Attitude Towards the Subject of Divorce.* comp. Universal House of Justice. Mona Vale, N.S.W.: Bahá'í Publications Australia, 1980, 1982, 1984, 1985. 14 p.
   See 4.92–4.93, 4.103.

4.120. *Education: Compilation Including Tablets, Prayers and Stories Taken from the Utterances of Baha'Ullah and Abdul Baha.* comp. Children's Educational Work Committee. [Chicago?]: Children's Educational Work Committee, 1923. 22 leaves.

4.121. *Enkindle the Souls: Raising the Quality of Teaching.* [Nairobi]: Continental Board of Counsellors in Africa, [1982] 36 p.

4.122. *Equality of Men and Women.* Auckland: National Spiritual Assembly of the Baha'is of New Zealand, n.d. [1985] 7 p. Quotations from 'Abdu'l-Bahá and Shoghi Effendi.

4.123. *The Establishment of the Universal House of Justice.* comp. Research Department of the Universal House of Justice. Oakham, Leics.: Bahá'í Publishing Trust, 1984. 60 p. (Bahá'í Publishing Trust Compilation Series; no. 16). Cover title: *The Universal House of Justice.*

4.124. *Excellence in All Things.* comp. Research Department of the Universal House of Justice. London: Bahá'í Publishing Trust, 1981. 18 p. (Bahá'í Publishing Trust Compilation Series; no. 13).

4.125. *idem.* Charlotte Amalie: National Spiritual Assembly of the Bahá'ís of the Virgin Islands, n.d. [1982] 11 p.

4.126. *idem.* New Delhi: Bahá'í Publishing Trust, 1982. 34 p.

4.127. *idem.* Mona Vale, N.S.W.: Bahá'í Publications Australia, 1982, 1983, 1984. 21 p.

4.127a. *idem.* 1st ed. n.p. [Kuala Lumpur]: Baha'i Publishing Trust Committee, Spiritual Assembly of the Baha'is of Malaysia, 1982. [4], 28 p.

4.128. *Family Life.* comp. Research Department of the Universal House of Justice. Mona Vale, N.S.W.: Bahá'í Publications Australia, 1982. 36 p.

4.129. *idem.* New Delhi: Bahá'í Publishing Trust, 1982, 67 p.

4.129a. *idem.* [Kuala Lumpur], Malaysia: Baha'i Publishing Trust Committee, Spiritual Assembly of the Baha'is of Malaysia, 1982. [4], 28 p.

4.130. *idem.* Auckland: National Spiritual Assembly of the Bahá'ís of New Zealand, 1982. 25 p.

4.131. *idem.* Lagos: Publishing Committee of the National Spiritual Assembly of the Bahá'ís of Nigeria, 1982, 51 p.

4.132. *idem.* Oakham; London: Bahá'í Publishing Trust, 1982. 34 p. (Bahá'í Publishing Trust Compilation Series; no. 14).

4.132a. *Fasting.* Auckland: National Spiritual Assembly of the Bahá'ís of New Zealand, 1983. Cover title: *The Fast.*

4.133. *The Fire Tablet; and, Prayer Revealed by 'Abdu'l-Bahá in Which Mention Is Made of Persecutions, the Martyred Friends and Their Relatives.* New Delhi: Bahá'í Publishing Trust, 1983, 17 p.

See 1.5, 1.30–1.34, 1.107–1.108, 1.128.

4.134. *Follow in Their Footsteps: Compilations of Texts About General Guidelines for Bahá'ís Engaged in the Teaching Work.* [St. Thomas]: National Spiritual Assembly of the Bahá'ís of the Leeward and Virgin Islands, 1977. 24 leaves.

See 4.136, 4.154, 4.280–4.281.

4.135. *The Garden of the Heart.* comp. Frances Esty. East Aurora, N.Y.: Roycrofters, 1930. 82 p. LC card 31–4542 rev.

4.136. *The Gift of Teaching.* London: Bahá'í Publishing Trust, 1977. 36 p. (Bahá'í Publishing Trust Compilation Series; no. 9).

See 4.134, 4.154, 4.280–4.281.

4.137. *The Glad Tidings of Bahá'u'lláh.* comp. George Townshend. London: John Murray, 1949, 1956. vi, 111 p. (Wisdom of the East Series). LC card 50–17711.

Compilation of Bahá'í sacred texts. Townshend wrote the introduction and several lines prefacing some of the selections.

4.138. *idem.* rev. ed. Oxford: George Ronald, 1975, 1978. vi, 116 p. LC card 76–380042.

4.139. *God's Eternal Legacy.* comp. Della Emery [et. al.]. Wilmette, Ill.: Bahá'í Publishing Committee, 1949. 97 leaves.

4.140. *A Guide to Parents in the Education and Training of Children.* Scarborough, Ont.: Bahá'í Publishing Committee, n.d. [196–] 19 p.

4.141. *The Heaven of Divine Wisdom.* London: Bahá'í Publishing Trust, 1978. 16 p. (Bahá'í Publishing Trust Compilation Series; no. 10).

Compilation on the subject of consultation.

See 4.9–4.10, 4.104–4.105, 4.267.

4.142. *'Hidden Words', and Communes from the Pens of Baha Ullah and Abdul Baha.* n.p., n.d. [190–?] 23 p.

See 1.3, 1.29, 1.49–1.73, 1.144.

4.143. *The Hidden Words of Bahá'u'lláh and Selected Holy Writings.* Kuala Lumpur: Baháí' [sic] Publishing Trust Committee, Spiritual Assembly of the Baháí's [sic] of Malaysia, 1985 (Penang: Ganesh Printing Works). 116 p.

See 1.3, 1.29, 1.49–1.73, 1.143.

4.144. *Holy Utterances Revealed by Baha'Ullah and the Master, Abdul Baha Regarding the Necessity for Steadfastness and Effort in the Present Time, that Thereby the Believers May Be Strengthened and Made Ready Under All Conditions to Stand Firm in the Covenant.* n.p. [Washington, D.C.: Remey], 1905. 10 leaves.

4.145. *Huqúqu'lláh.* comp. Research Department of the Universal House of Justice. Auckland: National Spiritual Assembly of the Bahá'ís of New Zealand, 1985. 39 p. Cover title: *Huqúqu'lláh, 'the Right of God'.*

4.145a. *Huqúqu'lláh.* comp. Research Department of the Universal House of Justice. n.p. [Kuala Lumpur]: Spiritual Assembly of the Baha'is of Malaysia, 1985. [2], 27 p.

4.146. *Imithandazo Yebantfwana = Children's Prayer Book.* [Mbabane]: National Spiritual Assembly of the Bahá'ís of Swaziland, 1982. 16 p. English and Swati text.

4.147. *The Importance of Deepening Our Knowledge and Understanding of the Faith.* [Kuala Lumpur]: Bahá'í Publishing Trust Committee,

Spiritual Assembly of the Bahá'ís of Malaysia, 1983. ii, 44 p.
See 4.159, 4.185, 4.197–4.198.

4.148. *idem.* Thornhill, Ont.: Bahá'í Community of Canada, 1983. iii, 53 p.

4.148a. *idem.* Wilmette, Ill.: Bahá'í Publishing Trust, 1983. iii, 53 p.

4.149. *idem.* Lagos: Publishing Committee of the National Spiritual Assembly of the Baha'is of Nigeria, 1983. 36 p.

4.150. *The Importance of Prayer, Meditation and the Devotional Attitude.* comp. Universal House of Justice. New Delhi: Bahá'í Publishing Trust, 1980. 46 p.
See 4.102, 4.208, 4.269–4.270.

4.151. *idem.* [Kingston]: National Spiritual Assembly of the Bahá'ís of Jamaica, 1980. 29 p.

4.152. *idem.* [Auckland]: National Spiritual Assembly of the Bahá'ís of New Zealand, 1980. 24 p.

4.153. *In Praise of God: Prayers for Bahá'ís.* Wilmette, Ill.: Bahá'í Publishing Trust, 1974, 1978. 11 p.

4.154. *The Individual and Teaching: Raising the Divine Call.* Wilmette, Ill.: Bahá'í Publishing Trust, 1977, June 1977. 40 p. LC card 77–155004.
See 4.134, 4.136, 4.280–4.281.

4.155. *idem.* Thornhill, Ont.: Bahá'í Community of Canada, 1977. 40 p.

4.156. *Inspiring the Heart: Selections from the Writings of the Báb, Bahá'u'lláh and 'Abdu'l-Bahá.* London: Bahá'í Publishing Trust, n.d. [1981] 200 p.

4.156a. *The Institution of the Hands of the Cause of God: Its Origin and Unfoldment, Auxiliary Boards, Relation to National Spiritual Assemblies.* n.p. [United States], n.d. [1957?] 9 leaves.

4.157. *Investing in the Children's Future: What Parents and Assemblies Can Do: Excerpts from the Bahá'í Writings from the Compilation on Bahá'í Education by the Universal House of Justice.* comp. Chellie Sundram. n.p. [Kuala Lumpur: Bahá'í Publishing Trust, Malaysia], n.d. [1983] 30 p.

4.158. *Justice & Peace: A Compendium of Quotations from the Bahá'í Writings.* n.p. [Paddington?, N.S.W.]: National Spiritual Assembly of the Bahá'ís of Australia, n.d. [1968] 6 leaves.

4.159. *Keys to Success: The Importance of Deepening Our Knowledge & Understanding of the Faith.* comp. Universal House of Justice. Auckland:

National Spiritual Assembly of the Bahá'ís of New Zealand, 1983. 36 p.
See 4.147–4.149, 4.185, 4.197–4.198.

4.160. *Kukambirana kwa Bahá'i = Baha'i Consultation.* Limbe: Spiritual Assembly of the Baha'is in Malawi, 1978. 14 p.

4.161. *Kuphunzitsa, Udindo Wathu Wokakamizidwa = Teaching, Our Sacred Obligation.* comp. Shidan Fathe-Aazam. Limbe: Spiritual Assembly of the Baha'is in Malawi, n.d. [1977] 23 p. Chichewa and English text.

4.162. *Let Thy Breeze Refresh Them: Bahá'í Prayers and Tablets for Children.* Oakham, England: Bahá'í Publishing Trust, 1976. 46 p.

4.163. *Life After Death.* comp. Barbara Mason. Honolulu: Hawaii Baha'i Press, 1976. ii, 34 p.

4.164. *Life Eternal: Extracts from the Writings of Bahá'u'lláh and 'Abdu'l-Bahá.* comp. Mary Rumsey Movius. East Aurora, N.Y.: Roycroft Shops, 1936, 1937. 178 p. LC card 37–2811 rev.

4.165. *Lights of Guidance: A Bahá'í Reference File.* comp. Helen Hornby. New Delhi: Bahá'í Publishing Trust, 1983. lvii, 547 p.
Collection of passages from Bahá'u'lláh, 'Abdu'l-Bahá, Shoghi Effendi and the Universal House of Justice on many topics. An excellent reference source arranged by topic, with each quote numbered. With an index.
See 4.241–4.243.

4.166. *Local Spiritual Assemblies.* comp. the Universal House of Justice. London: Bahá'í Publishing Trust, n.d. [197–] 20 p. (Bahá'í Publishing Trust Compilation Series; no.1].
See 4.167–4.168, 4.267.

4.167. *The Local Spiritual Assembly.* comp. the Universal House of Justice. n.p. [Toronto, Ont.]: National Spiritual Assembly of the Bahá'ís of Canada, 1970. 24 p.
See 4.166, 4.168, 4.267.

4.168. *The Local Spiritual Assembly: An Institution of the Bahá'í Administrative Order.* comp. Universal House of Justice. Wilmette, Ill.: Bahá'í Publishing Trust, n.d. [1970] 29 p.
See 4.166–4.167, 4.267.

4.169. *The Love of God: An Introductory Selection of Bahá'í Prayers.* London: Bahá'í Publishing Trust, 1972. 24 p.

4.169a. *The Love of God: An Introductory Selection of Bahá'í Prayers.* Manchester, U.K.: Bahá'í Faith Manchester Centre, n.d. [198–] [12] p.

4.170. *Magnified Be Thy Name: Prayers and Thoughts for Children from the Bahá'í Holy Writings.* comp. Child Education Committee of the National Spiritual Assembly of the Bahá'ís of the United Kingdom. London: Bahá'í Publishing Trust, 1956, 1976. 58 p.

4.171. *Meditation.* n.p. [Freetown: National Spiritual Assembly of the Bahá'ís of Sierra Leone], n.d. [1984] 4 p.

4.172. *The Mention of God: A Selection of Bahá'í Prayers.* Wilmette, Ill.: Bahá'í Publishing Trust, 1971. 11 p.

4.173. *idem.* [Kingston]: National Spiritual Assembly of the Bahá'ís of Jamaica, n.d. [1980?] 25 p.

4.174. *A Mighty River.* comp. Audrie Reynolds. Wilmette, Ill.: Bahá'í Publishing Trust, 1977, 1980. 53 p.

4.175. *The Most Great Peace.* Boston: Tudor Press, 1916. 46 p. LC card 18–1791 rev.

4.176. *The Most Great Peace.* New York: Local Spiritual Assembly of the Bahá'ís of the City of New York, n.d. [193–?] 16 p.

4.177. *My Prayer Book.* [Mbabane]: National Children's Committee of the Bahais of Swaziland, Lesotho, Mocambique. n.d. [before 1974] 30 p.

4.178. *New Day: Prophecies and Precepts from the Utterances of Baha'o'llah and Abdul Baha.* comp. Isabel F. Chamberlain. New York: The Fellowship Press Service, n.d. [191–]

4.179. *A New Kind of People.* comp. Continental Board of Counsellors of the Baha'i Faith in Africa. [Nairobi]: Continental Board of Counsellors of the Baha'i Faith in Africa, May 1984. 63 p.

4.180. *Ngaahi Lotu Ma'ae Fānau = Prayers for Children: in Tongan and English.* Auckland: National Spiritual Assembly of the Baha'is of New Zealand, 1985. 15 [i.e. 30] p.

4.181. *The Nineteen Day Feast, a Compilation.* Lusaka: National Spiritual Assembly of the Bahá'ís of Zambia, 1977. 22 p.
See 4.19, 4.250.

4.182. *Nineteen Programmes of Worship for Daily Devotions and Readings at 19 Day Feasts.* prepared by Irene Bennett, v.2. Kampala, Uganda: Bahá'í Publishing Trust, n.d. [1975] [44] p.

4.183. *O God, Guide Me!: A Selection of the Prayers Revealed by Bahá'u'lláh, the Báb, and 'Abdu'l-Bahá.* Wilmette, Ill.: Bahá'í Publishing Trust, 1974, 1976. v, 38 p.; 1978, 1980. v, 39 p.

4.184. *O God, My God . . .: Bahá'í Prayers and Tablets for Children and Youth.* Wilmette, Ill.: Bahá'í Publishing Trust, 1984. [93] p. Text in English and Persian.

4.185. *The Ocean of My Words: The Importance of Deepening Our Knowledge and Understanding of the Faith.* Extracts from the Writings of Bahá'u'lláh, the Writings and Utterances of 'Abdu'l-Bahá, the Letters of Shoghi Effendi and Letters Written on Behalf of Shoghi Effendi. comp. The Research Department of the Universal House of Justice. Mona Vale, N.S.W.: Bahá'í Publications Australia, 1983. 52 p.
See 4.147–1.149, 4.159, 4.197–4.198.

4.186. *The Oneness of Mankind.* New York: Bahá'í Publishing Committee, 1927. v, 58 p.

4.187. *The Onward March of the Faith.* London: Bahá'í Publishing Trust, 1975. 15 p. (Bahá'í Publishing Trust Compilation Series; no. 6).
Compilation about opposition to, and persecution of, the Bahá'í Faith.

4.188. *The Pattern of Bahá'í Life.* London: Bahá'í Publishing Trust, 1948. 55 p.
A selection of passages dealing with Bahá'í moral teachings and personal qualities, arranged under categories of purity, kindliness and radiance.

4.189. *idem.* 2nd ed. London: Bahá'í Publishing Trust, 1953. 64 p.

4.190. *idem.* 3rd ed. London: Bahá'í Publishing Trust, 1963, 1968, 1970, 1973, 1983. 63 p.

4.191. *Peace.* extracts from the writings of Bahá'u'lláh and 'Abdu'l-Bahá. n.p. [Banjul: National Spiritual Assembly of the Bahá'ís of Gambia], n.d. [1985] 2 p.

4.192. *Peace.* extracts from the writings and utterances of Bahá'u'lláh, the writings and utterances of 'Abdu'l-Bahá, the writings of Shoghi Effendi and letters written on his behalf, letters of the Universal House of Justice and letters written on its behalf; comp. Research Department of the Universal House of Justice. Mona Vale, N.S.W.: Bahá'í Publications Australia, 1985. 63 p.

4.193. *Peace.* comp. Research Department of the Universal House of Justice. n.p. [Manila: National Spiritual Assembly of the Bahá'ís of the Philippines], 1985. 34 p.

4.194. *Peace.* comp. Research Department of the Universal House of Justice. New Delhi: Bahá'í Publishing Trust, 1985. 98 p.

4.195. *Peace.* comp. Research Department of the Universal House of Justice, Bahá'í World Centre. Oakham, Leics.: Bahá'í Publishing Trust, 1985. v, 46 p. (Bahá'í Publishing Trust Compilation Series; no.17).

4.195a. *Peace.* comp. Research Department of the Universal House of Justice. n.p. [Kuala

4.196. *Peace, a Divine Creation: Excerpts from the Writings of Bahá'u'lláh, 'Abdu'l-Bahá. Statement on World Order.* by Shoghi Effendi. Wilmette, Ill.: National Spiritual Assembly of the Bahá'ís of the United States and Canada, 1943. 26 p.

4.197. *Pearls of Wisdom: A Compilation on Deepening.* [comp.] by the Universal House of Justice. [Karachi]: Bahá'í Publishing Trust, 1983. 118 p.
See 4.147–4.149, 4.159, 4.185, 4.198.

4.198. *Pearls of Wisdom: The Importance of Deepening Our Knowledge and Understanding of the Faith.* comp. Research Department of the Universal House of Justice. New Delhi: Bahá'í Publishing Trust, 1983. 124 p.
See 4.147–4.149, 4.159, 4.185, 4.197.

4.199. *Pioneering and Travel Teaching.* [Santurce]: Puerto Rico Bahá'í Teaching Committee, 1975. 14 leaves.

4.200. *Pioneers and Pioneering.* [Karachi]: National Youth Committee of the Baha'is of Pakistan, 142 B.E. [1985] 12 p.

4.201. *The Power of Divine Assistance.* comp. Research Department of the Universal House of Justice. Mona Vale, N.S.W.: Bahá'í Publications Australia, 1981. 27 p.
See 4.288, 4.290.

4.202. *idem.* New Delhi: Bahá'í Publishing Trust, 1981. 48 p.

4.203. *idem.* Oakham; London: Bahá'í Publishing Trust, 1981. iii, 24 p. (Bahá'í Publishing Trust Compilation Series; no. 12).

4.204. *idem.* [Thornhill, Ont.]: National Spiritual Assembly of the Bahá'ís of Canada, 1982. iv, 82 p.
Also includes selected prayers.

4.205. *The Power of the Covenant.* Wilmette, Ill.: Bahá'í Publishing Trust, 1956. 14 p.

4.206. *idem.* rev. ed. Wilmette, Ill.: Bahá'í Publishing Trust, 1972. 22 p.

4.207. *A Prayer Book for Children.* Sydney: National Spiritual Assembly of the Bahá'ís of Australia and New Zealand, n.d. [195– or 196–] 9 p.

4.208. *Prayer, Meditation and the Devotional Attitude.* comp. the Universal House of Justice. Mona Vale, N.S.W.: Bahá'í Publications Australia, 1980. 27 p.
See 4.102, 4.150–4.152, 4.269–4.270.

4.209. *Prayer of Bahá'u'lláh. Prayers and Tablets*

of 'Abdu'l-Bahá. trans. Shoghi Effendi. Boston, 1923. 32 p.

4.210. *idem.* 2nd ed. New York: Bahá'í Publishing Committee, 1924. 31 p.

4.211. *idem.* 3rd ed. New York: Bahá'í Publishing Committee, 1926. 32 p.

4.212. *[Prayers].* n.p., n.d. [between 1899 and 1901?]. [14] p.
Prayers and a note on the Ascension of Bahá'u'lláh. Untitled.

4.213. *Prayers.* n.p. [Thornhill, Ont.: National Spiritual Assembly of the Bahá'ís of Canada], n.d. [1984] [4] p.
Three prayers, one each by Bahá'u'lláh, the Báb and 'Abdu'l-Bahá. In English and Inuit.

4.214. *Prayers and Meditations.* Bahá'u'lláh, 'Abdu'l-Bahá; comp. at request of National Spiritual Assembly of the Bahá'ís of the United States and Canada. New York: Bahá'í Publishing Committee, 1929. ix, 210 p. Cover title: *Baha'i Prayers.*

4.215. *idem.* New York: Bahá'í Publishing Committee, 1931. 37 p. Cover title: *Daily Prayers.*

4.216. *Prayers for Children.* Nuku'alofa: National Spiritual Assembly of the Bahá'ís of Tonga and the Cook Islands, n.d. [1973?] 19 p.

4.217. *Prayers for Children.* Oakham, Leics.: Bahá'í Publishing Trust, n.d. [1985] 19 p.

4.218. *Prayers for Morning, Noon and Night.* [Victoria]: National Teaching Committee of the National Spiritual Assembly of the Bahá'ís of Cameroon, n.d. [1981]. 13 p.

4.219. *Prayers of the Báb, Bahá'u'lláh, 'Abdu'l-Bahá.* n.p. [Davison, Mich.: Louhelen Ranch?], n.d. [193–?]. 31 p. Cover title: *Bahai Prayers and Meditations.*
Inside front and back covers are photos of Louhelen Ranch.

4.220. *Prayers Revealed by Bahá'u'lláh, the Báb, and 'Abdu'l-Bahá.* trans. Shoghi Effendi. New York: Bahá'í Publishing Committee, 1939. 24 p.

4.221. *Prayers, Tablets, Instructions, and Miscellany Gathered by American Visitors to the Holy City During the Summer of 1900.* Chicago: The Adair Press, 1900. 91 p.

4.222. *Prescription for Teaching.* comp. from the Bahá'í writings. Peterborough, Eng.: The Arcade Agency, n.d. [197–?] [8] p.

4.223. *The Principle of Knowledge.* comp. and duplicated by Helen M. Gidden. n.p. [United States]: Helen M. Gidden, 1966. 4 p.

4.223a. *Proclaiming the Faith: A Compilation of*

Quotations from the Bahá'í Writings. comp. Office of Public Affairs. n.p. [Wilmette, Ill.]: Office of Public Affairs, Bahá'í National Center, 1982. [2], 24 p.

4.224. *Prohibition of Intoxicating Drinks.* Lagos: Publishing Committee of the National Spiritual Assembly of the Bahá'ís of Nigeria, 1982. 21 p.

4.225. *idem.* Nairobi: Baha'i Publishing Agency, n.d. [1985] 21 p.

4.226. *Purify My Heart: Bahá'í Prayers for Children.* [Tainan]: Bahá'í Publishing Trust of the National Spiritual Assembly of the Bahá'ís of Taiwan, 1983. 14 [i.e. 28] p.

4.227. *The Purpose of Man's Creation.* Port-of-Spain: National Spiritual Assembly of the Bahá'ís of Trinidad and Tobago, 1980. 5 leaves.

4.228. *Quotations from the Baha'i Writings on Prayer.* comp. Jenabe Caldwell. [Anchorage]: National Spiritual Assembly of the Bahá'ís of Alaska, 1973. 28 p.

4.229. *Racial Amity.* comp. M.H. and M.M. [Mariam Haney and Mountfort Mills]. n.p. [United States]: M.H. and M.M., 1924. 20 p.

4.230. *Rays from the Sun of Truth.* prepared by Ida A. Finch. Riverton, N.J.: New Era, 71 B.E. [1920–21] 16 p.

4.231. *The Reality of Brotherhood: Excerpts from the Bahá'í Writings: The New Principle of Human Relations.* Wilmette, Ill.: Bahá'í Public Relations, 1946. [3] p.

4.232. *The Reality of Man.* New York: Bahá'í Publishing Committee, 1931. viii, 61 p.

A popular compilation from Bahá'í scripture on the subject of man's spiritual reality and his relation to the universe.

4.233. *idem.* 2nd ed. New York: Bahá'í Publishing Committee, 1935. viii, 61 p.

4.234. *idem.* 3rd ed. New York: Bahá'í Publishing Committee, 1939. viii, 61 p.

4.235. *idem.* 4th ed. Wilmette, Ill.: Bahá'í Publishing Committee, 1942. viii, 61 p.

4.236. *idem.* 5th ed. Wilmette, Ill.: Bahá'í Publishing Committee, 1945. viii, 61 p.

4.237. *idem.* 6th ed. Wilmette, Ill.: Bahá'í Publishing Committee, 1947. viii, 61p.

4.238. *idem.* 7th ed. Wilmette, Ill.: Bahá'í Publishing Trust, 1956. viii, 61 p.

4.239. *idem.* 1962 ed. Wilmette, Ill.: Bahá'í Publishing Trust, 1962, 1966, 1969, 1972, 1975, 1979. viii, 61 p. LC card 62–52261.

4.240. *idem.* Indian ed. New Delhi: Bahá'í Publishing Trust, 1971. viii, 61 p.

4.241. *Reference File.* comp. Helen Hornby. Quito: Approved by National Spiritual Assembly of the Bahá'ís of Ecuador, 1981. lviii, 445, [2] p.
  See 4.165, 4.242–4.243.

4.242. *Reference File for Bahá'í Spiritual Assemblies, Pioneers and Teachers.* comp. Helen Hornby. Quito: Approved by National Spiritual Assembly of the Bahá'ís of Ecuador, 1973. 181, 7 p.
  See 4.165, 4.241.

4.243. *idem.* Quito: National Spiritual Assembly of the Bahá'ís of Ecuador, 1977. 479 p.

4.244. *Remembrance of God: A Short Selection of Bahá'í Prayers.* New Delhi: Bahá'í Publishing Trust, n.d. [196–] 28 p.

4.245. *idem.* 3rd rev. ed. New Delhi: Bahá'í Publishing Trust, 1979. 56 p.

4.246. *idem.* New Delhi: Bahá'í Publishing Trust, 1980. 39 p.

4.247. *idem.* n.p. [Thornhill, Ont.]: National Spiritual Assembly of the Bahá'ís of Canada, 1979. [23] p.

4.248. *Revealed at Akka by the Blessed Perfection, A Tablet from Our Lord, Abbas Effendi.* presented by Abdel Karim Effendi to the American Beloved. n.p. [United States], n.d. [190–] [2] p.

4.249. *The River of Life: A Selection from the Teachings of Baha Ullah and Abdul Baha.* trans., with explanatory notes and preface by Yūhannā Dāwūd. London: Cope & Fenwick, 1914 [preface] 62 p.

4.250. *Seeking the Light of the Kingdom: Compilations Issued by the Universal House of Justice on the Nineteen-Day Feast and Bahá'í Meetings.* London: Bahá'í Publishing Trust, 1977. 32 p. (Bahá'í Publishing Trust Compilation Series; no. 8).
  See 4.19, 4.181.

4.251. *Selected Bahá'í Prayers.* [London]: Bahá'í Publishing Trust, n.d. [1974] 18 p.

4.252. *Selected Writings on Bahá'í Administration (Nepali).* n.p. [Kathmandu: National Spiritual Assembly of the Bahá'ís of Nepal], n.d. [1984?] 108 p. Parallel English and Nepali texts.

Quotations from the works of Shoghi Effendi and the Universal House of Justice, with a few from Bahá'u'lláh.

4.253. *A Selection of Bahá'í Prayers and Holy Writings.* enl. ed. [Kuala Lumpur]: Bahá'í Publishing Trust Committee, Spiritual Assembly of the Bahá'ís of Malaysia, 1983. 119 p.

4.254. *idem.* 4th ed. Kuala Lumpur: Bahá'í Publishing Trust Committee, Spiritual Assembly of the Bahá'ís of Malaysia, 1984. 119 p.

4.255. *idem.* rev. ed. Kuala Lumpur: Bahá'í Publishing Trust Committee, Spiritual Assembly of the Bahá'ís of Malaysia, 1985 (Penang: Ganesh Printing Works). 128 p.

4.256. *Selections from Baha'i Holy Writings.* Limbe: Spiritual Assembly of the Baha'i in Malawi, 1982. 13 p.

4.257. *Selections from Bahá'í Scripture.* comp. and ed. David Hofman. Manchester, U.K.: Bahá'í Publishing Trust, 1941. 334 p. LC card A 43–3387.
Selections conveniently arranged by topic, from the writings of Bahá'u'lláh, the writings and talks of 'Abdu'l-Bahá, and prayers and devotions by Bahá'u'lláh, the Báb and 'Abdu'l-Bahá.

4.258. *Selections from Bahá'í Writings for Use at Declarations.* comp. National Teaching Committee. n.p. [Africa?], n.d. [196–?] 9 p.

4.259. *Selections from the Holy Utterances on the Subject of Unity.* n.p. [Washington, D.C.: Remey?], n.d. [191–?] 8 leaves.

4.260. *Some Aspects of Health and Healing: Selections from the Bahá'í Writings.* comp. the Universal House of Justice. [Auckland]: National Spiritual Assembly of the Bahá'ís of New Zealand, 1981. 18 p.

4.261. *Some Marriage Prayers and Readings from the Writings of the Bahá'í Faith: In English and Zulu.* n.p. [Mbabane: National Spiritual Assembly of the Bahá'ís of Swaziland], n.d. [197–] [12] p.

4.262. *Some Prayers for Children.* London: National Spiritual Assembly of the Bahá'ís of the United Kingdom, n.d. [1979]. 4 p.

4.263. *Some Quotations from the Baha'i Writings Relating to Socio-Economic Development and Human Progress.* n.p. [Banjul: National Spiritual Assembly of the Bahá'ís of the Gambia], 1984. 8 p.

4.264. *Some Special Bahá'í Prayers and Tablets.* London: Bahá'í Publishing Trust, 1945.

4.265. *Spirit Lifters: Selected from the Writings of the Bahá'í Faith.* n.p. [Toronto, Ont.: Vera Raginsky], n.d. [195–?] 6 p.

4.266. *idem.* n.p. [United States], n.d. [195– or 196–]. 20 p.

4.267. *Spiritual Assemblies and Consultation.* New Delhi: Bahá'í Publishing Trust, 1978. 136 p.
Includes compilations of the Universal House of Justice on Local Spiritual Assemblies, National Spiritual Assemblies and consultation.

See 4.9–4.10, 4.104–4.105, 4.141, 4.166–4.168, 5.103–5.104.

4.268. *Spiritual Enrichment.* n.p. [Kuala Lumpur: Spiritual Assembly of the Bahá'ís of Malaysia], n.d. [1983] 19 p.

4.269. *Spiritual Foundations: Prayer, Meditation and the Devotional Attitude.* comp. Research Department of the Universal House of Justice. Wilmette, Ill.: Bahá'í Publishing Trust, 1980. iii, 20 p.
See 4.102, 4.150–4.152, 4.208.

4.270. *idem.* Thornhill, Ont.: Bahá'í Community of Canada, 1980. iii, 20 p.

4.271. *Spiritual Sustenance: Bahá'í Prayers.* Kampala, Uganda: Bahá'í Publishing Trust, 1972. 27 p.

4.272. *The Splendour of God: Being Extracts from the Sacred Writings of the Bahais.* with an introduction by Eric Hammond. New York: E.P. Dutton, 1910. 124 p. (The Wisdom of the East Series).
An introduction to the sacred scriptures of the Bahá'ís, combined with remarks on several specific works and an overview of Bahá'í belief.

4.273. *idem.* London: John Murray, 1909, 1910, 1911. 124 p. (The Wisdom of the East Series).

4.274. *The Straight Path: Dedicated to Shoghi Effendi, First Guardian of the Bahá'í Faith on the Occasion of the Twenty-Fifth Anniversary of the Inception of the Guardianship.* comp. Mary Magdalene Wilkin. n.p. [United States]: Wilkin, 1947. 32 leaves.

4.275. *The Supreme Gift of God to Man: Selections from the Bahá'í Writings on the Value, Development and Use of the Intellect.* Wilmette, Ill.: Bahá'í Publishing Trust, 1973, 1973, 1977, 1980. ix, 21 p. (Bahá'í Comprehensive Deepening Program).

4.276. *Tablet of Aḥmad. Prayer for Canada.* n.p. [Canada], n.d. [197–] 6 p.

4.277. *Tablets, Communes and Holy Utterances.* n.p., n.d. [1897]. 23 p.

4.278. *Tablets Revealed by the Blessed Perfection and Abdul Beha Abbas, Brought to This Country by Haji Mirza Hassan, Mirza Assad'Ullah and Mirza Hussien* [sic]. New York: Board of Counsel, 1900. 13 p.

4.279. *Tablets Revealed in Honor of the Greatest Holy Leaf.* New York: National Spiritual Assembly of the Bahá'ís of the United States and Canada, 1933 (New York: J.J. Little and Ives). 9 p.

4.279a. *Teaching the Cause: Cornerstone of the*

Foundation of All Baha'i Activity. New Delhi: Baha'i Publishing Trust, 1977. 189 p.

4.280. *Teaching, the Greatest Gift of God.* comp. the Universal House of Justice. [Mona Vale, N.S.W.]: Bahá'í Publications Australia, 134 [1977] 39 p.
See 4.134, 4.136, 4.154.

4.281. *idem.* n.p. [Lusaka: National Spiritual Assembly of the Bahá'ís of Zambia], n.d. [1978?] 19 p.

4.282. *The Throne of the Inner Temple.* comp. Elias Zohoori. Kingston, Jamaica; approved by the National Spiritual Assembly of the Bahá'ís of Jamaica, 1985 (Kingston: University Printery and School of Printing, University of the West Indies). 97 p.
A compilation on the interrelationship of spiritual and physical health.

4.283. *To Know Thee and to Worship Thee.* n.p. [Ponape: National Spiritual Assembly of the Bahá'ís of North West Pacific Ocean], n.d. [1977] 6 p.

4.284. *The Training and Education of Children.* [Thornhill, Ont.]: National Spiritual Assembly of the Bahá'ís of Canada, 1976. v, 78 p.

4.285. *The True Nobility of Man.* n.p., n.d. [1924 or later] [2] p.

4.286. *(Túshih Rahmání: Majmú'ih az Áthár-i-Mubárakih bá Tarjumih Inglísí) = Selections of Original Tablets and Prayers with Approved Translations in English.* comp. Fattaneh Assassi Scott. n.p. [Wilmette, Ill.: Persian Affairs Committee], n.d. [1980] [203] p.

4.287. *Tusi Tatalo Bahá'í mo Tamaiti = Bahá'í Prayers for Children.* [Apia]: National Spiritual Assembly of the Bahá'ís of Samoa, 1971, 1978. 46 p. English and Samoan text.

4.288. *Ultimate and Complete Victory: The Power of Divine Assistance: A Compilation.* comp. Research Department of the Universal House of Justice. [Auckland]: National Spiritual Assembly of the Bahá'ís of New Zealand, 1981. 16 p.
See 4.201–4.204, 4.290.

4.289. *Universal Principles of the Bahai Movement: Social, Economic, Governmental.* Washington, D.C.: Persian-American Bulletin, 1912. 60 p. LC card 18–15940 rev. 2.

4.290. *The Unseen Divine Assistance.* comp. Universal House of Justice. [Auckland]: National Spiritual Assembly of the Bahá'ís of New Zealand, 1977. 22 p.
See 4.201–4.204, 4.288.

4.291. *Unto Him Shall We Return: Selections from the Bahá'í Writings on the Reality and Immortality*

of the Human Soul. comp. Hushidar Motlagh. Wilmette, Ill.: Bahá'í Publishing Trust, 1985. xiii, 143 p. LC card 84–24608.

4.292. *Victory Promises.* Honolulu: National Spiritual Assembly of the Bahá'ís of the Hawaiian Islands, 1978. 30 p.

4.293. *Waging Peace: Selections from the Bahá'í Writings on Universal Peace.* comp. of words of Bahá'u'lláh, 'Abdu'l-Bahá, Shoghi Effendi. Los Angeles: Kalimát Press, 1984. ix, 96 p. LC card 84–29715.

4.294. *What Modern Man Must Know About Religion: Selected Bahá'í Teachings.* Wilmette, Ill.: Bahá'í Publishing Committee, 1948. 29 leaves.

4.295. *Why Our Cities Burn: Views on the Racial Crisis in the United States from the Writings of the Bahá'í Faith.* Wilmette, Ill.: Bahá'í Publishing Trust, n.d. [1968] 24 p.

4.296. *Woorde om te Onthou = Words to Remember = Amazwi Okukhunjulwa = Mafoko a go Gopolwa.* n.p. [Johannesburg?: National Spiritual Assembly of the Bahá'ís of South and West Africa?], n.d. [197–] [4] p. English, Afrikaans, Xhosa and Sesotho text.

4.297. *Words about the Word: Selections from the Writings of Bahá'u'lláh about His Word: His Guidance in Our Study: Together with passages from the Writings of Muhammad, the Báb, 'Abdu'l-Bahá, Shoghi Effendi, and the Universal House of Justice.* n.p., 1977. ii, 45 leaves.

4.298. *Words of God: A Compilation of Prayers and Tablets from the Bahá'í Writings.* [Haifa]: Bahá'í World Centre, 1981. 34 p.

4.299. *idem.* n.p. [Charlotte Amalie: National Spiritual Assembly of the Bahá'ís of the Virgin Islands], n.d. [1981] 34 p.

4.300. *idem.* n.p. [Seoul: Bahá'í Publishing Trust of Korea], n.d. [1981] 34 p.

4.301. *idem.* New Delhi: Bahá'í Publishing Trust, 1982. 34 p.

4.302. *idem.* n.p. [Nairobi: Bahá'í Publishing Trust], n.d. [1982?] 34 p.

4.303. *idem.* n.p. [St. John's, Antigua: National Spiritual Assembly of the Bahá'ís of the Leeward Islands], 1981 [i.e. 1982?] 34 p.

4.304. *idem.* n.p. [Lagos]: National Spiritual Assembly of the Bahá'ís of Nigeria, 1982. 34 p.

4.305. *idem.* n.p. [Georgetown: National Spiritual Assembly of the Bahá'ís of Guyana], 1981 [i.e. 1983] 34 p.

4.306. *idem.* n.p. [Harare: National Spiritual Assembly of the Bahá'ís of Zimbabwe], 1981 [i.e. 1983] 34 p.

4.307. *idem*. n.p. [Wilmette, Ill.: Bahá'í Publishing Trust], 1981 [i.e. 1984] 34 p.

4.308. *idem*. n.p. [Haifa]: Bahá'í World Centre [i.e. Port of Spain: National Spiritual Assembly of the Bahá'ís of Trinidad and Tobago], 1981 [i.e. 1985?] 34 p.

4.309. *World Commonwealth of Bahá'u'lláh.* Kuala Lumpur: Malaya Bahá'í Society, n.d. [196–?] [12] p.

4.310. *idem*. New Delhi: National Spiritual Assembly of the Bahá'ís of India, 1968. 14 p.

4.311. *idem*. New Delhi: Bahá'í Publishing Trust, n.d. [197–] 16 p.

V
The Writings of Shoghi Effendi

'ABDU'L-BAHÁ, in his Will and Testament, appointed his grandson, Shoghi Effendi Rabbani (1897–1957), as Guardian of the Cause of God. The Guardian, as Head of the Bahá'í Faith, has as one of his duties the interpretation of the Bahá'í scriptures. Shoghi Effendi's interpretation within his assigned sphere is regarded as divinely guided and therefore infallible. During his tenure as Guardian (1921–57) Shoghi Effendi wrote extensively on the meaning of the Bahá'í scriptures, both in their broad implications and in the details of specific passages. Among the major tasks of his tenure as Guardian was to lay the framework of the Bahá'í administrative order and to guide the development of Bahá'í institutions – a task amply reflected in the content of his work. Shoghi Effendi wrote his letters in Persian and in impeccable and masterful English. The overwhelming majority of these works are therefore not translations.

5.1. *The Advent of Divine Justice*. New York: Bahá'í Publishing Committee, 1939, May 1939. 77 p. LC card 39–9338.

A book-length letter, written by the Guardian of the Bahá'í Faith in 1939 to the believers of the United States and Canada, outlining the spiritual prerequisites necessary for the North American Bahá'í community's prosecution of its tasks.

5.2. *idem.* Wilmette, Ill.: Bahá'í Publishing Committee, 1940, 1948. 77 p.

5.3. *idem.* Wilmette, Ill.: Bahá'í Publishing Trust, 1956. 90 p.

5.4. *idem.* 1st rev. ed. Wilmette, Ill.: Bahá'í Publishing Trust, 1963. v, 90 p. LC card 63–21643.

5.5. *idem.* 1969 ed. Wilmette, Ill.: Bahá'í Publishing Trust, 1969, 1971, 1974. v, 90 p.

5.6. *idem.* [1984 ed.] Wilmette, Ill.: Bahá'í Publishing Trust, 1984. x, 104 p. LC card 84–436.

5.7. *idem.* Indian ed. New Delhi: Bahá'í Publishing Trust, n.d. [between 1970 and 1977] v, 90 p.

5.8. *America and the Most Great Peace*. New York: Bahá'í Publishing Committee, 1933. 26 p.

5.9. *idem.* New York: Bahá'í Publishing Committee, 1933 [i.e. 1938] pp. 71–94.

5.10. *American Bahá'ís in Time of World Peril: A World Crusade Message from the Guardian*. Wilmette, Ill.: National Spiritual Assembly of the Bahá'ís of the United States, 1954. [5] p.

5.11. *Arohanui: Letters from Shoghi Effendi to New Zealand*. Suva, Fiji: Bahá'í Publishing Trust, 1982. xiii, 111 p.

5.12. *The Ascension of 'Abdu'l-Bahá*. comp. prepared in January 1922 by Lady Blomfield and Shoghi Effendi. London: Bahá'í Publishing Trust, n.d. [1985?] (Oakham, Leics.: Magnum Offset). 30 p.

See 5.106–5.108.

5.13. *Bahá'í Administration*. New York: Bahá'í Publishing Committee, 1928. viii, 155 p.

The Bahá'í administrative institutions, the instruments for channelling the spiritual dynamic of the Bahá'í Faith, were ordained by Bahá'u'lláh, elaborated by 'Abdu'l-Bahá and finally brought into existence by Shoghi Effendi. This collection of messages to the American Bahá'ís and their national institutions outlines the foundations on which the administrative institutions were to be established.

5.14. *idem.* 2nd ed. New York: Bahá'í Publishing Committee, 1933. viii, 188, [97] p.

Appended are three of the 'world order' letters and the declaration of trust and by-laws.

5.15. *idem.* 3rd ed. New York: Bahá'í Publishing Committee, 1936. viii, 221 p.

5.16. *idem.* 4th ed. Wilmette, Ill.: Bahá'í Publishing Committee, 1941. viii, 197 p.

5.17. *idem.* 5th ed. Wilmette, Ill.: Bahá'í Publishing Committee, 1945. x, 197 p. LC card 46–12026.

5.18. *idem.* 5th rev. ed. Wilmette, Ill.: Bahá'í Publishing Trust, 1960. x, 197 p.

5.19. *idem.* 1968 ed. Wilmette, Ill.: Bahá'í Publishing Trust, 1968. x, 209 p.

5.20. *idem.* 1974 ed. Wilmette, Ill.: Bahá'í Publishing Trust, 1974, [1980] x, 209 p.

5.21. *The Bahá'í Faith, 1844–1944: Information Statistical and Comparative*. Haifa, 1944 (Haifa: Warhaftig's Press). 26 p.

See 5.156.

5.22. *The Bahá'í Faith, 1844–1950: Information Statistical and Comparative*. Wilmette: Ill.:

Bahá'í Publishing Committee, 1950. 35 p. LC card 50–34896.

5.23. *The Bahá'í Faith, 1844–1952: Information Statistical and Comparative.* London: Bahá'í Publishing Trust, 1952. 74 p. LC card 54–20066.

5.24. *idem.* Wilmette, Ill.: Bahá'í Publishing Committee, 1953. 74 p. LC card 53–33412.

5.25. *Bahá'í Funds and Contributions.* comp. the Universal House of Justice. [Thornhill, Ont.]: National Spiritual Assembly of the Bahá'ís of Canada, 1970, 1974. 24 p.
    See 5.52, 5.83.

5.26. *The Bahá'í Life.* comp. the Universal House of Justice. Wilmette, Ill.: Bahá'í Publishing Trust, 1981. 22 p.
    See 5.51, 5.87–5.92.

5.27. *Bahá'í Youth: A Compilation.* comp. National Spiritual Assembly of the Bahá'ís of the United States. Wilmette, Ill.: Bahá'í Publishing Trust, 1973. 33 p. LC card 73–176465.

5.27a. *Bahá'u'lláh's Ground Plan of World Fellowship.* London: World Congress of Faiths, n.d. [1936] 15 p.

5.27b. *idem.* London: World Congress of Faiths, n.d. [1938] (World Fellowship through Religion. Pamphlet; no.17). 15 p.

5.28. *The Beloved of God and the Handmaids of the Merciful throughout the West, July 17, 1932.* [United States], 1932. 16 p. and envelope.
    Facsimile of Shoghi Effendi's message on the passing of the Greatest Holy Leaf.

5.29. *Call to the Nations.* comp. the Universal House of Justice. Haifa: Bahá'í World Centre, 1977. xviii, 69 p. LC card 82–210421.
    A selection from Shoghi Effendi's letters pertaining to 'that Divine Civilization, the establishment of which is the primary mission of the Bahá'í Faith'.

5.30. *idem.* Haifa: Bahá'í World Centre, 1977 [i.e., New Delhi: Bahá'í Publishing Trust, 1977?] xviii, 69 p.

5.31. *Centers of Bahá'í Learning.* comp. the Universal House of Justice. Wilmette, Ill.: Bahá'í Publishing Trust, 1980. iii, 20 p.

5.32. *idem.* Thornhill, Ont.: Bahá'í Community of Canada, 1980. iii, 20 p.

5.33. *Challenge: Messages to Bahá'í Youth = Défi: Messages aux Jeunes Bahá'ís.* Thornhill, Ont.: National Spiritual Assembly of the Bahá'ís of Canada, 1975. 20, 20 p.

5.34. *The Challenging Requirements of the Present Hour.* Wilmette, Ill.: National Spiritual Assembly of the Bahá'ís of the United States and Canada, 1947. 36 p.

5.35. *Charter of a Divine Civilization: A Compilation.* Wilmette, Ill.: National Spiritual Assembly of the Bahá'ís of the United States, 1956. 14 p.

5.36. *Citadel of Faith: Messages to America, 1947–1957.* Wilmette, Ill.: Bahá'í Publishing Trust, 1965, 1970, 1980. ix, 178 p. LC card 66–2270.
    The final collection of messages to America from the Guardian of the Bahá'í Faith, further outlining the position and responsibilities of the American Bahá'í community.

5.37. *The Citadel of the Faith of Bahá'u'lláh.* Wilmette, Ill.: National Spiritual Assembly of the Bahá'ís of the United States, 1948. 7 p.

5.38. *Continental Boards of Counsellors.* comp. the Universal House of Justice. London: Bahá'í Publishing Trust, n.d. [1971] 20 p. (Bahá'í Publishing Trust Compilation Series; no.2). First page title: *The Functions of the Institutions of the Continental Boards of Counsellors and Their Auxiliary Boards.*
    See 5.55, 5.76–5.77.

5.39. *idem.* 2nd ed. London: Bahá'í Publishing Trust, 1973. 24 p. (Bahá'í Publishing Trust Compilation Series; no.2). First page title: *The Functions of the Institutions of the Continental Boards of Counsellors and Their Auxiliary Boards.*

5.40. *Dawn of a New Day.* New Delhi: Bahá'í Publishing Trust, n.d. [1970?] xii, 233 p. Cover title: *Dawn of a New Day: Messages to India. 1923–1957.*
    Messages and cables from the Guardian to believers of the Indian subcontinent. Their range encompasses a wide variety of topics from teaching plans and goals to the application of Bahá'í principles. Includes a good index.

5.41. *The Destiny of America.* New York: Bahá'í Publishing Committee, 1940, 1941, 1944. 7 p. (Bahá'í Reprint; no. 6).

5.42. *The Destiny of the American Nation: To Proclaim the Unity of Mankind.* Wilmette, Ill.: Bahá'í Publishing Committee, 1947. 6 p.

5.43. *Directives from the Guardian.* comp. Gertrude Garrida. New Delhi: Bahá'í Publishing Trust, 1973. xiii, 92 p.
    A compilation of passages from the Guardian's letters on a number of topics which were published in the *Bahá'í News* of the United States. Arranged alphabetically by topic.

5.44. *idem.* New Delhi: Bahá'í Publishing Trust, n.d. [after 1973] (New Delhi: Arcee Press). x, 80 p.

5.45. *idem*. New Delhi: Bahá'í Publishing Trust for the National Spiritual Assembly of the Bahá'ís of the Hawaiian Islands, 1973. xiii, 92 p.

5.46. *The Dispensation of Bahá'u'lláh*. New York: Bahá'í Publishing Committee, 1934, 1937, 1940. 65 p.

This document clarifies the nature and mission of the Central Figures of the Bahá'í Faith and its administrative order. It is also included among the letters which constitute *The World Order of Bahá'u'lláh*.

5.47. *idem*. Wilmette, Ill.: Bahá'í Publishing Committee, 1943, 1947. 65 p.

5.48. *idem*. Wilmette, Ill.: Bahá'í Publishing Trust, 1960, 1970, 1975, 1981. 65 p.

5.49. *idem*. London: Bahá'í Publishing Trust, 1947, 1981. 69 p.

5.50. *idem*. 1st Indian ed. New Delhi: Bahá'í Publishing Trust, 1977. 65 p. LC card 81–903446.

5.51. *Excerpts from the Writings of the Guardian on the Bahá'í Life*. comp. the Universal House of Justice. Toronto, Ont.: National Spiritual Assembly of the Bahá'ís of Canada, 1973. 22 p.
See 5.26, 5.87–5.92.

5.52. *Extracts from the Guardian's Letters on Bahá'í Funds and Contributions*. comp. the Universal House of Justice. n.p. [Victoria?: National Spiritual Assembly of the Bahá'ís of the Cameroon Republic?], n.d. [1970] 14 p.
See 5.25, 5.83.

5.53. *The Faith of Bahá'u'lláh, a World Religion*. Wilmette, Ill.: Bahá'í Publishing Committee, 1947. 8 p.

Succinct statement of Bahá'í belief presented to the United Nations Special Committee on Palestine.

5.53a. *idem*. Wilmette, Ill.: Bahá'í Publishing Committee; Geneva, Switzerland: Bahá'í International Bureau, Bahá'í European Teaching Committee, 1947. 8 p.

5.54. *idem*. Wilmette, Ill.: Bahá'í Publishing Trust, 1959, 1966, 1971. 20 p; 1980. 21 p.

5.55. *The Functions of the Institutions of the Continental Boards of Counsellors and Their Auxiliary Boards*. comp. Research Department of the Universal House of Justice. 2nd ed. (reprinted with additional material). London: Bahá'í Publishing Trust, 1981. 23 p. Cover title: *Continental Board of Counsellors*.
See 5.38–5.39, 5.76–5.77.

5.56. *The Future World Commonwealth*. Wilmette, Ill.: National Spiritual Assembly of the Bahá'ís of the United States and Canada, 1936. 16 p.

5.57. *The Generation of the Half-Light: A Compilation for Bahá'í Youth*. comp. Arjun Rastogi. New Delhi: Bahá'í Publishing Trust, 1974. ix, 63 p.

5.58. *The Goal of a New World Order*. [New York]: National Spiritual Assembly of the Bahá'ís of the United States and Canada, 1931 (New York: J.J. Little and Ives). 28 p. LC card 43–18814.

5.59. *idem*. New York: National Spiritual Assembly of the Bahá'ís of the United States and Canada, Bahá'í Publishing Committee [distributor], n.d. [1938] 28 p.

5.60. *idem*. Wilmette, Ill.: Bahá'í Publishing Trust, 1971, 1976. 24 p.

5.61. *A God Given Mandate*. Wilmette, Ill.: Bahá'í Publishing Committee, 1946.

5.62. *God Passes By*. Wilmette, Ill.: Bahá'í Publishing Committee, 1944, 1945. xxiii, 412 p. LC card 44–51036 rev. 2.
Review:
The Christian Century (Chicago) v. 62 (Jan. 31, 1945), p. 146.
A lengthy spiritual-historical essay commemorating the centenary of the inception of the Bábí dispensation and the inauguration of the Bahá'í era. This work can be viewed as an authoritative interpretation of the meaning of Bahá'í history. Introduction is by George Townshend. Includes an index but no footnotes to the innumerable historical allusions.

5.63. *idem*. Wilmette, Ill.: Bahá'í Publishing Company, 1950. xxiii, 412, [22] p.

5.64. *idem*. Wilmette, Ill.: Bahá'í Publishing Trust, 1957, 1965, 1970. xxiii, 412, 22 p.

5.65. *idem*. [rev. ed.] Wilmette, Ill.: Bahá'í Publishing Trust, 1974, 1979. xxiii, 436 p. LC card 75–318019.

5.66. *The Golden Age of the Cause of Bahá'u'lláh*. New York: Bahá'í Publishing Committee, 1932. 20 p.

5.67. *The Greatest Holy Leaf: A Tribute to Bahíyyih Khánum*. London: National Spiritual Assembly of the Bahá'ís of the United Kingdom, n.d. [1980?] [4] p.

5.68. *The Guardian's Message for the Centenary of the Martyrdom of the Báb*. n.p. [United States?], 1950. [4] p.

5.69. *Guidance for Today and Tomorrow*. comp. National Spiritual Assembly of the Bahá'ís of the British Isles. London: Bahá'í Publishing Trust, 1953, 1973. xi, 273 p.

Extracts from letters by the Guardian (published in full in other volumes) dealing with a number of broad Bahá'í topics.

5.70. *Guidance for Youth.* comp. National Spiritual Assembly of the Bahá'ís of the United Kingdom. London: Bạhá'í Publishing Trust, n.d. [between 1963 and 1969] 11 p.; 1969. 12 p.

5.71. *The Heart of the Entire Planet.* London: National Spiritual Assembly of the Bahá'ís of the British Isles, n.d. [1939 or 1940?] 6 leaves.

5.72. *High Endeavors: Messages to Alaska.* [Anchorage]: National Spiritual Assembly of the Bahá'ís of Alaska, n.d. [1975?] xi, 112 p.

5.73. *High Endeavours: Messages to Alaska.* [Anchorage]: National Spiritual Assembly of the Bahá'ís of Alaska, 1976. ix, 85 p. LC card 77–151932.
    Letters written by and on behalf of the Guardian to individuals and Bahá'í institutions in Alaska. Includes an index and appended short extracts on specific topics.

5.74. *Importance and Methods of Close Collaboration Amongst the Institutions of the Faith.* n.p.: Continental Board of Counsellors in Africa, 1982. 13 p.

5.75. *The Importance of Teaching Indigenous People.* comp. the Universal House of Justice. [Toronto, Ont.]: National Spiritual Assembly of the Bahá'ís of Canada, 1968. 35 p.
    See 5.120, 5.132.

5.76. *The Institution of the Continental Boards of Counsellors.* [Toronto, Ont.]: National Spiritual Assembly of the Bahá'ís of Canada, n.d. [1970] 17 p.
    See 5.38–5.39, 5.55.

5.77. *idem.* [Thornhill, Ont.]: National Spiritual Assembly of the Bahá'ís of Canada, 1974. 17 p.

5.78. *Launching the World-Embracing Spiritual Crusade.* n.p. [Wilmette, Ill.]: National Spiritual Assembly, 1952. [4] p.

5.79. *Letter from Shoghi Effendi to the Bahais of America.* n.p. [United States], 1922. [7] p.

5.80. *Letters from Shoghi Effendi, January 21, 1922 – November 27, 1924.* New York: Bahá'í Publishing Committee, 1925. 24 p.

5.81. *Letters from Shoghi Effendi to the Believers of Central America and the Antilles from March 28, 1949 to October 6, 1957.* n.p. [San José, Costa Rica: National Spiritual Assembly of the Bahá'ís of Central America and the Antilles], n.d. [196–?] [77] leaves; mimeographed.

5.82. *Letters from the Guardian to Australia and New Zealand, 1923–1957.* Sydney, N.S.W.: National Spiritual Assembly of the Bahá'ís of

Australia and New Zealand, 1970, 1971. viii, 140 p.
    An unindexed chronological compilation of letters written by and on behalf of Shoghi Effendi to believers and institutions in these two countries.

5.83. *Lifeblood of the Cause.* comp. the Universal House of Justice. London: Bahá'í Publishing Trust, 1970. 19 p. (Bahá'í Publishing Trust Compilation Series; no.3).
    See 5.25, 5.52.

5.84. *idem.* 2nd ed. London: Bahá'í Publishing Trust, 1975. 20 p. (Bahá'í Publishing Trust Compilation Series; no.3).

5.85. *The Light of Divine Guidance: The Messages from the Guardian of the Bahá'í Faith to the Bahá'ís of Germany and Austria.* Hofheim-Langenhain: Bahá'í-Verlag, 1982. 311 p.
    Letters covering the period 1922–57 addressed to the national Bahá'í institutions of Germany and Austria and to some important local communities and individuals.

5.86. *The Light of Divine Guidance, Second Volume: Letters from the Guardian of the Bahá'í Faith to Individual Believers, Groups and Bahá'í Communities in Germany and Austria.* Hofheim-Langenhain: Bahá'í-Verlag, 1985. 136 p.

5.87. *Living the Baha'i Life.* [Manila]: National Spiritual Assembly of the Bahá'ís of the Philippines, 1980. 22 p.
    See 5.26, 5.51, 5.88–5.92.

5.88. *Living the Life.* comp. the Universal House of Justice. Kingston: National Spiritual Assembly of the Bahá'ís of Jamaica, n.d. [197–] 44 p.
    See 5.26, 5.51, 5.87, 5.92.

5.89. *idem.* New Delhi: Bahá'í Publishing Trust, n.d. [1972?] 52 p. [1978] 51 p.

5.90. *idem.* n.p. [Johannesburg: National Spiritual Assembly of the Bahá'ís of South and West Africa], n.d. [1972] 8 p.

5.91. *idem.* Karachi: Bahá'í Publishing Trust, 135 B.E. [1978–1979] 39 p.

5.92. *Living the Life.* London: Bahá'í Publishing Trust, 1974, 1984. 52 p.
    Two compilations, one of guidance given by the Guardian and the second of guidance given by the Universal House of Justice.
    See 5.26, 5.51, 5.87–5.91.

5.93. *Living the Life: A Compilation.* n.p. [Africa?], n.d. [1972 or later] 11 p.

5.94. *The Means of Triumph.* Dar Es Salaam: National Spiritual Assembly of the Bahá'ís of Tanzania, n.d. [197–] 1 p.

5.95. *Messages from the Guardian: Letters and Cablegrams Received by the National Spiritual Assembly from June 21, 1932 to July 21, 1940.* New York: Bahá'í Publishing Committee, 1940. 78 p.

'Compiled from Bahá'í News'; 'taken from the postscript of letters written through the Guardian's secretary, the postscripts being in Shoghi Effendi's own hand, and, from cablegrams likewise written by him over his own signature.'

5.96. *Messages from the Guardian Taken from Bahá'í News.* comp. James Heggie. [Australia]: James Heggie, 1972. 97 p.

5.97. *Messages to America: Selected Letters and Cablegrams Addressed to the Bahá'ís of North America, 1932–1946.* Wilmette, Ill.: Bahá'í Publishing Committee, 1947. iii, 118 p. LC card 48–13775.

Messages of the Guardian to Bahá'í institutions in North America during the upheavals preceding and during World War II. Includes a section of 'Notes and glossary' and a poor index.

5.98. *Messages to Canada.* [Toronto, Ont.]: National Spiritual Assembly of the Bahá'ís of Canada, 1965. xiii, 78 p.

Shoghi Effendi's letters to the Canadian Bahá'í community, 1923–57. Includes introduction by Hand of the Cause of God John A. Robarts, two pages of notes and an inadequate index of slightly over one page.

5.99. *Messages to the Bahá'í World 1950–1957.* Wilmette, Ill.: Bahá'í Publishing Trust, 1958. viii, 130 p. LC card 58–13187.

First collection bringing together letters of the Guardian addressed to the entire Bahá'í world. The Ten Year Crusade, launched in 1953, was the first worldwide Bahá'í teaching plan and most of the messages deal with the prosecution of this plan.

5.100. *idem.* Wilmette, Ill.: Bahá'í Publishing Trust, 1971. viii, 182 p. LC card 79–23900.

Appends a number of messages not included in the 1958 edition.

5.101. *A Mysterious Dispensation of Providence: A Message from the Guardian on the Persecution of the Bahá'ís in Irán.* Wilmette, Ill.: National Spiritual Assembly of the Bahá'ís of the United States, 1955. [7] p.

5.102. *The National Convention: A Handbook on the Functions, Significance, Principles and Procedures Involved in Baha'i National Conventions.* comp. from the writings of Shoghi Effendi and the Universal House of Justice by Organizing Committee of the National Convention of Malaysia. [Kuala Lumpur]: Organizing Committee, 129 B.E. [1973] [3], 8 leaves.

5.103. *The National Spiritual Assembly.* comp. the Universal House of Justice. Wilmette, Ill.: Bahá'í Publishing Trust, 1972, 1975. 61 p. Cover has subtitle: *An Institution of the Bahá'í Administrative Order.*
See 4.267.

5.104. *idem.* 2nd enl. ed. London: Bahá'í Publishing Trust, 1973. 40 p. (Bahá'í Publishing Trust Compilation Series; no.5).

5.105. *O le Uiga Moni o Filifiliga Baha'i = The Nature of Baha'i Elections.* [Apia]: National Spiritual Assembly of the Bahá'ís of Samoa, n.d. [1980?] [2] leaves. Samoan and English text.

5.106. *The Passing of 'Abdu'l-Bahá.* co-author Lady Blomfield. Haifa: Rosenfeld Brothers, 1922. 36 p.
Shoghi Effendi's record of the passing and funeral of his grandfather.
See 5.12.

5.107. *idem.* London: Bahá'í Publishing Trust, n.d. [196–?] 29 p.

5.108. *idem.* Stuttgart, Germany: Wilhelm Heppeler, n.d. [1922?] 32 p.

5.109. *The Passing of the Greatest Holy Leaf: A Tribute.* n.p. [Haifa?], 1932, 12 p.

5.110. *A Pattern for Future Society.* Wilmette, Ill.: Bahá'í Publishing Committee, 1940, 1941, 1945, 1946, 1948. 3 p. (Bahá'í Reprint; no.5).

5.111. *idem.* Wilmette, Ill.: Bahá'í Publishing Trust, [1957] 5 p.

5.112. *idem.* Manchester, U.K.: Bahá'í Publishing Trust, n.d. [194– or 195–] [4] p.

5.113. *idem.* New Delhi: Bahá'í Public Relations, n.d. [195–?] [3] p.

5.114. *Political Non-Involvement and Obedience to Government: A Compilation of Some of the Messages of the Guardian and the Universal House of Justice.* comp. Peter J. Khan. n.p. [Mona Vale, N.S.W.]: Bahá'í Publications Australia, 1979, 1980, 1984. 31 p.

5.115. *Principles of Bahá'í Administration.* 1st ed. London: Bahá'í Publishing Trust, 1950. 125 p. LC card 52–43414.

A compilation of Bahá'í procedure for use by assemblies, groups and individuals. 'The attempt has been made to keep the compilation as free as possible from restrictive and perhaps temporary regulations because in an evolving organism like the present Bahá'í community the processes of its procedure must also be kept fluid. The contents of the book are therefore of an impermanent nature and will require to be superseded at some future date.' [Preface]

5.116. *idem.* 2nd ed. London: Bahá'í Publishing Trust, 1963. xiv, 109 p.

5.117. *idem.* 3rd ed. London: Bahá'í Publishing Trust, 1973. xii, 116 p.

5.118. *idem.* 4th ed. London: Bahá'í Publishing Trust, 1976. xii, 116 p.

5.119. *idem.* New Delhi: Bahá'í Publishing Trust, 1982. xii, 116 p.

5.120. *Principles of Mass Teaching.* comp. the Universal House of Justice. n.p. [Toronto, Ont.]: National Spiritual Assembly of the Bahá'ís of Canada, 1971. 27 p.
    See 5.75, 5.132.

5.121. *The Promised Day Is Come.* Wilmette, Ill.: Bahá'í Publishing Committee, 1941, 1943, 1951. 136 p. LC card 41–18937.
    In the middle of World War II the Guardian of the Bahá'í Faith addressed this long letter to the Bahá'ís of the West in which he analyzed the disintegration of nations, societies and religions. 'Shoghi Effendi looks at history in the light of its essence: the relationship between temporal man and eternal God.' [Preface]

5.122. *idem.* 1961 ed. Wilmette, Ill.: Bahá'í Publishing Trust, 1961, 1967. x, 136 p. LC card 61–12434.

5.123. *idem.* rev. ed. Wilmette, Ill.: Bahá'í Publishing Trust, 1980. vi, 137 p. LC card 79–23981.

5.124. *idem.* Bombay, India: Bahá'í Assembly of Bombay, 1942. 176 p.

5.125. *idem.* 2nd Indian ed. New Delhi: Bahá'í Publishing Trust, 1976. vii, 136 p.

5.126. *Religion a Living Organism.* New York: Bahá'í Publishing Committee, 1940, 1941. 7 p. (Bahá'í Reprint; no.4).

5.127. *The Rising World Commonwealth.* [London]: Bahá'í Publishing Trust, 1945. 30 p.

5.128. *Rock-Bottom Requirements: Shoghi Effendi's Last Letter to the British Bahá'í Community.* London: National Spiritual Assembly of the Bahá'ís of the United Kingdom, n.d. [1981?] [3] p.

5.129. *The Sacred Epistles of the Beloved Guardian (Shoghi Effendi) Addressed to the Late Revered Hand of the Cause of God, Janab-i-Syyed Mustapha Roumie.* Rangoon: National Spiritual Assembly of the Bahá'ís of Burma, n.d. [196–?] [2], 40 p.

5.130. *Selected Writings of Shoghi Effendi.* Wil-mette, Ill.: Bahá'í Publishing Committee, 1942. 45 p.

5.131. *idem.* rev. ed. Wilmette, Ill.: Bahá'í Publishing Trust, 1975. vii, 37 p.

5.132. *A Special Measure of Love: The Importance and Nature of the Teaching Work Among the Masses.* Wilmette, Ill.: Bahá'í Publishing Trust, 1974. v, 33 p.
    See 5.75, 5.120.

5.133. *Spiritual Potencies of That Consecrated Spot.* New York: Bahá'í Publishing Committee, 1940. 7 p.

5.134. *Spiritualization of Our Social Relations = Boitshephiso jwa Botsalanojwa Rona.* n.p. [Mmabatho: National Spiritual Assembly of the Bahá'ís of Bophuthatswana], n.d. [1984] 1 p.
    Excerpts from *The Advent of Divine Justice* and another letter of Shoghi Effendi's.

5.135. *The Transformation of Human Society: A Bahá'í Commentary on the Current World Crisis.* Wilmette, Ill.: Bahá'í Public Relations, 1947. 11 p.

5.136. *Unfolding Destiny of the British Bahá'í Community: A Compilation of Some of the Letters and Cables of the Beloved Guardian Addressed to the British Bahá'í Community.* London: National Spiritual Assembly of the Bahá'ís of the British Isles, 1962. 41 leaves.

5.137. *idem.* Oakham, Eng.: Bahá'í Publishing Trust, 1976. 41 p.

5.138. *The Unfolding Destiny of the British Bahá'í Community: The Messages from the Guardian of the Bahá'í Faith to the Bahá'ís of the British Isles.* London: Bahá'í Publishing Trust, 1981. xviii, 529 p. LC card 82–124826.
    In addition to letters to the national institutions, this compilation includes letters to Spiritual Assemblies and individuals. Appended is a valuable section of biographical notes on important individuals mentioned. Extensive index.

5.139. *The Unfoldment of World Civilization.* New York: Bahá'í Publishing Committee, 1936. 46 p. LC card 44–12393.

5.140. *idem.* 1st British ed. n.p. [London]: Bahá'í Publishing Trust, n.d. [1936] 46 p.
    Reproduced photographically from the 1936 New York ed.

5.141. *idem.* Wilmette, Ill.: Bahá'í Publishing Committee, 1945. pp. 161–206.

5.142. *World Government & Collective Security: A Collection of Some Bahá'í Quotations.* New Delhi: National Spiritual Assembly of the Bahá'ís of India, Pakistan & Burma, 1953 (Delhi: National Printing Works). 15 p.

5.143. *The World Moves on to Its Destiny.* Wilmette, Ill.: Bahá'í Publishing Committee, n.d. [194–] 4 p.

5.144. *The World Order of Bahá'u'lláh.* New York: National Spiritual Assembly of the Bahá'ís of the United States and Canada, 1929 (New York: J.J. Little and Ives Co.). 12 p.

5.145. *The World Order of Bahá'u'lláh.* New York: Bahá'í Publishing Committee, 1938. xiv, 234 p. LC card 38–12104 rev.

Seven lengthy letters from the Guardian to the American Bahá'í community during the period 1929–36 presenting a dynamic exposition of the world mission of the Bahá'í Faith and clarifying the deeper implications of the Bahá'í teachings.

5.146. *idem.* Wilmette, Ill.: Bahá'í Publishing Committee, 1944. xvi, 234 p.

5.147. *idem.* Wilmette, Ill.: Bahá'í Publishing Trust, 1955. xvi, 234 p. LC card 56–17685.

5.148. *idem.* rev. ed. Wilmette, Ill.: Bahá'í Publishing Trust, 1965, 1969, vii, 234 p.

5.149. *The World Order of Bahá'u'lláh: Selected Letters.* 2nd rev. ed. Wilmette, Ill.: Bahá'í Publishing Trust, 1974, 1980, 1982. xiii, 234 p. LC card 75–311794.

Subtitle added with this edition.

5.150. *The World Order of Bahá'u'lláh, Further Considerations.* New York: National Spiritual Assembly of the Bahá'ís of the United States and Canada, 1930. 14 p.

5.151. *World Order Unfolds: Excerpts from Messages of Shoghi Effendi.* comp. National Spiritual Assembly of the Bahá'ís of the United States. Wilmette, Ill.: Bahá'í Publishing Committee, 1952. ii, 46 p.

5.152. *The World Religion: A Summary of Its Aims, Teachings and History.* New York: New York Bahá'í Center, n.d. [192–?] 7 p.

One of Shoghi Effendi's two classic summaries of the Bahá'í Faith (the other being *The Faith of Bahá'u'lláh*).

5.153. *idem.* New York: Bahá'í Publishing Committee, n.d. [before 1938], 1938. 7 p.

Two variants of 1938 printing: one with blank inside front cover; other with words 'For complete catalog of Bahá'í literature . . .'

5.154. *idem.* Wilmette, Ill.: Bahá'í Publishing Committee, 1941. 7 p.

5.155. *idem.* Karachi: Baha'i Spiritual Assembly of Karachi, n.d. [between 1923 and 1947] 7 p.

5.156. *A World Survey, the Bahá'í Faith, 1844–1944.* comp. Shoghi Effendi. Wilmette, Ill.: Bahá'í Publishing Committee, 1944. 24 p.

See 5.21.

5.157. *Worship in the Completed Temple.* n.p. [Wilmette, Ill.: National Spiritual Assembly of the Bahá'ís of the United States], n.p. [1950] 1 p.

VI
Works and Messages of the Universal House of Justice

THE Universal House of Justice, the international governing council of the Bahá'í administrative order, was ordained by Bahá'u'lláh, and its method of election and general duties defined by 'Abdu'l-Bahá. The Universal House of Justice legislates on all matters not dealt with in the Bahá'í sacred texts or in the interpretations of 'Abdu'l-Bahá and Shoghi Effendi. Its decisions within this sphere of authority are defined as infallible. These decisions, however, are subject to amendment or abrogation by the Universal House of Justice as conditions in society change.

6.1. *Analysis of the Five Year International Teaching Plan 1974–1979.* Haifa: Universal House of Justice, 1975. 103 p. LC card 82–178664.
A detailed overview of the goals of the third global teaching campaign.

6.2. *Analysis of the Nine Year International Teaching Plan 1964–1973.* Wilmette, Ill.: Bahá'í Publishing Trust, 1964. 38 p.
A detailed geographical analysis of the goals of the second international plan for the expansion of the Bahá'í Faith.

6.3. *Analysis of the Seven Year Plan, 1979–1986: Second Phase Goals, 1981.* Haifa: Universal House of Justice Statistics Department, 1981. iii, 128 p.

6.4. *The Bahá'í Faith, Statistical Information 1844–1968: Including the Current Status of the Goals of the Nine Year International Teaching Plan, 1964–1973.* Haifa: Universal House of Justice, 1968. 104 p.

6.5. *The Bahá'í Faith (Statistical Information), 1844–1968: Showing Current Status and Outstanding Goals of the Nine Year International Teaching Plan, 1964–1973.* Haifa: Universal House of Justice, 1968. 168 p.

6.6. *The Bahá'í Holy Places at the World Centre.* Haifa: Bahá'í World Centre, 1968. xi, 89 p. LC card 78–15969.
Originally a set of mimeographed sheets clipped together for use by Bahá'í pilgrims, this volume is enlarged and printed with illustrations and background on the 21 holy sites described.

6.7. *Canada and the Five Year Plan = Le Canada et le Plan de Cinq Ans.* Thornhill, Ont.: National Spiritual Assembly of the Bahá'ís of Canada, 1974. 18, 18, [10] p.

6.8. *The Constitution of the Universal House of Justice.* Haifa: Bahá'í World Centre, 1972. 16 p.
The 'Most Great Law', the constitutional charter for the supreme administrative institution of the Bahá'í Faith, touching also upon other levels of the Bahá'í order.

6.9. *The Continental Boards of Counselors: Letters, Extracts from Letters, and Cables from the Universal House of Justice. An Address by Counselor Edna M. True.* comp. National Spiritual Assembly of the Bahá'ís of the United States. Wilmette, Ill.: Bahá'í Publishing Trust, 1981. vi, 81 p. LC card 83–192912.

6.10. *The Five Year Plan: Messages from the Universal House of Justice to the Bahá'ís of the World and of the United States. Naw-Rúz 1974 Announcing the Objectives of the Third Global Teaching Campaign.* Wilmette, Ill.: Bahá'í Publishing Trust, 1974. 11 p.

6.11. *Five Year Plan Given to the Baha'is of East & West Malaysia.* [Kuala Lumpur: National Spiritual Assembly of the Bahá'ís of Malaysia], 1974. [8] p.

6.12. *The Five Year Plan, 1974–1979: Statistical Report, Riḍván 1978.* Haifa: Bahá'í World Centre, 1978. 60 p.
Progress report on the third global teaching campaign, first made available at the fourth International Bahá'í Convention.

6.13. *The Five Year Plan, 1974–1979: Statistical Report, Riḍván 1979.* Haifa: Bahá'í World Centre, 1979. 116 p.
Detailed summary of the results of the third global teaching campaign.

6.14. *Local Spiritual Assemblies: Further Extracts Issued with the Naw-Rúz Message 1979.* n.p. [London: National Spiritual Assembly of the Bahá'ís of the United Kingdom], n.d. [1979?] 6 p.

6.15. *A Message to the Attendants at the Canadian National Bahá'í Native Council, April 26–29,*

1981. n.p. [Thornhill, Ont.: National Spiritual Assembly of the Bahá'ís of Canada], n.d. [1981] [3] p.

6.15a. *Message to the Baha'i Youth in Every Land.* n.p. [Sydney, N.S.W.: National Spiritual Assembly of the Bahá'ís of Australia], 1966 (Mudgee, N.S.W.: Links Print). 6 p.

6.16. *Messages from the Universal House of Justice 1968–1973.* Wilmette, Ill.: Bahá'í Publishing Trust, 1976. x, 139 p. LC card 75–11795.

A sequel to *Wellspring of Guidance.* Consists of letters from the Universal House of Justice spanning that institution's second five-year term, covering Bahá'í developments during the second half of the Nine Year Plan and elucidating diverse questions confronting the Bahá'í community.

6.17. *Messages to the Bahá'í Youth of the World.* n.p. [Toronto, Ont.: National Spiritual Assembly of the Bahá'ís of Canada], n.d. [1969?] [6] p.

6.18. *The Nine Year Plan, 1964–1973: Statistical Report, Riḍván 1973.* Haifa: Universal House of Justice, 1973. 56 p.

6.19. *O le Fuafuaga o le Lima Tausaga i Bahá'í uma i Samoa, i Bahá'í o le Lalolagi = Five Year Plan to the Bahá'ís of Samoa, to the Bahá'ís of the World.* Apia: Niusipepa Bahá'í Samoa, 1974. 12 p. Samoan and English text.

6.20. *Perjanjian Keamanan Sedunia = The Promise of World Peace.* n.p. [Kuala Lumpur: National Spiritual Assembly of the Bahá'ís of Malaysia], 1985. 51 p. Malay and English text.
See 6.23–6.48, 6.52, 6.55.

6.21. *El Plan de Cinco Años, 1974–1979 = The Five Year Plan, 1974–1979.* [San Juan: National Spiritual Assembly of the Bahá'ís of Puerto Rico, 1974] 20, 20 p. English and Spanish text.

6.22. *Politics, the Bahá'í Viewpoint.* London: National Spiritual Assembly of the Bahá'ís of the United Kingdom, [1979] 11 p.

6.23. *[The Promise of World Peace]* [Presentation ed.] n.p. [Haifa: Bahá'í World Centre; Canada: Committee for Printing Deluxe Edition], 1985. 13 p., boxed, bound in leather, signed by the Universal House of Justice.

The first message addressed by the Universal House of Justice to the peoples of the world. Released in October 1985 to mark the beginning of the United Nations International Year of Peace and presented to many heads of state, heads of government, leaders of thought and dignitaries. The statement analyzes the paralysis of human will that has prevented the establishment of peace, some of the causes of war and the

steps necessary to reach the permanent cessation of hostilities.
See 6.20, 6.52, 6.55.

6.24. *The Promise of World Peace.* Haifa: Bahá'í World Centre [Canada: Committee for Printing Deluxe Edition], 1985. 13 p.
Presentation paper edition, oxblood cover.

6.25. *idem.* Haifa: Bahá'í World Centre, 1985. 21 p.
Several printings were done in both England and the United States.

6.26. *idem.* n.p. [Mona Vale, N.S.W.]: Bahá'í Publications Australia, 1985 (Canberra, CPN Publications). 21 p.
Includes on last page a guide to contents.

6.27. *idem.* n.p. [Mona Vale, N.S.W.]: National Spiritual Assemblies [sic] of the Baha'is of Australia, 1985. 21 p.
Brown cover with gold stamping.

6.28. *idem.* n.p. [Mona Vale, N.S.W.]: National Spiritual Assemblie [sic] of the Baha'is of Australia, 1985. 21 p.
Includes 2 p. insert introductory letter from the National Spiritual Assembly and a guide to contents.

6.29. *idem.* Belize: National Spiritual Assembly of the Bahá'ís of Belize, 1985. 21 p.

6.30. *idem.* Roseau: National Spiritual Assembly of the Bahá'ís of the Commonwealth of Dominica, 1985. 21 p.

6.31. *idem.* New Delhi: Bahá'í Publishing Trust, 1985. 21 p.

6.32. *idem.* Nairobi: Baha'i Publishing Agency, 1985 (Nairobi: Acme Press (K) Ltd.). 21 p.

6.33. *idem.* [Kuala Lumpur: National Spiritual Assembly of the Bahá'ís of Malaysia], 1985. 21 p.

6.34. *idem.* Auckland, N.Z.: National Spiritual Assembly of the Bahá'ís of New Zealand, 1985. 16 p.

6.35. *idem.* Auckland, N.Z.: National Spiritual Assembly of the Bahá'ís of New Zealand, 1985. 23 p. In glossy and matte covers.

6.36. *idem.* n.p. [Manila: National Spiritual Assembly of the Bahá'ís of the Philippines], 1985. 10 p.

6.37. *idem.* Johannesburg: National Spiritual Assembly of the Bahá'ís of South and West Africa, 1985. 21 cm.

6.38. *idem.* Port-of-Spain: National Spiritual Assembly of the Bahá'ís of Trinidad and Tobago, 1985. 28 p. Includes index.

6.39. *idem.* n.p. [London: National Spiritual Assembly of the Bahá'ís of the United Kingdom], 1985 (Cranleigh, Surrey: EntaPrint Ltd.). 28 p. White cover.

6.40. *idem.* n.p. [London: National Spiritual Assembly of the Bahá'ís of the United Kingdom], 1985 (Cranleigh, Surrey: EntaPrint Ltd.). [4], 28 p. Blue cover; includes preface and index.

6.41. *idem.* Wilmette, Ill.: Bahá'í Publishing Trust, 1985. 40 p. paper ed.

6.42. *idem.* Wilmette, Ill.: Bahá'í Publishing Trust, 1985. 40 p. Hard cover deluxe ed.

6.43. *The Promise of World Peace = (al-Salám al-'Álamí Wa'd Ḥaqq).* Rio de Janeiro: Editora Baha'i-Brasil [i.e. Beirut, Lebanon: Bahá'í Publishing Trust], 1985. 21, 27 p. English and Arabic text.

6.44. *The Promise of World Peace = (Vishwa Shanti Da Vada).* Chandigarh: State Publishing Committee of the Baha'is of Punjab, 1985. 22, 22 p. Text in English and Punjabi.

6.45. *The Promise of World Peace = O le Folafolaga o le Filemu mo le Lalolagi.* [Apia]: Fono Faaleagaga tau Atunuu a Bahai Samoa, 1985. 21, 18 p. Text in English and Samoan.

6.46. *The Promise of World Peace = Isithembiso Soxolo Lwelizwe.* Umtata: National Spiritual Assembly of the Bahá'ís of Transkei, Oct. 1985. 25 p. English and Xhosa text.

6.47. *The Promise of World Peace: A Message to the Peoples of the World.* Kansas City, Mo.: Baha'i Office of Public Affairs, 1985, 24 p.

6.48. *The Promise of World Peace: A Plan of Action.* Bethany, Okla.: Western Oklahoma District Baha'i Information Service, 1985. 16 p.

6.49. *Seven Year Plan.* n.p. [New Delhi: National Spiritual Assembly of the Bahá'ís of India], 1979. 14 p.

6.50. *The Seven Year Plan.* Wilmette, Ill.: Bahá'í Publishing Trust, 1980, 1981. 23 p.

The messages from the Universal House of Justice to the Bahá'ís of the world announcing the objectives of the fourth international teaching plan, published along with the message to the Bahá'ís of the United States. Appended is a set of 'Guidelines adopted by the National Spiritual Assembly of the Bahá'ís of the United States for the execution of the first phase of the Seven Year Plan'.

6.51. *The Seven Year Plan, 1979–1986: Statistical Report, Riḍván 1983.* Haifa: Bahá'í World Centre, 1983. 110 p.

6.52. *(Shì Jiè Hé Píng Dē Chéng Nuò) = The Promise of World Peace.* Hong Kong: National Spiritual Assembly of the Baĥ'ís [sic] of Hong Kong, 1985, Dec. 1985. 41 p. Text in Chinese and English.
   See 6.20, 6.23–6.48, 6.55.

6.53. *The Straight Path.* n.p. [Wilmette, Ill.: Bahá'í Publishing Trust], n.d. [1974] 4 p.

6.54. *Synopsis and Codification of the Laws and Ordinances of the Kitáb-i-Aqdas.* Haifa: Bahá'í World Centre, 1973. ix, 66 p. Title page title: *A Synopsis and Codification of the Kitáb-i-Aqdas, the Most Holy Book of Bahá'u'lláh.*

A comprehensive presentation, in outline form, of the laws and ordinances which appear in the *Kitáb-i-Aqdas* and in the appendix to that book known as the *Questions and Answers.* Contents include: introduction by the Universal House of Justice; passages from the *Kitáb-i-Aqdas* translated by Shoghi Effendi; synopsis and codification; notes and references. The passages which appear in this volume from the *Kitáb-i-Aqdas,* apart from a very few passages which have been translated and published in letters of the Universal House of Justice, are the only authoritative translation of this book from a Bahá'í viewpoint.
   See 1.18, 1.27–1.28, 1.75.

6.55. *(Va'dih-yi Ṣulḥ-i Jahání) = The Promise of World Peace.* n.p. [Karachi: National Spiritual Assembly of the Bahá'ís of Pakistan], 1985 (Hyderabad: Qurayshí Printing Press). 36, 21 p. Text in Sindhi and English.
   See 6.20, 6.23–6.48, 6.52.

6.56. *Wellspring of Guidance: Messages 1963–1968.* Wilmette, Ill.: Bahá'í Publishing Trust, 1969, 1970. viii, 159 p. LC card 72–261400.

Messages of the Universal House of Justice during its first term of office, touching particularly on the prosecution of the Nine Year Plan and on a number of questions about the implications of the death of Shoghi Effendi and the resulting absence of a living Guardian.

6.57. *idem.* 1st rev. ed. Wilmette, Ill.: Bahá'í Publishing Trust, 1976. viii, 150 p. LC card 76–129996.

VII
Works on the Bábí and Baháʾí Faiths

A

7.1. *A Klemechel a Baháʾuʾlláh = The Message of Baháʾuʾlláh*. Honolulu: National Spiritual Assembly of the Baháʾís of the Hawaiian Islands, 1985. 11 p. English and Palauan text.

7.2. Abasi, M.U. *A Brief Survey of Bahaʾi Movement*. Karachi: Asphandiar K.B. Bukhtair for the Bahaʾi Spiritual Assembly of Karachi, n.d. [192–?] 26 p.

Two variants, one with green cover, one with grey mottled cover.

7.3. *ʿAbduʾl-Bahá*. n.p.: Curtis D. Kelsey, n.d. [196–?] [4] p.

7.4. *ʿAbduʾl-Bahá*. n.p. [Apia: National Spiritual Assembly of the Baháʾís of Samoa], n.d. [197–] 4 p.

7.5. *ʿAbduʾl-Bahá*. Taipei: National Spiritual Assembly of the Baháʾís of Taiwan, 1978. 11, 19 p. (Kindled with the Fire of His Love). Text in Chinese and English.

7.6. *ʿAbduʾl-Bahá, 1844–1921, Fiftieth Anniversary Commemoration of the Passing of ʿAbduʾl-Bahá*. Colombo: National Spiritual Assembly of the Baháʾís of Ceylon, 1971. 30 p.

7.7. *ʿAbduʾl-Bahá, Fiftieth Anniversary of His Passing*. Wilmette, Ill.: World Order Magazine, 1971. 84 p.

Specially bound Fall 1971 issue of *World Order*, containing photos of ʿAbduʾl-Bahá and essays on his life, writings and books about him.

7.8. *ʿAbduʾl-Bahá, the Perfect Exemplar*. n.p., n.d. [197–?] 20 p.

7.9. *ʿAbduʾl-Baháʾs Visit to California, October 1912: A Compilation of Quotations and Commentary*. prepared by Charleen R. Maghzi. San Francisco: Spiritual Assembly of the Baháʾís of San Francisco, 1982. [4], 9, [7] p.

7.10. Abdul Hussein, Mirza. *Letter Written by Mirza Abdul Hussein on Behalf of the 'Friends' of Isfahan, Persia, to the American believers, April 25th, 1902*. trans. Mirza Ameen ʾUllah (Fareed). Chicago: Bahais Supply and Publishing Board, 1902. [4] p.

7.11. ʿAbduʾl-Karím Ṭihrání. *Addresses by Abdel Karim Effendi Teherani, Delivered Before the New York & Chicago Assemblies*. trans. by Anton F. Haddad. Chicago: Behais Supply and Publishing Board, 1900. 102 p. LC card 4–32684.

Abdel Karim Teherani (ʿAbduʾl-Karím Ṭihrání) was sent to the United States by ʿAbduʾl-Bahá to strengthen the believers after their former leader, Ibrahim Kheiralla, had sought to create a breach in the ranks of the Baháʾís. These essays were part of Abdel Karim's programme for keeping the Baháʾís steadfast.

7.12. Abuʾl-Faḍl Gulpáygání, Mírzá. *The Bahai Proofs, Hujajʾul Behäyyeh*. trans. Ishtael-ebn-Kalenter [Ali Kuli Khan]. 2nd ed. Chicago: The Grier Press, 1914. 288 p.

A classic introduction to Baháʾí teachings, written for an American Christian audience. 'Mírzá Abuʾl-Faḍl brought his own rationalist bent to bear on the problems of religion. He emphasized his logical proof for the religions, which held that the ability to endure and spread demonstrated their truth more effectively than did miracle stories.' [Foreword to 1983 facsimile ed.]

See 7.18.

7.13. —— *idem*. 3rd ed. New York: Baháʾí Publishing Committee, 1929. 288 p.

7.14. —— *The Baháʾí Proofs (Hujajaʾl-Bahíyyih); and A Short Sketch of the History of the Lives of the Leaders of This Religion*. trans. Ali-Kuli Khan (Ishtiʿal Ibn-i-Kalántar); introduction by Juan Ricardo Cole. Facsimile ed. of 1929 ed. Wilmette, Ill.: Baháʾí Publishing Trust, 1983. xiii, 305 p. LC card 83–22486.

7.15. —— *The Brilliant Proof, Burhäne Lämé*. Chicago: Bahai News Service, 1912. 37, 35 p. LC card 21–19953 rev.

Written in response to published attacks on the Baháʾí religion by the British clergyman Peter Z. Easton.

7.16. —— *idem*. Sydney: National Spiritual Assembly of the Baháʾís of Australia and New Zealand, 1949. 32 p.

7.17. —— *idem.* Wilmette, Ill.: Bahá'í Publishing Committee, 1949. 12 leaves.

7.18. —— *Hujaj'ul Beheyyeh, (The Behai Proofs).* trans. Ali Kuli Khan. New York: The J.W. Pratt Co., 1902. 310 p. LC card 2–24729 rev. *See 7.12–7.14.*

7.19. —— *Knowing God Through Love and Farewell Address of Mirza Abul Fazl.* Washington: Bahai Assembly of Washington D.C., 1904. 16 p.

7.20. —— *Letters and Essays, 1886–1913.* trans. Juan R.I. Cole. Los Angeles: Kalimát Press, 1985. xv, 193 p. LC card 85–18069.
A collection of essays and letters on diverse subjects by the most accomplished Bahá'í scholar of the first century of the Bahá'í Faith, selected from the Persian collection *Rasá'il va Raqá'im.* 'What is remarkable about the nature of Abu'l-Fadl's responses is that they are firmly based upon meticulous and prodigious historical inquiry and encyclopedic knowledge of sources, aided by full and free use of deductive reasoning.' [Introduction]

7.21. —— *Miracles and Metaphors.* trans. and annotated by Juan Ricardo Cole. Los Angeles: Kalimát Press, 1981. xx, 210 p. LC card 82–15309.
Reviews:
Kazemi, Farhad, *International Journal of Middle East Studies* (Cambridge, Eng.), v.16 no.2 (May 1984), pp. 280–281.
Lawson, B. Todd. *Religious Studies Review* (Macon, Ga.), v.11 no.2 (Apr. 1985), p. 206.
Royster, James E., *The Muslim World* (Hartford, Conn.), v.72 nos.3–4 (July–Oct. 1982), pp. 282–283.
Collection of essays and short commentaries by one of the most renowned of early Bahá'í scholars which sheds light on the doctrines of Christianity and Islam from a Bahá'í perspective.

7.22. —— *Translation of a Letter of Instruction from Mirza-Abul-Fazl. Twelfth Talk Given by Mrs. Isabella D. Brittingham. Teachings by Mirza Assad'Ullah.* New York: C.E. Sprague, n.d. [1904?] 12 leaves. Cover reads 'Volume 4'.

7.23. *Accompany Me In This Journey.* Haifa: William Collins, 1979. 28 p.

7.24. Accouche, Calneh. *Sublime Drama of Shoghi Effendi, Guardian of the Baha'i Faith.* [Mahé]: National Spiritual Assembly of the Baha'is of Seychelles, n.d. [1982] 25 p. Adapted from *The Priceless Pearl.*

7.25. *Activity of the Local Spiritual Assembly.* [Nairobi]: National Education Committee of the Bahá'ís of Kenya, 1973. (The Local Spiritual Assembly; 3). 9 p.

7.26. *Addenda to Statistical Information Published by the Hands of the Cause in the Holy Land in Ridván 1963: Countries Opened to the Faith of Bahá'u'lláh and Supplementary Accomplishments.* n.p. [Haifa: Bahá'í World Centre], n.d. [1964] 8 p.

7.27. *A-de-rih-wa-nie-ton On-kwe-on-we Neh-ha = A Message to the Iroquois Indians.* trans. Charles A. Cook. Toronto, Ont.: Bahá'í Publishing Committee, n.d. [195–] 11 p. English and Mohawk text.

7.28. *Administration.* ed. Advisory Committee on Education. Wilmette, Ill.: Bahá'í Publishing Trust, 1966. (Bahá'í Teacher's Handbook, v.4). 78 p.

7.29. *Administration: Functions of the Local Spiritual Assembly.* n.p. [Freetown: National Spiritual Assembly of the Bahá'ís of Sierra Leone], n.d. [1984] 2, 2 p.

7.30. *Administration Handbook.* [Limbe]: National Spiritual Assembly of the Bahá'ís of Malawi, n.d. [1975?] 6 p.

7.31. *idem.* [Harare]: National Spiritual Assembly of the Baha'is of Zimbabwe, 1984. [3], 5 p.

7.32. *An Adventure in Interfaith Understanding.* Toronto, Ont.: Canadian Bahá'í Community, 1967. 6 p.

7.33. Afnan, Ruhi. *Mysticism and the Baha'i Revelation.* New York: Bahá'í Publishing Committee, 1934. 80 p. LC card 35–3986 rev.
Written while the author was secretary to Shoghi Effendi. A comparison of Christian and Islamic mysticism with the Bahá'í approach to the subject. It is recognized that religion is fundamentally mystical in character and that the Christian, Islamic and Bahá'í traditions have common elements. The principles that prevent individual Bahá'ís from claiming mystic revelation are explained.

7.34. *Africa, Africa.* Lesotho: National Baha'i Convention, 1975. 16 p.

7.35. Afsharian, Payam. *Directory of Bahá'í Book Collectors, Bibliophiles, & Researchers.* Los Angeles: [Afsharian], 1984. 48 p.

7.36. —— *Directory of Collectors, Bahá'í Books and References, January 1981.* [Los Angeles]: Afsharian, 1981. 6 p.

7.37. Afshín, Mahnáz. *The Blessed Beauty Bahá'u'lláh.* n.p. [India]: Afshín, 1980 (New Delhi: Rakesh Press). 108 p.
Children's book.

7.38. —— *Let's Go to Heaven*. il. Chandrasekhar Joshi. n.p. [India]: Mrs Mahnáz Afshín, 1982 (Pune: Navyug). 27 p.
Children's book.

7.39. —— *The Story of Baha'u'llah*. New Delhi: Hemkunt Press, 1984. 72 p.
Children's book.

7.40. Ala'i, Lilian. *A Tribute to the Hands of the Cause of God*. n.p. [Manurewa, N.Z.]: Continental Board of Counsellors in Australasia, 1983. 10 p.

7.41. *Alaska!* n.p. [Anchorage: National Spiritual Assembly of the Bahá'ís of Alaska], 1978. pp. [8]–[13] Reprint from *Bahá'í News* (U.S.), (July 1978).

7.42. Alexander, Agnes Baldwin. *History of the Bahá'í Faith in Japan 1914–1938*. n.p. [Osaka]: Bahá'í Publishing Trust, Japan, 1977. 110 p.
Hand of the Cause of God Agnes Alexander's outline of Japanese Bahá'í history in which she was a significant participant. Includes photographs, an appendix of references to Japan in Bahá'í literature and some historical notes.

7.43. —— *Personal Recollections of a Bahá'í Life in the Hawaiian Islands: Forty Years of the Bahá'í Cause in Hawaii, 1902–1942*. Honolulu: National Spiritual Assembly of the Bahá'ís of the Hawaiian Islands, n.d. [1971?] 113 p.
Agnes Alexander, one of the first Hawaiian Bahá'ís, writes of Hawaii's Bahá'í history from personal experience.

7.44. —— *idem*. rev. ed. Honolulu: National Spiritual Assembly of the Bahá'ís of the Hawaiian Islands, 1974. 50 p.

7.45. Ali, Maulana Muhammad. *History and Doctrines of the Babi Movement*. Lahore: Ahmadiyya Anjuman Isha'at-i-Islam, 1933. ii, 94 p. LC card 72–204741.

7.46. Ali, Moulvi Mohammad. *The Babi Religion*. Lahore: The Mohammadan Tract and Book Depot, Punjab, n.d. [192–?] (Lahore: Central Printing Works). 52 p.

7.47. Ali, U. *Babism and Bahaism Examined*. New Kotwali, Agra: S.R. & Bros., 1956. 69 p.

7.48. Ali Kuli Khan. *On 'The Epistle to the Son of the Wolf': Notes and Brief Interpretations on the Course of Lectures Given at Green Acre Summer School at Eliot, Maine in August 1941*. n.p., n.d. [1941?] 32 leaves.

7.49. Alkany, Mohammed Ali. *Lessons in Religion*. trans. Edith Roohie Sanderson. Boston: Tudor Press, 1923. 97 p. LC card 24–6752.

7.50. Alpert, Carl. *Another Religion Calls Israel Home*. Wilmette, Ill.: Bahá'í Publishing Trust, n.d. [after 1963] [4] p. Reprint from *The Reconstructionist*, v.21 no.6.

7.51. Alter, S. Neale. *Studies in Bahaism*. Beirut: American Press, 1923. 72 leaves. LC card 49–42539.
Published version of the author's Ph.D. dissertation, which tends to be unfavourable to the Bahá'í Faith and to repeat standard Christian criticisms.

7.52. *Amaculo Ama = Baha'i Songs*. Umtata: National Spiritual Assembly of the Bahá'ís of Transkei, 1982. 16 p.

7.52a. *America, 200 Years of Imperishable Hope*. Editorial statement from *World Order* magazine. Wilmette, Ill.: Bahá'í Information Office, 1976. [8] p.

7.53. *America's Challenge: World Peace Through Racial Unity*. n.p. [Wilmette, Ill.]: NTC [i.e. National Teaching Committee], 1985, 1985. [8] p.

7.54. *And Did Those Feet*. London: Bahá'í Publishing Trust, 1970. 12 p.

7.55. *Åndelig Vekst*. n.p. [Oslo: National Spiritual Assembly of the Bahá'ís of Norway], n.d. [1982?] 15 p. Title page title: *A Plan Evolved by the Continental Board of Counsellors and the National Spiritual Assembly Comprising, 1. Insights into the Spiritualization of the Community, 2. A Plan of Action for Teaching*.

7.55a. Anderson, Angela. *Valley of Search*. Penzance, Cornwall: Wordens of Cornwall Limited, 1968. 158 p.
Autobiography of a British Bahá'í.

7.56. Anderson, Doreen. *World Unity: Children's Colouring and Study Book*. Port of Spain: National Spiritual Assembly of the Bahá'ís of Trinidad and Tobago, 1982. 5 [i.e. 10] leaves.

7.57. Anderson, Doreen; Billington, Joy. *Children's Colouring & Study Book*. Port of Spain, Trinidad: National Spiritual Assembly of the Bahá'ís of Trinidad and Tobago, 1983. [1], 5, 5 leaves. (Bahá'í Life; Book 1).

7.58. —— *Lesson Material for Children's Colouring & Study Book B*. n.p. [Port of Spain, Trinidad: National Spiritual Assembly of the Bahá'ís of Trinidad and Tobago], n.d. [1983] [10] p. (Bahá'í Life; Book 1).

7.59. Anderson, Norris. *Bahá'í, a Problem of Logic*. Manila: OMF, 1976. 10 p.
Anti-Bahá'í work from Christian viewpoint.

7.60. Andrews, Edna. *Bahá'í Youth Play, 'Qurratu'l-'Ayn'*. music arrangement by Earl M. Andrews. n.p., n.d. [1947?] 26 leaves.

7.61. Anglican Church of Canada. Diocese of Fredericton. *Bahá'í.* Fredericton, N.B.: Diocese of Fredericton, 1971. 9 p.
Anti-Bahá'í work from Christian viewpoint.

7.62. *An Anthology for Bahá'í Children.* [comp.] Abbás Afnán. London: Bahá'í Publishing Trust, 1979. 48 p.

7.63. *Appreciations of the Bahá'í Faith: Reprinted from The Bahá'í World. Vol. VIII.* Wilmette, Ill.: Bahá'í Publishing Committee, 1941. 66 p.

7.64. *Appreciations of the Bahá'í Faith: Reprinted from The Bahá'í World. Vol. VIII and IX.* Wilmette, Ill.: Bahá'í Publishing Committee, 1947. 69 p.

7.65. Arbab, Farzam. *I Am a Bahá'í.* n.p. [Bogotá]: National Spiritual Assembly of the Bahá'ís of Colombia, 1982. 27 p.

7.66. *'Arise to Further My Cause and to Exalt My Word Amongst Men . . .'* n.p. [Johannesburg: National Spiritual Assembly of the Bahá'ís of South and West Africa], n.d. [1984] 5 p.

7.67. Armstrong-Ingram, R.J. *Singers to the King.* n.p. [Mishawaka, Ind.]: Aubade, 1985. 13 p.
History of the first Bahá'í chorus, the Vahid Choral Society of Chicago.

7.68. As͟hraf, Farámarz. *A Short Essay on Baha'i Faith.* n.p. [Iran], n.d. [1974] 71 p.

7.69. *idem.* trans. Ninous As͟hraf. n.p. [Kelowna, B.C.: As͟hraf], n.d. [1985] 131 leaves.

7.69a. Ashton, Beatrice. *American Baha'is in the Time of World Peril: A World Crusade Message from the Guardian, Dated July 28, 1954.* outline prepared by Mrs Beatrice Ashton. Wilmette, Ill.: Bahá'í Publishing Committee, n.d. [1954?] 5 leaves.

7.70. —— *Outline of Course on the World Crusade.* n.p., n.d. [between 1957 and 1963] i, 14 leaves.

7.71. Assad'Ullah, Mirza. *Explanations Concerning Sacred Mysteries.* trans. Dr Fareed. Chicago: Behais Supply and Publishing Board, 1902. 159 p. Cover title: *Sacred Mysteries.*
Explanation of a number of topics of interest to Christians.

7.72. —— *Instructions Concerning Genesis and the Mystery of Baptism.* trans. Alla Khuli [sic] Khan. n.p., n.d. [190–] 32 p.

7.73. —— *The Mystery of Baptism.* trans. Mirza Ali Kuli Khan. n.p., n.d. [190–] 4 p.

7.74. —— *The School of the Prophets.* trans. Ameen Ullah Fareed; with an introduction by Edwin Harley Pratt. Chicago: Bahai Publishing Society, 1907. 163 p. LC card 7–42319.
An introductory text discussing the results of the coming of the Prophets and the basic teachings of the Bahá'í Faith. The work grew out of private correspondence which was not originally intended to become a book.

7.75. Association for Bahá'í Studies (Ottawa, Ont.). *Association d'Études Bahá'íes = Association for Bahá'í Studies.* Ottawa, Ont.: Association for Bahá'í Studies, n.d. [1983] [8] p.

7.76. —— *First International Symposium on the Bahá'í Faith and Islam: March 23–25, 1984, McGill University, Montreal, Québec, Canada.* Ottawa: Ont.: Association for Bahá'í Studies, 1984. [8] p.

7.77. Association for Bahá'í Studies – Australia: Annual Conference (4th: 1985: Yerrinbool, N.S.W.). *Proceedings of the Fourth Annual Conference of the Association for Baha'i Studies – Australia 1985, Yerrinbool, N.S.W..* Willeton, W.A.: Association for Bahá'í Studies – Australia, 1985. 159 p.

7.78. Association for Social and Economic Development in Southern Africa. *Proceedings of Their First Conference, Mbabane, Swaziland, 18–19 August 1984.* Mbabane: Association for Social and Economic Development in Southern Africa, 1984. 72 leaves.

7.79. *Attacks on Bahá'ís in Iran.* [Wilmette, Ill.]: U.S. Bahá'í Information Office, 1979. 2 p.

7.80. *Audio-Visual Library.* Wilmette, Ill.: National Teaching Committee, n.d. [196–] [6] p. folder.

7.81. *Auguste Forel and the Bahá'í Faith with Commentary by Peter Mühlschlegel.* Oxford: George Ronald, 1978. 60 p. LC card 79–670255.
Letter of the eminent psychiatrist and entomologist to 'Abdu'l-Bahá, the latter's lengthy reply treating of several scientific issues and supplementary information. 'Abdu'l-Bahá's reply led to Forel's stating in 1921, 'I have become a Bahá'í'.

7.82. Austin, Elsie. *Above All Barriers: The Story of Louis G. Gregory.* Wilmette, Ill.: Bahá'í Publishing Trust, 1964, 1965, 1969. 18 p.; 1976. iv, 18 p.

7.83. —— *The Story of Louis G. Gregory.* Wilmette, Ill.: Bahá'í Publishing Trust, 1955. 22 p.

7.84. —— *The Story of Louis G. Gregory, First Negro Hand of the Cause of Bahá'u'lláh.* n.p. [Wilmette, Ill.?], n.d. [195–] [6] p.

7.85. Australia. Parliament. *Persecution of Members of the Bahá'í Faith in Iran: Extracts from the*

Proceedings of the Australian Federal Parliament . . . n.p. [Mona Vale, N.S.W.]: Bahá'í Publications Australia, 1981. 18 p.

7.86. Australia. Parliament. Legislative Research Service. Foreign Affairs Group. *Notes on the Persecution of the Baha'is in Iran*. n.p. [Canberra, A.C.T.]: Legislative Research Service, 1984. 10 p.

7.87. Axford, Emily M. *The Baha'i Faith: The World Order of Baha'u'llah: Radio Talks*. n.p. [Australia], n.d. [194–] (Sydney: G.A. Jones (Sydney) Pty. Ltd. Print). [13] p.

7.88. Ayman, Iraj. *Significance of Sacrifice*. Setapak, Malaysia: Bahá'í Publishing Trust Committee, 1985. [4], 25 p.

B

7.89. *B*. n.p. [Belize City: Children and Family Life Committee], n.d. [1984] 8 p. Songbook.

7.90. *B.E. 130, 1973–1974*. New Delhi: Bahá'í Publishing Trust, 1973. [98] p.

7.91. *B.E. 135–136 Bahá'í History Calendar: 1979 International Year of the Child*. Honolulu: National Spiritual Assembly of the Bahá'ís of the Hawaiian Islands, 1978. [32] p. (Bahá'í History Calendar).

7.92. *The Báb*. n.p., n.d. [197–] 8 p.

7.93. *The Báb*. [Apia]: National Spiritual Assembly of the Bahá'ís of Samoa, n.d. [197–].

7.94. *The Báb*. Georgetown, Guyana: National Baha'i Office, n.d. [1977?]

7.95. *The Báb*. Taipei: National Spiritual Assembly of the Bahá'ís of Taiwan, 1979. 11, 30 p. (Kindled with the Fire of His Love).

7.96. *The Bab*. n.p. [Victoria: National Spiritual Assembly of the Bahá'ís of Cameroon], n.d. [1980] 6 p.

7.97. *The Bab*. n.p. [Freetown: National Spiritual Assembly of the Bahá'ís of Sierra Leone], n.d. [1984] 6 p.

7.98. Bach, Marcus. *Baha'i, a Second Look*. n.p. [Wilmette, Ill.: Bahá'í Publishing Trust, between 1957 and 1965] 3 p. Reprint from *The Christian Century*.

7.99. *idem*. Wilmette, Ill.: Bahá'í Publishing Trust, n.d. [196–?] 8 p.

7.100. —— *Shoghi Effendi, an Appreciation*. New York: Hawthorn Books, 1958. 42 p. LC card 58–10005.
Revision of chapter 3 of *The Circle of Faith*.

7.101. Backwell, Richard. *The Christianity of Jesus*. Portlaw, Ireland: Volturna Press, 1972. 128 p. LC card 73–330996.
The author attempts to reconstruct, from a Bahá'í perspective, what Jesus taught. Although some conclusions may be called into question,

the work is a valuable examination of essential Gospel teaching from a Bahá'í viewpoint.

7.102. *idem*. Peterhead, Scotland: Volturna Press, 1973. 128 p.

7.103. *idem*. Hythe, Kent: Volturna Press, 1977. 128 p.

7.104. *Badí'*. [Toronto]: National Spiritual Assembly of the Bahá'ís of Canada, n.d. [196–] [8] p.

7.105. Badí'í, Hooshmand. *The Baha'i Fund: A Time for Sacrifice*. Dhaka: National Spiritual Assembly of the Baha'is of Bangladesh, 1984. 43 p.

7.106. Badi'Ullah, Mirza. *Epistle to the Bahai World*. trans. Dr Ameen'Ullah Fareed. Chicago: Bahai Publishing Society, 1907. 28 p.
Badí'u'lláh was a brother of 'Abdu'l-Bahá, and of Muḥammad-'Alí, who opposed 'Abdu'l-Bahá. Badí'u'lláh turned away from Muḥammad-'Alí and in this letter exposed the latter's tactics and machinations against the Head of the Bahá'í Faith.

7.107. Bagley, Florence. *Your Participation in Bahá'í Programs*. n.p. [Wilmette, Ill.]: National Teaching Committee, 1969 [8] p.

7.108. *Bahá'í*. Honiara: National Spiritual Assembly of the Bahá'ís of the Solomon Islands, 1978. 8 p.

7.109. *Bahá'í*. il. Marcia J. Moore; comp. Kats and Happy Tamanaha. Honolulu: National Spiritual Assembly of the Bahá'ís of the Hawaiian Islands, 1973. 38 p.

7.110. *Bahá'í*. London: Bahá'í Publishing Trust, 1968. [8] p.

7.111. *Bahá'í*. n.p. [Auckland]: National Spiritual Assembly of the Bahá'ís of New Zealand, n.d. [196–?] [8] p.

7.112. *Bahá'í*. Bromley, Kent: Christian Information Centre, n.d. [197–] [11] p.

Anti-Bahá'í pamphlet from the viewpoint of the Children of God.

7.113. *Bahá'í.* n.p. [Wilmette, Ill.]: [National Teaching Committee], 1985, 1985. [8] p. Sometimes listed with title: *Bahá'í, Perhaps You've Heard of Us . . .*

7.114. *Bahá'í, a New Concept: The Earth One Country.* London: N.S.A. of the Baha'is of the United Kingdom, n.d. [197–?] [6] p.

7.115. *Bahá'í, a New Day: 7th Australian Bahá'í Youth Conference, 1976, Song Book.* n.p. [Sydney?, N.S.W.]: National Youth Committee, 1976. 36 p.

7.116. *Bahá'í, a New World Order.* Noumea, New Caledonia: Centre Bahá'í, n.d. [196–] 4 p.

7.117. *Bahá'í, a World Faith.* New Delhi: National Spiritual Assembly of the Bahá'ís of India, n.d. [195– or 196–] 17 p.

7.118. Bahá'í Academy (Panchgani, India). *Report Book, Eighteenth Course for Principles* [sic] *& Teachers of Baha'i Nursery & Primary Schools, 9th through 23rd June, 1985.* Panchgani: Bahá'í Academy, 1985. [12] p.

7.119. —— *Report Book, Nineteenth Course for Persian Pioneers, 23rd June through 21st July 1985.* Panchgani: Bahá'í Academy, 1985. [12] p.

7.120. —— *Report Book, 20th Course Research Group, 8th through 28th September 1985.* Panchgani: Bahá'í Academy, 1985. [4] p.

7.121. —— *Report Book, 21st Course for Travel Teachers, State Permanent Institute Coordinators, Social and Economic Development Coordinators and State Librarians.* Panchgani: Bahá'í Academy, n.d. [1985] [8] p.

7.122. —— *Report Book, 21st Course for Travel Teaching State Permanent Institute Coordinators, Social & Economic Development Coordinators, and State Librarians.* Panchgani: Bahá'í Academy, n.d. [1985] 8 p.

7.123. —— *Report Book, Twentysecond Course for Members of the Higher Institutions of the Faith (24 November – 9 December 1985).* Panchgani: Bahá'í Academy, 1985. 8 p.

7.124. —— *Report Book, Twentythird Course for Editors.* Panchgani: Bahá'í Academy, n.d. [1985] 8 p.

7.124a. *A Baha'i Address at Cross Street Chapel, Manchester, Sunday Evening, March 11th, 1923.* Manchester, U.K.: 1, Norton St., Hr. Broughton, 1923. [4] p.

7.125. *Bahá'í Anniversaries, Festivals and Days of Fasting.* n.p., n.d. [Wilmette: Bahá'í Publishing Committee, 195–]. [4] p. each.

Published with nearly the same text over a period of more than a decade, with various typefaces, colours and pagings.

7.126. *Bahá'í Answers.* Stanley, Falkland Islands: Local Spiritual Assembly of the Bahá'ís of Stanley, 1980. 15 p.

7.127. *Bahá'í Answers.* Wilmette, Ill.: Bahá'í Publishing Trust, 1957, 1965, 1967. 19 p.

7.128. *idem.* 1st rev. ed. Wilmette, Ill.: Bahá'í Publishing Trust, 1972, 1976, 1979, 1983. 23 p.

7.129. *Baha'i Answers.* Monrovia: National Spiritual Assembly of the Bahá'ís of Liberia, n.d. [1985] 8 p.

7.130. *The Baha'i Attitude Toward War.* San Francisco, Calif.: San Francisco Bahá'í Assembly, n.d. [191–] 4 p.

7.131. *(Bahá'ī Bhajana) = Baha'i Folk Songs: Part One.* Gwalior, India: STC North M.P., 1984. 34 p.

7.132. *Bahá'í Burial.* n.p. [Johannesburg]: National Spiritual Assembly of the Bahá'ís of South and West Africa, n.d. [1962?] 9 p.

7.133. *idem.* n.p. [Mbabane]: National Spiritual Assembly of the Baha'is of Swaziland, n.d. [1982?] 19, 20 p. English and Swati text.

7.134. *Bahá'í Calendar, 125, 1968/69.* Hellerup, Denmark, 1968. 22 p.

7.135. *Baha'i Calendar, 132 B.E.* n.p. [Lusaka: National Spiritual Assembly of the Bahá'ís of Zambia], 132 [1975] [15] p.

7.136. *Baha'i Calendar, 139–140 B.E., 1983.* n.p. [Bangkok]: Kamal Pars-Siam Co., Ltd., [1982] 1 p. with 6 calendar sheets.

7.137. *Bahá'í Calendar, 142 B.E., 1985–86.* n.p. [Gaborone: National Spiritual Assembly of the Bahá'ís of Botswana], 1985. [2] p.

7.138. *Bahá'í Calendar 1938.* n.p. [Wilmette, Ill.]: National Spiritual Assembly of the Bahá'ís of the United States and Canada, 1938. [7] p.

7.139. *Bahá'í Calendar 1939.* n.p. [Wilmette, Ill.]: National Spiritual Assembly of the Bahá'ís of the United States and Canada, 1939. [8] p.

7.140. *Bahá'í Calendar, Year 102 Combined with Gregorian Calendar.* n.p., n.d. [1945?] 20 p.

7.141. *The Bahá'í Cause: 'Abdu'l-Bahá's Message to Humanity in This Hour of Universal Change.* n.p. [New York?]: National Baha'i Assembly of United States and Canada, 1924, 1925. 8 p.

7.142. *The Bahá'í Centenary 1844–1944: A Record of America's Response to Bahá'u'lláh's Call to the Realization of the Oneness of Mankind* *to Commemorate the One Hundredth Anniversary of the Birth of the Bahá'í Faith*. Wilmette, Ill.: Bahá'í Publishing Committee, 1944. xix, 254 p. LC card 44–51037.

Essays, letters, photographs and other documentation of America's response to the message of Bahá'u'lláh.

7.143. *Bahá'í Centenary, 1844–1944, Washington, D.C..* Washington D.C., 1944. [4] p.

7.144. Bahá'í Centenary (1944: Chicago). *Bahá'í Centenary 1844–1944 All America Program: May 19th to May 24th, 1944, Bahá'í House of Worship, Wilmette, Illinois, May 25th, 1944, Hotel Stevens, Chicago.* Wilmette, Ill.: National Spiritual Assembly of the Bahá'ís of the United States and Canada, 1944. 15 p.

7.145. Bahá'í Centenary (1944: London). *The Centenary of the Bahá'í Faith. May 23rd 1944.* London: Bahá'í Centre, 1944. 12 p.

7.146. Bahá'í Centenary (1953: Chicago). *Centenary Birth of the Bahá'í Revelation, 1853–1953: Public Program, Chicago, Winnetka and Wilmette, April 29, May 1, 2, 3 and 6, 1953.* n.p. [Wilmette, Ill.]: National Spiritual Assembly of the Bahá'ís of the United States, 1953. [10] p.

7.147. *Bah'a'i [sic] Children Colouring Book.* il. Aartiste Services, Accra. [Accra]: National Spiritual Assembly of the Bahais of Ghana, 1984. [14] p.

7.148. *Bahá'í Children's Art Calendar, 134–135 B.E., 1978.* Victor, N.Y.: International Bahá'í Audio-Visual Centre, [1977] [16] p.

7.149. Bahá'í Children's Fair (3rd: 1985: Uttar Pradesh). *3rd Baha'i Children's Fair, 1985.* Uttar Pradesh: Bahá'í Tutorial Schools, 1985. [30] p.

7.150. *Bahá'í Classes for Children.* Nairobi: National Education Committee, 1973, 1974. 38 p.

7.151. *The Bahá'í Club of Howard University.* Washington, D.C.: Bahá'í Club of Howard University, n.d. [1982?] [6] p.

7.152. Bahai Committee of Investigation. *General Letters, Kirchner Affair. 1917–1918.* n.p. [Washington D.C.?]: Committee of Investigation, [1918] 13 leaves.

7.153. —— *Report of the Bahai Committee of Investigation, 1917–1918.* n.p. [Washington, D.C.?]: Committee of Investigation, [1918] 51 leaves.

Report on alleged covenant-breaking in Chicago in 1917–18.

7.154. *Bahá'í Community Life.* Taipei: National Spiritual Assembly of the Bahá'ís of Taiwan,

1978. 11, 20 p. (Kindled with the Fire of His Love).

7.155. *Bahá'í Community Life.* Wilmette, Ill.: Bahá'í Publishing Trust, 1976. v, 18 p. (Star Study Program).

7.155a. *The Bahá'í Community of Manchester Centenary Programme: June 17th–25th, 1944.* Manchester, U.K.: Bahá'í Community of Manchester, 1944. [4] p.

7.156. Bahai Conference and Congress, Western States Region (2nd: 1924: San Francisco). *Second Annual Bahai Conference and Congress, Western States Region: September 26, 27 and 28, 1924: California Club, 1750 Clay Street, San Francisco.* San Francisco, Calif.: Bahai Western Regional Committee, 1924. 4 p.

7.157. *Bahai Congress: Held by the Bahai Temple Unity for the Exposition of the Universal Principles, Economic, Social and Religious of the Bahai Movement.* Washington, D.C.; Chicago: Bahai Congress Committee, 1916. [16] p.

7.158. *Baha'i Curriculum for Children.* n.p. [Dublin]: National Spiritual Assembly of the Baha'is of the Republic of Ireland, 1985. [240] leaves in binder.

7.159. *Bahá'í Date Book.* Wilmette, Ill.: Bahá'í Publishing Trust, 19–. Published yearly.

7.160. *idem.* [Kingston]: National Spiritual Assembly of the Bahá'ís of Jamaica, 1981– .

7.161. *Bahá'í Desk Calendar, 134 B.E..* Wilmette Ill.: Bahá'í Publishing Trust, 1977. 24 p.

7.162. *Bahá'í Desk Calendar, 135 B.E..* Wilmette, Ill.: Bahá'í Publishing Trust, 1978. [22] leaves.

7.163. *Bahai Diary, 101 B.E.. 1944–1945.* New Delhi: National Spiritual Assembly of the Bahá'ís of India and Burma, 1944. [228] p.

7.164. *The Bahá'í Electoral Process.* Wilmette, Ill.: Bahá'í Publishing Trust, 1973, 1973, 1980. xi, 48 p. (Bahá'í Comprehensive Deepening Program).

7.165. Bahá'í European Teaching Conference (1st: 1948; Geneva). *Record of First Bahá'í European Teaching Conference, Geneva, Switzerland, May 22–27, 1948.* n.p.: European Teaching Committee of the American NSA, 1948. 33 leaves.

7.166. *The Bahá'í Faith.* Manchester, U.K.: Bahá'í Publishing Trust, n.d. [195–], 1954. 16 p.

See 7.220–7.220b.

7.167. *idem.* London: National Spiritual Assembly of the Bahá'ís of the British Isles, n.d. [ca. 1960] 16 p.

7.168. *Bahá'í Faith*. London: National Spiritual Assembly of the Bahá'ís of the United Kingdom, n.d. [196– or 197–] [6] p.

7.169. *Bahá'í Faith*. New Delhi: Bahá'í Public Information Deptt. [sic], n.d. [197–?] 8 p.

7.170. *idem*. New Delhi: Bahá'í Public Information Dept., 1972. 4 p.

7.171. *Baha'i Faith*. n.p. [New Delhi: Bahá'í Publishing Trust], n.d. [197–?] [8] p. folder.

7.172. *The Baha'i Faith*. New Delhi: Baha'i Publishing Trust, n.d. [197–?] (Darya Ganj, Delhi: Prabhat Offset Press). [6] p. folder.

7.173. *The Bahá'í Faith*. n.p. [Freetown: National Spiritual Assembly of the Bahá'ís of Sierra Leone], n.d. [197–] [2] p.

7.174. *The Bahá'í Faith*. Vandalia, Ohio: Presidential Art Medals, 1971. [16] p. (Great Religions of the World Art Medal Series).

7.175. *Bahai Faith*. Kuala Lumpur: National Spiritual Assembly of the Baha'is of Malaysia, n.d. [before 1974] [6] p.

7.176. *Bahá'í Faith*. Port of Spain: National Bahá'í Centre, n.d. [1976?] 2 p. folded to 6 p.

7.177. *Bahá'í Faith*. n.p. [Belize City: National Spiritual Assembly of the Bahá'ís of Belize], n.d. [1976] [6] p.; [1978] [13] leaves.

7.178. *The Bahá'í Faith*. Wilmette, Ill.: Bahá'í Publishing Trust, 1978, 1980, n.d. [1982] [24] p. Illustrated teaching booklet.

7.179. *idem*. Thornhill, Ont.: Bahá'í Canada Publications, 1979, n.d. [1980], n.d. [1984] [24] p. Illustrated teaching booklet. Accompanying material: *How to Use Your New Teaching Book*.

7.180. *Bahá'í Faith*. prepared by the Auxiliary Board of the Bahá'ís in Malawi. Limbe: Spiritual Assembly of the Bahá'ís in Malawi, 1979. 4 p.

7.181. *The Baha'i Faith*. n.p. [New Delhi: National Spiritual Assembly of the Bahá'ís of India], n.d. [1980] [8] p. Pamphlet used during the Indian Bahá'í centenary.

7.182. *The Baha'i Faith*. Lagos: National Spiritual Assembly of the Baha'is of Nigeria, 1981. [4] p.

7.183. *The Baha'i Faith*. Limbe, Malawi: Public Information Committee, n.d. [1982?] [2] p.

7.184. *The Bahá'í Faith*. Oakham, Leics.: Bahá'í Publishing Trust, n.d. [1983?] [6] p.

7.185. *The Bahá'í Faith*. London: Bahá'í Publishing Trust, n.d. [1984] [24] p. Illustrated teaching booklet.

7.186. *The Bahá'í Faith*. Roseau, Dominica: Bahá'í Faith [i.e. National Spiritual Assembly of the Bahá'ís of Dominica], n.d. [1984] [6] p. folder.

7.187. *The Baha'i Faith*. Singapore: Baha'i Centre, n.d. [1984] [6] p.

7.188. *The Bahá'í Faith*. London: National Spiritual Assembly of the Bahá'ís of the United Kingdom, n.d. [1985] [8] p.

7.189. *The Baha'i Faith, a Faith for Unity*. [London]: National Spiritual Assembly of the Bahá'ís of the British Isles, 1953. 11 leaves.

7.190. *The Baha'i Faith, a Magnificent Challenge*. n.p. [Wilmette, Ill.]: Radio Service Committee, 1960. 7 leaves.

7.191. *Bahá'í Faith, a Pattern for Future Society*. New Delhi: Bahá'í Public Information Department, n.d. [1972?] [4] p.

7.192. *The Baha'i Faith, a Summary of Its Aims, Purposes, History, Fundamental Teachings and Administrative Order*. West Englewood, N.J.: National Spiritual Assembly of the Bahá'ís of the United States and Canada, n.d. [192– or 193–] [3] p.

7.193. *Baha'i Faith, a Universal Religion*. Calcutta: Baha'i Spiritual Assembly, n.d. [193– or 194–] [2] p.

7.194. *The Baha'i Faith, a Universal Religion for Today's World: A New T.V. Series in the Chinese Language (Mandarin)*. San Fernando, Calif.: Light Years International, n.d. [1982] [4] p.

7.195. *The Bahá'í Faith, a World-Wide Cause for the Realization of the Oneness of Mankind*. New York: Bahá'í Publishing Committee, n.d. [193–] 11 p.

7.196. *The Bahá'í Faith, an Independent World Religion*. n.p. [Pacific Ocean], n.d. [197–] 4 p.

7.196a. *Bahá'í Faith, an Introduction*. Auckland: National Spiritual Assembly of the Baha'i [sic] of New Zealand, n.d. [197–?] [4] p.

7.197. *The Bahá'í Faith, an Introduction*. Seoul: Bahá'í Publishing Trust; Shirazi Enterprises, 1981. 37 p.

7.198. *The Bahá'í Faith and Christianity*. Lagos: National Spiritual Assembly of the Bahá'ís of Nigeria, n.d. [1981] [2] p.

7.199. *The Bahá'í Faith and Its World Community*. n.p. [Thornhill, Ont.]: National Spiritual Assembly of the Bahá'ís of Canada, 1982. 2 p.

7.200. *idem*. Hong Kong: National Spiritual Assembly of the Bahá'ís of Hong Kong, Oct. 1985. [2] p.
Omits Hong Kong statistics.

7.201. *idem.* Hong Kong: National Spiritual Assembly of the Bahá'ís of Hong Kong, Oct. 1985. [2] p.
Includes Hong Kong statistics.

7.202. *idem.* n.p. [Dublin]: National Spiritual Assembly of the Bahá'ís of the Republic of Ireland, 1985. [2] p.

7.203. *The Bahá'í Faith and the Arts.* Paddington: N.S.W.: National Spiritual Assembly of the Bahá'ís of Australia, n.d. [196–], n.d. [1985] [6] p.

7.204. *Baha'i Faith, Call to Mankind.* n.p. [Canada?], n.d. [196–?] [4] p.
Quotation from Bahá'u'lláh, 12 principles and notification of Bahá'í meeting which can be filled in by local communities.

7.205. *The Bahá'í Faith Fact Sheet.* Thornhill, Ont.: National Spiritual Assembly of the Bahá'ís of Canada, 1977. 16 p.
See 7.900.

7.206. *Baha'i' [sic] Faith Forging Links of Unity Around the World . . .* Dehilawa, Ceylon: L.S.A. of the Baha'is of Dehilawa-Mt. Lavinia, n.d. [1969?] [6] p.

7.207. *Bahá'í Faith, Fort Lauderdale.* Fort Lauderdale, Fla., n.d. [196–] 4 p.

7.208. *The Bahá'í Faith, God's Great Plan.* Lusaka, Zambia: Bahá'í Faith, n.d. [1978?], 1979. 6 p.

7.209. *The Baha'i Faith, God's Message for World Unity.* Limbe [Cameroon]: The Bahai Faith, n.d. [1983?] 8 p.

7.210. *The Bahá'í Faith: God's New Message.* Lagos: National Spiritual Assembly of the Bahá'ís of Nigeria, 1981. 19 leaves.

7.211. *The Baha'i Faith in Guyana, Silver Jubilee.* Georgetown, Guyana: National Bahá'í Centre, 1980. 6 p.

7.212. *The Bahá'í Faith in Russia: Two Early Instances.* Thornhill, Ont.: Canadian Association for Studies on the Bahá'í Faith, 1979. 21 p. (Bahá'í Studies; v.5).
Essays on the Bahá'ís in Ishqábád, by A.A. Lee, and on Leo Tolstoy's interest in the religion, by A.M. Ghadirian.

7.213. *The Bahá'í Faith Information Folder.* Mona Vale, N.S.W.: Bahá'í Publications Australia, n.d. [1979?], n.d. [1985 rev. reprint] 8 p.

7.214. *idem.* Nassau: National Spiritual Assembly of the Bahá'ís of the Bahamas, n.d. [1985] ˙8 p.

7.215. *The Baha'i Faith Information Folder.*

Lusaka: National Spiritual Assembly of the Baha'is of Zambia, n.d. [after 1976] 8 p.

7.216. *The Bahá'í Faith Information Folder.* Kuala Lumpur: Spiritual Assembly of the Bahá'ís of Malaysia, n.d. [1985] [10] p. folder.

7.216a. *Baha'i Faith, . . . 'O Ye Children of Men!'* Honolulu: National Spiritual Assembly of the Bahá'ís of the Hawaiian Islands, n.d. [197–?] (Delhi: Prabhat Offset Press Darya Ganj). [8] p. folder.

7.217. *The Bahá'í Faith Offers Convincing Answers to Your Questions About . . .* Wilmette, Ill.: Bahá'í Publishing Trust, 1962. 26 p.

7.218. *The Bahá'í Faith, Pathway to Peace.* Hofheim-Langenhain: Bahá'í-Verlag, n.d. [1985] 31 p.

7.219. *The Bahá'í Faith, Persecution in Iran.* London: National Spiritual Assembly of the Bahá'ís of the United Kingdom, 8 July 1981. 4 leaves; 25 November 1981. 5 leaves.

7.220. *The Bahá'í Faith: Religion Renewed and the World United.* London: Bahá'í Publishing Trust, 1954 (Norwich: Gildengate Press). 16 p.
See 7.166–7.167.

7.220a. *idem.* London: Bahá'í Publishing Trust, 1954 (Nottingham: Desa, [197–? printing]). 16 p.

7.220b. *idem.* London: Bahá'í Publishing Trust, 1954 (Nottingham: Desa, 1979). 16 p.

7.221. *The Bahá'í Faith: Spreading Love & Unity Day by Day, Invitation.* n.p. [Bangor, Wales: Audio Visual Centre], n.d. [1980?] [4] p.

7.222. *Baha'i Faith Symbolizes Unity; Observes Centenary with Plans for World Spiritual Crusade.* n.p., 1953. [4] p. Reprinted from *Color* magazine, Sept. 1953.

7.223. *The Bahá'í Faith, Ten Basic Teachings.* Bombay: Baha'i Centre, n.d. [196–?] 12 p.

7.224. *The Bahá'í Faith: The Earth Is But One Country, and Mankind Its Citizens.* Wilmette, Ill.: National Bahá'í Centre, n.d. [1984?] 8 p. folder.

7.225. *idem.* Dallas, Tex.: Baha'i Office of Public Affairs, Dallas/Fort Worth, 1985. 8 p. folder.

7.226. *The Bahá'í Faith, the Promise and the Challenge.* Logan, Utah: Spiritual Assembly of the Bahá'ís of Logan, n.d. [1981] [8] p.

7.227. *The Bahá'í Faith, the Promise and the Challenge.* n.p. [Wilmette, Ill.]: National Spiritual Assembly of the Bahá'ís of the United States, n.d. [197–] [4] p.

7.228. *Bahá'í Faith, the Spirit Way.* Wilmette,

Ill.: Bahá'í Publishing Trust, n.d. [1972], 1976, 1979. 29 p.

7.229. *Baha'i Faith, the Universal Religion.* Lagos: National Spiritual Assembly of the Bahá'ís of Nigeria, 1981. [6] p.

7.230. *Bahá'í Faith: There Is an Old Saying: 'When You See a Track or a Footprint That You Do Not Know, Follow It to the Point of Knowing'.* Thornhill, Ont.: National Spiritual Assembly of the Bahá'ís of Canada, n.d. [1984] 6, 8 p. English and Inuit text.

7.231. *The Bahai Faith Today: A Brief Summary.* Limbe, Malawi: Public Information Committee, n.d. [1979?] [36] p.

7.231a. *The Bahá'í Faith Unifies Mankind.* St Louis, Mo.: [National Spiritual Assembly of the Bahá'ís of the United States], n.d. [1974?] [8] p.
Includes programme and words to a 'mini-opera' performed at the St Louis National Teaching Conference (1974: St Louis, Mo.).

7.232. *The Baha'i Faith, Unity in Diversity.* Auckland: Public Relations Committee of the Baha'is of New Zealand, n.d. [1985] [12] p.

7.233. *The Baha'i Faith, Unity in Diversity: A Colourful Motion Picture Capturing the Diversity of People from Forty-Four Countries Gathered at the Bahá'í International Conference, Canberra, Australia.* Auckland, N.Z.: Ark Productions, n.d. [1984] [6] p.

7.234. *The Baha'i Faith, World Faith.* n.p. [New Delhi: National Spiritual Assembly of the Bahá'ís of India], n.d. [1980] [8] p.

7.235. *The Bahá'í Faith: You Are Invited to . . .* n.p. [Bangor, Wales: Audio Visual Centre], n.d. [1980?] [4] p.

7.236. *The Baha'i Fast.* n.p. [Nairobi]: National Education Committee of the Baha'is of Kenya, 1973. [4] p.

7.237. *The Bahá'í Feast.* n.p. [Apia]: National Spiritual Assembly of the Bahá'ís of Samoa, n.d. [196–] 4 p.

7.238. *Baha'i Founders.* n.p. [Wilmette Ill.: Child Education Committee?], n.d. [1940?] [18] leaves.

7.239. *The Baha'i Fund.* n.p. [Lagos]: National Spiritual Assembly of the Bahá'ís of Nigeria, 1982 (Jos: Adakula Printing Press). [4] p.

7.240. *The Bahá'í Fund.* n.p. [Nairobi]: National Education Committee of Kenya, n.d. [1973] [4] p.

7.241. *The Bahá'í Fund.* n.p. [Apia]: National Spiritual Assembly of the Bahá'ís of Samoa, n.d. [197–] 4 p.

7.242. *The Baha'i Fund.* n.p. [Bhubaneswar]: [Bahá'í] State Teaching Committee [of Orissa], n.d. [1984] 5 leaflets (2 p. each).

7.243. *The Bahá'í Fund.* n.p. [Freetown: National Spiritual Assembly of the Bahá'ís of Sierra Leone], n.d. [1984] 2 p.

7.244. *The Bahá'í Fund, an Orientation for Newly Enrolled Bahá'ís.* n.p. [Wilmette, Ill.: Office of the Treasurer], n.d. [1981?] [4] p.

7.245. *Bahá'í Funds Practical Guide: Where to Send Donations, What to Send Donations for.* n.p. [London]: National Spiritual Assembly [of the Bahá'ís of the United Kingdom], n.d. [1981] 9 p. At head of title in small type: *Practical Guide.*

7.246. *The Bahai God.* Tehran: P.O. Box 865, n.d. [1964?] iii, 25 p.
Anti-Bahá'í work. Same as 7.846.

7.247. *Bahá'í History Calendar.* 1978–1982. Honolulu: National Spiritual Assembly of the Bahá'ís of the Hawaiian Islands. 1978, 32 p.; 1979, [32] p.; 1980, 28 p.; 1981, 32 p.; 1982, [32] p.
Calendars after 1982 have separate titles. See index under (Bahá'í History Calendar).

7.248. *Bahá'í Holy Days: Bahá'í School Lesson Plans, Grades 1–9.* ed. Advisory Committee on Education. Wilmette, Ill.: Bahá'í Publishing Trust, 1968, 1976. 167 p.

7.249. *Bahá'í House of Worship.* n.p., n.d. [195–?] 3 p.

7.250. *Bahá'í House of Worship.* Wilmette, Ill.: Bahá'í Publishing Committee, 1947. 6 p.

7.251. *Bahá'í House of Worship.* Wilmette, Ill.: Bahá'í Publishing Committee, 1953. 8 p.

7.252. *idem.* Wilmette, Ill.: National Spiritual Assembly of the Bahá'ís of the United States, c1953. [8] p.

7.253. *The Bahá'í House of Worship.* Wilmette, Ill.: National Bahá'í Administrative Headquarters, n.d. [196–?] 11 p.

7.254. *Bahá'í House of Worship.* Wilmette, Ill.: Bahá'í Publishing Trust, 1965. 21 p.

7.255. *The Bahá'í House of Worship.* Paddington: N.S.W.: National Bahá'í Office, n.d. [between 1961 and 1963?] [6] p.

7.256. *The Bahá'í House of Worship: An Institution of the World Order of Bahá'u'lláh.* New York: Bahá'í Publishing Committee, n.d. [ca. 1930] 10 p.

7.257. *idem.* New York: Bahá'í Publishing Committee, n.d. [193–] 15 p.

Two variants, one showing the address of the New York Bahá'í Center, the other without it.

7.258. *idem.* Wilmette, Ill.: Bahá'í Publishing Committee, 1940, 1941. 15 p.

7.259. *Bahá'í House of Worship, Kikaya Hill, Kampala, Uganda.* Kampala, Uganda, n.d. [1963?] (Kampala: Uganda Argus). [4] p.

7.260. *idem.* n.p. [Kampala, Uganda]: Bahá'i Publishing Trust, n.d. [1971?] (Kampala: Consolidated Printers). 3 [i.e. 4] p.

7.261. *The Bahá'í House of Worship, Sydney, Australia.* Paddington, N.S.W.: National Bahá'í Office, n.d. [between 1961 and 1963?] (three printings of undetermined date within this time span, one with a drawing of the temple on the cover, [6] p.; one with a photo of the temple with no trees in the foreground, 11 p.; and a third with trees in the foreground, 11 p. – all without reference to the Universal House of Justice); n.d. [between 1963 and 1970] 11 p. (Cover shows temple with trees in foreground; text mentions election of the Universal House of Justice in 1963).

7.262. *idem.* n.p. [Mona Vale, N.S.W.]: Bahá'í Publications Australia, n.d. [1981?] [4] p.

7.263. *idem.* Mona Vale, N.S.W.: Bahá'í House of Worship, n.d. [1982?] [6] p.

7.264. *Bahá'í House of Worship, Sydney, Australia, Dedication Programme.* Paddington, N.S.W.: National Bahá'í Office, 1961. [8] p.

7.265. *The Bahá'í House of Worship: The First Universal Religious Edifice in the Western World.* New York: Bahá'í Publishing Committee, n.d. [1931?] 8 p.

7.266. *Bahá'í House of Worship, Wilmette, Illinois.* Wilmette, Ill.: Bahá'í National Center, n.d. [after 1953], n.d. [1973], n.d. [1977] 12 p.

2.267. *Bahá'í House of Worship, Wilmette, Illinois: You Are Invited to the Bahá'í House of Worship, Weekly Meetings in Praise of God.* Wilmette, Ill., 1970. [4] p.

7.268. Bahá'í Intercontinental Conference (1953: Chicago; Wilmette, Ill.). *Baha'i International Teaching Conference, Chicago and Wilmette, Illinois. U.S.A., May 3 – May 6, 1953.* n.p. [Wilmette, Ill.], 1953. 4 leaves, 4 p.

7.269. Bahá'í Intercontinental Conference (1953: Kampala, Uganda). *Bahá'í Inter-continental Conference, Kampala, Uganda: Held at the Hazíratu'l-Quds, 4 Kagera Road, Kampala, 6 to 12 Mulk 109, 12 to 18 February 1953.* Kampala, Uganda, 1953 (Welwyn Garden City, Herts.: Broadwater Press). 11 p.

7.270. Bahá'í Intercontinental Conference (1953: New Delhi). *Baha'i Centenary 1853–1953: 4th Intercontinental Conference, 7th–15th Oct. 1953, Publ c [sic] Lectures Programme, New Delhi, 8th & 12th October 1953.* New Delhi, 1953. [4] p.

7.271. —— *Baha'i Inter Continental Teaching Conference, New Delhi–India, Oct. 7 – Oct. 15, 1953.* New Delhi: National Bahá'í Headquarters, 1953. 16 p. Cover title: *4th Inter-continental Bahá'í Conference, October 7 to 15, New Delhi, India, 1953.*

7.272. Bahá'í Intercontinental Conference (1953: Stockholm). *Bahá'í Inter-continental Teaching Conference, Stockholm, Sweden, 1953.* Stockholm, 1953. [4] leaves, 4, 4, 4 p. Title inside reads: *Bahá'í International Teaching Conference.*

7.273. Bahá'í Intercontinental Conference (1958: Chicago: Wilmette, Ill.). *Bahá'í Intercontinental Conference, Chicago and Wilmette, Illinois: May 2, 3, 4, 1958.* n.p. [Wilmette, Ill.]: National Spiritual Assembly of the Bahá'ís of the United States, 1958. 15 p.

7.274. —— *Bahá'í Intercontinental Conference, May 2, 3, 4, 1958. Information Bulletin.* Chicago, 1958. [6] p.

7.275. Bahá'í Intercontinental Conference (1958: Kampala, Uganda). *Bahá'í Inter-continental Conference, Kampala, Uganda.* Kampala, Uganda: [National Spiritual Assembly of the Bahá'ís of Central and East Africa], 1958. 8, 12 p.

7.276. Bahá'í Intercontinental Conference (1958: Sydney, N.S.W.). *Second Intercontinental Bahá'í Conference, March 20–24, 1958.* Paddington, N.S.W.: National Spiritual Assembly of the Bahá'ís of Australia, 1958. [9] p.

7.276a. Bahá'í Intercontinental Conference (1967: Chicago; Wilmette, Ill.). *Bahá'í Centenary, 1867–1967: Commemorating the 100th Anniversary of Bahá'u'lláh's Tablets to the Kings.* n.p. [Wilmette, Ill.: National Spiritual Assembly of the Bahá'ís of the United States], 1967. [12] p.

7.277. Bahá'í Intercontinental Conference (1967: Kampala, Uganda). *Bahá'í Intercontinental Conference, Kampala, Uganda, 4th–8th October 1967.* Kampala, 1967. [8] p.

7.278. Bahá'í Intercontinental Conference (1967: New Delhi). *Intercontinental Bahá'í Conference, Asia, New Delhi, India, October 7 to 11, 1967.* New Delhi: National Spiritual Assembly of the Bahá'ís of India, 1967. 76 p.

7.279. —— *Intercontinental Bahá'í Conference, Asia, New Delhi, India, October 7–11, 1967.* New Delhi: National Spiritual Assembly of the Bahá'ís of India, 1967. 28 p.

7.280. Bahá'í Intercontinental Conference (1967: Panama). *La Fe Bahá'í, Conferencia Intercontinental, Ciudad de Panamá, República de Panamá. octubre 7, 8, 9, 10, 1967.* Panamá: Asamblea Espiritual Nacional de los Bahá'ís de la República de Panamá, 1967. 12 p. Spanish and English text.

7.281. Bahá'í International Community. *Appeal to the United Nations by the Bahá'í International Community.* New Delhi: National Spiritual Assembly of the Bahá'ís of India, Pakistan and Burma, 1955. 4 p.

7.282. —— *Bahá'í Appeal for Religious Freedom in Iran.* Wilmette, Ill.: Bahá'í International Community, 1955. 21 p.

7.283. —— *idem.* Wilmette, Ill.: Bahá'í Publishing Trust, 1956. 21 p.

7.284. —— *The Bahá'í International Community and the United Nations.* New York: Bahá'í International Community, Sept. 1985. 10 p.

7.285. —— *Bahá'í International Community Statements at the 39th Session of the United Nations Commission on Human Rights, January–March 1983.* New York: Bahá'í International Community, 1983. 28 p.

7.286. —— *The Bahá'ís in Iran: A Report on the Persecution of a Religious Minority.* New York: Bahá'í International Community, 1981. [68] p.
Documentation of the persecution of the Bahá'í community of Iran and its basis in religious intolerance.

7.287. —— *idem.* rev. and updated. New York: Bahá'í International Community, July 1982. 86 p.

7.288. —— *Building a Unified Community.* Thornhill, Ont.: National Spiritual Assembly of the Bahá'ís of Canada, 1976. 6 p.

7.289. —— *idem.* rev. ed. Wilmette, Ill.: Bahá'í Publishing Trust, 1980, Sept. 1980. 6 p.

7.290. —— *idem.* Bangor, [Wales]: Copycat, for the Audio Visual Centre, Spiritual Assembly of the Bahá'ís of Arfon, n.d. [1983?] [6] p.

7.291. —— *Chronological Summary of Individual Acts of Persecution Against Bahá'ís in Iran (from August 1978).* New York: Bahá'í International Community, 1981. 34 p.

7.292. —— *Divine Law, Source of Human Rights.* Wilmette, Ill.: Bahá'í Publishing Trust, 1973, 1976, 1983. 8 p.

7.292a. —— *Eighth Session of the United Nations Commission on Human Settlements: Kingston, Jamaica, 19 April–10 May 1985.* Statement submitted by the Bahá'í International Community.

n.p. [New York]: Bahá'í International Community, 1985. 3 p.

7.293. —— *The Environment and Human Values: A Bahá'í View.* New York: Bahá'í International Community, n.d. [before 1974] 6 p.

7.294. —— *idem.* rev. ed. Wilmette, Ill.: Bahá'í Publishing Trust, 1974. 6 p.

7.295. —— *idem.* 2nd rev. ed. Wilmette, Ill.: Bahá'í Publishing Trust, 1977, 1980, 1983. [6] p.

7.296. —— *Equality of Men and Women: A New Reality.* Wilmette, Ill.: Bahá'í Publishing Trust, 1975, 1979, 1983. 8 p.

7.296a. —— *idem.* n.p. [Wilmette, Ill.]: National Spiritual Assembly of the Bahá'ís of the United States, c1975 (New Delhi: Arcee Press). [12] p. Indian printing.

7.297. —— *Global Cooperation and the Environment.* n.p. [New York]: Bahá'í International Community, 1977. 3 p.

7.298. —— *Imposition by Iranian Government of Legal Ban on Bahá'í Activities in Iran.* New York: Bahá'í International Community, 1983. 8 leaves.

7.299. —— *Major Developments, July 1982–July 1983: The Bahá'ís in Iran, a Report on the Persecution of a Religious Minority.* New York: Bahá'í International Community, July 1983. 32 p.

7.300. —— *One World, One People: A Bahá'í View.* New York: Bahá'í International Community, c1974. [6] p. folder.

7.301. *idem.* rev. ed. New York: Bahá'í International Community, 1976. 6 p.

7.302. —— *idem.* rev. ed. Wilmette, Ill.: Bahá'í Publishing Trust, 1980. 6 p.

7.303. —— *Oral Statement Presented to the Second Special Session of the United Nations General Assembly Devoted to Disarmament, 24 June 1982.* New York: Bahá'í International Community, 1982. 3 p.

7.304. —— *A Pattern for Justice.* New York: Bahá'í International Community, 1974. 13 p.

7.305. —— *idem.* New Delhi: National Spiritual Assembly of the Bahá'ís of India, 1974. 10 p.

7.306. —— *Persecution of the Bahá'ís in Iran, 1979–1985: A 6-Year Campaign to Eliminate a Religious Minority.* New York: Bahá'í International Community, 1985. 10 p.

7.307. —— *The Promise of Disarmament and Peace.* New York: Bahá'í International Community, 1978. 6 p.; 1982. 7 p.

7.308. —— *idem.* n.p. [London, Ont.: Local Spiritual Assembly of the Bahá'ís of London, Ontario], 1982 [i.e. 1983] [6] p.

7.309. —— *idem.* Mona Vale, N.S.W.: National Spiritual Assembly of the Bahá'ís of Australia, n.d. [1983?] 7 p.

7.310. —— *idem.* n.p. [Mona Vale, N.S.W.]: Bahá'í Publications Australia, 1984 (Mudgee: Lynx Print), n.d. [1985] 8 p.

7.311. —— *idem.* Auckland: National Spiritual Assembly of the Baha'is of New Zealand, 1984. [8] p.

7.312. —— *Proposals for Charter Revision Submitted to the United Nations by the Bahá'í International Community.* Wilmette, Ill.: National Spiritual Assembly of the Bahá'ís of the United States, n.d. [1955?] 14 p.; n.d. [after 1955?] 15 p.; 1961. 15 p.

7.313. —— *Science and Technology for Human Advancement.* n.p. [New York: Bahá'í International Community], 1979. 4 p.

7.314. —— *Second World Conference to Combat Racism and Racial Discrimination, United Nations, Geneva, 1–12 August 1983: Statement Submitted by the Bahá'í International Community.* New York: Bahá'í International Community, 1983. 5 p.

7.315. —— *The Spiritual Basis of Equality.* n.p. [New York]: Bahá'í International Community, 1985. 3 leaves.

7.315a. —— *The Spiritual Basis of Equality.* n.p. [New York]: Bahá'í International Community, 1985. [4] p.

7.316. —— *Statement Submitted by the Bahá'í International Community to the Sixth Session of the United Nations Commission on Human Settlements, 26 April 1983, Helsinki, Finland.* n.p. [New York: Bahá'í International Community], 1983. [6] p.

7.316a. —— *Statements to United Nations Regional Preparatory Meetings for the 1985 World Conference to Review and Appraise the Achievements of the United Nations Decade for Women: Equality, Development and Peace, Arusha, Tanzania, 8–12 October 1984, Havana, Cuba, 19–23 November 1984.* n.p. [New York]: Bahá'í International Community, 1984. [12] p.

7.317. —— *Systematic Torture of Baha'is in Iranian Prisons.* New York: Bahá'í International Community, Oct. 1984. 15 p.

7.318. —— *Towards Universal Tolerance in Matters Relating to Religion or Belief: Submission by the Bahá'í International Community to the Seminar on the Encouragement of Understanding, Tolerance and Respect in Matters Relating to Freedom of Religion or Belief.* Geneva, Switzerland: Bahá'í International Community, 1984. ii, 27 p.

7.319. —— *Universal Values for the Advancement of Women.* n.p. [New York: Bahá'í International Community], n.d. [1980], n.d. [1983] 5 p.

7.320. —— *Update, the Bahá'ís in Iran: A Report on the Persecution of a Religious Minority.* New York: Bahá'í International Community, November 1981. i, 18 p.

7.321. —— *The Work of Bahá'ís in Promotion of Human Rights: A Statement Prepared for the United Nations Conference on Human Rights, Geneva, Switzerland, May 19–20, 1948.* Wilmette, Ill.: Bahá'í International Community, 1948. 1 p.

7.321a. —— *World Conference to Combat Racism and Racial Discrimination: Geneva, Switzerland, 14–25 August 1978.* n.p. [New York?]: Bahá'í International Community, 1978. 3 p.

7.322. Bahá'í International Conference (1976: Helsinki). *Conference News.* Helsinki, Finland: Bahá'í International Conference, 1976. 52 p.

7.323. Bahá'í International Conference (1977: Bahia, Brazil). *International Bahá'í Teaching Conference, January 27 to 30, 1977, Salvador, Brazil.* Salvador: Comité de Conferência Bahá'í de Bahia, 1977. [8] p.

7.323a. Bahá'í International Conference (1982: Canberra, A.C.T.). *Japan, Australia and the Spiritual Axis.* n.p. [Tokyo]: National Spiritual Assembly of the Bahá'ís of Japan; n.p. [Sydney: N.S.W.]: National Spiritual Assembly of the Bahá'ís of Australia, 1982. [4] p.

7.324. Bahá'í International Conference (1982: Lagos, Nigeria). *Conference Programme.* Lagos, Nigeria: Bahá'í International Conference, 1982. 16 p.

7.325. Bahá'í International Conference (1982: Montreal). *Bahá'í International Conference, Montreal, 1982: September 3–5, 1982, the Velodrome at Olympic Park = Bahá'í Internationale Conférence, Montréal, 1982: du 3 au 5 septembre 1982, Vélodrome du Parc Olympique.* n.p. [Thornhill, Ont.: Bahá'í Canada Publications], 1982. [24] p. English and French text.

7.326. —— *Cashier's Manual: Baha'i Montreal International Conference 1982.* n.p. [Toronto, Ont.: Bahá'í Distribution Service], 1982. [17] p.

7.326a. *Baha'i International Teaching Conferences, 1976–1977: Helsinki, Anchorage, Paris, Nairobi, Hong Kong, Bahia, Merida, Auckland.* n.p. [New York]: Bankers Trust Travel Service, 1976. [8] p.

7.327. Bahá'í International Youth Conference (1974: Hilo, Hawaii). *Where Eagles Soar: Martha Root, Agnes Alexander, Dr Augur*. comp. Kay Ruggles. Honolulu: National Spiritual Assembly of the Bahá'ís of the Hawaiian Islands, 1974. [16] p.

7.328. *Baha'i, It's a Revelation*. Walla Walla, Wash.: DTC of Northern Idaho and Eastern Washington, n.d. [1983] [6] p.

7.329. *Bahá'í Jubilee Souvenir*. London: National Spiritual Assembly of the Bahá'ís of the British Isles, 1953. 20 p.

7.330. *Baha'i Kalenda 142 B.E.. 1985–1986*. n.p. [Lae: National Spiritual Assembly of the Bahá'ís of Papua New Guinea], n.d. [1985] [2] p.

7.330a. Bahai-Kongress (3rd: 1924: Stuttgart). *Bahai-Kongress Stuttgart 1924*. Stuttgart: German Bahai-Bund, 1924. 15 p. First page title: *Report of the Bahai-Congress from the 20th to the 22nd of Sept. 1924*. German title, English text.

7.331. *Bahá'í Law: A Deepening Course for Bahá'ís*. comp. Beatrice C. Rinde, John B. Cornell. n.p. [Honolulu]: National Spiritual Assembly of the Bahá'ís of the Hawaiian Islands, n.d. [1974] ii, 80 p.
See 7.2418, 7.2515.

7.332. *Bahá'í Laws*. Wilmette, Ill.: Bahá'í Publishing Trust, 1976, 1979. v, 17 p. (Star Study Program).

7.332a. *idem*. n.p. [Lusaka: National Spiritual Assembly of the Bahá'ís of Zambia], n.d. [1980?] 14 p.

7.333. *Baha'i Laws and Obligations*. n.p. [Freetown: National Spiritual Assembly of the Bahá'ís of Sierra Leone], n.d. [1983?] [2] p. Title on p.2 is: *What Baha'is Believe*.

7.334. *Baha'i Laws and Teachings*. Lagos: Publishing Committee of the National Spiritual Assembly of the Baha'is of Nigeria, 1983. [19] leaves.

7.334a. Bahai Lending Library (London). *Bahai Lending Library, London: Rules and Terms*. London: Bahai Lending Library, n.d. [190–?] [6] p.

7.335. [*Bahá'í Lesson Plans for Children's Classes*] London: Bahá'í Education Committee, 1982. 42 p. Untitled.

7.336. *Bahá'í Lesson Plans, Level One*. n.p. [Georgetown: National Spiritual Assembly of the Bahá'ís of Guyana], n.d. [1982] 55 p.

7.337. *Bahá'í Lesson Plans, Level One*. New Delhi: National Bahá'í Education Committee, 1974. 54 p.; 1975. 59 p.

7.338. *idem*. Lusaka: National Spiritual Assembly of the Bahá'ís of Zambia, 1977. 54 p.

7.339. *Bahá'í Lesson Plans, Level Two*. New Delhi: National Bahá'í Education Committee, 1975. 79 p.

7.340. *Bahá'í Lesson Plans, Level Three*. New Delhi: National Bahá'í Education Committee, 1978. 88 p.

7.341. *Baha'i Lessons for Children: A Compilation, 30 Lessons*. comp. National Teaching Committee. Manila: National Spiritual Assembly of the Baha'is of the Philippines, 1985. vi, 88 p.

7.342. *Baha'i Lessons for Children: Baha'i History*. n.p. [Lagos, Nigeria: National Children's Committee], n.d. [1983?] 11 p.

7.343. *Baha'i Lessons for Children: Baha'i Teachings*. n.p. [Lagos, Nigeria: National Children's Committee], n.d. [1983?] 10 p.

7.344. *Baha'i Lessons for Children: Living the Baha'i Life*. n.p. [Lagos, Nigeria: National Children's Committee], n.d. [1983?] 10 p.

7.345. *The Bahá'í Life*. n.p.: [Africa Committee of National Spiritual Assembly of the Bahá'ís of the British Isles?], 1953. iv, 41 p.

7.346. *Bahá'í Life: A Handbook on Deepening*. n.p. [Sydney, N.S.W.]: National Spiritual Assembly of the Bahá'ís of Australia, 129 B.E. [1972] 61 p.

7.347. *idem*. comp. John A. Davidson. 3rd ed. Mona Vale, N.S.W.: Bahá'í Publishing Trust Australia, 133 B.E. [1976] 100 p.

7.348. *Baha'i Marriage*. n.p. [Nairobi]: National Education Committee of the Baha'is of Kenya, 1973. [4] p.

7.349. *Bahá'í Marriage*. n.p. [Johannesburg]: National Spiritual Assembly of the Bahá'ís of South and West Africa, n.d. [1962?] 12 p.

7.350. *Baha'i Marriage*. Lae: National Spiritual Assembly of the Bahais of Papua and New Guinea, 1983 (Alor Setar, Malaysia: Modern Press). 15 p.

7.351. *Bahá'í Memorial Service for Mr Amoz Gibson, Universal House of Justice Member, 1963–1982*. n.p. [Port-of-Spain: National Spiritual Assembly of the Bahá'ís of Trinidad and Tobago], 1982. [8] p.

7.352. *The Baha'i Message*. Manila: National Teaching Committee of the Baha'is of the Philippines, n.d. [196–?] [8] p.

7.353. *idem*. New Delhi: Bahá'í Publishing Trust, n.d. [196–?] (s.l.: Bright Printing Press). [8] p.

7.354. *idem.* New Delhi: Baha'i Publishing Trust, n.d. [196–?] (New Delhi: Arcee Press). [8] p. folder.

7.355. *idem.* New Delhi: Bahá'í Publishing Trust, n.d. [1980?] (New Delhi: Javee and Company). 8 p.

7.356. *The Baha'i Message, the Dawn of a New Day.* Sydney, N.S.W.: Bahai Centre, n.d. [193– or 194–] [6] p.

7.357. *The Bahai Movement.* Agra, India: Khattrya Printing Press, n.d. [1908?] 1 p.

7.358. *The Baha'i Movement: Aims and Purposes of the Baha'i Faith, Outline of History, Principles of Administration, Excerpts from Sacred Writings, Reading List.* New York: Bahá'í Publishing Committee, 1931. 47 p.

7.359. *idem.* Bombay: Bombay Baha'i Spiritual Assembly, 1932. 60 p.

7.360. *Bahai Movement. Baha U'llah.* n.p., n.d. [192– or 193–] 4 p. Text begins: 'The great orientalist, Professor Edward G. Browne, of the University of Cambridge . . .'

7.361. *The Bahai Movement Offers a Universal Programme.* Manchester, U.K.: Manchester Bahai Assembly, n.d. [191–?] [4] p.

7.362. *The Bahai Movement: Rapidly Spreading Throughout the World, and Attracting the Attention of Scholars, Savants and Religionists of All Countries – Oriental and Occidental.* n.p., n.d. [191–?] [2] p.

7.362a. *The Bahai Movement, the Reform of Islam from within: A Brief Outline of the Bahai Teaching.* Edinburgh: Macniven and Wallace, n.d. [1912] 12 p.

7.363. *Bahá'í Movement – The Truth Behind It!* Yarmouth, Eng.: Upper Room Tracts, n.d. [1984] 1 p.

7.364. Bahá'í Oceanic Conference (1970: Mauritius). *Baha'i Oceanic Conference, Queen Elizabeth College, 13 to 16 August 1970.* [Port Louis]: Baha'i Oceanic Conference, 1970 (Port Louis: Paul Mackay). 4 p.

7.365. —— *The Unfoldment of the Divine Plan.* [Port Louis]: Bahá'í Oceanic Conference, 1970 (Port Louis: Paul Mackay). 28 p. Cover title: *Bahá'í Oceanic Conference, 14 to 16 August 1970.*

7.366. Bahá'í Oceanic Conference (1971: Sapporo, Japan). *Bahá'í North Pacific Oceanic Conference.* n.p. [Sapporo], 1971. [6] p.

7.367. *The Bahá'í Peace Program.* Wilmette, Ill.: National Spiritual Assembly of the Bahá'ís of the United States and Canada, 1945. 16 p.

7.368. *idem.* Wilmette, Ill.: Bahá'í Publishing Trust, 1960, 1962, 1967, 1970, 1975. 21 p.

7.369. *Bahá'í Personal Transformation Program: (Originally Titled Bahá'í Comprehensive Deepening Program).* n.p. [Wilmette, Ill.]: Bahá'í National Education Committee, 1984. xi, 343 p. LC card 85–196420.

7.370. *Bahá'í Perspective.* Johannesburg, South Africa: National Information Centre, n.d. [1985] [7] leaves.

7.371. *Bahá'í Plan for World Order.* New York: New York Bahá'í Community, 1946. [4] p.

7.372. *Bahá'í Planning Calendar 1985.* Thornhill, Ont.: National Spiritual Assembly of the Bahá'ís of Canada, 1984. [25] p.

7.373. *Baha'i Pocket Diary: B.E. 142/143, 1986.* n.p. [Mona Vale, N.S.W.]: Baha'i Publications Australia, [1985] [64] p. Cover title: *B.E. 142/143, 1986.*

7.374. *Bahai Precepts.* n.p. [London]: The Selkirk Press, n.d. [191–?] 1 p.

7.375. *Bahá'í Principles: A Course for the Child of Intermediate Age.* Wilmette, Ill.: Bahá'í Publishing Committee, 1946. 19 leaves.

7.375a. Bahá'í Public Conference (1928: Chicago). *Baha'i Public Conference: Arranged by the Baha'is of the United States and Canada.* Chicago: Baha'is of the United States and Canada, 1928. [4] p.

7.376. *Bahá'í Public Relations: Reference Material in Chronological Order.* London: National Spiritual Assembly of the Bahá'ís of the United Kingdom, n.d. [1980] 30 p.

7.377. *Baha'i Publicity in the Berwyn-Cicero Life Newspaper, 1979–1980.* Berwyn, Ill.: Monroe C. Ioas, 1980. 20 leaves.

3.378. Bahai Publishing Society (Chicago). *Price List of the Bahai Publications.* Chicago: Bahai Publishing Society, n.d. [between 1902 and 1924] 60 p.

Only the first page has a listing of publications; the remainder of the booklet contains Bahá'í teachings on various subjects.

7.379. Bahai Publishing Society (Rangoon, Burma). *Publications of the Bahai Revelation.* Rangoon: Bahai Publishing Society, n.d. [191–?] [8] p.

7.380. Bahá'í Publishing Trust of the United States. *A Handbook for Bahá'í Librarians.* Wilmette, Ill.: Bahá'í Publishing Trust, 1978. 21 p.

7.381. Bahá'í Publishing Trust of the United States. *Rhythm of Growth, 1, 5, 9, 15, 30+:*

Catalog. Wilmette, Ill.: Bahá'í Publishing Trust, 1981. 16 p.

7.382. *A Bahá'í Puzzle Book for Children and Youth*. n.p. [Honolulu]: National Child Education Committee, 125 B.E. [1968–69] [18] leaves.

7.383. *A Bahá'í Puzzle Book for Young People from 8 to 80*. n.p. [Honolulu]: National Child Education Committee, 1974. iv, 60 p.

7.384. *Bahá'í Readings for the Pacific Week Ecumenical Service at the University of the South Pacific, 8th August 1978*. n.p. [Suva, Fiji]: Bahá'í Club at the University, 1978. 8 p.

7.385. *Baha'i References to Bible Verses*. n.p. [United States]: National Reference Library Committee, n.d. [196–] 24 p.

7.386. *The Bahā'ī Religion: Papers Read at the Conference on Some Living Religions Within the British Empire, 1924*. New York: Bahā'ī Publishing Committee, 1925. 23 p. Papers presented by Horace Holley and Ruhi Afnan.

7.387. *idem*. London: Bahā'ī National Spiritual Assembly for England, 1925. 23 p.

7.388. *The Bahai Revelation*. Chicago: Miss Mary Lesch, n.d. [191–?] 16 p.
Same as the 'Number 9' or 'Big Ben' compilation.

7.389. *idem*. n.p. [United States], n.d. [191–?] 16 p.

7.390. *The Baha'i Revelation Is the Spirit of This Age*. Washington, D.C.: Bahai Assembly, n.d. [191–?] [2] p.

7.391. *Bahá'í School Lesson Plans, Grade K: History, Teachings for the Individual, Social Teachings*. ed. Advisory Committee on Education. Wilmette, Ill.: Bahá'í Publishing Trust, 1968, 1976. 103 p. (Bahá'í Teacher's Handbook).

7.392. *Bahá'í School Lesson Plans Grade K: Social Teachings*. n.p. [Wilmette, Ill.: Bahá'í Publishing Trust], n.d. [196–] 6, 5, 5, 7, 4, 6 p. Cover title: *Baha'is Around the World*.

7.393. *Bahá'í School Lesson Plans Grade 1: History, Teachings for the Individual, Social Teachings*. ed. Advisory Committee on Education. Wilmette, Ill.: Bahá'í Publishing Trust, 1968, 1976. 105 p. (Bahá'í Teacher's Handbook).

7.394. *Bahá'í School Lesson Plans Grade 2: History, Teachings for the Individual, Social Teachings*. ed. Advisory Committee on Education. Wilmette, Ill.: Bahá'í Publishing Trust, 1968. 89 p.

7.395. *Bahá'í School Lesson Plans Grade 3: His-*

tory, Teachings for the Individual, Social Teachings. ed. Advisory Committee on Education. Wilmette, Ill.: Bahá'í Publishing Trust, 1970. 109 p.

7.396. *Bahá'í School Lesson Plans Grade 4: History, Teachings for the Individual, Social Teachings*. ed. Advisory Committee on Education. Wilmette, Ill.: Bahá'í Publishing Trust, 1970. 92 p.

7.397. *Bahá'í School Lesson Plans Grade 5: History, Teachings for the Individual, Social Teachings*. ed. Advisory Committee on Education. Wilmette, Ill.: Bahá'í Publishing Trust, 1970. 90 p.

7.398. *Bahá'í School Lesson Plans Grade 6: History, Teachings for the Individual, Social Teachings*. ed. Advisory Committee on Education. Wilmette, Ill.: Bahá'í Publishing Trust, 1968. 93 p.

7.399. *Bahá'í School Lesson Plans Grade 7: History, Teachings for the Individual, Social Teachings*. ed. Advisory Committee on Education. Wilmette, Ill.: Bahá'í Publishing Trust, 1968. 131 p.

7.400. *Bahá'í School Lesson Plans Grade 8: History, Teachings for the Individual, Social Teachings*. ed. Advisory Committee on Education. Wilmette, Ill.: Bahá'í Publishing Trust, 1968. 104 p.

7.401. *Bahá'í School Lesson Plans Grade 9: History, Teachings for the Individual, Social Teachings*. ed. Advisory Committee on Education. Wilmette, Ill.: Bahá'í Publishing Trust, 1970. 92 p.

7.402. *Bahá'í School Programs, 1941*. n.p. [Wilmette, Ill.?], 1941. [6] p.

7.403. *Bahá'í Schools, Summer Schedule, 1981*. n.p. [Wilmette, Ill: The American Bahá'í], 1981. [8] p.

7.404. *(Bahai Shinkyo Yōgū Shā)* = *Glossary of Bahá'i Terms English–Japanese*. n.p. [Tokyo: Local Spiritual Assembly of the Bahá'ís of Tokyo], showa 28 [1953] 10 p.

7.405. *Bahá'í Song Book*. comp. Sylvia Benatar. [Johannesburg?]: National Music Committee of South and West Africa, n.d. [196–?] 15 p.

7.406. *Baha'i Song Book*. Lagos: Publishing Committee of the National Spiritual Assembly of the Baha'is of Nigeria, 1983. 39 p.

7.407. *Baha'i Song Book*. Thailand: Regional Teaching Committee of Southern Thailand, Apr. 1985. 17 leaves.

7.408. *Bahá'í Songbook: Songs from Africa and*

Around the Bahá'í World. n.p. [Mbabane?: National Spiritual Assembly of the Bahá'ís of Swaziland and Mozambique?], n.d. [196–] 32 p.

7.409. *idem.* n.p. [Mbabane: National Spiritual Assembly of the Bahá'ís of Swaziland and Mozambique], n.d. [between 1971 and 1974] 23 p.

7.410. *Baha'i Songs.* n.p., n.d. [after 1970] 4 p.

7.411. *Bahá'í Songs.* n.p., n.d. [1972] [2] p.

7.412. *Bahá'í Songs.* rev. ed. Lusaka; National Spiritual Assembly of the Bahá'ís of Zambia, 1977. 15 p.

7.413. *Bahá'í Songs, Book 1.* comp. National Music Committee of the Bahá'ís of South and West Africa, n.p. [Johannesburg]: National Spiritual Assembly of the Bahá'ís of South and West Africa, 1982. [37] p.

7.414. *The Baha'i Speakers Bureau of the Hawaiian Islands.* Hawaii: Baha'i Speakers Bureau of the Hawaiian Islands, n.d. [1980?] 6 p.

7.414a. *The Baha'i Story.* prepared by Baha'i pioneers serving in the Navajo Indian Reservation. Wilmette, Ill.: American Indian Service Committee, a Committee of the National Spiritual Assembly of the Baha'is of the United States, 1961. 88 p.

7.415. Bahai Students' Union (American University of Beirut: Lebanon). *The Program of the Weekly Meetings of the Bahai Students of Beirut, Syria, 1930–1931.* Beirut: Bahai Students of Beirut, Syria, 1930. [36] p.

7.416. Bahá'í Studies Conference (1st: 1982: Yerrinbool, N.S.W.). *Baha'i Studies Conference, Yerrinbool, N.S.W., April 9th–12th, 1982.* Lindisfarne, Tas.: University of Tasmania Baha'i Society, 1982. 104 p.

Published proceedings of the conference includes ten essays on Bahá'í history and teachings.

7.417. Bahá'í Studies Conference (2nd: 1983: Yerrinbool, N.S.W.). *Proceedings of the Second Baha'i Studies Conference: Held at Baha'i School, Yerrinbool, N.S.W., Australia, on April 1st–4th 1983.* n.p. [Lindisfarne, Tas.]: University of Tasmania Baha'i Society, 1983. 189 p.

7.418. Bahá'í Studies Conference (3rd: 1984: Yerrinbool, N.S.W.). *Proceedings of the Third Baha'i Studies Conference.* n.p. [Lindisfarne, Tas.]: University of Tasmania Baha'i Society, 1984. 194 p.

7.419. *Bahá'í Studies, Études Bahá'ís, 1976: Six Papers Presented at the First Annual Meeting of the Association for Studies on the Bahá'í Faith.*

Held at Cedar Glen, Bolton, Ont., January 2–4, 1976. Thornhill, Ont.: Canadian Association for Studies on the Bahá'í Faith, 1976. 157 p. (Bahá'í Studies; v.1).

7.420. *Bahá'í Study Course.* Pittsburgh, Pa: Bahá'í Study Committee, 1932. 36 lessons.

7.421. *Bahá'í Teachings.* il. Tushar Kanti-Paul. n.p. [Mona Vale, N.S.W.]: Bahá'í Publishing Trust Australia, 134 B.E. [1977] 20 p.

7.422. *idem.* il. Tushar Kanti-Paul. rev. n.p. [Mona Vale, N.S.W.]: Bahá'í Publications Australia, 1985. 20 p.

7.423. *Bahá'í Teachings.* n.p. [Freetown: National Spiritual Assembly of the Bahá'ís of Sierra Leone], n.d. [1984] 7 p. in various pagings.

7.424. *Bahá'í Teachings for a World Faith.* Wilmette, Ill.: National Spiritual Assembly of the Bahá'ís of the United States and Canada, 1943, c1943 [after 1943] (aquamarine cover with green lettering), c1943 [195–?] (blue cover with dark blue lettering). 16 p.

7.425. *idem.* Wilmette, Ill.: Bahá'í Publishing Committee, c1943 [195–] 22 p.

7.426. *idem.* New Delhi: Bahá'í Publishing Trust, n.d. [195– or 196–] (blue cover), n.d. [196–] (green cover). 16 p.

7.427. *idem.* Wilmette, Ill.: Bahá'í Publishing Trust, n.d. [196–?], n.d. [197–?] 22 p.; 1972, 1976, 1978, 1982. 24 p.

7.428. *The Baha'i Temple.* n.p. [Wilmette, Ill.?]: Reprinted for National Bahá'í Assembly by Portland Cement Association, [195–?] 4 p. Reprint from *Architectural Concrete*, no date given.

7.429. Bahai Temple Convention (1909: Chicago). *Record of the Bahai Temple Convention Held March 22 and 23, 1909, at Chicago, Illinois.* Chicago: Bahai Temple Convention, 1909. [8] p.

7.430. *The Bahá'í Temple, House of Worship of a World Faith: Commemorating Completion of Exterior Ornamentation 1942.* Wilmette, Ill.: National Spiritual Assembly of the Bahá'ís of the United States and Canada, 1942. 34 p. LC card 43–16287.

7.431. *Bahá'í Temple, Mashriqu'l-Adhkár: In Course of Erection on a 9-Acre Tract on the Lake Shore in Wilmette, Illinois, 14 Miles North of Chicago.* n.p. [Chicago, Ill.]: The Research Service, Managing and Supervising Engineers, n.d. [193–?] 1 p.

7.432. *Bahá'í Temple Samoa: Dedication.* n.p. [Apia, Western Samoa: National Spiritual Assembly of the Bahá'ís of Samoa], n.d. [1984] 4 p. folder, in English and Samoan.

7.433. *The Bahá'í Temple, the House of Worship of a World Faith.* Wilmette, Ill.: Bahá'í Publishing Committee, 1944. 14 p.

7.434. Bahai Temple Unity. *Eleventh Annual Mashrekol-Azkar Convention and Bahai Congress.* New York: Bahai Temple Unity, n.d. [1918] 16 p.

7.435. ——— *Mashriq'ul-Adhkar Report, 1909–1925.* Chicago: Bahai Temple Unity, 1925. 31 p.

7.436. Bahai Temple Unity Convention (1912: Chicago). *Program, Bahai Temple Unity Convention, Chicago, April 27th to May 2nd 1912.* Chicago: Bahai Temple Unity, 1912. [4] p.

7.436a. Bahai Temple Unity Convention (15th: 1923: Chicago). *Bahai Congress and Fifteenth Annual Convention of the Bahai Temple Unity.* Chicago: Bahai Temple Unity, 1923. [4] p.

7.437. *Bahá'í, the Coming of World Religion.* Wilmette, Ill.: National Spiritual Assembly of the Bahá'ís of the United States, 1946. 12 leaves.

7.438. *Baha'i, the Harmony of Science, Faith and Reason.* Kumasi, Ghana: Local Spiritual Assembly of the Baha'is of Kumasi, n.d. [196–?] [6] p.

7.439. *The Baha'i Tutorial School: A Manual for Local Spiritual Assemblies.* n.p. [Accra]: National Spiritual Assembly of the Bahá'ís of Ghana, n.d. [198–?] 2 p.

7.440. *Bahá'í Unites Mankind.* Mona Vale, N.S.W.: National Spiritual Assembly of the Bahá'ís of Australia, n.d. [between 1965 and 1975] 5 p.

7.441. *idem.* Mona Vale, N.S.W.: Bahá'í Publications Australia, n.d. [1985] [10] p.

7.442. *Bahá'í Unity Calendar Diary, B.E. 130, 1973–1974.* Victor, N.Y.: International Bahá'í Audio-Visual Centre, 1973. 44 p.

7.443. *Bahá'í Victory Calendar Diary.* Victor, N.Y.: International Bahá'í Audio-Visual Centre, 1972. 44 p.

7.444. *The Bahá'í Viewpoint.* n.p. [Wilmette, Ill.]: Radio Service Committee, 1959. 4 scripts (No. 1, *The Meaning of Life*; no. 2, *God and Human Society*; no. 3, *The Return of Christ*; no. 4, *Religion and Churchdom*).

7.445. *The Bahá'í Way.* rev. ed. n.p. [Kingston]: National Spiritual Assembly of the Bahá'ís of Jamaica, 1971. 14 p.

7.446. *idem.* new ed. n.p. [Kingston]: National Spiritual Assembly of the Bahá'ís of Jamaica, 1978. 18 p.

7.447. *Bahá'í Week, Albert Pick Motel, March 21–30, 1969.* n.p. [Huntsville, Ala.: Florence Bagley], 1969. [12] p.

7.448. *Baha'i Week in Connecticut, April 22–April 29: Souvenir Edition, Connecticut Baha'i Bulletin.* Hartford, Conn.: Bahá'í Center, 1966. 4 p.

7.449. *The Bahá'í World.* vol.1 (1925–1926), [called *Bahá'í Year Book*] New York: Bahá'í Publishing Committee, 1926. 174 p.; vol. 2 (1926–1928), New York: Bahá'í Publishing Committee, 1928. xvi, 303 p.; vol. 3 (1928–1930), New York: Bahá'í Publishing Committee, 1930. xv, 377 p.; vol. 4 (1930–1932), New York: Bahá'í Publishing Committee, 1933. xvii, 547 p.; vol. 5, (1932–1934), New York: Bahá'í Publishing Committee, 1936. xix, 711 p.; vol. 6 (1934–1936), New York: Bahá'í Publishing Committee, 1937. xxvii, 771 p.; vol. 7 (1936–1938), New York: Bahá'í Publishing Committee, 1939, xxiii, 891 p.; vol. 8 (1938–1940), Wilmette, Ill.: Bahá'í Publishing Committee, 1942. xxxvii, 1039 p.; vol. 9 (1940–1944), Wilmette, Ill.: Bahá'í Publishing Committee, 1945. xxvi, 1003 p.; vol. 10 (1944–1946), Wilmette, Ill.: Bahá'í Publishing Committee, 1949. xxv, 880 p.; vol. 11 (1946–1950), Wilmette, Ill.: Bahá'í Publishing Committee, 1952. xxiii, 893 p.; vol. 12 (1950–1954), Wilmette, Ill.: Bahá'í Publishing Trust, 1956. xxvii, 996 p.; vol. 13 (1954–1963), Haifa: The Universal House of Justice, 1970, 1971, 1980. xxxix, 1228 p.; vol. 14 (1963–1968), Haifa: The Universal House of Justice, 1974, 1975. xxiii, 672 p.; vol. 15 (1968–1973), Haifa: Bahá'í World Centre, 1976. xxi, 824 p.; vol. 16 (1968–1976), Haifa: Bahá'í World Centre, 1979. xix, 740 p.; vol. 17 (1976–1979), Haifa: Bahá'í World Centre, 1982. xx, 652 p. LC card 27–5882 rev.

Review:

v.3. 'A Universal Religion: League of Nations and Bahaism: A New Religious Yearbook', *Inquirer & Christian Life* (London), no. 4637 (May 16, 1931), p. 239.

v.9. *Religious Education* (Mount Morris, Ill.), (Aug. 1946), pp. 242–3.

The volumes of this reference work constitute a survey of international progress of the Bahá'í Faith, as well as providing a source of basic information on Bahá'í scriptures, history and governing structure. The volumes are well illustrated with photographs and also include crucial source documents, essays, articles *in memoriam*, poetry and music, bibliographies and statistical information.

See 7.724.

7.450. *idem.* Wilmette, Ill.: Bahá'í Publishing Trust, 1980–1981. Volumes 1–12 reprinted.

7.451. *The Bahai World.* Tsimshatsui, Hong Kong: Bahai National Centre, n.d. [1981] [4] p.

7.452. Bahá'í World Centre. *Bahá'í Pilgrimage.* Haifa: Bahá'í World Centre, Jan. 1970. 10 p.; [Aug. 1971], Nov. 1972. 11 p.

7.453. —— *The Bahá'í Visitor: Information and Guidelines.* Haifa: Bahá'í World Centre, 1975. 10 p.

7.454. —— *idem.* new ed. Haifa: Bahá'í World Centre, 1978. 7 p.

7.455. —— *Information About Bahá'í Pilgrimage.* Haifa: Bahá'í World Centre, n.d. [1974?] 12 p.

7.456. —— *idem.* Haifa: Bahá'í World Centre, 1975–76. 4 p.

7.457. —— *idem.* Haifa: Bahá'í World Centre, [1983] [6] p.

7.458. —— *Information for Bahá'í Pilgrims.* Haifa: Bahá'í World Centre, 1969. 8 p.

7.459. —— *Information on Hotels and Transportation for Bahá'í Pilgrims.* n.p. [Haifa: Bahá'í World Centre], 1980, 1983. [4] p.

7.460. —— *Program of Pilgrimage and Other Useful Information.* Haifa: Bahá'í World Centre, 126 B.E. [1969] 18 p.; 127/128 B.E. [1970], 128/129 B.E. [1971], 129/130 B.E. [1972], 130/131 B.E. [1973] 19 p.; 131/132 B.E. [1974], 132/133 B.E. [1975] 18 p.; n.d. [1980] ii, 18 p.; n.d. [1984] ii, 18 p.

7.461. —— *The World Center of the Bahá'í Faith.* n.p. [Haifa: Bahá'í World Centre], n.d. [1965?] 4 p.

7.462. —— *The World Centre of the Bahá'í Faith.* Haifa: Bahá'í World Centre, 1969. 6 p.; 1975. 5 p.

7.463. —— *The World Centre of the Bahá'í Faith.* n.p. [Haifa: Bahá'í World Centre], n.d. [1984] [6] p. folder.

7.464. *Bahá'í World Community: The New Life.* Scarborough, Ont.: National Spiritual Assembly of the Bahá'ís of Canada, 1962. [6] p.

7.465. Bahá'í World Congress (1963: London). *Bahá'í World Congress, April 28–May 2, 1963.* London: Bahá'í Congress Arrangements Committee, 1963. 16 p.

7.466. —— *Programme, Bahá'í World Congress, Riḍván 120, 28 April–2 May 1963.* n.p. [London: Bahá'í Congress Arrangements Committee], 1963 (Welwyn Garden City, Herts.: Broadwater Press). 8 p.

7.467. —— *Programme of Speakers.* n.p. [London: Bahá'í Congress Arrangements Committee], 1963. 4 p.

7.468. *Bahá'í World Faith: A Summary of Its History, Teachings and Administrative Order.* Wilmette, Ill.: Bahá'í Publishing Trust, 1955, 1964. 8 p.

7.469. *The Bahá'í World Faith Announces the Second Annual World Religion Day, Sunday, January 21, 1951.* Wilmette, Ill.: Bahá'í Public Relations, 1951. 4 p.

7.470. *Baha'i World Faith Basic Information.* Stanford, Calif.: Baha'i College Bureau, Jan. 1958. 16 p.

7.471. *Bahá'í World Faith: Divine Revelation Is Progressive.* New Delhi: National Spiritual Assembly of the Bahai's [sic], n.d. [197–?] [2] p.

7.472. *Bahá'í World Faith Forging Links of Unity Around the World.* Kuala Lumpur, Malaysia: National Bahá'í Information Service, n.d. [196–] 5 p.

7.473. Baha'i World Fellowship Prayer Unity. American Branch. *Prayer for . . .* Lansing, Mich.: Miss Helen Whitney; Fowler, Ind.: Mrs Dana Wells, 1927–1928. 1 page sheets issued each month during 1927 and part of 1928.

7.474. *Baha'i World Peace Day Celebrations Souvenir, September 25, 1983.* Secunderabad: Ravinder Auluck (Secretary, Steering Committee of the World Peace Day Celebrations) on behalf of the Local Spiritual Assembly of the Baha'is of Hyderabad and Secunderabad, 1983. 14 p.

7.475. *Bahá'í Youth.* [Nairobi]: National Education Committee of the Baha'is of Kenya, 1973. 9 p.

7.476. Bahá'í Youth Academy (Panchgani, India). *Fourth Course for New Era Students, the Future Pioneers: 1st April through 8th May 1983.* Panchgani: Bahá'í Youth Academy of India, 1983. [8] p.

7.477. —— *Fifth Course for Rabbani Students: 27th May through 26th June 1983.* Panchgani: Bahá'í Youth Academy of India, 1983. [8] p.

7.478. —— *Report Book, Ninth Course for Assistants, 5th January through 12th February 1984.* Panchgani: Bahá'í Youth Academy of India, 1984. [8] p.

7.479. —— *Report Book, Tenth Course for Baha'i Women, 12th through 26th February 1984.* Panchgani: Bahá'í Youth Academy of India, 1984. [8] p.

7.480. —— *Sixth Course for Youth and Pioneers: 26th June through 24 July 1983.* Panchgani: Bahá'í Youth Academy of India, 1983. [12] p.

7.481. —— *Third Course for Baha'i Women, 6th*

Through 27th February 1983. Panchgani: Bahá'í Youth Academy, 1983. [8] p.

7.481a. *Baha'i Youth Hawaii!* Honolulu, Hawaii: National Youth Committee, 1984. [8]p.

7.482. *Baha'i Youth in Baha'i History.* n.p. [Gaborone]: Spiritual Assembly of the Bahá'ís of Botswana, 1973. 9 p.

7.482a. *Baha'i Youth Study Guide.* n.p. [United States], n.d. [195–] 4 leaves.

7.483. *Bahá'í Youth Year Book, 130 B.E.* n.p. [Karachi]: National Bahá'í Youth Committee, 1974. 121, 39 p.

7.484. *The Baha'is.* Croydon, S. Australia: St. Barnabas Church, 1959. 2 leaves. (Modern Heresies; no.10).
Anti-Bahá'í work from Christian viewpoint.

7.485. *Bahá'ís.* Thornhill, Ont.: Bahá'í Community of Canada, n.d. [1985] [6] p.

7.486. *Bahais and Believers.* by a Friend of Abdul Baha. n.p., n.d. [191–?] 8 p.
Discusses the difference between those who live by Bahá'í ideals, and those who are Bahá'í in name only. Attacks attempts to 'organize' the Bahá'í Faith.

7.487. *Baha'is in Harmony.* Georgetown: National Spiritual Assembly of the Bahá'ís of Guyana, 1978. 44 p.

7.488. *The Bahá'ís of Australia Welcome You to a Service to Celebrate International Year of the Child.* Mona Vale, N.S.W.: Bahá'í House of Worship, 1979. 4 p.

7.489. *Baha'is Sing Saam.* Windhoek, South West Africa: National Teaching Committee, n.d. [1981] [16] p. Songs in English, Nama and Afrikaans.

7.490. *Baha'ism.* St. Louis, Mo.: Concordia Tract Mission, n.d. [196–] 16 p.
Anti-Bahá'í work from Christian viewpoint.

7.491. *Bahaism, Its Origins and Its Role.* The Hague: [Nashr-i-Farhang-i-Inqiláb-i-Islámí], n.d. [1983?] 56 p. LC card 85–595232.
Official attack on the Bahá'ís by the authorities of the Islamic Republic of Iran.

7.492. *Bahá'u'lláh.* Wilmette, Ill.: Bahá'í Publishing Trust, 1974, 1977. v, 17 p. (Star Study Program).

7.493. *idem.* Suva, Fiji: Bahá'í Publishing Trust, 1977. vii, 36 p. (Star Study Program). In English and Ponapean.

7.494. *Bahá'u'lláh.* Taipei: National Spiritual Assembly of the Bahá'ís of Taiwan, 1979. 11, 18 p. (Kindled with the Fire of His Love).

7.495. *Bahá'u'lláh.* Georgetown: [National Spiritual Assembly of the Bahá'ís of Guyana], n.d. [1977 or 1978] [4] p.

7.496. *Bahá'u'lláh.* [Apia]: National Spiritual Assembly of the Bahá'ís of Samoa, n.d. [197–] 4 p.

7.497. *Bahá'u'lláh and Shri Krishna.* Egerton, England: The Peregrine Press, 1959. 8 p.

7.498. *Bahá'u'lláh and the Holy Bible.* Kingston: National Spiritual Assembly of the Bahá'ís of Jamaica, n.d. [1980] 31 p.

7.499. *Bahá'u'lláh: His Call to Mankind.* Toronto, Ont.: Canadian Bahá'í Community, 1967. 30 p.

7.500. *Baha'u'llah Is Calling You! = Baha'u'llah oa go bitsa!* Gaborone: Lekgotla la Mowa la Sechaba la Baha'i ba Botswana, n.d. [1977] [8] p. Text in English and Tswana.

7.501. *Baha'u'llah oa go bitsa!!! = Baha'u'llah Is Calling You!!!* Gaborone: National Spiritual Assembly of the Bahá'ís of Botswana, n.d. [1983] [6] p. Text in English and Tswana.

7.502. *Bahá'u'lláh Proclaims . . .* New Delhi: Bahá'í House, 1967. 12 p.

7.503. *Bahá'u'lláh: Reference Guide for Teachers.* n.p. [Arecibo, P.R.: CIRBAL], n.d. [1982] [13] leaves.

7.504. *Bahá'u'lláh, the Glory of God, the Promised One of All Ages.* n.p., n.d. [197–?] 11 leaves.

7.505. *idem.* n.p. [Port-of-Spain: National Spiritual Assembly of the Bahá'ís of Trinidad and Tobago], n.d. [1978?] 24 p.

7.506. *idem.* St Michael: National Spiritual Assembly of the Bahá'ís of Barbados and the Windward Islands, n.d. [1979] 31 p.

7.507. *Bahá'u'lláh, the Glory of God, the Promised One of All Ages, Messenger of God, Founder of the Bahá'í Faith.* Port of Spain, Trinidad: Baha'i Centre, n.d. [1978] 28 p.

7.508. *Bahá'u'lláh, the Glory of God, Who Is He?* Maseru: [National Spiritual Assembly of the Bahá'ís of Lesotho], n.d. [1981?] [2] p.

7.509. *Bahá'u'lláh, the Promised One of All Ages.* n.p. [Bogotá]: National Spiritual Assembly of the Bahá'ís of Colombia, 1982. 10 p.

7.510. *Bahá'u'lláh, the Promised One of All Ages: Theme 2, Level 1.* n.p. [Bogotá]: National Teaching Committee of the National Spiritual Assembly of the Bahá'ís of Colombia, 1983. 14 p.

7.511. *Baha'u'llah, 12th November 1817 to 29th May 1892.* n.p. [Lusaka?: National Spiritual

Assembly of the Bahá'ís of Zambia?], n.d. [197–] 6 leaves.

7.512. *Bahíyyih Khánum, the Greatest Holy Leaf.* n.p. [London: National Spiritual Assembly of the Bahá'ís of the United Kingdom], n.d. [1982] [4] p.

7.513. *Bahíyyih Khánum, the Greatest Holy Leaf: A Compilation from Bahá'í Sacred Texts and Writings of the Guardian of the Faith and Bahíyyih Khanum's Own Letters.* Haifa: Bahá'í World Centre, 1982. xix, 252 p.

Bahíyyih Khánum, the daughter of Bahá-'u'lláh and sister of 'Abdu'l-Bahá, lived a saintly life and was devoted to her brother and to Shoghi Effendi. Immediately after the death of 'Abdu'l-Bahá, Shoghi Effendi went into seclusion for several months. He entrusted the affairs of the Bahá'í community to this beloved aunt. Included in the compilation are letters to and about Bahíyyih Khánum from Bahá'u'lláh, 'Abdu'l-Bahá and Shoghi Effendi; the large portion of the work is comprised of Bahíyyih Khánum's own letters.

7.514. Baker, Dorothy. *The Path to God.* New York: Bahá'í Publishing Committee, n.d. [193–], c1937. 23 p.

7.515. —— *idem.* Wilmette, Ill.: Bahá'í Publishing Committee, c1937 [i.e. after 1940] 23 p.

7.516. —— *idem.* n.p., n.d. [194–? or 195–?] 24 p.

7.517. —— *Religion Returns.* Wilmette, Ill.: Bahá'í Publishing Committee, 1945, 1947, 1953. 28 p.

7.518. —— *The Victory of the Spirit.* Wilmette, Ill.: Bahá'í Publishing Committee, 1943. 28 p.

7.519. Balyuzi, H.M. *'Abdu'l-Bahá, the Centre of the Covenant of Bahá'u'lláh.* London: George Ronald, 1971, 1972, 1973. xiii, 560 p. LC card 72–196284.
Reviews:
'A Baha'i Here Below', *Times Literary Supplement* (London), (Apr. 7, 1972), p. 397.
Chelkowski, Peter. *Middle East Journal* (Washington, D.C.), v.26 (Autumn 1972), pp. 464–465.
Choice (Middletown, Conn.), (Sept. 1972), p. 827.
Elwell-Sutton, L.P. *Journal of the Royal Asiatic Society* (London), no.2 (1973), pp. 166–168.
Morgan, Dewi. *Books and Bookmen* (London), v.18 (Dec. 1972) p. 104.
The first full-scale study of the life of the son of and successor to the Founder of the Bahá'í Faith. Persian and English secondary source materials were used. Fully half of the volume is

dedicated to 'Abdu'l-Bahá's journey in Europe and North America in 1911–13.

7.520. —— *The Báb, the Herald of the Day of Days.* Oxford: George Ronald, 1973, Apr. 1973, 1974, 1975. xiv, 256 p. LC card 73–167688.
Reviews:
Choice (Middletown, Conn.), (Oct. 1973), p. 1216.
Elwell-Sutton, L.P. *Journal of the Royal Asiatic Society* (London), no.1 (1975), p. 67.
Theology Digest, v.22 no.3 (Autumn 1974), p. 262.
The first full-length biography in English of the Prophet of Shíráz, whose mission as founder of the Bábí religion and as forerunner of Bahá'u'lláh caused a social and political upheaval in mid-nineteenth-century Iran. The author consulted official documents of government archives and material gathered from records of the family of the Báb accessible to the author by dint of his kinship to the Báb.

7.521. —— *Bahá'u'lláh.* London: Bahá'í Publishing Trust, 1938. 34 p.

7.522. —— *Bahá'u'lláh: A Brief Life: Followed by an essay on the Manifestation of God Entitled The Word Made Flesh.* London: George Ronald, 1963, 1968, 1970, 1972. 134 p. LC card 71–261408.
Published for the centenary of Bahá'u'lláh's declaration of his mission, this book offers a short account of his life. The second half of the book is an essay examining the station of the Manifestation and his relationship to God.

7.523. —— *idem.* Oxford: George Ronald, 1973, 1974, 1976, 1984. 134 p.

7.524. —— *Bahá'u'lláh, the King of Glory.* Oxford: George Ronald, 1980, 1980, 1980. xiii, 539 p. LC card 81–134965.
Reviews:
Smith, Peter. *International Journal of Middle East Studies* (New York), v.13 no.3 (1981), pp. 369–370.
Beautifully printed and lavishly illustrated biography of the Founder of the Bahá'í Faith, based upon secondary sources and the unpublished memoirs of two companions, Áqá Husayn-i-Ashchí and Áqá Ridáy-i-Qannád-i-Shírází. Includes addenda on 'The Disastrous Reign of Násiri'd-Dín-Sháh', 'Representations to Consuls at the Time of Bahá'u'lláh's Banishment to 'Akká', 'The Aftermath of the Siege of Plevna', 'General Gordon in 'Akká and Haifa', 'Bibliographical Notes', a glossary, bibliography and a good index.

7.525. —— *Edward Granville Browne and the Bahá'í Faith.* Oxford: George Ronald, 1970,

1975, 1980. ix, 142 p. LC card 75–572111.
Reviews:
Armajani, Yahya. *Middle East Journal* (Washington, D.C.), v.25 (Spring 1971), p. 269.
Choice (Middletown, Conn.), (July/Aug. 1971), p. 686.
Elwell-Sutton, L.P. *Journal of the Royal Asiatic Society* (London), (1972), pp. 70–71.
—— *Royal Central Asian Journal* (London), v.58 no.1 (Feb. 1971), p. 123.
A review of the career of the Cambridge orientalist whose major interest was the history of the Bábí and Bahá'í Faiths. Browne was the only westerner to leave a record of his meeting with Bahá'u'lláh. Balyuzi deals with a number of historical controversies with tact and fairness.

7.526. —— *Eminent Bahá'ís in the Time of Bahá'u'lláh: with Some Historical Background.* Oxford: George Ronald, 1985. xvii, 381 p.
A companion volume to Balyuzi's *Bahá'u'lláh, the King of Glory*, this work includes biographies of several important believers of the late 19th century.

7.527. —— *A Guide to the Administrative Order of Bahá'u'lláh.* 2nd ed. London: Bahá'í Publishing Trust, 1947. 23 p.

7.528. —— *Khadíjih Bagum, the Wife of the Báb.* Oxford: George Ronald, 1981, 1982. xii, 35 p. LC card 81–212838.
The first published account in English of the life of the Báb's wife.

7.529. Barney, Laura Clifford. *God's Heroes.* London: Kegan Paul Trench Trubner & Co.; Philadelphia: Lippincott, 1910. xii, 106 p. LC card 10–23654.
A drama about the early days of the Bábí religion.

7.530. Barr, Lulu. *The Way to Happiness: Twelve Lessons Adaptable to All Ages.* Toronto, Ont.: National Spiritual Assembly of the Bahá'ís of Canada, n.d. [196–?] 14 p.

7.531. *Basic Bahá'í Beliefs.* Orange [N.S.W.]: Bahá'í Assembly, n.d. [1972?] 3 p.

7.532. *Basic Facts About the Bahá'í Faith: Questions and Answers (A Study Outline).* Apia: National Spiritual Assembly of the Bahá'ís of Samoa, 1984. 22 p.

7.533. *Basic Facts of the Baha'i Faith.* Freetown: [National Spiritual Assembly of the Bahá'ís of Sierra Leone], 1976. 1 p.

7.534. *Basic Facts of the Baha'i Faith.* Lagos, Nigeria: Bahá'í Publishing Trust, 1984. [4] p.

7.535. *Basic Techniques.* ed. Advisory Committee on Education. Wilmette, Ill.: Bahá'í Publishing Trust, 1966. 58 p. (Bahá'í Teacher's Handbook; v.2).

7.536. Bayne, E.A. *Bahais Again: The Larger Question: Speculations on the Significance of the Bahai Religious Sect in Iran.* New York: American Universities Field Staff, 1955. 10 p.

7.537. *Be As I Am: A Compilation.* comp. Elias Zohoori. n.p. [Kingston]: National Spiritual Assembly of the Bahá'ís of Jamaica, n.d. [1983] 60 p.
Anecdotes about 'Abdu'l-Bahá.

7.538. *Be As I Am, 'Abdu'l-Bahá.* Kuala Lumpur, Malaysia: National Baha'i Youth Committee, n.d. [1981] [42] p.

7.539. *Be Fair in Your Judgement.* London: National Spiritual Assembly of the Bahá'ís of the United Kingdom, 1979. 4 p.

7.540. Bean, Jack. *Bahá'u'lláh, 'The Divine Youth', 'Chief of the Monarchs of Love': A Comparison and Contrast of Theosophy with the Bahá'í Faith.* Brisbane, Qld.: Bean, 1949. 122 leaves.

7.541. Bebertz, Terry L. *Baha'i Callbook for the United States of America.* n.p. [Vassar, Mich.]: Bebertz, 138 B.E. [1981] [9] leaves.

7.542. Beckwith, Francis. *Baha'i.* Minneapolis, Minn.: Bethany House Publishers, 1985. 63 p.
Christian polemic against the Bahá'í Faith. The author claims that Bahá'í institutions have attempted to 'cover up' the supposed non-fulfilment of a prophecy of 'Abdu'l-Bahá's by making changes to the text of Esslemont's *Bahá'u'lláh and the New Era.*

7.543. *Becoming a Bahá'í: An Invitation.* Thornhill, Ont.: Bahá'í National Centre, n.d. [1985] [6] p.

7.544. Beecher, Ellen V. *Copy of a Letter Answering the Question: What is the Difference Between the Metaphysical Teaching of the Present Day, and that of the Bahai Revelation?.* n.p., n.d. [191–?] viii p.

7.545. *Being a Bahá'í.* Oakham, U.K.: Bahá'í Publishing Trust, 1972. (7 cards in portfolio).

7.545a. *Benevolence and Teaching.* Montclair, N.J.: World Fellowship Gardens, n.d. [192–] [1] p. (Service Leaflet; no.1).

7.546. Bennett, Lerone. *Bahá'í, a Way of Life for Millions.* Wilmette, Ill.: Bahá'í Publishing Trust, n.d. [1965 or later], 1977. 8 p.
Reprint from *Ebony.*

7.547. *Best Compliments, Local Spiritual Assembly of the Baha'is of Belgaum.* Belgaum, India: Local Spiritual Assembly of the Baha'is of Belgaum, n.d. [1985] [iv, 38] p.

7.547a. *The Best News on Earth: The Destiny of America.* Wilmette, Ill.: National Bahá'í Center, 1977. [2] p.

7.548. *Beyond National Sovereignty: World Peace Through a New World Order.* n.p. [Wilmette, Ill.]: NTC [i.e. National Teaching Committee], 1985, 1985. [8] p.

7.549. Bhagwandas, Mr. *The Bahai Songs (Part 1).* Rohri, Pakistan: Bhagwandas, 1943. 16 p.

7.550. Bhagwandas Nandusingh. *World Faith of Baha'u'llah.* 2nd ed. Poona, India: Shri Bhagwandas Nandusingh, 1964. [36] p.

7.551. Bishop, Helen Pilkington. *Talks by 'Abdu'l-Bahá Given in Paris: Supplementary Historical Note and Introduction.* London, 1936. xii p.

7.552. Bjorling, Joel. *The Baha'i Faith: A Historical Bibliography.* New York; London: Garland Publishing 1985. xi, 168 p. (Sects and Cults in America: Bibliographical Guides; v.6) (Garland Reference Library of the Humanities; v.223). LC card 83–49294.

While the author claims that this work is 'comprehensive', there are many errors, an inordinate emphasis on obscure works by opponents and excommunicants, and a large gap in the coverage of the worldwide published literature in English. It has been useful, nevertheless, in the absence of any fuller bibliographical treatments of the religion.

7.553. Blomfield, Lady [Sara Louisa]. *The Chosen Highway.* London: Bahá'í Publishing Trust, n.d. [1940] x, 265 p. LC card 44–1890.

This chronicle of some aspects of the lives of Bahá'u'lláh, the Báb and 'Abdu'l-Bahá relies heavily on testimonies of sources closely acquainted with the subjects: Bahíyyih Khánum, daughter of Bahá'u'lláh; Munírih Khánum, wife of 'Abdu'l-Bahá; Túbá Khánum, daughter of 'Abdu'l-Bahá; other early believers; and the author herself, who accompanied 'Abdu'l-Bahá during his sojourn in Britain. Includes 'The World Religion' by Shoghi Effendi, pp. 261–264, and 'Some Bahá'í Literature', p. 265.

7.553a. —— *idem.* London: Bahá'í Publishing Trust; Wilmette, Ill.: Bahá'í Publishing Committee, n.d. [1940] x, 265 p.

7.554. —— *idem.* Wilmette, Ill.: Bahá'í Publishing Committee, n.d. [194–?] x, 264 p.

Includes 'The World Religion' by Shoghi Effendi, pp. 261–264.

7.555. —— *idem.* Wilmette, Ill.: Bahá'í Publishing Trust, n.d. [between 1954 and 1966], 1967, 1970, 1975. x, 260 p. LC card 67–16026.

Does not include pp. 261–5 which appeared in 1940 editions.

7.556. —— *The First Obligation.* London: Caledonian Press, n.d. [1921] 16 p.

7.557. Bloodworth, Keith. *The Day of Peace.* St Michael: National Spiritual Assembly of the Bahá'ís of Barbados and the Windward Islands, 1979. 16 p.

7.558. Bluett, Margaret. *Development Ideas for Baha'i Communities in Papua New Guinea: Book One.* n.p. [Lae]: Spiritual Assembly of the Baha'is of Papua New Guinea, n.d. [1984] 18 p.

7.559. —— *Sampela Piksa Long Baha'i Titsing.* Lae: National Spiritual Assembly of the Bahá'ís of Papua New Guinea, 1977. 16 leaves. Text in English, Motu and Pidgin.

7.560. Bordewich, Fergus M. *Their 'Crime' is Faith.* Pleasantville, N.Y.: Reader's Digest Association, 1984. 6 p. Reprinted from Dec. 1984 *Reader's Digest.*

7.561. Bosch Bahá'í School (Santa Cruz, Calif.). *Auditorium: Educational Building Complex, Bosch Bahai School.* n.p. [Santa Cruz, Calif.]: Bosch Bahai School, Dec. 1984. [5] p.

7.562. —— *Bosch Bahá'í School, Fall-Winter 1984.* Santa Cruz, Calif.: Bosch Bahá'í School, 1984. [16] p.

7.563. —— *Bosch Bahá'í School, Summer 1984: From Creative Word to Creative Action.* Santa Cruz, Calif.: Bosch Bahá'í School, 1984. [16] p.

7.564. Bosch Bahá'í School (Santa Cruz, Calif.). *Bosch Bahá'í School, Summer 1985: Teach Ye the Cause of God.* Santa Cruz, Calif.: Bosch Bahá'í School, 1985. [16] p.

7.565. —— *Fall 1983: Thanksgiving, the Silent Teacher, November 24–27.* Santa Cruz, Calif.: Bosch Bahá'í School, 1983. [8] p.

7.566. —— *Promulgation of Universal Peace: Bosch Bahá'í School, Featuring 11 Sessions, June 18 through September 1.* Santa Cruz, Calif.: Bosch Bahá'í School, [1983] [12] p.

7.567. —— *Some Answered Questions, Summer 1982.* Santa Cruz, Calif.: Bosch Bahá'í School, 1982 [8] p.

7.568. —— *Winter-Spring 1984, Bosch Bahá'í School, Featuring Sessions January through May.* Santa Cruz, Calif.: Bosch Bahá'í School, 1984. [12] p.

7.569. Bourgeois, Louis. *The Bahai Temple: Press Comments, Symbolism.* Chicago, 1921. 31 p.

Two variants, one with sepia printing on cover, one with black printing on cover.

7.570. Bowes, Eric. *Great Themes of Life*. Wilmette, Ill.: Bahá'í Publishing Trust, 1958. xii, 83 p. LC card 58–8698.

A series of five 'sermons' delivered by this Bahá'í speaker at a Congregational Church in Australia, presenting the Bahá'í Faith for a Christian audience.

7.571. —— *These Things Shall Be*. Sydney, N.S.W.: Bahá'í Publications Australia, 1980. viii, 151 p.

A series of essays on the twelve principles of the Bahá'í social programme.

7.572. Boxer, Bonnie. *The Queen of Carmel*. [Israel]: Reprinted with permission of Avmag Aviation Magazine Ltd., 1982. [4] p. Reprinted from article appearing in *Israelal* (Tel Aviv), (Spring 1982) with by-line Malkah Gan-Or.

7.573. Boykin, John. *The Baha'i Faith*. Downers Grove, Ill.: Inter-Varsity Press, 1982. 32 p.

Christian polemical work on the Bahá'í Faith.

7.574. Boyle, Louise D. *The Laboratory of Life*. New York: Bahá'í Publishing Committee, c1937. 30 p.

7.575. Bradley, Fuchsia. *Bahá'í Flip Chart: Introductory Lessons to the Bahá'í Faith*. il. Claudia Talcott, n.p. [Anchorage]: National Child Education Committee of Alaska, n.d. [1984?] 31 leaves.

7.576. Braun, Eunice. *Bahá'u'lláh, His Call to the Nations: A Summons to World Order*. Wilmette, Ill.: Bahá'í Publishing Trust, 1967. 19 p.

7.577. —— *A Crown of Beauty: The Bahá'í Faith and the Holy Land*. concept and design by Hugh Chance. Oxford: George Ronald, c1982, 1982. 103 p.

An amply illustrated introduction to the Bahá'í teachings and the Bahá'í presence in the Holy Land.

7.578. —— *Dawn of World Peace: Commemorating the Public Declaration of Bahá'u'lláh, Founder of the Bahá'í Faith, April 21–May 2, 1963*. Wilmette, Ill.: Bahá'í Publishing Trust, 1963. 6 p.

7.579. —— *From Strength to Strength: The First Half Century of the Formative Age of the Bahá'í Era*. Wilmette, Ill.: Bahá'í Publishing Trust, 1978, Oct. 1978. viii, 74 p. LC card 78–9424.

Historical essay on the Bahá'í Faith from 1921 to the 1970s.

7.580. —— *idem*. New Delhi: Bahá'í Publishing Trust, 1979. viii, 74 p.

7.581. —— *Know Your Bahá'í Literature: A Study Course*. Wilmette, Ill.: Bahá'í Publishing Trust, 1959. 37 p.

7.582. —— *The March of the Institutions: A Commentary on the Interdependence of Rulers and Learned*. Oxford: George Ronald, 1984. xiii, 98 p.

The author examines the role of the 'learned' institutions of the Bahá'í Faith (those institutions of the Bahá'í order in which the members act primarily as individuals) in inspiring the Bahá'í community, nurturing the nascent administrative institutions and protecting the Bahá'í cause. These learned institutions include the Hands of the Cause of God, the International Teaching Centre, the Continental Boards of Counsellors, their Auxiliary Boards and the assistants to Auxiliary Board members.

7.583. Breneman, Steven Bret. *Fly Away Home*. il. Carol Joy. Evanston, Ill.: Bellwood Press, 1984. Children's book. 74 p. LC card 84–6252.

7.584. *A Brief History of the Baha'i Faith*. n.p. [Freetown: National Spiritual Assembly of the Bahá'ís of Sierra Leone], n.d. [1984?] 3 p. Printed versions are missing at least one page at the end.

7.585. *Bring in the Harvest*. n.p.. [Honolulu: National Spiritual Assembly of the Bahá'ís of the Hawaiian Islands], n.d. [1972?] 24 leaves.

7.586. Brittingham, Isabella D. *The Proof of the Manifestation of God in Baha'Ullah, from the Prophecies of Jesus Christ*. n.p.: Brittingham, 1904. 5 leaves.

7.587. —— *The Revelation of Bahä-ulläh in a Sequence of Four Lessons*. Chicago: Bahai Publishing Society, 1902; 5th ed. n.d. [191–], 8th ed. n.d. [191–], 9th ed. 1920. 33 p. (There were a large number of editions [i.e. printings] of this, with small variations).

7.588. Brittingham, James F. *The Message of the Kingdom of God*. n.p., n.d. [190–] 12 p.

7.589. —— *idem*. 2nd ed. n.p., 1909. 13 p.

7.589a. Brown, Charles E. *The Ghost of Mohammedanism (Bahaism)*. Anderson, Ind.: Gospel Trumpet Company, n.d. 32 p. [Bjorling 830]

7.590. Brown, Ramona Allen. *Memories of 'Abdu'l-Bahá: Recollections of the Early Days of the Bahá'í Faith in California*. Wilmette, Ill.: Bahá'í Publishing Trust, 1980. xxiii, 144 p. LC card 79–16412.

Recollection of the growth of the Bahá'í Faith in California, the visit of 'Abdu'l-Bahá, and of the life of the author who was herself one of the earliest Bahá'ís in the San Francisco Bay area.

7.591. Brown, Vinson. *The Song of Songs*. Happy Camp, Calif.: Naturegraph, n.d. [197–] 7 p. Reprint from *World Order* (Oct. 1946).

7.592. Browne, Edward Granville. *Materials for the Study of the Bábí Religion*. Cambridge: Cambridge University Press, 1918, 1961. xxiv, 380 p. LC card 19–2790.

A compendium of a number of documents on the Bahá'í Faith, some of it of dubious value. This work should be seen in light of Browne's other works and later scholarship. See *Edward Granville Browne and the Bahá'í Faith* by H.M. Balyuzi.

7.593. *The Bugle*. Toronto, Ont.: Canadian Bahá'í Community, 1975. 4 p.

7.594. *Building Bridges: A Bahá'í Songbook*. comp. Peggy Caton, Dale Nomura, under the direction of the Bahá'í National Education Committee. Los Angeles: Kalimát Press, 1984. xxii, 72 p.

7.595. *Building Bridges: Lyrics*. comp. Peggy Caton, Dale Nomura, under the direction of the Bahá'í National Education Committee, Los Angeles: Kalimát Press, 1984. xi, 79 p.

7.596. *Building the Bahá'í Community: Second Bahá'í European Teaching Summer School, Amsterdam, Holland, September 4 through 9, 1951*. n.p. [Wilmette, Ill.]: European Teaching Committee of the National Spiritual Assembly of the United States, 1951. 27 leaves.

7.597. *Building the Kingdom of God*, n.p. [Kingston: National Spiritual Assembly of the Bahá'ís of Jamaica], n.d. [1974?] 18 p.

7.598. *Building World Peace: Notes for Study of the Issue by the Bahá'í Community of Canada*. Thornhill, Ont.: National Spiritual Assembly of the Bahá'ís of Canada; Bahá'í Canada Publications, 1983. 6 p.

7.599. Burnside, George. *Why I Am Not a Baha'i*. n.p. [Australia: Burnside], n.d. [197–?] 8 p.

Anti-Bahá'í work from Seventh Day Adventist viewpoint.

C

7.600. Caby, Philippe. *The Baha'i Faith Explained and Refuted*. with a preface and postscript by Rev Fr Harry Peeters. Bambui, Cameroon: Regional Major Seminary, n.d. [197–] ([Cameroon]: Catholic Mission Mankon). [4], 28 p.

7.600a. Cadwalader, Robert E. *A Bibliography of Some Bahá'í Books and Booklets Needed by the Bosch Bahá'í School Library, January 1981*. Santa Cruz, Calif.: Bosch Bahá'í School, 1981. 11 p.

7.601. [*Calendar*] n.p. [United States] n.d. [1917?] ca. 120 p.

7.602. *Calendar 1932*. n.p. [Wilmette, Ill.: National Spiritual Assembly of the Bahá'ís of the United States and Canada], 1932. 12 leaves.

7.603. *Calendar for the 19 Day Baha'i Fast*. Evanston, Ill.: Deepening Committee of the Spiritual Assembly of the Baha'is of Evanston, Illinois, 1984. [48] p.

7.604. *Calendar of 19-Day Feasts: Twenty Important Facts Every Baha'i Should Know: Special Baha'i Days*. n.p., n.d. [196–?] 6 p.

7.605. *The Call of Bahá'u'lláh*. London: Bahá'í Publishing Trust, 1970. 38 p.

7.606. *Call to Youth*. Paddington, N.S.W.: National Bahá'í Office, n.d. [196–?] 8 p.

7.607. Cameron, Kenneth Walter. *Transcendentalists in Transition: Popularization of Emerson, Thoreau and the Concord School of Philosophy in the Greenacre Conferences and the Monsalvat School (1894–1909): The Role of Charles Malloy and Franklin Benjamin Sanborn Before the Triumph of the Baha'i Movement in Eliot, Maine*. Hartford, Conn.: Transcendental Books, 1980. 263 leaves.

A survey of the survival of transcendentalism at Greenacre, including a year by year record of the Greenacre Conferences and the Monsalvat School for the Comparative Study of Religion, and reproductions of the school's announcements of sessions. The author appears to side with those who believed that Sarah Farmer's property was taken over by the Bahá'ís against her expressed wishes.

7.608. *Campaign of Spiritualization and Intensified Individual Teaching Plan for Switzerland*. n.p. [Bern: National Spiritual Assembly of the Bahá'ís of Switzerland], 1983. [3] leaves.

7.609. Campbell, E.S. *The Books of God Are Open*. Wilmette, Ill.: Bahá'í Publishing Committee, 1950. 13 leaves.

7.610. —— *idem*. Wilmette, Ill.: Bahá'í Publishing Committee, 1953. 24 p.

7.611. Campbell, Helen. *The Bahai Movement in*

Its Social-Economic Aspect. 2nd ed. Chicago: Bahai Publishing Society, 1915, 22 p.
  See 7.612.

7.612. —— *Bahaism in Its Social-Economic Aspect.* Chicago: Bahai Publishing Society, 1910. 22 p.
  See 7.611.

7.613. Campbell, Myrtle W. *The Continuity of the Prophets.* New York: The Pageant Press, 1952. 169 p. LC card 52–14507.

7.614. *The Canadian Bahá'í Community.* n.p. [Thornhill, Ont.]: National Spiritual Assembly of the Bahá'ís of Canada, n.d. [1983] [4] p.

7.615. *¡Canta Esa Melodia! = Sing this Melody!* Vienna, Va.: Images International, 1979. 16 p.

7.616. Carden, Hugh. *Bahá'í Writings, A Concordance.* [Auckland]: National Spiritual Assembly of the Bahá'ís of New Zealand, Feb. 1975, Aug. 1975, Jan. 1976, Sep. 1976, 1979. 180 p.
  One of the first concordances to Bahá'í writings. It does not make a claim to comprehensiveness and as there is no standard referencing system to most Bahá'í scriptures, new editions of sacred texts have made this concordance become out of date. The 1979 printing is 21 cm., the others 29 cm.

7.617. —— *Concordance for Selections from the Writings of 'Abdu'l-Bahá.* Auckland: National Spiritual Assembly of the Bahá'ís of New Zealand, 1981. 116 p.

7.618. Caribbean Radio Television Workshop (1975: Mayaguez, P.R.). *Bahá'í Faith Caribbean Radio Television Workshop '75.* n.p. [San Juan: Comite de Radio-TV de Puerto Rico], n.d. [1976] 56 p.

7.619. Carnegie Steel Company (Pittsburgh). *The Jewel-Like Design of the Baha'i Temple, National Church of Mashreq'ul Adhkar at Wilmette.* Washington, D.C.: Research Service, n.d. [193–?] 1 p.

7.620. *A Celebration of the Life and Work of Richard St Barbe Baker 1889–1982.* n.p. [London: National Spiritual Assembly of the Bahá'ís of the United Kingdom], 1982. [8] p.

7.621. *Centenary of a Universal Religion.* n.p. [Wilmette, Ill.]: Radio Service Committee, 1960. 7 leaves.

7.622. *The Centenary of a World Faith: The History of the Bahá'í Faith and Its Development in the British Isles.* London: Bahá'í Publishing Trust, 1944. 63 p. LC card A 45–3908.

7.623. *Centenary of the Baha'i Faith in India, 1880–1980.* Bombay: Spiritual Assembly of the Bahá'ís of Bombay, 1980. 16 p.

7.624. Central States Bahá'í Summer School (1935: Louhelen Ranch, Davison, Mich.). *A Vacation with a Purpose.* Davison, Mich.: Central States Bahá'í Summer School, 1935. 6 p.

7.625. Centro para Intercambio Radiofónico Bahá'í de América Latina. *Amoz Gibson Training Centre for Bahá'í Media.* Arecibo, P.R.: CIRBAL, 1983. 1 p. folded to 6 p.

7.626. Chamberlain, Isabel Fraser. *From the World's Greatest Prisoner to His Prison Friends.* Boston: The Tudor Press, 1916. 22 p. (Cover title: *Divine Common Sense*).

7.627. —— *From the World's Greatest Prisoner to His Prison Friends: Prophecies and Precepts from the Utterances of Baha'o'llah and Abdul Baha.* with an introduction by Isabel F. Chamberlain. New York: Fellowship Press Service, n.d. [between 1916 and 1921]. 32 p.

7.628. —— *idem.* Boston: The Tudor Press, 1921.

7.629. Chase, Thornton. *The Bahai Revelation.* Chicago: Bahai Publishing Society, 1909, 1913, 1919. vi, 181 p. LC card 12–28373.
  An introductory exposition of Bahá'í teachings for a Christian audience by the first American Bahá'í.

7.630. —— *The Bahá'í Revelation.* New York: Bahá'í Publishing Committee, [1928] (New York: J.J. Little & Ives Company). [10], vi, 181 p.

7.631. —— *Before Abraham Was I Am.* Chicago: Bahai Publishing Society 1902 [i.e. 1903] 16 p.
  See 7.631a, 7.632.

7.631a. —— *Extract from a Letter.* n.p. [British Isles?], n.d. [1912?] 12 p. Text is that of *Before Abraham Was I Am.*
  See 7.631, 7.632.

7.632. —— *The Reality of the Return of Christ.* Toronto, Ont.: Bahá'í Publishing Committee, n.d. [195–?] 10 p.
  See 7.631, 7.631a.

7.632a. —— *The Serpent.* n.p. [Chicago], n.d. [1899 or 1900] 18 p.

7.633. —— *What Went Ye Out For to See?* n.p. [Chicago: Bahai Publishing Society], n.d. [1904] 5 p.

7.634. Chase, Thornton; Agnew, Arthur S. *In Galilee and In Spirit and In Truth.* Chicago: Bahai Publishing Society, 1908. 83 p.
  Record of a pilgrimage to the Holy Land during the time of 'Abdu'l-Bahá. Includes photographs.

7.635. —— *In Galilee and In Wonderland.* 2nd

ed. Chicago: Bahai Publishing Society, 1921. 71, 10 p.
Later ed. of 7.634.

7.636. —— *In Galilee. In Wonderland.* Los Angeles: Kalimát Press, 1985. xii, 83 p. LC card 85–9888.

7.637. Cheney, Elisabeth H. *Prophecy Fulfilled.* Wilmette, Ill.: Bahá'í Publishing Committee, 1944, 1945, 1948, 1950, 1952. 32 p.

7.638. —— *idem.* Wilmette, Ill.: Bahá'í Publishing Trust, 1955, 1963, 1968. 22 p.; 1972. 23 p.; 1974. 21 p.; 1978, 1980, 1983. 23 p.

7.639. —— *idem.* n.p. [Rarotonga?: National Teaching Committee of the Bahá'ís of the Cook Islands?], n.d. [1978?] 11 p.

7.640. Cheyne, Thomas Kelly. *The Reconciliation of Races and Religions.* London: Adam and Charles Black, 1914. xx, 260, [4] p. LC card 15–6117 rev.
Cheyne (1841–1915), English Bible scholar who introduced German biblical criticism to England, writes of the Bahá'í Faith as an answer to the critical needs of the Christian West.

7.641. Child, C.W. *Hands of Famous Men: Their Significance.* London: C.W. Child, n.d. [1914?] 9 p. Title inside is: *A Reading of the Hands of His Excellency Abdul Baha*, reprinted from *The International Psychic Gazette* (London).
A reading of 'Abdu'l-Bahá's palms.

7.642. *Child Education Training Manual.* n.p. [Mbabane: National Spiritual Assembly of the Bahá'ís of Swaziland], n.d. [1982?] 26 p.

7.643. *A Child of the Kingdom: Baha'i Lessons for Children's Classes.* n.p. [Salisbury]: National Spiritual Assembly of the Bahá'ís of Rhodesia, 1979. 32 p.

7.644. *A Child of the Kingdom: Baha'i Lessons for Children's Classes, Book 2.* n.p. [Harare]: National Spiritual Assembly of the Baha'is of Zimbabwe, 1982. 38 p.

7.645. *Children Class Teachers' Training Course.* Kuching, Sarawak: Bahá'í Centre, 1979. 45 p.

7.646. *Children Class Teachers' Training Course, 2nd Book.* Kuching, Sarawak: Child Education Committee, 1980. 35 p.

7.647. *Children's Classes: Crafts, Games and Songs.* ed. Advisory Committee on Education. Wilmette, Ill.: Bahá'í Publishing Trust, 1968. 63, 65 p. (Bahá'í Teacher's Handbook; v.5–6).

7.648. *The Children's Hour: A Bahai Leaflet for Children and Their Friends.* no.1–? Montclair, N.J.: World Fellowship, n.d. [192–?]

7.649. [*Children's Lessons*] Accra North: National Spiritual Assembly of the Bahá'ís of Ghana, n.d. [1981] 13 p.

7.650. *Children's Materials: A Compilation.* n.p. [Manila, Philippines]: National Child Education Committee, n.d. [1980?] 81 p.
Contents: *Flowers of One Garden* (G. Faizi); *Baha'i Principles for Children* (R.E. Ford); *Stories for Children* (Jacqueline Mehrabi); *The Nineteen Day Feast.*

7.650a. *Choosing Your Career.* n.p. [Wilmette, Ill.]: National Spiritual Assembly of the Bahá'ís of the United States, 1977. 16 p.

7.651. Christensen, Deborah. *God and Me.* il. John Solarz. Wilmette, Ill.: Bahá'í Publishing Trust, 1980. 16 p. (Sunflower Books for Young Children; no.3).

7.652. —— *I Am a Bahá'í: Includes – My Bahá'í Community, My Bahá'í Feasts, Our Bahá'í Holy Days and Holidays, Our Bahá'í House of Worship.* designed and il. Pepper Oldziey; il. John Solarz. Wilmette, Ill.: Bahá'í Publishing Trust, 1984. [64] p. (Sunflower Activity Books for Young Children; no. 5–8). Includes: *A Message to Parents*, [8] p.

7.653. —— *My Bahá'í Book.* il. John Solarz. Wilmette, Ill.: Bahá'í Publishing Trust, 1980. 20 p. (Sunflower Books for Young Children; no.1).

7.654. —— *My Favorite Prayers and Passages.* il. John Solarz. Wilmette, Ill.: Bahá'í Publishing Trust, 1980. 16 p. (Sunflower Books for Young Children; no.2).

7.655. —— *Our Bahá'í Holy Places.* il. John Solarz. Wilmette, Ill.: Bahá'í Publishing Trust, 1980. 20 p. (Sunflower Books for Young Children; no. 4).

7.656. Christensen, Deborah; Hein, Delane. *Creating a Spiritual Home: Mother's Book.* Nairobi: Baha'i Publishing Agency, 1985. 40 p. (A Baha'i Programme for Mothers).

7.657. —— *Creating a Spiritual Home: Teacher's Guide.* Nairobi: Baha'i Publishing Agency, 1985. 40 p. (A Baha'i Programme for Mothers).

7.658. *Learning at Home and at School: Mother's Book.* Nairobi: Baha'i Publishing Agency, 1985. 48 p. (A Baha'i Programme for Mothers).

7.659. —— *Learning at Home and at School: Teacher's Guide.* Nairobi: Baha'i Publishing Agency, 1985. 48 p. (A Baha'i Programme for Mothers).

7.660. —— *Raising Healthy Children: Mother's Book.* Nairobi: Baha'i Publishing Agency, 1985. 110 p. (A Baha'i Programme for Mothers).

7.661. —— *Raising Healthy Children: Teacher's Guide*. Nairobi: Baha'i Publishing Agency, 1985. 110 p. (A Baha'i Programme for Mothers).

7.662. —— *Teaching about Religion: Mother's Book*. Nairobi: Baha'i Publishing Agency, 1985. 62 p. (A Baha'i Programme for Mothers).

7.663. —— *Teaching about Religion: Teacher's Guide*. Nairobi: Baha'i Publishing Agency, 1985. 64 p. (A Baha'i Programme for Mothers).

7.663a. —— *Teaching Good Character: Mother's Book*. Nairobi: Baha'i Publishing Agency, n.d. [1985] 63 p. (A Baha'i Programme for Mothers).

7.663b. —— *Teaching Good Character: Teacher's Guide*. Nairobi: Baha'i Publishing Agency, 1985. 63 p. (A Baha'i Programme for Mothers).

7.664. —— *Using Good Discipline: Mother's Book*. Nairobi: Baha'i Publishing Agency, 1985. 55 p. (A Baha'i Programme for Mothers).

7.665. —— *Using Good Discipline: Teacher's Guide*. Nairobi: Baha'i Publishing Agency, 1985. 56 p. (A Baha'i Programme for Mothers).

7.666. Christian, Roberta K. *A Bahá'í Child's ABC*. il. Rochelle Boonschaft. Wilmette, Ill.: Bahá'í Publishing Committee, 1944, 1946. 29 leaves.

7.667. —— *idem*. Wilmette, Ill.: Bahá'í Publishing Trust, 1957, 1965. 29 leaves.

7.668. —— *A Bahá'í Child's Song Book*. verses Roberta K. Christian, music Eugene Babcock, il. E. Butler McHenry. Wilmette, Ill.: Bahá'í Publishing Committee, 1948, 1953. [27] p.

7.669. Christian, William Kenneth. *Baha'i World Faith, the Divine Truth for Today: Basic Facts*. Seremban, Malaya: Local Spiritual Assembly, n.d. [1965?] [6] p.
See 7.670–7.685.

7.670. —— *Basic Facts of the Bahá'í Faith*. Wilmette, Ill.: Bahá'í Publishing Committee, n.d. [195–] [2] p.

7.671. —— *idem*. Wilmette, Ill.: Bahá'í Publishing Trust, n.d. [195– or 196–], n.d. [197–], n.d. [1982] [6] p.

7.672. —— *idem*. Karachi: National Bahá'í Office, n.d. [196–] [4] p.

7.673. —— *idem*. Hong Kong, n.d. [197–?] 6 p.

7.674. —— *idem*. Dacca, Bangladesh: Spiritual Assembly of the Bahá'ís of Dacca, n.d. [197–?] [6] p.

7.675. —— *idem*. Kuala Lumpur: Bahá'í Publishing Trust Committee, n.d. [197–] 6 p.

7.676. —— *idem*. Paddington, N.S.W.: National Spiritual Assembly of the Bahá'ís of Australia, 127 B.E. [1970–1] 6 p.

7.677. —— *idem*. Christchurch, Devon: Local Spiritual Assembly of the Bahá'ís of Christchurch, 127 B.E. [1970–1] [6] p.

7.678. —— *idem*. n.p. [Monrovia, Liberia]: National Spiritual Assembly of the Bahá'ís of West Africa, 1971. [6] p.

7.679. —— *idem*. Kampala, Uganda: Bahá'í Publishing Trust, n.d. [1972 or 1973] [6] p.

7.680. —— *idem*. Mona Vale, N.S.W.: Bahá'í Publications Australia, 133 B.E. [1976–7], [1985] 6 p.

7.681. —— *idem*. Accra North, Ghana: Bahá'í Faith, n.d. [1980], [1981] 6 p.

7.682. —— *idem*. n.p. [Manila]: National Spiritual Assembly of the Bahá'ís of the Philippines, n.d. [197–?] [6] p.

7.683. —— *idem*. Kampala, Uganda: Bahá'í Publishing Trust, n.d. [1972 or 1973] [6] p.

7.684. —— *idem*. Freetown, Sierra Leone: National Bahai Centre, n.d. [1983?] [6] p.

7.685. —— *idem*. Lagos: Baha'i Publishing Trust, Nigeria, 1984. [4] p.

7.686. —— *Classification of Bahá'í Study Sources: A Selected Bibliography for the Student of the Bahá'í Faith*. Wilmette, Ill.: Bahá'í Publishing Committee, 1941. 7 p.; 1947. 8 p. LC card 43–49557.

7.687. —— *Two Roads We Face*. Wilmette, Ill.: Bahá'í Publishing Committee, 1946, 1949. 31 p.

7.688. Christie, W.J. *The Reality of Life*. Parry Sound, Ont.: W.J. Christie, 1975. 19 leaves.

7.689. Ciné Bahá'í. *Invitation*. Thornhill, Ont.: Ciné Bahá'í, n.d. [1977?] 6 p.

7.690. *Circle of Peace: Reflections on the Bahá'í Teachings*. ed. Anthony A. Lee. Los Angeles: Kalimát Press, 1985. xxi, 214 p. LC card 85–23287.
A collection of nine essays on peace-related issues, including American peace movements, human rights, women, youth and personal experience in the Vietnam War.

7.691. *Circle of Unity: A Proclamation to the Native Americans from the Bahá'í Faith*. Wilmette, Ill.: Bahá'í Publishing Trust, 1980. 14 p.

7.692. *Circle of Unity: Bahá'í Approaches to Current Social Issues*. ed. Anthony A. Lee. Los Angeles: Kalimát Press, 1984. xviii, 258 p. LC card 84–11203.
A collection of ten essays expressing the

authors' views of how the Bahá'í Faith sheds light on such topics as disarmament and nuclear weapons, women's issues, peace and Marxism. A stimulating and ground-breaking volume.

7.693. Claus, Ted. *New Light on the Spirit Path.* Wilmette, Ill.: Bahá'í Publishing Trust, 1966. iv, 57 p. LC card 66–22165.

7.694. Cobb, Stanwood. *The Destiny of America.* Wilmette, Ill.: Bahá'í Publishing Trust, 1958, 1970. 22 p.

7.695. —— *Finding Assurance in a World of Turmoil.* New York: Bahá'í Publishing Co., n.d. [193–?] [8] p.

7.696. —— *Homoculture: Principles of Bahá'í Education.* New York: Bahá'í Publishing Committee, n.d. [193–] 23 p.

7.697. —— *The Joy of Existence.* Washington, D.C.: Avalon Press, n.d. [197–] [4] p.

7.698. —— *Life with Nayan.* Washington, D.C.: Avalon Press, 1969. 62 p.

7.699. —— *Memories of 'Abdu'l-Bahá.* Washington, D.C.: The Avalon Press, 1962, n.d. [197–] 24 p.

7.700. —— *A Saga of Two Centuries: Autobiography.* n.p.: Cobb, 1979. 172 p.
Includes a description of how Cobb became a Bahá'í.

7.701. —— *Security for a Failing World.* Washington, D.C.: Avalon Press, 1934. xviii, 202 p. LC card 35–4241.
An overview of the influence of religion on the world and its relation to modern problems. Bahá'í precepts are included in the text without the work being a strictly introductory work on the Bahá'í Faith.

7.702. —— *idem.* New York: Bahá'í Publishing Committee, 1934. xvi, 140 p. LC card 42–45054.

7.703. —— *idem.* Indian ed. New Delhi: Bahá'í Publishing Trust, 1971. 202 p.

7.704. —— *idem.* 2nd ed. New Delhi: Bahá'í Publishing Trust, 1977. xvi, 205 p.

7.705. —— *Security for a Failing World: A Condensation.* Wilmette, Ill.: Bahá'í Publishing Committee, 1934. 16 p.

7.706. —— *Tomorrow and Tomorrow.* Washington, D.C.: Avalon Press, c1951. 103 p. LC card 51–40208.
Essays addressing the challenge of the new international situation following World War II.

7.707. —— *idem.* Wilmette, Ill.: Bahá'í Publishing Company, 1951. 82 p.

7.708. —— *idem.* Wilmette, Ill.: Bahá'í Publishing Committee, c1951. 82 p.

7.709. —— *idem.* n.p. [Wilmette, Ill.: Bahá'í Publishing Committee], c1952. 103 p.

7.710. —— *idem.* Wilmette, Ill.: Bahá'í Publishing Trust, 1960. 82 p.

7.711. —— *idem.* New Delhi: Bahá'í Publishing Trust, 1970. 82 p.
Three variants: one with pink cover; one with yellow cover with black lettering; one with black and magenta cover and series Service to Universities.

7.712. —— *What is a Bahá'í?* Wilmette, Ill.: Bahá'í Publishing Trust, n.d. [between 1955 and 1957], n.d. [1967?] 8 p.; n.d. [after 1967?] 6 p. Reprint from *Washington Daily News.*

7.713. Coker, Lynn. *The Little Stars Coloring Book.* n.p. [Davison, Mich.: Louhelen Bahá'í School], n.d. [1984] [35] leaves.

7.714. Cole, Juan Ricardo. *The Concept of Manifestation in the Bahá'í Writings.* Ottawa, Ont.: Association for Bahá'í Studies, 1982. 38 p. (Bahá'í Studies; v.9).
Scholarly examination of the essential Bahá'í doctrine of God's self-manifestation in the persons of the great founding prophets of religions – Moses, Buddha, Jesus, Muhammad, the Báb and Bahá'u'lláh. The author's knowledge of original sources as yet untranslated gives added depth to the exposition.

7.715. Coleman, Alonzo W.; Coleman, Sandra; Petit, Diane Bogolub. *Hands On!: Activities for the Education of Children.* Davison, Mich.: Louhelen Baha'i School, 1984. 175 p. (looseleaf in binder).

7.716. Coles, Claudia Stuart. *Allaho Abha: Thoughts and Prayers for the Mashrak-al-Azcar, 1909.* Washington, D.C.: Coles, 1909. 4 p.

7.717. Collins, Amelia. *A Tribute to Shoghi Effendi.* Wilmette, Ill.: Bahá'í Publishing Trust, n.d. [1960?] 12 p.

7.718. Collins, Charles. *Temple of Light: Bahá'í Edifice on Chicago North Shore, One of the Lovely Wonders of Architectural World.* n.p. [Wilmette, Ill.?: Bahá'í Publishing Committee?], 1953. [4] p. Reprint from *Chicago Sunday Tribune,* May 3, 1953.

7.719. *Commemorating the Visit of Amatu'l-Baha Ruhiyyih Khanum from the World Centre, Haifa, Israel, 31st August to 6th September 1961 to Federation of Malaya & Singapore.* Malacca: National Teaching Committee of Malaya & Singapore, 1961. [12] p.

7.720. *Commemorative Meeting to Observe the 50th Anniversary of an Address Delivered by 'Abdu'l-Bahá at Earl Hall, Columbia University, June 22, 1962.* New York, 1962. 8 p.

7.720a. *Comment from the American Press on the Baha'i House of Worship . . . Wilmette, Illinois.* n.p. [Wilmette, Ill.], n.d. [194–] [2] p.

7.721. *Comments and Excerpts: More than Twenty-Five Years of War, Revolution and Social Upheaval.* n.p., n.d. [ca. 1950?] 4 p. On cover: photograph of 'Abdu'l-Bahá; on back: Social and spiritual principles of the Bahá'í Faith.

7.722. *Communication Needs Co-operation: The Bahá'í Faith.* New Delhi: Bahá'í Publishing Trust, n.d. [1981] [4] p.

7.723. *idem.* London: National Spiritual Assembly of the Bahá'ís of the United Kingdom, n.p. [1981] [2] p.

7.724. *A Compendium of Volumes of the Bahá'í World, an International Record, I-XII, 82–110 of the Bahá'í Era (1925–1954).* comp. Roger White. Oxford: George Ronald, 1981. xxi, 790 p. LC card 82–168937.
See 7.449–7.450.

7.725. *Compilation of Excerpts on the Covenant and Administration for Use in Conference Institutes.* Wilmette, Ill.: Bahá'í Publishing Committee, 1950. 90 leaves.
See 7.758–7.759.

7.726. *Concert of Man: In Tribute to the Oneness of Mankind = Concert des Hommes: En Hommage à l'Unicité de l'Humanité.* n.p. [Thornhill, Ont.: National Spiritual Assembly of the Bahá'ís of Canada, n.d. [1978?] 8 p. English and French text.

7.727. Conference for Inter-Racial Amity (1928?: Green Acre, Eliot, Me.). *Conference for Inter-Racial Amity.* Eliot, Me.: National Inter-Racial Committee of the Baha'is of the United States and Canada, n.d. [1928?] [4] p.

7.728. Conference for Inter-Racial Amity (1930: Philadelphia). *Conference for Inter-Racial Amity.* arranged by Inter-Racial Amity Committee of the Bahá'ís of Philadelphia. Philadelphia, Pa.: Inter-Racial Amity Committee of the Bahá'ís of Philadelphia, 1930. [4] p.

7.729. Conference for Interracial Amity (1930: Portsmouth, N.H.; Eliot, Me.). *Conference for Interracial Amity.* arranged by the National Teaching Committee of the Baha'is of the United States and Canada, Portsmouth, N.H., August 21, Green Acre, Eliot, Maine, August 22, 23 and 24, 1930. n.p.: National Teaching Committee of the Baha'is of the United States and Canada, 1930. [4] p.

7.730. *Conference for Persian Bahá'ís in the United States.* n.p. [Wilmette, Ill.], 1978. 3 p.

7.731. Conference for the Education of Children (1985: Lake Isle, Alta.). *Conference for the Education of Children.* n.p. [Spruce Grove, Alta.]: National Baha'i Schools Committee, 1985. [6] p.

7.732. Conrader, Constance. *Women, Attaining Their Birthright.* Wilmette, Ill.: Bahá'í Publishing Trust, 1975, 1975, 1976, 1979. 36 p.
The two printings in 1975 are called the 'second' and 'third' printings. The first printing was in *World Order*, v.6 no.4 (Summer 1972), pp. 43–59.

7.733. *The Conspiracy to Destroy the Bahá'í Community in Iran.* n.p. [Port-of-Spain]: National Spiritual Assembly of the Bahá'ís of Trinidad and Tobago, n.d. [1981] 1 p.

7.734. *Consultation, Consultation, Consultation.* n.p. [Nairobi]: National Education Committee of the Baha'is of Kenya, 1973. [4] p.

7.735. *The Continental Board of Counsellors, Auxiliary Board Members and Their Assistants.* n.p.: Continental Board of Counsellors in Southern Africa, 1974. 14 p.

7.736. Continental Board of Counsellors in Africa. *O Ye Apostles of Baha'u'llah! To Each and Every Pioneer Resident on the Continent of Africa and Its Neighbouring Islands.* Nairobi: Baha'i Publishing Agency, n.d. [1985] 21 p.

7.737. Continental Board of Counsellors in Central America. *Supplementary Manual for Pioneers.* n.p.: Continental Board of Counsellors in Central America, 1973. 5 p.

7.738. Continental Board of Counsellors in Southern Africa. *Facts About Southern Africa for Prospective Pioneers.* n.p.: Continental Board of Counsellors in Southern Africa, n.d. [197–] 20 p.

7.739. —— *Information for International Traveling Teachers and a Few Facts for Pioneers in the Region of Southern Africa and the Islands of the Indian Ocean.* n.p.: Continental Board of Counsellors in Southern Africa, 1974. 18 leaves.

7.740. *Convention: A Compilation.* Auckland: National Spiritual Assembly of the Bahá'ís of New Zealand, 1980. 31 p.

7.741. *Convention for Amity between the Colored and White Races* (1921: Washington, D.C.). *Convention for Amity between the Colored and White Races Based on Heavenly Teachings, May 19, 20 and 21, Congregational Church, 10th and G Streets N.W., Washington, D.C.* Washington, D.C., 1921. 4 p.

7.742. Convention for Amity between the Colored

and White Races (1927: Eliot, Me.). *Convention for Amity between the Colored and White Races.* arranged by the National Inter-Racial Committee of the Baha'is of the United States and Canada. n.p. [New York]: National Inter-Racial Committee of the Baha'is of the United States and Canada, 1927. [6] p.

7.743. Convention for Amity in Inter-Racial Relations (1927: Washington, D.C.). *Convention for Amity in Inter-Racial Relations.* arranged by the Inter-Racial Committee of the Baha'is of Washington, D.C. Washington, D.C.: Inter-Racial Committee of the Baha'is of Washington, D.C., 1927. 6 p.

7.744. Convention of the Bahá'ís of Iceland (7th: 1978: Reykjavík). *Sjöunda Landsthing Bahá'ía á Íslandi.* n.p. [Reykjavík: National Spiritual Assembly of the Bahá'ís of Iceland], n.d. [1978] 16 p.

7.745. Convention of the Bahá'ís of Iceland (12th: 1983: Reykjavík). *12. Landsthing Bahá'ía, 27, 28 og 29 Mai, 1983, Reykjavík.* English ed. Reykjavík: [National Spiritual Assembly of the Bahá'ís of Iceland], 1983. 38 p.

7.746. Convention of the Bahá'ís of Iceland (14th: 1985: Kópavogur). *14. Landsthing Bahá'ía: 26, 27 og 28 April 1985, Kópavogur = 14th National Convention of the Bahá'ís of Iceland.* n.p. [Reykjavík]: National Spiritual Assembly, 1985. 44 p.

7.746a. Convention of the Bahá'ís of New Zealand (1st: 1957: Auckland). *Souvenir Programme. First National Convention of the Baha'is of New Zealand, 25th–28th April, 1957.* n.p. [Sydney?]: National Spiritual Assembly of the Bahá'ís of Australia and New Zealand, 1957 [Sydney?]: Bahá'í Press Committee). [8] p.

7.747. Convention of the Bahá'ís of Singapore (14th: 1985: Singapore). *14th National Convention B.E. 142 (Singapore, 26–28 April 1985).* Singapore: Spiritual Assembly of the Baha'is of Singapore, 1985. 119 p.

7.747a. Convention of the Bahá'ís of the United States and Canada (19th: 1927: Montreal). *Feast of Ridván Commemorating the Declaration Made by Bahá'u'lláh [sic] in the Garden of Ridván [sic], Baghdad, April 21, 1863: Hotel Windsor, Montreal, April 28th, 1927.* Montreal, 1927. [4] p.

7.747b. Convention of the Bahá'ís of the United States and Canada (36th: 1944: Wilmette, Ill.). *Baha'i Centenary Convention: Thirty-Sixth Annual Convention of the United States and Canada with Participation of Representatives of the Baha'i Communities of Central and South America.* Wilmette, Ill.: [National Spiritual Assembly of the Bahá'ís of the United States and Canada], 1944. [8] p.

7.748. Cook, Agnes. *The Bahai Movement Briefly Explained.* Cape Town, South Africa: Cape Town Bahai Circle, 1912. 8 p.

7.749. Cookson, Alexe. *Te Marama = The Light.* il. Nancy Chambers. Auckland: National Spiritual Assembly of the Bahá'ís of New Zealand, n.d. [196–?] 15 p.

7.750. Cooper, Roger. *The Baha'is of Iran.* London: Minority Rights Group, 1982. 16 p. (Minority Rights Group Reports; no.51). LC card 82–141690.

7.751. —— *idem.* with revisions by the Minority Rights Group. rev. and updated ed. London: Minority Rights Group, Aug. 1985. 16 p. (Minority Rights Group Reports; no.51).

7.752. Corre, Jay. *Music for Mankind.* n.p. [Wilmette, Ill.?]: Special Projects Committee, 1973. 7 leaves.

7.753. Cortazzi, Theodore. *Reincarnation.* New Delhi: Bahá'í Publishing Trust, n.d. [196–?] 39 p.

7.754. Council Fire (2nd: 1983: Lummi Reservation, Wash.). *Council Fire, Lummi Reservation, Washington State, Aug. 83.* Bellingham, Wash.: Bahá'ís of Bellingham, 1983. [6] p.

7.755. *The Country Is the World of the Soul.* Thornhill, Ont.: Bahá'í National Centre, n.d. [1977] [6] p.

7.756. *'The Country Is the World of the Soul . . .'* Wilmette, Ill.: Bahá'í National Center, n.d. [1984?] [2] p. and seeds in plastic bag.

7.757. *Course of Twelve Lessons on the Bahá'í Movement: 'The Dawn of the Universal Civilization' by Mirza Ahmad Sohrab . . . at the Bahá'í Center . . . New York City.* New York: Bahá'í Center, 1928. 3 p.

7.758. *The Covenant and Administration.* Wilmette, Ill.: Bahá'í Publishing Committee, 1950, 1951. 90 p.
See 7.725.

7.759. *idem.* Wilmette, Ill.: Bahá'í Publishing Trust, n.d. [after 1954] 90 p.; 1969. 93 p.

7.760. *The Covenant and the Universal House of Justice.* n.p. [Lomé: National Spiritual Assembly of the Bahá'ís of Togo], n.d. [1977?] 11 p.

7.761. *The Covenant, Part One.* n.p. [Lagos, Nigeria: Bahá'í Publishing Trust], n.d. [1984] [3] p.

7.762. *The Covenant, Part Two.* n.d. [Lagos,

Nigeria: Bahá'í Publishing Trust], n.d. [1984] [3] p.

7.763. *The Covenants of God.* n.p. [Kingston: National Spiritual Assembly of the Bahá'ís of Jamaica], n.d. [196–?] 28 p.

7.764. Cox, Alice; Musacchia, Evelyn. *Bahá'í Teaching Guide: A Practical Guide for the Education of Children: Intermediate.* comp. Alice Cox and Evelyn Musacchia. il. Lynn Hutchinson. Wilmette, Ill.: Bahá'í Publishing Trust, 1966. v, 221 p. Cover title: *Bahá'í Teaching Guide for Children.*

7.765. —— *Bahá'í Teaching Guide: A Practical Guide for the Education of Children: Intermediate: Teacher's Manual.* comp. Alice Cox and Evelyn Musacchia. Wilmette, Ill.: Bahá'í Publishing Trust, 1966. xiii, 223 p.

7.766. —— *Bahá'í Teaching Guide: A Practical Guide for the Education of Children: Pre-Primary.* comp. Alice Cox and Evelyn Musacchia. il. Lynn Hutchinson. Wilmette, Ill.: Bahá'í Publishing Trust 1966. v, 101 p. (Cover title: *Bahá'í Teaching Guide for Children*).

7.767. —— *Bahá'í Teaching Guide: A Practical Guide for the Education of Children: Pre-Primary, Primary: Teacher's Manual.* comp. Alice Cox and Evelyn Musacchia. Wilmette, Ill.: Bahá'í Publishing Trust, 1966. xii, 223 p. (Cover title: *Bahá'í Teaching Guide for Children*).

7.768. —— *Bahá'í Teaching Guide: A Practical Guide for the Education of Children: Primary.* comp. Alice Cox and Evelyn Musacchia. il. Lynn Hutchinson. Wilmette, Ill.: Bahá'í Publishing Trust, 1966. v, 142 p. (Cover title: *Bahá'í Teaching Guide for Children*).

7.769. Coy, Genevieve L. *The Bahá'í House of Worship: An Institution of the World Order of Bahá'u'lláh.* New York: Bahá'í Publishing Committee, n.d. [193–], 1939. 10 p.

7.770. —— *Counsels of Perfection: A Bahá'í Guide to Mature Living.* Oxford: George Ronald, 1978. 186 p. LC card 79–310123.

A self-help volume for Bahá'ís, covering such topics as self, achievement, use of money, education and fairness to oneself and others.

7.770a. —— *Hidden Words of Baha'u'llah: (This Course Was Given at Green Acre Baha'i School, 1955).* n.p. [Wilmette, Ill.]: American National Teaching Committee, 1956. 4 leaves.

7.771. —— *How You and I Can Become Better Teachers.* Suva, Fiji: National Spiritual Assembly of the Bahá'ís of the South Pacific Ocean, n.d. [between 1959 and 1970] 11 p.

7.772. —— *Improving Our Bahá'í Consultation.* Suva, Fiji: National Spiritual Assembly of the Bahá'ís of the South Pacific Ocean, n.d. [between 1967 and 1970] 6 p.

7.773. Cranmer, Elsie. *Continuity.* Bournemouth, U.K.: Cranmer, n.d. [194– or 195–] [23] p.

7.774. *'Create in Me a Pure Heart, O My God . . .' Baha'u'llah.* n.p., n.d. [198–] [10] p. Songs in English and Chinese.

7.775. *The Creative Plan of God: Comprehensive Study Outline for Teaching Children.* comp. National Baha'i Child Education Committee. rev. ed. Wilmette, Ill.: Bahá'í Publishing Trust, 1958. 70 p.

7.776. *Crece con Nosotros: Una Neuva Serie de Televisión de 12 Semanas, en Castellano, sobre la Fe Bahá'í = Grow with Us: A New 12-Week Spanish-Language Television Series about the Bahá'í Faith.* San Fernando, Calif.: Light Years International, n.d. [1983?] [6] p. Spanish and English text.

7.777. Crist, Mrs Gene. *God's Everlasting Covenant.* n.p. [United States], n.d. [196–?] [8] leaves.

7.778. —— *Progressive Revelation.* n.p. [Wilmette, Ill.]: [Bahá'í National Reference Library Committee?], n.d. [196–?] [9] leaves.

7.779. —— *Prophecy.* n.p. [Wilmette, Ill.]: Bahá'í National Reference Library Committee, n.d. [196–?] 10 leaves.

7.780. —— *The Return of Christ.* n.p. [United States], n.d. [196–?] 9 leaves.

7.781. Crittall Casement Window Company (Detroit). *A Temple of Light.* Detroit, Mich.: Crittall Casement Window Company, n.d. [193–] 1 p.

7.782. *Cult of the Month, Bahá'í.* Chicago: Jesus People USA, 1976. [8] p.

Anti-Bahá'í work from Christian viewpoint.

7.783. *idem.* Chicago: Jesus People USA, c1979. 7 p. Reprinted from *Cornerstone.*

7.784. Curzon, George N. *The Baha'i Movement.* n.p., n.d. [190– or 191–?] 1 p. Excerpts from *Persia and the Persian Question.*

D

7.785. Dahl, Arthur L. *Bahá'í, World Faith for Modern Man*. Wilmette, Ill.: Bahá'í Publishing Trust, 1960. 22 p.

The 1960 edition lists author as Arthur Dahl; revised edition lists Arthur L. Dahl.

7.786. —— *idem*. rev. ed. Wilmette, Ill.: Bahá'í Publishing Trust, 1972, 1975. 23 p.

7.787. Dale, John. *Unity and a Universal Language: World Means to World Peace*. Ceará, Brazil: Eldono de Bahaa Esperanto-Ligo, 1976. 30 p.

7.788. Danesh, Hossain B. *The Violence-Free Society: A Gift for Our Children*. Thornhill, Ont.: Canadian Association for Studies on the Bahá'í Faith, 1979. 44 p. (Bahá'í Studies; v.6). LC card 81–463911.

Examination of the influence of violence on modern society and some steps toward lessening it.

7.789. —— *idem*. 2nd ed. Ottawa, Ont.: Canadian Association for Studies on the Bahá'í Faith, 1979. 40 p. (Bahá'í Studies; v.6).

7.790. Danklefsen, Bob. *The Founding of the Baha'i Cult*. South Bend, Ind.: South Bend School of Personal Evangelism, n.d. [1973?] 3 p.

Anti-Bahá'í work from Christian viewpoint.

7.791. Davidson, John. *Gemstone: A Project to Develop Individual Capacities and Talents*. Mona Vale, N.S.W.: National Baha'i Community Development Committee, n.d. [1983?] 8 pts. (29 p.) in folder.

7.792. Davison Bahá'í School (Davison, Mich.). *Davison Bahá'í Summer School Present 'Unity in Diversity', August 5, 1976*. Davison, Mich.: Davison Bahá'í School, 1976. 4 p.

7.793. *Dawn of a New Age: An Illustrated History of the Baha'i Faith*. rev. ed. Suva, Fiji: Bahá'í Publishing Trust, 1981. 50 p.

7.794. *Dawn of the New Day*. New York: Bahá'í Publishing Committee, n.d. [193–] 16 p.

7.795. *idem*. Bombay: Spiritual Assembly of the Baha'is of Bombay, n.d. [193–?] 16 p.

7.796. *Dawn of World Civilization*. Geneva: Bahá'í International Bureau, n.d. [after 1945], n.d. [195–] (probably two printings were done in the 1950s). 16 p.

7.797. *Dawn Song, Choral Music*. sel. by Bahá'í Committee on Music; il. Joan Ucello. Wilmette, Ill.: Bahá'í Publishing Trust, 1969. 74 p.

7.798. *The Dawning Place of the Pacific: Baha'i House of Worship*. Apia: National Spiritual Assembly of the Bahá'ís of Samoa, 1985 (Apia: Commercial Printers). [36] p. Includes *Bahá'í House of Worship Samoa Dedication and Teaching Conference*, 12 p.

7.799. *Day of Prayer for Iranian Baha'is*. Guam: National Spiritual Assembly of the Bahá'ís of the Mariana Islands, 1982. [4] p.

7.800. *A Day of Prayer, May 23, 1982, at the Suva Civic Auditorium (and throughout Fiji)*. Suva, Fiji: Bahá'í Publishing Trust, 1982. 15 p.

7.801. *Day-Star, Bahá'í Faith*. Washington [State], n.d. [1979?] 4 p.

7.802. *Days to Remember: (Bahá'í Holy Days)*. comp. Dr Baher Forghani. Mona Vale, N.S.W.: Bahá'í Publications Australia, 1983. vii, 169 p.

Compilation of passages from Bahá'í scriptures and histories on all the Bahá'í holy days, arranged by holy day.

7.803. De Corrales, Jeanne Frankel. *Nine Days to Istanbul*. Los Angeles: Kalimát Press, 1981. vi, 111 p. (Pioneer Paperback Series). LC card 81–12410.

Personal narrative of an adventurous trip on the Orient Express en route to Bahá'í pilgrimage in the Holy Land.

7.804. Dealy, Paul Kingston. *The Dawn of Knowledge and the Most Great Peace*. New York: Bahai Board of Counsel, 1903. 40 p.

Published lectures introducing Bahá'í history and teachings in relation to Biblical prophecy.

7.805. —— *idem*. 2nd ed. n.p. [New York?: Bahai Board of Counsel?], n.d. [between 1903 and 1908] iv, 58 p.

7.806. —— *idem*. 3rd ed. Chicago: Bahai Publishing Society, 1908. 60 p.

Two variants, one saying 'Price 15 cents', the other 'Price 25 cents'.

7.807. Dean, S.I. *52 Bahá'í Talks for All Occasions*. Kuala Lumpur: National Spiritual Assembly of the Bahá'ís of Malaysia, n.d. [1970] 208 p.

Talks on a variety of Bahá'í topics, arranged for each week in the year and intended for use on radio or in other Bahá'í teaching and proclamation activities.

7.808. —— *idem*. rev. ed. Kuala Lumpur: Bahá'í Publishing Trust of Malaysia, 1977. iv, 208 p.

7.809. *Dedication and Official Opening of the*

Australian National Ḥazíratu'l-Quds, Sunday, 20th October 1974, Bahá'í Temple Gardens, Ingleside, Sydney. Ingleside, N.S.W.: [National Spiritual Assembly of the Bahá'ís of Australia], 1974 (Mudgee: Lynx Print). [5] leaves.

7.810. Deibert, Alvin N. *B. J. and the Language of the Woodland.* il. Carol Joy. Evanston, Ill.: Bellwood Press, 1983. 49 p. LC card 82–24422.

Children's tale of a frog who learns the languages of the other animals. Illustrates unity in diversity and the need for a common language.

7.811. Demas, Kathleen Jamison. *From Behind the Veil: A Novel About Táhirih.* Wilmette, Ill.: Bahá'í Publishing Trust, 1983. 130 p. (Gateway Series). LC card 83–6337.

Fictional account of the life of Ṭáhirih, the Báb's only woman disciple, written for teenagers.

7.812. *Description of the Proposed Site for the Mashrak-el-Azkar.* n.p. [Chicago?], n.d. [191–] 1 p.

7.813. *The Dispensation of Bahá'u'lláh: A Study Outline.* New York: Bahá'í Publishing Committee, 1938. 14 leaves.
See 7.1977.

7.814. Dive, Dulcie. *4th Inter-continental Baha'i Conference, New Delhi, India, October 7–15, 1953.* New Delhi: National Spiritual Assembly of the Bahá'ís of India, Pakistan & Burma, 1953. 60, 4 p.

7.815. *The Divine Secret for Human Civilization.* Geneva, Switzerland: Quo Vadis?, n.d. [191–?] 30 p.

7.816. *idem.* Geneva, Switzerland: Quo Vadis?, 1928. 96 p.

7.817. *Do You Know in What Day You Are Living?* Kampala: National Spiritual Assembly of the Bahá'ís of Central and East Africa, n.d. [between 1956 and 1964] 6 p.

7.818. *idem.* Toronto, Ont.: National Spiritual Assembly of the Bahá'ís of Canada, n.d. [between 1960 and 1969] 5 p.

7.819. Dobrochowski, Nancy. *The Rainbow System: A Teacher's Handbook.* n.p. [Tauranga, New Zealand: Dobrochowski], n.d. [1984] 126 p.

7.820. Dodge, Arthur Pillsbury. *The Truth of It: The Inseparable Oneness of Common Sense, Science, Religion.* New York: Mutual Publishing, 1901. 155 p. LC card 38–19163.

Introduction of the Bahá'í Faith to Christian readers as fulfilling the requirements of common sense, true science and true religion.

7.821. —— *Whence? Why? Whither? Man!*

Things! Other Things! Westwood, Mass.: The Ariel Press, G.E. Littlefield, 1907. 269 p. LC card 8–1000.

Examination of biblical prophecy and its fulfilment in the Bahá'í Faith.

7.822. Dominey, Kel. *Flickerings.* Mona Vale, N.S.W.: National Spiritual Assembly of the Bahá'ís of Australia, 1980, 1984. 20 leaves.

7.823. *The Drama of Salvation: Days of Judgment and Redemption: Institute-Study.* Wilmette, Ill.: Bahá'í Publishing Committee, 1951. 134 p. LC card 53–26415.

A study course outline containing a large number of quotations from Bahá'í Central Figures and the Guardian on the subject of the Bahá'í era as the Day of God/Day of Judgement.

7.824. Dreyfus, Hippolyte. *The Universal Religion: Bahaism.* London: Cope & Fenwick, 1909. 175 p.

English translation of *Essai sur le Béhaïsme* written by a well-known French Bahá'í and orientalist.

7.825. —— *idem.* Chicago: Bahai Publishing Company, 1909. 175 p. Cover title: *Bahaism, the Universal Religion.*

7.826. Dugdale, Dorothy M. *Bahá'í Viewpoint: A Collection of Talks on Various Subjects from the Viewpoint of a Bahá'í.* n.p. [Australia]: Dugdale, 1972. 112 p.

7.826a. Duncan, Charles. *Finding God: Is God But a Supposition? Here Is Scientific Proof of the Existence of God.* Kowloon: Local Spiritual Assembly of the Bahá'ís of Hongkong, n.d. [196–] 18 p.

7.827. Dunlop, Evangeline Elizabeth Crowell. *The Bounties of the Kingdom: A Fairy Play.* Washington, D.C.: Dunlop, 1916 (Riverton, N.J.: Press of the New Era). 31 p.

7.828. Dyar, Aseyeh Allen. *Introduction to the Bahai Revelation: Being a Series of Talks Given During the Summer of 1919 on a Trip through the Northwest Introductory to a Statement of the Message of the Bahai Revelation.* Washington, D.C., 1920. 111 p. LC card 20–13266 rev.

7.828a. Dyar, Aseyeh Allen; Dyar, Harrison G. *The Bahai Revelation as Presented in Five Short Talks.* Washington, D.C., 1919, 28 p.

7.829. —— *Short Talks on the Practical Application of the Bahai Revelation.* Washington, D.C., 1922. 104 p. LC card 23–4475.

Talks on many aspects of the Bahá'í teachings. Several of these addresses express a very personal view on such subjects as birth control and race relations which are not in full accord with Bahá'í belief.

7.830. *The Dynamic Force of Example.* Wilmette, Ill.: Bahá'í Publishing Trust, 1974, 1977, 1980. xv, 215 p. (Bahá'í Comprehensive Deepening Program). LC card 74–198175.

A course in spiritual development, using 'Abdu'l-Bahá as a model.

7.830a. *Dynamics of Prayers.* n.p., n.d. [197–?] 1 p.

E

7.831. *Each One Teach One: A Call to the Individual Believer.* Wilmette, Ill.: Bahá'í Publishing Trust, 1975. 19 p.

7.832. *Each One Teach One Calendar: National Teaching Conferences.* n.p. [Wilmette, Ill.: Bahá'í Publishing Trust], n.d. [1976] [2] p. folded to [6] p.

7.833. *Early Bahá'ís.* Taipei: National Spiritual Assembly of the Bahá'ís of Taiwan, 1978. 11, 23 p. (Kindled with the Fire of His Love).

7.834. *The Earth Is but One Country and Mankind Its Citizen [sic].* Apia: National Spiritual Assembly of the Bahai's of Samoa, 1985. [3] p.

7.835. *The Earth Is But One Country and Mankind Its Citizens.* Seattle, Wash.: Bahá'í Public Affairs Committee, n.d. [1983] 6 p.

7.836. Eastern Shore Multi-Cultural Festival (1982: University of Maryland, Eastern Shore). *Unity in Diversity, Saturday, October 9, 1982. University of Maryland, Eastern Shore, Princess Anne, Maryland.* Maryland: Eastern Shore Multi-Cultural Festival Committee, 1982. [6] p.

7.837. Edge, Clara A. *Ṭáhirih.* Grand Rapids, Mich.: Edgeway Publishing Company, 1964. viii, 193 p.

A novel about Ṭáhirih that takes many liberties with history.

7.837a. *Edith Miller Danielson as She Began Her Pioneering in 1953: Knight of Bahá'u'lláh.* Bellevue, Wash.: Bahá'í Community of Bellevue, 1984. 3 p.

7.838. Edwards, John. *Christ Has Returned.* Arfon, Wales: Audio Visual Centre of the Spiritual Assembly of the Bahá'ís of Arfon, n.d. [1983?] (Bangor: Copycat). [8] p.

7.839. —— *Seek and Ye Shall Find: A Baha'i View of the Return of Christ.* Poole, Eng.: Spiritual Assembly of the Baha'is of Poole, n.d. [1980?] [12] p.

7.840. Ehsani, Mehraz. *Manual for Auxiliary Board Assistants.* n.p. [Nairobi, Kenya]: Continental Board of Counsellors in Central and East Africa, [1977] 127 p.

7.841. *Eighty Golden Years: The Bahá'í Faith in Hawaii, 1901–1981.* Honolulu: National Spiritual Assembly of the Bahá'ís of the Hawaiian Islands, 1981. 20 p.

7.842. *Eko Bahá'í Mokandinlogun Fun Omode = 19 Baha'i Lessons for Children.* n.p. [Lagos]: National Spiritual Assembly of the Bahá'ís of Nigeria, 1979. 40 p. Text in Yoruba and English.

7.843. *Election of the Local Spiritual Assembly.* n.p. [Nairobi]: National Education Committee of the Baha'is of Kenya, 1973. 6 p. (Local Spiritual Assembly; 2).

7.844. *Elements of a World Faith: Teachings of Bahá'u'lláh.* New York: New York Bahá'í Center, 1935. 1 p.

7.845. *Emerging from Obscurity.* n.p. [Wilmette: Office of the Treasurer], n.d. [1982] [6] p. Cover title: *The Fund.*

7.846. *An Enquiring Letter Written by a Friend to the Bahai Community.* Tehran: P.O. Box 865, n.d. [between 1964 and 1973] iii, 25 p.
Same as 7.246.

7.847. Entzminger, Albert P. *The Manifestation.* New York: Bahá'í Publishing Committee, 1937. 32 p.
See 7.849–7.850.

7.848. —— *idem.* Wilmette, Ill.: Bahá'í Publishing Committee, c1937. 32 p.

7.849. —— *Manifestation, Not Incarnation: The Reality of Christ.* Wilmette, Ill.: Bahá'í Publishing Trust, 1968. 21 p.; 1974. 19 p.
See 7.847, 7.850.

7.850. —— *The Reality of Christ.* Wilmette, Ill.: Bahá'í Publishing Trust, [1980] 19 p.
See 7.847–7.849.

7.851. *Equal Rights for Women and Men.* n.p. [Limbe]: National Women's Committee of the Baha'is of Cameroon, Aug. 1985. [6] p.

7.852. *Erstes europäisches Bahá'í Haus der Andacht = First European Bahá'í House of Worship.* Hofheim-Langenhain: Nationale Geistige Rat der Bahá'í in Deutschland, n.d. [1977] [8] p. Text in German and English.

7.853. *Erstes europäisches Haus der Andacht der Bahá'í = First European Bahá'í House of Worship: Langenhain im Taunus bei Frankfurt am Main*. Frankfurt/Main: Nationale Geistige Rat der Bahá'í in Deutschland, n.d. [between 1964 and 1977] [8] p. Text in German and English.

7.854. Esslemont, John Ebenezer. *Bahá'u'lláh and His Message*. London: National Baha'i Assembly of England, 1924. 24 p.

7.855. —— *Bahá'u'lláh and His Message*. London: National Spiritual Assembly of the Bahá'ís of the British Isles, 1938. 39 p.

7.856. —— *idem*. New York: Bahá'í Publishing Committee, n.d. [after 1924], n.d. [193–] (Chicago: Hammond Press). 32 p.

7.857. —— *Bahá'u'lláh and the New Era*. London: George Allen & Unwin Ltd., 1923, 1924. 236 p.
Reviews:
'The Bahais', *The Palestine Weekly* (Jerusalem), v.5 no.46 (Nov. 30th, 1923), pp. 440–441.
'More About the Bahais', *The Friend* (London), (Jan. 18, 1924), p. 53.
'Near East Bookshelf: The Bahai Cult', *The Near East* (London), v.24 no.649 (Oct. 18, 1923), p. 405.
The classic introduction to the Bahá'í Faith which Shoghi Effendi said would inspire generations yet unborn. Primarily directed to a Christian audience. Revised in 1937, 1950 and 1970 to update the book in light of new developments 'with a minimum of alteration to the text, and chiefly by use of footnotes and of an epilogue giving current statistics'.

7.858. —— *idem*. New York: Brentano's, n.d. [1923], n.d. [1926?] (for Bahá'í Publishing Committee). 236 p. LC card 33–1576 rev.
Review:
Zwemer, Samuel M. *The Moslem World* (Hartford, Conn.), v.14 no.2 (Apr. 1924), pp. 212–213.

7.859. ——*Bahá'u'lláh and the New Era*. New York: Bahá'í Publishing Committee, 1927. 307 p.
Review:
Pacific Affairs, v.4 no.11 (Nov. 1931), p. 1026.

7.860. —— *idem*. rev. ed. New York: Bahá'í Publishing Committee, 1937, [1938] viii, 349 p. LC card 40–30297.
The 1938 reprint is indistinguishable from the 1937 first printing because no reprint statement was included.

7.861. —— *idem*. rev. 2nd ed. London: George Allen & Unwin for the Bahá'í Publishing Trust, 1940. 300 p. LC card 41–5568.

Review:
Slater, A.R. *London Quarterly and Holborn Review*, v.165 (1940), p. 495.

7.862. —— *idem*. rev. ed. New York: Bahá'í Publishing Committee, 1940, [1942] viii, 349 p.
The 1940 is erroneously called the 'second printing', there having been a reprint in 1938 which was not identified as such on the book itself. The 1942 printing is indistinguishable from the 1940 printing because no reprint statement was included.

7.863. —— *idem*. rev. ed. Wilmette, Ill.: Bahá'í Publishing Committee, 1944, 1946, 1948, 1950, 1953. xii, 349 p. LC card 50–2289.

7.864. —— *idem*. Indian ed. New Delhi: Publishing Committee of the National Spiritual Assembly of the Bahá'ís of India & Burma, n.d. [1945] viii, 348 p. LC card 47–22666.

7.865. —— *idem*. rev. 3rd ed. London: Bahá'í Publishing Trust, 1952. 311 p. LC card 56–45326.

7.866. —— *idem*. rev. ed. Wilmette, Ill.: Bahá'í Publishing Trust, 1956. xii, 349 p.

7.867. —— *idem*. 2nd rev. ed. Wilmette, Ill.: Bahá'í Publishing Trust, 1960, 1966. xii, 349 p.

7.868. —— *idem*. Indian ed. New Delhi: Bahá'í Publishing Trust, 1969. xiii, 399 p.

7.869. —— *idem*. 3rd rev. ed. Wilmette, Ill.: Bahá'í Publishing Trust, 1970. xiii, 301 p. LC card 73–112794.
Review:
Theology Digest, v.20 no.4 (Winter 1972), p. 349.

7.870. —— *idem*. 3rd rev. ed. Wilmette, Ill.: Bahá'í Books, published by Pyramid Publications for Bahá'í Publishing Trust, 1970. 302 p.

7.871. —— *idem*. 3rd rev. ed. Pyramid ed. New York: Pyramid Books, 1970. 302 p.

7.872. —— *idem*. Indian ed. This ed. New Delhi: Bahá'í Publishing Trust, 1971. ix, 301 p.

7.873. —— *idem*. rev. 4th ed. London: Bahá'í Publishing Trust, 1974. xi, 269 p.

7.874. —— *idem*. 4th rev. ed. Wilmette, Ill.: Bahá'í Books, published by Pyramid Publications for Bahá'í Publishing Trust, 1976, 1978. 301 p. LC card 73–112791.

7.875. —— *idem*. This ed. New Delhi: Bahá'í Publishing Trust, 1978. xi, 269 p.

7.876. —— *idem*. 4th rev. ed. Cloth ed. Wilmette, Ill.: Bahá'í Publishing Trust, 1980. xiv, 300 p. LC card 79–21937.

7.877. —— *idem*. 5th rev. paperback ed. Wilmette, Ill.: Bahá'í Publishing Trust, 1980. xiv, 300 p.

7.878. —— *idem.* 4th ed. Karachi: Bahá'í Publishing Trust Pakistan, 1980. 302 p.

7.879. ——*Equation of Bahai 96 with Gregorian 1939–1940 Calendar.* Shanghai: Ouskouli, [1939] 4 p.

7.880. —— *Equation of Bahai & Gregorian Calendar.* Shanghai: Ouskouli, n.d. [1938?] 4 p.

7.881. —— *The Message of Bahá'u'lláh.* rev. ed. Manchester, U.K.: Bahá'í Publishing Trust, 1945, 1949, 1960. 30 p. Size of item in each printing varies.

7.882. —— *idem.* Karachi: Bahá'í Publishing Trust, 1976. 30 p.

7.883. —— *One World, One Faith.* New Delhi: Bahá'í Publishing Trust, n.d. [1976] 28 p.

7.884. —— *idem.* 2nd ed. New Delhi: Bahá'í Publishing Trust, 1979. 28 p.

7.885. —— *What Is a Bahai?* London: Kenneth Mackenzie, 1919 (West Kensington: The Malvina Press). 31 p.

7.886. —— *idem.* American ed. Chicago: Louis Bourgeois, 1921. 41 p.

7.887. Esslemont, Peter. *A Life Plan.* Wheatley, U.K.: George Ronald, 1953. 84 p.

7.888. *The Eternal Covenant of God.* n.p. [Bogotá]: National Spiritual Assembly of the Bahá'ís of Columbia, 1982. 9 p.

7.889. *The Eternal Covenant of God: Theme 1, Level 1.* n.p. [Bogotá]: National Teaching Committee of the National Spiritual Assembly of the Bahá'ís of Colombia, 1983. 14 p.

7.890. European Bahá'í Youth Conference (1983: Innsbruck, Austria). *Setting Aglow the Hearts.* Innsbruck, Austria: European Bahá'í Youth Conference, 1983. [4] p.

7.891. European Teaching Conference (1st: 1948: Geneva, Switzerland). *First Bahá'í European Teaching Conference, May 22–27, 1948, Geneva, Switzerland.* n.p. [Wilmette, Ill.?: European Teaching Committee?], 1948. 65 leaves.

7.892. European Teaching Conference (2nd: 1949: Brussels, Belgium). *Second Bahá'í European Teaching Conference, August 5, 6, and 7, 1949.* n.p. [Wilmette, Ill.?: European Teaching Committee?], 1949. 94 leaves.

7.893. European Teaching Conference (3rd: 1950: Copenhagen). *Third Bahá'í European Teaching Conference, Copenhagen, Denmark, July 24 through 27, 1950.* n.p. [Wilmette, Ill.?]: European Teaching Committee of the National Spiritual Assembly of the Bahá'ís of the United States, 1950. [3] p.

7.894. —— *Third Bahá'í European Teaching Conference, July 24–30, 1950, Copenhagen, Denmark.* n.p. [Wilmette, Ill.?: European Teaching Committee?], 1950. 95, [3] leaves.

7.895. European Teaching Summer School (1st: 1950: Copenhagen). *First Bahá'í European Teaching Summer School, Copenhagen, Denmark, July 28 through 30, 1950.* n.p. [Wilmette, Ill.?]: European Teaching Committee of the National Spiritual Assembly of the Bahá'ís of the United States, 1950. [3] p.

7.896. Evans, Winston. *Lord of the New Age.* Wilmette, Ill.: Bahá'í Publishing Trust, 1956. 18 p.; 1956. 21 p.

7.897. —— *idem.* Wilmette, Ill.: Bahá'í Publishing Trust, n.d. [196–] 8 p.

7.897a. —— *The Promised Day of God.* Toronto, Ont.: Bahá'í Publishing Committee, n.d. [195–] 11 p.

7.898. *Explanation of Spiritual Evolution As Taught from the Bahá'í Teachings.* comp. C.D. Kelsey. West Englewood, N.J.: Audio-Visual Education Committee, 1958. [7] leaves.

7.899. *Extract from a Tablet of Baha'u'llah. Enoch, the Messenger.* n.p., n.d. [196–?] [4] p.
Includes quotation from Bahá'u'lláh: 'Thou hast associated with Me and hast seen the Sun of the Heaven of My Wisdom . . .' followed by accounts of the ascent of Enoch into the heavens and his meeting with a holy being who was to descend to earth.

F

7.900. *Fact Sheet, Bahá'í Faith.* Thornhill, Ont.: Bahá'í National Centre, n.d. [1977?] 16 leaves. *See* 7.205.

7.901. *Facts About the Bahá'í Faith.* London:

National Spiritual Assembly of the Bahá'ís of the British Isles. n.d. [195– or 196–] [2] p.

7.902. *Faith Called Baha'i.* St John's, Antigua: Baha'i Centre, n.d. [1978] [6] p.

7.903. *Faith for Freedom.* New York: New York Bahá'í Assembly, 1944. [24] p.

7.904. *idem.* 2nd ed. New York: New York Baha'i Assembly, 1945. 22 p.

7.905. *idem.* Wilmette, Ill.: Bahá'í Publishing Committee, 1947, 1948. 21 p.; 1951, 1954. 24 p.

7.906. *idem.* Wilmette, Ill.: Bahá'í Publishing Trust, 1958. 24 p.; 1964. 23 p.; 1968, 1971. 22 p.

7.907. *Faith in Action: A Compilation for Bettering Human Relations.* Wilmette, Ill.: Bahá'í Publishing Committee, 1954. 36 p.

7.908. *The Faith in India, Rhodesia, Malawi, Swaziland, Lesotho and Mozambique, and in the Indian Ocean Region.* n.p., n.d. [1970?] 9 p.

7.909. *The Faith of Baha'u'llah.* [Bathurst, Gambia]: National Spiritual Assembly of the Bahá'ís of Upper West Africa, 1972. 27 p.

7.910. Faizi, Abu'l-Qásim. *Bahá'í Lessons: The Recorded Talks of Hand of the Cause of God, Mr A.Q. Faizi, Given During His Visit to Australia, November 1969.* n.p. [Sydney, N.S.W.]: National Spiritual Assembly of the Bahá'ís of Australia, 1969. 50 leaves.

7.911. —— *Explanation of the Emblem of the Greatest Name.* Wilmette, Ill.: Bahá'í Publishing Trust, 1975, 1977, 1980. 5 p.
　　See 7.913.

7.912. —— *Explanation of the Emblem of the Greatest Name. The Narcissus to 'Akka.* New Delhi: Bahá'í Publishing Trust, n.d. [197–?] 37 p.

7.913. —— *Explanation of the Symbol of the Greatest Name.* New Delhi: Bahá'í Publishing Trust, n.d. [between 1970 and 1977] 20 p. Cover title: *Symbol of the Greatest Name.*
　　See 7.911–7.912.

7.914. —— *A Flame of Fire.* New Delhi: Bahá'í Publishing Trust, 1969. 23 p.; 1973. 20 p.

7.915. —— *From Adrianople to 'Akká.* London: Bahá'í Publishing Trust, n.d. [1969]. 30 p.; 1974. 32 p.
　　A talk given at the Bahá'í Oceanic Conference, Palermo, Sicily, August 1968, concerning the exile journeys of Bahá'u'lláh.

7.916. —— *A Gift of Love Offered to the Greatest Holy Leaf.* comp. and ed. by Gloria Faizi. n.p.: Gloria A. Faizi, 1982. 39 p.
　　A tribute to the sister of 'Abdu'l-Bahá with recollections of Shoghi Effendi.

7.917. —— *Milly, A Tribute to the Hand of the Cause of God Amelia E. Collins.* Oxford: George Ronald, 1977. x, 41 p. LC card 83–839365.

An appreciation of the life's work of the Hand of the Cause of God and vice-president of the first International Bahá'í Council (forerunner of the Universal House of Justice), called by Shoghi Effendi the 'outstanding benefactress of the Faith'.

7.918. —— *Narcissus to Akka.* New Delhi: Bahá'í Publishing Trust, n.d. [196–] 12 p.
　　Story of believers from the village of Sayessan who took pots of narcissus to Bahá'u'lláh.

7.919. —— *idem.* New Delhi: Bahá'í Publishing Trust, n.d. [1970?] 17 p. Includes section on Thomas Breakwell.

7.920. —— *Our Precious Trusts.* New Delhi: Bahá'í Publishing Trust, 1973. 28 p.

7.921. ——*The Prince of Martyrs: A Brief Account of the Imám Ḥusayn.* Oxford: George Ronald, 1977. [6], 68 p. LC card 78–315052.
　　Account for Western readers of the impact of the martyrdom of the grandson of Muḥammad on the fortunes of Islám.

7.922. —— *Three Meditations on the Eve of November the Fourth.* London: Bahá'í Publishing Trust, 1970, 1972. 32 p. Cover title: *Meditations on the Eve of November 4th.*
　　Shoghi Effendi, Guardian of the Bahá'í Faith, died on 4th November 1957. These meditations were those of 'Abu'l-Qásim Faizi as he stood on the shores of the Straits of Magellan on the anniversary of the Guardian's passing and are addressed to the Bahá'í pioneers.

7.923. —— *The Wonder Lamp.* New Delhi: Bahá'í Publishing Trust, 1975. 23 p.
　　A parable about the need for the renewal of religion.

7.924. Faizi, Gloria. *Bahá'í Dharma.* New Delhi: Bahá'í Centre, 1975. 6 p.

7.925. —— *The Bahá'í Faith, An Introduction.* Lebanon, 1971. 130 p. LC card 76–26809.
　　A brief encapsulation of the fundamentals of Bahá'í belief. Sections on the Central Figures, basic tenets and the administration are included, each accompanied by extracts from the Bahá'í sacred texts.

7.926. —— *idem.* 2nd ed. Lebanon, 1972. 130 p.

7.927. —— *idem.* 2nd Indian ed. New Delhi: Bahá'í Publishing Trust, c1971. 130 p.

7.928. —— *idem.* rev. ed. United States, 1972. 121 p. LC card 72–84825.

7.929. —— *idem.* rev. ed. Wilmette, Ill.: Bahá'í Publishing Trust, 1972, 1975, 1978. v, 122 p.

7.930. —— *Fire on the Mountain-Top.* London: Bahá'í Publishing Trust, 1973. x, 141 p.

A collection of inspirational and historical vignettes about the lives of early Bahá'ís in Iran.

7.931. —— *Flowers of One Garden*. India: Faizi, 1977 (Poona: Kirloskar Press). 56 p.

7.932. —— *Man and His Creator*. New Delhi: Bahá'í Publishing Trust, 1975. 26 p.

7.933. —— *The Manifestations of God*. New Delhi: Bahá'í Publishing Trust, 1975. 29 p.

7.934. —— *Prayer and Meditation*. New Delhi: Bahá'í Publishing Trust, 1975. 22 p.

7.935. —— *The Promise of Lord Krishna*. Bangalore: Baha'i Centre, 1975. 24 p.

7.935a. —— *24 Picture-Lessons*. n.p. [New Delhi: Bahá'í Publishing Trust], n.d. [197–] 24 p. Includes guide: *How to Use the 24 Picture-Lessons*.

7.936. *The Family*. Manila, Philippines: Baha'i Publishing Trust, n.d. [1985] 16 p.

7.937. *The Farmer Comes First*. Thornhill, Ont.: Bahá'í National Centre, [1977] [4] p.

7.938. *The Farmer Comes First: The Destiny of the Farmer in the Unfoldment of God's Plan for Today*. Thornhill, Ont.: Bahá'í National Centre, n.d. [1984?] [4] p.

7.939. *The Fast*. n.p. [Lusaka: National Spiritual Assembly of the Bahá'ís of Zambia], n.d. [1971] [5] p.

7.940. Fathea'zam, Hushmand. *The New Garden*. New Delhi: Bahá'í Publishing Trust, 1958.
A widely-used introductory text, now translated into many languages, based upon notes prepared for a Bahá'í teaching institute in India.

7.941. —— *idem*. New Delhi: Baha'i Publishing Trust, n.d. [196–] (Delhi: Navchetan Press Private Limited). 176 p.

7.942. —— *idem*. New Delhi: Bahá'í Publishing Trust, 1963.

7.943. —— *idem*. 4th ed. New Delhi: Bahá'í Publishing Trust, 1970. 171 p.

7.944. —— *idem*. 5th ed. New Delhi: Bahá'í Publishing Trust, 1971. 171 p.

7.945. —— *idem*. Manila: [National Spiritual Assembly of the Bahá'ís of the Philippines], n.d. [197–?] 171 p.

7.946. —— *idem*. Dacca: National Spiritual Assembly of the Bahá'ís of Bangladesh, n.d. [1978?] 171 p.

7.947. —— *idem*. 6th ed. New Delhi: Bahá'í Publishing Trust, 1980. 134 p.

7.948. —— *idem*. 7th ed. New Delhi: Bahá'í Publishing Trust, 1985. [6], 124 p.

7.949. Fazel, Mirza Jenabe. *Lectures Giving the Solution of the World's Problems from a Universal Standpoint. Series 1–5*. trans. Mirza Ahmad Sohrab. Seattle, Wash.: Bahai Literature Center, n.d. [1921] Series 1, 63 p.; Series 2–5, 64 p. each. Title page title: *Lectures Delivered Under Auspices of Seattle Bahai Assembly*.
Five small pamphlets comprising lectures on many social problems.

7.950. *The Feast of 'Alá' (Loftiness), March 2*. n.p. [Wilmette, Ill.?: Community Development Institute Task Force], 1972. [18] p.

7.950a. *idem*. n.p. [Wilmette, Ill.?: Community Development Institute Task Force], 1972. [24] p.

7.950b. *The Feast of 'Azamat (Grandeur), May 17*. n.p. [Wilmette, Ill.?]: Community Development Institute Task Force, 1972. [20] p.

7.950c. *The Feast of Bahá (Splendor), March 21*. n.p. [Wilmette, Ill.?: Community Development Institute Task Force], 1972. [20] p.

7.950d. *The Feast of Masá'il (Questions), Dec. 12*. n.p. [Wilmette, Ill.?]: Community Development Institute, 1972. 19 p.

7.950e. *The Feast of Núr (Light), June 5*. n.p. [Wilmette, Ill.?]: Community Development Institute Materials Task Force, 1972. [20] p.

7.950f. *The Feast of Qudrat (Power), Nov. 4*. n.p. [Wilmette, Ill.?]: Community Development Institute Materials, 1972. [18] p.

7.950g. *The Feast of Sharaf (Honor), December 31*. n.p. [Wilmette, Ill.?]: Community Development Institute Materials, 1972. [20] p.

7.950h. *The Feast of Sovereignty*. n.p. [Wilmette, Ill.?]: Community Development Institute Materials, 1973. [20] p.

7.951. Ferraby, John. *All Things Made New: A Comprehensive Outline of the Bahá'í Faith*. London: George Allen & Unwin, 1957, 1960. 318 p. LC card 58–22511.
This book gives a comprehensive outline of the history and teachings of the Bahá'í Faith. Though complex subjects are simplified and some topics are not covered, this still serves as one of the best introductory texts.

7.952. —— *idem*. rev. American ed. Wilmette, Ill.: Bahá'í Publishing Trust, 1960, 1963. 318 p.

7.953. —— *idem*. rev. ed. London: Bahá'í Publishing Trust, 1975. 319 p.

7.954. —— *idem*. 1st Indian ed. New Delhi: Bahá'í Publishing Trust, 1977. 319 p.

7.955. —— *Bahá'í Teachings on Economics.* Manchester, U.K.: Bahá'í Publishing Trust, n.d. [1954] 16 p.

7.956. —— *idem.* London: Bahá'í Publishing Trust, n.d. [1966], n.d. [1970], 1979. 16 p.

7.957. —— *Progressive Revelation.* Manchester, U.K.: Bahá'í Publishing Trust, n.d. [1954?] 23 p.

7.958. —— *idem.* London: Bahá'í Publishing Trust, n.d. [between 1954 and 1966] 23 p.

7.959. —— *idem.* rev. ed. London: Bahá'í Publishing Trust, 1966, 1975. 16 p.

7.960. *A Few Facts About the Bahá'í Faith.* n.p. [Wilmette, Ill.: National Teaching Committee?], n.d. [196–?] 1 leaf.

7.961. *A Few Facts Concerning the Bahai Movement.* n.p., n.d. (two versions, both 2 pp., one 12 cm., the other 15 cm.).

7.962. *Fiftieth Anniversary of the Passing of Bahíyyih <u>Kh</u>ánum, the Greatest Holy Leaf.* Wilmette, Ill.: [National Spiritual Assembly of the Bahá'ís of the United States], 1982. [4] p.

7.963. *The Fiftieth Anniversary of the Passing of Bahíyyih <u>Kh</u>ánum, 'The Greatest Holy Leaf', Daughter of Bahá'u'lláh.* n.p. [Port of Spain: National Spiritual Assembly of the Bahá'ís of Trinidad and Tobago], 1982. [12] p.

7.964. *50th Anniversary of the Passing of the Greatest Holy Leaf.* n.p. [Guam]: National Spiritual Assembly [of the Bahá'ís of the Mariana Islands], 1982. [4] p.

7.965. *Fifty Years Ago a Great World Teacher Came from the East.* n.p. [Wilmette, Ill.: National Spiritual Assembly of the Bahá'ís of the United States], n.d. [1962] [4] p.

7.966. *The Final Year.* n.p. [Thornhill, Ont.]: National Spiritual Assembly of the Bahá'ís of Canada, n.d. [1978] [8] p.

7.967. Finke, Olga. *The Chief Shepherd.* Lakemont, Ga.: Tarnhelm Press, 1973. 92 p.
Introduction to Bahá'u'lláh as the fulfilment of Christian prophecies.

7.968. *First Centenary of the Declaration of Baha'u'llah (21 April 1863 – 21 April 1963).* Karachi: National Spiritual Assembly of the Baha'is of Pakistan, 1963. 9 p. First five pages are Shoghi Effendi's *The Faith of Bahá'u'lláh, a World Religion.*

7.969. *The First Centenary of the Martyrdom of the Radiant Bab.* Karachi, Pakistan: Baha'i Hall, 1950. 29 p.

7.970. *First Introduction Into the Bahá'í Faith.* n.p. [Johannesburg]: National Spiritual Assembly of the Bahá'ís of South and West Africa, 1973. 6 p.

7.971. *First Latin-American Session.* Colorado Springs, Colo.: Bahá'í Inter-America Committee, 1940. [4] p.

7.972. *First Steps in the Baha'i Spiritual Community.* New Delhi: National Spiritual Assembly of the Bahá'ís of India, n.d. [197–?] 11 p.

7.973. Fitz-Gerald, Nathan Ward. *The Light of God: The Glorious Revelation.* Los Angeles: Fitz-Gerald, 1916. 12 p.

7.974. —— *The New Revelation: Its Marvelous Message.* Tacoma, Wash., 1905. 288 p.
A pot-pourri of introductory materials on the Bahá'í Faith, which includes much misinformation. Includes an early translation of *The Hidden Words.* Typography includes considerable amounts of bold typeface.

7.975. Fleming, Gordon. *The Real You-th.* n.p. [Anchorage, Alaska: National Spiritual Assembly of the Bahá'ís of Alaska], 1983. [4], 81, [3] p.

7.976. Fletcher, F. *To Make Your 'Lotto' Game.* n.p. [Mbabane, Swaziland: National Tutorial School Committee], n.d. [1982?] [18] leaves.
Two games for teaching English.

7.977. [*Flip Chart for Youth*] Salisbury, Rhodesia: National Bahá'í Youth Committee, 1976. [18] leaves.

7.978. *A Floral Messenger from the Holy Land.* n.p., n.d. [191–?] 4 p.

7.979. *Flowers Culled from the Rose Garden of Acca.* n.p., [1910] 40 p.
Notes taken while on pilgrimage 'by the three pilgrims Mrs. Ida A. Finch, Miss Fanny A. Knobloch, Miss Alma S. Knobloch'.

7.980. *Food for Thinking Christians.* Washington, D.C.: Bahai Assembly, n.d. [191–] 11 p.

7.981. *For a Drop of the Lover's Blood.* n.p. [Wilmette, Ill.]: National Persian/American Affairs Committee, 1985. [16] p.
Manual to accompany a video-cassette presentation to assist the integration of Iranian believers into American society.

7.982. Ford, Mary Hanford. *The Oriental Rose or the Teachings of Abdul Baha.* New York: Broadway Publishing Company, 1910. 213 p.
Introductory work on Bahá'í history and teachings as expounded by 'Abdu'l-Bahá. Of the two printings of the New York edition the first has a seriffed monogram on the spine, the second a 'bulls-eye' monogram.

7.983. —— *idem.* Chicago: Bahai Publishing

Society, 1910 [actually printed at a later date] 213 p. LC card 25–2273 rev.

7.984. —— *Secret of Life.* San Francisco, Calif.: Press of A. Carlisle and Co., Upham and Rutledge Inc., 1933. 265 p. LC card 37–39725.

A novel, the main characters of which become involved in the Bahá'í Movement.

7.985. ——*The World of Abdul Baha.* New York: Reality Publishing Company, 1921. 46 p.

Overview of 'Abdu'l-Bahá's teachings, particularly in relation to the socialism then in vogue.

7.986. —— *idem.* 2nd ed. New York: Reality Publishing Company, 1921. 46 p.

7.987. —— *idem.* 3rd ed. n.p., n.d. [after 1921] 64 p.

7.988. —— *idem.* 4th ed. New York: J.J. Little & Ives, n.d. [193–?] 64 p.

7.989. Ford, R.E. *Bahá'í Principles for Children.* il. E. Povey, n.p. [London]: Bahá'í Publishing Trust, 1974. 13 p.

7.990. *The Formation of a Local Spiritual Assembly.* Harare: National Spiritual Assembly of the Bahá'ís of Zimbabwe, Baha'i Distribution Service, 1984. 5 p.

7.991. *A Fortress for Well-Being: Bahá'í Teachings on Marriage.* Wilmette, Ill.: Bahá'í Publishing Trust, 1973, 1973, 1974, 1977, 1980, 1984. xi, 86 p. (Bahá'í Comprehensive Deepening Program).

Of the two 1980 printings, one is paper, the other a smaller hardcover version.

7.992. *The Foundation: A Baha'i Deepening Course.* n.p.: Continental Board of Counsellors of the Bahá'í Faith in Southern Africa, 1976. 32 p.

7.993. *Foundations of the Local Spiritual Assembly.* n.p. [Nairobi]: National Education Committee of the Baha'is of Kenya, 1973. 10 p. (The Local Spiritual Assembly; 1).

7.993a. *4th List of Gardens of Abdu'l Baha.* Montclair, N.J.: World Fellowship, n.d. [192–] 1 p.

7.994. Fozdar, Jamshed. *Buddha Maitreya Amitabha Has Appeared.* New Delhi: Bahá'í Publishing Trust, 1976. 591 p. LC card 75–6131.

Review:

Reyna, Ruth. *Hinduism: Journal of the Bharat Sevashram Sangha* (London), no.84 (Spring 1979), pp. 30–32.

An exhaustive work quoting extensively from Buddhist (and Hindu) scriptures to demonstrate the fulfilment of Buddhist prophecies in the Bahá'í Faith.

7.995. —— *The Fallacy of Ancestor Worship.* Bombay, 1965. 64 p. LC card SA 66–7067.

An attempt to place ancestor worship and the doctrine of karma into the context of Bahá'í teachings. Framed as an argument to disprove.

7.996. —— *Karma and the Fallacy of Reincarnation.* Kuala Lumpur, Malaysia: Bahá'í Publishing Trust Committee, 1977. 115 p.

Essay on subjects which Fozdar covers more thoroughly and with more tact in *The God of Buddha* and *Buddha Maitreya Amitabha Has Appeared.*

7.997. Fozdar, Shirin. *Buddha and Amitabha.* Calcutta: Daw Sen & Co., n.d. [between 1957 and 1964] (Calcutta: Anna Art Press Private Ltd.) 34 p.

See 7.1000.

7.998. —— *idem.* n.p., n.d. [197–] (New Delhi: Arcee Press). 34 p.

7.999. —— *I Found God.* Calcutta: Daw Sen & Co., n.d. [between 1957 and 1964] 21 p.

7.1000. —— *Lord Buddha and Amitabha.* New Delhi: Bahá'í Publishing Trust, n.d. [195–?] 48 p.

Essay on the fulfilment of prophecy concerning the coming of the Fifth Buddha.

See 7.997–7.998.

7.1001. —— *Reincarnation Explained.* Ahmedabad: Sastu Sahitya Mudranalaya, n.d. [194–?] 27 p.

7.1002. —— *The Way to Peace.* Ahmedabad: Local Spiritual Assembly, 1948. 27 p.

7.1003. —— *idem.* Singapore: Fozdar, 1976. 28 p.

7.1004. Frain, Marie M. Kershaw. *Spiritual Perspective.* n.p. [Wilmette, Ill.]: World Order, 1940. [4] p. Reprinted from *World Order,* (Jan. 1940).

7.1005. Frederics, Annette. *La Luz de Bahá-'u'lláh = The Light of Bahá'u'lláh.* n.p. [Panama: National Spiritual Assembly of the Bahá'ís of Panama], n.d. [1967?] [13] leaves.

Coloring book.

7.1006. *Freedom of Religion on Trial in Morocco: The Nador Case.* New York: Bahá'í International Community, 1963. 32 p.

7.1007. Freeman, Dorothy. *From Copper to Gold: The Life of Dorothy Baker.* researched by Louise B. Matthias. Oxford: George Ronald, 1984. xii, 320 p.

The life story of a woman who viewed herself as a rather ordinary housewife but who was later placed in Bahá'í public life because of her appointment as a Hand of the Cause of God in

1951. Told in a popular and inspirational style with dramatic reconstructions of conversations and events.

7.1008. *Fresno Mayor Ted Wills Proclaims March 29–April 6 as Bahá'í Week*. Fresno, Calif.: [Local Spiritual Assembly of the Bahá'ís of Fresno?], 1974. 8 p.

7.1009. Friends of Louhelen (Davison, Mich.). *The Friends of Louhelen*. Davison, Mich.: Louhelen Bahá'í School, n.d. [1982] [2] p.

7.1010. *From Iran East and West*. ed. Juan R. Cole and Moojan Momen. Los Angeles: Kalimát Press, 1984. xiii, 205 p. (Studies in Bábí and Bahá'í History; v.2). LC card 83–227.
Six solid scholarly essays covering Bahá'í history in Iraq, Iran, North America and India.

7.1011. *From One Parent to Another*. [Mona Vale, N.S.W.]: Bahá'í Publishing Trust Australia, 133 B.E. [1976] [4] p.

7.1012. *idem*. Manila: Bahá'í Publishing Trust of the Phils., n.d. [1984?] [4] p.

7.1013. *Fundamentals of the Baha'i Faith*. n.p.: Area Teaching Committee of Southern Rhodesia and Northern Moçambique, 115 B.E. [1958–1959] 22 p.

7.1014. Furútan, 'Alí-Akbar. *The Human Soul and Its Immortality*. New Delhi: Bahá'í Publishing Trust, n.d. [ca. 1970] (New Delhi: Everest Press). 23 p.
Essay providing rational and scientific evidence for the immortality of the soul.

7.1015. —— *idem*. New Delhi: Bahá'í Publishing Trust, n.d. [after 1970] (New Delhi: Skylark Printers). 23 p.

7.1016. —— *Mothers, Fathers, and Children: Practical Advice to Parents*. Oxford: George Ronald, 1980, 1982, 1984. ix, 270 p. LC card 82–204916.
A 'how-to' book for parents. The writing bears the marks of the Persian culture to which it was originally addressed but provides many valuable suggestions.

7.1017. —— *Raising the Tent of Unity*. New Delhi: Bahá'í Publishing Trust, n.d. [before 1972] (Delhi: Kirpal Printing Press), 1972. 12 p.

7.1018. —— *Science and Religion*. New Delhi: Bahá'í Publishing Trust, 1970 (New Delhi: Everest Press). 25 p.

7.1019. —— *idem*. New Delhi: Bahá'í Publishing Trust, n.d. [after 1970] (New Delhi: Skylark Printers). 25 p.

7.1020. —— *The Source of Glory*. New Delhi: Bahá'í Publishing Trust, n.d. [after 1970] (two variant printings, one with text enclosed in black border). 6 p.

7.1021. —— *The Story of My Heart: Memoirs of 'Alí-Akbar Furútan = Hikáyat-i-Dil*. trans. Mahnaz Aflatooni Javid. Oxford: George Ronald, 1984. xvi, 219 p.
Translated from Persian. The early chapters on Furútan's life in the Iranian and Turkistan Bahá'í communities are the book's chief interest. Later chapters are a catalogue of places and topics of talks.

G

7.1022. Gail Marzieh. *Atomic Mandate*. New Delhi: Bahá'í Publishing Trust, n.d. [after 1950] 7 p.

7.1023. —— *Bahá'í Glossary*. Wilmette, Ill.: Bahá'í Publishing Trust, 1955, 1957, 1965, 1969, 1973, 1976. 56 p. LC card 55–36988.
Transliteration and definitions of several hundred Persian and Arabic terms appearing in Bahá'í writings. Included are numeric values of the letters of the Arabic/Persian alphabet as well as simple guides to pronunciation.

7.1024. —— *Dawn Over Mount Hira and Other Essays*. Oxford: George Ronald, 1976. vii, 245 p. LC card 77–351197.
A collection of essays drawn from the wide

literary output of the author, covering many Bahá'í topics in a very personal testimony.

7.1025. —— *He Has Come to the Nations*. Wilmette, Ill.: Bahá'í Publishing Committee, 1946. 8 p.; 1947. [12] p.

7.1026. —— *Headlines Tomorrow*. New York: New York Baha'i Assembly, 1944. [6] p.

7.1027. —— *idem*. Wilmette, Ill.: Bahá'í Publishing Committee, 1944, 1945, 1946. 4 p.

7.1028. —— *idem*. Manchester, U.K.: Bahá'í Publishing Trust, n.d. [195–?] [8] p.

7.1029. —— *Khánum, the Greatest Holy Leaf*. Oxford: George Ronald, 1981, 1982. 40 p.

The author's childhood impressions of Bahíyyih Khánum.

7.1030. —— *Other People, Other Places*. Oxford: George Ronald, 1982. vii, 275 p.
Excerpts from the author's diary and collected literary pieces giving glimpses of many famous individuals (Bahá'í and non-Bahá'í) and covering a range of topics.

7.1030a. —— *Primer for Bahá'í Assemblies*. n.p. [London]: Assembly Development Committee, n.d. [194–] 6 leaves.

7.1031. —— *The Sheltering Branch*. London: George Ronald, 1959, 1974. 101 p.
A portrait of 'Abdu'l-Bahá, based largely upon his talks in the West, with references to the diary of Florence Khánum, the author's mother.

7.1032. —— *idem*. Oxford: George Ronald, 1978. 102 p.

7.1033. —— *idem*. Wilmette, Ill.: Bahá'í Publishing Trust, 1970. 101 p. LC card 78–314341.

7.1034. —— *Six Lessons on Islám*. Wilmette, Ill.: Bahá'í Publishing Committee, 1953. 34 p.

7.1035. —— *idem*. Wilmette, Ill.: Bahá'í Publishing Trust, 1969, 1973. 34 p.

7.1036. Garcia, David. *Welcome to the Bahá'í Faith*. [Umtata]: National Spiritual Assembly of the Bahá'ís of Transkei, May 1983. 41 p.

7.1037. Garis, M.R. *Martha Root, Lioness at the Threshold*. Wilmette, Ill.: Bahá'í Publishing Trust, 1983. xv, 578 p. (Champion Builder Books). LC card 83–3913.
The first biography of Martha Root, the archetypal Bahá'í itinerant teacher. Many sources could not be consulted in the writing of this biography, making this the first of what will no doubt be many studies of Martha Root's life.

7.1038. Garlington, William N. *Fire and Blood: A Novel*. Los Angeles: Kalimát Press, n.d. [1984] 213 p. (Pioneer Paperback Series). LC card 84–3882.
Fictional account of early days of the Bábí Faith.

7.1039. Gash, Andrew. *Stories from 'Star of the West'*. il. Tushar Kanti-Paul. Mona Vale, N.S.W.: Bahá'í Publications Australia, 1985. 64 p.

7.1040. Gaver, Jessyca Russell. *The Bahá'í Faith*. New York: Award Books; London: Tandem Books, 1968, 1969. 222 p.
Same as 7.1041.

7.1041. —— *The Bahá'í Faith: The Dawn of a New Day*. New York: Hawthorn Books Inc., 1967. 223 p. LC card 66–15248.
A popular, although not always accurate, introduction for American readers.

7.1042. *Gemmer le Pouvoir! = Tapping the Power!* n.p. [Thornhill, Ont.: National Spiritual Assembly of the Bahá'ís of Canada], 1977. [8] p.
Brochure for a series of conferences on prayer, with Hand of the Cause John A. Robarts.

7.1043. Geyserville Bahá'í School (Geyserville, Calif.). *Bahá'í Summer School, June 21, 1952 through August 2, 1952*. Geyserville, Calif.: Geyserville Bahá'í School, 1952. [6] p.

7.1044. —— *Geyserville Bahá'í School Teaches World Citizenship: July 7–September 1, 1963: Thirty-fifth Season*. Geyserville, Calif.: Geyserville Bahá'í School, 1963. [12] p.

7.1045. Ghadirian, Abdu'l-Missagh. *In Search of Nirvana: A New Perspective on Alcohol and Drug Dependency*. Oxford: George Ronald, 1985. 77 p.
One Bahá'í psychiatrist's perspective on the psychology and prevention of substance abuse.

7.1046. Giachery, Ugo. *One God, One Truth, One People: Some Thoughts on the Peace Encyclical of Pope John XXIII*. Wilmette, Ill.: Bahá'í Publishing Trust, 1965. 23 p.; 1967. 22 p.

7.1047. —— *Shoghi Effendi, Recollections*. Oxford: George Ronald, 1973, 1974. x, 238 p. LC card 74–174543.
Dr Giachery visited Haifa on several occasions and worked with the Guardian himself in the erection of the superstructure of the Shrine of the Báb on Mt Carmel. Giachery here shares his personal reminiscences of Shoghi Effendi.

7.1048. Gift, Maye Harvey. *God and His Manifestations: Outline for Study of the Baha'i Movement*. n.p. [New York?]: Baha'i Committee on Publications, 1925. 20 p.

7.1049. Ginn, Henry. *God's Great Plan*. Wilmette, Ill.: Bahá'í Publishing Trust, 1968. 26 p.

7.1050. *idem*. rev. ed. Wilmette, Ill.: Bahá'í Publishing Trust, 1983. iv, 28 p.

7.1051. *Giving the Baha'i Message*. n.p.: Curtis D. Kelsey, n.d. [196–?] [4] p.

7.1052. *The Glory of God*. Windhoek: National Spiritual Assembly [of the Bahá'ís of South West Africa/Namibia], [1984] [4] p.

7.1053. Glory School (Shantiniketan, West Bengal). *Prospectus*. Shantiniketan: Glory School, n.d. [1982?] [14] p.

7.1054. *Glossary of Bahá'í Terms*. Tokyo: Pub-

lishing Committee of the Bahá'ís of Japan, n.d. [1956?] 71 p.
English-Japanese glossary of Bahá'í terms.

7.1055. *The Goal Is World Civilization.* Wilmette, Ill.: Bahá'í Committee on Public Relations, n.d. [194–?] 4 leaves.

7.1056. *God, His Mediator and Man: A Study of Comparative Religion.* Wilmette, Ill.: Bahá'í Publishing Trust, 1958. 39 p.
Contents: The Scriptures of Different Faiths (Pritam Singh); The Oneness of Religion (Doris McKay).

7.1057. *God Is Man's Goal.* Wilmette, Ill.: Bahá'í Publishing Committee, n.d. [after 1947] 7 p.

7.1058. *God Is 1, Man Is 1, All the Religions Are 1: Grenadian Baha'i Song Book.* St George's: National Spiritual Assembly of the Baha'is of Grenada, n.d. [1985] 24 p.

7.1059. *God Speaks Again.* Toronto, Ont.: National Spiritual Assembly of the Bahá'ís of Canada, n.d. [ca. 1958] 12 p.

7.1060. *God Speaks Again.* Roseau, Dominica: Baha'i Faith, n.d. [1983] [2] p.

7.1061. *God's Gift to You.* comp. Women & Children's Committee of Monrovia. Monrovia: National Spiritual Assembly of the Bahá'ís of Liberia and Guinea, 1977. [20] p.

7.1062. *God's Great Plan.* n.p. [Port of Spain: National Spiritual Assembly of the Bahá'ís of Trinidad and Tobago], n.d. [1976?] 2 p.

7.1063. *God's Message Is Renewed.* Hong Kong: Baha'i National Centre, n.d. [1981] [8] p.

7.1064. *God's New Age.* n.p. [Wilmette, Ill.]: National Teaching Committee of the National Spiritual Assembly of the Bahá'ís of the United States, 1970. 15 p.

7.1065. *idem.* Nairobi: National Spiritual Assembly of the Bahá'ís of Kenya, n.d. [197–] (Nairobi: Acme Press). 15 p.

7.1066. *idem.* Wilmette, Ill.: Bahá'í Publishing Trust, n.d. [after 1970], n.d. [1976] 15 p.

7.1067. *idem.* n.p. [Sydney, N.S.W.]: National Spiritual Assembly of the Bahá'ís of Australia, 1971. 16 p.

7.1068. *idem.* n.p. [Bangkok: National Spiritual Assembly of the Bahá'ís of Thailand], n.d. [1983] 8 p. English and Khmer text.

7.1069. *God's Plan for a United World: A Panel Presentation of the Bahá'í World Faith.* n.p. [Wilmette, Ill.]: Radio Service Committee, 1959. [2], 15 leaves.

7.1070. *God's Plan for Man Revealed by Baha'o'llah.* Karachi, Pakistan: Spiritual Assembly, n.d. [192–?] 1 p.

7.1071. *God's Purpose Progressively Revealed: Religion Renewed and the World United.* London: Bahá'í Publishing Trust, n.d. [1969], 1980. [8] p.

7.1072. Goldstein, Kit. *The Light on Singing Mountain.* n.p. [Panama City]: National Spiritual Assembly of the Bahá'ís of Panama, n.d. [1973] 17 p.

7.1073. Goodall, Helen S.; Cooper, Ella Goodall. *Daily Lessons Received at Acca, January 1908.* Chicago: Bahai Publishing Society, 1908, 1917. 101 p.
Early American Bahá'ís had neither a vast corpus of literature, nor Bahá'í administrative institutions such as exist today. They were sustained by the visits of believers to 'Abdu'l-Bahá, the oral and written accounts of their experiences, and the letters received from 'Abdu'l-Bahá. This is an account of the authors' pilgrimage to the Holy Land and what they heard from the Head of their Faith.

7.1074. —— *Daily Lessons Received at 'Akká, January 1908.* rev. ed. Wilmette, Ill.: Bahá'í Publishing Trust, 1979. xii, 98 p. LC card 79–19806.

7.1075. *Grand Opening Ceremony, Radio Bahá'í, WLGI FM 90.9: March 23, 1985, the Louis G. Gregory Baha'i Institute, Hemingway, South Carolina, 2:00 p.m.* Hemingway, S.C.: Louis G. Gregory Baha'i Institute, 1985. [16] p.

7.1076. *The Great Announcement.* Kingston: National Teaching and Distribution Committee of the National Spiritual Assembly of the Bahá'ís of Jamaica, n.d. [197–?] 5 p.

7.1077. *The Greatest Gift.* n.p. [Willowdale, Ont.]: Canadian Bahá'í Community, 1970. 15 p.

7.1078. *'The Greatest Holy Leaf', Bahíyyih Khánum, Daughter of Bahá'u'lláh.* n.p. [Accra: National Spiritual Assembly of the Bahá'ís of Ghana], n.d. [1982] 4 p.

7.1079. *The Greatness of the Local Spiritual Assembly: A Dramatic Sketch for Five Readers and One Other.* n.p. [Victoria: National Spiritual Assembly of the Bahá'ís of Cameroon], n.d. [1981] 5 p.

7.1080. Green Acre Bahá'í School, *Green Acre Bahá'í School, 1984.* Eliot, Me.: Green Acre Bahá'í School, 1984. 4 p.

7.1081. —— *Green Acre 1954 Season.* Eliot, Me.: Green Acre School Committee, 1954. 11 p.

7.1082. —— *Green Acre Program, July–August*

1931. Eliot, Me.: Green Acre Committee, 1931. 7 p.

7.1083. —— *Thirty-sixth Season, 1930*. Eliot, Me.: Green Acre Fellowship, 1930. 4 p.

7.1084. Green Acre Bahá'í Summer School (1946: Eliot, Me.). *Green Acre Bahá'í Summer School, June 29–Septemeber [sic] 2, 1946*. Eliot, Me.: Green Acre, 1946. 14 p.

7.1085. *Green Acre, Eliot, Maine: A Focal Center of Devotional and Humanitarian Activity*. Eliot, Me.: Green Acre Fellowship, n.d. [192–?] 4 p.

7.1085a. Green Acre Fellowship. *Charter and By-Laws of Green Acre Fellowship*. [Eliot], Maine: Green Acre Fellowship, 1922. [3] p.

7.1086. —— *A General Call to All Forward Looking Men and Women in the Bahai Cause Throughout the World*. Eliot, Me.: Board of Trustees of Green Acre Fellowship, n.d. [1919] 8 p.

7.1087. Green Acre Institute of World Unity. *Creating the New World Outlook*. Eliot, Me.: Green Acre Institute for World Unity, 1927. 11 p.

7.1088. Green-Acre-on-the-Piscataqua. *Program of the Eleventh Season of Summer Conferences*. Eliot, Me.: Green-Acre, 1904. 28 p. Cover title: *Peace*.

7.1089. —— *Program of the Ninth Season of Summer Lectures*. Eliot, Me.: Green-Acre, 1902. 20 p.

7.1090. —— *Programme of the Fourth Season of Summer Conferences*. Eliot, Me.: Green-Acre, 1903. 28 p. Cover title: *Tenth Season, Green Acre Conferences*.

7.1091. Green Lake Bahá'í Conference (23rd: 1982: Green Lake, Wis.). *Points of Light: 23rd Annual Green Lake Bahá'í Conference*. Menomonee, Wis.: Green Lake Bahá'í Conference Planning Committee, 1982. [4] p.

7.1092. Greg & Malini (Singing Group). *Journey's End*. n.p. [Wilson, W.A.]: Gemsongs, 1984 (Penang, Malaysia: Ganesh Printing Works). [36] p.

7.1093. Gregory, Louis G. *Bahá'í to Jew*. Wilmette, Ill.: Bahá'í Publishing Committee, n.d. [194–?] 4 p.

7.1094. —— *A Heavenly Vista*. Washington, D.C.: R.L. Pendleton, 1911. 32 p. LC card 72–196756.

7.1095. —— *The Races of Men: Many or One*. New York: Bahá'í Publishing Committee, 1929. 40 p.

7.1096. Grossman, Hartmut. *The Secret of Setting Aglow the Hearts*. pt.1. n.p. [Helsinki: National Spiritual Assembly of the Bahá'ís of Finland], n.d. [1984] 11 p.

7.1097. —— *Teaching the Bahá'í Faith: An Introduction to the Compilation 'The Individual and Teaching', Also Known as 'The Gift of Teaching'*. n.p. [Helsinki: National Spiritual Assembly of the Bahá'ís of Finland], n.d. [1982?] (n.p: Gillet Oy pikapaino). 17 p.

7.1098. *Growing Toward 20,000*. n.p. [Wilmette, Ill.: Office of the Treasurer], n.d. [1982] [4] p.

7.1099. Grundy, Julia M. *Ten Days in the Light of Acca*. Chicago: Bahai Publishing Society, 1907, n.d. [after 1907] 111 p. LC card 39–24772.
Pilgrims' notes of the author's visit in 1905 to 'Abdu'l-Bahá, with personal glimpses of life in the 'Holy Household'.

7.1100. —— *Ten Days in the Light of 'Akká*. rev. ed. Wilmette, Ill.: Bahá'í Publishing Trust, 1979. 107 p. LC card 79–12177.

7.1101. *The Guardian's Seven Year Plan for the American Bahá'ís, 1946–1953*. Wilmette, Ill.: National Spiritual Assembly of the Bahá'ís of the United States and Canada, n.d. [1946] 13 p.

7.1102. *Guidance One: Bahá'í Prayers and Teachings*. n.p. [Port-of-Spain]: National Spiritual Assembly of the Bahá'ís of Trinidad and Tobago, n.d. [197–] 23 p.

7.1103. *Guidance One: Selected Baha'i Prayers, Nineteen Day Feast Days, Divine Revelators, What Every Baha'i Knows*. Kuala Lumpur, Malaysia: National Spiritual Assembly, n.d. [196– or 197–] 28 p. Parallel Chinese and English text.

7.1104. *Guidelines to Planned Giving: Do You Need Financial Planning?* Wilmette, Ill.: Office of the Treasurer, n.d. [1981?] 16 p.

7.1105. *Guidelines to Planned Giving: Estate Planning in the 80s*. Wilmette, Ill.: Office of the Treasurer, 1980. 16 p.

7.1106. *Guidelines to Planned Giving: Gifts of Appreciated Property*. Wilmette, Ill.: Office of the Treasurer, n.d. [1981?] 15 p.

7.1107. *Guidelines to Planned Giving: Investments and Taxes*. Wilmette, Ill.: Office of the Treasurer, n.d. [1981?] 16 p.

7.1108. *Guidelines to Planned Giving: Minimizing Your Income Taxes*. Wilmette, Ill.: Office of the Treasurer, n.d. [1981?] 15 p.

7.1109. *Guidelines to Planned Giving: Tax Plan-*

ning Ideas for Executives and Professionals. Wilmette, Ill.: Office of the Treasurer, n.d. [1981?] 16 p.

7.1110. *Guidelines to Planned Giving: The Pooled Income Fund*. Wilmette, Ill.: Office of the Treasurer, n.d. [1981?] 16 p.

H

7.1111. *'Ha' 'Hu' in 9 Days*. n.p. [Addis Ababa]: National Spiritual Assembly of the Bahá'ís of Ethiopia, 1979. 33 leaves.

7.1112. Haddad, Anton F. *Divine Revelation the Basis of All Civlization*. New York: Board of Counsel, 1902. 24 p.

7.1113. —— *The Maxim of Bahaism*. New York: Board of Counsel, n.d. [ca. 1900] 24 p.

7.1113a. —— *idem*. n.p. [Rangoon, Burma]: Bahai Publishing Society, n.d. [1910?] 24 p.

7.1114. —— *A Message from Acca*. n.p., 1900. 16 p.

7.1115. —— *A Message from Akka*. New York: Board of Counsel, 1900. 16 p.

7.1116. —— *The Station of the Manifestation and the Greatness of the Day*. New York: Board of Counsel, 1901. 16 p.

7.1117. Hainsworth, Philip. *Bahá'í Focus on Human Rights*. London: Bahá'í Publishing Trust, 1985. viii, 64 p.
   Reviews:
Palin, Iain S. *World Federalist Newsletter* (Littlehampton, U.K.), (1985/2), pp. 5, 21.
Scharf, Betty. *New World* (London), (Sept./Oct. 1985).

7.1118. —— *Marriage, a Bahá'í View*. London: National Spiritual Assembly of the Bahá'ís of the United Kingdom, 1978. 6 p.

7.1119. Hall, Mrs Basil. *The Drama of the Kingdom: A Pageant Play, the Plan for Which Was Given by Abdul Baha Abbas in London, 17th January 1913*. London: The Weardale Press, 1933. viii, 66 p.

7.1120. Hall, E.T. *Baha'i Reflections, 1925*. Manchester, U.K.: Hall, 1925. [3] p.

7.1121. —— *The Beginning of the Bahá'í Cause in Manchester*. Manchester, U.K.: Manchester Bahá'í Assembly, 1925. 37 p. (Cover title: *The Bahá'í Dawn, Manchester*).

7.1122. —— *Continuation of 'The Bahá'í Dawn: Manchester'*. n.p. [Manchester?], Nov. 1933. 8 leaves.

7.1123. —— *The Divine Tablets: A Retrospect for*

the Manchester Bahais. Higher Broughton, U.K.: E.T. Hall, 1922. 21 p.

7.1124. —— *Meditations of a Bahai Christian*. Manchester, U.K.: C.E. Bennet and Company, 1912.

7.1125. —— *Thoughts on the Glorious Ideal of Baha'ullah*. Manchester, U.K.: Hall, 1929. 10 p.

7.1125a. —— *The Universal Religion (Its Principles & Purpose)*. Manchester, U.K.: For the Manchester Bahá'í Assembly, passed for publication by the British Bahá'í Spiritual Assembly, 1927. 18 p.

7.1126. *The Handbook for Summer Garden Baha'i School: (A Daily Summer School Program for Children)*. n.p. [Wilmette, Ill.]: National Education Committee, n.d. [1984] ii, 69 p.

7.1127. *Hands of the Cause of God*. Taipei: National Spiritual Assembly of the Bahá'ís of Taiwan, 1979. 11, 16 p. (Kindled with the Fire of His Love).

7.1128. Hands of the Cause of God. *A Message from the Hands of the Cause to the Bahá'í World*. Wilmette, Ill.: National Spiritual Assembly of the Bahá'ís of the United States, 1961. 6 p. Message of Nov. 5, 1961.

7.1129. Hands of the Cause of God Residing in the Holy Land. *The Bahá'í Faith, 1844–1963*: Information Statistical and Comparative. Haifa: Hands of the Cause of God Residing in the Holy Land, 1963 (Ramat Gan: Peli-P.E.C. Printing Works). 128 p.

7.1130. Handy, Carol. *The Dragons of Rizvania*. il. Louise Taylor. Oxford: George Ronald, 1984. 58 p.
   The story of a boy who attains maturity by fighting dragons that represent his inner weaknesses and strengths.

7.1131. *Hanma Iyange = Every Day*. n.p. [Lagos: National Spiritual Assembly of the Bahá'ís of Nigeria], n.d. [1982] [9] leaves. English and Tiv text.

7.1132. Hannen, Jospeh H. *Akka Lights*. n.p., 1909. 15 p.

7.1133. —— *The Bahai Teaching*. n.p., n.d.

[1917?] 1 p. Reprinted from *New York Globe*, May 1, 1917.

7.1134. Harmon, W.W. *Divine Illumination*. Boston: Bahai Movement, 1915. 72 p.

An introduction to Bahá'í spiritual life under such chapter headings as 'Spiritual Illumination', 'The Plane of the Mind'.

7.1135. Harper, Orrol L. *A Bird's Eye View of the World in the Year 2000*. n.p. [United States], n.d. [191–?] 8 p.

7.1135a. Harris, W. Hooper. *History and Teachings of Bahaism*. Rangoon, Burma: Bahai Publishing Society, 1907 (Burma: K.L.V. Press). 12 p. First page title: *Bahaism, Its History and Teachings*.

7.1136. —— *Lessons on the Beha Revelation*. Bayonne: N.J.: Charles E. Sprague, n.d. [1901] 67 p.

A series of lessons based on Christian prophecies, used for teaching the Bahá'í Faith in the early days of the religion in the United States.

7.1137. Hatcher, John S. *Ali's Dream: The Story of Bahá'u'lláh*. il. Jean MacNeill. Oxford: George Ronald, 1980. xi, 248 p.

A fictionalized account of Bahá'í history, written for young people.

7.1138. —— *From the Auroral Darkness: The Life and Poetry of Robert Hayden*. Oxford: George Ronald, 1984. xii, 342 p.

Reviews:

Blount, Marcellus. *Black American Literature Forum* (Terre Haute, Ind.), v.19 no.4 (Winter 1985), pp. 169–171.

O'Meally, R.G. *Choice* (Middletown, Conn.), (July/Aug. 1985), p.174.

Literary biography and analysis of one of America's outstanding twentieth century poets. Important in bringing to light the value and importance of Bahá'í symbolism in Hayden's work, while setting that symbolism in the context of the wider spiritual content of Hayden's writing.

7.1139. —— *The Metaphorical Nature of Physical Reality*. Thornhill, Ont.: Canadian Association for Studies on the Bahá'í Faith, 1977. 27 p. (Bahá'í Studies; v.3).

7.1140. Hatcher, William S. *The Concept of Spirituality*. Ottawa, Ont.: Association for Bahá'í Studies, 1982. iii, 35 p. (Bahá'í Studies; v.11).

7.1140a. —— *Development of Local Spiritual Assemblies*. n.p. [Kuala Lumpur]: Baha'i Publishing Trust Committee of Malaysia, 1982 [i.e. 1983?] [2], 18 p.

7.1141. —— *The Science of Religion*. Thornhill,

Ont.: Canadian Association for Studies on the Bahá'í Faith, 1977. 45 p. (Bahá'í Studies; v.2).

7.1142. —— idem. 2nd ed. Thornhill, Ont.: Canadian Association for Studies on the Bahá'í Faith, 1980. 45 p. (Bahá'í Studies; v.2).

7.1143. Hatcher, William S.; Martin, J. Douglas. *The Bahá'í Faith: The Emerging Global Religion*. San Francisco, Calif.: Harper & Row, 1984, 1984, 1985, 1985. xvii, 226 p. LC card 84–42743.

Reviews:

Piehl, Mel. *Library Journal* (New York), v.110 no.4 (Mar. 1, 1985), pp. 94–95.

Ruthven, Malise, 'Beyond the Islamic State', *Times Literary Supplement* (London), (Oct. 25, 1985), p. 1214.

Booklist (Chicago), v.81 no.17 (May 1, 1985), p. 1220.

Pucelik, T.M., *Choice* (Middletown, Conn.), (Sept. 1985).

An introductory work relating the Bahá'í Faith to current social and spiritual concerns. The 1985 printings contain a frontispiece of the Shrine of the Báb.

7.1144. *Haus der Andacht: Grundsteinlagung = Mother Temple of Europe: Laying of Cornerstone*. Langenhain: Nationale Geistige Rat der Bahá'í in Deutschland, 1960. 4 p.

7.1145. *Have They Been Fulfilled?* New York: David, n.d. [190–] [4] p.

7.1146. *Have You Heard of Bahá'u'lláh?* n.p., n.d. [197–?] [12] p.

7.1147. Ḥaydar-'Alí, Ḥájí Mírzá. *Bahai Martyrdoms in Persia in the Year 1903 A.D.* Chicago: Bahai Publishing Society, 1904. 28 p.

7.1148. —— idem. trans. Dr Youness Khan. 2nd ed. Chicago: Bahai Publishing Society, 1917: 28 p.

7.1149. —— idem. n.p. [Mishawaka, Ind.]: Aubade, 1985. 27 p.

7.1150. —— *Stories from the Delight of Hearts: the Memoirs of Ḥájí Mírzá Ḥaydar-'Alí*. trans. A.Q. Faizi. Los Angeles: Kalímat Press, 1980, 1980. vi, 168 p. LC card 79–91219.

These memoirs of one of the foremost early believers were first published in Bombay in Persian in 1913. This abridged translation offers a glimpse into the experiences of Bahá'ís in Iran, Palestine and Egypt during the lifetime of Bahá'u'lláh.

7.1151. *He Is Abdul-Baha, the Servant of the Glory of God!* n.p., n.d. [191–?] 1 p.

7.1152. Heard, Geoffrey N. *The Kingdom Comes*. Lae: National Spiritual Assembly of the Bahá'ís of Papua New Guinea, n.d. [1975?], n.d. [1981] 19 p.

7.1153. *Hearts on Fire: A Campaign of Spiritualisation and Personal Teaching.* n.p. [Reykjavík]: National Spiritual Assembly of the Bahá'ís of Iceland, 1982. no. 1, [16] p.; no. 2, [20] p.; no. 3, [16] p.; no. 4, [16] p.; no. 5 [20] p.; no. 6, [20] p.

7.1154. Hebrew Assembly of Bahais. *Translation of a Letter Written by the Hebrew Assembly of Bahais in Teheran, Persia to the House of Spirituality, Chicago, Ill. for the Perusal of All American Friends.* New York: Bahai Board of Counsel, n.d. [1904?] [6] p.

7.1155. Heggie, James. *Bahá'í Scriptural Index.* n.p. [Australia]: Heggie, 1971. 544 p.
Mimeographed, bound, limited quantity production. Selective concordance to major scriptural texts.

7.1156. —— *Index, God Passes By.* [Sydney, N.S.W.]: National Spiritual Assembly of the Bahá'ís of Australia, 1976. 976 p.
Mimeographed, bound concordance to Shoghi Effendi's history.

7.1157. —— *An Index of Quotations from the Bahá'í Sacred Writings.* Oxford: George Ronald, 1983, 1984. xii, 811 p. LC card 84–135154.
Published selective concordance to major passages in Bahá'í scriptures. For those familiar with Bahá'í literature, there are many important passages missing. However, it is the first work of its kind and scope and thus very valuable until more detailed concordances become available.

7.1158. —— *An Index of Quotations from the Writings of Shoghi Effendi.* n.p. [Australia]: Heggie, n.d. [1984] 3 v. (1469 mimeographed leaves). Spine title: *Quotations from Writings of Shoghi Effendi.*

7.1159. —— *Index to the Writings of Shoghi Effendi.* n.p. [Australia]: Heggie, 1972. 606 p. (Baha'i Concordance; v. 2).

7.1160. —— *Muhammad and Islam: A Bahá'í Qur'ánic Study: Rodwell's Translation.* n.p. [Australia]: Heggie, 1972. 84 p.

7.1160a. —— *Qur'anic Study Index: Rodwell's Translation.* Paddington, N.S.W.: Authorized by the National Spiritual Assembly of the Bahá'ís of Australia, 1957. xi, 63 leaves.

7.1161. Hellaby, William; Hellaby, Madeline. *Prayer, a Bahá'í Approach.* Oxford: George Ronald, 1985. 117 p.
A detailed study of prayer and its dynamics, by two well-known British Bahá'ís. William Hellaby was a Christian clergyman before accepting the Bahá'í Faith.

7.1162. Heller, Wendy. *Clementine and the Cage.* il. Rex John Irvine. Los Angeles: Kalimát Press, 1980. 32 p. LC card 79–28063.
Children's story about life after death using 'Abdu'l-Bahá's image of the 'bird' of the soul being freed from the 'cage' of the body.

7.1163. —— *Lidia: The Life of Lidia Zamenhof, Daughter of Esperanto.* Oxford: George Ronald, 1985. xvi, 260 p.
Review:
Auld, William. *La Brita Esperantisto* (London), 81a Jaro, N-ro 866 (Septembro-Oktobro 1985), p. 71.
A thorough biography of the daughter of the founder of Esperanto, herself an accomplished Esperantist and a Bahá'í.

7.1164. —— *My Name is Nabil.* il. Rex John Irvine. Los Angeles: Kalimát Press, 1981. [45] p. LC card 81–3703.
Children's introduction to the Bahá'í Faith and Bahá'í family and community life.

7.1165. —— *The Sunshine Tree and Other Tales from Around the World.* il. Brian O'Neill. Oxford: George Ronald, 1982. viii, 85 p. Includes *Parents' and Teachers' Guide to the Sunshine Tree.*
Nineteen folk tales illustrating the qualities of kindness, perseverance and unity.

7.1166. *Help to Establish Universal Peace: Are These Sentimentalists or Thinkers?* n.p. [Karachi, Pakistan?], n.d. [195–?] [2] p.

7.1167. Hendry, Derald E. *In the Hollow of His Hand: The Story of Ethel Murray.* n.p. [Morgantown, N.C.]: Derald E. Hendry, 1984. [4], 79 leaves.

7.1168. Herbert, Leonard. *Paintings on the Holy Land and the Bahá'í Faith.* Honolulu: National Spiritual Assembly of the Bahá'ís of the Hawaiian Islands, 1976. [4] p.

7.1169. *Heroic Age of the Bahá'í Faith.* [Nuku-'alofa]: National Spiritual Assembly of the Bahá'ís of Tonga and the Cook Islands, 1973. 21 p. (Study Guide; no.1).

7.1170. Herrick, Elizabeth. *Unity Triumphant: The Call of the Kingdom: An Introduction to the Bahá'í Teachings and a Testimony of Faith in the Revelation of Bahá'u'lláh.* London: Kegan Paul Trench Trubner & Company, 1923. vi, 226 p.

7.1171. —— *idem.* 2nd ed. London: Unity Press, 1925. 226 p.

7.1172. *Hi Bahai's.* Johore Bahru, Malaysia: [Local Spiritual Assembly of the Bahá'ís of Johore Bahru], 1972. [6] leaves.

7.1173. *The Highest Wish of True Lovers.* Auckland: National Spiritual Assembly of the Bahá'ís of New Zealand, 1981. i, 19 p.

7.1174. Himalayan Bahá'í Teaching Conference (2nd: 1983: Tadong, Sikkim). *II Himalayan Baha'i Teaching Conference, 19th, 20th, and 21st Oct. 1983.* Tadong: [National Spiritual Assembly of the Bahá'ís of Sikkim], 1983. [10] p.

7.1175. Himes-Cox, Florence. *The Dawn-Breakers: Chronological Study Outline.* n.p. [Wilmette, Ill.?]: Study Outline Committee, n.d. [195–?] 15 [i.e. 39] leaves.

7.1176. Historical Records Survey (New Jersey). *Inventory of the Church Archives of New Jersey: Baha'i Assemblies.* Newark, N.J.: Historical Records Survey, 1940. 28 p. LC card 41–20125.

7.1177. *The History of the Bab.* 1st Eng. ed. Calí: National Teaching Committee of the National Spiritual Assembly of the Bahá'ís of Colombia, Oct. 1983. 10 leaves.

7.1178. Hoagg, H. Emogene. *Conditions of Existence: Servitude, Prophethood, Deity.* New York: Bahá'í Publishing Committee, 1938. 40 leaves.

7.1179. —— *The Three Worlds: Introductory to the Revelation of Bahá'u'lláh.* New York: Bahá'í Publishing Committee, 1938. 40 leaves.

7.1180. Hofman, David. *Commentary on the Will and Testament of 'Abdu'l-Bahá.* London: George Ronald, 1943. 28 p.

A study of one of the three 'charters' of the Bahá'í administrative order.

7.1181. —— *idem.* 2nd ed. London: Bahá'í Publishing Trust, 1947. 29 p.

7.1182. —— *idem.* 3rd ed. rev. Oxford: George Ronald, 1955. 30 p.

7.1183. —— *idem.* 4th ed. rev. with epilogue. Oxford: George Ronald, 1982. 53 p.

7.1184. —— *George Townshend, Hand of the Cause of God (Sometime Canon of St Patrick's Cathedral, Dublin, Archdeacon of Clonfert).* Oxford: George Ronald, 1983. xiv, 404 p.
Review:
Church of Ireland Gazette (Dublin), (11 May 1984).

A literary biography of this important Bahá'í figure – a former official of the Church of Ireland who renounced his ecclesiastical office to devote himself to furthering the Bahá'í cause. Illustrated, good index. Hofman is Townshend's literary executor.

7.1185. —— *God and His Messengers.* il. Geoffrey Rideout. Oxford: George Ronald, 1953, 1958, 1967. 60 p.

Stories of the Founders of the world's great religions told for young children.

7.1186. —— *idem.* il. Zohreh Zahra'i. rev. ed. Oxford: George Ronald, 1973. 55 p.

7.1187. —— *The Renewal of Civilization.* London: George Ronald for the Bahá'í Publishing Trust, c1945 [i.e. Apr. 1946] v, 96 p. LC card 46–18454.

An introductory work which 'gives a brief account of the history, teachings and aims of the Bahá'í Faith, emphasizing the religious foundation of civilization and its progressive evolution towards a world society'. [Cover of 1972 rev. Talisman ed.]

7.1188. —— *idem.* 2nd ed. London: George Ronald for the Bahá'í Publishing Trust, 1946 [Aug.] v, 96 p.

The 1953 fifth impression shows that this was the second impression.

7.1189. —— *idem.* 3rd ed. London: George Ronald for the Bahá'í Publishing Trust, 1947 [Apr.] v, 96 p.

Cover title spells 'civilization' with a 'z'; title-page title spells it with an 's'. The 1953 fifth impression shows that this was the third impression.

7.1189a. —— *idem.* 4th ed. London: George Ronald for the Bahá'í Publishing Trust, 1949 [May] v, 96 p.

The 1953 fifth impression shows that this was the fourth impression.

7.1190. —— *idem.* Wheatley, U.K.: George Ronald, 1953, 1954. v, 96 p.

7.1191. —— *idem.* Indian ed. New Delhi: Baha'i Publishing Trust, 1959. 122 p.

7.1192. —— *idem.* This new ed. London: George Ronald, 1960. 126 p. (Talisman Books; no.3).

7.1193. —— *idem.* rev. ed. London: George Ronald, 1969. 143 p. LC card 73–490733.

7.1194. —— *idem.* 1st American ed. Wilmette, Ill.: Bahá'í Publishing Trust, 1970, 1972. 143 p. LC card 70–15555.

7.1195. —— *idem.* rev. Talisman ed. London: George Ronald, 1972. 143 p.

7.1196. —— *idem.* rev. Talisman ed. Oxford: George Ronald, 1981. 143 p.

7.1197. Holley, Horace, 1887–1960. *The Bahá'í Faith.* New York: Bahá'í Publishing Committee, 1933. 14 p.; n.d. [after Feb. 1934], n.d. [1934?], 1939. 13 p.

7.1198. —— *The Bahá'í Faith.* n.p., 1952. 1 p. Reprinted from *Encyclopaedia Britannica.*

7.1199. —— *The Baha'i Faith: A New Spiritual Creation.* n.p., n.d. [194–?] 4 leaves.

7.1200. —— *The Bahá'í Principle of Civilization.* Wilmette, Ill.: Bahá'í Publishing Committee, 1943, 1945, 1947. 32 p.

7.1201. —— *Bahai, the Spirit of the Age.* London: Kegan Paul Trench Trubner & Co., 1921. xi, 212 p.

An introduction which seeks to distil the Bahá'í message as it speaks to various religions and philosophies. Included are chapters on Christianity, Judaism, science, politics and economics, Christian Science, Theosophy. Includes a 'constructive reading list'.

7.1202. —— *idem.* New York: Brentano's, 1921. xi, 212 p. LC card 21–21146 rev.
Review:
Labaree, Robert M. *The Moslem World* (Hartford, Conn.), v. 12 no.2 (Apr. 1922), pp. 208–209.

7.1203. —— *Bahaism, the Modern Social Religion.* London: Sidgwick & Jackson, Ltd.; New York: Mitchell Kennerly, 1913. xi, 223 p. LC card A 14–2588.

An introduction to the Bahá'í social programme. Appended are Holley's 'A Pilgrimage to Thonon' and a bibliography.
See 7.1219a.

7.1204. —— *Bahá'u'lláh's Book of Certitude: A Study Guide.* Wilmette, Ill.: Bahá'í Publishing Committee, 1954. 6 leaves.

7.1205. —— *Challenge to Chaos: The Mission of the Bahá'í Faith.* Wilmette, Ill.: Bahá'í Publishing Committee, 1954. 22 p.

7.1206. —— *Deepening the Spiritual Life: Bahá'í References Suitable for Group Discussion or Individual Meditation.* New York: Bahá'í Publishing Committee, n.d.[1940?]. 40 leaves.

7.1207. —— *idem.* 2nd ed. Wilmette, Ill.: Bahá'í Publishing Commitee, 1944. 3 leaves.

7.1208. —— *Economics as Social Creation.* New York: Bahá'í Publishing Committee, 1937. 30 p.

7.1209. —— *God Passes By: Study Guide.* Wilmette, Ill.: Bahá'í Publishing Trust, 1961. 5 leaves.

7.1210. —— *idem.* Wilmette, Ill.: Bahá'í Publishing Trust, 1977. 21 p.

7.1211. —— *The God Who Walks With Men.* Wilmette, Ill.: Bahá'í Publishing Committee, 1954. 31 p.

7.1212. —— *idem.* Wilmette, Ill.: Bahá'í Publishing Trust, n.d. [1955 or later], 1967. 28 p.

7.1213. —— *idem.* Wilmette, Ill.: Bahá'í Publishing Trust, 1976. 19 p.

7.1214. —— *Green Acre, a Focal Center of Devotional and Humanitarian Activity.* n.p., 1926. 8 p. Reprint from *The Bahá'í Magazine,* (July 1926).

7.1215. —— *The Kitáb-i-Íqán: A Study Guide.* Wilmette, Ill.: Bahá'í Publishing Committee, 1942. 6 leaves.

7.1216. —— *idem.* Wilmette, Ill.: Bahá'í Publishing Trust, 1957. 9 p.

7.1217. —— *The Meaning of Worship: The Purpose of the Bahá'í House of Worship.* Wilmette, Ill.: Bahá'í Publishing Committee, 1953. 6 p.

7.1218. —— *idem.* Wilmette, Ill.: Bahá'í Publishing Trust, n.d. [196–] [8] p.

7.1219. —— *idem.* Wilmette, Ill.: Bahá'í Publishing Trust, 1980. 12 p.

7.1219a. —— *The Modern Social Religion.* London; Toronto: Sidgwick & Jackson, Ltd., 1913. xi, 223 p.
See 7.1203.

7.1220. —— *A Pilgrimage to Thonon.* Letchworth, Herts.: Garden City Press, Ltd., 1911. 7 p.

7.1221. —— *The Present-Day Administration of the Bahá'í Faith.* Wilmette, Ill.: Bahá'í Publishing Committee, 1947. 17 p.

7.1222. —— *Religion for Mankind.* London: George Ronald, 1956. 248 p. LC card 57–3663.

A collection of cogent essays on several aspects of the Bahá'í social programme and the dynamic of community and administrative life.

7.1223. —— *idem.* This ed. London: George Ronald, 1966. 248 p. LC card 67–88848.

7.1224. —— *idem.* 1st American ed. Wilmette, Ill.: Bahá'í Publishing Trust, 1967. 248 p. LC card 67–5023.
Reviews:
Heiser, W. Charles, *Theology Digest*, v.16 no.3 (Autumn 1968), p. 276.
Gardner, Aurora W., *Library Journal* (New York), (June 1, 1967).

7.1225. —— *idem.* Talisman ed. London: George Ronald, 1969. 248 p. (Talisman Books; no. 9).

7.1226. —— *idem.* Oxford: George Ronald, 1976. 248 p.

7.1227. —— *Religious Education for a Peaceful Society.* Wilmette, Ill.: Bahá'í Public Relations, n.d. [195–] 25 p.

7.1228. —— *The Revelation of Bahá'u'lláh.* Wilmette, Ill.: Bahá'í Publishing Committee, 1946. 16 p.

7.1229. —— *The Social Principle.* New York: L.J. Gomme, 1915.

7.1229a. —— *Stenographic Notes of Talk Given by Mr. Horace Holley, at the Los Angeles Baha'i Center, October 23, 1948.* ed. by Horace Holley, approved for use in Western states. n.p. [Los Angeles?]: Stencilled by L. Johnson, 1948. 4 p.

7.1229b. ——*A Study Aid: Christ and Baha'u'llah by George Townshend.* n.p. [Wilmette, Ill.: National Spiritual Assembly of the Bahá'ís of the United States], n.d. [1957] 8 p.

7.1230. —— *Study Outline, God Passes By.* Wilmette, Ill.: Bahá'í Publishing Committee, 1945. 4 leaves.

7.1231. —— *The World Economy of Bahá'u'lláh.* New York: Bahá'í Publishing Committee, 1931. 28 p. LC card 32–4879 rev.

7.1232. —— *The World Order of Bahá'u'lláh: A Study Outline.* New York: Bahá'í Publishing Committee, n.d. [1940?] 5 leaves.

7.1233. —— *idem.* Wilmette, Ill.: Bahá'í Publishing Trust, 1968. 9 p. Cover title: *The World Order of Bahá'u'lláh: Study Guide.*

7.1234. Holley, Marion. *The Most Great Peace: A New Phase of Human Thought.* New York: Bahá'í Publishing Committee, n.d. [193–] 23p.
Two variant printings, one showing 'printed in U.S.A.'.

7.1235. Hopson, Eliane A. *Creation and Evolution: A Baha'i Perspective.* New York: Newscope Productions, 1982. ii, 38 p.

7.1236. Hornby, Helen. *Heroes of God: History of the Bahá'í Faith in Ecuador, 1940–1979.* Quito, Ecuador: Helen Bassett Hornby, 1984 (Quito: Arqtelier). xi, 321 p.

7.1236a. *House of Worship Statistics.* rev. n.p. [Wilmette, Ill.: National Spiritual Assembly of the Bahá'ís of the United States], 1977. [3] p. folder.

7.1237. *How?* n.p. [Pakistan?], n.d. [196–?] [12] p. folder. Title on back cover: *Join Us.*

7.1238. *'How Profuse the Blood . . .'* Guam: National Spiritual Assembly of the Bahá'ís of the Mariana Islands, n.d. [1984?] [14] p.

7.1239. *How to Find Out More About the Bahá'í Faith.* Thornhill, Ont.: Bahá'í National Centre, n.d. [1980?] [3] p.

7.1240. Huddleston, John. *The Earth Is But One Country.* London: Bahá'í Publishing Trust, 1976. 185, [21] p.
Reviews:
Choice (Middletown, Conn.), (July/Aug. 1979), p. 683.

Littlefield, David W. *Library Journal* (New York), (Oct. 1, 1978), p. 1993.
A comprehensive introduction to the Bahá'í Faith, directed to those interested in current world conditions. Appendices document the languages into which Bahá'í literature had been translated, minority groups and tribes represented in the Bahá'í community, and independent nations, significant territories and islands with Bahá'í communities.

7.1241. —— *idem.* 2nd ed. London: Bahá'í Publishing Trust, 1980. 185, [23] p.

7.1242. Hughes, Emma. *Unity of Mankind.* n.p., n.d. [191–?] 15 p.

7.1243. *Human Relations for World Unity.* Wilmette, Ill.: Bahá'í Publishing Committee, n.d. [between 1947 and 1955] 8 p.

7.1244. *Human Rights Are God-Given Rights.* Wilmette, Ill.: Bahá'í Publishing Trust, 1976, 1980. 4 p.

7.1245. *idem.* Addis Ababa: N.S.A. Baha'is of North East Africa, 1968. [2] p.

7.1246. *Humanity Has Two Wings: The Bahá'í Faith.* London: National Spiritual Assembly of the Bahá'ís of the United Kingdom, n.d. [1981] [2] p.

7.1247. *idem.* New Delhi: Bahá'í Publishing Trust, n.d. [1981] [4] p.

7.1247a. *Humble Fellowship – Loving Consultation.* Montclair, N.J.: World Fellowship Gardens, n.d. [192–] [1] p. (Service Leaflet; no. 2).

7.1248. Hunt, Arnold D. *Who Are the Bahá'ís?* Melbourne, Vic.: The Methodist Publishing House, 1968. 24 p.
Anti-Bahá'í work from Christian viewpoint.

7.1249. Hunt, Ethel M.M. *A Journey from Judaism to the Baha'i Faith.* with a statement on the spread of the Baha'i teachings among the Jews in Persia, by A.J. Weinburg. n.p., n.d. [1941?] [8] p.

7.1250. Ḥusayn of Hamadán, Mírzá. *The New History (Táríkh-i-Jadíd) of Mírzá 'Alí Muhammed, the Báb.* Amsterdam: Philo Press, 1975. lii, 459, 26 p. LC card 76–379785.

7.1251. —— *The Táríkh-i-Jadíd: or, New History of Mírza 'Ali Muḥammad the Báb.* trans. Edward Granville Browne. Cambridge, Eng.: Cambridge University Press, 1893. lii, 459, 26p. LC card 49–43545.
Reviews:
Goldsmid, F.J. *Journal of the Royal Asiatic Society,* (1894), pp. 640–646.
The Spectator (London), v. 73 (Aug. 11, 1894), p. 185.

'Decades of suppression and persecution suffered by Babis caused a sense of disillusion and frustration in the scattered communities throughout Iran which in turn led to the temporary neglect of their historical past, both in oral and written forms. Toward the 1880's . . . the revival of the Babi circles in Iran demonstrated a . . . need for the compilation of new general narratives . . . in a different language and style and with an emphasis on historical events that could satisfy the new ideological orientation of these groups [Bahá'ís and Azalís].' (Amanat, 'The Early Years of the Babi Movement', 1981). This history was written by Mírzá Ḥusayn of Hamadán, under the patronage of Mánakjí Limjí Hataria, and with assistance from

Mírzá Abu'l-Faḍl Gulpáygání. Browne's harsh criticisms of what he regarded as Bahá'í 'distortions and deviations' may be questioned, for it is not yet known whether other versions of an earlier history (published by Browne as the *Kitáb-i-Nuqtatu'l-Káf*) were in existence. *See also* Balyuzi, *Edward Granville Browne and the Bahá'í Faith*.

7.1252. Hussey, Arlene. *Three Stories to Read and Color.* Honolulu: National Spiritual Assembly of the Bahá'ís of the Hawaiian Islands, 1978. [64] p.

7.1253. Hutchens, Eleanor S. *The Power of Prayer*. Wilmette, Ill.: Bahá'í Publishing Trust, 1975, 1978. 19 p.

I

7.1254. *I Am a Bahá'í.* n.p. [Wilmette, Ill.: Bahá'í Publishing Trust], n.d. [196–]. (7 cards in folder).

7.1255. *I Am a Bahá'í.* Ottawa, Ont.: National Public Relations Committee of the Bahá'ís of Canada, n.d. [ca. 1950] [4] p.

7.1256. *Imiyalezo.* n.p. [Umtata]: Ibalwe Liqumru Lesizwe Sase Transkei [i.e. National Spiritual Assembly of the Bahá'ís of Transkei]. no. 1, [1981] 32 p.; no.2, 1981. 10 p.; no.3, 1981. 19 p.; no.4, [1982] 22 p.; no.5, [1982] 19 p.

7.1257. *In an Age of Frustration and Uncertainty, We Can Still Be Happy.* Thornhill, Ont.: Bahá'í National Centre, n.d. [1980?] [6] p.

7.1258. *In Celebration of the Victorious Completion of the Nine Year International Teaching Plan, 1964–1973: Banquet, Orrington Hotel, Evanston, Illinois, May 19, 1973.* Evanston, Ill., 1973. 6 p.

7.1259. *In Commemoration of the 50th Anniversary of the Ascension of 'Abdu'l-Bahá, American Samoa and Western Samoa, November 26–28, 1971.* Samoa: [National Spiritual Assembly of the Bahá'ís of Samoa], 1971. 4 p.

7.1260. *In Defence of the Faith.* comp. Spiritual Assembly of Malaysia. n.p. [Kuala Lumpur]: National Spiritual Assembly of Malaysia, 1983. 39, [28] p.

7.1261. *In Memoriam, Counsellor Raúl Pavón: Observances, Tobago Baha'i School, National Baha'i Centre, January 8th, 5.00 p.m.* n.p. [Port of Spain: National Spiritual Assembly of the Bahá'ís of Trinidad and Tobago], n.d. [1984] [8] p.

7.1262. *In Memoriam, Hand of the Cause of God Mr Paul Haney.* Woodbrook: National Spiritual Assembly of the Bahá'ís of Trinidad and Tobago, 1983. [4] p.

7.1263. *In Memoriam, Mrs Sylvia Ioas.* n.p. [Woodbrook: National Spiritual Assembly of the Bahá'ís of Trinidad and Tobago], 1983. [8] p.

7.1264. *In Memoriam, Ruth Fuhrman, 1899–1925.* n.p., 1925. 8 p.

7.1265. *In Memory of Miss Martha Root (August 10, 1872–September 1939).* New Delhi: National Spiritual Assembly of the Bahá'ís of India, Pakistan and Burma, n.d. [after 1955] 8 p.

7.1266. *Incwadzi Yekufak Imibala Yemabahayi = Baha'i Colouring Book.* n.p. [Mbabane]: Women's and Children's Committee of the National Spiritual Assembly of the Bahá'ís of Swaziland, 1982. 22 leaves. Swati and English text.

7.1267. *Index, Bahá'í News.* v.1., No.1 to No. 172. comp. May Prentiss Stebbins. Wilmette, Ill.: Bahá'í Publishing Trust, 1956. 102 p.; v.2, No.173 to No.322. comp. May Prentiss Stebbins. Wilmette, Ill.: Bahá'í Publishing Trust, 1959. 134 p.; v.3, No.323 to No.393. comp. Amine DeMille. Wilmette, Ill.: Bahá'í Publishing Trust, 1966. 69 p.; v.4, No.394 to No.453. comp. Amine DeMille. Wilmette, Ill.: Bahá'í Publishing Trust, 1970. 89 p.; v.5, No.454 to No.513. Wilmette, Ill.: Bahá'í Publishing Trust, n.d. [1978] 59 p.
See 9.70.

7.1268. *Index, Bahá'í News: December 1923 to November 1933, no. 1 to no. 79.* prepared by a committee under the supervision of the National Spiritual Assembly. New York: Bahá'í Publishing Committee, 1934. 58 leaves.
See 9.70.

7.1269. *Index, Bahá'í News: January 1934–December 1936, numbers 80 to 104.* prepared by a committee under the supervision of the National Spiritual Assembly. New York: Bahá'í Publishing Committee, 1937. 25 leaves.
See 9.70.

7.1270. *Index, God Passes By.* Wilmette, Ill.: Bahá'í Publishing Company, 1948. 24 p.

7.1271. *Individual and Teaching.* Taipei: National Spiritual Assembly of the Bahá'ís of Tawian, 1978. 11, 15 p. (Kindled with the Fire of His Love).

7.1272. *The Individual Believer and the Bahá'í Fund.* n.p. [Wilmette, Ill.: Office of the Treasurer], n.d. [1984] [4] p.

7.1273. *Individual Goal.* New Delhi: National Spiritual Assembly of the Bahá'ís of India, n.d. [1981?] 10 p. (Proclamation Series; 3).

7.1274. *The Individual in Action.* Wilmette, Ill.: National Teaching Committee, 1982. 8 p.

7.1275. Industria dei Marmi Vicentini. *S.U.H.I. [sic] Project, Bahá'í World Centre.* Chiampo, Italy: Industria dei Marmi Vicentini, 1978. 8 p.

7.1276. *Information About the Baha'i House of Worship, Wilmette, Illinois, for the Use of Temple Model Exhibitors.* comp. Temple Guides Committee. Wilmette, Ill.: Bahá'í Publishing Committee, 1942. iv, 20 leaves.

7.1277. *Information Brief on the Bahá'í Faith.* n.p. [Mona Vale, N.S.W.: National Spiritual Assembly of the Bahá'ís of Australia], n.d. [1985] [2] p.

7.1278. *Information for Guides of the Baha'i House of Worship, Wilmette, Illinois.* Wilmette, Ill.: Bahá'í Publishing Committee, 1947. 37 leaves.

7.1279. *Institute Activity Report: To Be Read During the Feast Day.* n.p. [Kuala Lumpur: National Spiritual Assembly of the Bahá'ís of Malaysia], n.d. [1982] [10] p.

7.1280. *Institute Deepening Course.* n.p. [Salisbury, Rhodesia]: National Spiritual Assembly of the Bahá'ís of South Central Africa, 1966. 38 p.

7.1281. *Institute Reference File for Consolidation, Teaching and Expansion.* n.p. [Wilmette, Ill.]:

American National Teaching Committee, 1962. ii, 49 p.

7.1282. *Instructions for Travelling Teachers.* n.p. [Salisbury, Rhodesia]: National Spiritual Assembly of the Bahá'ís of South Central Africa, 1966. 3 p.

7.1283. *Inter-American Baha'i Bulletin, 1938–1939.* n.p. [Wilmette, Ill.?]: Inter-America Committee, 1939. 27 p.

7.1284. Inter-Coordination Conference (1984: Windhoek, Southwest Africa/Namibia). *Inter-Coordination Conference of National Spiritual Assembly for National Teaching Committee, Women's & Children's Committee, National Youth Committee, Publications Committee, Audio-Visual Committee, Auxiliary Board Members.* Windhoek: National Spiritual Assembly of the Bahá'ís of Southwest Africa/Namibia, 1984. [4] p.

7.1285. International Bahá'í Council. *Report of the International Bahá'í Council to the Friends Throughout the World: Received with Covering Letter, on the above Letterhead.* London: National Spiritual Assembly of the Bahá'ís of the British Isles, 1951. 13 p.

7.1286. International Bahá'í School (Temerity Ranch, Colorado Springs, Colo.), *First Bahá'í Latin-American Session, 1940.* n.p.: International School Committee, 1940. 40 leaves.

7.1287. —— *First Four Latin American Sessions, Teaching Notes.* Colorado Springs, Colo.: International School, Temerity Ranch, 1944. 94 leaves.

7.1288. —— *International Bahá'í School Session of 1945, Temerity Ranch, Colorado Springs: Notes on 'God Passes By' by Shoghi Effendi.* n.p. [Wilmette, Ill.]: Approved by the Reviewing Committee of the National Spiritual Assembly of the Bahá'ís of the United States and Canada, 1945. 13, [3] leaves. Cover title: *Notes, International School Session, 1945.*

7.1289. —— *Third Bahá'í Latin-American Session, 1942.* n.p.: International School Committee, 1942. 51 leaves.

7.1290. International Chinese Teaching Committee. *Chinese Teaching Manual.* n.p. [Selangor, Malaysia]: International Chinese Teaching Committee, 1985. ii, [2], 33 leaves.

7.1291. International Teaching Centre. *Bahá'í Scholarship.* Auckland: National Spiritual Assembly of the Bahá'ís of New Zealand, 1985. 8 p.

7.1292. *International Year of Peace: The Bahá'í*

Faith. Wilmette, Ill.: Bahá'í National Center, n.d. [1985] [6] p.
Orange cover; on education.

7.1293. *idem.* Wilmette, Ill.: Bahá'í National Center, n.d. [1985] [6] p.
Blue cover; on elimination of prejudice.

7.1294. *idem.* Wilmette, Ill.: Bahá'í National Center, n.d. [1985] [6] p.
Green cover; on extremes of wealth and poverty.

7.1295. *idem.* Wilmette, Ill.: Bahá'í National Center, n.d. [1985] [6] p.
Purple cover; on spiritual renewal.

7.1296. *idem.* Wilmette, Ill.: Bahá'í National Center, n.d. [1985] [6] p.
Red cover; on women.

7.1297. *International Year of Youth: Special Service for Youth, 14th April 1985. Ingleside*, N.S.W.: Bahá'í House of Worship, 1985. [8] p.

7.1298. *Intone (Bahá'í Song Book).* Kuching, Malaysia: Administrative Committee of the Baha'i Religious Community of Sarawak, n.d. [1974] 99 p.

7.1299. *Introduction to a Study of the Qur'án: With Additional References from Several Bahá'í Texts.* Wilmette, Ill.: Bahá'í Publishing Trust, 1956, 1971. 21 p.

7.1300. *An Introduction to Baha'i Faith.* Dacca: National Spiritual Assembly of the Bahá'ís of Bangladesh, n.d. [1980] 16 p.

7.1301. *An Introduction to the Baha'i Faith.* n.p. [United States], n.d. [195–?] 8 leaves.

7.1302. *An Introduction to the Baha'i Faith: A Course of Study in Nineteen Lessons.* Vancouver, B.C.: Baha'is of Vancouver, n.d. [193–?] [4] p.

7.1303. *Introduction to the Study of the Qur'án.* Wilmette, Ill.: Bahá'í Publishing Committee, 1942. 25 leaves.

7.1304. *An Invitation to Investigate Baha'i.* Manila, Philippines: National Baha'i Information Service, n.d. [197–?] 5 p.

7.1305. *Invitation to Learning: The Bahá'í Faith.* Wilmette, Ill.: Bahá'í Publishing Trust, 1961. 32 p.

7.1306. Iran. Ministry of Foreign Affairs. *Some Facts about the 'Bahais' in Iran.* n.p., n.d. [1984?] 6, 9 p.

7.1307. *Iran, the Facts.* Mona Vale, N.S.W.: National Spiritual Assembly of the Bahá'ís of Australia, 1981. [4] p.

7.1308. *Iranian Martyrs Project: Phase 2.* n.p. [Johannesburg: National Spiritual Assembly of the Bahá'ís of South and West Africa], n.d. [1984] 1 p.

7.1309. Irwin, Beatrice. *Heralds of Peace.* n.p.: Irwin, 1938. 44 p.

7.1310. *Is Democracy a Failure: The Causes and Cure of Human Exploitation.* Washington, D.C.: Baha'i Magazine, 1933. 8 p.

7.1311. *Islam, a Pathway to the Bahá'í Faith.* n.p. [Bathurst, Gambia]: Bahá'í Publishing Committee of the National Spiritual Assembly of the Bahá'ís of Upper West Africa, 1972. 12 p.

7.1312. *Islands: Excerpts from Bahá'í Writings on the Significance of Islands.* London: National Spiritual Assembly of the Bahá'ís of the United Kingdom, n.d. [1980?] [4] p.

7.1313. Ives, Howard Colby. *Portals to Freedom.* New York: E.P. Dutton & Co., 1937. 253 p. LC card 37–5965 rev.
A first-hand account of the experiences of this Unitarian minister upon meeting 'Abdu'l-Bahá in New York in 1912.

7.1314. —— *idem.* 2nd ed. Cynthiana, Ky.: The Hobson Press, 1943. 266 p.

7.1315. —— *idem.* Northampton, U.K.: George Ronald, 1943. 253 p. LC card 50–44482.

7.1316. —— *idem.* Birmingham, Eng.: George Ronald, 1948. 253 p.

7.1317. —— *idem.* Birmingham, Eng.: George Ronald; Wilmette, Ill.: Bahá'í Publishing Committee, 1948. 253 p.

7.1318. —— *idem.* Oxford: George Ronald, 1953, 1976, 1983. 253 p.

7.1319. —— *idem.* London: George Ronald, 1962. 253 p.

7.1320. —— *idem.* Wilmette, Ill.: Bahá'í Publishing Trust, 1967, 1970. 253 p. LC card 67–9801.

7.1321. —— *The Song Celestial.* Portland, Ore.: Shankle Printing, 1938. 62 p.

7.1322. —— *idem.* Chicago: The Landon Press, 1938 [i.e. 1962, 1973] 62 p. LC card 38–37251.
These are actually reprints of the Shankle printing, with frontispiece [1962] and in reduced size [1973].

J

7.1323. Jackson, Betty M. *Creative Thinking and Group Consultation: Notes on a Workshop Held in Fiji.* n.p.: Continental Board of Counsellors, South-Eastern Asia, n.d. [1978?] 8 p. No.2 in a series.

7.1324. Jackson, D. Thelma. *Your Role in the Nine Year Plan.* Wilmette, Ill.: Bahá'í Publishing Trust, 1969. 21 p.

7.1325. Jackson, James F. *Inharmonic.* Tehran: P.O. Box 1606, n.d. [196–] 33 p.
Anti-Bahá'í work.

7.1326. Jání Káshání, Ḥájí Mírzá. *Kitáb-i-Nuqṭatu'l-Káf: Being the Earliest History of the Bábís.* ed. Edward G. Browne. Leyden: E.J. Brill; London: Luzac & Co., 1910. xcv, [76], 297 p. (E.J.W. Gibb Memorial Series; xv). Introduction in English; text in Persian.
There are references in Bahá'í works to an 'old history' which covered the events of the early years of the Bábí cause, probably written by Ḥájí Mírzá Jání Káshání. Browne's edition of the *Kitáb-i-Nuqṭatu'l-Káf* is thought to be nearest to this yet untraced 'old history'. Much controversy surrounds the authenticity of some of its passages, the possibility of later distortions, and the real identity of the author. (Amanat, 'The Early Years of the Babi Movement', 1981). See Balyuzi, *Edward Granville Browne and the Bahá'í Faith*; MacEoin, *Revised Survey of the Sources for Early Bábí Doctrine and History*, 1977).

7.1327. *Japan Will Turn Ablaze: Tablets of 'Abdu'l-Bahá, Letters of Shoghi Effendi and Historical Notes About Japan.* n.p. [Osaka, Japan]: Bahá'í Publishing Trust 1974. 90 p.
A compilation of sources on the growth and history of the Bahá'í Faith in Japan.

7.1328. *Jenabe Fazel, Philosopher and Lecturer of Persia.* n.p. [United States], n.d. [1921] [4] p.

7.1329. Johnson, Lowell. *The Baha'i Faith in Africa: The Early Days.* n.p., n.d. [196–] 30 p.

7.1330. —— *The Covenants of God.* n.p., n.d. [196–] 18 p.

7.1331. —— *idem.* Toronto, Ont.: National Spiritual Assembly of the Bahá'ís of Canada, n.d. [1960?] 18 p.

7.1332. —— *Mullá Ḥusayn.* Toronto: Ont.: National Spiritual Assembly of the Bahá'ís of Canada, n.d. [196–] 26 p. (Golden Crown Series).
The story of Mullá Ḥusayn told for children.

7.1333. —— *idem.* rev. ed. Johannesburg: National Spiritual Assembly of the Bahá'ís of South and West Africa, 1982. 44 p. (Golden Crowns Series).

7.1334. —— *Quddús.* n.p. [Toronto: National Spiritual Assembly of the Bahá'ís of Canada], n.d. [196–] [3], 22 p. (Five Golden Crowns Series).
The story of Quddús told for children.

7.1335. —— *idem.* Toronto, Ont.: National Spiritual Assembly of the Bahá'ís of Canada, [196–] 22 p. (Golden Crown Series).

7.1336. —— *idem.* rev. ed. Johannesburg: National Spiritual Assembly of the Bahá'ís of South and West Africa, 1982. 38 p. (Golden Crowns Series).

7.1337. —— *Remember My Days: The Life-Story of Bahá'u'lláh.* Johannesburg: National Spiritual Assembly of the Bahá'ís of South and West Africa, n.d. [196–?] 40 p.

7.1338. —— *idem.* Johannesburg: National Spiritual Assembly of the Bahá'ís of South and West Africa, n.d. [196–?] 49 p.

7.1339. —— *idem.* rev. ed. Johannesburg: National Spiritual Assembly of the Bahá'ís of South and West Africa, 1980. 41 p.

7.1340. —— *idem.* rev. ed. Johannesburg: National Spiritual Assembly of the Bahá'ís of South and West Africa, 1980 reprint with corrections. 41 p.

7.1341. —— *idem.* 2nd rev. ed. Johannesburg: National Spiritual Assembly of the Bahá'ís of South and West Africa, 1985. 68 p.

7.1342. —— *Ṭáhirih.* Toronto, Ont.: National Spiritual Assembly of the Bahá'ís of Canada, n.d. [196–] 23 p. (Golden Crown Series).
The story of Ṭáhirih told for children.

7.1343. —— *idem.* rev. ed. Johannesburg: National Spiritual Assembly of the Bahá'ís of South and West Africa, 1982. 38 p. (Golden Crowns Series).

7.1344. —— *Your High Destiny.* Johannesburg: National Spiritual Assembly of the Bahá'ís of South and West Africa, n.d. [1979 or 1980] 130 p.
'The Duplication and distribution of this book has been approved for experimental and review purposes.'

7.1345. Jordan, Daniel C. *Becoming Your True Self: How the Bahá'í Faith Releases Human*

Potential. Wilmette, Ill.: Bahá'í Publishing Trust, 1968, 1971, 1978. 22 p.; 1980. 19 p.

7.1346. —— *In Search of the Supreme Talisman: A Bahá'í Perspective on Education*. Wilmette, Ill.: Bahá'í Publishing Trust, 1980. 17 p.

7.1347. —— *Knowledge, Volition, and Action: The Steps to Spiritual Transformation*. Wilmette, Ill.: Bahá'í Publishing Trust, 1973, Dec. 1973, 1977, 1980. v, 18 p. (Bahá'í Comprehensive Deepening Program).

7.1348. —— *The Meaning of Deepening: Gaining a Clearer Apprehension of the Purpose of God for Man*. Wilmette, Ill.: Bahá'í Publishing Trust, 1973, Dec. 1973, 1977, 1980. ix, 86 p. (Bahá'í Comprehensive Deepening Program). LC card 74–84824.

7.1349. —— *O Son of the Supreme: From the Hidden Words of Bahá'u'lláh* [music]. Cardiff,

Wales: George Ronald, 1956. 3 p.

7.1350. —— *O Son of the Wondrous Vision: From the Hidden Words of Bahá'u'lláh* [music]. Cardiff, Wales: George Ronald, 1956. 4 p.

7.1351. *Journey to Bahá'u'lláh: 165th Anniversary Celebration of the Birth of Bahá'u'lláh*. n.p. [Thornhill, Ont.]: Inter-Assembly Planning Committee for the Birth of Bahá'u'lláh, 1977. [4] p.

7.1352. *Jubilee Celebration, Bahá'ís of the United States, April 29–May 6, 1953*. Wilmette, Ill.: National Spiritual Assembly of the Bahá'ís of the United States, 1953. 46 p.

7.1353. Jubilee of the Year Nine (1953: London). *Devotional Programme for the Jubilee of the Year Nine, Jalál 13th, 110, April 21st, 1953*. n.p. [London: Centenary Committee], n.d. [1953] 4 p.

K

7.1354. Kazemzadeh, Firuz. *The Bahá'í Faith: A Summary Reprinted from the Encyclopaedia Britannica*. Wilmette, Ill.: Bahá'í Publishing Trust, 1976, 1977, 1982. 13 p.

7.1355. —— *idem*. Large type ed. Wilmette, Ill.: Bahá'í Publishing Trust, 1977. 19 p.

7.1356. —— *Universal and Lasting Peace: Commentary on 'Abdu'l-Bahá's Tablet to the Hague*. Wilmette, Ill.: Bahá'í Publishing Trust, 1970. 22 p.

7.1357. Kean, William C. *Stirrings of the Heart*. Mona Vale: N.S.W.: Bahá'í Publications Australia, 1985. ii, 25 p.

7.1358. Kelsey, Curtis D. *The Future of Mankind*. Wilmette, Ill.: Bahá'í Publishing Trust, n.d. [196–] Reprinted from *Weekend Magazine, Bergen Evening Record* (Hackensack, N.J.).

7.1359. Kelsey, Olivia. *Two Shall Appear*. n.p., 1943. 56 p.

7.1360. —— *idem*. rev. 2nd ed. Independence, Mo.: Lambert Moon, 1943. 56 p.

7.1361. Kern, Margaret. *The Rustle of His Robe: A Vision of the New Day*. Akron, Ohio: Sun Publishing Co., 1901. 94 p.

7.1362. *Key to the Pronunciation of Persian and Arabic Words*. n.p., n.d. [195–?] 2 p.

7.1363. *The Keystone: The Bahá'í Faith*. London: Bahá'í Publishing Trust, n.d. [195–] 6 p.

7.1364. Khan, Peter. *The Promised Day Is Come Study Guide*. Wilmette, Ill.: Bahá'í Publishing Trust, 1967. 25 p.

7.1365. Kheiralla, Ibrahim George. *Bab-Ed-din, the Door of True Religion: 1, Za-ti-et Al-lah, 2, El Fi-da: Revelation from the East: Rational Argument*. Chicago: Chas. H. Kerr and Company, 1897. 84 p.

The second and most complete published version of the lessons used by Kheiralla in teaching the Bahá'í Faith in the United States. The book does not contain direct reference to the Faith, nor does it include the final lesson in which seekers were given the 'Greatest Name'.

7.1366. —— *Za-Ti-Et Al-Lah: The Identity and the Personality of God*. Chicago: Grant's Printery, 1896. 44 p. LC card 40–24467.

The first published version of part of the lessons given by Kheiralla in the classes he instituted for teaching the Bahá'í Faith.

7.1367. Kheiralla, Marian. *Extract from Mrs Marian Kheiralla's Letter to Mrs Herron, June 20th, 1900*. n.p., 1900. [3] p.

7.1368. Khoreshi, S.H. *The Baha'i Faith and Islam*. New Delhi: National Spiritual Assembly of the Bahá'ís of India and Burmh [sic], 1946. 49 p.

7.1369. *Khumbula Isivumelwano = Remember the Covenant*. n.p. [Mbabane]: National Spiritual

Assembly of the Bahá'ís of Swaziland, 1978. 16 p. English and Zulu text.

7.1369a. Kim-Farley, Robert. *Career Planning: In Search of a Spiritually Satisfying Career.* n.p. [United States: Kim-Farley], 1981. [2], 32, [2] p.

7.1369b. Kirsting, Fritz. *Musical Inspirations.* Denton, Tex.: Ancient Root Pub., 1980. [4], 16, [4] p.

7.1370. *Kitab-i-Aqdas.* n.p. [Kuala Lumpur?: National Spiritual Assembly of the Bahá'ís of Malaysia?], n.d. [1973] [1], 28 p.

7.1371. *The Kitab-i-Aqdas, the Most Holy Book of Bahá'u'lláh.* [Nairobi]: National Education Committee of the Baha'is of Kenya, 1973. 4 p.

7.1372. *Kitty Barten Carpenter, 1900–1983.* n.p. [New Zealand], 1983. [9] p.

7.1373. *Know Thou of a Certainty that Love Is the Secret of God's Holy Dispensation.* Georgetown: National Spiritual Assembly of the Bahá'ís of Guyana, 1980. 15 p.

7.1374. *'Ko Wai Au?' = 'Who Am I?'.* Auckland: National Spiritual Assembly of the Bahá'ís of New Zealand, 1985. 19 p.

7.1375. Kolstoe, John. *Consultation: A Universal Lamp of Guidance.* Oxford: George Ronald, 1985. viii, 199 p.

The author analyzes the Bahá'í process of decision-making and conflict resolution known as consultation.

7.1376. Kolstoe, John; Simple, Peter. *Bahá'í Teachings.* Anchorage: National Spiritual Assembly of the Bahá'ís of Alaska, n.d. [1964] 15 p.

7.1377. *Kote Ra Te Whetu o Tona Kororia Nui = The Day-Star of His Glory.* Auckland: National Spiritual Assembly of the Bahá'ís of New Zealand, n.d. [1967?] 32 leaves. Maori and English text.

7.1378. *Kwagh Aondo u Bahá'í = Bahá'í Faith: Bahá'í Teaching Book in Tiv.* n.p. [Lagos, Nigeria]: Bahá'í Publishing Committee, 1982. [15] leaves. English and Tiv text.

L

7.1379. Labíb, Muḥammad. *The Seven Martyrs of Hurmuzak.* trans. by Moojan Momen. Oxford: George Ronald, 1981. xiii, 63 p. LC card 82–182575.

Report of an incident which occurred in an Iranian village in 1955 when seven Bahá'ís were killed.

7.1380. Lane, Byron S. *A Key to the Important Things in the Bible.* Kenosha, Wis.: B.S. Lane, 1900. 87 p.

7.1381. Latimer, George Orr. *The Call of God.* Chicago: Bahai Publishing Society, n.d. [1914?] 20 p.

7.1382. —— *The Lesser and the Most Great Peace.* Wilmette, Ill.: Bahá'í Publishing Committee, 1944, 1945, 1947. 29 p.

7.1383. —— *The Light of the World.* by a group of pilgrims. Boston: George Orr Latimer, 1920. 148 p.

Daily diary of Latimer's pilgrimage to the Holy Land in 1919, including reports of the words of 'Abdu'l-Bahá.

7.1384. *Laws and Teachings of Bahá'u'lláh = Ezinye Zezi Fundiso Nemithetho ka Baha'u'llah.* n.p. [Mbabane: National Spiritual Assembly of

the Bahá'ís of Swaziland], n.d. [1982?] 39 p. Text in English and Swati.

7.1385. Leach, Bernard. *My Religious Faith.* n.p. [St. Ives, Cornwall?]: Leach, n.d. [1953?] 5 p.

7.1386. —— *idem.* London: National Spiritual Assembly of the Bahá'ís of the United Kingdom, n.d. [1979?] 3, [3], 5 p.

7.1387. Leach, Jim. *Death Sentences of Baha'is in Iran Must Be Commuted.* n.p. [Washington, D.C.]: Jim Leach, 1983. 1 p.

7.1388. Lee, Anthony A. *The Black Rose: A Story About 'Abdu'l-Bahá in America.* il. Rex John Irvine. Los Angeles: Kalimát Press, 1979. 24 p.

7.1389. —— *The Cornerstone: A Story About 'Abdu'l-Bahá in America.* il. Rex John Irvine. Los Angeles: Kalimát Press, 1979. 24 p.

7.1390. —— *The Proud Helper: A Story About 'Abdu'l-Bahá in the Holy Land.* il. Rex John Irvine. Los Angeles: Kalimát Press, 1979. 24 p.

7.1391. —— *The Scottish Visitors: A Story About 'Abdu'l-Bahá in Britain.* il. Rex John Irvine. Los Angeles: Kalimát Press, 1980. [24] p.

7.1392. —— *The Unfriendly Governor: A Story About 'Abdu'l-Bahá in the Holy Land.* il. Rex John Irvine, Los Angeles: Kalimát Press, 1979. 24 p.

7.1393. *'Let All Rejoice'.* Honolulu: National Spiritual Assembly of the Bahá'ís of the Hawaiian Islands, n.d. [1984] [18] p.

7.1394. *'Let All Rejoice': Bahá'í History Calendar, 1984, 140–141 B.E.* Honolulu: National Spiritual Assembly of the Bahá'ís of the Hawaiian Islands. [32] p. (Bahá'í History Calendar).

7.1395. *Let Us Strive with Heart and Soul that Unity May Dwell in the World.* n.p., n.d. [190– or 191–?] 4 p.

7.1396. *Let's Get Cooking: Recipes for All Bahá'í Occasions: Dedicated to the Louis G. Gregory Bahá'í Institute Radio Station.* Wilmette, Ill.: From the Office of the Treasurer, 1983. 123 p.

7.1397. *Letters to Christians.* Toronto: Ont.: Bahá'í Publishing Committee, n.d. [between 1957 and 1963] 15 p.

7.1398. Lieber, Joel. *The Embrace of the Baha'i.* n.p., 1964. 4 p. Reprint from *Kiwanis Magazine*, (Oct. 1964).

7.1399. *Life After Death.* n.p.: National Teaching Committee, 1959. 4 p.

7.1400. *The Life of the Master, Abdu'l Baha.* Jacksonville, Fla.: Baha'i Assembly, n.d. [1937] 8 p.

7.1401. Liggitt, Joyce. *Baha'i Family Life* n.p. [Salisbury]: National Spiritual Assembly of the Bahá'ís of Rhodesia, 1975. 8 p.

7.1401a. —— *idem.* n.p. [Lusaka]: National Spiritual Assembly of the Bahá'ís of Zambia, 1980. 13 p.

7.1402. —— *Community Deepening Programme.* n.p. [Limbe]: Spiritual Assembly of the Bahá'ís of Malawi, 1985. 30 lessons.

7.1403. —— *Wealth Without Gold.* Lusaka: National Spiritual Assembly of the Bahá'ís of Zambia, n.d. [1969], n.d. [ca. 1975] 8 p.

7.1404. *The Light of Bahá'u'lláh: An Introduction to the Bahá'í Faith.* Wilmette, Ill.: Bahá'í Publishing Trust, 1982. vi, 138 p. LC card 83–166774.
Star Study Program booklets published as one volume.

7.1405. Lindstrom, Janet. *The Kingdoms of God.* il. Anna Stevenson. Wilmette, Ill.: Bahá'í Publishing Trust, 1961. 41 p. LC card 61–8040.
An introduction for children to the Bahá'í concept of creation.

7.1406. —— *idem.* rev. ed. Wilmette, Ill.:

Bahá'í Publishing Trust, 1974. 41 p. LC card 75–332328.

7.1407. Lippitt, Marian Crist. *The Divine Art of Living: Seven Round Table Discussions.* Wilmette, Ill.: Bahá'í Publishing Trust, 1977. 21 p.

7.1408. —— *Round Table Discussions Based on The Divine Art of Living.* Wilmette, Ill.: Bahá'í Publishing Trust, 1956. vii p.

7.1409. —— *idem.* Wilmette, Ill.: Bahá'í Publishing Trust, 1972. 21 p.

7.1410. —— *A Study of the Divine Art of Living in Seven Discussion Periods.* Wilmette, Ill.: Bahá'í Publishing Committee, 1950. vii leaves.

7.1410a. Littrell, Eileen. *A Private Baha'i School for Children of All Nationalities, Races, Creeds.* Spenard, Alaska: Littrell; Spenard Baha'i L.S.A., n.d. [196–?] 32 p.

7.1411. Littrel, Eileen; Main, Katy. *Stories of the Master: A Collection of Stories for Children.* by National Child Education Committee of Alaska; stories by Eileen Littrel & Katy Main; il. Katy Main; ed. Eugene B. Van Zanten. n.p. [Anchorage, Alaska]: National Child Education Committee, 1977. iii, 49 p.

7.1412. *Living the Baha'i Life.* New Delhi: National Spiritual Assembly of the Baha'is of India, n.d. [197–?] [4] p.

7.1413. *Living the Life.* New Delhi: National Spiritual Assembly of the Baha'is of India, n.d. [197–?] [4] p.

7.1414. *Living the Life.* n.p., n.d. [197–] [4] p. Pink, with sketch of sunrise coming over hills.

7.1415. *The Local Spiritual Assembly.* Wilmette, Ill.: Bahá'í Publishing Trust, 1975, 1979. v, 18 p. (Star Study Program).

7.1416. *idem.* Ponapean ed. Honolulu: National Spiritual Assembly of the Bahá'ís of the Hawaiian Islands for the National Spiritual Assembly of the Bahá'ís of the Caroline Islands, 1978. 45 p. (Star Study Program). Parallel English and Ponapean text.

7.1417. *The Local Spiritual Assembly.* n.p. [Anchorage: National Spiritual Assembly of the Bahá'ís of Alaska], n.d. [between 1965 and 1975] [39] p.

7.1418. *The Local Spiritual Assembly.* n.p. [Lomé: National Spiritual Assembly of the Bahá'ís of Togo], n.d. [1977?] [13] p.

7.1419. *idem.* n.p. [Victoria: National Spiritual Assembly of the Bahá'ís of Cameroon], n.d. [1978?] 13 p.

7.1420. *The Local Spiritual Assembly: A Guide-*

book for Kenya. n.p. [Nairobi]: National Education Committee of the National Spiritual Assembly of the Bahá'ís of Kenya, 1973. 25 p.

7.1421. Local Spiritual Assembly of the Bahá'ís of Bombay (India). *Genocide: Final Phase in the Conspiracy to Destroy the Baha'i Community in Iran.* Bombay: Spiritual Assembly of the Bahá'ís of Bombay, 1981. 25 leaves.

7.1422. —— *Mr. Collis Featherstone, Hand of the Cause of God and Representative of the Baha'i World Centre, Meets the Press on 7th April 1983.* Bombay: Spiritual Assembly of the Baha'is of Bombay, 1983. 15 leaves.

7.1423. —— *World Religion Day, 20th January 1977.* Bombay: Spiritual Assembly of the Bahá'ís of Bombay, 1977. [6], 18 p.

7.1424. —— *World Religion Day, 1983.* Bombay: Spiritual Assembly of the Bahá'ís of Bombay, 1983. 11 p.

7.1425. Local Spiritual Assembly of the Bahá'ís of Brighton (England). *An Invitation to People of Modern Thought.* Brighton: Spiritual Assembly of the Bahá'ís of Brighton, n.d. [1952?] 6 p.

7.1426. Local Spiritual Assembly of the Bahá'ís of Calabar (Nigeria). *The Baha'is in Iran: A Report on the Persecution of a Religious Minority.* Calabar: Local Spiritual Assembly of the Bahá'ís of Calabar, 1981. 8 p.

7.1426a. Local Spiritual Assembly of the Bahá'ís of Cork (Ireland). *Memorandum and Articles of Association of the Spiritual Assembly of the Bahá'ís of the City of Cork.* Dublin: Hugh J. O'Hagan Ward & Co., Solicitors, 1979. 13, [1] p.

7.1427. Local Spiritual Assembly of the Bahá'ís of Denison (Tex.). *The Baha'i Community of Denison.* Denison, Tex.: Baha'i Community of Denison, n.d. [1984] 2 p.

7.1427a. Local Spiritual Assembly of the Bahá'ís of Hong Kong. *Memorandum and Articles of Association of the Spiritual Assembly of the Bahá'ís of Hong Kong: Incorporated the 28th Day of November, 1969.* Hong Kong: Brutton & Steward, 1969. 30 p.

7.1428. Local Spiritual Assembly of the Bahá'ís of Lucknow (India). *Report on Bahá'í Proclamation, Lucknow (India), 1975.* Lucknow: Local Spiritual Assembly of the Bahá'ís of Lucknow, 1975. 40 p.

7.1428a. Local Spiritual Assembly of the Bahá'ís of Manchester (U.K.). *Certificate of Incorporation, Memorandum and Articles of Association of the Spiritual Assembly of the Bahá'ís of Manchester.* Manchester: Spiritual Assembly of the Bahá'ís of Manchester, 1980, 6, 8 p. At head of title:

The Companies Acts, 1948–1980: An Unlimited Company without a Share Capital.

7.1429. Local Spiritual Assembly of the Bahá'ís of New York (N.Y.). *New York Baha'i Community Pilgrimage to Commemorate the Fiftieth Anniversary of the Ascension of 'Abdu'l-Bahá, November 26–28, 1971.* New York: Spiritual Assembly of the Bahá'ís of New York, 1971. [4] p.

7.1430. Local Spiritual Assembly of the Bahá'ís of Niagara Falls (N.Y.). *50th Anniversary Abdu'l Baha's Visit to the 'Mighty Waters of the Niagara', September 1912–1962.* Niagara Falls, N.Y.: Spiritual Assembly of the Bahá'ís of Niagara Falls, 1962. [8] p.

7.1431. Local Spiritual Assembly of the Bahá'ís of Peterborough (England). *For You.* Peterborough: Local Spiritual Assembly of the Bahá'ís of Peterborough, n.d. [between 1970 and 1978] [12] p.

7.1432. Local Spiritual Assembly of the Bahá'ís of Philadelphia (Pa.). *Baha'i Center and Reading Room.* Philadephia, Pa.: Baha'is of Philadelphia, n.d. [193–?] [4] p.

7.1433. Local Spiritual Assembly of the Bahá'ís of Shanghai (China). *Circular Letter from the Shanghai Baha'is.* Shanghai, n.d. [193–?] 8 p. English, Persian and Chinese text.

7.1434. Local Spiritual Assembly of the Bahá'ís of Tempe (Ariz.). Greater Phoenix Bahá'í Media Committee. *Media: Friend or bstacle.* Tempe, Ariz.: Greater Phoenix Bahá'í Media Committee, n.d. [1980?] [45] leaves in various pagings.

7.1435. Local Spiritual Assembly of the Bahá'ís of Wilmette (Illinois). *Memorial to Louis Bourgeois.* Wilmette, Ill.: Local Spiritual Assembly of the Bahá'ís of Wilmette, 1930. 9 leaves.

7.1436. Longyear, Marion H. *The Goal Is World Order.* Wilmette, Ill.: Visual Education Committee, 1948. 13 leaves.

7.1437. *A Look at the Baha'i Faith and Its Great Plan.* El Cajon, Calif.: Universal Evangelism, n.d. [196–?] [4] p.
Anti-Bahá'í work from Christian viewpoint.

7.1438. *The Lord Our God, the Lord Is One.* London: Bahá'í Publishing Trust, 1960. 12 p.

7.1439. Los Angeles Bahá'í History Conference (1st: 1983: Los Angeles). *Proceedings of the UCLA Baha'i History Conference, August 5–7, 1983.* comp. David Piff, n.p., n.d. [1984] 88, [56] leaves.

7.1440. —— *idem.* 1st revision. comp. David Piff, n.p., n.d. [1984] 88, [32] leaves.

7.1441. Louhelen Bahá'í School (Davison, Mich.). *Fall, 1984 Programs.* Davison, Mich.: Louhelen Bahá'í School, 1984. [4] p.

7.1442. —— *Fall Schedule 1982.* Davison, Mich.: Louhelen Bahá'ı School, 1982. [8] p.

7.1443. —— *Fall, Winter, Spring 1985–86 Programs.* Davison, Mich.: Louhelen Bahá'í School, 1985. 6 p.

7.1444. —— *1983 Fall Schedule.* Davison, Mich.: Louhelen Bahá'í School, 1983. [16] p.

7.1445. —— *1983 Spring-Summer Schedule for Louhelen Bahá'í School.* Davison, Mich.: Louhelen Bahá'í School, 1983. [12] p.

7.1446. —— *Spring, 1984 Programs.* Davison, Mich.: Louhelen Bahá'í School, 1984. [6] p.

7.1447. —— *Summer, 1984 Programs.* Davison, Mich.: Louhelen Bahá'í School, 1984. [4] p.

7.1448. —— *Summer 1985 Programs.* Davison, Mich.: Louhelen Bahá'í School, 1985. [6] p.

7.1449. —— *Summer Program 1947.* Davison, Mich.: Louhelen Bahá'í School, 1947. [8] p.

7.1450. —— *Winter-Spring-Summer 1985 Programs.* Davison, Mich.: Louhelen Baha'i School, 1985. [6] p.

7.1451. Louis G. Gregory Bahá'í Institute (Hemingway, S.C.). *Louis G. Gregory Bahá'í Institute.* Hemingway, S.C.: Louis G. Gregory Bahá'í Institute, n.d. [1982?] [6] p.

7.1452. —— *The Louis G. Gregory Bahá'í Institute 1977 Summer Program.* Hemingway, S.C.: Louis G. Gregory Bahá'í Institute, 1977. [16] p.

7.1452a. —— *Louis G. Gregory Bahá'í Institute Program of Dedication.* n.p. [Hemingway, S.C.]: Louis G. Gregory Bahá'í Institute, 1972. [6] p.

7.1453. *Love and Unity in the Bahá'í Community.* n.p. [Bogotá]: National Spiritual Assembly of the Bahá'ís of Colombia, 1982. 20 p.

7.1454. *Love and Unity in the Bahá'í Community: Theme 3, Level 1.* [Bogotá]: National Teaching Committee of the National Spiritual Assembly of the Bahá'ís of Colombia, 1983. 21 p.

7.1455. 'Love of God'. n.p. [St John's, Antigua: National Spiritual Assembly of the Bahá'ís of the Leeward Islands], n.d. [1984?] [5] p. (Spiritual Education for Children, Teacher's Manual).

7.1456. *Love That Child: Bahá'í Faith, International Year of the Child.* Wilmette, Ill.: National Spiritual Assembly of the Bahá'ís of the United States, 1979. 6 p.

7.1457. *Loyalty to Government.* Wilmette, Ill.: National Spiritual Assembly of the Bahá'ís of the United States, n.d. [196–?] 1 p.

7.1457a. *idem.* [Tunis]: National Spiritual Assembly of the Baha'is of Northwest Africa, n.d. [196–] [3] p.

7.1458. *idem.* New Delhi: National Spiritual Assembly of the Bahá'ís of India, n.d. [197–?] [2] p. English and Hindi text.

7.1459. *idem.* n.p. [Nairobi]: National Education Committee of the Baha'is of Kenya, 1973. [4] p.

7.1460. *idem.* Freetown: Spiritual Assembly of the Baha'is of Sierra Leone, n.d. [1984?] [3] p.

7.1461. *Loyalty to Government = Getrouheid aan Regering.* Johannesburg: National Spiritual Assembly of the Bahá'ís of South and West Africa, 1979. 6 p. English and Afrikaans text.

7.1462. *Loyalty to Government = Loaloapwoat ong Government: En Bahá'í Ire.* Agana, Guam: Mwomwohdishon Baha'i = National Bahá'í Public Information Office, n.d. [1980?] [2] p. English and Ponapean text.

7.1463. *Loyalty to Government: The Bahá'í Viewpoint.* Wilmette, Ill.: National Spiritual Assembly of the Bahá'ís of the United States, n.d. [197–?] 1 p.

7.1464. *idem.* Dar es Salaam: National Spiritual Assembly of the Bahá'ís of Tanzania, n.d. [1976] 1 p.

7.1465. *idem.* Mona Vale, N.S.W.: National Spiritual Assembly of the Bahá'ís of Australia, n.d. [1983?], n.d. [1985] 1 p.

7.1466. *idem.* Tsimshatsui: National Spiritual Assembly of the Bahá'ís of Hong Kong, n.d. [1985] 1 p.

7.1467. *Loyalty to Government: The Bahá'í Viewpoint = Ko e Vakai 'a e Tui Baha'i: Talangofua Kakato ki he Pule'anga.* Nuku'alofa: National Spiritual Assembly of the Bahá'ís of Tonga, n.d. [1984] [2] p. English and Tongan text.

7.1468. *Loyalty to Government: The Bahá'í Viewpoint = Kumvera Boma: Mfundo za ChiBaha'i.* Limbe: Spiritual Assembly of the Baha'is in Malawi, n.d. [1982] [2] p. English and Chichewa text.

7.1469. *Loyalty to Government = UkuThobela uMbuso.* Johannesburg: National Spiritual Assembly of the Bahá'ís of South and West Africa, 1979. 6 p. English and Xhosa text.

7.1470. *Loyalty to Government = Ukwethembeka Embusweni.* [Johannesburg]: National Spiritual Assembly of the Bahá'ís of South and West Africa, n.d. [197–] [8] p. English and Zulu text.

7.1471. *Loyalty to Government = Vhuluvha kha Muvhuso.* Johannesburg: National Spiritual Assembly of the Bahá'ís of South and West Africa, 1983. [10] p. English and Venda text.

7.1472. Lucas, Mary L. *A Brief Account of My Visit to Acca.* Chicago: Bahai Publishing Society, 1905. 42 p.

M

7.1473. Ma'ani, Kamal. *Badí'.* Thailand: Ma'ani, 1977 ([Bangkok]: (Kamal) Pars-Siam Co.). 24 p.

7.1474. McClelland, Robert. *The Promise of World Peace: A Study Guide on the Message from the Universal House of Justice to the Peoples of the World.* [Honolulu]: National Spiritual Assembly of the Bahá'ís of the Hawaiian Islands, n.d. [1985] 10 leaves.

7.1475. McCormick, Jim. *The History and Doctrines of the Baha'i Faith.* Belfast, Northern Ireland: Great Joy Publications; Edinburgh: Messrs. B. McCall Barbour [distributors]; Belfast: Breda Centre [distributors], n.d. [1985] 20 p.
Anti-Bahá'í Christian polemic.

7.1476. McCormick, Margery. *Aids for Teaching the Bahá'í Faith.* Wilmette, Ill.: Bahá'í Distribution and Service Department, 1963. 28 p.

7.1477. —— *Aids for Understanding and Teaching the Fundamentals of the Bahá'í Faith.* n.p.: McCormick, n.d. [195–?] 15 leaves.

7.1478. McDaniel, Allen Boyer. *Progress Schedule, Dome Ornamentation, Baha'i Temple.* Washington, D.C.: Research Service, 1933. 1 p.

7.1479. —— *The Spell of the Temple.* New York: Vantage Press, 1953. 96 p. LC card 54–814.
The first book-length treatment of the project to build a Bahá'í temple in Wilmette, Illinois.

7.1480. —— *A Temple of Light.* Cambridge, Mass.: Technology Review, 1930. 4 p. Reprint from *Technology Review* (Boston), v.33 no.1 (Oct. 1930).

7.1481. Macdonald, Charles R. *Community Development Programme: An Expansion and Modification of the Assembly Development Programme Issued in 1977.* New Delhi: National Spiritual Assembly of the Baha'is of India, Mar. 1984. 159 p.

7.1482. MacGregor, Lorri. *The Bahá'í Faith and Christianity.* Mt Gravatt, Qld.; Delta, B.C.: MacGregor Ministries, 1984. 12 p.
Christian polemical work.

7.1483. McLaughlin, Robert W. *These Per-*

spicuous Verses: A Passage from the Writings of Bahá'u'lláh. Oxford: George Ronald, 1982. 94 p. LC card 82–185503.
Detailed analysis of one passage from Bahá'u'lláh's *Epistle to the Son of the Wolf.*

7.1484. MacNutt, Howard. *Unity Through Love.* from notes of Hooper Harris. Chicago: Bahai Publishing Society, 1906. 32 p.

7.1485. —— *idem.* 2nd ed. Chicago: Bahai Publishing Society, 1908. 32 p.

7.1486. Maharashtra State Bahá'í Annual Planning Conference (1984: Bombay). *Maharashtra State Bahá'í Annual Planning Conference (Bombay) 15th and 16th September 1984. B.E. 141: Graced by the Presence of Beloved Hand of the Cause of God Amatu'l-Bahá Ruhiyyih Khanum.* Bombay: Bahá'í State Teaching Committee of Maharashtra, 1984. 28 p.

7.1487. Mahmoudi, Jalil. *A Concordance to the Hidden Words of Bahá'u'lláh.* Wilmette, Ill.: Bahá'í Publishing Trust, 1980. vii, 88 p. LC card 80–21346.

7.1488. —— *The Story As Told.* Healdsburg, Calif.: Naturegraph, 1973. 63 p. LC card 73–605.
Introduction to the unity of religions through quotations from the world's scriptures.

7.1489. —— *idem.* rev. ed. Los Angeles: Kalimát Press, 1979. il. Russell Roberts. 80 p. LC card 79–65925.

7.1490. *The Maid-Servants of God: A Compilation.* n.p. [Nairobi]: National Education Committee of Kenya, 1973. 17 p.

7.1491. *Making News, Ways of Getting Media Coverage: A Scrapbook.* Thornhill, Ont.: Bahá'í National Centre, 1980. 44 p.

7.1492. *Malawi Baha'i Faith Men Attend Israel Meet.* Limbe: Auxiliary Board of the Baha'is in Malawi, approved by the Spiritual Assembly of the Baha'is in Malawi, 1979. 4 p. Reprinted from *Malawi News* and *Daily Times.*

7.1493. *Man of the Trees, Richard St. Barbe Baker, In Memoriam.* Saskatoon, Sask.: Spiritual Assembly of the Bahá'ís of Saskatoon, 1982. [16] p.

7.1494. *Man One Family.* Wilmette, Ill.: Bahá'í Publishing Committee, 1943. 8 p.

7.1495. *idem.* Wilmette, Ill.: Bahá'í Publishing Trust, 1957, 1967. 22 p.; 1970, 1976. 20 p.

7.1496. *Man, the Supreme Talisman.* Wilmette, Ill.: Bahá'í Publishing Committee, n.d. [between 1947 and 1955] 7 p.

7.1496a. *Manchester Bahá'í Assembly, 16 Lily Street, Hr. Crumpsall.* Manchester: Manchester Bahá'í Assembly, 1930–31 (London: Hudson & Kearns Ltd.). [4] p. Title inside: *A Course of Six Addresses by E.T. Hall on the Bahá'í Teaching for the Individual and the Community.*

7.1497. *Mankind Is One = La Humanidad Es Una.* n.p. [Malabo: National Spiritual Assembly of the Bahá'ís of Equatorial Guinea], n.d. [197–] [12] p.
Text in Spanish and English.

7.1498. Mann, Fritz A. *Celtic Departure, 1912: A New Fine Art Print by Fritz A. Mann.* Colorado Springs, Colo.: Globetown Art Communications, 1985. [4] p.

7.1499. Manocha, Kishan. *A Commentary on the Declaration of Human Rights.* London: National Spiritual Assembly of the Bahá'ís of the United Kingdom, 1984. 29 p. At head of title: International Youth Year Project. Title on first page: *The Universal Declaration of Human Rights: A Commentary.*

7.1500. *Man's Unique Distinction.* n.p.: Continental Board of Counsellors in Southern Africa, 1976. 38 leaves.

7.1501. *A Manual for Teachers of Children's Classes.* n.p. [Mbabane]: National Spiritual Assembly of the Bahá'ís of Swaziland, Mozambique and Angola, n.d. [1977] 39 p.

7.1502. *Many People Are Confused and Frustrated.* Thornhill, Ont.: Bahá'í National Centre, n.d. [1980?] [5] p.

7.1503. Marangella, Philip A. *Bahá'u'lláh.* Nikoo, Japan: Asia N.T.C., 1955. 2 p. Poem, text in Japanese and English.

7.1504. Marie of Romania. *By Dowager Queen Marie of Rumania = (Bi Qalam-i-'Ulyá Ḥaḍrat-i-Márí Malikiy-i-Rúmányá).* n.p. [Iran?], n.d. [194–?] 8, 11 p. English and Persian text.

7.1505. —— *A Queen's Talk to American Women = (Naṣíḥat Malikah).* Egypt: (al-Maḥfil al-Markazí al-Rúḥání li-Iqlím, Miṣr), 1926. 6, 12 p. English and Arabic text.

7.1506. *Marion Jack, Immortal Heroine.* Thorn-

hill, Ont.: Bahá'í Canada Publications, 1985. 13 p.

7.1507. *Mark Tobey, Art and Belief.* by Arthur L. Dahl and others. Oxford: George Ronald, 1984. vii, 119 p. LC card 84–215357.
Collection of essays about Tobey's art and his religious faith as a Bahá'í. Some illustrations in colour.

7.1508 Marrella, Giustino; Busato, Gigi. *Angeline Giachery.* n.p. [Italy], n.d. [1982] [6] p.

7.1509. *Marriage.* n.p. [Dakar: National Spiritual Assembly of the Bahá'ís of Senegal], n.d. [1984] 3 p.

7.1510. Marsella, Elena Maria. *The Quest for Eden.* New York: The Philosophical Library, 1966. 275 p. LC card 66–16172.
The Eden myth and its expected fulfilment in a future promised age. Marsella associates its fulfilment with the appearance of the Bahá'í Faith and its awaited 'golden age'.

7.1511. *Martha Root, Herald of the Kingdom: A Compilation.* comp. Kay Zinky; ed. A. Baram. New Delhi: Bahá'í Publishing Trust, 1983. xx, 438 p.
Almost entirely made up of essays from *The Bahá'í World* relating to Martha Root.

7.1512. Martin, Douglas. *The Persecution of the Bahá'ís of Iran, 1844–1984.* Ottawa, Ont.: Association for Bahá'í Studies, 1984. v, 86 p. (Bahá'í Studies; v.12/13).

7.1513. —— *The Spiritual Revolution.* Thornhill, Ont.: Canadian Bahá'í Community, 1974. 19 p.

7.1514. Martin, Walter R. *The Bahá'í Faith.* Wayne, N.J.: Christian Research Institute, n.d. [197–] 18 p.
Anti-Bahá'í work from Christian viewpoint.

7.1515. *The Martyr-Prophet of a World Faith: Commemorating the Centenary of the Martyrdom of the Bab, July 9, 1850 – July 9, 1950.* New Delhi: National Spiritual Assembly of the Bahá'ís of India, Pakistan and Burma, 1950. 63 p. LC card 74–182197.

7.1516. *Martyrdom Centenary of Tahirih, Qurratu'l-'Ayn, 1852–1952.* New Delhi: Bahá'í Public Relations, 1952 (Delhi: National Printing Works). [6] p.

7.1517. *Martyrdom of the Báb, 1850–1950: Commemorating the One Hundredth Anniversary of the Martyrdom of the Báb.* Sydney, N.S.W.: National Spiritual Assembly of the Bahá'ís of Australia and New Zealand, 1950 (Sydney: Edgar Bragg & Sons). 24 p. Cover title: *Martyrdom of the Báb, 1850–1950: A Centenary Commemoration.*

7.1518. Masih Farhangi Academy (Karachi, Pakistan). *Report Book: First Course for Baha'i Youth 142 B.E., 8th June through 10th August 1985.* Karachi: Masih Farhangi Academy, 1985. [12] p.

7.1519. —— *Report Book: Second Course for Baha'i Youth 142 B.E., 11th September through 30th October 1985.* Karachi: Masih Farhangi Academy, 1985. 12 p.

7.1520. Masson, Jean. *The Bahai Movement.* Chicago: Ill.: Bahai Assembly, n.d. [191–?] [4] p.

7.1521. —— *Mashreq'ul-Azkar and the Bahai Movement.* Chicago: Executive Board Bahai Temple Unity, 1921. 39 p.

7.1522. —— *idem.* 2nd ed. Chicago: Executive Board Bahai Temple Unity, 1921. 39 p.

7.1523. *Material and Divine Civilization.* Geneva, N.Y.: Outline Bureau of the National Teaching Committee of the Baha'is of the United States and Canada 1930. 10 leaves.

7.1524. Mathews, Loulie A. *Not Every Sea Hath Pearls.* Milford, N.H.: The Cabinet Press, 1951. vii, 173 p. LC card 52–16005.

Personal reminiscences of one who devoted great energies to travelling the world on behalf of the Bahá'í Faith. Early printings have title imprinted on spine.

7.1525. —— *The Outposts of a World Religion.* n.p., n.d. [after 1935] 11 leaves.

7.1526. —— *Whence Comes the Light?* New York: Bahá'í Publishing Committee, 1929. 84 p. (Bahá'í Studies).

7.1527. Mathews, Loulie A., et al. *Studies in Jewish Mysticism.* n.p., n.d. [1952?] 41 p.

7.1528. Matthisen, Nina B. *The Lonely Stranger: Duet.* lyrics Rena M.O. Pettersen, music Nina B. Matthisen. Chicago: Nina B. Matthisen, 1931. 3 p.

7.1529. —— *The Making of the Temple: Duet.* lyrics Janet Bolton, music Nina B. Matthisen. Chicago: Nina B. Matthisen, 1931. 5p.

7.1530. Maung Sein. *The Brief Account of the School of H.H. Abdu'l Baha, in His Village, Daidanaw, Kalazoo . . . 1935–1936.* Daidanaw, Burma: The Educational Committee, 1936 (Mandalay: M.B.T. Printing Works). 6 p.

7.1531. Maxwell, May. *An Early Pilgrimage.* Chicago: Bahai Publishing Society, 1917. 33 p.

May (Bolles) Maxwell was among the first group of western pilgrims to visit 'Abdu'l-Bahá in 'Akká in 1898. This booklet is her recollection of that pilgrimage.

7.1532. —— *idem.* Wheatley, U.K.: George Ronald, 1953. 43 p.

7.1533. —— *idem.* London: George Ronald, 1969. 43 p.

7.1534. —— *idem.* Oxford: George Ronald, 1974, 1976. 43 p.

7.1535. *Meeting of Edinburgh Citizens to Greet Abdul Baha (Abbas Effendi).* arranged by the Edinburgh Esperanto Society. Edinburgh: Edinburgh Esperanto Society, 1913. [4] p.

7.1536. Mehrabi, Jackie. *Nine Holy Days.* London: Bahá'í Publishing Trust, 1975. 48 p.

Children's booklet describing Bahá'í holy days.

7.1537. Mehrabi, Jacqueline. *Remember the Rainbow.* il. Brian Parsons. Oxford: George Ronald, 1985. [6], 33 p.

Children's book about evolution.

7.1538. —— *The Song in the Ground.* Oxford: George Ronald, 1985. [48] p.

The story of Bahá'u'lláh told for children.

7.1539. —— *Stories for Children.* London: Bahá'í Publishing Trust, 1970. [32] p.

7.1540. —— *idem.* new ed. London: Bahá'í Publishing Trust, 1985. 29 p.

7.1541. —— *Stories of 'Abdu'l-Bahá.* London: Bahá'í Publishing Trust, 1984. 48 p.

7.1542. Mehta, Mani H. *A Challenging Letter to Ghandi & Jinnah: A Unique Revelation.* Bombay: A. Parthasarathi, 1944. 13 p. LC card 45–7234.

7.1543. *A Memorable Feast, Abdul Baha the Host.* n.p., n.d. [1912?] [8] p.

7.1544. *A Memorial Day Meditation or New Light on the Life Hereafter.* n.p. [Wilmette, Ill.]: Radio Service Committee, 1959. 6 leaves.

7.1545. *A Memorial for Robert Hayden, poet.* Ann Arbor, [Mich.]: Ann Arbor Baha'i Community, 1980. [4] p.

7.1546. *A Memorial Gathering for the Hand of the Cause of God Dr Rahmatu'llah Muhajir.* Port-of-Spain: National Spiritual Assembly of the Bahá'ís of Trinidad and Tobago, 1980. 6 p.

7.1547. *Memorial Service for Daood Toeg, Beloved Servant of God, Born 1897, Died 1974.* Thornhill, Ont., 1974. [4] p.

7.1548. *Memorial Service for Hand of the Cause of God Mr Enoch Olinga. His Beloved Wife Elizabeth, and Their Three Children, Badi, Lennie, Tahirih.* [Port of Spain]: National Spiritual Assembly of the Bahá'ís of Trinidad and Tobago, 1979. 8 p.

7.1549. *A Memorial Service for the Hand of the Cause of God Shu'á'u'lláh 'Alá'í (1888–1984).* n.p. [Thornhill, Ont.: National Spiritual Assembly of the Bahá'ís of Canada], 1984. [4] p.

7.1550. *Memorial Service in Tribute to Hand of the Cause of God Mr Enoch Olinga, His Wife Elizabeth, Children Badi, Lennie, Tahirih.* Monrovia: National Spiritual Assembly of the Bahá'ís of Liberia and Guinea, 1979. 3 p.

7.1551. *The Memorial Services of Abdul-Baha on Mount Carmel, Palestine: Accounts from Letters and Newspapers.* received and trans. Dr Zia Bagdadi. Chicago, 1922. 8 p.

7.1552. *A Message for Mankind: The Bahá'í Faith.* n.p. [London: National Spiritual Assembly of the Bahá'ís of the United Kingdom], n.d. [1981] [2] p.

7.1553. *The Message of Bahá'u'lláh.* Wilmette, Ill.: Bahá'í Publishing Trust, n.d. [1968?] [12] p.

7.1554. *idem.* n.p., n.d. [between 1968 and 1975] [12] p.

7.1555. *idem.* n.p. [Bangkok: National Spiritual Assembly of the Bahá'ís of Thailand], n.d. [1983] 3 leaves. English and Khmer text.

7.1556. *Message of Bahá'u'lláh to the Rulers.* n.p. [New Delhi?], n.d. [1968?] [2] p.

7.1557. *The Messengers of God Are One: Religion Renewed and the World United.* London: Bahá'í Publishing Trust, n.d. [1969], 1980. [8] p.

7.1558. *Meta Baha'i?* [Honolulu]: National Spiritual Assembly of the Bahá'ís of the Hawaiian Islands, 1965. 16 p. Trukese and English text.

7.1559. Meyer, Ray. *Bahá'í, Follower of the Light.* il. Pamela Poulter. n.p. [Mona Vale, N.S.W.]: National Spiritual Assembly of the Bahá'ís of Australia, 1972. iv, 71 p.

7.1560. —— *idem.* 1st American ed. Wilmette, Ill.: Bahá'í Publishing Trust, 1976. 71 p.

7.1561. —— *idem.* rev. American ed. Wilmette, Ill.: Bahá'í Publishing Trust, 1979. 72 p.
Review:
New Review of Books and Religion (New York), v.3 no.9 (May 1979), p. 27.

7.1562. —— *idem.* ev. n.p. [Mona Vale, N.S.W.]: Bahá'í Publications Australia, 1984 (Mudgee: Lynx Print). iv, 72 p.

7.1563. Meyer, Zoe. *Children's Stories from the Dawn-Breakers.* il. Carl Scheffler. Wilmette, Ill.: Bahá'í Publishing Trust, 1955, 1964, 1976. 66 p. LC card 56–21319.
Stories from *Nabil's Narrative* simplified and adapted for children.
See 7.1564.

7.1564. —— *Stories from the Dawn-Breakers.* il. Carl Scheffler. Wilmette, Ill.: Bahá'í Publishing Trust, 1970. 66 p.
See 7.1563.

7.1565. Miller, Grant Hindin. *Sing O Carmel.* Auckland, N.Z.: Grant Hindin Miller, 1984. [16] p.

7.1566. Miller, William McElwee. *The Bahá'í Faith: Its History and Teachings.* South Pasadena, Calif.: William Carey Library, 1974, 1984. xix, 443 p. LC card 74–8475.
Reviews:
Choice (Middletown, Conn.), (Dec. 1975), p. 1323.
Donaldson, Dwight M. *The Muslim World* (Hartford, Conn.], v.65 no.4 (Oct. 1975), pp. 298–299.
Elwell-Sutton, L.P. *Journal of the Royal Asiatic Society* (London), no.2 (1976), pp. 157–158.
Ellwood, Robert S. *Missiology* (Scottsdale, Pa.), v.3 (July 1975), pp. 387–389.
Geijbels, M. *Bulletin of the Christian Study Centre* (Rawalpindi, Pakistan), (1976), pp. 153–154.
Goodpasture, Henry McKennie. *The Presbyterian Outlook* (Richmond, Va.), (Sept. 22, 1975), p. 15.
Presbuteros (Baltimore, Md.), (Nov. 1974), p. 4.
　A version of the development of the Bahá'í Faith by a former Protestant missionary in Iran. The author, himself unsympathetic to the Bahá'í Faith, relies heavily on an inveterate enemy of the Bahá'í movement, Jalal Azal, for documentation. While presenting an air of scholarly detachment, the survey is directed so as to present the Bahá'í Faith in as unfavourable a light as possible. See Douglas Martin, 'The Missionary as Historian', *Bahá'í Studies*, v.4 (Dec. 1978), pp. 1–29; *World Order*, v.10 no.3 (Spring 1976), pp. 43–63.

7.1567. —— *Bahá'ism: Its Origin, History and Teachings.* New York: Fleming Revell Co., 1931. 214 p. LC card 31–25646.
Reviews:
Book Review Digest (New York), (1931), pp. 729–730.
Garrison, W.E. 'Oriental Cult or Universal Religion', *The Christian Century* (Chicago), (Dec. 9, 1931), pp. 1559–1560.
Haydon, A. Eustace. 'The Religion of Bahá'í', *World Tomorrow* (New York), v.15 (Jan. 1932), p. 27.
Vail, Albert. 'Baha'ism Defended', *The New Humanist* (Chicago), v.6 no.1 (Jan.–Feb. 1933), pp. 40–42.
Zwemer, Samuel M. *The Moslem World* (Hartford, Conn.), v.22 no.1 (Jan. 1932), p. 91.
　Standard Christian anti-Bahá'í polemic.

7.1568. —— *What Is the Bahá'í Faith?* Grand

Rapids, Mich.: Eerdmans, 1977. 151 p. LC card 77–8063
Condensation of 7.1566.

7.1568a. —— *What Is the Baha'i World Faith?* Santa Ana, Calif.: Christian Apologetics, Research and Information Service, 1977. 23 p. [Bjorling]

7.1569. *Minor Terminology and Words Used in the Bahá'í Faith.* Athens: National Spiritual Assembly of the Bahá'ís of Greece, 1980. 34 leaves.
English-Greek dictionary of Bahá'í terms.

7.1570. *Miss Martha Root, World Traveller, Peace Advocate, Baha'i Lecturer.* n.p., n.d. [after 1931] [44] p.
One large sheet, folded, with reproductions of letters of introduction and clippings about Martha Root. Probably used by Miss Root as an introductory brochure about herself during her travelling teaching tours.

7.1571. *Mission of Youth.* n.p. [Wilmette, Ill.: Bahá'í Publishing Trust], n.d. [1981] [4] p.

7.1572. Mitchell, Bahia Deloomy. *Alcohol and Alcoholism: An Overview.* Wilmette, Ill.: National Spiritual Assembly of the Bahá'ís of the United States, 1975. p. 27–47. Reprinted from *World Order*, v.8 no.3.

7.1573. Mitchell, Glenford E.; Jordan, Daniel C. *What Is Race?: Questions and Answers on the Most Challenging Issue.* Wilmette, Ill.: Bahá'í Publishing Trust, 1967, 1969, 1978. 22 p.

7.1574. Moffett, Ruth J. *Do'a: On Wings of Prayer.* Des Moines, Ia.: Wallace Homestead Co., 1974. xiv, 96 p.

7.1575. —— *Do'a: The Call to Prayer.* Chicago, 1933, 1938. 125 p. LC card 35–2677.
A broad Bahá'í approach to prayer and meditation or 'the practice of the presence of the Spirit of God', using quotations from the Bahá'í Faith and other religions.

7.1576. —— *idem.* Wilmette, Ill.: Bahá'í Publishing Committee, 1953. 125 p.

7.1577. —— *Du'á, On Wings of Prayer.* rev. and ed. Keven Brown. Prism ed. Happy Camp, Calif.: Naturegraph Publishers, 1984. 94 p. LC card 84–3486.

7.1578. —— *New Keys to the Book of Revelation.* New Delhi: Bahá'í Publishing Trust, 1977. 199 p. At head of title: *God Speaks Again.*
Popular review of the Book of Revelation in light of various Bahá'í interpretations. Not always accurate in attribution of statements to Shoghi Effendi.

7.1579. —— *idem.* 2nd ed. New Delhi: Bahá'í Publishing Trust, 1980. xxi, 199 p.

7.1580. —— *A Pilgrimage to the Holy Land.* Ruhaniyyih Ruth Moffett. n.p. [Honolulu: National Spiritual Assembly of the Bahá'ís of the Hawaiian Islands], n.d. [1980] 52 leaves. Cover title: *Revealing Haifa Notes and Directives by Our Guardian in 1954.*

7.1581. Momen, Moojan. *The Bábí and Bahá'í Religions, 1844–1944: Some Contemporary Western Accounts.* Oxford: George Ronald, 1981. xxx, 572 p. LC card 81–214657.
Review:
MacEoin, Denis. *Religion* (London), v.12 (1982), pp. 405–408.
Collection of published and unpublished documents arranged chronologically, with editorial commentary. Includes a valuable introduction to western scholarship on the Bahá'í Faith and a section of biographical notes on significant individuals mentioned.

7.1582. —— *Dr John Ebenezer Esslemont, M.B., Ch.B., SBEA, Hand of the Cause of God.* London: Bahá'í Publishing Trust, 1975. 45 p.
A brief appreciation of one of the most notable early Bahá'ís, whose *Bahá'u'lláh and the New Era* remains the standard introductory work on the Bahá'í Faith in English.

7.1583. Momen, Wendi. *Call Me Riḍván.* il. Ed Povey. Oxford: George Ronald, 1982. 60 p.
Story of a Bahá'í child who learns about being different and the importance of diversity.

7.1583a. Monypenny, Leslie. *Bahai Temple, Huge Symbol of 9 Religions in 1: Unique Edifice Depicts 'Glory of God'.* Wilmette, Ill.: Baha'i Public Relations, [1949] [2] p. Reprint from: *The Chicago Daily Tribune*, Feb. 26, 1949.

7.1584. Moore, Peter. *God Made the Stars.* n.p. [Los Angeles: Kalimát Press], 1981. [32] p.
Very simple book about creation for small children.

7.1585. Morrison, Gayle. *To Move the World: Louis G. Gregory and the Advancement of Racial Unity in America.* Wilmette, Ill.: Bahá'í Publishing Trust, 1982, [1983] xxvii, 399 p. (Champion Builder Books). LC card 81–22763.
A scholarly biography and social commentary on the life and work of Louis Gregory, the first black member of the National Spiritual Assembly of the Bahá'ís of the United States and Canada and a pioneer for the cause of racial amity. Morrison chronicles 'the social and racial forces at work in the United States . . . and the dynamics of the Bahá'í Faith that were shaping . . . a community unequivocally committed to the oneness of mankind and the elimination of racial prejudice'.

7.1586. Moses David [pseud.] *Bahai Shrine*

Prophecy. Dallas, Tex.: Children of God, n.d. [197–?] [4] p.

7.1587. —— *The Temple Prophecy*. London: Children of God Trust, 1973. 4 p.

7.1588. Moshrefzadeh, M. *Prejudice in Iran*. [Peoria], Arizona: Moshrefzadeh, 1984. [2], 55 leaves.

7.1589. Moslem Students' Association in the US & Canada, Persian Speaking Group. *What You Should Know About Bahaism*. n.p.: Moslem Students' Association in the US & Canada, 1982. 6 leaves.
Anti-Bahá'í work from an Islamic viewpoint.

7.1590. *The Most Challenging Issue: The Baha'i Community and Racial Prejudice: A Compilation*. Wilmette, Ill.: Most Challenging Issue Seminar Committee, Spiritual Assembly of the Baha'is of Wilmette, Illinois, 1982. 41, [3], [1] p.

7.1591. *The Mother Temple of Africa, Kampala, Uganda: Dedication*. Kampala, Uganda: [National Spiritual Assembly of the Bahá'ís of Central and East Africa], 1961 (Kampala: Uganda Argus Ltd.). [4] p.

7.1592. Motlagh, Hushidar. *Touching the Heart: A Guide to Teaching*. n.p. [Mt Pleasant, Mich.]: Motlagh, n.d. [1982] xix, 351 p.

7.1593. *The Mountain of the Lord: A Baha'i Compilation*. comp. Robert L. Ferguson; artwork, Barbara R. Ferguson. n.p. [Glenview, Ill.: Ferguson], n.d. [1984] 16 p.

7.1594. *Mui Koh Baha'i Sintor Saw Engkai Chaia' = What Every Baha'i Should Know*. Penang, Malaysia: Area Teaching Committee of the Baha'is of Penang, 1972. 20 p. English and Hokkien Chinese text.

7.1595. Munírih Khánum. *Episodes in the Life of Moneereh Khanum*. trans. Ahmad Sohrab. Los Angeles: Persian-American Publishing Co., 1924. 31 p. LC card 25–8078.

7.1596. Munje, H.M. *1844 A.D., Pinpoint Target for All Faiths*. [Kuala Lumpur]: Spiritual Assembly of the Bahá'ís of Malaysia, 1982. 18 p.

7.1596a. —— *Baha'i, the Reunited Humanity*. Mysore, India: Local Spiritual Assembly of the Baha'is, n.d. [196–] 18, [1] p.

7.1596b. —— *Baha'i World Faith*. Kanpur, India: H.M. Munje, n.d. [197–?] [6] p. folder.

7.1597. —— *The Whole World Is But One Family*. New Delhi: Bahá'í Publishing Trust, n.d. [196–?] 55, iv p.

7.1598. —— *The World Is But One Family*. n.p. [Kuala Lumpur]: Spiritual Assembly of the Baha'is of Malaysia, n.d. [1983] 55, iii p.

7.1599. Munro, W. Fraser. *Baha'i-ism, a Mixture of Religions*. Toronto, Ont.: Board of Evangelism and Social Service, United Church of Canada, n.d. [197–?] 8 p.
Anti-Bahá'í work from Christian viewpoint.

7.1600. Murchie, Guy. *I Am a Bahá'í*. Wilmette, Ill.: Bahá'í Publishing Trust, 1958, 1976. 4 p. Reprinted from *Chicago Sunday Tribune*, July 13, 1958.

7.1601. Murray, Fred. *The Story of Fred Murray*. a report told to Howard Harwood. Mona Vale, N.S.W.: National Spiritual Assembly of the Bahá'ís of Australia, n.d. [1984] [6] p.

7.1602. Musacchia, Evelyn. *A Bahá'í Picture-Coloring Book: Bahá'í Holy Places Around the World*. n.p. [Honolulu]: National Spiritual Assembly of the Bahá'ís of the Hawaiian Islands, 1971. 18 p. (Cover title: *Bahá'í Holy Places Around the World*).

7.1603. —— *A Bahá'í Teaching Guide for Children: A Practical Program for the Education of Children: Intermediate Workbook (8–12 Years)*. Honolulu, Hawaii: National Bahá'í Printing Committee, 1964. 31 leaves.

7.1604. —— *A Bahá'í Teaching Guide for Children (Series no.1): A Practical Program for the Education of Children: Preschool Workbook (2–5 Years)*. Honolulu, Hawaii: National Bahá'í Printing Committee, 1964. 27 leaves.

7.1605. —— *A Bahá'í Teaching Guide for Children (Series no.1): A Practical Program for the Education of Children: Elementary Workbook (6–8 Years)*. Honolulu: Hawaii: National Bahá'í Printing Committee, 1964. 33 leaves.

7.1606. —— *A Bahá'í Teaching Guide for Children (Series no.1): A Practical Programme for the Education of Children: Teacher's Manual*. Honolulu, Hawaii: National Bahá'í Printing Committee, 1964. 22 leaves.

7.1607. —— *Coloring Book, Bahá'í Places Around the World*. comp. Evelyn Musacchia; il. Dorrine Sadilek, n.p. [Honolulu]: National Child Education Committee of the National Spiritual Assembly of the Bahá'ís of the Hawaiian Islands, 1975, 1983. 48 p. Title page title: *A Baha'i Coloring Book*.

7.1608. *Music for Bahá'ís: Choral Music, Packet One*. n.p. [Wilmette, Ill.]: Committee on Music and the Distribution & Service Department, 1965. [38] p.

7.1609. Muṣṭafá Rúmí, Siyyid. *A Short Thesis of Bahai Faith*. Rangoon, Burma: Bahai Publishing Society, 1911. 19 p.

7.1610. *My Baby Book*. Wilmette, Ill.: National

Spiritual Assembly of the Bahá'ís of the United States, 1980. 32 p.

7.1611. *'My Calamity Is My Providence': An Anthology of Poetry Mostly Written by Contemporary Baha'i Poets in Response to the Persecution of Baha'is in Iran.* comp. and organized by Tahirih Khodadoust Foroughi. Wilmette, Ill. [i.e. Reno, Nev.]: Tahirih Khodadoust Foroughi, 1984. 84 p.

N

7.1612. Nabíl-i-A'ẓam. *The Dawn-Breakers: Nabíl's Narrative of the Early Days of the Bahá'í Revelation.* trans. Shoghi Effendi. New York: Bahá'í Publishing Committee, 1932. lxiii, 685 p. LC card 32–8946.
Reviews:
Vail, Albert. *Religious Education* (Mount Morris, Ill.), v.27 no.7 (Sept. 1932), pp. 665–667.
Zwemer, Samuel M., *The Moslem World* (Hartford, Conn.), v.22 no.4 (Oct. 1932), p. 415.
Shoghi Effendi edited and translated from Persian the first portion of this exhaustive account, by a contemporary and participant, of the origins of the Bábí movement. Included are a valuable introduction written by George Townshend, facsimiles of writings of the Báb, copious photographs of places discussed in the text, a bibliography of works consulted by Shoghi Effendi and a guide to transliteration.

7.1613. —— *idem.* New York: Bahá'í Publishing Committee, 1932. lxiii, 685 p.
A limited edition specially bound numbering 150 copies autographed by the translator.

7.1614. —— *idem.* Wilmette, Ill.: Bahá'í Publishing Committee, 1953. lxiii, 685 p.

7.1615. —— *idem.* 1st British ed. London: Bahá'í Publishing Trust, 1953, 1975. xxxv, 507 p.
British editions lack photographs and notes.

7.1616. —— *idem.* Wilmette, Ill.: Bahá'í Publishing Trust, 1962, 1970, 1974. lxiii, 685 p. LC card 77–14837.
Review:
Theology Digest, v.19 no.3 (Autumn 1971), p. 280.

7.1617. [Nagle] Breda; [Keane], Alan; [Ó Hannracháin], Seán. *Bahá'í Song Book.* Ireland, 1982. [16] leaves.

7.1618. Nakhjavání, 'Alí. *A Flame within Us.* n.p. [Thornhill, Ont.: National Teaching Committee], n.d. [1984] [16] p.

7.1619. Nakhjavání, Bahíyyih, et. al. *Artist, Seeker and Seer* (Bahíyyih Nakhjavání). *The Heroic Soul and the Ordinary Self* (Geoffrey Nash). *A Calico Courage* (Roger White). *The Effect of Revelation on Artistic Expression* (Otto Donald Rogers). Ottawa, Ont.: Association for Bahá'í Studies, 1982. 59 p. (Bahá'í Studies; v.10).

7.1620. Nakhjavání, Bahíyyih. *Four on an Island.* Oxford; George Ronald, 1983. viii, 136 p.
Literary study of the four Bahá'ís who were exiled to Cyprus in 1868 and how their exile is a metaphor for each individual's internal spiritual and psychological exile from his true self.

7.1621. —— *Response.* Oxford: George Ronald, 1981. x, 134 p. LC card 82–149457.
The dual nature of human relationships and the need for response to the partner in each relationship. The author suggests that the fundamental premise of the Bahá'í Faith is the integration and resolution of the conflicts that tend to limit our response.

7.1622. —— *When We Grow Up.* Oxford: George Ronald, 1979. 112 p. LC card 82–185488.
Addresses problems faced by Bahá'í parents in bringing up children in a world with values at variance with Bahá'í spiritual principles.

7.1623. Nakhjavání, Violette. *Amatu'l-Bahá Visits India.* New Delhi: Bahá'í Publishing Trust, n.d. [1966?] 196 p. LC card 79–906069.
An affectionate diary of the journey through India in 1964 by the widow of Shoghi Effendi. The author was with Amatu'l-Bahá Rúhíyyih Khánum for most of the 55,000 miles and more than 70 villages visited. *See 7.2176.*

7.1624. —— *idem.* 2nd ed. New Delhi: Bahá'í Publishing Trust, 1984. xix, 180 p.
Adds an index of the examples and stories used in Amatu'l-Bahá's talks.

7.1625. Nash, Geoffrey. *Iran's Secret Pogrom: The Conspiracy to Wipe Out the Bahá'ís.* Suffolk, U.K.: Neville Spearman, 1982. 156 p. LC card 82–196608.
Review:
Petrossian, Vahe. *Middle East Economic Digest* (London), v.26, no.30, p. 47.

Overview of the situation of the Bahá'ís in Iran in the earlier stages of the wave of terror unleashed against the Bahá'ís in 1979.

7.1626. —— *The Phoenix and the Ashes: The Bahá'í Faith and the Modern Apocalypse.* Oxford: George Ronald, 1984. ix, 148 p.
Review:
Campbell, Donald. *University of Edinburgh Journal* (Scotland), v. 32 no. 2 (Dec. 1985), p. 59.
Five essays, beginning with the 19th century expectation of a new age and the apparent disappointment of that hope. The author contrasts subsequent disillusionment and disintegration with the Bahá'í belief in a spiritual rebirth that is as yet unperceived by the mass of humanity.

7.1627. National Bahá'í Teaching Conference (1978: Port of Spain, Trinidad). *National Bahá'í Teaching Conference, January 15th 1978.* Port of Spain: Trinidad National Bahá'í Centre, 1978. 9 leaves.

7.1628. National Bahá'í Youth Conference (3rd: 1973: Oklahoma City, Okla.). *Third National Bahá'í Youth Conference, Oklahoma City, June 20–24, 1973.* n.p. [Wilmette, Ill.: National Spiritual Assembly of the Bahá'ís of the United States], 1973. 12 p.

7.1628a. National Bahá'í Youth Conference (4th: 1977: Urbana, Ill.). *Program, 4th Bahá'í National Youth Conference, 6/29–7/3, '77.* n.p. [Wilmette, Ill.: National Spiritual Assembly of the Bahá'ís of the United States], 1977. 14, [2] p.

7.1629. National Bahá'í Youth Conference (1977: Trinidad and Tobago). *National Baha'i Youth Conference, 8–11 April, 1977.* Trinidad and Tobago, 1977. [14] leaves.

7.1630. National Conference on Human Rights (1968: Chicago). *National Conference on Human Rights, September 13, 14 and 15, 1968.* Wilmette, Ill.: North American Bahá'í Office for Human Rights, 1968. [8] p.

7.1631. *National Deepening Institute, July 1985. 'The Local Spiritual Assembly'.* n.p. [Mona Vale, N.S.W.]: National Spiritual Assembly of the Baha'is of Australia, 1985. 17 p.

7.1632. *National Deepening Institute, 'The Secret of Divine Civilization', July 1984.* n.p. [Mona Vale, N.S.W.]; National Spiritual Assembly of the Bahá'ís of Australia, 1984. 32 p.

7.1633. *The National Spiritual Assembly: A Deepening Course.* n.p.: Continental Board of Counsellors in Southern Africa, 1971. 20 p.

7.1634. National Spiritual Assembly of the Bahá'ís of Alaska. *Alaska Bahá'í Directory.*

Anchorage: National Spiritual Assembly of the Bahá'ís of Alaska. 1959–60. [2] p.; 1960–61. [2] p.; 1961–62. [2] p.; 1962–63. [2] p.; 1963–64. [2] p.; 1964–65. [2] p.; 1965–66. [4] p.; 1966–67. [4] p.; 1967–68. [4] p.; 1968–69. [4] p.; 1969–70. [4] p.; 1970–71. [4] p.; 1971–72. [4] p.
Listed are only those years when the directory was published. It also appeared in mimeographed, dittoed and typed forms of various kinds.

7.1635. —— *Local Spiritual Assembly Guidelines for Alaska.* Anchorage: National Spiritual Assembly of the Bahá'ís of Alaska, 1979. ix, 158 p.

7.1636. National Spiritual Assembly of the Bahá'ís of Australia. *Bahá'í Chairman's Manual.* n.p. [Mona Vale, N.S.W.]: Bahá'í Publications Australia, 1982 (Mudgee; Lynx Print), 1985. 24 p.

7.1637. —— *Bahá'í Public Information Officer's Manual.* n.p. [Mona Vale, N.S.W.]: Bahá'í Publishing Trust Australia, 1976. 24 p.

7.1638. —— *Bahá'í Secretary's Manual.* n.p. [Mona Vale, N.S.W.]: Bahá'í Publishing Trust Australia, 1976, 1977, 1978, 1981, 1982, 1984, 1985. 12 p.

7.1639. —— *Bahá'í Treasurer's Manual.* n.p. [Mona Vale, N.S.W.]: National Spiritual Assembly of the Bahá'ís of Australia, 130 B.E. [1973–74], 1977, 1981, 1982, 1984, 1985. 20 p.

7.1640. —— *Declaration of Trust and By-Laws of a National Spiritual Assembly, By-Laws of a Local Spiritual Assembly.* n.p. [Mona Vale, N.S.W.]: National Spiritual Assembly of the Bahá'ís of Australia], 1975. 26 leaves.

7.1641. —— *The Five Year Plan,* B.E. 131–136: *Goals for Australia.* n.p. [Mona Vale, N.S.W.]: National Spiritual Assembly of the Bahá'ís of Australia, 1974. 15 p.

7.1642. —— *Handbook for Local Spiritual Assemblies in Australia.* n.p. [Mona Vale, N.S.W.]: National Spiritual Assembly of the Bahá'ís of Australia, 1980. v, 74 p.

7.1643. —— *[Local Spiritual Assembly Manual]* n.p. [Mona Vale, N.S.W.: National Spiritual Assembly of the Bahá'ís of Australia], n.d. [ca. 1976] [88] leaves.

7.1644. —— *The National Spiritual Assembly of the Bahá'ís of Australia, 1934–1984.* n.p. [Mona Vale, N.S.W.]: National Spiritual Assembly of the Bahá'ís of Australia, 1984. 16 p.

7.1645. —— *The Nine Year Plan, Supplement, 1964–1973.* n.p. [Sydney, N.S.W.]: National

Spiritual Assembly of the Bahá'ís of Australia, 1964. 12 p.

7.1645a. National Spiritual Assembly of the Bahá'ís of Australia. National Teaching Committee. *'The Promise of World Peace' – a National Proclamation Plan.* Dapto, N.S.W.: National Bahá'í Teaching Committee for Australia, 1985. [4] p.

7.1646. National Spiritual Assembly of the Bahá'ís of Australia. National Teaching Committee. *The Baha'i Faith and Christendom.* n.p. [Sydney, N.S.W.]: National Teaching Committee of the Bahá'ís of Australia, 1963. 7 p.

7.1647. National Spiritual Assembly of the Bahá'ís of Australia. Public Information Office. *The Bahá'í Faith.* Mona Vale, N.S.W.: Public Information Office of the Bahá'ís of Australia, n.d. [197–] 2 leaves.

7.1648. National Spiritual Assembly of the Bahá'ís of Australia and New Zealand. *The Crucial Year: A Message of Paramount Importance to Every Bahá'í.* Sydney: N.S.W.: National Spiritual Assembly of the Bahá'ís of Australia and New Zealand, 1952. 15 p.

7.1649. National Spiritual Assembly of the Bahá'ís of the Bahamas. National Teaching Committee. *Individual Goals.* n.p. [Nassau: National Teaching Committee], n.d. [1984] [6] leaves.

7.1650. National Spiritual Assembly of the Bahá'ís of Bangladesh. *7–Year Plan.* [Dhaka]: National Spiritual Assembly of the Bahá'ís of Bangladesh, Jan. 1985. 63 p.

7.1651. National Spiritual Assembly of the Bahá'ís of Belize. National Children and Family Life Committee. *Children's Study Course.* San Ignacio, Cayo: Baha'i National Children and Family Life Committee, n.d. [1984] [2] leaves.

7.1652. National Spiritual Assembly of the Bahá'ís of Bermuda. *Bermudian Baha'i Community Directory.* Hamilton: National Spiritual Assembly of the Bahá'ís of Bermuda, 1984. [12] p.

7.1653. National Spiritual Assembly of the Bahá'ís of the British Isles. *Annual Report.* London: National Spiritual Assembly of the Bahá'ís of the British Isles. 109, 1952. 16 p.; 110, 1953. 16 p.; 111, 1954. 16 p.; 112, 1955. 15 p.; 113, 1956. 18 p.; 114, 1957. 19 p.; 121, 1964–65. 16 p.; 122, 1965–66. 20 p.; 123, 1966–67. 17 p.; 124, 1967–68. 19 p.; 125, 1968–69. 16 p.; 127, 1970–71. 15 p.
See also 7.1828.

7.1653a. —— *Memorandum and Articles of Association.* London: J. Hampson Fogg, 1939. 20 p.

At head of title: The Companies Act, 1929 – An unlimited company without a share capital.

7.1654. —— *Some Aspects of Bahá'í Procedure.* n.p. [London]: National Spiritual Assembly of the Bahá'ís of the British Isles, 1947. 8 p.

7.1655. —— *Some Hints for Baha'i Communities.* n.p. [London]: National Spiritual Assembly of the Bahá'ís of the British Isles, n.d. [195–?] 6 leaves.

7.1656. —— *Statement on the Acceptance of New Believers.* n.p. [London]: National Spiritual Assembly of the Bahá'ís of the British Isles, 1947. 5 leaves.

7.1657. —— *The Ten Year Crusade: A Programme of Action for the Second Year.* London: National Spiritual Assembly of the Bahá'ís of the British Isles, 1954. 4 p.

7.1658. National Spiritual Assembly of the Bahá'ís of the British Isles. National Teaching Committee. *Teaching and Consolidation Handbook.* n.p. [London]: National Teaching Committee of the National Spiritual Assembly of the Bahá'ís of the British Isles, 1957, 1961. 50 p.

7.1659. —— *Teaching Manual.* n.p. [London]: National Teaching Committee, 1948. 37 leaves.

7.1660. National Spiritual Assembly of the Bahá'ís of the British Isles. Public Relations Committee. *Suggestions for Press Correspondents.* n.p. [London]: Public Relations Committee, n.d. [195–?] 6 p.

7.1661. National Spiritual Assembly of the Bahá'ís of Burma. *Bulletin of the First National Spiritual Assembly of the Bahá'ís of Burma.* Rangoon: National Spiritual Assembly of the Bahá'ís of Burma, 1959. 14 p.

7.1662. National Spiritual Assembly of the Bahá'ís of Cameroon. *Bahá'í.* Victoria: National Spiritual Assembly of the Bahá'ís of Cameroon, n.d. [1978?] 15 p.

7.1663. —— *The Bahá'í Faith.* Victoria: National Spiritual Assembly of the Bahá'ís of Cameroon, 1980. 7 p.

7.1664. —— *Declaration of Loyalty to Government.* n.p. [Victoria]: National Spiritual Assembly of the Bahá'ís of Cameroon Republic, n.d. [1968?] 5 p.

7.1665. —— *Guide Lines for Organizing and Arranging a Baha'i Book Exhibition.* n.p. [Victoria]: National Spiritual Assembly of the Bahá'ís of Cameroon, n.d. [1979] 4 p.

7.1666. —— *How to Organize a Public Meeting.* n.p. [Victoria]: National Spiritual Assembly of the Bahá'ís of Cameroon, n.d. [1979] 4 p.

7.1667. —— *How to Organize a Week-End Conference.* n.p. [Victoria]: National Spiritual Assembly of the Bahá'ís of Cameroon, n.d. [1979] 2 p.

7.1668. —— *A Manual for the Election of Local Spiritual Assemblies.* n.p. [Victoria]: National Spiritual Assembly of the Bahá'ís of Cameroon, n.d. [1978?] 6 p.

7.1669. —— *Unit Convention and National Convention.* n.p. [Victoria]: National Spiritual Assembly of the Bahá'ís of Cameroon, n.d. [1979] 10 p.

7.1670. National Spiritual Assembly of the Bahá'ís of Cameroon. Consolidation Committee. *The Local Spiritual Assembly.* Victoria: National Spiritual Assembly of the Bahá'ís of Cameroon, n.d. [1979] 31 p.

7.1671. National Spiritual Assembly of the Bahá'ís of Cameroon. National Teaching Committee. *Officers of the Local Spiritual Assembly.* n.p. [Victoria]: National Teaching Committee, n.d. [1981] 6 p.

7.1672. —— *Setting Individual Teaching Goals: A Few Guide Lines.* Victoria: National Teaching Committee, 1981. 7 p.

7.1673. National Spiritual Assembly of the Bahá'ís of Canada. *Assembly Resource Compilation.* n.p. [Thornhill, Ont.: National Spiritual Assembly of the Bahá'ís of Canada], 1979. 71 p.

7.1674. —— *Bahá'í Assemblies: Incorporation and By-Laws (Canada).* Thornhill, Ont.: National Spiritual Assembly of the Bahá'ís of Canada: Bahá'í Canada Publications, 1978. 35 p.

7.1675. —— *By-Laws of the National Spiritual Assembly and the Act to Incorporate the National Spiritual Assembly of the Bahá'ís of Canada, and of a Local Spiritual Assembly.* Toronto, Ont.: [National Spiritual Assembly of the Bahá'ís of Canada], 1950. 22 p.

7.1676. —— *Canada and the Five Year Plan: Domestic Goals = Le Canada et le Plan de Cinq Ans: Buts Domestiques.* Thornhill, Ont.: National Spiritual Assembly of the Bahá'ís of Canada, 1975. 54 p.

7.1677. —— *The Future of Canada: A Bahá'í Perspective.* A brief presented to the Royal Commission on the Economic Union and Development Prospects of Canada. Thornhill, Ont.: Bahá'í Canada Publications, 1984. 32 p.

7.1678. —— *Guidelines for Proclamation-Teaching Projects in Canada.* n.p. [Thornhill, Ont.: National Spiritual Assembly of the Bahá'ís of Canada], n.d. [1974] 7 p.

7.1679. —— *A Message to the Indians.* Toronto, Ont.: Bahá'í Publishing Committee, n.d. [195–?] [6] p.

7.1680. —— *A Presentation by the Canadian Baha'i Community to the Participating Organizations of the Canadian Conference on Human Rights, Ottawa, December 1–3, 1968.* Toronto, Ont.: National Spiritual Assembly of the Bahá'ís of Canada, 1968. 3, 32 leaves.

7.1681. —— *Secretary's Handbook.* n.p. [Thornhill, Ont.]: National Spiritual Assembly of the Bahá'ís of Canada, 1974. 15 p.; 1978. 17 p.

7.1682. —— *Selections from the Assembly Resource Kit.* Thornhill, Ont.: National Teaching Committee, n.d. [ca. 1979] 21 p.

7.1683. —— *The Seven Year Plan and Canada's Goals for Phase I and II.* n.p. [Thornhill, Ont.: Bahá'í Canada Publications], n.d. [1981?] 40 p.

7.1684. —— *The Seven Year Plan and Canada's Goals for the First Two Years.* Thornhill, Ont.: Bahá'í Canada, 1979. 24 p.

7.1685. —— *Threshold of Oneness: The Bahá'í Faith and French-English Relations in Canada.* Thornhill, Ont.: National Spiritual Assembly of the Bahá'ís of Canada, 1978. 10, 9 p.

7.1686. —— *idem.* 2nd ed. Thornhill, Ont.: National Spiritual Assembly of the Bahá'ís of Canada, 1981. 10, 9 p.

7.1687. National Spiritual Assembly of the Bahá'ís of Canada. National Indian Reserves Teaching Committee. Indians of Canada, Looking to the Future: A Guide for Bahá'ís in Contact with Indians. n.p.: National Indian Reserves Teaching Committee, 1964. 20 p.

7.1688. National Spiritual Assembly of the Bahá'ís of Canada. National Pioneer Committee. *Career/Study Choices for International Service.* n.p. [Thornhill, Ont.]: National Pioneer Committee of the Bahá'ís of Canada, Mar. 1985. 26 p.

7.1689. —— *Finding Work Overseas: An Introduction to International Employment for Professionals and Technicians.* n.p. [Thornhill, Ont.]: National Pioneer Committee, 1981. [40] p.

7.1690. —— *idem.* 2nd ed. Thornhill, Ont.: National Pioneer Committee of Canada, Jan. 1984. 36 p.
  Two variants, one with blue light paper covers, the other with white stiff paper covers.

7.1691. National Spiritual Assembly of the Bahá'ís of Canada. National Teaching Committee. *The Final Year.* Thornhill, Ont.: National Teaching Committee, 1978. [40] p.

7.1692. —— *A Series of Three Lessons on the*

Baha'i Faith. Thornhill, Ont.: National Teaching Committee, n.d. [1983] Lesson 1, 6 p.; Lesson 2, 4 p.; Lesson 3, 5 p.

7.1693. National Spiritual Assembly of the Bahá'ís of Canada. National Treasury. *Bahá'í Fund Education Resource Book*. Thornhill, Ont.: National Spiritual Assembly of the Bahá'ís of Canada, 1979. 1 vol. (loose-leaf).

7.1694. —— *The Bahá'í Fund in the Five Year Plan, 1974–1978: A Progress Report*. n.p. [Thornhill, Ont.]: National Treasury, 1978. 12 p.

7.1695. —— *The Fund: Local, National, Continental, International*. n.p. [Thornhill: National Treasury], n.d. [1977] [8] p.

7.1696. —— *Treasurer's Handbook*. Thornhill, Ont.: National Treasury, 1974.

7.1697. National Spiritual Assembly of the Bahá'ís of Canada. Saskatchewan Bahá'í Schools Committee. *Weekend Learning Event*. Saskatoon, Sask.: Saskatchewan Bahá'í Schools Committee, 1985. [6] p.

7.1698. National Spiritual Assembly of the Bahá'ís of the Caroline Islands. *Electing Delegates to Your National Convention*. Ponape: National Spiritual Assembly of the Bahá'ís of the Caroline Islands, n.d. [1980?] 14 leaves. English and Palauan.

7.1699. National Spiritual Assembly of the Bahá'ís of Central and East Africa. *Intercontinental Conference for Africa, Kampala, Uganda, 22nd–28th January, 1958*. n.p. [Kampala, Uganda]: National Spiritual Assembly of the Bahá'ís of Central and East Africa, 1958. 19 p.

7.1699a. National Spiritual Assembly of the Bahá'ís of Ceylon. *Memorandum and Articles of Association of the Spiritual Assembly of the Baha'is of Ceylon*. n.p. [Colombo]: Spiritual Assembly of the Baha'is of Ceylon, n.d. [196–?] 4, 6 p.

7.1700. —— *Three Months Teaching Plan*. Colombo: National Spiritual Assembly of the Bahá'ís of Ceylon, 1972. 25 p.

7.1701. National Spiritual Assembly of the Bahá'ís of Colombia. *Pioneering Oportunities [sic] for Students in South America: Information About South American Universities and Scholarships*. n.p. [Bogotá?]: National Spiritual Assembly of the Bahá'ís of Colombia, n.d. [ca. 1970] 100 leaves.

7.1702. National Spiritual Assembly of the Bahá'ís of Denmark. *Pioneering in Denmark*. n.p. [Hellerup: National Spiritual Assembly of the Bahá'ís of Denmark], 1977. 5 leaves.

7.1703. —— *Pioneering in Greenland*. n.p.

[Hellerup: National Spiritual Assembly of the Bahá'ís of Denmark], n.d. [1977?] 10 leaves.

7.1704. National Spiritual Assembly of the Bahá'ís of Ethiopia. *50, Baha'i Faith in Ethiopia: A Time to Remember, 1933–1983*. Addis Ababa: National Spiritual Assembly of the Bahá'ís of Ethiopia, 1983. 16 leaves.

7.1705. National Spiritual Assembly of the Bahá'ís of the Fiji Islands. *The Bahá'í Faith*. Suva: National Spiritual Assembly of the Bahá'ís of the Fiji Islands, 1977. 12 leaves.

7.1706. —— *The Bahá'í Faith*. Suva: National Spiritual Assembly of the Bahá'ís of the Fiji Islands, n.d. [1985] 27, [12] p.

7.1707. —— *Welcome Into the Bahá'í World Community*. Suva: National Spiritual Assembly of the Bahá'ís of the Fiji Islands, n.d. [1974] 6 p.

7.1708. —— *Year of Victory: Teaching Plans of the National Spiritual Assembly of the Bahá'ís of the Fiji Islands*. Suva: National Spiritual Assembly of the Bahá'ís of the Fiji Islands, 1977. 25 p.

7.1709. National Spiritual Assembly of the Bahá'ís of the Fiji Islands. National Teaching Committee. *Guidelines for Pioneers and Travelling Teachers to the Fiji Islands*. Suva: Bahá'í Publishing Trust, 1982. 13 p.

7.1710. National Spiritual Assembly of the Bahá'ís of the Fiji Islands. Peace/Proclamation Committee. *Study Guide and Commentary: The Promise of World Peace*. Suva: Peace/Proclamation Committee under the guidance of the National Spiritual Assembly of the Bahá'ís of the Fiji Islands, 1985. 34 p.

7.1711. National Spiritual Assembly of the Bahá'ís of the Gilbert Islands and Tuvalu. *What Is a Baha'i!!: Basic Duties and Responsibilities of a Baha'i*. Tarawa: National Spiritual Assembly of the Bahá'ís of the Gilbert Islands and Tuvalu, 1978. 16 p.

7.1712. National Spiritual Assembly of the Bahá'ís of Guyana. *Calendar of Major Events, May 1984–May 1985*. Georgetown: National Spiritual Assembly of the Bahá'ís of Guyana, 1984. [2] p.

7.1713. National Spiritual Assembly of the Bahá'ís of the Hawaiian Islands. *Local Spiritual Assembly Administration: A Handbook for Deepening & Training*. Honolulu: National Spiritual Assembly of the Bahá'ís of the Hawaiian Islands, 1980. 58 p.

7.1714. —— *75th Anniversary Banquet of the Bahá'í Faith in Hawaii*. Honolulu: National Spiritual Assembly of the Bahá'ís of the Hawaiian Islands, 1976. [8] p.

7.1715. National Spiritual Assembly of the Bahá'ís of Hong Kong. *The Bahá'í Faith Reference File*. Hong Kong: National Spiritual Assembly of the Bahá'ís of Hong Kong, 1979. 28 p.

7.1716. —— *In Memory of the Bahá'í Martyrs in Iran, 135–139 B.E.: Hong Kong, 23 May 1982*. Hong Kong: National Spiritual Assembly of the Bahá'ís of Hong Kong, 1982. 7, [1] p.

7.1717. National Spiritual Assembly of the Bahá'ís of Iceland. *Information Bulletin: Update on the Persecutions of the Bahá'ís in Iran, March-June 1982*. Reykjavík: National Spiritual Assembly of the Bahá'ís of Iceland, 1982. 3 leaves.

7.1717a. National Spiritual Assembly of the Bahá'ís of India. *Declaration of Trust & By-laws adopted by the National Spiritual Assembly of the Bahá'ís of India. By-laws of a Local Spiritual Assembly*. New Delhi: National Baha'i Office, 1968 (Delhi: Everest Press). 29 p.

7.1718. —— *Nine Year Plan for the Bahá'ís of India, 1964–1973*. New Delhi: National Spiritual Assembly of the Bahá'ís of India, n.d. [1964?] 48 p.

7.1719. National Spiritual Assembly of the Bahá'ís of India. National Teaching Committee. *Assembly Development Programme*. New Delhi: National Teaching Committee, n.d. [1976?] xv, 148 p.

7.1720. —— *The Teaching Structure: Aims, Implementation and First Results*. New Delhi: National Teaching Committee, n.d. [1980] 9 leaves.

7.1721. National Spiritual Assembly of the Bahá'ís of India. National Youth Committee. *Baha'i Youth Guidelines*. n.p. [New Delhi]: National Baha'i Youth Committee of India, n.d. [1981] 5 leaves.

7.1722. —— *Bahá'í Youth Plans*. New Delhi: National Youth Committee, n.d. [1972?] 43 p.

7.1723. —— *idem*. New Delhi: National Youth Committee, 1974. 31 p.

7.1724. —— *Bahá'í Youth Plans Ending Ridvan 72*. Bombay: National Youth Committee of India, n.d. [1971?] 20 p.

7.1725. National Spiritual Assembly of the Bahá'ís of India and Burma. *Baha'i Directory India and Burma*. New Delhi: National Spiritual Assembly of the Bahá'ís of India and Burma. 1958–59. [8] p.

7.1726. —— *Declaration of Trust, Memorandum of Association and By-Laws of the National Spiri-tual Assembly of the Baha'is of India and Burma*. 2nd ed. Lahore: Pritam Singh, 1933. 16, 2 p.

7.1727. —— *idem*. 3rd ed. n.p.: Rustom Khos-rove, 1934–35 (Poona: P.M. Modi at the 'Israelite Press'). 18 p.

7.1728. National Spiritual Assembly of the Bahá'ís of India, Pakistan and Burma. *Annual Report*. New Delhi: National Spiritual Assembly of the Bahá'ís of India, Pakistan and Burma. 1949–50. 13 p.; 1951–52. 52 p.
Listed are only those annual reports known to have been published.

7.1729. —— *Declaration of Trust & By-Laws, By-Laws of a Local Spiritual Assembly*. New Delhi: National Baha'i Office, 1950. 22 p.

7.1730. National Spiritual Assembly of the Bahá'ís of Iran. *The Banning of Bahá'í Religious Institutions in Iran: An Open Letter*. n.p. [Wilmette, Ill.]: National Spiritual Assembly of the Bahá'ís of the United States, 1983. 8 p.

7.1731. —— *For the Crime of Belief: A Reprint of an Open Letter Sent to the Officials of the Islamic Revolutionary Government Following the Banning of the Baha'i Administration in Iran in 1983*. Auckland: National Spiritual Assembly of the Baha'is of New Zealand, 1984. [8] p.

7.1732. —— *An Open Letter from the National Spiritual Assembly of the Bahá'ís of Iran About the Banning of the Bahá'í Administration*. n.p. [Freetown: National Spiritual Assembly of the Bahá'ís of Sierra Leone], n.d. [1983] 13 p.

7.1733. —— *Voice of a Persecuted People: An Open Letter from the National Spiritual Assembly of the Bahá'ís of Iran*. London: National Spiritual Assembly of the Bahá'ís of the United Kingdom, n.d. [1984] 12 p.

7.1734. National Spiritual Assembly of the Bahá'ís of the Republic of Ireland. *Annual Report*. Dublin: National Spiritual Assembly of the Bahá'ís of the Republic of Ireland. 1976–77. [4] p.; 1979–80. 15 p.; 1980–81. 14 p.; 1982–83. 15 p.; 1983–84. 20 p.; 1984–85. 17 p.

7.1735. —— *The Bahá'í Faith*. Dublin: National Spiritual Assembly of the Bahá'ís of the Republic of Ireland, n.d. [1981] [2] p. [with 16 fold out pages]

7.1736. —— *'Examine Our Cause'*. Dublin: National Spiritual Assembly of the Bahá'ís of the Republic of Ireland, n.d. [1984] 12 p.

7.1737. —— *Guidance to Local Spiritual Assemblies for International Peace Year*. n.p. [Dublin: National Spiritual Assembly of the Bahá'ís of the Republic of Ireland], n.d. [1985] 10 p.

7.1737a. —— *Memorandum and Articles of Asso-*

ciation of the National Spiritual Assembly of the Bahá'ís of the Republic of Ireland: Incorporated the 30th Day of January 1973. Dublin: Herman Good & Co., 1973. 17 p. At head of title: Companies Act 1963 – An unlimited company not having a share capital.

7.1737b. —— *Memorandum and Articles of Association of the National Spiritual Assembly of the Bahá'ís of the Republic of Ireland: Incorporated the 30th Day of January, 1973 (as adopted by the special resolution dated the 18th day of July 1981).* n.p. [Dublin]: Registrar of Companies, 1981. 20 p. At head of title: Companies Acts, 1963 to 1977 – an unlimited company not having a share capital.

7.1738. —— *A Teaching Campaign for the Individual.* Dublin: National Spiritual Assembly of the Bahá'ís of the Republic of Ireland, 1980. 4 p.

7.1739. National Spiritual Assembly of the Bahá'ís of Jamaica. *A Statement: The Bahá'í Faith.* Kingston: National Spiritual Assembly of the Bahá'ís of Jamaica, n.d. [1980] 17 p.

7.1740. —— *Twenty-Fifth Anniversary of the Establishment of the National Spiritual Assembly of the Bahá'ís of Jamaica, 1961–1985.* n.p. [Kingston: National Spiritual Assembly of the Bahá'ís of Jamaica], n.d. [1985] 27 p.

7.1741. National Spiritual Assembly of the Bahá'ís of Kenya. *Death and Burial.* Nairobi: Baha'i Publishing Agency, n.d. [1985] 21 p.

7.1742. National Spiritual Assembly of the Bahá'ís of Kenya. National Education Committee. *Bahá'í Classes for Women.* n.p. [Nairobi]: National Spiritual Assembly of the Bahá'ís of Kenya, 1975. 27 p.

7.1743. National Spiritual Assembly of the Bahá'ís of Kenya. National Teaching Committee. *Regional Teaching Committee: A Suggested Guideline.* Nairobi: National Teaching Committee, n.d. [1973?] 18 p.

7.1744. National Spiritual Assembly of the Bahá'ís of Kenya. National Youth Committee. *Conference Workshop-Materials: Dating, Marriage & Family Life.* n.p. [Nairobi]: National Baha'i Youth Committee, n.d. [1984] 5 p.

7.1745. —— *Conference Workshop Materials: Planning Personal Service.* n.p. [Nairobi]: National Baha'i Youth Committee, n.d. [1984] 4 p.

7.1746. —— *Four Month Youth Programme (December 1983–April 1984) Presented at Nakuru Youth Conference, December 11th 1983.* Nairobi: National Baha'i Youth Committee of the Baha'is of Kenya, 1984. 2 leaves.

7.1746a. National Spiritual Assembly of the Bahá'ís of the Leeward Islands. *Memorandum and Articles of Association of the National Spiritual Assembly of the Baha'is of the Leeward Islands.* St John's, Antigua: Time H. Kendall, Barrister & Solicitor, 1983. 14 leaves. At head of title: Antigua and Barbuda, The Companies Act, Cap. 358 – an unlimited company without a share capital.

7.1747. National Spiritual Assembly of the Bahá'ís of Liberia. *Views of the National Spiritual Assembly of Liberia on the Subjects Chosen for General Consultation in Five Plenary Sessions of the 1983 International Convention in Haifa-Israel.* Monrovia: National Spiritual Assembly of Liberia, 1983 (Monrovia: Baha'i Printery). [6] leaves.

7.1748. National Spiritual Assembly of the Bahá'ís of Liberia & Guinea. *The Plight of the Baha'i Faith in Iran: A Religious Community Under Threat of Extermination.* Monrovia: National Spiritual Assembly of the Bahá'ís of Liberia & Guinea, n.d. [1981] 14 p.

7.1749. National Spiritual Assembly of the Bahá'ís of Luxemburg. *Vers la Victoire = Toward Victory: Teaching Plan of the National Spiritual Assembly of the Bahá'ís of Luxembourg Grand-Duchy.* Luxembourg: National Spiritual Assembly of the Bahá'ís of Luxembourg Grand-Duchy, 1977. 7 leaves. Text in English.

7.1750. National Spiritual Assembly of the Bahá'ís of Malawi. *Committee Terms of Reference.* Limbe: National Spiritual Assembly of the Bahá'ís of Malawi, 1979. [21] p.

7.1751. —— *Guidance for Local Spiritual Assemblies: A Guide to Bahá'í Administration.* Limbe: National Spiritual Assembly of the Bahá'ís of Malawi, 1974. 25 p.

7.1752. National Spiritual Assembly of the Bahá'ís of Malawi. Women and Children Committee. *Bahá'í Lessons for Children.* n.p. [Limbe]: Women and Children Committee, 1978. [13] leaves.

7.1753. National Spiritual Assembly of the Bahá'ís of Malaysia. *Annual Report.* Kuala Lumpur: Spiritual Assembly of the Bahá'ís of Malaysia. 132, 1975–76. 109 p.; 134, 1977–78. 149 p.; 136, 1979–80. 6, 51, 57, 22 p., [6] leaves; 138, 1981–82. 2, 16, 5, 18, 14, 7, 9, 10, 15, 5, 12 p., [2] leaves; 140, 1983–84. 3, 13, 5, 6, 11, 3, 11, 6, 9 p.

7.1754. —— *The Bahá'í Faith.* n.p. [Kuala Lumpur]: National Spiritual Assembly of the Bahá'ís of Malaysia, n.d. [1979]. [2] p. [with several small flip-out pages]

7.1755. —— *5 Month Plan, Nov. 21 1976 to Apr. 21 1977.* [Kuala Lumpur]: Spiritual Assembly of Malaysia, 1976. [4] p.

7.1756. —— *Memorandum and Articles of Association of the Spiritual Assembly of the Bahá'ís of Malaysia.* n.p. [Kuala Lumpur: National Spiritual Assembly of the Bahá'ís of Malaysia], 1974 (Kuala Lumpur: Premier Press Sdn. Bhd.). 8 p.

7.1757. —— *Proclamation Plans, 1967–1973; Based on Dr R. Muhajer's Pattern for Teaching & Proclamation, 12th July, 1967.* n.p. [Kuala Lumpur]: N.S.A. Malaysia, 1967. 19 leaves.

7.1758. —— *2nd Year, 7 Year Plan.* Kuala Lumpur: Spiritual Assembly of the Baha'is of Malaysia, 1980. [16] p.

7.1759. —— *7 Year Plan Final Phase: Blue-Print for Individual and Community Life.* n.p. [Kuala Lumpur: National Spiritual Assembly of the Bahá'ís of Malaysia], 1984. 40 p.

7.1760. —— *7 Year Plan of the Universal House of Justice for Malaysia: 2nd Phase, April 1981–April 1983* [sic]. Kuala Lumpur: Spiritual Assembly of the Baha'is of Malaysia, 1981. 24 leaves.

7.1761. —— *Update Report, Goals of the Second Phase of the Seven Year Plan.* n.p. [Kuala Lumpur]: Spiritual Assembly of the Bahá'ís of Malaysia, Oct. 1982. 25 leaves.

7.1762. National Spiritual Assembly of the Bahá'ís of Malaysia. Child Education Committee. *Let's Have a Children's Class, Part 1.* n.p. [Kuala Lumpur, Malaysia: Child Education Committee], n.d. [198–] [4] leaves.

7.1763. —— *Let's Have a Children's Class, Part 2.* n.p. [Kuala Lumpur: Child Education Committee], n.d. [198–] [31] leaves.

7.1764. National Spiritual Assembly of the Bahá'ís of Malaysia. Child Education Committee of East Malaysia. *Lesson Books for Age 4 & Grade 1.* Kuching: Child Education Committee of East Malaysia, n.d. [1981] [82] p.

7.1765. —— *Lesson Book for Age 7 & Grade 4.* Kuching: Child Education Committee of East Malaysia, n.d. [1981] [78] p.

7.1766. —— *Lesson Book for Age 10 & Grade 7.* Kuching: Child Education Committee of East Malaysia, n.d. [1981] [112] p.

7.1767. National Spiritual Assembly of the Bahá'ís of Malaysia. Community Development Committee. *5 Year Global Plan.* n.p. [Kuala Lumpur]: National Community Development Committee of the National Spiritual Assembly of the Baha'is of Malaysia, 1974. 24 p.

7.1768. National Spiritual Assembly of the Bahá'ís of Malaysia. National Youth Committee of Peninsular Malaysia. *Youth Mobile Plan, B.E. 136.* Kuala Lumpur: National Bahai Youth Committee of Peninsular Malaysia, 1979. 17 p.

7.1769. National Spiritual Assembly of the Bahá'ís of Malaysia. National Coordinating Unit. *The New Age: Do You Know In What Day You Are Living? A Deepening Course.* Kuala Lumpur: National Spiritual Assembly of the Bahá'ís of Malaysia, n.d. [196–?] 27 p.

7.1770. National Spiritual Assembly of the Bahá'ís of Malaysia. National Youth Council. *The Council's Gift: Our Humble Token of Love to All the Friends Attending the First Regional Youth Convention for the Central Zone.* n.p. [Kuala Lumpur]: National Youth Council, 1970. 15 p.

7.1771. —— *Souvenir Presented by the National Baha'i Youth Council of Malaysia on the Occasion of the Oceanic Conference Held in Singapore, 1–3 January L971* [sic]. Singapore: National Baha'i Youth Council of Malaysia, 1971. [110] p.

7.1772. National Spiritual Assembly of the Bahá'ís of Malaysia. Secretariat. *Secretariat Report.* [Kuala Lumpur]: Department of the Secretariat, Spiritual Assembly of the Baha'is of Malaysia. BE 137, month of July & August. [11] leaves; BE 139, November & December 1982. [14] leaves; January–February 1983 BE 139. [28] p.

7.1773. National Spiritual Assembly of the Bahá'ís of Mauritius. *Baha'i.* Port Louis: National Spiritual Assembly of the Baha'is of Mauritius, n.d. [1985] [1], 12, [3] p.

7.1774. National Spiritual Assembly of the Bahá'ís of New Hebrides. *Goals for 1977–78 (B.E. 134) = Olgeta Gol Long 1977–78 (Yia Namba 134 Long Baha'i Kalenda) = Les Buts pour l'Année 1977–78 (Année 134 de l'ère Bahá'íe).* n.p. [Port Vila]: National Spiritual Assembly of the Baha'is of New Hebrides, 1977. [16] p. English, Bislama and French text.

7.1775. —— *Handbook for Local Spiritual Assemblies = Tok Tok Blong Kadedem ol Lokal Spiritul Assembli = Manuel de Guidance pour les Assemblées Spirituelles Locales.* n.p. [Port Vila]: National Spiritual Assembly of the Bahá'ís of New Hebrides, 1978. 61 p.

7.1776. —— *The New Hebrides: Information for Prospective Bahá'í Pioneers and Travel-Teachers.* rev. ed. n.p. [Port Vila]: National Spiritual Assembly of the Bahá'ís of New Hebrides, 1977. 5 p.

7.1777. National Spiritual Assembly of the Bahá'ís of New Zealand. *Guidelines for Local*

Spiritual Assemblies. n.p. [Auckland]: National Spiritual Assembly of the Bahá'ís of New Zealand, 1981. vii, 142 p.

7.1778. —— *Miss Shahin Delvand Hanged in Shiraz, Iran, 18 June 1983: Crime – Being a Bahá'í.* n.p. [Auckland]: National Spiritual Assembly of the Bahá'ís of New Zealand, n.d. [1983] [4] p.

7.1779. —— *Role and Responsibilities of Local Spiritual Assemblies Assisting New Immigrants Sponsored by the National Spiritual Assembly of the Baha''is of New Zealand.* Auckland: National Spiritual Assembly of the Baha''is of New Zealand, 1985. 16 leaves.

7.1780. —— *A Study Guide to the Letter of the Universal House of Justice to the Bahá'ís of the World, 20 October, 1983.* Auckland: National Spiritual Assembly of the Bahá'ís of New Zealand, 1984. 3 leaves.

7.1781. National Spiritual Assembly of the Bahá'ís of New Zealand. Community Development Committee. [*National Deepening Programme, Phase I*]: *'What Is Baha'u'llah's Purpose for the Human Race?'* n.p. [Auckland, N.Z.: Community Development Committee], n.d. [1980?] 12 p. (Study Guide; no.1).

7.1782. —— *National Deepening Programme, Phase II: For What Ends Did Bahá'u'lláh Submit to the Appalling Cruelties and Indignities Heaped Upon Him?* Auckland, N.Z.: Community Development Committee, 1981. 18 p.

7.1783. —— *[National Deepening Programme, Phase III]: What Does He Mean by a New Race of Men?* n.p. [Auckland, N.Z.: Community Development Committee], n.d. [1982?] 16 p.

7.1784. —— *National Deepening Programme, Phase IV, Part One: 'The Use of the Daily Obligatory Prayer'.* n.p. [Auckland, N.Z.]: Bahá'í Community Development Committee, 1983. ii, 15 p.

7.1785. —— *National Deepening Programme, Phase IV, Part Two: 'The Observance of the Fast'.* n.p. [Auckland, N.Z.]: Bahá'í Community Development Committee, 1983. ii, 14 p.

7.1786. —— *National Deepening Programme, Phase IV Part Three: 'The Reading of the Divine Verses Every Evening and Morning, Especially at Dawn'.* n.p. [Auckland, N.Z.]: Baha'i Community Development Committee, 1984. iv, 14 p.

7.1787. National Spiritual Assembly of the Bahá'ís of New Zealand. National Child Education Committee. *Curriculum for Baha'i Children's Classes.* n.p. [Auckland, N.Z.]: National Child Education Committee, 1984 (Dunedin: Progress Print). 23 p.

7.1788. —— *Manual for the Bahá'í Education of Children.* n.p. [Auckland]: National Spiritual Assembly of the Bahá'ís of New Zealand, 1981 (Dunedin: Progress Print). ii, 40 p.

7.1789. National Spiritual Assembly of the Bahá'ís of Nigeria. *The Bahá'í Faith.* Lagos: National Spiritual Assembly of the Bahá'ís of Nigeria, 1980. 19 p.

7.1790. —— *The Bahá'í Faith.* Lagos: National Spiritual Assembly of the Bahá'ís of Nigeria, 1984. 20 p.

7.1791. National Spiritual Assembly of the Bahá'ís of Norway. National Pioneer Committee. *Pioneering to Norway.* Oslo, Norway: National Pioneer Committee, 1982. 23 p.

7.1792. National Spiritual Assembly of the Bahá'ís of Norway. National Teaching Committee. *Pioneering to Norway.* Oslo, Norway: National Teaching Committee, 1979. 11 p.

7.1792a. National Spiritual Assembly of the Bahá'ís of Pakistan. *Souvenir: A Brief History of the Baha'i Faith in Pakistan.* Karachi: National Spiritual Assembly of the Bahá'ís of Pakistan, 1957 (Karachi: Process Pakistan). 48 p. At head of title: *First National Spiritual Assembly of the Bahá'ís of Pakistan.*

7.1793. National Spiritual Assembly of the Bahá'ís of Papua New Guinea. *Annual Report.* Lae: Spiritual Assembly of the Bahá'ís of Papua New Guinea. 141, 1984–85. [44] p.

7.1794. —— *The Bahá'í Faith.* Lae: National Spiritual Assembly of the Bahá'ís of Papua New Guinea, n.d. [1978?] 16 p.

7.1795. —— *The Bahá'í Faith.* Lae: Spiritual Assembly of the Bahá'ís of Papua New Guinea, n.d. [1985] 22 p.

7.1796. —— *Teaching Committees.* n.p. [Lae]: Spiritual Assembly of the Bahá'ís of Papua New Guinea, n.d. [1985] 30 p.

7.1797. National Spiritual Assembly of the Bahá'ís of the Philippines. *The Bahá'í Faith Reference File.* Manila: National Spiritual Assembly of the Bahá'ís of the Philippines, 1977. [22] p.

7.1798. —— *The Baha'i Marriage, the Baha'i Children and Birth Certificate, the Baha'i Burial Service: A Guide for the Use of Local Spiritual Assemblies.* Manila: National Spiritual Assembly of the Bahá'ís of the Philippines, 1984. 28 p.

7.1799. —— *Philippine One Year Teaching Plan Goals, Ridvan 1965 (Nov.-Apr.).* n.p. [Manila]: National Spiritual Assembly, 1965. [4] p.

7.1800. National Spiritual Assembly of the

Bahá'ís of Puerto Rico. Teaching Committee. *Goals for the Third Year of the Five Year Plan = Metas para el Tercer Año del Plan de Cinco Años*. San Juan, P.R.: Teaching Committee, n.d. [1976] [56] p.

7.1801. National Spiritual Assembly of the Bahá'ís of Rhodesia. *Building the Baha'i Community*. n.p. [Salisbury]: National Spiritual Assembly of the Bahá'ís of Rhodesia, 1970. 5 p.

7.1802. National Spiritual Assembly of the Bahá'ís of Rhodesia. National Women's Committee. *Baha'i Lessons for Women's Clubs*. n.p. [Salisbury, Rhodesia]: National Women's Committee, 1976. 22 p.

7.1803. National Spiritual Assembly of the Bahá'ís of St Lucia. *The Duties and Responsibilities of Delegates to the National Baha'i Convention*. n.p. [Castries]: National Spiritual Assembly of the Baha'is of St Lucia, n.d. [1985] [8] p.

7.1804. National Spiritual Assembly of the Bahá'ís of Samoa. *The Bahá'í Faith*. Apia: National Spiritual Assembly of the Bahá'ís of Samoa, 1977. 13 leaves.

7.1805. —— *Bahá'í House of Worship, Guide's Manual*. n.p. [Apia, Western Samoa]: National Spiritual Assembly of the Bahá'ís of Samoa, n.d. [1985] 15 p.

7.1806. —— *Falelauasiga Bahá'í = Bahá'í Burial*. Apia: National Spiritual Assembly of the Bahá'ís of Samoa, 1977. 12 p. English and Samoan text.

7.1807. —— *Welcome Into the Bahá'í World Community*. Apia: National Spiritual Assembly of the Bahá'ís of Samoa, n.d. [197–] 6 p.

7.1808. National Spiritual Assembly of the Bahá'ís of Sierra Leone. Children's Education Committee. *Baha'i Children's Classes: Lesson Plans, Level Two*. Freetown: The Children's Education Committee, a committee of the National Spiritual Assembly of the Baha'is of Sierra Leone, 1985. 36 p.

7.1809. National Spiritual Assembly of the Bahá'ís of Sierra Leone. National Childrens' Committee. *The Baha'i Children's Booklet*. n.p. [Freetown, Sierra Leone]: National Children's Committee, 1982. 33 p.

7.1810. National Spiritual Assembly of the Bahá'ís of Singapore. *Annual Report*. Singapore: Spiritual Assembly of the Bahá'ís of Singapore. 132–3, 1975–76. 33 p.; 133, 1976–77. 53 p.; 134, 1977–78. 46 p.; 135, 1978–79. 46 p.

7.1810a. —— *Memorandum and Articles of Association of the Spiritual Assembly of the Baha'is of Singapore: Incorporated on the 4th Day of Oct., 1976*. Singapore: Spiritual Assembly of the Baha'is of Singapore, 1976. 13 p. At head of title: The Companies Act, Cap.185, Republic of Singapore – Company limited by guarantee.

7.1811. —— *Victory Hand-book, 2nd Phase, 7 Year Plan, BE 138–140*. Singapore: National Spiritual Assembly of the Bahá'ís of Singapore, 1981. 36 p.

7.1812. National Spiritual Assembly of the Bahá'ís of Singapore. National Youth Committee. *Ninety-Day Plan, 27th May–24th August: The Baha'i Youth, Singapore*. Singapore: The Baha'i Youth, n.d. [1984] [4] p.

7.1813. National Spiritual Assembly of the Bahá'ís of South and West Africa. *The Bahá'í Faith and Political Parties*. Johannesburg: National Spiritual Assembly of the Bahá'ís of South and West Africa, 1983. 1 p. card.

7.1814. —— *Guidance for Local Spiritual Assemblies: A Guide to Bahá'í Administration*. Johannesburg: National Spiritual Assembly of the Bahá'ís of South and West Africa, 1975. 24 p.

7.1815. —— *Shu'á'u'lláh 'Alá'í*. n.p. [Johannesburg]: National Spiritual Assembly of the Bahá'ís of South and West Africa, 1984. [2] p.

7.1816. —— *Welcome Into the Bahá'í World Community*. n.p. [Johannesburg]: National Spiritual Assembly of the Bahá'ís of South and West Africa, n.d. [196–?], n.d. [1979] 6 p.

7.1816a. —— *Welcome Into the Bahá'í World Community*. Windhoek: National Spiritual Assembly of the Bahá'ís of SWA/Namibia, n.d. [1985] [6] p.

7.1817. National Spiritual Assembly of the Bahá'ís of South and West Africa. Creative Planning Committee. *Institute Outline for the Covenant and Administration*. Johannesburg: Creative Planning Committee of the National Assembly of South and West Africa, n.d. [196–?] 31 leaves.

7.1818. National Spiritual Assembly of the Bahá'ís of South Central Africa. *About Being a Bahá'í: A Concentrated Study Course*. n.p. [Salisbury, Rhodesia]: National Spiritual Assembly of the Bahá'ís of South Central Africa, 1964. 43 leaves.

7.1819. National Spiritual Assembly of the Bahá'ís of Sri Lanka. *Final Year of the Second Phase of the Seven Year Plan: Baha'i Year 140. Ridvan 1983–Ridvan 1984*. Colombo: National Spiritual Assembly of the Baha'i Faith in Sri Lanka, 1983. 16 p.

7.1820. National Spiritual Assembly of the

Bahá'ís of Swaziland, Lesotho & Mozambique. *On Becoming a Bahá'í*. n.p. [Mbabane]: National Spiritual Assembly of the Bahá'ís of Swaziland, Lesotho & Mozambique, 1970. 9 p. Based on U.S. pamphlet of same name.
See 7.1866.

7.1821. National Spiritual Assembly of the Bahá'ís of Tonga. *The Bahá'í Faith*. Nuku'alofa: National Spiritual Assembly of the Bahá'ís of Tonga, 1979. 18 leaves.

7.1822. —— *Victory Plan of the National Spiritual Assembly of the Bahá'ís of Tonga*. n.p. [Nuku'alofa]: National Spiritual Assembly of the Bahá'ís of Tonga, 1977. 13 leaves.

7.1823. National Spiritual Assembly of the Bahá'ís of Tonga and the Cook Islands. *Administrative Handbook for Local Spiritual Assemblies*. Nuku'alofa: National Spiritual Assembly of the Bahá'ís of Tonga and the Cook Islands, 1974. 68 p.

7.1824. —— *Guidance for Bahá'í Visitors, Traveling Teachers, and Pioneers to Tonga, Niue Island, Cook Islands*. n.p. [Nuku'alofa]: National Spiritual Assembly of the Bahá'ís of Tonga and the Cook Islands, 1975. 19 p.

7.1825. National Spiritual Assembly of the Bahá'ís of Transkei. *Some Guidelines for the Chairman, Secretary and Treasurer*. n.p. [Umtata]: National Spiritual Assembly of the Bahá'ís of Transkei, n.d. [1980] 9 p.

7.1826. National Spiritual Assembly of the Bahá'ís of Trinidad and Tobago. *Hand of the Cause of God Shu'a'u'llah 'Ala'i*. Port of Spain: National Spiritual Assembly of the Bahá'ís of Trinidad and Tobago, n.d. [1984] 1 p.

7.1827. National Spiritual Assembly of the Bahá'ís of Uganda. *The Baha'i Faith in Uganda, 1951–1976*. Kampala, Uganda: Bahá'í Publishing Trust, 1976. 38 p.

7.1828. National Spiritual Assembly of the Bahá'ís of the United Kingdom. *Annual Report*. 130, 1973–74. 12 p.; 131, 1974–75. 15 p.; 132, 1975–76. 15 p.; 133, 1976–77. 26 p.; 134, 1977–78. 33 p.; 135, 1978–79. 33 p.; 136, 1979–80. 43 p.; 140, 1982–83. 43 p.; 141, 1983–84. 36 p.
See also 7.1653.

7.1829. —— *[Area Goals for the First Year of the Second Phase of the Seven Year Plan]* London: National Spiritual Assembly of the Bahá'ís of the United Kingdom, 1981. [48] p.

7.1830. —— *Bahá'í*. London: National Spiritual Assembly of the Bahá'ís of the United Kingdom, 1979. 22 p.

7.1831. —— *Beyond Disarmament*. London:

National Spiritual Assembly of the Bahá'ís of the United Kingdom, Apr. 1983 (Bangor [Wales]: Copycat). 22 p.

7.1832. —— *Goals, Current Situation*. n.p. [London: National Spiritual Assembly of the Bahá'ís of the United Kingdom], n.d. [1982] [48] p.

7.1833. —— *Irán, Persecution of the Bahá'í Faith*. London: National Spiritual Assembly of the Bahá'ís of the United Kingdom, 1980. [27] leaves.

7.1834. —— *idem*. rev. London: National Spiritual Assembly of the Bahá'ís of the United Kingdom, 1980. [31] leaves.

7.1835. —— *National Directory*. London: National Spiritual Assembly of the Bahá'ís of the United Kingdom. July 1981. [16] p.; January 1982. [16] p.; June 1982. [18] p.

7.1836. —— *New Shock for Bahá'ís As House of Commons Considers Issue 'Matter of Deep Concern'*. London: National Spiritual Assembly of the Bahá'ís of the United Kingdom, 1985. 2 leaves.

7.1837. —— *Notes for Guidance for Local Spiritual Assemblies*. London: National Spiritual Assembly of the Bahá'ís of the United Kingdom, 1981. 118 p.

7.1838. —— *The Opening Phase of the Seven Year Plan*. London: National Spiritual Assembly of the Bahá'ís of the United Kingdom, 1979. 81 p.

7.1839. —— *Programme for Victory*. n.p. [London: National Spiritual Assembly of the Bahá'ís of the United Kingdom], 1976. 20 p.

7.1840. —— *Teaching and Consolidation Manual*. 2nd rev. ed. London: Bahá'í Publishing Trust, 1976. 42 p.

7.1841. —— *Voice of Protest: An Open Letter to the Iranian Embassy*. London: National Spiritual Assembly of the Bahá'ís of the United Kingdom, n.d. [1984] 12 p.

7.1842. National Spiritual Assembly of the Bahá'ís of the United Kingdom. National Consolidation Committee. *Books for Children*. n.p. [London]: National Consolidation Committee, n.d. [1982] 16 p.

7.1843. National Spiritual Assembly of the Bahá'ís of the United Kingdom. National Proclamation Committee. *Proclamation Handbook*. n.p. [London]: National Proclamation Committee, n.d. [1984] 1 v. (looseleaf).

7.1844. National Spiritual Assembly of the Bahá'ís of the United Kingdom. National Teaching Committee. Travel Teaching Department. *Arise in His Name: A Guide for Travel Teachers*. n.p. [London]: Travel Teaching Department of the National Teaching Committee of the National Spiritual Assembly of the Bahá'ís of the United Kingdom, n.d. [197–?] 10 [i.e. 12] p.

7.1845. National Spiritual Assembly of the Bahá'ís of the United Kingdom. National Youth Committee. *Bahá'í Youth and the 2nd Phase*. n.p. [London]: National Youth Committee, July 1981. 27 p.

7.1846. National Spiritual Assembly of the Bahá'ís of the United States. *Bahá'í Annual Reports*. Wilmette, Ill.: National Spiritual Assembly of the Bahá'ís of the United States. 1952–53. 29 p.; 1953–54. 39 p.; 1954–55. 44 p.; 1955–56. 33 p.; 1956–57. 36 p.; 1957–58. 31 p.; 1958–59. 30 p.; 1959–60. 36 p.; 1960–61. 40 p.; 1961–62. 32 p..; 1962–63. 29 p. 1963–64. 17 p.; 1964–65. p.; 1965–66. 26 p.; 1966–67. 31 p.; 1967–68. 29 p.

7.1847. —— *The Bahá'í Community: A Summary of Its Organization and Laws*. rev. ed. Wilmette, Ill.: Bahá'í Publishing Trust, 1963. vi, 57 p. LC card 63–24765.
   See 7.1950–7.1951.

7.1848. —— *A Bahá'í Declaration of Human Obligations and Rights*. Wilmette, Ill.: National Spiritual Assembly of the Bahá'ís of the United States, n.d. (two variants, both probably in the 1960's). 8 p.

7.1849. —— *The Bahá'í Group: Its Purpose and Operation*. Wilmette, Ill.: Bahá'í Publishing Trust, 1958. 20 p.

7.1850. —— *Bahá'í Literature for More Effective Teaching Among Christians*. n.p. [Wilmette, Ill.]: National Spiritual Assembly of the Bahá'ís of the United States, 1957. [3] p.

7.1851. —— *The Bahá'í Position on Military Service: A Public Statement*. Wilmette, Ill.: National Spiritual Assembly of the Bahá'ís of the United States, n.d. [196–?] 1 p.

7.1852. —— *Bahá'í Principles of Education*. Wilmette, Ill.: National Spiritual Assembly of the Bahá'ís of the United States, n.d. [1955?] 1 p.

7.1853. —— *The Bahá'í Revelation and Christendom*. Wilmette, Ill.: National Spiritual Assembly of the Bahá'ís of the United States, 1959. [4] p.

7.1854. —— *A Call to the American Bahá'ís for Unity and Sacrifice During Year Three of the Seven Year Plan*. Wilmette, Ill.: National Spiritual Assembly of the Bahá'ís of the United States, 1948. [4] p.

7.1855. —— *A Community Study Guide on The Promise of World Peace*. n.p. [Wilmette, Ill.]: National Spiritual Assembly of the Bahá'ís of the United States, Aug. 1985. 13 p.

7.1856. —— *Declaration of Trust and By-Laws of the National Spiritual Assembly of the Bahá'ís of the United States. By-Laws of a Local Spiritual Assembly*. Wilmette, Ill.: National Bahá'í Office, 1949. 20 p.
   The national and local constitutions of Bahá'í institutions in the United States, which have served as models for constitutional foundation of all Bahá'í institutions around the world.
   See 7.1961–7.1962

7.1857. —— *idem*. Wilmette, Ill.: Bahá'í Publishing Trust, c1949 [i.e. 195–?] 20 p.; 1964. 22 p.; 1965, 1969. 21 p.; 1975. 31 p.

7.1858. —— *The Development of Local Spiritual Assemblies*. Wilmette, Ill.: Bahá'í Publishing Trust, 1975. xiv, 365 p. (Bahá'í Comprehensive Deepening Program).
   A course for helping Local Spiritual Assemblies become mature in handling community affairs.

7.1859. —— *Elimination of Prejudice: The Bahá'í Attack*. Wilmette, Ill.: National Spiritual Assembly of the Bahá'ís of the United States, n.d. [195–?] 1 p.

7.1860. —— *Guidelines for Local Spiritual Assemblies*. Wilmette, Ill.: Bahá'í Publishing Trust, 1976. ix, 154 p.

7.1861. —— *Handbook of Information for the National Convention Dedication of the House of Worship, and the Second International Teaching Conference*. n.p. [Wilmette, Ill.: National Spiritual Assembly of the Bahá'ís of the United States], n.d. [1953] 22 p.

7.1862. —— *Local Spiritual Assembly Secretary's Manual*. Wilmette, Ill.: National Spiritual Assembly of the Bahá'ís of the United States, 1972. 1 vol. (loose-leaf).

7.1863. —— *Manual for Training Teams*. Wilmette, Ill.: Bahá'í Publishing Trust, 1975. v, 154 leaves. (Bahá'í Comprehensive Deepening Program).

7.1863a. —— *The Meaning of Covenant-Breaking*. Los Angeles: Los Angeles Spiritual Assembly, 1958. 4 leaves.

7.1864. —— *National Spiritual Assembly of the Bahá'ís of the United States*. Wilmette, Ill.: National Spiritual Assembly of the Bahá'ís of the United States, 1975. 16 p.
   Brochure on the national Bahá'í institution at the time of its 50th anniversary.

7.1865. —— *National Spiritual Assembly of the Bahá'ís of the United States.* Wilmette, Ill.: National Spiritual Assembly of the Baha'ís of the United States, 1983. 16 p.

Report to the national convention on the financial condition of the American Bahá'í community.

7.1866. —— *On Becoming a Bahá'í: Basic Responsibilities and Privileges of Bahá'í Membership.* Wilmette, Ill.: Bahá'í Publishing Trust, n.d. [1969], c1969, 1970. 21 p. LC card 71–6140.

7.1867. —— *idem.* rev. ed. Wilmette, Ill.: Bahá'í Publishing Trust, 1980. 22 p.

7.1868. —— *idem.* Freetown: National Spiritual Assembly of the Bahá'ís of Sierra Leone, n.d. [1983?] 21 p.

7.1869. —— *The Published Works of the Guardian.* n.p. [Wilmette, Ill.]: National Spiritual Assembly of the Bahá'ís of the United States, n.d. [1954?] 1 p.

7.1870. —— *The Religion of Humanity: The Meaning of the Bahá'í World Faith.* Wilmette, Ill.: National Spiritual Assembly of the Bahá'ís of the United States, n.d. [after 1953] 6 p.

7.1871. —— *Religious Liberty, Basis of World Peace.* Wilmette, Ill.: National Spiritual Assembly of the Bahá'ís of the United States, n.d. [195–?] 1 p.

7.1872. —— *Sequoyah: Tribute to a Servant of Mankind from the Bahá'í Faith to the Cherokee Nation.* Wilmette, Ill.: National Spiritual Assembly of the Bahá'ís of the United States, 1976. 12 p.

7.1873. —— *Trustees of the Merciful: The Station, Responsibilities and Duties of the Local Spiritual Assembly.* Wilmette, Ill.: Bahá'í Publishing Trust, 1958. 27 p.

7.1874. —— *United States Bahá'í Directory.* Wilmette, Ill.: National Spiritual Assembly of the Bahá'ís of the United States. 1933/34, Nov. 1933. 7 p.; 1940/41. 5 p.; 1944/45. 5 p.; 1945/46. 8 p.; 1946/47. 8 p.; 1947/48. 8 p.; 1948/49. 8 p.; 1950/51. 8 p.; 1951/52. 10 p.; 1952/53. 10 p.; 1953/54. 7 p.; 1954/55. 8 p.; 1955/56. [8] p.; 1956/57. [8] p.; 1957/58. [12] p.; 1959/60, pt. 1. [4] p./pt. 2. [8] p.; 1960/61, pt. 1. [6] p./pt. 2. [8] p.; 1961/62, pt. 1. [6] p./pt. 2. [8] p.; 1962/63, pt. 1. [8] p.; 1963/64, pt. 1. [11] p./pt. 2. [4] p.; 1964/65, pt. 1. [11] p./pt. 2. [4] p.; 1965/66, pt. 1. [11] p./pt. 2. [4] p.; 1966/67, pt. 1. [12] p./pt. 2. [8] p.; 1967/68, pt. 1. [12] p./pt. 2. [8] p.; 1968/69, pt. 1. [12] p.; 1969/70. [16] p.; 1970/71. [20] p.; 1975/76 [Aug. 1975]. [28] p./Sept. 1975. [28] p./Jan. 1976. [20] p.; 1976/77, Jan. 1976 [i.e. 1977. [20] p.; 1977/78, July 1977.

[20] p. Title varies: *Bahá'í Directory* to 1944/45, and 1947/48 – 197–; *American Bahá'í Directory,* 1945/46, 1946/47; *United States Bahá'í Directory,* 197–?

Includes only directories published by type-setting and printing. It is not clear which years are missing or have only been reproduced by mimeograph or photocopying.

7.1875. —— *The Will and Testament of 'Abdu'l-Bahá: Charter of a Divine Civilization.* Wilmette, Ill.: National Spiritual Assembly of the Baha'ís of the United States, n.d. [after 1948] 9 p.

7.1876. National Spiritual Assembly of the Bahá'ís of the United States. African Teaching Committee. *Affician [sic] Areas in the Ten Year Spiritual Crusade of the Bahá'í World Faith.* n.p. [Wilmette, Ill.]: African Teaching Committee, 1953. 41 p.

7.1877. National Spiritual Assembly of the Bahá'ís of the United States. American Indian Service Committee. *Teaching Brochure of the American Indian Service Committee.* Wilmette, Ill.: American Indian Service Committee, n.d. [after 1948] [43] p.

7.1877a. National Spiritual Assembly of the Bahá'ís of the United States. Area Teaching Committee of the Western States. *Launching the World-Embracing Crusade: Outline: The Guardian's Proclamation to the Baha'i World Community.* n.p. [Los Angeles]: Area Teaching Committee, Western States, n.d. [1952] 4 pp.

7.1878. National Spiritual Assembly of the Bahá'ís of the United States. Bahá'í Committee for the United Nations. *Human Rights, Basis for World Peace.* Wilmette, Ill.: National Spiritual Assembly of the Bahá'ís of the United States, 1968. [12] p.

7.1879. National Spiritual Assembly of the Bahá'ís of the United States. Bahá'í House of Worship Activities Committee. *House of Worship Special Visit Program.* Wilmette, Ill.: Bahá'í House of Worship Activities Committee, n.d. [1975] 8 p.

7.1880. National Spiritual Assembly of the Bahá'ís of the United States. Child Education Committee. *Manual of Suggestions for Organizing a Bahá'í Children's Hour.* Wilmette, Ill.: Bahá'í Publishing Committee, n.d. [194–] 5 leaves.

7.1881. National Spiritual Assembly of the Bahá'ís of the United States. Committee for the United Nations. *Bahá'ís at the United Nations.* Wilmette, Ill.: Bahá'í Publishing Trust, n.d. [196–?] 4 p.

7.1882. National Spiritual Assembly of the Bahá'ís of the United States. Community

Development Committee. *Manual for Bahá'í Teachers Assisting Local Spiritual Assemblies*. Wilmette, Ill.: Community Development Committee, n.d. [1966?] 62 p.

7.1883. National Spiritual Assembly of the Bahá'ís of the United States. Interracial Teaching Committee. *Baha'i Inter-Racial Teaching Program, 1956–1957*. n.p. [Wilmette, Ill.: Baha'i Inter-Racial Teaching Committee], 1956. 13 [i.e. 14] leaves.

7.1884. —— *Baha'i Inter-Racial Teaching Program, 1957–1958*. Wilmette, Ill.: Bahá'í Inter-Racial Teaching Committee, 1957. 7 leaves.

7.1885. National Spiritual Assembly of the Bahá'ís of the United States. National Archives Committee. *Guide to the Holdings of the National Bahá'í Archives, Bahá'í National Center, Wilmette, Illinois*. Wilmette, Ill.: National Bahá'í Archives, 1983. 19 p.

7.1886. —— *Guidelines for Bahá'í Archives*. Wilmette, Ill.: National Bahá'í Archives, 1983. v, 59 p. LC card 84–160425.

7.1887. National Spiritual Assembly of the Bahá'ís of the United States. National Bahá'í Schools Committee. *Bahá'í Schools: A Manual of Organization and Operation*. n.p. [Wilmette, Ill.]: National Bahá'í Schools Committee, n.d. [1970] iii, 47 p.

7.1888. National Spiritual Assembly of the Bahá'ís of the United States. National Education Committee. *Bahá'í Curriculum Guide*. Wilmette, Ill.: National Education Committee, 1982. xiii, 11 p.

7.1889. —— *Bahá'í Parent Program*. Wilmette, Ill.: National Education Committee, n.d. [1980] [49] p.

7.1890. —— *Child Education Teacher Training Handbook*. Wilmette, Ill.: National Spiritual Assembly of the Bahá'ís of the United States, 1979. 194 p.

7.1891. —— *Children's Programs for Baha'i Schools: Director's Resource Guide*. n.p. [Wilmette, Ill.]: National Education Committee of the Bahá'ís of the United States. n.d. [1983?] 30 p.

7.1892. —— *Guidelines for Organizing a Bahá'í Children's Class Program*. n.p. [Wilmette, Ill.]: National Education Committee of the Baha'is of the United States, n.d. [1983?] 15 p.

7.1893. —— *Objectives for a Bahá'í Education Program*. n.p. [Wilmette, Ill.]; National Education Committee of the Bahá'ís of the United States, n.d. [1983?] 13 p.

7.1894. —— *Unity Celebration: A Consolidation Activity: Coordinator's Guide*. n.p. [Wilmette, Ill.]: National Education Committee of the Bahá'ís of the United States, n.d. [1983?] 6 p.

7.1895. National Spiritual Assembly of the Bahá'ís of the United States. National Programming Committee. *A New Approach to Bahá'u'lláh and the New Era*. Wilmette, Ill.: Bahá'í Publishing Committee, 1949, n.d. [1950?] 46 p.

7.1896. National Spiritual Assembly of the Bahá'ís of the United States. National Projects Committee. *Two Year Program of Preparation, 1951–1953*. Wilmette, Ill.: Bahá'í Publishing Committee, 1951. [37] p.

7.1897. National Spiritual Assembly of the Bahá'ís of the United States. National Public Information Office. *Public Information Kits for Bahá'í Special Event Days, Bahá'í Holy Days and Other Events*. Wilmette, Ill.: National Bahá'í Public Information Office, 1972. 23, [14] p.

7.1898. National Spiritual Assembly of the Bahá'ís of the United States. National Reference Library Committee. *A Compilation: The Mashriqu'l-Adhkár*. n.p. [Wilmette, Ill.?]: National Reference Library Committee, n.d. [194–?] 5 leaves.

7.1899. —— *Subject Index: Will and Testament of 'Abdu'l-Bahá*. n.p. [Wilmette, Ill.]: National Reference Library Committee of the National Spiritual Assembly of the Bahá'ís of the U.S., n.d. [196–?] 20 p.

7.1900. —— *Subject Index: Writings of Bahá'u'lláh in Bahá'í World Faith and Gleanings*. n.p. [Wilmette, Ill.?]: National Reference Library Committee, n.d. [195–?] [2], 71 leaves.

7.1901. —— *Universal House of Justice: A Compilation*. n.p. [Wilmette, Ill.?]: National Reference Library Committee, 1958. 15 leaves.

7.1902. —— *The Worlds of God: Basic Classifications of Existence as Defined in the Bahá'í Writings: A Compilation*. n.p. [Wilmette, Ill.?]: National Reference Library Committee, 1965–1971 [i.e. 1971] iv, 105 p.

Analyzes the nature of reality according to Bahá'í categories: the world of Deity, the world of Prophethood, the world of servitude.

7.1903. National Spiritual Assembly of the Bahá'ís of the United States. National Teaching Committee. *Consolidation: Guidelines for Integrating the Mass Teaching and Mass Consolidation Processes*. Wilmette, Ill.: Bahá'í Teaching Committee, 1978. 12 p.

7.1904. —— *Design for Victory, 1976–1979: Goals for Individuals and Communities During the*

Five Year Plan. Wilmette, Ill.: Bahá'í Publishing Trust, 1976. vi, 162 p.

7.1905. —— *District Teaching Committee Manual.* Wilmette, Ill.: National Teaching Committee, 1974. 1 vol. (loose-leaf).

7.1906. —— *Effective Teaching: Instructor's Guide.* n.p. [Wilmette, Ill.]: National Teaching Committee, Dec. 1985. ii, 39 p.

7.1907. —— *Effective Teaching: Workbook: Connecting Hearts with Bahá'u'lláh.* n.p. [Wilmette, Ill.]: National Teaching Committee, Dec. 1985. 59 p.

7.1908. —— *The Greatest Gift: A Community Enrichment Program on Teaching the Cause of God.* Wilmette, Ill.: Bahá'í Publishing Trust, 1974. ii, 12 p.

7.1909. —— *The Homefront Pioneer.* Wilmette, Ill.: National Teaching Committee, Apr. 1984. [20] p.

7.1910. —— *A New Race of Men.* Wilmette, Ill.: Bahá'í Publishing Trust, 1970, 1973. 29 p. (Deepening Portfolio; no.2).

7.1911. —— *A New World Order,* Wilmette, Ill.: Bahá'í Publishing Trust, 1970, 1977. 48 p. (Deepening Portfolio; no.1).

7.1912. —— *1983–1984 Plan for Growth.* Wilmette, Ill.: National Teaching Committee, May 1983. [6] p.

7.1913. —— *Remembrance of God.* n.p. [Wilmette, Ill.: National Teaching Committee], n.d. [1970] 32 p.

7.1914. —— *Seven Year Plan, the Final Phase.* Wilmette, Ill.: National Teaching Committee, n.d. [1984] [6] p.

7.1915. —— *The Suffering of Bahá'u'lláh.* Wilmette, Ill.: Bahá'í Publishing Trust, 1974. 32 p. (Deepening Portfolio; no.3).

7.1916. —— *Suggested Guidelines for Teaching the Masses.* Wilmette, Ill.: Bahá'í Publishing Trust, 1971. 39 p.

7.1916a. — *Suggestions for Opening a New City to the Baha'i Faith.* rev. n.p. [Wilmette, Ill.]: American National Teaching Committee, 1952. 4 p.

7.1917. —— *Teaching Through Friendship Teams: 1983–1984 Plan for Growth.* Wilmette, Ill.: National Teaching Committee, n.d. [1983] [6] p.

7.1918. —— *Youth Can Move the World!: 1985 Summer Projects.* Wilmette, Ill.: National Teaching Committee, 1985. [4] p.

7.1919. National Spiritual Assembly of the Bahá'ís of the United States. National Youth Committee. *Great Great Deeds: Action Manual for Bahá'í College Clubs.* n.p. [Wilmette, Ill.]: National Youth Committee, 1982. x, 59 p.

7.1920. —— *Youth Three Year Phase.* Wilmette, Ill.: National Youth Committee, 1981. [8] p.

7.1921. National Spiritual Assembly of the Bahá'ís of the United States. Office of the Treasurer. *Accounting Procedures for Bahá'í Treasurers.* Wilmette, Ill.: National Spiritual Assembly of the Bahá'ís of the United States, 1976. 38 p.

7.1922. —— *Accounting Records for Local Treasurers.* n.p. [Wilmette, Ill.: Office of the Treasurer], n.d. [196–?] 21 leaves (portfolio ring binder). Binder title: *Treasurer, Local Spiritual Assembly.*

7.1923. —— *America's Spiritual Destiny.* Wilmette, Ill.: Office of the Treasurer, Sept. 1983. 104 p.

7.1924. —— *America's Spiritual Destiny: A Guide for Personal or Group Study.* Wilmette, Ill.: Bahá'í Publishing Trust, 1984, Nov. 1984. vii, 104 p.

7.1925. —— *The Fund: Treasurer's Report, National Bahá'í Convention, 1975.* Wilmette, Ill.: Office of the Treasurer, 1975. 13 p.

7.1926. —— *The Fund: Treasurer's Report, National Bahá'í Convention, 1976.* Wilmette, Ill.: Office of the Treasurer, 1976. 12 p.

7.1927. —— *The Fund: Treasurer's Report, National Bahá'í Convention, 1979.* Wilmette, Ill.: Office of the Treasurer, 1979. 8 p.

7.1928. —— *The Fund: Treasurer's Report, National Bahá'í Convention, 1982.* Wilmette, Ill.: Office of the Treasurer, 1982. 8 p.

7.1929. —— *The Generating Impulse: A Community Enrichment Program on the Bahá'í Fund.* Wilmette, Ill.: Office of the Treasurer, 1973. 12 p.

7.1930. —— *The Individual Believer and the Rhythm of Growth.* n.p. [Wilmette, Ill.]: Office of the Treasurer, 1982. v, 83 p.

7.1931. —— *Local Bahá'í Fund Audit Procedure.* rev. ed. n.p. [Wilmette, Ill.]: Office of the Treasurer, Mar. 1983. 8 p.

7.1932. —— *The Mystery of Sacrifice.* n.p. [Wilmette, Ill.]: Office of the Treasurer, 1980. 84 p.

7.1933. —— *The National Bahá'í Fund.* Wilmette, Ill.: National Bahá'í Fund, n.d. [1985] [12] p.

7.1934. —— *Questions and Answers for Bahá'í*

Treasurers. n.p. [Wilmette, Ill.]: Office of the Treasurer, n.d. [197–] 37 p.

7.1935. —— *The Secret of Wealth: A Course on Personal Resource Management.* n.p. [Wilmette, Ill.]: National Spiritual Assembly of the Bahá'ís of the United States, 1979. iii, 85 p.

7.1936. —— *The Surest Way.* n.p. [Wilmette, Ill.]: Office of the Treasurer, 1978. v, 76 p.

7.1937. —— *Task Force Reports: Seventh National Treasurer's Representatives Training Institute.* n.p. [Wilmette, Ill.]: Office of the Treasurer, 1984. [8] p.

7.1938. —— *Training Manual for National Treasurer's Representatives.* n.p. [Wilmette, Ill.]: National Spiritual Assembly of the Bahá'ís of the United States, 1976. 40, [26] p.

7.1939. —— *Treasurer's Report, St Louis Bahá'í Conference, 1974.* n.p. [Wilmette, Ill.: Office of the Treasurer], 1974. [12] p.

7.1940. —— *Where There's a Will . . .* n.p. [Wilmette, Ill.]: Office of the Treasurer, 1983. 29 p.

7.1941. National Spiritual Assembly of the Bahá'ís of the United States. Projects Development Committee. *Suggestions for the Conduct of Institutes on the Covenant and Administration.* Wilmette, Ill.: Projects Development Committee, n.d. [1951] 4 leaves.

7.1942. National Spiritual Assembly of the Bahá'ís of the United States. Public Information Office. *Bahá'í Faith Fact Sheet.* Wilmette, Ill.: Public Information Office, n.d. [1972], n.d. [1976], n.d. [1977] 14 leaves.

7.1943. —— *Who is Bahá'u'lláh?* Wilmette, Ill.: Public Information Office, 1966 n.d. [1972?] n.d. [1978] 4 leaves.

7.1944. National Spiritual Assembly of the Bahá'ís of the United States. Study Aids Committee. *An Aid to the Study of the Administrative Order of the Faith of Bahá'u'lláh.* Wilmette, Ill.: Bahá'í Publishing Committee, 1948. 16 leaves.

7.1945. —— *The Covenant: An Outline for Study.* Wilmette, Ill.: Bahá'í Publishing Committee, 1948. 28 leaves.

7.1946. —— *The Fireside Teaching Method: A Manual for Bahá'ís.* Wilmette, Ill.: Bahá'í Publishing Committee, n.d. [after 1948] 7, [3] leaves.

7.1947. —— *Outline to Accompany What Modern Man Must Know About Religion.* Wilmette, Ill.: Bahá'í Publishing Committee, 1948. [5] leaves.

7.1948. National Spiritual Assembly of the Bahá'ís of the United States and Canada. *Annual Bahá'í Reports.* Wilmette, Ill.: National Spiritual Assembly of the Bahá'ís of the United States and Canada. 1938/39. 42 p.; 1939/40. 42 p.; 1940/41. 40 p.; 1941/42. 57 p.; 1942/43. 39 p.; 1943/44. 59 p.; 1944/45. 39 p.; 1945/46. 62 p.; 1946/47. 57 p.

6.1949. —— *The Bahá'í Case Against Mrs Lewis Stuyvvesant Chanler and Mirza Ahmad Sohrab: A Statement Prepared for the Members of the American Bahá'í Community.* Wilmette, Ill.: National Spiritual Assembly of the Bahá'ís of the United States and Canada, 1941. 22 p.

7.1950. —— *The Baha'i Community: A Summary of Its Foundation and Organization.* Wilmette, Ill.: Bahá'í Publishing Committee, 1947, 1954. vii, 70 p. LC card 47–7788.
   See 7.1847.

7.1951. —— *idem.* New Delhi: Bahá'í Publishing Trust, 1960, 1964. vii, 68 p.

7.1952. —— *A Bahá'í Declaration of Human Obligations and Rights.* Wilmette, Ill.: Bahá'í Public Relations, 1947. 8 p.

7.1953. —— *idem.* n.p. [Egypt], n.d. [1947?] (Alexandria: Ompr. Ramses). 14, 12 p. English and Arabic text.

7.1954. —— *Bahá'í Persecutions in Persia: An Appeal Addressed to His Imperial Majesty Reza Shah Pahlavi.* New York: Bahá'í Publishing Committee, 1926. 31 p.

7.1955. —— *Bahá'í Procedure.* New York: Bahá'í Publishing Committee, 1937. 78 leaves.
   A compilation treating selected Bahá'í administrative and procedural matters. Passages cited are from Shoghi Effendi or the National Spiritual Assembly of the Bahá'ís of the United States and Canada, with a few sections having no attributions.

7.1956. —— *idem.* 2nd ed. Wilmette, Ill.: Bahá'í Publishing Committee, 1942. ix, 115 p. LC card 42–8515.

7.1957. —— *Bahá'í State and Province Conventions, February 10, 1946: Convention Call and Directions.* n.p. [Wilmette, Ill.]: National Spiritual Assembly, 1946. [4] p.

7.1958. —— *The Bahá'í Teachings on Universal Peace.* New York: Bahá'í Publishing Committee, 1939. 11 p.

7.1959. —— *The Basis of the Baha'i Community: A Statement Concerning the New History Society.* Wilmette, Ill.: National Spiritual Assembly of the Bahá'ís of the United States and Canada, 1941. 5 leaves.

7.1960. —— *Communication from the National Spiritual Assembly of the Bahai Temple Unity,* *and Reports of Various National Committees to the High Assemblies of the United States and Canada.* n.p. [Chicago?]: National Spiritual Assembly of the Bahá'ís of the United States and Canada, 1923. 12 p.

7.1961. —— *Declaration of Trust. By-Laws of a Local Spiritual Assembly.* New York: Bahá'í Publishing Committee, 1933. 23 p.
  See 7.1856–7.1857.

7.1962. —— *idem.* Wilmette, Ill.: National Bahá'í Office, 1945. 20 p.

7.1963. —— *A New Plan of Unified Action to Complete the Bahá'í Temple and Promote the Cause in America.* n.p. [New York?]: National Spiritual Assembly of the Bahá'ís of the United States and Canada, n.d. [1931?] 4 p.

7.1964. — *A Plan of Unified Action to Spread the Bahá'í Cause Throughout the United States and Canada, January 21, 1926–December 31, 1928.* S. Eliot, Me.: National Spiritual Assembly of the Bahá'ís of the United States and Canada, 1925. 15 p.

7.1965. —— *A Prodigious Bahá'í Effort.* n.p. [Wilmette, Ill.: National Spiritual Assembly of the Bahá'ís of the United States and Canada], n.d. [1947] [2] p.

7.1966. —— *Statement on the Will and Testament of 'Abdu'l-Bahá, Charter of a Divine Civilization.* Wilmette, Ill.: National Spiritual Assembly of the Bahá'ís of the United States and Canada, 1942. 7 p.

7.1967. —— *The World Faith of Bahá'u'lláh: A Summary of Its Aims, Teachings, History and Administrative Order.* Wilmette, Ill.: National Spiritual Assembly of the Bahá'ís of the United States and Canada, 1943, 1944. 4 p.; 1944. [8] p.

7.1968. National Spiritual Assembly of the Bahá'ís of the United States and Canada. Bahá'í Publishing Committee. *Bahá'í Sacred Writings and Literature of the Bahá'í Cause.* Wilmette, Ill.: Bahá'í Publishing Committee, 1929. 16 p.

7.1969. —— *Literature of the Bahá'í Religion, Published by the Bahá'í Publishing Committee, New York, N.Y., U.S.A.* Poona, India: Bahá'í Book Stall, n.d. [1932] 15 p. Book prices listed in rupees.

7.1970. National Spiritual Assembly of the Bahá'ís of the United States and Canada. Child Education Committee. *Comprehensive Study Outline for Children.* New York: Bahá'í Publishing Committee, 1940. 53 leaves.

7.1971. —— *Manual of Suggestions for Organizing a Bahá'í Children's Hour.* Wilmette, Ill.:

Bahá'í Publishing Committee, n.d. [ca. 1945] 5 leaves.

7.1972. —— *Study Course for Bahá'u'lláh and the New Era.* Wilmette, Ill.: Bahá'í Publishing Committee, 1942. [35] leaves.

7.1973. National Spiritual Assembly of the Bahá'ís of the United States and Canada. National Teaching Committee. *Training for Bahá'í Teaching.* Wilmette, Ill.: Bahá'í Publishing Committee, 1943. 8 leaves.

7.1973a. National Spiritual Assembly of the Bahá'ís of the United States and Canada. Public Relations Committee. *A Bahá'í Declaration of Human Obligations and Rights.* Wilmette, Ill.: Bahá'í Public Relations, 1947. 1 leaf. Reprint from: *The Manitoban* (Winnipeg), v.33 no.40 (Mar. 7, 1947).

7.1974. National Spiritual Assembly of the Bahá'ís of the United States and Canada. Publicity Committee. *Bahá'í Publicity for Use by Spiritual Assemblies and Committees.* New York: Publicity Committee, 1929. [22] leaves.

7.1975. National Spiritual Assembly of the Bahá'ís of the United States and Canada. Study Aids Committee. *An Aid to the Study of the Administrative Order of the Faith of Bahá'u'lláh.* Wilmette, Ill.: Bahá'í Publishing Committee, 1946. 17 leaves.

7.1976. National Spiritual Assembly of the Bahá'ís of the United States and Canada. Study Outline Committee. *The Advent of Divine Justice: Study Guide.* Wilmette, Ill.: Bahá'í Publishing Trust, 1961. 21 leaves; 1969. 19 p.
  See 7.1981.

7.1977. —— *The Dispensation of Bahá'u'lláh: A Study Outline.* Wilmette, Ill.: Bahá'í Publishing Committee, 1943. 8 leaves.
  See 7.813.

7.1978. —— *Fundamentals of Bahá'í Membership: A Teaching and Study Outline.* New York: Bahá'í Publishing Committee, n.d. [1940?] 44 leaves.

7.1979. —— *idem.* rev. Wilmette, Ill.: Bahá'í Publishing Committee, 1943. 10 leaves.

7.1980. —— *Muhammad and the Founding of Islám: A Study Outline Based on Bahá'í Literature.* Wilmette, Ill.: Bahá'í Publishing Committee, 1942, 1946. 53 leaves.

7.1981. —— *Study Outline and Aids for The Advent of Divine Justice.* Wilmette, Ill.: Bahá'í Publishing Committee, 1941. 26 leaves.
  See 7.1976.

7.1982. —— *Study Outline on Public Speaking.*

New York: Bahá'í Publishing Committee, 1937. 4 leaves.

7.1983. —— *Study Outline on the Essential Principles of Creative Writing.* New York: Bahá'í Publishing Committee, 1937. 6 leaves.

7.1984. —— *Study Outline, The Book of Certitude (Tablet of Iqán).* New York: Bahá'í Publishing Committee, 1933. 14 leaves.

7.1985. —— *Study Outlines and Aids for World Order Letters of Shoghi Effendi.* New York: Bahá'í Publishing Committee, [1940]. vii, 64 p.

7.1986. —— *Twenty Lessons in Bahá'í Administration.* New York: Bahá'í Publishing Committee, 1935. 28, [14] leaves.

7.1986a. National Spiritual Assembly of the Bahá'ís of the United States and Canada. Temple Guides Committee. *Information About the Baha'i House of Worship, Wilmette, Illinois: For the Use of Temple Model Exhibitors.* Wilmette, Ill: Baha'i Publishing Committee, 1942. iv, 20 leaves.

7.1987. National Spiritual Assembly of the Bahá'ís of the Virgin Islands. *The Wine of Astonishment: A Study Course on Christian Doctrines.* n.p. [Charlotte Amalie, U.S. Virgin Islands]: National Spiritual Assembly of the Bahá'ís of the Virgin Islands, n.d. [1985] 12 leaves.

7.1988. National Spiritual Assembly of the Bahá'ís of Zambia. *The Baha'i Faith.* Lusaka: National Spiritual Assembly of the Bahá'ís of Zambia, n.d. [1981?] [2] p. [with 14 flip-up leaves].

7.1989. —— *A Guide to Establishing Local Endowments.* Lusaka: National Spiritual Assembly of the Bahá'ís of Zambia, 1977. 4 p.

7.1990. National Spiritual Assembly of the Bahá'ís of Zimbabwe. *Guidance for Local Spiritual Assemblies: A Guide to Bahá'í Administration.* Harare: National Spiritual Assembly of the Baha'is of Zimbabwe, 1984. 27 p.

7.1991. National Youth Conference (1981: Albury, Victoria). *National Youth Conference Booklet, Albury '81.* Mona Vale, N.S.W.: National Youth Committee, 1981. 12 p.

7.1992. *Neda.* n.p. [Panchgani, India], n.d. [1983?] 13 leaves.

7.1993. *The Needs of the Present Hour.* comp. Continental Board of Counsellors in Southern Africa. n.p. [Johannesburg, S. Afr.]: Continental Board of Counsellors in Southern Africa, 1974. 45, 20 p.

7.1994. Nelson, Lee; Nelson, Miriam G. *Concordance to Epistle to the Son of the Wolf.* Los

Angeles: Kalimát Press, 1985. xvi, 282 p. LC card 85–5780.

7.1995. —— *Concordance to the Kitáb-i-Íqán.* Los Angeles: Kalimát Press, 1984. xiv, 322 p. LC card 84–7855.

7.1996. Nelson, Lee; Towfiq, Miriam G. *Concordance to Gleanings from the Writings of Bahá'u'lláh.* Los Angeles: Kalimát Press, 1983. xvi, 504 p. LC card 83–6162.
  Review:
Sweetland, James H., *American Reference Books Annual,* v.17 (1985), p. 483.

7.1997. *Never Tell a Bad Thing.* n.p. [Port of Spain: National Spiritual Assembly of the Bahá'ís of Trinidad and Tobago], n.d. [1979] [8] leaves.

7.1998. *New Attacks on the Bahá'ís in Iran: Canada Responds = Nouvelles Attaques contre les Bahá'ís en Iran: le Canada Répond.* Thornhill, Ont.: National Spiritual Assembly of the Bahá'ís of Canada, 1980. 8 p. Number two in a series entitled: *Update on Iran.*

7.1998a. *The New Day.* London: N.S.A. of the Baha'is of the British Isles, n.d. [196–] [4] p.

7.1999. *A New Day Comes.* Wilmette, Ill.: American Indian Service Committee, 1954. 6 p.

7.2000. *A New Day Is Dawning: A Bahai Musical Fireside.* Penang: Spiritual Assembly of the Bahais of Malaysia, 1974. 35 p.

7.2001. New Era High School (Panchgani, India). *An International Bahá'í School: New Era High School, Panchgani, India.* Panchgani: New Era High School, n.d. [197–] [8] p.

7.2001a. —— *The New Era High School: Prospectus for Primary, Secondary, and Higher Secondary.* Panchgani, India: New Era High School, n.d. [197–?] 11 p., [9] p. of plates.

7.2002. —— *Prospectus.* Panchgani: New Era High School, n.d. [196–?] 15 p.

7.2003. —— *Rustom M. Sohaili Auditorium, New Era High School, Panchgani.* Panchgani: New Era High School, n.d. [1978] 12 p.

7.2004. —— *Souvenir Brochure, the New Era School, Panchgani 412 805, Maharashtra, India.* Panchgani: New Era School, n.d. [1981] [12] p.

7.2005. —— *35th Anniversary Souvenir Brochure.* Panchgani: New Era High School, 1980. [8] p.

7.2006. New Era Press (Limassol, Cyprus). *An Introduction to New Era Press.* Limassol: New Era Press, 1984. [4] p.

7.2007. New Era Singers (Panchgani, India).

Unity in Diversity. Panchgani, Maharashtra: New Era High School, 1985. 21 p.

7.2008. *New Horizons of Unity.* n.p., n.d. [195–?] 6 p.

7.2009. *The New Life.* Port of Spain, Trinidad: Bahá'í Community, n.d. [1979?] [6] p. folder.

7.2010. *A New Race of Men.* New Delhi: Bahá'í Publishing Trust, 1972. 35 p.

7.2011. *A New Way of Life: What It Means to Be a Bahá'í Youth.* rev. ed. Wilmette, Ill.: Bahá'í Publishing Trust, 1965, 1967, 1971. 24 p.

7.2012. *A New Way to Bring People Together: The Bahá'í Faith.* n.p. [Wilmette, Ill.: National Spiritual Assembly of the Bahá'ís of the United States], n.d. [197–] [4] p.

7.2013. *A New Wind: A 30 Minute Color Film About the Bahá'í Faith.* Wilmette, Ill.: National Baha'i Headquarters, 1969. [6] p.

7.2014. *A New Wind Blowing.* il. Anna Stevenson. Wilmette, Ill.: Bahá'í Publishing Trust, 1970. 50 p.
Songbook.

7.2015. *A New World Family.* London: National Spiritual Assembly of the Bahá'ís of the United Kingdom, n.d. [1981?] 2 p. folded to 6.

7.2016. *A New World Order.* West Englewood, N.J.: National Spiritual Assembly of the Bahá'ís of the United States and Canada, [193–?].
Series of deepening leaflets, 2 p. each through 1936, 4 p. from 1937.

7.2017. *New World Order Diary for 1946.* London: Bahá'í Publishing Trust, 1946. [132] p.

7.2018. Newman, Winifred Barnum. *The Secret in the Garden.* Wilmette, Ill.: Bahá'í Publishing Trust, 1980. 32 p. LC card 81–123472.
Children's story about unity in diversity.
Reviews:
Henze, Sandra, *Library Journal* (New York), (Nov. 15, 1981).
Henze, Sandra, *School Library Journal* (New York), (Nov. 1981).
Hoffman, Lyla, *Interracial Books for Children Bulletin*, v.12 nos.4 & 5 (1981), p. 38.

7.2019. —— *The Spotlessly Leopard.* Evanston, Ill.: Bellwood Press, 1983. 41 p. LC card 82–24423. Children's book.

7.2020. *News Features on the Bahá'í Faith.* n.p. [Wilmette, Ill.: National Bahá'í Public Information Department], n.d. [1968?] [4] p.

7.2021. *Nhlumba Bertha Mkhize, 1889–1981.* Johannesburg: National Spiritual Assembly of the Bahá'ís of South and West Africa, 1982. [6] p.

7.2022. Niaz, A.Q. *The Babee and Bahaee Religion.* Rabwah, Pakistan: Ahmadiyya Muslim Foreign Missions Office, 1960. 87 p.
Anti-Bahá'í work from Ahmadiyya Muslim viewpoint.

7.2023. —— *idem.* Qadian, Punjab, India: Mirza Wasim Ahmad, 1975. 77 p.

7.2024. *Nine Pointed Star Study Guide on Introduction to the Baha'i Faith.* [Kuala Lumpur]: Spiritual Assembly of the Bahá'ís of Malaysia, n.d. [197–] 3 p.

7.2025. *The Nineteen Day Feast.* Canada: Produced by N.I.T.C. under the National Spiritual Assembly of the Bahà'ìs [sic] of Canada, n.d. [196–?] [8] p.

7.2026. *Nineteen Day Feast* [Star Study Flip Chart]. Wilmette, Ill.: Bahá'í Publishing Trust, 1974. 46 p. (Star Study Program).

7.2026a. *The Nineteen Day Feast = Osivilo So Mafiku Omulongo Na Tano Nane = Ofeste Roomurongo Namuviu = Disi-khoese a Tsedi di Kai-kais = Die Neentien Dae-fees.* n.p. [Windhoek: National Spiritual Assembly of the Bahá'ís of South West Africa/Namibia], n.d. [1985] 30 p. In English, Kuanyama, Herero, Nama and Afrikaans.

7.2027. *A 1953 Prescription for Living.* Baltimore, Md.: Mrs H. Morton Langrall, 1953. [4] p.

7.2028. *19 Themes on the 'Dispensation'.* Kuala Lumpur: Spiritual Assembly of the Bahá'ís of Malaysia, 1982. 24 p.

7.2029. *The Non-Political Character of the Baha'i Faith.* Lagos, Nigeria; Accra, Ghana; Lomé, Togo: National Spiritual Assembly of the Bahá'ís of West Central Africa, n.d. [between 1967 and 1970] 6 leaves.

7.2030. Norquay, James Rupert. *The Norquay Script: A Phonetic Alphabet of Befitting Beauty for English.* 2nd ed. n.p. [Canada]: Norquay, 1984. [6] p.

7.2031. —— *Rújano!: A Phonetic Script for English of Befitting Beauty.* n.p. [Victoria, B.C.]: Norquay, 1983. [6] p.

7.2032. Norris, Daniel. *Flip Book: Images Inspired by the Bahá'í Writings.* n.p. Norris, 1980. [127] leaves.

7.2033. —— *Igualdad del Hombre y la Mujer = Equality of Man and Woman.* n.p. [Sendoi City, Japan]: Daniel Norris, n.d. [1983] [53] leaves.

7.2034. North, A. *A Christian Looks at the Baha'i World Faith.* New South Wales: Standing Committee of the Presbyterian Church of Australia

in the State of N.S.W., n.d. [1963?] (Marrickville, N.S.W.: Dalnor Press). [12] p.
Christian polemic.

7.2035. North American Bahá'í Office for Human Rights. *Education for the New Age.* Wilmette, Ill.: North American Bahá'í Office for Human Rights, 1970. 64 p.

7.2036. —— *Human Rights Are God-Given Rights: Report of Activities in Observance of International Human Rights Year, 1968.* Wilmette, Ill.: North American Bahá'í Office for Human Rights, 1968. 102 p.

7.2037. *North American Bahá'í Radio, WLGI, Louis Gregory Institute.* n.p. [Hemingway, S.C.: Louis Gregory Institute], n.d. [1983] [6] p.

7.2038. Northquist, R.A. *Difficult Structural Concrete Work Placed in Baha'í Temple.* Chicago: Robert W. Hunt Company, 1931. [4] p. Reprinted from *Concrete* (May 1931).

7.2038a. *Notes for Authors.* Oxford: George Ronald, 1985. 16 p.

7.2039. *Notes of Love.* n.p. [Kuala Lumpur]: Spiritual Assembly of the Bahais of Malaysia, 1974. 49 p.

7.2040. *Notes on Mass Teaching.* New Delhi: [National Spiritual Assembly of the Bahá'ís of India], 1964. 20 p.

7.2041. *Now You're a Bahá'í: An Outline of the*

Responsibilities and Privileges of a Bahá'í. Mona Vale, N.S.W.: Bahá'í Publishing Trust Australia, 134 B.E. [1977] 20 p.

7.2042. *idem.* rev. n.p. [Mona Vale, N.S.W.]: Bahá'í Publications Australia, 1984 (Mudgee: Lynx Print). 20 p.

7.2043. [*Number 9 Compilation*]. [U.S.], n.d. [190–?], n.d. [191–], n.d. [before 1921] (two different versions, one has blue cover with uncut edges, the other has dark blue-purple cover); New York: Bahá'í Publishing Committee, n.d. [after 1925], n.d. [1926], n.d. [after 1926] 16 p.
This is the small introductory pamphlet with the number 9 on the cover which was printed with several small variations in text and was translated into a number of languages in the first three decades of the 20th century. Also known as 'Big Ben' and 'Little Ben'.

7.2044. *idem.* n.p. [Tokyo: National Spiritual Assembly of the Bahá'ís of Japan], n.d. [1971] 52 p. Souvenir of 1971 Sapporo conference.

7.2045. Núrí, Allama Yahya. *Finality of Prophethood and a Critical Analysis of Babism, Bahaism, Qadiyanism.* Tehran: Madrasih Shohada, 1981. 60, 44, 110 p. English and Persian text. LC card 84–931332.
Anti-Bahá'í work from Islamic viewpoint.

7.2046. —— *idem.* Tihrán: Majma'-i Mutáli'át va Taḥqíqat-i Islámí va Majma'-i Ma'árif-i Islámí, 1360 [1981–82] xiii, 65, 106 p.

O

7.2047. *O Fa'amatalagaotooto o le Pulega o le Fa'atuatuaga Bahá'í = An Outline of Bahá'í Administration.* rev. and updated. Apia, Western Samoa: Fono Fa'aleagaga a Bahá'í o Samoa = National Spiritual Assembly of the Bahá'ís of Samoa, 1982. 26, 20 p. Samoan and English text.

7.2048. *O God Educate These Children: Baha'i Lessons for Children's Classes.* n.p. [Lusaka]: National Spiritual Assembly Zambia, Child Education Committee, 1977. 54 p.

7.2049. *O My Friends! Walk Ye In the Ways of the Good Pleasure of the Friend . . .* Malaysia: National Baha'i Youth Committee, 137 B.E. [1980–81] 28 p.

7.2049a. *O Son of being! Make mention of Me on My earth, that in My heaven I may remember thee . . .* Paddington, N.S.W.: National Spiritual

Assembly of the Baha'is of Australia and New Zealand, 1953. [4] p. Each page has a different title: *Diffuse the Glad-Tidings; The Guardian's Cable; The Plan Position on the 15th February, 1953.*

7.2050. *The Oath of the Prophet Mohammed to the Followers of the Nazarene.* trans. Anton F. Haddad. New York: Board of Counsel, 1902. 7 p.

7.2051. *Official Documentation Testifying to Discrimination Against the Bahá'í Community Since the Creation of the Islamic Republic of Iran.* New York: Bahá'í International Community, 1981. [53] leaves.

7.2052. *Okí! Nitsítapee: A Message to the Blackfeet Indians.* Toronto, Ont.: Bahá'í Publishing Committee, n.d. [195–?] 11 p.

7.2053. Olafsson, Jean. *Color the Wild Flowers of Pioneer Goals.* n.p. [Canada], n.d. [1983?] 19 leaves.

7.2054. *On the Bahá'í Faith.* New Delhi: Bahá'í Publishing Trust, n.d. [196–?] [7] p.

7.2055. *On the Spiritual Significance of Living a Pure and Clean Life.* n.p. [Lagos]: National Spiritual Assembly of the Bahá'ís of Nigeria, n.d. [1982] 2 p.

7.2056. *On Wings of the Soul = (Yŏng Hŭn Ui Nalgae).* n.p. [Seoul: National Spiritual Assembly of the Bahá'ís of Korea], n.d. [1981] 64 p. Korean and English text.

7.2057. *Once to Every Man and Nation: Stories about Becoming a Bahá'í.* ed. Randie and Steven Gottlieb. Oxford: George Ronald, 1985. 146 p.
An inspirational collection of personal narratives by American believers relating how they became Bahá'ís.

7.2058. *One Common Faith: World Peace Through the Oneness of Religion.* n.p. [Wilmette, Ill.]: N.T.C. [i.e. National Teaching Committee], 1985, 1985. [8] p.

7.2059. *101 Teaching Ideas: 'Bahá'í, a Way of Life'.* n.p. [Mona Vale, N.S.W.?: National Teaching Committee?], n.d. [1984] [4] leaves.

7.2060. *163rd Commemoration of the Birth of Baha'u'llah, Saturday Afternoon, 15 November 1980. Department of Special Collections, KSU University Library.* n.p. [Kent, Ohio: Kent State University Library], 1980. [4] p. Bibliography of items on Queen Marie of Romania.

7.2061. *One Planet, One People . . . Please: Bahá'í Faith.* Los Angeles: Los Angeles Baha'i Center, n.d. [1977] [4] p.

7.2062. *idem.* n.p., n.d. [1980?] [2] p.

7.2063. *One Planet, One People . . . Please: Bahá'í Faith: Bahá'í Week in Los Angeles, November 12th–November 20th 1977.* Los Angeles: Spiritual Assembly of the Bahá'ís of Los Angeles, 1977. [4] p.

7.2064. *One Universal Faith.* Wilmette, Ill.: Bahá'í Publishing Trust, n.d. 6 p. (numerous printings with slight variations from the 1960s to present).

7.2065. *idem.* Mona Vale, N.S.W.: Bahá'í Publications, Australia, n.d. [197–], n.d. [1985] 6 p.

7.2066. *idem.* Ponape: National Spiritual Assembly of the Bahá'ís of North West Pacific Ocean, 1976. 4 p. English and Trukese text.

7.2067. *idem.* Manila: National Spiritual Assembly of the Bahá'ís of the Philippines, n.d. [197–?], n.d. [1985] [6] p.

7.2068. *idem.* Port-of-Spain: [National Spiritual Assembly of the Bahá'ís of Trinidad and Tobago], n.d. [1979] [6] p.

7.2069. *One World, One Family: The Bahá'í Faith.* Wilmette, Ill.: Bahá'í Publishing Trust, n.d. (numerous printings, 1950s and 1960s with small variations some 2 p., some 6 p.).

7.2070. *One World Sings.* Wilmette, Ill.: Bahá'í Publishing Trust, n.d. [196–] 96 p.

7.2071. *The Oneness of Mankind: Basic Principle of the Bahá'í Faith.* Wilmette, Ill.: Bahá'í Publishing Trust, n.d. [196–] [2] p.

7.2072. *The Oneness of the World of Humanity.* Tehran: P.O. Box, 1606, n.d. [197–] 21 p.
Anti-Bahá'í work.

7.2073. Ong, Henry. *Uncle Yankee.* California: Ong Publications, 1979. [18], 116 p.
Biography of Yan Kee Leong, a professional cartoonist and Counsellor of the Bahá'í Faith in Asia.

7.2074. *The Open Door.* Wilmette, Ill.: Bahá'í Publishing Committee, 1947, 1952. 5 p.
Booklet describing the Bahá'í teachings on life after death.

7.2075. *idem.* Wilmette, Ill.: Bahá'í Publishing Trust, 1976. 19 p.

7.2076. *idem.* rev. ed. Wilmette, Ill.: Bahá'í Publishing Trust, 1979. 22 p.

7.2077. *An Open Door to a New and Greater Life.* Wilmette, Ill.: Bahá'í Publishing Trust, n.d. [196–?] 19 p.

7.2078. *Operation Befriend . . . Not Secret.* n.p. [Wilmette, Ill.: National Spiritual Assembly of the Bahá'ís of the United States], n.d. [1980] [12] p.

7.2079. *The Origin of Baha'ism.* Tehran: P.O. Box 1606, n.d. [197–] 40 p.
Anti-Bahá'í work.

7.2080. *idem.* Shiraz: P.O. Box 468, n.d. [197–?] 34 p.

7.2081. Ostovar, Terry. *Fly Through the Bahá'í Year.* Los Angeles: Kalimát Press, 1980. 40 p.
Illustrated children's story in verse about Bahá'í holy days and calendar.

7.2082. *Our Children – a Bahá'í View.* Sydney, N.S.W.: Bahá'í Publications Australia, 1979, 1985. 6 p.

7.2082a. Ouskouli. *World Crisis: Religion Is the Remedy.* China, 1941. 1 leaf. Reprint from: *North-China Daily News* (Mar. 9, 1941).

7.2083. *An Outline of Bahá'í Administration.* Kampala, Uganda: National Spiritual Assembly of the Bahá'ís of Central and East Africa, n.d. [between 1956 and 1964], n.d. [196–?] 18 p.; n.d. [before 1964?] 20 p.

7.2084. *An Outline of Bahá'í History.* n.p. [Kampala, Uganda]: National Spiritual Assembly of the Bahá'ís of Central and East Africa, n.d. [195–] 20 p.

7.2085. *idem.* Kampala, Uganda: Bahá'í Publishing Trust, n.d. [196–] 24 p.

7.2086. *idem.* n.p. [Kampala, Uganda]: Approved by National Spiritual Assembly of the Bahá'ís of Uganda and Central Africa, n.d. [between 1964 and 1970?] 22 p.

7.2087. *idem.* n.p. [Salisbury, Rhodesia]: National Spiritual Assembly of the Bahá'ís of South Central Africa, n.d. [between 1964 and 1970] 7 p.

7.2088. *idem.* n.p. [Salisbury, Rhodesia]: National Spiritual Assembly of the Bahá'ís of South Central Africa, 1969. 21 p.

7.2089. *idem.* n.p., n.d. [1978?] 23 p.

7.2090. *idem.* n.p. [Harare]: National Spiritual Assembly of the Bahá'ís of Zimbabwe, 1982. 16 p.

7.2091. *An Outline of Bahá'í History, Laws, Administration.* Kampala, Uganda: Bahá'í Publishing Trust, 1973. 79 p.

7.2092. *An Outline of Bahá'í Teachings and Laws.* Scarborough, Ont.: National Spiritual Assembly of the Bahá'ís of Canada, Bahá'í Publishing Committee, n.d. [196–?] 20 p.

7.2093. *An Outline of the Sacred Will and Testament of 'Abdu'l-Bahá.* n.p. [Wilmette, Ill.]: Approved by the Reviewing Committee of the National Spiritual Assembly of the Bahá'ís of the United States and Canada, n.d. [194–?] 53 leaves.

7.2094. *Overcoming Self.* n.p. [Port-of-Spain: National Spiritual Assembly of the Bahá'ís of Trinidad and Tobago], n.d. [1980] 4 leaves.

P

7.2095. P[aine], M[abel] H[yde]. *Tribute to Bertha Hyde Kirkpatrick.* n.p., n.d. [1948?] 4 leaves.

7.2096. Pakistan Bahá'í Summer School (1946: Karachi). *Ninth Sessions, Bahá'í Summer School, 1946.* Karachi: Bahá'í Summer School, 1946. [4] p.

7.2097. *The Palo Altan, Volume X, No. 43, November 1, 1912.* Palo Alto, Calif., n.d. [1971] 4 p.
Reprint of the issue of *The Palo Altan* which reported the visit of 'Abdu'l-Bahá.

7.2098. *Panduan Pertama = Guidance One.* n.p. [Kuala Lumpur: National Spiritual Assembly of the Bahá'ís of Malaysia], n.d. [1970] 29 p. Malay and English text.

7.2099. Panton, D.M. *Bahaism, the Universal Religion.* London: Chas. J. Thynne & Jarvis Ltd., n.d. [192–?] 8 p. (Satanic Counterfeits of the Second Advent; no.7).
Anti-Bahá'í Christian polemical tract.

7.2100. *Paragraph Summary, Promise of World Peace.* Johannesburg, South Africa: Bahá'í National Information Centre, n.d. [1985] 1 p.

7.2101. *Part of the Bahá'í History of the Family of Charles and Maria Ioas.* by the five living children of Charles and Maria Ioas. n.p. [Berwyn, Ill.: Monroe Ioas], 1978. [10], 24, [2] leaves.

7.2102. *Pattern for a New World Order: Its Individual Ethics, Its New Democracy, Its World Federalism.* New Delhi: Bahá'í Jubilee Celebrations Committee, n.d. [1953] 12 p.

7.2103. *A Pattern for Future Society.* Wilmette, Ill.: Bahá'í Publishing Trust, n.d. [196–], 1974. 6 p.

7.2104. Peeke, Margaret B. *My Visit to Abbas-Effendi in 1899.* Cleveland, Ohio: Dr Pauline Barton-Peeke, 1911 (Chicago: The Grier Press). 23 p.

7.2105. Pellegrino, R.A. *Baha'u'llah and the Holy Bible.* St. Vincent: National Spiritual Assembly of the Baha'i's [sic] of St. Vincent and the Grenadines, n.d. [1985] 13 p. (End Times/Open Book; Series 1).

7.2106. Penfold, Saxby Vouler. *Mrs Eddy's Successor: An Analysis of the Causes of the Discovery of Christian Science with an Authentic Forecast of the Future of the Christian Science Movement.* New Canaan, Conn.: New Canaan Publications, 1938. 17 p.
Fulfilment of Christian Science in the Bahá'í Faith.

7.2107. *People Are Asking . . .: The Persecution of the Bahá'ís in Iran.* Thornhill, Ont.: Bahá'í Canada Publications, n.d. [1980] 8 p.

7.2108. *idem.* London: National Spiritual Assembly of the Bahá'ís of the United Kingdom, n.p. [1981] 6 p.

7.2109. *idem.* Thornhill, Ont.: Canadian Bahá'í Community, n.d. [1985?] [8] p.

7.2110. Perigord, Emily McBride. *Translation of French Foot-Notes of the Dawn-Breakers.* New York: Bahá'í Publishing Committee, n.d. [1939] 83 p.

7.2111. —— *idem.* Wilmette, Ill.: Bahá'í Publishing Trust, 1970, 1973, 1977. 83 p.

7.2112. Perkins, Mary; Hainsworth, Philip. *The Bahá'í Faith.* London: Ward Lock Educational, 1980, 1981, 1982, 1985. (Living Religions Series). 96 p.
Introductory booklet published by a prominent British publisher of educational materials on religion.

7.2113. *Perpetual Bahá'í Calendar.* designed by Edna Morgan McKinney. n.p. [New York?]: Bahá'í Publishing Committee, n.d. [192–?] 1 p.

7.2114. *Persecution of the Bahá'ís in Iran: People Are Asking.* Gangtok: National Spiritual Assembly of the Bahá'ís of Sikkim, n.d. [1983] 8 p.

7.2115. *Persian-American Educational Society, Incorporation Statement and Constitution and By-Laws.* Washington, D.C.: Persian-American Educational Society, 1910.

7.2116. *Personal Teaching: How to Make It a Way of Life: A Personal Teaching & Fireside Resource.* Thornhill, Ont.: Bahá'í Canada Publications, n.d. [1981] 35 p.

7.2117. *idem.* Thornhill, Ont.: Bahá'í Canada Publications [i.e. Canberra, Australia: National Teaching Committee], n.d. [1981] 35 p.

7.2118. Phelps, Myron H. *The Life and Teachings of Abbas Effendi.* New York: G.P. Putnam's Sons: The Knickerbocker Press, 1903, 1904. xliii, 259 p. Cover title: *Abbas Effendi, His Life and Teachings.* LC card 3–81985 rev.
Reviews:
Arena (Boston, Mass.), v.32 (Nov. 1904), pp. 556–558.
The Nation (New York), v.78 (Apr. 7, 1904), pp. 277–278.
Phelps spent a lengthy period with 'Abdu'l-Bahá in 'Akká in 1902 and left this full account of 'Abdu'l-Bahá and his family. Inaccurate in many particulars but valuable for its contemporary atmosphere.

7.2119. —— *idem.* 2nd rev. ed. New York; London: G.P. Putnam's Sons, 1912. xlvii, 243 p.
Review:
The Theosophist (Madras), v.34 no.11 (Aug. 1913), pp. 777–778.
Tisdall, W. St Clair. *The Moslem World* (Hartford, Conn.), v.3 no.2 (Apr. 1913), pp. 206–210.

7.2120. —— *The Master in 'Akká.* rev. & annotated by Marzieh Gail. Los Angeles: Kalimát Press, 1985. xlii, 161 p.
Reprinted portions of *The Life and Teachings of Abbas Effendi* including the spoken chronicle of the Greatest Holy Leaf.

7.2121. Pickering, Ernest. *The Ecumenical Cult – Bahaism.* Minneapolis: Minn.: Religion Analysis Service, n.d. [between 1957 and 1963?] [10] p.
Anti-Bahá'í work from Christian viewpoint.

7.2122. —— *idem.* Minneapolis, Minn.: Religion Analysis Service; Belfast, Northern Ireland: Breda Centre [distributor], n.d. [1985?] [10] p.

7.2123. *The Pilgrimage.* Thornhill, Ont.: Bahá'í Distribution Service, n.d. [1980] [4] p.

7.2124. *Pilgrimage: Bahá'í History Calendar, 1983, 139–140 B.E.* Honolulu; National Spiritual Assembly of the Bahá'ís of the Hawaiian Islands, 1982. [32] p. (Bahá'í History Calendar).

7.2125. Pinchon, Florence E. *Bahá'í Teachings on Life After Death.* Manchester, U.K.: Bahá'í Publishing Trust, n.d. [194–?] 20 p.

7.2126. —— *idem.* Wilmette, Ill.: Bahá'í Publishing Committee, c1954. (at least two variants with this copyright date, one 22 p., the other 23 p.).

7.2127. —— *idem.* London: Bahá'í Publishing Trust, n.d. [ca. 1960] 23 p.

7.2128. —— *The Coming of 'the Glory': (As Described in the Bahai Writings).* London: Simpkin Marshall Ltd., 1928. 144 p.
Essay on the Bahá'í Faith as the fulfilment of Christian promises and as the beginning of a new golden age.

7.2129. *[Pioneering and Culture Shock].* n.d. [Toronto?]: National Pioneer Committee of Canada, n.d. [1972 or 1973] 20 p.

7.2130. Piper, Raymond Frank. *Ways to Wholeness.* Wilmette, Ill.: Bahá'í Publishing Committee, 1944. 22 p.

7.2131. *The Plan: Sharing Our Happiness: Accomplishing the Joy of Universal Participation.* n.p.: Continental Board of Counsellors in Southern Africa, 1972. 19 leaves.

7.2132. *A Plan Evolved by the Continental Board of Counsellors and the National Spiritual Assembly Comprising, 1. Insights Into the Spiritualization of the Community, 2. A Plan of Action for Teaching.* Dublin: National Spiritual Assembly of the Bahá'ís of the Republic of Ireland, 1982. [1], 12, [5] p.
See 7.2463.

7.2132a. *The Plan of God: (The Ancient Covenant of God).* n.p. [United States], n.d. [ᵃ95–] 4 leaves.

7.2133. *A Portrait: The Montana Bahá'í Community.* Great Falls, Mont.: Montana Bahá'í District Teaching Committee, n.d. [197–] 8 p.

7.2134. *The Power of the Covenant.* Thornhill, Ont.: National Spiritual Assembly of the Bahá'ís of Canada, v.1, *Bahá'u'lláh's Covenant with Mankind.* Feb. 1976, 1977, 1982. iii, 37 p.; v.2, *The Problem of Covenant-Breaking.* Oct. 1976, 1982. iv, 48 p.; v.3, *The Face of Opposition.* Apr. 1977. iv, 72 p.
A three-part examination of the Bahá'í covenant, the instrument intended to preserve the unity of the Bahá'í Faith.

7.2135. *idem.* New Delhi: Bahá'í Publishing Trust, 1979.
Same volumes and paging as 7.2134.

7.2136. *Power to Renew the World: A Challenge to Christians.* Wilmette, Ill.: Bahá'í Publishing Trust, 1965. 24 p.

7.2137. *'Prayer'.* Cali, Colombia: National Teaching Committee of the Baha'is of Colombia, 1976 [i.e. St. John's, Antigua: National Spiritual Assembly of the Bahá'ís of the Leeward Islands, 1984?] [5] p. (Spiritual Education of Children, Teacher's Manual).

7.2138. *Prayer Is a Key.* n.p. [Wilmette, Ill.]: Radio Service Committee, 1959. 5 leaves.

7.2139. *Prejudice.* n.p. [Kuala Lumpur?: National Spiritual Assembly of the Bahá'ís of Malaysia?], n.d. [1973] 4, 4, [1] p.

7.2140. *Preparation for Pioneering: A Pioneer's Manual.* Wilmette, Ill.: International Goals Committee, n.d. [196–]. 40 p.; 1976. [43] p.

7.2141. *Press Acclaims Centenary of Universal Religion, 1853–1953.* Chicago: Bahá'í Centenary News Service, 1953. [4] p. that fold out into one poster.

7.2142. *Press and Eminent People Acclaim Bahá'í World Faith Centenary, 1853–1953.* New Delhi: Bahá'í Jubilee Celebrations Committee, 1953. 16 p.

7.2143. *The Priceless Pearl: A Tribute to Shoghi Effendi.* London: National Spiritual Assembly

of the Bahá'ís of the United Kingdom, n.d. [1980?] [4] p.

7.2144. *The Principle of Truthfulness.* comp. and duplicated by Helen M. Gidden. n.p.: Gidden, 1966. [4] p.

7.2145. *The Principles of Child Education in the Bahá'í Faith.* Wilmette, Ill.: Bahá'í Publishing Trust, n.d. [196–?] (two variants, one has sketch of Wilmette Temple on cover), n.d. [1976], n.d. [1977] 6 p.

7.2146. *Principles of the Bahá'í Faith.* New York: Bahá'í Publishing Committee, n.d. [193–?] 16 p.

7.2147. *idem.* Wilmette, Ill.: Bahá'í Publishing Committee, 1941. 16 p.

7.2148. Pritam Singh. *The Second Coming of Shri Krishna.* New Delhi: Bahá'í Publishing Trust, n.d. [195– or 196–] 16 p.

7.2149. —— *The Two Bridges.* Lahore: Pritam Singh, 1944. 22 p.

7.2150. *Proclamation of Bahá'u'lláh.* Kuala Lumpur: Technical College Bahá'í Society, n.d. [1967?] 6 p.

7.2151. *Proclamation of Bahá'u'lláh to Mankind, 1867–1967: Bahá'í Intercontinental Conference, Kampala.* Kampala, Uganda: Uganda Argus, 1967. 4 p.

7.2152. *Proclamation to the Kings & Rulers: Bahá'í Faith, 1867–1967.* Honolulu: National Spiritual Assembly of the Bahá'ís of the Hawaiian Islands, 1967. 8 p.

7.2153. *Progressive Revelation.* n.p., n.d. [197–] 8 p.

7.2154. *The Promise Kept: Bahá'u'lláh Has Come: The Bahá'í Faith.* n.p. [United Kingdom], n.d. [197–?] [6] p.

7.2155. *The Promise of World Peace: An Overview.* n.p. [London: National Spiritual Assembly of the Bahá'ís of the United Kingdom], 1985 (Cranleigh, Surrey: EntaPrint Ltd.). 7 p.

7.2156. *The Promise of World Peace: Bahá'í History Calendar, 1986, 142–143 B.E.* Honolulu: National Spiritual Assembly of the Bahá'ís of the Hawaiian Islands, 1985. [28] p. (Bahá'í History Calendar).

7.2157. *The Promised Day of God.* Wilmette, Ill.: Bahá'í Publishing Committee, 1953. 9 p.

7.2158. *Prophecies and Warnings.* New York; Washington, D.C.; Chicago: Bahai Assembly, n.d. [190–] [4] p.

7.2159. *Prophecies, Signs of the Coming of the 'Son of Man'.* New York: David, n.d. [190–] 4 p.

7.2160. *A Proposal for an Educational Centre Governed by Bahá'í Principles.* Gwynedd, Wales: Judd, n.d. [1985] ([Bangor]: Copycat). [4] p.

7.2161. *The Protective Shadow of His Word: A Compilation on Protection.* comp. Gertrude V. Garrida, assisted by Gary L. Morrison. n.p.: Garrida, n.d. [1980?] 34, [10] p.

7.2162. *Purpose and Meaning of the Bahá'í Ringstone Symbol.* n.p., n.d. [1983?] 1 p.

Q

7.2163. *Questions and Answers About the Bahá'í World Faith.* Manchester, U.K.: Bahá'í Publishing Trust, n.d. [between 1950 and 1958] 6 p.

7.2164. *idem.* London: Bahá'í Publishing Trust, 1959. 6 p.

7.2165. *Questions and Answers on the Attitude of Baha'is to Government and Politics.* Suva: National Spiritual Assembly of the Bahá'ís of the Fiji Islands, n.d. [between 1970 and 1975] 4 p.

7.2166. *Questions and Answers: The Administrative Order Based on the Will and Testament of 'Abdu'l-Bahá, 'His Greatest Legacy to Posterity'.* n.p., 1948. 45 leaves.

7.2167. *Questions Often Asked.* Manila, Philippines: Bahá'í Publishing Trust Committee, n.d. [1977?] 16 p.

7.2168. *Questions the World Is Asking.* Wilmette, Ill.: Bahá'í Publishing Committee, n.d. [early 1950s] 5 pts (1. *Has Religion Failed?* [4] p.; 2. *Why This World Upheaval?* [4] p.; 3. *Is There a World Leader?* [4] p.; 4. *Can Peace Be Maintained?* [4] p.; 5. *Can Human Nature Be Changed?* [4] p.).

7.2169. *Quickeners of Mankind: Pioneering in a World Community.* Thornhill, Ont.: Bahá'í Canada Publications, 1980. 129 p.

R

7.2170. Rabbani, Hussein. *The Oneness of Mankind.* New York: Bahá'í Publishing Committee, n.d. [193–] 23 p.

7.2171. —— *idem.* Wilmette, Ill.: Bahá'í Publishing Committee, 1944. 22 p.

7.2172. Rabbani, Rúḥíyyih. *Bahíyyih Khánum, the Greatest Holy Leaf.* Malawi: Bahá'í International Summer School, Malawi, 1982 (Lilongwe: Extension Aids Branch, Ministry of Agriculture). ix p.

7.2173. —— *The Desire of the World: Materials for the Contemplation of God and His Manifestation for This Day.* Oxford: George Ronald, 1982, 1984. 186 p.
Compilation of selections from Bahá'í scripture, arranged with commentary by Amatu'l-Bahá Rúḥíyyih Khánum. Includes a section on the titles of God and Bahá'u'lláh.

7.2174. —— *The Good Message.* New Delhi: Bahá'í Publishing Trust, n.d. [196–?] 70 p. LC card 63–709.

7.2175. —— *The Hand of the Cause Enoch Olinga, 'In Memoriam'.* Freetown: National Spiritual Assembly of the Bahá'ís of Sierra Leone, n.d. [1984] [3], 14 p.

7.2176. —— *A Manual for Pioneers.* New Delhi: Bahá'í Publishing Trust, 1974. 227 p.
'Pioneers' are self-supporting Bahá'í settlers in foreign lands. One of the most widely-travelled Bahá'ís is the author, the widow of Shoghi Effendi. She here shares her ideas and observations about pioneering from many years of personal experience observing pioneers and travelling for the Faith.

7.2177. —— *idem.* This ed. New Delhi: Bahá'í Publishing Trust, 1981. 227 p.

7.2178. —— *A Message to the Indian and Eskimo Bahá'ís of the Western Hemisphere.* Toronto, Ont.: National Spiritual Assembly of Canada, 1969. 14 p.

7.2179. —— *idem.* 2nd ed. Thornhill, Ont.: Bahá'í Canada Publications, 1982. [28] p.

7.2180. —— *The Passing of Shoghi Effendi.* in

collaboration with John Ferraby. London: Bahá'í Publishing Trust, 1958. 25 p.

7.2181. —— *Prescription for Living.* Oxford: George Ronald, 1950. xii, 194 p. (an edition of 300 copies in dark blue cloth serial numbered and autographed by the author).

A straight-forward discussion of mankind's present unhappiness, confusion and uncertainty, and the possible solutions presented by the Bahá'í Faith.

7.2182. —— *idem.* Oxford: George Ronald, 1950. xii, 194 p. (regular edition). LC card 51–3528.

7.2183. —— *idem.* rev. ed. London: George Ronald, 1960. 205 p.; 1969, 1970, 1975. 204 p.

7.2184. —— *idem.* 1st Talisman ed. Oxford: George Ronald, 1972, 1977. 204 p.

7.2185. —— *idem.* 2nd rev. ed. Oxford: George Ronald, 1978. 272 p.

7.2186. —— *The Priceless Pearl.* London: Bahá'í Publishing Trust, 1969. 482 p. (an edition of 1500 copies bound in red cloth, serial numbered and signed by the author).

An appraisal of Shoghi Effendi's life and work by Rúḥíyyih Rabbani (née Mary Sutherland Maxwell) who, after her marriage to the Guardian served as his personal secretary and was appointed by him a Hand of the Cause of God. The view she brings to her subject is therefore unique in its depth and understanding.

7.2187. —— *idem.* London: Bahá'í Publishing Trust, 1969. 482 p. (regular edition).

7.2188. —— *A Spiritual Assembly's Growing Pains.* New Delhi: Bahá'í Publishing Trust, n.d. [196–?] 28 p.

7.2189. —— *idem.* 1st Australian ed. [Mona Vale, N.S.W.]: Bahá'í Publishing Trust Australia, 1976. 32 p.

7.2190. —— *The Story of Enoch Olinga.* [Umtata]: National Spiritual Assembly of the Bahá'ís of Transkei, Apr. 1984. 38 p.

7.2191. —— *Success in Teaching: An Intimate Talk with Bahá'ís Who Long to Serve the Faith.* Wilmette, Ill.: Bahá'í Publishing Trust, n.d. [196–?] 7 p. Author's name misspelled as 'Rúḥíyyh' on cover.

7.2192. —— *idem.* Wilmette, Ill.: Bahá'í Publishing Trust, 1970. 24 p.

7.2193. —— *idem.* n.p. [Mona Vale, N.S.W.]: Bahá'í Publications Australia, n.d. [1985] (Mudgee: Lynx Printing Service). 24 p.

7.2193a. —— *Teaching Problems.* Manchester, U.K.: Bahá'í Publishing Trust, 1949. 16 p.

7.2194. —— *Twenty-Five Years of the Guardianship.* Wilmette, Ill.: Bahá'í Publishing Committee, 1948. 27 p.

7.2195. Rabbani School (Gwalior, India). *Rabbani School.* Gwalior, India: [National Spiritual Assembly of the Bahá'ís of India], n.d. [1977?] [4] p.

7.2196. *Race and Man: A Compilation.* comp. Maye Harvey Gift and Alice Simmons Cox. Wilmette, Ill.: Bahá'ı Publishing Committee, 1943, 1945. xx, 134 p. LC card 43–17009.

7.2197. *Radio and TV within Your Reach.* Maracaibo, Venezuela: Cirbal, 1985. [8] p.

7.2198. Radley, Gail. *Second Birth: The Goal of Life.* il. Richard Morgan. London: Bahá'í Publishing Trust, 1984. [30] p.

Explanation of life after death for children.

7.2199. —— *Special Strengths.* il. Joe Boddy. Evanston, Ill.: Bellwood Press, 1984. [8], 56 p. LC card 84–21658.

Children's story about spiritual strengths.

7.2200. —— *Zahra's Search.* il. Winifred Barnum Newman. Wilmette, Ill.: Bahá'í Publishing Trust, 1982. [32] p. LC card 82–11583.

Children's story illustrating the importance of ardour in seeking.

7.2201. Raj, Veni. *A Diamond in the Darkness.* il. Tushar Kanti-Paul. Oxford: George Ronald, 1984. 30 p.

True story of a blind boy from Sarawak who became a Bahá'í.

7.2202. Rajah, K. *The Creative Power Behind All Existence.* Seremban, Malaysia: K. Rajah, 1976 (Penang: Ganesh Printing Works). 36 p.

7.2203. —— *God Is the All Knowing Power of the Universe.* Seremban, Malaysia: Rajah, n.d. [196–?] 15 p.

7.2204. —— *Poverty to Plenty.* Seremban, Malaysia: K. Rajah, 1975 (Penang: Ganesh Printing Works). 20 p.

7.2205. Raman, S.P. *My Quest for the Fulfillment of Hinduism.* Wilmette, Ill.: Bahá'í Publishing Trust, 1974. 22 p.

7.2205a. —— *idem.* Wilmette, Ill.: Bahá'í Publishing Trust, n.d. [i.e. Kuala Lumpur: National Spiritual Assembly of the Bahá'ís of Malaysia, 1985] 22 p.

7.2206. *The Realization of World Unity: A Public Meeting in Commemoration of the Twenty-Fifth Anniversary of the Arrival of 'Abdu'l-Bahá in America, 1912: Held in the Bahá'í House of Worship. Sunday, April 11, 1937.* Wilmette, Ill.:

[National Spiritual Assembly of the Bahá'ís of the United States and Canada], 1937. [4] p.

7.2207. *Recurring Cycles.* West Englewood, N.J.: National Spiritual Assembly of the Bahá'ís of the United States and Canada, n.d. [192–] [4] p.

7.2208. Reed, Betty. *Could This Be Your Hope, Your Dream?* London: National Spiritual Assembly of the Bahá'ís of the United Kingdom, n.d. [1981] [2] p.

7.2209. —— *idem.* London: National Spiritual Assembly of the Bahá'ís of the U.K., n.d. [1983?] [4] p.

7.2210. —— *The Eternal Covenant.* London: Bahá'í Publishing Trust, 1973. 4 p.

7.2211. —— *Pokka's Stories.* Oakham, Eng.: Bahá'í Publishing Trust, n.d. [1976] 32 p. Cover title: *Stories of Bahá'u'lláh as Told by Pokka.*
Illustrated children's stories of Bahá'u'lláh.

7.2212. Regional Conference on Education and Human Rights (1968: Cleveland, Ohio). *Regional Conference on Education and Human Rights, June 14–15, 1968, Cleveland, Ohio.* Cleveland, Ohio: Regional Conference on Education and Human Rights, 1968. [6] p.

7.2213. Regional Conference on Prejudice and Human Rights (1968: Memphis, Tenn.). *Regional Conference on Prejudice and Human Rights, June 7–8, 1968, Memphis, Tennessee.* Memphis, Tenn.: Regional Conference on Prejudice and Human Rights, 1968. [6] p.

7.2214. Regional Conference on Youth and Human Rights (1968: Richmond, Calif.). *Regional Conference on Youth and Human Rights, June 7–8, 1968, Richmond, California.* Richmond, Calif.: Regional Conference on Youth and Human Rights, 1968. [6] p.

7.2215. *Releasing Women's Potential: A Continuing Forum: Peter Clark Hall, University Centre, University of Guelph, May 29th, June 5, June 12, June 19, 1983.* Guelph, Ont.: Baha'i Community of Guelph, 1983. [8] p.

7.2216. *Religion in Life Emblem: Bahá'í Faith.* Canada: Girl Guides of Canada, Boy Scouts of Canada, n.d. [1977?] 6 p.

7.2217. *The Religion of the Future: An Introduction to the Bahai Faith.* Accra North: National Spiritual Assembly of the Bahá'ís of Ghana, n.d. [1971?] 9 p.

7.2218. *The Religion of World Unity.* Wilmette, Ill.: Bahá'í Publishing Committee, n.d. [after 1947] 7 p.

7.2219. Remey, Charles Mason. *Architectural Compositions in the Indian Style. Designs for*

Temples and Shrines. Newport, R.I.: Remey, 1923. 87 p. LC card 24–17887.

7.2220. —— *Architectural Design for the Baha'i Temple to Be Built Upon Mount Carmel.* Washington, D.C.: Remey, 1948. 21, [22] leaves. (Bahá'í Reminiscences, Diary, Letters and Other Documents).

7.2221. —— *An Architectural Design for the Building to Enshrine the Archives of the Baha'i Faith.* n.p. [Washington, D.C.]: Remey, 1954. 6, 24, [9] leaves.

7.2222. —— *Architectural Exhibition of a Series of Preliminary Designs by Charles Mason Remey for the Mashrak El Azkar (Bahai Temple).* n.p. [Washington, D.C.]: Remey, n.d. [191–] [8] p.

7.2223. —— *The Bahai Library of Constructive Religion: The Peace of the World.* Chicago: Bahai Publishing Society, 1919. 46 p. Cover title: *The Peace of the World.* LC card 20–2685.
This booklet 'is merely a synthesis of the Baha'i constructive peace propaganda as already approved and set forth in the literature of this movement'.

7.2224. —— *Bahai Manuscripts: Suggestions for Their Preservation and Arrangement.* Newport, R.I.: Remey, 1923. 20 p. LC card 24–24845.

7.2225. —— *The Bahai Movement: A Series of Nineteen Papers Upon the Bahai Movement.* Washington, D.C.: J.D. Milans and Sons, 1912. 115 p.

7.2226. —— *idem.* 2nd ed. Washington, D.C.: J.D. Milans & Sons, 1912. 115 p. LC card 12–15705 rev.

7.2227. —— *The Bahai Movement: A Teaching of Peace: Address Made Before the Third National Peace Congress, Baltimore Maryland, U.S.A., Saturday, May 6, 1911 by Charles Mason Remey.* [1st ed.?] Chicago: Bahai Assembly of Chicago; New York City: Bahai Assembly of New York; Washington, D.C.: Bahai Assembly of Washington, 1911. 16 p. Cover title: *Peace.* LC card 17–28574.

7.2228. —— *The Bahai Movement: A Teaching of Peace: Address Made by Charles Mason Remey Before the Third National Peace Congress, Baltimore, Maryland, U.S.A., Saturday, May 6, 1911.* [2nd ed.?] Chicago: Bahai Assembly of Chicago; New York City: Bahai Assembly of New York; Washington, D.C.: Bahai Assembly of Washington, 1911. 16 p. Cover title: *Peace.*

7.2229. —— *The Bahai Movement: A Teaching of Peace: Address Made by Charles Mason Remey Before the Third National Peace Conference, Baltimore, Maryland, U.S.A., Saturday, May 6, 1911.* 3rd ed. Washington, D.C.: Bahai Assembly of Washington, 1911. 16 p. Cover title: *Peace*.

7.2230. —— *The Bahai Movement for Universal Religion*. n.p., n.d. [1919?] [4] p. Reprinted from *The New Era* (Riverton, N.J.), Aug. 1, 1919.

7.2231. —— *The Bahai Movement for Universal Religion, Brotherhood and Peace: A Sketch of Its History and Teachings*. Washington, D.C.: Persian-American Bulletin, 1912. 16 p. LC card 19–5547.

7.2232. —— *The Bahai Religion*. n.p., n.d. [1919?] [3] p. Reprinted from *The New Era* (Riverton, N.J.), July 25, 1919.

7.2233. —— *The Bahai Religion and World Peace*. n.p., n.d. [1919?] [4] p. Reprinted from *The New Era* (Riverton, N.J.), August 22, 1919.

7.2234. —— *The Bahai Religion and World Unity*. n.p., n.d. [1919?] [4] p. Reprinted from *The New Era* (Riverton, N.J.), September 5, 1919.

7.2235. —— *Bahá'í Reminiscences, Diary, Letters and Other Documents*. Washington, D.C.: Remey, 1938. (56 volume set of personal archives reproduced in a limited number of typescripts).

7.2236. —— *The Bahai Revelation and Reconstruction*. Chicago: Distributed by Bahai Publishing Society, 1919. 88 p. LC card 20–2686.

Sketches the history and the spiritual, social and economic principles of the Bahá'í Movement and describes the possible effects of their application in post-World War I reconstruction.

7.2237. —— *Bahai Teaching: Quotations from the Bahai Sacred Writings and Several Articles upon the History and Aims of the Teachings*. Washington, D.C.: J.D. Milans & Sons, 1917. [ca. 100] p. LC card 18–2925.

Seven pamphlets bound together under one title, the contents focusing on unity and peace; the covenant God has established with mankind, the latest chapter of which is the Revelation of Bahá'u'lláh; and introductory essays on Bahá'í teachings and principles.

7.2238. —— *The Bahai Temple*. n.p., n.d. [1919?] [4] p. Reprinted from *The New Era* (Riverton, N.J.), August 8, 1919.

7.2239. —— *Constructive Principles of the Bahai Movement*. Chicago: Bahai Publishing Society, 1917 (Washington, D.C.: J.D. Milans & Sons). 63 p. LC card 18–1731.

A general introduction for Americans. Includes a section dealing with the embryonic 'Mashrak-el-Azkar' (Bahá'í House of Worship) in Wilmette, Ill., for which Remey submitted designs.

7.2240. —— *The Covenant*. Washington, D.C.: Bahai Assembly of Washington, D.C., 1912. 32 p. LC card 19–5548 rev.

7.2241. —— *The Daily Diary of Charles Mason Remey*. Washington, D.C.: Remey,, 1940–1948. 13 v. (Bahá'í Reminiscences, Diary, Letters and Other Documents).

7.2242. —— *Description of a Design in the Indian Style of Architecture for the First Mashrekol-Azkar to Be Erected in America*. Washington, D.C.: Remey, 1920. [3] leaves.

7.2243. —— *Firmness in the Covenant*. n.p. [Washington, D.C.: Remey], 1918. 5 leaves.

7.2244. —— *Five Preliminary Designs for the Mashrak-el-Azkar, Showing Varying Treatments in Different Styles of Architecture*. n.p. [Washington, D.C.]: C.M.R., n.d. [1916] 16 leaves. Cover title: *Mashrak-el-Azkar*.

7.2245. —— *Illustrated Description of a Design in the Persian-Indian Style of Architecture for the First Mashrak-El-Azkar (Bahai Temple) to Be Erected in America*. Humbly Offered to the Center of the Covenant through the Bahai Temple Unity by C.M.R. April 26–28, 1920. Washington, D.C.: C.M.R., 1920. 8, [1], [3] p., 16 leaves. LC card 21–15733.

7.2246. —— *The Indian Style of Architecture: A Brief Sketch of Its History and Development, with a Design for a Temple*. Boston, 1925. 8 p. LC card 25–24410.

7.2247. —— *Journal Diary of a Bahá'í Teacher in Latin America, 1946–1947*. Washington, D.C.: Remey, n.d. [1949?] 119 leaves. LC card 49–3130.

7.2248. —— *Journal Diary of Bahá'í Travels in Europe, 1947*. Washington, D.C.: Remey, n.d. [1949?] 291 leaves. LC card 49–3827.

7.2249. —— *Journal Diary of European Bahá'í Travels, April–November 1948*. Washington, D.C.: Remey, 1949. 338 leaves. LC card 49–3129.

7.2249a. —— *Mashrak-el-Azkar*. Washington, D.C.: Remey, n.d. [191–]8, [1], 2 leaves, [15] leaves of plates.

7.2250. —— *Mashrak-el-Azkar, Descriptive of the Bahai Temple and Illustrative of an Exhibition of Preliminary Designs for the First Mashrak-el-Azkar to be Built in America, Showing Nine Varying Treatments in Different Styles of Architecture*. Washington: J.D. Milans & Sons, 1917. 120 p. LC card 18–2513.

Describes requirements for the Bahá'í centre of worship. The author, himself an architect, presents plans and sketches for nine different stylistic treatments for the structure.

7.2251. —— *The Message of Unity: The Bahai*

Movement. Washington, D.C.: Bahai Assembly of Washington, 1908. 16 p.

7.2252. —— *The New Day: The Bahai Revelation, a Brief Statement of Its History and Teachings*. Chicago: Bahai Publishing Society [distributor], 1919. 27 p. LC card 20–2687 rev.

7.2253. —— *A Nonagonal Temple in the Indian Style of Architecture*. Italy: Remey, 1927. 22 p., 10 leaves. LC card 28–2679.

7.2254. —— *Observations of a Bahai Traveller*. Washington, D.C.: Carnahan Press, n.d. [1909] 94 p. LC card 18–13653.
Narrative of travels in 1908 among the Bahá'ís of the Holy Land, Iran and Turkestan.

7.2255. —— *idem*. 2nd ed. Washington, D.C.: J.D. Milans and Sons, 1915. 133 p. LC card 15–6116 rev.
Contains an added section on the Central Figures and origins of the Bahá'í Faith.

7.2256. —— *An Open Letter to the Bahais in America*. n.p. [Washington, D.C.], 1918. 8 leaves.

7.2257. —— *An Outline of the Bahai' [sic] Teachings*. n.p. 1905. 7 p.

7.2258. —— *A Prospectus: A Series of Five Lectures Upon the Universal Religious and Social Principles of the Bahai Movement*. Washington, D.C.: Remey, 1919. 8 p. LC card 24–24931.

7.2259. —— *The Protection of the Cause of God*. n.p., 1918. 28 leaves.

7.2260. —— *The Relation of the Bahai Movement to the Religions of the Past*. n.p., n.d. [1919?] [4] p. Reprinted from *The New Era* [Riverton, N.J.), August 29, 1919.

7.2261. ——*Reminiscences and Letters*. Washington, D.C.: Remey, n.d. [after 1940] (100 volumes produced in several typescript, bound copies).

7.2262. —— *Reminiscences of the Summer School, Green-Acre, Eliot-Maine*. n.p.: Remey, 1949. 2v. (Remey Family Records). Cover title: *Reminiscences of Green Acre*. LC card 58–3335.

7.2263. —— *Report of a Tour of Bahá'í Assemblies, October 1923–April 1924*. n.p., 1924. 34 p.

7.2264. —— *Report to Abdul Baha of the Bahai Activities in the States of North Carolina, South Carolina, Georgia and Florida U.S.A.* n.p., 1919. 28 p.

7.2265. —— *Reports of Bahá'í Travels and Teaching Activities*. Washington, D.C.: Remey, n.d. [1947?] [151] leaves.

7.2266. —— *The Revelation of Baha'ullah [sic]*.

Washington, D.C.: Remey, 1906. 11 p. Cover title: *Religious Unity*.

7.2267. —— *A Series of Twelve Articles Introductory to the Study of the Bahá'í Teachings: Treating Briefly of the Revelation of Bahá'u'lláh History, Organization, Religious and Secular Doctrines and Institutions*. New York: Bahá'í Publishing Committee, 1925. 184 p. LC card 25–27648.

7.2268. —— *Service in the Kingdom*. n.p., 1906. [4] p.

7.2269. —— *Seven Articles Upon the Bahai Religious Movement*. Riverton, N.J., 1919, 30 p. Reprinted from *The New Era*. LC card 24–24843.

7.2270. —— *Some Tenets Taught by the Bahai Religion*. n.p., n.d. [1919?] [4] p. Reprinted from *The New Era* (Riverton, N.J.), August 15, 1919.

7.2271. —— *Suggestions for the Arrangement of a Bibliography and Reference Indexes to the Bahá'í Teachings, with Practical Explanations of How to Build up Bahá'í Index Systems*. n.p., 1923. 16 p. Cover title: *Bahá'í Indexes*. LC card 24–24932.

7.2272. —— *Suggestions for the United Prayer*. Washington, D.C.: Remey, n.d. [191–?] 2 p.

7.2273. —— *A Teacher of the Bahá'í Faith in South America, 1945–1946*. Washington, D.C.: Remey, n.d. [1949?] 208 leaves. LC card 49–3128.

7.2274. —— *Through Warring Countries to the Mountain of God*. Washington, D.C.: Charles Mason Remey, 1915. 111 leaves. LC card 18–11713.
'An account of some of the experiences of two American Baha'is in France, England, Germany and other countries, on their way to visit Abdul Baha in the Holy Land.'

7.2275. —— *Unity: The Revelation of Bahá-'u'lláh*. n.p., 1905. [8] p.

7.2276. —— *The Universal Consciousness of the Bahá'í Revelation: A Brief Treatise Introductory to the Study of the Bahá'í Religion*. Florence, Italy: Charles Mason Remey; Chicago Bahá'í Publishing Committee [distributor], 1925 (Firenze: Tipografia Sordamoti). 60 p. LC card 25–24154.

7.2277. *A Reply to Rev. H.C. Gurney, C.M.S. Missionary in Persia*. Adelaide, S. Aust.: Baha'i's of Adelaide, n.d. [192–?] (Adelaide, S. Aust.: Advertiser Printing Office). [4] p.

7.2278. *Reports of Proceedings of Meetings in New York City and Chicago, Illinois*. Chicago: Press of Hollister Bros., 1900. 16 p.
Reports of meetings in which 'Abdu'l-Karím Ṭihrání confronted Ibrahim Kheiralla over Kheiralla's renunciation of 'Abdu'l-Bahá and

defection to Muḥammad-'Alí ('Abdu'l-Bahá's half-brother who opposed the written will of Bahá'u'lláh).

7.2279. *Response to the Revelation: Poetry by Bahá'ís.* Thornhill, Ont.: Canadian Association for Studies on the Bahá'í Faith, 1980. 43 p. (Bahá'í Studies; v.7).

7.2280. *The Return of Christ.* Suva, Fiji: Bahá'í Publishing Trust, 1978. 23 p.

7.2281. Reveal, Pamela. *Bahá'í Ideas.* n.p. [Honolulu: Hawaii Bahá'í National Library?], n.d. [1981] [7, 8] leaves.

7.2282. —— *Bahá'í Ideas!* Honolulu: Hawaii Bahá'í National Library, 1984. 5 p., [17] leaves.

7.2283. —— *idem.* Lusaka: National Child Education Committee of the National Spiritual Assembly of the Baha'is of Zambia, 1985. [22] p.

7.2284. —— *To the Heart.* Honolulu: Hawaii National Bahá'í Library, 1984. [24] p. Cover title: *To the Heart: A Children's Pilgrimage to the Baha'i World Center.*

7.2285. —— *To the Heart: A Children's Pilgrimage to the Baha'i World Center.* Hawaii: National Child Development Committee, 1982. 11 [i.e. 20.] p.

7.2286. [Revell], Ethel. *My Master.* Sister Ethel. n.p., n.d. [191–?] 2 p.

7.2287. Rexford, Orcella. *Radiant Acquiescence.* New York: Bahá'í Publishing Committee, 1937. 16 p.

7.2288. —— *idem.* Wilmette, Ill.: Bahá'í Publishing Committee, 1941. 14 p.

7.2289. *Richard St. Barbe Baker, O.B.E., L.L.D.: Born 9 October, 1889 Near Southampton, England, Died 9 June, 1982 Saskatoon, Canada.* n.p. [Saskatoon: Local Spiritual Assembly of the Bahá'ís of Saskatoon], n.d. [1982] [8] p.

7.2290. Richards, J.R. *Baha'ism.* London: S.P.C.K., 1965. 21 p. (Christian Knowledge Booklets; no.5).
Anti-Bahá'í work from Christian viewpoint.

7.2291. —— *The Religion of the Baha'is.* London: Society for the Promotion of Christian Knowledge, 1932. xx, 242 p. LC card 34–7591.
Review:
Zwemer, Samuel M. *The Moslem World* (Hartford, Conn.), v.23 no.3 (July 1933), p. 311.
Richards faults the Bahá'ís for inadequate concepts of sin and on the oft-cited grounds that Bahá'ís do not place Jesus Christ above the other messengers.

7.2292. *Riḍván Greetings from Bahá'ís of Nagasaki, Japan, April 21, 1959.* Nagasaki: Bahá'ís of Nagasaki, 1959. 8 p.

7.2293. Riggs, Robert F. *The Apocalypse Unsealed.* New York: Philosophical Library, 1981. xvi, 312 p. LC card 80–81698.
Riggs studies many interrelated esoteric disciplines and their relation to the Apocalypse – zodiac, gemmatria, geometric symbolism. Includes appendices listing references to the Book of Revelation in Bahá'í works.

7.2294. *The Right to an Identity.* Toronto, Ont.: Canadian Bahá'í Community, n.d. [between 1967 and 1976] [16] p.

7.2995. Robarts, Ella M. *The Children of the Kingdom: The Bahai Junior Movement.* Boston: The Huntington Press, 1922. [6] p.

7.2296. Robarts, John A. *Letter to Bahá'ís.* n.p., 1960 [12] p.

7.2297. Robinson, Gertrude. *Bahá'u'lláh and the New Era: A Course of Study.* Wilmette, Ill.: Bahá'í Publishing Trust, 1971. 20 p.

7.2298. —— *Course of Study Based on 'Bahá'u'lláh and the New Era' by J.E. Esslemont.* Wilmette, Ill.: Bahá'í Publishing Committee, 1942. 18 leaves.

7.2299. —— *idem.* Wilmette, Ill.: Bahá'í Publishing Trust, 1955. 22 p.

7.2300. *The Role of Parents in the Education of Children.* n.p. [Thornhill, Ont.]: Canadian Bahá'í Community, 1978. 52 p.

7.2301. *The Role of the Auxiliary Board Member: A Compilation.* Harare: Continental Board of Counsellors of the Baha'i Faith in Africa, Harare Office, 1982. 28 p.

7.2302. *The Role of Women in the New World Order.* comp. Manigeh Cannon and Sunni DaVar. Mayaguez, P.R.: Spiritual Assembly of the Bahá'ís of Mayaguez, 1975. 9 leaves.

7.2303. [Romer, Harry H.] *Ancient Persia was the Home of a Wonderful Art* . . . London: [Romer], n.d. [192–?] 1 p.

7.2304. Root, Martha L. *Bahá'i Circular Letter from Martha L. Root.* n.p., n.d. [1930?] 8 p.

7.2305. —— *Baha'i Letter About India and Burma.* Rangoon: Rangoon Standard Press, n.d. [between 1930 and 1939?] 20 p.

7.2306. —— *Second List of Friends in China to Send Bahai Literature (the First List Was of Peking Friends).* n.p., n.d. [193–?] 4 p.

7.2307. —— *Táhirih the Pure: Iran's Greatest Woman.* Karachi: Martha L. Root, 1938

(Karachi: Haji Nazir-ud-Din Hafiz Abdul Karim Babar at the Civil & Military Press). xvi, 113 p. LC card 75-327899.

Journalistic portrayal of the Bábí heroine, one of the first disciples of the Báb, a poet and scholar in Islamic doctrine and law. She is recorded as having removed her veil at the conference of Badasht and she later suffered a martyr's fate.

7.2308. —— idem. Karachi: National Spiritual Assembly of the Bahá'ís of Parkistan, c1938 [i.e. ca. 1970] xvi, 101 p.

7.2309. —— idem. rev. ed. with an introductory essay by Marzieh Gail. Los Angeles: Kalimát Press, 1981. v, 146 p. LC card 80-39945.

7.2310. —— What the Baha'i Faith Can Do for Poverty. n.p., 1938 (Indore: Holkar Govt. Press). 15 p.

7.2311. Roozbehyan, F. The Paradise on Earth. n.p. [Iran: Roozbehyan], n.d. [after 1960] 88 p.

7.2312. Rosenberg, Ethel J. A Brief Account of the Bahai Movement. Hampstead: The Priory Press; London: J.M. Watkins for the Bahai Society of London, 1911. 29 p.

7.2313. —— A Brief Sketch of Behaism. London: R.F. Hunger, 310 Euston Rd., N.W., 1905. 12 p.

7.2314. Ross-Enfield, Louis. How a Member of the Jewish Faith Became a Bahá'í. London: Bahá'í Publishing Trust, n.d. [between 1970 and 1977] 1 p.

7.2315. Rost, H.T.D. The Brilliant Stars: The Bahá'í Faith and the Education of Children. Oxford: George Ronald, 1979. ix, 182 p. LC card 80-670096.
   Review:
Dotts, M. Franklin. Religious Education (New Haven, Conn.), v.75 no.4 (July–Aug. 1980), pp. 501–502.

Bahá'í educational precepts, with a considerable number of quotations from Bahá'í works. Based partly upon the author's doctoral dissertation.

7.2316. Roushaná'í, Illumination: Anthology of Nine Bahá'í Writers. Detroit, Mich.: Trans-Love Energies, 1968. 144 p.

7.2317. Ruhe, David S. Door of Hope: A Century of the Bahá'í Faith in the Holy Land. Oxford: George Ronald, 1983. 247 p. LC card 83-184956.
   Review:
Mazzaoui, Michel M. Journal of the American Oriental Society (New Haven, Conn.), v.105 no.2 (1985), pp. 360–362.

A guide to the historical sites associated with the Bahá'í Faith in the Holy Land, arranged by location rather than purely chronologically. Dr Ruhe relates Bahá'í sites to earlier historical events. Indispensable for understanding Bahá'í pilgrimage. Illustrated with many black and white photographs.

7.2318. Ruhe, Margaret. Guidelines for Parents. n.p. [Wilmette, Ill.]: Bahá'í National Education Committee of the United States, n.d. [1985] 28 p.

7.2319. —— Some Thoughts on Marriage. Los Angeles: Kalimát Press, 1982. 13 p.

7.2320. Ruhi Institute (Puerto Tejada, Cauca, Colombia). History Course 1: The Life of the Báb. Puerto Tejada: Ruhi Institute, n.d. [1983] 35 p.

7.2321. —— Laws and Ordinances, Course 1: Prayer. Puerto Tejada: Ruhi Institute, n.d. [1983] 18 p.

7.2322. —— Laws and Ordinances, Course 2: Understanding the Bahá'í Writings. Puerto Tejada: Ruhi Institute, n.d. [1983] 13 p.

7.2323. —— Laws and Ordinances, Course 3: The Joy of Teaching. Puerto Tejada: Ruhi Institute, n.d. [1983] 17 p.

7.2324. —— idem, n.p. [Freetown: National Spiritual Assembly of the Bahá'ís of Sierra Leone], n.d. [1984] 6 p.

7.2325. —— Principles and Beliefs, Course 1: Life and Death. Puerto Tejada: Ruhi Institute, n.d. [1983] 36 p.

7.2326. —— Principles and Beliefs, Course 2: Some Principles of Bahá'í Education. Puerto Tejada: Ruhi Institute, n.d. [1983] 32 p.

7.2327. —— Service, Course 1: Deepening Booklets. Puerto Tejada: Ruhi Institute, n.d. [1983] 21 p.

7.2328. —— Service, Course 2: I Am a Bahá'í. Puerto Tejada: Ruhi Institute, n.d. [1983] 23 p.

7.2329. —— Service, Course 3: Bahá'í Classes for Children. Puerto Tejada: Ruhi Institute, n.d. [1983?] 88 p.

7.2330. Rules of the Road for Latin America. n.p. [Lima, Peru], n.d. [1950?] 8 leaves.

7.2331. Rutstein, Nathan. He Loved and Served: The Story of Curtis Kelsey. Oxford: George Ronald, 1982, 1982. 185 p. LC card 82-147132.

Biography of a simple man who, though he never went to college or gained worldly fame, was asked by 'Abdu'l-Bahá to come to Haifa in 1921 to install the first electrical lighting for the Shrine of the Báb.

7.2332. —— *Teaching the Bahá'í Faith: Spirit in Action.* Oxford: George Ronald, 1984. iv, 188 p. LC card 82–253287.

A practical book for overcoming some of the fears or misconceptions Bahá'ís may have about sharing their religious beliefs with others.

S

7.2333. Sabet, Huschmand. *The Heavens Are Cleft Asunder.* Oxford: George Ronald, 1975. 153 p. LC card 76–356048.

An assessment of the older religions (particularly Christanity) and their apparent inability to meet the needs of mankind today. When first published in German this book aroused considerable interest among theologians and thinkers.

7.2334. *Sacrifice.* n.p. [London: National Spiritual Assembly of the Bahá'ís of the United Kingdom], n.d. [1982] 49 p.

7.2335. Ṣahbá, Fáriburz. *The Green Years.* trans. Betsy R. Berz, K. Mesbáh; il. H. Seyḥoún. New Delhi: Bahá'í Publishing Trust, 1982. 107 p.

Children's stories of events during the heroic early days of the Bábí and Bahá'í Faiths. Originally written for the Persian children's magazine *Varqá.*

7.2336. Sala, Emeric. *This Earth One Country.* Boston: Bruce Humphries Inc.; Toronto, Ont.: The Ryerson Press, 1945. 185 p. LC card 46–776.

Post World War II introduction to the Bahá'í Faith emphasizing the religion's internationalism and goal of world order.

7.2337. Salmání, Ustád Muḥammad 'Alí. *My Memories of Bahá'u'lláh.* trans. Marzieh Gail. Los Angeles: Kalimát Press, 1982. xi, 148 p. LC card 82–13100.

Review:

Mazzaoui, Michel M. *Journal of the American Oriental Society* (New Haven, Conn.), v.105 no.2 (1985), pp. 360–362.

The memoirs of an unschooled man of humble origins who accompanied Bahá'u'lláh on his exile from Baghdád to Constantinople, Edirne and finally 'Akká. Little new information of substance is revealed in this work; its interest lies in the picture of simple devotion that it conveys.

7.2338. *Samandari House, Open House, Saturday, 14th July 1984, 10 a.m.–4 p.m.* n.p. [Thames, New Zealand: Diane Scott], 1984. [3] p.

Restored house named after Farámarz Samandarí, giving information about him and the persecution of Bahá'ís.

7.2339. Samandari Travel Agency. *Tours to the*

Holy Land Specially Arranged for Bahá'í Pilgrims and Visitors. Genève, Switzerland: Samandari Travel Agency, 1976. 8 p.

7.2340. *Samoa, Bahá'í House of Worship: The Dawning Place of the Mention of God in the Heart of the Pacific.* Apia, W. Samoa: Baha'i Information Service, n.d. [1984] 6 p.

7.2341. Santillana, Rosa. *Rosa Santillana in English.* Santiago, Chile: Primavera Productions, n.d. [1985] 13 p.

English translation of lyrics to Spanish Bahá'í songs.

7.2342. Sassi, Gabriel. *An Investigation of Bahaism: An Address Concerning the Bahais Religion, Delivered at the Paris Exposition of 1900, Before an Assembly of Learned and Prominent Men.* trans. Honore J. Jaxon. Chicago: Behais Supply and Publishing Board, 1901. 27 p. Cover and running title: *Martinist's Report.*

7.2343. *Saucer-Dish Dated 1878, Diameter 10 in.: An Exact Reproduction of the Original, Which Was Obtained from the Afnan Family for the Mottahedeh Collection.* Evanston, Ill.: International Goals Committee, n.d. [1982] 1 p.

7.2344. Scaramucci, Mrs. *The Bahai Revelation.* London: The Priory Press, 1911.

7.2345. Scatcherd, Felicia R. *A Wise Man from the East.* London: The Unity Press, 1912. 7 p.

7.2346. Schaefer, Udo. *The Imperishable Dominion: The Bahá'í Faith and the Future of Mankind.* trans. Janet Rawling-Keitel, David Hopper, Patricia Crampton. Oxford: George Ronald, 1983. xvii, 301 p. LC card 83–237382.

An analysis of current social, political, legal and moral trends, and the approach taken by the Bahá'í Revelation. Translated from the German.

7.2347. —— *The Light Shineth in Darkness: Five Studies in Revelation after Christ.* trans. Hélène Momtaz Neri, Oliver Coburn. Oxford: George Ronald, 1977, 1979, 1980. viii, 195 p. LC card 78–320332.

Reviews:

Choice (Middletown, Conn.), (Oct. 1978), pp. 378–379.

Littlefield, David W. *Library Journal* (New

York), (Oct. 1, 1978), p. 1993.
Theology Digest, v.27 no.1 (Spring 1979).

A translation from the German of five essays that (1) defend the Bahá'í Faith in the face of an attack by a Protestant theologian, (2) show the relationship of the Bahá'í Faith to Islam and (3) defend Islam against the misrepresentations of Westerners. Selected by *Choice* as one of the 200 outstanding academic books of 1978. The 1980 printing includes added material on the Bahá'í view of St Paul.

7.2348. *A School of World Religion.* Wilmette, Ill.: Bahá'í Public Relations, n.d. [194– or 195?] [4] p.

7.2349. Schopflocher, Lorol. *Sunburst.* London: Ryder & Co., 1937. 320 p.

The author, prominent socialite and wife of the Hand of the Cause of God Siegfried Schopflocher, recounts her own life story and her many travels on behalf of the Bahá'í Faith.

7.2350. Scott, Nina; Staudt, Dawn. *My Bahá'í ABC Book.* Drogheda, Ireland: Dawn Staudt, 1985. [28] p.

7.2351. Scrutton, Robert J. *The Message of the Masters.* ed. Kenneth Johnson. Jersey: Neville Spearman, 1982. xix, 261 p. LC card 82–196602.

Introduction to the Bahá'í Faith geared toward those interested in occult knowledge. Several pages of specific predictions of future events are appended. Much of the supposed 'scientific' information and 'prophecies' lack any confirmation or support in the Bahá'í writings or in science.

7.2352. *The Search for Truth: The Bahá'í Faith.* New Delhi: Bahá'í Publishing Trust, n.d. [1981] [2] p.

7.2353. *idem.* London: National Spiritual Assembly of the Bahá'ís of the United Kingdom, n.d. [1981] [4] p.

7.2354. Sears, William. *All Flags Flying!* il. Robert Reedy. Johannesburg: National Spiritual Assembly of the Bahá'ís of South and West Africa, 1985. 350 p.

Hand of the Cause William Sears continues the story of his life that he began in *God Loves Laughter*. Written in a rapid-fire speaking style. This is not, strictly speaking, a biography, but a series of personal vignettes, perhaps not all 'factual'.

7.2355. —— *Birth of World Religion.* n.p. [Wilmette, Ill.]: Radio Service Committee, 1960. 8 leaves.

7.2356. —— *A Cry from the Heart: The Bahá'ís in Iran.* Oxford: George Ronald, 1982. 219 p. LC card 82–196613.

William Sears's 'personal cry of indignation at what is happening to the Bahá'ís of Iran' following the deposing of the S͟háh and the creation of Khomeini's Islamic Republic. Dramatic narratives recount the increasing persecution and human suffering undergone by the Iranian Bahá'ís. Appended are a list of Bahá'ís killed in Iran since 1978, and cable messages of the Universal House of Justice reporting incidents that occurred after the manuscript was completed.

7.2357. —— *God Loves Laughter.* London: George Ronald, 1960, 1961, 1964, 1968, 1970. viii, 181 p.

The unpretentious and witty story of the author's youth and conversion to the Bahá'í Faith. Sears left broadcasting to travel the world expounding the Bahá'í Cause.

7.2358. —— *idem.* Oxford: George Ronald, 1974, 1977, 1979, 1984. viii, 181 p.

7.2359. —— *The Majesty and Greatness of the Local Spiritual Assembly.* New Delhi: Bahá'í Publishing Trust, n.d. [1977] 28 p.

7.2360. —— *The Martyr-Prophet of a World Faith.* Wilmette, Ill.: Bahá'í Publishing Committee, 1950. 19 p.

7.2361. —— *Message to Africa, 4 August 1981.* Umtata: National Spiritual Assembly of the Bahá'ís of Transkei, Apr. 1982. 11 p.

7.2362. —— *Message to Africa, 23 May 1981.* Umtata: National Spiritual Assembly of the Bahá'ís of Transkei, Apr. 1982. 9 p.

7.2363. —— *Message to Africa, 31 December 1981.* Umtata: National Spiritual Assembly of the Bahá'ís of Transkei, Apr. 1982. 17 p.

7.2364. —— *New Interpretation of History.* n.p. [Wilmette, Ill.]: Radio Service Committee, 1959. 9 leaves.

7.2365. —— *New Life for the World.* n.p. [Wilmette, Ill.]: Radio Service Committee, 1959. 10 leaves.

7.2366. —— *A New Satellite Is Born: The Assistants to the Auxiliary Boards, Its Significance and Implications.* Petaling Jaya, Malaysia: Auxiliary Board Members in Malaysia, 1976. 6 leaves.

7.2367. —— *The Prisoner and the Kings.* Toronto, Ont.: General Publishing Company, Ltd., 1971. 240 p. LC card 72–184434.

A dramatic and popular recounting of Bahá'u'lláh's proclamation of his mission to the kings and leaders of his day and the results of their unwillingness to heed.

7.2368. —— *The Promised One of All Religions.*

n.p. [Wilmette, Ill.]: Radio Service Committee, 1959. 9 leaves.

7.2369. —— *Radio Script: Subject, the Martyr-Prophet of a World Faith*. Wilmette, Ill.: Bahá'í Publishing Committee, 1950. 4 leaves.

7.2370. —— *Release the Sun*. New Delhi: Bahá'í Publishing Trust, 1957. 317 p.
A history, in the style of an adventure novel, of the days of the Báb. Appendices deal with a number of proofs, particularly from a Christian viewpoint, of the validity of the missions of the Báb and Bahá'u'lláh.

7.2371. —— *idem*. Wilmette, Ill.: Bahá'í Publishing Trust, 1960, 1964, 1968, 1970, 1971, 1975. v, 250 p. LC card 60–8220.

7.2372. —— *Study Course on Prophecies Fulfilled by the Coming of Bahá'u'lláh*. Palm Springs, Calif.: Sears, 1971.
Script to accompany tape recordings.

7.2373. —— *Thief in the Night, or The Strange Case of the Missing Millennium*. London: George Ronald, 1961, 1964, 1968, 1969, 1971, 1972. xiv, 304 p. (Talisman Books; no.5). LC card 63–3110.
Traditional proofs, mostly from the Bible, to show that Bahá'u'lláh fulfils the prophecies of Christianity (and other world religions). Based upon the author's own search for scriptural support for Bahá'í claims.

7.2374. —— *idem*. Oxford: George Ronald, 1976, 1977, 1978, 1985. xiv, 304 p. (Talisman Books; no.5).

7.2375. —— *idem*. 1st cased ed. Oxford: George Ronald, 1980. xiv, 304 p.

7.2376. —— *The Wine of Astonishment*. London: George Ronald, 1963, 1970, 1983. 194 p. (Talisman Books; no.9 [i.e. no.10 on back cover])
A consideration, for general audiences, of the Bahá'í understanding of several Christian doctrines.

7.2377. —— *WLGI Bahá'í Radio*. n.p. [Wilmette, Ill.: National Spiritual Assembly of the Bahá'ís of the United States], 1983. 4 p.

7.2378. —— *World Religion and the Law of Love*. n.p. [Wilmette, Ill.]: Radio Service Committee, 1959. 9 leaves.

7.2379. Sears, William; Quigley, Robert. *The Flame*. Oxford: George Ronald, 1972, 1973. 141 p. Cover title: *The Flame: The Story of Lua*. LC card 72–188629.
An inspirational biographical essay on one of the most renowned early Bahá'ís: the 'Mother Teacher of the West', Lua Getsinger.

7.2380. *Second Steps in the Baha'i Spiritual Com-munity*. New Delhi: National Spiritual Assembly of the Bahá'ís of India, n.d. [197–?] 25 p.

7.2381. *Selected Baha'i Stories*. arr. Mariette Leong. n.p. [Lae]: Spiritual Assembly of the Bahá'ís of Papua New Guinea, 1979. 72 p.

7.2382. Sell, Edward. *The Báb and the Bábís*. Vepery, Madras: SPCK Press, 1895. 51 p.

7.2383. —— *Baháism*. London; Madras; Colombo: Christian Literature Society for India, 1912. [4], 50, [2] p. (The Islam Series).
Examines Bahá'í history and doctrine from a negative but not vituperative viewpoint.

7.2383a. Seminars on Education for a New Age (1985: Castries, St. Lucia). *Education, a New Perspective: Papers from a Series of Seminars on Education for a New Age*. Castries, St. Lucia: National Spiritual Assembly of the Baha'is of St. Lucia, 1985. [130] p. in various paginations.
Sixteen papers presented at a Baha'i education conference.

7.2384. *A Service Marking the Conclusion of United Nations Week, Sunday, 31st October, 1976*. Ingleside: N.S.W.: Bahá'í House of Worship, 1976. 4 p.

7.2385. *Service of Public Dedication, Bahá'í House of Worship, Wilmette, Illinois, May 2, 1953*. Wilmette, Ill.: Bahá'í House of Worship, 1953. [4] p.

7.2386. *Service, Our Heritage: For the Rededication of Our Efforts to Win the Goals of the Five Year Plan*. n.p.: Continental Board of Counsellors in Southern Africa, 1977. 8 leaves.

7.2387. *A Service to Celebrate Race Unity Day: Bahá'í House of Worship, Ingleside, Sunday, 10th June, 1984*. Ingleside, N.S.W.: Bahá'í House of Worship, 1984. [8] p.

7.2388. *A Service to Commemorate the United Nations Year of Communication: Bahá'í House of Worship, Ingleside, Sunday, 23rd October, 1983*. Ingleside, N.S.W.: Bahá'í House of Worship, 1983. [10] p.

7.2389. *A Service to Commemorate World Religion Day 1982: Sunday, 24th January, 1982, Bahá'í House of Worship, Ingleside*. Ingleside, N.S.W.: Bahá'í House of 'Vorship, 1982. [4] p.

7.2390. *A Service to Commemorate World Religion Day, Sunday, 15th January, 1984, Bahá'í House of Worship, Ingleside*. Ingleside, N.S.W.: Bahá'í House of Worship, 1984. [8] p.

7.2391. Seto, Mamie L. *Introduction to the Bahá'í Teachings: A Ten Lesson Study Course*. Wilmette, Ill.: Bahá'í Publishing Committee, 1943. 13 leaves.

7.2392. —— *Spiritual and Social Teachings for a New Age.* Wilmette, Ill.: Bahá'í Publishing Trust, 1960. 14 leaves; 1962, 1966. 23 p.

7.2393. —— *The Spiritual Meaning of Adversity.* Wilmette, Ill.: Bahá'í Publishing Committee, 1944, 1949. 25 p.; 1953. 24 p.

7.2394. —— *Tests – Their Spiritual Value.* New York: Bahá'í Publishing Committee, n.d. [193–] 16 p.

7.2395. —— *idem.* Wilmette, Ill.: Bahá'í Publishing Committee, n.d. [between 1940 and 1954] 15 p.

7.2396. *7 Year Plan in Devon & Cornwall.* n.p. [United Kingdom], 1979. [35] p.

7.2397. Shah, K.T. *Religion of the Future.* New Delhi: National Spiritual Assembly of the Bahá'ís of India and Burma, n.d. [between 1923 and 1947] 39 p.

7.2398. Shapiro, David. *For Unity of Mankind.* Brooklyn, N.Y.: Shapiro, 1942. 24 p.

7.2399. —— *idem.* 2nd ed. New York: Skilprint, 1943. 24 p. LC card A44–1899.

7.2400. ——*idem.* 4th ed. Brooklyn, N.Y.: Shapiro, 1944. 24 p. LC card 46–12865.

7.2401. Shaw, R. Gregory; Jorgensen, Ann. *The Baha'i Radio Production Studio Buying Guide.* Maracaibo: CIRBAL Bahá'í Mass Media Centre, Jan. 1983. [5] p.

7.2402. Shirazi, M.R. *Twenty-One Days with Abdul Baha in the Holy Land.* n.p. [Karachi?]: The 'Sind Observe' Press, n.d. [1914?] 22 p.

7.2403. *Shoghi Effendi.* Taipei: National Spiritual Assembly of the Bahá'ís of Taiwan, 1978. 11, 14 p. (Kindled with the Fire of His Love).

7.2404. Shook, Glenn A. *Mysticism, Science and Revelation.* Oxford: George Ronald, 1953, 1974, 1976. x, 145 p. LC card 54–30009.

A phenomenological study of religious and scientific worldviews from a Bahá'í perspective. The subject is abstruse but Shook writes clearly for the layman.

7.2405. —— *idem.* Wheatley, U.K.: George Ronald, 1954. x, 145 p.

7.2406. —— *idem.* London: George Ronald, 1964. x, 145 p.

7.2407. —— *idem.* 1st American ed. Wilmette, Ill.: Bahá'í Publishing Trust, 1967, 1970. x, 145 p. LC card 67–9571.

7.2408. *Should Religion Be Taught in Schools? What Do You Think?* Toronto, Ont.: Canadian Bahá'í Community, n.d. [196–] 4 p.

7.2409. Shrestha, Anand Lal. *Declaration of Bab, May 23rd.* Birganj, Nepal: Shyam Press, n.d. [1974?] [4] p. English and Nepali text.

7.2410. *The Shrines and Gardens of the Bahá'í Faith, Mount Carmel, Haifa.* n.p. [Haifa: Bahá'í World Centre], n.d. [195–?] 4 p.

7.2411. *The Silver Jubilee of the Bahá'í Faith in the District of Franklin, 1978–79.* Frobisher Bay, N.W.T.: Bahá'í of Frobisher Bay, N.T., 1979. 8 p.

7.2412. Simple, Peter. *Bahá'í Teachings.* Wilmette, Ill.: American Indian Service Committee, n.d. [196–?] 12 p.

7.2413. Simple, Peter; Kolstoe, John. *Bahá'í Teachings, Light for All Regions.* Zimbabwean ed. Harare: National Spiritual Assembly of the Bahá'ís of Zimbabwe, Bahá'í Distribution Service, 1984. 7 p.

7.2414. —— *Light for All Regions.* Wilmette, Ill.: Bahá'í Publishing Trust, 1969. 24 p. Cover title: *Bahá'í Teachings, Light for All Regions.*

7.2415. Simpson, G. Palgrave. *The Bahai Faith: What It Is and What It Teaches.* London, 1920. 32 p.

7.2416. *Sing a New Song: Bahá'í Songs for Children.* comp. Bahá'í Committee on Music; il. Anna Stevenson. Wilmette, Ill.: Bahá'í Publishing Trust, 1968. 44 p.

7.2417. *Singles Session: Men and Women in a New Age.* Santa Cruz, Calif.: Bosch Bahá'í School, 1985. [2] p.

7.2418. *Six Lessons on Bahá'í Law: A Deepening Course for Bahá'ís.* comp. Beatrice C. Rinde and John B. Cornell, rev. ed. Honolulu: National Spiritual Assembly of the Bahá'ís of the Hawaiian Islands, 1976. ii, 80 p.

See 7.331, 7.2515.

7.2419. *Six Lessons on the Procedure and Spirit of Baha'i Elections.* n.p., n.d. [197–] 17 p.

7.2420. Skrine, Francis Henry. *Bahaism, the Religion of Brotherhood and Its Place in the Evolution of Creeds.* London: Longmans Green and Company, 1912. 72 p. LC card 12–9517 rev.

7.2421. *Skysongs Song Book.* Santiago, Chile: Primavera Productions, n.d. [1985] [3], 21, [2] p.

7.2422. Smith, Beatrice. *Teaching from Home: Suggestions of Ways & Opportunities to Teach the Faith, for Those Who Stay at Home.* Londonderry: Northern Ireland Teaching Committee, n.d. [1981?] 14 p.

7.2423. Smith, Herbert H. *Herbert's Diary: An Account of Trailer Travels Among Some Centers of*

Baha'i Teaching. ed. Charles Mason Remey. n.p. [Washington, D.C.?]: Remey, 1940. 57 leaves. (Bahá'í Reminiscences, Diary, Letters and Other Documents).

7.2424. *So I'm a Bahá'í, Now What?* n.p. [United States], n.d. [196–] 21 p.

7.2425. Social and Economic Development Conference (1985: Chattanooga, Tenn.). *Bahá'í Parenting: Creating a Bahá'í Identity*. Chattanooga, Tenn.: Spiritual Assembly of the Bahá'ís of Chattanooga, 1985. [6] p.

7.2426. Society of the Bahai Students of Beirut (Lebanon). *The Program of the Society of the Bahai Students, 1928–1929*. Beirut: American University, 1928. [32] p. English and Persian text.

7.2427. —— *The Program of the Society of the Bahai Students of Beirut, 1929–1930*. Beirut: Society of the Bahai Students of Beirut, 1929. [50] p. English and Persian text.

8.2428. Sohrab, Ahmad. *Abdul Baha in Egypt*. New York: J.H. Sears and Co. for the New History Foundation, 1929. xxxiii, 390 p. LC card 29–8817 rev. 2.

Sohrab was one of 'Abdu'l-Bahá's secretaries and interpreters during 'Abdu'l-Bahá's missionary journey to the West. Sohrab recorded these reminiscences of 'Abdu'l-Bahá's sojourn in Egypt during 1913.

7.2429. —— *idem*. London: Ryder & Co., n.d. [1929?] xxxiii, 390 p.

7.2430. —— *Letter from Mirza Ahmad Sohrab to the Meeting Held in Miss Juliet Thompson's Studio*. n.p. [New York], 1913. 12 leaves.

Description of the Committee of Investigation that had been sent by the Ottoman government to the Holy Land.

7.2431. —— *The New Humanity: A Compendium of the Ideals of Universal Civilization*. Los Angeles: Persian American Pub. Co., 1927. xvi, 308 p. LC card 27–24605 rev.

7.2432. —— *Tablets, Instructions and Words of Explanation Revealed by Abdul Baha Abbas for the Assemblies and Meetings of the Bahais of the United States and Canada*. New York, 1919. 82 p. Cover title: *Unveiling of the Divine Plan*.
See 3.16, 3.154–3.156.
Proceedings of several meetings at which the Tablets of the Divine Plan were read for the first time to the American believers. There is considerable commentary and introductory material by Sohrab.

7.2433. *Some Aspects of Baha'i Family Life*. comp. Beth Witham. n.p. [Johannesburg:

National Spiritual Assembly of the Bahá'ís of South and West Africa], n.d. [1978] 16 p.

7.2434. *Some Bahá'í Principles & Procedures Concerning Marriage, Birth & Death*. Accra, Ghana: National Spiritual Assembly of the Bahá'ís of Ghana, 1983. 16 p.

7.2435. *Some Baha'i Proofs Based on the Holy Qur'an*. n.p. [Port-of-Spain: National Spiritual Assembly of the Bahá'ís of Trinidad and Tobago], n.d. [1979?] 25 p.
See 7.2440.

7.2436. *Some Notes on Bahá'í Proofs Based on the Bible*. n.p., n.d. [196–?] 12 p. (mimeographed).

7.2437. *idem*. Kampala, Uganda: Bahá'í Publishing Trust of the Bahá'ís of Central and East Africa, 1963. (Kampala: Uganda Argus, Ltd.). 16 p.

7.2438. *idem*. Kampala, Uganda: Bahai Publishing Trust of Uganda and Central Africa, 1966. 16 p.

7.2439. *idem*. Bangalore, India: Baha'i Centre, n.d. [1977?] 47 p.

7.2440. *Some Notes on Bahá'í Proofs Based on the Qur'án*. n.p., n.d. [196–] 25 leaves.
See 7.2435.

7.2441. *Some of the Teachings and Laws of Bahá'u'lláh*. n.p. [Kampala, Uganda]: National Spiritual Assembly of the Bahá'ís of Central and East Africa, n.d. [between 1956 and 1964] 19 p.

7.2442. *idem*. n.p. [Port Louis, Mauritius]: National Spiritual Assembly of the Bahá'ís of the Indian Ocean, n.d. [between 1964 and 1972] 22 p.

7.2443. *Some Practical Aspects of the Bahai Teaching*. Rangoon, Burma: Rangoon Mail Press, n.d. [after 1922] 8 p.

7.2444. *Some Principles of the Bahá'í Faith*. New York: Bahá'í Publishing Committee; Shanghai, P.O. Box 551, n.d. [192– or 193–] 16 p.

7.2445. *Some Teachings We Should Know*. Nairobi: National Community Development Committee, n.d. [1983] 6, 7 p. English and Swahili text.

7.2445a. *Song of Peace Festival, 26th October, 1985, 7 p.m.–10 p.m., at Tshung Tsin School Hall*. Kota Kinabalu, Sabah, Malaysia: Local Spiritual Assembly of the Baha'is of Kota Kinabalu, 1985. 24 p.

7.2446. *Songs Bahá'ís Sing*. n.p. [Port of Spain]: National Spiritual Assembly of the Bahá'ís of Trinidad and Tobago, 1977. [16] p.

7.2447. *Songs of Prayer and Praise.* Chicago: Bahai Publishing Society, 1903. 9 p.

7.2448. *idem.* Chicago, 1912. 16 p.

7.2449. Sorabjee, Zena. *Nabíl's Narrative Abridged.* New Delhi: Bahá'í Publishing Trust, 1974. 176 p.

7.2450. —— *idem.* New Delhi: Bahá'í Publishing Trust, 1976. 152 p.

7.2451. South Africa Bahá'í Summer School (1st: 1982: Ciskei). *The National Youth Task Force Host the First South African Baha'i Summer School in Ciskei.* n.p. [Johannesburg: National Spiritual Assembly of the Bahá'ís of South and West Africa], n.d. [1982] [6] p.

7.2452. South East Asia Regional Conference (2nd: 1978: Kuching, Sarawak). *Second South East Asia Regional Conference, 16th–19th Dec. '78, Kuching, Sarawak, Eastern Malaysia.* Kuching: South East Asia Regional Conference, 1978. [4] p.

7.2453. *A Special Service to Commemorate United Nations Week, Bahá'í House of Worship, Ingleside, Sunday, 21st October, 1984.* Ingleside, N.S.W.: Bahá'í House of Worship, 1984. 7 p.

7.2454. *A Special Service to Extol the Memory of the Bahá'ís in Írán Who Have Been Executed for Their Faith and to Pray for Those Remaining Who Are Faced with Grave Dangers: Bahá'í House of Worship, Mona Vale, Ingleside, 18th April, 1982 at 11.00 a.m.* Mona Vale, N.S.W.: Bahá'í House of Worship, 1982. [4] p.

7.2455. *A Special Service to the Memory of Mrs Sylvia Ioas, Member of the International Bahá'í Council: Baha'i House of Worship, Sydney, Friday, 9th December, 1983, 7:30 p.m.* Sydney, N.S.W.: Baha'i House of Worship, 1983. [4] p.

7.2456. *Spectacular Landmark at the Crossroads.* Wilmette, Ill.: National Bahá'í Public Information Department, n.d. [1967?] 4 p.
Reprinted from *Illinois Public Opinion* (Jan.–Feb. 1967).

7.2457. *The Spirit of Hospitality.* comp. Peter Senior. [Kingston]: National Spiritual Assembly of the Bahá'ís of Jamaica, n.d. [197–] 20 p.

7.2458. *The Spiritual Destiny of Africa.* Lagos: National Spiritual Assembly of the Bahá'ís of Nigeria, n.d. [1981]. 32 p.

7.2459. *idem.* Lagos: Baha'i Publishing Committee of the National Spiritual Assembly of the Baha'is of Nigeria, 1982. iv, 26 p.

7.2460. *Spiritual Enrichment.* n.p. [Kuala Lumpur: National Spiritual Assembly of the Bahá'ís of Malaysia], n.d. [1983] 19 p.

7.2461. *The Spiritual Revolution Has Already Begun . . . on T.V. Sets Across the Nation.* San Fernando, Calif.: Light Years International, n.d. [1982] [8] p.

7.2462. *Spiritual Teachings.* Wilmette, Ill.: Bahá'í Publishing Trust, 1976. v, 15 p. (Star Study Program).

7.2463. *Spiritualization of the Bahá'í Community.* n.p. [Kuala Lumpur: Spiritual Assembly of the Bahá'ís of Malaysia], n.d. [1983] 24 p.
See 7.2132.

7.2464. Sprague, Sidney. *The Story of the Bahai Movement, a Universal Religion.* Hampstead: The Priory Press; London: John M. Watkins, 1907. 22 p. (Mayle's Penny Series).

7.2465. —— *idem.* 2nd ed. rev. Hampstead: The Priory Press; London: John M. Watkins, 1908. 20 p. (Mayle's Penny Series).

7.2466. —— *idem.* Hampstead: The Priory Press, distributed by Bahai Publishing Society, n.d. [1907 or 1908?] 20 p.

7.2467. —— *A Year with the Bahais in India and Burma.* London: The Priory Press; Chicago: Distributed by the Bahai Publishing Society, 1908, 1908. 53 p.

7.2468. Sreenivasan, M.M. *The Miracle.* Malaysia: Baha'i Publication released by Family Systems Sdn. Bhd., n.d. [1985?] (Petaling Jaya, Selangor: Koperasi Percetkan Malaysia Berhad). 39 p.

7.2469. St Louis National Teaching Conference (1974: St Louis, Mo.). *First National Bahá'í Conference of the Five Year Plan: Conference Program and Guide.* n.p. [Wilmette, Ill.]: National Spiritual Assembly of the Bahá'ís of the United States, 1974. 28 p.

7.2470. Starkes, M. Thomas. *American Bahais and the Baptist Witness.* Atlanta, Ga.: Home Mission Board, n.d. [196–] [12] p.
Anti-Bahá'í work from Christian viewpoint.

7.2471. State Bahá'í Women's Conference (2nd: 1984: Tumkur, Karnataka). *State Baha'i Womens' Conference, April 14 & 15, 1984, Tumkur, Karnataka, India.* n.p. [Bangalore, India: State Baha'i Women's Committee], 1984. [10] p.

7.2472. Stebbins, May P. *Reading List for Study of the Covenant.* Wilmette, Ill.: Bahá'í Publishing Committee, 1948. 4 leaves.

7.2473. Stendardo, Luigi. *Leo Tolstoy and the Bahá'í Faith.* Oxford: George Ronald, 1985. [10], 75 p.
Explores the Russian author's interest in and contact with the Bábí and Bahá'í Faiths, uncovering Tolstoy's profound appreciation for,

and partial misunderstanding of, the new religion.

7.2474. Stephens, K. Dean. *Transmit Thy Knowledge*. San Salvador, El Salvador: C.I.R.B.A.L., 1977. 16 p. (Mass Media Guidelines Booklets Series).

7.2475. Stephens, Kenneth D. *So Great a Cause: A Surprising New Look at the Latter Day Saints*. Healdsburg, Calif.: Naturegraph Publishers, 1973. 215 p. LC card 72–13406.
  Attempt to show that the Bahá'í Faith is the fulfilment of the hopes and beliefs of Latter-day Saints (Mormons). Nearly half the book is questions with answers from the Bible and Mormon standard works.

7.2476. Stevens, E.S. *The Mountain of God*. 3rd ed. London: Mills & Boon, 1911. 380 p. LC card 11–1435.
  A novel about the Bahá'ís in 'Akká at the time of 'Abdu'l-Bahá.

7.2477. Stevenson, Don. *The Wonderlamp*. from a story by Abu'l-Qásim Faizi; verse by Hugh Featherstone Blyth. Los Angeles: Kalimát Press, c1981 [i.e. 1983] [43] p. LC card 81–23648.
  Illustrated adaptation of A.Q. Faizi's story of the need to love and follow the light in whatever lamp it may shine.

7.2478. Stirrat, Charlotte. *Bahá'í Marriage, Naming the Baby, Making a Will, Bahá'í Burial: A Manual for Local Spiritual Assemblies*. Windhoek: National Spiritual Assembly of the Bahá'ís of SWA/Namibia, n.d. [1984?] 25 p.

7.2479. Stockman, Robert H. *The Bahá'í Faith in America*. v.1, Wilmette, Ill.: Bahá'í Publishing Trust, 1985. xxix, 277 p. LC card 84–28214.
  Reviews:
  The Christian Century (Chicago), (Sept. 25, 1985), p. 843.
  Pucelik, T.M. *Choice* (Middletown, Conn.), v.23 no.4 (Dec. 1985), p. 619.
  The first scholarly study of American Bahá'í history, with much information gleaned from Bahá'í archives, particularly the well-organized National Bahá'í Archives in Wilmette, Ill. Well-illustrated.

7.2480. *Stories About 'Abdu'l-Bahá*. ed. G. Faizi. New Delhi: Bahá'í Publishing Trust, 1981, 1982. viii, 35 p.

7.2481. *Stories for Children, number 5: Bahá'u'lláh and the Egyptian Merchant*. n.p. [Wilmette, Ill.]: National Spiritual Assembly of the Bahá'ís of the United States, Child Education Committee, n.d. [195–?] 4 p.

7.2482. *Stories from the Life of Bahá'u'lláh*. n.p. [Salisbury, Rhodesia]: National Spiritual

Assembly of the Bahá'ís of South Central Africa, n.d. [between 1964 and 1970] 7 p.

7.2483. *The Story of Bahá'í, World's Newest Religion*. Lagos; National Spiritual Assembly of the Bahá'ís of Nigeria, 1978. 1 folded sheet. Reprinted from *The Sunday Standard*, May 28, 1978.

7.2484. *The Story of Mona, 1965–1983*. Thornhill, Ont.: Bahá'í Canada Publications, 1985. 38 p.
  The story of Mona Mahmudnizhad and those who were martyred with her given as background for the video 'Mona with the Children'.

7.2485. *The Story of Ridvan*. n.p. [Port-of-Spain: National Spiritual Assembly of the Bahá'ís of Trinidad and Tobago], n.d. [1981] [7] p.

7.2486. *The Story of the Bahá'í House of Worship*. Wilmette, Ill.: Bahá'í National Center, 1976. 1 sheet folded to [8] 'pages'.

7.2487. *The Story of the Bahá'ís and Their Unique Temple of Worship*. Wilmette, Ill.: Bahá'í Publishing Committee, n.d. [1945?] [3] p. Reprinted from *Chicago Sunday Tribune*, June 17, 1945.

7.2488. *idem*. Wilmette, Ill.: Bahá'í Public Relations, 1945. [3] p.

7.2489. *Story Supplement for 'God Passes By'*. Wilmette, Ill.: Bahá'í Publishing Committee, 1948. 95 p.

7.2490. *The Structure of Unity: An Introduction to the Bahá'í Community in the United States*. Wilmette, Ill.: Bahá'í Office of Public Affairs, 1979. 13 p.

7.2491. *Studies in Bábí and Bahá'í History*. ed. Moojan Momen. Los Angeles: Kalimát Press, 1982. x, 337 p. (Studies in Bábí and Bahá'í History; v.1) LC card 83–227.
  Reviews:
  Lawson, B. Todd. *Religious Studies Review* (Macon, Ga.), v.11, no.2 (Apr. 1985), p. 206.
  Mazzaoui, Michel M. *Journal of the American Oriental Society* (New Haven, Conn.), v.105 no.2 (1985), pp. 360–362.
  The Middle East Journal (Washington, D.C.), v.27 (Autumn 1983), p. 721.
  Five essays on Bábí-Bahá'í history, three of them on the American community.

7.2492. *Study Aid on the Essential Verities of the Bahá'í Faith*. Wilmette, Ill.: Bahá'í Publishing Committee, 1947. 28 leaves.

7.2493. *Study Classes*. ed. Advisory Committee on Education. Wilmette, Ill.: Bahá'í Publishing Trust, 1966. 110 p. (Bahá'í Teacher's Handbook; v.3).

7.2494. *Study Course on the Bahá'í Faith*. n.p.

[London]: Study Course Committee, n.d. [194– or 195–?] [14] p.

7.2495. *idem.* n.p. [London]: National Teaching Committee of the National Spiritual Assembly of the Bahá'ís of the British Isles, Feb. 1958. 15, [1] p.

7.2496. *A Study Guide to The Dawn-Breakers, Nabíl's Narrative of the Early Days of the Bahá'í Revelation.* n.p. [New York]: National Teaching Committee, 1932. 30 leaves.

7.2497. *idem.* Wilmette, Ill.: Bahá'í Publishing Committee, 1946. 30 p.; 1953. 35 p.

7.2498. *idem.* Wilmette, Ill.: Bahá'í Publishing Trust, 1959, 1967, 1978. 35 p.

7.2499. *Subject Index of Bahá'í Writings: Hidden Words, Bahá'u'lláh.* n.p. National Reference Library Committee, 1961. 8 p.

7.2500. *Subject Index of Bahá'í Writings: 'Seven Valleys and Four Valleys', Bahá'u'lláh.* n.p. [Charleston, W.Va.]: National Reference Library Committee, n.d. [ca. 1960] 7 leaves.

7.2501. *Subject Index, Writings of Bahá'u'lláh in the Kitáb-i-Íqán.* n.p.: National Reference Library Committee, n.d. [ca. 1960?] 46 leaves.

7.2502. *Suggestions for Teachers of Baha'i Children's Classes.* St John's, Antigua: National Children's Committee, 1982. [12] leaves.

7.2503. *Suggestions for the Conduct of Institutes on the Covenant and Administration.* Wilmette, Ill.: Bahá'í Publishing Trust, 1969. [4] p.

7.2504. *Suggestions for the Teacher.* n.p. [Cali]: Teaching Committee of the National Spiritual Assembly of the Baha'is of Colombia [i.e. St John's, Antigua: National Spiritual Assembly of the Bahá'ís of the Leeward Islands], n.d. [1984?] 22 p. (Spiritual Education of Children).

7.2505. Sultani, Mujtaba. *Baha'ism, a Sect at the Service of Colonialism.* Tehran: Islamic Propagation Organization, 1985. 52 p.
Shí'í polemical work on the Bahá'í Faith.

7.2506. *A Summary of Bahá'í History.* Anchorage: National Spiritual Assembly of the Bahá'ís of Alaska, 1980. 16 p.

7.2507. *A Summary of the Statement on Peace by the Universal House of Justice to the Peoples of the World.* n.p. [Manila: National Spiritual Assembly of the Bahá'ís of the Philippines], 1985. [3] leaves.

7.2508. Sundram, Chellie J. *Analysing Performance Problems.* n.p.: Continental Board of Counsellors, Southeastern Asia, n.d. [1978?]. 8 p. (No. 6 in a series).

7.2509. —— *The Asrama for Mentawei Bahá'í*

Children, Padang, Indonesia. n.p.: Continental Board of Counsellors, Southeastern Asia, 1980. 34 p.

7.2510. —— *The Bahá'í Fund and the Individual.* n.p.: Continental Board of Counsellors, Southeastern Asia, n.d. [1978?] 28, 10 p. (No. 7 in a series).

7.2511. —— *Group Appreciation of Selected Sacred Writings.* n.p. Continental Board of Counsellors, Southeastern Asia, n.d. [1978?] 4 leaves. (No. 3 in a series).

7.2512. —— *Media and Selected Audio-Visual Equipment.* n.p.: Continental Board of Counsellors, Southeastern Asia, n.d. [1978?] 31 leaves.

7.2513. —— *Problem-Solving the Bahá'í Way for the Individual and the Community.* n.p.: Continental Board of Counsellors, Southeastern Asia, n.d. [1978?] 4 leaves. (No. 5 in a series).

7.2514. —— *The Seven-Day Glow: One Method of Structuring a Learning/Teaching Experience Using Concepts from the Sacred Writings of the Bahá'í Faith.* n.p.: Continental Board of Counsellors, Southeastern Asia, n.d. [1978?] 3 leaves. (No. 4 in a series).

7.2515. *Supplementary Material to Support a Course on Bahá'í Law: An Advanced Class for Bahá'ís.* comp. Beatrice C. Rinde. n.p., 1967. ii, 59 p.
See 7.331, 7.2418.

7.2516. *Supplementary Stories to Accompany 'An Outline of Baha'i History'.* n.p. [Kampala, Uganda]: National Spiritual Assembly of the Baha'is of Central and East Africa, n.d. [between 1959 and 1964] 13 p.; n.d. [197–?] 14 p.

7.2517. *idem.* Zambia ed. Lusaka: National Spiritual Assembly of the Baha'is of Zambia, 1981. 24 p.

7.2518. *Sweet Melody: A Collection of Bahá'í Songs.* Kingston: National Spiritual Assembly of the Bahá'ís of Jamaica, 1980. 54 p.

7.2519. *A Symbol of Man's Hope for a Better World: Bahá'í World Faith.* Wilmette, Ill.: [National Spiritual Assembly of the Bahá'ís of the United States], n.d. [195–?] 6 p.

7.2520. *Synergy: 'The Whole Is Greater than the Sum of Its Parts'.* n.p. [Thornhill, Ont.: National Teaching Committee], n.d. [1984] [4] p.

7.2521. Szanto-Felbermann, Renée. *Rebirth: The Memoirs of Renée Szanto-Felbermann.* London: Bahá'í Publishing Trust, 1980. 185 p.
Autobiography of a woman of Jewish heritage who was the first Hungarian Bahá'í. Particularly interesting is the period as a Jewish-Bahá'í in Hungary during the Nazi era.

T

7.2522. Taafaki, Irene. *The Horse of the Moonlight.* il. Jeff Wakeford. Oxford: George Ronald, 1981. [38] p.
Stories for children in which the steeds associated with the Báb and Bahá'u'lláh recount their experiences.

7.2523. Taherzadeh, Adib. *Are You Interested in the Secret of Becoming a Successful Bahá'í and Winning the Goals?: Perhaps You Will Find this Short Article by Adib Taherzadeh of Interest.* n.p. [Windhoek, s.w.a./Namibia: National Publications Committee], n.d. [1982?] 19 p.

7.2524. —— *The Revelation of Bahá'u'lláh.* v.1, 1853–1863, Oxford: George Ronald, 1974, 1975. xvi, 363 p.; v.2, 1863–1868, Oxford: George Ronald, 1977. xvi, 476 p.; v.3, 1868–1877, Oxford: George Ronald, 1983. xviii, 483 p. LC card 75–305657.
Review:
v.2. *Choice* (Middletown, Conn.), (Feb. 1976), p. 1591.
Using both authentic English translations and original sources, the author describes the contents of most of Bahá'u'lláh's major Tablets. Taherzadeh adds considerable historical and biographical background. Illustrated.

7.2525. —— *Trustees of the Merciful.* London: Bahá'í Publishing Trust, 1972. 79 p.

7.2526. Taherzadeh, Habib. *The Coming of the Lord.* Porto Alegre, Brazil, 1967 (Porto Alegre: Gráfica Editora a Nação). 26 p.

7.2527. *Ṭáhirih, the First Woman Suffrage Martyr.* n.p. [Port of Spain]: National Spiritual Assembly of the Bahá'ís of Trinidad and Tobago, 1977. [12] p.

7.2527a. Tamadun ul Molk [Tamaddunu'l-Mulk]. *Report of an Address on the Bahai Movement.* given at the City Temple on Sunday Afternoon, Oct. 16th, 1910 by Tamadun ul Molk. East Sheen, Eng.: Bahai Press, 1910. 11 p.

7.2528. Te Pakaka Tawhai. *Adaptations. The Marae.* [Auckland]: National Spiritual Assembly of the Bahá'ís of New Zealand, 1983. 3, 6 p.

7.2529. *Te Whakatikenga Pahai Te Aonga Ake O Te Ra Hou = The Bahai Cause, the Dawn of a New Day.* Auckland: N.z.: M. Smethurst, 1933. 16 p. Maori and English text.

7.2530. *Teach Where You Are.* n.p. [Nairobi]: Published for the Kenya National Teaching Conference [by the National Education Committee], 130 B.E. [1973] 8 p.

7.2530a. *Teacher Training Course.* n.p. [Suva, Fiji]: Regional Spiritual Assembly of the Baha'is of the South Pacific, n.d. [between 1959 and 1970] 20 p.

7.2531. *Teacher's Guide for Children's Classes.* n.p. [Port-of-Spain: National Spiritual Assembly of the Bahá'ís of Trinidad and Tobago], n.d. [1982] [8] leaves.

7.2532. *Teaching: It Is Better to Guide One Soul Than to Possesss All That Is on Earth.* London: National Spiritual Assembly of the Bahá'ís of the United Kingdom, n.d. [1980?] [4] p.

7.2533. *Teaching Reference File.* rev. n.p. [Wilmette, Ill.]: American National Teaching Committee, Dec. 1962. 23, xiii p.

7.2534. *idem.* rev. Wilmette, Ill.: National Teaching Committee, 1965. 13 leaves.

7.2535. *Teaching the Bahá'í Faith: Direct Teaching.* n.p. [Wilmette, Ill.]: Teaching Committee, n.d. [1952?] [5] leaves.

7.2536. *Teaching the Bahá'í Faith: The Fireside Method.* n.p. [Wilmette, Ill.]: National Teaching Committee, 1952. 4 leaves.

7.2536a. Tehrani, Noreen. *God Cares.* London: Bahá'í Publishing Trust, 1979. [12] p.

7.2536b. —— *God Loves.* London: Bahá'í Publishing Trust, 1979. [16] p.

7.2536c. —— *God Made.* London: Bahá'í Publishing Trust, 1979. [12] p.

7.2536d. —— *Help Me.* London: Bahá'í Publishing Trust, 1979. [12] p.

7.2536e. —— *I Am Happy.* London: Bahá'í Publishing Trust, 1979. [12] p.

7.2536f. —— *Please God.* London: Bahá'í Publishing Trust 1979. [12] p.

7.2536g. —— *Show Me.* London: Bahá'í Publishing Trust, 1979. [12] p.

7.2536h. *The Temple Garden of God.* n.p. [United States]: Published by permission of the National Spiritual Assembly of America, n.d. [1922] 8 p. Directory of believers in several countries.

7.2537. *A Temple of Light.* n.p., 1930. 4 p.

7.2538. *A Temple of Light: Baha'i Temple at Wilmette, Illinois.* n.p., n.d. [1930?] 8 p. Includes article by Allen McDaniel from *Technology Review* (Boston), Oct. 1930.

7.2539. *Temple of Unique Design Taxes Ingenuity of Form Builders.* Washington, D.C.: The Research Service, 1931. [4] p.
Reprint from *Construction Methods* (Aug. 1931).

7.2540. *Temple Photographs.* Chicago: Baha'i Temple Librarian and Sales Committee, H.E. Walrath, n.d. [193–?] 1 leaf.

7.2541. *Thai Baha'i Song Book.* n.p. [Thailand]: Area Teaching Committee of Southern Thailand, 1983. 13 leaves. Thai and English songs.

7.2542. *That I May Improve the Quality of My Bahá'í Life, I Hereby Resolve in the Memory of These Courageous Souls* . . . n.p. [London: National Spiritual Assembly of the Bahá'ís of the United Kingdom], n.d. [1981 or 1982] [2] p.

7.2543. *These Things Shall Be.* London: Bahá'í Publishing Trust, 1970. 16 p.

7.2544. *These Thinkers' Thoughts Are Greatly Valued.* Karachi, Pakistan: Public Relations Committee, n.d. [195–?] [2] p.

7.2545. *They Are All But One.* London: National Spiritual Assembly of the Bahá'ís of the United Kingdom, n.d. [1981] [2] p.

7.2546. *idem.* New Delhi: Bahá'í Publishing Trust, n.d. [1981] [4] p.

7.2547. *Third Steps in the Baha'i Spiritual Community.* New Delhi: National Spiritual Assembly of the Bahá'ís of India, n.d. [197–?] 28 p.

7.2548. *This Is Bahaaism.* n.p., n.d. [197–] 32 p.
Islamic document attacking the Bahá'í Faith. Filled with numerous inaccuracies and falsehoods.
See 7.2700.

7.2549. *idem.* Tripoli, Libya: Islamic Call Society, n.d. [1980?] 32 p.

7.2550. *idem.* Qum: Centre of Islamic Studies, n.d. [1980?] 32 p. Cover title: *What is Bahai'ism?*

7.2551. Thompson, Juliet. *'Abdu'l-Bahá the Center of the Covenant.* Wilmette, Ill.: Bahá'í Publishing Committee, 1948. 28 p.

7.2552. —— *Abdul Baha's First Days in America.* East Aurora, N.Y.: The Roycrofters, n.d. [192–?] 40 p. (Diary entries shown as 1924, should be 1912).

7.2553. —— *The Diary of Juliet Thompson.* with a preface by Marzieh Gail. Los Angeles: Kalimát Press, 1983, 1983. xxiii, 393 p. LC card 83–10540.
The diary of one of the earliest Bahá'ís of New

York, covering her many hours with 'Abdu'l-Bahá in 1909, 1911, 1912. A vivid personal account of spiritual love and the tests of her faith.

7.2554. —— *I, Mary Magdalen.* New York: Delphic Studios, 1940. xvi, 224 p. LC card 40–13809.
Novel which is a semi-autobiographical account of Thompson's contact with 'Abdu'l-Bahá.

7.2555. *Thou Art My Lamp and My Light Is in Thee, Bahá'u'lláh.* London: National Spiritual Assembly of the Bahá'ís of the United Kingdom, 1983. 17 p.

7.2556. *Thoughts on Teaching Indians.* White-horse, Yukon: National Eskimo and Indian Bulletin Committee, n.d. [195–] 10 p.

7.2556a. *Thoughts on the Bahá'í Fund.* Oxford: Holywell Press, 1960. [4] p.

7.2557. *Three Accounts of Love Sacrificed.* trans. from the Persian by Amin Banani, n.p. [Wilmette, Ill.]: National Spiritual Assembly of the Bahá'ís of the United States, c1982. pp. 9–35. Reprint from *World Order*, v.17 no.1 (Fall 1982).

7.2558. *3 Simple Steps Why Bahai Philosophy Is Not the Answer.* n.p. [St. Louis, Mo.], n.d. [1975] 1 p.
Anti-Bahá'í work from Christian viewpoint.

7.2559. *Three Studies on Bahá'í History.* Thornhill, Ont.: Canadian Association for Studies on the Bahá'í Faith, 1978. 43 p. (Bahá'í Studies; v.4).
Essays on the writings of William McE. Miller (inveterate opponent of the Bahá'ís), introduction of the Bahá'í Faith into Poland, and Auguste Forel.

7.2559a. *Through the Silence.* Montclair, N.J.: World Fellowship Gardens, n.d. [192–] [1] p. (Service Leaflet; no.3).

7.2560. *Thy Heavenly Army.* n.p. [Thornhill, Ont.]: National Spiritual Assembly of the Bahá'ís of Canada, n.d. [between 1971 and 1975] 40 p.

7.2561. *Time Line of the Heroic Age and the Formative Age of the Baha'i Faith.* based on an idea of Michael Woodward; designed by Evelyn Musacchia. Honolulu: National Spiritual Assembly of the Bahá'ís of the Hawaiian Islands, 1975. [4 p.] Pages may be put together to form 1 sheet.

7.2562. *Tingomá temáBahá'í.* [Mbabane]: National Spiritual Assembly of the Bahá'ís of Swaziland, n.d. [1982?] 60 p.

Songs, mostly in English, with a few in African languages.

7.2563. *To Be a Bahá'í.* Wilmette, Ill.: Bahá'í Publishing Trust, n.d. [1976] 8 cards in pocket.

7.2564. *To Follow a Dream Time: Father and Mother Dunn, the Spiritual Conquerors of a Continent: Commemorating the Fiftieth Anniversary of the Arrival of the Bahá'í Faith in Australia 18 April 1970.* Paddington, N.S.W.: National Spiritual Assembly of the Bahá'ís of Australia, 1970. 24 p.

7.2565. *Today's Dilemma: More Law, Less Order.* London: Bahá'í Publishing Trust, 1974. [6] p.

7.2566. Tomlin, Viva B.M. *Sadratu'l-Muntahá, the Tree Beyond Which There Is No Passing.* Oxford: Stephen Tomlin, 1982. 43 p. (Edition of 50 copies).

7.2567. Tony Lease Tours (Laguna Beach, Calif.). *Historic First Oceanic Conference, Bahá'í World, Palermo, Sicily: A 17 Day Tour for Bahá'ís Only Including Palermo and Haifa.* Laguna Beach, Calif.: Tony Lease Tours, 1968. [10] p.

7.2568. *Toosahyuuauk Eneupanune = Message to the Eskimos.* Anchorage: Alaska Teaching Committee, 1954. [22] p. English and Eskimo text.

7.2569. *Torture: The Anguish of the Bahá'ís in Iran.* London: National Spiritual Assembly of the United Kingdom, n.d. [1984] [8] p.

7.2570. Townshend, George. *Abdul Baha, a Study of a Christlike Character.* Reprinted from the *Church of Ireland Gazette* by request; and *The Hidden Words of Bahaullah.* n.p., n.d. [195–?] 26 p.

7.2571. —— *Christ and Bahá'u'lláh.* London: George Ronald, 1957, May 1957, 1963. 116 p. LC card A 58–3699.

The author resigned his Orders after forty years in the Church of Ireland in order to proclaim his conviction that Christ had returned in Bahá'u'lláh. This book was deemed by Shoghi Effendi to be Townshend's 'crowning achievement'.
Review:
The Southern Presbyterian Journal, v.16 no.30 (Nov. 20, 1957).

7.2572. —— *idem.* Wilmette, Ill.: Bahá'í Publishing Trust, 1966, 1967. 116 p. LC card 68–168.

7.2573. —— *idem.* rev. ed. London: George Ronald, 1966, 1967. 116 p. (Talisman Books; no.11). LC card 66–70761.

7.2574. —— *idem.* This ed. Oxford: George Ronald, 1971, 1972. 116 p.

7.2575. —— *idem.* rev. Talisman ed. Oxford: George Ronald, 1976. 116 p.

7.2576. —— *idem.* rev. ed. Oxford: George Ronald, 1977, 1983, 1985. 116 p.

7.2577. —— *idem.* n.p. [Missoula, Mont.]: This Stone with Seven Eyes, 134 B.E. [1977–78] 116 p.

7.2578. —— *The Covenant: An Analysis.* Manchester, U.K.: Bahá'í Publishing Trust, 1950. 15 p.

7.2579. —— *The Heart of the Gospel: Being a Restatement of the Teaching of the Bible in Terms of Modern Thought and Modern Need.* London: Lindsay Drummond, 1939. 188 p.

Another presentation of the Bahá'í Faith as the fulfilment of Christianity by this former clergyman of the Church of Ireland. The theme of this volume is the Bible's documentation of the reality of the spiritual evolution of mankind.

7.2580. —— *idem.* New York: Bahá'í Publishing Committee, 1940. vii, 184 p.

7.2581. —— *The Heart of the Gospel: or, The Bible and the Bahá'í Faith.* rev. ed. Oxford: George Ronald, 1951. 164 p. LC card 52–25585 rev.

7.2582. —— *idem.* rev. ed. London; Cardiff: George Ronald, 1955. 164 p.

7.2583. —— *idem.* This ed. London: George Ronald, 1960. 158 p. (Talisman Books; no. 2).

7.2584. —— *idem.* This ed. Oxford: George Ronald, 1972. [ix], 150 p.

7.2585. —— *idem.* Wilmette, Ill.: Bahá'í Publishing Trust, 1972. [ix], 150 p.

7.2586. —— *The Hidden Words of Bahá'u'lláh: A Reflection.* n.p.: Townshend, n.d. [1952?] 6 p.

7.2587. —— *The Mission of Bahá'u'lláh.* Wilmette, Ill.: Bahá'í Publishing Committee, 1944. 23 p.

7.2588. —— *The Mission of Bahá'u'lláh and Other Literary Pieces.* Oxford: George Ronald, 1952, 1976. 154 p. LC card 53–18030.

A collection of Townshend's essays, most of them on the Bahá'í Faith.

7.2589. —— *idem.* London: George Ronald, 1965. 154 p.

7.2590. —— *idem.* 1st American ed. Wilmette, Ill.: Bahá'í Publishing Trust, 1967. 154 p.

7.2591. —— *The Old Churches and the New World-Faith.* London: National Spiritual Assembly of the Bahá'ís of the British Isles, n.d. [1949?] (Birmingham: The Templar Press). 19 p.

7.2592. —— *The Promise of All Ages.* London: Simpkin Marshall, n.d. [1934] 254 p. Christophil shown as author. LC card 35–3597.

An introduction to the Bahá'í Faith, of high literary quality, intended primarily for a Christian audience, in which the author surveys mankind's spiritual evolution culminating in the Bahá'í Revelation.

7.2593. —— *idem.* New York: Bahá'í Publishing Committee, n.d. [1935], n.d. [1938] 254 p. Christophil shown as author. LC card 35–6449.

7.2594. —— *idem.* Wilmette, Ill.: Bahá'í Publishing Committee, 1944. 254 p.

7.2595. —— *idem.* rev. ed. n.p.: George Ronald, 1948. 163 p.; 1957. vii, 163 p. LC card 53–21577.

7.2596. —— *idem.* This ed. London: George Ronald, 1961. 178 p. (Talisman Books; no.4).

7.2597. —— *idem.* This rev. ed. Oxford; George Ronald, 1972. x, 181 p. LC card 74–164972.

7.2598. —— *idem.* Wilmette, Ill.: Bahá'í Publishing Trust, 1973. x, 181 p.

7.2599. —— *Questions About the Second Coming Asked by Bahá'ís of Kampala, Uganda, Africa: Answers by George Townshend.* Wilmette, Ill.: Bahá'í Publishing Committee, 1953. 10 p.

7.2600. —— *Religion and the New Age.* New York: Bahá'í Publishing Committee, 1938. 23 p. Author listed as A.G.B.

7.2601. —— *idem.* Wilmette, Ill.: Bahá'í Publishing Committee, 1943, 1945. 19 p.

7.2602. *Trail of Light.* Otavalo, Ecuador: Editorial Gallo Capitán, n.d. [1983] 2 p. folded to 6 p.

7.2603. *Training to Teach: A Manual.* n.p. [Santurce]: Puerto Rico Bahá'í Teaching Committee, 1975. 28 leaves.

7.2604. Treadwell, Dorothy; Boddy, Patricia Treadwell. *Plants of Thine Orchard: Baha'i Lessons for Children: A Simplified Version of 'Flores de Tu Prado'.* n.p. [Lima]: National Spiritual Assembly of the Bahá'ís of Peru, 1979. [41] leaves.

7.2605. *A Tribute.* n.p. [Colombo, Sri Lanka]: World Religion Day Committee, n.d. [1985] (Ratmalana: Sarvodaya Vishva Lekha). 82 p.

7.2606. *A Tribute to Bahá'u'lláh on the Day of His Birth.* Anne Elise Schaaf, Anne Atkinson, with the assistance of the House of Worship Activities Committee. n.p. [Wilmette, Ill.]: House of Worship Activities Committee, 1984. [4] p.

7.2607. Tritt, Jessie A. *Baha'ism in America.* Los Angeles: American Prophetic League, 1956. 6 p.

7.2608. [True, Edna M.] *The Divine Plan of 'Abdu'l-Bahá.* comp. for the Third European Summer School, Luxembourg. n.p. [Wilmette, Ill.?: European Teaching Committee?], 1952. 18 leaves.

7.2609. True, Marguerite. *A Junior's Book of Religion.* Wilmette, Ill.: Bahá'í Publishing Committee, 1945. 12 leaves.

7.2610. —— *Living Today for Tomorrow's World: A Junior's Book of Religion.* il. Jean Hutchinson. Wilmette, Ill.: Bahá'í Publishing Trust, 1956. 21 p.; 1977. 22 p.

7.2610a. *The True Spirit.* Manchester, U.K.: Manchester Bahá'í Assembly, 1927. [4] p. Inside title: *What Is Bahá'i-ism?*

7.2611. Truesdell, A.I. *The Baha'i Faith by a Methodist Layman.* New York: Bahá'í Publishing Committee, 1925. 16 p.

7.2612. *Truk Travel Teaching Tour, December 11–14, 1976: We're Looking for YOU!: Take Time, Travel Teach Truk.* Ponape: National Teaching Committee of the Eastern Caroline Islands, 1976. 4 p.

7.2613. *The Trusted Ones of God: The Local Spiritual Assembly.* Wilmette, Ill.: Bahá'í Publishing Trust, 1972. 47 p.

7.2614. *Tuimbe Pamoja, Baadhi ya Nyimbo za Bahá'í.* Nairobi: National Spiritual Assembly of the Bahá'ís of Kenya, n.d. [1973?] 24 p. English and Swahili songs.

7.2615. *Twelve Bahá'í Teachings = Koyeruwa Bahá'í 12.* n.p. [Lagos: National Spiritual Assembly of the Bahá'ís of Nigeria], n.d. [1981] 2 p. English and Hausa text.

7.2616. *Twelve Bahá'í Teachings = Ukpep ñkpo Baha'i duopeba.* n.p. [Lagos, Nigeria: Bahá'í Publishing Trust], n.d. [1985?] 2 p. English and Efik text.

7.2617. *Twelwe* [sic] *Bahá'í Teachings = Awon Eko Bahá'í.* n.p. [Lagos: National Spiritual Assembly of the Bahá'ís of Nigeria], n.d. [1981] 2 p. English and Yoruba text.

7.2618. *Twenty Lessons in the Bahá'í Revelation.* New York: Bahá'í Publishing Committee, n.d. [before 1940] 20 leaves.

7.2619. *Two Roads We Face.* n.p. [Wilmette, Ill.]: Radio Service Committee, 1960. 8 leaves.

U

7.2620. *The Ulster Problem: A New Approach.* Londonderry: N[orthern] I[reland] Committee of the National Spiritual Assembly of the Baha'is of the United Kingdom, n.d. [1981] 10 p.

7.2621. *The Ultimate Reality.* Hong Kong: Bahá'í National Centre, n.d. [1981] [8] p. At head of title: *The Baha'i World.*

7.2622. *Umngcwabo WesiBaha'i = Baha'i Burial: Imithandazo, Nezifundo.* n.p. [Mbabane: National Spiritual Assembly of the Bahá'ís of Swaziland], n.d. [197–?] 7, 6 p. Zulu and English text.

7.2623. *United Nations Day Service Held as a Memorial Service to Dr R. St Barbe Baker: Bahá'í House of Worship, Mona Vale Road, Ingleside, Sunday, 24th October, 1982.* Ingleside, N.S.W.: Bahá'í House of Worship, 1982. [6] p.

7.2624. *United Nations Year of Peace Service.* Tiapatata, Western Samoa: Bahá'í House of Worship, 1985. 15 p.

7.2625. United States. Bureau of the Census. *Bahá'ís: Statistics, History, Doctrine and Organization.* Washington, D.C.: United States Government Printing Office, 1929. 11 p. (Census of Religious Bodies; 1926). LC card 29–26052.

7.2626. —— *Bahá'ís: Statistics, Denominational History, Doctrine and Organization.* Washington, D.C.: United States Government Printing Office, 1939. iv, 7 p. (Census of Religious Bodies; 1936).

7.2626a. United World School (Lucknow, India). *Prospectus 1985–86.* founded by Lucknow Baha'i Education Society. Lucknow: United World School, 1985. [2], 10 p.

7.2627. *Unity from Diversity.* Wilmette, Ill.: Bahá'í Publishing Trust, n.d. [before 1972] 4 p.

7.2628. *Unity in the Baha'i Family.* n.p. [Roseau]: National Spiritual Assembly of the Bahá'ís of the Commonwealth of Dominica, 1984. [4] p.

7.2629. *Unity of the Human Race.* Cali, Colombia: National Teaching Committee of the Baha'is of Colombia, May 1975 [i.e. St John's, Antigua: National Spiritual Assembly of the Bahá'ís of the Leeward Islands, 1984?] [4] p. (Spiritual Education of Children, Teacher's Manual).

7.2630. *Universal Compulsory Education: A Principle of the Bahá'í Faith.* n.p. [Auckland]: National Spiritual Assembly of the Bahá'ís of New Zealand, n.d. [196–] [5] p.

7.2631. *Universal Guidance Renewed: Religion Renewed and the World United.* London: Bahá'í Publishing Trust, n.d. [1969], 1980. [8] p.

7.2632. *The Universal House of Justice.* n.p. [Nairobi]: National Education Committee of Kenya, n.d. [1973] [4] p.

7.2633. *The Universal House of Justice.* n.p. [Kuala Lumpur?: National Spiritual Assembly of the Bahá'ís of Malaysia?], n.d. [1973] [1], 26 p.

7.2634. *The Universal House of Justice Is the Supreme Institution of the Baha'i Faith.* n.p. [Nairobi: Baha'i Publishing Agency], n.d. [1985] 1 p.

7.2635. *Universal Peace: More than an End to War.* n.p. [Wilmette, Ill.]: NTC [i.e. National Teaching Committee], 1985, 1985. [8] p.

7.2636. *Universal Peace: More than an End to War.* Santa Cruz, Calif.: Bosch Baha'i School, 1985. [8] p.

7.2637. *Universal Religion.* Surat: Vakil, 1914. 30 p.

7.2638. *A Universal Religion.* n.p. [Wilmette, Ill.]: Radio Service Committee, 1959. 7 leaves.

7.2639. *Universality, Human Rights, Peace: The Baha'i Faith.* London: National Spiritual Assembly of the Bahá'ís of the United Kingdom, n.d. [ca. 1980] [6] p. folder.

7.2640. *Unrestrained as the Wind: A Life Dedicated to Bahá'u'lláh.* Wilmette, Ill.: Bahá'í Publishing Trust, 1985, 1985. ix, 191 p.
A compilation of Bahá'í scripture, interpretation, historical passages and inspirational stories for youth.

7.2641. *Update on Iran, no.1.* Thornhill, Ont.: Canadian Association for Studies on the Bahá'í Faith, n.d. [1979?] 4 p.

7.2642. *Update on Iran [no.3].* Thornhill, Ont.: National Spiritual Assembly of the Bahá'ís of Canada, 1981. [6] p.

7.2643. *Update on Iran, vol. 4.* Thornhill, Ont.: National Spiritual Assembly of the Bahá'ís of Canada, Apr. 1983. [6] p.

V

7.2644. Vader, John Paul. *For the Good of Mankind: August Forel and the Bahá'í Faith*. Oxford: George Ronald, 1984. x, 114 p.

August Forel was one of Switzerland's and Europe's major scientific and social thinkers of the early twentieth century. This short sketch of Forel examines his association with the Bahá'í Faith. Based upon the author's doctoral dissertation.

7.2645. Vail, Albert R. *The Bahai Movement: Its Spiritual Dynamic*. n.p., n.d. [after 1914] 11 p. Reprinted from *Harvard Theological Review* (Cambridge, Mass.), v.7 (July 1914).

7.2646. Vail, Virgie V. *The Glorious Kingdom of the Father Foretold*. New York: Bahá'í Publishing Committee, 1940. xii, 262 p. LC card 40–33653 rev.
Review:
Miller, William McElwee. *The Moslem World* (Hartford, Conn.), v.31 no.1 (Jan. 1941), pp. 90–91.

Fulfilment of Christian prophecies – the Bahá'í Faith as the promised Kingdom of God.

7.2647. Vajdi, K.H. *Human Happiness*. Ujjain: Vajdi, n.d. [196–?] 109 p.

7.2648. —— *Youth on Trial*. Ujjain: Vajdi, n.d. [197–] 66 p.

7.2649. The Varqa School (Ahmednagar, India). *The Varqa School*. Ahmednagar, M.S.: The Varqa School, n.d. [1985?] 13 p.

7.2650. Vaswani, T.L. *The Baha'i Faith and the Modern World*. Karachi: S.L. Shahani at Motherland Press, n.d. [after 1938] 13 p.

7.2651. Vea, J. *The Baha'i Faith Answered by Christianity*. Niua Toputapu, Tonga: Free Wesleyan Church of Niua Toputapu, 1973. 9 p.

Anti-Bahá'í work from Christian viewpoint.

7.2652. *Very Important: Please Read Before You Throw Away*. Katong, Singapore: Spiritual Assembly of the Baha'is of Katong, n.d. [197–?] 2 p.

7.2653. *Victory Bulletin*. n.p. [South Carolina]: Deep South Committee, 1970. 8 p.

7.2654. *Victory Bulletin*. Souvenir ed. Wilmette, Ill.: National Teaching Committee, 1966. 4 p.

7.2655. *Vietnamese Bahaism*. Saigon: Comnavsuppac, n.d. [between 1964 and 1974] 8 p. (A Survey of the Religions of Vietnam) (Navy Personal Response Handout Series; C–1).

7.2656. *Views of Acca, Haifa, Mount Carmel and Other Holy Places*. Chicago: Behais Supply and Publishing Board, n.d. [between 1900 and 1902] 20 leaves.

7.2657. *idem*. Chicago: Bahai Publishing Society, n.d. [between 1903 and 1921] 20 leaves.

7.2658. *Vignettes from the Life of 'Abdu'l-Bahá*. collected and ed. by Annamarie Honnold. Oxford: George Ronald, 1982. xi, 199 p.

'A compilation of inspiring anecdotes pertaining to the Bahá'í way of life as demonstrated by 'Abdu'l-Bahá.' Its 'index to anecdotes' is organized under headings which describe the spiritual qualities of 'Abdu'l-Bahá.

7.2659. *Visit the Bahá'í House of Worship. Sheridan Road at Linden Avenue, Wilmette, Illinois*. Wilmette, Ill.: National Bahá'í Headquarters, n.d. [196–?] 2 p.

7.2660. *Visit the Bahá'í House of Worship, Wilmette, Illinois*. n.p. [Wilmette, Ill.: National Spiritual Assembly of the Bahá'ís of the United States], n.d. [1981] 2 p.

7.2661. *Visiting the Grave of the Beloved Guardian, Shoghi Effendi, New Southgate Cemetery*. n.p. [London: National Spiritual Assembly of the Bahá'ís of the United Kingdom], n.d. [1980?] 4 p.

W

7.2662. Wade, John. *World Unity*. London: National Spiritual Assembly of the Bahá'ís of the British Isles, n.d. [196–?] 8 p.

7.2663. Waite, Louise R. *Bahai Hymns and Poems*. Chicago: Bahai Publishing Society, 1904. 31 p.

7.2664. —— *Bahai Hymns of Peace and Praise*. n.p. [Chicago], L.R. Waite, 1908. 16 p.

Details of the printings of this booklet are contained in R.J. Armstrong-Ingram's *Music, Devotions and Mashriqu'l-Adhkár*. (Los Angeles: Kalimát Press, 1987), pp. 39–44.

7.2664a. —— *idem.* n.p. [Chicago]: L.R. Waite, c1908 [i.e. 1910 or 1911].

7.2664b. —— *idem.* n.p. [Chicago]: L.R. Waite, c1908 [i.e. between 1913 and 1915].

7.2664c. —— *idem.* n.p. [Chicago]: L.R. Waite [i.e. Mary Lesch], c1908 [i.e. 1917].

7.2664d. —— *idem.* 2nd ed. n.p. [Chicago]: L.R. Waite, 1927.

7.2665. —— *idem.* introd. & notes by R. Jackson Armstrong-Ingram. n.p. [Mishawaka, Ind.]: Aubade, 1984. [17], 4–17 p.

7.2666. —— *Prelude and Benediction.* Hollywood, Calif.: Waite, 1930. 5 p.

7.2667. —— *Song of the Covenant.* n.p., n.d. [1913] [2] p.

7.2667a. —— *Unity of the Manifestations: (All Mouthpieces of God).* Address delivered at the 1936 session of the Geyserville Summer School. n.p. [Geyserville, Calif.?], 1936. 10 p.

7.2668. —— *Words of Abdul Baha in Regard to the Mashrak-el-Azkar in Chicago.* from notes taken by Louise R. Waite, October 1909. n.p., n.d. [1909?] 3 p. Two variants, one on green paper, the other on white paper.

7.2669. Waite, Stephen. *Rabbani: Towards a Relevant Education.* Gwalior, India: Rabbani School, n.d. [1980?] [6] p.

7.2670. Walcott, Cynthia K. *The Gift.* il. Lynn Hutchinson-Reynolds. Wilmette, Ill.: Bahá'í Publishing Trust, 1976. 37 p. LC card 76–5476.
Children's story using animals to tell the story of the revelation of a new message from God.

7.2671. Walsh, Walter. *Living Religions and the Bahai Movement.* London: Free Religious Movement Towards World-Religion and World-Brotherhood, 1924. 15 p. (Free Religious Addresses; no.236).

7.2672. Ward, Allan L. *The Ten-Year Crusade: Seven Thousand Years in Retrospect.* Wilmette, Ill.: Bahá'í Publishing Trust, 1960. 22 p.

7.2673. —— *239 Days, 'Abdu'l-Bahá's Journey in America.* Wilmette, Ill.: Bahá'í Publishing Trust, 1979. 218 p. LC card 79–14713.
The author follows 'Abdu'l-Bahá on his tour of North America, making extensive use of contemporary newspaper reports.

7.2674. Watson, Albert Durrant. *The Dream of*

God. Chicago: Bahai Publishing Society, 1922. [48] p.

7.2675. —— *idem.* Toronto, Ont.: The Banner Press, 1922. [46] p.

7.2676. Watson, Marie A. *My Pilgrimage to the Land of Desire.* New York: Bahá'í Publishing Committee, 1932. 23 p.

7.2677. Waves of One Sea (Singing Group). *Yes, I Believe You.* n.p. [Lagos?]: National Spiritual Assembly of the Bahá'ís of Nigeria, n.d. [1974?] 20 p.

7.2678. *Way to Universal Brotherhood.* Bombay, India: Bahai Spiritual Assembly, n.d. [ca. 1920] 24 p.

7.2679. *We Should Know.* Nairobi, Kenya: National Education Committee, n.d. [197–?] 11 p.

7.2680. *We Will Have a School: Louhelen.* East Lansing, Mich.: Spiritual Assembly of the Baha'is of East Lansing, 1981. [20] p.

7.2681. Webster, Lecile. *Bahá'í Pilgrimage to the Bahá'í World Centre, Haifa.* Columbia, Md.: International Travel Consultant, n.d.[1980] [8] p.

7.2682. Wegener, Daniel Nelson. *Divine Springtime: Louise Caswell Recalls the Early Years of the Bahá'í Faith in Central America and Panama.* Tegucigalpa, Honduras: Union Press, 1977. II, 135 p.

7.2683. Weil, Henry A. *Closer Than Your Life Vein.* Anchorage: National Spiritual Assembly of the Bahá'ís of Alaska, 1978. vi, 114 p.
A course in spiritual regeneration and development.

7.2684. Weinberg, A.J. *The Epidemic of the Persian Jews.* with accompanying notes by Edward Dewing; also an address given in Temple Emmanuel, San Francisco by 'Abdu'l-Bahá. Montreal, Que.: Spiritual Assembly of the Bahá'ís of Montreal, n.d. [ca. 1950] [4] p.

7.2685. Weinberg, Arthur M. *The Refuge & the Cave.* il. Mary Jane Rostami. London: Bahá'í Publishing Trust, 1982. 111 p.
A novel for teenagers about an interracial group of youth who travel to the past and to the future to see the evolution of religion and the future glory of the Bahá'í commonwealth.

7.2686. Weinberg, Seymour. *The Lord Is One.* Wilmette, Ill.: Bahá'í Publishing Trust, 1963, [1967], 1976. 23 p.

7.2687. *Welcome to the Bahá'í House of Worship.* Wilmette, Ill.: Bahá'í National Center, n.d. [1979?] 6 p.

7.2688. Weller, Rachel Fort. *'The Earth Is But One Country'*. Wilmette, Ill.: Bahá'í Publishing Trust, n.d. [after 1968] 6 p. Reprint from *Friends Journal* (Philadelphia), (March 1, 1968).

7.2689. Wells, Bruce. *From Discontent: The Biography of a Mystic*. Oxford: George Ronald, 1985. 204 p.
Fictional account of a 'seeker' coming to find the Bahá'í Faith.

7.2689a. West African Centre for Bahá'í Studies (Lagos, Nigeria). *The West African Centre for Bahá'í Studies = Le Centre d'Afrique Occidentale pour les Etudes Bahaíes*. Lagos: National Spiritual Assembly of the Bahá'ís of Nigeria, n.d. [1985].

7.2690. Whalen, William J. *Baha'i*. Chicago: Claretian Publications, 1966. 23 p.
Written from Christian (Catholic) viewpoint.

7.2691. *What Are the Baha'i Teachings on Evil?* n.p. [Roseau]: National Spiritual Assembly of the Bahá'ís of the Commonwealth of Dominica, 1984. [2] p.

7.2692. *What Are the Baha'i Teachings on Heaven and Hell?* n.p. [Roseau]: National Spiritual Assembly of the Bahá'ís of the Commonwealth of Dominica, 1984. [4] p.

7.2693. *What Are the Baha'i Teachings on Life After Death?* n.p. [Roseau]: National Spiritual Assembly of the Bahá'ís of Commonwealth of Dominica, 1984. [2] p.

7.2694. *What Are the Principles of the Baha'i Faith?* n.p., n.d. [197–] 8 p.

7.2695. *idem.* n.p. [Nairobi: National Education Committee of Kenya], n.d. [1973] 8 p.

7.2696. *What Baha'is Believe*. Windhoek: National Spiritual Assembly [of the Bahá'ís of South West Africa/Namibia], n.d. [1984] [4] p.

7.2697. *What Faiths Believe About Future Life*. Wilmette, Ill.: Bahá'í Publishing Trust, 1966. 1 p.
Reprint from *Chicago's America* (Apr. 10, 1966).

7.2698. *What Is a Baha'i?* Accra North: National Spiritual Assembly of the Bahá'ís of Ghana, 1980, [1981] 6 p.

7.2699. *What Is a Bahá'í?* Roseau, Dominica: Baha'i Faith, n.d. [1982?] [4] p.

7.2700. *What Is Baha'ism?* Rome: Islamic European Cultural Centre, 1985. 51 p.
See 7.2548–7.2550.

7.2701. *What Is Iran Afraid Of?* n.p. [London]: National Spiritual Assembly of the Bahá'ís of the United Kingdom, 1983. 15 p.

7.2702. *idem.* Dublin: National Spiritual Assembly of the Bahá'ís of the Republic of Ireland, n.d. [1983?] 16 p.

7.2703. *What Is the Bahá'í Faith?* New York: Bahá'í Publishing Committee, n.d. [after 1921], 1939. 8 p.

7.2704. *idem.* Toronto, Ont.: National Spiritual Assembly of the Bahá'ís of Canada, n.d. [1958] 11 p.

7.2705. *idem.* Huntsville, Ala.: Local Spiritual Assembly of the Bahá'ís of Huntsville, Alabama, n.d. [197–?] 19 p.

7.2706. *idem.* n.d. [Mbabane: National Spiritual Assembly of the Bahá'ís of Swaziland], n.d. [197–?] 10 p.

7.2707. *idem.* Salisbury, Rhodesia n.d. [ca. 1970] (Salisbury: African Newspapers Ltd.). 19 p. Two variants, one blue cover 19 cm, one pink cover 18 cm.

7.2708. *idem.* Lusaka: National Spiritual Assembly of the Bahá'ís of Zambia, n.d. [1975?] 12 p.

7.2709. *idem.* Colombo: National Spiritual Assembly of the Bahai's [sic] of Sri Lanka, 1977. 6 p.

7.2710. *idem.* rev. ed. n.p. [Johannesburg]: National Spiritual Assembly of the Bahá'ís of South and West Africa, 1978. 30 p.

7.2711. *idem.* Kingston: National Spiritual Assembly of the Bahá'ís of Jamaica, n.d. [1979 or 1980] [12] p.

7.2712. *idem.* n.p. [Lagos]: National Spiritual Assembly of the Bahá'ís of Nigeria, 1981. [12] p.

7.2713. *idem.* Kingston: National Spiritual Assembly of the Bahá'ís of Jamaica, n.d. [1982?] 16 p.

7.2714. *idem.* Saint George's, Grenada: The Baha'i Centre, n.d. [1985] [4] p.

7.2715. *idem.* rev. ed. Johannesburg: National Spiritual Assembly of the Bahá'ís of South and West Africa, 1985 (Cape Town: Budd and Thomson). 30 p.

7.2716. *What Is the Baha'i Faith*. Auckland, N.Z.: False Prophets Project, c1976. 8 p.
Anti-Bahá'í work from Christian viewpoint.

7.2717. *What Is the Bahá'í Faith*. Kingston: National Spiritual Assembly of the Bahá'ís of Jamaica, n.d. [198–?] 12 p.

7.2718. *What Is the Baha'i Movement?* 4th ed. London: Hudson & Kearns, 1926. 7 p.

7.2719. *What Is the Bahá'í Movement?* New York: Bahá'í Publishing Committee, n.d. [193–?] 8 p.

Various printings, some list Bahá'í assemblies on last page, some do not.

7.2720. *idem.* Shanghai: P.O.B. 551, n.d. [193–?] 8 p.

7.2721. *idem.* Montreal, Que.: Bahá'í Assembly of Montreal, n.d. [193–?] 8 p.

7.2722. *idem.* New York, n.d. [1931?] 4 p.

7.2723. *What Is the Bahá'í Religion?* n.p. [United Kingdom?], n.d. [ca. 1980] [4] p.

7.2724. *What Is the Bahá'í World Faith: A World Religion Day Script for 2 Voices.* n.p. [Wilmette, Ill.]: Radio Service Committee, 1960. 8 leaves.

7.2725. *What Is This Faith Called Bahá'í?* n.p. [St Thomas: National Spiritual Assembly of the Bahá'ís of the Leeward and Virgin Islands], n.d. [1979?] 4 p. Reprinted from *The Virgin Islander*, v.2 no.6.

7.2726. *What It Means to Be a Bahá'í.* London: Bahá'í Publishing Trust, 1971. [6] p.

7.2727. *idem.* London: Bahá'í Publishing Trust, 1972. 10 p.

7.2728. *What Others Say About the Bahá'í Faith.* Kingston: National Spiritual Assembly of the Bahá'ís of Jamaica, n.d. [before 1974] 18 p.

7.2729. *What to Remember: A Souvenir of Your Visit to the Bahá'í Temple.* Wilmette, Ill.: National Spiritual Assembly of the Bahá'ís of the United States, n.d. [1951 or 1952] 4 p.

7.2730. *Where Do I, As a Baha'i, Fit in with the Peace Movement?* n.p. [Auckland]: National Spiritual Assembly of the Bahá'ís of New Zealand, 1984. 10 p.

7.2731. White, Roger. *Another Song, Another Season.* Oxford: George Ronald, 1979. 172 p. LC card 82–102385.
Reviews:
Ewart, Gavin. *British Book News* (London), (Jan. 1980), p. 51.
McCann, Paul. *Quarry* (Kingston, Ont.), v.30 no.1 (Winter 1981), pp. 74–78.
Phillips, Hilda. *Artlook* (Australia), v.6 no.11, p. 52.
—— *Outrigger* (Auckland, N.Z.), (1980), pp. 1–4.
Roger White's first volume of collected poetry, includes many portrayals of Bahá'í martyrs, teachers and ordinary believers.

7.2732. —— *Different Perspectives: Poems.* Haifa: White, 1979. ii, 49 p. Chapbook.

7.2733. —— *Old Songs, New Songs: Poems.* Haifa: White, 1977. 38 p. Chapbook.

7.2734. —— *The Shell and the Pearl: An Account*

of the Martyrdom of 'Alí-Aṣghár of Yazd. Oxford: George Ronald, 1984. 26 p.

7.2735. —— *Sketches of 'Abdu'l-Bahá Adapted from the Diary of Juliet Thompson.* Haifa: White, n.d. [between 1971 and 1973] 11 p. Chapbook.

7.2736. —— *A Sudden Music.* Oxford: George Ronald, 1983. 191 p.
Review:
Phillips, Hilda. *Signature* (New Zealand), (Sept.–Oct. 1984), p. 79.
Fictionalized account of the beginnings of the Bahá'í community in Paris, as told in the letters of a young woman.

7.2737. —— *Whitewash: Poems by Eileen Vail's Brother.* n.p. [Haifa]: White, 1982. 35 p. Chapbook.

7.2738. —— *The Witness of Pebbles.* Oxford: George Ronald, 1981. xv, 217 p. LC card 82–185469.
The author's second volume of collected poems.

7.2739. Whitehead, O.Z. *Some Bahá'ís to Remember.* Oxford: George Ronald, 1983. 272 p.
Biographical sketches of some 15 early Bahá'ís and an essay on the early days of the Bahá'í Faith in Manchester, England.

7.2740. —— *Some Early Bahá'ís of the West.* Oxford: George Ronald, 1976, 1977. x, 227 p. LC card 77–367477.
A collection of short biographical sketches of 24 early Bahá'ís of the western world.

7.2741. Whitmore, Bruce W. *The Dawning Place: The Building of a Temple, the Forging of the North American Bahá'í Community.* Wilmette, Ill.: Bahá'í Publishing Trust, 1984. xi, 331 p. LC card 83–25852.
Review:
Theology Digest, v.32 no.1 (Spring 1985).
William, P.W. *Choice* (Middletown, Conn.) (Feb. 1985), p. 832.
The story of the construction of the Bahá'í House of Worship in Wilmette, Ill. In detailing the story of this building's construction, the author also covers important events of twentieth century American Bahá'í history. Considerable use was made of primary materials in the National Bahá'í Archives.

7.2742. Whittle, Margaret. *Report on Iran and the Bahais.* Geneva, Switzerland: Friends World Committee for Consultation, Quaker United Nations Office, Nov. 1982. 3 p.

7.2743. *Who Are the Bahá'ís?* n.p. [Thornhill,

Ont.: National Spiritual Assembly of the Bahá'ís of Canada], n.d. [1984?] [4] p.
Promotional flyer for the film 'The Bahá'ís'.

7.2744. *Whoso Readeth Let Him Understand.* New York: David, n.d. [190–?] 32 p.

7.2745. *idem.* New York: Roy, n.d. [190–?] 32 p.

7.2746. *Why Bahá'u'lláh?* Wilmette, Ill.: Bahá'í Publishing Trust, 1971. 14 p.

7.2747. *Why Don't Baha'is Baptise with Water?* n.p. [Roseau]: National Spiritual Assembly of the Baha'is of the Commonwealth of Dominica, 1984. [2] p.

7.2748. *Why Morality?* n.p. [Johannesburg]: National Spiritual Assembly of the Bahá'ís of South and West Africa, pt.1, 1983. 10 p.

7.2749. Wilhelm, Roy. *The Golden Rule.* New York: Roy, n.d. [191–?] [4] p.

7.2750. [Wilhelm, Roy] *idem.* n.p., n.d. [191–?] [4] p.

7.2751. Wilhelm, Roy; Mills, Mountfort J. *Glimpses of Abdul Baha Prior to 1908 A.D.* by 'Roy' and M.J.M. n.p., 1908. 16 p.

7.2752. —— *Knock and It Shall Be Opened to You.* by 'Roy' and M.J.M. New York: Roy, n.d. [190–] 16 p.

7.2753. Wilkin, Mary Magdalene. *Verities of the Bahá'í Faith.* n.p. [United States]: Mary Magdalene Wilkin, n.d. [1938 or later] 20 p.

7.2754. Williams, Basil. *A Brief Sketch of the Rise and Development of Babism.* London: Eyre and Spottiswoode, 1914.

7.2755. Wilson, Robert. *Workshop: How to Recognize the Manifestation of God.* Lake Forest Park, Wash.: Wilson, 1981. 8 p.

7.2756. Wilson, Robert George. *True Believer.* Seattle, Wash., 1980. 34 leaves.

7.2757. Wilson, Samuel Graham. *Bahaism and Its Claims.* New York: Fleming Revell Co., 1915. 298 p. LC card 15–2507.
Reviews:
Buchanan, C.M. *The Moslem World* (Hartford, Conn.), v.6 no.3 (July 1916), pp. 325–326.
Moore, George Foot. *Harvard Theological Review* (Cambridge, Mass.), v.10 (July 1917), pp. 296–302.
A Protestant missionary's polemical view of the history and tenets of the Bahá'í movement. Wilson was familiar with much early source material in English on the Faith, which he used only when it could be quoted or misquoted to suit his purpose of impugning the character of the Bahá'í Central Figures and proving Christianity superior.

7.2758. —— *idem.* New York: AMS Press, 1970. 298 p. LC card 79–131493.

7.2759. *The Wind Is Singing in the Mountains.* Salisbury: National Youth Committee of the National Spiritual Assembly of the Bahá'ís of Rhodesia, 1979. 8 p.

7.2760. Winterburn, Mr and Mrs George T. *Table Talks with Abdul Baha in February, 1904.* trans. Mirza Youness Khan. Chicago: Bahai Publishing Society, 1908, 1915. 32 p.

7.2761. Witham, Elizabeth M. *Bahá'í Colouring Book 1.* n.p. [Johannesburg]: National Spiritual Assembly of the Bahá'ís of South and West Africa, 1983. 20 [i.e. 40] p. English, Afrikaans and Xhosa text.

7.2762. —— *Bahá'í Colouring Book 2.* Johannesburg: National Spiritual Assembly of the Bahá'ís of South and West Africa, 1983. 20 p. English, Afrikaans and Xhosa text.

7.2763. —— *Bahá'í Colouring Book 3.* Johannesburg: National Spiritual Assembly of the Bahá'ís of South and West Africa, 1984. 20 p. English, Afrikaans and Xhosa text.

7.2764. —— *Colouring Book of Baha'i Quotations for Parents and Children.* il. Gretchen K. Border. n.p. [Johannesburg]: National Spiritual Assembly of the Bahá'ís of South and West Africa, Children and Parent Education Committee, n.d. [1970] 46 leaves.

7.2765. Wittman, Debbie D. *The Birth of the Bahá'í Faith.* Wilmette, Ill.: Bahá'í Publishing Trust, 1980. 23 p.
Introduction in 'comic strip' format.

7.2766. Witzel, Donald R. *Buddha, Krishna, Zoroaster.* n.p. [Maracaibo?: Witzel], n.d. [197–?] [42] leaves in various foliations.

7.2767. Wolcott, Charles. *Blessed Is the Spot. O Thou By Whose Name: Two Prayers of Bahá'u'lláh.* music by Charles Wolcott. Wilmette, Ill.: Bahá'í Publishing Trust, 1957. [7] p.

7.2768. —— *From the Sweet-Scented Streams: A Prayer of Bahá'u'lláh.* music by Charles Wolcott. Wilmette, Ill.: Bahá'í Publishing Committee, 1954. [11] p.

7.2769. Women for One World (Boulder, Colo.). *What's Cookin'? in the World.* Lenexa, Kan.: Cookbook Publishers, Inc., 1982. [2], 73 p.

7.2770. *Women in Art: Music, Dance, Poetry & Visuals Inspired by the Bahá'í Revelation: Studio Theatre, Annenberg Center, University of Pennsylvania, November 23, 1982.* n.p. [Philadelphia, Pa.]: Studio Theatre, 1982. [12] p.

7.2771. Woolson, Gayle. *Divine Symphony*. New Delhi: Bahá'í Publishing Trust, 1971. 120 p.
Résumé of the lives and teachings of the founders of the major world religions.

7.2772. —— *idem*. rev. ed. New Delhi: Bahá'í Publishing Trust, 1976. 138 p.; 1977. 132 p.

7.2773. *The Work of Assistants to Auxiliary Board Members: A Simplified Compilation*. n.p. [Manurewa, N.Z.]: Continental Board of Counsellors in Australasia, 1982. [10] p.

7.2774. *idem*. n.p. [Manurewa, N.Z.]: Continental Board of Counsellors in Australasia, 1982. [28] p. English and Pidgin text.

7.2775. *The Work of the Auxiliary Boards: A Simplified Compilation*. n.p. [Manurewa, N.Z.]: Continental Board of Counsellors in Australasia, 1982. [21] p.

7.2776. *Working Together the Bahá'í Way: A Compilation*. Harare, Zimbabwe: Continental Board of Counsellors of the Baha'i Faith in Africa, Harare Office, 1982. 14 p.

7.2777. *World Developments of the Faith: A Study Outline in Six Parts*. n.p. [London]: National Spiritual Assembly of the Bahá'ís of the British Isles, 1952. 46 p.

7.2778. *A World Faith*. Wilmette, Ill.: National Bahá'í Assembly, n.d. [194– or 195–] [2] p. (No.4).

7.2779. *A World Faith: Studies in the Teachings of Bahá'u'lláh*. New York: Bahá'í Publishing Committee, 1936. 67 p. LC card 37–4286 rev.

7.2780. *World Herarld* [sic]. n.p., 1971. 4 p.

7.2781. World Order (Wilmette, Ill.). *Coming to Terms with Death*. n.p. [Wilmette, Ill.: Bahá'í Publishing Trust], 1974. 1 p.

7.2782. —— *Disarming for Universal Peace*. n.p. [Wilmette, Ill.: Bahá'í Publishing Trust], 1974. 1 p.

7.2783. —— *idem*. Bangor [Wales]: Copycat, n.d. [1983?] 1 p.

7.2784. —— *The Ecology Within*. n.p. [Wilmette, Ill.: Bahá'í Publishing Trust], 1974. 1 p.

7.2785. —— *From Alienation to World Peace*. n.p. [Wilmette, Ill.: Bahá'í Publishing Trust], 1974. 1 p.

7.2786. —— *Rebellious Youth: Toeing Their Elders' Mark*. n.p. [Wilmette, Ill.: Bahá'í Publishing Trust], 1974. 1 p.

7.2787. —— *Women: Striking the Balance*. n.p. [Wilmette, Ill.: Bahá'í Publishing Trust], 1974. 1 p.

7.2788. —— *idem*. Bangor [Wales]: Copycat, n.d. [1983?] 1 p.

7.2789. *World Order and World Peace? or Never Ending World Turmoil: The Burning Question of the Day!* Bombay, India: Bahai Spiritual Assembly of Bombay, n.d. [1942?] [2] p.

7.2790. *World Religion*. n.p. [Wilmette, Ill.]: Radio Service Committee, 1960. 9 leaves.

7.2791. *A World Religion*. n.p. [Wilmette, Ill.]: Radio Service Committee, 1960. 10 leaves.

7.2792. World Religion Conference (1977: Lucknow). *World Religion Conference, to Celebrate 160th Birthday of His Holiness Bahá'u'lláh: Ravindralaya, Lucknow, India, 12th November, 1977*. Lucknow, India: Local Spiritual Assembly of the Bahá'ís of Lucknow, 1977. vi, 59, 19 p.

7.2793. *World Religion Day*. Wilmette, Ill.: Bahá'í House of Worship, 1985. [4] p.

7.2794. *World Religion Day 1985*. n.p. [Hong Kong: National Spiritual Assembly of the Bahá'ís of Hong Kong], 1985. 4 p.

7.2795. World Religion Day Observance (5th: 1985: Colombo, Sri Lanka). *World Religion Day 5th Annual Observance in Sri Lanka: Theme, Spiritual Standards for a Peaceful Society*. n.p. [Colombo]: World Religion Day Committee, 1985. [4] p.

7.2796. *World Unity*. n.p. [Nairobi]: National Education Committee of the Baha'is of Kenya, 1973. [4] p.

7.2797. World Unity Conference (1926: Buffalo, N.Y.). *The World Unity Conferences: October 22, 23, and 24, 1926, Buffalo, N.Y.* Worcester, Mass.: World Unity Conferences, 1926. [6] p.

7.2797a. World Unity Conference (1926: Cleveland, Ohio). *The World Unity Conferences – Promoting the Oneness of Mankind: Cleveland, November 26, 27 and 28, 1926*. Worcester, Mass.: World Unity Conference Committee, 1926. [6] p.

7.2798. World Unity Conference (1927: Chicago). *The World Unity Conferences – to Create Harmony and Understanding Among Religions, Races, Nations and Classes: Morrison Hotel, Chicago, January 21, 22 and 23, 1927*. n.p. [Worcester, Mass.: World Unity Conference Committee], 1927. [6] p.

7.2798a. World Unity Conference (1927: Hartford, Conn.). *The World Unity Conferences – to Create Harmony and Understanding Among Religions, Races, Nations and Classes: Hotel Bond, Hartford, June 1, 2, 3, 1927*. Worcester, Mass.:

World Unity Conference Committee, 1927. [6] p.

7.2798b. World Unity Conference (1927: Montreal, Quebec). *The World Unity Conferences – to Create Harmony and Understanding Among Religions, Races, Nations and Classes: Montreal 1927, April 29th, Ritz Carlton Hotel, April 30th, McGill University, May 1st, Church of the Messiah.* Worcester, Mass.: World Unity Conference Committee, 1927. [6] p.

7.2799. World Unity Conference (1927: New Haven, Conn.). *The World Unity Conferences – to Create Harmony and Understanding Among Religions, Races, Nations and Classes: Hotel Taft, New Haven, March 25, 26, 27, 1927.* New Worcester, Mass.: World Unity Conference Committee, 1927. [6] p.

7.2799a. World Unity Conference (1927: New York). *The World Unity Conferences – Promoting the Oneness of Mankind: New York, February 25, 26, 27, 1927.* Worcester, Mass.: World Unity Conferences Committee, 1927. [6] p.

7.2799b. World Unity Conference (1927: New York). *The World Unity Conferences – to Create Harmony and Understanding Among Religions, Races, Nations and Classes: 1927, February 25th/26th/27th.* Worcester, Mass.: World Unity Conferences Committee, 1927. [3] p.

7.2799c. World Unity Conference (1927: Portsmouth, N.H.). *The World Unity Conferences – to Creat Harmony and Understanding Among Religions, Races, Nations and Classes: Portsmouth, N.H., February 18, 19, 20, 21, 1927.* n.p. [Worcester, Mass.: World Unity Conference Committee], 1927. [6] p.

7.2800. *World Unity, the Paramount Need: Essays, Today's Youth Write for Peace.* Essay competition organised by Local Baha'i Youth Committee Baroda. Lucknow, India: Baha'i Proclamation Committee, n.d. [1982] 60 p.

7.2800a. *The Writings of 'Abdu'l-Bahá: A Studied Approach.* London: National Consolidation Committee of the National Spiritual Assembly of the Baha'is of the United Kingdom, n.d. [1978?]. 12 p.

X–Z

7.2801. Yazdi, Marion Carpenter. *Youth in the Vanguard: Memoirs and Letters Collected by the First Bahá'í Student at Berkeley and at Stanford University.* Wilmette, Ill.: Bahá'í Publishing Trust, 1982. xx, 267 p. LC card 82–6793.

These memoirs include considerable historical information on other early Bahá'ís in California, and on the development of the religion in that state. Illustrated with index.

7.2802. Young, Patrick. *'God's Little Lemon Squeezer': Why the Bustling Baha'is Feel Their Religion's Day Has Come.* Wilmette, Ill.: National Baha'i Public Information Department, n.d. [1966?] 1 p. Reprinted from: *National Observer*, Monday, May 2, 1966.

7.2803. *Your Experience As a Bahá'í.* Wilmette, Ill.: Bahá'í Publishing Committee, 1948, 1954. 11 p.

7.2804. *idem.* Wilmette, Ill.: Bahá'í Publishing Trust, 1963, 1970. 12 p.

7.2805. *Your Future Is Glorious.* Pennant Hills, [Australia?]: Bahá'í Community of Hornsby, Shire, n.d. [196–?] 6 p.

7.2806. *Your New Life: The Baha'i Community.*

Roseau, Dominica: Baha'i Faith, n.d. [1980] 6 p.

7.2807. *Youth and Development.* n.p. [Thornhill, Ont.]: National Spiritual Assembly of the Baha'is of Canada, n.d. [1985] 31 p.

7.2808. *Youth Can Move the World!* Thornhill, Ont.: Bahá'í Youth Movement, n.d. [1985] [4] p.

7.2809. *Youth Can Move the World.* n.p. [Karachi]: National Youth Committee of the Baha'is of Pakistan, 142 B.E. [1985] 10 p.

7.2810. *Youth Can Move the World: A Bahá'í View.* Maseru: National Spiritual Assembly of the Bahá'ís of Lesotho, 1985. [6] p.

7.2811. *Youth Can Move the World: Bahá'í History Calendar, 1985, 141–142 B.E.* Honolulu: National Spiritual Assembly of the Bahá'ís of Hawaii, 1984. 28 p. (Bahá'í History Calendar).

7.2812. Youth for One World (Redlands, Calif.). *Coordinator's Manual.* Redlands, Calif.: Spiritual Assembly of the Bahá'ís of Redlands, Ca., 1980. 52 leaves.

7.2813. ——— *YOW Member Manual.* Redlands,

Calif.: Spiritual Assembly of the Bahá'ís of Redlands, Ca., 1980. 116 p.

7.2814. *Youth Month in California: Sponsored by the Bahá'í Faith, December 15–January 12.* California, 1974. 8p.

7.2815. *Youth Supplement.* n.p., n.d. [1981] [31] p.

7.2816. Yukon Bahá'í Institute (Lake Labarge, Yukon). *Yukon Bahá'í Institute.* Whitehorse, Yuk.: Yukon Bahá'í Institute, n.d. [1985] [6] p.

7.2817. *Yumi Song Book.* Lae, Papua New Guinea: Songbook Committee, n.d. [1985?] [2], 15, [4] leaves.

7.2818. Zeine, Ramsey. *Deepening in Groups.* n.p. [Beirut?], 1977. 20 p.

7.2819. Zohoori, Elias. *Bahá'í Character Lessons for Children's Classes.* n.p. [Kingston: National Spiritual Assembly of the Bahá'ís of Jamaica], n.d. [1978] 2 pts.

VIII
Braille Materials

BRAILLE publications and other services to the blind have been provided by the Bahá'í community for several decades. The Bahá'í Service for the Blind in the United States has operated successively from Schenectady, New York, Los Angeles, California, Tucson, Arizona, and Wilmette, Illinois since the 1940s. The Bahá'í community of the United Kingdom also has a Service for the Blind. The compiler is aware that what is listed here is only a portion of the materials produced. Many more items are listed, for example, in *The Bahá'í World*, volume XIII, pp. 1112–6; however, nearly all of them are unavailable at the Bahá'í World Centre or anywhere else and the listings themselves are not complete enough to be useful for entry in this bibliography. Shoghi Effendi indicated in correspondence with the National Spiritual Assembly of the Bahá'ís of the United States on 3 May 1954 that some 110 titles had been published in Braille. The bibliographer has no clear record of any of these other than the titles included here.

8.1. 'Abdu'l-Bahá. *Christ's Promise Fulfilled.* transcribed by Mary Francis Baral. n.p. [Los Angeles]: Bahá'í Service for the Blind, 1963, ix, 81 leaves.

8.2. —— *Foundations of World Unity.* transcribed by Mary Francis Baral, n.p. [Tucson, Ariz.]: Bahá'í Service for the Blind, 1965, 2 v.

8.3. —— *Memorials of the Faithful.* transcribed by Gertrude D. Schurgast. n.p. [Tucson, Ariz.]: Bahá'í Service for the Blind, 1973. 4 v.

8.4. —— *Paris Talks.* London: Bahá'í Service for the Blind, 1975. 3 v.

8.5. —— *idem.* transcribed by Barbara Willson. n.p. [Tucson, Ariz.]: Bahá'í Service for the Blind, 1976, 3 v.

8.6. —— *The Secret of Divine Civilization.* transcribed by Mary Francis Baral. n.p. [Los Angeles]: Bahá'í Service for the Blind, 1962. 2 v.

8.7. —— *Selections from the Writings of 'Abdu'l-Bahá.* transcribed by Barbara Willson. n.p. [Tucson, Ariz.]: Bahá'í Service for the Blind, 1980–81. 5 v.

8.8. —— *Some Answered Questions.* n.p. [Los Angeles]: Bahá'í Service for the Blind, 1962. 5 v.

8.9. —— *Tablets of the Divine Plan.* transcribed by Mary Francis Baral and Kent Dana. n.p. [Tucson, Ariz.]: Bahá'í Service for the Blind, 1973, xv, 79 leaves.

8.10. —— *The Wisdom of 'Abdu'l-Bahá.* transcribed by C.M. Rodman. Batavia, N.Y.: Genesee County Chapter, American Red Cross, 1936, 4 v.

8.11. —— *World Order Through World Faith.* n.p. [Los Angeles]: Bahá'í Service for the Blind, 1947.

8.12. —— *idem.* n.p. [Tucson, Ariz.]: Bahá'í Service for the Blind, 1966. [60] leaves.

8.13. —— *Writings of 'Abdu'l-Bahá* (taken from *Inspiring the Heart*). Stevenage, Eng.: Service for the Blind Committee, 1982. 83 leaves.

8.14. *'Abdu'l-Bahá, Fiftieth Anniversary of His Passing.* transcribed by Gertrude D. Schurgast. n.p. [Tucson, Ariz.]: Bahá'í Service for the Blind, 1973. 3 v.

8.15. The Báb. *Selections from the Writings of the Báb.* comp. Research Department of the Universal House of Justice and translated by Habib Taherzadeh with the assistance of a Committee at the Bahá'í World Centre; transcribed by Mary Francis Baral. n.p. [Tucson, Ariz.]: Bahá'í Service for the Blind, 1977. 3 v.

8.16. —— *Writings of the Báb* (taken from *Inspiring the Heart*). Stevenage, Eng.: Service for the Blind Committee, 1982. 79 leaves.

8.17. *The Bahá'í Electoral Process.* transcribed by Barbara Willson, n.p. [Tucson, Ariz.]: Bahá'í Service for the Blind, 1975. v, 61 leaves. (Bahá'í Comprehensive Deepening Program).

8.18. *The Bahá'í Faith: What Is the Bahá'í Faith?* n.p. [Stevenage, Eng.: Service for the Blind Committee], n.d. [ca 1980] [10] leaves.

8.19. *The Bahá'í House of Worship.* n.p. [Los Angeles]: Bahá'í Service for the Blind, 1952. [20] p.

8.20. *Bahá'í Miscellany.* n.p. [Tucson, Ariz.: Bahá'í Service for the Blind], n.d. [197–]. 7 v.

8.21. *The Bahá'í Story.* prepared by Bahá'í pioneers serving the Navajo Indian Reservation; transcribed by Mary Francis Baral. n.p. [Los

Angeles]: Bahá'í Service for the Blind, 1962. 2 v.

8.22. *Bahá'í Teachings for a World Faith.* n.p. [Los Angeles]: Bahá'í Service for the Blind, 1954.

8.23. *idem.* n.p. [Tucson, Ariz.]: Bahá'í Service for the Blind, 1967. [28] p.

8.24. Bahá'u'lláh. *Braille Transcription of the Words of Bahá'u'lláh Inscribed Over the Nine Entrances to the Bahá'í House of Worship.* n.p., n.d. [before 1947]. [8] p.

8.25. —— *Epistle to the Son of the Wolf.* retranscribed by Barbara Willson. n.p. [Tucson, Ariz.]: Bahá'í Service for the Bind, 1969. 3 v.

8.26. —— *The Fire Tablet.* n.p. [Tucson, Ariz.; Bahá'í Service for the Blind], n.d. [1980]. [9] leaves.

8.27. —— *idem.* London: Bahá'í Service for the Blind, n.d. [1985]. 8 leaves.

8.28. —— *Gleanings from the Writings of Bahá'u'lláh.* n.p. [Los Angeles]: Bahá'í Service for the Blind, 1958.

8.29. —— *idem.* retranscribed by Mary Francis Baral. n.p. [Tucson, Ariz.]: Bahá'í Service for the Blind, 1967. 5 v.

8.30. —— *Gleanings from the Writings of Bahá'u'lláh: Selections.* transcribed by C.M. Rodman. Batavia, N.Y.: Genesee County Chapter, American Red Cross, 1940.

8.31. —— *The Hidden Words of Bahá'u'lláh.* transcribed by C.M. Rodman. Batavia, N.Y.: Genesee County Chapter, American Red Cross, 1936.

8.32. —— *idem.* embossed F.A. Baker, Los Angeles, 1943.

8.33. —— *idem.* n.p. [Los Angeles]: Bahá'í Service for the Blind, 1953.

8.34. —— *idem.* Tucson, Ariz.: Bahá'í Service for the Blind, 1968. 60 p.

8.35. —— *The Kitáb-i-Íqán.* Los Angeles: American Brotherhood of Free Reading for the Blind, 1935. 2 v.

8.36. —— *idem.* transcribed by C.M. Rodman. Batavia, N.Y.: Genesee County Chapter, American Red Cross, 1938. 4 v.

8.37. —— *idem.* Wilmette, Ill.: Bahá'í Publishing Committee; [Los Angeles]: Braille Institute of America for Bahá'í Service for the Blind, a committee of the National Spiritual Assembly of the Bahá'ís of the United States, 1961. 2 v.

8.38. —— *Long Healing Prayer.* London: Bahá'í Service for the Blind, n.d. [1981]. 9 leaves.

8.39. —— *The Mission of Bahá'u'lláh.* n.p. [Los Angeles]: Bahá'í Service for the Blind, 1953.

8.40. —— *idem.* n.p. [Tucson, Ariz.]: Bahá'í Service for the Blind, 1977. [36] p.

8.41. —— *Prayers and Meditations by Bahá'u'lláh.* retranscribed by Mary Francis Baral. n.p. [Tucson, Ariz.]: Bahá'í Service for the Blind, 1966–7. 4 v.

8.42. —— *The Proclamation of Bahá'u'lláh to the Kings and Leaders of the World.* transcribed by Mary Francis Baral. n.p. [Tucson, Ariz.]: Bahá'í Service for the Blind, 1968. x, 87 leaves.

8.43. —— *Selected Writings of Bahá'u'lláh.* transcribed by Mary Francis Baral. n.p. [Los Angeles]: Bahá'í Service for the Blind, 1959. 62 leaves.

8.44. —— *Tablets of Bahá'u'lláh Revealed After the Kitáb-i-Aqdas.* comp. by the Research Department of the Universal House of Justice and translated by Habib Taherzadeh with the assistance of a Committee at the Bahá'í World Centre; transcribed by Mary Francis Baral. n.p. [Tucson, Ariz.]: Bahá'í Service for the Blind, 1979. 3 v.

8.45. —— *Writings of Bahá'u'lláh* (taken from *Inspiring the Heart*). Stevenage, Eng.: Service for the Blind Committee, 1982. 2 v.

8.46. Bahá'u'lláh, 'Abdu'l-Bahá. *Bahá'í Occasional Prayers.* n.p. [Tucson, Ariz.]: Bahá'í Service for the Blind, 1972. [68] p.

8.47. —— *Bahá'í Occasional Prayers.* Stevenage, Eng.: Service for the Blind Committee, 1981. 51 leaves.

8.48. —— *Bahá'í Prayers.* n.p. [Tucson, Ariz.]: Bahá'í Service for the Blind, 1972. [80] p.

8.49. —— *Bahá'í Prayers* [U.K. 1975 ed.]. Stevenage, Eng.: Service for the Blind Committee, 1981. 99 leaves.

8.50. —— *The Bahá'í Revelation.* London: Bahá'í Service for the Blind, 1977. 7 v.

8.51. —— *Bahá'í World Faith.* n.p. [Los Angeles]: Bahá'í Service for the Blind, 1961.

8.52. —— *idem.* retranscribed by Mary Francis Baral. n.p. [Tucson, Ariz.]: Bahá'í Service for the Blind, 1965–6. 10 v.

8.53. —— *Communion with God.* n.p. [Los Angeles]: Bahá'í Service for the Blind, 1947.

8.54. —— *idem.* n.p. [Tucson, Ariz.: Bahá'í Service for the Blind], n.d. [1966]. [24] p.

8.55. —— *The Divine Art of Living*. transcribed by Mary Francis Baral. n.p. [Los Angeles]: Bahá'í Service for the Blind, 1962. 3 v.

8.56. —— *Let Thy Breeze Refresh Them: Bahá'í Prayers and Tablets for Children*. London: Bahá'í Service for the Blind, 1981. 22 leaves.

8.57. —— *The Reality of Man*. Wilmette, Ill.: Bahá'í Publishing Committee, 1946.

8.58. —— *idem*. transcribed by Eudora Adkins. n.p. [Tucson, Ariz.]: Bahá'í Service for the Blind, 1969, iv. 80 leaves.

8.59. Bahá'u'lláh, 'Abdu'l-Bahá, Shoghi Effendi. *Bahá'í Education*. Stevenage, Eng.: Service for the Blind Committee, 1982. 2 v.

8.60. —— *Bahá'í Writings on Music*. Stevenage, Eng: Service for the Blind Committee, 1981. 23 leaves.

8.61. —— *The Gift of Teaching*. London: Bahá'í Service for the Blind, 1980. 67 leaves.

8.62. —— *The Heaven of Divine Wisdom*. London: Service for the Blind, 1980. 38 leaves (Bahá'í Publishing Trust Compilation Series; no. 10).

8.63. —— *The Individual and Teaching: Raising the Divine Call*. transcribed by Kent Dana. Wilmette, Ill.: Bahá'í Service for the Blind, 1981. vii, 61 leaves.

8.64. —— *The Onward March of the Faith*. Stevenage, Eng.: Service for the Blind Committee, 1982. 1 v.

8.65. —— *Seeking the Light of the Kingdom*. Stevenage, Eng.: Service for the Blind Committee, 1981. 55 leaves.

8.66. Bahá'u'lláh, the Báb, 'Abdu'l-Bahá. *Bahá'í Prayers*. transcribed by William D. Peary. Wilmette, Ill.: Bahá'í Service for the Blind, 1985. 3 v.

8.67. Bahá'u'lláh, the Báb, 'Abdu'l-Bahá, Shoghi Effendi. *The Importance of Prayer, Meditation and the Devotional Attitude*. Stevenage, Eng.: Service for the Blind Committee, 1982. 38 leaves. (Bahá'í Publishing Trust Compilation Series; no. 11).

8.68. —— *The Power of Divine Assistance*. Stevenage, Eng.: Service for the Blind Committee, 1985. 46 leaves. (Bahá'í Publishing Trust Compilation Series; no. 12).

8.69. Bahá'u'lláh, the Báb, 'Abdu'l-Bahá, Shoghi Effendi, the Universal House of Justice. *Family Life*. Stevenage, Eng.: Service for the Blind Committee, 1982. 61 leaves. (Bahá'í Publishing Trust Compilation Series; no. 14).

8.70. —— *Spiritual Foundations: Prayers [sic], Meditation, and the Devotional Attitude*. transcribed by William D. Peary. Wilmette, Ill.: Bahá'í Service for the Blind, 1985. 37 leaves.

8.71. Balyuzi, H.M. *'Abdu'l-Bahá, The Centre of the Covenant of Bahá'u'lláh*. Stevenage, Eng.: Service for the Blind Committee, 1981. 12 v.

8.72. —— *Bahá'u'lláh: The Word Made Flesh*. London: Bahá'í Service for the Blind, 1977. 3 v.

8.73. —— *Khadíjih Bagum, the Wife of the Báb*. transcribed by Kent Dana. n.p. [Tucson, Ariz.]: Bahá'í Service for the Blind, 1982. iii, 34 leaves.

8.74. —— *idem*. Stevenage, Eng.: Service for the Blind Committee, 1982. 43 leaves.

8.75. Blomfield, Lady [Sara Louisa]. *The Chosen Highway*. London: Bahá'í Service for the Blind, 1980. 5 v.

8.76. Cheney, Elisabeth H. *Prophecy Fulfilled*. n.p. [Los Angeles]: Bahá'í Service for the Blind, 1956. [24] p.

8.77. Collins, William P. *The Bahá'í Faith and Mormonism: A Preliminary Survey*. transcribed by William D. Peary. n.p. [Tucson, Ariz.]: Bahá'í Service for the Blind, 1982. ii, 49 leaves.

8.78. *The Dynamic Force of Example*. transcribed by Barbara Willson. n.p. [Tucson, Ariz.]: Bahá'í Service for the Blind, 1975–6. 3 v. (Bahá'í Comprehensive Deepening Program).

8.79. Esslemont, John Ebenezer. *Bahá'u'lláh and the New Era*. n.p., 1932, 3 v.

8.80. —— *idem*. n.p. [Los Angeles]: Bahá'í Service for the Blind, 1957. 3 v.

8.81. —— *idem*. transcribed by Mary Francis Baral. n.p. [Tucson, Ariz.]: Bahá'í Service for the Blind, 1973. 5 v.

8.82. *Faith for Freedom*. n.p. [Los Angeles]: Bahá'í Service for the Blind, 1947.

8.83. Faizi, Abu'l-Qásim. *Milly, a Tribute to the Hand of the Cause of God Amelia E. Collins*. n.p. [Stevenage, Eng.: Service for the Blind Committee], n.d. [1980]. 52 leaves.

8.84. —— *Narcissus to 'Akká*. London: Bahá'í Service for the Blind, 1980. 21 leaves.

8.85. —— *The Prince of Martyrs*. Stevenage, Eng.: Service for the Blind Committee, 1982. 78 leaves.

8.86. Faizi, Gloria. *The Bahá'í Faith, an Introduction*. transcribed by Barbara Willson. n.p. [Tucson, Ariz.]: Bahá'í Service for the Blind, 1974, 2 v.

8.87. Fathea'zam, Hushmand. *The New Garden.* London: Bahá'í Service for the Blind, 1980. 3 v.

8.88. Ferraby, John. *All Things Made New: A Comprehensive Outline of the Bahá'í Faith.* transcribed by Mary Francis Baral. Tucson, Ariz.: Bahá'í Service for the Blind, 1967–8. 6 v.

8.89. —— *idem.* London: Service for the Blind Committee, 1977, 6 v.

8.90. Ford, R.E. *Bahá'í Principles for Children.* Stevenage, Eng.: Service for the Blind Committee, 1982. 17 leaves.

8.91. *A Fortress for Well-Being: Bahá'í Teachings on Marriage.* transcribed by Barbara Willson, n.p. [Tucson, Ariz.]: Bahá'í Service for the Blind, 1975. v, 77 leaves. (Bahá'í Comprehensive Deepening Program).

8.92. Gail, Marzieh. <u>Kh</u>ánum, *The Greatest Holy Leaf.* Stevenage, Eng.: Service for the Blind Committee, 1982. 44 leaves.

8.93. —— *The Sheltering Branch.* n.p. [Tucson, Ariz.]: Bahá'í Service for the Blind, 1981. 102 leaves.

8.94. Gaver, Jessyca Russell. *The Bahá'í Faith: The Dawn of a New Day.* transcribed by Barbara Willson. n.p. [Tucson, Ariz.]: Bahá'í Service for the Blind, 1973. 5 v.

8.95. Ḥaydar-'Alí, Ḥájí Mírzá. *Stories from the Delight of Hearts: The Memoirs of Ḥájí Mírzá Ḥaydar-'Alí.* translated & abridged by A.Q. Faizi; transcribed by William D. Peary. n.p. [Tucson, Ariz.]: Bahá'í Service for the Blind, 1982. 3 v.

8.96. Hellaby, Madeline. *Death, the Messenger of Joy.* Stevenage, Eng.: Service for the Blind Committee, 1985. 65 leaves.

8.97. Hofman, David. *The Renewal of Civilization.* n.p. [Los Angeles]: Bahá'í Service for the Blind, 1948, 1954, 1957, 1962.

8.98. Holley, Horace. *God Passes By, a Study Guide.* transcribed by Mary Francis Baral. n.p. [Tucson, Ariz.]: Bahá'í Service for the Blind, 1965. i, 13 leaves.

8.99. —— *The God Who Walks With Men.* n.p. [Los Angeles]: Bahá'í Service for the Blind, 1954.

8.100. —— *Religion for Mankind.* transcribed by Gertrude D. Schurgast. n.p. [Tucson, Ariz.]: Bahá'í Service for the Blind, 1970–1. 5 v.

8.101. Huddleston, John. *The Earth is But One Country.* Stevenage, Eng.: Service for the Blind Committee, 1985. 5 v.

8.102. *Indexes to the Priceless Pearl by Rúḥíyyih Rabbani.* London: Bahá'í Service for the Blind, n.d. [1979]. 2 v.

8.103. Ives, Howard Colby. *Portals to Freedom.* London: Bahá'í Service for the Blind, 1980. 5 v.

8.104. Jordan, Daniel C. *Knowledge, Volition and Action: The Steps to Spiritual Transformation; and, The Supreme Gift of God to Man.* transcribed by Barbara Willson. n.p. [Tucson, Ariz.]: Bahá'í Service for the Blind, 1975. v, 39 leaves. (Bahá'í Comprehensive Deepening Program).

8.105. —— *The Meaning of Deepening: Gaining a Clearer Apprehension of the Purpose of God for Man.* transcribed by Barbara Willson. n.p. [Tucson, Ariz.]: Bahá'í Service for the Blind, 1974. ix, 94 leaves. (Baha'í Comprehensive Deepening Program).

8.106. *Library Catalogue.* Stevenage, Eng.: Service for the Blind Committee, 1982. 38 leaves.

8.107. *The Light of Bahá'u'lláh: An Introduction to the Bahá'í Faith.* transcribed by William D. Peary. Wilmette, Ill.: Bahá'í Service for the Blind, 1983. 2 v.

8.108. Maxwell, May. *An Early Pilgrimage.* Stevenage, Eng.: Service for the Blind Committee, 1982. 38 leaves.

8.109. Mehrabi, Jacqueline. *Nine Holy Days.* London: Bahá'í Service for the Blind, 1980. 47 leaves.

8.110. Nabíl-i-A'ẓam. *The Dawn-Breakers.* London: Bahá'í Service for the Blind, n.d. [197–]. 13 v.

8.111. National Spiritual Assembly of the Bahá'ís of the United States. *The Bahá'í Community: A Summary of Its Organization and Laws.* transcribed by Mary Francis Baral. Los Angeles: Bahá'í Service for the Blind, 1963. 2 v.

8.112. *One Universal Faith.* Los Angeles: Bahá'í Service for the Blind, 1957.

8.113. *The Open Door.* Los Angeles: Bahá'í Service for the Blind, 1952. [11] p.

8.114. *The Power of the Covenant.* transcribed by Kent Dana. Wilmette, Ill.: Bahá'í Service for the Blind, 1979. 3 pts.

8.115. *The Power of Divine Assistance.* transcribed by Barbara Willson. n.p. [Tucson, Ariz.]: Bahá'í Service for the Blind, 1982. i, 40 leaves.

8.116. *Principles of the Bahá'í Faith.* n.p. [Schenectady, N.Y.]: Bahá'í Service for the Blind, 1943.

8.117. *The Proclamation Campaign.* Stevenage,

Eng.: Service for the Blind Committee, 1982. 18 leaves.

8.118. Rabbani, Rúḥíyyih. *Prescription for Living.* transcribed by Gertrude D. Schurgast. n.p. [Tucson, Ariz.]: Bahá'í Service for the Blind, 1971-2. 4 v.

8.119. —— *idem.* Stevenage, Eng.: Service for the Blind Committee, 1983. 4 v.

8.120. —— *The Priceless Pearl.* London: Bahá'í Service for the Blind, 1979. 12 v.

8.121. Sabet, Huschmand. *The Heavens are Cleft Asunder.* transcribed by William D. Peary. n.p. [Tucson, Ariz]: Bahá'í Service for the Blind, 1982. 3 v.

8.122. Sears, William. *Thief in the Night.* Stevenage, Eng.: Service for the Blind Committee, 1984. 5 v.

8.123. —— *The Wine of Astonishment.* Stevenage, Eng.: Service for the Blind Committee, 1984. 3 v.

8.124. Shoghi Effendi. *The Advent of Divine Justice.* transcribed by Mary Francis Baral. n.p. [Los Angeles]: Bahá'í Service for the Blind, 1962. 2 v.

8.125. —— *Bahá'í Administration.* transcribed by Gertrude D. Schurgast. n.p. [Tucson, Ariz.]: Bahá'í Service for the Blind, 1967-9. 4 v.

8.126. —— *Citadel of Faith: Messages to America, 1947-1957.* transcribed by Barbara Willson. Wilmette, Ill.: Bahá'í Service for the Blind, 1978. 4 v.

8.127. —— *The Dispensation of Bahá'u'lláh.* transcribed by Mary Francis Baral, n.p. [Los Angeles]: Bahá'í Service for the Blind, 1963. 2 v.

8.128. —— *Excerpts from the Writings of the Guardian on Bahá'í Life.* transcribed by Mary Francis Baral. n.p. [Tucson, Ariz.]: Bahá'í Service for the Blind, 1975. [49] p.

8.129. —— *The Faith of Bahá'u'lláh.* n.p. [Los Angeles]: Bahá'í Service for the Blind, 1960.

8.130. —— *The Goal of a New World Order.* transcribed by Melba B. King. n.p. [Los Angeles]: Bahá'í Service for the Blind, 1949.

8.131. —— *God Passes By.* transcribed by Mary Francis Baral. n.p. [Tucson, Ariz.]: Bahá'í Service for the Blind. 1963-5. 12 v.

8.132. —— *Guidance for Today and Tomorrow.* Stevenage, Eng.: Service for the Blind Committee, 1976. 5 v.

8.133. —— *Lifeblood of the Cause.* Stevenage, Eng.: Service for the Blind Committee, 1981. 44 leaves.

8.134. —— *The National Spiritual Assembly.* transcribed by Kent Dana. n.p. [Tucson, Ariz.]: Bahá'í Service for the Blind, 1973. iii. 95 leaves.

8.135. —— *The Promised Day Is Come.* retranscribed by Mary Francis Baral. n.p. [Tucson, Ariz.]: Bahá'í Service for the Blind, 1967-8, 3 v.

8.136. —— *The World Order of Bahá'u'lláh.* transcribed by Barbara Willson. n.p. [Tucson, Ariz.]: Bahá'í Service for the Blind, 1970-1. 5 v.

8.137. Shoghi Effendi, Universal House of Justice. *A Special Measure of Love: The Importance and Nature of the Teaching Work Among the Masses.* transcribed by Kent Dana. n.p. [Tucson, Ariz.]: Bahá'í Service for the Blind, 1975. iv, 56 p.

8.137a. Taherzadeh, Adib. *The Revelation of Bahá'u'lláh: Adrianople, 1863-1868.* London: Bahá'í Service for the Blind, 1979. 10 v.

8.138. —— *The Revelation of Bahá'u'lláh: 'Akká, The Early Years: 1868-1877.* Stevenage, Eng.: Service for the Blind Committee, 1985. 10 v.

8.139. —— *The Revelation of Bahá'u'lláh: Baghdád: 1853-1863.* London: Bahá'í Service for the Blind, 1978. 8 v.

8.140. —— *Trustees of the Merciful.* London: Bahá'í Service for the Blind, 1977. 92 leaves.

8.141. Universal House of Justice. *Messages from the Universal House of Justice: Taken from Bahá'í News and Inserts.* transcribed by Barbara Willson. n.p. [Tucson, Ariz.]: Bahá'í Service for the Blind, 1967- . 6 v.

8.142. —— *A Synopsis and Codification of the Kitáb-i-Aqdas, the Most Holy Book of Bahá'u'lláh.* Tucson, Ariz.: Bahá'í Service for the Blind, 1975. xv, 70 leaves.

IX
Periodicals

LARGE numbers of English-language periodicals are published by Bahá'í institutions in printed, mimeographed, dittoed, cyclostyled and photo-copied formats. Many are primarily intended for internal use of the Bahá'í community itself. Although thorough bibliographic control has not yet been established, it was felt that a beginning could be made by listing those national, inter-national, scholarly and special-interest Bahá'í periodicals which have been catalogued in the International Bahá'í Library, regardless of method of reproduction. Later supplements will list newly-established English-language periodicals, and those older periodicals not included in this present instalment which will be catalogued in future by the International Bahá'í Library. Where a '?' appears this indicates uncertainty of date of first issue or of date of closure of a periodical which appears to have ceased publication. In some cases, where a periodical with several title and number-ing changes is actually a run of a single periodical, this periodical is included in a single entry. The title index includes all variant titles.

9.1. *Ablaze!: Japan Bahá'í Youth Newsletter.* no.1 (7 [i.e. July] 1984)– . Tokyo: NYC [Na-tional Youth Committee] Issues 1–3 are bilingual English-Japanese.

9.2. *The Aesthete: A Quarterly Arts Publication.* v.1 no.1 (Spring 1976)–v. 1 nos. 3–4 (Fall 1976–Winter 1977). Ottawa, Ont.: A. Ouimet, R. Landau.

9.3. *Africa News.* African ed. no.1 (Nov. 1951) – ?. n.p. [London]: Africa Committee of the National Spiritual Assembly of the Bahá'ís of the British Isles.

9.4. *Africa News.* English ed. no.1 (Oct. 1950) – ?. n.p. [London]: Africa Committee of the National Spiritual Assembly of the Bahá'ís of the British Isles.

9.5. *African Highlights.* no.1 (Sept. 1981)– . Nairobi: Continental Board of Counsellors of the Bahá'í Faith in Africa.

9.6. *Alaska Baha'i Dawn Patrol Newsletter.* no.1 (Jan. 1979)–no.9 (Jan.–Feb. 1980). Fairbanks.

9.7. *Alaska Bahá'í News.* no.1 (Aug. 1957)– . Anchorage: National Spiritual Assembly of the Bahá'ís of Alaska.

9.8. *Alaska Baha'i Teaching Bulletin.* no.1 (Sept. 1980)– ?. Anchorage: National Teaching Com-mittee.

9.9. *Alaska Baha'i Youth Newsletter,* v.1 no.1 (1980)– ?. Kenai, Alaska: Youth Advisory Committee. Some published by Central Penin-sula Baha'i Youth Group.

9.10. Alaska Teaching Committee. *Bulletin.* [no. 1] (Aug. 1945)–[no.87] (Apr. 1957). Anchor-age: Alaska Teaching Committee.

9.11. *The American Bahá'í.* no.1 (Jan. 1970)– . Wilmette, Ill.: National Spiritual Assembly of the Bahá'ís of the United States.

9.11a. *Anis: Bulletin for Baha'i Children.* no.1 (21 Apr. 1978)– ?. Victoria: National Spiritual Assembly of the Bahá'ís of Cameroon, National Child Magazines Committee.

9.12. *The Arctic Quarterly: A Bulletin for the Bahá'í Circumpolar Community.* [v.1 no.1] (Dec. 1974)– ?. n.p. [Wakefield, Que.]: National Arctic Teaching Committee. Succeeds: *The Polar Bear Press.*
   See 9.423.

9.13. *Arise.* v.1 no.1 (Aug.–Sept. 1982)– . n.p. [Nairobi?]: National Youth Committee of the National Spiritual Assembly of the Bahá'ís of Kenya.

9.14. *Arise: The Bahá'í News of the Windward Islands.* v.1 no.1 (Jamal-Azamat 138, May 1981)–v.2 no.6 (Mar. 1983). n.p. [Kingstown, St Vincent]: National Spiritual Assembly of the Bahá'ís of the Windward Islands.

9.15. *Arise for Victory.* v.1 no.1 (15 Dec. 1977) – ?. Kumasi: National Teaching Committee of the National Spiritual Assembly of the Bahá'ís of Ghana.

9.16. *Arise to Assist: The Quarterly News Bulletin of the Auxiliary Board Members in Kenya.* no.1 (Oct. 1985)– . Kenya: Auxiliary Board Mem-bers in Kenya.

9.17. *Art of Living.* no.1 ([Jan.? 1985])– . Lusaka, Zambia: Social and Economic Develop-ment Committee.

9.18. *Asia Pioneer News.* v.1 no.1 (Mar. 1985)– . Singapore: Continental Pioneer Committee for Asia.

9.19. *The Assistants: A Bahá'í Bulletin for the Assistants to Auxiliary Board Members in A.P.* no.1 (14 May 1982)– ?. Secunderabad, Andhra Pradesh: Pirooz Fazli.

9.20. *Assistants Bulletin for the Board of Protection in Bangladesh.* no.1 (Mulk 141, Feb. 1985)– . Dhaka: Mr. Amjad Ali.

9.21. *Assistants Newsmagazine.* v.1 no.1 (July 1983)– . n.p. [Sri Lanka]: K. Selowarajoo.

9.22. Association for Bahá'í Studies (Ottawa). *Bulletin.* no.1 (June 1975)– . Ottawa, Ont.: Association for Bahá'í Studies.

The Association was originally called The Canadian Association for Studies on the Bahá'í Faith.

9.23. Association for Bahá'í Studies – Australia. *Newsletter.* no.1 (Apr. 1985)– . Willeton, W.A.: Association for Baha'i Studies – Australia.

9.24. *Australian Bahá'í Bulletin.* no.1 (Oct. 1953)– . Sydney: National Spiritual Assembly of the Bahá'ís of Australia. Title varies: *National News Item,* no.1–no.7; *Bahá'í News Bulletin,* no.8–no.9; *Bahá'í Bulletin,* no.10–no.34. Succeeds: *Bahá'í Bulletin.*
See 9.32.

9.25. *Baha'i Academy News Letter.* no.1 (25 Oct. 1985)– . Panchgani, India: Baha'i Academy.

9.26. Bahá'í Administrative Committee for Thailand. *Bulletin.* (?1976)– ?. Bangkok: Baha'i Administrative Committee.

9.27. *Baha'i Africa Newsletter.* no.1 (Mar. 1958) – ?. Salisbury, So. Rhodesia: Regional National Spiritual Assembly of South and West Africa.

9.28. *Bahá'í Audio-Visual Bulletin = Le Bulletin Audio-Visuel Bahá'í.* (?)– ?. n.p. [Victor, N.Y.]: International Bahá'í Audio-Visual Centre.

9.29. *(Bahai Balatan).* v.1 no.1 (?)– . n.p. [Dhaka: National Spiritual Assembly of the Bahá'ís of Bangladesh] Bengali and English text.

9.30. *Baha'i Berichten.* English ed. no.1 (1 Aug. 1979)– ?. 's-Gravenhage [Netherlands]: Nationale Geestelijke Raad.

9.31. *The Bahai Bulletin.* v.1 no.1 (Sept. 1908)– v.1 no.6 (Apr.–May 1909). New York: Bahai Publishing Society.

9.32. *Bahá'í Bulletin.* no.1 (June 1948)–no.65 (Sept. 1953). n.p. [Sydney, N.S.W.: National Spiritual Assembly of the Bahá'ís of Australia and New Zealand] Title varies: *Bahá'í News Bulletin,* no.1–36. Succeeds: *Bahá'í Quarterly.*

Succeeded by: *Australian Bahá'í Bulletin.*
See 9.24, 9.136.

9.33. *Baha'i Bulletin.* v.1 no.1 (Nov. 1959)– ?. Suva, Fiji; National Spiritual Assembly of the Bahá'ís of the South Pacific Ocean. Title varies: *South Sea Islands News,* v.1 no.1 (Nov. 1959)–v.2 no.1 (July 1960).

9.34. *Baha'i Bulletin.* no.1 (Sept. 1964)– ?. n.p. [Honiara]: National Spiritual Assembly of the Bahá'ís of the South West Pacific Ocean.

9.35. *Bahá'í Bulletin.* no.1 (Jan.–Feb. 1971)– . Port of Spain: National Spiritual Assembly of the Bahá'ís of Trinidad and Tobago. Title varies: *News Bulletin of Trinidad and Tobago,* no.1– ?; *Trinidad & Tobago Bulletin,* ?–no.5; *Bulletin of Trinidad and Tobago,* no.6–48.

9.36. *Baha'i Bulletin for the Eastern Caroline Islands.* v.1 no.1 (Jan. 1983)– . Ponape: National Teaching Committee of the Eastern Caroline Islands. Title varies: *Baha'i Bulletin,* v.1 no.1 (Jan. 1983)–v.2 no.10–12 (Oct.–Dec. 1984).

9.37. *Bahá'í Bulletin for the Western Caroline Islands.* v.1 no.1 (Masa'il-Mulk 142 [Dec. 1985–Feb. 1986])– . Colonia, Yap: National Spiritual Assembly of the Western Caroline Island[s] Succeeds: *Baha'i Newsletter of the Western Caroline Islands.*

9.38. *Bahá'í Bulletin of North East Asia.* no.1 (July 1957)– ?. Tokyo: National Spiritual Assembly of the Bahá'ís of North East Asia.

9.39. *Bahá'í Bulletin of the French Antilles.* no.0 (Dec. 1977)–no.19 (Mar.-Apr. 1981). Point-à-Pitre: National Spiritual Assembly of the Bahá'ís of the French Antilles.

9.40. *Bahá'í Bulletin: Territory of Papua and New Guinea.* v.1 no.1 (May 1969)–no.3 (July 1969). n.p. [Lae]: National Spiritual Assembly of the Bahá'ís of Papua New Guinea.

9.41. *Bahá'í Canada* [old series]. no.290 (Dec. 1975)–no.316 (June 1978). Thornhill, Ont.: National Spiritual Assembly of the Bahá'ís of Canada. Continues: *Canadian Bahá'í News.*
See 9.196.

9.42. *Bahá'í Canada* [new series]. [v.1] no.1 (Sept. 1978)– . Thornhill, Ont.: National Spiritual Assembly of the Bahá'ís of Canada. Title varies: *Bulletin,* no.1–no.8.

9.43. *Baha'i Child-Life.* v.1 no.1 (?)– . Victoria, B.C.: Children's Bulletin Committee.

9.44. *Baha'i Coast News.* no.1 (?)– ?. Mombasa, Kenya: R.T.C. of the Coast.

9.45. Bahá'í Computer User's Association. *News-*

letter. [no.1] (11 May 1982)– ? Navajo, N.M.: Roger Coe.

9.46. *Bahá'í Digest.* v.1 no.1 (May 1973)– ?. Wilmette, Ill.: National Spiritual Assembly of the Bahá'ís of the United States.
  Newsletter for Bahá'ís in corrective institutions.

9.47. *Baha'i Echos.* v.1 no.1 (Oct. 122 [1965]) – ?. Monrovia, Liberia: NSA of West Africa.

9.48. *Bahá'í Family Life.* no.1 (Dec. 1976)– ?. Auckland, N.Z.: Family Life Committee.

9.49. *Baha'i Feast Letter.* (25 Aug. 1984)– . Limbe: Spiritual Assembly of the Baha'is in Malawi. Continues: *Nineteen Day Feast Letter.*

9.50. *Baha'i Feast Letter = Incwadi Yesidlo Samabaha'i.* no.1 (14 June 1974)– ?. Mbabane, Swaziland: [National Spiritual Assembly of the Bahá'ís of Swaziland]. Title varies: *Feast Letter*, no.1 (14 June 1974).

9.51. *(Bahai fisto letah) = NSA News Letter, Feast Letter.* no.1 (1974. 8.1)– . n.p. [Tokyo: National Spiritual Assembly of the Bahá'ís of Japan] Mostly Japanese, some pages in English.

9.52. *Baha'i Flash News.* v.1 no.1 (Aug. 12, 1977)– ?. Quezon City: National Spiritual Assembly of the Bahá'ís of the Philippines with assistance of the Local Spiritual Assembly of Quezon City.

9.53. *The Bahai Fortnightly.* v.1 no.1 (Jan. 7, 1931)– ?. Lahore: Pritam Singh. Title varies: *The Bahai Weekly*, v.1 no.1 (Jan. 7, 1931)–v.2 no.?. LC card 44–10111.

9.54. *Bahá'í Gazette.* no.1 (Oct. 1957)– . Kampala: National Spiritual Assembly of the Bahá'ís of Uganda. Published successively by the National Spiritual Assemblies of Central & East Africa, and Uganda & Central Africa; numbering restarts with National Spiritual Assembly of Uganda. Title varies: *National Bahá'í Newsletter*, no.1 (Oct. 1971)–no.12 (Nov.–Dec. 1973); *Bahá'í Gazette*, no.1 (Oct. 1957)–no.46 (Feb. 1971), no.13 (May–June 1974)– ?.

9.55. *Bahá'í Geppo.* English ed. (Nov. 1955)– (June 1972). n.p. [Tokyo]: National Spiritual Assembly of the Bahá'ís of North East Asia.

9.56. *Baha'i Infro-Expo 75.* no.1 (Mar. 1975)– no.4 (July 1975). Honolulu: Public Information Office.

9.57. *Bahá'í International Community and the United Nations Newsletter.* no.1 (May 1977)– no.2 (Aug. 1977). New York: Bahá'í International Community.

9.58. *Bahá'í International Health Agency. Bulletin.* no.1 (Apr. 1983)– . Ottawa, Ont.: Bahá'í International Health Agency.

9.59. *Bahá'í International News Service.* no.1 (Dec. 1967)– . Haifa: Bahá'í World Centre. Title varies: no.3–12 called *Release of News Items*.

9.60. *The Baha'i Islander: A News-Letter for the Baha'is of Trinidad, Tobago, Curacao, Aruba and Bonaire.* no.1 (Mar. 1965)– ?. Caracas: National Spiritual Assembly of the Baha'is of Venezuela.

9.61. *Baha'i Jeevan = Bahá'í Life.* ([June 1973])– . n.p. [Kanpur: State Teaching Committee of Uttar Pradesh] Title varies: Some issues do not have *Bahá'í Life* on cover. Publisher varies: [Kanpur: State Teaching Committee of Uttar Pradesh] until 1986; [Lucknow: State Bahá'í Council of Uttar Pradesh] thereafter.

9.62. *Bahá'í Journal.* no.1 (Sept. 1936)–no.250 (Apr./May 1979). London: National Spiritual Assembly of the Bahá'ís of the United Kingdom.

9.63. *The Bahá'í Journal.* v.1 no.1 ([Mar. 1984])– . London: National Spiritual Assembly of the Bahá'ís of the United Kingdom.

9.64. *Baha'i Jubilee: Spiritual Preparation, Readings for Nineteen-Day Feasts.* bulletin #1 (?1952)– ? n.p. [Wilmette, Ill.?]: Jubilee Committee of the National Spiritual Assembly.

9.65. *Baha'i Kundu: Niusipepa Bilong ol Baha'i.* v.1 no.1 (May 1969)– . Lae: National Spiritual Assembly of the Bahá'ís of Papua New Guinea. Title varies: *Baha'i Bulletin*, no.1–3. From no.19, Motu and Pidgin editions were published separately from the English.

9.66. *Baha'i Lesotho Litaba Newsletter.* ?– . n.p. [Maseru: National Spiritual Assembly of the Bahá'ís of Lesotho] Title varies: *Leselinyana Lesotho Newsletter*, (June 1975); *Litaba Lesotho Newsletter*, (Aug. 1975)–(Nov.–Jan. 1977–78); *Baha'i Lesotho Litaba Newsletter*, (Mar.–Apr. 1978)– . Text in English and Sesotho.

9.67. *Baha'i Life Better Life.* v.1 no.1 ([Mar.] 1985)– . n.p. [Lagos]: Baha'i Women/Children's Education Committee of National Spiritual Assembly of the Baha'is of Nigeria.

9.68. *Bahá'í Mediagram: Bahá'í Radio-Television Newsletter.* no.1 (Oct. 1979)– . Maracaibo, Venezuela: Centro par Intercambio Radiofónico Bahá'í de América Latina.

9.69. *Bahá'í Monthly News Service.* v.1 no.1 (Sept. 1979)–(Mar. 1984). London: National

Spiritual Assembly of the Bahá'ís of the United Kingdom. Title varies: *Bahá'í Monthly News Service*, v.1 no.1 (Sept. 1979)–no.12 (Aug. 1982); *Bahá'í News Services*, (Oct. 1982)–(Mar. 1984).

9.70. *Bahá'í News*. no.1 (Dec. 1924)– . Wilmette, Ill.: National Spiritual Assembly of the Bahá'ís of the United States. Title varies: *Bahá'í News Letter*, 1924–1929. LC card 78–640732.

For indexes, *see* 7.1268–7.1270. For *Bahá'í News U.S. Supplement* see 9.112.

9.71. *Bahai News*. no.1 (June 1928)– ?. Cairo: National Spiritual Assembly of the Bahá'ís of Egypt. Title varies: *Bulletin*, (1928–1929); *Bahai News Letter*, (1930–1935). Text in English and Arabic.

9.72. *Baha'i News*. no.1 (May–Aug. 1957)– ?. Djakarta: Regional Spiritual Assembly of the Baha'is of South East Asia.

9.73. *Baha'i News*. no.1 (Apr. 1958)– ?. Karachi: National Spiritual Assembly of the Baha'is of Pakistan.

9.74. *Bahá'í News*. [no.1] (Apr.–July 1961)– . Kingston: National Spiritual Assembly of the Bahá'ís of Jamaica.

9.75. *Bahá'í News*. no.1 (? 1965)– ?. Dar es Salaam: National Spiritual Assembly of the Bahá'ís of Tanzania. Numbering begins anew with Oct. 1971; early issues contain some Swahili.

9.76. *Bahá'í News*. no.1 (June 1970)– . n.p. [Harare]: National Spiritual Assembly of the Bahá'ís of Zimbabwe. Title varies: *Bahá'í News of Rhodesia*, no.1–42. No.1–65 published by National Spiritual Assembly of the Bahá'ís of Rhodesia.

9.77. *Baha'i News*. no.1 (July 1977)– . Vila: National Spiritual Assembly of the Bahá'ís of Vanuatu. No.1–27 published by National Spiritual Assembly of the Bahá'ís of the New Hebrides.

9.78. *Baha'i News*. no.1 (Oct. 1984)– . n.p. [St George's]: National Spiritual Assembly of the Bahá'ís of Grenada. Title varies: *Monthly Newsletter*, no.1 (Oct. 1984)–no.3 (Dec. 1984); *Baha'i Newsletter*, no.4 (Jan. 1985); *Baha'i News*, no.5 (Feb. 1985)– .

9.79. *Bahá'í News*. ? – . Georgetown: National Spiritual Assembly of the Bahá'ís of Guyana. Title varies: *Baha'i News Letter* / *Baha'i Newsletter*, no.7 (Oct.–Dec. 1977)–no.13 (June–Aug. 1979); *Bahá'í News Guyana*, no.14 (Sept. 1979)–v.13 no.2 (Sept.–Nov. 1981); *Bahá'í News*, v.1 ([May 1983])– .

9.80. *Bahá'í News*. ? – ?. n.p. [Reykjavík]: National Spiritual Assembly of the Bahá'ís in Iceland.

9.81. *Bahá'í News*. ? – ?. St. Thomas, v.1.: [National Spiritual Assembly of the Bahá'ís of the Leeward and Virgin Islands].

9.82. *Bahá'í News and Reviews*. no.1 (Apr. 1947)– ?. n.p. [Tihran]: National Spiritual Assembly of the Bahá'ís of Iran.

9.83. *Bahá'í News = Bahá'í Tidhindi*. no.1 (? 1972)– . Reykjavík: National Spiritual Assembly of the Bahá'ís of Iceland = Andlegt Thjódhradh Bahá'ía á Íslandi. Bilingual English/Icelandic.

9.84. *Baha'i News Bangladesh*. ? – . n.p. [Dhaka]: National Spiritual Assembly of the Bahá'ís of Bangladesh.

9.85. *Bahá'í News Bulletin*. no.1 (?)– . Colombo: National Spiritual Assembly of the Bahá'ís of Ceylon.

9.86. *Bahá'í News Bulletin*. ? – ?. Addis Ababa: National Spiritual Assembly of the Bahá'ís of North East Africa.

9.87. *Bahá'í News Bulletin*. no.100 (Asma, Aug. 20, 1982)– . n.p. [Banjul]: National Spiritual Assembly of the Bahá'ís of the Gambia. Numbering begins at 100 so as to avoid any confusion with earlier newsletters of the Gambia.

9.88. *Baha'i News Dominica*. (Aug. 1983)– . Roseau: National Spiritual Assembly of the Bahá'ís of Dominica. Title varies: *Newsletter from the National Spiritual Assembly of the Bahá'ís of Dominica*, (Aug. 1983).

9.89. *Baha'i News from Other Lands*. ? – ? . n.p. [New Delhi]: National Spiritual Assembly of the Bahá'ís of India & Burma.

9.90. *Bahá'í News from South and West Africa*. no.1 (Mar. 1958)– . n.p. [Johannesburg]: National Spiritual Assembly of the Bahá'ís of South and West Africa. Title varies: *Baha'i African Newsletter*, 1958–1960; *Bahá'í Newsletter of South and West Africa*, 1960–1964; *Bahá'í Newsletter*, 1964–1967, 1974–1975; *South and West Afrika*, 1970; *Bahá'í News, South and West Africa*, 1970; *Bahá'í News for South and West Africa*, 1971; *Bahá'í News of South and West Africa*, 1972–1973; current title from 1975.

9.91. *Bahá'í News India*. no.1 (Sept./Oct. 1972) – . New Delhi: National Spiritual Assembly of the Bahá'ís of India.

9.92. *Baha'i News = Izindaba Zamabaha'i*. no.1 (24 June 1974)– . Mbabane: National Spiritual Assembly of the Bahá'ís of Swaziland. English and Swati text.

9.93. *Baha'i News-Letter.* no.1 (? 1938)– ?. Baghdad: National Spiritual Assembly of the Baha'is of 'Iraq.

9.94. *Baha'i News-Letter.* (20 Aug. 1980)– . Colombo: Spiritual Assembly of the Baha'i Faith in Sri Lanka. Title varies: Some issues called *Bahá'í Monthly News Service, Bahá'í Monthly News Sri Lanka, Baha'i Newsletter* and *19 Day Feast Newsletter.*

9.95. *Baha'i News Letter.* ? – ?. Caracas: National Spiritual Assembly of the Baha'is of Venezuela.

9.96. *Baha'i News Letter for Taiwan.* (Mercy 2, 142 [24 June 1985])– . Hsin Ying, Taiwan: Danel Boone.

9.97. *Baha'i News Letter = Lalolagi Fou.* ? – ?. n.p. [Funafuti: National Spiritual Assembly of the Bahá'ís of Tuvalu] Title varies: Early issues called *Lalolagi Fou = Baha'i Newsletter of Tuvalu.*

9.98. *Bahá'í News Letter of the Gilbert and Ellice Islands.* no.1 (June 1967)– ?. n.p. [Tarawa: National Spiritual Assembly of the Bahá'ís of the Gilbert and Ellice Islands].

9.99. *Bahá'í News of Barbados.* v.1 no.1 (June 1981)– . St Michael: National Spiritual Assembly of the Bahá'ís of Barbados. Succeeds: *Bahá'í News of Barbados and the Windward Islands.*

9.100. *Bahá'í News of Barbados and the Windward Islands.* convention issue (Ridvan 129 [Apr. 1972])–v.9 no.8 (Mar.–Apr. 1981). St Michael: National Spiritual Assembly of the Bahá'ís of Barbados and the Windward Islands. Title varies: *Bahá'í News of the Windward Islands,* no.1– ?.

9.101. *Baha'i News of Lesotho.* ? – . n.p. [Maseru]: National Spiritual Assembly of the Baha'is of Lesotho. Succeeds bilingual ed. *Litaba Tsa Baha'i = Baha'i News Lesotho.*

9.102. *The Baha'i News of Panama.* yr. 1 no.1 (Jan. 1961)– ?. Panama: National Spiritual Assembly of the Baha'is of the Republic of Panama. Title varies: *Panamanian Baha'i Bulletin,* yr. 1 no.1 (Jan. 1961)– ?; *The Baha'i News of Panama,* [no.1 (Apr.–May 1961]– ?.

9.103. *Bahá'í News of South Central Africa.* no.1 (June 1964)–no.62 (Mar. 1970). Salisbury, Rhodesia: National Spiritual Assembly of the Bahá'ís of South Central Africa.

9.104. *Bahá'í News of Southwest Africa/Namibia.* no.1 (June 24, 1981)– . Windhoek: National Spiritual Assembly of the Bahá'ís of South West Africa/Namibia.

9.105. *Baha'i News of Swaziland and Mozambique.* [no.1] ([Oct. 1971])–(Mar./Apr. 1974). Mbabane: National Spiritual Assembly of the Bahá'ís of Swaziland and Mozambique.

9.106. *Baha'i News of the Greater Antilles.* no.1 (?1958)– ?. Kingston, Jamaica: National Spiritual Assembly of the Baha'is of the Greater Antilles.

9.107. *Bahá'í News of the Lesser Antilles.* no.1 (May 1967)– ?. Grenada: Bahá'í News [i.e. St Thomas: National Spiritual Assembly of the Bahá'ís of the Leeward, Windward and Virgin Islands].

9.108. *Bahá'í News of the Philippines.* no.1 (?) – ?. Manila: National Spiritual Assembly of the Bahá'ís of the Philippines. Succeeded by: *Philippines Baha'i News.*

9.109. *Bahá'í News Sheet of the Tanganyika-Zanzibar Teaching Committee.* no.1 (?)– ?. Tanga, Tanganyika: Tanganyika-Zanzibar Teaching Committee.

9.110. *Baha'i News – Sri Lanka.* no.1 (Feb. 1973)–(? 1975). n.p. [Colombo]: National Spiritual Assembly of the Bahá'ís of Sri Lanka. Title varies: some short-term changes to *Sri Lanka Baha'i News* and *Baha'i News – Sri Lanka (Ceylon).*

9.111. *Baha'i News Swaziland, Lesotho, Mozambique.* [no.1] (May 1967)–(Dec. 1970–Feb. 1971). Mbabane: National Spiritual Assembly of the Bahá'ís of Swaziland, Lesotho and Mozambique. Title varies: *Regional Baha'i News of Swaziland, Lesotho and Mozambique,* no.1–3; *Baha'i News of the Region of Swaziland, Lesotho and Mozambique,* no.4; *Bahá'í News,* no.5–126 no.3 (Oct. 1969).

9.112. *Bahá'í News U.S. Supplement.* no.1 (1958)–no.118 (1967). Wilmette, Ill.: National Spiritual Assembly of the Bahá'ís of the United States.

9.113. *Baha'i News Worldwide.* ? – ?. n.p. [Anchorage: National Spiritual Assembly of the Bahá'ís of Alaska] Title varies, interspersed throughout run: *Baha'i International News Service, Baha'i World News Bulletin, Alaska Baha'i Worldwide, Baha'i News Worldwide.* Reproduction of *Bahá'í International News Service.*

9.114. *Bahá'í Newsfront.* no.1 (Sept. 1975)– no.18 (Apr. 1979). Lae: National Spiritual Assembly of the Bahá'ís of Papua New Guinea.

9.115. *The Bahá'í Newsletter.* ? – ?. Haifa: Spiritual Assembly of Haifa.

9.116. *Baha'i Newsletter.* ? – ?; no.1 (Dec. 31, 1966)– ?; v.1 no.1 (Jan. 15, 1970)– ? New Delhi: National Spiritual Assembly of the Bahá'ís of India. Title varies: *Baha'i News*

Letter, through 1967; *Baha'i News Bulletin*, no.68 (May 1954)–no.74 (Jan. 1955), with a *Baha'i News Letter*, numbered 68–75 (Feb.–Mar. 1955); *Baha'i Newsletter*, v.1 no.1 (Jan. 15, 1970)– ?

9.117. *Bahá'í Newsletter.* v.1 no.1 (Oct. 1969) – ?. n.p. [Georgetown]: National Spiritual Assembly of the Bahá'ís of Guyana, Surinam and French Guiana.

9.118. *Baha'i Newsletter.* v.1 no.1 (June 1970) – . n.p. [Victoria]: National Spiritual Assembly of the Bahá'ís of Seychelles. Title varies: Some issues are *Seychelles Baha'i News* or *Baha'i News Letter*.

9.119. *Bahá'í Newsletter.* v.1 no.1 (31 Oct. 1971)–v.1 no.4 (Jalal 128–29/1972). Ath Cliath: National Teaching Committee of the Republic of Ireland.

9.120. *Baha'i Newsletter.* v.1 no.1 (Aug. 1972) – . Addis Ababa: National Spiritual Assembly of the Bahá'ís of Ethiopia.

9.121. *Bahá'í Newsletter.* no.1 (May 1975)– . Freetown: National Spiritual Assembly of the Bahá'ís of Sierra Leone. Some numbers called *Bahá'í News Letter*.

9.122. *Baha'i Newsletter.* no.1 (June 1982)– . Juba, Sudan: Regional Teaching Committee Southern Region.

9.123. *Baha'i Newsletter.* no.1 (Jan. 1984)– . Monrovia: National Spiritual Assembly of the Bahá'ís of Liberia.

9.124. *The Bahá'í Newsletter of the Caroline Islands.* v.1 no.1 (Mar. 1982). Ponape: National Spiritual Assembly of the Bahá'ís of the Caroline Islands. Only one number published.

9.125. *Bahá'í Newsletter of the Falkland Islands.* ? – . Stanley, Falkland Is.: Spiritual Assembly of the Baha'is of Stanley. Title varies: Some issues called *Falkland Bahá'í Newsletter*.

9.126. *Baha'i Newsletter of the National Spiritual Assembly of the Baha'is of West Central Africa.* no.1 (May 1964)– ?. Lagos, Nigeria: National Spiritual Assembly of the Baha'is of West Central Africa.

9.127. *Baha'i Newsletter of the South Pacific Islands.* no.1 (June 1966)– ?. n.p. [Honiara]: National Spiritual Assembly [of the Bahá'ís of the South West Pacific Ocean].

9.128. *Baha'i Newsletter of the Spiritual Assembly of the Baha'is of Ghana.* ? – ?. Accra North: Spiritual Assembly of the Baha'is of Ghana. Continued by: *Ghana Baha'i News*.

9.129. *Baha'i Newsletter of the Western Caroline Islands.* v.1 no.1 (Baha 40, Mar. 21–Apr. 8, 1983)– ?. Koror, Palau: Bahá'í Administrative Committee of the Western Caroline Islands. Succeeded by: *Bahá'í Bulletin for the Western Caroline Islands.*

9.130. *Bahá'í North.* v.1 no.1 (Mar.–May 1985) – . Chandigarh: Editorial Board of the State Teaching Committee of the Baha'is of Punjab.

9.131. *Bahá'í Public Relations.* ? – ?. Wilmette, Ill.: Baha'í Public Relations Committee.

9.132. Bahá'í Publishing Trust of the United Kingdom. *Broadsheet.* no.1 (Oct. 1983)– . Oakham, Leics., Eng.: Bahá'í Publishing Trust.

9.133. Bahá'í Publishing Trust of the United States. *News Bulletin: For Customers Outside the Continental United States.* (June 1979)–(Nov. 1979). Wilmette, Ill.: Bahá'í Publishing Trust.

9.134. —— *Update.* (19 June 1979)–(June/July 1982?). Wilmette, Ill.: Bahá'í Publishing Trust. Title varies: *News bulletin*, through end of 1980.

9.135. *Bahá'í Pulse.* (Nov. 1980). Georgetown, Guyana: National Youth Committee. Only one number published.

9.136. *Bahá'í Quarterly.* no.1 (Oct. 1936)–no.48 (July 1948). Adelaide: National Spiritual Assembly of the Bahá'ís of Australia and New Zealand. Succeeded by: *Bahá'í Bulletin.* See 9.32.

9.137. *Bahá'í Samáchár.* ? – ?. Bombay: National Baha'i Youth Committee.

9.138. *Baha'i Sikkim.* v.1 no.1 (? 1980)– . Tadong, Gangtok: National Spiritual Assembly of the Baha'is of Sikkim.

9.139. *The Bahá'í Star: The Magazine for Bahá'í Youth of Zimbabwe.* no.1 (Sept. 1983)– . Harare: The Magazine Committee.

9.140. *Bahá'í Studies.* v.1 (1976)– . Ottawa, Ont.: Association for Bahá'í Studies. Monographic series; each volume is listed separately. See index under (Bahá'í Studies).

9.141. *Baha'i Studies Bulletin.* v.1 no.1 (June 1982)– . Newcastle upon Tyne, Eng.: Stephen Lambden.

9.142. *Bahá'í Studies Notebook.* I no.1 (Dec. 1980)– . Ottawa, Ont.: Association for Bahá'í Studies.

9.143. *Baha'i Sunshine.* ? – ?. Nassau: National Spiritual Assembly of the Bahá'ís of the Bahamas.

9.144. *The Bahá'í Teacher.* v.1 no.1 (July 1924) – ?. Montclair, N.J.: First International Home

Station. 'Published for Baha'i Study Classes of World Fellowship Gardens.'

9.144a. *Bahá'í Temple News Bulletin.* no.1 (Mar. 1948)– ?. Evanston, Ill.: Bahá'í Temple Program Committee.

9.145. *Bahá'í Tidhindi.* [Eng. ed.] (? 1972)– ?. Reykjavík: Andlegt Thjódhradh Bahá'ía á Íslandi.

9.146. *Baha'i Toktok.* ? – ?. Rabaul, Papua New Guinea: Area Teaching Committee.

9.147. *Bahá'í Tuvalu.* no.1 (June 1981)– . Funafuti: National Spiritual Assembly of the Bahá'ís of Tuvalu. Text in English and Tuvaluan.

9.148. *Bahá'í-Uutiset = Bahá'í News: Suomi-Finland.* v.128 no.3 (June 1971)– . Helsinki: Suomen Bahá'íen Kansallinen Henkinen Hallintoneuvosto. Continues: *Bahá'í Sanoma.* Text in Finnish and English.

9.149. *Bahá'í-Uutiset = Bahá'í-Nytt: English Suppliment* [sic]. no.1 (Joulukuu/December 1984)– . Helsinki: Suomen Bahá'íden Henkisen Hallintoneuvoston Julkaisu = Ansvarig Utgivare Nationella Andliga Rådet för Finlands Bahá'íer.

9.150. *Bahá'í Vanuatu: Nius, Nouvelles, News.* no.55 (Apr.–May 1985)– . Port Vila: National Spiritual Assembly of the Bahá'ís of Vanuatu. Continues: *Bahá'í Nius* and *Bahá'í News.*

9.151. *Bahá'í Wolbo: English Supplement.* ? – ?. Seoul: National Spiritual Assembly of the Bahá'ís of Korea. Title varies: some issues *The Wolbo (Korean Baha'i News); Korean Baha'i News.*

9.152. *Bahá'í Yng Nghymru.* no.1 (Sept. 1968) – ?. Pontypridd, Wales: Welsh Goals Committee.

9.153. *Bahá'í Youth.* no.1 (Sept. 1973)– ?. Kingston: National Youth and Child Education Committee of the Baha'is of Jamaica.

9.154. *Baha'i Youth Academy Bulletin.* no.1 (1 Oct. 1982)– . Panchgani, India: Baha'i Youth Academy.

9.155. *Baha'i Youth Activities.* no.1 (July 1972) – ?. Lushoto, Magamba, Tanzania: National Baha'i Youth Centre.

9.156. *Baha'i Youth: An International Bulletin.* ? – ?. New York: National Spiritual Assembly of the Baha'is of the United States and Canada.

9.157. *Baha'i Youth Broadsheet: Youth Community of the British Isles.* v.1 no.1 (Aug.–Sept. 109 [1952])– ?. Bournemouth: Youth Committee.

9.158. *Bahá'í Youth Bulletin.* ? – ?. New Delhi: National Baha'i Youth Committee of India, Pakistan & Burma. Publisher varies: Youth Committee of the National Spiritual Assembly of the Bahá'ís of India & Burma (Poona); Regional Youth Committee of India of the National Spiritual Assembly of the Baha'is of India, Pakistan and Burma (Bombay); National Baha'i Youth Committee of the India, Pakistan & Burma (New Delhi).

9.159. *Bahá'í Youth Bulletin.* v.1 no.1 (Sept. 1946)– ?. London: National Youth Committee of the National Spiritual Assembly of the Bahá'ís of the British Isles.

9.160. *Baha'i Youth Bulletin.* no.1 (? 1978)– ?. Nairobi: National Youth Committee of the National Spiritual Assembly of the Baha'is of Kenya.

9.161. *Bahá'í Youth Bulletin.* ? – ?. Wilmette, Ill.: National Baha'i Youth Committee of the United States of America.

9.162. *The Baha'i Youth Bulletin.* (Nov. 1978) – ?. Johannesburg, South Africa: National Youth Committee.

9.163. *Baha'i Youth Bulletin.* v.1 no.1 (Dec. 1950)–v.5 no.8 (May 1957). Wilmette, Ill.: United States Baha'i Youth Committee.

9.164. *Bahá'í Youth Letter.* v.1 no.1 (Knowledge 103 [Oct. 1946]–no.55 (July 1961). Semaphore, S.A.: N.Y.C. of the N.S.A. of Aus. [National Youth Committee of the National Spiritual Assembly of the Bahá'ís of Australia].

9.165. *Bahá'í Youth Magazine.* v.1 no.1 (Aug. 1958)– ?. Auckland: Youth Co-ordinating Committee of the Bahá'ís of New Zealand. At head of title: New Zealand.

9.166. *Baha'i Youth Newsletter.* ? – ?. London: National Baha'i Youth Committee of the British Isles.

9.167. *Baha'i Youth: The Youth Bulletin of the United States.* ? – ?. n.p. [Wilmette, Ill.]: National Bahá'í Youth Committee.

9.168. *Bahà'ì* [sic] *Youth: Youth Bulletin for Rhodesia.* ? – ?. Salisbury: Youth Bulletin Committee.

9.169. *The Bangladeshi Bahá'í.* [no.1] (Naw Rúz 138 [Mar. 1981])– ?. Dacca: National Spiritual Assembly of the Bahá'ís of Bangladesh.

9.170. *Be.* no.1 (Jan. 1982)– . Iowa City, Iowa: University of Iowa Baha'i Club.

9.171. *The Bedrock.* no.1 (June 1974)– ?. Thornhill, Ont.: National Spiritual Assembly of the Bahá'ís of Canada.

9.172. *Belize Bahá'í News.* [no.1] (Oct.–Dec. 1976)– ?. Belize City: National Spiritual Assembly of the Bahá'ís of Belize.

9.173. *Belize Baha'i Newsletter.* [no.1] (Jan. 1984)– . Belize City: [National Spiritual Assembly of the Bahá'ís of Belize].

9.174. *Benelux Bahá'í Bulletin.* English ed. no.1 (May–July 1961)– ?. Esch-sur-Alzette, Luxemburg: National Spiritual Assembly of the Bahá'ís of Benelux.

9.175. *Berita Baha'i.* ? – ?. n.p. [Kuala Lumpur: National Spiritual Assembly of the Bahá'ís of Malaysia].

9.176. *Bermuda Bahá'í Newsletter.* ? – ?. Bermuda: National Spiritual Assembly of the Bahá'ís of Bermuda.

9.177. *The Best Seller: The Bahá'í Distribution Service Newsletter.* v.1 no.1 (Oct. 1984)– . n.p. [Wilmette, Ill.]: Bahá'í Distribution Service.

9.178. *Billabong.* no.1 (Winter 1983, Núr 140 B.E.)– . Singleton, N.S.W.: The Billabong Team.

9.179. *Board Activity News Pakistan: A Bulletin for Exchange of Information Between Auxiliary Board Members in Pakistan.* (Aug. 1985)– . Pakistan: Auxiliary Board Members in Pakistan.

9.180. *Boletín Bahá'í = Bahá'í Bulletin.* no.1 (May 1975)– ?. Panama: National Spiritual Assembly of the Bahá'ís of the Republic of Panama. Succeeded by *Carta Noticiosa Bahá'í.* Text in English and Spanish.

9.181. *Boletín Bahá'í.* (junio 1981)– . Panamá: Asamblea Espiritual Nacional de los Bahá'ís de la República de Panamá. Succeeds: *Carta Noticiosa Bahá'í.* Text in Spanish and English.

9.182. *Bomake Nebantfwana.* no.1 (July 1974) – . Mbabane: National Woman's and Children's Committee, under the auspices of the National Spiritual Assembly of the Baha'is of Swaziland.

9.183. *Bophuthatswana Bahá'í Newsletter = Lokwalo Dikgang.* no.1 (July 1981)– . Mafikeng: National Spiritual Assembly of the Bahá'ís of Bophuthatswana.

9.184. *Bosch Bahá'í School Session Update.* ?– . Santa Cruz, Calif.: Bosch Bahá'í School. Title may be read as *Session Update.*

9.185. *Botswana Baha'i.* ? – ?. Gaborone: Spiritual Assembly of the Baha'is of Botswana. Bilingual ed.

9.186. *Botswana Baha'i.* (Apr. 1984)– . n.p. [Gaborone]: Spiritual Assembly of the Baha'is of Botswana. English ed.

9.187. *Bravo Europe: Baha'i Radio & Audio-Visual Opportunities: A Newsletter.* no.0 (May 1983)– . Utzigen, Switzerland: Bravo Europe.

9.188. *Brilliant Star.* v.15 no.1 (Mar./Apr. 1983)– . Hixson, Tenn.: National Spiritual Assembly of the Bahá'ís of the United States. Continues: *Child's Way.*
See 9.207.

9.189. *Brilliant Star: Children's School News.* (Nov. 1, 1981)– . n.p. [Mahé]: National Education Committee of the National Spiritual Assembly of the Baha'is of Seychelles.

9.190. *Brilliant Stars.* no.1 (July 1985)– . Dhaka: National Women Committee of the Baha'is of Bangladesh.

9.191. *Bulletin, Alaska Teaching Committee.* [no.1] (Aug. 1945)–[no.87] (Apr. 1957). Anchorage: Alaska Teaching Committee. Title varies: *News Flashes from Alaska,* no.1; *Alaska Regional Bulletin,* no.2–3, 5; *Regional Bulletin,* no.4; *Bulletin of Alaska Bahá'í Religion Teaching Committee,* no.6–23; *Alaska Bahá'í Regional Teaching Bulletin,* no.24; *Alaskan News Bulletin,* no.26–43; *Regional Bulletin for Alaska,* no.44–48, 50–53; *Bahá'í Bulletin for Alaska,* no.49; *Alaska Regional Bulletin,* no.54; *Alaska News Bulletin,* no.61–67.

9.192. *Bulletin Bahá'í.* ? – ?. Noumea: National Spiritual Assembly of the Baha'is of the South West Pacific. Bilingual French and English.

9.193. *Bulletin Baha'i News.* Ed. bilingue = Bilingual ed. ? – ?. Yaounde: Assemblee Spirituelle Nationale des Baha'is du Cameroun =National Spiritual Assembly of the Bahá'ís of Cameroon. Title varies: *Baha'i News of Cameroon,* v.1 no.1 (?)– ?; *Baha'i News Cameroon,* v.8 no.2 (June/July 1975)–v.9 no.1 (Mar./Apr. 1976); *Baha'i News of Cameroon = Nouvelles Baha'is du Cameroun,* v.9 no.2 (May/July 1976)– ?; *Bulletin Baha'i du Cameroun = Baha'i News of Cameroon,* ? – ?; *Bulletin Baha'i News,* v.12 no.3 (Sept./Oct. 1980)– ?. Continued by separate English and French editions.

9.194. *Bulletin Baha'i News.* English ed. v.13 no.1 (May/Aug. 1981)– . Limbe: National Spiritual Assembly of the Bahá'ís of Cameroon.

9.195. *Canadian Administrative Bulletin.* ? – ?. Thornhill, Ont.: National Spiritual Assembly of the Bahá'ís of Canada.

9.196. *Canadian Bahá'í News.* no.1 (May 1948)–no.289 (Nov. 1975). Thornhill, Ont.: National Spiritual Assembly of the Bahá'ís of Canada. Continued by: *Bahá'í Canada* [old series] Title varies: *Bahá'í News,* no.41–151.
See 9.41.

9.197. Canadian Bahá'í International Development Service. *Newsletter.* no.1 (Oct. 1983)– . Ottawa, Ont.: Canadian Bahá'í International Development Service.

9.198. *CC News Release.* ? – ?. n.p. [London, Eng.]: Consolidation Committee. Title varies: some are *C. C. News Release.*

9.199. *Center Lights: The Bahá'í National Center Newsletter.* ? – ?. n.p. [Wilmette, Ill.]: Office of Personnel Affairs.

9.200. *Children's Chapter: Supplement to New Zealand Baha'i Newsletter.* no.1 (Sept. 1962)–133 no.2–3 (Apr. 1976). n.p. [Auckland: National Spiritual Assembly of the Bahá'ís of New Zealand].

9.201. *Children's Feastletter.* ? – . n.p. [Dublin, Ireland]: Child Education Committee.

9.202. *Children's Glad Tidings.* ? – ?. n.p. [Monrovia]: NSA of Liberia.

9.203. *Children's Journal.* (June 1983)– . n.p. [Colombo, Sri Lanka: National Bahá'í Child Education Committee].

9.204. *Children's New Dawn.* no.1 (Jan.–Feb. 1974)– ?. n.p. [Nuku'alofa]: National Spiritual Assembly of the Bahá'ís of Tonga and the Cook Islands.

9.205. *Children's 19 Day Feast Newsletter.* ? – ?. n.p. [London]: Child Education Advisory Committee of the National Spiritual Assembly of the Bahá'ís of the United Kingdom.

9.206. *The Child's Way* [old series]. v.1 no.1 (?, 1949)–no.118 (July–Aug. 1968). Wilmette, Ill.: Child's Way Editorial Committee.

9.207. *Child's Way* [new series]. v.1 no.1 (Jan.–Feb. 1969)–v.14 no.6 (Jan./Feb. 1983). Wilmette, Ill.: Bahá'í Subscriber Service. Continued by: *Brilliant Star.*
    See 9.188.

9.208. *Chrysalis: Alabama Bahá'í Schools Committee Newsletter.* ? – ?. Birmingham, Ala.: Alabama Bahá'í Schools Committee.

9.209. *CommUNITY Life.* [no.1] (Kamál 137 [Aug. 1980])– ?. Londonderry: Northern Ireland Teaching Committee.

9.210. *Consolidation & Expansion: Journal of the South-West Wales Region.* no.1 (Summer 1950) – ?. Birmingham, Eng. [etc.]: South-West Wales Regional Committee.

9.211. Continental Board of Counsellors in Asia. *Newsletter.* no.1 (Mar. 1985)– . n.p. [New Delhi]: Continental Board of Counsellors in Asia.

9.212. Continental Board of Counsellors in Asia. Continental Pioneer Committee. *General Circular.* no.1 (8 Mar. 1983)– . Singapore: Continental Pioneer Committee for Asia.

9.213. Continental Board of Counsellors in Australasia. *News Bulletin.* [no.1] ([Dec. 1983])– . n.p.: Suhayl Ala'i.

9.214. Continental Board of Counsellors in South Central Asia. *Quarterly Bulletin.* no.1 (Feb. 1978)–no.7 (Spring 1980). New Delhi: Continental Board of Counsellors in South Central Asia.

9.215. Continental Board of Counsellors in Southern Africa. *Newssheet.* no.1 (July 1977)–no.15 (Dec. 1980). n.p.: Continental Board of Counsellors in Southern Africa.

9.216. Continental Board of Counsellors in Western Africa. *Newsletter.* no.1 (Dec. 1976) – ?. n.p.: Continental Board of Counsellors in Western Africa.

9.217. *Cook Islands Bahá'í Newsletter.* no.1 ([Aug. 1978])– . Rarotonga: National Spiritual Assembly of the Bahá'ís of the Cook Islands. Title varies: *Nuti Pepa Baha'i Kuki Airani,* no.1–no.3. Publisher varies: National Teaching Committee of the Cook Islands, no.1 (Aug. 1978)–(Aug. 1985).

9.218. *The Dawn: A Monthly Bahai Journal of Burma.* v.1 no.1 (Sept. 1923)–v.6 no.10 (June 1929). Rangoon, Burma: M.S. Desai.

9.219. *Dawnbreaker: The Baha'i Newsletter of the Fiji Islands.* v.1 no.1 (Asma 133 [Aug. 1976]) – ?. n.p. [Suva]: National Spiritual Assembly of the Baha'is of the Fiji Islands.

9.220. *The Dawning Light: Baha'i News Letter for Taiwan.* (Mercy 2, 142 [24 June 1985])– . Hsin Ying, Taiwan: Danel Boone. Title varies: *Baha'i News Letter for Taiwan,* (Mercy 2, 142)–(July 26, 1985); *The Dawning Light,* no.3 (Aug. 28, 1985)– .

9.221. *Day Spring.* no.1 (Jan. 1984)– . Corbridge, Northumberland: National Consolidation Committee of the National Spiritual Assembly of the Bahá'ís of the United Kingdom.

9.222. *The Day-Star.* no.1 (Oct. 1983)– . n.p. [Kampala?, Uganda]: National Women's Committee.

9.222a. *Development Directline.* no.1 (May 1982)– . Wilmette, Ill.: National Teaching Committee. Title varies: *DTC Directline,* no.1 (May 1982)–(Oct. 1985).

9.223. *The Divine Pearls: A Periodical for the Study of the Baha'i Faith.* no.1 (Nov./Dec.

1983)– . Colombo: Spiritual Assembly of the Baha'i Faith in Sri Lanka.

9.224. *Echo.* no.1 (14–20 Nov. 1977)– ?. Luxembourg: Assemblée Spirituelle Nationale des Bahá'ís du Luxembourg. Text in German, French and English.

9.225. *Eighteen Forty Four = 1844.* issue 1 (Winter 1985)– . Canterbury, Eng.: Eighteen Forty Four.

9.226. *Emerald News.* no.1 (Feb. 1968)– ?. Derry: Irish Goals Committee.

9.227. *Eskimo and Indian Baha'i News.* ? – ?. Whitehorse, Yukon: National Eskimo and Indian Bulletin Committee.

9.228. *European Bahá'í News.* (Feb. 1985)– . Peseux, Switzerland: Continental Board of Counsellors for the Protection and Propagation of the Bahá'í Faith in Europe.

9.229. *The Facilitator.* v.1 no.1 (? 1979)– . n.p. [Wilmette, Ill.]: National Education Committee. Title varies: *The Dynamic Force of the Facilitator*, v.1 no.1 (? 1979)–v.3 no.4 (? 1982); *The Facilitator*, v.4 no.1 (Jan.–Feb. 1983)– .

9.230. *(al-Fajr al-Badí').* no.1 (Sept. 1972)– ?. n.p. [Beirut: National Spiritual Assembly of the Bahá'ís of the Near East].

9.231. *Feast Letter for All Local Spiritual Assemblies.* ? – ?. Kolonia, Yap: National Spiritual Assembly of the Bahá'ís of the North West Pacific Ocean.

9.232. *Fiji Bahá'í News.* no.1 (Oct. 1970)– . Suva: National Spiritual Assembly of the Bahá'ís of the Fiji Islands. Numbering begins anew in July 1980.

9.233. *Flash!* communique no.1 ([July 1984]). Colombo: Spiritual Assembly of the Baha'i Faith in Lanka (Ceylon). Only one issue.

9.234. *Flowers of the Rose Garden.* ? – ?. Witfield, Boksburg, S. Afr.: National Child Education Committee.

9.235. *Friends: A Newsletter for Single Bahá'ís.* v.1 no.1 (1985?)– . Matairie, La.

9.236. *From the n.s.a. Table: Newsletter.* ? – ?. n.p. [Reykjavík]: n.s.a. [i.e. National Spiritual Assembly of the Bahá'ís of Iceland].

9.237. *Fundamentals: A Bulletin for Local Treasurers from the National Treasurer's Office.* inaugural issue (Oct.–Nov. [1984])– . n.p. [Wilmette, Ill.]: National Treasurer's Office.

9.238. *Gambia Bahá'í News.* v.1 no.1 (5 June 1971)– . Banjul: National Spiritual Assembly

of the Bahá'ís of the Gambia. Title varies: *Bahá'í Newsletter*, v.1 no.1 (5 June 1971)–v.2 no.12 (May 1973); *Bahá'í News = Nouvelles Bahá'íes*, v.3 no.1 (June 1973)–v.4 no.3 (Feb. 1975); *Gambian Bahá'í News*, v.5 no.1 (Apr. 1975); *Bahá'í News*, v.5 no.2–3 (May–July 1975)–v.5 no.9 (Apr.–May 1976); *Gambia Bahá'í News*, v.6 mo. 1 (May-June 1976)– .

9.239. *Geneva Bureau News Exchange.* ? – ?. Geneva: International Bahá'í Bureau.

9.240. *Ghana Bahá'í Bulletin.* no.1 (Feb. 1959) – ?. Accra: Regional Teaching Committee [of Ghana].

9.241. *Ghana Baha'i News.* v.1 no.1 (Qawl, Masa'il 134 [23 Nov.–11 Dec. 1977])– . Accra: Spiritual Assembly of the Bahá'ís of Ghana.

9.242. *Glad Tidings.* no.1 (June 1975)– . Monrovia: National Spiritual Assembly of the Bahá'ís of Liberia and Guinea.

9.243. *The Global Communicator: A Quarterly Newsletter from the U.S. Bahá'í Publishing Trust to Its Overseas Accounts.* v.1 no.1 (Spring 1985)– Wilmette, Ill.: Bahá'í Publishing Trust.

9.244. *Glory.* ? – ?. Karachi: National Deepening & Fine Arts Sub-Committee.

9.245. *Glory: Bahá'í Youth Magazine.* v.1 no.1 (Dec. 1966)– . Panchgani: National Bahá'í Youth Committee of India. Title varies: *Bahá'í Youth Magazine*, v.1 no.1 (Dec. 1966)–v.4. no.1 (Aug. 1971).

9.246. *Grass Roots.* no.1 (Nov. 1977)–no.3 (June 1978). Pago Pago: Continental Board of Counsellors for Australasia.

9.247. *The Green Door: A Magazine of Arts and Studies*, v.1 no.1 (July 1981)– v.1 no.2 (Feb. 1982). St Niklaas, Belgium: The Green Door.

9.248. *Guidelines to Planned Giving.* inaugural issue [no.1] (Summer 1979)– ?. Wilmette, Ill.: Office of the Treasurer.

9.249. *Habari za Kibaha'i Tanzania.* (June 1975)– ?. Dar-es-Salaam: Baraza la Kiroho la Kitaifa la Wabaha'i wa Tanzania. Swahili and English text.

9.250. *Handmaids of Baha.* no.1 (Nov. 23, 1983) – . Dhaka, Bangladesh: National Women Committee.

9.251. *Handog.* v.1 no.1 (June 1974)– ?. Manila: National Youth Committee of the Bahá'ís of the Philippines.

9.252. Hands of the Cause of God residing in Europe. *Newsletter for Board Members.* [no.1] ([Dec. 1967])–[no.5] ([June 1968]). [Europe]: European Hands.

9.253. *Happy Family = Vuvale Mamarau.* no.1 (1981)– ?. n.p. [Suva: National Spiritual Assembly of the Bahá'ís of the Fiji Islands, Bahá'í Family Life Committee].

9.254. *Harmony Baha'i Magazine.* [no.1] (Oct. 1979)– ?. Peradeniya; Matale; Kandy: Auxiliary Board Members for Sri Lanka.

9.254a. *The Hawaii Bulletin.* no.1 (Aug. 1951)–(May 1958). Honolulu, Hawaii: Hawaii Teaching Committee. Title varies: *Bulletin,* no.1 (Aug. 1951); *Territory of Hawaii, Regional Teaching Committee Bulletin,* no.2 (Oct. 1951); *Hawaii News Bulletin,* no.3 (Nov. 1951)–no.6 (Apr. 1952); *Bulletin, Hawaii Regional Teaching Committee,* (July 1952); *Regional Teaching Bulletin,* (Sept./Oct. 1952); *Hawaii R.T.C. Bulletin,* (Dec. 1952); *Bulletin, Regional Teaching Committee,* (Mar. 1953); *Hawaii Bulletin,* (Mar. 1955)–(Feb./Mar. 1957); *The Hawaii Bulletin,* (Mar. 1958)–(May 1958).

9.255. *Hellenic Baha'i Newsletter.* v.1 no.1 (Jan. 1981)– ?. Thessaloniki: [National Spiritual Assembly of the Bahá'ís of Greece].

9.255a. *Helping Hand: Parenting Resource Network.* v.1 no.1 (May/June [1985])– v.1 no.4 (Nov./Dec. 1985). Honolulu: National Child Education Committee of the Hawaiian Islands.

9.256. *Herald.* no.1 (? 1979)– . Karachi: National Youth & Education Committee of the Baha'is of Pakistan.

9.257. *Herald of the East.* v.1 no.1 (Mar. 1921)–v.4 no.7–8 (Nov./Dec. 1924). Cawnpore: Edited and Published for National Spiritual Assembly of India and Burma by Professor Pritam Singh.

9.258. *Herald of the South.* [series 1] v.1 trial no.(Sept. 1925)–v.28 no.2 (July 1960); [series 2] v.28 no.1 (n.d. [1964?])–v.34 no.2 (Sept. 1970); [series 3] v.1 no.1 (Autumn 131 [Apr. 1974])–v.2 no.4 (Summer 132 [Jan. 1976]). Sydney, N.S.W.: National Spiritual Assembly of the Bahá'ís of Australia.

9.259. *Herald of the South.* [New series] v.1 (Oct. 1984)– . Canberra, A.C.T.: National Spiritual Assemblies of the Bahá'ís of Australia and New Zealand.

9.260. *Highpoints.* no.1 (Nov. 16, 1981)– . n.p. [Thornhill: National Spiritual Assembly of the Bahá'ís of Canada].

9.261. *The Home Front: A News Bulletin.* [no.1] (July 1956)– ?. n.p. [London]: National Teaching Committee of the National Spiritual Assembly of the Bahá'ís of the British Isles.

9.262. *Hong Kong Baha'i News.* ?– . Kow-loon, Hong Kong: National Spiritual Assembly of the Baha'is of Hong Kong.

9.263. *Hong Kong Baha'i Newsletter.* no.1 (?) – ?. Hong Kong: [Local Spiritual Assembly of the Bahá'ís of Hong Kong].

9.264. *Hup: The Magazine for Bahá'í Youth in the United Kingdom.* v.1 no.1 (Mar. 1985)– . n.p. [Newcastle-upon-Tyne]: National Youth Committee of the National Spiritual Assembly of the Bahá'ís of the United Kingdom.

9.265. *I Read the News Today.* no.1 (1979)– ?. Wilmette, Ill.: George Dannells.

Excerpts from newspapers, magazines, government reports, illustrating acceptance of Bahá'í principles.

9.266. Images International Audio-Visual Productions. *Newsletter.* ?– . Vienna, Va.: Images International Audio-Visual Productions.

9.267. *In Tune.* (? 1972)– ?. London: National Youth Committee of the NSA of the Baha'is of the United Kingdom.

9.268. *Indaba ZamaBahá'í = The Bahá'í News of Transkei.* v.1 no.1 ([Mar. 1981])– . Umtata: National Spiritual Assembly of the Bahá'ís of Transkei. Text in English and Xhosa.

9.269. *India This Month: A Review of Baha'i News by the National Teaching Committee.* (? 1979)– ?. New Delhi: Vasudevan Nair on behalf of the National Teaching Committt.

9.270. *Intercom-Bahá'í.* no.1 (Sept.? 1975)–no.45 (July 1979). London: National Spiritual Assembly of the Bahá'ís of the United Kingdom.

9.271. *Intermedia.* v.1 no.1 (June 1982)–v.1 no.8 (Sept. 1983). n.p. [Wilmette, Ill.]: Bahá'í Office of Public Affairs.

9.272. International Bahá'í Audio-Visual Centre. *Newsletter.* no.1 (Feb. 1981)–no.3 (Feb. 1982); v.1 no.1 (Jan. 1984)– . Thornhill, Ont.: International Bahá'í Audio-Visual Centre.

9.273. International Bahá'í Bureau. *Bulletin.* no.1 ([1928?]– ?. Genève: International Baha'i Bureau.

9.274. *The Island Bahá'í.* v.1 no.1 (July 1972) – ?. St Thomas: National Spiritual Assembly of the Bahá'ís of the Leeward and Virgin Islands.

9.275. *Island Baha'i.* no.1 (May–June 1981)– . St Thomas: National Spiritual Assembly of the Bahá'ís of the Virgin Islands.

9.276. *J & K Baha'i Bulletin.* v.1 no.1 (? 1984) – . n.p. [Jammu]: State Teaching Committee of the Baha'is of Jammu. Text in English, Hindi and Urdu.

9.277. *Jeunes Bahá'í Youth.* v.1 no.1 ([June?] 1978)–v.1 no.5 ([July?] 1979). Dartmouth, N.S.: Committee for the Guidance of Youth. Text in English and French.

9.278. *Junior Youth.* ? – ?. n.p. [Wilmette, Ill.?]: National Baha'i Child Education Committee.

9.279. *Kenya Bahá'í Gazette.* no.1 (Dec. 1964) – . Nairobi: National Spiritual Assembly of the Bahá'ís of Kenya.

9.280. *Koala News.* no.1 (May 1954)–no.63 (May 1959). Semaphore, S. Aust.: A[sian] T[eaching] C[ommittee] of the N.S.A. of Aust.

9.281. *Kokua (Help!).* v.1 (Sept. 1978)–v.3 (Dec. 1978). Honolulu, Hawaii: National Teaching Committee.

9.282. *The Lamplighter.* no.1 (? 1965)– . Honolulu: National Child Education Committee.

9.283. *Landegg Info.* 1/85 (Ja. 1985)– . Landegg, Switzerland: Tagungszentrum Landegg.

9.284. *Lasten 19 Päiven Juhlan Uutislehti = Children's 19 Day Feast Newsletter = 19 Dagsfest Barnens Tidning.* (Dec. 31, 1978)– ?. n.p. [Finland]: National Child Education Committee. Text in Finnish and English.

9.285. *Latin American Baha'i Bulletin: Newsletter from the Hands of the Cause of the Western Hemisphere – South American Zone.* no.1 (? 1966)– ?. n.p.: Hands of the Cause of the Western Hemisphere – South American Zone.

9.286. *The Leeward Link.* v.1 no.1 (Sept. 1981) – . n.p. [St John's, Antigua]: National Spiritual Assembly of the Bahá'ís of the Leeward Islands.

9.287. *Lesotho Bahá'í News.* no.1 (Jan.–Feb. 1972)– ?. Maseru: National Spiritual Assembly of the Bahá'ís of Lesotho.

9.288. *The Light: Baha'i Bulletin for the Assistants to Auxiliary Board Members in A.P.* no.1 (Kamal 140, 1 Aug. 1983)– . Vijayawada, Andra [sic] Pradesh: Z. Muniandy, Baha'i Centre.

2.289. *Light of the Age.* v.1 no.1 (Jan. 1971)– ?. Bagan Jerma, Butterworth: National Spiritual Assembly of the Baha'is of Malaysia.

9.290. *Light of the East.* [v.1 no.1] ([Aug.?] 1974)– . Hong Kong: National Publishing Committee of Hong Kong and Macau.

9.291. *The Light of the Pacific.* no.1 (Aug. 1964) – . Honolulu: National Spiritual Assembly of the Bahá'ís of the Hawaiian Islands.

9.292. *Litaba Tsa Baha'i = Baha'i News Lesotho.* ? – ?. n.p. [Maseru]: Lekhotla la Sechaba la Moea la Baha'i ba Lesotho, National Spiritual Assembly of the Baha'is of Lesotho. Sesotho and English text. Succeeded by separate editions for Sesotho and English.
See 9.101

9.293. *The Little Circular.* no.1 (Aug. 1980)– . n.p. [Dublin]: Child Magazine Committee of the National Spiritual Assembly of the Bahá'ís of the Republic of Ireland.

9.294. *The Little Journal: A Bahá'í Magazine.* no.1 (? 1965)– ?. n.p. [London]: 'Little Journal' Subcommittee of the Child Education Committee of the National Spiritual Assembly of the Baha'is of the United Kingdom.

9.295. *The Little Journal: A Bahá'í Magazine.* Series II no.1 (Summer 1975)– . London: Bahá'í Education Committee of the National Spiritual Assembly of the Bahá'ís of the United Kingdom.

9.296. *El Lucero.* [Eng. ed.] ? – ?. Santurce: Spiritual Assembly of the Bahá'ís of Puerto Rico.

9.297. *Luxembourg Baha'i Newsletter.* no.1 (June 1962)–v.4 no.5 (May 1966). n.p. [Luxembourg-Ville: National Spiritual Assembly of the Bahá'ís of Luxemburg].

9.298. *The Magazine of the Children of the Kingdom.* v.1 no.1 (Dec. 1919)–v.5 no.3 (June 1924). Boston: Ella M. Robarts.

9.299. *The Magnet.* v.1 no.1 (Fall 1980)– ?. Greenfield, Ind.: National Spiritual Assembly of the Bahá'ís of the United States, District Teaching Committee of Indiana.

9.300. *Malawi Bahá'í News.* (July 1978)– . Limbe: Spiritual Assembly of the Bahá'ís in Malawi. Bilingual English/Chichewa from no 24 (Apr.–Aug. 1983).

9.301. *Malaysia Baha'i Bulletin.* [v.1] no.1 (Apr.–May 1975)– ?. Seremban: Spiritual Assembly of the Baha'is of Malaysia. Title varies: *Berita Baha'i = Malaysian Baha'i Bulletin*, [v.1] no.1 (Apr.–May 1975)–v.2 no.2–3 (June–Sept. 1976); *Malaysia Baha'i Bulletin*, (Jan.–Apr. 1977)– .

9.302. *Malaysian Baha'i News.* v.1 no.1 (? 1965)–v.9 no.4 (Dec. 1973–July 1974). Penang: National Spiritual Assembly of the Baha'is of Malaysia.

9.303. *Malta Bahá'í Journal.* no.1 (1980)– no.6 (Apr.–May 1982). Malta: Bahá'í Community of Malta.

9.304. *Marianas Baha'i News.* v.1 no.1 (June 1978)– . n.p. [Agana, Guam]: National Spiritual Assembly of the Bahá'ís of the Mariana Islands.

9.305. *Mashriqu'l-Adhkár Leaflet.* ? – ?. Montclair, N.J.: [Victoria Bedikian], reviewed by the National Spiritual Assembly of America. Title varies: some early issues called *Mashriqu'l-Adhkár*.

9.306. *Media Means.* [v.1 no.1] (Nov. 1978) – ?. Wilmette, Ill.: Bahá'í National Information Committee.

9.307. *Message from the Auxiliary Board Members.* 1st newsletter (Qudrat 141 [Nov. 1984])– . Ghana: Auxiliary Board.

9.308. *Micronesian Bahá'í News.* v.1 no.1 (Apr. 1972)– ?. Guam; Saipan: National Spiritual Assembly of the Bahá'ís of the N.W. Pacific Ocean. Places of publication vary. Title varies: *Micronesian Baha'i Mirror*, v.1 no.1 (Apr. 1972)–v.1 no.4 (Dec. 1972); *Micronesian Bahá'í News*, v.1 no.5 (Apr. 1973)– ?.

9.309. *More 'Great Great Deeds'.* (Winter 1983) – ?. n.p. [Wilmette, Ill.]: Baha'i National Youth Committee.

9.310. *[N.S.A. Newsletter].* ? – . Nairobi: National Spiritual Assembly of the Baha'is of Kenya. Title varies; *N.S.A. Newsletter*, (several issues in 1984); *A Baha'i Newsletter to Be Read at 19-Day Feasts*, (Apr. 1984); no title, (2 Aug. 1984)– .

9.311. *NAHBOHR Bulletin.* no.1 (Sept. 1977). Honolulu: National Assembly of Hawaiian Bahá'ís Office for Human Rights. One issue published.

9.312. *National Baha'i Bulletin.* no.1 (Nov. 19, 1919)–(Sept. 15, 1924). Washington, D.C.: Teaching Committee of the National Spiritual Assembly. Title varies: *Teaching Bulletin*, no.1 (Nov. 19, 1919); *Bulletin*, no.1 ([June 1920])– ([June 1923]); *National Baha'i Bulletin*, no.1 (Oct. 15, 1923)–(Sept. 15, 1924).

9.313. *National Baha'i Bulletin.* no.1 (Jan. 1975) –no.18 (Jan.–Feb. 1977). Yate, New Caledonia: Baha'i Bulletin Committee [of the National Spiritual Assembly of the Bahá'ís of the South West Pacific Ocean]. Title varies: *Baha'i Bulletin*, no.1 (Jan. 1975); *Light of Unity*, no.8 (Oct. 1975)–no.15 (July–Aug. 1976).

9.314. *National Bahá'í Review.* no.1 (Jan. 1968) –no.121 (Jan. 1983). Wilmette, Ill.: National Spiritual Assembly of the Bahá'ís of the United States. No. 112 not published. Continued after no.121 as pages of *The American Bahá'í* with the paging of that periodical. Title may be read as *Bahá'í National Review* from no.96 (Jan. 1976).

9.315. *National Baha'i Youth Magazine.* v.1 no.1 (Jan. 1967)– ?. n.p. [Kampala: National Spiritual Assembly of the Bahá'ís of Uganda and Central Africa].

9.316. National Spiritual Assembly of the Bahá'ís of Barbados. *Feast Letter.* ? – ?. n.p. [Bridgetown]: National Spiritual Assembly of the Baha'is of Barbados.

9.317. National Spiritual Assembly of the Bahá'ís of the British Isles. *News Letter.* ? – (Oct. 1964). London: National Spiritual Assembly of the Bahá'ís of the British Isles.

9.318. National Spiritual Assembly of the Bahá'ís of the British Isles. Northern Teaching Committee. *Northern Regional Bulletin.* no.1 (26 Nov. 1951)– ?. n.p.: Northern Teaching Committee.

9.319. National Spiritual Assembly of the Bahá'ís of Burma. *News Letter.* ? – ?. Rangoon: National Spiritual Assembly of the Baha'is of Burma.

9.320. National Spiritual Assembly of the Bahá'ís of Cameroon. *Nineteen Day Feast of . . . ?* – . n.p. [Limbe: National Spiritual Assembly of the Bahá'ís of Cameroon].

9.321. National Spiritual Assembly of the Bahá'ís of Canada. Bahá'í Education Resource Committee. *Newsletter.* v.1 no.1 (Dec. 1985) – . Thornhill, Ont.: Baha'i Education Resource Committee.

9.322. National Spiritual Assembly of the Bahá'ís of the Caroline Islands. *Feast Letter.* ? – ?. n.p. [Ponape]: National Spiritual Assembly of the Bahá'ís of the Caroline Islands. Title varies: *Feast Letter for the Bahá'ís*, (July 1979).

9.323. National Spiritual Assembly of the Bahá'ís of Central and East Africa. *Newsletter.* ? – ?. Kampala, Uganda: National Spiritual Assembly of the Bahá'ís of Central and East Africa. Title varies: *National Assembly Newsletter*, no.1 (?) – ?.

9.324. National Spiritual Assembly of the Bahá'ís of Cyprus. *Newssheet of the National Spiritual Assembly of the Baha'is of Cyprus.* (Rahmat [June] 1978)– . n.p. [Nicosia]: National Spiritual Assembly of the Baha'is of Cyprus.

9.325. National Spiritual Assembly of the Bahá'ís of Ghana. *Letter for the Feast of . . . ?* – . n.p. [Accra North]: National Spiritual Assembly of the Baha'is of Ghana.

9.326. National Spiritual Assembly of the Bahá'ís of Grenada. *Monthly Newsletter.* no.1

(Oct. 1984)– . n.p. [St George's]: National Spiritual Assembly of the Bahá'ís of Grenada.

9.327. National Spiritual Assembly of the Bahá'ís of Iceland. *Newsletter.* (24 June 1975) – ?. Reykjavík: National Spiritual Assembly of the Bahá'ís of Iceland.

9.328. National Spiritual Assembly of the Bahá'ís of India. State Teaching Committee of Himachal Pradesh. *News Letter.* ? – . Mandi: Baha'is S.T.C. of Himachal Pradesh.

9.329. National Spiritual Assembly of the Bahá'ís of the Republic of Ireland. *Feast Newsletter.* (24.6.1972)– . Dublin: National Spiritual Assembly of the Bahá'ís of the Republic of Ireland.

9.330. National Spiritual Assembly of the Bahá'ís of Kenya. *The Newsletter of the National Spiritual Assembly of the Bahá'ís of Kenya.* (10 June 1976)– ?. n.p. [Nairobi]: National Spiritual Assembly of the Bahá'ís of Kenya.

9.331. National Spiritual Assembly of the Bahá'ís of Malaysia. Child Education Committee. [*Newsletter*] [no.1] (June 1981)– . Kuala Lumpur: Child Education Committee. Each issue has different title, indicating the theme.

9.332. National Spiritual Assembly of the Bahá'ís of Malaysia. National Teaching Committee. *NTC Newsletter of the National Teaching Committee of the Baha'is of Malaysia.* (13.6.1973)– ?. Kuala Lumpur: National Teaching Committee of the Baha'is of Malaysia.

9.333. National Spiritual Assembly of the Bahá'ís of the Mariana Islands. *Feast of . . . ?* – . Guam: National Spiritual Assembly of the Bahá'ís of the Mariana Islands.

9.334. National Spiritual Assembly of the Bahá'ís of the Netherlands. *Newsletter.* no.1 (June 1962)– ?. Voorburg: National Spiritual Assembly of the Bahá'ís of the Netherlands.

9.335. National Spiritual Assembly of the Bahá'ís of Nigeria. *Bulletin.* no.76–11–1 (Nov. 1976)– . Lagos: National Spiritual Assembly of the Bahá'ís of Nigeria.

9.336. National Spiritual Assembly of the Bahá'ís of the South West Pacific Ocean. *Monthly Newsletter.* (1 June 1976)–(3 Apr. 1977). Vila: National Spiritual Assembly of the Bahá'ís of the South West Pacific Ocean.

9.337. National Spiritual Assembly of the Bahá'ís of Sri Lanka. *General Circular.* ? – ?. Colombo: Spiritual Assembly of the Bahá'ís of Sri Lanka.

9.338. National Spiritual Assembly of the Bahá'ís of the Sudan. National Teaching and Deepening Committee. *Newsletter.* no.1 (Sept. 1980)– ?. Khartoum: National Teaching and Deepening Committee.

9.339. National Spiritual Assembly of the Bahá'ís of Thailand. *English Newsletter.* ? – ?. Bangkok: National Spiritual Assembly of the Baha'is of Thailand.

9.340. National Spiritual Assembly of the Bahá'ís of the United Kingdom. National Teaching Committee. *N.T.C. News.* no.1 (Kalimát 141 [July 1984])– . London: National Teaching Committee.

9.341. National Spiritual Assembly of the Bahá'ís of the United Kingdom. Service for the Blind Committee. *SFB Newsletter.* no.1 (Dec. 1977)– . Stevenage, Herts.: Service for the Blind Committee.

9.342. National Spiritual Assembly of the Bahá'ís of the United States. National Programming Committee. *Bulletin.* ? – ?. n.p. [Wilmette, Ill.]: National Programming Committee.

9.343. National Spiritual Assembly of the Bahá'ís of the United States. National Teaching Committee. *Newsletter.* (? 1981)– ?. n.p. [Wilmette, Ill.]: National Teaching Committee of the National Spiritual Assembly of the Bahá'ís of the United States.

9.344. National Spiritual Assembly of the Bahá'ís of the United States. Office of the Treasurer. [*Newsletter*] (Nov. 13, 1970)– . Wilmette, Ill.: Office of the Treasurer.

9.345. National Spiritual Assembly of the Bahá'ís of West Africa. *News from Your National Spiritual Assembly.* no.1 (May 21, 1974)– ?. n.p. [Monrovia, Liberia]: National Spiritual Assembly.

9.346. National Spiritual Assembly of the Bahá'ís of Zambia. *Newsletter.* no.1 (June 1971)–no.2 (Aug. 1971). Lusaka: National Spiritual Assembly of the Bahá'ís of Zambia. Combined with: *Teacher.* Title varies: *Newsletter of the Baha'is of Zambia*, no.1 (June 1967); *Newsletter, Baha'is of Zambia*, no.2 (Aug. 1967)–no.6 (21 Mar. 1968); *Newssheet*, no.1 (Aug. 1968); *Baha'i Newsletter.* (Jan.–Feb. 1971)–(Apr.–May 1972).

9.347. *National Teaching Committee Newsletter.* no.1 (? 1978)– ?. n.p. [Reykjavík, Iceland]: National Teaching Committee.

9.348. *National Treasurer's Bulletin.* no.1 ([Apr. 1972])–no.2 (1 July 1972). n.p. [Honolulu]: National Spiritual Assembly of the Bahá'ís of the Hawaiian Islands. Only two numbers produced.

9.349. *National Treasurer's Newsletter.* ? – . Ponape, Eastern Caroline Islands: National Baha'i Office.

9.350. *The National Treasurer's Representative Bulletin.* no.1 (Oct. 1976)– . n.p. [Wilmette, Ill.: Office of the Treasurer]

9.351. *National Youth Bulletin.* v.1 no.1 (Sept. 1982)– . Mymensingh: National Baha'i Youth Committee of Bangladesh. Title varies: *Youth Page*, v.1 no.1 (Sept. 1982)–v.2 no.3 (Nov. 1983); *National Youth Bulletin*, v.2 no.4 (Apr. 1984)– .

9.352. *National Youth Bulletin for West Africa.* (19 Mar. 1967)– ?. Monrovia, Liberia: National Youth Committee of the N.S.A.

9.353. *Native American Baha'i Institute Newsletter.* v.1 no.1 (July 1984)– . Houck, Ariz.: Native American Baha'i Institute.

9.354. *Navajo-Hopi Bahá'í Newsletter.* (Nov. 1984)– . Window Rock, Ariz.: NHDTC.

9.355. *New Bases: Bahá'í Public Affairs Committee Newsletter.* v.1 no.1 (Oct. 4, 1981)– . Seattle, Wash.: Bahá'í Public Affairs Committee. Title varies: *Bahá'í Media Northwest*, v.1 no.1– ?

9.356. *The New Dawn.* no.1 (July 1973)– ?. n.p. [Nuku'alofa]: National Spiritual Assembly of the Bahá'ís of Tonga. Text in English and Tongan.

9.357. *The New Dawn.* no.1 (1976)–no.11 (July–Sept. 1979). Trinidad: National Bahá'í Youth Committee.

9.358. *The New Day.* ? – ?. Red Deer Alta.: Western Indian Reserves Teaching Committee.

9.359. *The New Day.* v. 1 no.1 (July–Aug. [1975] 132)– . Georgetown: Bahá'í Youth Committee of Guyana.

9.360. *New Day.* v.1 no.1 (May 1972)– . Dublin: National Spiritual Assembly of the Bahá'ís of the Republic of Ireland.

9.361. *The New Day.* v.1 no.1 (Apr.–Aug. 1977)– ?. Majuro: National Spiritual Assembly of the Bahá'ís of the Marshall Islands.

9.362. *New Era.* ed. S. Hishmatulla. [no.1] (1936)– ?. Karachi: Bahai Hall.

9.363. *New World Order.* v.1 no.1 (?). n.p. [United States] Privately printed, no more published?

9.364. *New World Order.* v.1 no.1 (Dec. 1938) – ?. London: National Spiritual Assembly of the Bahá'ís of the British Isles. Title varies: early issues entitled *The New World Order.*

9.365. *New Zealand Bahá'í Newsletter.* v.2 no.1 (May 1957)– . Auckland: National Spiritual Assembly of the Bahá'ís of New Zealand.

9.366. *News Bulletin for Auxiliary Board Assistants from Auxiliary Board Members in Bangladesh.* [Eng. ed] ? – ? . Myensingh: Auxiliary Board Members in Bangladesh.

9.367. *News from Louhelen.* v.1 no.1 ([Dec. 1982])– . Davison, Mich: Louhelen Baha'i School.

9.368. *News from the Secretariat.* no.1 (? 1984) – . Lae: Spiritual Assembly of the Baha'is of Papua New Guinea.

9.369. *News from the World Centre.* (Feb. 1960)– no.6 (Nov. 1966). Haifa: Bahá'í World Centre.

9.370. *News Letter from Baha'is of the British Isles.* (July 1929)– ?. n.p. [London]: National Spiritual Assembly.

9.371. *Newsflash.* (Ilm 142 [Oct. 1985])– . Auckland: National Spiritual Assembly of the Bahá'ís of New Zealand.

9.371a. *Newsheet for the Baha'is of Cyprus (South).* ('Azamat = May 17th, 1984)–(Nur = June 5th, 1984). n.p. [Nicosia: National Spiritual Assembly of the Bahá'ís of Cyprus].

9.372. *Newsletter for Auxiliary Board Members.* no.1 (Mar. 1982)–no.5 (Mar. 1983). Immenstaad, Germany: Continental Board of Counsellors for Protection and Propagation of the Bahá'í Faith in Europe. Succeeds: *Newsletter for Board Members.*
   See 9.373.

9.373. *Newsletter for Board Members.* no.1 ([Sept. 1968])–no.77 (Feb. 1, 1981). n.p.: Continental Board of Counsellors for the Protection and Propagation of the Bahá'í Faith in Europe. Succeeded by: *Newsletter for Auxiliary Board Members.*
   See 9.372.

9.374. *Newsletter NZ Baha'i Youth.* [no.1] (Aug. 1968)– ?. n.p. [Auckland, N.Z.]: National Bahá'í Youth Committee. Cover title varies: *Bahá'í Youth Newsletter*, [no.1] (Aug. 1966)– (July 1970); *Newsletter NZ Baha'i Youth* (Summer 1971). Title page title varies: *Baha'i Youth Magazine*, [no.1] (Aug. 1968), (Summer 1971); *Baha'i Youth News Letter/Baha'i Youth Newsletter*, no.2 (Sept. 1968)–no.4 (May 1969), no.13 (Feb.-Mar. 1970); *Baha'i Youthletter*, no.10 (Aug., 1969)–no.12 (Dec. 1969–Jan. 1970); *N.Z. Baha'i Youth Newsletter*, (July 1970).

9.375. *The Newsletter of the Auxiliary Board Members in Zambia.* ? – ?. Zambia: Auxiliary Board Members.

9.376. *Nigerian Bahá'í News.* v.1 no.1 (May 1970)– . Lagos: National Spiritual Assembly of the Bahá'ís of Nigeria.

9.377. *Nightingale.* v.1 no.1 ([July 1966])– ?. Colombo: National Spiritual Assembly of the Baha'is of Ceylon. Title varies: *Nightingale of the Emerald Isle*, v.1 no.1 ([July 1966])–v.1 no.7 ([July 1967]).

9.378. *Nightingale: A Baha'i Magazine for Youth = Le Rossignol: Un Journal Baha'i pour les Jeunes.* English ed. 138 no.1 (138 [Mar. 1982])– n.p. [Limbe]: National Youth Committee of Cameroon.

9.379. *Nineteen-Day Bahá'í Feast Newsletter.* no.1 (Aug. 1, 1976)– . n.p. [Port-of-Spain]: National Spiritual Assembly of the Bahá'ís of Trinidad and Tobago.

9.380. *The Nineteen-Day Feast Bulletin.* (29 Jan. 1979)– . Georgetown: National Spiritual Assembly of the Bahá'ís of Guyana.

9.381. *Nineteen-Day Feast Circular.* (27 Sept. 1971)– . Colombo: Spiritual Assembly of the Bahá'ís of Sri Lanka. Title varies: *19–Day Feast Newsletter*, (8 Sept. 1978)–(31 Dec. 1979).

9.382. *Nineteen Day Feast Communication: From the Desk of the National Secretary.* no.1 (Will 15, 127 [Sept. 1970])– ?. Addis Ababa: National Spiritual Assembly of the Bahá'ís of North East Africa.

9.383. *19 Day Feast Letter.* ? – . New Delhi: National Spiritual Assembly of the Baha'is of India. Title varies: *Nineteen Day Feast Circular*, (1966–1974); *Nineteen-Day Feast Newsletter*, (1975); *19 Day Feast Letter*, (1976–).

9.384. *Nineteen Day Feast Letter.* ? – ?. Kuala Lumpur: National Spiritual Assembly of the Baha'is of Malaysia.

9.385. *19 Day Feast Letter.* (20 Aug. 1979)– ?. Lae: National Spiritual Assembly of the Baha'is of P.N.G. [Papua New Guinea]

9.386. *Nineteen Day Feast Letter.* (June 5, 1980) – ?. Reykjavík: National Spiritual Assembly of the Bahá'ís of Iceland.

9.387. *Nineteen Day Feast Letter.* [no.1] ('Izzat 140, 8 Sept. 1983)–(20 Aug. 1984). Limbe: Spiritual Assembly of the Baha'is in Malawi. Continued by: *Baha'i Feast Letter.*

9.388. *19 Day Feast Letter of the French Antilles = Lettre de la Fête des 19 Jours des Antilles Françaises.* ? – ?. Point-à-Pitre, Guadeloupe: Spiritual Assembly of the Bahá'is of the French Antilles.

9.389. *19 Day Feast News Letter.* (Aug. 1978)

– . Dhaka: National Spiritual Assembly of the Bahá'ís of Bangladesh.

9.390. *19 Day Feast News Letter.* ? – . n.p. [Bombay]: State Teaching Committee of the Baha'is of Maharashtra.

9.391. *Nineteen-Day Feast Newsletter.* ? – ?. n.p. [Georgetown: Guyana]: National Spiritual Assembly of the Baha'is of Guyana, Surinam and French Guiana.

9.392. *19 Day Feast Newsletter.* ? – . Hong Kong: National Spiritual Assembly of the Baha'is of Hong Kong. Title varies: *Bahá'í 19; 19 Bahá'í News; 5 News 19; 19 Day Feast Newsletter.*

9.393. *Nineteen Day Feast Newsletter.* ? – . Kuching: National Teaching Committee of the Baha'is of East Malaysia.

9.394. *Nineteen Day Feast Newsletter.* [no.1] (23 Nov. 1968]– . London: National Spiritual Assembly of the Bahá'ís of the United Kingdom. Title varies: *Newsletter*, (23 Nov. 1968); *19 Newsletter/19 News Letter*, (Masa'il 1968)–(9 Apr. 1977); *19 Day Feast Message*, (21 Mar. 1980)–(27 Sept. 1982); *Nineteen Day Feast Newsletter*, (16 Oct. 1982)– .

9.395. *Nineteen Day Feast Newsletter.* no.1 (Sug. 28, 1969)– . n.p. [Manila]: National Spiritual Assembly of the Baha'is of the Philippines.

9.396. *19 Day Feast Newsletter.* [no.1] (28 Apr. 1972)– . Singapore: National Spiritual Assembly of the Bahá'ís of Singapore.

9.397. *19 Day Feast Newsletter.* no.1 (30 June 1977)– ?. Suva: National Spiritual Assembly of the Bahá'ís of the Fiji Islands.

9.398. *19 Day Feast Newsletter.* (June 5, 1981) – . Port Blair: National Spiritual Assembly of the Andaman and Nicobar Islands. Publisher varies: Baha'i State Teaching Committee of Andaman & Nicobar Islands.

9.399. *19 Day Feast Newsletter Supplement.* (Nov. 1981)– ?. n.p. [Kuala Lumpur]: Spiritual Assembly of Bahais of Malaysia.

9.400. *19 Day Star.* [no.1] ([Jan.? 1972])– ?. Panchgani, Maharashtra: Student Deepening Department. Publisher varies: Some issues published by Baha'i Committee for College Teaching, West India. Title varies; *Name Me*, [no.1] (Jan.?, 1972]).

9.401. *Nineteen Day Star: National Baha'i Women and Children's Newsletter.* no.1 (Dec. 31, 1975)– ?. Kampala: N.S.A. of the Baha'is of Uganda.

9.402. *19 Days Newsletter for Baha'is Only.*

[no.1] (5 June 1977)– ?. Gangtok: National Spiritual Assembly of the Bahá'ís of Sikkim.

9.403. *Nkhani za aBaha'i = Malaŵi Baha'i News*. ? – ?. Blantyre: Spiritual Assembly of the Baha'is in Malawi. Text in English and Chichewa. Succeeded by separate editions in English and Chichewa.

9.404. *Nordisk Bahá'í Bulletin*. ? – ?. Enskede [Sweden]: Nationella Andliga Rådet. Text in English, Norwegian, Swedish, Finnish.

9.405. *Northern Lights: Alaska Baha'i Children's Bulletin*. v.1 no.1 (Sept. 1973)– ?. McGrath, Alaska: Northern Lights Bulletin Committee. Title varies: *Alaska Baha'i Children's Newsletter*, v.1 nos. 1, 2.

9.406. *Northern Province Baha'i News*. ? – ?. Kasama, Zambia.

9.407. *Northwest Africa Baha'i Bulletin*. v.1 no.1 (? 1959)– ?. n.p. [Tunis, Tunisia]: National Spiritual Assembly of the Baha'is of Northwest Africa.

9.408. *Noticias Bahá'ís*. English ed. ? – ?. n.p. [San José, Costa Rica]: National Spiritual Assembly of the Baha'is of Central America.

9.409. *NSA Bulletin*. no.1 (Dec. 1983)– . n.p. [Bangkok]: Spiritual Assembly of the Baha'is of Thailand.

9.410. *NTC Bulletin of the Eastern Carolines*. v.1 no.1 (Apr. 1982). Ponape: National Teaching Committee of the Eastern Carolines.

9.411. *Nusipepa Bahá'í-Samoa*. [no.1] (July 1970)– . n.p. [Apia]: National Spiritual Assembly of the Bahá'ís of Samoa. Includes subtitle, for nos. 1–7, *Samoa Bahá'í News*. English and Samoan text.

9.412. *Ocean*. ? – . n.p. [Karachi]: National Baha'i Youth Committee of Pakistan. Title varies: *Baha'i Youth News*, to 1973; *Ocean*, no.1 (8 Jan. 1974)– .

9.413. *Old and New*. v.1 no.1 (Nov. 1905). Seattle, Wash.: Nathan Ward Fitz-Gerald. Only one number published.

9.414. *Orient-Occident Unity Bulletin*. v.1 no.1 (Oct. 1911)– ?. Washington, D.C.: Orient-Occident Unity. Title and publisher varies: *Bulletin of the Persian American Educational Society*, v.1 no.1 (Oct. 1911)–v.1 no.5 (Feb. 1912).

9.415. *Pacific Pioneer*. ? – ?. Maryborough, Qld.: Australian Pioneer Committee.

9.416. *Panama Baha'i News*. English ed. no.1 (July 1968)– ?. Panama: National Spiritual Assembly of the Bahá'ís of the Republic of Panama. Title varies: *Baha'i News from Panama, Crossroads of the World*, no.1 (July 1968)–no.10 (Apr. 1969); *Baha'i News*, no.12 (June 1969)–no.36 (Mar. 1974); *Panama Baha'i News*, no.37 (Apr. 1974)– .

9.417. *Peace-Setters Newsletter*. v.1 no.1 (? 1985)– . Seattle, Wash.: Baha'i Public Affairs Committee NW.

9.418. *Peacegram*. no.1 ([Nov. 1985])– . n.p. [Auckland, N.Z.]: International Year of Peace Committee.

9.419. *The Pearl*. [no.1] ([June] 1972)– ?. Singapore: National Bahá'í Youth Committee of Singapore.

9.420. *Philippine Baha'i News*. v.1 no.1 (? 1969)– . Baguio City: National Spiritual Assembly of the Baha'is of the Philippines. Succeeds: *Baha'i News of the Philippines*.

9.421. *Philippine Bahá'í Youth Bulletin*. v.1 no.1 ([May? 1972])– ?. Manila: Student Affairs Co-ordinating Council of the Bahá'ís of the Philippines.

9.422. *Pioneer Post*. v.1 no.1 (Sept. 1978)– . Wilmette, Ill.: International Goals Committee of the National Spiritual Assembly of the Bahá'ís of the United States.

9.423. *The Polar Bear Press*. v.1 (Feb. 1973)– [v.2] (Feb. 1974). Lucerne, Que.: National Arctic Committee. Succeeded by: *The Arctic Quarterly*.
See 9.12

9.424. *Project East–West, Kerala, India*. no.1 (July 30, 1975)– ?. n.p. [New Delhi: National Youth Committee of India]

9.425. *Public Information Newsletter*. v.1 no.1 (? 1966)– ?. n.p. [Wilmette, Ill.]: National Bahá'í Public Information Office.

9.426. *Public Information Newsletter*. no.1 (July 1973)–no.80–2 (Aug. 1980). Honolulu: Public Information Office of the National Spiritual Assembly of the Bahá'ís of the Hawaiian Islands.

9.427. *Publications in English Bulletin: An International Biannual Report of Books, Pamphlets and Magazines of Interest to Bahá'ís*. no.1 (Autumn 1984)– . Oxford: George Ronald, Publisher.

9.428. *Pulse of the Pioneer = Le Pouls du Pionnier*. no.1 (Sept. 1972)– . Thornhill, Ont.: National Pioneer Committee of Canada. English and French text.

9.429. *The Quarterly Señal of Radio Bahá'í*. v.1 no.1 (Feb. 1981)– ?. n.p. [Quito]: National Spiritual Assembly of the Bahá'ís of Ecuador.

9.430. *Radio Bahá'í Bulletin.* v.1 no.1 (Winter 1980)– ?. Quito: National Spiritual Assembly of the Bahá'ís of Ecuador.

9.431. *Reflections.* no.1 (Nov. 1976)– ?. St Johns, Nfld: Committee for the Education of Children.

9.432. *The Regional Bahá'í News: Quarterly Review.* no.1 (Oct. 1959)– ?. n.p. [Campbellville, British Guiana]: Regional Teaching Committee for the Guianas, Barbados and Trinidad.

9.433. *Rising Stars of Africa.* [no.1] (1981–82) – . St Helena, Venda: National Teaching Committee of the Baha'is of South & West Africa.

9.434. *Rong en Bahá'í = Bahá'í News.* ? – . n.p. [Ponape, Caroline Islands: National Teaching Committee].

9.435. *Le Rossignol: Journal des Jeunes Bah'ais* [sic] *du Cameroun.* Bilingual ed. ? – . n.p. [Limbe]: Comité National des Jeunes du Cameroun. Text in French and English.

9.436. *Round Robin.* ? – ?. Ottawa, Ont.: New Territories Committee. Title is within text of newsletter. Masthead shows simply 'New Territories Committee'.

9.437. *Ruhi Institute Bulletin.* no.1 (Oct. 1983) – . Cali, Colombia: Ruhi Institute Committee.

9.438. *Saint Lucia Baha'i News.* v.1 no.1 (July 1983)– . Castries, St Lucia: Baha'i News.

9.439. *Schools = Écoles.* ?–(June 1984). n.p. [Thornhill, Ont.]: Bahá'í Schools Committee. Also titled: *R.S.C. Activity Bulletin.*

9.440. *Scottish Newsletter.* (May 1950)– ?. Kilmarnack, Ayrshire: Scottish Teaching Committee. Title varies: *Scottish R.T.C. Newsletter,* (May 1950)– ?; Scottish Baha'i Newsletter, ? – ? ; *Scottish Newsletter, ? – ?.*

9.441. *The Search.* ? – ?. Bombay: National Baha'i Youth Committee of India.

9.442. *A Selection of News Items from the Universal House of Justice and the Hands of the Cause Residing in the Holy Land.* ? – ?. n.p. [Nairobi: National Spiritual Assembly of the Bahá'ís of Kenya].

9.443. *Shining Stars.* v.1 [no. 1] (Feb.–Mar. 1981)– . Zaria, Nigeria: National Children's Committee.

9.444. *Shiraz.* ? – ?. Singapore: Baha'i Society, University of Singapore.

9.445. *Shiraz.* v.1 no.1 (May 1970)– ?. n.p. [Kuala Lumpur]: Baha'i Society, University of Malaya.

9.446. *Siam Scene.* ? 139 ([? 1983])– . n.p. [Bangkok, Thailand]: National Pioneering Committee.

9.447. *Solomon Islands National Baha'i Newsletter.* no.1 (? 1971)– . n.p. [Honiara]: National Spiritual Assembly of the Baha'is of the Solomon Islands. Title varies: *B.S.I.P. Baha'i News; Baha'i News Letter, Baha'i Monthly Newsletter, Monthly Newsletter, Newsletter, National Spiritual Assembly Newsletter, Solomon Baha'i News, Solomon Islands Bahá'í Newsletter, Baha'i Newsletter for the Solomon Islands, National Baha'i News of Solomon Islands, National Baha'i News, News Bulletin, NSA Newsbulletin, Solomon Islands National Baha'i Newsletter,* interspersed with frequent changes.

9.448. *South Carolina Pulseline: News Bulletin.* no.1 ([1984?])– ?. Hemingway, S.C.: Regional Teaching Committee.

9.449. *Southern Teaching Journal: News Letter of Southern Teaching Committee of British Isles.* no.1 (Oct. 1951)– ?. Cardiff: Southern Teaching Committee.

9.450. *Spiritual Mothering Journal.* v.1 no.1 (Jan.–Feb. 1981)– . Dover, N.H.: Melinda Armstrong.

9.451. *Star of the West.* v.1 no.1 (Mar. 21, 1910)– v.25 no.12 (Mar. 1935). Chicago: Baha'i News Service. Title varies: *Baha'i News,* v.1; *The Bahá'í Magazine,* v.21–v.25. LC card 13–9982.

9.452. *idem.* v.1 no.1 (Mar. 21, 1910)–v.14 no.12 (Mar. 1924). Oxford: George Ronald, 1978, 1984. Reprinted in 8 bound volumes.

9.453. *Starfall: The Quarterly Newsletter of the Australian Baha'i Youth.* ? – ?. Brisbane, Qld.: [National Youth Committee?]

9.454. *Stars of the New World.* [no.1] (June 1980)– ?. Elandsfontein, Transvaal: National Teaching Committee.

9.455. *Suomen Ruusutarha.* no.1 ([Apr. 1982]) – . Naantali: Gerry Nolen [for the National Spiritual Assembly of the Bahá'ís of Finland]. English and Finnish text.

9.456. *Supplement to Noticias Baha'is.* no.1 (Feb. 1979)– ?. Caracas: National Spiritual Assembly of the Baha'is of Venezuela. Title varies: *Venezuelan Bahá'í English Language Bulletin,* no.1; current title from no.2.

9.457. *Surat Gawai 19 Hari = 19 Day Feast Newsletter.* (5 June 1972)– . n.p. [Kuching, Sarawak]: National Teaching Committee [of East Malaysia]

9.458. *Surat Kenduri Hari 19 = 19 Day Feast*

Newsletter. ? – ?. Kuala Lumpur: Spiritual Assembly of the Baha'is of Malaysia.

9.459. *SVG Baha'i News Letter.* (Nur 141 [June 1984])– . n.p. [Kingstown, St Vincent: National Spiritual Assembly of the Bahá'ís of St Vincent and Grenada]

9.460. *Taiwan Baha'i News.* ? – ?. n.p. [Taipei]: National Spiritual Assembly of the Baha'is of Taiwan. Title varies: *English News Bulletin of the National Spiritual Assembly of the Bahá'ís of Taiwan, Taiwan English Baha'i News.*

9.461. *Taiwan Baha'i News Bulletin.* ? – ?. n.p. [Taipei]: National Administrative Committee of the Baha'is of Taiwan, Free China. Title varies: *Taiwan Baha'i Newsletter.*

9.462. *Talking Leaves.* ? – ?. Phoenix, Ariz.: American Indian Service Committee.

9.463. *Tamilnadu 19 Day Feast Letter.* v.1 no.1 (Núr 130, 5 June 1973)– . Madras: Baha'i State Teaching Committee of Tamilnadu. Title varies: *19 Day Feast Letter*, v.1 no.1 (5 June 1973)– ?.

9.464. *Tanganyika/Zanzibar Baha'i News Sheet.* ? – ?. Tanga, Tanganyika: Tanganyika/Zanzibar Teaching Committee.

9.465. *Te Bong Ae Boou.* [no.1] (May–June 1977)– . n.p. [Bikenibeu, Tarawa: National Spiritual Assembly of the Bahá'ís of Kiribati and Tuvalu] Title varies: *The New Day = Te Ota Ae Bou*, [no.1] (May–June 1977); *The New Day = Te Bong Ae Bou*, no.2 (July–Aug. 1977)– ?; *The New Day*, ? – (Jan. 1979); *Te Bong Ae Boou*, (Feb.–Mar. 1979)– .

9.466. *Te Ota Ae Bou.* ? – ?. Tarawa: National Spiritual Assembly of the Baha'is of the Gilbert Islands & Tuvalu. At head of title: *English Translation of Baha'i Newsletter of the National Spiritual Assembly of the Baha'is of the Gilbert Islands & Tuvalu.*

9.467. *Te Whanaketanga = Time of Youth.* v.1 (Mar. 1984)– . Hastings, N.Z.

9.468. *Teach.* v.1 no.1 (Dec. 1972)– ?. Mangalore: National Teaching Committee of South India.

9.469. *Teach: Voice of Youth.* ? – ?. Karachi, Pakistan: Baha'i Youth Committee.

9.470. *Teacher.* (24 June 1968)–(1 Aug. 1971). Lusaka: National Spiritual Assembly of the Bahá'ís of Zambia. Succeeded by: *Zambian Lion.*

9.471. *Teaching Bulletin of the Nine Year Plan.* no.1 (Nov. 1964)–no.30 (Aug. 1967). Wilmette, Ill.: National Teaching Committee.

9.471a. *Teaching Flash!* (1 Apr. 1985)–(1 June 1985). Harare, Zimbabwe: Continental Board of Counsellors in Africa.

9.472. *Teaching in the Marianas.* (June 1983)–(July 1983). n.p. [Guam]: National Teaching Committee, a Committee of the National Spiritual Assembly of the Bahá'ís of the Mariana Islands.

9.473. *Temple Bulletin.* [no.1] (Nov. 1960)–no.3 (Mar. 1962). Frankfurt/M.: National Spiritual Assembly of the Bahá'ís of Germany.

9.474. *Ten Year World Crusade.* 6/120 ([June 1963])– ? Northampton: National Spiritual Assembly of the Bahá'ís of the British Isles, National Teaching Committee.

9.475. *The Thai Bahai News.* (July–Aug. 1972) – ?. Bangkok: National Spiritual Assembly of the Baha'is of Thailand. Title varies: *Bahai News Thailand*, (July–Aug. 1972); *Baha'i News of Thailand*, v.2 [i.e. no.2] (Sept. 1972); *The Thai Bahai News*, v.3 [i.e. no.3] (Feb. 1973)– ?.

9.476. *Tidal Wave: Philippine Baha'i News.* ? – ?. n.p. [Manila]: National Spiritual Assembly of the Baha'is of the Philippines. Publisher varies: before April 1964, published by the National Teaching Committee of the Baha'is of the Philippines.

9.477. *Timoun: Developpement de l'Éducation Bahá'íe en Haiti = Development of Bahá'í Education in Haiti.* no.1 (Spring 1984)– . Lilavois, Haiti: International Board of Directors of the Anis Zunuzi Bahá'í School. Title varies: *Ti Mun*, no.1 (Spring 1984).

9.478. *Torch: Baha'i Youth Magazine.* (Oct. 1958)– ?. New Delhi: National Baha'i Youth Committee of India, Burma & Ceylon.

9.479. *Travelling Fellowship.* under direction of Zoraya [sic] Chamberlain. [no.1] (1 Aug. 1919) – . New York: Fellowship Press.

9.480. *Treasury Newsletter.* no.1 (Nov. 1981)– ?. n.p. [Thornhill, Ont.]: National Spiritual Assembly of the Bahá'ís of Canada.

9.481. *The Trumpet Blast of the Louis G. Gregory Bahá'í Institute.* v.1 issue 1 (?)– . Hemingway, S.C.: Louis G. Gregory Bahá'í Institute.

9.482. *The Trumpet: Uganda Baha'i Youth News.* v.1 no.1 (Jan. 1971)– ?. Kampala, Uganda: National Youth Committee.

9.483. *U.S. Bahá'í Report: A Quarterly News and Information Service.* v.1 no.1 (Spring 1985)– . Wilmette, Ill.: National Spiritual Assembly of the Bahá'ís of the United States.

9.484. *The Ubiquitist.* v.1 no.1 (Sept. 1976)– ?.

Wilmette, Ill.: National Bahá'í Youth Committee.

9.485. *Uganda Bahá'í News.* (? 1963)– ?. Kampala: Uganda Teaching Committee.

9.486. *Unified Actions: An Information Newsletter.* (24 Jan. 1985)– . Wilmette, Ill.: National Spiritual Assembly of the Bahá'ís of the United States.

9.487. *United States Africa Bulletin.* ? – ?. n.p. [Wilmette, Ill.?]: U.S. African Teaching Committee.

9.488. *Unity: Newsletter of the National Baha'i Youth Committee, Malaysia.* v.1 no.1 (? 1968) – ?. Kuala Lumpur: National Baha'i Youth Committee.

9.489. *Update International Chinese Teaching.* no.1 (October [19]85)– . n.p.: International Chinese Teaching Committee.

9.490. *'Utho Jawano' Monthly.* yr. 1 ed. 1 (? 1968)– ?. Lucknow, India: Local Bahai Spiritual Assembly.

9.491. *Uttar Pradesh Baha'i Tutorial Schools Monthly Bulletin.* no.1 (Oct. 1984)– . Uttar Pradesh: Baha'i Tutorial Schools (Kanpur: Kumar Printers). In English and Hindi.

9.492. *Varqá: The Children's Magazine.* Eng. ed. v.1 no.1 (Mar./Apr. 1981)– . New Delhi: Varqá.

9.493. *Victory Fingers: News Letter for Assistants to Auxiliary Board Members in Tamil Nadu.* (Jan. 1984)– . Tamil Nadu: Auxiliary Board Members in Tamil Nadu. Title varies: *Matchless Fingers of the Vital Arm: Baha'i Monthly Newsletters for Assistants to the Auxiliary Board Member.* (Jan 1984)– ?; *Victory Fingers* (or sometimes *Victorious Fingers*), (June 1985)– .

9.494. *Vienna Baha'i News.* ? – ?. Vienna, Austria: Franz Poellinger.

9.495. *The Voice of Youth.* ? – ?. London National Bahá'í Youth Committee of the British Isles.

9.496. *Wena.* v.1 no.1 (? 1985)– . Umtata: Baha'i National Youth Development Committee for the Baha'i Youth of Transkei.

9.497. *West African Bahá'í Newsletter.* ? – ?. Monrovia, Liberia: National Spiritual Assembly of the Bahá'ís of West Africa. Title varies: *National Spiritual Assembly of the Bahá'ís of West Africa, Newsletter*, through Apr. 1970; *West African Bahá'í Newsletter/West African Bahá'í News Letter*, (May 1970)– ?.

9.498. West African Centre for Bahá'í Studies (Lagos, Nigeria). *Newsletter.* no.1 (Mar. 1985) – . Lagos, Nigeria: The West African Centre for Bahá'í Studies = Le Centre d'Afrique Occidentale pour les Etudes Bahá'íes.

9.499. *What's Happening in Singapore.* ? – ?. Singapore: Area Teaching Committee, State of Singapore.

9.500. *Wind of Bahá.* v.1 no.1 (? 1980)– ?. Anchorage: Alaska.: Wind of Baha Committee of the National Spiritual Assembly of the Baha'is of Alaska.

9.501. *Wings: Magazine for Baha'i Women.* no.1 (June 1980)– ?. n.p. [Limbe: National Spiritual Assembly of the Bahá'ís of Cameroon].

9.502. *World Citizen.* v.1 no.1 (Jan./Feb. 1980)– v.2 no.1 (1st Quarter, 1981). Houston, Tex.: World Citizen.

9.503. *World Fellowship for the Children of the Kingdom.* v.1 no.1 (Mar. 1923)– ?. Montclair, N.J.: First International Home Station. Title varies: *World Fellowship*, v.1 no.1 (Mar. 1923)–v.1 no.9/10 (Aug. 1924); *Bahá'í World Fellowship*, v.1 no.11 (Sept./Oct. 1924)–v.2 no.1 (Apr./June 1925). Title page title on v.2 no.2 (Sept. 1925) is *The Magazine of the Children of the Kingdom*.

9.504. *World Order* [old series]. v.1 no.1 (Apr. 1935)–v.14 no.12 (Mar. 1949). New York: Bahá'í Publishing Committee. Succeeded: *World Unity* and *Star of the West*. LC card 37–18666.

9.505. *World Order* [new series]. v.1 no.1 (Fall 1966)– . Wilmette, Ill.: National Spiritual Assembly of the Bahá'ís of the United States LC card 64–18.

9.506. *World Unity.* v.1 no.1 (Oct. 1927)–v.15 no.6 (Mar. 1935). New York: World Unity Publishing Corp. Edited by Horace Holley. Succeeded by: *World Order.* LC card 31–9575 rev.

9.507. *The Y.O.W. Log.* (Dec. 1969)– ?. Wilmette, Ill.: National Teaching Committee, Youth and Student Activities.

9.508. *Young Baha'i.* [no.1] (15 Dec, 1983)– . n.p. [Banjul?, The Gambia: National Spiritual Assembly of the Bahá'ís of the Gambia?]

9.509. *Youth.* [no.1] (Sharaf 137 [Dec. 1980])– ?. n.p. [Kuala Lumpur]: National Bahá'í Youth Committee.

9.510. *Youth = Jeunes.* (15 Dec. 1984)– . Thornhill, Ont.: National Youth Teaching Committee. Title is the committee's stationery. Other titles include: *To all information groups in the Baha'i Youth Movement*; *Youth Can Move the World*; Bahá'í Youth Movement, *Newsletter*.

9.511. *The Youth Flame.* ? – . Christie Road: National Youth Task Force of the Baha'is of South and West Africa.

9.512. *Youth Focus.* (Jan.–Feb. 1985)– . San Juan, Trinidad and Tobago: Bahá'í Youth of Trinidad and Tobago.

9.513. *Youth Hotline.* v.1 no.1 ([Feb. 1981])– . Wilmette, Ill.: Bahá'í National Youth Committee.

9.514. *Youth News Update.* ? – ?. Wilmette, Ill.: Bahá'í National Youth Committee.

9.515. *Youth Newsletter.* ? – ?. n.p. [London?, Eng.: National Youth Committee?]

9.516. *Zambian Lion.* no.1 (Sept. 1971)–no.7 (June 1972). Lusaka: National Spiritual Assembly of the Bahá'ís of Zambia. Succeeds: *Teacher.*

9.517. *Zambian Baha'i News.* no.1 (Sept. 1972) – . Lusaka: National Spiritual Assembly of the Bahá'ís of Zambia. Title varies: *Zambian Baha'i Newsletter*, no.1 (Sept. 1972)–no.2 (Oct. 1973); *Baha'i Newsletter*, 131 no.2 (June 1974)–131 no.4 ([Nov. 1974]); *Zambian National Baha'i Newsheet*, (Oct. 1975)–(Mar. 1976).

9.518. *Zenith.* (Sharaf 118 [Jan. 1962])– ?. Belfast: Irish Bahai Youth Committee. Title varies: *Guth an óige.*

9.519. *(Zhōng huá líng xī) = Baha'i News.* no.1 (Feb. 1971)– . n.p. [Taipei]: National Spiritual Assembly of the Baha'is of Taiwan Republic of China.

X
Works Containing Reference to the Bábí and Bahá'í Faiths

WITHIN a specialized subject bibliography such as this one, it is not common practice to grant space to the large number of works on other topics that deal cursorily with the subject of the bibliography. What is interesting in the case of these references to the Bahá'í Faith in books on other subjects is that their significance may outstrip the brevity of the references themselves. Cursory mentions of the Bahá'í religion may reveal important information about the way it is commonly perceived. Facts unavailable elsewhere sometimes appear in a one-sentence gloss in a larger work. Further data is available to the student who analyzes the broader subject content of these publications in which the Bahá'ís are mentioned.

The works containing references to the Bahá'í Faith during the period 1844 to 1985 fall into a number of broad categories:

1. General works on religion; sociological studies of religion; selections from the sacred scriptures of the world's religions

A great many of these treat the Bahá'ís in a very cursory manner, the most frequent statements being that it is a Muslim sect with some following in the West; and that it is 'syncretistic', that is, it has borrowed teachings from all other religions and put them together into a new one. Occasionally it is seen as an object worthy of sophisticated derision as in Peter Rowley's *New Gods in America* [10.1258]. Generally it is portrayed with sympathy in the company of some errors of fact, as in the works of the American professor of religion Marcus Bach [10.101–10.105]. In a few cases it is dealt with factually and with a freshness of view that is striking as with Robert S. Ellwood's work on new religious movements [10.474] in which he concludes that the Bahá'í Faith is an independent religion that does not belong in a book on cults. Bahá'í texts have more and more been included in collections of holy scriptures, as it has come to be recognized as a religion possessing a body of sacred literature as meaningful as those of other great faiths.

2. Works on the history, politics, customs and social life of Iran

The classic such work is E.G. Browne's *A Year*

Amongst the Persians [10.271], along with essential accounts by Chirol [10.332], Curzon [10.401], Sykes [10.413], Bassett [10.144–10.145], Rice [10.1236], Ross [10.1255–10.1256] and Sheil [10.1327]. Many orientalists and academics have been exposed to the Bábís and Bahá'ís through reading rather than through personal experience. Generally this has led to expressions of sympathy for the hardships faced by the Iranian Bahá'í community but a poor grasp of Bahá'í doctrine, which was often described in early works as pantheistic [10.1105]. There was also a tendency in many of these works to report hearsay as though it were fact. This was especially true with regard to speculation about the Bahá'í central figures. Works on current Iranian affairs have focused particularly on the origin and meaning of the persecutions of the Bahá'ís under both the Pahlavi and Islamic Revolutionary governments.

3. Works on Palestine, Israel and the Middle East

Many of these works in the early twentieth century were written about travel experiences during which the authors met 'Abdu'l-Bahá, Shoghi Effendi or some of the Bahá'ís in the Holy Land. A.L. Pemberton's *A Modern Pilgrimage to Palestine* [10.1140] is a good example, as are the works of Ashbee [10.84], Boddy [10.218], Coleman [10.372], Curtis [10.400], Dunning [10.452], Holmes [10.706] and Whittingham [10.1560]. Recent works set the Iranian persecutions in the wider context of Middle Eastern affairs or mention the presence of the Bahá'í World Centre in Israel as a central factor in Islamic political repression of the Bahá'ís in many Middle Eastern countries. There are also a very large number of guidebooks to Israel that mention the existence of the Bahá'í spiritual and administrative centres in the Haifa-'Akká (Acre) area.

4. Works on Islam

Christian authors often deal with the Bahá'í religion either as a minor sect or as a mitigating influence on the harshness of Islam. Academic writers and orientalists are more concerned with the Bábí and Bahá'í Faiths insofar as they shed light on Islamic – particularly Shí'í – history, but not generally as a subject of academic study in its own right. The assessment of Islamic apologists such as Syed Hossein Nasr [10.1056–10.1059] is that the Bahá'í Faith, for good or ill, introduced western secular ideas to the Islamic world in a religious guise.

5. Works by Christian missionaries and Christian apologetic works

The first mention of the Báb in any Western book was Henry A. Stern's *Dawning of Light in the East* [10.1391], itself a report of missionary journeys to the Jews in Iran and nearby countries. Christian approaches to the Bábí and Bahá'í religions have been ambivalent. In an early stage of western Christian writing on the religions, Christian missionaries speculated that the Bahá'í teachings would free Iranians and Arabs from Islam, thus preparing them for conversion to Christianity. There were some, even then, who considered the Bahá'ís a danger to missionary activity, such as Isaac Adams [10.9–10.10], Mooshie G. Daniel [10.403–10.404] and Samuel K. Nweeya [10.1092–10.1095], and there have been others through the years with the same view, particularly William McElwee Miller [10.1011], Samuel Graham Wilson [10.1579–10.1581] and Samuel M. Zwemer [10.1639–10.1645]. Evangelical crusaders Walter R. Martin [10.195, 10.970–10.972] and Jan Karel Van Baalen [10.1487–10.1490], among others, have dedicated themselves to fighting 'cults', among which they list the Bahá'í religion as one of the most dangerous. Many writers of the liberal Christian tradition have sought to find 'christian spirit' in Bahá'í beliefs, approaching them from an ecumenical perspective; yet even Paul Tillich's [10.1428] ecumenism only goes up to a certain point.

6. Reference books

Encyclopaedias, dictionaries and handbooks have enjoyed varying degrees of success at purveying correct information. Editions of the *Encyclopaedia Britannica* early in this century and the *Encyclopaedia of Religion and Ethics* contained articles on Bábism by E.G. Browne. By the 1950s the Bahá'ís had become established enough to make representations to publishers of general encyclopaedias that resulted in Bahá'í authorship or review of articles on the religion, for instance, the inclusion of a full article by Dr Firuz Kazemzadeh in the 15th edition of the *Britannica* [10.1067] in 1975. In some works, however, other biases operated. The *Twentieth Century Encyclopedia of Religious Knowledge* [10.1456], which speaks from a Protestant evangelical viewpoint, accused the Bahá'ís of seeking world dictatorship under the Universal House of Justice. The *Academic American Encyclopedia* [10.8] contained an article which used as its primary source William McElwee Miller's *The Bahá'í*

Faith – Its History and Teachings – a source that is difficult to rate as a scholarly and unbiased treatment. A similar caveat has to be made about the article 'Baha'ism' in *A Handbook of Living Religions* [10.645], whose author Denis MacEoin is a former Bahá'í who became disaffected. An interesting example of enthusiasm is the *World Christian Encyclopedia* [10.1601] which attempted estimates of Bahá'í membership and growth patterns worldwide; it is very close in many particulars but also wildly exaggerated in others. A recent major work is the *Encyclopaedia Iranica* [10.484] which, when completed, will contain a large number of academic articles on the religion, most of them by Bahá'ís trained in academic disciplines.

7. Biographies

Biographies of well-known individuals have occasionally mentioned their contacts with Bahá'ís, as in the cases of Benjamin Jowett [10.1], Alain Locke [10.21] (himself a declared Bahá'í), Marie of Romania [10.1118], Cornelius Vanderbilt, Jr [10.1494], Cosima Wagner [10.1527] and Dunduzu K. Chisiza [10.1156]. Mention of the Bahá'ís occurs frequently in the biographies of Iranians of the late 19th and early 20th centuries [e.g. 10.28].

8. Fiction

Bahá'í characters have sometimes been used to add colour to novels and short stories. Prominent writers of fiction such as Saul Bellow [10.163], Lloyd C. Douglas [10.442], Sinclair Lewis [10.913a–10.913b], James Michener [10.997], Muriel Spark [10.1364] and Gore Vidal [10.1501] have all referred to Bahá'ís in at least one novel. This has not always been in a favourable light, as evidenced in what by Bahá'í standards would be considered a scurrilous reference in Vidal's *Myra Breckenridge*. Carol Bergé's short story 'The Farm Woman' may also be considered unflattering, as its main character is portrayed as a disturbed woman who uses her faith as a Bahá'í to ill effect. There are a number of references that have appeared in science fiction novels [10.58, 10.424, 10.1326].

9. New Age; Occultism; Astrology; UFOs

The New Age movement's emphasis on exotic spiritual experimentation has resulted in a number of brief references in new age guides to spiritual groups. Prolific authors in these fringe areas include W. Tudor Pole [10.1167–10.1173] on spiritualism, Dane Rudhyar [10.1260–10.1268] on astrology, Robert Scrutton [10.1299–10.1301] on lost continents and esoteric spirituality, and George Hunt Williamson [10.1568–10.1570] on UFOs. Of interest is the question of what attraction the Bahá'í religion would hold for this group, considering the profound Bahá'í emphasis on scientific and rational thought.

10. Architecture, Art and Literature

Bahá'í temples have long been an attractive topic for architectural writers. The Bahá'í House of Worship in Wilmette, Illinois, has been the most frequently mentioned in books, no doubt due to its being the oldest Bahá'í temple in existence. In art, two major artists account for the vast majority of references to the Bahá'ís in this context: Mark Tobey and Otto Donald Rogers. Literary studies have usually turned to early Persian Bahá'í poets, in particular Ṭáhirih, as well as Nabíl and Na'ím.

11. Social issues

Peace, human rights (particularly in the context of the Iranian persecutions) and racism are the three major areas in which books were likely to make reference to the Bahá'í religion up to 1985. Two major works on the race question in the United States [10.447, 10.1044] refer specifically to the Bahá'í community as embracing a wide diversity and encouraging interracial marriage. In the context of social issues should also be mentioned studies of Marxism and socialism that touch upon the Bahá'í Faith and how it was viewed in the

Soviet Union during the period. [10.723, 10.869, 10.1426].

12. Extremist publications

The Bahá'í Faith, with its progressive social programme and international viewpoint, was bound to engender opposition from forces seeking a more narrow, nationalist, authoritarian order. Works by the U.S. Labor Party founded by Lyndon LaRouche [10.247, 10.448] dredge up and promote the Islamic Revolutionary charges that the Bahá'ís are Zionist and British spies. Others during the 1950s placed the Bahá'ís among 'communist sympathizer' groups [10.434]. Still others, in league with the politically-involved Christian right, attack the Bahá'í approach to world federation and international cooperation as a tool of the devil and a plot of the anti-Christ [10.385].

The listing here is clearly quite incomplete, comprising perhaps upwards of one-half the works in English that actually refer to the Bábí and Bahá'í religions during the 1844–1985 period. During the 1980s, the task of remaining abreast of such brief references has been exceedingly difficult due to the sheer number of publications that include such mentions. No attempt has been made to provide annotations for these references. A few major items have significant details of content noted.

A

10.1. Abbott, Evelyn; Campbell, Lewis. *The Life and Letters of Benjamin Jowett*. London: John Murray, 1897. II:466.

10.2. *ABC News 20/20, July 28, 1983*. New York: ABC News, 1983. 'In the Name of Islam', pp. 7–10.

10.3. Abdul Rahman ben Hammad al Omar. *Islam the Religion of Truth*. Riyadh: al Farazdak Press, 1390 [i.e. 1970] p. 59.

10.4. Aberly, John. *An Outline of Missions*. Philadelphia, Pa.: Muhlenberg Press, 1945. p. 15.

10.5. Abimbola, Wande. *An Address by the Vice-Chancellor of the University of Ife, Professor Wande Abimbola, Delivered at the Sixteenth Convocation Ceremony, Saturday, 14th December, 1985*. Ile-Ife, Nigeria: University of Ife, 1985 (n.p.: Anchorprint). pp. 12, 17.

10.6. *Abingdon Dictionary of Living Religions*. Keith Crim, general ed. Nashville, Tenn.: Abingdon, 1981. Adams, C.J., ' 'Abdu'l-Bahá',

p. 1; 'Báb', p. 86; 'Bahā'ī', pp. 87–9; 'Bahā-'ullāh', p. 89; 'Shoghi Effendi', p. 687.

10.7. Abrahamian, Ervand. *Iran Between Two Revolutions*. Princeton, N.J.: Princeton University Press, 1982. pp. 12, 16–17, 24, 25, 54, 62, 90, 163, 174, 385, 421, 432, 514, 532.

10.8. *Academic American Encyclopedia*. Princeton, N.J.: Arete Publishing Company, 1981. II: 7. Willem A. Bijlefeld, 'Babism' and 'Baha'i'.
Makes use of William McE. Miller's *The Bahá'í Faith, Its History and Teachings*.

10.9. Adams, Isaac. *Darkness and Daybreak*. Grand Rapids, Mich.: Dickinson Bros., Published in the Interests of the Persian Mission, 1898. pp. 204–17.

10.10. —— *Persia By a Persian: Personal Experiences, Manners, Customs, Habits, Religious and Social Life in Persia*. n.p. [Chicago?], 1900. pp. 453–90.

10.11. Addison, James Thayer. *The Christian*

Approach to the Moslem: A Historical Study. New York: Columbia University Press, 1942. pp. 176, 189–90.

10.12. —— *idem.* New York: AMS Press, 1966. pp. 176, 189–90.

10.12a. Afkhami, Gholam R. *The Iranian Revolution: Thanatos on a National Scale.* Washington, D.C.; Middle East Institute, 1985. p. 206.

10.13. *African Encyclopedia.* London: Oxford University Press, 1974. p. 74.

10.13a. *Afro-American Religious History: A Documentary Witness.* ed. Milton C. Sernett. Durham, N.C.: Duke University Press, 1985. p. 375.

10.14. Ahlstron, Sydney E. *A Religious History of the American People.* New Haven, Conn. [etc.]: Yale University Press, 1972. pp. 1049–50.

10.15. —— *idem.* Garden City, N.Y.; Image Books, 1975. II: 564–565.

10.16. Ahmad, al-Haj Khwaja Nazir. *Paraclete: from 'Jesus in Heaven on Earth'.* Woking, U.K.: Woking Muslim Mission Literary Trust; Lahore, Pakistan: Azeez Manzil; Mansfield, Oh.: Reproduced for Distribution by the Islamic Centre of America, 1956. 'The Bahai Creed', pp. 41–56.

10.17. Akhavi, Shahrough. *Religion and Politics in Contemporary Iran: Clergy-State Relations in the Pahlavi Period.* Albany: State University of New York Press, 1980. p. 33; 'The Anti-Baha'i Campaign' [of 1955], pp. 76–87.

10.18. *Akko.* Jerusalem: Ministry of Industry, Trade and Tourism, 1978. pp. 5–6.

10.19. *idem.* Jerusalem: Israel Ministry of Tourism, 1983. p. 5.

10.20. Al-i Ahmad, Jalal. *Occidentosis: A Plague from the West.* trans. Robert Campbell; annot. and introd. Hamid Algar. Berkeley, Calif.: Mizan Press, c1984. (Contemporary Islamic Thought. Persian Series). pp. 45, 57n, 143 n42.

10.21. *Alain Locke: Reflections on a Modern Renaissance Man.* ed. Russell J. Linnemann. Baton Rouge, La.; London: Louisiana State University, 1982. pp. 13n, 33n.

10.22. *The Alawi Complex in Syria.* Jerusalem: Media Analysis Center, July 24, 1984. (Contemporary Mideast Backgrounder; no. 190). p. 5.

10.23. Albanese, Catherine L. *America: Religions and Religion.* Belmont, Calif.: Wadsworth Publishing Co., 1981. pp. 189, 190, 201–3, 218.

10.24. Alder, Lory; Dalby, Richard. *The Dervish of Windsor Castle: The Life of Arminius Vambery.*

London: Bachman & Turner, 1979. pp. 482, 484.

10.25. Alec-Tweedle, Mrs. *Mainly East.* New York: E.P. Dutton, 1922. pp. 252–3.

10.26. —— *idem.* London: Hutchinson & Co., 1922. pp. 252–3.

10.27. *Alfred Adler: His Influence on Psychology Today.* ed. Harold H. Mosak. Park Ridge, N.J.: Noyes Press, 1973. Erik Blumenthal, 'Individual Psychology and Bahá'í', pp. 228–37.

10.28. Algar, Hamid. *Mīrzā Malkum Khān: A Study in the History of Iranian Modernism.* Berkeley: University of California Press, 1973. pp. 11, 46, 58–9, 213–6, 221–5, 227, 306.

10.29. —— *Religion and State in Iran, 1785–1906: The Role of the Ulama in the Qajar Period.* Berkeley: University of California Press, 1969. pp. 136, 138–44, 146–51.

10.30. —— *The Roots of the Islamic Revolution.* London: The Open Press, 1983. pp. 58, 68, 104, 107.

10.31. Ali, Maulana Muhammad. *The Founder of the Ahmadiyya Movement: A Short Study.* 3rd ed. Newark, Calif.: Ahmadiyya Anjuman Isha'at Islam, Lahore, Inc., 1984. pp. 51, 58.

10.32. —— *The Religion of Islam: A Comprehensive Discussion of the Sources, Principles and Practices of Islam.* New Delhi: S. Chand & Company, n.d. [196–?] p. 422.

10.33. Ali, Syed Ameer. *The Spirit of Islam: A History of the Evolution and Ideals of Islâm, with a Life of the Prophet.* London: Christophers, 1922. pp. 357–9, 482, 491.

10.34. Allan, John; Butterworth, John; Langley, Myrtle. *A Book of Beliefs.* One vol. paperback ed. Tring, Herts.: Lion Publishing, 1983. pp. 108–11.

10.35. Allen, Cady H. *The Message of the Book of Revelation.* Nashville, Tenn.: Cokesbury Press, 1939. p. 118n.
'Abdu'l-Bahá's explanation of Revelations 12 from *Some Answered Questions*, with a Christian refutation.

10.36. Allen, Devere. *The Fight for Peace.* New York: Macmillan Co., 1930. pp. 619, 628.

10.37. Allen, Richard. *Imperialism and Nationalism in the Fertile Crescent: Sources and Prospects of the Arab-Israeli Conflict.* New York: Oxford University Press, 1974. p. 244n.

10.38. Allen, Thomas; Sachtleben, William. *Across Asia on a Bicycle.* New York: Century Co., 1903. pp. 87–9.

10.39. Allworth, Edward. *Nationalities of the Soviet East: Publications and Writing Systems: A Bibliographical Directory and Transliteration Tables for Iranian and Turkic-Language Publications, 1818–1945 Located in U.S. Libraries.* New York: Columbia University Press, 1971. p. 66.

10.40. American Academy of Religion. Society of Biblical Literature. *Abstracts, Annual Meeting, 1983.* n.d. [Chico, Calif.]: Scholars Press, 1983. p. 86.

10.41. *American Painting, 1900–1970.* Nederland: Time-Life International, c1970, c1973. p. 131.

10.42. *American Poets Since World War II.* ed. Donald J. Greiner. Detroit, Mich.: Gale Research, 1980. (Dictionary of Literary Biography; v. 5). 'Robert Hayden'/James Mann, pp. 310–18; Bahá'í, pp. 311, 312, 317.

10.43. American University (Washington, D.C.). Foreign Area Studies. *Iran, a Country Study.* ed. Richard F. Nyrop. 3rd ed. Washington, D.C.: American University, 1978. pp. 109, 131, 132, 134, 157.

10.44. American University of Beirut. Alumni Association. *Who's Who, 1870–1923.* Beirut: American Press, 1924. 'Shawki Hadi Rabbani', p. 142.

10.45. *The Americana Annual, 1984.* n.p. [Danbury, Conn.]: Grolier, 1984. pp. 248, 438.

10.46. Amnesty International (London). *Amnesty International Report, 1982.* London: Amnesty International Publications, 1982. p. 326.

10.47. —— *Amnesty International Report, 1983.* London: Amnesty International Publications, 1983. pp. 305, 306, 307, 308.

10.48. —— *Amnesty International Report, 1984.* London: Amnesty International Publications, 1984. pp. 333, 335.

10.49. —— *Amnesty International Report, 1985.* London: Amnesty International Publications, 1985. p. 310.

10.50. —— *Political Killings by Governments.* London: Amnesty International, 1983. p. 19.

10.51. Amnesty International USA. *Amnesty International Documentation on Iran.* New York: Amnesty International, U.S. Section, 1982. pp. 13–14.

10.52. Anderson, Norman. *Christianity and Comparative Religion.* Leicester, U.K.: Intervarsity Press, 1970, 1976. pp. 9, 14, 48–9.

10.53. Anderson, Wing. *Prophetic Years 1947–1953.* Los Angeles: Kosmon Press, 1946. p. 103.

10.54. —— *Seven Years That Changed the World, 1941–1948.* Los Angles: Kosmon Press, 1940. p. 15.

10.55. Andrews, Fannie Fern Phillips. *The Holy Land Under Mandate.* Boston: Houghton Mifflin Co., 1931. I: 200–1.

10.55a. —— *idem.* Hyperion reprint ed. Westport, Conn.: Hyperion Press, 1976. I: 200–1.

10.56. *Anglo-Palestine Yearbook.* F.J. Jacoby, ed. London: Anglo-Palestine Publications, 1946. p. 344; 1947–8. pp. 33, 323.

10.57. *Annual Act of Dedication for Peace.* Cambridge, Eng.: United Nations Association, Cambridge Branch: Cambridge Community Relations Council, 1982. p. 3.

10.58. Anthony, Piers. *God of Tarot.* New York: Berkeley Books, 1983. p. 105.

10.59. *Antichrist, Does Such a Person Exist?* Benoni, S. Afr.: Latter Rain Assemblies of South Africa, n.d. [197–] p. 6.

10.60. *The Aquarian Guide to Occult, Mystical, Religious, Magical London and Around.* Françoise Strachan, ed. London: Aquarian Press, 1970. pp. 5–6.

10.61. *The Arab World: A Handbook.* ed. Hassan S. Haddad, Basheer K. Nijim. Wilmette, Ill.: Medina Press, 1978. p. 68. (Aaug Monograph Series; 9).

10.62. *Arabic Literature to the End of the Umayyad Period.* ed. A.F.L. Beeston, T.M. Johnstone, R.B. Serjeant and G.R. Smith. Cambridge, U.K.: Cambridge University Press, 1983. (The Cambridge History of Arabic Literature). p. 213.

10.63. *The Arabs: People and Power.* editors of Encyclopaedia Britannica. New York: Bantam, 1978. pp. 154–5.

10.64. Arasteh, A. Reza; Arasteh, Josephine. *Man and Society in Iran.* Leiden: E.J. Brill, 1970. pp. 4, 57, 99.

10.65. Arberry, Arthur John. *British Orientalists.* London: William Collins, 1943. p. 24.

10.66. —— *Oriental Essays: Portraits of Seven Scholars.* London: George Allen & Unwin, 1960. pp. 168–71, 175.

10.67. —— *Persian Books.* London: Printed by Order of the Secretary of State for India, 1937. (Catalogue of the Library of the India Office; v.2 pt.6). pp. 1, 59, 63, 78, 232, 317.

10.68. —— *Shiraz, Persian City of Saints and Poets.* Norman, Okla.: University of Oklahoma

Press, 1960. (Centers of Civilization Series; Book 2). pp. xii, 25–8.

10.69. *Area Handbook for Iraq.* Harvey W. Smith [et al.] Washington, D.C.: U.S. Government Printing Office, 1971. p. 157.

10.70. *Area Handbook for the Hashemite Kingdom of Jordan.* Howard C. Reese [et al.] Washington, D.C.: U.S. Government Printing Office, 1969. p. 138.

10.71. Arguelles, Jose; Arguelles, Miriam. *Mandala.* Boulder, Colo.: Shambhala, 1972. p. 110.

10.72. Arielli, A.D. *Israel.* New York: Doubleday, 1960. p. 54.

10.73. Arjomand, Said Amir. *The Shadow of God and the Hidden Imam: Religion, Political Order, and Societal Change in Shi'ite Iran from the Beginning to 1890.* Chicago; London: University of Chicago Press, 1984. pp. 22, 245, 253–7, 269, 324n. (Publications of the Center for Middle Eastern Studies; no.17).

10.74. Armajani, Yahya. *Iran.* Englewood Cliffs, N.J.: Prentice-Hall, 1972. pp. 115–7.

10.75. —— *Middle East Past and Present.* Englewood Cliffs, N.J.: Prentice-Hall, 1970. pp. 10, 42, 224, 252–4.

10.76. Arnold, Arthur. *Through Persia by Caravan.* New York: Harper & Bros., 1877. pp. 278–80.

10.77. Arnold, Matthew. *Essays in Criticism.* London: Macmillan & Co., 1893. 'A Persian Passion Play', pp. 226–7.

10.78. —— *idem.* New York: A.L. Burt Co., n.d. pp. 166–7.

10.79. —— *idem.* Chicago: University of Chicago, 1968. pp. 137–8.

10.80. Arnot, Robert. *The Sufistic Quatrains of Omar Khayyam.* New York: M. Walter Dunne, 1903. p. xxii.

10.81. Arnson, Cynthia; Dagget, Stephen; Klare, Michael. *Background Information on the Crisis in Iran.* Washington, D.C.: Institute for Policy Studies, Mar. 1979. p. 1.

10.82. Art Gallery of Peterborough (Ont.). *Atmospheric Synthesis: Paterson Ewen, Otto Rogers, Gathie Falk, David Bierk, October 22– November 17, 1985.* Peterborough, Ont.: Art Gallery of Peterborough, 1985. pp. 3, 7.

10.83. Aschner, Ernest; Server, Zachery. *Journal to Israel: A Pictorial Guide.* New York:

Monde, 1956. p. 83, photograph of the Shrine of the Báb.

10.84. Ashbee, C.R. *A Palestine Notebook 1918– 1923.* Garden City, N.Y.: Doubleday, Page & Co., 1923. pp. 116–20; 173.

10.85. Ashford, Douglas F. *National Development and Local Reform: Morocco, Tunisia and Pakistan.* Princeton, N.J.: Princeton University Press, 1967. pp. 314–5.

10.86. Asimov, Isaac. *The Near East – 10,000 Years of History.* Boston: Houghton Mifflin, 1968. p. 252.

10.87. *The Atheist's Handbook:* USSR. Washington, D.C.: U.S. Joint Publications Research Service, 1961. pp. 58–9.

10.88. Atherton, Gertrude. *Julia France and Her Times.* New York: Macmillan Co., 1912. pp. 277–8, 280, 298, 331.

10.89. Atiyeh, George N. *The Contemporary Middle East, 1948–1973: A Selective and Annotated Bibliography.* Boston: G.K. Hall, 1975. pp. 525–6, item 5986.

10.90. Atkins, Gaius Glenn. *Modern Religious Cults and Movements.* New York: Fleming Revell, 1923. pp. 328–35.

10.91. Atkins, Gaius Glenn; Braden, C.S. *Procession of the Gods.* New York: Richard R. Smith, 1930. p. 451.

10.92. —— *idem.* London: Constable, 1931. p. 454.

10.93. —— *idem.* New York: Harper & Bros., 1936. p. 454.

10.94. *Atlas of Israel: Cartography, Physical Geography, Human and Economic Geography, History.* Jerusalem: Ṣurvey of Israel; Amsterdam: Elsevier, 1970. part XV/5.

10.95. *Australian Women Photographers, 1890– 1950.* Parkville, Vict.: George Paton Gallery, 1981. pp. 10, 28.

10.96. Aven, Gene. *My Search.* Seattle, Wash.: Life Messengers, n.d. [196–?] p. 28.

10.97. Avery, Peter. *Modern Iran.* London: Ernest Benn, 1965, 1967. pp. 44, 52–67, 76, 80, 81, 91, 97, 110, 114–5, 121, 132, 276, 277, 279, 280, 469.

10.98. Avi-Yonah, Michael. *The Holy Land.* New York: Holt, Rinehart & Winston, 1972. pp. 221, 225, photograph of Shrine of the Báb.

10.99. Ayres, Lew. *Altars of the East.* Garden City, N.Y.: Doubleday & Co., 1956. pp. 258–9.

B

10.100. Bach, Ira J. *A Guide to Chicago's Historic Suburbs on Wheels & on Foot*. Chicago; Athens, Ohio; London: Swallow Press: Ohio University Press, 1981. p. 535.

10.101. Bach, Marcus. *The Circle of Faith*. New York: Hawthorn Books, 1957. 'Shoghi Effendi', pp. 47–84; 186, mention on dust cover.

10.102. —— *Let Life Be Like This!* Englewood Cliffs, N.J.: Prentice-Hall, 1963. p. 195.

10.103. —— *Report to the Protestants*. Indianapolis, Ind.: Bobbs-Merrill Co., 1948. pp. 180, 181, 184–5, 187, 191–2, 193, 199–200, 205, 212, 217, 218, 219, 231.

10.104. —— *Strangers at the Door*. Nashville, Tenn.: Abingdon Press, 1971. pp. 74–95.

10.105. —— *They Have Found a Faith*. Indianapolis, Ind.: Bobbs-Merrill Co., 1948. pp. 189–221, 229, mention on dust cover.

10.106. Bacharach, Jere L. *A Middle East Studies Handbook*. rev. ed. Seattle, Wash.: University of Washington Press, 1984. p. 63.

10.106a. —— *A Near East Studies Handbook*. Seattle, Wash.: University of Washington Press, 1974, 1976. p. 122.

10.107. Baedeker, Karl. *Baedeker's Palestine and Syria with Routes Through Mesopotamia and Babylonia and the Island of Cyprus*. 5th ed. Leipzig: K. Baedeker; New York: C. Scribner's Sons, 1912. p. 235.

10.108. *Baedeker's Israel*. Englewood Cliffs, N.J.: Prentice-Hall, n.d. [1982?] pp. 28, 105, 106, 109.

10.109. Baer, Gabriel. *Population and Society in the Arab East*. New York: Praeger, 1964. pp. 91, 146.

10.110. Bagdadi, Zia M. *Treasures of the East: The Life of Nine Oriental Countries*. Chicago, 1929. pp. 67–91.

10.111. Bahm Archie J. *The World's Living Religions*. New York: Dell Publishing Co., 1964. pp. 333–4, 356, 368.

10.112. —— *idem*. Carbondale, Ill.: Southern Illinois University Press; London: Feffer & Simons, 1978. pp. 333–4, 356, 368.

10.113. Bahuth, J.J. *Glimpses of Palestine*. n.p., 1941. p. 26.

10.114. Baigell, Mathew. *Dictionary of American Art*. New York: Harper & Row, 1979. pp. 354–5 about Mark Tobey.

10.115. Bainbridge, William. *Around the World Tour of Christian Missions*. Boston: D. Lathrop, 1882. pp. 360, 368.

10.116. Baker, Richard St Barbe. *Famous Trees of Bible Lands*. London: H.H. Greves, 1974. pp. 32, 141.

10.117. —— *I Planted Trees*. London: Lutterworth, 1944. pp. 147–50.

10.118. —— *Kamiti: A Forester's Dream*. London; Cardiff: George Ronald, 1958. pp. 65–6.

10.119. —— *Land of Tané: The Threat of Erosion*. London: Lutterworth Press, 1956. p. 133.

10.120. —— *Men of the Trees: In the Mahogany Forests of Kenya & Nigeria*. New York: Dial Press, 1931. p. 204.

10.121. —— *My Life, My Trees*. London: Lutterworth, 1970. pp. 64, 74, 78, 114–15, 133, 148.

10.122. —— *idem*. 1st paperback ed. Findhorn, Moray, Scotland: Findhorn Publications, 1979. pp. 61, 66, 71, 74, 110–1, 128, 129, 130, 142, 143.

10.122a. —— *idem*. 2nd ed. Forres, Scotland: Findhorn Press, 1985. Same page references as 10.122.

10.123. *Baker Lake, N.W.T., 1870–1970*. Baker Lake, N.W.T., 1970. pp. 74–7.

10.124. *Baker's Pocket Dictionary of Religious Terms*. Donald T. Kauffman, ed. Grand Rapids, Mich.: Baker Book House, 1967. pp. 10, 55, 56, 57.

10.125. Bakhash, Shaul. *Iran: Monarchy, Bureaucracy and Reform Under the Qajars, 1858–1896*. London: Ithaca Press, 1978. pp. 24, 324.

10.126. —— *The Reign of the Ayatollahs: Iran and the Islamic Revolution*. London: I.B. Tauris & Co., 1985. pp. 24, 26, 87, 113, 221.

10.126a. Balfour, Edward. *The Cyclopaedia of India and of Eastern and Southern Asia*. 3rd ed. London: Bernard Quaritch. 1885. "Babi." I:216.

10.126b. —— *idem*. Graz, Austria: Akademische Druk- u. Verlaganstalt, 1967. "Babi." I:216.

10.127. Balfour, J.M. *Recent Happenings in Persia*. Edinburgh; London; William Blackwood and Sons, 1922. pp. 51–3.

10.128. Ball, John. *The Fourteenth Point.* Boston: Little Brown & Co., 1973. pp. 32, 67, 95, 153, 207, 231, 276, 296, 312. Novel.

10.129. Bamdad, Badr-ol-Moluk. *From Darkness into Light: Women's Emancipation in Iran.* Hicksville, N.Y.: Exposition Press, 1977. p. 23.

10.130. Banani, Amin. *The Modernization of Iran, 1921–1941.* Stanford, Calif.: Stanford University Press, 1961. pp. 25–7, 42, 95–7.

10.131. Bancroft, Anne. *The New Religious World.* London: Macdonald, 1985. pp. 26–9, 42, 43, 44.

10.132. Barbour, G.F. *The Life of Alexander Whyte, D.D..* New York: George H. Doran Co., 1923, 1925. pp. 554–5.

10.133. Bardsley, Graham F. *Cults, Christianity, and Its Distortion.* Falls Church, Va.: PS Services, 1977. pp. 61–70.

10.134. Barnes, Frank. *How to Detect a False Religion.* Spokane, Wash.: Barnes, n.d. [1980?] Short pamphlet with passing reference.

10.135. Barnett, Stephen; Bogard, Mel. *Alternative Auckland: A Survival Guide.* Auckland, N.Z.: Alternative Publishing, 1978. p. 194.

10.136. Barr, Margaret. *The Great Unity: A New Approach to Religious Education.* Boston: Beacon Press, 1951. pp. 83–5, 95.

10.137. Barrows, John Henry. *Christianity the World-Religion.* Chicago: A.C. McClurg & Co., 1897. pp. 38–9.

10.138. Barthold, W. *An Historical Geography of Iran.* trans. Svat Soucek. Princeton, N.J.: Princeton University Press, 1984. pp. 168, 213, 220.

10.139. Barton, George, A. *The Religions of the World.* 4th ed. Chicago: University of Chicago Press, 1917. p. 111.

10.140. —— *idem.* New York: Greenwood Press, 1969. p. 111.

10.141. Barton, James L. *The Christian Approach to Islam.* Boston: Pilgrim Press, 1918. pp. 197–200.

10.141a. Barton, Louis. *Land of Promise.* London: Werner Laurie, 1956. p. 23, facing p. 48.

10.142. Baseman, Bob. *The Holy Land: Pictorial Guide and Souvenir.* Jerusalem: Palphot, n.d. [197–] pp. 59–60.

10.143. Basio, R.G. *The Moths.* Manila, Philippines: Basio, 1981 (Manila: Mss Printers). Back cover.

10.144. Bassett, James. *Persia, Eastern Mission.* Philadelphia, Pa., 1890. pp. 51, 182–3.

10.145. —— *Persia, the Land of the Imams: A Narrative of Travel and Residence, 1871–1885.* New York: Charles Scribner's Sons, 1886. pp. 77, 213–4, 229, 297–300, 338.

10.146. Bat Haim, Hadassah. *Galilee and Golan.* Jerusalem; London: Weidenfeld and Nicolson, c1973. (Weidenfeld Colour Guides to Israel). pp. 44–5.

10.147. Bates, Francis Van Ness Howe. *Christianity and Cosmopolitan Civilization.* Boston: Christopher Publishing House, 1966. p. 359.

10.148. Baudouin, Charles. *Contemporary Studies.* trans. E. and C. Paul. New York: E.P. Dutton, 1925. 'Bahaism: A Movement Toward the Community of Mankind', pp. 131–46.

10.149. —— *idem.* Freeport, N.Y.: Books for Libraries Press, 1969. 'Bahaism: A Movement Toward the Community of Mankind', pp. 131–46.

10.150. Bausani, Alessandro. *The Persians from the Earliest Days to the Twentieth Century.* London: Elek, 1971. pp. 166–7.

10.151. *Baxter Dictionary of Dates and Events.* ed. Mark Napier. Toronto; London; New York: Baxter Publishing, 1963. pp. 21, 22.

10.152. Bayat, Mangol. *Mysticism and Dissent: Socioreligious Thought in Qajar Iran.* Syracuse, N.Y.: Syracuse University Press, 1982. pp. 58, 79–81, 87–131, 179–80.
Review:
Amanat, Abbas. *Iranian Studies* (New York), v.17 no.4 (Autumn 1984), pp. 467–75. Bábí/Bahá'í, pp. 468–74.

10.153. Bayne, E.A. *Persian Kingship in Transition.* New York: American Universities Field Staff, 1968. pp. 45–6, 247.

10.154. *Bazak Guide to Israel, 1975–1976.* Tel Aviv: Bazak, 1975. pp. 320–4, 334, 351.

10.154a. *Bazak Guide to Israel.* prod. by Avraham Levi. Jerusalem: Bazak Israel Guidebook Publishers, 1978. pp. 294, 304.

10.155. *Bazak Guide to Israel, 1983–84.* Jerusalem: Bazak Israel Guidebook Publishers, 1983. pp. 81–2, 362, 364–5, 386, 389, 394.

10.156. *Bazak Israel Guide.* Tel Aviv; Jerusalem; New York: Bazak Israel Guidebook Publishers, c1972. pp. 23–4, 313, 318, 319, 341, 345.

10.157. *Be Here Now: Remember.* New York: Crown Publishing, 1978. p. 76 of 'Cookbook' section.

10.158. Bell, Archie. *The Spell of the Holy Land.* Boston: Page Co., 1915. pp. 258, 304–21. Full page photograph: Abbas Effendi, p. 304 facing page.

10.159. Bell, Gertrude. *The Desert and the Sown.* London: W. Heinemann, 1907. pp. 149–50, 193. Picture of Mishkín-Qalam, p. 149.

10.160. —— *idem.* New York: E.P. Dutton, 1907. pp. 149–50, 193. Picture of Mishkín-Qalam, p. 149.

10.161. —— *The Letters of Gertrude Bell.* London: Ernest Benn, 1927. I: 131–2.

10.162. —— *idem.* New York: Boni & Liveright, 1927. I: 131–2.

10.163. Bellow, Saul. *The Adventures of Augie March.* Greenwich, Conn.: Fawcett Publications, c1953. Bahá'í temple, p. 253.

10.164. Ben-Horin, Eliahu. *The Middle East: Crossroads of History.* New York: W.W. Norton, 1943. p. 70.

10.165. Benard, Cheryl; Khalilzad, Zalmay. *'The Government of God': Iran's Islamic Republic.* New York: Columbia University Press, 1984. p. 133. (The Modern Middle East Series; no.15).

10.166. Benjamin, S.G.W. *Persia and the Persians.* Boston: Ticknor & Co., 1887. p. 353–5.

10.167. Bennigsen, Alexandre; Quelquejay, Chantal. *The Evolution of the Muslim Nationalities of the USSR and Their Linguistic Problems.* Oxford: Central Asian Research Centre, 1961. p. 39.

10.168. —— *Islam in the Soviet Union.* London: Pall Mall Press, 1967. pp. 4, 19, 172.

10.169. Bentley, Sid. *Religions of Our Neighbors.* Victoria, B.C.: Province of British Columbia, Ministry of Education, 1983. I: 2, 9; VIII: 24–32.

10.170. Bentwich, Norman. *Fulfilment in the Promised Land, 1917–1937.* Westport, Conn.: Hyperion Press, 1976. pp. 91–2.

10.171. —— *Israel.* New York: Toronto: McGraw-Hill, 1952. pp. 183–4.

10.172. —— *Israel and Her Neighbours: A Short Historical Geography.* London: Rider and Company, 1955. pp. 89–90.

10.173. —— *Israel Resurgent.* London: Ernest Benn, 1960. p. 206.

10.174. —— *Mandate Memories, 1918–1948.* London: Hogarth Press, 1965. pp. 40, 46.

10.174a. ——. *idem.* New York: Schocken Books, 1965. pp. 40, 46.

10.175. —— *My 77 Years: An Account of My Life and Times, 1883–1960.* Philadelphia, Pa.: Jewish Publication Society of America, 1961. 'Abdu'l-Bahá, pp. 57–8.

10.176. —— *Palestine.* London: Ernest Benn, 1934. (The Moslem World: A Survey of Historical Forces). pp. 234–5.

10.177. —— *The Religious Foundations of Internationalism.* London: George Allen & Unwin, 1933. pp. 178–9, 241.

10.178. —— *A Wanderer in the Promised Land.* New York: Charles Scribner's Sons, 1933. pp. 78–80.

10.179. —— *Wanderer in War, 1939–45.* London: Victor Gollancz, 1946. p. 181.

10.180. Berenson, Mary. *A Modern Pilgrimage.* New York: D. Appleton, 1933. pp. 30–2.

10.181. Bergé, Carol. *A Couple Called Moebius.* Indianapolis, Ind.: Bobbs-Merrill, 1972. 'The Farm Woman', pp. 23–34.

10.182. Berrett, Lamar C. *Discovering the World of the Bible.* Nashville, Tenn.: Thomas Nelson Publishers, 1979. pp. 333–5.

10.183. Berry, Gerald L. *Religions of the World.* New York: Barnes & Noble, 1947, 1956, 1965, 1968. p. 126.

10.184. Berry, W.J. *A Brief Survey of Present-Day Cults, False Teachings, Satanic Deceptions, with a Warning to God's People.* Elon College, N.C.: Primitive Publications, 1970. pp. 24–5. [Bjorling 828]

10.185. Bethmann, Erich W. *Bridge to Islam: A Study of the Religious Forces of Islam and Christianity in the Near East.* London: George Allen & Unwin, 1953. p. 162.

10.186. —— idem. Nashville, Tenn.: Southern Publishing Association, 1950. p. 192.

10.187. Bettany, G.T. *Mohammedanism and Other Religions of Mediterranean Countries.* London: Ward Lock & Co., 1892. pp. 167–9.

10.188. —— *The World's Religions: A Popular Account of Religions Ancient and Modern.* London; New York; Melbourne: Ward, Lock & Co., 1890. pp. 574–5.

10.189. —— *The World's Religions: A Comprehensive Popular Account of All the Principal Religions of Civilized and Uncivilized Peoples.* New York: Christian Literature Company, 1891. pp. 574–5.

10.190. Bevington, Colin. *New Light from the*

East. London: Falcon Booklets, 1974. pp. 19–23.

10.191. *Beyond the Blues: New Poems by American Negroes*. Selected and introduced by Rosey E. Pool. Lympne, Kent: Hand and Flower Press, 1962. p. 111.

10.192. Bhagavan Das. *The Essential Unity of All Religions*. Wheaton, Ill.: Theosophical Press, 1966. p. 525.

10.193. Bharati, Agehananda. *The Light at the Center: Context and Pretext of Modern Mysticism*. Santa Barbara, Calif.: Ross-Erikson, 1976. pp. 219, 233.

10.194. Bibesco, Princess V. (Marthe Lucie). *The Eight Paradises*. trans. from French. New York: E.P. Dutton & Co., 1923. pp. 31–6.

10.195. Bible. English. Authorized. 1981. *Walter Martin's Cults Reference Bible; King James Version with Reference Notes, Topical Index, Bibliography, a Guide to the Major Cults, and Other Study Helps*. Santa Ana, Calif.: Vision House, c1981. pp. 4, 5, 13–19, 793n, 17, 23, 25–6, as well as various references throughout the New Testament in notes stating the 'cultic misuse' of the verses.

10.196. *The Bible of Mankind*. comp. and ed. Mirza Ahmad Sohrab. New York: Universal, 1939. pp. 590–731, 735–6.
   Review:
Calverley, Edwin E., *The Moslem World* (Hartford, Conn.), v.30 no.2 (Apr. 1940), pp. 200–2.

10.197. *Bibliographical Guide to Iran: The Middle East Library Committee Guide*. ed. L.P. Elwell-Sutton. Brighton, Sussex: Harvester Press; Totowa, N.J.: Barnes & Noble Books, 1983. MacEoin, Denis, 'Shaikhism, Babism, Baha'ism', pp. 79–84.

10.198. Bier, Aharon. *Eretz Israel: A Jewish Pilgrim's Companion*. Jerusalem: Department for Torah Education and Culture in the Diaspora of the World Zionist Organization, 1976. p. 174.

10.199. Bill, James Alban. *The Politics of Iran: Groups, Classes, and Modernization*. Columbus, Ohio: Charles E. Merrill Pub. Co., 1972. pp. 45n, 61.

10.200. Bill, James Alban; Leiden, Carl. *The Middle East: Politics and Power*. Boston: Allyn and Bacon, 1974. pp. 26, 57, 90n.

10.201. —— *Politics in the Middle East*. 2nd ed. Boston; Toronto: Little, Brown and Company, 1984. pp. 39, 73.

10.202. Binder, Leonard. *Iran: Political De-velopment in a Changing Society*. Berkeley,

Calif.: University of California Press, 1962. pp. 74, 161–3, 243, 296.

10.203. —— *Revolution in Iran: Three Essays*. New York: American Academic Association for Peace in the Middle East, 1980. (Middle East Review Special Studies; no.1). p. 62.

10.204. Binder, Louis Richard. *Modern Religious Cults and Society: A Sociological Interpretation of a Modern Religious Phenomenon*. Boston, 1933. p. 46.

10.205. —— *idem*. New York: AMS Press, 1970. p. 46.

10.206. Binning, Robert B.M. *A Journal of Two Years' Travel in Persia, Ceylon, etc*. London: W.H. Allen & Co., 1857. I: 403–8.

10.207. *A Biographical Dictionary of Artists*. London: Macmillan, 1983. p. 676.

10.208. Bishop, Mrs (Isabella L. Bird). *Journeys in Persia and Kurdistan*. New York: G.P. Putnam's Sons, 1891. I: 273.

10.209. —— *idem*. London: John Murray, 1891. I: 273.

10.210. Bishop, Peter D. *Words in World Religions*. London: SCM Press, 1949. p. 120.

10.211. Blaiklock, E.M. *Eight Days in Israel*. London: Ark Publishing, 1980. p. 119.

10.212. Bliss, Frederick Jones. *Religions of Modern Syria and Palestine*. New York: Charles Scribner's Sons, 1912. pp. 19–20.

10.213. —— *idem*. New York: AMS Press, 1972. pp. 19–20.

10.214. Bliss, Kathleen. *The Future of Religion*. Harmondsworth, Middlesex: Penguin Books, 1972. p. 14.

10.215. Bloomfield, Bernard. *Israel Diary*. New York: Crown Publishers, 1950. pp. 3–4.

10.216. Blunt, Wilfred. *A Persian Spring*. London: James Barrie Books, 1957. p. 251.

10.217. —— *Secret History of the English Occupation of Egypt: Being a Personal Narrative of Events*. New York: Knopf, 1922. p. 63.

10.218. Boddy, Alexander A. *Days in Galilee and Scenes in Judaea: Together with Some Account of a Solitary Cycling Journey in Southern Palestine*. London: Gay & Bird, 1900. pp. 17–20.

10.219. Boeckel, Florence Brewer. *Between War and Peace*. New York: Macmillan Co., 1928. pp. 102–3.

10.220. Bogue, R.H. *Compounds in Portland Cement Revealed by High-Temperature Research Upon Cement Compounds*. Washington, D.C.:

Portland Cement Association Fellowship at the National Bureau of Standards, 1935. pp. 2, 11.

10.221. Bolitho, Hector. *A Biographer's Notebook*. New York: Macmillan Co., 1950. p. 22.
Queen Marie's letter to 'an American friend' in 1934 in which she seems to deny that she was a Bahá'í at the time.

10.222. —— *idem*. London: Longman's, Green, n.d. [1950] p. 22.

10.223. Bolus, E.J. *The Influence of Islam: 'A Study of the Effects of Islam Upon the Psychology & Civilization of the Races Which Profess It'*. London: Temple Bar Publishing Co., 1932. pp. 34, 84–5.

10.224. *A Book of Daily Readings: Passages in Prose and Verse for Solace and Meditation*. Selected and arranged by G.F. Maine. London; Glasgow: Collins, n.d. [195–?] Quotes from Abbas Effendi ('Abdu'l-Bahá), pp. 63, 113.

10.225. *Botswana '82 Year Book*. Gaborone, 1982. p. 155.

10.226. Boulton, Marjorie. *Zamenhof, Creator of Esperanto*. London: Routledge and Kegan Paul, 1960. pp. 211–12.

10.227. Bouquet, A.C. *Comparative Religion*. Harmondsworth, Middlesex, Eng.; New York: Penguin Books, 1941. p. 214.

10.228. —— *idem*. 4th rev. ed. Melbourne; London; Baltimore: Penguin Books, 1953. p. 282.

10.229. —— *Sacred Books of the World: A Companion Source-Book to Comparative Religion*: Harmondsworth: Penguin, 1954, 1967. pp. 312–14.

10.230. Bowyer, Mathew J. *Encyclopedia of Mystical Terminology*. South Brunswick; New York: A.S. Barnes; London: Thomas Yoseloff, 1979. p. 16.

10.231. Boyce, Mary. *Zoroastrians: Their Religious Beliefs and Practices*. London: Routledge and Kegan Paul, 1979. p. 212.

10.232. Braden, Charles S. *Jesus Compared*. Englewood Cliffs, N.J.: Prentice-Hall, 1957. p. 86.

10.233. —— *The Scriptures of Mankind: An Introduction*. New York: Macmillan Co., 1952. pp. 472–3, 485.

10.234. —— *Spirits in Rebellion: The Rise and Development of New Thought*. Dallas, Tex.: Southern Methodist University Press, 1963. p. 395.

10.235. —— *These Also Believe: A Study of Modern American Cults & Minority Religious Move-*

ments. New York: Macmillan, 1949. p. 464.

10.236. —— *The World's Religions*. Nashville, Tenn.: Cokesbury Press, 1939. p. 233.

10.237. —— *idem*. New York; Nashville, Tenn.: Abingdon Press, 1954. p. 233.

10.238. Bradley, David G. *Circle of Faith: A Preface to the Study of World Religions*. New York: Abingdon Press, 1966. p. 21.

10.239. Bradshaw, Jane. *Eight Major Religions in Britain*. London: Edward Arnold, 1979. pp. 155–70.

10.240. Brandreth, Gyles. *Brandreth's Party Games: 150 Games for Adults*. London: Eyre Methuen, 1972. p. 83.

10.241. Brasch, R. *The Eternal Flame*. Sydney, N.S.W.: [etc.]: Angus and Robertson, 1958. pp. 80–1, photograph of Shrine of the Báb opposite p. 178.

10.242. Breese, David. *Know the Marks of Cults*. Wheaton, Ill.: Victor Books, 1975. p. 48.
Refers erroneously to Meher Baba as leader of the 'Bahai cult'.

10.243. Brelvi, Mahmud. *The Muslim Neighbors of Pakistan*. Lahore, Pakistan: Ripon Printing Press, 1950. p. 39.

10.244. Brick, Daniel; Riwkin-Brick, Anna. *Palestine*. Cleveland, Ohio: World Publishing Co., n.d. [1949?] p. [60].

10.245. Brightman, Edgar S. *Personality and Religion*. New York: Abingdon Press, 1934. p. 108.

10.246. —— *idem*. New York: AMS Press, 1979. p. 108.

10.247. *Britain's Opium War Against the U.S.* New York: U.S. Labor Party, 1978. pp. 24–5.

10.248. *Britannica Book of the Year*. Chicago: Encyclopaedia Britannica. 1983, p. 592; 1984, pp. 593, 601; 1985, p. 358.

10.249. *The Britannica Encyclopedia of American Art*. Chicago: Encyclopaedia Britannica, n.d. [1973] p. 563 in reference to Mark Tobey.

10.249a. *Britannica Junior Encyclopaedia for Boys and Girls*. Chicago: Encyclopaedia Britannica, 1975. 'Baha'i Faith', III:19–20.

10.250. British Empire Exhibition (1924: London). *Palestine Pavilion Handbook and Tourist Guide*. ed. Palestine Pavilion Organisation Committee. London: Fleetway Press, 1924. p. 42.

10.250a. *The British Encyclopaedia*. London: Odhams Press Limited, 1933. 'Babism', I: 441.

10.251. British Museum. Department of Oriental Printed Books and Manuscripts. *Catalogue of Arabic Books in the British Museum.* by A.G. Ellis. [London]: Trustees of the British Museum, 1967. I: 264, 655.

10.252. —— *Second Supplementary Catalogue of Arabic Printed Books in the British Museum.* comp. Alexander S. Fulton, Martin Lings. London: Trustees of the British Museum, 1959. col. 24, 71, 332, 536, 573.

10.253. —— *Third Supplementary Catalogue of Arabic Printed Books in the British Library, 1958–1969.* comp. Martin Lings and Yasim Hamid Safadi. London: Published for the British Library Board by British Museum Publications, 1977. I: 12, 170, 183; IV: 744.

10.254. British Refugee Council. *Refugee Report 1984: An International Survey.* ed. Jeff Crisp and Clive Nettleton. London: British Refugee Council, 1984. p. 56.

10.255. Brockelmann, Carl. *History of the Islamic Peoples.* trans. Joel Carmichael and Moshe Perlmann. New York: Putman's, 1947. p. 326, 424–7.

10.256. —— *idem.* New York: Capricorn Books, 1960. pp. 326, 424–7.

10.257. Broderick, Robert C. *Historic Churches of the United States.* New York: Wilfred Funk, 1958. pp. 186–91.

10.258. Brown, Arthur Judson. *One Hundred Years: A History of the Foreign Missionary Work of the Presbyterian Church in the U.S.A., with Some Account of Countries, Peoples and the Policies and Problems of Modern Missions: Book One.* New York: Fleming H. Revell Co., 1936. pp. 480–1.

10.259. Browne, Edward Granville. *A Brief Narrative of Recent Events in Persia: Followed by a Translation of 'The Four Pillars of the Persian Constitution'.* London: Luzac, 1909. p. 10.

10.260. —— *A Descriptive Catalogue of the Oriental MSS. Belonging to the Late E.G. Browne.* completed and ed. with a memoir of the author and a bibliography of his writings by Reynold A. Nicholson. Cambridge: University Press, 1932. 'Shaykhí and Bábí MSS'. pp. 53–87.
Review:
Zwemer, Samuel M., *The Moslem World* (Hartford, Conn.), v.23 no.2 (Apr. 1933), p. 211.

10.261. —— *A History of Persian Literature in Modern Times, (A.D. 1500–1924).* Cambridge: Cambridge University Press, 1924. pp. 121, 122, 147, 149–51, 153–4, 156, 162, 187n, 194–220, 329, 411, 415, 420–30, 446. (A Literary History of Persia, v.4).

10.262. —— *A History of Persian Literature Under Tartar Dominion (A.D. 1265–1502).* Cambridge: Cambridge University Press, 1920. pp. 432, 452, 465, 470. (A Literary History of Persia; v.3).

·10.263. —— *A Literary History of Persia.* 4 vols. Cambridge: Cambridge University Press, n.d. [1928–1930] I: 86, 98, 99, 100, 101, 130, 165, 170, 172, 311, 312, 407, 410, 415, 423; II: 41, 70, 89, 187, 202, 460; III: 432, 452, 465, 470; IV: 121, 122, 147, 149–51, 153–4, 156, 162, 187n, 194–220, 329, 411, 415, 420–30, 446.

10.264. —— *Of the Culminating Event of This My Journey, Some Few Words at Least Must Be Said* . . . n.p., n.d. [19--] Taken from the introduction to *A Traveller's Narrative*; includes Browne's pen-portrait of Bahá'u'lláh. 1 p.

10.265. —— *The Persian Revolution of 1905–1909.* Cambridge: Cambridge University Press, 1910. pp. xvi-xvii, xxii, 11, 45, 60–2, 106–7, 148, 424–9.

10.266. —— *idem.* New York: Barnes & Noble, n.d. [1966] pp. xvi-xvii, xxii, 11, 45, 60–2, 106–7, 148, 424–9.

10.267. —— *idem.* London: Cass, 1966. pp. xvi-xvii, xxii, 11, 45, 60–2, 106–7, 148, 424–9.

10.268. —— *Press and Poetry in Modern Persia.* Cambridge: Cambridge University Press, 1914. pp. 18n, 59, 235–6, 294, 310.

10.269. —— *idem.* Los Angeles: Kalimát Press, 1982. pp. 18n, 59, 235–6, 294, 310.
Review:
Sprachman, Paul. *MELA Notes* (Los Angeles), no.3 (Fall 1984), pp. 19–21. Baha'í Faith: p. 19.

10.270. —— *A Supplementary Handlist of the Muhammadan Manuscripts Including All Those Written in the Arabic Character Preserved in the Libraries of the University and Colleges of Cambridge.* Cambridge: Cambridge University Press, 1922. pp. 35, 239, 240.

10.271. —— *A Year Amongst the Persians.* London: Adam and Charles Black, 1893. pp. 58–66, 74, 100–2, 148–53, 173, 194, 203, 205–18, 228–9, 232, 269–71, 275, 294, 297–339, 367, 394–409, 421, 437, 440, 443–5, 450–2, 457–8, 463–6, 469–70, 475–9, 481–96, 499–533, 535, 540–8, 550, 562–3, 566.
Reviews:
The Critic (New York), v.24 (n.s. 21) (Jan. 13, 1894), p. 16.
Athenaeum (London), v.103 (Jan. 20, 1894), pp. 76–8.
The Nation (New York), v.58 (Apr. 26, 1894), pp. 317–18.

The Spectator (London), v.72 (Apr. 28, 1894), pp. 559–60.

10.272. —— *idem.* New York: Macmillan; Cambridge: University Press, 1926. *See* 10.271 for paging.

10.273. —— *idem.* intro. by Denis MacEoin. London: Century Publishing; New York: Hippocrene Books; Toronto: Lester & Oppen Dennys Deneau Marketing Services, 1984. pp. xi-xiii, 64–72, 81, 110–12, 162–7, 189, 212, 221–39, 253, 317, 321, 326–71, 373, 399, 401–2, 403, 431–48, 452–3, 457, 460–1, 475, 478, 485–7, 492–5, 500–1, 504, 509–10, 514, 520–42, 545–82, 584–5, 587, 590–9, 601, 604, 608, 612, 614–15, 617–19.

10.274. Browne, Laurence E. *The Prospects of Islam.* London: S.C.M. Press, 1944. pp. 17, 84–7, 89, 116, 199.

10.275. Bundy, E.C. *Collectivism in the Churches.* Wheaton, Ill.: Church League of America, 1960. pp. 234, 241.

10.276. Bunge, Martin L. *The Story of Religion from Caveman to Superman.* Pasadena, Calif.: Fellowship Publishing House, 1931. pp. 209–10.

10.277. Burr, Nelson R. *Religion in American Life.* New York: Appleton-Century-Crofts,

1971. (Goldentree Bibliographies in American History). pp. 46–7.

10.278. Burton, Ursula; Janice Dolley. *Christian Evolution: Moving Towards a Global Spirituality.* Wellingborough, U.K.: Turnstone Press, 1984. p. 96.

10.279. Bushnell, George D. *Wilmette – a History.* Wilmette, Ill.: Village of Wilmette, 1984. pp. 95, 100, 101, 103, 162.

10.280. Butler, Donald G. *Many Lights.* London: Geoffrey Chapman, 1975. pp. 157–61.

10.281. Butterworth, John. *Cults and New Faiths.* Tring, Herts.: Lion Publishing, 1981. (A Book of Beliefs). pp. 44–7.

10.282. *By Word and Deed: Sacred Writings.* selected and arr. Elsie Cranmer. London: Mitre Press, 1973. pp. 65–75.

10.283. Byford-Jones, W. *Quest in the Holy Land.* London: Robert Hale, 1961. p. 130.

10.284. Byng, Edward J. *The World of the Arabs.* Boston: Little, Brown & Co., 1944. pp. 270, 307.

10.285. Byrne, Dymphna. *Israel & the Holy Land: Welcome to Israel and the Holy Land.* Glasgow; London: Collins, 1985. pp. 32, 36.

C

10.286. Calef, Noël [text and captions]; Molinard, Patrice [photographs]. *The Israel I Love.* New York: Tudor Publishing Company, 1966. pp. 26–7, colour photograph of the Shrine of the Báb.

10.287. Calef, Noël. *The Israel I Love.* Israel: Leon Amiel Publisher, 1977. p. 35.

10.288. *The Cambridge History of Islam.* ed. P.M. Holt, Ann K.S. Lambton, Bernard Lewis. Cambridge: University Press, 1970. I: 452, 454, 618–19.

10.289. Canada. Statistics Canada. *Census of Canada, 1981: Population, Ethnic Origin.* Ottawa, Ont.: Statistics Canada, 1984. pp. 5-1 – 5-32.

10.290. Canada House Cultural Centre Gallery (London, Eng.). *The Canadian Landscape: Paintings Selected from the Ontario Heritage Foundation, Firestone Art Collection.* London, Eng.: Canada House Cultural Centre Gallery,

1983. p. 29 in section on Bahá'í painter Otto Donald Rogers.

10.291. *Canadian Centennial Anthology of Prayer.* Canada: The Canadian Interfaith Conference, 1967. p. 118.

10.292. *The Canadian Encyclopedia.* Edmonton, Alta.: Hurtig Publisher, 1985. Martin, J. Douglas, 'Baha'i Faith', I: 127–8.

10.293. Canavarro, Marie de S. *Insight Into the Far East.* Los Angeles: Wetzel, 1925. pp. 156–7, 165–6, 168.

10.294. Canney, Maurice. *An Encyclopaedia of Religions.* London: G. Routledge & Sons, 1921. 'Babism', pp. 48–9; 'Bahaism', pp. 49–50.

10.295. —— *idem.* Detroit, Mich.: Gale Re-search Co., 1970. pp. 48–9, 49–50.

10.296. —— *idem.* Delhi: NAG Publishers, 1976. pp. 48–9, 49–50.

10.297.   Carey, Iskandar. *Orang Asli: The Aboriginal Tribes of Peninsular Malaysia*. Kuala Lumpur: Oxford University Press, 1976. pp. 325–6, 329, 337.

10.298.   Carlsen, Robin Woodsworth. *The Imam and His Islamic Revolution: A Journey into Heaven and Hell*. Victoria, B.C.: Snow Man Press, 1982. pp. 16, 156, 160–2, 182–3, 191.

10.299.   Carmody, Denise Lardner; Carmody, John Tulley. *Ways to the Center: An Introduction to World Religions*. 2nd ed. Belmont, Calif.: Wadsworth Publishing Company, 1984. p. 333.

10.300.   Carpenter, Edward. *Pagan and Christian Creeds: Their Origin and Meaning*. New York: Blue Ribbon Books, 1920. pp. 153, 214–17.

10.301.   —— idem. New York: Harcourt, Brace & Co., 1920. pp. 153, 214–17.

10.302.   Carpenter, J. Estlin. *Comparative Religion*. New York: Henry Holt & Co.; London: Williams and Norgate, n.d. pp. 70–1, 188.

10.303.   Carpenter, J. Estlin; Wicksteed, P.H. *Studies in Theology*. London: J.M. Dent, 1903. pp. 254–6.

10.304.   Carpenter, Johonet Halsted. *The Well of Understanding*. Durham, N.H.: Sophia Press, 1982. *passim*.

10.305.   Carroll, Michael. *From a Persian Tea-House*. London: John Murray, 1960. p. 15.

10.306.   *Carta's Official Guide to Israel and Complete Gazetteer to All Sites in the Holy Land*. Jerusalem: Ministry of Defence Publishing House: Carta, 1983. pp. 62, 69–70, 90, 173, 176.

10.306a.   Carter, Paul. *The Spiritual Crisis of the Gilded Age*. Dekalb, Ill.: Northern Illinois University Press, 1971. pp. 218–19, 221.

10.307.   Carus, Paul. *Philosophy as a Science*. Chicago: Open Court Publishing Co., 1909. p. 98.

10.308.   —— *The Pleroma: An Essay on the Origin of Christianity*. Chicago: Open Court Publishing Co., 1909. p. 111.

10.309.   Cash, W. Wilson. *Christiandom and Islam*. New York: Harper & Bros., 1937. pp. 68, 133.

10.310.   —— *The Expansion of Islam*. London: Church Missionary Society, 1928. pp. 8, 117–21.

10.311.   —— *Persia Old and New*. London: Church Missionary Society, 1929. pp. 12–13.

10.312.   Catarivas, David. *Israel*. London: Edward Hulton, 1959. p. 32.

10.313.   Cave, Sydney. *An Introduction to the Study of Some Living Religions of the East*. London: Duckworth & Co., 1921. pp. 234–5.

10.314.   —— idem. New York: Charles Scribner's Sons 1923. pp. 234–5.

10.315.   —— *Living Religions of the East*. New York: Charles Scribner's Sons, 1922. pp. 234–5, 247.

10.316.   Cavendish, Richard. *The Great Religions*. New York: Arco Publishing Co., 1980. pp. 238, 239, photograph of Shrine of the Báb.

10.317.   *The Century Cyclopedia of Names: A Pronouncing and Etymological Dictionary of Names in Geography, Biography, Mythology, History, Ethnology, Art, Archaeology, Fiction, etc.* New York: Century Co., 1894. 'Bab', 'Babi', pp. 104–5.

10.318.   *A Century of Mission Work in Iran (Persia), 1834–1934: A Record of the Work of the Iran (Persia) Mission of the Board of Foreign Missions of the Presbyterian Church in the U.S.A.* Beirut: American Press, n.d. [1936] pp. 131, 138.

10.319.   Cerminara, Gina. *Insights for the Age of Aquarius*. Englewood Cliffs, N.J.: Prentice-Hall, 1973. p. 245.

10.320.   —— *Many Lives, Many Loves*. New York: William Sloane Associates, 1963. p. 216.

10.321.   Chambers, Grant; Chambers, Bayley. *This Age of Conflict*. New York: Harcourt, Brace & Co., 1943. p. 680.

10.321a.   *Chambers Biographical Dictionary*. ed. J.O. Thorne, T.C. Collocott. rev. ed. Edinburgh: Chambers, 1984. 'Abdu'l-Bahá, p. 2; Bahá'u'lláh, p. 81.

10.322.   *Chamber's Encyclopaedia: A Dictionary of Universal Knowledge*. New ed. London and Edinburgh: William & Robert Chambers; Philadelphia: Lippincott, 1901. I: 628.

10.323.   *Chambers's Encyclopaedia*. New rev. ed. London: International Learning Systems, n.d. [1966]. Alessandro Bausani, 'Babi-Baha'i', II: 20.

10.324.   Champion, Selwyn Gurney. *The Eleven Religions and Their Proverbial Lore*. New York: E.P. Dutton 1946. pp. xiii, 172, 181, 184–8, 192, 193, 196–200, 337, 339.

10.325.   *Change and the Muslim World*. ed. Philip H. Stoddard, David C. Cuthbell, Margaret W. Sullivan. Syracuse, N.Y.: Syracuse University Press, 1981. pp. 118–19.

10.325a.   Chanler, Julie. *His Messengers Went Forth*. il. Olin Dows. New York: Coward-McCann, 1948. pp. 53–64.

10.326. Chatwin, Bruce. *In Patagonia.* London: Picador, 1979. pp. 34–6.

10.327. Chicago World Flower and Garden Show (6th: 1964: Chicago). *Official Guide Book.* Chicago, 1964. pp. 11, 17, 28, 29.

10.328. Chicago World Flower and Garden Show (7th: 1965: Chicago). *The Chicago World Flower and Garden Show, March 20–28, 1965.* Chicago, 1965. pp. 9, 16–17.

10.329. Child, C.W. *Your Hand Read by Post.* London: C.W. Child, n.d. [1914?] 'Abdu'l-Bahá listed as one whose palm has been read.

10.330. *Childcraft: The How and Why Library.* Chicago: World Book, 1976. 'Gift of Stone', X: 72–3. Temple in Wilmette, Ill.

10.331. Chirol, Valentine. *Fifty Years in a Changing World.* New York: Harcourt, Brace and Company, 1928. p. 152.

10.332. —— *The Middle Eastern Question, or Some Problems of Indian Defence.* London: John Murray, 1903. pp. 113–28.

10.333. *Christians and the Holy Spirit: Pupil's Book.* ed. Sister Rachel Dagenais, Cynthia Mackay. 2nd ed. Kampala, Uganda: Centenary Publishing House, 1982. (Pupil's Book Primary; no.7). p. 43.

10.334. Christie, Ella R. *Through Khiva to Golden Samarkand: The Remarkable Story of a Woman's Adventurous Journey Alone Through the Deserts of Central Asia to the Heart of Turkestan.* Philadelphia, Pa.: J.B. Lippincott Co., 1925. pp. 26, 66.

10.335. —— *idem.* London: Seeley, Service & Co., 1925. pp. 26, 66.

10.336. Christopher, John B. *The Islamic Tradition.* New York: Harper & Row, 1972. pp. 83–5.

10.337. *The Church at Work in the Modern World.* ed. William C. Bower. Chicago: University of Chicago Press, 1935. p. 276.

10.338. *idem.* Freeport, N.Y.: Books for Libraries Press, n.d. [1967] p. 276.

10.339. Church of the Ascension (New York). *First Sunday in Advent, November 28, 1971.* New York: Church of the Ascension, 1971. Includes section on 'Baha'is to Visit Ascension on November 28', and 3 p. insert of 'Abdu'l-Bahá's talk delivered in 1912.

10.340. Church Peace Union. *Universal Religious Peace Conference.* New York: Church Peace Union, n.d. [1928?] p. 39.

10.341. *Churches and States: The Religious Institution and Modernization.* Victor D. Du Bois [et al.] New York: American Universities Field Staff, 1967. pp. 128n, 183.

10.342. *Circle of Voices: A History of the Religious Communities of British Columbia.* ed. Charles P. Anderson, Tirthankar Bose, Joseph I. Richardson. Lantzville, B.C.: Oolichan Books, 1983. pp. 2, 19–26, 285.

10.343. *City of Acre, Israel.* 'Aco: 'Aco Rotary Club, 1955. p. 6.

10.344. Clare, Israel Smith. *Library of Universal History.* New York: R.S. Peale: J.A. Hill, 1899. X: 325.
The Bábís referred to as assassins of Náṣiri'd-Dín Sháh.

10.345. —— *The World's History Illuminated.* St Louis, Mo.: Western Newspaper Syndicate, 1897. 8 vols. VIII: 3251.

10.346. Clark, Elmer T. *The Small Sects in America.* Nashville, Tenn.: Cokesbury Press, 1937. pp. 29, 183.

10.347. —— *idem.* rev. ed. New York; Nashville, Tenn.: Abingdon-Cokesbury Press, 1949. pp. 18, 147, 233.

10.348. Clarke, John I. *The Iranian City of Shiraz.* Durham, Eng.: Department of Geography, University of Durham, 1963. p. 51.

10.349. *Classical America IV.* William A. Coles, ed. New York: W.W. Norton, 1977. pp. 150–1.
Design for Bahá'í temple in Ṭihrán.

10.350. Clawson, Mary. *Letters from Jerusalem.* London: Abelard-Schuman, 1957. p. 95.

10.351. Clemen, Carl. *Religions of the World: Their Nature and Their History.* trans. Rev. A.K. Dallas. New York: Harcourt, Brace & Co., 1931. pp. 469–70.

10.352. —— *idem.* Freeport, N.Y.: Books for Libraries Press, 1969. pp. 469–70.

10.353. Cobb, Stanwood. *Character: A Sequence in Spiritual Psychology.* Washington, D.C.: Avalon Press, 1938, 1971. *passim.*

10.354. —— *Dermatoglyphics: Scientific Study of the Hand, Based on 60 Years of Research and Experience.* Washington, D.C.: Avalon Press, 1974. pp. 44–5.

10.355. —— *Develop Your Spiritual Power: A Call to Action: Man's Fulfillment on the Planet Earth.* Washington, D.C.: Avalon Press, 1977. *passim.*

10.356. —— *Discovering the Genius Within You.* Metuchen, N.J.: Scarecrow Reprint, 1960. *passim.*

10.357. —— *Islamic Contributions to Civilization.*

Washington, D.C.: Avalon Press, 1963, 1965. p. 81.

10.358. —— *The Meaning of Life*. Washington, D.C.: Life Guidance Society, 1932. p. 15.

10.359. —— *Patterns in Jade of Wu Ming Fu*. Washington, D.C.: Avalon Press, 1935. p. 2.

10.360. —— *Radiant Living*. Washington, D.C.: Avalon Press, 1970. *passim*.

10.361. —— *The Real Turk*. Boston: Pilgrim Press, 1914. pp. 217–27.

10.362. —— *Symbols of America*. Washington, D.C.: Avalon Press, 1046. pp. 27–32.

10.363. —— *Thoughts on Education and Life*. Washington, D.C.: Avalon Press, 1975. *passim*.

10.364. —— *Wings of the Spirit*. Washington, D.C.: Avalon Press, 1971. *passim*.

10.364a. —— *The Wisdom of Wu Ming Fu*. New York: Henry Holt and Company, 1931. pp. 11, 12.

10.365. Cogley, John. *Religion in a Secular Age: The Search for Final Meaning*. New York: New American Library, 1968. p. 173.

10.366. —— *idem*. New York: Frederick A. Praeger, 1968. p. 118.

10.367. Cohen, Hayim J. *The Jews of the Middle East, 1860–1972*. New York: John Wiley & Sons; Jerusalem: Israel Universities Press, 1973. pp. 54, 162–3.

10.368. Cohen, Mark I.; Hahn, Lorna. *Morocco – Old Land, New Nation*. London: Pall Mall Press, 1966. pp. 141–2, 146.

10.369. Cohen, Ruth. *Our Visit to Israel: Audio Visual Programme*. Jerusalem: Holyviews Ltd., n.d. [197–?] pp. 38–9.

10.370. Coke, Richard. *The Heart of the Middle East*. London: Thornton Butterworth, 1925. p. 211.

10.371. Colange, L. *Zell's Popular Encyclopedia: A Universal Dictionary of English Language, Science, Literature, and Art*. Philadelphia, Pa.: T. Ellwood Zell, 1875. pp. 190–2.

10.372. Coleman, Henry R. *Light from the East: Travels and Searches in Bible Lands in Pursuit of More Light on Masonry*. Louisville, Ky., 1890. pp. 347–9.

10.373. *Colliers Encyclopedia*. New York: Macmillan Educational: (P.F. Collier Inc.). Hugh E. Chance, 'Baha'i Faith', Ill.: 460–1.

10.374. *The Columbia-Viking Desk Encyclopedia*. 2nd ed. New York: Viking Press, 1960. 'Babism', p. 95; 'Bahaism', p. 99.

10.375. Comay, Joan. *Everyone's Guide to Israel*. Garden City, N.Y.: Doubleday, 1962. pp. 273, 285.

10.376. —— *Introducing Israel*. London: Methuen & Co., 1963. pp. 191–2, 196, 199.

10.377. —— *Israel: An Uncommon Guide*. New York: Random House, 1969. pp. 257–8, 270–1.

10.378. *Comparative Religion*. ed. Amarjit Singh Sethi, Reinhard Pummer. New Delhi [etc.]: Vikas Publishing House, 1979. J. Douglas Martin, 'The Bahai Faith and Its Relation to Other Religions', pp. 150–68.

10.379. *Compton's Encyclopedia and Fact-Index*. Chicago: F.E. Compton Company, 1983. 'Baha'i Faith', III: 19–20.

10.379a. *The Concise Columbia Encyclopedia*. ed. Judith S. Levey and Agnes Greenhall. New York: Columbia University Press, 1983. 'Babism', p. 59; 'Baha'ism', p. 61; 'Baha Ullah', p. 61.

10.379b. *Concise Dictionary of the Christian World Mission*. ed. Stephen Neill, Gerald H. Anderson, John Goodwin. London: United Society for Christian Literature: Lutterworth Press, 1971. Stephen Neill, 'Baha'i Religion or Bābism', p. 49.

10.380. Condit, Carl W. *Chicago, 1910–1929: Building, Planning and Urban Technology*. Chicago: University of Chicago Press, 1973. p. 230.

10.381. *Contemporary Artists*. 2nd ed. London: Macmillan Publishers, 1983. Ron Glowen, 'Tobey, Mark', pp. 922, 924.

10.382. Convention on Human Rights and Civil Liberties in Iran (1982: Chicago). *Human Rights in the Islamic Republic of Iran: Papers Presented at the Convention on Human Rights and Civil Liberties in Iran, Chicago, May 22, 1982*. Flossmoor, Ill.: Iran Committee for Democratic Action and Human Rights, 1982. pp. 11–12; Martin, Douglas, 'The Baha'is of Iran under the Revolutionary Regime, 1979–1982', pp. 33–49.

10.383. Cooley, John K. *Baal, Christ, and Mohammed: Religion and Revolution in North Africa*. New York: Holt, Rinehart and Winston, 1965. pp. 322–3.

10.383a. Copeland, E. Luther. *Christianity and World Religions*. Nashville, Tenn.: Convention Press, 1963. pp. 127–9.

10.383b. —— *World Mission, World Survival: The Challenge and Urgency of Global Missions Today*. Nashville, Tenn.: Broadman Press, n.d. [1985] pp. 68, 69, 118.

10.383c. *Corpus Dictionary of Western Churches*.

ed. T.C. O'Brien. Washington, D.C.; Cleveland, Ohio: Corpus Publications, 1970. pp. 64–5.

10.384. Cottam, Richard W. *Nationalism in Iran.* Pittsburgh, Pa.: University of Pittsburgh Press, 1979. pp. 87–9, 342, 357.

10.385. Cotter, John. *A Study in Syncretism: The Background and Apparatus of the Emerging One World Church.* n.p. [Flesherton, Ont.]: Canadian Intelligence Publications, 1980, 1983. pp. 9, 10, 28–34, 39, 69, 70, 93.
  Attacks Bahá'ís as supporting a communistic, syncretistic, revolutionary, totalitarian religion.

10.386. Coulter, Carol. *Are Religious Cults Dangerous?* Dublin; Cork: The Mercier Press, 1984. p. 13. (Make Up Your Mind Series).
  Bahá'í Faith declared not to be a cult.

10.387. Cousins, James H.; Cousins, Margaret E. *We Two Together.* Madras, India: Ganesh & Co., 1950. Shoghi Effendi mentioned, p. 577.

10.388. Cousins, Norman. *The Celebration of Life.* New York: Harper & Row, 1974. pp. 24, 28.

10.389. ——*In Place of Folly.* New York: Harper & Bros., 1961. p. 191.

10.390. —— *Who Speaks for Man?* New York: Macmillan Co., 1953. pp. 232, 234, 236–7, 239, 241.

10.391. Cowles, Alton House. *The Conquering Horseman.* Boston: Christopher Publishing House, 1923. p. 68n.

10.392. Cragg, Kenneth. *The Call of the Minaret.* New York: Oxford University Press, 1956. p. 133.

10.393. —— *The House of Islam.* Encino, Calif.: Dickenson Publishing Co., 1975. p. 81.

10.394. Cresson, W.P. *Persia – the Awakening East.* Philadelphia, Pa.; London: J.B. Lippincott, 1908. pp. 130–5.

10.394a. Cribb, James. *Treasures of the Sea: Marine Life in the Pacific Northwest.* Toronto, Ont.: Oxford University Press, 1983. Quotation from Bahá'u'lláh's *The Seven Valleys* in preliminary material.

10.394b. Cribb, James; Cousteau, Jacques-Yves; Suchanek, Thomas H. *Marine Life in the Caribbean.* Toronto, Ont.: Skyline Press, 1984. Mention in preface.

10.395. *Critical Perspectives on Modern Persian Literature.* ed. and comp. Thomas M. Ricks. Washington, D.C.: Three Continents Press, 1984. pp. 113, 228, 374.

10.396. Cron, Frederick W. *The Man Who Made Concrete Beautiful: A Biography of John Joseph Earley.* Ft. Collins, Colo.: Centennial Publications, 1977. pp. 38–48, 62, back cover.

10.397. Cross, Tony. *St. Helena: Including Ascension Island and Tristan da Cunha.* Newton Abbot; London: David & Charles, 1980. p. 99.

10.398. Crowe, Keith J. *A History of the Original Peoples of Northern Canada.* Montreal; London: Arctic Institute of North America, McGill-Queen's University Press, 1974. p. 149.

10.399. Culligan, Emmett J. *Triumphant Peace.* San Bernardino, Calif.: Crestline Book Company, 1956. pp. 36–7, 40–1.
  Negative references from a Catholic viewpoint.

10.399a. Cumbey, Constance E. *A Planned Deception: The Staging of a New Age 'Messiah'.* East Detroit, Mich.: Pointe Publishers, 1985. pp. 29–30.

10.400. Curtis, William Eleroy. *To-Day in Syria and Palestine.* Chicago: Fleming Revell Co., 1903. pp. 219–22.

10.401. Curzon, George N. *Persia and the Persian Question.* 2 vols. London: Longmans, Green & Co., 1892. I: 43, 269, 414, 417, 496–504; II: 43, 103.

10.401a. —— *idem.* London: Frank Cass & Co., 1966. Same paging as 10.401.

10.402. Cust, Lionel. *Jerusalem, a Historical Sketch.* London: A. & C. Black, 1924. p. 208.

D

10.403. Daniel, Mooshie G. *Modern Persia.* Wheaton, Ill.: Wheaton College Press, 1897. 'Bobeism', pp. 145–52.

10.403a. —— *idem.* Toronto, Ont.: Henderson & Co., 1898. pp. 131, 154–61.

10.404. —— *idem.* Toronto, Ont.: Carswell Co. Limited, 1901. pp. 154–61.

10.405. Däniken, Erich von. *The Stones of Kiribati: Pathways to the Gods?* London: Souvenir Press, 1982. p. 28.

10.406. Danner, Margaret. *The Down of a Thistle: Selected Poems, Prose Poems and Songs.* Waukesha, Wis.: Country Beautiful, 1976.
Several poems about the Bahá'í Faith are included.

10.407. Danner, Margaret; Randall, Dudley. *Poem Counterpoem.* 2nd rev. ed. Detroit, Mich.: Broadside Press, 1969. p. [24]

10.408. Das Gupta, Kedarnath. *Essence of Religions.* New York: World Fellowship of Faiths, 1941. pp. 10, 135–9.

10.409. Dashti, Ali. *In Search of Omar Khayyam.* trans. L.P. Elwell-Sutton. New York: Columbia University Press, 1971. pp. 257, 264.

10.410. Davidson, Abraham A. *The Story of American Paintings.* New York: Harry N. Abrams Publishers, 1974. p. 140.

10.411. Davis, John Tyssul. *A League of Religions.* London: Lindsay Press, 1926. pp. 100–9.

10.412. Day, Harvey. *Occult Illustrated Dictionary.* London: Kaye & Ward; New York: Oxford University Press, 1975. pp. 17–18.

10.413. De Bunsen, Victoria. *The Soul of a Turk.* London: John Lane; New York: John Lane Company, 1910. pp. 205, 207, 251, 257.

10.414. De Paul, Vincent. *Jesus Christ, Son of God, Will Return During 1980's.* n.p., 1978. pp. 119–22.

10.415. *Death.* ed. John Prickett. Guildford; London: Lutterworth Educational, 1980. Chapter by Philip Hainsworth, pp. 33–40.

10.416. *Definite Signs of This Age Closing.* by 'a Business man'. 3rd ed. Westport, Conn.; Antwerp, Ohio: G. Elgin Keefer, 1925. pp. 44–5, title page.

10.417. Dehan, Emmanuel. *Our Visit to Israel.* Tel Aviv: Dehan, 1981. (Jerusalem: Steimatzky's Agency Ltd.). pp. 191, 193, 198.

10.418. *Democracy in Israel.* Jerusalem: Keter Publishing House, 1974. p. 49.

10.419. Dennis, James S. *The New Horoscope of Missions.* New York: Fleming H. Revell, 1908. p. 94.

10.420. Dennis-Jones, K. *Israel-Collins Holiday Guide.* New York: Rand McNally, 1970. p. 67.

10.421. Detzer, J.E. *Man's Search for Faith.* Aberdeen, S.D.: North Plains Press, 1970. pp. 235, 254, 326–9, 353, 354, 359, 373.

10.422. Dexter, Harriet Harmon. *What's Right with Race Relations.* New York: Harper Bros., 1958. pp. 195–6.

10.422a. *Dialogue in Art: Japan and the West.* ed. Chisaburoh Yamada. Tokyo: Kodansha International, 1976. pp. 303–5.
Interview with Mark Tobey.

10.423. Dichter, B. *Akko, a Bibliography.* Akko: Akko Municipality, 1970. pp. 20–1.

10.424. Dick, Philip K. *Eye in the Sky.* New York: Ace Books, c1957.
Science fiction novel which includes lengthy section on followers of 'The Second Bab'.

10.425. Dicks, Brian. *The Israelis: How They Live and Work.* Newton Abbot, U.K.: David & Charles, 1975. p. 31.

10.426. *A Dictionary of Comparative Religion.* general ed. S.G.F. Brandon. New York: Scribner's, 1970. pp. 124–6.

10.427. *Dictionary of National Biography, 1912–1921.* Oxford: Oxford University Press, 1922. Peacke, A.S., 'Cheyne, Thomas Kelly (1841–1915)', pp. 119–20.

10.428. *Dictionary of National Biography, 1922–1930.* London: Oxford University Press, 1937. Ross, E. Denison, 'Browne, Edward Granville (1862–1926)', p. 123.

10.429. *Dictionary of Philosophy.* ed. Dagobert Runes. New York: Philosophical Library, 1983. p. 49.

10.430. *A Dictionary of Religion and Ethics.* Shailer Mathews and Gerald Birney Smith, eds. New York: The Macmillan Co., 1921, 1923. M. Sprengling, 'Bahaism', p. 46.

10.431. *idem.* Detroit, Mich.: Gale Research Co., 1973. p. 46.

10.432. *A Dictionary of Religious Education.* ed. John M. Sutcliffe. London: SCM Press, Christian Education Movement, 1984. p. xii; Stephen Lambden, 'Bahá'í', pp. 36–9.

10.433. *Dictionary of South African Biography.* Pretoria, S. Afr.: Butterworth's for the Human Sciences Research Council, 1982. IV: 667–8. Lowell Johnson, 'Turvey, Reginald Ernest George'.

10.434. Dilling, Elizabeth. *The Red Network: A 'Who's Who' and Handbook of Radicalism for Patriots.* Kenilworth, Ill.: Dilling, 1934. p. 128.

10.435. Dodd, Edward M.; Fose, Wilson Dodd. *Mecca and Beyond.* Boston: Central Committee on United Study of Foreign Missions, 1937. p. 146.

10.436. Donaldson, Dwight M. *The Shí'ite Religion: A History of Islam in Persia and Irak.* London: Luzac Co., 1933. pp. 359–69.

10.437. —— *idem.* New York: AMS Press, [1984] pp. 359–69.

10.438. Donaldson, St. Clair. *The Call from the Moslem World.* London: Press and Publication Board of Church Assembly, 1926. p. 40.

10.439. Dooley, Tom. *Dr. Tom Dooley's Three Great Books: Deliver Us from Evil, The Edge of Tomorrow, The Night They Burned the Mountain.* New York: Farrar, Straus & Cudahy, n.d. pp. 308–9.

10.440. —— *The Night They Burned the Mountain.* New York: Farrar, Straus & Cudahy, 1960. pp. 87–8.
    Refers to Dr Taeed, a Bahá'í pioneer in Laos.

10.441. Dos Passos, John. *Journeys Between Wars.* New York: Harcourt, Brace, 1939. pp. 132–3.

10.442. Douglas, Lloyd C. *Magnificent Obsession.* New York: Houghton Mifflin Co., 1929, 1957, 1963. p. 5.

10.443. Douglas, William O. *Strange Lands and Friendly People.* New York: Harper & Bros., 1951. p. 51.

10.444. —— *West of the Indus.* New York: Doubleday & Co., 1958. pp. 254, 272, 279–80, 417–18, 427.

10.445. *'The Down of a Thistle Is as Soft as the Petal of a Rose': A Tribute to Margaret Danner Cunningham from Her Friends and Family.* Chicago: [DuSable Museum?], 1984. *passim.*

10.446. Drake, Durant. *Problems of Religion.* Boston: Houghton Mifflin, 1916. pp. 211, 231.

10.447. Drake, St. Clair; Cayton, Horace R. *Black Metropolis: A Study of Negro Life in a Northern City.* rev. and enl. ed. New York: Harcourt, Brace & World, 1970. 2 v. I: 139, 146, 148, 152–3; II: 530.

10.448. Dreyfuss, Robert. *Hostage to Khomeini.* New York: New Benjamin Franklin House, 1980. pp. 115–18, 120–2, 125.

10.449. Dubin, Joseph W. *The Green Star.* Philadelphia, Pa.: National Institute of Esperanto, 1944. 46, 114, 127, 274.

10.450. Duff, Mountstuart Elphinstone Grant. *Notes from a Diary, 1886–1888.* London: John Murray, 1900. I: 251; II: 20–1.

10.451. *The Dune Encyclopedia.* comp. Dr Willis E. McNelly. New York: Berkeley Books, 1984. 'Orange Catholic Bible, Faiths Responsible for', mentions 'Galactic Spiritual Assembly of Bahais', p. 409.

10.452. Dunning, H.W. *To-Day in Palestine.* New York: James Pott & Co., 1907. pp. 164–6.

10.453. Dutcher, George M. *Modern Persia.* New York: P.F. Collier & Son Co., 1928. pp. 362–3, 401. (The History of Nations; v.5).

10.454. Duveneck, Josephine Whitney. *Life on Two Levels: An Autobiography.* Los Altos, Calif.: William Kaufmann, 1978. p. 49.
    Author's impression of a talk given in London by 'Abdu'l-Bahá.

10.455. Dwight, H.G. *Persian Miniatures.* Garden City, N.Y.: Doubleday, Page & Co., 1917. p. 176.

10.456. Dwight, Henry Otis. *Constantinople and Its Peoples: Its Peoples, Customs, Religions and Progress.* New York: Fleming Revell Co., 1901. p. 83.

E

10.457. Easterman, Daniel. *The Last Assassin.* London: Hodder and Stoughton, 1984. pp. 371–3.

10.458. Eastwick, Edward B. *Journal of a Diplomate's* [sic] *Three Years' Residence in Persia.* London: Smith, Elder & Co., 1864. p. 206.

10.459. —— *idem.* Tehran: Imperial Organization for Social Services, 1976. p. 206.

10.459a. Eban, Abba. *Promised Land.* foreword Leon Uris; text Abba Eban; paintings Gordon Wetmore. Nashville, Tenn.; New York: Thomas Nelson, 1978. pp. 118–19, 166.

10.459b. Ebtehaj, G.H. *Guide Book on Persia.* Tehran: Printed at the Parliament Press, n.d. [1931] p. 21.

10.460. *The Echo of the Faithful, 25th Issue.* [Malaysia]: Religious Organisation of the Royal Malaysian Air Force of Butterworth, n.d. [1982] pp. 2, 10–11.

10.461. Eddy, (George) Sherwood. *God in History.* New York: Association Press, 1947. p. 169.

10.462. —— *A Portrait of Jesus: A Twentieth Century Interpretation of Christ.* London: George Allen & Unwin, 1945. p. 83.

10.463. Edelman, Lily. *Israel*. Edinburgh: Thomas Nelson & Sons, 1958. p. 42.

10.464. —— *Modern Israel: New People in an Old Land*. Hollywood, Calif.: Wilshire Book Co., 1969. pp. 51–3.

10.465. —— *New People in a New Land*. New York: Thomas Nelson & Sons, n.d. p. 42.

10.466. Edwards, A. Cecil. *A Persian Caravan*. New York: Harper & Bros., 1928. pp. 14–23.

10.466a. —— *idem*. London: Duckworth, 1928. pp. 14–23.

10.466b. —— *idem*. Freeport, N.Y.: Books for Libraries, 1970. pp. 14–23.

10.467. Edwards, David L. *Religion and Change*. New York: Harper and Brothers, 1969. p. 264.

10.468. Edwards, Dawn. *Journey Into Consciousness*. Los Angeles: The Philosophical Forum, 1955. p. 198.

10.469. Eells, George. *Robert Mitchum*. New York: Franklin Watts, 1984. p. 241.

10.470. *Eerdman's Handbook to the World's Religions*. Grand Rapids, Mich.: Willie B. Eerdman's Publishing Co., 1982. Werner Schilling, 'Unity and Peace: The Bahá'í Faith', pp. 268–70; 395.
See 10.1614.

10.471. Ehrenpreis, Marcus. *The Soul of the East*. New York: Viking Press, 1928. p. 206.

10.472. Ellis, Harry B. *Heritage of the Desert: The Arabs and the Middle East*. New York: The Ronald Press Company, 1956. p. 193.

10.473. Ellwood, Charles A. *The Reconstruction of Religion*. New York: Macmillan Co., 1922. p. 68.

10.474. Ellwood, Robert S. *Religious and Spiritual Groups in Modern America*. Englewood, Cliffs, N.J.: Prentice-Hall, 1973. pp. 275–81.
Ellwood concludes that the Bahá'í Faith is an independent religion in the prophetic tradition and should not really be included in a book on cults.

10.474a. Elston, Roy. *The Traveller's Handbook for Palestine and Syria*. new ed. rev. Harry Charles Luke. London: Simkin Marshall; Hamilton, Kent: Thos. Cook & Son. 1924. p. 263. (Cook's Traveller's Handbooks). Cover title: *Cook's Traveller's Handbook, Palestine and Syria*.

10.475. Elston, Roy. *The Traveller's Handbook for Palestine and Syria*. 2nd ed. rev. by Harry Charles Luke. London: Simpkin Marshall Ltd., 1929. p. 274. Cover title: *Cook's Traveller's Handbook, Palestine and Syria*.

10.476. Elwell-Sutton, L.P. *A Guide to Iranian Area Study*. Ann Arbor, Mich.: Published for the American Council of Learned Societies by J.W. Edwards, 1952. pp. 76–7, 80–1, 145–6, 167, 172.

10.477. —— *Modern Iran*. London: George Rutledge Sons, 1941, 1942. pp. 60–1.

10.478. Emanuel, W.V. *The Wild Asses: A Journey Through Persia*. London: Jonathan Cape, 1939. pp. 88, 109.

10.479. —— *idem*. New York: AMS Press, 1974. pp. 88, 109.

10.480. Emerson, Edwin, Jr. *A History of the Nineteenth Century Year by Year*. New York: P.F. Collier & Son, 1900. II: 1131.

10.481. *Encyclopaedia Britannica*. 11th ed. Cambridge, 1910. Edward G. Browne, 'Babiism', III: 94–95.

10.482. *idem*. 24 vols. Chicago: Encyclopaedia Britannica; William Benton Publisher, 1959. 'Báb', II: 838; Horace Holley, 'Bábiism', II: 840–41; Horace Holley, 'Bahá'í Faith', II: 928.

10.483. *idem*. Chicago, 1972. Charles Joseph Adams, 'Bab', 'Babism', 'Baha'i Faith', 'Baha'u'llah', II: 943, 946–7, 1030, 1032–3.

10.484. *Encyclopaedia Iranica*. ed. Ehsan Yarshater. London: Routledge & Kegan Paul, 1982– . Bausani, A.; MacEoin, D., 'Abd al-Bahā', I: 102–4; M. Momen, 'Abu'l-Fażl Golpāyegānī', I: 289–90; M. Momen, 'Adib Tālaqānī', I: 461; M. Momen, 'Afnān', I: 567–9; M. Momen, ' 'Alī Akbar Sahmīrzādī', I: 857; D. MacEoin, ' 'Alī Bestāmī', I: 860; M. Momen, 'Amīn', Hājjī', I: 938–9. Other mentions: I: 484, 674, 960, 966–7.

10.485. *The Encyclopaedia of Islam*. ed. M. Th. Houtsma, T.W. Arnold, R. Basset and R. Hartmann. Leiden: E.J. Brill, 1913–1938. Clément Huart, 'Bāb', I: 544–6 and 'Bābī', II: 548.

10.486. *idem*. new ed. Leiden: E.J. Brill; London: Luzac, 1960– . A. Bausani, 'Bāb', I: 833–5, 'Bābīs', I: 846–7, 'Bahā' Allāh', I: 911–12, 'Bahā'īs', I: 915–18; 'Azalī', I: 809; T.W. Haig, 'Kāshānī, Hādidjī Mīrzā Djanī', I: 696; H. Algar, 'Kādzim Rashtī', IV: 854; L.P. Elwell-Sutton, D. MacEoin, 'Kurrat al-'Ayn', V: 102; other references, I: 263, 304, 1099; III: 325; IV: 39, 51; V: 698, 1172; Suppl.: 53–4, 71, 77, 94–5.

10.487. *Encyclopaedia of Religion and Ethics*. ed. J. Hastings. Edinburgh: Clark; New York: Scribner, 1908–[1928] Edward Granville Browne, 'Báb, Bábís', II: 299–308.

10.488. *The Encyclopedia Americana*. Danbury, Conn.: Americana Corp., 1979. Articles:

' 'Abdu'l-Bahá', I: 29; 'Babism', III: 7; 'Bahá'í Faith', III: 54; 'Bahá'u'lláh', III: 57.

10.489. *Encyclopedia Canadiana.* Toronto, Ont.: Grolier of Canada, 1970. Winnifred I. Harvey, 'Baha'i World Faith', I: 279–80.

10.490. *Encyclopedia International.* New York: Grolier, 1971. 'Babi', II: 293.

10.491. *Encyclopedia Judaica.* Jerusalem: Encyclopedia Judaica: Keter Publishing House, 1972. IX: 923–4.

10.491a. McClintock, John; Strong, James. *Cyclopaedia of Biblical, Theological, and Ecclesiastical Literature.* New York: Harper & Brothers, 1871. "Babi, or Babists," I:593–594.

10.491b.—— *idem.* New York: Arno Press, 1969. "Babi, or Babists," I: 593–594.

10.492. *Encyclopedia of Associations.* 18th ed. Detroit, Mich.: Gale Research Company, 1984. IV: 317.

10.493. *idem.* 19th ed. Detroit, Mich.: Gale Research Company, 1985. I: 1346.

10.493a. *Encyclopedia of Black America.* W. Augustus Low, ed.; Virgil A. Clift, assoc. ed. New York: Macmillan, 1981. p. 147.

10.493b. *idem.* New York: Da Capo Press, 1984. p. 147.

10.494. *Encyclopedia of Newfoundland and Labrador.* editor in chief Joseph R. Smallwood; managing editor Robert D.W. Pitt. St. John's, Nfld: Newfoundland Book Publishers, 1981. Rae Perlin, 'Baha'i Faith', I: 108.

10.494a. *Encyclopedia of Occultism & Parapsychology.* ed. Leslie Shepard. 2nd ed. Detroit, Mich.: Gale Research Company, 1984. I: 125.

10.494b. *An Encyclopedia of Religion.* ed. Vergilius Ferm. Westport, Conn.: Greenwood Press, 1976. p. 52.

10.495. *An Encyclopedia of World History: Ancient, Medieval and Modern.* comp. & ed. William L. Langer. 5th ed. Boston: Houghton Mifflin, 1978. p. 895.

10.495a. *Encyclopedia of Zionism and Israel.* ed. Raphael Patai. New York: Herzl Press; McGraw-Hill, 1971. "Bahai Community in Israel," p. 101.

10.495b. *Encyclopedic Dictionary of Religion.* ed. Paul Kevin Meagher, Thomas C. O'Brien, Sister Consuelo Maria Aherne. Washington, D.C.: Corpus Publications, 1979. pp. 333–334.

10.495c. Engel, Lyle. *Israel.* New York: Cornerstone Library, 1963. pp. 149, 151, 153.

10.496. English, Paul Ward. *City and Village in Iran: Settlement and Economy in the Kirman Basin.* Madison, Wis.: University of Wisconsin Press, 1966. p. 56.

10.496a. *Enhancing Global Human Rights.* Jorge I. Domínguez [et. al.] New York: McGraw-Hill, 1979. p. 138.

10.496b. Entwisle, Frank. *Abroad in England.* New York; London: W.W. Norton, 1983. pp. 99–100.

10.496c. Erskine, Beatrice [Mrs Steuart]. *Palestine of the Arabs.* London [etc.]: George G. Harrap & Co., 1935. pp. 235–6.

10.497. Eskelund, Karl. *Behind the Peacock Throne.* London: Alvin Redman, 1965. pp. 75–85.

10.498. Esposito, John L. *Islam and Politics.* Syracuse, N.Y.: Syracuse University Press, 1984. pp. 123, 230.

10.499. Esslemont, Peter. *Zamenhof and Esperanto.* Sandgate, Eng.: Edmund Ward Pub. Ltd., n.d. [between 1945 and 1960] pp. [13]–[14]

10.500. Estes, Joseph. *A Baptist Look at Islam.* Atlanta, Ga.: Home Mission Board, n.d. pp. 2–3.

10.501. *Everybody's Cyclopedia.* New York: Syndicate Publishing, 1912. 'Bâbi', volume 1 (unpaged).

10.502. *Everyman's Encyclopaedia.* 6th ed. London: J.M. Dent, 1978. 'Bahá'í', I: 644–5; 'Shoghi Effendi', XI: 59.

F

10.502a. *Facts About Israel.* Jerusalem: Ministry for Foreign Affairs, Information Division, 1963. pp. 34, 55.

10.502b. *idem.* Jerusalem: Ministry for Foreign Affairs, Information Division, 1967. pp. 40, 63.

10.503. *idem.* . Newcomer's ed. [Jerusalem]: The Information and Publications Division, 1968. pp. 64, 70.

10.503a. *idem.* Jerusalem: Ministry for Foreign Affairs, Information Division, 1968, pp. 43, 71, 72.

10.503b. *idem.* Jerusalem: Ministry for Foreign Affairs, Information Division, 1969, pp. 46, 69, 70.

10.503c. *idem.* Jerusalem: Ministry for Foreign Affairs, Information Division, 1970, pp. 47, 71, 72.

10.503d. *idem.* Jerusalem: Keter Publishing House, 1971. pp. 38, 60.

10.503e. *idem.* Jerusalem: Keter Publishing House, 1972. pp. 38, 60.

10.503f. *idem.* Jerusalem: Division of Information, Ministry for Foreign Affairs, 1973. pp. 76–77.

10.503g. *idem.* Jerusalem: Division of Information, Ministry for Foreign Affairs, n.d. [1974]. pp. 76–77.

10.504. *idem.* Jerusalem: Ministry of Foreign Affairs, 1979. p. 7.

10.504a. *idem.* Jerusalem: Covenant Marketing Association, Ministry of Foreign Affairs, 1979. Colour photograph of shrine between pp. 84–5.

10.504b. *idem.* Jerusalem: Ministry of Foreign Affairs, Information Division, 1985. p. 92.

10.505. *Facts About the Township of Teaneck, a Residential Community, Bergen County, New Jersey.* Teaneck, N.J.: Teaneck Board of Commerce, 1941. pp. [19–20]

10.506. *Faith and the United Nations: A Call from Religious Leaders.* London: United Nations Association, n.d. [197–] p. 6.

10.507. Falk, Richard. *Human Rights and State Sovereignty.* New York; London: Holmes & Meier Publishers, 1981. pp. 211, 212.

10.508. Farah, Caesar E. *Islam – Beliefs and Observances.* Woodbury, N.Y.: Barron's Educational Series, 1970. pp. 220, 243–8, 274, 277.

10.509. Farman, Hafez F. [Farman-Farmayan, Hafez]. *Iran: A Selected and Annotated Bibliography.* New York: Greenwood Press, 1968. Items 6, 336, 340, 349.

10.510. Fawcett, Millicent. *Easter in Paradise, 1921–1922.* London: T. Fisher Unwin, 1926. pp. 56–7.

10.511. —— *idem.* New York: Frank-Maurice Inc., [1926] pp. 56–7.

10.512. Ferguson, Charles W. *The Confusion of Tongues: A Review of Modern Isms.* Garden City, N.Y.: Doubleday, Doran & Co., 1928. pp. 5, 6, 13, 231–50, 450–1.

10.513. —— *The New Books of Revelation.* Garden City, N.Y.: Doubleday, Doran & Co., 1929. pp. 13, 231–50, 450–1. Same as above, retitled.

10.514. Ferguson, John. *War and Peace in the World's Religions.* New York: Oxford University Press, 1978. pp. 149–55.

10.515. Ferm, Vergilius. *Living Schools of Religion.* Ames, Ia.: Littlefield, Adams & Co., 1958. pp. 308–14.

10.516. Ferré, Nels F.S. *The Finality of Faith: and, Christianity Among the World Religions.* New York: Harper & Row, 1963. pp. 88, 104.

10.517. —— *idem.* Westport, Conn.: Greenwood Press, 1979. pp. 88, 104.

10.518. —— *Know Your Faith.* New York: Harper Bros., 1959. p. 34.

10.519. —— *Making Religion Real.* New York: Harper Brothers, 1955. p. 42.

10.520. —— *Strengthening the Spiritual Life.* London: Collins, 1956. p. 54.

10.520a. Fertow, Fred. M. *Robert Hayden.* Boston: Twayne Publishers, 1984. (Twayne's United States Authors Series; 471). pp. [xii], 15, 59, 61, 107, 114, 115, 116, 128.

10.521. Festival of Faith (1955: San Francisco). *A Festival of Faith: A Service of Prayer for Peace and Divine Guidance to the United Nations, June 19, 1955. 3:30 p.m. San Francisco Cow Palace.* San Francisco, Calif.: Dettner's Printing House, 1955.
Includes Bahá'í prayers.

10.522. Filmer, Henry. *The Pageant of Persia: A Record of Travel by Motor in Persia with an Account of Its Ancient and Modern Ways.* Indianapolis, Ind.: Bobbs-Merrill Co., 1936. pp. 27, 28, 196–200, 202–3.

10.522a. Finbert, Elian J. *Israel.* Paris: Hachette, 1956. pp. 55, 166, 181–182.

10.523. Fischer, Michael M.J. *Iran, from Religious Dispute to Revolution.* Cambridge, Mass.; London: Harvard University Press, 1980. pp. 69, 101, 150, 184, 185, 186, 187, 206, 229, 247(n7), 280(n5).

10.524. Fisher, Sydney Nettleton. *The Middle East, a History.* New York: Alfred A. Knopf, 1979. p. 379.

10.525. Fisher, W.B. *The Middle East: A Physical, Social and Regional Geography.* 6th ed. London: Metheun & Co., 1971. p. 127.

10.526. —— *idem.* 7th ed. London: Methuen, 1978. p. 123.

10.527. Fitch, Florence Mary. *Allah, the God of Islam.* New York: Lothrop, Lee & Shepard Co., 1950. p. 136.

10.528. *Fodor's Islamic Asia: Iran, Afghanistan, Pakistan.* ed. Eugene Fodor, William Curtis. New York: David McKay Company, 1974. pp. 88, 110–11.

10.529. *Fodor's Israel.* New York: D. McKay, 1969, 1970. pp. 341, 351, 355, 363; 1971, 1972, 1973, 1974, 1975. pp. 340, 350, 354, 362; 1977, 1978, 1979. pp. 191, 196–7, 201, 206; 1980. pp. 177, 182, 187, 191–2; 1981, 1982. pp. 260, 270.

10.530. *Fodor's Israel 1985.* London: Hodder and Stoughton, 1985. pp. 252, 256, 261–2, 268.

10.531. *The Fontana Biographical Companion to Modern Thought.* ed. Alan Bullock and R.B. Woodings. London: Fontana Paperbacks, 1983. Denis MacEoin, 'Bahá'Allāh (Bahá'u'lláh) Mīrzā Ḥusayn 'Alī Nūrī', p. 36; 'Shoghi Effendi Rabbani', p. 701.

10.532. *The Fontana Dictionary of Modern Thought.* ed. Alan Bullock, Oliver Stallybrass. London: Fontana-Collins, 1977. p. 50.

10.533. *For All Who Go Down to the Sea in Ships.* Washington, D.C.: Office of the Chief of Naval Operations, 1985. Bahá'í prayers, pp. 89–90.

10.534. Forbes, D. *Heart of Iran.* London: Robert Hale, 1963. pp. 125–6.

10.535. Forbes, Murray. *Hollow Triumph.* Chicago: Ziff-Davis Publishing Co., c1946. pp. 215, 233–4, 267.

10.536. Forbes, Rosita. *Conflict: Angora to Afghanistan.* New York: Frederick A. Stokes Co., 1931. pp. 75, 126, 184, 210–11.

10.537. —— *idem.* London: Cassell and Company, 1931. pp. 69–70, 116–17, 168.

10.538. Forbis, William H. *Fall of the Peacock Throne: The Story of Iran.* New York: Harper & Row, 1980. pp. 163–4.

10.539. Forel, August. *Out of My Life and Work.* trans. Bernard Miall. New York: W.W. Norton, 1937. p. 342.

10.540. Forlong, J.G.R. *Faiths of Man: A Cyclopaedia of Religions.* London: Bernard Quaritch, 1906. I: 223–4.

10.541. —— *Faiths of Man: Encyclopedia of Religions.* New Hyde Park, N.Y.: University Books, 1964. I: 223–4.

10.542. Forman, Henry James; Gammon, Roland. *Truth Is One.* New York: Harper & Bros., 1954. pp. 218–20, 222. Photographs: Bahá'í House of Worship, Wilmette, p. 218; Dr Hushang Javid and Horace Holley, p. 218.

10.543. Forster, Peter G. *The Esperanto Movement.* The Hague: Mouton Publishers, 1982. (Contributions to the Sociology of Language; 32). pp. 38, 107, 324, 401.

10.544. Fozdar, Jamshed. *The God of Buddha.* New York: Asia Publishing House, 1973. pp. 2, 20.

10.545. Fradenburgh, J.N. *Living Religions, or The Great Religions of the Orient.* Cincinnati, Ohio: Cranston & Stowe, 1888. pp. 476–7.

10.546. Frankfurt Book Fair (34th: 1982: Frankfurt am Main). *Religion: Yesterday's Religion in Today's World: World Religions.* Frankfurt am Main: Ausstellungs-und Messe-GmbH des Bösenvereins des Deutschen Buchhandels, 1982. pp. 299–302.

10.547. Fraser, David. *Persia and Turkey in Revolt.* Edinburgh; London: William Blackwood and Sons, 1910. p. 271.

10.548. Frasnay, Daniel. *The Artist's World.* London: J.M. Dent & Sons, 1969. pp. 142, 149 in article on Mark Tobey.

10.549. *Freedom in the World: Political Rights and Civil Liberties, 1981.* ed. Raymond D. Gastil; with essays by Richard W. Cottam [et al.] Oxford: Clio Press, 1981. p. 360.

10.550. Freeman, Cynthia. *No Time for Tears.* Toronto, Ont.: Bantam Books, 1982. pp. 171, 268.

10.551. Freeman, Hobert E. *Occult Oppression and Bondage.* Warsaw, Ind.: Freeman, n.d. [1984?] p. [4]

10.552. Freiburger, Paul; Swaine, Michael. *Fire in the Valley: The Making of the Personal Computer.* Berkeley, Calif.: Osborne-McGraw-Hill, 1984. p. 217.

10.553. Friedman, Paul Jay. *Biochemistry.* Boston: Little, Brown and Company, 1977. p. vii.

10.554. *From Buffalo Chips to Natural Gas.* New Brigden, Alta.: New Brigden Community Association, 1984. Jean Doolan, 'The Baha'i Faith in the Local Community,' pp. 86, 212.

10.555. *From Nationalism to Revolutionary Islam.* ed. Said Amir Arjomand. London: Macmillan, in association with St Anthony's College Oxford, 1984. pp. 205, 211.

10.556. Frye, Richard N. *The Heritage of Persia.* Cleveland, O.: World Publishing Co., n.d. p. 212.

10.557. —— *idem.* New York: New American Library, 1963. p. 250.

10.558. —— *Iran.* New York: Henry Holt & Co., 1953. pp. 11, 66.

10.559. —— *Persia.* rev. ed. London: Allen & Unwin, 1968. pp. 20, 55, 64, 80–1, 83, 97.

10.560. *Funk & Wagnalls New Standard Encyclopedia of Universal Knowledge.* New York; London: Funk & Wagnalls, 1934. 'Babism', II: 309.

10.561. *Funk & Wagnalls New Standard Encyclopedia Year Book for 1949.* ed. Henry E. Vizetelly. New York: Funk & Wagnells, 1950. p. 57.

10.562. Futterer, A.F. *Palestine Speaks.* by the Pioneer Golden Ark Explorer. Los Angeles: A.F. Futterer Organizer of Ancient World Tours, 1931. p. 443.

10.563. Fyvel, T.R.; Kwaldo, Boris. *This Is Israel.* Tel-Aviv: Tevel Publishing Co., n.d. pp. 49, 54.

G

10.564. Gabrielle, Rúhíyyih [Rosenwald, Ruth]. *Time Capsule 1982: The Crimson Ark.* San Marcos, Calif.: Time Capsule, 1980.
Contains many poems with direct and indirect reference to the Bahá'í Faith.

10.565. Gack, Christoph G.; Wobcke, Manfred. *Israel and the Occupied Territories.* Victoria, Australia: Lonely Planet Publications, 1981. p. 119.

10.566. Gacek, Adam. *Catalogue of the Arabic Manuscripts in the Library of the School of Oriental and African Studies, University of London.* London: School of Oriental and African Studies, University of London, 1981. MS. of the Kitáb-i-Aqdas, item 158.

10.567. Gaer, Joseph. *The Wisdom of the Living Religions.* New York: Dodd, Mead & Co., 1956. p. 224.

10.567a. Gafni, Shlomo, S.; Heyden, A. van der. *The Glory of the Holy Land.* Jerusalem: Steimatzky: The Jerusalem Publishing House, 1982. p. 226.

10.568. Gail, Marzieh. *Avignon in Flower, 1309–1403.* Boston: Houghton Mifflin, 1965. p. 180.

10.569. —— *Persia and the Victorians.* London: George Allen & Unwin, 1951. pp. 55–8.
Reviews:
Young, T. Cuyler, *The Middle East Journal* (Washington, D.C.), v.6 (Winter 1952), pp. 102–3.
Khoobyar, Helen, *The Muslim World* (Hartford, Conn.), v.42 no.2 (Apr. 1952), p. 151.

10.570. —— *The Three Popes: An Account of the Great Schism, When Rival Popes in Rome, Avignon and Pisa Vied for the Rule of Christendom.* New York: Simon & Schuster, 1969. pp. 94, 247.

10.571. Gairdner, W.H.T. *The Reproach of Islam.* London: Student Volunteer Missionary Union, 1909. p. 351.

10.572. Galvin, Kathleen M.; Brommel, Bernard J. *Family Communication: Cohesion and Change.* Glenview, Ill.: Scott, Foresman and Company, 1982. p. 287.

10.573. Gardet, Louis. *Mohammedanism.* New York: Hawthorne, 1961. p. 113.

10.574. Garrison, Winfred E. *The March of Faith: The Story of Religion in America Since 1865.* New York: Harper & Brothers, 1933. pp. 275, 281–3.

10.575. —— *idem.* Westport, Conn.: Greenwood Press, 1971. pp. 275, 281–3.

10.576. Gartler, Marion; Laikin, Judith; Hall, George. *Understanding Israel.* Sacramento, Calif.: California State Series, 1964. Colour photograph, Shrine of the Báb, on cover.

10.576a. Gaudefroy-Demombynes, Maurice. *Muslim Institutions.* London: George Allen & Unwin, 1950. pp. 45–6.

10.577. Geden, A.S. *Comparative Religion.* London: Society for Promoting Christian Knowledge, 1917. p. 107.

10.578. Geden, Alfred S. *Studies in Comparative Religion.* London: Charles H. Kelly, 1898. pp. 291–300.

10.579. Geisendorfer, James V. *Religion in America: A Directory.* Leiden: E.J. Brill, 1983. p. 21.

10.580. Gelhorn, Eleanor Cowles. *McKay's Guide to the Middle East.* New York: David McKay Co., 1965. pp. 160–1.

10.581. Germanus, Julius. *Modern Movements in*

Islam. Calcutta: Visva-Bharati Book Shop, 1932. pp. 54–78.

10.581a. —— *Modern Movements in the World of Islam.* Lahore: Al-Biruni, 1978. pp. 54–78.

10.582. Gerstner, John H. *Survey of the Major Cults.* Chicago: Moody Press, 1965. 1 p. laminated.

10.583. —— *The Theology of the Major Sects.* Grand Rapids, Mich.: Baker Book House, 1963. p. 16, 178.

10.584. Ghosh, A. *The Koran and the Kafir, Islam and the Infidel: All That an Infidel Needs to Know About the Koran But Is Embarrassed to Ask.* Houston, Tex.: A. Ghosh, 1983. p. xi.

10.584a. Ghulamali Ismail Naji. *Zehra Bano.* Karachi: Peermahomed Ibrahim Trust, 1972. 'Tahirih', pp. 100–101.

10.585. Gibb, Hamilton A.R. *Modern Trends in Islam.* New York: Octagon Books, c1947. p. 12.

10.586. —— *Mohammedanism: An Historical Survey.* London: Oxford University Press, 1949. pp. 164, 186.

10.587. Gibbon, David. *Chicago: A Picture Book to Remember Her By.* n.p.: Crescent Books, 1979. Picture of Wilmette Temple, pp. [62–63].

10.588. —— *The Holy Land: A Picture Book to Remember Her By.* Great Britain: Crescent Books, 1978. p. 16, photograph of Shrine of the Báb.

10.589. Gibbons, Herbert Adams. *Wider Horizons: The New Map of the World.* New York: The Century Co., 1930. pp. 104, 299.

10.590. Gibbons, John. *The Road to Nazareth: Through Palestine Today.* London: Robert Hale, 1936. pp. 45–6.

10.591. Gibran, Jean; Gibran, Kahlil. *Kahlil Gibran: His Life and World.* Boston: New York Graphic Society, 1947. pp. 273, 287–8.

10.592. —— *idem.* New York: Avenel Books, 1981. pp. 273, 287–8.

10.593. Gibran, Kahlil; Haskell, Mary. *Beloved Prophet: The Love Letters of Kahlil Gibran and Mary Haskell, and Her Private Journal.* ed. and arr. Virginia Hilu. New York: Knopf, 1972. pp. 74, 77.

10.594. Gillespie, Dizzy. *To Be or Not . . . To Bop: Memoirs.* with Al Fraser. Garden City, N.Y.: Doubleday, 1979. pp. 185, 287–8, 430–1, 460–1, 463–4, 473–6, 479–80, 493.

10.595. Glenbow-Alberta Institute (Calgary). *New Paintings by Otto Rogers.* Calgary, Alta.:

Glenbow-Alberta Art Gallery, n.d. [1973] p. [10]

10.596. *Glimpses of the Mother's Life.* comp. Nilima Das; ed. K.D. Sethna. Pondicherry, India: Sri Aurobindo Ashram, 1978. I: 104–9.
Meeting of 'The Mother' (Mira Richard) with 'Abdu'l-Bahá.

10.597. Glover, Robert H.; Kane, Herbert J. *Progress of World-Wide Missions.* New York: Harper and Brothers, 1960. p. 235.

10.597a. Glover, T.R. *The Ancient World: A Beginning.* Cambridge: Cambridge University Press, 1935. p. 74.

10.597b. —— *idem.* London: New York: Penguin Books, 1944. p. 74.

10.598. *Goals for Mankind: A Report to the Club of Rome on the New Horizons of Global Community.* Ervin Laszlo [et. al.] New York: E.P. Dutton, 1977. pp. 368–9.

10.599. *A Golden Treasury of Persian Poetry.* [comp.] Hadi Ḥasan. 2nd rev. ed. New Delhi: Indian Council for Cultural Relations, 1972. Poetry of Ṭáhirih, pp. 412–15.

10.600. Goldziher, Ignaz. *Introduction to Islamic Theology and Law.* trans. Andras and Ruth Hamori. Princeton, N.J.: Princeton University Press, 1981. pp. 245–9.

10.601. *Good Words for 1884.* ed. Donald Macleod. London: Isbister & Co., 1884. W. Robertson Smith, 'Mohammedan Mahdis', p. 624.

10.602. Goodwin-Gill, Guy S. *The Refugee in International Law.* Oxford: Clarendon Press, 1983. pp. 28, 43n.

10.603. Gordis, Robert. *A Faith for Moderns.* rev. and augm. ed. New York: Block Publishing, 1971. p. 46.

10.604. Gordon, Cyrus H. *Lands of the Cross and Crescent: Aspects of Middle Eastern and Occidental Affairs.* Ventnor, N.J.: Ventnor Publishers, 1948. p. 137.

10.605. Gordon, David C. *Lebanon, the Fragmented Nation.* London: Croom Helm; Stanford, Calif.: Hoover Institution Press, 1980. p. 40.

10.606. Gordon, Thomas Edward. *Persia Revisited (1895): with Remarks on H.I.M. Mozuffer-ed-Din Shah, and the Present Situation in Persia (1896).* London; New York: Edward Arnold, 1896: pp. 81–91.

10.607. Gowen, Herbert H. *A History of Religion.* London: Society for Promoting Christian Knowledge, 1934. pp. 5, 550–1.

10.608. Grabbe, Paul. *The Story of Orchestral Music and Its Times*. New York: Grosset & Dunlap, 1960. p. 68.

10.609. Graham, Jory. *Chicago, an Extraordinary Guide*. Chicago: Rand McNally & Co., 1967. p. 402.

10.610. Graham, Robert. *Iran, the Illusion of Power*. London: Croom Helm, 1979. pp. 97, 221–2, 225.

10.611. Gratus, Jack. *The False Messiahs*. London: Gollancz, 1975. pp. 209–11.

10.612. —— *idem*. New York: Taplinger Publishing Co., 1976. pp. 209–11.

10.613. Grayzel, Solomon. *A History of the Jews from the Babylonian Exile to the Present, 5728–1968*. rev. ed. New York: New American Library, 1968. p. 633.

10.614. *Great Religions of the World*. Herbert Giles [et. al.] New York: Harper & Bros., 1901. E. Denison Ross, 'Babism', pp. 187–215.

10.615. *idem*. rev. ed. New York: Harper & Bros., 1912. pp. 187–215.

10.616. *The Great Soviet Encyclopedia*. New York: Macmillan, 1973. 'Bab', II: 516; M.S. Ivanov, 'Babism', II: 521; M.S. Ivanov, 'Babi Uprisings', II: 521; Klimovich, L.I., 'Bahaism', III: 10.

10.617. *The Great Thoughts*. comp. George Seldes. New York: Ballantine Books, 1985. p. 31.

10.618. Green, Gerald. *The Stones of Zion: A Novelist's Journal in Israel*. New York: Hawthorn Books, 1971. pp. 305–7, 318.

10.619. Green, Jerrold D. *Revolution in Iran: The Politics of Countermobilization*. New York: Prayer, 1982. pp. 56, 97, 102, 123, 157.

10.620. Green, Philip Leonard. *Pan-American Progress*. New York: Hastings House, 1942. p. 177.

10.621. Groseclose, Elgin. *Introduction to Iran*. New York: Oxford University Press, 1947. p. 14.

10.622. Gross, Ronald. *High School*. New York: Simon and Schuster, 1972. pp. 274, 276.

10.623. Gruber, Ruth. *Israel Today: Land of Many Nations*. New York: Hill and Wang, 1958. p. 17.

10.624. Gruss, Edmonnd C. *Cults and the Occult*. rev. ed. Grand Rapids, Mich.: Baker Book House, 1980. pp. 93–102.

10.625. —— *Cults and the Occult in the Age of Aquarius: An Introduction*. Grand Rapids, Mich.: Baker Book House, 1974. pp. 84–91.

10.625a. —— *idem*. Nutley, N.J.: Presbyterian and Reformed Publishing Co., 1974. pp. 84–91.

10.626. Guérard, Albert Léon. *Education of a Humanist*. Cambridge, Mass.: Harvard University Press, 1949. p. 250.

10.626a. *A Guide-Book to Central Palestine, Samaria and Southern Galilee: Including Nablus, Arsuf, Haifa, Acre, Nazareth, Tiberias and Their Districts*. based upon Baedeker's Palestine & Syria. n.p. [Jerusalem]: The Palestine News, 1918. p. 38.

10.627. *A Guide to Cults & New Religions*. Ronald Enroth & others. Downers Grove, Ill.: InterVarsity Press, 1983. John Boykin, 'The Bahá'i Faith', pp. 25–41.

10.627a. *Guide to Palestine and Syria*. 3rd ed. London: Macmillan and Co., 1905. p. 108.

10.628. Guillaume, Alfred. *Islam*. 2nd rev. ed. Baltimore, Md.; Harmondsworth, Middlesex: Penguin, 1956. p. 124.

10.629. Gundry, D.W. *Religions: A Preliminary Historical and Theological Study*. London; Macmillan & Co. Ltd.; New York: St. Martin's Press, 1958. pp. 141–2.

10.630. Gurdon, Hugo. *Iran, the Continuing Struggle for Power*. Wisbech, Cants.: Menas Press, 1984. p. 15.

H

10.631. Haas, William S. *Iran*. New York: Columbia University Press, 1946. pp. 90–1.

10.632. —— *idem*. New York: AMS Press, 1966. pp. 90–1.

10.633. Haddad, George M. *Revolutions and Military Rule in the Middle East: The Northern Tier*. New York: Robert Speller & Sons, 1965. p. 84.

10.634. Hadley, Earl I. *The Magic Powder: History of the Universal Atlas Cement Company and* *the Cement Industry.* New York: Putnam, 1945. pp. 200–1. Frontis.: Photograph of Bahá'í House of Worship, Wilmette; facing page 197, photograph House of Worship detail.

10.635. *Haifa, Israel.* Haifa: Haifa Municipality and EL AL Israel Airlines, n.d. [196–?] *passim.*

10.636. *idem.* Haifa: Ministry of Tourism and Haifa Municipality, n.d. [196–?] *passim.*

10.637. *Haifa, Israel: Where to Go and What to Do.* Jerusalem: Published for the Ministry of Tourism by Youval Tal Adv. Ltd., 1965. p. 4.

10.638. Haines, Charles Reginald. *Islam as a Missionary Religion.* London: Society for Promoting Christian Knowledge, 1889. pp. 201–2.

10.639. Hairi, Abdul-Hadi. *Shi'ism and Constitutionalism in Iran: A Study of the Role Played by the Persian Residents of Iraq in Iranian Politics.* Leiden: E.J. Brill, 1977. pp. 27, 69, 71, 76–7, 109–11, 178.

10.639a. Hall, E.T. *The Isles Unveiled: The British Isles.* Wick, U.K.: Peter Reid & Co., n.d. [1933?] 4 leaves, includes reference to 'Abdu'l-Baha.

10.640. Hall, William H. *The Near East – Crossroads of the World.* New York: Interchurch Press, 1920. p. 66.

10.641. Hamel, Guy F. Claude. *Humanity at a Glance.* Ottawa, Ont.: Editions Stencil, n.d. [1977] pp. 33–8.

10.642. Hamilton, Elizabeth. *Put Off Thy Shoes: A Journey Through Palestine.* New York: Scribner's, 1957. p. 86.

10.643. —— *idem.* London: A. Deutsch, 1957. p. 86.

10.644. Hammett, Ralph W. *Architecture in the United States: A Survey of Architectural Styles Since 1776.* New York: John Wiley & Sons, 1976. p. 307.

10.645. *A Handbook of Living Religions.* ed. John R. Hinnells. Harmondsworth, U.K.: Viking, 1984. pp. 14, 156; Denis MacEoin, 'Baha'ism', pp. 475–98.

10.646. *The Handbook of Palestine.* Harry Charles Lukach, Edward Keith-Roach, eds. London: Macmillan & Co., 1922. pp. 33, 58–9, 105, 107.

10.647. *The Handbook of Palestine and Trans-Jordan.* ed. Sir Harry Luke and Edward Keith-Roach. London: Macmillan, 1930. pp. 37, 70–1, 132, 404.

10.648. *idem.* 3rd ed. London: Macmillan, 1934. pp. 38, 72–3, 132, 438.

10.648a. *Handbook of the World's Religions.* ed. A.M. Zehavi. New York: Franklin Watts, 1973. 'Babi', p. 176.

10.649. Handley-Taylor, Geoffrey. *Bibliography of Iran.* Chicago: St James Press, 1969. pp. 104, 107, 108, 109.

10.650. Handy, Robert T. *A History of the Churches in the United States and Canada.* Oxford: At the Clarendon Press, 1976. p. 340.

10.651. Hansen, Dorothy Lee. *Cedar Berries: Poems of Pioneer Texas & American Indian Heritage.* Napa, Calif.: Adinkra Press, 1985. pp. 18–23.

10.652. Har Dayal, Lala. *Hints for Self-Culture.* Bombay; Delhi; Bangalore: Jaico Publishing House, 1961. pp. 97, 110, 114, 115.

10.653. Hardinge, Arthur H. *A Diplomatist in the East.* London: Jonathan Cape, 1928. p. 262.

10.654. Hardon, John A. *Religions of the World.* Westminster, Md.: Newman Press, 1963. pp. 368–9.

10.655. —— *Religions of the World.* New York: Image Books, 1968. II: 97.

10.656. Harman, John William. *Man & Religion.* Parson, W.Va.: Advance Publishing Co., 1934. pp. 137–40.

10.657. Harris, Bill. *Israel, the Promised Land.* New York: Mayflower Books, 1980. pp. 310–11, 316–17.

10.658. Harris, Erdman. *God's Image and Man's Imagination.* New York: Charles Scribner's Sons, 1959. p. 120.

10.659. Harris, George L. *Iraq – Its People, Its Society, Its Culture.* New Haven, Conn.: Human Relations Area Files Press, 1958. pp. 51, 64. (Survey of World Cultures).

10.660. —— *Jordan: Its People, Its Society, Its Culture.* New Haven, Conn.: Human Relations Area Files Press, 1958. p. 28. (Survey of World Cultures).

10.660a. Harris, Maxwell Henley. *The Vegetative Eye.* Melbourne, Vic.; Adelaide, S. Aust.: Reed & Harris, 1943. Ṭáhirih, pp. 18–24, 29–31, 48, 73.

10.661. Harris, Warren G. *Gable and Lombard.* New York: Simon & Schuster, 1974. pp. 137, 153.

10.662. Harrison, Marguerite Elton (Baker). *There's Always Tomorrow.* New York: Farrar & Rhinehart, 1935. p. 644.

10.663. Harry, Miriam. *A Springtide in Palestine.*

London: Ernest Benn; Boston: Houghton Mifflin, 1924. pp. 25–6.

10.664. Hart, Walter C. *First Course in Algebra.* Boston: D.C. Heath, 1947. p. 76.

10.665. Hartman, William C. *Hartman's Who's Who in Occult, Psychic and Spiritual Realms.* New York: Occult Press, 1925. pp. 17, 33, 85–7, 165, 187.

10.666. —— *Who's Who in Occultism, New Thought, Psychism and Spiritualism.* Jamaica, N.Y.: Occult Press, 1927. pp. iv, vi-viii, 1–2, 7, 11, 13, 16, 18, 39, 51–2, 58, 60, 77, 177, 226, 230, 235, 241, 251–3.

10.667. Harvard University Library. *Catalogue of Arabic, Persian and Ottoman Turkish Books.* Cambridge, Mass.: Harvard University Library, 1968. V: 97, 99–100.

10.668. Hasan-e-Fasa'i. *History of Persia Under Qajar Rule.* trans. Heribert Busse. New York: Columbia University Press, 1972. pp. 277, 290–4, 302–4.

10.669. Haug, Arthur [photographs]; Cromie, Robert [text]. *Chicago.* Chicago: Ziff Davis Publishing Co., 1948. p. 67.

10.670. Hawi, Khalil S. *Khalil Gibran: His Background, Character & Works.* Beirut: American University of Beirut, 1963. p. 113.

10.671. Hayden, Robert. *Angle of Ascent: New and Selected Poems.* New York: Liveright, 1975. pp. 15, 39, 61–2, 79, 80, 116, 117.

10.672. —— *Collected Poems.* ed. Frederick Glaysher. New York: Liveright, 1985. pp. 7, 46, 47, 99–100, 138, 159, 180, 197.

10.673. —— *Collected Prose.* ed. Frederick Glaysher. Ann Arbor: University of Michigan Press, 1984. pp. vii, 60, 71, 73, 82, 84, 86, 110–12, 197, 200.

10.674. —— *Words in the Mourning Time.* New York: October House, 1970. pp. 15, 50–1.

10.675. Hayes, Carlton Joseph Huntley. *A Political and Cultural History of Modern Europe.* New York: Macmillan Co., 1917, 1924, 1939. II: 450.

10.676. Hebrew University of Jerusalem. Institute of Contemporary Jewry. Oral History Division. *Oral History Division, Catalogue No. 3.* Jerusalem: Keter Publishing House, 1970. p. 38.
　Listing for interview with Salman Hougi Aboudi, mention of Jewish Bahá'ís in Baghdad.

10.677. Heckethorn, Charles William. *The Secret Societies of All Ages and Countries.* New Hyde Park, N.Y.: University Books, 1965. II: 263–9.

10.678, Hedges, Sid G. *Prayers and Thoughts from World Religions.* Richmond, Va.: John Knox Press, 1970, 1972. *passim.*

10.679. Hefley, James C. *The Youthnappers.* Wheaton, Ill.: Victor Books, 1977. pp. 89–90.

10.680. Heikal, Mohamed. *Iran, the Untold Story.* New York: Pantheon Books, 1982. p. 69.

10.681. —— *The Return of the Ayatollah: The Iranian Revolution from Mossadeq to Khomeini.* London: André Deutsch, 1981. p. 69.

10.682. Helms, Cynthia. *An Ambassador's Wife in Iran.* New York: Dodd, Mead & Co., 1981. p. 43.

10.683. Helprin, Mark. *Refiner's Fire: The Life and Adventures of Marshall Pearl, a Foundling.* New York: Dell Publishing Co., 1977. p. 11.

10.684. Herod, F.G. *What Men Believe.* London: Methuen Educational, 1968. p. 140.

10.685. Herrick, George F. *Christians and Mohammedans: A Plea for Bridging the Chasm.* New York: Fleming Revell Co., 1912. p. 145.

10.686. Herzel, Theodor. *Altneuland: Old-New Land: Novel.* Haifa: Haifa Publishing Company, 1964. pp. 66, 99.

10.686a. Hewitt, Gordon. *The Problems of Success: A History of the Missionary Society, 1910–1942.* London: SCM Press, 1971. I: 387.

10.687. Higgins, Harold H. *Shadows to the Unseen.* North Montpelier, Vt.: Driftwood Press, 1937. p. 52.

10.688. Hill, George H. *Airwaves of the Soul: The Influence and Growth of Religious Broadcasting in America.* Saratoga, Calif.: R & E Publishers, 1983. pp. 18, 27, 29.

10.689. Hindus, Maurice. *In Search of a Future: Persia, Egypt, Iraq, and Palestine.* Garden City, N.Y.: Doubleday, 1949. p. 21.

10.690. Hippchen, Leonard J.; Yim, Yong. *Terrorism, International Crime & Arms Control.* Springfield, Ill.: Charles C. Thomas Publisher, 1982. pp. 49, 64, 263, 272, dedication.

10.691. Hiro, Dilip. *Iran Under the Ayatollas.* London: Routledge & Kegan Paul, 1985. pp. 38, 39–40, 75, 78, 243.

10.692. *The Historians' History of the World.* 25 vols. London: Hooper & Jackson, 1904. XXIV: 493–4, 499.

10.693. *History of Nations.* ed. Henry Cabot Lodge. 25 vols. New York: P.F. Collier & Son, 1928. *India and Modern Persia,* vol. 5, pp. 362–3, 401.

10.694. Hitti, Philip K. *History of Syria, Including Lebanon and Palestine.* London: Macmillan, 1951. pp. 60, 585.

10.695. —— *The Near East in History.* Princeton, N.J.: D. Van Nostrand Co., 1961. pp. 391, 403–7, 415.

10.696. —— *The Origin of the Druze People & Religion: With Extracts from Their Sacred Writings.* New York: AMS Press, 1966. pp. 30, 48.

10.697. —— *Short History of the Near East.* New York: D. Van Nostrand Company, c1966. pp. 191–2, 195.

10.698. Hoade, Eugene. *A Short Guide to the Holy Land.* 2nd ed. Jerusalem: Franciscan Printing Press, 1973. p. 174.

10.699. Hocking, William Ernest. *Living Religions and a World Faith.* New York: Macmillan Co., 1940. pp. 180, 212.

10.700. Hodgson, Marshall G.S. *The Order of the Assassins.* 's-Gravenhage, Netherlands: Mouton & Co., 1955. pp. 276, 291.

10.701. —— *The Venture of Islam: Conscience and History in a World Civilization.* Chicago: University of Chicago Press, 1974. III: 304–7, 310.

10.702. Hoffman, Daniel P. *India's Social Miracle.* Healdsburg, Calif.: Naturegraph Co., 1961. pp. 40, 68, 95.

10.702a. Holbach, Maude M. *Bible Ways in Bible Lands: An Impression of Palestine.* London: Kegan Paul, Trench, Trubner, 1912. pp. 5–10.

10.703. *Holiday Magazine Travel Guide, Israel.* New York: Random House, 1973. pp. 91, 94. Photograph of Shrine of the Báb and International Archives Building, page 91.

10.704. Holisher, Desider. *The House of God.* New York: Crown Publishers, 1946. p. 171. Photograph of Bahá'í House of Worship, Wilmette, page 171.

10.705. Holm, Jean. *The Study of Religions.* London: Sheldon Press, c1977. p. 20.

10.706. Holmes, John Haynes. *Palestine To-Day and To-Morrow.* New York: Macmillan Co., 1929. pp. 32–6.

10.706a. —— *idem.* London: George Allen & Unwin, 1930. pp. 32–6.

10.707. —— *idem.* New York: Arno, 1977. pp. 32–6.

10.708. *The Holy Land.* Jerusalem: Franciscan Printing Press, 1973. pp. 18–19.

10.709. *Home Town Tour.* Chicago: Marshall Field & Co., 1943. 'Baha'i Temple', p. 10.

10.710. Hoover, W.I.T. *Religionisms and Christianity.* Boston: Stratford Co., 1924. pp. v, 165–78.

10.711. Hopfe, Lewis M. *Religions of the World.* Beverly Hills, Calif.: Glencoe Press, 1976. pp. 294–9.

10.712. Hopkins, E. Washburn. *The History of Religions.* New York: Macmillan Co., 1918, 1926. pp. 479, 482.

10.713. —— *Origin and Evolution of Religion.* New Haven, Conn.: Yale University Press, 1923, 1924. p. 71.

10.714. —— *idem.* New York: Cooper Square Publishers, 1969. p. 71.

10.715. Hoult, Thomas Ford. *The Sociology of Religion.* New York: The Dryden Press, 1958. pp. 90, 128, 129.

10.716. Hourani, Albert. *Arabic Thought in the Liberal Age, 1798–1839.* London: Oxford University Press, issued under the auspices of the Royal Institute of International Affairs, 1962, 1967. p. 124.

10.717. House, David. *The Biogas Handbook.* Culver City, Calif.: Peace Press, 1978, 1981. pp. 258–9.

10.718. Howard, David; Ayers, John. *China for the West: Chinese Porcelain and Other Decorative Arts for Export from the Mottahedeh Collection.* London: Sotheby Parke Bernet, 1978. II: 481, 483.

10.719. Howe, Mark Anthony de Wolfe. *Holmes-Pollock Letters, 1874–1932.* Cambridge, Mass.: Harvard University Press, 1941, 1946. I: 206.

10.720. —— *John Jay Chapman and His Letters.* Boston: Houghton Mifflin, 1937. 'Abdu'l-Bahá, p. 260.

10.721. Howells, Rulon S. *Do Men Believe What Their Church Prescribes.* Salt Lake City, Utah: Deseret Book Co., 1932. p. 160.

10.722. Howen, Herbert H. *Asia, a Short History from Earliest Times to the Present.* Boston: Little, Brown & Co., 1936.

10.723. Hoxha, Enver. *Reflections on the Middle East, 1958–1983.* Tirana, Albania: The Institute of Marxist-Leninist Studies of the Central Committee of the Party of Labour of Albania: The '8 Nëntori' Publishing House, 1984. p. 369.

10.724. Huart, Clément. *Ancient Persia and Iran-*

ian Civilization. New York: Barnes and Noble, 1972. p. 79.

10.725. —— *A History of Arabic Literature*. London: W. Heinemann, 1903. p. 212.

10.726. —— *idem*. New York: D. Appleton & Co., 1903. p. 212.

10.727. Hubbard, Elbert. *Hollyhocks and Golden Glow*. East Aurora: N.Y.: Roycrofters, 1912. pp. 21–40.

10.728. —— *Selected Writings*. New York: Wm. H. Wise & Co., 1928. This volume entitled: *Hundred-Point Men*. X: 320–32. Photograph of 'Abdu'l-Bahá, p.320.

10.729. Hudson, Dale L. *Children Must be Taught How to See: A Practical Guide for Parents and Teachers*. Suva, Fiji: United International Publications, 1985. p. iii.

10.730. Hudson, Winthrop S. *Religion in America*. New York: Charles Scribner's Sons, 1973. p. 287.

10.731. *Hudūd al-'Ālam: The Regions of the World: A Persian Geography, 372 A.H., 982 A.D.* trans. V. Minorsky. 2nd ed.; with pref. by V.V. Barthold trans. from Russian by Minorsky; ed. C.E. Bosworth. London: Luzac & Co. for the Trustees of the E.J.W. Gibb Memorial, 1970. (E.J.W. Gibb Memorial Series. New Series; xi). pp. xlii–xliv.

10.732. Huebener, Theodore; Voss, Carl. *This Is Israel – Palestine. Yesterday, Today and Tomorrow*. New York: Philosophical Library, 1956. p. 110.

10.733. Hughes, Thomas Patrick. *Dictionary of Islam*. London: W.H. Allen & Co., 1865. p. 579.

10.734. Human Rights Internet (Washington, D.C.). *North American Human Rights Directory*. ed. Laurie S. Wiseberg and Hazel Sirett. Washington, D.C.: Human Rights Internet, 1984. p. 172.

10.735. Humana, Charles. *World Human Rights Guide*. New York: Pica Press, 1984. p. 164.

10.736. Hume, Robert Ernest. *The World's Living Religions*. New York: Charles Scribner's Sons, 1924. p. 212.

10.737. —— *idem*. Completely rev. New York: Charles Scribner's Sons, 1959. pp. 13, 14, 221, 240–1.

10.738. Hume-Griffith, M.E. *Behind the Veil in Persia and Turkish Arabia*. Philadelphia, Pa.: Lippincott, 1909. pp. 116–19.

10.739. —— *idem*. 2nd ed. London: Seeley & Co., 1909. pp. 116–19.

10.740. Hunt, Paul. *Inside Iran*. Tring, Herts.: Lion, 1981. p. 107.

10.741. Hunter, Stanley Armstrong. *Temple of Religion and Tower of Peace at the 1939 Golden Gate International Exposition*. San Francisco: Temple of Religion and Tower of Peace, 1940. pp. 10, 54, 85.

10.742. Hussain, Asaf. *Islamic Iran: Revolution or Counter Revolution*. London: Frances Pinter, 1985. p. 79.

10.743. —— *Islamic Movements in Egypt, Pakistan and Iran: An Annotated Bibliography*. London: Mansell Publishing Limited, 1983. p. 128.

10.744. *Hutchinson's History of the Nations: A Popular, Concise, Pictorial, and Authoritative Account of Each Nation from the Earliest Times to the Present Day*. ed. Walter Hutchinson. London: Hutchinson & Co., n.d. [1914?] pt. 24 p. 998, pt. 25 pp. 1001.

10.745. Hutchison, John A. *Paths of Faith*. New York: McGraw-Hill, 1969. pp. 185, 599, 606.

10.746. —— *idem*. 3rd ed. New York: McGraw-Hill, 1981. pp. 516, 526–7.

10.747. Huxley, Julian. *Knowledge, Morality and Destiny*. New York: Mentor Books, 1957, 1960. p. 241.

10.748. Hyamson, Albert M. *Palestine Old and New*. New York: Robert M. McBride, 1928. pp. 14, 233–4.

10.749. Hyre, K.M.; Goodman, Eli. *Price Guide to the Occult and Related Subjects*. Los Angeles, Calif.: Reference Guide Inc., 1967. pp. 11, 120, 161, 310.

I

10.750. *I Believe: The Place of Faith in World Religions*. London: Christian Education Movement, 1978. pp. 1–4.

10.751. *Ibrahim Yazdi Interview*. New York: WNET/Thirteen, 1979. (MacNeil-Lehrer Report; transcript no.1048 show no.5068).

10.752. *An Illustrated History of the World's Religions.* ed. Geoffrey Parrinder. Feltham, Middlesex: Newnes, 1983. pp. 378, 507, 515.

10.753. Inchbold, A.C. *Under the Syrian Sun: The Lebanon, Baalbek, Galilee, and Judaea.* London: Hutchinson & Co., 1906. II: 356–62.

10.754. India. Persian Boundary Commission. *Eastern Persia: An Account of the Journeys of the Persian Boundary Commission, 1870–71–72.* London: Macmillan and Co., 1876. I: 108.

10.755. Indian National Congress (55th Session: 1948: Jaipur). *The Indian National Congress Souvenir, 55th Session, Jaipur, 1948.* ed. R.B. Vasudev. Delhi: Hindustan Publicity Corporation, 1948. Shoghi Effendi, 'A Pattern for Future Society', pp. [64–5]

10.756. *Initiation Rites.* ed. John Prickett. London: Lutterworth Educational, 1978. pp. 27–8.

10.757. Inlow, E. Burke. *Shahanshah: A Study of the Monarchy of Iran.* Delhi: Motilal Banarsidass, 1979. pp. 127–30.

10.758. *Instead of Violence: Writings by the Great Advocates of Peace and Nonviolence Throughout History.* ed. Arthur and Lila Weinberg. New York: Grossman, 1963. pp. 295–7.

10.759. *Inter-Faith Service in Observance of International Youth Year, 1985.* n.p. [Port-of-Spain], Trinidad: Religious Fraternity in Trinidad & Tobago: National Coordinating Committee of the IYY, 1985. pp. 3, 4.

10.760. International Biographical Centre (Cambridge, U.K.). *Personal Information Card, Sverre Ryen Holmsen.* Cambridge: International Biographical Centre, n.d. [1969?] Reference to Holmsen being a Bahá'í.

10.761. International Conference on the Application of Mini- and Micro-Computers in Information, Documentation, and Libraries (1983: Tel Aviv). *The Application of Mini- and Micro-Computers in Information, Documentation and Libraries.* edited by Carl Keren and Linda Perlmutter. Amsterdam [etc.]: North-Holland, 1983. Kathleen Keenan, 'Use of Relational Databases for Information Retrieval', pp. 153–8.
Describes the Bahá'í World Centre's computerized document indexing system.

10.762. International Congress of Human Sciences in Asia and North Africa (31st: 1983: Tokyo). *Proceedings of the Thirty-First International Congress of Human Sciences in Asia and North Africa, Tokyo-Kyoto, 31st August–7th September 1983.* ed. Yamamoto Tatsuro. Tokyo: Toho Gakkai, 1984. pp. 275, 279–80.
Abstract of Amin Banani's paper on 'Religion

or Foreign Intrigue: The Case of the Babi-Baha'i Movements in Iran'.

10.763. International Congress of World Fellowship of Faiths (1956: Tokyo). *Sessions and Proceedings.* Tokyo: World Fellowship of Faiths, 1956. pp. 12, 15, 29–31.

10.764. International Solidarity Front for the Defense of Iranian People's Democratic Rights. *The Crimes of Khomeini's Regime: A Report on Violations of Civil and Political Rights by the Islamic Republic of Iran.* Berkeley, Calif.: ISF Iran, 1982. pp. 51–3, 139, 152, 156, 175.

10.765. —— *Report on ISF Iran's Lobbying Activities, 38th Session of the UN Human Rights Commission.* Paris; Berkeley, Calif.: ISF Iran, 1982. pp. 4–6, 8, 10, 28–9.

10.765a. International Symposium on Asian Studies (2nd: 1980). *Proceedings of the Second International Symposium on Asian Studies.* Hong Kong: Asian Research Service, 1980. Garrigues, Steven L., 'Universalization of Religious Identity: The Expansion of the Bahá'í Faith beyond the Islamic Environment', pp. 619–32.

10.766. *Interreligous Calendar, 1983.* Los Angeles: Interreligious Council of Southern California, 1983. pp. 3–5.

10.767. *Interreligious Calendar, 1984.* Los Angeles: Interreligious Council of Southern California, 1984. pp. 3–5.

10.768. Ioannides, Christos P. *America's Iran: Injury and Catharsis.* Lanham, Md.; New York; London: University Press of America, 1984. p. 152.

10.769. Iqbal, Muhammad. *The Development of Metaphysics in Persia: A Contribution to the History of Muslim Philosophy.* Lahore, Pakistan: Bazin-Iqbal, 1964. pp. 125, 143–4.

10.770. —— *The Reconstruction of Religious Thought in Islam.* London: Oxford University Press, 1934. p. 145.

10.771. —— *idem.* Lahore, Pakistan: Muhammad Ashraf, 1958. p. 152.

10.771a. —— *Six Lectures on the Reconstruction of Religious Thought in Islam.* Lahore: Kapur Art Printing Works, 1930. p. 214.

10.772. *Iran.* Herbert H. Vreeland, research chairman and editor [et. al.] New Haven, Conn.: Human Relations Area Files, 1957. (Country survey series; v.3). pp. 101, 254, 296, 297.

10.772a. *Iran – a Revolution in Turmoil.* ed. Haleh Afshar. Basingstoke, Hants.; London: Macmillan, 1985. p. 134.

10.773. *Iran and Islam: In Memory of the Late Vladimir Minorsky.* C.E. Bosworth, ed. Edinburgh: University Press, 1971. pp. 48, 56.

10.774. *Iran, Background Notes.* Washington, D.C.: Department of State, Dec. 1976. p. 1.

10.775. *idem.* Washington, D.C.: Department of State, May 1982. pp. 1, 4.

10.776. Iran Committee for Democratic Action and Human Rights. *Human Rights & Civil Liberties in Iran, May 1980–July 1981.* Flossmoor, Ill., 1981. pp. 9–10.

10.777. *Iran, in Defense of Human Rights.* n.p. [Paris?]: National Movement of the Iranian Resistance, 1983. pp. 38, 40, 90, 91, 95, 104, 106, 137, 156.

10.778. *The Iran-Iraq War: New Weapons, Old Conflicts.* ed. Shirin Tahir-Kheli, Shaheen Ayubi. New York: Praeger, 1983. (Foreign Policy Issues). Nikki R. Keddie, 'The Minorities Question in Iran', pp. 90, 91, 105–6, 107, 108.

10.778a. *Iran Since the Revolution: Internal Dynamics, Regional Conflict, and the Superpowers.* ed. Barry M. Rosen. Boulder, Colo.: Social Science Monographs; New York: Columbia University Press [distributor], 1985. pp. 14, 15, 85.

10.779. *Iranian Civilization and Culture: Essays in Honour of the 2,500th Anniversary of the Founding of the Persian Empire.* ed. Charles J. Adams. Montreal: McGill University Institute of Islamic Studies, 1972. p. 10.

10.780. *Iranian Nationalism and the Great Powers.* New York: Middle East Research & Information Project, May 1975. p. 5. (MERIP Reports; no.37).

10.781. *Iranian Refugees: New Phenomena.* n.p. [United States]: Commission to Aid Iranian Refugees, 1984. pp. 4–5, 6, 23, 58.

10.782. *Iranian Revolution in Perspective.* Farhad Kazemi, ed. Chestnut Hill, Mass.: Society for Iranian Studies, 1981. pp. 67–8, 71, 78, 96. This is v.13 no.1–4 of *Iranian Studies.*

10.783. *Iranians in the U.K.* London: UKCOSA, July 1982. pp. 13–14.

10.784. *Iraq and the Persian Gulf.* n.p. [London]: Naval Intelligence Division, 1944. (Geographic Handbook Series). pp. 316, 330.

10.785. Iraq Petroleum Company. *Handbook of the Territories Which Form the Theatre of Operations of the Iraq Petroleum Company Limited and Its Associated Companies.* London: Iraq Petroleum Company, 1948 (London: St. Clements Press). pp. 25, 110.

10.786. Irfani, Suroosh. *Iran's Islamic Revolution: Popular Liberation or Religious Dictatorship?* London: Zed Books Ltd., 1983. pp. 5–6, 48, 71.
Bahá'ís not to blame for acts of Bábís; 'imperialists' used popular fear of Bahá'ís to achieve their ends in Iran.

10.787. Irving, Clive. *Crossroads of Civilization: 3000 Years of Persian History.* London: Weidenfeld and Nicolson, 1979. pp. 184, 186.

10.788. —— *Promise the Earth.* New York: Ballantine Books, 1982. pp. 47, 208–9.
Historical novel of British colonialism in the Middle East, with references to the Bahá'í Faith.

10.789. Irwin, Beatrice. *The New Science of Colour.* London: William Rider, 1923. pp. 12, 116–17.

10.790. Ishaque, M. *Four Eminent Poetesses of Iran.* Calcutta: Iran Society, 1950. pp. 28–35.

10.791. —— *Modern Persian Poetry.* Calcutta: Mir Mohammed Israil, 1943. pp. 2, 39.

10.792. Ishmael, Woodi. *The Power of Faith.* New York: Pocket Books, 1965. p. 23.

10.793. *Islam and Development: Religion and Socio-Political Change.* ed. John L. Esposito. Syracuse, N.Y.: Syracuse University Press, 1980. (Contemporary Issues in the Middle East). p. 16.

10.794. *Islam and Russia: A Detailed Analysis of An Outline of the History of Islamic Studies in the USSR by N.A. Smirnov.* Oxford: Central Asian Research Centre in Association with St Anthony's College (Oxford) Soviet Affairs Study Group, 1956. pp. 35, 44, 54–5, 61, 63, 65, 66, 68, 69, 70, 75, 77, 83, 85.

10.795. *Islam in Africa.* ed. James Kritzeck, William H. Lewis. New York; London: Van Nostrand-Reinhold, 1969. p. 234.

10.796. *Islam in India and the Middle East.* comp. S.M. Ahmed. Allahabad: Abbas Manzil Library, n.d. [1951?] (Islamic Series; no.5). pp. 161–2.

10.797. *Islam in the Modern World.* ed. Denis MacEoin, Ahmed al-Shahi. London; Canberra: Croom Helm, 1983. pp. 95–6, 103.

10.798. *Islam To-Day.* ed. A.J. Arberry, Rom Landau. London: Faber and Faber, 1943. pp. 173n, 177.

10.799. *Islamic Dilemmas: Reformers, Nationalists and Industrialization: The Southern Shore of the Mediterranean.* ed. Ernest Gellner. Berlin; New

York; Amsterdam: Mouton Publishers, 1985. (Religion and Society; 25). p. 13.

10.800. *Israel.* Berne: Hallweg: Steimatzky's Agency in Israel, 1967. pp. 13, 24–5.

10.801. *Israel.* Paris; Geneva; New York; Karlsruhe: Nagel Publishers, 1954. (Nagel Travel Guide Series: English). pp. 155–6. Cover title: *Nagel's Israel Travel Guide.* Spine title: *Nagel's Israel.*

10.802. *Israel: Its Role in Civilization.* ed. Moshe Davis. New York: The Seminary Israel Institute, 1956. p. 171.

10.803. *idem.* New York: Arno Press, 1977. p. 171.

10.804. *Israel Pocket Atlas and Handbook.* comp. Hermann M.Z. Meyer. Jerusalem: The Universitas, 1961. p. 60.

10.805. *Israel Travel Agents Manual, 1983–84.* Jerusalem: Israel Economist Publishing Service, 1983. p. 113.

10.806. *Issues in the Islamic Movement, 1981–82 (1401–1402).* ed. Kalim Siddiqui. London: The Open Press Limited, 1983. p. 251.

10.807. *Issues in the Islamic Movement.* ed. Kalim Siddiqui. London: The Open Press, 1984. Yaqub Zaki, 'Reagan Blows the Baha'i Cover', pp. 347–9.

J

10.808. Jack, Homer A. *Nuclear Disarmament, the Priority for Humanity.* Chicago: World Without War Publications, 1984. p. 8.

10.809. Jackson, A.V. Williams. *Persia, Past and Present.* New York; London: Macmillan & Co., 1906. pp. 28, 48–50, 119, 273, 328, 375.

10.810. —— *idem.* New York; AMS Press, 1975. pp. 28, 48–50, 119, 273, 328, 375.

10.811. Jamali, Mohammed. *The New Iraq: Its Problem of Bedouin Education.* New York: Teacher's College, Columbia University, 1934. p. 109.

10.812. Jamalzadeh, Mohammed Ali. *Isfahan Is Half the World: Memories of a Persian Boyhood.* trans. W.L. Heston. Princeton, N.J.: Princeton University Press, 1983. pp. 53, 54, 56–63, 214–27, 252, 287, 288.
Review:
Betteridge, Anne H. *The Muslim World* (Hartford, Conn.), v.75 no.3–4 (July–Oct. 1985), pp. 183–4. Bábís, p. 184.

10.813. James, George Wharton. *Singing Through Life with God.* Pasadena, Calif.: Radiant Life Press, 1920. pp. 400–1.

10.814. Japan Religious Conference (1928: Tokyo). *The Japan Religious Conference Held at Tokyo, June 5–8, 1928.* Tokyo: The Japan Religious Association, 1928. Agnes Alexander, Bahá'í representative, pp. 11–12.

10.815. Jennings, Gary. *March of the Gods.* New York: Association Press, 1976. pp. 155–6.

10.816. *Jerusalem 1918–1920: Being the Record of the Pro-Jerusalem Council During the Period of the British Mandate.* ed. C.R. Ashbee. London: John Murray, 1921. 'Sir Abbas Eff. Abd-el-Baha, K.B.E.', p. 74.

10.817. *Jerusalem – the Future of the Holy City for Three Monotheisms: Hearing Before the Subcommittee on the Near East of the Committee on Foreign Affairs, House of Representatives.* Washington, D.C.: U.S. Government Printing Office, 1971. pp. 205–6.

10.818. Jessup, Henry Harris. *Fifty-Three Years in Syria.* 2 vols. New York: Fleming Revell, 1910. I: 329; II: 605, 636–8, 687–8.

10.819. *The Jews – Their History, Culture and Religion.* ed. Louis Finkelstein. 3rd ed. n.p. [Philadelphia, Pa.]: Jewish Publication Society of America, 1960. II: 1186.

10.820. Jiggetts, J. Ida. *Israel to Me: A Negro Social Worker, Inside Israel.* New York: Bloch Publishing Co., 1957. pp. 90, 92.

10.821. Johnson, Gail Cook. *High-Level Manpower in Iran: From Hidden Conflict to Crisis.* New York: Praeger, 1980. p. 81.

10.822. Johnson, Paul. *A History of Christianity.* London: Weidenfeld and Nicolson, 1976. p. 497.

10.823. Johnson, R.P. *Middle East Pilgrimage.* New York: Friendship Press, 1958. p. 144.

10.824. Joint Committee on the Survey of Christian Literature for Moslems. *Christian Literature in Moslem Lands: A Study of the Activities of the Moslem and Christian Press in All*

Mohammedan Countries. New York: George H. Doran, 1923. pp. 55, 105–6.

10.825. Jones, Allen K. *Iranian Refugees: The Many Faces of Persecution*. Washington, D.C.: U.S. Committee for Refugees, 1984. pp. 4–6, 15, 17, 18. (USCR Issue Paper).

10.826. Jones, L. Bevan. *The People of the Mosque*. Calcutta, India: Association Press, Y.M.C.A., 1932. pp. 141–6.

10.827. Jordan, David Starr. *The Days of a Man: Being Memories of a Naturalist, Teacher, and Minor Prophet of Democracy*. Yonkers, N.Y.:

World Book Company, 1922. II: 414.

10.828. Jordan, Louis Henry. *Comparative Religion: Its Adjuncts and Allies*. London: Humphrey Milford: Oxford University Press, 1915. pp. 288–93, 421.
  Review of Hermann Roemer's *Die Babi-Behai;* anti-Bahá'í work from a Christian viewpoint.

10.829. *Joy of Knowledge Library*. London: Mitchell Beazley Encyclopaedias Ltd., 1968. 'Baha'i Faith', 'Bahaullah', Fact index A-K, p. 68.

K

10.830. Kahn, E.J., Jr. *Who, Me?* New York: Harper, 1949. p. 178–9.

10.831. Kalmykov, Andrei Dmitrievich. *Memoirs of a Russian Diplomat: Outposts of the Empire, 1893–1917*. ed. Alexandra Kalmykow. New Haven, Conn.; London: Yale University Press, 1971. (Yale Russian and East European Studies; no.10). 'Ishqábád Temple, pp. 151–3.

10.832. Kamshad, Hassan. *Modern Persian Prose Literature*. Cambridge, U.K.: University Press, 1966. pp. 48, 51, 194.

10.833. Karmon, Yehuda. *Israel – a Regional Geography*. London: Wiley Interscience, 1971. pp. 79, 212.

10.834. Katouzian, Homa. *The Political Economy of Modern Iran: Despotism and Pseudo-Modernism, 1926–1979*. London: Macmillan, 1981. pp. 62, 70, 90, 209.

10.834a. Kauffman, Donald T. *The Dictionary of Religious Terms*. London: Marshall, Morgan & Scott, 1967. 'Bab, The', p. 55; 'Babi', 'Babism', p. 56; 'Bahaism', 'Baha Ullah', p. 57.

10.835. Kay, C.M. *A Story of Stories*. 2nd ed. with an additional chapter on the Bahá'í religion. Hythe, Kent: Volturna Press, 1985. pp. 97–105.

10.836. Kazemzadeh, Firuz. *Russia and Britain in Persia, 1864–1914: A Study in Imperialism*. New Haven, Conn.: Yale University Press, 1968. pp. 188, 445–6, 513, 585.

10.837. Keddie, Nikki R. *Iran – Religion, Politics and Society: Collected Essays*. London: Cass, 1980. pp. 15–23, 24, 26, 27, 28, 34–5, 36, 38, 43, 47, 48, 49, 50, 62, 69, 94–5, 115, 151.

10.838. —— *An Islamic Response to Imperialism: Political and Religious Writings of Sayyid Jamāl ad-Dīn 'al-Afghānī'*. Berkeley, Calif.: University of California, 1968. pp. 10–11, 30, 43, 158.

10.839. —— *Religion and Rebellion in Iran: The Tobacco Protest of 1891–1892*. London: Frank Cass & Co., 1966. pp. 56, 71, 72, 102, 107–9, 113, 132, 136, 143, 144.

10.840. —— *Roots of Revolution: An Interpretive History of Modern Iran*. New Haven, Conn.; London: Yale University Press, 1981. pp. 22, 48–52, 64, 242.

10.841. —— *Sayyid Jamal ad-Din 'al-Afghani': A Political Biography*. Berkeley, Calif.: University of California, 1972. pp. 19–22, 275, 378.

10.841a. *Keesing's Contemporary Archives, Record of World Events*. London: Longman, 1955– . 1983: 3400; 1984: 32690–1; 1985: 33950.

10.842. Keeton, Morris. *Values Men Live By*. New York: Abingdon Press, 1960. p. 26.

10.843. Kellett, E.E. *A Short History of Religions*. London: Victor Gollancz, 1933. pp. 364–72.

10.844. Kendrick, Lorna Langton. *Lorna*. ed. Patricia Kendrick Rothman. n.p.: Conrad Rothman, 1975. p. 24.

10.845. Kennedy, J.M. *The Religions and Philosophies of the East*. London: T. Werner Laurie, n.d. [1911] pp. 169–84.

10.846. —— *idem*. New York: John Lane Company, 1911. pp. 169–84.

10.847. Kennedy, Richard. *The International Dictionary of Religion: A Profusely Illustrated*

Guide to the Beliefs of the World. New York: Crossroad, 1984. pp. 24–5, 247.

10.847a. Ketko, Shlomo. *Project: A Guide for Participants in Youth and Student Programmes in Israel.* 3rd ed. Jerusalem: Youth and Hechalutz Department, the Jewish Agency, 1970. p. 78.

10.848. Keyan, Rostam. *Being and Alienation.* New York: Philosophical Library, 1981. pp. 167, 233, 234, 240, 369–73.
   Bahá'í Faith described as 'neo-Zoroastrian'; makes claim that Bahá'u'lláh was 'converted to Mazdaism' by Manikji Limji Hataria.

10.849. Keyserling, Hermann. *The Travel Diary of a Philosopher.* 2 vols. New York: Harcourt, Brace & Co., 1925. I: 160, 178; II: 273.

10.850. Khomeini, Ruhu'llah. *A Clarification of Questions.* trans. J. Borujerdi. Boulder, Colo.; London: Westview Press, 1984. pp. 410, 413, 432.

10.851. —— *Imam Khomeini's Message for (the 5th of June/15th of Khordad).* Tehran: Council for the Celebrations of the Third Anniversary of the Victory of the Islamic Revolution, 1982. pp. 21–2.

10.852. —— *Islam and Revolution.* trans. and annotated Hamid Algar. Berkeley, Calif.: Mizan Press, 1981. pp. 128, 152 n28, 161 n151.

10.853. *Khomeini & the Opposition.* New York: Middle East Research & Information Project, Mar.–Apr. 1982. pp. 5, 11. (MERIP Reports; no.104).

10.854. Khouri, Rami G. *The Jordan Valley: Life and Society Below Sea Level.* London: New York; Longman, published in association with the Jordan Valley Authority, 1981. p. 79.

10.855. Kidron, Michael; Segal, Ronald. *The New State of the World Atlas.* New York: Simon and Schuster, 1984. Map 56.

10.856. Kikabhai, Madhuri. *Whither India?* Siramban, India: Mathruwani Press, n.d. [between 1945 and 1960] p. 44.

10.856a. Kim, Young Oon. *World Religions, volume 1: Living Religions of the Middle East.* New York: Golden Gate Publishing Co., 1976, pp. 115, 262–3.

10.857. King, Winston. *Introduction to Religion.* New York: Harper & Row, 1954. p. 485.

10.858. *The Kingdom of Christ Is in Sight!* n.p. [Ireland], n.d. [1985?] 31 p. p. 6.

10.859. Kirkpatrick, Clifford. *Religion in Human Affairs.* London: John Wiley & Sons; London: Chapman & Hall, 1929. pp. 212, 291, 307, 487.

10.860. Kisch, Frederick Hermann. *Palestine Diary.* London: V. Gollancz, 1938. p. 133.

10.861. —— *idem.* New York: AMS, 1975. p. 133.

10.862. Klein, F.A. *The Religion of Islam.* London: Curzon Press; New York: Humanities Press, 1979. pp. 238–41.

10.863. Klimovich, Lyutsian Ippolitovich. *Islam International.* Washington, D.C.: U.S. Department of Commerce, Joint Publications Research Service, 1966. pp. 158–64, 186–7.

10.864. Kloss, Heinz; McConnell, G.D. *The Written Languages of the World: A Survey of the Degree and Modes of Use.* Québec: Presses de l'Université Laval, 1978. I:451.

10.865. Knanishu, Joseph. *About Persia and Its People: A Description of Their Manners, Customs, and Home Life, Including Engagements, Marriages, Modes of Traveling, Forms of Punishments, Superstitions, etc.* Rock Island, Ill.: Lutheran Augustana Book Concern, 1899. p. 206.

10.866. Koeper, Frederick. *Illinois Architecture from Territorial Times to the Present: A Selective Guide.* Chicago; London: University of Chicago Press, 1968. Bahá'í House of Worship, pp. 294–5.

10.867. Kohn, Hans. *A History of Nationalism in the East.* New York: Harcourt Brace, 1929. pp. 15, 20, 31–5, 36, 320, 328, 430.

10.868. —— *idem.* Grosse Point, Mich.: Scholarly Press, 1969. pp. 15, 20, 31–5, 36, 320, 328, 430.

10.869. Kolarz, Walter. *Religion in the Soviet Union.* London: Macmillan & Co.; New York: St Martin's Press, 1966. pp. 470–3, 497.

10.869a. Konikoff, A. *Trans-Jordan – An Economic Survey.* Jerusalem: Jewish Agency for Palestine, 1943 p. 20.

10.869b. —— *Transjordan – An Economic Survey.* Jerusalem: Economic Research Institute of the Jewish Agency for Palestine, 1946. p. 21.

10.869c. Kraemer, Hendrik. *World Cultures and World Religions: The Coming Dialogue.* Philadelphia, Pa.: Westminster Press, 1960. p. 269.

10.870. Kubie, Nora. *Israel.* New York: Franklin Watts, 1975. pp. 26, 38.

10.871. Kudsi-Zadeh, A. Albert. *Sayyid Jamal al-Din al-Afghani: An Annotated Bibliography.* Leiden: E.J. Brill, 1970. pp. 7, 32, 81.

10.872. Kulvinskas, Viktoras. *Survival into the 21st Century: Planetary Healers Manual.* Woodstock Valley, Conn.: 21st Century Publications, 1975. p. 21.

10.873. Kuper, Leo. *The Prevention of Genocide*. New Haven, Conn.; London: Yale University Press, 1985. pp. 152–3, 163–4, 170, 222, 223.

10.874. Kurian, George Thomas. *Encyclopedia of the Third World*. rev. ed. London: Mansell, 1982. II: 837, 857, 1205.

L

10.875. Ladjevardi, Habib. *Labor Unions and Autocracy in Iran*. Syracuse, N.Y.: Syracuse University Press, 1985. (Contemporary Issues in the Middle East). p. 149.

10.876. Laffin, John. *The Dagger of Islam*. London: Sphere Books, 1979. pp. 90, 128.

10.877. —— *idem*. rev. Bantam ed. New York: Bantam, 1981. pp. 93, 132.

10.878. —— *Know the Middle East*. Gloucester, U.K.: Alan Sutton, 1985. pp. 13–14.

10.879. Lake Mohonk Conference on International Arbitration (18th: 1912). *Report*. Lake Mohonk, N.Y., 1912. pp. 42–3.
Talk by 'Abdu'l-Bahá.

10.880. Lammens, Henri. *Islam – Beliefs and Institutions*. trans. E. Denison Ross from the French. London: Methuen & Co., 1929. pp. 189–96.

10.881. —— *idem*. New York: E.P. Dutton & Co., 1929. pp. 189–96.

10.882. Landau, Rom. *Search for Tomorrow*. London: Weidenfeld and Nicolson, 1938. Shoghi Effendi, pp. 211–16.

10.883. Landis, Benson Y. *Religion in the United States*. New York: Barnes & Noble, 1968. pp. 3–4, 104.

10.884. —— *World Religions: A Brief Guide to the Principal Beliefs and Teaching of the Religions of the World and to the Statistics of Organized Religion*. New York: Dutton, 1957. pp. 24–5.

10.885. Landor, A. Henry Savage. *Across Coveted Lands*. 2 vols. New York: Charles Scribner's Sons, 1903. I: 391.

10.886. Lapide, Pinchas E. *A Pilgrim's Guide to Israel*. London: George G. Harrap, 1966. p. 103.

10.887. Lapidus, Ira M. *Contemporary Islamic Movements in Historical Perspective*. Berkeley, Calif.: Institute of International Studies, University of California, 1983. p. 36. (Policy Papers in International Affairs; no.18).

10.888. Laqueur, Walter Z. *Middle East in Transition*. New York: Frederick A. Praeger, 1958. p. 202.

10.888a. Larned, J.N. *History for Ready Reference*. rev. & enl. ed. Springfield, Mass.: C.A. Nichols Co., Publisher, 1901. 'Bâb, The', I: 245.

10.889. Larsen, Elaine. *Israel*. New York: Hasting House, 1976. pp. 71, 78–9, 80–1.

10.890. Larson, Bob. *Larson's Book of Cults*. Wheaton, Ill.: Tyndale House Publishers, 1982. pp. 261–4.

10.891. Lazarus-Yafeh, Hava. *Some Religious Aspects of Islam: A Collection of Articles*. Leiden: E.J. Brill, 1981. (Studies in the History of Religions). pp. 12, 103, 161.

10.892. Leach, Bernard. *The Art of Bernard Leach*. ed. Carol Hogben. London: Boston; Faber and Faber, 1978. p. 46.

10.893. —— *Beyond East and West: Memoirs, Portraits and Essays*. London; Boston: Faber and Faber, 1978, 1985. pp. 164–5, 215–16, 234, 278, 282, 284, 285, 291–3, 301–3, 304, 305, 307.

10.894. —— *Drawings, Verse and Belief*. London: Jupiter Books, 1973. pp. 8–11.

10.895. —— *A Potter in Japan, 1952–1954*. London: Faber and Faber, 1960. p. 76.

10.896. Leach, Jim. *Congressman Jim Leach Washington Report (March 28, 1984)*. Washington, D.C.: Jim Leach, 1984. p. 2.

10.897. —— *Congressman Jim Leach Washington Report (July 17, 1985)*. Washington, D.C.: Jim Leach, 1985. pp. 1–2.

10.898. Ledeen, Michael; Lewis, William. *Debacle: The American Failure in Iran*. New York: Knopf, 1981. pp. 30, 103, 106.

10.899. Lee, James. *The Final Word!: An American Refutes the Sayings of Ayatollah Khomeini*. New York: Philosophical Library, 1984. p. 65.

10.900. Leete, Frederick De Land. *Palestine – Its Scenery, Peoples and History*. London: Skeffington & Son, 1933. pp. 161, 180.

10.901. —— *Palestine – Land of Light*. Boston: Houghton Mifflin, 1932. p. 170.

10.901a. *The Legacy of Islam*. ed. Jospeh Schacht with C.E. Bosworth. 2nd ed. Oxford: At the Clarendon Press, 1974. p. 57.

10.902. *The Legacy of Persia*. ed. A.J. Arberry. Oxford: At the Clarendon Press, 1953. p. 80.

10.903. Lemesurier, Peter. *The Armageddon Script: Prophecy in Action*. Salisbury, Wilts.: Element Books, 1981. pp. 206–7.

10.904. Lenczowski, George. *The Middle East in World Affairs*. Ithaca, N.Y.: Cornell University Press, 1952. pp. 205, 374.

10.905. —— *idem*. 4th ed. Ithaca, N.Y.; London: Cornell University Press, 1980. pp. 200, 228.

10.906. Lengyel, Emil. *World Without End: The Middle East*. New York: John Day, 1953. pp. 212, 227–8.

10.907. *Let's Go: The Budget Guide to Greece, Israel and Egypt, 1983*. Gary Marx, ed. New York: St Martin's Press, 1983. pp. 405, 410, 414, 420.

10.908. Levi, Avraham. *Bazak Guide to Israel, 1977–1978*. New York: Harper & Row, 1977. pp. 285, 299, 307, 311, 322, 327. Colour photograph of the Shrine of the Báb, page 314; colour photograph of the Shrine, pages 296–7; drawing of Shrine of the Báb, page 302.

10.909. Levy, Reuben. *The Persian Language*. New York: Philosophical Library, 1951. p. 106.

10.910. —— *The Social Structure of Islam*. London: Cambridge University Press, 1957. p. 39.

10.911. Lewensohn, Avraham. *Massada Guide to Israel*. Givatayim, Israel: Massada, 1985. pp. 59, 188.

10.912. Lewis, Bernard. *The Jews of Islam*. Princeton, N.J.: Princeton University Press, 1984. p. 20.

10.913. Lewis, John. *The Religions of the World Made Simple*. New York: Doubleday & Co., 1958. p. 90.

10.913a. Lewis, Sinclair. *Babbitt*. New York: Harcourt, Brace & World, 1922. p. 358.

10.913b. —— *Main Street*. New York: Harcourt, Brace & World, 1920. p. 308.

10.914. Leymarie, Jean. *Watercolours from Dürer to Balthus*. London: Weidenfeld & Nicolson, 1985. Mark Tobey as a Bahá'í, p. 109.

10.915. Library of Congress. Subject Cataloging Division. *Classification Class B, Part II,*

BL-BX: Religion. 2nd ed. Washington, D.C.: Library of Congress, 1962. p. 81.

10.916. Lincoln, C. Eric. *The Black Muslims in America*. Boston: Beacon Press, 1961. pp. 29, 215.

10.917. Ling, Trevor. *A History of Religion East and West: An Introduction and Interpretation*. London: Macmillan & Co.; New York: St Martin's Press, 1968. pp. 388–9, 419.

10.918. —— *idem*. New York: Harper & Row, 1980. pp. 388–9.

10.919. Linklater, Eric. *The Man on My Back: An Autobiography*. London: Macmillan & Co., 1941. pp. 137–8.

10.920. Linton, J.H. *Persian Sketches*. London: Church Missionary Society, 1923. p. 100.

10.921. Lipnack, Jessica; Stamps, Jeffrey. *Networking: The First Report and Directory*. Garden City, N.Y.: Doubleday & Company, 1982. p. 177.

10.922. Lippel, Israel. *The All Faith Book of Feasts in the Holy Land, 1982*. Jerusalem: Jerusalem Institute for Interreligious Relations and Research, 1982. Includes description of Bahá'í calendar and a listing of holy days.

10.923. Littell, Franklin H. *A Pilgrim's Inter-Faith Guide to the Holy Land*. Jerusalem: Carta and the Jerusalem Post, 1981. pp. 26–7.

10.924. Lochhaas, Philip H. *How to Respond to Islam*. St Louis, Mo.: Concordia Publishing House, 1981. p. 21.

10.925. Loeb, Laurence D. *Outcaste: Jewish Life in Southern Iran*. New York: Gordon and Breach, 1977. pp. 32, 74–5, 174, 189.

10.926. *Longman's English Larousse*. Harlow, U.K.: Longmans, 1968. pp. 1, 84, 87.

10.927. Longrigg, Stephen H. *Iraq, 1900 to 1950: A Political, Social and Economic History*. Beirut: Librairie du Liban, 1968. p. 192.

10.928. —— *The Middle East: A Social Geography*. London: Gerald Duckworth, 1963. p. 95.

10.929. —— *idem*. Chicago: Aldine Publishing Co., 1963. p. 95.

10.930. —— *idem*. rev. ed. London: Gerald Duckworth, 1970. p. 95.

10.931. —— *idem*. rev. ed. Chicago: Aldine Publishing Co., 1970. p. 95.

10.932. Lorey, Eustache de; Sladen, Douglas. *Queer Things About Persia*. London: Eveleigh Nash, 1907. pp. 268, 307–17.

10.933. Lorimer, John Gordon. *Gazetteer of the*

Persian Gulf, 'Oman, and Central Arabia. Calcutta: Superintendent of Government Printing, 1915. v. 1 pt. 2, pp. 2350n, 2384–5.

10.934. —— *idem*. Farnborough, Hants., U.K.: Gregg International Publishers; Shannon: Irish University Press, 1970. v. 1 pt. 2, pp. 2350n, 2384–5.

10.935. Löwenthal, Rudolf. *Russian Materials on Islam and Islamic Institutions: A Selective Bibliography*. Washington, D.C.: Department of State, 1958. pp. 15–16.

10.936. Lukach, Harry Charles; Jardine, Douglas James. *The Handbook of Cyprus*. London:

Edward Stanford, 1913. pp. 48–9.

10.937. Luke, Harry Charles. *An Eastern Chequerboard*. London: Lovat Dickson, 1934. p. 71.

10.938. —— *The Fringe of the East: A Journey Through Past and Present Provinces of Turkey*. London: Macmillan, 1913. pp. 263–7. Includes photographs of Ṣubḥ-i-Azal and his funeral.

10.939. —— *Prophets, Priests and Patriarchs: Sketches of the Sects of Palestine and Syria*. London: Faith Press, n.d. [1927] pp. 70–2.

10.940. Lumby, Christopher. *Cook's Traveller's Handbook to Palestine, Syria and Iraq*. London: Simpkin Marshall, 1934. pp. 248, 254.

M

10.941. MacCallum, Elizabeth P. *The Nationalist Crusade in Syria*. New York: Foreign Policy Association, 1928. pp. 263, 271.

10.942. McCulloch, Kenneth C. *Mankind, Citizen of the Galaxy*. La Pas, Man.: Rings of Saturn Publishing, 1985. pp. 232, 236–7, 259–60.

10.943. McDaniel, Robert A. *The Shuster Mission and the Persian Constitutional Revolution*. Minneapolis, Minn.: Bibliotheca Islamica, 1974. p. 54.

10.944. Macdonald, Barrie. *Cinderellas of the Empire: Towards a History of Kiribati and Tuvalu*. Canberra: Australian National University Press, 1982. p. 213.

10.944a. MacDonald, Duncan B. *Development of Muslim Theology, Jurisprudence and Constitutional Theory*. London: George Routledge & Sons, 1903. (The Semitic Series; no.9). p. 5.

10.945. McGlinn, Sen. *Feeding Harbour: Selected Poems, 1973–1983*. Christchurch, N.Z.: McGlinn, 1984. p. 48n.

10.946. MacIntosh, Douglas Clyde. *The Pilgrimage of Faith in the World of Modern Thought*. Calcutta, India: University of Calcutta, 1931. p. 33.

10.947. McKibbin-Harper, Mary. *The Doctor Takes a Holiday*. Cedar Rapids, Ia.: Torch Press, 1941. p. 52.

10.948. *Macmillan Concise Dictionary of World History*. comp. Bruce Wetterau. New York: Collier Books, Macmillan Publishing Company, 1983. pp. 61, 63.

10.949. MacMunn, George. *The Religions and*

Hidden Cults of India. London: Sampson Low, Marston & Co., n.d. [1932] p. 200.

10.950. —— *idem*. Delhi: Oriental Publishers & Distributors, 1975. p. 200.

10.951. MacNeil-Lehrer Report. *Khomeini's Islamic Government: February 8, 1979*. New York: MacNeil-Lehrer Report, 1979. *passim*.

10.952. Maguire, John; Dunn, Mary Lee. *Hold Hands and Die: The Incredibly True Story of the People's Temple and the Reverend Jim Jones*. New York: Dale Books, 1978. pp. 239, 247.

10.953. *Mahmehr Golestaneh, Virginia Miller Galleries, December 1–19, 1981*. Coral Gables, Fla.: Virginia Miller Galleries, 1981. p. [3]

10.954. Mahmud, Sayyid Fayyaz. *The Story of Islam*. Karachi: Oxford University Press, 1959. p. 290.

10.955. Malcolm, Napier. *Five Years in a Persian Town*. New York: E.P. Dutton, 1907. pp. 86–96.

10.956. —— *idem*. London: John Murray, 1908. pp. 86–96.

10.957. *Man, Myth & Magic: An Illustrated Encyclopedia of the Supernatural*. n.p. [London]: Purnell, n.d. [1970?] M. Saunders, 'Bahais', pp. 208–9.

10.957a. *Man, Myth & Magic: The Illustrated Encyclopedia of Mythology, Religion and the Unknown*. ed. Richard Cavendish. New York: Marshall Cavendish, 1985. M. Saunders, 'Bahais', II: 224–5.

10.958. *Man of the Trees, Richard St. Barbe*

Baker. ed. Hugh Locke. Saskatoon, Sask.: Richard St. Barbe Baker Foundation, 1984. pp. 27, 30, 32.

10.959. *Man, State and Society in the Contemporary Middle East*. ed. Jacob M. Landau. New York: Praeger Publishers, 1972. p. 265.

10.960. Mann, Sylvia. *This is Israel: Pictorial Guide and Souvenir*. Herzlia, Israel: Palphot Ltd., 1982. pp. 141–2.

10.960a. *The Many Faces of Religion and Society*. ed. M. Darrol Bryant, Rita T. Mataragnon. New York: Paragon House Publishers, 1985. Olusola Olukunle, 'Social Uses and Abuses of Religion in Developing Countries', pp. 100–101, Bahá'í, p. 100.

10.960b. *The Many Ways of Being: A Guide to Spiritual Groups and Growth Centres in Britain*. ed. Stephen Annett. London: Abacus, 1976. pp. 81–3, 252, 276, 277, 278, 279.

10.961. *Mark Tobey, April 10 to May 1, 1976*. New York: M. Knoedler & Co., 1976. pp. 13, 14, 16.

10.962. Margoliouth, David S. *Mohammedanism*. New York: Henry Holt and Company; London: Williams and Northgate, n.d. [1916?] p. 191. (Home University Library of Modern Knowledge).

10.963. Markham, Clements R. *A General Sketch of the History of Persia*. London: Longmans, Green & Co., 1874. pp. 495–6.

10.964. —— *idem*. Nendeln, Liechtenstein: Kraus Reprint, 1977. pp. 495–6.

10.965. Marlowe, John. *Iran – a Short Political Guide*. New York: Praeger, 1963. pp. 9, 104.

10.965a. Marnham, Patrick. *So Far from God: A Journey to Central America*. London: Jonathan Cape, 1985. pp. 141–2.

10.966. *Marriage and the Family*. ed. John Prickett. Cambridge, U.K.: Lutterworth Press, 1985. pp. 33–45.

10.967. Marshall, Edward A. *Christianity and Non-Christian Religions Compared*. Chicago: Bible Institute Colportage Association, 1910. p. 68.

10.968. Martin, Alfred W. *Comparative Religion and the Religion of the Future*. New York: Appleton & Co., 1926. pp. 81–91.

10.969. Martin, James. *A Plain Man in the Holy Land*. Edinburgh: Saint Andrew Press, 1978. p. 85.

10.970. Martin, Walter R. *The Christian and the*

Cults. Grand Rapids, Mich.: Zondervan, 1956. pp. 30–3.

10.971. —— *The Kingdom of the Cults*. Minneapolis, Minn.: Bethany Fellowship, 1965; rev. ed., 1968, 1977. pp. 252–8, 351, 438.

10.971a. —— *idem*. rev. & exp. ed. Minneapolis, Minn.: Bethany House Publishers, 1985. pp. 271–278.

10.972. —— *Rise of the Cults*. rev. ed. Santa Ana, Calif.: Vision House, 1980. pp. 117–24.

10.973. Marty, Martin E. *A Nation of Behavers*. Chicago; London: University of Chicago Press, 1976. p. 141.

10.973a. Marty, Martin E. *Pilgrims in Their Own Land: 500 Years of Religion in America*. Boston: Little, Brown and Company, 1984; New York: Penguin Books, 1985. pp. 346, 452–3.

10.974. *The Maryknoll Catholic Dictionary*. comp. & ed. Albert J. Nevins. New York: Grosset & Dunlap, 1965. p. 65.

10.975. Massé, Henri. *Islam*. trans. from French by Halide Edib. New York: G.P. Putnam's Sons, 1938. pp. 217, 248, 255–9.

10.976. *Masterpieces of Mystery: The Seventies*. n.p.: Davis, 1979. Florence V. Mayberry, 'In the Secret Hollow', p. 231.

10.977. Mathison, Richard R. *Faiths, Cults and Sects of America*. Indianapolis, Ind.: Bobbs-Merrill, 1960. pp. 104–6.

10.977a. Matson, G. Olaf. *The Palestine Guide, Including Trans-Jordan*. 5th ed. Jerusalem: Joshua Simon, n.d. [1946] p. 323.

10.978. Maud, Constance E. *Sparks Among the Stubble*. London: P. Allen & Co., 1924. pp. 26–7, 81–112. Portrait of 'Abdu'l-Bahá facing p. 83.

10.979. Maxwell, William. *Parenting*. Suva, Fiji: I.Q. Company, 1978. pp. 7, 8.

10.980. Maxwell, William; Maxwell, Mary Elizabeth. *52 Ways to Raise the IQ of a Child*. Suva, Fiji: I.Q. Company, 1979. pp. 49–50.

10.981. Mayer, F.E. *The Religious Bodies of America*. St Louis, Mo.: Concordia Publishing House, 1954. pp. 560–1.

10.982. Mbiti, John S. *Introduction to African Religion*. New York: Praeger, 1975. pp. 188–9.

10.982a. Mbuy, Tatah H. *The Impact of Religious Sects Among Anglophone Students of Cameroon*. Cameroon, n.d. [ca. 1985] pp. 20. 60–2, 86.

10.983. Mead, Frank S. *Handbook of Denomina-*

tions in the United States. New York: Abingdon–Cokesbury Press, 1951. pp. 24–5, 185.

10.984. —— *idem*. 5th ed. Nashville, Tenn.: Abingdon Press, 1970. pp. 29–31, 221, 237.

10.985. —— *idem*. 7th ed. Nashville, Tenn.: Abingdon Press, 1980. pp. 32–4, 259, 277.

10.986. —— *idem*. new 8th ed. Nashville, Tenn.: Abingdon Press, 1985. pp. 33–4.

10.986a. Meade, F.H.M.; Zimmermann, A.W.; Whaling, F. *Religions of the World*. Edinburgh: Holmes McDougall Ltd., 1985. pp. 90–1, 92, 94, 95.

10.986b. Means, Pat. *The Mystical Maze*. United States: Campus Crusade for Christ, 1976. p. 211.

10.987. Mears, I.; Mears, L.E. *Creative Energy*. London: John Murray, 1931. pp. 144–5.

10.988. Mehdevi, Anne Sinclair. *Persia Revisited*. New York: Alfred A.Knopf, 1964. p. 6.

10.989. Meisler, Benjamin; Yeivin, Samuel. *Palestine Guide for Navy, Army and Air Force*. Tel-Aviv: Edition Olympia, 1940. p. 252.

10.990. Meister, Charles W. *Year of the Lord: A.D. Eighteen Forty-Four*. Jefferson, N.C.; London: McFarland & Company, 1983. pp. 2, 218–45, 248–9.

10.990a. Meistermann, Barnabas. *Guide to the Holy Land*. new rev. ed. London: Burns Oates & Washbourne, 1923. p. 628.

10.990b. —— *New Guide to the Holy Land*. London: Burns & Oates, 1907. p. 551.

10.991. Melton, J. Gordon. *The Encyclopedia of American Religions*. Wilmington, N.C.: McGrath, 1978. II: 351–4.

10.992. —— *The Encyclopedia of American Religions: First Edition Supplement*. Detroit, Mich.: Gale Research Company, 1985. pp. 73–5.

10.992a. Meluch, R.M. *Jerusalem Fire*. New York: New American Library, 1985.

10.993. Mensching, Gustav. *Tolerance and Truth in Religion*. University, Ala.: University of Alabama Press, 1971. pp. 8–9.

10.994. Meredith-Owens, G.M. *Handlist of Persian Manuscripts, 1895–1966*. London: Trustees of the British Museum, 1968. p. 33–6.

10.995. Merritt-Hawkes, O.A. *Persia – Romance & Reality*. London: Ivor Nicholson & Watson, 1935. pp. 115–17, 144–5, 152, 251, 268–9, 295.

10.995a. Mertens, A. *What, When, Where in the Holy Land*. Jerusalem: Franciscan Printing Press, 1977. p. 51. Cover title: *Guide Yourself*.

10.995b. Meysels, Theodor F. *Israel in Your Pocket*. Tel Aviv: Ben-Dor Israel Publishing, 1955. pp. 17–18, 42–44.

10.996. Meysels, Theodor F. *Israel in Your Pocket*. 10th anniversary ed. Tel Aviv: Ben Dor Israel Pub. Co., 1958. pp. 21–2, 56–8.

10.997. Michener, James. *The Source*. New York: Random House, 1965. p. 3.

10.998. —— *idem*. Greenwich, Conn.: Fawcett Publications, 1965. p. 11.

10.999. *The Middle East: A Political and Economic Survey*. London; New York: Royal Institute of International Affairs, 1950. pp. 202, 240, 277, 279.

10.1000. *idem*. ed. Sir Reader Bullard. 3rd ed. London: Oxford University Press, 1958. p. 371.

10.1001. *Middle East Contemporary Survey, Volume 2, 1977–78*. ed. Colin Legum. New York; London: Holmes & Meier Publishers, 1979. pp. 472, 522.

10.1002. *Middle East Contemporary Survey, Volume 6, 1981–82*. ed. Colin Legum, New York; London: Holmes & Meier Publishers, 1984. pp. 551–2.

10.1003. *Middle East Contemporary Survey, Volume 7, 1982–83*. ed. Colin Legum, New York; London: Holmes & Meier Publishers, 1985. p. 538.

10.1004. *The Middle East – the Arab States in Pictures*. coordinating ed. E.W. Egan; research eds. Camille Mirepoix, Eugene Gordon, Jon Teta. New York: Sterling Publishing Co.; London: Oak Tree Press, 1980. p. 179.

10.1005. Mill, George Oxford; Tull, Delena. *Texas Parks and Campgrounds: North, East, and Coastal Texas*. Austin: Texas Monthly Press, 1984. Bahá'u'lláh's prayer 'Blessed is the spot' on display page.

10.1006. *Millennialism and Charisma*. ed. Roy Wallis. Belfast, N. Ireland: The Queen's University, 1982. Peter Smith, 'Millenarianism and the Babi and Baha'i Religions', pp. 231–84.

10.1007. Miller, Henry. *The Air-Conditioned Nightmare*. New York: New Directions, 1970. p. 57.

10.1008. Miller, Herbert A. *The Beginnings of To-morrow: An Introduction to the Sociology of the Great Society*. New York: D.C. Heath and Company, 1933. pp. 249–50.

10.1009. Miller, Janet. *Camel Bells of Baghdad*. Boston: Houghton Mifflin, 1934. pp. 218, 220, 264.

10.1010. Miller, Milton G.; Schwartzman, Sylvan D. *Our Religion and Our Neighbors.* New York: Union of American Hebrew Congregations, 1963. pp. 6, 209–10, 273.

10.1011. Miller, William McElwee. *Ten Muslims Meet Christ.* Grand Rapids, Mich.: William B. Eerdmans, 1969. pp. 37, 45, 107–11, 125–31.

10.1012. Mills, Dorothy. *Beyond the Bosphorus.* Boston: Little, Brown & Co., 1926. pp. 97–100.

10.1013. Minorsky, Vladimir. *Iranica: Twenty Articles.* Tehran: University of Tehran, 1964. pp. 254, 259.

10.1014. *The Mission of Israel.* ed. Jacob Baal-Teshuva. New York: Robert Speller & Sons, 1963. p. 64.

10.1015. Moazzam, Anwar. *Jamāl al-Dīn al-Afghāni, a Muslim Intellectual.* New Delhi: Concept Publishing Company, 1984. p. 92, 133.

10.1016. *The Modern Encyclopedia: A New Library of World Knowledge.* 7th ed. New York: Grosset & Dunlap: Wm. H. Wise, 1935. 'Bahaism', p. 97.

10.1017. *Modern Iran: The Dialectics of Continuity and Change.* Michael E. Bonine, Nikki R. Keddie, eds. Albany: State University of New York Press, 1981. pp. 4, 14, 45–7, 49–51, 55, 85, 331, 343, 397.

10.1018. *The Mohammedan World of To-Day.* ed. S.M. Zwemer, E.M. Wherry, James L. Barton. Indian ed. Allahabad: Chugh Publications, 1976. pp. 17, 115, 116, 117–18, 121, 129–30.

10.1018a. *The Mohammedan World of Today.* ed. S.M. Zwemer, E.M. Wherry, James L. Barton. New York: Fleming Revell, 1903. pp. 17, 115, 116, 117–18, 121, 129–30.

10.1019. Momen, Moojan. *An Introduction to Shi'i Islam: The History and Doctrines of Twelver Shi'ism.* New Haven, Conn.; London: Yale University Press, 1985. pp. 135, 136–7, 138, 140, 141, 229, 231–2, 237, 248, 253, 261, 285–6, 294, 296, 297, 303, 341–2.
Reviews:
MacEoin, Denis. 'Roots of Revolution', *Times Higher Educational Supplement* (London), (Sept. 20, 1985), p. 21.
This book was extensively reviewed but only MacEoin's mentions the Bahá'í Faith.

10.1019a. —— *idem.* Oxford: George Ronald, 1985. Same paging as in 10.1019.

10.1020. Moncrieff, A.R. Hope. *The World of To-Day: A Survey of the Lands and Peoples of the Globe as Seen in Travel and Commerce, Volume II.* London: Gresham Publishing Company, n.d. [1905] pp. 107–8n.

10.1020a. Monsalvat School for the Comparative Study of Religion (Eliot, Me.). *The Monsalvat School for the Comparative Study of Religion: At Greenacre, Eliot, York Co., Maine, U.S.: Sixth Annual Session, July–August, 1901.* Eliot, Me.: Monsalvat School for the Comparative Study of Religion, 1901. pp. [3], 7, 10, 12, [13].

10.1021. Montagu, Edwin S. *An Indian Diary.* Edited by Venetia Montagu. London: Heinemann, 1930. pp. 64, 99.

10.1022. Moore, George Foot. *History of Religions.* New York: Scribner's Sons, 1919. II: 509–19.

10.1023. Moppett, George. *Otto Rogers: A Survey, 1973–1982.* Saskatoon, Sask.: Mendel Art Gallery, 1982. pp. 7, 11, 22, 29, 32, 35.

10.1024. Morris, James Winston. *The Wisdom of the Throne: An Introduction to the Philosophy of Mulla Sadra.* Princeton, N.J.: Princeton University Press, 1981. p. 50. (Princeton Library of Asian Translations). (UNESCO Collection of Representative Works. Arabic Series).

10.1025. Morrison, J.A. *Middle East Tensions: Political, Social, Religious.* New York: Harper & Bros., 1954. p. 110.

10.1026. Mortimer, Edward. *Faith and Power: The Politics of Islam.* New York: Random House, 1982. pp. 110, 314, 352.

10.1026a. —— *idem.* New York: Vintage Books, 1982. pp. 110, 314, 352.

10.1027. Moshiri, Farrokh. *The State and Social Revolution in Iran: A Theoretical Perspective.* New York; Berne; Frankfurt am Main: Peter Lang, 1985. (American University Studies: Series 10, Political Science; v.5). pp. 100, 186.

10.1028. *The Moslem World of To-Day.* ed. John R. Mott. London: Hodder and Stoughton, 1925. pp. 305, 307, 310, 314.

10.1029. Mott, Francis John. *Christ the Seed.* Boston: A.A. Beauchamp, 1939; London: Gate Publishing Co., 1939. p. 19.

10.1030. Mottahedeh, Roy P. *The Mantle of the Prophet: Religion and Politics in Iran.* New York: Simon and Schuster, 1985. pp. 68, 102, 104, 238–40, 244, 360–1, 388–9, 394.

10.1031. Moulvi, A.M. *Modern Iran.* Bombay, India: Saif Azad, 1938. p. 46.

10.1032. Mounsey, Augustus H. *A Journey Through the Caucasus and the Interior of Persia.* London: Smith, Elder & Co., 1872. pp. 103–7.

10.1033. Mulholland, John F. *Hawaii's Religions.* Rutland, Vt.; Tokyo: Charles E. Tuttle, 1970. pp. 303–5.

10.1034. Muller, Robert. *Most of All, They Taught Me Happiness.* Garden City, N.Y.: Doubleday, 1978. p. 55.

10.1035. Mumford, Lewis. *The Conduct of Life.* New York: Harcourt, Brace & Co., 1951. p. 117.

10.1036. —— *idem.* London: Secker & Warburg, 1957. p. 117.

10.1037. —— *idem.* New York: Harcourt Brace Jovanovich, 1970. p. 117.

10.1038. Murchie, Guy. *The Seven Mysteries of Life: An Exploration in Science & Philosophy.* Boston: Houghton Mifflin, 1978. pp. ix, 372, 459, 492–3, 495, 612–16, 624.

10.1039. —— *Song of the Sky.* Cambridge, Mass.: Riverside Press, 1954. pp. 327, 421.

10.1040. —— *idem.* London: Secker & Warburg, 1955. pp. 307, 392.

10.1041. *Muslim Peoples: A World Ethnographic Survey.* Richard V. Weekes, ed. Westport, Conn.: Greenwood Press, 1978. p. xxix.

10.1042. *The Muslim World: A Historical Survey.* Leiden: E.J. Brill, 1981. pt. 4 fasc. 1, pp. 63–4.

10.1043. *idem.* 2nd ed. rev. and exp. London: Aldwych Press, 1984. p. xxxiv.

10.1044. Myrdal, Gunnar. *An American Dilemma: The Negro Problem and Modern Democracy.* New York: Harper & Row, 1962. p. 871n.

10.1045. *Myths and Facts 1982: A Concise Record of the Arab-Israeli Conflict.* ed. Leonard J. Davis and Moshe Decter. Washington, D.C.: Near East Report, 1982. pp. 2, 141–2.

N

10.1046. Naamani, Israel T. *Israel – a Profile.* London: Pall Mall Press, 1972. pp. 9, 78.

10.1047. Naficy, Hamid. *Iran Media Index.* Westport, Conn.; London: Greenwood Press, 1984. (Bibliographies and Indexes in World History; no.1). pp. 115–16.

10.1048. *Nagel's Encyclopedia-Guide, Israel.* 4th ed. Geneva; Paris; Munich: Nagel Publishers, 1978. p. 287.

10.1049. *Nahariyya.* Jerusalem: Ministry of Tourism, n.d. [1982] (Israel: Where to Go and What to See). p. 6.

10.1050. Naipaul, V.S. *Among the Believers: An Islamic Journey.* New York: Alfred A. Knopf, 1981. pp. 16–19.

10.1051. Nakosteen, Mehdi; Kragh, Agnes. *In the Land of the Lion and the Sun: The Country, Customs and Cultures of My People.* Denver, Colo.: World Press, 1937. pp. 79–80.

10.1052. Naor, Mordechai. *Please Meet Israel: All You Wanted to Know About People and Places in Israel.* Tel Aviv: Dahlia Pelled Publishers, 1983. p. 77, 80. Photograph of Shrine of the Báb on p. 5 of plates.

10.1053. Nariman, G.K. *Persia and Parsis.* Bombay: Published under the patronage of the Iran League, 1925. pp. 34–5.

10.1054. Nash, Ogden. *The Pocket Book of Ogden Nash.* introd. Louise Untermeyer. New York: Pocket Books, 1962. 'The Seven Spiritual Ages of Mrs Marmaduke Moore', p. 100.

10.1054a. —— *Selected Verse of Ogden Nash.* New York: Random House Modern Library, 1945. pp. 10–12.

10.1055. Nashat, Guity. *The Origins of Modern Reform in Iran, 1870–80.* Urbana, Ill.: University of Illinois Press, 1982. p. 19.

10.1056. Nasr, Seyyed Hossein. *Iran (Persia).* Tehran: Offset Press, 1973. p. 61.

10.1057. —— *Islam and the Plight of Modern Man.* London: Longman, 1975. pp. 118, 119.

10.1058. —— *Islamic Life and Thought.* Albany, N.Y.: State University of New York Press, 1981. p. 14.

10.1059. —— *Three Muslim Sages: Avicenna, Suhrawardi, Ibn 'Arabi.* Delmar, N.Y.: Caravan Books, 1964. p. 154.

10.1059a. *The National Cyclopaedia of American Biography. Volume XX.* New York: James T. White & Company, 1929. "Hall, Albert Heath," p. 67.

10.1060. *Neely's History of the Parliament of Religions and Religious Congresses at the World's Columbian Exposition.* Walter R. Houghton, ed. Chicago: F.T. Neely, 1893. pp. 640–1.

10.1061. Neligan, A.R. *Hints for Residents and Travellers in Persia.* London: John Bale, Sons & Danielsson, Ltd., 1914. p. 2.

10.1062. Nelson, Lesley. *Vegetarian Restaurants in England*. Harmondsworth, Middlesex: Penguin Books, 1982. p. 192.

10.1062a. Nevill, Ralph. *Unconventional Memories: Europe, Persia, Japan*. London: Hutchinson & Co., 1923. 'Baabism', p. 149.

10.1062b. *The New Age Encyclopaedia*. ed. Sir Edward Parrott [et. al.] London; Edinburgh; New York: Thomas Nelson and Sons, Ltd., 1920–21. 'Babi and Babiism', I: 430.

10.1063. *New Catholic Encyclopedia*. 17 vols. New York: McGraw-Hill, 1967. Philip K. Hitti, 'Babism', II: 2–3; James Kritzeck, 'Baha'ism', II: 14–15.

10.1064. *The New Century Cyclopedia of Names*. Englewood Cliffs, N.J.: Prentice-Hall, 1954. I: 12, 289, 291, 306–7.

10.1065. *The New Columbia Encyclopedia*. ed. William H. Harris, Judith S. Levey. 4th ed. New York: Columbia University Press, 1975. pp. 202, 209.

10.1066. *The New Consciousness Sourcebook: Spiritual Community Guide #5*. Berkeley, Calif.: Spiritual Community/NAM, 1982. pp. 17, 36, 194.

10.1067. *The New Encyclopaedia Britannica*. 15th ed. Chicago: Encyclopaedia Britannica, 1975. Micropaedia: ' 'Abd ol-Baha', p. 13; 'Azalis', I: 696; 'Bab', I: 704–5; 'Babism', I: 708–9; 'Baha Allah', I: 731; 'Baha'i Faith', I: 731; 'Mashriq al-Adhkar', VI: 668; 'Shoghi Effendi Rabbani', IX: 161; 'Spiritual Assemblies', IX: 428–9. Macropaedia: Firuz Kazemzadeh, 'Baha'i Faith', 2: 587–90.

10.1068. *The New International Dictionary of the Christian Church*. ed. J.D. Douglas. Grand Rapids, Mich.: Zondervan Publishing House, 1974. Eric J. Sharpe, 'Baha'i', p. 96.

10.1069. *New Religions: Based on Papers Read at the Symposium on New Religions Held at Åbo on the 1st–3rd of September 1974*. ed. Haralds Biezais. Stockholm: Almqvist & Wiksell International, 1975. p. 112 (Scripta Instituti Donneriani Aboensis; 7).

10.1070. *The New Schaff-Herzog Encyclopedia of Religious Knowledge*. Grand Rapids, Mich.: Baker Book House, 1949. George W. Gilmore, 'Babism', I: 394–6; Margaret B. Peeke, 'Behaism', II: 30–1.

10.1071. New South Wales. Anti-Discrimination Board. *Discrimination and Religious Conviction*. Sydney, N.S.W.: New South Wales Anti-Discrimination Board, 1984. pp. 60, 336, 338.

10.1072. *The New Standard Jewish Encyclopedia*.

Cecil Roth, Geoffrey Wigoder, eds. in chief. new rev. ed. Jerusalem: Massada, 1970. pp. 219, 822–3.

10.1073. Newman, E.M. *Seeing Egypt and the Holy Land*. New York; London: Funk & Wagnalls Co., 1928. pp. 164–5, 171–2, 204. Photograph of 'Abdu'l-Bahá, page 204.

10.1074. Nicholson, Reynold A. *The Mystics of Islam*. Beirut, Lebanon: Khayats, 1966. p. 89.

10.1075. —— *idem*. London: Routledge and Kegan Paul, 1975. p. 89.

10.1076. Nigosian, S.A. *World Religions*. Vancouver, B.C.: Copp Clark Publishing, 1974. p. 101.

10.1077. Nilsson, Anna T. *ABC of the Peace Movement: Dates and Facts*. 2nd ed. Genève, Switzerland: International League of Youth, Geneva Section, c1931, 1932. p. 31.

10.1078. Nima, Ramy. *The Wrath of Allah: Islamic Revolution and Reaction in Iran*. London; Sydney: Pluto Press, 1983. pp. 61, 110.

10.1078a. *Nineteenth Century Religious Thought in the West*. ed. Ninian Smart, John Clayton, Steven Katz, Patrick Sherry. Cambridge, Cambridge University Press, 1985. II: 202.

10.1079. Nir, Dov. *New Guide to Israel*. London: Ward Lock Limited, 1973. pp. 195–6, 208.

10.1080. Nöldeke, Theodor. *Sketches from Eastern History*. London; Edinburgh: Adam and Charles Black, 1892. pp. 101–2.

10.1081. *Non-Christian Religions A to Z*. ed. under supervision of Horace L. Friess; based on work of Helmuth von Glasenapp. New York: Grosset & Dunlap, 1963. pp. 19–21.

10.1082. Norden, Hermann. *Under Persian Skies: A Record of Travel by the Old Caravan Routes of Western Persia*. Philadelphia, Pa.: Macrae, Smith Co., n.d. [ca. 1930] pp. 51–2, 127, 208, 226–7, 243.

10.1083. Norder, Cordelia A. *The Eternal Voice: The Word Made Flesh Down Through the Ages*. Rhinelander, Wis.: Legacy Press, 1972. pp. 2, 51–62, 69, 75–7, 81, 83.

10.1084. —— *idem*. rev. ed. Rhinelander, Wis.: Legacy Press, 1974. pp. 2, 55–69, 77, 81, 83–5, 89, 91, 93–5.

10.1085. —— *idem*. 3rd ed. Lac du Flambeau, Wis.: Blue Winds Printing & Design, Inc., 1982. pp. 2, 55–69, 77, 83–5, 91.

10.1086. North, C.R. *An Outline of Islam*. London: The Epworth Press, 1934. pp. 98–100.

10.1087. Noss, John B. *Man's Religions*. New York: Macmillan, 1949. p. 556.

10.1088. —— *idem*. 6th ed. New York: Macmillan; London: Collier Macmillan, 1980. pp. 543–4.

10.1088a. *Notable American Women, 1607–1950: A Biographical Dictionary*. ed. Edward T. James [et al.] Cambridge, Mass.: Belknap Press of Harvard University Press, 1971. Ross E. Paulson, "Campbell, Helen Stuart," pp. 280–281.

10.1089. *Notable Women of Hawaii*. ed. Barbara Bennett Peterson. Honolulu: University of Hawaii Press, 1984. Duane Troxel, 'Alexander, Agnes', pp. 1–4.

10.1090. Novak, Michael; Schifter, Richard. *Rethinking Human Rights: Volume II: One Standard, Many Methods*. Washington, D.C.: Foundation for Democratic Education, 1982. p. 61.

10.1090a. Nuseibeh, Hazem Zaki. *The Ideas of Arab Nationalism*. Ithaca, N.Y.: Cornell University Press, 1956. Babi movement, p. 41.

10.1091. *The Nuttall Encyclopaedia*. ed. G. Elgie Christ and A.L. Haydon. New ed. London; New York: Frederick Warne, 1930. p. 41.

10.1092. Nweeya, Samuel K. *Persia and the Moslems: An Historical and Descriptive Account of Persia from the Earliest Ages to the Present Time*. St Louis, Mo.: Press of Von Hoffmann, 1924. pp. [15], 149–74.

10.1093. —— *Persia the Land of the Magi, or the Home of the Wise Men*. Indianapolis: Press of Wood-Weaver Printing Co., 1904. pp. 91–6 (chap. 11: 'The Kurds and Bobes').

10.1094. —— *idem*. Philadelphia, Pa.: John C. Winston Co., 1910. pp. 213–35 (chapter 13: 'Babism').

10.1095. —— *idem*. Philadelphia, Pa.: John C. Winston Co., 1916. pp. 226–48 (chap. 12: 'Babism, Its Relation to Mohammedism and Christianity').

The later editions are expanded and include Nweeya's long exchange with Bahá'ís about proofs of Bahá'u'lláh's claims.

O

10.1095a *Of Gods and Men: New Religious Movements in the West*. ed. Eileen Barker. Macon, Ga.: Mercer University Press, 1983. Frederick William Bird, William Reimer, "Participation Rates in New Religions and Parareligious Movements," pp. 217, 220, 223, 229; Christine E. King, "Strategies for Survival: Experience in the Third Reich," p. 241.

10.1096. Ojike, Mbonu. *My Africa*. London: Blandford Press, 1955. p. 149.

10.1097. Oken, Alan. *Alan Oken's Complete Astrology*. rev. Bantam trade ed. Toronto; New York; London; Sydney: Bantam Books, 1980. 'Abdu'l-Bahá, pp. 565–6; Bahá'í Faith, p. 549.

10.1098. O'Leary, DeLacy Evans. *Islam at the Crossroads: A Brief Survey of the Present Position and Problems of the World of Islam*. London: Kegan Paul, Trench, Trubner & Co., 1923; New York: E.P. Dutton & Co., 1923. pp. 110–19.

10.1099. Oliphant, Laurence. *Haifa, or Life in Modern Palestine*. Edinburgh: William Blackwood, 1887. pp. 103–7.

10.1100. —— *idem*. New York: Harper & Bros., 1887. pp. 103–7.

10.1101. —— *idem*. new ed. Jerusalem: Canaan Publishing House, 1976. pp. 129–35.

10.1101a. Olmstead, Clifton E. *History of Religion in the United States*. Englewood Cliffs, N.J.: Prentice-Hall, 1960. p. 524.

10.1102. O'Malley, Desmond. *'I Stand by the Republic': Address to Dail Eireann on Feb. 20th, 1985*. n.p. [Ireland], 1985. p. 6.

10.1103. *One in All: An Anthology of Religion from the Sacred Scriptures of the Living Faiths*. comp. Edith B. Schnapper. London: John Murray, 1952. pp. xv, 15–16, 30–1, 45–6, 62–3, 78, 92–3, 109–10, 126–7, 142–3, 149. (Wisdom of the East Series).

10.1104. Oneida Pow-Wow (11th: 1983: Oneida, Wis.). *11th Annual Oneida Pow-Wow, Festival of Performing Arts, July 1, 2, 3, 4, 1983: Souvenir Program*. n.p. [Oneida, Wis.]: Pow-Wow Committee, 1983. p. [2].

10.1105. *Oriental Life: An Account of Past and Contemporary Conditions and Progress in Asia, excepting China, India and Japan*. ed. Ethlyn T. Clough. Detroit, Mich.: Bay View Reading Club, 1910. pp. 10, 27.

10.1106. Orni, Ephraim; Efrat, Elisha. *Geography of Israel*. Jerusalem: Israel Program for Scientific Translations, 1964. p. 197.

10.1106a. —— *idem*. 2nd ed. Jerusalem: Israel Program for Scientific Translations, 1966. pp. 217–18. Photograph of Shrine of the Báb, p. 218.

10.1107. —— *idem*. 3rd rev. ed. Jerusalem: Israel Universities Press, 1971. p. 284.

10.1107a. —— *This is Israel: A Guide Book*. Jerusalem: Achiasaf Publishing House, 1962. pp. 64, 85, 144, 311.

10.1108. Osborne, Christine. *An Insight and Guide to Jordan*. Harlow, U.K.: Longman, 1981. p. 15.

10.1109. Osmańczyk, Edmund Jan. *The Encyclopedia of the United Nations and International Agreements*. Philadelphia, Pa.; London: Taylor and Francis, 1985. p. 65.

10.1110. Ovington, Mary White. *The Walls Came Tumbling Down*. New York: Harcourt, Brace & Co., 1947. pp. 125–7.

10.1111. —— *idem*. New York: Arno Press, 1969. pp. 125–7.

10.1112. —— *idem*. New York: Schocken Books, 1970. pp. 125–7.

10.1113. Owen, Rosamond Dale. *My Perilous Life in Palestine*. London: George Allen & Unwin, 1928. pp. 230–41.

10.1114. *The Oxford Book of Prayer*. General ed. George Appleton. Oxford: Oxford University Press, 1985. pp. 15, 344–7.

10.1115. Oxford University. Balliol College. *Balliol College Annual Record, 1983*. Oxford: The College, 1983. Shoghi Effendi: pp. 76–7.

10.1115a. Oxford University. Balliol College. *The Balliol College Register, 1833–1933*. ed. Sir Ivo Elliott. 2nd ed. Oxford: Printed for Private Circulation by John Johnson at the University Press, 1934. Shoghi Effendi, p. 383.

10.1116. —— *The Balliol College Register, 1900–1950*. ed. Sir Ivo Elliott. 3rd ed. Oxford: Printed for Private Circulation by Charles Batey, at the University Press, 1953. Shoghi Effendi: p. 222.

P

10.1117. *Paintings from the Falkland Islands by Duffy Sheridan: An Exhibition, the Royal Festival Hall, London, S.E.I.* London: Royal Festival Hall, n.d. [1983] *passim*.

10.1118. Pakula, Hannah. *The Last Romantic: A Biography of Queen Marie of Roumania*. New York: Simon and Schuster, 1984. p. 337.

10.1119. Palestine. *A Survey of Palestine*. Palestine: Government Printer, 1946. II: 926.

10.1120. *Palestine and Transjordan*. n.p. [Oxford]: Naval Intelligence Division, 1943. pp. 134, 143, 144, 299, 303, 465, 469. Written mainly by Albert M. Hyamson [et. al.]

10.1121. *Palestine Annual*. Cairo: A. Reid & Son, n.d. [1922?] pp. 43–5, 103.

10.1122. Palmer, Bernard. *Understanding the Islamic Explosion*. Beaverlodge, Alta.: Horizon House, 1980. pp. 91–2, 179–82.

10.1123. Palmer, Edward Henry. *Oriental Mysticism: A Treatise on the Sufistic and Unitarian Theosophy of the Persians*. 2nd ed. London: Luzac & Co., 1938. p. 44.

10.1124. *Parents Underground to Free Our Children*. Vancouver, Wash.: PUTFOC, n.d. [1978?]
Includes Bahá'í Faith in list of 'enemy' groups.

10.1125. Parkes, James. *A History of Palestine from 135 A.D. to Modern Times*. London: Victor Gollancz, 1949. pp. 251–2.

10.1126. —— *Whose Land?: A History of the Peoples of Palestine*. rev. ed. Harmondsworth: Penguin, 1970. pp. 217–18.

10.1127. Parrinder, E. Geoffrey. *A Book of World Religions*. Amersham, U.K.: Hulton Educational, 1965. pp. [ii], 148, 149, 151.

10.1128. —— *Comparative Religion*. New York: Macmillan Co., 1962. pp. 23, 82, 108.

10.1129. —— *idem*. London: George Allen & Unwin, 1962. pp. 23, 82, 108.

10.1130. —— *A Dictionary of Non-Christian Religions*. Philadelphia, Pa.: Westminster Press, 1971. pp. 7, 38–9.

10.1131. —— *What World Religions Teach*. London: Harrap, 1968. pp. 107–9, 140, 190.

10.1132. Parrish, Maude. *Nine Pounds of Luggage*. Philadelphia, Pa.: J.B. Lippincott Co., 1939. pp. 368–73.

10.1133. Patai, Raphael. *Israel Between East and West: A Study in Human Relations*. Philadelphia, Pa.: Jewish Publication Society of America, 1953. p. 234.

10.1134. —— *idem*. Westport, Conn.: Greenwood Publishing Corporation, 1970. p. 234.

10.1134a. Pavri, P. *The Coming World Teacher: (In Questions and Answers)*. 2nd ed. Adyar, Madras: Indian Star Headquarters, 1923. p. 55.

10.1135. Payne, Robert. *The Holy Sword: The Story of Islam from Muhammad to the Present*. London: Robert Hale, 1959. pp. 255–7.

10.1136. —— *The Splendor of Persia*. New York: Alfred Knopf, 1957. pp. 227–8.

10.1137. Pearlmann, Moshe; Yannai, Yaacov. *Historical Sites in Israel*. rev. and enl. 4th ed. Jersualem: Steimatzky's Agency; Ramat-Gan: Massada Publishing, 1978. p. 120.

10.1138. Pearson, J.D. *Index Islamicus*. London: Mansell, 1958– . Each issue contains sections on the Bahá'í Faith.

10.1139. Peeke, Margaret B. *Number & Letters, or The Thirty-Two Paths of Wisdom*. de luxe ed. New York: Broadway Publishing, 1908. p. iii.

10.1139a. Peerbhai, Adam. *Verdict on Perdu*. Durban, [S. Afr.]: Universal Printing Works, n.d. [1956?] 'Bahai Movement': pp. 51–3.

10.1140. Pemberton, L.B. *A Modern Pilgrimage to Palestine*. Philadelphia, Pa.: Dorrance & Co., 1925. pp. 67, 73, 74–104, 105, 111–13, 142, 149, 155, 156, 189, 190–7, 263–4. Illustrations: drawing of Bahá'í House of Worship, Wilmette, Louis Bourgeois' model, dust cover and frontispiece; Garden of 'Rizwan, Near Haifa', p. 92; 'Abdu'l-Bahá, p. 100.

10.1140a. *The Penguin Dictionary of Religions*. ed. John R. Hinnells. Harmondsworth, U.K.: Penguin Books, 1984. pp. 59, 60, 226.

10.1141. Penrose, Stephen B.L. *That They May Have Life: The Story of the American University of Beirut, 1866–1941*. Beirut: American University, 1970. pp. 130, 219.

10.1142. Perelman, S.J. *The Rising Gorge*. London; Melbourne; Toronto: Heinemann, 1961. p. 170.

10.1143. Perry, Glenn E. *The Middle East: Fourteen Islamic Centuries*. Englewood Cliffs, N.J.: Prentice-Hall, Inc., 1983. pp. 162, 300.

10.1144. *Persia*. n.p. [Oxford]: Naval Intelligence Division, 1945. pp. 295, 326, 330–1, 527, 534, 541.

10.1145. *A Persian Anthology*. being translations from the Persian by Edward Granville Browne, ed. E. Denison Ross. London: Methuen & Co., 1927. pp. 26, 38–40, 59–60, 68–73.

10.1146. *A Persian Bibliography: A Catalogue of the Library of Books and Periodicals in Western Languages on Persia (Iran) in the Diba Collection*. London: TNR Productions, 1981.
Includes a number of Bahá'í volumes.

10.1146a. *The Persian Gulf States: A General Survey*, ed. Alvin J. Cottrell. Baltimore, Md.: Johns Hopkins University Press, 1980. pp. 311, 529.

10.1147. Peseschkian, Nossrat. *In Search of Meaning: A Psychotherapy of Small Steps*. Heidelberg; Berlin: Springer-Verlag, 1985. pp. viii, xiii, 27, 40–43, 51, 62, 65, 145.

10.1148. —— *The Merchant and the Parrot: Mideastern Stories as Tools in Psychotherapy*. New York: Vantage Press, 1982. pp. 49, 51, 55, 56, 58, 59, 157, 161.

10.1149. Petersen, William J. *Those Curious New Cults*. New Canaan, Conn.: Keats Publishing, 1975. pp. 207–18.

10.1150. —— *Those Curious New Cults in the 80s*. rev. ed. New Canaan, Conn.: Keats Publishing, 1982. pp. 190–201.

10.1150a. Petersen, William J.; Harvey, Joan. *A Study Guide for Those Curious New Cults*. New Canaan, Conn.: Keats Publishing, 1973. pp. 40–2.

10.1151. Pfleiderer, Otto. *Religion and Historic Faiths*. New York: B.W. Huebsch, 1907. p. 286.

10.1152. *Phaidon Dictionary of Twentieth-Century Art*. London: Phaidon, 1975. p. 384.

10.1153. Phelan, M. *Handbook of All Denominations*. 4th ed. Nashville, Tenn.: Cokesbury Press, 1927. p. 6.

10.1154. Phelips, Vivian. *The Churches and Modern Thought: An Inquiry into the Grounds of Unbelief and an Appeal to Candour*. 2nd ed. London: Watts, 1934. pp. 212, 277. (The Thinkers Library; 20).

10.1155. Philby, H. StJ.B. *A Pilgrim in Arabia*. London: Robert Hale Limited, 1946. pp. 169–70, 180–3.

10.1156. Phiri, D.D. *Dunduzu K. Chisiza*. Blantyre, Malawi: Longman (Malawi) Ltd., 1974. pp. 9–10, 65. (Malawians to Remember).

10.1156a. Phoenix [Pseudonym]. *His Holiness.* Lahore: Islamic Literature Publishing House, 1935, 1958, 1970. pp. xiii, 165–82.

10.1157. Picton, J. Allanson. *The Religion of the Universe.* London: Macmillan and Co., 1904. pp. 210, 230.

10.1158. Piggot, John. *Persia Ancient and Modern.* London: H.S. King & Co., 1874. pp. 99–100, 104–6, 109–10, 159–61.

10.1159. Pike, E. Royston. *Encyclopedia of Religion and Religions.* London: George Allen & Unwin, 1951. pp. 42–3.

10.1160. —— *idem.* New York: Meridian Book, 1958. pp. 42–3.

10.1161. —— *Ethics of the Great Religions: With Some Account of Their Origins, Scriptures & Practices.* London: Watts & Co., 1948. pp. 212–13.

10.1162. *A Pilgrim's Guide to Planet Earth: Traveler's Handbook & Spiritual Directory.* ed. Parmatma Singh Khalsa. San Rafael, Calif.: Spiritual Community Publications; London: Wildwood House, 1984. pp. 40, 48, 77, 172, 173, 254.

10.1163. *Pilgrims to Tehran and Beyond.* ed. James Prior. Argenta, B.C.: Argenta Friends School Press, 1983. [Bjorling 818]

10.1164. Pingry, Patricia A. *Houses of Worship.* Milwaukee, Wis.: Ideals Publishing, 1977. pp. 60–1.

10.1165. Podger, Shirin. *Poetry, 1979–1982.* Haifa: [Podger], 1982.
Several poems using the Bahá'í Faith as theme.

10.1166. *Poems from the Persian.* Edward G. Browne [ed.] London: Ernest Benn, n.d. [193–?] Ṭáhirih (Qurratu'l-'Ayn), p. 30.

10.1167. Pole, Wellesley Tudor. *My Dear Alexias: Letters from Wellesley Tudor Pole to Rosamond Lehmann.* ed. Elizabeth Gaythorpe. Jersey: Neville Spearman, 1979. pp. 206–7.

10.1168. —— *Private Dowding: A Plain Record of the After-Death Experiences of a Soldier Killed in Battle, and Some Questions on World Issues Answered by the Messenger Who Taught Him Wider Truths.* 4th ed. London: J.M. Watkins, 1918. (Deeper Issues Series). pp. 84–5.

10.1169. —— *idem.* New York: Dodd, Mead & Co., 1919. pp. 84–5.

10.1170. —— *The Silent Road.* London: Neville Spearman, 1960. pp. 24–6, 75–80, 90.

10.1171. —— *Some Deeper Aspects of the War.* Bristol, England: Taylor Bros., 1914. pp. 5, 7.

10.1172. —— *Writing on the Ground.* London: Neville Spearman, 1968. pp. 135–72, mention on flap of dust cover. Photograph of 'Abdu'l-Bahá facing page 135.

10.1173. Pole, Wellesley Tudor; Lehmann, Rosamond. *A Man Seen from Afar.* London: Neville Spearman, 1965. pp. 53, 77.

10.1174. *Political Dictionary of the Middle East in the 20th Century.* ed. Yaacov Shimoni, Evyatar Levine. Jerusalem: Jerusalem Publishing House, 1972. Shaul P. Colbi, 'Baha'is', p. 63.

10.1175. *The Political Role of Minority Groups in the Middle East.* ed. R.D. McLaurin. New York: Praeger, 1979. pp. 10, 271, 273, 290, 294.

10.1176. *The Population of Iran: A Selection of Readings.* ed. Jamshid A. Momeni. Honolulu: East-West Population Center; Shiraz: Pahlavi Population Center, 1977. p. 87.

10.1177. *Populations of the Middle East and North Africa: A Geographical Approach.* edited by J.I. Clarke and W.B. Fisher. New York: African Publishing Company; London: University of London Press, 1972. pp. 72, 191.

10.1178. Port, Wymar. *Chicago the Pagan.* Chicago: Judy Publishing Co., 1953. pp. 167–8, Wilmette temple.

10.1179. *Pot Wars: More Arms for Salvador?: Baha'i Murders in Iran.* New York: WNET/Thirteen, Nov. 16, 1983. (The MacNeil/Lehrer News Hour; Transcript no.2123). Interview with Firuz Kazemzadeh, pp. 9–12.

10.1180. Potter, Charles Francis. *The Faiths Men Live By.* New York: Prentice-Hall, 1954. pp. 307–8.

10.1181. *Preface to Philosophy: Book of Readings.* Ross Earle Hoople, Raymond Frank Piper, William Pearson Tolley, [comp.] New York: The Macmillan Company, 1946. pp. 379–84.

10.1182. *Preface to Philosophy: Textbook.* William Ernest Hocking [et. al.] New York: Macmillan Co., 1946. p. 399.

10.1183. Premadasa, Ranasinghe. *Address of the Hon. R. Premadasa, M.P., Prime Minister of the Democratic Socialist Republic of Sri Lanka at the Fifth Observance in Sri Lanka of World Religion Day on 20th January, 1985.* n.p. [Colombo]: Government Press, 1985. pp. [1], [5].

10.1184. Price, Willard. *Adventures in Paradise: Tahiti and Beyond.* New York: John Day, 1955. pp. 180–1.

10.1185. —— *Adventures in Paradise: Tahiti, Samoa, Fiji.* London: Heinemann, 1956. pp. 180–1.

10.1186. *Problems and Methods of the History of Religions.* ed. U. Bianchi, C.J. Bleeker, A. Bausani. Leiden: Brill, 1972. (Studies in the History of Religions; xix). pp. 57, 63.

10.1187. Public Relations Society of America. *25th Annual Silver Anvil Awards.* New York: Public Relations Society of America, 1969. p. 6.

10.1188. Purdom, C.B. *The God-Man: The Life, Journeys and Work of Meher Baba with an Interpretation of His Silence and Spiritual Teachings.* Crescent Beach, S.C.: Sheriar, 1971. p. 85.

10.1189. Purton, Rowland. *Dear God.* Oxford: Basil Blackwell, 1984. Bahá'í prayers pp. 121, 189.

Q

10.1190. *Qajar Iran: Political, Social and Cultural Change, 1800–1925.* ed. Edmund Bosworth and Carole Hillenbrand. Edinburgh: Edinburgh University Press, 1983. pp. 4, 13, 49, 55, 69, 148–9, 150–1, 250, 256, 257, 259, 260.

10.1191. Quale, G. Robina. *Eastern Civilizations.* New York: Appleton, Century, Crofts, 1966. pp. 90, 91, 96.

10.1192. —— *idem.* 2nd ed. Englewood Cliffs, N.J.: Prentice-Hall, 1975. pp. 57–8.

10.1193. Queen, Richard. *Inside and Out: Hostage to Iran, Hostage to Myself.* New York: G.P. Putnam's Sons, 1981. p. 29.

10.1194. *Quinlan Terry.* ed. Frank Russell. London: Architectural Design, 1981. Tihrán Bahá'í temple, pp. xxiv–xxvii, xliv–xlv, xlviii.

R

10.1195. Rabino, H.L. *Mázandarán and Astarábád.* London: Luzac, 1928. (E.J.W. Gibb Memorial Series. New Series; vii). p. 14.

10.1196. Rabinovich, Abraham. *Akko, St. Jean d'Acre: Palphot Pictorial Guide & Souvenir.* n.p. [Herzlia, Israel]: Palphot Ltd., n.d. [1982?] pp. [6], [35].

10.1197. Radford, Ruby L. *Many Paths to God.* Wheaton, Ill.: Theosophical Publishing House, 1970. pp. 2, 122–5, 127.

10.1198. Radhakrishnan, Sarvepalli. *Eastern Religions and Western Thought.* Oxford: Clarendon Press, 1939. p. 340.

10.1199. —— *idem.* London: Oxford University Press, 1951. p. 340.

10.1200. —— *idem.* New York: Oxford University Press, 1959. p. 340.

10.1201. Radji, Parviz C. *In the Service of the Peacock Throne: The Diaries of the Shah's Last Ambassador to London.* London: Hamish Hamilton, 1983. pp. 214, 218, 224.

10.1202. Rahman, Fazlur. *Islam.* 2nd ed. Chicago; London: University of Chicago Press, 1979. p. 179.

10.1203. Raisin, Jacob S. *Gentile Reactions to Jewish Ideals, with Special Reference to Proselytes.* New York: Philosophical Library, 1953. pp. 433–5.

10.1204. Ramati, Alexander. *Israel Today.* London: Eyre & Spottiswoode, 1962. pp. 162–7; photograph of the Shrine of the Báb.

10.1205. Rand, Abby. *The American Traveller's Guide to Israel.* New York: Charles Scribner's Sons, 1972. pp. 13, 74, 199. Photograph of the Shrine of the Bab, p. 196.

10.1206. Randall, John Herman. *The Meaning of Religion for Man.* New York: Harper & Row, 1968. p. 114.

10.1207. Rasooli, Jay M.; Allen, Cady H. *The Life Story of Dr. Sa'eed of Iran: Kurdish Physician to Princes and Peasants, Nobles and Nomads.* 2nd ed. Grand Rapids, Mich.: Grand Rapids International Publications, 1958. pp. 90, 92, 103, 115.

10.1208. Rathbone, Eliza E. *Mark Tobey – City Paintings.* Washington, D.C.: National Gallery of Art, 1984. pp. 20–1, 30, 51, 52, 55, 57, 60, 67, 72, 73, 95, 96, 97, 98, 99, 106, 108.

10.1209. *Reator Nuclear a Leito Fluidizado = Fluidized Bed Nuclear Reactor.* Porto Alegre, R.S., Brazil: Eberle S.A.: n.d. [1984] p. 6.

10.1210. Rees, Ronald. *Land of Earth and Sky: Landscape Painting of Western Canada.* Saskatoon, Sask.: Western Producer Prairie Books, 1984. p. 52.

10.1211. Reese, William L. *Dictionary of Philosophy and Religion: Eastern and Western Thought.* Atlantic Heights, N.J.: Humanities Press; Sussex: Harvester Press, 1980. p. 49.

10.1211a. Reeves, Minou. *Behind the Peacock Throne.* London: Sidgwick & Jackson, 1986. pp. 55–6.

10.1212. Reinach, Salomon. *Orpheus: A General History of Religions.* London: W. Heinemann; New York: G.P. Putnam Sons, 1909. p. 169.

10.1213. —— *Orpheus: A History of Religions.* New York: Liveright, 1930, 1933. pp. 179–80.

10.1214. Reitlinger, Gerald. *A Tower of Skulls: A Journey Through Persia and Turkish Armenia.* London: Duckworth, 1932. pp. 139–41, 146–7, 185.

10.1214a. *Religion and Culture in Canada = Religion et Culture au Canada: Essays by Members of the Canadian Society for the Study of Religion.* ed. Peter Slater. Canada: Canadian Corporation for Studies in Religion, 1977. Fred Bird, "Rituals Used by Some Contemporary Movements," p. 456.

10.1215. *Religion and Politics in Iran: Shi'ism from Quietism to Revolution.* ed. Nikki R. Keddie. New Haven, Conn.: Yale University Press, 1983. pp. 8, 17, 42, 65, 68, 76.

10.1216. *Religion and Politics in the Middle East.* ed. Michael Curtis. Boulder, Colo.: Westview Press, 1981. p. 368.

10.1217. *Religion and Rural Revolt.* ed. J.M. Bak, A. Benecke. Manchester, U.K.: Manchester University Press, 1984. Kurt Greussing, 'The Babi Movement in Iran, 1844–1852: From Merchant Protest to Peasant Revolution', pp. 256–69.

10.1218. *Religion in South Asia.* G.A. Oddie, ed. London: Curzon Press, 1977. William N. Garlington, 'The Baha'i Faith in Malwa', pp. 101–17.

10.1219. *Religion in the Middle East: Three Religions in Concord and Conflict.* gen. ed. A.J. Arberry; subject ed. C.F. Beckingham. Cambridge: Cambridge University Press, 1969. I: 115–16, 173, 196; II: 64, 96n, 117, 155, 338, 633–4.

10.1220. *Religion in the Twentieth Century.* ed. Vergilius Ferm. New York: Philosophical Library, 1948. pp. 307–14.

10.1220a. *Religion North American Style.* ed. Patrick H. McNamara. 2nd ed. Belmont, Calif.: Wadsworth Publishing Company, 1984. pp. 282, 285–8.

10.1220b. *Religion Today: A Challenging Enigma.* ed. Arthur L. Swift. New York; London: Whittlesey House, 1933. pp. 44, 52.

10.1221. *Religions of the Empire: A Conference on Some Living Religions Within the Empire: Held at the Imperial Institute, London, September 22nd to October 3rd, 1924. Under the Auspices of the School of Oriental Studies (University of London) and the Sociological Society.* ed. William Loftus Hare. New York: Macmillan, 1925. 'The Bahá'í Cause'/read by Mountford [sic] Mills; 'The Bahá'í Influence on Life'/Ruhi Afnan, pp. 304–28.

10.1222. *idem.* London: Duckworth, 1925. pp. 304–28.

10.1223. *Religious Books, 1876–1982.* New York: R.R. Bowker Company, 1983. I: 122; II: 125–30.

10.1224. *Religious Cooperation in the Pacific Islands.* Suva, Fiji: University of the South Pacific, 1983. Irene Williams, 'The Baha'i Faith', pp. 49–60.

10.1225. *The Religious Dimension.* A selection of essays presented at a Colloquium on Religious Studies held at the University of Auckland, New Zealand in August 1975, ed. John C. Hinchliff. Auckland: Rep Prep, 1976. Linda Ramer, 'Education Based on the Religious Definition of Man', pp. 101–3.

10.1226. *The Religious Heritage of Southern California: A Bicentennial Survey.* Los Angeles: Interreligious Council of Southern California, 1976. p. 114.

10.1227. *Religious Life and Communities.* Jerusalem: Keter Books, 1974. pp. 86–9, 155. (Israel Pocket Library).

10.1228. *Religious Requirements and Practices of Certain Selected Groups: A Handbook for Chaplains.* Washington, D.C.: Department of the Army, 1978. pp. VII-11 – VII-16.

10.1229. *Religious Systems of the World: A Contribution to the Study of Comparative Religion.* 5th ed. London: Swann Sonnenschein, 1901. E.G. Browne, 'Babiism', pp. 333–53.

10.1230. *idem.* London: Swann Sonnenschein, 1905. E.G. Browne, 'Bahaism', pp. 333–55.

10.1231. Remey, Charles Mason. *Houses in Which the Remey Family, Their Forebears and Children Have Lived: A Family Chronicle.* n.p. [Washington, D.C.]: Remey, 1957. (Remey Family Records). I: 11, 31, 43–4; II: [7], [9], [10], [27]–[32].

10.1232. —— *Specifications for the Completion of the Reméum.* n.p. [Washington, D.C.]: Remey, 1953, 1960 [introd.] (Remey Family Records). p. 20.

10.1233. Renan, Ernest. *The Apostles.* trans. William G. Hutchison. London: Watts & Co., 1905. p. 134.

10.1234. Rexford, Orcella. *The Voice of Nature: The Wonders of Plant Life in Their Service to Man, Afield with the Wild Flowers and Plants.* San Francisco: Rexford, 1934. pp. 153, 154.

10.1235. Rice, Clara C. *Mary Bird in Persia.* London: Church Missionary Society, 1916. pp. 37–40, 71, 102, 107, 143, 191.

10.1236. —— *Persian Women and Their Ways.* London: Seeley, Service & Co., 1923. pp. 21, 24, 155–6, 275–6.

10.1237. —— *idem.* Tehran: Imperial Organization for Social Services, 1976. pp. 21, 24, 155–6, 275–6. (Pahlavi Commemorative Reprint Series).

10.1238. Rice, Edward. *Eastern Definitions: A Short Encyclopedia of Religions of the Orient.* Garden City, N.Y.: Doubleday, 1978. pp. 44–6.

10.1239. —— *Ten Religions of the East.* New York: Four Winds Press, 1978. pp. 2–3, 127, 133–41.

10.1240. Richard St Barbe Baker Foundation. *Founding Conference Proceedings.* ed. by Kate M. Lindsay. Toronto, Ont.: Richard St Barbe Baker Foundation, 1984. pp. 5, 25.

10.1241. Richards, Fred. *A Persian Journey: Being an Etcher's Impressions of the Middle East with Forty-Eight Drawings.* New York: Jonathan Cape Smith, 1932. pp. 216, 230.

10.1242. Richards, J.R. *The Open Road in Persia.* London: Church Missionary Society, 1933. pp. 20, 25, 29, 30, 39, 44, 66.

10.1242a. Richter, Julius. *A History of Protestant Mission in the Near East.* Edinburgh; London: Oliphant, Anderson & Ferrie, 1910. pp. 286–91.

10.1243. Rieu, Charles. *Catalogue of the Persian Manuscripts in the British Museum: Supplement.* London: Trustees of the British Museum, 1977. items 12–15.

10.1244. Ringgren, Helmer; Strom, Ake V. *Religion of Mankind, Today & Yesterday.* Philadelphia, Pa.: Fortress Press, 1967. p. 206.

10.1245. Rix, Herbert. *Sermons and Essays.* London: Williams and Norgate, 1907. 'The Persian Bab', pp. 295–325.

10.1246. Rizvi, Saiyid Athar Abbas. *Iran – Royalty, Religion and Revolution.* Canberra: Ma'rifat Publishing House, 1980. pp. 99, 138–41, 197, 199, 201, 345.

10.1247. Robertson, Irvine. *What the Cults Believe.* Chicago: Moody Press, 1966. pp. 80–1.

10.1248. Robertson, John M. *Pagan Christs.* London: Watt & Co., 1911. pp. xvi-xviii.

10.1249. Rosen, Barbara; Rosen, Barry. *The Destined Hour: The Hostage Crisis and One Family's Ordeal.* Garden City, N.Y.: Doubleday & Company, 1982. pp. 58, 79.

10.1250. Rosen, Friedrich. *Oriental Memories of a German Diplomatist.* New York: E.P. Dutton, 1930. pp. 147, 284–5.

10.1251. —— *idem.* London: Methuen, n.d. [1930] pp. 147, 284–5.

10.1252. Rosenbaum, Maurice. *Israel: A Concise Guide to Israel.* London: Geographia, 1981. (Thornton Cox Travellers Guides). pp. 106–7

10.1253. Rosenberg, Stuart E. *Great Religions of the Holy Land: An Historical Guide to Sacred Places and Sites.* South Brunswick; New York: A.S. Barnes and Company; London: Thomas Yoseloff, 1971. Photograph of the Shrine of the Báb, p. 151.

10.1254. Ross, Dana Fuller. *Yankee.* New York: Dell Publishing Co., 1982. p. 24.
'Temples for the B'hai faith of the Persians' are said to be located in Constantinople in 1789.

10.1255. Ross, E. Denison. *Both Ends of the Candle.* London: Faber & Faber, 1943. pp. 54–60, 77, 81, 85, 201.

10.1256. —— *The Persians.* Oxford: Clarendon Press, 1931. pp. 67–9, 75, 76.

10.1257. Ross, Emory; Ross, Myrta. *Africa Disturbed.* New York: Friendship Press, 1959. p. 169.

10.1257a. Rotthier, Mary B. *Ancient and Modern Palestine.* 4th ed. New York: Meany Printing Co., 1898. II:474.

10.1258. Rowley, Peter. *New Gods in America: An Informal Investigation into the New Religions of American Youth Today.* New York: David McKay Co., 1971. pp. 3, 8, 12–17, 205.

10.1259. Rubin, Morton. *The Walls of Acre: Intergroup Relations and Urban Development in*

Israel. New York: Holt, Rinehart and Winston, 1974. pp. 30, 35, 39.

10.1260. Rudhyar, Dane. *The Astrological Houses.* New York: Doubleday, 1972. p. 184.

10.1261. —— *Astrological Timing.* New York: Harper & Row, 1972. pp. 42, 53, 63–4, 109, 114, 139–40, 141, 142–3, 151.

10.1262. —— *The Astrology of Personality.* New York: Lucis Publishing Co., 1936. pp. 209–10, 233, 238, 246, 272, 322, 421.

10.1263. —— *idem.* Garden City, N.Y.: Doubleday, 1970. pp. 240–1, 268, 274, 282–3, 312–13, 374, 490.

10.1264. —— *Birth Patterns for a New Humanity: A Study of Astrological Cycles Structuring the Present Worldcrisis.* The Netherlands: Servire-Wassenar, 1969. pp. 42, 53, 102, 114, 139, 142–4, 151, 191, 211.

10.1265. —— *New Mansions for New Men.* New York: Lucis Publishing Co., 1938. p. 236.

10.1266. —— *idem.* n.p. [Claremont, Calif.]: Hunter House, 1978. p. 236.

10.1267. —— *Rania, an Epic Narrative.* San Francisco: Unity Press, 1973. pp. 176–8.

10.1268. —— *The Sun Is Also a Star.* New York: E.P. Dutton, 1975. p. 97.

10.1269. Rumble, Leslie; Carty, Charles Mortimer. *Radio Replies in Defense of Religion.* 3 vols. St Paul, Minn.: Radio Replies Press, 1942. III: 42.

10.1270. Russell, John. *Mark Tobey, May–June 1968.* London: Hanover Gallery, 1968. p. [2]

10.1271. Russell, Lao. *God Will Work with You But Not for You: A Living Philosophy.* 4th ed. Waynesboro, Va.: University of Science and Philosophy, 1973. pp. 70–3.

10.1272. Ruthven, Malise. *Islam in the World.* Harmondsworth, Middlesex: Penguin, 1984. p. 206.

10.1273. Rutland, Jonathan. *Looking at Israel.* London: Adam & Charles Black; Philadelphia, Pa.: J.B. Lippincott Co., 1970. p. 27; photograph of the Shrine of the Báb, title page and p. 27.

10.1274. Rypka, Jan. *History of Iranian Literature.* Dordrecht, Holland: D. Reidel Publishing Co., 1968. pp. 77, 374.

S

10.1275. Ṣabá,, Mohsen. *English Bibliography of Iran.* n.p. [Tehran]: Centre for Studies and Research on the Iranian Civilization, n.d. [1965] (Bank Melli Iran Press). (Centre for Studies and Research on the Iranian Civilization. Publication; no.1). pp. xxiv, 18–19.

10.1276. *Sacred Texts of the World: A Universal Anthology.* ed. Ninian Smart, Richard D. Hecht. London: Macmillan Reference Books, 1982. pp. viii, 369, 379, 407.

10.1277. *idem.* New York: Crossroad, 1982. pp. viii, 369, 379, 407.

10.1278. *The Saga of Haifa, City of Carmel.* n.p. [Haifa], n.d. [1969] p. [9], photographs on pp. 710, 711.

10.1279. Saghaphi, Mirza Mahmoud Khan. *In the Imperial Shadow.* Garden City, N.Y.: Doubleday, Doran & Co., 1926. p. 400.

10.1280. Said, Kurban. *Ali & Nino.* New York: Pocket Books, 1972. pp. 110, 112.

10.1281. Sailer, T.H.P. *The Moslem Faces the Future: An Introduction to the Study of the Moslem World.* New York: Missionary Education Movement of the United States and Canada, 1926. p. 99.

10.1282. Salisbury, W. Seward. *Religion in American Culture: A Sociological Interpretation.* Homewood, Ill.: Dorsey Press, 1964. p. 62.

10.1283. Sampson, A.C.M. *The Neglected Ethic: Cultural and Religious Factors in the Care of Patients.* London: McGraw-Hill Book Co., 1982. pp. 47–9.

10.1284. Samson, Ruth Bjorkman. *Seven Steps to Peace.* New York: Exposition Press, 1956. pp. 29, 55, 56, 101, 119.

10.1284a. Samuel, Edwin Herbert. *A Lifetime in Jerusalem.* London; New York; Toronto: Abelard-Schuman, 1970. p. 132.

10.1285. Samuel, Herbert. *Belief and Action: An Everyday Philosophy.* London: Cassel & Co., 1937. p. 87.

10.1286. Sanasarian, Eliz. *The Women's Rights*

Movement in Iran: Mutiny, Appeasement, and Repression from 1900 to Khomeini. New York: Praeger, 1982. pp. 6–7, 41, 47, 136, 148.

10.1287. Saroyan, William. *Places Where I've Done Time.* New York: Praeger Publishers, 1972. 'The Bahai Temple, Haifa, 1961', pp. 60–2.

10.1288. Sasek, Miroslav. *This Is Israel.* New York: Macmillan, 1962, 1966. 27, 33. Children's book of drawings with captions: Shrine of the Báb, page 27; view of Bay of Haifa from Mt Carmel showing Shrine of the Báb and Bahá'í Archives building which are not identified.

10.1289. Saskatchewan Arts Board. *Five from Saskatchewan = Cinq Artistes de la Saskatchewan.* Saskatchewan: Saskatchewan Arts Board, 1983. Bahá'í artist Otto Donald Rogers, pp. [3], [4].

10.1290. Saurat, Denis. *A History of Religions.* London: Jonathan Cape, 1934. pp. 258, 259.

10.1291. Savage, Minot J. *The Passing and the Permanent in Religion.* New York: G.P. Putnam's Sons, 1901. p. 147.

10.1292. Schimmel, Annemarie. *Islam in the Indian Subcontinent.* Leiden; Köln: E.J. Brill, 1980. pp. 186, 223. (Handbuch der Orientalistik).

10.1292a. Schmidt, Roger. *Exploring Religion.* Belmont, Calif.: Wadsworth, 1980. p. 285.

10.1293. Schmied, Wieland. *Tobey.* New York: Abrams, n.d. [1966?] p. 7.

10.1294. Schneider, Herbert Wallace. *Religion in 20th Century America.* Cambridge, Mass.: Harvard University Press, 1952. p. 23.

10.1295. —— *idem.* rev. ed. New York: Atheneum, 1964. p. 27.

10.1296. Schoen, Elin. *Widower.* New York: William Morrow and Company, 1984. pp. 45–6, 51, 97, 109, 160.

10.1297. *Scholars, Saints, and Sufis: Muslim Religious Institutions in the Middle East Since 1500.* ed. Nikki R. Keddie. Berkeley, Calif.: University of California Press, 1978. p. 216.

10.1298. Schoonmaker, Ann. *Me, Myself & I: Everywoman's Journey to Herself.* New York: Harper & Row, 1977. pp. [v], 109, 118, 130.

10.1299. Scrutton, Robert J. *Eating Right is Beautiful: Nature's Way.* London: Neville Spearman, 1976. pp. 31, 156–70.

10.1300. —— *The Other Atlantis.* Jersey: Neville Spearman, 1977. pp. 31, 83, 131, 146–8.

10.1301. —— *Secrets of Lost Atland.* ed. Ken Johnson. Jersey: Neville Spearman, 1978. pp. 147, 179, 197, 198–9, 202, 208, 210.

10.1302. Seals, James. *The Music of Seals & Crofts Made Easy for Guitar by Brent Phillips.* New York: Dawnbreaker Music Co.: Exclusive Selling Agent for the United States and Canada, Warner Bros. Publications, 1976. pp. 59–60.

10.1303. —— *Seals & Crofts Complete.* New York: Warner Brothers, 1977. Includes several songs with mention of the Faith.

10.1304. —— *Seals & Crofts Retrospective.* 2 vols. New York: Dawnbreaker Music: Exclusive Selling Agent for the United States and Canada, Warner Bros. Publications, 1974. I: 71–3, 84–5; II: 33.

10.1305. —— *Summer Breeze.* New York: Dawnbreaker Music Co.: Exclusive Selling Agent for the United States and Canada, Warner Bros. Publications, 1971. pp. [2], 27.

10.1306. —— *Unborn Child.* New York: Dawnbreaker Music Co.: Exclusive Selling Agent for the United States and Canada,, Warner Bros. Publications, 1974. pp. [9], back cover.

10.1307. *The Search for God.* David Manning White [ed.] New York: Macmillan; London: Collier Macmillan, 1985. pp. 73–7.

10.1308. Searight, Sarah. *The British in the Middle East.* London: Weidenfeld & Nicholson, 1969. p. 81–2, 142.

10.1309. —— *idem.* New York: Atheneum, 1969. pp. 81–2, 142.

10.1310. —— *idem.* London: The Hague; East-West Publications in association with Livres de France, Cairo, 1979. pp. 100, 101, 191, 227.

10.1311. Seaver, George. *Francis Younghusband, Explorer and Mystic.* London: John Murray, 1952. p. 341.

10.1312. Secrist, Henry T. *Comparative Studies in Religion: An Introduction to Unitarianism.* Boston: American Unitarian Association, 1909. p. 16.

10.1313. Sedych, Andrei. *This Land of Israel.* New York: Macmillan, 1967. pp. 68–71. Photograph of the Shrine of the Báb, pages 69 and 86.

10.1314. Seitz, William C. *Abstract Expressionist Painting in America.* Cambridge, Mass.; London: Published for the National Gallery of Art by Harvard University Press, 1983. (The Alisa Mellon Bruce Studies in American Art). pp. 5, 66, 111, 116, 136, 145, 160 (all in relation to Mark Tobey's art).

10.1315. —— *Mark Tobey.* New York: Museum

of Modern Art, 1962. pp. 10, 12–15, 44, 45, 47, 50, 90, 91.

10.1316. Sell, Edward. *The Faith of Islam*. London: Society for the Promotion of Christian Knowledge, 1920. pp. 184–209.

10.1317. —— *idem*. 4th ed. Wilmington, Del.: Scholarly Resources, 1976. pp. 184–209.

10.1317a. —— *Ithna 'Asharíyya or the Twelve Shí'ah Imáms*. Madras [etc.]: Christian Literature Society for India, 1923. (The Islam Series). p. 57.

10.1318. Seminar on Excellence in Education (1984: Lucknow). *Seminar on Excellence in Education: Discussing the Need of All Round Excellence in Education*. organized by City Montessori School, Lucknow. Lucknow, India: City Montessori School, 1984. Inside covers, back cover, p. 22 of fourth numbered section.

10.1319. *Service of Celebration on the Occasion of the Tenth Anniversary Independence, National Stadium, Suva, Sunday, 12th October, 1980*. Suva: Dominion of Fiji, 1980. p. 13.

10.1320. *Service to Commemorate the 40th Anniversary of the Signing of the Charter of the United Nations on 26 June 1945*. [London]: Westminster Abbey, 1985. p. 11.

10.1321. Shabaz, Absalom D. *Land of the Lion and the Sun: Personal Experiences, the Nation of Persia, Their Manner, Customs and Their Belief*. Madison, Wis.: Shabaz, 1901 and n.d. pp. 49–51. 1901 edition has photograph of 'Abdu'l-Bahá, page 51. Undated edition has an illustration of 'Mohammed and the Koran' on page 51 in its place.

10.1322. Shamuyarira, Nathan M. *Crisis in Rhodesia*. New York: Transatlantic Arts, 1966. p. 27.

10.1323. Sharabi, H.B. *Governments and Politics of the Middle East in the Twentieth Century*. Princeton, N.J.: D. Van Nostrand Company, 1962. p. 7.

10.1324. Sharma, Roshan Lal. *Holy Men and Holy Cows*. New York: Exposition Press, 1968. pp. 163–4.

10.1325. Shearer, Tony. *Lord of the Dawn: Quetzalcoatl, the Plumed Serpent of Mexico*. Healdsburg, Calif.: Naturegraph, 1971. pp. 183, 189–90, bibliography.

10.1326. Sheckley, Robert. *Mindswap*. New York: Ace Books, 1978. pp. 3, 205.

10.1327. Sheil, Lady. *Glimpses of Life and Manners in Persia*. London: John Murray, 1856. pp. 175–81, 272–82.

Review:
Quarterly Review (London), no.202 (Mar. 1857), pp. 501–41.

10.1328. —— *idem*. New York: Arno Press, 1973. pp. 175–81, 272–82.

10.1329. Shepard, Judy; Rosenfeld, Alvin. *Ticket to Israel*. New York: Rhinehart & Co., 1952. pp. 202, 218, 230.

10.1330. Sherman, Arnold; Brilliant, Sylvia. *Israel on $15 a Day*. 1978–79 ed. New York: Arthur Frommer Inc., 1978. pp. 178, 208.

10.1331. *Le Shî'isme Imâmite: Colloque de Strasbourg (6–9 Mai 1968)*. Paris: Presses Universitaires de France, 1970. Lambton, A.K.S., 'The Persian 'Ulamā and Constitutional Reform', pp. 252–3.

10.1331a. *Shorter Encyclopaedia of Islam*. ed. H.A.R. Gibb, J.H. Kramers. Leiden: E.J. Brill, 1953. pp. 52–3, 55.

10.1331b. *idem*. Ithaca, N.Y.: Cornell University Press, c1953. pp. 52–3, 55.

10.1331c. *idem*. Leiden: E.J. Brill; London: Luzac, 1961. pp. 52–3, 55.

10.1331d. Shulman, Albert M. *The Religious Heritage of America*. San Diego, Calif.: A.S. Barnes, 1981. pp. 350–2.

10.1332. Shuster, W. Morgan. *The Strangling of Persia*. New York: Century Co., 1912. pp. 21–2.

10.1333. —— *idem*. New York: Greenwood Press, 1968. pp. 21–2.

10.1334. Siddiqi, Aslam. *Modernization Menaces Muslims*. Lahore, Pakistan: Sh. Muhammad Ashraf, 1974. pp. 63, 277.

10.1335. —— *idem*. 2nd ed. Lahore, Pakistan: Sh. Muhammad Ashraf, 1981. pp. 63, 277.

10.1336. Silberstein, Joan. *Hosteling through the Holy Land*. Jerusalem: Weidenfeld and Nicholson together with Steimatzky's Agency, 1973. p. 57.

10.1337. Sinclair, Upton. *The Profits of Religion: An Essay in Economic Interpretation*. Pasadena, Calif.: Upton Sinclair, 1918. p. 254.

10.1338. —— *idem*. New York: Vanguard Press, 1927. p. 254.

10.1339. —— *idem*. New York: AMS Press, 1970. p. 254.

10.1340. Singer, Caroline; Baldridge, Cyrus LeRoy. *Half the World Is Isfahan*. New York; London: Oxford University Press, 1936. p. 36.

10.1341. Singh, Sawan. *Spiritual Gems: Extracts from Letters to Seekers and Disciples*. 6th ed. Beas,

Punjab: Radha Soami Satsang, 1980. pp. 130–1 (no.90).

10.1341a. Sirof, Harriet. *The Junior Encyclopedia of Israel.* photographs by Neil Tepper. Middle Village, N.Y.: Jonathan David Publishers, 1980. pp. 51, 173, 350.

10.1342. Siwatibau, Suliana; Williams, B. David. *A Call to a New Exodus: An Anti-Nuclear Primer for Pacific People.* Suva, Fiji: Pacific Conference of Churches; Lotu Pasifika Productions, 1982. p. 63.

10.1343. Skinner, Clarence R. *A Religion for Greatness.* Boston: Murray Press, 1945. p. 11.

10.1344. Sluglett, Peter. *Theses on Islam, the Middle East and North-West Africa, 1880–1978, Accepted by Universities in the United Kingdom and Ireland.* London: Mansell Publishing Limited, 1983. p. 114 item 2820.

10.1345. Smart, Ninian. *Background to the Long Search.* London: British Broadcasting Corporation, 1977. p. 19.

10.1346. —— *The Religious Experience.* 2nd ed. New York: Charles Scribner's Sons, 1976. pp. 22, 435–6.

10.1347. —— *The Religious Experience of Mankind.* New York: Charles Scribner's Sons, 1969. pp. 22, 417–18.

10.1348. Smith, Barry R. *Warning.* n.p. [New Zealand]: Smith Family Evangelism, 1983. p. 138.

10.1349. Smith, Ethel Sabin. *God and Other Gods: Essays in Perspective on Persisting Religious Problems.* New York: Exposition Press, 1973. pp. 154–7.

10.1349a. Smith, Margaret. *Rābiʿa the Mystic & Her Fellow-Saints in Islām: Being the Life and Teaching of Rābiʿa Al-ʿAdawiyya Al-Qaysiyya of Basra Together with Some Account of the Place of the Women Saints in Islām.* introd. Annemarie Schimmel. Cambridge; London [etc.]: Cambridge University Press, 1984. Ṭáhirih, pp. 158–63.

10.1350. Smith, R. Bosworth. *Mohammed and Mohammedanism.* London: Smith Elder & Co., 1874. pp. xiv, 218.

10.1351. —— *idem.* New York: Harper & Bros. 1875. p. 244.

10.1352. —— *idem.* 2nd ed. London: Smith Elder & Co., 1876. p. 319.

10.1353. —— *idem.* 3rd ed. London: J. Murray, 1889. pp. 269–70.

10.1354. Smith, Wilfred Cantwell. *Islam in Mod-ern History.* Princeton, N.J.: Princeton University Press, 1957. pp. 135n, 153.

10.1355. —— *idem.* New York: New American Library, 1963. pp. 140n, 158.

10.1356. Snouck Hurgronje, C. *Mohammedanism: Lecture on Its Origin, Its Religious and Political Growth and Its Present State.* New York: G.P. Putnam's Sons, 1916. p. 88.

10.1357. Soffer, Arnon; Kipnis, Baruch. *Atlas of Haifa and Mount Carmel.* Haifa: Applied Scientific Research Co., University of Haifa, 1980. p. 79.

10.1358. Solomon, Victor. *A Handbook of Conversions to the Religions of the World.* New York: Stravon Educational Press, 1965. pp. 362–7. Photograph of the Baháʾí International Archives and the Shrine of the Báb, page 364 and House of Worship, Wilmette, page 366.

10.1359. Soper, Edmund Davidson. *The Religions of Mankind.* rev. ed. New York: Abingdon-Cokesbury, 1938. pp. 311–12.

10.1360. —— *idem.* 3rd ed. rev. New York: Abingdon, 1951. p. 223.

10.1361. Sourdel, Dominique. *Islam.* New York: Walker, 1962. pp. 93, 143.

10.1362. Southern Alberta Art Gallery (Lethbridge). *Otto Rogers, New Paintings and Sculpture, 1977–78.* Lethbridge, Alta.: Southern Alberta Art Gallery, 1978. pp. [4], [6]–[10].

10.1363. *The Soviet Union and the Middle East: the Post-World War II Era.* ed. Ivo J. Lederer, Wayne S. Vucinich. Stanford, Calif.: Hoover Institution Press, 1974. p. 228.

10.1363a. Sox, David. *The Gospel of Barnabas.* London: George Allen & Unwin, 1984. pp. 127, 151.

10.1364. Spark, Muriel. *The Mandelbaum Gate.* London: Macmillan London Limited, 1965. p. 26.

10.1365. Spear, Percival. *India – a Modern History.* new ed., rev. and enl. Ann Arbor, Mich.: University of Michigan Press, 1972. p. 98.

10.1366. Speer, Robert E. *The Finality of Jesus Christ.* Westwood, N.J.: Fleming H. Revell Co., 1933. pp. 59, 270.

10.1367. —— *The Light of the World: A Brief Comparative Study of Christianity and Non-Christian Religions.* West Medford, Mass.: Central Committee on the United Study of Missions, 1911. pp. 213–16.

10.1368. —— *Missions and Modern History: A Study of the Missionary Aspects of Some Great*

Movements of the Nineteenth Century. New York: Fleming H. Revell Co., 1904. I: 119–82; II: 659, 671.

10.1368a. —— *idem.* Philadelphia; New York; Chicago: Westminster Press, 1904. I: 119–82; II: 659, 671.

10.1369. —— *Missions and Politics in Asia: Studies in the Spirit of the Eastern Peoples, the Present Making of History in Asia, and the Part Therein of Christian Missions.* New York: Fleming H. Revell, 1898. pp. 32–4.

10.1370. —— *The Unfinished Task of Foreign Missions.* New York: Fleming H. Revell Co., 1926. pp. 196–8.

10.1371. Spengler, Oswald. *The Decline of the West: Perspectives of World History.* 2 vols. New York: Alfred Knopf, 1926–1928. II: 228. The later abridged edition has no Bahá'í mention.

10.1372. Spicer-Simpson, Theodore. *A Collector of Characters.* [Miami, Fla.]: University of Miami Press, 1962. 'Abdu'l-Bahá medal: pp. 60–1, [106].

10.1373. Spiegelberg, Frederic. *Living Religions of the World.* Englewood Cliffs, N.J.: Prentice-Hall, 1956. pp. 419–21.

10.1374. *Spirit of Toronto, 1834–1984.* ed. Margaret Lindsay Holton. Toronto, Ont.: Image Publishing, 1983. Mary Gray, 'The Baha'i Faith', pp. 168–79.

10.1375. *The Spirit of Truth and the Spirit of Error: What God Has Said on Seven Fundamentals, and What Men Are Now Saying.* comp. Keith L. Brooks. 2nd rev. ed. Chicago: Moody Press, 1976. p. [6]

10.1376. Spittler, Russell P. *Cults and Isms: Twenty Alternates to Evangelical Christianity.* Grand Rapids, Mich.: Baker Book House, 1962. pp. 93–5, 130, 132.

10.1377. Spring Rice, Cecil. *The Letters and Friendships of Sir Cecil Spring Rice.* ed. Stephen Gwynn. London: Constable, 1929. I: 298.

10.1378. Sri Lanka. Postmaster-General's Office. *Issue of a Stamp to Mark World Religion Day, 1985.01.20.* Colombo: Postmaster-General's Office, 1985.

10.1379. St. John, Robert. *Israel.* New York: Time Inc., 1962. pp. 129–31.

10.1380. Stamp, L. Dudley. *Asia, a Regional and Economic Geography.* 10th ed. London: Methuen, 1959. p. 127.

10.1381. *Stamp Bulletin no.168: Commemorative Issue, World Religion Day.* Colombo, Sri Lanka: Philatelic Bureau, Department of Posts, 1985.

10.1382. Stanford University. *Religion at Stanford, 1984–85.* Stanford, Calif.: Stanford University, 1984. p. [6]

10.1383. Stark, Freya. *Baghdad Sketches.* New York: E.P. Dutton, 1938. pp. 12–14.

10.1384. —— *idem.* London: John Murray, 1939. pp. 12–14.

10.1385. —— *The Valleys of the Assassins and Other Persian Travels.* London: John Murray, 1975. pp. 202, 335.

10.1385a. Stark, Rodney; Bainbridge, William Sims. *The Future of Religion: Secularization, Revival and Cult Formation.* Berkeley; Los Angeles; London: University of California Press, 1985. pp. 238, 241–2, 244–5, 257, 445, 451, 464.

10.1385b. Starkes, M. Thomas. *No Man Goes Alone.* Atlanta, Ga.: Home Mission Board, Southern Baptist Convention, 1972. pp. 4, 45, 75–6, 80–1.

10.1386. Starkes, M. Thomas. *Today's World Religions.* New Orleans, La.: Insight Press, 1978. pp. 147–51.

10.1387. Steinbacher, John. *Robert Francis Kennedy – the Man, the Mysticism, the Murder.* Los Angeles: Impact Publishers, 1968. pp. 15–17.

10.1388. Steiner, M.J. *Inside Pan-Arabia.* Chicago: Packard, 1947. p. 211.

10.1389. *Stella – the Story of Stella Jane Reekie, 1922–1982.* comp. Jessie Adamson, Kay Ramsay, Maxwell Craig. Glasgow: South Park Press, 1984. pp. ix, 27, 29, 30.

10.1390. Sterling, Martie; Sterling, Robin. *Last Flight from Iran.* New York: Bantam, 1981. pp. 207–208.

10.1391. Stern, Henry A. *Dawnings of Light in the East: With Biblical, Historical, and Statistical Notices of Persons and Places Visited During a Mission to the Jews, in Persia, Coordistan, and Mesopotamia.* London: Charles H. Purday: Wetheim and Macintosh, 1854. pp. 261–2.
First book in the West to mention the Báb.

10.1392. Stevens, Roger. *The Land of the Great Sophy.* 3rd ed. London: Eyre Methuen, 1979. pp. 47–8.

10.1393. Stevenson, Dwight Eshelman. *Faiths That Compete for My Loyalty.* St Louis, Mo.: Christian Board of Publication, 1948. pp. 71–2.

10.1394. Stewart, George Rippey. *American Way of Life.* Garden City, N.Y.: Doubleday, 1954. pp. 67, 69.

10.1394a. —— *idem.* New York: Russell & Russell, 1971. pp. 67, 69.

10.1395. Stock, Eugene. *The History of the Church Missionary Society: Its Environment, Its Men and Its Work.* London: Church Missionary Society, 1899–1916. III: 753; IV: 135.

10.1396. Stoddard, Lothrop. *The New World of Islam.* New York: Charles Scribner's Sons, 1921. p. 324.

10.1397. Storer, Jacob. *The Spirit of Reality: Its Manifold Reflections in Spiritual Thoughts: For Daily Reading and Meditation.* Buffalo, N.Y.: Humboldt Publishing Co., 1931. Quotations from Bahá'u'lláh and 'Abdu'l-Bahá throughout.

10.1397a. —— *Thoughts That Build, for Daily Reading and Meditation.* New York: Macmillan Company, 1924. p. v., and quotations from Baha'o'llah [sic] and Abdul Baha throughout.

10.1398. Storey, C.A. *Persian Literature: A Bio-Bibliographical Survey.* London: Luzac, 1972. I: 339, 346, 385, 1054, 1060, 1061, 1182, 1285–6, 1287–8.

10.1398a. Storrs, Ronald. *Lawrence of Arabia: Zionism and Palestine.* Harmondsworth, U.K.; New York: Penguin Books, 1940. p. 14.

10.1399. —— *The Memoirs of Sir Ronald Storrs.* New York: G.P. Putnam's Sons, 1937. pp. 67, 322, 332.

10.1400. —— *idem.* New York: Arno, 1972. (World Affairs, National and International Viewpoints). pp. 70, 328, 337.

10.1401. —— *Orientations.* London: Ivor Nicholson & Watson, 1937. pp. 72, 365, 375–6. Ruhi, the agent mentioned on many pages throughout the book, is identified by Storrs in *Lawrence of Arabia* as a Persian Bahá'í agent.

10.1401a. —— *idem.* London: Readers Union by arrangement with Ivor Nicholson & Watson, 1939. pp. 67, 322, 332.

10.1402. *Studies in Islamic Society: Contributions in Memory of Gabriel Baer.* ed. Gabriel R. Warburg, Gad G. Gilbar. Haifa: Haifa University Press, 1984. p. 99.

10.1403. Super Sky International, Inc. *Annual Report 1985.* Mequon, Wis.: Super Sky International Inc., 1985. cover, pp. 4–7.

10.1403a. *Supplement to the Oxford English Dictionary.* Oxford: At the Clarendon Press, 1961. p. 53.

10.1403b. *A Survey of Persian Art: From Prehistoric Times to the Present.* ed. Arthur Upham Pope; asst. ed. Phyllis Ackerman. London: Oxford University Press, 1938–1939. I: 105, IV: 1741–2.

10.1403c. *idem.* 2nd ed. Shiraz: Asia Institute, 1964. I: 105, IV: 1741–2.

10.1403d. *idem.* 3rd ed. Tehran: Shahbanu Farah Foundation: National Iranian Radio and Television, 1977. I: 105, IV: 1741–2.

10.1403e. *idem.* 3rd ed. Ashiya, Japan: Sopa; New York: Maxwell Aley Literary Associates, 1981. I: 105, IV: 1741–2.

10.1404. Sutter, Frederic Koehler. *Scenes of Samoa.* Apia, Western Samoa: Commercial Printers, 1983. plate 32: photograph of Samoa temple.

10.1405. Sweet, William Warren. *The Story of Religion in America.* New York: Harper & Brothers, 1939. p. 626.

10.1406. —— *The Story of Religions in America.* New York: Harper & Brothers, 1930. p. 544.

10.1407. Swietochowski, Tadeusz. *Russian Azerbaijan, 1905–1920: The Shaping of National Identity in a Muslim Community.* Cambridge, Eng.: Cambridge University Press, 1985. (Soviet and East European Studies). p. 72.

10.1408. Swindell, Larry. *Screwball: The Life of Carole Lombard.* New York: William Morrow and Company, 1975. pp. 25–6.

10.1409. Swingle, Charles Manning. *The Keep-Well Book, with Something of the Philosophy of Well-Being.* Cleveland, Ohio: By the author, 1914. pp. 13, 228.

10.1410. Sykes, Ella C. *Persia and Its People.* London: Methuen, 1910. pp. 36, 140–3.

10.1411. Sykes, Mark. *The Caliph's Last Heritage.* New York: Arno Press, 1973. (The Middle East Collection). p. 558.

10.1412. —— *The Caliph's Last Heritage: A Short History of the Turkish Empire.* London: Macmillan and Co., 1915. p. 558.

10.1413. Sykes, Percy Molesworth. *A History of Persia.* London: Macmillan & Co., 1915. II: 443–7.

10.1414. —— *idem.* rev. ed. London: Macmillan & Co., 1930. II: 341–5.

10.1415. —— *Persia.* Oxford: Clarendon Press, 1922. pp. 127–9. Spine title: *A History of Persia.*

10.1416. —— *Ten Thousand Miles in Persia or Eight Years in Iran.* London: John Murray, 1902. pp. 195–6.

10.1417. —— *idem.* New York: Scribner's Sons, 1902. pp. 195–6.

10.1417a. Székely, Edmond. *Cosmos, Man and Society: A Paneubiotic Synthesis.* trans. & ed.

L. Purcell Weaver. 2nd ed. (rev.). London: C.W. Daniel Company, 1937. p. 31.

T

10.1418. Ṭabáṭabá'í, Muḥammad Ḥusayn. *Shi'ite Islam.* Albany, N.Y.: State University of New York Press, 1975. p. 76.

10.1419. Taleghani, Ayatullah Sayyid Mahmud. *Society and Economics in Islam.* trans. R. Campbell. Berkeley, Calif.: Mizan Press, 1982. (Contemporary Islamic Thought, Persian Series). pp. 90, 106 n15.
Reviews:
Bayat, Mangol. *Middle East Studies Association Bulletin* (Seattle, Wash.), v.18 no.2 (Dec. 1984), pp. 227–30. Bahá'í Faith: p. 229.
Choice (Middletown, Conn.), (June 1983), p. 1476.

10.1420. *Tell the American People: Perspectives on the Iranian Revolution.* ed. David H. Albert. Philadelphia, Pa.: Movement for a New Society, 1980. pp. 89–90.

10.1421. *Themes of Islamic Civilization.* ed. John Alden Williams. Berkeley, Calif.: University of California Press, 1971. pp. 242–3.

10.1422. Thielmann, Max von. *Journey in the Caucasus, Persia and Turkey in Asia.* London: John Murray, 1875. I: 262; II: 52, 90–1.

10.1423. *This I Believe: The Living Philosophies of One Hundred Thoughtful Men and Women in All Walks of Life.* foreword Edward R. Murrow; ed. Edward P. Morgan. New York: Simon and Schuster, 1952. William Sears, pp. 167–8.

10.1424. Thomas, Lewis V.; Frye, Richard N. *The United States and Turkey and Iran.* n.p.: Archon Books, 1971. p. 208.

10.1425. Thomsen, Harry. *The New Religions of Japan.* Rutland, VT.: Charles E. Tuttle, 1963. pp. 130, 149.

10.1426. Thrower, James. *Marxist-Leninist 'Scientific Atheism' and the Study of Religion and Atheism in the USSR.* Berlin: Mouton Publisher, 1983. (Religion and Reason; 25). p. 448.
Mentions Ivanov's *Babidskie Vosstaniia v Irane* and its Marxist analysis of the Bábí upheavals.

10.1427. Tierney, Martin. *The New Elect: The Church and New Religious Groups.* Dublin, Ireland: Veritas Publications, 1985. pp. 86–7.

10.1428. Tillich, Paul. *My Search for Absolutes.*

New York: Simon & Schuster, 1967. p. 138. (Credo Perspectives).

10.1429. Tillyard, Aelfrida. *Spiritual Exercises and Their Results: An Essay in Psychology and Comparative Religion.* New York: Macmillan Co., 1927. pp. 12, 22.

10.1430. ——— *idem.* London: Society for Promoting Christian Knowledge, 1927. pp. 12, 22.

10.1431. Tippett, Maria. *Emily Carr, a Biography.* Harmondsworth, Middlesex: Penguin Books, 1982. p. 163.

10.1432. Titus, Murray T. *The Young Moslem Looks at Life.* New York: Friendship Press, 1937. pp. 61–2.

10.1433. Tobey, Mark. *Mark Tobey Paintings from the Collection of Joyce and Arthur Dahl.* Palo Alto, Calif.: Stanford University, 1967. pp. 7, 13, 15.

10.1434. ——— *Mark Tobey Retrospective Exhibition: Paintings and Drawings, 1925–1961.* London: Whitechapel Gallery, 1962. p. 9.

10.1435. ——— *Tobey.* Basel, Switzerland: Editions Beyler, 1971. pp. 19–20, 98.

10.1436. ——— *Tobey's 80: A Retrospective.* Seattle, Wash.; London: Seattle Art Museum; University of Washington Press, 1970. pp. 5, 7.

10.1437. Tolstoy, Alexandra. *Tolstoy: A Life of My Father.* New York: Harper, 1951. p. 472.

10.1438. ——— *idem.* London: Victor Gollancz, 1953. p. 472.

10.1439. Tolstoy, Leo. *Kingdom of God. What Is Art? What Is Religion?* New York: Thomas Y. Crowell, 1899. p. 353.

10.1440. ——— *What Is Religion?* New York: Thomas Y. Crowell, 1902. pp. 146–7.

10.1441. ——— *What Is Religion? and Other New Articles and Letters.* trans. V. Tchertkoff and A.C. Fifield. London: Free Age Press, 1902. p. 174.

10.1442. Toronto (Ont.). Board of Education. *Readings and Prayers for Use in Toronto Schools.* Toronto: Board of Education for the City of

Toronto, 1985. pp. 12, 17, 23–30, 172, 173, 176, 178, 179.

10.1443. *Towards a Modern Iran: Studies in Thought, Politics and Society.* ed. Elie Kedourie, Sylvia G. Haim. London: Cass, 1980. pp. 70–2, 75, 91–2, 98, 113.

10.1444. *Towns and Villages in Israel.* ed. Zeev Meljon. Tel Aviv: Immanuel Blauschild and Arie Nuernberg, 1966. pp. 82–3, 85, 88–9, 163.

10.1445. Townsend, Meredith. *Asia and Europe.* Westminster, Eng.: Archibald Constable, 1901. p. 262. (Constable's Indian and Colonial Library).

10.1446. Toy, Crawford Howell. *Introduction to the History of Religions.* Boston: Ginn and Co., 1913. pp. 552–3.

10.1447. —— *idem.* New York: AMS Press, 1970. pp. 552–3.

10.1448. Toynbee, Arnold J. *Christianity Among the Religions of the World.* New York: Charles Scribner's Sons, 1957. p. 104.

10.1449. —— *idem.* London: Oxford University Press, 1957. p. 104.

10.1450. —— *Civilization on Trial.* New York: Oxford University Press, 1948. p. 204.

10.1451. —— *A Study of History.* London: Oxford University Press, 1948–1961. V: 174–6; VII: 417, 418; VIII: 117; IX: 461; XII: 97, 212.

10.1452. *Trees: Sixty Years Toward the Future.* Crawley, Sussex: The Men of the Trees, 1982. p. 19.

10.1453. Tritton, A.S. *Islam – Beliefs and Practices.* London: Hutchinson University Library, 1951. pp. 157–8.

10.1454. —— *idem.* Westport, Conn.: Hyperion Press, 1981. pp. 157–8.

10.1455. Trout, David M. *Religious Behavior.* New York: Macmillan Co., 1931. pp. 281–2.
Horace Holley's meeting with 'Abdu'l-Bahá.

10.1456. *Twentieth Century Encyclopedia of Religious Knowledge: An Extension of the New Schaff-Herzog Encyclopedia of Religious Knowledge.* ed. Lefferts A. Loetscher. Grand Rapids, Mich.: Baker Book House, 1955. Edwin E. Calverley, 'Bahaism', I: 104; Dwight M. Donaldson, 'Babism', I: 101–2.
Calverley asserts that the Bahá'í goal is to raise a worldwide dictatorship under the Universal House of Justice.

10.1457. *Twentieth-Century Iran.* ed. Hossein Amirsadeghi; assisted by R.W. Ferrier. New York: Holmes & Meier, 1977. pp. 2, 5, 80, 186–7.

U

10.1458. Ullman, James Ramsey. *Where the Bong Tree Grows; The Log of One Man's Journey in the South Pacific.* Cleveland, Ohio; New York: World Publishing Company, 1963. p. 127.

10.1459. Underhill, Evelyn. *The Life of the Spirit and the Life of To-Day.* London: Methuen & Co., 1922. p. 286.

10.1460. —— *idem.* New York: E.P. Dutton, 1922, 1928. p. 286.

10.1461. Underhill, Helen. *God Speaks, and Other Poems.* Newtown, Pa.: Helen Underhill, 1985. pp. [3], 44–7, 67–8.

10.1462. *Understanding the New Religions.* ed. Jacob Needleman, George Baker. New York: The Seabury Press, 1978. pp. xix, 19, 36.

10.1463. Underwood, Alfred C. *Conversion – Christian and Non-Christian: A Comparative and Psychological Study.* New York: Macmillan, 1925. p. 89.

10.1464. UNDO, Inc. (Miami, Fla.). *UNDO, Order Out of Chaos.* Miami, Fla.: UNDO, Inc., 1968. p. 28.

10.1465. United States. Bureau of the Census. *Religious Bodies, 1906.* Washington, D.C.: Government Printing Office, 1910. II: 41–2.

10.1466. —— *Religious Bodies 1916.* 2 vols. Washington, D.C.: Department of Commerce, Bureau of Census, 1919. I: 36, 74, 78, 142, 154–5, 164, 165, 182–3, 184–5, 198–9, 202–3, 208–9, 214–15, 228–9, 232–3, 358–9, 378–9, 380–1, 430–1, 448–9, 478–9, 490–1, 494–5, 512–13, 526–7; II: 43–5.

10.1467. —— *Religious Bodies 1926.* 2 vols, Washington, D.C.: Department of Commerce, Bureau of Census, 1930. I: 10, 82–3, 92, 97, 102, 112, 117, 122–3, 148–9, 166–7, 192–3, 194–5, 216–17, 220–1, 230–1, 270–1, 276–7, 296–7, 360, 369, 374, 378, 381, 389, 392, 394, 406, 408, 446, 451, 457, 468, 470, 472, 475, 477,

482, 486, 490, 496, 502, 507, 510, 515, 521, 536, 540, 548, 563, 572; II: 70–6.

10.1468. —— *Religious Bodies 1936.* 3 vol. Washington, D.C.: Department of Commerce, Bureau of Census. 1941. I: 12, 86–7, 98, 110, 116, 126, 136–7, 146–7, 176–7, 190–1, 198–9, 224–5, 226–7, 232–3, 248–9, 254–5, 264–5, 300–1, 306–7, 314–15, 316–17, 350–1, 440, 442, 448, 455, 461, 464, 466, 470, 472, 480, 483, 485, 488, 490, 497, 499, 502, 505, 515, 520, 528, 542, 546, 553, 555, 560, 564, 565, 566, 568, 574, 581, 584, 585, 589, 592, 594, 595, 600, 605, 610, 617, 621, 623, 626, 630, 632, 634, 635, 640, 646, 652, 655, 666, 669, 673, 678, 679, 681, 686, 691, 692, 700, 713, 715; II, pt. 1: 76–82.

10.1469. United States. Congress. House of Representatives. Subcommittee on Human Rights and International Organizations. *Religious Persecution as a Violation of Human Rights.* Washington, D.C.: U.S. Government Printing Office, 1983. pp. 149–250, 890–8, numerous other single references.

10.1470. —— *Religious Persecution of the Baha'is in Iran: Hearing Before the Subcommittee on Human Rights and International Organizations of the Committee on Foreign Affairs, House of Representatives, Ninety-Eighth Congress, Second Session, May 2, 1984.* Washington, D.C.: U.S. Government Printing Office, 1984. iii, 108 p.

10.1471. —— *Review of the 38th Session and Upcoming 39th Session of the U.N. Commission on Human Rights.* Washington, D.C.: U.S. Government Printing Office, 1983. pp. 6, 11, 47, 63.

10.1472. United States. Department of State. *Country Reports on Human Rights Practices.* Washington, D.C.: U.S. Government Printing Office, 1981. p. 989.

10.1473. —— *Country Reports on Human Rights Practices for 1981.* Washington, D.C.: U.S. Government Printing Office, 1982. pp. 979, 987–8.

10.1474. —— *Country Reports on Human Rights Practices for 1982.* Washington, D.C.: U.S. Government Printing Office, 1983. pp. 1139, 1143, 1152.

10.1475. —— *Country Reports on Human Rights Practices for 1983.* Washington, D.C.: U.S. Government Printing Office, 1984. pp. 1255–6, 1262–3.

10.1476. United States National Commission for UNESCO. *A World to Gain: A Handbook for International Education Year, 1970.* Washington, D.C.: National Education Association, 1969. pp. 33, 37, 41, back cover.

10.1477. *Unity and Variety in Muslim Civilization.* Armand Abel [et al]; ed. Gustave E. von Grunebaum. Chicago: University of Chicago Press, 1955. pp. 197–8, 206n.

10.1478. Universal Atlas Cement Company. *Architectural Concrete Slabs: A Modern Medium for Architectural Expression Made with Exposed Aggregates, Welded Reinforcing, and Atlas White Cement.* New York: The Producer's Council, 1939. [4] p. (Bulletin of the Producer's Council; no.31). Includes photograph of Wilmette House of Worship.

10.1479. —— *Beauty and Permanence with Concrete.* New York: Universal Atlas Cement Company, 1939. p. 8.

10.1480. —— *The Story of Universal Atlas Cements.* n.p. [New York]: Universal Atlas Cement Company, n.d. [193–] Cover.

10.1481. University of Pennsylvania. Middle East Research Institute. *Iran.* London; Dover, N.H.: Croom Helm, 1985. p. 4. (MERI Reports).

10.1482. Upton, Joseph M. *The History of Modern Iran: An Interpretation.* Cambridge, Mass.: Harvard Centre for Middle Eastern Studies: distributed by Harvard University Press, 1970. (Harvard Middle Eastern Monographs; v.2). pp. 10–11.

10.1483. Uris, Leon. *Exodus Revisited.* New York: Doubleday, 1960. Photograph of the Bahá'í International Archives building, page 32.

10.1484. Ussher, John. *A Journey from London to Persepolis: Including Wanderings in Daghestan, Georgia, Armenia, Kurdistan, Mesopotamia and Persia.* London: Hurst and Blackett, 1865. pp. 627–9.

V

10.1485. Vail, Albert R.; Vail, Emily McClellan. *Heroic Lives.* Boston: Beacon Press, 1917. pp. 289–303.

10.1486. Vambery, Arminius. *Western Culture in Eastern Lands: A Comparison of the Methods Adopted by England and Russia in the Middle*

East. London: John Murray, 1906. pp. 334–7.

10.1487. Van Baalen, Jan Karel. *The Chaos of Cults*. Grand Rapids, Mich.: William B. Eerdman's Publishing Co., 1947. pp. 96–109.

10.1488. —— *The Chaos of Cults: A Study in Present-Day Isms*. 4th rev. & enl. ed. Grand Rapids, Mich.: Eerdmans, 1973. pp. 146–61.

10.1489. —— *Christianity Versus the Cults*. Grand Rapids, Mich.: William B. Eerdman's Publishing Co., 1958. pp. 66–71.

10.1490. —— *Our Birth Right and the Mess of Meat*. Grand Rapids, Mich.: William B. Eerdman's Publishing Co., 1929. pp. 169–77.

10.1490a. Vander Werff, Lyle L. *Christian Mission to Muslims*. South Pasadena, Calif.: William Carey Library, 1977. pp. 139, 141, 165–6, 243.

10.1491. Van Hoof, Mary Ann. *Revelations and Messages as Given through Mary Ann Van Hoof at Necedah, Wisconsin, volume I*. Necedah, Wis.: Van Hoof, 1966. pp. 22, 212–14, 309–10, 412–13.
Defines the 'Bahai Temple' as the 'Hub of Evil' in the world.

10.1492. Van Paassen, Pierre. *Days of Our Years*. New York: Hillman-Curl, 1939, 1940. p. 30.

10.1493. Van Sommers, Tess. *Religions in Australia*. Adelaide, S. Austr.: Rigby, 1966. pp. 17–23. Photograph of interior of Bahá'í House of Worship, Sydney, Australia, page 17.

10.1494. Vanderbilt, Cornelius, Jr. *Man of the World: My Life on Five Continents*. New York: Crown Publishers, 1959. pp. 311–12, 317–18, 320–1.
Pilgrim notes about prophecies of world destruction set for 1960; Larry Hautz, pioneer in South Africa.

10.1495. —— *idem*. London: Hutchinson of London, 1959. pp. 311–12, 317, 318, 320.

10.1496. Vaswani, T.L. *The Brotherhood of Religions*. Lahore, India: Mercantile Press, 1912. p. 29.

10.1497. Vaughan, George. *Temple and Towers (A Survey of the World's Moral Outlook)*. Boston: Meador Publishing Co., 1941. pp. 429–31, 551–2.

10.1498. Vaughan, John Gaines. *Religion, a Comparative Study*. Cincinnati, Ohio: Printed for the author by Abingdon Press, 1919. pp. 321–3.

10.1498a. Viator. *A Knapsack Guide to Palestine*. London: Standard Press, n.d. [1914–1918] p. 107.

10.1499. Vicedom, Georg F. *The Challenge of World Religions*. Philadelphia, Pa.: Fortress Press, 1963. pp. 9, 54, 90, 92, 106.

10.1500. Victory Foundation. *The Victory Foundation: A Philanthropic Institution Devoted to Education for World Peace and Unity*. Wilmette, Ill.; Los Angeles: The Victory Foundation, 1982. pp. [5], [8].

10.1501. Vidal, Gore. *Myra Breckenridge*. New York: Bantam, 1968. pp. 86–91.

10.1502. *The Viking Portable Library World Bible*. Robert O. Ballou, ed. New York: Viking Press, 1944. pp. 448–9.

10.1503. Vilnay, Zev. *The Changing Face of Acco*. Acco: Tambour, n.d. [197–?] p. 32.

10.1504. —— *The Guide to Israel*. Jerusalem: Vilnay, 1958, 1960. pp. 28, 346–7, 359.

10.1505. —— *idem*. 7th ed. Jerusalem: Vilnay, 1964. pp. 346, 361, 364, 552.

10.1505a. Vilnay, Zev. *The Guide to Israel*. 13th ed. rev. Jerusalem: Steimatzky, 1970. pp. 30, 37, 346, 361, 364.

10.1506. —— *idem*. 19th ed. rev. Jerusalem: Steimatzky, 1977. pp. 387, 405.

10.1507. —— *Israel Guide*. 2nd ed. Jerusalem: Central Press, 1958. pp. 341, 353, 357–8.

10.1507a. —— *The New Israel Atlas: Bible to Present Day*. Jerusalem: Israel Universities Press, 1968. pp. 26, 27, 38.

10.1508. —— *Steimatzky's Palestine Guide*. Jerusalem: Steimatzky Publishing Company, 1935. pp. 24–6, 37.

10.1508a. —— *Steimatzky's Palestine Guide*. Jerusalem: Steimatzky Publishing Co., 1942. pp. lxiv, lxx, 168–169, 176, 179.

10.1509. —— *idem*. Jerusalem: Steimatzky Publishers, 1941. pp. lxiv, 162–3, 170, 173.

10.1510. *Visions: Contemporary Art in Canada*. essays Alvin Balkind [et. al.]; ed. Robert Bringhurst [et. al.] Vancouver, B.C.; Toronto: Douglas & McIntyre, 1983. p. 99.

10.1511. Visser't Hooft, W.A. *No Other Name: The Choice Between Syncretism and Christian Universalism*. London: SCM Press Ltd., 1963. pp. 35, 43, 88, 114.

10.1512. *The Vital Forces of Christianity and Islam*. J.H. Golden, ed. London: Humphrey Milford, 1915. W.A. Shedd, 'Second Study', pp. 51–2, 57, 62, 63, 74.

10.1513. *Voices Israel, 1979. Vol. 7*. Haifa: Haifa Publications, 1979. pp. 55–6, 74.

10.1514. *Voices Israel, Volume 10, 1982*. Haifa: Endeavour Publication, 1982. pp. 145, 148, 150, 155

10.1515. *Voices Israel, 1983, Volume 11*. Haifa: Endeavour Publications for the VOICES Group, 1983. pp. ii, 98.

10.1516. *Volcano Island Guide, Island of Hawaii*. Hawaii, 1968. p. 41.

10.1517. Voll, John Obert. *Islam – Continuity and Change in the Modern World*. Boulder, Colo.: Westview Press; Essex, Eng.: Longman, 1982. p. 108.

10.1518. Voss, Carl Hermann. *In Search of Meaning: Living Religions of the World*. Cleveland, Ohio: World Publishing Co., 1968. pp. 158–9.

10.1519. —— *Living Religions of the World: Our Search for Meaning*. Cleveland, Ohio: William Collins & World Publishing Co., 1977. pp. 158–9.

10.1520. —— *Rabbi and Minister: The Friendships of Stephen S. Wise and John Haynes Holmes*. Buffalo, N.Y.: Prometheus Books, 1964.

10.1521. —— *The Universal God*. Cleveland, Ohio: World Publishing Co., 1953. p. 269. Quotations from Bahá'u'lláh's words to Browne.

W

10.1522. Waamani, Israel T. *Israel – a Profile*. New York: Praeger, 1972. pp. 9, 78.

10.1523. Wach, Joachim. *Sociology of Religion*. Chicago: University of Chicago Press, 1971. pp. 132, 138, 201, 342.

10.1524. Wadia, Ardaser Sorabjee N. *The Message of Mohammed*. London: J.M. Dent & Sons, 1923. p. 141.

10.1525. Wagar, W. Warren. *Building the City of Man*. New York: Grossman Publishers, 1971. p. 56.

10.1526. —— *The City of Man: Prophecies of a World Civilization in Twentieth-Century Thought*. Boston: Houghton Mifflin Co., 1963. pp. 7, 63, 117–20, 300.

10.1527. Wagner, Cosima Liszt. *Cosima Wagner's Diaries*. ed. Martin Gregor-Dellin, Dietrich Mack; trans. Geoffrey Skelton. London: Collins, 1980. II: 678–9.

10.1528. Wallis, Wilson D. *Messiahs, Christian and Pagan*. Boston: Richard G. Badger, 1918. pp. 111–16, 228–9.

10.1529. —— *Messiahs: Their Role in Civilization*. Washington, D.C.: American Council on Public Affairs, 1943. pp. 96–9, 193.

10.1530. Walstrum, Mary Price. *The Nineteenth and Twentieth Centuries: Reminiscences*. Philadelphia, Pa.: Dorrance & Company, 1934. pp. 16, 24–5, 43.

10.1531. Ward, John. *The Hansard Chronicles: A Celebration of the First Hundred Years of Hansard in Canada's Parliament*. Canada: Deneau and Greenberg, 1980. p. 170.

10.1532. Warren, Edith. *Important American Poets and Songwriters*. New York: Valiant House, 1947. [IV]: 141.

10.1533. Washington, M. Bunch. *The Art of Romare Bearden: The Prevalence of Ritual*. New York: Abrams, n.d. [1973?] Introduction: *passim*.
   Review:
Marr, Warren. 'Black Artist Illumined', *The Crisis* (New York), v.81 no.3 (Mar. 1974). Mentions Bahá'í Faith.

10.1534. Waterbury, John. *The Commander of the Faithful: The Moroccan Political Elite – A Study in Segmented Politics*. London: Weidenfeld and Nicolson, 1970. pp. 292–3.

10.1535. Waterfield, Robin E. *Christians in Persia: Assyrians, Armenians, Roman Catholics and Protestants*. London: George Allen & Unwin, 1973. pp. 113, 114, 118, 158–9, 163.

10.1535a. Watson, Albert Durrant. *Birth Through Death: The Ethics of the Twentieth Plane*. New York: James A. McCann Company, 1920. 'Abdu'l-Bahá, p. 254.

10.1536. —— *The Poetical Works of Albert Durrant Watson*. Toronto, Ont.: The Ryerson Press, 1924. pp. 101, 113, 233–61.

10.1537. —— *The Twentieth Plane: A Psychic Revelation*. Philadelphia, Pa.: George W. Jacobs, 1919. pp. 60, 208.

10.1538. Watson, Robert Grant. *A History of Persia: From the Beginning of the Nineteenth Century to the Year 1858*. London: Smith Elder & Co., 1866. pp. 347–52, 360–2, 385–95, 407–10.

10.1539. —— *idem*. Tehran: Imperial Organization for Social Services, 1976. Same paging as 1866 ed.

10.1540. Watt, W. Montgomery. *Islamic Philosophy and Theology*. Edinburgh; University Press, 1972, 1979. pp. 171, 188. (Islamic Surveys; v.1).

10.1541. —— *Truth in the Religions: A Sociological and Psychological Approach*. Edinburgh: Edinburgh University Press, 1963. pp. 11, 76, 162.

10.1542. Watts, Alan. *In My Own Way: An Autobiography, 1915–1965*. London: Jonathan Cape, 1973. p. 252.

10.1543. Watts, Harold H. *The Modern Reader's Guide to Religion*. New York: Barnes & Noble, 1964. pp. 501, 584.

10.1543a. *The Way of Life*. n.p. [Cameroon?], n.d. [ca. 1985] pp. 14–15. (The Christian Way Series; Book 1).

10.1544. *Way to Peace: A Compendium of Spiritual and Moral Principles of Various World Religions*. Lucknow, India: Lucknow Publishing House, 1980. pp. 145–58.

10.1545. *idem*. Lucknow, India: Lucknow Publishing House, 1981. pp. 181–205, 273–4.

10.1546. Weber, Julius A. *Religions and Philosophies in the United States of America*. Los Angeles: Wetzel Publishing Co., 1931. pp. 255–60.

10.1547. Wedeck, Harry E. *Dictionary of Spiritualism*. New York: Philosophical Library, 1971. p. 48.

10.1548. *Week of Prayer for World Peace: For All Faiths in One World, 20–27 October 1985*. Lower Hutt, N.Z.: WPWP Committee, 1985. p. [6]

10.1549. Weigel, Gustave. *Churches in North America*. Baltimore, Md.: Helicon Press, 1961. pp. 132–3.

10.1550. Weiner, Herbert. *The Wild Goats of Ein Gedi: A Journal of Religious Encounters in the Holy Land*. Garden City, N.Y.: Doubleday, 1961. p. 19.

10.1551. Welch, Anthony. *Calligraphy in the Arts of the Muslim World*. Austin: University of Texas Press in cooperation with the Asia Society, 1979. pp. 168–9.

10.1552. *Welcome to Haifa!* Haifa: Haifa Municipality, n.d. [1951] pp. [6], [16].

10.1552a. Wetterau, Bruce. *Concise Dictionary of World History*. London: Robert Hale, 1984. pp. 61, 63, 64, 713.

10.1553. Whalen, William J. *Faiths for the Few: A Study of Minority Religions*. Milwaukee, Wis.: Bruce Publishing Co., 1963. pp. v, vii, 36–41; mention on dust cover.

10.1554. —— *Minority Religions in America*. rev. ed. New York: Alba House, 1982. pp. 15–25.

10.1554a. —— *Minority Religions in America*. New York: Alba House, 1972. 'The Baha'is', pp. 15–28.

10.1555. ——*Separated Brethren: A Survey of Protestant, Anglican, Eastern Orthodox and Other Denominations in the United States*. 3rd rev. ed. Huntingdon, Ind.; Our Sunday Visitor, 1979. pp. 230–7.

10.1556. White, E.B. *Everyday Is Saturday*. New York; London: Harper & Brothers, 1934. pp. 45–6.

10.1557. White, Lyman Cromwell. *International Non-Governmental Organizations*. New York: Greenwood Press, 1968. p. 165.

10.1558. White, Roger. *One Bird, One Cage, One Flight: Homage to Emily Dickinson*. Happy Camp, Calif.: Naturegraph Publishers, 1983. Includes some quotations from Bahá'í writings.
Review:
Warren, Michael, *Poetry Toronto*, no.109 (Jan. 1985), pp. 21–22. Bahá'í Faith, p. 22.

10.1559. *Whither Islam?: A Survey of Modern Movements in the Moslem World*. ed. H.A.R. Gibb. New York: AMS Press, 1973. p. 169.

10.1559a. Whitten, Thaya. *The Mending Wing*. Montral: Studio Kolbé, 1985. p. 25.

10.1560. Whittingham, George Napier. *The Home of Fadeless Splendours, or Palestine of To-Day*. New York: E.P. Dutton & Co., n.d. [1921] pp. 234–6. Photograph of the knighting of 'Abdu'l-Bahá facing page 234.

10.1561. Widgery, Alban B. *Living Religions and Modern Thought*. New York: Round Table Press, 1936. pp. 212–20.

10.1562. Wilber, Donald N. *Contemporary Iran*. New York: Frederick A. Praeger, 1963. pp. 7, 34, 61.

10.1563. —— *Iran, Past and Present*. 4th ed. Princeton, N.J.: Princeton University Press, 1958. pp. 77, 128.

10.1563a. —— *Iran, Past and Present: From Monarchy to Islamic Republic*. 9th ed. Princeton, N.J.: Princeton University Press, 1981. p. 162.

10.1564. Wilkinson, Charles. *Holy Land Pilgrimage*. Ancaster, Ont.: Pilgrim Paperbacks, 1984. pp. 109–12.

10.1565. Willcox, K.M. *Your Guide to Israel.* London: Alvin Redman, 1966. pp. 37, 227, 245, 248.

10.1566. Williams, David Rhys. *World Religions and the Hope for Peace.* Boston: Beacon Press, 1951. pp. 142–51, 203, 218, mention on dust cover.

10.1567. Williams, E. Crawshay. *Across Persia.* London: Edward Arnold, 1907. pp. 269–72.

10.1568. Williamson, George Hunt. *Road in the Sky.* London: Neville Spearman, 1959. pp. 241–2.

10.1569. —— *The Saucers Speak: A Documentary Report of Interstellar Communication by Radio-telegraphy.* Los Angeles: New Age Publishing Co., 1954. p. 110.

10.1570. —— *idem.* London: Neville Spearman, 1963. p. 110.

10.1571. Wills, C.J. *In the Land of the Lion and the Sun, or Modern Persia: Being Experiences of Life in Persia from 1866 to 1881.* new ed. London: Ward Lock & Co., 1891. pp. 144, 153–6, 164, 201, 272, 317, 339.

10.1572. —— *Persia As It Is.* London: Sampson, Low, Marston, Serle & Rivington, 1887. pp. 7–8.

10.1573. *Wilmette's Nautical Heritage: A Pictorial History.* Wilmette, Ill.: Sheridan Shore Yacht Club, 1982. pp. iv, 98–9, 113.

10.1574. Wilson, Arnold T. *A Bibliography of Persia.* Oxford: At the Clarendon Press, 1930. Frequent entries for works on the Bábí and Bahá'í Faiths.

10.1575. —— *Persia.* New York: Charles Scribner's Sons, 1933. pp. 29, 50, 171, 188.

10.1576. —— *S.W. Persia: Letters and Diaries of a Young Political Officer, 1907–1914.* n.p. [London]: Readers Union Limited by arrangement with Oxford University Press, 1942. pp. 121–2.

10.1577. Wilson, Howard A. *Invasion from the East.* Minneapolis, Minn.: Augsburg, 1928. p. 19.

10.1578. Wilson, J. Christy. *Introducing Islam.* New York: Friendship Press, n.d. [196–?] p. 52.

10.1579. Wilson, Samuel Graham. *Modern Movements Among Moslems.* New York: Fleming Revell Co., 1916. pp. 62, 74, 116–32, 133, 138–9, 146, 153, 155, 169, 243, 244.

10.1580. —— *Persian Life and Customs: With Scenes and Incidents of Residence and Travel in the Land of the Lion and the Sun.* New York: Fleming H. Revell Co., 1895. pp. 12, 62, 146, 185–6, 221.

10.1580a. —— *idem.* Edinburgh; London: Oliphant Anderson and Ferrier, 1896. pp. 12, 62, 146, 185–6, 221.

10.1581. —— *idem.* New York: AMS Press, 1973. pp. 12, 62, 146, 185–6, 221.

10.1582. Wismer, Don. *The Islamic Jesus: An Annotated Bibliography of Sources in English and French.* New York: Garland Publishing Co., 1977. p. 254.

10.1583. Witt, J.C. *Portland Cement Technology.* 2nd ed. New York: Chemical Publishing Co., 1966. pp. 288–9, photograph of Wilmette Temple.

10.1584. Wolcott, Leonard; Wolcott, Carolyn. *Religions Around the World.* Nashville, Tenn.: Abingdon Press, 1967. pp. 171, 174–5, 182.

10.1585. Wollaston, Arthur N. *The Sword of Islam.* London: John Murray, 1905. pp. 471–6.

10.1586. *Women and Family in the Midde East: New Voices of Change.* ed. Elizabeth Warnock Fernea. Austin, Tex.; University of Texas Press, 1985. Ṭáhirih, p. 317.

10.1587. *Women and Revolution in Iran.* ed. Guity Nashat. Boulder, Colo.: Westview Press, 1983. pp. 20, 270.

10.1588. *Women and the Family in Iran.* ed. Asghar Fathi. Leiden, Neth.: E.J. Brill, 1985. (Social, Economic and Political Studies of the Middle East; v.38). p. 6; Hoda Mahmoudi, 'Tahira, an Early Iranian "Feminist" ', pp. 79–85.

10.1589. *Women in the Muslim World.* ed. Lois Beck, Nikkie Keddie. Cambridge, Mass.; London: Harvard University Press, 1978. pp. 190, 198, 206, 296.

10.1590. *Women Lawyers: Pespectives on Success.* ed. Emily Couric. New York: Law & Business: Harcourt Brace Jovanovich, 1984. pp. 207, 208, 209, 211, article on Dorothy W. Nelson.

10.1591. *Women of Iran: The Conflict with Fundamentalist Islam.* ed. Farah Azari. London: Ithaca Press, 1983. p. 171.

10.1592. Wons, Anthony. *Tony's Scrap Book, 1932–33.* Chicago: Reilly & Lee, 1932. p. 41.

10.1593. Wood, Clement. *The Outline of Man's Knowledge.* New York: Grosset & Dunlap, 1927. p. 517.

10.1594. Wood, M.M. *Glimpses of Persia.* London: Church Missionary Society, 1922. p. 30, 76.

10.1595. Wood, Nancy. *When Buffalo Free the Mountains.* Garden City, N.Y.: Doubleday, 1980. pp. 90, 96.

10.1596. *Words of Conscience: Religious Statements on Conscientious Objection.* ed. Shawn Perry. 9th ed. Washington, D.C.: National Interreligious Service Board for Conscientious Objectors, 1980. pp. 20–1.

10.1597. *idem.* ed. Beth Ellen Boyle. 10th ed. Washington, D.C.: National Interreligious Service Board for Conscientious Objectors, 1983. pp. 65–6.

10.1598. *World Bible.* ed. Robert O. Ballou. New York: Viking Press, 1944. pp. 448–9.

10.1599. *World Book Encyclopedia.* Chicago: Field Enterprises Educational, 1968. Hugh E. Chance, 'Bahá'ís', 'Bahá'u'lláh', II: 24.

10.1600. *idem.* Chicago: World Book, Inc., 1985. II: 25–6, X: 318b, XVI: 216.

10.1601. *World Christian Encyclopedia: A Comparative Study of Churches and Religions in the Modern World, AD 1900–2000.* ed. David B. Barrett. Nairobi, Kenya: Oxford University Press, 1982. Listings under nearly all countries.

10.1602. *World Encyclopedia of Political Systems & Parties.* ed. George E. Delury. New York: Facts on File Publications, 1983. pp. 489–90, 612.

10.1603. *World Fellowship: Addresses and Messages by Leading Spokesmen of All Faiths, Races and Countries.* ed. Charles Frederick Weller. New York: Liveright, 1935. pp. 20–1, 77–80, 157, 269–71, 570, 781–2.

10.1604. *World Minorities in the Eighties.* ed. Georgina Ashworth. Sunbury, U.K.: Quartermaine House, 1980. pp. 57, 60–1.

10.1605. *World Refugee Survey, 1982.* New York: ACNS, 1982. p. 5, 17.

10.1606. *World Religions: A Handbook for Teachers.* ed. W. Owen Cole. 2nd ed. London: The Community Relations Commission in conjunction with the SHAP Working Party on World Religions in Education, 1976. pp. 166–71.

10.1607. *idem.* 3rd ed. London: Commission on Racial Equality in conjunction with the SHAP Working Party on World Religions in Education, 1977. pp. 170–6.

10.1608. *World Religions: From Ancient History to the Present.* ed. Geoffrey Parrinder. rev. and updated ed. New York; Bicester, Eng.: Facts On File Publications, 1983. pp. 378, 507, 515.

10.1609. *The World Religions Speak on the 'Relevance of Religion in the Modern World'.* ed. Finley P. Dunne, Jr. The Hague: Dr W. Junk, 1970. (World Academy of Art and Science; 6). H.M. Munje, 'A Bahá'í Viewpoint', pp. 177–81.

10.1609a. *Worldmark Encyclopedia of the Nations.* ed. Moshe Y. Sachs. 4th ed. New York: Worldmark Press: Harper & Row, 1971. IV: 118, 138, 166.

10.1610. *The World's Great Religions.* New York: Time Incorporated, 1957. pp. 5, 118.

10.1611. *The World's Parliament of Religions: An Illustrated and Popular Story of the World's First Parliament of Religions.* ed. Rev. John Henry Barrows. Chicago: Parliament Pub. Co., 1893. II: 1125–6, in talk by Henry H. Jessup, 'The Religious Mission of the English Speaking Nations'.

10.1612. *The World's Religions.* ed. Sir Norman Anderson. Leicester, U.K.: Inter-Varsity Press, 1950. p. 132.

10.1613. *idem.* 4th ed. Leicester, U.K.: Inter-Varsity Press, 1975. p. 132.

10.1614. *The World's Religions.* Tring, Herts.: Lion Publishing, 1982. Werner Schilling, 'Unity and Peace: The Bahá'í Faith', pp. 268–70; 395.
See 10.470.

10.1615. *The World's Religions Against War.* Paris; New York; London: Church Peace Union, 1928. pp. 1, 100, 154, 155, 156, 157, 158, 160, 161, 162.

10.1616. Wratislaw, A.C. *A Consul in the East.* Edinburgh; London: William Blackwood and Sons, 1924. p. 246.

10.1617. Wright, Denis. *The English Amongst the Persians.* London: Heinemann, 1977. pp. 44, 120, 164.

10.1618. —— *The Persians Amongst the English: Episodes in Anglo-Persian History.* London: I.B. Tauris & Co., 1985. pp. 142, 146–8, 197.

10.1619. Wysner, Gloria M. *Near East Panorama.* New York: Friendship Press, 1950. pp. 59–60.

X, Y, Z

10.1620. Yassour, Yaakov. *Haifa in Israel's Tenth Year*. Haifa: Haifa Municipality Development Department, 1958. pp. 106–7.

10.1621. *Year Book and Almanac of the Holy Land*. A.P. Anthony, ed. Chicago: Holy Land Almanac, 1936. pp. 127–8.

10.1621a. Ye'or, Bat. *The Dhimmi: Jews and Christians Under Islam*. rev. & enl. English ed Rutherford [etc.], N.J.; Fairleigh Dickinson University Press; London; Toronto: Associated University Presses, 1985. p. 77.

10.1622. Yonan, Isaac Malek. *The Beloved Physician of Tehran*. Nashville, Tenn.: Cokesbury Press, 1934. pp. 88–90.

Dr Sa'eed Khan Kurdistani, convert to Christianity, describes his ability to quote from the Bayán in attempting to convert Bábís and Bahá'ís.

10.1623. *You Better Believe It: Black Verse in English*. ed. Paul Breman. Harmondsworth, Middlesex: Penguin Books, 1973. p. 102, 121.

10.1624. Young Barbara. *This Man from Lebanon: A Study of Kahlil Gibran*. New York: Alfred A. Knopf, 1945, 1961, 1979. pp. 68–9, 187.

10.1625. Young, T. Cuyler. *Near Eastern Culture and Society*. Princeton, N.J.: Princeton University Press, 1951. p. 136.

10.1626. Younghusband, Francis. *The Gleam*. London: John Murray, 1923. pp. 182–214.

10.1627. —— *Modern Mystics*. London: John Murray, 1935. pp. 97–142, 252.

10.1628. —— idem. New Hyde Park, N.Y.: University Books, 1970. pp. 97–142, 252.

10.1629. —— *A Venture of Faith: Being a Description of the World Congress of Faiths Held in London, 1936*. London: Michael Joseph, 1937. pp. 50, 152–6.

10.1630. *Your Guide in Haifa: 'Israel's City of the Future'*. Haifa: Development Department of the Haifa Municipality, n.d. [195–] pp. [8], [27].

10.1631. YWCA. *Peace: YWCA Peace Site*. San Anselmo, Calif.: YWCA, [1985] p. [4].

10.1632. Zabih, Sepehr. *Iran Since the Revolution*. London; Canberra; Croom Helm, 1982. p. 37.

10.1633. Zaheer, Ehsan Elahi. *Qadiyaniat: An Analytical Survey*. Lahore, Pakistan: Idara Tarjuman al-Sunnah, 1972. pp. 1A, 17, 326.

10.1634. Zeligs, Dorothy. *Story of Modern Israel*. New York: Bloch Publishing Co., 1961. pp. 12, 337.

10.1635. Zerubavel, Eviator. *The Seven Day Cycle: The History and Meaning of the Week*. New York: The Free Press; London: Collier Macmillan Publishers, 1985. pp. 48–50, 56, 74–5, 77, 141.

10.1635a. Ziff, William B. *The Rape of Palestine*. 1st British ed. London: St. Botolph's Publishing, 1948. p. 339.

10.1636. Ziring, Lawrence. *Iran, Turkey, and Afghanistan: A Political Chronology*. New York: Praeger, 1981. p. 32.

10.1637. —— *The Middle East Political Dictionary*. Santa Barbara, Calif.; Oxford, Eng.: ABC-CLIO Information Services, 1984. p. 145.

10.1638. Zonis, Marvin. *The Political Elite of Iran*. Princeton, N.J.: Princeton University Press, 1971. pp. 147, 148n, 274–6.

10.1639. Zwemer, Samuel M. *Across the World of Islam: Studies in Aspects of the Mohammedan Faith and in the Present Awakening of the Moslem Multitudes*. New York: Fleming H. Revell Company, 1929. pp. 284, 292, 293, 294.

10.1640. —— *Heirs of the Prophets: An Account of the Clergy and Priests of Islam, the Personnel of the Mosque and 'Holy Men'*. Chicago: Moody Bible Institute, 1946. p. 118.

10.1641. —— *Islam, a Challenge to Faith*. New York: Student Volunteer Movement for Foreign Missions, 1907. pp. 147–9, 248.

10.1642. —— idem. 2nd rev. ed. London: Marshall Bros., n.d. [1909?] pp. 147–9, 248.

10.1643. —— *The Law of Apostasy in Islam*. New Delhi: Amarko Book Agency, 1975. pp. 96–7.

10.1644. —— *The Moslem World*. New York: Young People's Missionary Movement of the United States and Canada, 1908. p. 200.

10.1645. Zwemer, Samuel M.; Brown, Arthur Judson. *The Nearer and Farther East*. New York: Macmillan Co., 1908. p. 98.

XI
Articles in Non-Bahá'í Periodicals

ARTICLES about the Bábí religion in periodicals – journals, magazines and newspapers – began appearing within months of the Báb's declaration in 1844. The first mention was a newspaper account in *The Times* (London) on 1 November 1845. As Bábism and the Bahá'í Faith became better known, some journals dedicated considerable space to them, particularly *The International Psychic Gazette* (London) which at one time included a Bahá'í article in nearly every issue; *Open Court* (Chicago), *The Moslem World* (Hartford, Conn.) and *The Missionary Review of the World* (Princeton, N.J.), the last two of which were concerned with defending Christianity; *The Journal of the Royal Asiatic Society* (London) in which most of E.G. Browne's articles appeared; and *The Christian Commonwealth* (London). As with references to the Bahá'í religion in non-Bahá'í monographs, the field is undoubtedly vast but covers many of the same areas in the following types of articles:

1. General introductions to Bahá'í teachings and history form the largest grouping

2. Christianity, Christian apologetic and missionary reports

A major purveyor of Christian polemic against the Bahá'í Faith has been the journal *The Moslem World* (Hartford, Conn.) (now titled *The Muslim World*). As the mouthpiece of a major theological seminary, its original intent was to show the inroads of Christianity in the Muslim world and the efficacy of Christian missions to the Muslims. Though this has changed in recent decades, the early years of this century saw a spate of anti-Bahá'í articles in this journal. This was matched by *The Missionary Review of the World* (Princeton, N.J.), some of the articles in which reached a level of scurrilousness that is not usually tolerated in such journals at the present time. Authors, many of them active or returned missionaries, who were frequent contributors to this polemical literature, included: Peter Z. Easton [11.357–11.358], whose articles caused Mírzá Abu'l-Faḍl to write *The Brilliant Proof*; William McElwee Miller [11.693–11.696]; J.R. Richards [11.861]; Robert P. Richardson [11.862–11.864]; J.H. Shedd and William A. Shedd [11.915–11.917]; Stoyan Krstoff Vatralsky [11.1044], who wrote about the beliefs and teaching methods of the Bahá'ís before the

community had openly revealed its existence; Samuel Graham Wilson [11.1095–11.1104], who exhibited a singlemindedness and rancor unequalled by any except Easton; and Samuel M. Zwemer [11.1127–11.1128].

3. Iranian Bahá'í history and the current situation in Iran

The single most prolific author of articles on Iranian Bahá'í history is E.G. Browne, whose many studies in *The Journal of the Royal Asiatic Society* and other journals constitute an extensive body of early Western knowledge and interpretation of the movement. Occasional articles on the persecution of the Iranian Bahá'í community appeared before 1979, but in the flood of reporting since that time five to ten percent of the articles make some reference to the Bahá'ís under the Islamic Revolutionary government. One result of this has been the appearance of stories on historical incidents relating to the Bahá'ís in Iran. One such story appeared in two different articles about Robert Whitney Imbrie, an American diplomat in Iran early in this century who was killed by a local mob that accused him of being a Bábí [11.463, 11.1050].

4. Islam, Islamic apologetic, Islamic revolutionary rhetoric

Much of the periodical literature on Islam was written from a Christian viewpoint and as such is dealt with in the sections on Christianity. However, a growing number of articles are concerned with attacking the Bahá'í Faith from a Muslim perspective on religious and political grounds [11.33, 11.101, 11.113, 11.152], particularly as a 'tool of Zionism and imperialism'.

5. Sociological studies and scholarly Bahá'í studies

Several of the articles on the sociology of religion are by well-known sociologists such as Peter Berger [11.194–11.195], Rodney Stark [11.957–11.958], Parratt [11.785] and Ebaugh and Vaughn [11.359–11.360], all dealing with cult/sect membership and the dynamics of conversion processes. Articles dealing solely with the Bahá'í religion from a sociological viewpoint cover various issues, such as possible differences in the Bahá'í community's level of commitment from that of other religions [11.198, 11.599–11.600], the social structure in early Bábism [11.705, 11.944], and a critique of the model used by Peter Berger in his study of the Bahá'í community [11.943]. Two articles also undertake a sociological treatment of Covenant-breaking (see Section XII): the 'Bahá'ís Under the Provisions of the Covenant' [11.174] and the Covenant-breakers of Acre in Israel [11.275].

6. Biographies

Articles that recount some aspects of the lives of individuals are not a large portion of this literature. They range from popular magazine accounts of entertainers such as Vic Damone [11.364] to frequent references to the life of Ṭáhirih (Qurratu'l-'Ayn).

7. New Age; Occultism; Astrology

This category does not seem to fill a large part of the periodical literature on the Bahá'í religion. Spiritualism plays a part again in the articles by Wellesley Tudor Pole [11.814–11.815], and there is an article by Dane Rudhyar on astrology [11.885] and one on C.W. Child's reading of 'Abdu'l-Bahá's palms [11.267].

8. Architecture, Art and Literature

As in the case of reference to the Bahá'í Faith in books on other topics, the references to architecture, art and literature are usually concerned with Bahá'í Houses of Worship, the artists Mark Tobey

and Otto Donald Rogers, and the poetry of Robert Hayden.

9. Social issues

A few articles deal with Bahá'í views on such issues as peace, women and human rights.

10. Extremist exposés

A minor selection of articles attacks the Bahá'í teachings from extremist positions, e.g. racism [11.616], communism [11.446] and Islamic fundamentalism [11.1124; see section on Islam above].

11. Covenant-breaker reports

Some periodical articles are by or about Covenant-breakers (see Section XII). A handful relate to the New History Society [e.g. 11.79, 11.1081] and to Ibrahim Kheiralla and the Behaists [11.606–11.609, 11.789].

The compiler has not included newspaper articles because of the vast quantity of newspaper coverage, inadequate indexing for most newspapers in the English-speaking world, and the minor nature of the great majority of newspaper accounts. The periodical articles listed here are from journals or magazines – publications appearing at regular or irregular intervals of from once a week to once a year. The items included in this section represent no more than 50% of the articles treating the Bahá'í Faith that have appeared in journals, both well-known and obscure.

A

11.1. 'A.I. Concerned with Executions in Iran', *Human Rights Internet Reporter* (Washington, D.C.), v.7 no.1 (Sept.–Oct. 1981), p. 167.

11.2. 'Abdu'l-Bahá. 'Abdul Baha on Reincarnation', *The International Psychic Gazette* (London), v.1 no.7 (Feb. 1913), p. 197.

11.3. —— 'Abdul Baha on Universal Peace', *The International Psychic Gazette* (London), no.13 (Aug. 1913), p. 5.

11.4. —— 'Abdul Baha on Universal Peace: Address Given to the Alliance Spiritualiste, Paris', *The International Psychic Gazette* (London), no.10 (May 1913), pp. 299–300.

11.5. —— 'Abdul Baha's Address to Cosmos Club, as Reported by Three Lady Disciples',

The International Psychic Gazette (London), no.8 (Mar. 1913), p. 220.

11.6. —— 'Abdul Baha's Thanks for New Year's Greeting', *The International Psychic Gazette* (London), no.23 (June 1914), p. 315.

11.7. —— 'America and World Peace', *The Independent* (New York), 73 (Sept. 12, 1912), pp. 606–9.

11.8. —— 'Aspects of Natural and Divine Philosophy', *The Christian Commonwealth* (London), (Jan. 22, 1913), pp. i–ii.

11.9. —— 'The Baha'i Faith, the True Modernism', *Woman* (St Vincent), (Sept.–Oct. 1982), p. 22. Extract from *Foundations of World Unity*.

11.10. —— 'The Brotherhood of Man', *The*

Crisis (New York), v.4 no.2 (June 1912), pp. 88–9.

11.11. —— 'A Letter from Abdul Baha', *Theosophy in Scotland*, v.4 no.6 (Oct. 1913), pp. 82–4.

11.12. —— 'The Lofty Summit of Unchanging Purpose: Words of Abdul-Baha to Lua Getsinger, Ramleh, Egypt, Aug. 19, 1913: From the Diary of Mirza Ahmad Sohrab', *The International Psychic Gazette* (London), no.18 (Jan. 1914), p. 18.

11.12a. —— 'A New Year's Greeting from Abdul Baha: Abdul Baha's Message to the Readers of the "Vahan"', *The Vahan* (London), v.22 no.6 (Jan. 1913), pp. 118–19.

11.13. —— 'On the Importance of Divine Civilization', translated from the original Persian by Mirza Ahmad Sohrab, *The Asiatic Quarterly Review* (London), new series v.1 no.2 (Apr. 1913), pp. 224–37.

11.14. —— 'One of the Meanings of Sacrifice: Talk by Abdul-Baha to One of His Friends', *The International Psychic Gazette* (London), no.19 (Feb. 1914), p. 202.

11.15. —— ['The Secret of Divine Civilization, Selections'], *Education Today* (Taipei), no.2 (17 Aug. 1984), p. 1.

11.16. —— 'A Short Summary of the Teachings of Baha'u'llah', *Contemporary Review* (London), no.101 (Mar. 1912), pp. 401–2.

11.17. —— 'Survival and Salvation', *The International Psychic Gazette* (London), no.24 (July 1914), pp. 341–2.

11.18. —— 'The Three Realities', *The Path* (London), v.3 no.8 (Feb. 1913), pp. 285–90.

11.19. —— 'Universal Peace', *The Christian Commonwealth* (London), v.33 no.1664 (Sept. 3, 1913), p. 838.

11.20. —— 'Unpublished Talks by 'Abdu'l-Baha', *The Sufi Quarterly* (Geneva), v.3 (1928), pp. 227–31.

11.21. 'Abdul Baha', *The Outlook* (London), v.129 (Dec. 21, 1921), pp. 632–3.

11.22. 'Abdul Baha at Bristol', *The Christian Commonwealth* (London), (Sept. 27, 1911), p. 898.

11.23. 'Abdul Baha at Oxford', *The Christian Commonwealth* (London), (Jan. 22, 1913), pp. i–ii.

11.24. 'Abdul Baha at the Higher Thought Centre', *The Christian Commonwealth* (London), (Jan. 22, 1918), p. ii.

11.25. 'Abdul Baha in England: Warm Welcome from His English Followers', *The Christian Commonwealth* (London), (Jan. 1, 1913), pp. 261–4.

11.26. Abrams, Elliott. 'Iran Under Khomeini', *The New York Times Magazine*, (Mar. 18, 1984), p. 110.

11.27. 'Action of UN Human Rights Commission', *Human Rights Internet Reporter* (Washington, D.C.), v.10 nos. 3–4 (Jan.–Apr. 1985), pp. 406–7. Bahá'í Faith: p. 407.

11.28. 'Activities of the World's Youngest Religion in Vietnam', *The Times of Viet-Nam* (Saigon), v.4 no.12 (Mar. 25, 1962), pp. 16–19.

11.29. Adams, Eric R. 'Baha'i Religion Gains Converts World Over', *Saturday Night* (Toronto), v.63 no.8 (25 Oct. 1957), p. 13.

11.30. Afnán, Muḥammad; Hatcher, William S. 'Western Islamic Scholarship and Bahá'í Origins', *Religion* (London), v.15 (1985), pp. 29–51.

11.31. 'After the Shah, Big New Worries for Iran's Minorities', *U.S. News & World Report* (Washington, D.C.), (Jan. 29, 1979), p. 32.

11.32. Agbabiaka, Tunde. 'Baha'i Religion for All Faiths', *Sunday Concord* (Ikeja, Nigeria), v.3 no.76 (Aug. 15, 1982), pp. 7–9.

11.33. Ahmad, Shahid. 'Criminals and Stooges Under the Bahai Cover', *Crescent International* (Markham, Ont.), v.2 no.10 (Aug. 1–15, 1983), p. 5.

11.34. 'Ahmadism and Bahaism in the Same Boat', *The Moslem World* (Hartford, Conn.), v.31 no.1 (Jan. 1941), pp. 94–5.

11.35. Akinrolabu, Fola. 'A New Faith Brought from Iran', *Spear* (Ikeja, Nigeria), (May 1984), pp. 4–5.

11.36. Al Haj Garba Isa. 'Opposed', *The Middle East* (London), no. 105 (July 1983), p. 5.

11.37. 'All Pilgrims Welcome', *News from Israel* (Bombay), v.19 no.8 (Apr. 15, 1972), p. 13.

11.38. Allderdice, Jacob. 'Cults, Sects, Religions', *Scholastic Update* (New York), v.117 no.1 (Mar. 1, 1985), p. 10.

11.39. Allen, Dwight. 'Baha'i, a Religion, a Way of Life', *Viewpoint* (Stanford, Calif.), v.2 no.1 (Autumn 1952), pp. 11–14.

11.40. Alpert, Carl. 'Another Religion Calls Israel Home', *The Reconstructionist* (New York), v.21 no.6 (Apr. 29, 1955), pp. 19–22.

11.41. —— Bahai, a Strange Religion', *Young Judaean* (New York), (Oct. 1958), pp. 18–19.

11.42. —— 'Bahai Helps Beautify Israel', *The Jewish Week* (New York), v.197 no.49 (Apr. 19, 1985), p. 2.

11.43. —— 'Bahai Religion Also Finds a Place in Israel', *Sentinel* (Chicago), (Apr. 4, 1968), p. 9.

11.44. —— 'The City of Haifa', *Middle Eastern Affairs* (New York), v.7 no.11 (Nov. 1956), pp. 377–83. Bahá'í Faith, p. 381.

11.45. 'Alternative Religions in Anchorage: a Guide to What's Different', *Anchorage Magazine* (Anchorage, Alaska), (Apr. 1979), pp. 13–15.

11.46. 'Alternatives II', *The Kentish Times* (Tasmania), (Mar. 1984), p. 6.

11.47. 'An American Babist and Her Fate', *Current Literature* (London), v.31 (July 1901), pp. 105–6.

11.48. Amnesty International. 'Amnesty International Statement on Human Rights Violations in Iran', *Human Rights Internet Reporter* (Washington, D.C.), v.9 no.4 (Mar.–June 1984), pp. 565–6.

11.49. 'Amnesty International Amasses Reports of Torture in Iran: Over 4,000 Executed Since Revolution', *Human Rights Internet Reporter* (Washington, D.C.), v.7 no.3 (Jan.–Feb. 1982), pp. 537–8.

11.50. 'Amnesty Testifies at Senate Hearings on Torture', *Amnesty Action* (New York), (July–Aug. 1984).

11.51. 'And More Ideas', *Guiding* (N.Z.), (Aug. 1984).

11.52. Andree, George. 'The Bahai Teachings in Relation to Theosophy', *The International Psychic Gazette* (London), no.11 (June 1913), p. 325.

11.53. Arbuthnot, Robert H. 'The Bab and Babeeism', *Contemporary Review* (London), no.11 (Aug. 1869), pp. 581–601; no.12 (Oct. 1869), pp. 245–66.
Distillation of information from Gobineau's *Les Religions et les Philosophies dans l'Asie Central* and Mirza Kazem Beg's *Bab et les Babis*.

11.54. 'Architectural Romance of Bahai Temple Told by Los Angeles Engineer in Book', *Southwest Builder and Contractor* (Los Angeles), (Nov. 6, 1925), pp. 42–3.
Recounts some of the story of the Wilmette Bahá'í House of Worship as told by L.B. Pemberton in *A Modern Pilgrimage to Palestine*.

11.55. 'Are Bahais Muslims?', *Arab News* (Jiddah, Saudi Arabia), (22 Nov. 1985).

11.56. 'Are Communism and Christianity Incompatible', *Town Meeting* (New York), v.13 no.6 (June 5, 1947), pp. 3–22. Reference to Bahá'ís on p. 16.

11.57. Arnold, Matthew. 'A Persian Passion Play', *The Cornhill Magazine* (London), v.24 (1871), pp. 668–87.

11.57a. 'Artists Workshop a Success', *Family Magazine* (Guyana), (May 3, 1981), p. xiii.

11.57b. 'At Bahai Temple in Wilmette, Ill.', *Ebony* (Chicago), (Dec. 1955).

11.58. Atkinson, Robert. 'Ba'hai's [sic] American Beginning in Maine', *East West Journal* (Brookline, Mass.), (Dec. 1977), pp. 78–83.

11.59. 'Attacks on Freedom of Religion: Baha'is and Muslim Fundamentalists', *Human Rights Internet Reporter* (Washington, D.C.), v.10 no.1–2 (Sept.–Dec. 1984), pp. 168–9.

11.60. 'Award New Contract for Baha'i Temple Work', *Winnetka Talk* (Winnetka, Ill.), v.26 no.30 (Oct. 21, 1937), p. 5.

B

11.61. 'The Bab', *The Oxford Magazine*, (May 25, 1892), p. 394.

11.62. 'The Bab and His Successors', *The Middle East* (London), (Apr. 1983), pp. 36–7.

11.63. 'Babism in New York', *The Missionary Review of the World* (Princeton, N.J.), v.29 (May 1906), p. 391.

11.64. 'Babism in Persia', *The Missionary Review*

of the World (Princeton, N.J.), v.11 n.s. (Jan. 1898), p. 55.

11.65. 'Babist Movement', *The Nation* (New York), v.87 (Dec. 24, 1908), p. 627.

11.66. 'The Bâbys', *The Church Missionary Intelligencer* (London), (June 1872), pp. 161–75.

11.67. Bach, Marcus. [Answer to Letter to the Editor], *Unity* (Unity Village, Mo.), (Aug.

1982), pp. 12–14.
Question about using a prayer of 'Abdu'l-Bahá's in public schools.

11.68. —— 'Baha'i, a Second Look', *The Christian Century* (Chicago), v.74 no.15 (Apr. 10, 1957), pp. 449–51.

11.69. —— 'The Bahai Faith', *Adult Student* (Nashville, Tenn.), v.15 no.10 (Oct. 1956), pp. 60–4.

11.70. —— 'He Changed My Life', *The Rotarian* (Evanston, Ill.), (Dec. 1968), pp. 18–19.

11.71. —— 'Paranormal Basis of Baha'i', *Fate* (Evanston, Ill.), (July 1968), pp. 92–100.

11.72. —— 'What's Happening on Church Street, U.S.A.?', *Better Homes and Gardens* (Des Moines, Iowa), v.34 (Oct. 1956), pp. 74–5, 154–5. Bahá'í Faith, p. 75.

11.73. Bagley, F.R.C. 'Religion and State in Iran', *Islamic Studies* (Pakistan), v.10 no.1 (Mar. 1971), pp. 1–22. Bahá'í Faith, p. 9.

11.74. 'Baha'i', *Time* (New York), (July 20, 1931), p. 48.

11.75. 'Bahai', *The Presbyterian Herald* (Belfast), (Sept. 1985), pp. 4–5.

11.76. 'Baha'i Ads for Awareness', *National Business Review* (Wellington, N.Z), (7 Oct. 1985).

11.77. 'Baha'i: An Odd-Looking Temple Outside Chicago Houses a High-Minded Faith', *Life* (New York), v.29 (Dec. 11, 1950), pp. 159–61.

11.78. 'Bahai Books', *The Theosophist* (Madras), (Jan. 1935), pp. 407–8.
Review of books published by the New History Society.

11.79. 'Bahai Bride', *Time* (New York), (Mar. 10, 1930), p. 70.
Marriage of Elsie Benkard, daughter of Julie Chanler, to Charles Clarke.

11.80. 'The Bahá'í Calendar', *Indo-Iranica* (Calcutta), v.5 no.2 (1951–2), p. 29.

11.81. 'The Bahai Church, a Mohammedan Sect', *Sunday Letter of Catholic Mission Mankon, Bamenda, Cameroon*, (Feb. 24, 1980), pp. [2–3]

11.82. *idem. Youth Tower* (Bamenda, Cameroon), (Mar. 1980), pp. [1–2]

11.82a. 'Baha'i Conference, Institute Ceremony Set for Oct. 20–22.' *Along the Coast* (Myrtle Beach, S.C.), v.18 no.30 (Oct. 1972), p. 18, cover. Cover title: 'Bahai Faith Conference'.

11.83. 'Baha'i Convention Opens Tonight', *Wilmette Life* (Wilmette, Ill.), (May 23, 1968), cover.

11.83a. 'Baha'i Delegation Meets Israel's Prime Minister', *India and Israel* (Bombay), v.4 no.2 (Aug. 1951), p. 32.

11.83b. 'The Baha'i Dispensation: The Coming of the Son of Man', *The Super-Man* (London), v.3 no.5 (June 1922), p. 62.

11.84. 'Baha'i Faith', *Mini World* (Paramaribo), no.21 (July–Aug. 1978), p. 22.

11.85. 'Baha'i Faith', *Orbit: The Magazine for Young Zambians*, v.6 no.3 (May–June 1978), pp. 26–7.

11.86. 'The Baha'i Faith', *Sinorama* (Taiwan), v.5 no.10 (10.1980), pp. 88–91.

11.87. 'The Bahá'í Faith', *The Harrow Community Church Bulletin* (Harrow, Eng.), (May 1981?).

11.88. 'Baha'i Faith', *Neucleus* (Armidale, N.S.W.), v.38, no.4 (June 1984), p. 16.

11.89. 'The Baha'i Faith', *Update* (Aarhus, Denmark), v.9 no.3 (Sept. 1985), pp. 3–8.

11.90. 'The Baha'i Faith', *Fair News* (London), (Oct. 1985), p. 15.
A leading 'anti-cult' group in the United Kingdom defends the Bahá'í Faith against the cult label.

11.91. 'The Bahá'í Faith: A New Way of Life for Bahamians', *Eye-Opener Magazine* (Bahamas), (Oct. 1979), pp. 14–15, 37.

11.92. 'The Bahai Faith, a Universal Religion: Spiritualisation of Power', *Woman* (St Vincent), (1983), pp. 16, 22.

11.93. 'The Bahá'í Faith and the New Age', *Chimo*, v.7 no.12 (1981), pp. 6–11.

11.94. 'Baha'i Faith Located in Kenosha', *Wisconsin Then and Now* (Madison), v.23 no.10 (May 1977), pp. 4–5, 7.

11.95. 'Baha'i Faith Makes Gains Among Rural Blacks in Southern U.S.', *The Christian Century* (Chicago), v.88 no.12 (Mar. 24, 1971), p. 368.

11.96. 'Baha'i Faith, Only Church in World That Does Not Discriminate', *Ebony* (Chicago), v.7 no.12 (Oct. 1952), pp. 39–46.

11.97. 'Baha'i Faith: Second in a Series on Other Creeds', *Ecumenews* (Hartford, Conn.), issue 3 (Apr. 1971), pp. [1]–[3].

11.97a. 'Baha'i Faith Symbolizes Unity: Observes Centenary with Plans for World Spiritual Crusade', *Color* (Charleston, W.Va.; Philadelphia, Pa.), (Sept. 1953), pp. 46–9.

11.98. 'Baha'i Faith Travel Teachers Call Here', *Nor'wester* (Cayman Island), (Dec. 1976), pp. 44–5.

11.99. 'Baha'i Faith Will Advertise', *The Christian Century* (Chicago), (Sept. 25, 1946), p. 1141.

11.100. 'A Bahai Farewell', *The International Psychic Gazette* (London), no.10 (May 1913), p. 300.
Farewell by London Bahá'ís for Mr & Mrs John Jenner, who were leaving for Tasmania. Includes a Tablet of 'Abdu'l-Bahá to the Jenners.

11.101. 'Baha'i File: The Politics of a Faith', *Arabia: The Islamic World Review* (East Burnham, nr. Slough, Bucks.), v.4 no.46 (June 1985), pp. 37–45.

11.102. 'Baha'i Funerals Follow No Formal Ritual', *The American Funeral Director* (New York), (May 1968), pp. 49–50.

11.103. 'The Baha'i House of Worship', *The Illustrated Weekly of India* (Bombay), v.74 no.16 (Apr. 19, 1953), p. 25.

11.104. 'The Baha'i House of Worship', *Turisguía* (Panamá), (Mayo 1982), pp. 13–15.

11.105. 'Bahá'í House of Worship at Wilmette, Illinois: Dedicated to the New World Order Revealed by Bahá'u'lláh, Based Upon Human Brotherhood without Prejudice of Race, Nationality or Creed', *The Christian Community* (Chicago), v.1 no.6 (Oct. 7, 1934), cover, p. 5.

11.106. 'Bahá'í House of Worship Dedication, May 2, 1953', *Wilmette Life* (Wilmette, Ill.), (Apr. 30, 1953).

11.107. 'Bahai House of Worship: Roof Restoration Preserves National Landmark Whose Exterior Is the First Precast, Concrete Lace Work in the U.S.', *Building Operating Management* (Milwaukee, Wis.), (July 1985), pp. 84, 86.

11.108. Bahá'í International Community. 'Baha'i's Give U.N. a Message', *World Peace News* (New York), v. 9 no.7 (Oct. 1978).

11.109. 'Baha'i International Community Recently Forwarded $5000.00 to UNDRO', *The Diplomatic World Bulletin* (New York), (Dec. 4, 1978).

11.110. 'Baha'i Leader Visits Taiwan Believers', *Zhōng Guó Gōng Shāng Lǚ Yóu Zá Zhì* (Taipei), no.47 (Apr. 1979), p. 16.

11.111. 'Baha'i Leaders Are Executed', *Amnesty International Newsletter* (London), v.12 no.2 (Feb. 1982), p. 6.

11.112. 'Bahai Members Executed', *The Forum* (Wichita, Kan.), (June 1981), p. 1.

11.113. 'Baha'i Members of the Espionage Network Executed', *Imam* (London), (Feb. 11, 1982), p. 22.

11.114. 'Baha'i Message to Humanity', *Broadcast* (Los Angeles), v.1 no.6 (Mar. 1932), pp. 6–9.

11.115. 'Baha'i Movement', *The Outlook* (London), v.101 (June 15, 1912), pp. 326–7.

11.116. 'The Bahai Movement', *The Inquirer and Christian Life* (London), no.4588 (June 7, 1938), pp. 275–6.
Letter from Charles Biggins and editorial reply from Griffith J. Sparham.

11.116a. 'Bahai Movement and the W.R.I.'. *The War Resister* (Enfield, Middlesex, Eng.), no.16 (May 1927), p. 8.

11.117. 'The Bahai Movement and World Peace', by a British Bahai, *The People's Weekly*, (Sept. 27, 1930), p. 5.

11.118. 'The Bahá'í Movement in England', *Town and Country News* (London), v.74 no.441 (Nov. 24, 1933), p. 10.

11.119. 'The Bahai Movement of Persia: Its Universal Aspect', *The Empress* (Calcutta), v.29 no.1 (Apr. 1914), pp. 10–11.

11.120. 'The Baha'i Movement: Official Statement', *The Occult Digest*, (Sept. 1927), pp. 11, 30.
Includes an inset with a letter from Horace Holley giving the Bahá'í view of capital punishment.

11.121. 'Bahai Museum for Mount Carmel', *The Israel Review* (Bangkok), v.1 no.6 (Aug. 1955), p. 6.

11.121a. 'Baha'i News', *India and Israel* (Bombay), special independence issue (20 Apr. 1953), p. 17. Includes subtitled sections: 'Baha'i Newsletter from Haifa', 'Baha'i Budgeteer'.

11.121b. 'Baha'i News', *India and Israel* (Bombay), v.5 no.12 (June 1953), p. 21. Includes subtitled sections: 'Newsletter from Haifa', 'Jubilee Week in Delhi'.

11.122. 'The Bahai Nightingale', *The International Psychic Gazette* (London), no.21 (Apr. 1914), p. 263.
About composer Louise R. 'Shahnaz' Waite.

11.123. 'Baha'i Notes', *The International Psychic Gazette* (London), v.1 no.6 (Jan. 1913), p. 179.

11.124. 'Bahai, 100 Years of a One-World Religion', *Pathfinder* (Chicago), (Nov. 19, 1952), pp. 56–7.

11.125. 'Baha'i Organization Awards Visually

Handicapped Man', *Ha'ilono Kina* (Hawaii), v.13 (Dec. 1980).

11.126. 'Baha'i Persecution in Persia', *The Near East* (London), v.30 no.807 (Nov. 4, 1926), p. 517.

11.127. 'Baha'i Religion Out', *The Church Around the World* (Wheaton, Ill.), v.12 no.7 (June 1982), p. [2]

11.128. 'The Bahai Shrine', *El Al Sales Digest*, no.50 (Oct. 1968), pp. 8–9.

11.129. 'Baha'i Shrine for the Western World: Baha'i Temple, Wilmette, Illinois, Louis J. Bourgeois, Architect', *The Architectural Record* (New York), v.96 (July 1944), p. 112.

11.130. 'Bahai Teens Will Get More Involved', *Topic Newsmagazine* (Bradford, Ont.), (Sept. 12, 1984).

11.131. 'The Baha'i Temple', *Journal of the American Concrete Institute* (Detroit, Mich.), v.4 no.5 (Jan. 1933), pp. 4–5.

11.132. 'The Baha'i Temple', *Chicago Calendar*, v.3 no.11 (Dec. 1–15, 1934), pp. 4, 15–17, 21.

11.133. 'The Baha'i Temple', *Architectural Concrete* (Chicago), v.10 no.2 ([1944]), pp. 20–3.

11.134. 'Bahá'í Temple', *The Pure Oil News* (Chicago), v.27 no.9 (Feb. 1945), pp. 6–8.

11.135. 'Baha'i Temple', *Turisguía* (Panama), (April, 1972), pp. 4–6.

11.136. 'Baha'i Temple Gardens Will Be Setting for Two Convocations', *Wilmette Life* (Wilmette, Ill.), (Apr. 24, 1958).

11.137. 'A Bahai Temple in Chicago', *The Outlook* (London), v.126 (Dec. 1, 1920), p. 579.

11.138. 'Bahai Temple, in Wilmette', *Bell Telephone News* (Chicago), v.27 no.2 (Feb. 1937), cover, inside front cover.

11.139. 'The Bahai Temple Model', *The Prompter* (New York?), (June 1920), pp. 62–3.

11.139a. 'Baha'i Temple, New Delhi: (First Project in India to Use Galvanized Rebar),' *Galvanizing* (Bombay), (Apr./June 1984), cover, p. 1.

11.140. 'Baha'i Temple, Third in the World, Being Built on Mona Vale Hilltop, Sydney', *Building, Lighting, Engineering* (Sydney, N.S.W.), (Sept. 24, 1958), pp. 38–9.

11.141. 'Baha'i Women Murdered in Iran', *Women's International Network News* (Lexington, Mass.), v.9 no.4 (Autumn, 1983), p. 42.

11.142. 'Baha'ia', *The Christian Century* (Chicago), v.74 (May 15, 1957), p. 625.
Letters by Chester Wafford and C.H. Allen.

11.143. 'The Bahá'ís', *Secretariat News* (New York), (31 Oct. 1978), p. 1.

11.144. 'Baha'is, a Model of Private Sponsorship', *Refuge* (Downsview, Ont.), v.2 no.1 (Sept.–Oct. 1982), pp. 1, 3.

11.145. 'Baha'is Appeal to Christians', *Church and Community News* (Abingdon, U.K.), (July 1983), p. 9.

11.146. 'Baha'i's [sic] Dedicate Temple', *News Bulletin* (Pago Pago, American Samoa), (Sept. 7, 1984), p. 2.

11.147. 'Bahais "Deviants", Tools of Zionists – Al-Azhar', *Al-Islam* (Colombo, Sri Lanka), (1984), p. 16.

11.148. 'Baha'is Die for Beliefs', *The United Church Observer* (Toronto), (Oct. 1983), pp. 40–1.

11.149. 'Baha'is Find Friends in Canada', *Panorama: The Staff Newspaper of Employment and Immigration Canada* (Ottawa), (Mar. 1983), p. 1.

11.150. 'Bahais Hanged in Iran', *One World* (Geneva), (19 May–6 July 1983), p. 6.

11.151. 'The Bahai's Horror in Iran: Is This the Brotherhood of Man?', *She* (Pakistan), (July 1984), pp. 20–1.

11.152. 'The Baha'is in Iran', *Imam* (London), v.2 no.5–6 (June–July 1982), pp. 20–1.

11.153. 'Baha'is in Iran', *Dialog* (Aarhus, Denmark), v.7 no.2 (1983), p. 30.

11.154. 'The Baha'is in Iran', *L'Echo des Iles* (Seychelles), no.9 (15 juin–1 juillet 1984), pp. 19–20.

11.155. 'Baha'is of All Americas to Hold Centenary', *Wilmette Life* (Wilmette, Ill.), (May 18, 1944).

11.156. 'The Baha'is of Iran', *Outsider* (London), no.22 (Dec. 1985), p. 4.

11.157. 'Baha'is of South Australia Celebrate 50th Anniversary of the Foundation of the Baha'i Faith in the State', *Messenger* (Port Adelaide, S. Aust.), (Nov. 21, 1973), 4 p. special supplement.

11.158. 'The Baha'is of the United States and Canada Hold Their Seventh [sic] Annual Convention and Congress at Green Acre, Eliot Maine: Prominent Colored People in Attendance', *The Spokesman* (New York), v.1 no.9 (Aug./Sept. 1925), pp. 12–14.

11.159. 'Baha'is 100th', *Newsweek* (New York), v.41 no.19 (May 11, 1953), p. 60.

11.160. 'Baha'is Report Increased Assemblies,

Doubling of Membership in the U.S.', *The Christian Century* (Chicago), v.88 (May 19, 1971), p. 616.

11.161. 'The Bahais Return to Israel: Eighty Persians Journey Back to Haifa and Acre, the Holy Towns of Their Creed', *The Sphere* (London), v.198 no.2583 (Aug. 6, 1949), p. 189.

11.161a. 'Baha'is See H Bomb Threat as World Spiritual Crisis', *Wilmette Life* (Wilmette, Ill.), (July, 1, 1954), p. 32.

11.162. 'Bahais: The Persecution Continues', *The Economist* (London), (Oct. 26, 1985), p. 52.

11.163. *idem. Le Nouvel Economiste* (Paris), (26 Nov. 1985).

11.164. 'Baha'is, the "Untouchables" of Iran', *The Illustrated Weekly of India* (Bombay), v.104 no.16 (May 8–14, 1983), pp. 16–17.

11.164a. 'Bahaism', *Evangelical Christendom* (London), (Nov./Dec. 1912), pp. 192–3.

11.165. 'Baha'ism', *Church News* (London), (May 1966), p. [16]

11.166. 'Baha'ism a False Cult', *The Sunday School Times* (Philadelphia, Pa.), (July 28, 1956), p. 594.

11.167. 'Bahaism in America', *The Moslem World* (Hartford, Conn.), v.14 no.2 (Apr. 1924), pp. 190–1.

11.168. 'Baha'ism: Pair, Third to Wed in Cult in the United States', *Newsweek* (New York), v.3 (Feb. 10, 1934), p. 31.
Wedding performed by Mirza Ahmad Sohrab of the New History Society.

11.169. Bahar, Jalil. 'The Theocrats Take Over: Iran', *Index on Censorship* (London), (5/81), pp. 2–3.

11.170. Bahareh. 'The Conversion: A Short Story About a Baha'i Family Which First Appeared in an Underground Paper in Iran', *Index on Censorship* (London), (5/83), p. 22.

11.171. —— 'The Day Light Came to Our House', *Liberty* (Washington, D.C.), v.79 no.2 (Mar.–Apr. 1984), pp. 3–4.

11.172. Bailey, Dennis. 'The Baha'i Religion: Tucked Away in Eliot for 50 Summers, an All-Encompassing Faith Has Drawn People to Maine', *Maine Times* (Topsham, Me.), v.14 no.45 (Aug. 27, 1982), pp. 2–4.

11.173. —— 'Iran and the Baha'is', *The Bulletin* (Sydney), (Nov. 18, 1980), p. 6.

11.174. Balch, Robert W.; Farnsworth, G.; Wilkins, S. 'When the Bomb Drops: Reactions to Disconfirmed Prophecy in a Millennial Sect', *Sociological Perspectives* (Beverly Hills, Calif.), v.26 no.2 (Apr. 1983), pp. 137–58.

11.175. Balise, David. 'The Baha'i Faith and the Divine Principle', *The Way of the World*, 9/10 (Sept.–Oct. 1974), pp. 35–45.
Implies that Sun Myung Moon, founder of the Unification Church, is 'He Whom God Shall Make Manifest' and that the Báb and Bahá-'u'lláh were his heralds.

11.176. Banuazizi, Ali. 'The Iranian Agony', *Commonweal* (New York), (25 Feb. 1983), pp. 107–8.

11.177. Barker, George. 'So That's What a Baha'i Feast Looks Like', *Picture Post* (London), (Apr. 15, 1944), pp. 14–15.

11.178. Barker, S. Louis. 'A North Palestine Station', *Church Missionary Gleaner* (London), (May 1892), pp. 74–5.
Missionaries visit with members of the family of Bahá'u'lláh.

11.178a. Barnea, Yoram. 'Haifa, a Beautiful City', *Apropo Israel* (Tel Aviv), (Nov.–Dec. 1983), pp. 14–15. Bahá'í: cover, p. 15.

11.179. Bartlett, Robert C. 'Winnetka Day at Baha'i Temple: A Guest Editorial', *Winnetka Talk* (Winnetka, Ill.), (Feb. 23, 1961), p. 8.

11.180. Batchelor, Thelma. 'The Baha'i Faith, Uniting the World One Heart at a Time', *The Mirror* (Nepal), (Jan. [1985]), pp. 4–5.

11.181. Bausani, Alessandro. 'Can Monotheism Be Taught?: Further Considerations on the Typology of Monotheism', *Numen* (Leiden), v.10 no.3 (1963), pp. 167–201. Bahá'í Faith, pp. 177, 199.

11.182. —— 'Modern Religious Trends in Islam', *East and West* (Rome), (1953), pp. 12–18, 87–90. Bábí and Bahá'í Faiths, pp. 13, 14, 87, 88, 89.

11.183. Bayat, Mangol. 'The Concepts of Religion and Government in the Thought of Mîrzâ Âqâ K͟hân Kirmânî, a Nineteenth-Century Persian Revolutionary', *International Journal of Middle East Studies* (New York), v.5 (1974), pp. 381–400.
Numerous references to Bábís and Azalís.

11.184. —— 'Mirza Aqa Khan Kirmani: A Nineteenth Century Persian Nationalist', *Middle Eastern Studies* (London), v.10 (1974), pp. 36–59.
Numerous references to Bábís and Azalís.

11.185. ——'A Phoenix Too Frequent: The Concept of Historical Continuity in Modern Iranian Thought', *Asian and African Studies*

(Haifa), v.12 (1978), pp. 203–20. Babism p. 204n.

11.186. Beach, B.B. 'One S-L-O-W Step Forward: The U.N. Declaration on Religious Liberty', *Liberty* (Washington, D.C.), (Nov.–Dec. 1981), p. 19.

11.187. 'Beauty in Concrete', *US Steel News* (Pittsburgh, Pa.), v.19 no.4 (Oct. 1954), back cover.

11.188. Bechtel, Stefan. 'Healing That's Free for All', *Prevention* (Emmaus, Pa.), v.35 no.4 (Apr. 1983), pp. 75–80. Reference to Bahá'í Faith, p. 79.

11.189. Beint, Mina. 'A Persian Martyr', *NHR National Newsletter* (Solihull, West Midlands, U.K.), (Autumn 1984), p. 29.

11.190. Ben-Galil, Dov. 'Reintroducing the Limelighters', *Top of Israel*, (May 82), pp. 1, 3–4. Bahá'í Faith, p. 4.

11.191. Bennett, Lerone. 'Bahá'í, a Way of Life for Millions', *Ebony* (Chicago), v.20 (Apr. 1965), pp. 48–50, 52–6.

11.192. Bent, J. Theodore. 'Village Life in Persia', *Review* (London), v.5 (Jul.–Dec. 1891), pp. 355–62. Reference to Bahá'ís, pp. 356–7.

11.193. Bentwich, Norman. 'Acre Old and New', *Contemporary Review* (London), v.188 no.1076 (Oct. 1955), pp. 233–5. Bahá'í Faith, pp. 234–5.

11.194. Berger, Peter L. 'Sectarianism and Religious Sociation', *The American Journal of Sociology* (Chicago), v.64 (1958), pp. 41–4. Bahá'í Faith, p. 44n.

11.195. —— The Sociological Study of Sectarianism', *Social Research* (New York), v.21 (1954), pp. 467–85. Bahá'í Faith, p. 468.

11.196. Berton, Gene. 'A Dome Like Hands in Prayer', *The Mentor* (New York), v.8 (Nov. 1920), p. 39.

11.197. 'The Besieged Bahais of Iran', *Asiaweek* (Hong Kong), (Apr. 3, 1981). p. 46.

11.198. Bharati, Agehananda. 'Baha'i Statistics and Self-Fulfilling Design: Comment on James J. Keene's "Redefinition of Religion" ', *Journal for the Scientific Study of Religion* (Jamaica, N.Y.), (Fall 1968), p. 281.

11.199. Biernacki, Conrad. 'Mottahedeh, Designer and Producer of Original and Reproduction Porcelain', *Antique Showcase* (Canfield, Ont.), v.19 no.7 (Jan. 1984), pp. 41–3. Bahá'í Faith, p. 42.

11.200. —— 'Report on ROM Lecture, "East Meets West in China": Mrs. Mildred Mottahedeh', *Antique Showcase* (Canfield, Ont.), v.19 no.8 (Feb. 1984), pp. 13–15. Bahá'í Faith, p. 13.

11.201. Bird, Frederick; Reimer, Bill. 'Participation Rates in New Religious and Para-Religious Movements', *Journal for the Scientific Study of Religion* (Jamaica, N.Y.), v.21 no.1 (1982), pp. 1–14. Bahá'í Faith, pp. 2, 3, 5, 6, 9.

11.202. Bishop, Joseph W. 'Rogues' Gallery: The Liberal Crack-Up, by R. Emmett Tyrell' [review], *Commentary* (New York), (Feb. 1985), pp. 69–70. Bahá'í Faith, p. 70.

11.203. Biven, Evelyn Lackey. 'The Baha'i World Faith and the International Language', *International Language Review*, v.5 (July–Dec. 1959), unpaged.

11.204. Bixby, James T. 'Babism and the Bab', *New World* (London), v.6 (Dec. 1897), pp. 722–50.

11.205. —— 'What Is Behaism?', *North American Review* (Boston), no.195 (June 1912), pp. 833–46.

11.206. Bjorling, Joel. 'Leland Jensen, the Prophet Who Cried "Wolf",' *Understanding Cults and Spiritual Movements* (Del Mar, Calif.), v.1 no.3 (1985), pp. 6–9.

11.207. Blake, Patricia. 'Terror in the Name of God: The Mullahs Impose Their Will with a Vengeance', *Time* (New York), (July 6, 1981), pp. 10–11.

11.208. 'A Blend of All Religions', *The Literary Digest* (New York), v.107 (Nov. 22, 1930), p. 20.

11.209. Bliss, Edwin E. 'Bab and Babism', *Missionary Herald* (Cambridge, Mass.), (May 1869), pp. 146–8.
American missionary in Istanbul, 1856–92, refers to the Bahá'í community in Adrianople and the exile to 'Akká.

11.210. Blomfield, Lady (Sara Louisa). 'The Baha'is', *The Sufi Quarterly* (Geneva), v.3 no.4 (Mar. 1928), pp. 206–26.

11.211. 'The Blossoming of a Dream', *Larsen & Toubro Limited Newsletter* (Bombay), v.26 no.2 (July–Sept. 1985), back cover.

11.212. Bois, Jules. 'The New Religions of America, III: Babism and Bahaism', *The Forum* (New York), v.74 no.1 (July 1925), pp. 1–10.

11.213. Bolton, Stanley. 'What Is a Bahá'í?', *Pix* (Sydney, N.S.W.), v.29 no.9 (May 2, 1953), pp. 33–5.

11.214. Bond, Constance. 'The Pastels of Alice

Barney', *The Smithsonian* (Washington, D.C.), (Feb. 1985), p. 168.

11.215. Borah, Leo A. 'Illinois, Healthy Heart of the Nation', *National Geographic Magazine* (Washington, D.C.), v.104 no.6 (Dec. 1953), pp. 781–820. Bahá'í Faith, p. 783.

11.216. Bordewich, Fergus M. 'The Baha'is, Their "Crime" Is Faith', *Reader's Digest* (Surry Hills, N.S.W.), v.126 no.757 (May 1985), pp. 61–5.

11.217. —— 'Their "Crime" Is Faith', *Reader's Digest* (Pleasantville, N.Y.), (Dec. 1984), pp. 61–8.

11.218. —— *idem. Reader's Digest* (Hong Kong), Asia ed., v.44 no.263 (Feb. 1985), pp. 92–6.

11.219. —— 'Torture of a Peaceful People: Refusing to Renounce Their Faith, the Baha'is in Iran Suffer Ruthless Cruelty', *Reader's Digest* (London), v.126 no.753 (Jan. 1985), pp. 97–100.

11.220. Bourne, John. 'Cults, the Counterfeit Church', *Seeds* (N.Z.), (1978), p. 6.

11.221. 'Boy Entertainer Grows Up', *The Manila Chronicle Entertainment Guide* (Manila), v.4 no.44 (Nov. 5, 1966), p. 22.
Story of Jack Davis, a Bahá'í.

11.222. Boyles, Ann. 'Women and the Baha'i Faith: The Religious Principle of Equality', *Canadian Woman Studies* (Scarborough, Ont.), v.5 no.2 (Winter 1983), pp. 16–18.

11.223. Braden, Charles S. 'Why Are the Cults Growing', *The Christian Century* (Chicago), (Jan. 12, 1944), pp. 45–7. Bahá'í Faith, p. 45.

11.224. Braswell, George W. 'Iran and Islam', *Theology Today* (Princeton, N.J.), v.36, no.4 (1980), pp. 523–33. Bahá'í Faith, pp. 528, 532.

11.225. Breneman, Bret. 'Those Braided Rings', *PHP* (Japan), (Aug. 1981), pp. 6–14. Bahá'í, pp. 9–10, 11.

11.226. Brenner, Fred. 'Khomeini's Dream of an Islamic Republic', *Liberty* (Washington, D.C.), v.74 no.4 (July/Aug. 1979), pp. 11–13. Bahá'í Faith, p. 13.

11.227. Brookhiser, Richard. 'The Evil of Banality', *National Review* (New York), v.37 no.3 (Oct. 4, 1985), pp. 47–9. Bahá'ís of Iran, p. 48.

11.228. Brooks, Gordon. 'Social Scenes', *This Month in Taiwan, Republic of China* (Taipei), v.12 no.1 (Jan. 1985), p. 123.

11.229. Browne, Edward Granville. 'The Assassination of Násiru'd-Dín Shah', *New Review* (London), v.14 (June 1896), pp. 651–9. Bahá'í Faith, pp. 651–4 *passim.*

11.230. —— 'The Bábís of Persia', *Journal of the Royal Asiatic Society* (London), v.21 (July 1889), pp. 486–526; (Oct. 1889), pp. 881–1009.

11.231. —— 'Catalogue and Descriptions of 27 Bábí Manuscripts', *Journal of the Royal Asiatic Society* (London), (July 1892), pp. 433–99, 637–710.

11.232. ——'The Literature of Persia', *Persia Society Publications* (London), (1912), pp. 33–4.

11.233. —— 'The Persian Constitutional Movement', *Proceedings of the British Academy*, v.8 (1917–18), p. 316.

11.234. —— 'The Persian Constitutionalists', *Proceedings of the Central Asian Society* (London), (1909), pp. 1–16. Bahá'ís, p. 12.

11.235. ——'The Religious Influence of Persia', *Persia Society Publications* (London), pp. 71–2.

11.236. —— 'Sir 'Abdu'l-Baha 'Abbas, Died 28th November 1921', *Journal of the Royal Asiatic Society* (London), (Jan. 1922), pp. 145–6.

11.237. —— 'Some Notes on the Literature and Doctrines of the Ḥurufi Sect', *Journal of the Royal Asiatic Society* (London), v.30 (1898), pp. 61–95. Bábís, pp. 71, 78, 83, 84, 87–9.

11.238. ——'Some Remarks on the Bábí Texts Edited by Baron Victor Rosen', *Journal of the Royal Asiatic Society* (London), (Apr. 1892), pp. 259–335.

11.239. ——'Three Recent Russian Contributions to Persian Scholarship by Professor V. Zhukovski and Captain A.G. Toumanski', *Journal of the Royal Asiatic Society* (London), (1900), pp. 351–7.

11.240. Bruce, Robert. 'News of the Month: In a Letter from Dr. Bruce of Persia . . .', *The Jewish Intelligence* (London), v.6 (Aug. 1890), p. 126.

11.241. 'Brunei Special Report', *Asiaweek* (Hong Kong), v.10 no.1 (6 Jan. 1984), pp. 18–43. Bahá'í Faith, p. 32.

11.242. Bull, J. 'Portrait', *Forum* (New York), v.74 (July 1925), front cover, portrait of 'Abdu'l-Bahá.

11.243. Burns, Kathleen. 'The Sea Dayaks in the Baram', *Sarawak Gazette* (Kuching), v.92 no.1297 (Mar. 31st, 1966), pp. 97–8.

11.244. Byrnes, Hazel Webster. 'Baha'i', *Modern Maturity* (Long Beach, Calif.), (Apr.–May 1967), pp. 42–3.

C

11.245. Cali, Grace. 'Paul Tillich's Concept of Revelation in Relation to the Baha'i Faith', *The Journal of Faith and Thought* (Montclair, N.J.), v.3 no.2 (Fall 1985), pp. 3–11.

11.246. Campbell, Duncan; Walker, Steve. 'Falklands: After the War Is Over,' *New Statesman* (London), (11 June 1982).
Mentions 'some 30 members of the Baha'i religion' who refused evacuation.

11.247. Campbell, Helen. 'A New Economic Movement and Young Persia', *Twentieth Century Magazine* (Boston), (Feb. 1910), pp. 456–63.

11.248. Campbell, Myrtle W. 'Is This the New Religion?', *Fate* (Evanston, Ill.), v.1 no.4 (Winter 1949), pp. 4–15.

11.249. 'Can There Be a Universal Religion?', *World's Work* (New York), v.24 (July 1912), p. 273.

11.250. Canaday, John. ' "Vibrant Space" of Mark Tobey', *The New York Times Magazine*, (Sept. 9, 1962), pp. 64–5, 70–2. Bahá'í, p. 64.

11.251. 'Captives in Iran', *Life and Work* (Edinburgh), (Dec. 1980). 'Prayers for Iranians', letter to the editor from Iain S. Palin, (Feb. 1981), p. 6.

11.252. Carroll, Patricia. 'Jim Schoppert, Minimal Sculptor', *Alaska Journal* (Anchorage), (Spring 1979), pp. 88–91 *passim*.

11.253. Cartwright, Garth. 'Singing a New Song: Feeling the Distances', *New Zealand Woman's Weekly* (Auckland), (Nov. 25, 1985), p. 99.

11.254. Carus, Paul. 'A New Religion – Babism'. *The Open Court* (Chicago), v.18 no.6 (June 1904), pp. 355–72; v.18 no.7 (July 1904), pp. 398–420.

11.255. Cassells, Louis. 'Baha'i World Faith Sees Word of God Revealed by Special "Manifestations" ', *The Lutheran* (Philadelphia), (Apr. 24, 1968), pp. 22–3.

11.256. 'Casting and Fitting Panels for Baha'i Temple Dome Shell', *Engineering News-Record* (New York), (Oct. 13, 1932), p. 430.

11.257. 'Centennial of a Faith', *Where Magazine* (Chicago), (Oct. 25, 1952), p. 7.

11.258. Chakravartty, Nikhil. 'Inside Iran Today', *Mainstream* (New Delhi), v.19 no.6 (Oct. 11, 1980), pp. 21–33. Bahá'í Faith, p. 24.

11.259. 'A Challenge to the Bahais', *The Moslem World* (Hartford, Conn.), v.15 no.2 (Apr. 1925), pp. 191–2.

11.260. Chambala, H. Kalebe. 'Baha'i Faith: Each Individual Must Investigate the Truth Himself', *This is Malawi* (Blantyre), v.13 no.2 (Feb. 1983), pp. 22–4.

11.261. Chamupati. 'Bahaism: A Study', *The Vedic Magazine* (Lahore), v.23 no.9, whole no.193, 3rd series no.9 (Nov. 1924), pp. 561–8.

11.262. Chanler, Lewis Stuyvesant. 'Identification', *More Light* (New York), v.1 no.3 (Mar. 1930), p. 8.

11.263. —— 'The Recurrent Message', *More Light* (New York), v.1 no.2 (Feb. 1930), p. 19.

11.264. 'Chasing Technology: Editorial', *Hydroscope* (Toronto), (Nov. 23, 1984), p. 2.

11.265. Chatwin, Bruce. 'The Marvels of Patagonia', *Geo* (Los Angeles), (July 1982), pp. 58, 62–3, 66, 68–9, 113. Bahá'í Faith, pp. 63, 66.

11.266. Chaudhri, A.R. 'Bahai Doctrine of Manifestation Examined', *The Islamic Review* (London), v.32 no.5 (May 1944), pp. 160–82.

11.266a. 'Chicago Beautiful,' *Chicago Sunday Tribune Magazine* (Jan. 6, 1946), p. 15.

11.267. Child, C.W. 'The Hands of Abdul Baha', *The International Psychic Gazette* (London), v.1 no.7 (Feb. 1913), pp. 199–200.

11.268. Chopra, Hira Lal. 'Baha'ism in India', *The Panjab Past and Present*, v.x–1 (Apr. 1976), pp. 85–94.

11.269. —— *idem. University of Calcutta Post-Graduate Dept. of Islamic History & Culture Magazine*, (1965), pp. 16–26.

11.270. Christian, William Kenneth. 'The Meaning of the Temple', *Third World* (Washington, D.C.), v.1 no.1 (Apr. 1975), p. 7.

11.271. Chryssides, George D. 'Baha'i: Uniting All or One More Division?', *Reform* (London), (Sept. 1979), p. 15.

11.272. Clad, James. 'The Deadly Victory: Khomeini's Revolution Brings Pride and Purpose But No Peace', *Far Eastern Economic Review* (Hong Kong), (4 July 1985), pp. 22–5. Bahá'í Faith, p. 23.

11.273. Clawson, Patrick. 'The Bahais', *The New York Review of Books*, v.29 no.4 (Sept. 23, 1982).

11.274. Cody, Sherwin. 'An Exotic Temple for a Chicago Suburb', *New York Times Book Review and Magazine*, (Aug. 1, 1920), p. 28.

11.275. Cohen, Erik. 'The Baha'i Community of Acre', *Folklore Research Center Studies* (Jerusalem), v.3 (1972), pp. 119–41.

11.276. Colbi, Paul S. 'The Religion of the Bahai', *Holy Land Review* (Jerusalem), v.5 no.3–4 (Autumn–Winter 1979), pp. 93–6.

11.277. Cole, Juan Ricardo. 'Rashid Rida on the Baha'i Faith: A Utilitarian Theory of the Spread of Religions', *Arab Studies Quarterly* (Shrewsbury, Mass.), v.5 no.3 (Summer 1983), pp. 276–91.

11.278. Collins, Charles. 'Temple of Light', *Chicago Sunday Tribune Grafic Magazine*, (May 3, 1953), pp. 9, 12.

11.279. Collins, William P. 'It Is Time That I Should Turn to Other Memories: Sherlock Holmes and Persia, 1893', *The Baker Street Journal* (Bronx, N.Y.), v.31 no.4 (Dec. 1981), pp. 213–23. Sherlock Holmes and the Bahá'í Faith, pp. 218–23.

11.280. —— 'Of Middlebury and the Baha'is', *Middlebury College Magazine* (Middlebury, Vt.), (Winter 1984), p. 13.
A letter to the editor replying to an in memoriam for Sharon Rickey Kazemi which had failed to note her Bahá'í services.

11.281. —— 'A Short Bibliographic History of Bahá'í Periodicals', *Collector's Network News* (Madison, Wis.), v.1 no.2 (Mar.–Apr. 1977), pp. 10–12.

11.282. —— 'Thoughts on the Mormon Scriptures: An Outsider's View of the Inspiration of Joseph Smith', *Dialogue: A Journal of Mormon Thought* (Salt Lake City, Utah), v.15 no.3 (Autumn 1982), pp. 49–59.

11.283. Comay, Joan. 'Israel's Fourth Religion', *Israel Speaks* (New York), v.6 no.22 (Dec. 19, 1952), p. 12.

11.284. 'A Coming Awakening', *Light* (London), (Jan. 7, 1911), p. 5.
Report of an address by Wellesley Tudor Pole on the Bahá'í Faith.

11.285. 'Composite Foundations for Large Temple Building', *Engineering News-Record* (New York), v.91 no.21 (Nov. 22, 1923), pp. 842–3.

11.286. 'Concern Continues Over Repression in Iran', *Matchbox* (New York), (Feb. 1981), p. 3.

11.286a. 'Concerning Arts and Crafts: News Items from the World's Scrapbook', *The Illustrated London News* (London), (Dec, 29, 1934),

p. 1105. Paragraph has title: 'A Temple of Peace at Wilmette, Chicago . . .'

11.287. Consoli, John. 'New UPI Owners Refuse to Reveal Financial Sources'. *Editor & Publisher* (New York), (June 12, 1982), pp. 11, 41 *passim*.

11.288. ——'UPI Sale', *Editor & Publisher* (New York), (Jan. 1, 1983), pp. 12, 14 *passim*.

11.289. Conway, J.D. 'What Would You Like to Know About the Church?', *The Catholic Digest* (St Paul, Minn.), (Jan. 1964), pp. 124–7.
Bahá'í Faith from a Catholic viewpoint.

11.290. Cooper, Ella Goodall. 'Bahai, Peace and Understanding', *Everywoman* (San Francisco), v.10 no.3 (June 1915), pp. 8–9, 31.

11.291. —— 'Unique Congress in Interests of Peace', *Everywoman* (San Francisco), v.10 no.1 (Apr. 1915), pp. 12–13.

11.292. ——'Universal Peace: Apex Toward Which the Bahai Movement Is Progressing', *Everywoman* (San Francisco), v.10 no.2 (May 1915), pp. 4, 16.

11.293. Cooper, Margaret. 'Mission to Iran: A Refugee from the Revolution Talks to Margaret Cooper', *Homeopathy Today* (London), v.1 no.16 (Summer 1984), pp. 9–10.

11.294. Cottrell, H. 'Babism', *The Academy* (Syracuse, N.Y.), v.47 no.1192 (Mar. 9, 1895), p. 220.

11.295. *Country Time & Tide* (Montagu, Mass.). v.1 no.1 (Jan. 1902)–v.11 no.3 (Feb. 1909).
Almost every issue has a report on Green Acre, Eliot, Maine, and its Bahá'í activities.

11.296. Cousins, Norman. 'Is God a Christian?', *Saturday Review* (New York), v.42 (Feb. 28, 1959), p. 22.

11.297. —— 'Think of a Man', *Saturday Review* (New York), v.39 (Aug. 4, 1956), pp. 9–14.
Bahá'í Faith, p. 14.

11.298. Cox, Harvey. 'Religion Is Again a Potent Social Force', *U.S. News & World Report* (Washington, D.C.), v.96 no.9 (Mar. 5, 1984), pp. 47–8. Bahá'ís in Iran, p. 48

11.299. Cranmer, E.M. Paterson. 'A Universal Religion', *Occult Review* (London), (Apr. 1938), pp. 128–32.

11.300. Cranmer, Elsie. 'The Prophet Who Warned Rulers', *Magazine Digest* (Sydney, N.S.W.), v.29 no.4 (July 1955), pp. 119–22.

11.301. Crawford, Theron C. 'The School of the Prophets: A Modern Zoroaster, Being a Talk with a Prophet-Sage of Today', *Mastery* (Lon-

don), v.2 no.2 (Aug./Oct. 1915), pp. 87–95. 'Bahaist', p. 93.
Interview with Mirza Assad 'U'llah.

11.302. Crisp, Lyndall. 'Crescent Moon Under the Southern Cross: The Muslims in Australia', *The National Times* (Broadway, N.S.W.), (Aug. 30–Sept. 5, 1985), pp. 9–12. Bahá'í Faith, p. 11.

11.303. 'Cross Section', *Preservation News* (Washington, D.C.), (Aug. 1985), pp. 8–9.

11.304. Crowther, Hal. 'A Cruel Fate for a Gentle People', *Spectator Magazine* (Raleigh, N.C.), v.4 no.15 (Feb. 25–Mar. 3, 1982), pp. 1, 5.

11.305. 'Cultic Deceit Revisited', *Shocks* (Iba-dan, Nigeria), (June 1983), p. 1.

11.306. Curtis, Michael. 'Khomeini's Thoughts on Jews and Israel', *Middle East Review* (New Brunswick, N.J.), (Spring 1979), pp. 57–8.

11.307. Cuthbert, Arthur. 'Bahai Love and Unity', *The International Psychic Gazette* (London), no.17 (Dec. 1913), p. 138.

11.308. —— 'The Message of the Bahai Movement', *The International Psychic Gazette* (London), no.6 (Jan. 1913), p. 160.

11.309. ——'Nauroz, the Bahai New Year Feast', *The International Psychic Gazette* (London), no.22 (May 1914), pp. 291–2.

D

11.310. Dahl, Hilbert E. 'Bahá'í Temple Gardens: The Landscape Setting of a Unique Architectural Monument', *Landscape Architecture* (Boston), v.43 no.4 (July 1953), pp. 144–9.

11.311. Dahlin, John E. 'Bahaism', *The Discerner*, v.2 no.9 (Jan./Mar. 1958), pp. 11, 15. [Bjorling 833]

11.312. Daly, Margaret. 'The Baha'i Faith', *Interrobang P* (University of the Americas, Cholula, Puebla, Mexico), v.1 no.3 (Mar. 10, 1982).

11.313. Daragahi, Haideh. 'The Shaping of the Modern Persian Short Story: Jamalzadih's "Preface" to *Yiki Bud, Yiki Nabud*', *The Literary Review* (Teaneck, N.J.), v.18 no.1 (Fall, 1974), pp. 18–37. Bahá'í Faith, p. 27.

11.313a. Darbinian, Reuben. 'The Newly-Discovered English-Language Journals or Work Books of Reuben Darbinian,' *The Armenian Review* (Boston), v.34 no.4–136 (Dec. 1981), pp. 389–402. Bahá'ís in Boston, Mass., pp. 392–398 *passim*. 400 (n138, n141, n148).

11.314. Davies, Derek. 'Traveller's Tales', *Far Eastern Economic Review* (Hong Kong), (11 Apr. 1985), p. 33.
World Religion Day stamp of Sri Lanka and Bahá'í responsibility for it.

11.315. Davis, Kortright. 'The Bahai Faith', *Vox Collegii* (Barbados), (1972), pp. 11–13.

11.316. Day, Michael. 'A Beacon of Unity', *Tusitala*, (Autumn 1985), pp. 32–3.

11.317. De Folo, Keith. 'Baha'i, World's Newest Faith', *Afro Magazine Section* (Baltimore, Md.), (Feb. 14, 1953), pp. 1, 11.

11.318. Dean, Frederic. ' 'Abd-ul Baha Abbas Effendi: A Personal Reminiscence', *The Independent and the Weekly Review* (New York), v.107 no.3797 (Dec. 24, 1921), p. 322.

11.319. Dearmer, Percy. 'Persia and Christianity: Freedom at Last', *The Church of England Newspaper* (London), (Mar. 6, 1931), p. 9.

11.320. 'Death Cuts Short Architect's Record of Great Baha'i Project', *Wilmette Life* (Wilmette, Ill.), (Dec. 12, 1930), pp. 32–3.

11.321. 'Death Inside Khomeini's Jails', *Newsweek* (New York), (June 18, 1984), p. 57, U.S. ed.

11.322. 'Death of Abdul Baha Abbas', *Light* (London), (Dec. 3, 1921), p. 786.

11.323. 'Dedicates Temple Site in 1912', *Wilmette Life* (Wilmette, Ill.), v.26 (May 13, 1937), pp. 24, 30.

11.324. Delloff, Linda Marie. 'Religious Repression in Khomeini's Iran', *The Christian Century* (Chicago), (Aug. 13–20, 1980), pp. 786–90. Bahá'í Faith, pp. 788–9.

11.325. Demos, Jan Paul. 'A New Life for Rob and Shiva Dosenbach', *Rostland Communiqué* (Phoenix), v.1 no.2 (Winter 1984), p. 10.
Two Bahá'ís leaving the U.S. for service at the Bahá'í World Centre.

11.326. Derrett, J. Duncan M. 'St. Thomas More As a Martyr', *The Downside Review* (Bath,

Eng.), no.344 (July 1983), pp. 187–93. Bahá'í Faith, pp. 189, 191.

11.326a. Despard, C. 'Towards Unity', *The Vote* (London), v.7 no.168 (Jan. 10, 1913), p. 180. Includes portrait of 'Abdu'l-Bahá on the cover.

11.327. Devine, Jim. 'Persecution of Religious Minority: Baha'is Deprived of Their Basic Human Rights', *Sun Magazine* (Brisbane, Qld.), (Nov. 20, 1983), p. 85.

11.328. DiBuono, Natalie M. 'The Baha'i Religion: Emphasis Is on Mankind's Oneness', *The Churchman* (New York), (Mar. 1969), p. 8.

11.329. —— 'One God, One Mankind, One Religion: Precepts of the Baha'i Faith', *The Register-Leader of the Unitarian Universalist Association*, v.149 no.9 (Nov. 1967), pp. 11–14.

11.330. Dickey, C.R. 'The World Religion', *Destiny* (Haverhill, Mass.), (Nov. 1953), pp. 375–80.

11.331. 'Died, Bahiyyih Khanum', *Time* (New York), v.20 no.5 (Aug. 1, 1931), p. 33.

11.332. Diehl, Valida Davila. 'Escondido: Negro History Week in Escondido', *Negro History Bulletin* (Washington, D.C.), (Apr. 1957), pp. 156–7.

11.333. Dime, Eric Adolphus. 'Is the Millennium Upon Us?: The Bahais Claim That This Is That "Great and Terrible Day of the Lord" ', *The Forum* (New York), v.58 no.2 (Aug. 1917), pp. 167–80.

11.334. 'Disciple of a Modern Prophet: Shirin Fozdar Is an Inspiration to Followers of Baha'i in Australia', *People* (Sydney, N.S.W.), v.4 no.14 (Sept. 9, 1953), pp. 35–7.

11.335. 'Discovering Unity in Religion: Theme of the World Religion Day Meet in Saigon', *The Times of Viet-Nam Magazine* (Saigon), v.5 no.5 (Feb. 3, 196–), pp. 13–16.

11.336. Dnar, Arye. 'Bahais Love Flowers and Beauty', *Hello Israel*, (8–14 Jan. 1974), p. 33 and cover.

11.337. 'Do All Worship the Same God?', *Awake!* (Brooklyn, N.Y.), (Jan. 22, 1974), pp. 17–19, *passim*.

11.338. Dobson, J.A. 'The Strangest Religion in New York', *Broadway Magazine* (New York), (Sept. 1906), pp. 481–7.

11.339. Dodge, Arthur Pillsbury. 'The Bahai Revelation', *The Open Court* (Chicago), v.19 (1905), pp. 56–63.

11.340. Dodge, Wendell Phillips. 'Arthur Pillsbury Dodge and His Motor Car', *New Hampshire Profiles* (Concord, N.H.), (Apr. 1971), pp. 40–1, 62–[84]. Bahá'í Faith, p. [84].

11.341. Donlin, John. 'There Stands Today on the Shore of Lake Michigan . . .', *The Plasterer* (Chicago), v. 27 no.4 (Apr. 1933), pp. 39, 41.

11.341a. Donnelly, Mary Rose. 'Nuclear Issues Aired at Hearings', *The United Church Observer* (Toronto, Ont.), (Jan. 1985).

11.342. 'Dorothy Lee Hansen', *West Africa* (London), (20 Dec. 1982). *passim*.

11.343. Douglas, William O. 'Station Wagon Odyssey: Baghdad to Istanbul', *National Geographic Magazine* (Washington, D.C.), v.115 (Jan. 1959), pp. 48–89. Bahá'ís, p. 73.

11.344. Dowden, Richard. 'In the Terror of Tehran', *The New York Review of Books*, v.31 no.1 (Feb. 2, 1984), pp. 8, 10, 12. Bahá'í Faith, p. 10.

11.345. Dowson, Peter. 'Did You Know', *Grantham Team News* (Grantham, Lincs.), (Sept. 1981).

11.346. 'Dr. Kelman on Bahai Teaching', *The Christian Commonwealth* (London), (Jan. 22, 1913), p. ii.

11.347. Drazen, Daniel J. 'The Bahais, Iran's Supreme Heretics', *Liberty* (Washington, D.C.), v.76 no.6 (Nov.–Dec. 1981), pp. 16–18.

11.348. Drecksler, Addie. 'The Baha'is: Now Classed As Criminals in Iran, This Community with Century-Old Strong Ties to Israel Faces a Threat of Annihilation Which, for All the Obvious Reasons, Evokes Strong Feelings of Sympathy Among Jews', *Newsview* (Tel Aviv), v.4 no.32 (Nov. 1, 1983), pp. 18–27.

11.349. 'Drift in Iran', *The Economist* (London), v.175 no.5835 (June 25, 1955), pp. 1135–6.

11.350. Dwyer, Cynthia. 'A Plea for the Baha'is: Former Prisoner Reports Iran Persecution', *The Episcopalian* (Philadelphia, Pa.), (Apr. 1982).

E

11.351. 'Each Man to His Own Beliefs: Freedom of Religion in the Federal Republic of Germany', *Scala* (Frankfurt), Nr. 4 (1980), pp. 40–3 *passim*.

11.352. Earl, David M. 'The Bahá'í Faith and World Government', *Common Cause: A Journal of One World* (Chicago), v.4 no.2 (Sept. 1950), pp. 92–9.

11.353. Earle, Irene. 'Abbas Effendi, Called Abdul Baha . . . Leader of the Bahai Movement, Arrived in America Recently'. *The Survey* (New York), v.28 (27 Apr. 1912), pp. 178–9.

11.354. Earley, John J. 'Architectural Concrete of the Exposed Aggregate Type', *Journal of the American Concrete Institute* (Detroit, Mich.), v.5 no.4 (Mar.–Apr. 1934), pp. 251–78.
Includes section on the Wilmette Temple.

11.355. —— 'Concrete Fulfills a Promise', *Architectural Concrete* (Chicago), v. 1 no.1 (1934), pp. 4–6.
Refers to Wilmette Temple.

11.356. ——'The Project of Ornamenting the Baha'i Temple Dome', *Journal of the American Concrete Institute* (Detroit, Mich.), (June 1933), pp. 403–11.

11.356a. 'An Eastern Prophet's Message: Abdul Baha Says, "There Is No Distinction: Men and Women are Equal" ', *The Vote* (London), v.7 no.168 (Jan. 10, 1913), pp. 181–2.

11.357. Easton, Peter Z. 'The Babis of Persia', *The Missionary Review of the World* (Princeton, N.J.), v.17 (June 1894), pp. 451–3.
American Presbyterian missionary in Iran delivers a vituperative attack, describes Babism as a 'devilish, satanic system'. '. . . the Babis richly deserve all they have been called upon to suffer'.

11.357a. —— 'Bahaism, a Warning', *Evangelical Christendom* (London), (Sept./Oct. 1911), pp. 166, 186–8.

11.357b. —— 'The Message of Bahaism', *The English Churchman and St. James's Chronicle* (London), no.3587 (Sept. 28, 1911), p. 626.

11.358. —— 'Wahabiism and Babism: Bibliography', *The Missionary Review of the World* (Princeton, N.J.), v.17 (July 1894), pp. 529–30.

11.359. Ebaugh, Helen Rose Fuch; Vaughn, Sharron Lee. 'Ideology and Recruitment in Religious Groups', *Review of Religious Research* (Storrs, Conn.), v.26 no.2 (Dec. 1984), pp. 148–57. Bahá'í Faith mentioned *passim*. pp. 149–55.

11.360. ——'Life Crises Among the Religiously Committed: Do Sectarian Differences Matter?' *Journal for the Scientific Study of Religion* (Jamaica, N.Y.), v.23 no.1 (1984), pp. 19–31. Bahá'í Faith referred to throughout.

11.361. 'Edward G. Browne', *Journal of the Royal Asiatic Society* (London), (Apr. 1926), pp. 378–85.

11.362. Edwards, A. Cecil. 'The Governor', *The Atlantic Monthly* (Boston), (Sept. 1926), pp. 376–80.

11.363. Edwards, Bill. 'A Baha'i Critic', *World Federalist Newsletter* (Littlehampton, U.K.), (1985/3), pp. 12–13.

11.364. Efron, Edith. 'Seeking the Right Note: Vic Damone, Again a Summer Replacement, Is Still Hoping to Hit the Top', *TV Guide* (Philadelphia), (June 3, 1967), pp. 11–14. Bahá'í Faith, pp. 12, 14.

11.365. 'Egyptian Court Rules Baha'i Marriages Invalid', *Human Rights Internet Reporter* (Washington, D.C.), v.10 nos. 3–4 (Jan.–Apr. 1985), p. 406.

11.366. Ehmann, Werner. 'Memories of Haifa and the Baha'i in the Past and Now', *The Templer Record*, no.385 (May 1979).

11.367. Eisler, Riane. 'Technology at the Turning Point: The Blade and the Chalice', *Women's International Network News* (Lexington, Mass.), v.10 no.3 (Summer 1984), pp. 22–4. Bahá'í Faith, p. 24.

11.368. Eitner, Lorenz. 'Mark Tobey and the Romantic Tradition', *Tobey* (Basel, Switzerland), Nr. 2 (Dez. 1980), pp. [1]–[4] Bahá'í Faith: p. [1]

11.369. Elder, John S. 'The Moral and Spiritual Situation in Iran', *The Muslim World* (Hartford, Conn.), v.38 no.2 (Apr. 1948), pp. 100–12. Bahá'í Faith, pp. 107–9.
Calls Bahá'í Faith a 'dictatorship'.

11.369a. Elwell-Sutton, L.P. 'Muḥammad and the Course of Islám, by H.M. Balyuzi . . .' *Journal of the Royal Asiatic Society* (London), (1977), p. 208.
Balyuzi's book made no reference to the Bahá'í Faith and has not been listed in this bibliography. Elwell-Sutton refers to Bahá'í, however, in this review.

11.370. 'Embassy Defends Baha'i Terror', *Am-*

nesty International Newsletter (London), (Oct./ Nov. 1983), p. 30.

11.371. Ennis, Michael. 'The Shape of Things to Come', *Texas Monthly* (Austin), (Aug. 1978), pp. 140–2.

Includes discussion of proposed Bahá'í National Archives Building in Wilmette.

11.372. Enright, Robert. 'Landscapes of the Soul', *Maclean's* (Toronto), (Oct. 11, 1982), p. 71.

11.373. Erlandson, Seth. 'How Baha'i Interprets the Bible and the Last Times', *The Discerner*, v.10 no.12 (Oct./Dec. 1982), pp. 10–12. [Bjorling 835]

11.374. Ertugrul, Irene. 'The Plight of a Troubled Minority', *The Middle East* (London), (Apr. 1983), pp. 35–7.

11.375. Esslemont, John Ebenezer. 'Baha'u'llah and the New Era: The Glad Tidings', *Sanj Vartaman* (Bombay), (Sept. 1934), pp. 100m, 100o, 100q.

11.376. —— 'Is Religious Unity Impossible?': A

Plea for More Tolerance in the East', *The Illustrated Weekly of India* (Bombay), v.55 no.51 (Dec. 23, 1934), p. 87.

11.377. Esslemont, Peter. 'Wanted, Universal Language: The Story of Esperanto', *Outlook: The Voice of the Brotherhood Movement*, (Apr. 1956), pp. 3–4 *passim*.

11.378. 'The Ethnic Religions and Their Expansion', *Current Literature* (London), v.31 (July 1901), pp. 104–6. [Bjorling 513]

11.379. Evans, E.P. 'Bab and Babism', *Hours at Home* (New York), v.8 (Jan. 1869), pp. 210, 222, 292.

11.380. —— 'A New Religion', *All the Year Round* (London), v.22 (July 17, 1869), pp. 149–54.

11.381. 'Executions Commonplace', *Canadian Jewish News* (Toronto), (Aug. 27, 1981).

11.382. 'Expect 900 to Attend Convention of Baha'is', *Wilmette Life* (Wilmette, Ill.), v.37 no.52 (Apr. 28, 1949), pp. 3, 19.

F

11.382a. 'Fabricated', *Time* (New York), (Jan. 16, 1939), p. 21.

11.383. 'The Faith of Baha'i', *Pathfinder* (Chicago), v.53 no.36 (Dec. 18, 1946), p. 33.

11.384. Farhang, Mansour. 'Iran, a Great Leap Backward: Khomeini's Revolution Devours Its Children', *The Progressive* (Madison, Wis.), (Aug. 1984), pp. 19–22. Bahá'í Faith, p. 19.

11.385. —— 'Khomeini's Reign of Terror', *The Nation* (New York), (Jan. 30, 1982), pp. 108–10. Letter from John Huddleston and Farhang's reply, (Feb. 27, 1982), p. 226.

11.386. 'Father of the Trees', *Earth Garden* (Epping, N.S.W.), no.32 (Nov. 1981–Jan. 1982), pp. 6–7 *passim*.

11.387. Fentress, David Wendell. 'Baha'i', *Lehigh Review* (Bethlehem, Pa.), v.9 no.4 (Dec. 1935), pp. 6–7.

11.388. Ferdowsi, Faran. 'In Iran, a Campaign of Terror Against Baha'is', *Matchbox* (New York), (Oct. 1983), pp. 11–12.

11.389. 'Figures Show Most Executions Are Politically Related', *Amnesty International Newsletter* (London), v.12 no.4 (Apr. 1982), p. 1.

11.390. Filson, Bruce K. 'Love of Trees Fostered Battle to Save Redwoods', *Western People* (Saskatoon), (Oct. 7, 1982), pp. 10–11. Bahá'í Faith, p. 10.

11.391. —— 'Man of the Trees', *For Every Child a Tree: Information Kit* (Toronto), (Spring 1983), pp. 13–15.

11.392. —— 'The Maxwell House: Montréal Architect's Home Is Now a Baha'i Shrine', *Canadian Collector* (Toronto), v.18 no.3 (May–June 1983), pp. 18–19.

11.393. Finke, Olga. 'The Challenge of Atheism', *Orion Magazine*, (July-Aug. 1968), pp. 17–18.

11.394. 'First in U.S.A.', *Jewel* (Chicago), v.38 no.12 (Nov. 1959), pp. 4–5.

11.395. Fischel, Walter. 'The Bahai Movement and Persian Jewry', *The Jewish Review* (London), (Mar. 1934), pp. 47–55.

11.395a. —— *idem*, *India and Israel* (Bombay), v.4 no.5 (Nov. 1951), p. 27.

11.396. Fischer, Alfred Joachim. 'In the Stranglehold of Teheran's Mullah Regime', *Contemporary Review* (London), (Apr. 1984), pp. 190–2.

11.397. 'Floods in Viet Nam', *ICVA News* (Geneva, Switzerland), no.80 (Jan. 1979), pp. 49–50. Bahá'í, p. 50.

11.397a. 'Flowering of a Faith,' *ECC Concord* (Bombay), v.3 no.3 (Oct./Dec. 1980), pp. 2–6.

11.398. 'Follower of Light: A Thoughtful Milwaukeean Turns His Thoughts to the Brotherhood of Man', *Protection* (Hartford, Conn.), (Aug. 1954), pp. 8–9.
Article on Bahá'í Lawrence Hautz.

11.399. 'For a Song: Seals & Crofts Mix Music and Baha'i Faith to Earn Pennies for Heaven', *People Weekly* (New York), v.5 no.2 (Jan. 19, 1976), pp. 39–41.

11.400. Ford, Mary Hanford. 'The Bahai Movement: Baha Ollah's Exile and Stay in Akka', *The Prompter* (New York), (Dec. 1920), pp. 213–14.

11.401. —— 'The Bahai Movement: The Glorious Life of Baha Ollah', *The Prompter* (New York), (Nov. 1920), pp. 185–6.

11.402. —— 'The Bahai Movement: The Glory of God in the World', *The Prompter* (New York), (Oct. 1920), pp. 153–4.

11.403. —— 'The Significance of the Bahai Movement', *The Prompter* (New York), (Aug. 1920), p. 93.

11.404. 'Foreign Ministry Denounces Reagan Call on Baha'is', *Foreign Broadcast Information Service Daily Reports* (Washington, D.C.), (26 May 1983), section viii, p. 12.

11.405. 'A Forty-Year Phase of Wilmette History', *Wilmette Life* (Wilmette, Ill.), v.36 no.5 (June 5, 1947), p. 29.

11.406. 'The Founder of Bahaism', *Review of Reviews* (London), v.65 (Feb. 1922), p. 217.

11.407. 'The Fourth Annual Conference of the National Association for the Advancement of Colored People', *The Crisis* (New York), v.4 (June 1912).
Refers to 'Abdu'l-Bahá's talk to the conference.

11.408. '4th Humanitarian Awards of the Baha'i', *This Month in Taiwan, Republic of China* (Taipei), v.11 no.1 (Jan. 1984), p. 175.

11.409. Fozdar, Jamshed. 'The Bahai Faith', *New Outlook* (Los Angeles), (Aug. 1952), pp. 40–2.

11.410. Fozdar, John. 'The Baha'i Faith', *Sarawak Gazette* (Kuching), v.92 no.1305 (Nov. 30th, 1966).

11.411. Fozdar, Shirin. 'The Baha'i Faith in India', *The Modern Review* (Calcutta), v.133 no.1 (Jan. 1948), pp. 82–3.

11.412. —— 'The Bahai's [sic] Faith and World Peace', *Sarawak Gazette* (Kuching), v.93 no.1309 (Mar. 31st, 1967), pp. 56–7.

11.413. —— 'Qurratu'l Ayn, "Solace of the Eyes", the First Woman Suffragette', *The Illustrated Weekly of India* (Bombay), (Jan. 23, 1938), p. 50.

11.414. Frame, J. Davidson. 'Bahaism in Persia', *The Moslem World* (Hartford, Conn.), v.2 no.3 (July 1912), pp. 236–44.

11.415. Frankenberg, Naomi. 'I Love Your Little Country', *Orah* (Montreal), v.25 no.1 (Sept. 1985), pp. 21–2. Bahá'í, p. 21.

11.416. Fraser, Isabel. 'Abdul Baha on Music', *The International Pyschic Gazette* (London), no.14 (Sept. 1913), p. 39.

11.417. —— 'Christmas Day with Abdul Baha in London: Some Comments on Modern Observance', *Everywoman* (San Francisco), v.10 no.9 (Dec.–Jan. 1915–16), pp. 2–3.

11.418. Frazee, Charles. 'The Baha'is, One of the World's Newest Religions', *Catholic Near East* (New York), v.9 no.3 (Fall 1983), pp. 4–7.

11.419. Freeden, Herbert. 'Israel's Youngest Religion', *Congress Weekly* (New York), v.25 no.1 (Jan. 1958), pp. 8–9.

11.420. Frey, Dorothy A. 'Baha'is Report Successful Nationwide Negro History Week Observance', *Negro History Bulletin* (Washington, D.C.), v.21 no.1 (Oct. 1957), pp. 3–7.

11.421. 'From Allah's Earth', *The Economist* (London), (May 28, 1983), p. 61.

G

11.422. Gan-Or, Malkah. 'The Queen of Carmel', *Israelal* (Tel Aviv), (Spring 1982), pp. 14–16.

11.423. Gapp, Paul [text]; Osgood, Charles [photographs]. 'In Praise of the Great Indoors', *Chicago Tribune Magazine*, (Feb. 14, 1982), cover, pp. 10–15. Bahá'í House of Worship in

Wilmette, Ill. shown on cover, mentioned, p. 11.

11.424. 'Gemas de Sabiduria de las Escrituras Baha'i = Gems of Wisdom from the Baha'i Writings', *Alma Tica* (San José, Costa Rica), v.10 no.50 (Marzo 1942), pp. 18–20. Text in Spanish and English.

11.425. Geraci, Francine. 'An Iranian Purge of a Divergent Faith', *Maclean's* (Toronto), (July 13, 1981).

11.426. Germanus, Julius. 'Modern Movements in Islam: III, Persia', *The Visva-Bharati Quarterly* (Calcutta), v.8 (1931), pp. 74–98. Bahá'í Faith, pp. 77–98.

11.427. Ghobadian, A. 'The Denial of Human Rights in Iran', *Voice of Iran: Tribune of the National Movement of the Iranian Resistance 'NAMIR'* (London), no.19 (Nov./Dec. 1985), pp. 7–8.

11.428. Ghosh, Tirthankar. 'Persecuted for Their Faith?', *Sunday* (Calcutta), v.9 no.10 (Aug. 23, 1981), p. 43.

11.429. Giles, Diane. 'Keeping the Faith: A Historical Perspective', *The Midweek Bulletin* (Kenosha, Wis.), (July 31, 1984), (Aug. 7, 1984).

11.430. Gill, Sylvia. 'Her Royal Highness, the Doctor', *Fair Lady* (South Africa), (June 2, 1982), pp. 60–4, 66, 222–4.

11.431. Gilman, Jayne. 'One God, Many Faiths', *She* (London), (May 1984), pp. 100–101.

11.432. Gittings, James A. 'It's Still Dangerous to Believe', *A.D.* (New York), v.11 no.4 (Apr. 1982), pp. 14–16. Bahá'í Faith, p. 14.

11.433. 'The Glitter of Bahaism', *The Literary Digest* (New York), v.71 (Dec. 24, 1921), p. 30.

11.434. Glueck, Nelson. 'An Archeologist Looks at Palestine', *National Geographic Magazine* (Washington, D.C.), v.92 (Dec. 1947), pp. 739–52. Bahá'í Faith, p. 745.

11.435. Goering, Curt. 'The Baha'is of Iran: Persecution Is Government Policy', *Matchbox* (New York), (Nov. 1981), pp. 1, 5.

11.436. Goff, Victoria. 'Persecution in Iran', *Worldview* (New York), v.25 no.3 (Mar. 1982), pp. 11–12.

11.437. 'Gold Domed Shrine on Mt. Carmel Is Center of World-Wide Baha'i Faith', *Zim Lines Bulletin*, v.1 no.8 (Sept. 1955), pp. 1, 4.

11.438. Gopaul, V.S. 'The Earth Is But One Country and Mankind Its Citizens', *Journal of the University of Mauritius*, nos. 10 & 11 (July–Dec. 1981), pp. 1–4.

11.439. Gordon, T. Crouther. 'Bahaism and Christianity', *Expository Times* (Aberdeen; Edinburgh), (Apr. 1927), pp. 325–8.

11.439a. Gott, Francis. 'Bahá'í', *Newsweek* (New York), (June 15, 1953), p. 1.
Letter to the editor.

11.440. Gous, Fatimah. 'A Champion of Women's Rights', *Today* (Singapore), v.1 no.13 (Oct. 28, 1984), p. 11.

11.440a. 'Govt Takes Over Takuba Lodge', *Catholic Standard* (Georgetown, Guyana), v.81 no.23 (June 12, 1983). Mentions 'National Spiritual Assembly of Bahá'ís'.

11.441. 'Gramophile: Norman Bailey', *Hi-Fi News & Record Review* (Croydon, U.K.), (Sept. 1976), p. 100.

11.442. 'Gramophile: Norman Bailey', *Hi-Fi News & Record Review* (Croydon, U.K.), (Nov. 1979), p. 127.

11.443. 'Grand Match – the Two New Forces in the World', *Oomoto: Gazeto Esperanta* (Ayabe, Japan), unua jaro (Apr. 1925), pp. 31–6.
Bahá'í Faith and the Esperanto movement.

11.444. 'The Great Master: The Personality', *World Peace Through Spiritual Regeneration* (Calcutta), v.2 no.16–17 (Jan. 1 & 16, 1937), pp. 310–14.

11.445. Gregory, Louis G. 'The Baha'i Movement', *The Independent* (New York), v.72 (Apr. 11, 1912), pp. 770–2.

11.446. Grey, Hilary. 'The Brotherhood', *The American Mercury* (New York), (Mar. 1958), pp. 35–40. Bahá'í Faith, p. 35.
Claims that the Bahá'í Faith is part of a communist plot. Response in the Oct. 1958 issue by Grace Healley [i.e. Horace Holley] on behalf of the National Spiritual Assembly of the Bahá'ís of the United States.

11.447. Griffin, Lepel. 'Russia, Persia and England', *The Nineteenth Century* (London), v.41 no.233 (July 1896), pp. 1–18. Bábís, pp. 6–7.

11.448. 'Grim Toll of Executions in Iran', *Canadian Churchman* (Toronto), v.107 no.8 (Oct. 1981).

11.449. Gross, Jonathan. 'Meaningful Video', *Starweek* (Toronto), (July 20, 1985).

11.449a. Grossmann, Hermann. 'A Bahist's [sic] View of the W.R.I.', *The War Register* (Enfield, Middlesex, Eng.), no.16 (May 1927), p. 2.

11.450. Guardian in Chief (Halcyon Temple).

'The Behai', *The Temple Artisan* (Halcyon, Calif.), v.9 no.12 (May 1909), pp. 221–3.

11.451. Gulick, Robert L. 'Possible Economic Depression', *World Affairs Interpreter* (Los Angeles), v.18 no.4 (Winter 1948), pp. 361–6. Bahá'í Faith, p. 366.

H

11.452. Habibi, Ramin. 'Iran' [letter to the editor], *The Economist* (London), v.292 no.7359 (Sept. 15, 1984), p. 5.

11.453. Hackett, W.D.B. 'This New Faith Offers a New World Order', *Saturday Night* (Toronto), (Dec. 8, 1945), p. 31.

11.454. 'Haifa, Centre of the Bahai Faith', *Skyways* (Johannesburg, S. Afr.), (Oct. 1972).

11.455. Hainsworth, Philip. 'The Bahá'í Faith: What Is It?', *Contact* (U.K.), no.5 (Oct. 1975), p. 3.

11.456. Halliday, Fred. 'The Coalition Against the Shah', *New Statesman* (London), (Jan. 5, 1979), pp. 4–6. Bahá'í Faith, p. 5.

11.457. —— 'Inside the Iranian Opposition', *The Nation* (New York), (Sept. 26, 1981), pp. 257, 274–6. Bahá'í Faith, p. 275.

11.458. —— 'Lunch with Mohammed', *New Statesman* (London), (27 Jan. 1984), pp. 16–17. Bahá'í Faith, p. 17.

11.459. 'Hanging Heretics', *The Economist* (London), (June 25, 1983), p. 51.

11.460. 'Hanging On by Digging In', *The Economist* (London), (Sept. 23, 1978), pp. 83–4. Bahá'í Faith, p. 83.

11.461. Hansell, William H. 'The Spiritual Unity of Robert Hayden's Angle of Ascent', *Black American Literature Forum* (Terre Haute, Ind.), v.13 no.1 (Spring 1979), pp. 24–31. Bahá'í, pp. 24, 25, 27.

11.462. Haque, Serajul. 'Bahaiism, a Neo-Crusade', *The Islamic Times* (Dhaka, Bangladesh), v.3 no.14 (June 1984), pp. 5–7, 9–10, 30.

11.463. Hardcastle, Bruce. 'A Death in Tehran: More Adventures in Iranian Diplomacy', *The New Republic* (Washington, D.C.), (Dec. 29, 1979), pp. 10–12.

11.464. Hare, William Loftus. 'A Parliament of Living Religions: Some Modern Movements: The Bahai Cause', *The Open Court* (Chicago), v.38 no.12 (Dec. 1924), pp. 735–7.

11.465. Harris, Lisa. 'Artist Shares Canvas Concepts', *This Week on Okinawa*, (Oct. 20–27, 1985), pp. 3–5. Bahá'í Faith, p. 3.

11.466. 'Has Iran Moderated Its Treatment of Baha'is?', *Human Rights Internet Reporter* (Washington, D.C.), v.10 no.5 (May–Aug. 1985), p. 714.

11.467. 'Has Man Need of a Prophet?', *More Light* (New York), [v.1 no.1?] ([Jan. 1930?]), pp. 6–8.

11.468. Hashimi, Abdul Quddus. 'No. 19 Theory on the Qur'an Aids and Advances the Cause of Bahaism', *The Muslim Digest* (Durban, S. Afr.), (July–Aug. 1981), pp. 137–41.
Attacks tracts which show the Qur'an to be based on the number 19, as this 'plays into' the hands of the Bahá'ís.

11.469. Hashma Tullah, Mirza. 'Farewell Meeting to Mirza Ali Akbar', *The International Psychic Gazette* (London), no.18 (Jan. 1914), p. 177.

11.470. Hassall, Graham. 'Persecution of a Minority in Iran', *Union Recorder* (Sydney, N.S.W.), v.62 no.9 (28 June 1982), pp. 11, 14.

11.471. Hatcher, William S. 'A Logical Solution to the Problem of Evil', *Zygon: A Journal of Religion and Science* (Winter Park, Fla.), v.9 no.3 (Sept. 1974), pp. 245–55.

11.472. ——'Science and the Bahá'í Faith', *Zygon: A Journal of Religion and Science* (Winter Park, Fla.), v.14 no.3 (Sept. 1979), pp. 229–53.

11.473. Hauser, Ernest O. 'Can He Hold Back the Red Tide?', *Saturday Evening Post* (Philadelphia, Pa.), v.228 (Sept. 3, 1955), pp. 28–9, 70–2. Bahá'í Faith, p. 71.

11.474. Haweis, H.R. 'Talk with a Persian Statesman', *Contemporary Review* (London), v.70 (1896), pp. 73–7.

11.475. Heath, Terrance. 'The Cosmic Landscapes of Otto Rogers', *Artscanada* (Toronto), v.30 no.1, issue nos. 176–7 (Feb./Mar. 1973), pp. 28–33. Bahá'í, p. 32.

11.476. Hein, Kurt. 'Community Radio in Ecuador Meeting People's Needs', *Development*

Communication Report (Washington, D.C.), no.42 (June 1983).

11.477. —— 'Community Radio in Ecuador Playing Local Music, Strengthening Cultural Ties', *Development Communication Report* (Washington, D.C.), no.44 (Dec. 1983), p. [2].

11.478. —— 'Community Radio Thriving in Ecuador: Otavalo Indians Running Their Own Show', *Development Communication Report* (Washington, D.C.), no.40 (Dec. 1982), pp. 11, 13.
Description of Radio Bahá'í of Otavalo, Ecuador.

11.479. —— 'Popular Participation in Rural Radio: Radio Baha'i Otavalo, Ecuador', *Studies in Latin American Popular Culture*, v.3 (1984), pp. 97–104.

11.480. Henry, William A. 'Sometimes First, Always Second: Can U.P.I. the Avis of Wire Services, Keep Its Motor Running?', *Time* (New York), (Sept. 12, 1980), p. 60.

11.481. 'Heralds of the Saviour', *World Peace Through Spiritual Regeneration* (Calcutta), v.2 no.16–17 (Jan. 1 & 16, 1937), pp. 314–17.
Describes Bahá'í Central Figures as Heralds of the 'saviour' Dayananda.

11.482. 'Heretics in Islam', *Time* (New York), v.65 (June 6, 1955), pp. 40–1. [European edition?]

11.483. *idem.*, *Time* (New York), v.65 (June 6, 1955), p. 68.

11.484. Herrick, Elizabeth. 'Abdul Baha and Universal Peace', *The Super-Man and Psychic Monitor* (London), v.2 no.1 (Dec. 1921), pp. 15–16.

11.485. —— 'The Bahai Dispensation and the Coming of the Kingdom of God', *The Super-Man* (London), v.3 no.3 (Apr. 1922), pp. 31–2.

11.486. —— 'The Bahai Dispensation Is the Light of God's New Day', *The Super-Man* (London), (July/Aug. 1922), pp. 79–80.

11.487. —— 'The Feast of Rizwan: Its History and Its Celebration in London', *The International Psychic Gazette* (London), no.10 (May 1913), p. 301.

11.488. Hierseman, Judy. 'Baha'is Stress Unity, Service to Others', *Now: Green Bay Press-Gazette* (Green Bay, Wis.), (Oct. 14, 1979), pp. N1–N3, N7. Cover title: 'The Baha'is, Who Are They?'

11.489. Hift, Fred. 'Her Faith Fills Her Life: This Canadian Architect's Daughter Is Devoted to Her Work, Spreading the Beliefs of Baha'i',

Weekend Magazine (Montreal), v.11 no.31 (1961), pp. 10–11.

11.490. 'Highlighting Haifa', *This Week in Israel* (Tel Aviv), (May 27–June 2, 1982), p. 79.

11.491. 'The Hojjatiyeh Society: Its History, Advocates and Opponents', *Iran Press Digest* (Tehran), (28.9.1982), pp. 19–21; (5.10.1982), pp. 15–18; (12.10.1982), pp. 16–20; (26.10.1982), pp. 15–18; (2.11.1982), pp. 16–18.

11.492. Holbach, Maude M. 'The Bahai Movement, with Some Recollections of Meetings with Abdul Baha', *The Nineteenth Century Review* (London), v.77 (Feb. 1915), pp. 452–66.

11.493. 'Holier Than Khomeini', *The Economist* (London), v.286 no.7277 (Feb. 19, 1983), pp. 50, 53.

11.494. Holley, Horace. 'Abdul Baha', *Unity* (Chicago), v.88 no.15 (Dec. 22, 1921), pp. 232–3.

11.495. —— 'Aims and Purposes of the Baha'i Faith', *Sanj Vartaman* (Bombay), (Sept. 1935), pp. 107, 109.

11.496. —— 'The Bahá'í Faith', *Unity* (Chicago), v.112 no.13 (Feb. 19, 1934), pp. 214–17.

11.497. —— 'Education for World Order: The Story of the Bahá'í Faith', *Women, Inc.*, (Chicago), (Mar. 1936), pp. 30–6.

11.498. —— 'A Torchbearer of Unity: The Mind of Abdu'l-Baha', *The New Orient* (New York), v.3 no.1 (Dec. 1925), pp. 1–8.

11.499. —— 'The World Issue of Race', *The Crisis* (New York), v.43 no.7 (July 1936), p. 204.

11.500. Hollingsworth, Kim. 'My Calamity Is My Providence: The Faith and Sufferings of Iran's Baha'is', *Fellowship in Prayer* (Lawrenceville, Kan.), v.36 no.4 (Aug./Sept. 1985), pp. 3–7.

11.501. Holmes, John Haynes. 'Abdul Baha', *Unity* (Chicago), v.88 no.14 (Dec. 15, 1921), pp. 215–16.

11.502. 'The Holy Man of Baha'i', *Search* (Amherst, Mass.), (Dec. 1960).

11.503. Homayun, Sirus. 'The Baha'i Faith in Iran', *Mini-World* (Paramaribo), (Nov.–Dec. 1981), p. 17.

11.504. Hopkins, A.A. 'Exotic Temples for Our Two Greatest Cities', *Scientific American* (New York), v.123 no.7 (Aug. 14, 1920), p. 159.

11.505. Hosain, M. Hidayat, 'Edward Granville Browne (1862–1926)', *Asiatic Society of Bengal Journal* (Calcutta), v.NS23 (1927), pp. clxv–clxxi. Bahá'í Faith, p. clxvii.

11.506. Howard, Mike. 'The Tears of the Bahais', *The Plain Dealer Magazine* (Cleveland, Ohio), (Aug. 25, 1985), pp. 6–8, 11–12, 21, 23.

11.507. Hubbard, Elbert. 'Modern Prophet', *Hearst's Magazine* (New York), v.22 (July 1912), pp. 49–51.

11.508. Huddleston, John. 'Bahai', *The Economist* (London), (Oct. 14, 1978).

11.509. —— 'Pebble to Start a Landslide?', *Development/International Development Review* (Rome), v.22 no.1 (Feb. 1980).

11.510. Hughes, Barry Conn. '21 Ways to Find God', *Canadian Magazine* (Toronto), (Aug. 5, 1972), pp. 2–4, 6.

11.511. 'Human Rights Abuses in Iran', *Human Rights Internet Reporter* (Washington, D.C.), v.10 no.1–2 (Sept.–Dec. 1984), pp. 146–7.

11.512. 'Human Rights Caucus Fights for Freedoms', *Congressman Porter's Washington Report*, v.4 no.2 (Fall 1983).

11.513. 'Humanity Resurgent', *Health News* (Hollywood, Calif.), v.9 no.7 (Apr. 11, 1941), pp. 1, 15.

11.514. Hunton, Maryellen Rogers. 'A Temple for You and Me: And Yet Another Historical Narrative', *Suburban Home* (Evanston, Ill.), v.1 no.5 (Apr. 15, 1932), pp. 21, 38.

I

11.515. 'Illinois', *TWA Ambassador* (New York), (Summer 1961), p. 19.

11.516. 'Illinois in 1953', comp. James N. Adams, *Journal of the Illinois State Historical Society*, v.47 (Spring 1954), pp. 71–83. Bahá'í Faith, p. 76.

11.517. 'Ilona Rodgers: Baha'i', *New Idea* (Melbourne, Vic.), no.10 (2 Oct. 1982).

11.518. 'In an Oriental Mosque', *The Christian Commonwealth* (London), (Jan. 22, 1913), p. ii.

11.518a. 'In Holy Land', *Wilmette Life* (Wilmette, Ill.), v.43 no.16 (Aug. 19, 1954), pp. 4, 44.

11.519. 'In Iran, New Threats to the Baha'i', *Human Rights Internet Reporter* (Washington, D.C.), no.122 (Sept.–Nov. 1983), p. 247.

11.520. 'In Memoriam: The Tragic Death of Dr. Daniel C. Jordan in Connecticut', *International Journal of Peace and Prejudice Research* (Nürnberg), v.1 no.1 (July 1983), pp. 41–6.

11.521. 'In 1907, Long Before the Birth of Communism, a Holy Seer Abdul Baha Talked About the Payment of Bonus, the Establishment of Industrial Courts and Insurance for the Worker', *The Bitter Humour Fortnightly* (Bombay), v.1 no.1 (Oct. 20, 1953), pp. 4, 6.

11.522. 'In Our Country, These Women Would Have Been Honoured for Their Contribution to Society . . .: In Their Country, They Were Killed', *Time* (Montreal), (July 18, 1983).

11.523. 'In the Hands of the Hands', *Time* (New York), v.70 no.24 (Dec. 9, 1957), pp. 87–8.

11.524. 'In the News', *Secretariat News* (New York), (14 Sept. 1979), p. 3.
Bahá'í International Community activities reported.

11.525. 'Independent Frames Support Exterior and Interior Surfaces of Temple Dome', *Engineering News-Record* (New York), (Jan. 8, 1931), pp. 75–6.

11.526. 'Insured for More than Twenty Years', *The Saint Paul Letter* (St Paul, Minn.), (Aug. 1953), pp. 7, 6, 23.

11.526a. International Bahá'í Council. 'Baha'is Praise Religious Freedom in Israel', *India and Israel* (Bombay), v.4 no.1 (July 1951), p. 23.

11.527. International Conference on Religious Liberty (1985: Washington, D.C.). 'International Conference on Religious Liberty', *World Affairs* (Washington, D.C.), v.147 no.4 (Spring 1985), pp. 235–313. Bahá'í Faith, pp. 238, 242, 243–6, 307, 312.

11.528. 'International Youth Camp in GRI', *GRI News* (Gandhigram, India), v.12 no.7 (Sept. 1985), pp. 7–10. Bahá'í Faith, p. 7.

11.529. 'An Interview', *Burma Patriot* (Mandalay), (6 July 1927), pp. 7–9.
Interview with Munír Nabíl Zádih about the Bahá'í Faith. In English and Burmese.

11.530. 'Intolerance for the Tolerant', *The Economist* (London), (Sept. 13, 1980).

11.531. Ion. 'Abdul Baha, Teachings of Bahaism, Unity of All Religions, Universal Peace: Interview with Abbas Effendi, "the Servant of

God" ', *The Scots Pictorial* (Glasgow), (Jan. 18, 1913), p. 335.

11.532. 'Iran', *Human Rights Internet Reporter* (Washington, D.C.), (Mar.–May 1982), pp. 763–5.

11.533. 'Iran', *Human Rights Internet Reporter* (Washington, D.C.), v.8 no.2–3 (Dec. 1982–Mar. 1983), pp. 302–3.

11.534. 'Iran', *Index on Censorship* (London), (March 1985), p. 50.

11.535. 'Iran, a Respite from the Agony?', *The Nation* (New York), (Apr. 17, 1982), p. 455.

11.536. 'Iran, an Epidemic of Fear Among the Expatriates', *Business Week* (New York), (Dec. 11, 1978), pp. 71–2.

11.537. 'Iran, Baha'i Persecution', *Human Rights Internet Reporter* (Washington, D.C.), v.7 no.2 (Nov.–Dec. 1981), p. 423.

11.538. 'Iran, Baha'i Persecution Continues', *Amnesty Action* (New York), (Apr. 1984), p. 8.

11.539. 'Iran, Clerical Fascism Ahead?', *Church & State* (Silver Spring, Md.), v.32 no.2 (Feb. 1979), pp. 3, 6–7.

11.540. 'Iran Declares War on Infidels', *The Forthright Review* (Toronto), v.1 (Apr. 1984), p. 4.

11.541. 'Iran Envoy Denounces "Imperialist Myth of Human Rights" ', *Amnesty International Newsletter* (London), (Sept. 1982), p. 7.

11.542. 'Iran, Execution of Baha'i Members', *Human Rights Perspective* (New York), (Spring 1983), p. 4.

11.543. 'Iran: Executions of Baha'is Continue, Another 22 Executed', *Amnesty* (London), (June-July 1983), p. 29.

11.544. 'Iran, Execution Toll Over 4,400: Many Shot in Secret', *Amnesty International Newsletter* (London), v.12 no.7 (July 1982), p. 6.

11.545. 'Iran, Human Rights Reports', *Human Rights Bulletin* (Geneva, Switzerland), v.4 no.1 (July 1985), p. 22.

11.546. 'Iran: Kurds, Baha'is Hanged', *Amnesty International Newsletter* (London), v.13 no.8 (Aug. 1983), pp. 1, 6.

11.547. *Iran Newsletter* (Hong Kong), no.44 (Sept. 25, 1981), pp. 7–8.
Letter responding to a Hong Kong television programme on the Faith.

11.548. *idem.*, no.51 (Mar. 16, 1982), pp. 4–5.

11.549. *Iran Press Service* (London), no.1 (Jan. 1981)– . Numerous references to the Faith in each issue.

11.550. 'Iran Seeks to Suppress Baha'i Faith', *The Christian Century* (Chicago), v.72 (June 8, 1955), p. 677.

11.551. 'Iran Solidarity', *Human Rights Network Newsletter* (London), no.3, p. 5.

11.552. 'Iranian Authorities Are Continuing a Drive to Decimate Bahais', *Christianity Today* (Carol Stream, Ill.), (June 17, 1983).

11.553. 'Iranian Exiles Take French Leave', *U.S. News & World Report* (Washington, D.C.), (July 18, 1983), p. 9.

11.554. 'Iranian Lawyers Linked to Baha'i Community', *American Bar Association Network for Concerned Correspondents* (Washington, D.C.), (Nov. 1983), pp. 1–2.

11.555. 'Iranians Executed After Unfair Trials', *Amnesty International Newsletter* (Sydney, N.S.W.), (June 1980), p. 12.

11.555a. 'Iran's Secret Detention Centers: Sites of Torture, Mock Executions, Killings', *Amnesty Action* (New York), (Apr. 1985), pp. 1, 3.

11.556. 'IRNA Criticizes U.S. "Propaganda Tirade" on Baha'i', *Foreign Broadcast Information Service Daily Reports* (Washington, D.C.), (27 May 1983), section viii, pp. 11–12.

11.557. Irwin, Beatrice. 'The Bahai Movement', *Occult Review* (London), (1913), pp. 280–6.

11.558. 'Is Baha'i a Religion?', *Psychic Digest* (Toronto), v.1 no.1, p. 4.

11.559. Iseman, Frederick. 'Canons of the Cool: Robert Farris Thompson Was Destined to Become Another Stuffy Yale Intellectual – Until He Danced the Mambo', *Rolling Stone* (New York), (Nov. 22, 1984), pp. 23, 27–8, 81. Bahá'í Faith, p. 28.

11.560. Ishaque, M. 'Qurratu'l-'Ayn, a Babi Martyr', *Indo-Iranica* (Calcutta), v.3 no.1 (July 1948/9), pp. 1–8.

11.561. 'Israel, Sun and Fun', *Travel Bulletin Israel Travel Guide*, (1985/86), p. 14.

11.562. Issa, H. 'The Religion of Love', *The North Pointer Annual Magazine* (Darjeeling), (1983), pp. 49–50.

11.563. 'It Couldn't Be Done Today', *Concrete Quarterly* (Wexham Springs, Slough, Bucks.), (Apr. 1981), pp. 20–2.

11.564. Iyer, Pico. ' A Fever Bordering on Hysteria: After Five Years, Khomeini Still Seems in Full Control of Iran's Revolution', *Time* (New York), v.123 no.11 (12 Mar. 1984), pp. 36–9. Bahá'í Faith, p. 37.

J

11.565. Jacobs, Janet. 'The Economy of Love in Religious Commitment: The Deconversion of Women from Non-Traditional Religious Movements', *Journal for the Scientific Study of Religions* (Jamaica, N.Y.), v.23 no.2 (1984), pp. 155–71. Bahá'í Faith, pp. 159, 165.

11.566. Jahanpour, Ruhiyyih. 'Refusal to Give Up Her Faith Led to Imprisonment, Torture and Exile for an Iranian Baha'i', *People Weekly* (New York), v.23 no.11 (Sept. 1985), pp. 99–100, 102, 104.

11.567. Janner, Greville. 'Freedom of Speech', *New Life* (London), (16 Sept. 1983).

11.568. Javadi, Hasan, 'E.G. Browne and the Persian Constitutional Movement', *Iran: Journal of Persian Studies* (London), (1976), pp. 133–40. Bahá'í Faith, pp. 134–5.

11.569. Javid, Manucher J. 'Nursing Prescription', *The University of Wisconsin Nurse's Alumnae Bulletin* (Madison), (Nov. 1957), pp. 29–36. Quotations from Bahá'í Writings, pp. 34–6.

11.570. —— 'A Tale of Two Drugs: Urea and Chymopapain', *Neurosurgery* (Baltimore, Md.), v.13 no.2 (1983), pp. 211–13. Bahá'í Faith, p. 211.

11.571. Jawanmordi, Faridoon. 'The World-Religion', *Mira* [East & West] (Hyderabad), v.6 no.3–4 (June-July 1940), pp. 937–8, frontispiece, back cover.

11.572. Jeffery, Arthur. 'Geschichte der Behai-Bewegung, von Sydney Sprague' [review], *The Moslem World* (Hartford, Conn.), v.13 no.1 (Jan. 1923), p. 107.

11.573. —— 'Shoghi Effendi, das Hindscheiden Abdul-Bahas, von Sitarih Khanum' [review], *The Moslem World* (Hartford, Conn.), v.14 no.2 (Apr. 1924), p. 209.

11.573a. 'Jenabe Fazel Mazandarini [sic]', *Independent Protestant Church News* (Columbus, Ohio), v.11 no.14 (May 1923), pp. 1–2.

11.574. Jessup, Henry Harris. 'Babism and the Babites', *The Missionary Review of the World* (Princeton, N.J.), v.25 (Oct. 1902), pp. 771–5.

11.575. —— 'The Babites', *The Outlook* (London), v.68 (22 June 1901), pp. 451–6.

11.576. Johnson, Harold. 'Bahaism, the Birth of a World Religion', *Contemporary Review* (London), v.101 (Mar. 1912), pp. 391–402.

11.577. Johnson, Pat O'Malley. 'More Tragedies for Iran Baha'is', *The Forum* (Wichita, Kan.), (Sept. 1981).

11.578. Johnston, C. 'Ray from the East: Bahaism, a World Religion', *Harper's Weekly* (New York), v.56 (July 20, 1912), p. 9.

11.579. Jones, J.L.T.E. 'Bahaism – a Movement of Great Future Significance', *The Congregational Quarterly* (London), (July 1929), pp. 352–6.

11.580. Jones, Jenkin Lloyd. 'The Bahai Movement: A Free Religious Movement in the East', *Unity* (Chicago), v.79 no.25 (Feb. 28, 1918), pp. 410–14.

11.581. 'Just a Trouble-Shooter Now', *The Michigan Alumnus* (Ann Arbor). (Nov. 16, 1957), pp. 73–5. Bahá'í Faith, p. 75. About Charles Wolcott.

K

11.582. K., B. 'A Tobey Profile', *Art Digest* (New York), v.26 no.2 (Oct. 15, 1951), pp. 5, 26, 34. Bahá'í Faith, p. 26.

11.582a. Kalbag, Chaitanya. 'Iran, towards Islamic Medievalism?', *New Delhi*, (2 Apr. 1979), pp. 85–6. Bahá'í, p. 85.

11.583. Kale, Bhanu. 'Baha'is in Iran Face Persecution', *Himmat* (Bombay), (8 Aug. 1980).

11.584. Kang, Wi Jo. 'The Influence of Eastern Religions in America', *Currents in Theology and Mission* (St Louis, Mo.), (Aug. 1976), pp. 228–33. Bahá'í, pp. 232–3.

11.585. Kapsch, Richard J. 'Baha'i Shrine and Garden in Israel', *Travel & Leisure* (New York), (June 1984), p. 198.

11.585a. Katzander, Howard L. 'The Marvelous Mottahedeh Mark', *Town and Country* (New York), v.135 no.5017 (Sept. 1981), pp. 245–6. Bahá'í, p. 245.

11.586. Kazemi, Farhad. 'Some Preliminary

Observations on the Early Development of Babism', *The Muslim World* (Hartford, Conn.), v.53 no.2 (Apr. 1977), pp. 119–31.

11.587. Kazemzadeh, Firuz. 'Attack on the Bahais: The Persecution of the "Infidels" ', *The New Republic* (Washington, D.C.), (June 16, 1982), pp. 16–18.

11.588. —— 'Morocco's Little Inquisition: The Campaign Against Bahai', *New Leader* (New York), v.46 (29 Apr. 1963), pp. 11–12.

11.589. —— 'Plight of the Bahá'ís', *Freedom at Issue* (New York), no.78 (May/June 1984), pp. 30, back cover.

11.590. —— 'The Terror Facing the Bahais', *The New York Review of Books*, v.29 no.8 (May 13, 1982), pp. 43–4.

11.591. Keddie, Nikki R. 'Culture Traits, Fantasy, and Reality in the Life of Sayyid Jamal al-Din al-Afghani', *Iranian Studies* (New York), v.9 no.2–3 (Spring-Summer 1976), pp. 89–120. Bahá'í Faith, p. 100.

11.592. —— 'Iranian Politics 1900–1905: Background to Revolution', *Journal of Middle Eastern Studies* (London), v.5 (1969), pp. 3–31, 151–67, 234–50. Bahá'í Faith, pp. 153, 157, 162, 164, 242.

11.593. —— 'Is There a Middle East?', *International Journal of Middle East Studies* (New York), v.4 (1973), pp. 255–71. Bahá'í Faith, p. 267.

11.594. —— 'The Origins of the Religious-Radical Alliance in Iran', *Past and Present* (Oxford, U.K.), no.34 (July 1966), pp. 70–80. Azalí Bábís, p. 77.

11.595. —— 'The Pan-Islamic Appeal: Afghani and Abdülhamid II', *Middle Eastern Studies* (London), v.3 no.1 (Oct. 1966), pp. 46–67. Bábís, p. 64.

11.596. —— 'Religion and Irreligion in Early Iranian Nationalism', *Comparative Studies in Society and History* (Cambridge, U.K.), v.4 no.3 (1962), pp. 265–95. Bahá'í Faith, pp. 267–74, 277–9, 284–6.

11.597. —— 'Sayyid Jamal al-Din al Afghani's First Twenty-Seven Years: The Darkest Period', *Middle East Journal* (Washington, D.C.), v.20 no.4 (Autumn 1966), pp. 517–33. Bahá'í Faith, pp. 524–5.

11.598. —— 'The Tradition of Tyranny', *Times Literary Supplement* (London), (3 Dec. 1982), pp. 3–4. Azalí Bábís, p. 4 col. 3.

11.599. Keene, James J. 'Bahai World Faith: Redefinition of Religion', *Journal for the Scientific Study of Religion* (Jamaica, N.Y.), v.6 (fall 1967), pp. 221–35.

11.600. —— 'Religious Behavior and Neuroticism, Spontaneity, and Worldmindedness', *Sociometry* (Albany, N.Y.), v.30 no.2 (1967), pp. 137–57.

11.601. Kelsey, Curtis D. 'On the Bahai Faith', *Bergen Evening Record Week-end Magazine Section* (Hackensack, N.J.), (July 14, 1956), p. 5.

11.602. Kerridge, Roy. 'The Ulster Gospel', *New Society* (London), (24 Jan. 1985), pp. 137–8. Bahá'í Faith, p. 138.

11.603. Khan, Peter. 'The Baha'i Faith', *Witness* (Sydney, N.S.W.), v.68 no.3 (Mar. 1959), pp. 6–8.

11.604. Khan Bahadur Agha Mirza Muhammad. 'Some New Notes on Babiism', *Journal of the Royal Asiatic Society* (London), (July 1927), pp. 442–70.

11.605. Khavary, Morad. 'Iran', *The Economist* (London), (13 Oct. 1984).

11.606. Kheiralla, Ibrahim G. 'Behaism, In Reply to the Attack of Robert P. Richardson', *The Open Court* (Chicago), v.29 no.10 (Oct. 1915), pp. 633–40.

11.607. —— 'Behaism Is the Nucleus of All Religions', *The Occult Truth Seeker* (Lawrence, Kan.), v.2 no.3–4 (Aug.–Sept. 1902), pp. 56–62.

11.608. —— 'The Immortality of the Soul and Its Condition After Death', *The Occult Truth Seeker* (Enterprise, Kan.), v.2 no.12 (May 1903), pp. 260–3.

11.609. —— 'A Letter from the American Representative of Behaism', *The Open Court* (Chicago), (June 1904), pp. 374–6.

11.610. Khomeini, Ruhu'llah. 'Khomeini 28 May Speech on Baha'is, Tudeh Party', *Foreign Broadcast Information Service Daily Reports* (Washington, D.C.), (31 May 1983), section viii, pp. 11–12.

11.611. King, Sylvia. 'Symbolism and the Humanities', *Canadian Geographical Journal*, v.28 no.3 (Mar. 1944), pp. 146–9. About the Wilmette Temple.

11.612. Kirchner, Mrs Albert. 'A Bahaist Protest', *The Open Court* (Chicago), (Nov. 1915), pp. 702–3.

11.613. Kristol, Irving. 'The Common Sense of Human Rights', *Span* (India), (Sept. 1981), pp. 2–3. Bahá'í Faith, p. 3.

11.614. 'Kurds and Baha'is Executed', *Amnesty* (London), (Aug.-Sept. 1983), p. 3.

L

11.615. Labaree, Robert M. 'The Bahai Propaganda in America', *The Missionary Review of the World* (Princeton, N.J.), v.42 no.8 (Aug. 1919), pp. 591–6.

11.616. Lacy, Edward. 'Baha'is, Poisoners of the Racial Soul: Another Levantine Messiah Aims for White Moral Disarmament', *National Vanguard* (Washington, D.C.), (Aug. 1981).

11.616a. Lacy, Edward A. 'A Bahai Writes from Korea', *India and Israel* (Bombay), v.5 no.1 (July 1952), p. 38.

11.617. Lahuti, Abdulkasim. 'About Myself', *Soviet Literature* (Moscow), no.9 (1954), pp. 138–42. Bahá'í Faith, p. 139.

11.618. 'Lake Mohonk Conference', *Northwestern Christian Advocate* (Chicago), (May 1, 1912), pp. 556–7. 'Abdu'l-Bahá, p. 556.

11.619. 'Lake Mohonk Conference: Distinguished Men to Discuss International Arbitration', *The Peace Movement* (Berne), no.9 (May 15, 1912), pp. 140–1. 'Abdu'l-Bahá, p. 140.

11.620. Lambton, Ann K.S. 'Persian Society Under the Qájárs', *Journal of the Royal Asiatic Society* (London), v.48 (1961), pp. 123–39. Bahá'í Faith, p. 136.

11.621. Lando, Barry. 'Injured Iran: The Torture Continues', *The New Republic* (Washington, D.C.), (June 13, 1983), pp. 12–13.

11.622. Landreth, Gordon. 'Anthology of Multi-Faith Prayers', *The Church of England Newspaper* (London), (19 Apr. 1985).

11.623. Langwell, Robyn. 'Ilona Rodgers, Back in New Zealand Soon?', *New Zealand Woman's Weekly* (Auckland), (Mar. 14, 1983), pp. 4–6.

11.624. Latimer, George Orr. 'A World Faith: Studies in the Teachings of Bahá'u'lláh: A World Community', *Sanj Vartaman* (Bombay), (Sept. 1936), pp. 120I, 120K.

11.625. Law-Barrar, Roberta L. 'The Bahá'í Call for a World Constitution', *Disarmament Campaigns* (The Hague), no.50 (Dec. 1985), p. 24.

11.625a. 'Lead-Coated Sheet Copper on Novel Baha'i Temple,' *Bulletin of the Copper & Brass Research Association* (New York), no.73 (Oct. 1, 1932), p. 15.

11.626. Lee, Jeremy. 'False Christs – a Word of Warning', *The Canadian Intelligence Service* (Flesherton, Ont.), v.32 no.10 (Oct. 1982), pp. 1–5 (89–93). Bahá'í Faith, p. 3 (91).

11.627. Leiendecker, Harold. 'Baha'i Temple of Light', *Northwest Engineer* (Evaston, Ill.), v.10 no.3 (Sept. 1951), pp. 6, 18–19, 38.

11.628. Leonard, Arthur Glyn. 'Bahaism – Its Origin and Concept: A Cult of Universal Brotherhood and Divine Unity', *Imperial and Asiatic Quarterly Review* (Woking), series 3, v.29 (1910), pp. 139–53.

11.629. Leslie. 'Richard St. Barbe Baker, Man of the Trees', *Children of the Green Earth* (Umpqua, Ore.), no.1 (Spring 1983), p. [3]

11.629a. 'Letters to the Editor, Baha'i Faith', *Ebony* (Chicago), v.8 no.2 (Dec. 1952).
   Letters from Gisela B. Dyer , National Spiritual Assembly of the Bahá'ís of the United States, Marion Peterson and Jessyca Russell.

11.630. Levin, Gail. 'Marsden Hartley and Mysticism', *Arts Magazine* (New York), (Nov. 1985), pp. 17–21. Bahá'í, pp. 17, 20.

11.631. Lieber, Joel. 'The Embrace of the Baha'i', *The Kiwanis Magazine* (Chicago), (Oct. 1964), pp. 24–6, 53.

11.632. 'Like a Jewel, in Its Setting of Generous Foliage and Bright Summer Sky Is This World Famous Dome of the Baha'i Temple', *Wilmette Life* (Wilmette, Ill.), v.25 no.10 (July 16, 1936), cover.

11.633. Lincoln, Joany Millar. 'Warmest Greetings from Bangui', *Mills Quarterly* (Oakland, Cal.), (Spring 1981), pp. 4–5.

11.634. Littman, David. 'Jews Under Muslim Rule: The Case of Persia', *Wiener Library Bulletin* (London), v.32 n.s. no.49–50 (1979), pp. 2–15. Bahá'í Faith, pp. 2, 4, 5, 14–15n.

11.635. 'Local Woman Testifies', *Montezuma Valley Journal* (Cortez, Colo.), (May 9, 1984), p. 13B.

11.636. 'Local Woman Touched by Executions in Iran', *Montezuma Valley Journal* (Cortez, Colo.), (Aug. 24, 1983), p. 13A.

11.637. Lofton, John. 'Reagan Backslides on Issue of Religion', *Moral Majority Report* (Richmond, Va.), (Feb. 1984), pp. 3, 17. Bahá'í, p. 3.

11.638. Logue, Jacquelyne Heubel; Garvey, Eileen. 'Managerial Dilemmas in Home Health Care', *Family & Community Health* (Rockville, Md.), v.8 no.2 (1985), pp. 46–53. Bahá'í Faith, p. 47.

11.639. 'Lotus Blossom Shape for Indian Temple', *Engineers Australia* (St Leonards, N.S.W.), (Jan. 25, 1980), p. 22.

11.640. Low, Arthur E. 'The Concept as an Engineering Design', *Concrete* (London), v.6 no.11 (Nov. 1972), pp. 24–6.
Panama temple.

11.641. Lunin, B.V. 'The Life and Works of Academician Vasilii Vladimirovich Bartol'd', *Soviet Anthropology and Archeology* (Armonk, N.Y.), v.9 no.2 (Fall 1970), pp. 91–126. Bahá'í Faith, note 24.

11.642. 'Luxembourg Opens Doors to Bahá'ís', *Luxembourg News Monthly* (Luxembourg), no.2 (Feb. 1985), p. 21.

11.643. Lyles, Jean Faffey. 'An Olympic Minuet', *The Christian Century* (Chicago), (Oct. 26, 1983), pp. 955–6. Bahá'í Faith, p. 955.

M

11.644. McClory, Robert. 'New Time Religion', *Reader: Chicago's Free Weekly*, v.12 no.48 (Feb. 2, 1983), pp. 8–9, 22–5.

11.645. McConnell, Clyde. 'Otto Rogers', *Artscanada* (Toronto), v.28 no.1, issue no.152/153 (Feb./Mar. 1971), p. 52

11.646. McCormick, Jim. [Baha'is in Iran: Letter to the Editor], *Update* (Aarhus, Denmark), v.7 no.4 (Dec. 1983), pp. 76–7.

11.647. McDaniel, Allen B. [Letter to the editor], *The Plasterer* (Chicago), v.27 no.5 (May 1933), p. 15.
Wilmette temple.

11.648. —— 'The Temple of Light', *Journal of the American Concrete Institute* (Detroit, Mich.), v.4 no.9 (June 1933), pp. 397–401.

11.649. —— 'A Temple of Light', *Technology Review* (Boston), v.33 no.1 (Oct. 1930), pp. 23–4, 46, 48.

11.649a. MacEoin, Denis. 'Aspects of Militancy and Quietism in Imami Shi'ism,' *Bulletin of the British Society for Middle Eastern Studies* (Oxford), v.11 no.1 (1984), pp. 18–27. Bábís, pp. 23–24, 25–26.

11.650. —— 'The Babi Concept of Holy War', *Religion* (London), v.12 (1982), pp. 93–129.

11.651. —— 'From Babism to Baha'ism: Problems of Militancy, Quietism, and Conflation in the Construction of a Religion', *Religion* (London), v.13 (1983), pp. 219–55.

11.652. —— 'Iran's Troubled Minority', *Gazelle Review of Literature on the Middle East* (London), (1985), pp. 44–9.

11.652a. —— 'Nineteenth Century Babi Talismans', *Studia Iranica* (Paris) v.14 (1985), pp. 77–98.

11.653. 'Machined Marble Columns for Classic Style', *Stone Industries* (Maidenhead, Eng.), (Nov.–Dec. 1978), pp. 15–17.

11.654. McKay, Doris. [Letter to the editor], *Atlantic Monthly* (Boston), v.139 (Jan. 1927), pp. 141–2.

11.655. McKenty, Beth. 'Baha'is Commemorate Predictions and Warnings of Founder', *Ebony* (Chicago), v.23 (Apr. 1968), pp. 124–9.

11.656. MacNeice, Jill. 'Catch a Falling Giant: With New Owners and a High-Tech Fix, UPI Stumbles into Town', *Regardie's* (Washington, D.C.), (Aug.-Sept. 1983), pp. 25–6.

11.657. McWilliams, Carey. 'The Cults of California', *Reader's Digest* (Pleasantville, N.Y.), v.48 (May 1946), pp. 39–44. Bahá'í Faith, p. 41.

11.658. Mahdavi, Shireen. 'Women and Ideas in Qājār Iran', *Asian and African Studies* (Haifa), v.19 no.2 (July 1985), pp. 187–97, Bábí women, pp. 188–91.

11.659. 'Mohametan Schism'; *Ecletic Magazine of Foreign Literature, Science and Art* (New York; Philadelphia), (Jan.–Apr. 1846), p. 142.

11.660. *idem.*, *Literary Gazette and Journal of Belles Lettres, Arts, Sciences, etc.* (London), no.1504 (Nov. 15, 1845), p. 757.

11.661. Mahran, Mirza. 'The Rationale of Behaism', *East and West* (Bombay), v.7 (1908), pp. 1021–6.

11.662. 'The Maitatsine Phenomenon: A Special Report', *Radiance* (Samaru Zana, Nigeria), (Jan. 1983), pp. 36–40. Bahá'í, p. 37.

11.663. Maloney, Lawrence D. 'Plague of Religious Wars Around the Globe', *U.S. News & World Report* (Washington, D.C.), v.96 no. 25 (June 25, 1984), pp. 24–6. Bahá'í Faith, p. 25.

11.663a. 'Manhattan Marriage', *Time* (New York), (Feb. 12, 1934), pp. 26–7.

Wedding of Mary Yvette Nadeau and Hamad Obadie performed by Ahmad Sohrab.

11.664. Manji, H.M. 'Birth of a Golden Age: The Principles of the Baha'i Movement', *Kaiser-i-Hind* (Bombay), (Jan. 2, 1938), pp. 54, 56.

11.665. Mann, James. 'Iran's "Holy War" Against the Bahais', *U.S. News & World Report* (Washington, D.C.), (Aug. 29, 1983), p. 40.

11.666. Manocha, Kishan. 'In Pursuit of IYY Aims', *Scene* (Leicester, U.K.), (1985).

11.667. Manuchehri, Rokhsan. 'Religious Minorities, No Joy Ride', *The Iranian* (Tehran), v.1 no.16 (Oct. 17, 1979), pp. 6–7.

11.668. 'Many Religions, Their Influence Today', *Awake!* (Brooklyn, N.Y.), (Jan. 8, 1984), pp. 3–4. Bahá'í, p. 3.

11.669. Martin, Douglas. 'The Baha'is of Iran', *Cultural Survival Quarterly* (Cambridge, Mass.), v.7 no.3 (Fall 1983), pp. 5–7.

11.669a. —— 'The Baha'is of Iran Under the Islamic Republic, 1979–1983', *Middle East Focus* (Toronto), v.6 no.4 (Nov. 1983), pp. 17–27, 30–1.

11.670. —— 'The Baha'is of Iran Under the Pahlavi Regime, 1921–1979', *Middle East Focus* (Toronto), v.4 no.6 (Mar. 1982), pp. 7–17.

11.670a. —— 'The Uses and Abuses of Power: A Case Study', *The High School Journal* (Chapel Hill, N.C.), v.68 no.4 (Apr.–May 1985), pp. 316–26.

11.671. Martin, Owen. 'What Is the Baha'i Faith?', *Probe* (Jamaica), v.2 no.5 (June 1973), pp. 8–9.

11.672. Masefield, Morley. 'The Religion of Bahá'í', *Courier* (Oxford, Eng.), v.42 no.5 (May 1964), pp. 21–4.

11.673. Masliyah, Sadok. 'Persian Jewry: Prelude to a Catastrophe', *Judaism* (New York), v.29 (Fall 1980), pp. 390–403. 'Bahaism and the Persian Jews', pp. 401–2.

11.674. Masson, Jean. 'The "Bahaï Revelation" – Its Western Advance', *The American Review of Reviews* (New York), v.39 (Feb. 1909), pp. 214–16.

11.675. —— 'The Mashrak-el-Azkar and the Bahai Movement', *The Lake Shore News*, (Oct. 19, 1916).

11.676. Masujima, Rokuichiro. 'Bahaism and Buddhism: The Zeu [sic] Sect's Mission in This Mundane World: Story of Baha Orah, the Persian Prophet: Discrimination Must Go', *The Trans-Pacific* (Tokyo), v.13 (July 3, 1926), p. 3.

11.677. Maud, Constance E. ''Abdul Baha (Servant of the Glory)', *The Fortnightly Review* (London), v.97 (Apr. 1912), pp. 707–15.

11.678. ——'The First Persian Feminist', *The Fortnightly Review* (London), v.99 (June 1913), pp. 1175–82.

11.679. 'May 25 Program to Recount History of Baha'i in U.S.', *Ouilmette Heritage* (Wilmette, Ill.), (Spring 1983), p. [1].

11.680. Mayer, Alan James. 'The City of Immigrants: Some New Torontonians Talk About Their Adopted Home', *Quest* (Toronto), (Mar. 1984), pp. 29–37. Iranian Bahá'í refugees.

11.681. Mazlish, Bruce. 'The Hidden Khomeini', *New York*, (Dec. 24, 1979), pp. 49–54.

11.682. 'A Meeting', *World Peace Through Spiritual Regeneration* (Calcutta), v.2 no.16–17 (Jan. 1 & 16, 1937), pp. 320–2. Report of a talk on the Faith by Siegfried Schopflocher.

11.682a. Mehta, Mani H. 'Baha'u'llah – and the Indian Crisis', *Blitz Magazine* (Bombay), (19 Sept. 1942).

11.683. Mellgren, Doug-Harald. 'Blazing the Trail for Peace', *The Saga* (Stravanger, Norway), (31 Okt. 1985). Bahá'í pioneers in Norway.

11.684. Menon, Shashi. 'Baha'is Are Being Made Scapegoats by Khomeini: Dr. Marco G. Kappenberger', *Onlooker* (Bombay), v.44 no.4 (Feb. 16–28, 1982), p. 17.

11.685. —— 'Mullahs Exterminate the Bahais', *Onlooker* (Bombay), v.43 no.16 (Sept. 1–15, 1981), p. 41.

11.686. Merritt-Hawkes, O.A. 'The Plight of Persian Women', *Magazine Digest* (Toronto), v.8 no.6 (June 1934), pp. 88–91. Bahá'í Faith, p. 91.

11.687. 'The Message of a Martyr', *East and West Series* (Poona, India), no.66 special no.(Apr./June 1961), pp. 73–4.

11.688. Metta, Vasudeo B. 'The Modern Spirit in Women of Iran', *Woman's Outlook* (Manchester, Eng.), v.18 no.412 (Jan. 30, 1937), pp. 434–5. Features Ṭáhirih.

11.689. —— 'Riza Khan, Persia's New Dictator', *Current History* (New York), v.23 no.3 (Dec. 1925), pp. 367–70. Bahá'í, p. 370.

11.690. Meyer, Glenn A. 'Manucher J. Javid, M.D.', *Surgical Neurology* (Boston), v.18 no.4 (Oct. 1982), pp. 227–9.

Biography of a Bahá'í.

11.691. 'Midwest Taj Mahal', *Mainliner*, (Mar. 1959), no paging.

11.692. Miller, Karen Gray. 'Do Libraries Get Religion?', *Library Journal* (New York), v.107 no.18 (Oct. 15, 1982), pp. 1941–3. Bahá'í, p. 1942.

11.693. Miller, William McElwee. 'The Bahai Cause Today', *The Moslem World* (Hartford, Conn.), v.30 no.4 (Oct. 1940), pp. 379–404.

11.694. —— 'The Baha'i Cult', *Christianity Today* (Carol Stream, Ill.), v.10 (Feb. 18, 1966), pp. 24–5.

11.695. —— 'The Religious Situation in Iran', *The Muslim World* (Hartford, Conn.), v.41 no.1 (Jan. 1951), pp. 79–87. Bahá'í Faith, pp. 79, 87.

11.696. —— 'What Is the Baha'i World Faith?', *Incite* (Heidebeek, Heerde, Netherlands), v.2 no.1 (Dec. 1975), pp. 22–8.

11.697. Minorsky, V. '(Babidskie Vosstaniia v Irane)': [review], *Bulletin of the School of Oriental and African Studies* (London), v.11 (1943–6), pp. 875–83.
Review of M.S. Ivanov's book on the Bábí upheavals, which is written from a Marxist economic viewpoint.

11.698. 'Miss Farmer and Greenacre', *The Open Court* (Chicago), v.29 (Sept. 1915), p. 572.

11.699. 'Miss Root to Lecture in Poona: Education for World Peace', *The Illustrated Weekly of India* (Bombay), (Feb. 6, 1938).

11.700. Mitchell, Glenford E. 'The Baha'i Faith in Africa', *Africa Report* (New Brunswick, N.J.), (Oct. 1963), pp. 14–15.

11.701. Mitchell, J. Murray. 'A New Sect in India', *The Missionary Review of the World* (Princeton, N.J.), v.27 (Feb. 1904), pp. 97–100. Bábís, p. 97.

11.702. 'A Modern Fairy Tale: The Princess Who Became a Doctor', *Ndiza Natsi* (Manzini, Swaziland), v.1 no.2 (1984), pp. 2–3, 5, 7, 9.

11.703. 'Modern Man's Expression of Love for His Maker', *Woman's Voice* (Singapore), (June 1953), pp. 22–4.
Bahá'í temple, Wilmette, Ill.

11.704. 'A Modern Prophet: "The Times" on Abdul Baha', *The Christian Commonwealth* (London), (Sept. 24, 1919), p. 622.

11.705. Momen, Moojan. 'The Social Basis of the Babi Upheavals in Iran (1843–53): A Preliminary Analysis', *International Journal of Middle Eastern Studies* (Cambridge, U.K.), v.15 (1983), pp. 157–83.

11.706. —— 'The Trial of Mullā 'Alī Basṭāmī: A Combined Sunnī-Shī'ī Fatwā Against the Bāb', *Iran: Journal of Persian Studies* (London), v.20 (1982), pp. 113–43.

11.707. Moore, Arthur. 'The Making of a New Religion', *T.P.'s & Cassells Weekly* (London), v.1 no.1 (new series), (Oct. 27, 1923), pp. 28–9.

11.708. Moore, James. 'Baha'i, Religion of the Remote God', *The Christian Reader* (Sept./Oct. 1981), no paging.

11.709. —— 'A New Look at Baha'i', *His Magazine* (Chicago), (Feb. 1971), pp. 16–18.

11.710. 'Moqtada'i Denies Baha'i Persecution in Iran: LD311233 Tehran Domestic Service in Persian 1030 GMT 31 Jan 85', *Foreign Broadcast Information Service Daily Reports* (Washington, D.C.), (Feb. 1, 1985), p. 13.

11.710a. 'More About Bahais' [sic], *India and Israel* (Bombay), v.3 no.11 (May 1951), p. 55.

11.711. 'More from NGOs and Peace Researchers', *Disarmament Times* (New York), v.5 no.21 (9 July 1982), p. 3.
Includes report on Bahá'í International Community.

11.712. Morey, Frederick. '16th Annual Report of Higginson Press, the Literary Life, Yokes and Goals', *Higginson Journal* (Brentwood, Mass.), no.37 (Dec. 1983), pp. 11–24. Bahá'í Faith, pp. 12, 16.

11.713. Moribame, Samuel. 'Bahai', *Kutlwano: Mutual Understanding* (Gabarone, Botswana), v.18 no. 2 (Dec. 1980), pp. 22–7.

11.714. 'Mormons Are A-Building', *Pacific Islands Monthly* (Sydney, N.S.W.), (July 1983), Samoa Bahá'í temple, p. 39.

11.715. 'Moroccan Monarch Meets the Press', *The Christian Century* (Chicago), v.80 (Apr. 17, 1963), pp. 484–5.
Moroccan persecutions of 1962.

11.716. 'Morocco, a Question of Faith', *The Economist* (London), v.206 (Jan. 5, 1963), p. 26.

11.717. Mortimer, K.J. 'Catholics in Turbans', *The Catholic Digest* (St Paul, Minn.), (Oct. 1955), pp. 99–103. Bahá'ís, p. 99.

11.718. 'The Mother and Abdul Baha', *Bulletin of Sri Aurobindo International Centre of Education*, v.29 no.4 (Nov. 1977), pp. 50–63.

11.719. Mottahedeh, Mildred. 'Mrs. Mildred Mottahedeh: An Exclusive Interview with Conrad Biernacki', *Antique Showcase* (Canfield,

Ont.), v.19 no.8 (Feb. 1984), pp. 18–21. Bahá'í Faith, p. 18.

11.720. Moyal, Munir Abdallah. 'Post-Islamic Religions of the Near East', *The Aryan Path* (Bombay), v.16 no.8 (Aug. 1945), pp. 291–5. Bahá'í Faith, p. 292.

11.721. 'Mr. Browne in Persia', *The Spectator* (London), (Apr. 28, 1894), pp. 559–60.

11.722. 'Mr. Charles Mason Remey, Architect and Author', *Town and Country Life* (London), v.1 no.4 (July 1928).

11.723. 'Mrs. Mackwelung Passed Away', *The National Union* (Kolonia, Pohnpei), v.6 no.12 (June 30, 1985), p. 2.

11.724. 'Mrs. Rubiyyih [sic] Rabbani, Author,

Lecturer', *Typhoon* (Taipai), v.27 no.27 (Jan. 11, 1979), p. 1.

11.725. Muhammad, Don E. 'Childish Barbarism', *Newsweek* (New York), (May 5, 1980).

11.726. Munje, H.M. 'Sir Padampat, an Industrial Tycoon & Spiritually Noble', *J.K. Review* (New Delhi), v.41 no.1 (Mar. 1980), pp. 27–9.
Bahá'í Faith and Dr Munje's contact with Sir Padampat Singhania.

11.727. Murphy, Patricia. 'It Couldn't Be Done Today', *Modern Concrete* (Chicago), v.42 no.12 (Apr. 1979), pp. 40–5.
John J. Earley and the Wilmette temple.

11.728. 'Muslims Help, So Bahaiis [sic] Rejoice', *Al-Islam* (Colombo, Sri Lanka), v.2 no.1 (Dec. 1984–Jan. 1985), p. 1.

N

11.729. Naharoy, S. 'The Flowering of a Faith', *ECC Concord* (Bombay), v.8 no.3 (July-Sept. 1985), cover, pp. 2–8, back cover.

11.730. Nandi, S.K. 'A Monument to Faith: Structural Features and Construction of the Bahá'í House of Worship', *Architecture + Design* (New Delhi), v.1 no.2 (Jan.-Feb. 1985), pp. 26–7, 29, 31, 33.

11.731. Naqavi, Ali Raza. 'Babism and Baha-'ism: A Study of Their History and Doctrines', *Islamic Studies* (Islamabad, Pakistan), v.14 no.3 (Autumn 1975), pp. 185–217. Reply by Denis MacEoin, v.15 no.2 (Summer 1976), pp. 143–50.

11.731a. Nathaniels, Elizabeth. 'Towards a New Paradigm of Power', *Alternatives* (New York), v.9 no.4 (Dec. 1983), pp. 665–73. Bahá'í Faith, p. 673.

11.732. 'National Sovereignty', *The Friend* (London), (5, 12, 26 Nov. 1982).
Exchange of letters on the internationalism of the Bahá'í Faith.

11.733. 'Nature Collaborates on Temple's Architecture', *Engineering News-Record* (New York), (Nov. 15, 1979), p. 24. Richard Henderson, 'A Lesson on Bahaism': [letter to the editor], (Dec. 20, 1979), p. 16. Delhi, India temple.

11.734. Neil, James. 'Missionary Journey to Galilee', *The Jewish Intelligence* (London), (Dec. 1872), pp. 299–307. 'Abdu'l-Bahá, pp. 300–1.

11.734a. Neumann, H. 'The Baha'i Sanctuary at

Haifa: Haifa Engineer's Lecture before Bombay Baha'is', *India and Israel* (Bombay), v.5 no.8 (Feb. 1953), p. 43.

11.735. 'Never Walk Alone', *The New Republic* (Washington, D.C.), v.189 no.2 (Dec. 19, 1983), pp. 7–9. Bahá'í, p. 9.

11.736. New History Society. 'The New History Society', *World Peace Through Spiritual Regeneration* (Calcutta), v.2 no.18 (Feb. 1, 1937), p. [348].

11.737. 'The New History Society', *More Light* (New York), [v.1 no.1?] ([Jan. 1930?]), pp. 32–3.

11.738. [New History Society publications review], *Federated India* (Madras), (May 30, 1934), p. 6.

11.739. 'New Life?' *The Economist* (London), (20 Mar. 1982), p. 61.

11.740. 'New Prairie Architecture', *The Literary Digest* (New York), v.66 no.7 (Aug. 14, 1920), pp. 30–1.
Wilmette temple.

11.740a. 'A New Religion,' *The Nation* (New York), v.2 no.59 (June 22, 1866), pp. 793–5.

11.741. 'New Repressive Measure Against Baha'is', *Human Rights Internet Reporter* (Washington, D.C.), v.10 nos. 3–4 (Jan.-Apr. 1985), p. 408.

11.742. 'A New World Order', *The Illustrated*

Weekly of India (Bombay), v.56 no.52 (Dec. 29, 1935), pp. 25, 54.

11.743. 'New Year of Trees', *Christian Life in Israel* (Jerusalem), no.11 (Spring 1984), pp. 2–3. About Richard St Barbe Baker; includes reference to the Bahá'í Faith.

11.743a. Newcombe, Hanna. 'Alternative Approaches to World Government', *Peace Research Reviews* (Oakville, Ont.), v.5 no.3 [rev. v.1 no.2] (Feb. 1974), p. 55.

11.744. 'Nigeria, the Third Decade of Independence', *Radiance* (Samaru Zana, Nigeria), (Jan. 1983), pp. 7–13. Bahá'í Faith, p. 11.

11.745. Nijenhuis, John. 'Bahá'í, World Faith for Modern Man?', *Journal of Ecumenical Studies* (Philadelphia, Pa.), v.10 no.3 (Summer, 1973), pp. 532–51.

11.746. 'The Nine Hands', *Newsweek* (New York), v.55 (June 27, 1960), p. 94.

11.747. 'Nine-Sided Nonesuch', *Time* (New York), v.41 (May 24, 1943), p. 36.

11.748. '1985 Tucker Award Winners: Seat of the Universal House of Justice', *Building Stone Magazine* (New York), (Mar.-Apr. 1985), p. 24.

11.749. '1986 International Year of Peace', *The University This Week* (Lae, P.N.G.), (29 Nov. 1985), p. 1.

11.750. 'The Nonagon', *The Nation* (New York), v.196 (Feb. 16, 1963), pp. 130–1. Morocco persecutions.

11.751. Norman, J.D. 'Muslim March', *New Society* (London), (27 Sept. 1985).

11.752. 'A Note on the History of the Growth & Development of World Peace', *World Peace Through Spiritual Regeneration* (Calcutta), v.2 no.16–17 (Jan. 1 & 16, 1937), pp. 317–20. Bahá'í Faith, p. 318.

11.753. 'Notebook', *The New Republic* (Washington, D.C.), v.190 (May 28, 1984), pp. 9–10,

11.754. 'Noted Baha'i Leader to Address Congress', *Wilmette Life* (Wilmette, Ill.), v.37 no.52 (Apr. 28, 1949).

11.755. 'Notes for Home Editors', *The Christian Century* (Chicago), v.74 (July 24, 1957), p. 885. Portion of the "Editorial" for the issue.

11.756. Nowlan, Alden. 'A Bubble Dancer and the Wickedest Man in Carleton County', *The Fiddlehead* (Fredericton, N.B.), no.125 (Spring, 1980), pp. 74–7. Bahá'ís, p. 76.

11.757. Nowshadl, Farshid. 'Personal Announcement', *Impact International* (London), (23 Aug. 1984). Author announces he is not a Bahá'í.

O

11.758. 'O and E', *Sarawak Gazette* (Kuching), v.91 no.1292 (Oct. 31st, 1965), p. 326.

11.759. Ober, Harlan. 'In the Presence of Abdul Baha', *National Magazine* (Boston), v.50 (May 1922), pp. 548–51.

11.760. Oberling, Pierre. 'The Role of Religous Minorities in the Persian Revolution, 1906–1912', *Journal of Asian History* (Wiesbaden), v.12 no.2 (1978), pp. 1–29. Bábís, pp. 13–14.

11.761. Okite, Odhiambo. 'Bahai in Black Africa: A Force to Contend With', *Christianity Today* (Carol Stream, Ill.), v.14 no.53 (Mar. 13, 1970), p. 53.

11.762. Olaoye, Wole. 'Bahai, the Religion of All Religions', *Trust* (Lagos, Nigeria), (Oct. 1982), pp. 22–5.

11.763. Olson, Barbara; Olson, Eric. 'The Small World of Nossrat Scott', *Birmingham* (Birmingham, Ala.), v.25 no.3 (Mar. 1985), pp. 9–10, 12–14, 16–18. Bahá'í Faith, pp. 10, 17–18.

11.764. Olson, Cynthia R. 'The Baha'i Faith', *The American Swedish Monthly* (New York), (Feb. 1954), pp. 16–17, 24.

11.765. Omotoso, Adedayo. 'A White Poet with a Vision of Africa', *Trust* (Lagos, Nigeria), (Oct. 1982), pp. 27–8. Dorothy Lee Hansen, a Bahá'í poet.

11.765a. Onderdonk, Francis S. 'Possibilities of a Concrete Architecture', *The Michigan Technic* (Ann Arbor), (Jan. 1926), pp. 16, 24.

11.766. 'One Hundred Years Ago "the Bab" Proclaimed His Faith', *News Review* (London), v.17 no.22 (June 1, 1944), p. 22.

11.767. '110 Years Back a Persian Prophet Took the Road to Martyrdom', *Sunday Pictorial* (Colombo, Ceylon), v.1 no.29 (19 Dec. 1954), p. 11.

11.768. 'One World, One Faith', *Spotlight* (Kingston, Jamaica), v.13 no.11 (Nov. 1952), pp. 29–30.

11.769. 'Opening of Bahai House of Worship', *Savali* (Apia, Western Samoa), (Sept. 1984), pp. 10–11.

11.770. 'The Ordeal of a Central Banker: The Personal Story of Ali Reza Nobari, Governor, Central Bank of Iran, 1979–1981', *Euromoney* (London), (Feb. 1982), pp. 22–44. Bahá'í Faith, p. 29.

11.771. Orr, Fay. 'Beware of Cults Bearing Bibles', *Alberta Report* (Edmonton), (Nov. 7, 1983), p. 59.

11.772. Ostling, Richard N. 'Slow Death for Iran's Baha'is', *Time* (New York), v.123 no.8 (Feb. 20, 1984), p. 55.

11.773. 'Other Worldly', *The Economist* (London), (July 24, 1982), p. 43.

P

11.774. Pahlavi, Soraya. 'Soraya, Autobiography of a Princess', *McCall's* (New York), (June 1963), pp. 72–3, 164–72. Bahá'í Faith, p. 166.

11.775. 'Palestine Tomorrow: Major W. Tudor Pole on the Holy Land', *The Christian Commonwealth* (London), (Sept. 24, 1919), p. 614. 'Abdu'l-Bahá described in interview.

11.776. Palin, Elizabeth. 'Letters . . .', *Peace by Peace* (Northern Ireland), v.9 no.13 (Aug. 1984).

11.777. —— 'Modern Martyrs', *NHR National Newsletter* (Solihull, W. Midlands, U.K.), no. 38 (Spring 1985), p. 17.

11.778. Palin, Iain. 'The Bahais', *The Economist* (London), (Feb. 13, 1982).

11.779. —— 'Bahais', *The Economist* (London), v.288 no.7300 (30 July 1983), p. 6.

11.780. —— 'Healing and Medicine', *Arthritis News* (London), (Autumn 1985), p. 18.

11.781. —— [Letter to the Editor], *Newsweek* (New York), (Apr. 23, 1984).

11.782. —— 'Lifting the Sanctions', *Now!* (London), (Feb. 6, 1981), p. 30.

11.783. Palmer, Glenda. ' "Unity in Diversity" at the New Era International School', *Award World* (London), no.18 (18 Sept. 1984).

11.784. Parker, L.E. 'Baha'u'llah and Ramakrishna: A Comparative Study', *The Aryan Path* (Bombay), v.8 no.12 (Dec. 1937), pp. 540–3.

11.785. Parratt, J.K. 'Religious Change in Port Moresby', *Oceania* (Sydney, N.S.W.), (Dec. 1970), pp. 106–13. Bahá'í Faith, pp. 111–13.

11.786. Patton, Derek W. 'Mankind Is One: Where We Stand from an Historical Perspective', *Club Bulletin, Rotary Club of Taoyuan West, Taiwan, China*, v.7 (June 8, 1983), pp. 1–5.

11.787. Pearce, Chris. 'In the Name of God: Apostasy or Death for Iran's Baha'is', *East-West Photo Journal*, v.2 no.6 (Winter 1981), pp. 20–3.

11.788. Pearson, Virginia. 'Those Worlds Beyond the Sun', *Mind Digest* (Paradise, Pa.), (Nov. 1945), pp. 43–50. Author's vision of completed Wilmette temple before she knew anything of the Bahá'í Faith.

11.789. Pease, Frederick O. 'Dr. Ibrahim G. Kheiralla: A Biographical Sketch', *The Occult Truth Seeker* (Lawrence, Kan.), v.2 no.2 (July 1902), pp. 25–9.

11.790. Pederson, Larry. 'Iran's Prisons', *Newsweek* (New York), v.104 no.4 (July 23, 1984), p. 4.

11.791. 'People Are Asking: The Persecution of the Baha'is in Iran', *(Zhōng Guó Bào Dào)* (Taiwan), 933, pp. 36–2. Text in Chinese and English.

11.792. Pereira, Godfrey. 'Khomeini, the Baha'i Butcher', *Celebrity* (Bombay), v.3 no.4 (Feb. 1984), pp. 63–5.

11.793. 'Persecution of Baha'is', *Human Rights Internet Reporter* (Washington, D.C.), v.10 no.1–2 (Sept.–Dec. 1984), pp. 147–8.

11.794. 'Persecution of Bah'is [sic] in Iran', *Goa Today* (Panjim, Goa), v.16 no.7 (Feb. 1982), p. 21.

11.795. 'Persia in Illinois', *Quick* (New York), v.5 no.13 (Sept. 24, 1951), p. 29.

11.796. 'Persian Prophet', *The Independent* (New York), v.73 (July 18, 1912), pp. 159–60.

11.797. 'The Persian Rival to Jesus and His American Disciples', *The Moslem World* (Hartford, Conn.), v.6 no.2 (Apr. 1916), p. 203.

11.798. 'A Persian Teacher', *The Crisis* (New York), v.4 no.1 (May 1912), pp. 14–16.

11.799. 'Persia's Contribution to the Culture of the World', *The Modern Review* (Calcutta), (Feb. 1931), pp. 186–7.

11.800. Peters, Karl E. 'Editorial', *Zygon: A Journal of Religion and Science* (Winter Park, Fla.), v.14 no.3 (Sept. 1979), pp. 195–9. Bahá'í Faith, p. 197.

11.801. Petronus. 'Diplomatic Pouch', *The Diplomatic World Bulletin* (New York), v.9 no.6 (Mar. 19, 1979).

11.802. Petrossian, Vahe. 'Iran Takes a First Step Towards Solving "Bahai Problem"', *Middle East Economic Digest* (London), (9 Sept. 1983), p. 30.

11.803. Pettersen, Arild. 'Napoleon III and the Rites of Sovereign Nations', *World Peace News* (New York), v.16 no.6 (Oct. 1985), p. 8.

11.804. 'The Phenomenal Spread of Bahaism', *Current Literature* (London), v.51 (Sept. 1911), pp. 298–300.

11.805. Phillott, D.C. 'Edward Granville Browne', *Asiatic Society of Bengal Journal and Proceedings* (Calcutta), v.7 (Aug. 1911), pp. cxx–cxxi.

11.806. Pickering, Ernest. 'The Ecumenical Cult – Bahaism', *The Discerner*, v.4 no.7 (July/Sept. 1963), pp. 5–8.

11.807. Pitts, Brendan. 'Death in the Clinic', *AMA Gazette* (Glebe, N.S.W.), (May 1981), pp. 4–5.

11.808. —— 'Manuchir Hakim Murdered in Iran', *Medical Journal of Australia* (Glebe, N.S.W.), (May 16, 1981), p. 540.

11.809. Pitts, William Lee. 'Religious Cults in the United States', *Choice* (Middletown, Conn.), v.21 no.8 (Apr. 1984), pp. 1094–102. Bahá'í Faith, pp. 1098, 1099.

11.810. Pitzer, Pat. 'A Living Treasure of Hawaii', *Hawaii* (Honolulu), (Apr. 1982), pp. 34–6.
Juliette May Fraser wins Agnes Baldwin Alexander Award.

11.811. 'Plight of Iranian Baha'is', *Gist* (Washington, D.C.), (Oct. 18, 1984), pp. 1–2.

11.812. Podger, Ivan. [The Shrine of Bahai], *Calvert School Newsletter* (Baltimore, Md.), no.6 (Summer 1982), p. 4.

11.813. Pogorelske, Paulyne. 'A Face for All Series: That's Ilona Rodgers, Star of the Moment', *TV Week* (Melbourne, Vic.), (July 3, 1982), p. 73.

11.814. Pole, Wellesley Tudor. 'Abdu'l-Baha Abbas and the Baha'i Faith', *Light* (London), v.70 no.3368 (Dec. 1950), pp. 347–51.

11.815. —— 'Recollection of a Healing Incident: Sequel to 'Abdu'l-Baha Abbas and the Baha'i Faith', *Light* (London), v.71 no.3370 (Feb. 1951), pp. 398–400.

11.816. Pool, Rosey E. 'Robert Hayden, Poet Laureate: An Assessment', *Negro Digest* (Chicago), v.15 (June 1966), pp. 39–47. Bahá'í Faith, p. 43.

11.817. Popoff, Eli. 'Journey to the Holy Land', *Mir* (Grand Forks, B.C.), no. 15 (May 1977), pp. 38–59. Bahá'í Faith's relations to Doukhobors, pp.39–40.

11.818. Post, Constance J. 'Image and Idea in the Poetry of Robert Hayden', *College Language Association Journal* (Atlanta, Ga.), v.20 (1976), pp. 164–75. Bahá'í Faith, pp. 165–7, 174.

11.818a. Prakash, Padma. 'Right Now: An Interview with a Septuagenarian Suffragette, Shirin Fozdar, Who Was in India to Attend the First All Asian Baha'i Women's Conference Held in New Delhi Last Month,' *Femina* (Bombay), (Nov. 4–7, 1977).

11.819. 'Preliminary Background Report on Potential for Rural Development in the New Seventh Division of Sarawak with Special Emphasis on Survey Results of Iban Longhouses for the Year 1971–1972', *Sarawak Gazette* (Kuching), v.99 no.1383 (May 31st, 1973), pp. 99–115. Bahá'í Faith, pp. 104–15.

11.820. 'Preparing to Inherit the Earth', *Radio Times* (London), (12–18 Oct. 1985), pp. 10–11.

11.820a. 'President Weizmann's Death', *India and Israel* (Bombay), v.5 no.6 (Dec. 1952), pp. 8–11. On p. 9 Shoghi Effendi and Charles Mason Remey are barely visible in a funeral photograph.

11.821. Price, Ron. 'The World Order of Baha'u'llah', *Cosmos* (Lane Grove, N.S.W.), v.9 no.2 (Sept. 1981), pp. 3, 13.

11.822. Pritam Singh. 'The Place of the Bab in Bahaism', *The Hindustan Review* (Patna), (Sept.–Oct. 1919), pp. 245–8.

11.823. —— 'The Prophet of This Age, Baha Ollah', *The Hindustan Review* (Patna), (Apr. 1920), pp. 243–5.

11.824. —— 'The Rise of the Baha'i Faith in Iran', *The Visva-Bharati Quarterly* (Calcutta), (Feb. 1939), pp. 333–8.

11.825. 'Profile, Rae Perlin: Art Critic Also an Artist of Distinction', *The Newfoundland Herald* (St John's, Nfld.), (Aug. 30, 1989 [sic] [i.e. 1979?]), pp. 12–13.

11.826. 'Profiles' [John A. Robarts], *Axiom* (Halifax, N.S.), v.3 no.6 (Nov.–Dec. 1977), p. 32.

11.827. 'Propagande "Bahai" = Bahai Propaganda', *L'Écho des Îles* (Seychelles), (15 juillet 1971), pp. 238, 240. Text in French and English.

11.828. Propper, Michael. 'Campaign Protests Murdered Iranian MDs', *American Medical News* (Chicago), (May 3, 1985).

11.829. 'Prophecies Come True: Haifa's Rapid Development Was Fortold [sic] by Great Men of the Recent Past', *The Israel Export Journal* (Tel Aviv), v.6 no.4 (Apr. 1954), pp. 22–3.
  Photograph of the Shrine of the Báb and a quotation from 'Abdu'l-Bahá on the future of Haifa and 'Akká.

11.830. 'A Prophet from the East', *The Literary Digest* (New York), v.44 (May 4, 1912), pp. 955–7.

11.831. Pugh, Jeanne. 'Iran's Persecution of the Bahais', *Crossroads* (St Petersburg, Fla.), (Sept. 10, 1983), pp. 1, 4–5, 7, 10.

Q

11.832. Qasim, Seeme. 'A Young Indian Baha'i Speaks Out', *Eve's Weekly* (Bombay), (Oct. 17–23, 1981), p. 13.

11.833. 'Quartz in Concrete', *The Mineralogist* (Portland, Ore.), v.10 no.11 (Nov. 1942), pp. 348–50.

R

11.834. Rabbani, Rúhíyyih. 'No Pain, No Gain', *Education Today* (Taipei), no.2 (17 Aug. 1984), pp. 1–2.

11.835. 'Radio Baha'i, Ecuador', *Frequence* (Montreal), v.1 no.3 (15 May 1983), p. 7.

11.836. Rawat, H.M. 'Bahaism a Conspiracy Against Islam and Muslims', *The Muslim Digest* (Durban, S. Afr.), (Aug.–Sept. 1977), pp. 117–23.

11.837. 'Re in London', *Education* (London), (12 Oct. 1984).

11.838. 'Recant or Else', *The Economist* (London), (Jan. 23, 1982).

11.839. Rees, J.D. 'The Bab and Babism', *Littell's Living Age* (Boston), v.210 (Aug. 22, 1896), pp. 451–8.

11.840. —— idem., *The Nineteenth Century* (London), v.40 no.233 (July 1896), pp. 56–66.

11.841. —— 'Persia', *MacMillan's Magazine* (London), v.55 (1887), pp. 442–53. Bahá'í Faith, p. 444.

11.842. Rees, John. 'Where and Why the Communists Are Advancing', *American Opinion* (Bel-

mont, Mass.), (July–Aug. 1983), pp. 45–66. Bahá'ís in Iran, p. 49.

11.843. 'The Reform of Mohammedanism', *The Spectator* (London), (June 4, 1910), pp. 914–15.
  Review of a lecture by Bernard Temple on Bábís and Bahá'ís.

11.844. 'The Refugees It Doesn't Talk About', *The Economist* (London), (Feb. 13, 1982), pp. 50–1.

11.845. Reid, J.R. 'The Model for the Bahai Temple, Chicago, Louis J. Bourgeois, Architect', *The Architectural Record* (New York), v.47 (June 1920), pp. 501–5.

11.846. Reid, Tony. 'Crump Flags It Away', *New Zealand Listener* (Wellington), (Nov. 20, 1982), pp. 21–2, 25, 26.
  About Barry Crump, a New Zealand Bahá'í.

11.847. Rein, Peter. 'The Lotus That Will Blossom Over Delhi', *New Civil Engineer* (London), (20 Sept. 1979), pp. 22–3.

11.848. 'Religion and State in Morocco', *The Muslim World* (Hartford, Conn.), v.53 no.3 (July 1963), p. 265.
  Morocco persecutions.

11.849. 'A Religion Without Priests', *The Illustrated Weekly of India* (Bombay), v.57 no.22 (May 31, 1936), p. 53.

11.850. 'Religions in Micronesia', *Highlights* (Saipan, Mariana Is.), (July 1, 1978), p. 6.

11.851. 'Religions Within the Empire', *The Near East* (London), v.26 no.702 (Oct. 23, 1924), pp. 430–2.
Includes section on 'Bahaism'.

11.852. 'Religious Liberty Conference Spawns Controversy', *Religion & Democracy: A Newsletter of the Institute on Religion and Democracy* (Washington, D.C.), (May–June, 1985), pp. 1, 3, 4. Bahá'í Faith, p. 3.

11.853. 'Religious Persecution of the Baha'is in Iran', *Human Rights Internet Reporter* (Washington, D.C.), v.10 no.1–2 (Sept.–Dec. 1984), p. 148–9.

11.854. Remey, Charles Mason. 'The Great Global Catastrophe', *Search* (Amherst, Mass.), v.50 (Dec. 1962), pp. 34–40.

11.855. Renner, John. 'Explosive Act of Desperation', *Maclean's* (Toronto), v.94 no.28 (July 13, 1981), p. 23.

11.856. 'Report from Iran', *UN Chronicle* (New York), v.19 no.8 (Sept. 1982), pp. 52–8. Bahá'ís, pp. 53, 55, 56, 58.

11.857. 'Report on Alleged Violations of Human Rights in Iran', *UN Chronicle* (New York), v.22 (Mar. 1985), pp. 46–7. Bahá'ís, p. 47.

11.858. 'Repression of Religious Minorities: The Baha'is', *Human Rights Internet Reporter* (Washington, D.C.), v.9 no.7 (Dec. 1983–Jan. 1984), p. 376.

11.859. 'Rhodesian Delegates Attend Baha'is Spiritual Convocation', *Parade* (Salisbury, Rhodesia), (July 1978), p. 36.

11.860. Rice, W.A. 'A Babi Pamphlet', *The Church Missionary Intelligencer* (London), (Aug. 1902), pp. 564–73.

11.861. Richards, J.R. 'Baha'ism in Persia Today', *The Moslem World* (Hartford, Conn.), v.21 no.3 (Oct. 1931), pp. 344–51.

11.862. Richardson, Robert P. 'The Persian Rival to Jesus and His American Disciples', *The Open Court* (Chicago), v.29 (Aug. 1915), pp. 460–83.

11.863. —— 'The Precursor, the Prophet, and the Pope: Contributions to the History of the Bahai Movement', *The Open Court* (Chicago), v.30 no.10 (Oct. 1916), pp. 617–37; v.30 no. 11 (Nov. 1916), pp. 657–85.

Anti-Bahá'í article from Christian perspective.

11.864. —— 'The Rise and Fall of the Parliament of Religions at Greenacre', *The Open Court* (Chicago), v.46 no.3 (Mar. 1931), pp. 129–66.
Attack on the Bahá'í ownership of Greenacre Bahá'í School in Eliot, Maine.

11.865. Righter, Rosemary. 'Pogrom in Iran', *Education* (West Perth, W.A.), (May 24, 1982), p. 19.

11.866. Rihani, Amin. 'Dr. I.G. Kheiralla Dies in Syria', *The Syrian World* (New York), v.3 no.2 (May 1929), pp. 49–50.

11.867. Roberts, Florence. 'Who and What Are the Baha'is?', *The New Zealand Woman's Weekly* (Auckland), (May 29, 1952), pp. 10, 53–5.

11.868. Roberts, Tom. 'An Intimate Letter', *Northward Journal* (Moonbeam, Ont.), no.24 (1985), pp. 70–3. Bahá'í Faith, p. 71.

11.869. Robertson, Lloyd. 'Hard Eyed Hatred in Iran', *The Presbyterian Record* (Don Mills, Ont.), (Sept. 1983), p. 12.

11.870. Robinson, Catherine. 'The Baha'is in Iran', *The Friend* (London), (Feb. 19, 1982), p. 214.

11.871. Robinson, Davis R. 'Baha'i', *Iranian Assets Litigation Reporter* (Edgemont, Pa.), (Aug. 5, 1983).

11.872. Rogal, Kim. 'The Islamic Crusade: Blood, Oil and Politics', *Newsweek* (New York), v.103 no.11 (Mar. 12, 1984), pp. 21–6. Bahá'í Faith, p. 21.

11.873. Romarheim, Arild. 'Jesus & Baha'i', *Voice* (Dartington, U.K.), (1975).

11.874. Romer, Annie B. 'A Call from the East to Women', *Speaking of Women* (New York), v.1 no.1 (July 1936), p. 26.

11.875. Root, Martha L. 'Happiness from Bahai Viewpoint', *Roycroft* (East Aurora, N.Y.), v.10 no.4 (June 1922), pp. 131–3.

11.876. Rose, Leonie. 'A Temple Built of Light', *The World Observer* (New York), v.1 no.5 (Sept. 1937), p. 22.

11.877. Rosenberg, Ethel. 'Bahaism, Its Ethical and Social Teachings', *International Congress for the History of Religions (3rd). Transactions*, v.1 (1908), pp. 321–5.

11.878. Rosenburg, Harold. 'The Art Galleries: A Risk for the Intelligence', *The New Yorker*, (Oct. 27, 1962), pp. 152, 154, 157–63. Mark Tobey and Bahá'í, p. 162.

11.879. Roshni, 'Tahira the Pure, Poet and Martyr', *Eve's Weekly* (Bombay), (Oct. 17–23, 1981), p. 39.

11.880. Ross, E. Denison. 'Babism', *North American Review* (Boston), v.172 no.533 (Apr. 1901), pp. 606–22.

11.881. —— *idem.*, *Current Literature* (London), v.31 (July 1901), pp. 104–5.

11.882. Ross, Howard S. 'National Spiritual Assembly of the Bahá'ís of Canada', *The Canada Gazette = La Gazette du Canada* (Ottawa), v.83 no.6 (Feb. 5, 1949), pp. 464, 522.

11.882a. Rothman, Steven. 'Make a Beginning: The Story of Wilmette's Baha'i Temple', *Omnibus* (Chicago), (May 1964), pp. 18–23.

11.883. 'RSTS User Has "Real Problem" ', *Computerworld* (Framingham, Mass.), v.17 no.34 (Aug. 22, 1983), p. 13.

Problems in computer application at the Bahá'í World Centre.

11.884. Rubin, Bonnie Miller. 'The Baha'i House of Worship', *Minneapolis Tribune Picture*, (June 24, 1979), pp. 4–5, 7, 9.

11.885. Rudhyar, Dane. 'The New Religion: 1940 to Mark the Beginning of a World-Wide Religious Revival', *American Astrology* (New York), v.7 no.9 (Nov. 1939), pp. 8–14.

11.886. Ruff, Ivan. 'Baha'i, the Invisible Community', *New Society* (London), v.29 no.623 (12 Sept. 1974), pp. 665–8.

11.887. Russell, George. 'Railing Against Racism', *Time* (New York), v.124 no.26 (Dec. 24, 1984), pp. 18–19. Bahá'í, p. 18.

11.888. Russell, John. 'The "White Writing" of Mark Tobey', *Dialogue* (Washington, D.C.), v.10 no.1 (1977), pp. 57–65. Bahá'í, p. 60.

S

11.889. Sabegeh, Joseph Osire. 'The Rise of Religious Cults', *Shocks* (Ibadan, Nigeria), (June 1983), p. 3.

11.890. Sabzevari, Hossein. 'Blacklist, Bias, Killing Mark "Ultra-Free" Voting', *Guardian* (New York), (May 23, 1984).

11.891. 'Saigon Baha'is Celebrate 145th Anniversary of the Birth of Their Prophet', *The Times of Viet-Nam Magazine* (Saigon), v.4 no.46 (Nov. 18, 1962), pp. 18–19.

11.892. 'Salatless "Saviours" of Islam?', *Al-Islam* (Colombo, Sri Lanka), v.2 no.2 (Feb./Mar. 1985), pp. 1, 6.

11.893. Salov, M. Baer. 'Regarding "Religionization of Mankind" by Yonousuke Nakano', *The Ananai* (Shimizu City, Japan), no.5 (May 1953), pp. 19–20.

11.894. Samandari, Anita. 'Death in Tabriz', *The Green and White: University of Saskatchewan Alumni Association Magazine*, (Winter 1980/81), pp. 12–14.

11.894a. Samuel, Herbert. 'The Baha'i Faith, a World Religion: Their Spiritual Centre Is Haifa', *India and Israel* (Bombay), v.3 no.9 (Mar. 1951), pp. 20–1. Articles in 'boxes' have titles: 'A Prophecy Comes True', 'An Epoch-Making Decision'.

11.895. Sanandaji, S.H.V. 'The Attack on

Baha'i', *The Spectator* (London), v.195 no.6627 (July 1, 1955), p. 15.

11.896. Scatcherd, Felicia R. 'A Wise Man from the East', *The International Psychic Gazette* (London), v.1 no.6 (Jan. 1913), pp. 158–9.

11.897. Schlatter, Franklin D. 'Baha'i Rift', *Ebony* (Chicago), (May 1965).
Letter to the editor.

11.898. Scott, Peggy. 'The Vanishing of the Veil: Abdul Baha at St. John's, Westminster', *The Christian Commonwealth* (London), v.31 no.1562 (Sept. 20, 1911).

11.899, Scully, Brendan. 'A Visit to the Holy Land', *INE Brief* (Dublin), (May 1980), pp. 14–16. Bahá'í Faith, p. 15.

11.900. 'Sculptor's Art Reproduced in Display Pieces', *Signs of the Times* (Cincinnati, Ohio), v.8 no.4 (Apr. 1938), p. 76.

11.901. Sechter, I. Aizic. 'Israeli Baha'i', *Omnibus* (Chicago), (Feb. 1965), p. 17.

11.902. Sefidvash, Farhang. 'Conceito de um Reator Nuclear de Potência para o Brasil', *Revista Basileira de Tecnologia* (Brasilia), v.11 (1980), pp. 145–58. Bahá'í Faith, p. 146. Title in Portuguese, article in English.

11.903. Sempich, Frederick. 'Change Comes to Bible Lands', *National Geographic Magazine*

(Washington, D.C.), v.74 no.6 (Dec. 1938), pp. 695–750. Bahá'í, p. 750.

11.904. Seoharvi, Abdurrahman. 'Bahaism', *The Calcutta Review*, v.124 (July 1907), pp. 409–27.

11.905. Seton, Delia Mary. 'Baha'is: Another View of the Middle East', *The Mediterranean and Eurafrica*, (June 1958), pp. 16–17.

11.906. 'Severe Persecution of Iranian Bahais Reported', *Daily Bulletin* (Bern, Switzerland), no.213 (Nov. 13, 1984), pp. 1, 2, cover.

11.907. Shafaat, Ahmad. 'A Look at Bahaism', *Al-Ittihad* (Plainsfield, Ind.), (Summer 1974), pp. 14–17, 21–3.

11.908. Shah, Ikbal Ali. 'Iran and Britain', *The Contemporary Review* (London), v.166 no.944 (Aug. 1944), pp. 91–4. Bahá'í, p. 93.

11.909. Shah, Ramnik. 'The Baha'is Protest', *New Delhi*, v.2 no.3 (30 April 1979), p. 5.

11.910. Shahabuddin, Syed. 'Iran, the Mullah and the Gun', *Sunday* (Calcutta), v.9 no.44 (18–24 Apr. 1982), pp. 36–7, 39, 41. Bahá'ís, p. 39.

11.911. Shapiro, Benjamin B. 'Structural Design of Baha'i Temple', *Journal of the American Concrete Institute* (Detroit, Mich.), v.30 (Jan.–Feb. 1934), pp. 239–46.

11.912. Sharma, Vichitra. 'Belief in a Universal Faith: The Baha'i Faith Celebrating a Proud Centenary', *Contour* (New Delhi), v.1 no.11 (18–24 May 1980), pp. 25–8.

11.912a. Sharpe, G. Coverdale. 'The Bahai Movement – Where Unitarians Are at One with It: For a Better Understanding', *Inquirer & Christian Life* (London), no.4584 (May 10, 1930), pp. 222–3.

11.913. 'She Spreads the Word', *New Idea* (Melbourne, Vic.), (Feb. 13, 1982), p. 31.
Bahá'í travelling teacher Mahvash Master.

11.914. 'She Was a Baha'i Pioneer', *Islander* (Agana, Guam), (June 24, 1979), pp. 3–4.
Story of Cynthia R. Olson.

11.915. Shedd, J.H. 'Babism: Its Doctrine and Relation to Mission Work', *The Missionary Review of the World* (Princeton, N.J.), v.17 (Dec. 1894), pp. 894–904.

11.915a. Shedd, William A. 'Bahaism, a warning', *Evangelical Christendom* (London), (Nov./Dec. 1911), p. 199.

11.916. —— 'Bahaism and Its Claims', *Missionary Review of the World* (Princeton, N.J.), v.34 (Oct. 1911), pp. 727–34.

11.916a. —— idem., *Evangelical Christendom* (London), (Nov./Dec. 1911), pp. 210–14.

11.917. —— 'An Interesting Document on the Bab', *The Moslem World* (Hartford, Conn.), v.5 no.1 (Jan. 1915), pp. 111–12.
Dr Cormick's description of the Báb.

11.918. Sherarji, Lionel. 'World Prophet Baha'u'llah', *Sunday Pictorial* (Colombo, Ceylon), v.1 no. 25 (21 Nov. 1954), p. 23.

11.919. Sheridan, Greg, 'Baha'is Victims of the Ayatollah's Drive', *The Bulletin* (Sydney, N.S.W.), (May 26, 1981), p. 32.

11.920. Shirazi, M.R. 'Bahai Movement and Its Principles', *Guldasta-i-Karachi*, (Dec. 1922), pp. 6–9.

11.921. Shoghi Effendi, 'The Faith of Baha'u-'llah', *India and Israel* (Bombay), v.5 no.6 (Dec. 1952), pp. 32–3.

11.922. —— 'The Goal of a New World Order', *Sanj Vartaman* (Bombay), (Sept. 1933), pp. 98c–98f.

11.923. 'The Shrine of the Báb', *World Faiths* (London), no.109 (Autumn 1979), cover, p. 6.

11.924. Shultz, George P. 'Human Rights and the Moral Dimension of U.S. Foreign Policy', *Department of State Bulletin* (Washington, D.C.), v.84, no. 5 (Apr. 1984), pp. 15–19. Bahá'ís, p. 17.

11.925. Siddiqui, M.A. 'Qurrat-ul-Ayn, a Profile in Courage', *Dawn Magazine* (Karachi), (4 Mar. 1973).

11.926. Sidersky, Phillip. 'Visit to the Prophet of Persia', *The Missionary Review of the World* (Princeton, N.J.), v.25 (Oct. 1902), pp. 775–6.

11.927. Sigler, Betty. 'The Baha'i Presence', *El Yam Log* (Israel), no.67 (Autumn 1979), pp. 28–31.

11.928. 'Sikkim and the Message', *Arabia: The Islamic World Review* (East Burnham, nr. Slough, Bucks.), no.35 (July 1984), p. 94.

11.929. Silgardo, Melanie. 'Recant or Die', *Imprint* (Bombay), v.21 no.6 (Sept. 1981), pp. 35–6, 41.

11.930. Singer, Henry A. [Letter to the editor], *The New York Times Magazine*, (29 June 1981), p. 62.
Persecutions in Iran.

11.931. Singerman, Philip. 'Reminiscence: What a Karate Bum Finds in Okinawa Is Fallibility, But Not Inspiration', *Sports Illustrated* (New York), (Nov. 19, 1979). *passim*.

11.932. 'Sioux Performer Tours Alaska', *Alaska Native News* (Juneau), (Dec. 1984), p. 32.
Kevin Locke.

11.933. Sivasamy, S. 'Ascension of the Expounder of Baha'i Faith, 'Abdu'l-Baha', *Sunday Pictorial* (Colombo, Ceylon), v.1 no.27 (Dec. 5, 1954), p. 9.

11.934. —— 'Birth of a World Religion', *Sunday Pictorial* (Colombo, Ceylon), v.1 no.52 (29 May 1955), p. 7.

11.935. Slack, Frederick A. 'Beha'u'llah (the Glory of God)', *The Occult Truth Seeker* (Lawrence, Kan.), v.1 no.12 (May 1902), pp. 209–11.

11.936. Slykhuis, John. 'Bahais Escape Terror in Iran', *Topic Newsmagazine* (Bradford, Ont.), (Aug. 7, 1984), pp. [1–2].

11.937. Smith, Colin. 'The Ayatollah's "Holy" War on Bahai Religion', *The Bulletin* (Sydney, N.S.W.), (July 12, 1983), pp. 101–2.

11.938. Smith, Donald B. 'Honoré Joseph Jaxon: A Man Who Lived for Others', *Saskatchewan History* (Saskatoon), v.34 no.3 (Autumn 1981), pp. 81–101. Bahá'í, pp. 91, 96.
Jaxon was a Bahá'í who broke the Covenant in 1918.

11.939. —— 'Ordered to Winnipeg: Varsity Men Fought Louis Riel, But One Served as His Secretary', *The Graduate* (Toronto), (Nov.–Dec. 1984), pp. 5–9.

11.939a. Smith, Maxine. 'No Colour Prejudice', *India and Israel* (Bombay), v.4 no.6 (Dec. 1951), p. 40.

11.940. Smith, Noel. 'The Baha'i Religion: The Baha'is Believe Their Day Has Come', *Baptist Bible Tribune*, v.21 no.11 (Sept. 4, 1970), pp. 3–7.

11.941. Smith, Peter. 'Additional Doctoral and Masters' Theses Relating to Babi and Baha'i Subjects', *Bulletin of the British Society for Middle Eastern Studies* (Oxford), v.9 no.1 (1982), pp. 89–90.

11.942. —— 'Bahá'í Studies, University of Lancaster, 7–8 April, 1979', *Bulletin of the British Society for Middle Eastern Studies* (Oxford), v.6 no.2 (1979), pp. 119–23.

11.942a. Smith, Peter. 'Doctoral and Masters Theses on Bahá'í Subjects (1923–1977).' *Bulletin of the British Society for Middle Eastern Studies* (Oxford), v.6 no.2 (1979), pp. 129–130.

11.943. —— 'Motif Research: Peter Berger and the Baha'i Faith', *Religion* (London), v.8 no.2 (Autumn 1978), pp. 210–34.

11.944. —— 'A Note on Babi and Baha'i Numbers in Iran', *Iranian Studies* (Cambridge,

Mass.), v.17 no.2–3 (Spring-Summer 1984), pp. 295–301.

11.945. Smith, Philippa. 'The Baha'i Faith', *The Friend* (London), (Apr. 17, 1981), pp. 477–8.

11.946. Smith, Terence. 'Iran – Five Years of Fanaticism', *The New York Times Magazine*, (Feb. 12, 1984), pp. 21–2, 24, 26, 28, 30, 32, 34, 36. Bahá'í Faith, p. 28.

11.947. Soffer, Clara. 'The Baha'is', *WIZO in Israel* (Spring 1952), pp. 8–9.

11.947a. ——'A Fourth World Religion in Israel', *Igeret Lagolah* (Jerusalem), nos. 31–2 (Dec.–Jan. 1951), pp. 16–20.

11.948. —— 'A Gold Dome Gleams on Mount Carmel', *WIZO in Israel* (Tel Aviv), no.52 Jan. 1954), p. 5.

11.948a. —— 'Modern Haifa: The Spiritual Centre of the Baha'is', *India and Israel* (Bombay), v.4 no.10 (Apr. 1952), pp. 16–17.

11.949. Sohrab, Ahmad. 'Abdul Baha on the Value of a Universal Language', *The International Psychic Gazette* (London), (Apr. 1913), pp. 250–1.

11.950. —— 'A Few Constructive Thoughts on Universal Love', *Broadcast* (Los Angeles), v.1 no.5 (Feb. 1923), pp. 12–15.

11.951. —— 'The Three Powers', *More Light* (New York), v.1 no.3 (Mar. 1930), pp. 43–4.

11.952. Sorabjee, Soli J. 'Whither Human Rights?', *Mainstream* (New Delhi), (Jan. 26, 1979), pp. 15–17. Bahá'í, p. 15.

11.953. Sorabjee, Zena. 'Persecution of the Baha'is in Iran', *Freedom First* (Bombay), (Aug. 1981), p. 7.

11.953a. Sparham, Griffith J. 'The Bahai Movement', *Inquirer & Christian Life* (London), no.4585 (May 17, 1930), p. 239.

11.954. 'A Spectacular View', *Wilmette Life* (Wilmette, Ill.), (Jan. 2, 1975), cover, p. 4.

11.955. St Rose, Milton Peter. 'The Bahai Faith, a Popular Movement for World Unity', *Customs Link* (Castries, St Lucia), v.1 no.2 (July 1983), p. 6.

11.956. Stannard, J. 'The Passing of a Great Leader of Men: Abdul Baha – an Appreciation', *The Sphinx* (Cairo), (Dec. 17, 1921), p. 195.

11.956a. —— 'Prof. Vambery and the Religion of Peace', *The International Psychic Gazette* (London), no.15 (Oct. 1913), p. 81.

11.957. Stark, Rodney. 'Cult Membership in the Roaring Twenties: Assessing Local Receptivity', *Sociological Analysis* (Chicago), v.42 no.2 (1981), pp. 137–62. Bahá'í Faith, pp. 140, 145, 155.

11.958. —— 'Secularization and Cult Formation in the Jazz Age', *Journal for the Scientific Study of Religion* (Jamaica, N.Y.), v.20 no.4 (1981), pp. 360–73. Bahá'í Faith, pp. 364, 365, 367.

11.958a. Stengel, Susan. ' "I'd Like to Tell You– " Baha'i Faith', *Transcendence* (Seattle, Wash.), v.1 no.1 (1982), p. 19.

11.959. Stephen, David. 'Britain, a Home from Home for Refugees?', *New Society* (London), (24 Feb. 1983), p. 298.

11.960. Stephens, Mitchell. 'Can UPI Be Turned Around?', *Columbia Journalism Review* (New York), (Oct. 1982), pp. 54–8. Bahá'í Faith, p. 55.

11.961. Stevens, E.S. 'Abbas Effendi – His Personality, Work and Followers', *The Fortnightly Review* (London), v.95 (June 1911), pp. 1067–84.

11.962. —— 'The Light in the Lantern', *Everybody's Magazine* (New York), v.25 (Dec. 1911), pp. 775–86.

11.963. Stewart, George Craig. 'The New Persian Temple in Illinois', *The Missionary Review of the World* (Princeton, N.J.), v.44 no.10 (Oct. 1921), pp. 792–6.

11.964. Stileman, Charles Harvey. 'A Week with the Babis', *The Church Missionary Intelligencer* (London), (July 1893), pp. 512–16.

11.965. Stiles, J. 'A World Religion and Universal Peace', *Plain Truth* (Liverpool, U.K.), v.23 no.260 (Jan. 1913), pp. 4–10.

11.966. Stirling, Pamela. 'How Nigh Is the End?', *New Zealand Listener* (Wellington), (Sept. 6, 1980), pp. 20ff. Bahá'í Faith, p. 21.

11.967. Stocking, Annie Woodman. 'The New Woman in Persia', *The Moslem World* (Hartford, Conn.), v.2 no.4 (Oct. 1912), pp. 367–72. Bahá'í, p. 372.

11.968. 'Strange Faith of Baha'i: Its Weddings Are Preacherless, Its Sacred Number Is 9', *Newsweek* (New York), v.15 (Feb. 19, 1940), p. 31.

11.969. 'The Strife of Tongues: Interview with Dr. L.L. Zamenhof', *The Christian Commonwealth* (London), v.33 no.1664 (Sept. 3, 1913), pp. 825–6.

11.970. Suche, Anne. 'Gallery: Otto Rogers', *Western Living* (Vancouver, B.C.), Saskatoon ed., v.2 no.2 (Feb. 1985), p. 86.

11.971. Sugar, Alfred. 'The Bahai Movement', *Inquirer & Christian Life* (London), no.4586 (May 24, 1930), p. 250.

11.972. Sugrue, Thomas. 'About the Front Cover . . .', *Land Reborn* (New York), v.2 no.4 (July–Aug. 1951), cover, p. 10.

11.973. 'Summary Executions Still Widespread, Commission's Special Rapporteur Reports', *UN Chronicle* (New York), v.22 (Mar. 1985), pp. 39–40. Bahá'ís, p. 39.

11.974. 'Survey of the Month', *Opportunity* (New York), v.5 no.8 (Aug. 1927), p. 247.
About Louis G. Gregory's election to the National Spiritual Assembly of the Bahá'ís of the United States.

11.975. Suter, Keith. 'Baha'is in Iran', *National Outlook* (Australia), (May 1982), p. 25.

11.976. Suthers, A.E. 'A Baha'i Pontiff in the Making', *The Moslem World* (Hartford, Conn.), v.25 no.1 (Jan. 1935), pp. 27–35.
Negative article about Shoghi Effendi.

11.977. Sutton, Horace. 'The Last Time I Saw Haifa', *Saturday Review* (New York), v.39 (Nov. 17, 1956), pp. 33–4.

11.978. Sykes, Christopher. 'The Bâb and Bahaism', *The Spectator* (London), v.185 no.6838 (July 14, 1950), pp. 42–3.

11.979. 'A Symphony in Stone', *Guest in Chicago*, v.1 no.12 (Apr. 1953), pp. 4–6.

T

11.980. Taheri, Amir. 'Divine Law and Human Rights', *Index on Censorship* (London), (5/83), pp. 19–21. Bahá'í, p. 20.

11.981. Takieddine, Randa. 'Ayatollah Khomeini's Policies: An Interview with Bani Sadr',

An-Nahar Arab Report & MEMO (Beirut), (29 Jan. 1979), pp. 5–7.
Misrepresents position of Iranian Bahá'í community.

11.982. 'The Talk of the Town: Notes and Com-

ments', *The New Yorker* (New York), (Feb. 4, 1985), pp. 31–2.
Persecutions in Iran.

11.983. Tammik, Heidi. 'Green Acre Baha'i School: A History of an Eliot, Maine Tradition', *Showcase: Foster's Weekly Feature Magazine* (Dover, N.H.), (Apr. 20, 1984), pp. 2–4, 20. Cover title: 'Green Acre Baha'i School: A Tradition in Eliot, Maine'.

11.984. Tavris, Carol. 'Religious Conversion: What People Seek in a New Faith', *Vogue* (New York), (Nov. 1982), p. 150.

11.985. Taylor, David L. 'The Willkie of Baghdad', *The Kiwanis Magazine* (Chicago), (June 1947), pp. 8–9.

11.986. 'The Teaching of the Babi', by J.K.M., *The Book Buyer* (New York), v.22 (June 1901), p. 416.

11.987. 'Tehran Radio Comments on Human Rights Criticism', *Foreign Broadcast Information Service Daily Reports* (Washington, D.C.), (9 Dec. 1985), section viii, pp. 15–16.

11.988. 'Tempest in a Temple', *Newsweek* (New York), v.45 (June 6, 1955), p. 50.

11.989. Temple, Bernard. 'Persia and the Regeneration of Islam', *Journal of the Royal Society of Arts* (London), (May 27, 1910), pp. 652–65.

11.990. 'Temple for Bahai Faith Uses God's Blueprints: New Delhi Structure Mimics Lotus Blossom', *Engineering News-Record* (New York), (Nov. 8, 1984), pp. 34–5, cover.

11.991. 'Temple Is Ultimate in Precast Art', *Cement Imagination* (Mississauga, Ont.), v.12 no.2 (June 1980), pp. [1, 3]

11.992. 'Temple of Light: The Intricate and Delicately Beautiful Baha'i Temple Demonstrates the Durable Versatility of Concrete', *Concrete Construction* (Addison, Ill.), v.28 no.2 (Feb. 1983), pp. 119–22.

11.993. 'Temple of Peace', *The Israel Export Journal* (Tel Aviv), (Nov. 1960), p. 16.

11.994. 'A Temple of Peace at Wilmette, Chicago, with a Translucent Dome, a Centre of Bahai Belief', *The Illustrated London News* (London), v.185 no. 4993 (Dec. 29, 1934), p. 1105.

11.995. 'Temple of Unique Design Taxes Ingenuity of Form Builders', *Construction Methods* (Chicago), (Aug. 1931).

11.995a. 'Temple Structure Lecture Theme', *Winnetka Talk* (Winnetka, Ill.), (Oct. 2, 1941), p. 55.

11.996. 'Terremoto en Guatemala', *Secretariat News* (New York), (31 Mar. 1976), p. 3.
Bahá'í International Community contributions to earthquake relief.

11.997. 'Terror in Iran', *Peace by Peace* (Northern Ireland), (Sept. 18, 1981), p. 6.

11.998. 'Terror in Iran', *Voice of the Martyrs* (Auckland, N.Z.), (Oct. 1981), p. [4]

11.999. 'Then Shall Appear the Sign of the Son of Man in Heaven?', *More Light* (New York), [v.1 no.1?], ([Jan. 1930?]), p. 19.
Quotation from Bahá'í scriptures.

11.1000. ' "They Can't Last Very Long": An Exiled President Speaks Out Against the Khomeini Regime', *India Today* (New Delhi), (Sept. 16–30, 1981), pp. 75–6. Bahá'í Faith, p. 76.

11.1001. 'The Third Reich and the Bahais', *AJR Information* (London), (Jan. 1984), p. 3.

11.1001a. '30 Years of Pioneering on Tyendinaga Honored,' *Tekawennake* (Brantford, Ont.), v.5 no.4 (May 23, 1979).

11.1002. Thompson, Juliet. 'Persian Reformer's View of Art', *Art World and Arts & Decoration*, v.1 (Mar. 1917), pp. 409, 412–14.

11.1003. Thompson, Kenneth W. 'Bahai Temple, Wilmette, Ill.', *US Steel News* (Pittsburgh, Pa.), (Mar. 1937), cover, p. 1.

11.1004. Tillotson, Peter. 'British Design for a Temple in Panama: A Symbolic Form in Concrete', *Concrete* (London) [Bulgarian ed.], v.6 no.11 (Nov. 1972), pp. 22–4.

11.1005. —— 'Nine Gateways to God: British Design for a Temple in Panama: A Symbolic Form in Concrete', *Concrete* (London), v.6 no.11 (Nov. 1972), pp. 22–4.

11.1006. 'Time to Speak Up', *Canadian Jewish News* (Toronto), (Nov. 19, 1981).

11.1007. Tinney, James S. 'Baha'i Doctrine Attracts Non-Whites', *The National Leader* (Philadelphia, Pa.), v.2 no.24 (Oct. 20, 1983), pp. 14, 21.

11.1008. Tisdall, W. St Clair. 'Die Babi-Beha'i, die jüngste muhammedanische Sekte, von Dr. Hermann Roemer' [review], *The Moslem World* (Hartford, Conn.), v.3 no.3 (July 1913), pp. 320–1.

11.1008a. 'To a Baha'i, the Most Important Prayer Is a Person's Daily Life,' *Champaign-Urbana Guide* (Champaign, Ill.), (July 1977), p. 11.

11.1009. 'To the Glory of God, a Work of Art in

Concrete', *PTL News* (Pittsburgh, Pa.), (Dec. 1954), pp. 6–9.

11.1010. Tobler, Emile. 'A Protest from the Bahaists', *The Open Court* (Chicago), v.30 no.8 (Aug. 1916), pp. 505–8.

11.1011. Tomlin, Viva. 'For God and Country', *New Internationalist* (Oxford, Eng.), (Oct. 1983), p. 13.

11.1012. 'Towards Spiritual Unity: An Interview with Abdul Baha: Dialogue Between Abbas Effendi and Rev. R.J. Campbell, M.A.', *The Christian Commonwealth* (London), v.31 no.1561 (Sept. 13, 1911), pp. 849–50.

11.1013. Townshend, George. 'The Bahai Faith: Abstract of an Address Delivered on Monday, April 17th, 1950', *Religions: Journal of the Society for the Study of Religions* (London), no.70 (Sept.–Dec. 1950), pp. 69–72.

11.1014. 'Tribunal Considers Baha'i Protest', *Iranian Assets Litigation Reporter* (Edgemont, Pa.), (Aug. 19, 1983).

11.1015. Trotter, Coutts. 'A New Religion', *Scottish Review* (London), v.19 (Apr. 1892), pp. 326–43.

11.1016. Truelove, Adrienne. 'Fanaticism in Iran', *Education: Journal of the New South Wales Teachers' Federation*, v.63 no.11 (July 5, 1982), p. 9.

11.1017. Tsao, Y.S. 'Reflections on the Chung San Cultural Foundation', *The China Critic* (Shanghai), v.6 no.21 (May 25, 1933), pp. 519–22

11.1017a. —— 'The Unity of Civilization and the Universality of Religion', *The Chinese Social and Political Science Review* (Peiping), (1927), pp. 610–25.

11.1018. Tu'itahi, Sione H. 'Women's Status Cited by Baha'i in Tonga Meet', *Pacific Magazine* (Honolulu, Hawaii), (Dec. 1985).

11.1019. 'Twelve Years' Persistence Sold This Job', *Portland Cement Association Newsletter* (Chicago), (Sept. 27, 1932).

11.1020. '20 International Conferences in 1963', *The Israel Export Journal* (Tel Aviv), (Jan. 1963).

Mentions first International Bahá'í Convention.

U

11.1021. 'U.S. Rival to Taj Mahal Is Dedicated Near Chicago', *Capper's Weekly* (Topeka, Kan.), (May 5, 1953).

11.1022. Ullman, Chana. 'Cognitive and Emotional Antecedents of Religious Conversion', *Journal of Personality and Social Psychology* (Washington, D.C.), v.43 no.1 (1982), pp. 183–92. Bahá'í Faith, pp. 185, 186, 188, 189, 191.

11.1023. Ullmann, Christian. 'Khomeini vs. the Bahais: "Official" Persecution Stalks Iran's "Heretics" ', *World Press Review* (New York), v.29 no.11 (Nov. 1982), p. 61.

11.1024. 'UN Sub-Commission on Discrimination and Minorities', *The Review* [International Commission of Jurists] (Geneva), no.27 (Dec. 1981), pp. 40–6. Bahá'í Faith, p. 46.

11.1025. ' "Undo the Evils of Bantu Education" Principal Says', *Ikonomi* (Mafikeng, Bophuthatswana), v.1 no. 5 (Dec. 1982), p. 15.

11.1026. 'Unholy War: Assault on Iran's Anglicans', *Time* (New York), (May 26, 1980), p. 62.

11.1027. 'Unicef Emergency Appeal', *Secretariat News* (New York), v.39 no.18 (Oct. 31, 1984), p. 8.

11.1028. 'El Único Templo Bahá'í en América Latina Está Ubicado en Panamá = Latin America's Only Bahá'í Temple Is Here in Panama', *Enfoque de Panamá = Focus on Panama*, v.12 no.1 (1982–1983), pp. 125–9.

11.1029. 'Union of Nations', *The Dawn* (Bombay), v.8 no.10 (15 Sept. 1942), p. 3.

11.1029a. 'Unity of Mankind', *Hindu Vishwa* (London), (Nov. 1925), p. 25.

11.1030. 'The Universal Gospel That Abdul Baha Brings Us', *Current Literature* (London), v.52 (June 1912), pp. 676–8.

11.1031. 'The Universal Races Congress', *The Christian Commonwealth* (London), v.31 no.1555 (Aug. 2, 1911), pp. 753–4.

11.1032. 'Unusual Structure to Be Built at Wilmette, Ill.', *Engineering News-Record* (New York), (Aug. 14, 1930), p. 269.

11.1033. 'Up Speckled to Wilhelm's Lodge: A

Worthwhile Jaunt from Kezar', *The Kezar Kat* (Kezar, Me.), v.1 no.2 (Aug. 1938). Back page.

11.1034. 'US Public Delegate to UN Reports

Executions of Baha'is in Iran', *Human Rights Internet Reporter* (Washington, D.C.), v.9 no.7 (Dec. 1983–Jan. 1984), p. 376.

V

11.1035. Vader, John Paul. 'August Forel Defends the Persecuted Persian Baha'is, 1925–27', *Gesnerus* (Aarau, Switzerland), no.41 (1984), pp. 53–60.

11.1036. Vail, Albert. 'Bahai, a Revelation of the Springtime of God', *The Herald of Asia* (Tokyo), v.9 no.19 (Aug. 7, 1920), pp. 522–3.

11.1037. —— 'The Baha'i Temple of Universal Peace', *The Open Court* (Chicago), v.45 no.7 (July 1931), pp. 411–17.

11.1038. —— 'Bahaism: A Study of a Contemporary Movement', *Harvard Theological Review* (Cambridge, Mass.), v.7 (July 1914), pp. 339–57.

11.1039. —— 'Making Brotherhood a Reality', *Abbott's Monthly* (Chicago), (Jan. 1931), pp. 27–8, 67, 71–2.

11.1039a. —— 'What Baha'i Means', *The Evanston Review* (Evanston, Ill.), v.4 no.47 (Apr. 25, 1929), p. 1.

11.1040. Vakil, N.R. 'The First Universal Religious Edifice in the Western World', *The Hindustan Review* (Patna), v.68 no.370 (Dec. 1935), pp. 387–8.

11.1041. Van den Hoonaard, Will. C. 'Emerging from Obscurity: The Response of the Iranian Baha'i Community to Persecution, 1978–1982', *Conflict Quarterly* (Fredericton, N.B.), v.3 no.1 (Fall 1982), pp. 5–16.

11.1042. Vashist, D.F. 'An Interview with Ruhiyyih Khanum, Wife of the Guardian of International Baha'is [sic] Faith', *Indian Promenade* (New Delhi), v.1 no.8–9 (Apr.–May. 1967), pp. 5–6.

11.1043. Vashitz, Joseph. 'Dhawāt and 'Isamiyyūn: Two Groups of Arab Community Leaders in Haifa During the British Mandate', *Asian and African Studies* (Haifa), v.17 no.1–3 (1983), pp. 95–120. Bahá'í, p. 99.

11.1044. Vatralsky, Stoyan Krstoff. 'Mohammedan Gnosticism in America: The Origin,

History, Character and Esoteric Doctrines of the Truth-Knowers', *American Journal of Theology* (Chicago), v.6 no.1 (Jan. 1902), pp. 57–78.

11.1045. Vaupel, Ouise. 'Changing a World', *The Open Court* (Chicago), v.45 no.7 (July 1931), pp. 418–24.

11.1046. —— 'What Is the Bahai Movement?: A Review of the Movement for World Brotherhood Founded by the Great Persian Seer', *Psychology* (New York), v.14 no.3 (May 1930), pp. 20–1, 66–8.

11.1047. Venable, Charles Leslie. 'Baha'i Temple Moves Toward Completion', *The Christian Century* (Chicago), v.58 (Oct. 22, 1941), p. 1316.

11.1048. Verma, Prakash. 'Iran's Persecuted Baha'is', *Sunday* (Calcutta), v.11 no.3 (7–13 Aug. 1983), pp. 38–9.

11.1049. 'Views and Reviews', *Mastery* (London), v.2 no.2 (Aug./Oct. 1915), pp. 139–56. Bahá'í Faith, Mirza Assad 'U'llah and Ameen 'U'llah Fareed, pp. 153–6.

11.1050. Villard, Henry S. 'Murder in Teheran', *Foreign Service Journal* (Washington, D.C.), (June 1982), pp. 24–7.
Murder in the 1920s in Ṭihran of U.S. diplomat Robert Whitney Imbrie who was accused of being a Bábí.

11.1051. 'A Violence Free Society', *Secretariat News* (New York), (January 16, 1980), p. 9.

11.1052. 'Visit of Abdul Baha to Great Britain', *The Moslem World* (Hartford, Conn.), v.3 no.2 (Apr. 1913), p. 196.

11.1053. Voliva, Wilbur Glenn. 'The Overlapping of Dispensations', *Leaves of Healing* (Zion, Ill.), v.48 no.9 (May 21, 1921), pp. 133–8. Bahá'í Faith, p. 137.
Bahá'í temple in Wilmette 'will have to go' during the millennium.

11.1054. 'Vote for the Mullah of Your Choice', *The Economist* (London), (Feb. 11, 1984).

W

11.1055. Wade, John T. 'Iran', *The Economist* (London), (29 Sept. 1984).

11.1056. Waite, Louise R. 'A Great Bahai Temple in America', *The International Psychic Gazette* (London), no.24 (July 1914), pp. 339–40.

11.1057. Walker, C.G. 'A New Aspect of Cut Stone', *The Exponent* (Des Moines, Ia.), v.1 no.2 (June 1940), pp. 6–7.

11.1058. Walker, John W. 'Epilogue Page', *Newcastle College Advanced Education* (Newcastle, N.S.W.), (Nov. 1984). Bahá'í Faith and Christianity.

11.1059. —— 'More from the Religious Smorgasbord: Bahá'í Faith', *Newcastle College Advanced Education* (Newcastle, N.S.W.), (Aug. 1984).

11.1060. Walton, Pauline. 'Fear Grips Bahái Doctors', *Doctor* (Surrey, U.K.), (Apr. 23, 1981).

11.1061. Walzer, William C. 'October 28, the Bahai Faith (World Service Sunday)', *Adult Teacher* (Nashville, Tenn.), v.9 no.10 (Oct. 1956), pp. 45–8. Christian criticism of Bahá'í doctrines.

11.1062. 'The War the World Forgot', *The Observer* (London), (26 June 1983), pp. 18–19, 21, 23–4. Bahá'í Faith, p. 24.

11.1063. Watkins, Bob. 'World Unity Is Bahá'i Vision', *Voice* (Dartington, U.K.), (Jan. 1984), pp. 2, 26.

11.1064. 'We Love All Religions', *Time* (New York), v.81 (Apr. 26, 1963), p. 69.

11.1065. *idem.*, p. 53 [European ed.]

11.1066. 'The Week: Indonesia', *Far Eastern Economic Review* (Hong Kong), (14 Mar. 1985), p. 11. Banning of the Bahá'í Faith in Indonesia.

11.1067. Weesit, Teresa D. 'The Baha'i Faith: Fostering Brotherhood and Kicking Away Human Foible and Folly "Like an Old Shoe" ', *Philippine Panorama*, (Nov. 29, 1981), pp. 20, 26–7, 32, 34, 54.

11.1068. Weil, Gotthold. 'Arnold Toynbee's Conception of the Future of Islam', *Middle Eastern Affairs* (New York), v.2 no.1 (Jan. 1951), pp. 3–17. Bahá'í Faith, pp. 10, 14.

11.1069. Weinstein, Alfred. 'Lady Doctor Heals the Indians', *The Atlanta Journal and Constitution Magazine*, (Apr. 3, 1960), pp. 40, 42.

Jennie Coe Taylor, Bahá'í pioneer in Guatemala.

11.1070. Weir, Clara E. 'Pageantry: The Messenger', *The Quarterly Journal of Speech* (Ann Arbor, Mich.), v.19 no.3 (June 1933), pp. 379–85. Ṭáhirih, pp. 383, 385; 'Abdu'l-Bahá, p. 383.

11.1071. Weiss, Gaea Laughingbird. 'Richard St. Barbe Baker, Savior of the Trees', *New Age* (Allston, Mass.), (Nov. 1982), pp. 56–7.

11.1072. Whalen, William J. 'Baha'i', *U.S. Catholic* (Chicago), (June 1966), pp. 41–4.

11.1073. —— 'Baha'ism', *Our Sunday Visitor* (Huntingdon, Ind.), (May 19, 1963).

11.1074. 'What Is Baha'ism?', *The Banner* (Grand Rapids, Mich.), (Apr. 20, 1973), p. 9.

11.1075. 'What Is the Baha'i Cause?', *Awake!* (Brooklyn, N.Y.), (Sept. 22, 1957), pp. 17–20. Statement from Jehovah's Witnesses viewpoint.

11.1076. 'What Is the Baha'i Faith', *World Peace Through Spiritual Regeneration* (Calcutta), v.2 no.18 (Feb. 1, 1937), pp. 342–5.

11.1077. 'What Is This Faith Called Bahá'í?', *The Virgin Islander*, v.2 no.6, pp. 25–8.

11.1078. Wheeler, Jenny. 'Breaking: Kiwi Kids Are Streets Ahead', *New Zealand Woman's Weekly* (Auckland), (Apr, 23, 1984), pp. 28–30. Bahá'í Faith, p. 30 and photograph.

11.1079. —— 'For Wheelchair Mother, a Fifth Child at 45', *New Zealand Woman's Weekly* (Auckland), (Sept. 7, 1981), pp. 4–5. About Anastasia Del Monte, a Bahá'í.

11.1080. 'When Baha'is Build a Temple', *The Highway Traveler* (Cleveland), v.9 no.5 (Oct.–Nov. 1937), pp. 24, 38.

11.1081. White, E.B. 'The Talk of the Town: Notes and Comment', *The New Yorker* (New York), (Mar. 22, 1930). Mentions Bahá'í marriage 'rite' in wedding of Elsie Benkard and Charles Clarke.

11.1082. White, Henry. 'How Babis Died for Their Faith in Persia', *Mercy and Truth* (London), (1903), pp. 275–6. Yazd upheaval of 1903.

11.1083. White, Roger. 'Guest Poet', *Seven Gates: Poetry from Jerusalem* (Jerusalem), v.1 [no. 1] (Winter 1985), pp. 93–6. Bahá'í Faith, p. 93.

11.1083a. —— 'My Religion, Baha'i, Is a Love Story', *Liberty* (Toronto, Ont.), v.32 no.4 (June 1955), p. 26.

11.1084. —— 'Sweetmeat', *White Wall Review* (Toronto), (1985), p. 14.

11.1085. —— 'Travelling Backward. Honoured. Soap Bubble Song. Belated Hanukka', *Arc* (Ramat Aviv, Israel), 1(1983), pp. 58–60.

11.1086. Whitehead, O.Z. 'Lillian', *George Spelvin's Theatre Book* (Newark, Del.), v.1 no.1 (Spring 1978), pp. 3–95. Bahá'í Faith, pp. 59–61, 68, 72, 75, 77, 80, 82, 83, 92–4.
Reminiscences of Whitehead's association with Lillian Gish.

11.1087. Whiteside, Eddie. 'Persecuted for Their Beliefs', *The Presbyterian Herald* (Belfast), no.484 (June 1985), p. 21.

11.1088. Wickman, George E. 'A Unique Temple Rises in Illinois', *G-E Contractor* (Bridgeport, Conn.), v.1 no.9 (Nov. 1931), pp. 12–13.

11.1089. 'Will Bahaism Unite All Religious Faiths?', *The American Review of Reviews* (New York), v.45 (June 1912), pp. 748–50.

11.1090. Williams, Val. 'No Let-Up in the Rule of Religious Hate', *Now!* (London), (Feb. 13, 1981).

11.1091. Williams, Wilburn. 'Covenant of Timelessness & Time: Symbolism & History in Robert Hayden's Angle of Ascent', *Massachussetts Review* (Amherst, Mass.), v.18 (Winter 1977), pp. 731–49. Bahá'í Faith, p. 744.

11.1092. Willson, Robert Z. 'The Baha'i World Faith', *Inward Light* (Wallingford, Pa.), no.49 (Fall 1955), pp. 35–7.
Author's story of conversion from the Quakers to the Bahá'í Faith.

11.1093. Wilson, Mary F. 'Story of the Bab', *Contemporary Review* (London), v.48 (Dec. 1885), pp. 808–29.

11.1094. —— *idem.*, *Littell's Living Age* (Boston, Mass.), v.168 (Jan. 16, 1886), pp. 151–63.

11.1095. Wilson, Samuel Graham. 'Babism, a Failure', *The Missionary Review of the World* (Princeton, N.J.), v.27 (Feb. 1904), pp. 91–7; (Mar. 1904), pp. 207–11.

11.1096. —— 'Bahaism, an Antichristian System', *Bibliotheca Sacra* (Oberlin, Ohio), v.72 (Jan. 1915), pp. 1–22.

11.1097. —— 'Bahaism and Religious Assassination', *The Moslem World* (Hartford, Conn.), v.4 no.3 (July 1914), pp. 231–45.

11.1098. —— 'Bahaism and Religious Deception', *The Moslem World* (Hartford, Conn.), v.5 no.2 (Apr. 1915), pp. 166–84.

11.1099. —— 'Bahaism and the Woman Question', *The Missionary Review of the World* (Princeton, N.J.), v.37 (Oct. 1914), pp. 739–45; (Dec. 1914), pp. 915–19.

11.1100. —— 'Bahaism in Its Relation to the State', *Church Missionary Review* (London), (Jan. 1915), pp. 19–26.

11.1101. —— 'Bahaism: Its Failure in Moral Conduct', *The Moslem World* (Hartford, Conn.), v.5 no.3 (July 1915), pp. 268–82.

11.1102. —— 'The Bayan of the Bab', *Princeton Theological Review* (Princeton, N.J.), v.13 no.4 (Oct. 1915), pp. 633–54.
Review of Nicolas's translation into French of the Persian Bayán.

11.1103. —— 'The Claims of Bahaism', *The East and the West* (London), v.12 (July 1914), pp. 249–70.

11.1104. —— 'Is Bahaism Anti-Christian?', *The Bible Magazine* (New York), (Aug. 1915), pp. 681–98.

11.1105. Winchester, Simon. 'This Defiant Breed', *Sunday Times Magazine* (London), (June 12, 1983), pp. 7, 30–5.
Exhibition by painter Duffy Sheridan, American Bahá'í pioneer in the Falkland Islands.

11.1105a. 'Windsor's Friends', *The New Yorker* (New York), (1939), p. 16.

11.1106. Winger-Bearskin, Michael. 'Baha'is in Iran Persecuted', *Tulsa Jewish Review* (Tulsa, Okla.), (Sept. 1983), pp. 27–8, 46.

11.1107. Winkler, Fredi. 'Beth-Shalom Guest House', *News from Israel* (West Columbia, S.C.), (Apr. 1982), pp. 16–17. Bahá'í Faith, p. 16.

11.1108. ' "Winnetka Day" Open House at Baha'i Temple to Feature Tours, Music, Exhibits, Service', *Winnetka Talk* (Winnetka, Ill.), (Feb. 23, 1961), cover, p. 29.

11.1108a. Wise, Anny. 'United Nations – General Assembly on Elimination of All Forms of Religious Intolerance', *Begrip Belgie* (Mechelen, Belgium), Nr. 2 (Winter 1983), pp. 8–13. Bahá'í, pp. 9–13.

11.1109. 'With Living Legend Dizzy Gillespie Topping the Bill, the Lesotho Jazz Festival Was One Hell of a Blow and All That Jazz', *Scope* (Mobeni, S. Afr.), (Jan. 20, 1978), pp. 85, 116–17.

11.1110. 'A Wonderful Movement in the East: A Visit to Abdul Baha at Alexandria', *The Chris-*

tian Commonwealth (London), (Dec. 28, 1910), p. 231.

11.1111. Woodlen, Etta. 'What Is the Baha'i World Faith', *Negro History Bulletin* (Washington, D.C.), v.23 no.1 (Oct. 1959), pp. 13–14.

11.1112. Woodward, Kenneth L. 'Iran's Holy War on Baha'is', *Newsweek* (New York), (Jan. 25, 1982), p. 63, European ed.

11.1113. —— idem., p. 73, U.S. ed.

11.1114. —— 'The Minority that Iran Persecutes', *Newsweek* (New York), (Mar. 24, 1980), p. 53, U.S. ed.

11.1115. —— idem., p. 61, European ed.

11.1116. Worku, Belete. 'The All-Male Club', *The Blue Nile Toastmaster*, 2192-U (1978?), pp. 16–17.

11.1117. 'World Religion Day', *Australian Stamp Monthly* (North Melbourne, Vic.), (Mar. 1985).

X, Y, Z

11.1118. Yacoob, M.H. 'Facts About the Bahaaee Religion', *Ahmadiyya or True Islam* (Trinidad and Tobago), (Apr.–June 1396 [1976]), p. 3.

11.1119. Yarjani, Javad. 'Iran Maligned', *The Bulletin* (Sydney, N.S.W.), (Nov. 4, 1980), p. 11.

11.1120. Young, F.S. 'Baha'i Temple Sparkling Tribute to Mineralogy', *Oregon Mineralogist* (Portland), v.2 no.1 (Jan. 1934), p. 8.

11.1121. —— 'The Five Billion Carat Gem Bahai Temple at Willmette [sic], Illinois', *The Mineralogist* (Portland, Ore.), v.4 no.1 (Jan. 1936), pp. 30–1, 54.

11.1122. Young, Patrick. 'The Growing Faith of Baha'i', *Dominion Magazine*, (Jan. 1967), pp. 29–33.

11.1123. Youngjohn, Lee. 'Baha'i's [sic] Persecuted and Martyred in Iran', *Das Tor* (Glendale, Ariz.), v.20 no.7 (Oct. 22, 1984), pp. 4, 8.

11.1124. Zaki, Yaqub. 'Reagan Blows the Baha'i Cover', *Crescent International* (Markham, Ont.), v.12 no.8 (July 1–15, 1983), pp. 1, 11.

11.1125. Zanjání, Áqá 'Abdu'l-Aḥad. 'Personal Reminiscences of the Bábí Insurrection at Zanján in 1850', *Journal of the Royal Asiatic Society* (London), v.29 (1897), pp. 761–827. Translated by Edward G. Browne.

11.1126. Zeine, Zeine N. 'The Attack on Baha'i', *The Spectator* (London), v.194 no.6623 (June 3, 1955), pp. 705–6.

11.1127. Zwemer, Samuel M. "Le Beyan Persan, by Seyyed Ali Mohammed . . .; Le Cheikhisme (Extrait), by A.L.M. Nicolas . . .; La Science de Dieu, by A.L.M. Nicolas' [review], *The Moslem World* (Hartford, Conn.), v.2 no.2 (Apr. 1912), p. 202.

11.1128. —— 'Persia Faces the Future', *Church Missionary Review* (London), (Mar. 1927), pp. 42ff.

XII
Works of Covenant-Breakers

THE Bahá'í Faith is seen by the Bahá'ís as the first of the world's religions to be invested with an instrument capable of ensuring the continued unity of the body of its followers. The Covenant established by Bahá'u'lláh provides for the Bahá'í Cause a centre to whom all Bahá'ís are required to turn for the resolution of difficult problems. Bahá'u'lláh appointed 'Abdu'l-Bahá as head of the Faith after him and interpreter of Bahá'í scriptures. 'Abdu'l-Bahá appointed Shoghi Effendi to be the Guardian of the Cause of God and interpreter of the holy texts, and laid down the necessary qualifications for any future Guardians after him. Bahá'u'lláh and 'Abdu'l-Bahá also created and delineated a series of elected bodies: Local Houses of Justice (presently termed Local Spiritual Assemblies), National or Secondary Houses of Justice (currently called National Spiritual Assemblies) and the Universal House of Justice. Bahá'ís are parties to this Covenant which requires obedience to the head and centre of the Faith and wholehearted support of and cooperation with its divinely-revealed order.

From time to time individuals within the Faith have attempted either to create a sect or following around their own personal interpretation or have opposed the person or body which is at the head of the Bahá'í Faith. In thus attempting to force Bahá'u'lláh's teachings into a personal mould, and in opposing the officially appointed head of their religion, such individuals have revealed their own ambition. The sanction for such 'breaking of the Covenant' is expulsion from the ranks of the faithful, who must have no social intercourse with the one so expelled.

Covenant-breaking is not the same thing as simple disaffection. Since no one is coerced into becoming, or remaining, a Bahá'í, no stigma is attached to those who cease to be Bahá'ís. Covenant-breaking is fundamentally different, involving those who from within the Bahá'í community attempt to manipulate the Bahá'í Faith to their own advantage or in accordance with their own concepts.

In the course of Bahá'í history there have been individuals and groups of Bahá'ís who have opposed Bahá'u'lláh's appointment of 'Abdu'l-Bahá, 'Abdu'l-Bahá's appointment of Shoghi Effendi, the administrative institutions or the election of the Universal House of Justice. Such individuals and groups have left a number of publications reflecting their viewpoints. Bahá'ís are not forbidden to read this material but they are strongly warned of the dangers of doing so without a thorough knowledge of the Faith's teachings and history.

The following works by or associated with Covenant-breakers are arranged as the other entries in this bibliography. Below is a list of some of the major Covenant-breaker groups, and the individuals associated with them, in a roughly chronological order:

1. Azalís in America

August J. Stenstrand was a partisan of Ṣubḥ-i-Azal (the half-brother of Bahá'u'lláh and the nominee of the Báb), probably the only westerner to give him allegiance.

2. Behaists (partisans of Muḥammad-'Alí)

Ibrahim G. Kheiralla repudiated the leadership of 'Abdu'l-Bahá and cast in his lot with Muḥammad-'Alí, who had opposed the provisions of Bahá'u'lláh's Will in which 'Abdu'l-Bahá was made head of the Faith. Kheiralla's followers, all located in America, were called Behaists. Among his lieutenants were J.G. Hamilton and F.O. Pease. A manuscript history of the Kheiralla episode, written by Anton Haddad, indicates that Kheiralla wished for personal leadership of the Bahá'ís in America and the acceptance of his own peculiar doctrines as the official teaching of the Bahá'í Faith (see *Baha'i Studies Bulletin*, v.2 no.3 (Dec. 1983), pp. 3–67).

3. Anti-organization 'Free Baha'is'

Ruth White personally opposed the Will and Testament of 'Abdu'l-Bahá and did everything in her power to defame the character of Shoghi Effendi before the Palestine authorities. Her accusations that Shoghi Effendi had forged the Will have recently been taken up again by Hermann Zimmer in Germany, a member of an organization called the 'Freie Bahai' (Free Bahais). Ruth White herself left the Bahá'í teachings entirely behind and became a follower of Meher Baba.

4. New History Society/Caravan of East and West

Ahmad Sohrab and Julie Chanler accepted Shoghi Effendi as Guardian but in effect refused to follow his wishes because of their personal abhorrence of the Bahá'í administrative order. When they set up the New History Society as a competing organization and showed continued disregard for the wishes of the Guardian in the matter, they were declared Covenant-breakers. They later founded another organization called The Caravan of East and West.

5. Remeyites

Charles Mason Remey was a Hand of the Cause of God and was appointed president of the International Bahá'í Council by Shoghi Effendi. When Shoghi Effendi died in 1957 without leaving a Will or naming a successor, Remey declared himself in 1960 to be the 'hereditary Guardian' on the basis of his position as president of the Council. Remey was cut off from all his former positions and became the leader of a small group known as 'Bahá'ís Under the Hereditary Guardianship'. One of Remey's early supporters was Mary Magdalen Wilkin. Joel Marangella, one of Remey's closest associates, was named by Remey in 1964 as the president of a new International Bahá'í Council; in 1969, more than four years before Remey's death, Marangella proclaimed himself 'third Guardian'. The Remeyites have broken into a number of groups:

(a) The 'Orthodox Bahá'í Faith, Mother Bahá'í Council' composed of those who followed Joel B. Marangella as 'third Guardian'.

(b) A small group following Donald Harvey as Marangella's rival in claiming to be the 'third Guardian' based upon written documents from Remey stating that Harvey was to succeed him. Francis C. Spataro operates the Charles Mason Remey Society, composed of Harvey supporters, from Jamaica, N.Y.

(c) The 'Orthodox Bahá'í Faith under the Regency' organized by Reginald King, who claimed to be regent for an as yet unnamed descendent of Bahá'u'lláh who would become the 'second Guardian'. This group now rejects Remey and those who claim guardianship in succession to him.

(d) The 'Bahá'ís Under the Provisions of the Covenant', a group founded by Leland Jensen, headquartered in Missoula, Montana. Jensen claims that Davidic kingship was inherited by Bahá'u'lláh, passed to 'Abdu'l-Bahá, who then passed the kingship to Charles Mason Remey by making Remey an 'adopted son'. The kingship was then passed again to Remey's adopted son, Joseph Pepe Remey. Jensen claims to be Joshua (spoken of in Zachariah 3) and to be the 'establisher of the kingdom of Bahá'u'lláh', as well as the fulfiller of American Indian prophecies. Supporters include Roger Caryl.

6. House of Mankind; Faith of God

John Carré was the spokesman for Jamshid Ma'ání, referred to as 'The Man'. 'The Man' also titles himself 'Samá'u'lláh' and claims to be the last and greatest of three Manifestations that began with the Báb and Bahá'u'lláh. Supporters include S.H. Khoreshi and Taj ud Din Chawdhuri.

7. Independent individuals

Ruhi Afnan, a cousin of Shoghi Effendi, was excommunicated for disobedience to Shoghi Effendi and for having contacts with other family members who had been expelled from the Faith. Afnan's works are largely philosophical and are generally not in conflict with Bahá'í concepts.

Interesting historical overviews of Covenant-breaker groups are provided in: Joel Bjorling, *The Baha'i Faith: A Historical Bibliography* (New York: Garland Publishing Company, 1985); and Vernon Elvin Johnson, 'An Historical Analysis of Critical Transformations in the Evolution of the Baha'i World Faith' (unpublished Ph.D. dissertation, Baylor University, 1974). Johnson shows considerable weakness in his grasp of the Bahá'í doctrine of the Covenant, but the historical information on the Covenant-breaker organizations helps to clarify their relationships and claims. Further information is available in *The Encyclopedia of American Religions* by J. Gordon Melton (Wilmington, N.C.: McGrath, 1978) and later editions of the same work published by Gale Research Inc. of Detroit.

12.1. Afnan, Ruhi Muhsen. *Baha'u'llah and the Bab Confront Modern Thinkers*. New York: Philosophical Library, 1977. xiv, 172 p. LC card 75–109166.
　　Review:
Choice, (Oct. 1978), p. 1066.
　　The second in a two-part philosophical treatise, this book by Shoghi Effendi's cousin and former secretary is subtitled: 'Book II: Spinoza: Concerning God'. Its principal concern is Spinoza's monism which was central to his concept of God. Revealed religion, especially in the teachings of the Báb and Bahá'u'lláh, is seen as avoiding the predicaments of Spinoza's approach to the Divinity.

12.2. —— *The Revelation of Bahá'u'lláh and the Báb*. New York: Philosophical Library, 1970. xiii, 222 p. LC card 75–109166.
　　Subtitled 'Book I: Descartes' Theory of Knowledge', this work considers the concepts central to the French philosopher's system in light of their treatment in the Bahá'í Revelation.

12.3. Apsey, Lawrence S. *I Resign*. New York:

New History Foundation, 1932. 6 p. [Bjorling 956]

12.4. *The Bahai Cause, Founded by Baha-o-llah, Is a Call to Spiritually Mature Men and Women.* New York: Caravan of the East and West, n.d. [194–?] [4] p.

12.5. *The Bahai Cause Is a Call to Spiritually Mature Men and Women.* New York: New History Society, n.d [1942] 4 p.

12.6. *A Bahá'í Study on Individual Investigation, Unity and the Covenant, Covenant-Breakers, the Guardianship.* Florence, Italy: Supporters of the 2nd Guardianship, 1963. 6 p.

12.7. *Bahá'í Teachings.* Las Vegas, N.M.: Orthodox Bahá'í Faith, n.d. [1984?] 9 sheets in folder.

12.8. Behai, Kamar. *A Statement on the Dispute Between the Behai Family.* n.p. [Haifa: Kemar Behai], n.d. [1953] 6 circulars, [12] leaves.

12.9. *Bible Prophecies Fulfilled Today.* Roswell, N.M.: Mother Baha'i Council of the United States, 1979. [3], 14 p.

12.10. *Biographical Sketch of Mirza Ahmad Sohrab, Director of the Caravan of East and West, Inc.* n.p., n.d. [1954?] 3 p.

12.11. Brand, Max. *The Gate: Scenic Oratorio for Soli, Chorus, and Orchestra in Two Parts (19 Scenes).* libretto Max Brand, Mirza Ahmad Sohrab and Julie Chanler; music Max Brand. New York: Associated Music Publishers, 1944. 61 p. LC card 44–36458.

12.12. The Caravan of East and West. *Call to a World Conference in Jerusalem, 1957.* New York: The Caravan of East and West, n.d. [1955?] 4 p.

12.12a. —— *A Code of Civilization.* resolutions presented by Mirza Ahmad Sohrab and passed unanimously by the members of the Caravan on Saturday afternoon, April 10th, 1954. New York: Caravan of East and West, 1954.

12.13. —— *One Hundred Years, 1844–1944.* New York: Caravan of East and West, 1944. 24 leaves.

12.14. —— *idem.* New York: Caravan of East and West, 1944. 46 p.

12.15. —— *The Plan of the Caravan for the Republic of Mankind.* New York: Caravan of East and West, n.d. [195–?] [4] p.

12.16. Carré, John. *The Appointed Interpreters of the Word of God.* n.p.: Carré, n.d. [197–?] [Bjorling 1040]

12.16a. —— *Confirmation Through Prophecy.* Lahore, Pakistan: M. Aslan Bajwa, Feb. 1971 (Lahore: ILMI Printing Press). 16 p.

12.16b. —— *Copy of the Letter Sent to Pope Paul VI.* n.p. [Mariposa, Calif.?]: John Carré, 1969. [1] leaf.

12.17. —— *The Covenant of God Under Attack.* n.p.: Carré, n.d. [197–?] [Bjorling, 1041]

12.18. —— *Dies Irae: Day of Wrath, Day of God.* Mariposa, Calif.: House of Mankind, 1977. 47 p.

12.18a. —— *A Gate – Thoughts About Life and Man.* Rawalpindi, Pakistan: Syed Zafar Imam, 1970. 6 leaves.

12.19. —— *An Island of Hope.* Mariposa, Calif.: House of Light, 1975. 24 p.

12.19a. —— *A New Race of Men: The Day of the End.* Julian, Calif.: Information-World Order, n.d. [between 1963 and 1970] [10] leaves.

12.20. —— *Spiritual Evolution and the New Age.* Mariposa, Calif.: n.d. [197–] 8 p.

12.20a. —— *idem.* Mariposa, Calif.: John Carré, n.d. [197–] (Lahore, Pakistan: M. Aslan Bajwa). 7, [1] p.

12.21. —— *Spiritual Purity.* n.p.: Carré, n.d. [197–?] 2 p. [Bjorling 1045]

12.21a. —— *Universal Man.* Mariposa, Calif.: John Carré, n.d. [1969?] [2] leaves.

12.22. —— *The Violation of the Baha'i Faith.* n.p.: Carré, n.d. [197–?] [Bjorling 1046]

12.22a. Caryl, Roger. *Principles of Faith for a New Era of Mankind: The Twelve Fundamental Principles of the Baha'i Faith.* Missoula, Mont.: Baha'i Center Under the Provisions of the Covenant, May 1985. [2], 25, [1] p.

12.23. Chanler, Julie Olin. *From Gaslight to Dawn: An Autobiography.* New York: New History Foundation, 1956. 413 p. LC card 56–27422.

12.24. —— *The Great Book.* New York: New History Society, n.d. [193–] 1 leaf.

12.25. —— *The Green International.* New York: Green International, n.d. [193–] 1 leaf.

12.26. *Charles Mason Remey: Taken from Who's Who in America (with a Few Added Explanations).* Florence, Italy, 1964. [2] p.

12.27. *Christ's Fulfillment of Old Testament Prophecies.* Roswell, N.M.: Mother Baha'i Council of the United States, 1981. [3], 13 p.

12.27a. Ewing, Galen W. *The Orthodox Bahá'í Faith.* n.p. [New Mexico?]: Ewing, 1982. 13 leaves.

12.28. *Facts for Behaists.* trans. and ed. I.G. Kheiralla. Chicago: Kheiralla, 1901. 64 p.

12.29. Gazvini, M.J. *A Brief History of Beha U'llah, the Founder of the Behai Religion.* Akka, Palestine: M.J. Gazvini, 1914 ([San Diego: G.E. Traub]). 91 p. LC card 16–2007 rev.

12.30. *God Wants You to Know the Truth.* n.p., n.d. [1961?] 4 leaves.

12.31. *The Guardianship.* Santa Fe, N.M.: Spiritual Assembly of the Baha'is of Santa Fe, Under the Hereditary Guardianship, n.d. [1963?] [4] p. Includes a letter from Samuel Smart.

12.32. Hamilton, Joseph George. *'The Days of Noah': Recensions.* Chicago: The Hamilton Press, 1933. 19 p.

12.33. —— *The Millennium Is Possible.* Chicago, 1918 (Chicago: I.V. Martesson). 28 p.

12.34. —— *The New Religion.* assisted by Frederick O. Pease. Chicago: N.A.U.R. Publishing Society, 1926. 23 p. LC card 44–46308.

12.35. —— *No More Darkness!: Short Sermons, Part 1.* Chicago: The Hamilton Press, 1934. 19 p.

12.36. —— *Some Seemly Explanations of Symbolism and Formalism: Short Sermons No. 3.* Chicago: The Hamilton Press, 1940. 24 p.

12.37. —— *Symbols and Signs: Recitations.* Chicago: Joseph G. Hamilton, 1932. 22 p.

12.38. *The Human Charter: Principles of Baha-ollah and Abdul Baha for the Founding of a World Society.* New York: New History Foundation, 1945. 85 p. LC card 45–7083.

12.39. *The Impending World Catastrophe.* Rawalpindi: National Spiritual Assembly of the Baha'is of Pakistan Under the Hereditary Guardianship, 1965. 12 p.

12.40. Ioas, Leroy; Chanler, Mrs Lewis Stuyvesant [Julie Chanler]; Sohrab, Ahmad. *Three Letters.* New York: Caravan of East and West, 1954. [11] leaves.

12.41. Jensen, Leland. *The Antichrist.* n.p. [Missoula, Mont?: Jensen], n.d. [197–?] 11 p. [Bjorling 1034]

12.42. —— *The Beast.* n.p. [Missoula, Mont.?: Jensen], n.d. [197–?] 18 p. [Bjorling 1035]

12.42a. —— *Dear Joseph Pepe Remey, Aghsan.* n.p. [Missoula, Mont: Leland Jensen], n.d. [1979?] 45, [1] p. + Introduction (9 leaves).
Long published letter to Joseph Pepe Remey, adopted son of Charles Mason Remey, intended to convince him that he should accept the post of guardian in succession to his adopted father. Includes also a lengthy exposition of Jensen's claim to be 'Joshua, the establisher of the kingdom of Bahá'u'lláh'.

12.43. —— *Jeane Dixon Was Right.* Missoula, Mont.: Jensen, 1980. vi, 130 p.

12.44. —— *The Most Mighty Document.* Missoula, Mont.: Joshua, n.d. [1980] 14, viii, 70 p.

12.45. Kheiralla, Ibrahim George. *Behá'u'lláh, the Glory of God.* assisted by Howard MacNutt. Chicago: Kheiralla, 1900. 545 p. LC cards 0–2417 rev., 33–24131.
Review:
Goodspeed, George S. *The American Journal of Theology* (Chicago), (Jan. 1902), pp. 184–5.
The work which was based upon the series of lessons used by Kheiralla to teach the Bahá'í Faith in the 1894–1900 period in the United States and which he hoped 'Abdul-Bahá would approve as the doctrinal standard for the Bahá'ís in America. Appears in two variants: in one volume and in two volumes.

12.46. —— *idem.* 2nd ed. Chicago: Goodspeed Press, 1915. 545 p.

12.47. —— *The Creator and What It Takes to Win the Peace.* Newark, N.J.: W.E. Dreyer, 1943. [Bjorling 936]

12.48. —— *An Epistle of Peace.* Chicago: National Association of the Universal Religion, 1918. 12 p.

12.49. —— *Immortality: Hereafter of Man's Soul and Mind: Man Never Dies.* New York: Syrian-American Press, 1928. 32 p. LC card 29–4336.

12.50. —— *Immortality Scientifically Demonstrated.* Evanston, Ill.: Kheiralla, 1914. 16 p.

12.51. —— *Miracles.* Newark, N.J.: W.E. Dreyer, 1943. 24 p.

12.52. —— *Ninety-Five Questions and Answers Concerning the Teachings of the Behai Religion, Which Is Organized as the Universal Religion of the World.* Kenosha, Wis.: Dr Ibrahim G. Kheiralla, 1925. 14 p.

12.53. —— *O Christians! Why Do Ye Believe Not on Christ?* Chicago: Goodspeed Press, 1917. 192 p. LC card 17–4994.
Includes a valuable and lengthy autobiographical section.

12.54. —— *Proof of the Existence and Immortality of the Soul from a Scientific and Logical Standpoint: The Mind, As Taught by the Society of Behaists.* Newark, N.J.: Wm. E. Dreyer, 1943. 34 p. LC card 72–224008.

12.55. —— *The Three Questions.* n.p. [Chicago], n.d. [191–?] 26 p.

12.56. —— *Universal Peace and Its Sole Solution.* n.p. [Evanston, Ill.], n.d. [1914] 18 p.

12.56a. Khoreshi, S.H. *The Riddle of One*

Thousand Years. n.p. [Pakistan]: S.H. Khoreshi, 1969. 11 p.

12.57.   King, Reginald. *The Birth of World Religion*. Las Vegas, N.M.: National Publishing Institute of the Orthodox Bahá'í Faith in the United States, 1976. [8] p.

12.58.   —— *The Mutilation of the Will and Testament of 'Abdu'l-Bahá*. Las Vegas, N.M.: Orthodox Bahá'í Faith, n.d. [1976?] [8] p.

12.59.   The Man [Jamshid Ma'ani]. *'God'*. trans. Taj-ud-Din, S.H. Khoreshi, and John Carré. Mariposa, Calif., n.d. [197–] (Chowchilla, Calif.: Bass Printing & Litho). [12] p.

12.59a.   —— *Heaven*. Mariposa, Calif., n.d. [197–?] 7 p. [Bjorling 1047]

12.59b.   —— *Prayers of the Man for All Mankind*. comp. J. Carré; trans. Ch. Taj ud Din. Lahore: Maj. Aslam Bajwa, Mar. 1970 (Lahore: Bengal Art Press). 15, [1] p.

12.60.   —— *The Reason of Man's Creation*. Mariposa, Calif., 1971. 5 p. [Bjorling, 1048]

12.61.   —— *The Sun of the World of Man*. Mariposa, Calif., 1971. 5 p. [Bjorling 1049]

12.61a.   —— *To the Baha'i Community Throughout the World*. Sedona, Ariz.: Vagabond House, 1967. 4, [1] p.

12.62.   —— *Universal Order*. Mariposa, Calif., 1971. 9 p. [Bjorling, 1050]

12.63.   Marangella, Joel B. *The Bahá'í Guardians: A Brief History from the Writings of the Third Guardian*. New York: National Bureau of the Orthodox Bahá'í Faith of the United States and Canada, 1972. 5 p.

12.64.   —— *A Brief History of the Violation of the Covenant of Bahá'u'lláh at the World Center of the Bahá'í Faith Following the Passing of the First Guardian of the Bahá'í Faith*. n.p.: Orthodox Bahá'í Faith, 1975. 35 p. (Herald of the Covenant; no.2).

12.65.   —— *Proclamation of the Third Guardian, Nov. 12, 1969*. Germany: Joel B. Marangella, 1969. 6, [2] p.

12.66.   —— *What Is the Meaning of Loyalty to the Covenant of Bahá'u'lláh and Who Are the Present-Day Covenant-Breakers?* Española, N.M.: Orthodox Bahá'í Faith, 1977. 43 p. (Herald of the Covenant; no.5).

12.67.   Meghnot, Jamshid. *The News of the Holy Land – Appendix to Bahai News no.327*. Lahore: National House of Pakistan, 6 Dec. 1972. 5 leaves.

12.67a.   ——*The Time for the Establishment of*

Bahá'u'lláh's Kingdom Has Come. Wayne, Mich.: The Servant of the Word of God, n.d. [197–] 64 p.

12.68.   Meyer, Marilyn. *Why I Like Being a Baha'i*. Roswell, N.M.: Mother Baha'i Council of the United States, 1979. 7 p.

12.69.   Mother Baha'i Council of the United States. *Articles of Incorporation of the Mother Baha'i Council of the United States*. Roswell, N.M.: Mother Baha'i Council of the United States, 1978. 5 p. [Bjorling 1022]

12.70.   —— *By-laws of the Local Baha'i Council*. Roswell, N.M.: Mother Baha'i Council of the United States, n.d. [197–] 4 p. [Bjorling 1024]

12.71.   —— *By-laws of the Mother Baha'i Council of the United States*. Roswell, N.M.: Mother Baha'i Council of the United States, 1979. 13 p. [Bjorling, 1025]

12.72.   National Association for the Universal Religion. *The Guide for the National Association of the Universal Religion and Its Branches*. Chicago: National Association for the Universal Religion, n.d. [1914?] 20 p.

12.73.   *A New Day Comes*. Las Vegas, N.M.: Orthodox Bahá'í Faith, n.d. [1984?] [8] p.

12.74.   New History Society. *The Plan of the New History Society for the Reconstruction of the Human Commonwealth*. New York: New History Society, n.d. [1939?] [4] p.

12.75.   *One People, One World, One God: An Introduction to the Baha'i Faith*. Las Vegas, N.M.: National House of Justice, Orthodox Baha'i Community of the United States and Canada, 1984. 31 p.

12.76.   *Opening of Bahai Library*. New York: Caravan of East & West, 1953. [2] leaves.

12.76a.   *The Orthodox Baha'i Faith: The Cause for Universal Religion, Brotherhood and Peace: A Sketch of Its History and Teachings*. Roswell, N.M.: Mother Baha'i Council of the United States, 1981. 10 p. Cover title: *The Orthodox Baha'i Faith: An Introduction*.

12.77.   Pease, Leslie E. *A Short History of Religion*. Appleton, Wis.: Leslie E. Pease, n.d. [193–?] 13 p.

12.78.   *The Pleasure of Your Company Is Requested at the Opening of Bahai Library at 132 East 65th Street, New York 21, N.Y., Tuesday Evening, April 21st, 1953 at Eight O'clock*. New York: Caravan [of East and West], 1953. [6] p. folder.

12.79.   *Project for the Celebration of the Bahai Centennial in May, 1944, the One Hundredth*

Anniversary of the Founding of the Bahai Cause. New York: Caravan of East and West, 1944. [4] p.

12.79a. *References to the Guardianship.* comp. and annotated by LaVonne DeHainaut. [Las Vegas, N.M.]: National Teaching Institute of the Orthodox Baha'i Faith in the United States, 1972. [1], 11 leaves.

12.80. *Reincarnation, or the Return of the Soul.* Newark, N.J.: [Wm. E. Dreyer], 1943. 23 p.

Includes an essay by I.G. Kheiralla and quotation from Bahá'u'lláh.

12.81. Remey, Charles Mason. *Announcement to the Hands of the Faith from Mason Remey, the Second Guardian of the Bahá'í Faith, of His Appointment of Guardianship by the First Guardian of the Faith.* Florence, Italy; Washington, D.C.: Remey, 1960. 65 leaves.

12.82. —— *Another Appeal to the Hands of the Faith.* Washington, D.C.: Remey, 1960. 39, 2, [2] leaves.

12.83. —— *An Appeal to the Hands of the Faith.* Washington, D.C.: Remey, 1960. 7, [1], 2, [2] leaves.

12.84. —— *Appeals Made to the Hands of the Faith.* Washington, D.C.: Remey, 1960. 7, 28, 62 leaves.

See 12.81–12.83, 12.93.

12.85. —— *Baha'i Proclamation to the Government of Israel.* Washington, D.C.: Remey, 1960. [124] p.

12.86. —— *Daily Observations of the Bahá'í Faith Made to the Hands of the Faith in the Holy Land.* n.p.: Remey, 1960. 4 v.

12.87. —— *I Encyclical to the Baha'i World from Mason Remey, Guardian of the Baha'i Faith.* Washington, D.C.: Remey, n.d. [1960] [3] p.

12.88. —— *II Encyclical to the Baha'i World from Mason Remey, Guardian of the Baha'i Faith.* Washington, D.C.: Remey, n.d. [1960] 3 p.

12.89. —— *III Encyclical to the Baha'i World from Mason Remey, Guardian of the Baha'i Faith.* Washington, D.C.: Remey, n.d. [1960] 10 p.

12.90. —— *The End of the World of Man and the Coming of God's Kingdom Upon Earth.* Santa Fe, N.M.: Baha'is [sic] of Santa Fe, 1962. [2] p.

12.91. —— *The Great Global Catastrophe.* Santa Fe, N.M.: Baha'is of Santa Fe Under the Hereditary Guardianship, n.d. [after 1961] 6 p.

12.92. —— *Greetings to the Baha'is of the Occi-*

dent and the Orient from the Guardian of the Faith. Florence, Italy: Remey, 1964. 4 p.

12.92a. —— *A Last Appeal to the Hands of the Baha'i Faith: A Private and Secret Document to Be Read Only by the Hands of the Faith.* n.p. [Santa Fe, N.M.: Baha'is of Santa Fe, Under the Hereditary Guardianship], 1960 [i.e. 196–] [2], 52 p. Cover title: *A Last Appeal to the Hands of the Faith.*

No imprint shown on the pamphlet: there is a stamp on the last page indicating that it is distributed by Baha'is of Santa Fe, Under the Hereditary Guardianship. The text was originally distributed in a multiple-copy typescript form in 1960 but the present version is fully typeset and printed, probably during the 1960s.

See 12.93.

12.93. —— *A Last Appeal to the Hands of the Faith.* Washington, D.C.: Remey, 1960. 77, 2, [2] leaves.

See 12.92a.

12.94. —— *The Last Message from the Guardian of the Faith to the Former Hands of the Faith.* Washington, D.C.: Remey, 1962. [2] p.

12.95. —— *Letter from the Guardian.* Florence, Italy: Remey, Jan. 1967. [2], 3 leaves.

12.96. —— *A Naw Ruz Greeting Message to the Baha'i World.* Florence, Italy: Remey, 120 B.E. [1963] 2 p.

12.97. —— *Open Letter to the 'Custodian Hands' in Haifa.* Florence, Italy: Mason Remey, n.d. [1963] [4] p.

12.98. —— *Proclamation to the Bahá'ís of the World.* Washington, D.C.: Remey, 1960. [50] leaves.

Includes 12.87–12.88.

12.99. *Proclamation to the Bahá'ís of the World Through the Annual Convention of the Bahá'ís of the United States of America Assembled at Wilmette, Illinois.* Washington, D.C.: Remey, 117 B. [1960] 5 p.

12.100. —— *The Question of the Guardianship of the Bahá'í Faith: Several Letters Received by the Hands of the Faith in the Holy Land Relative to the Continuation of the Guardianship of the Baha'i Faith.* Washington, D.C.: Remey, 117 B. [1960] [136] p.

12.101. —— *A Statement by the Second Guardian of the Baha'i World Faith.* Santa Fe, N.M.: Baha'is of Santa Fe Under the Hereditary Guardianship, n.d. [1960?] 10 leaves.

12.102. *The Revolt of Youth: Prize Papers in Five Competitions Offered by the New History Society to the Youth of the United States, Europe, Latin*

America, Asia, Africa, Australia, Canada and New Zealand. New York: New History Society, n.d. [1931?] 32 p.

12.103. Schlatter, Frank; Schlatter, Carole. *Partial Update on Abdu'l-Baha's Visit to This Country.* Roswell, N.M.: Mother Baha'i Council of the United States, 1982. 11 p. [Bjorling 1030]

12.104. Sohrab, Ahmad. *Abdul Baha's Grandson: Story of a Twentieth Century Excommunication.* New York; Universal Pub. Co. for the New History Foundation, 1943. 178 p. LC card 43–9919.
Review:
Wilson, J. Christy. *The Moslem World* (Hartford, Conn.), v.33 no.4 (Oct. 1934), p. 300.
Biography of Ruhi Afnan and the story of his expulsion from the Faith.

12.105. —— *Baha-o-llah: An Address by Mirza Ahmad Sohrab.* New York: Caravan of East and West, 1947. 11 leaves.

12.106. —— *Broken Silence: The Story of Today's Struggle for Religious Freedom.* New York: New History Foundation, 1942. 608 p. LC card 42–5289.
Review:
Wilson, J. Christy. *The Moslem World* (Hartford, Conn.), v.33 no.2 (Apr. 1943), p. 145.
The story of the New History Society and the expulsion of Sohrab and Julie Chanler from the Bahá'í Faith. Stridently polemical and a strong personal attack on Shoghi Effendi.

12.107. —— *I Heard Him Say: Words of Abdul Baha as Recorded by His Secretary Mirza Ahmad Sohrab.* New York: New History Foundation, 1937. x, 126 p.

12.108. —— *Living Pictures in the Great Drama of the 19th Century.* New York: New History Foundation, 1933. 95 p. LC card 34–264 rev.
Review:
New York Times Book Review, (Jan. 14, 1934), p. 12.

12.109. —— *The Message of the New History Society to the Youth of Europe.* New York: New History Society, n.d. [193–] 24 p. [Bjorling 963]

12.110. —— *My Bahai Pilgrimage: Autobiography from Childhood to Middle Life.* New York: Universal Publishing Company, 1959. 131 p.

12.110a. —— *My Faith.* New York: Caravan of East and West, n.d. [195–?] [4] p.

12.111. —— *The New Eden.* il. Leiton Haring. New York: New History Society, 1957. 181 p. LC card 58–26294.

12.112. —— *A Persian Rosary of Nineteen Pearls.* New York: New History Society, n.d. [1939] [4] p.

12.113. —— *idem.* New York: Caravan of East & West, n.d. [194–?] [4] p.

12.114. —— *idem.* New York: Caravan of East and West, n.d. [195–?] [4] p.

12.115. —— *Renaissance.* New York: New History Foundation, 1930. 26 p.

12.116. —— *Second Bahai Pilgrimage from July 7th to August 8th, 1954: Diary Letter.* New York: Caravan of East and West, 1954. 59 leaves.
Includes information on Covenant-breakers in the Holy Land whom Sohrab met during his trip.

12.117. —— *The Song of the Caravan.* New York: New History Foundation, 1930 (New York: The Grayzel Press). xii, 410 p. LC card 30–20213 rev.

12.117a. —— *idem.* New York: Published for the New History Foundation by George Dobsevage, 1930 (New York: The Grayzel Press). xii, 410 p.

12.118. —— *The Story of the Divine Plan: Taking Place During, and Immediately Following World War I.* New York: New History Foundation, 1947. 120 p.

12.119. —— *The Will and Testament of Abdul Baha, an Analysis.* New York: Universal Publishing Co. for the New History Foundation, 1944. 125 p. LC card 45–14773.
Reviews:
Christian Century (Chicago), v.61 (Aug. 16, 1944), p. 951.
Wilson, J. Christy, *The Moslem World* (Hartford, Conn.), v.36 no.1 (Jan. 1946), p. 83.

12.120. Spataro, Francis C. *From Christ to Baha'u'llah.* n.p. [Bellerose, N.Y.?]: Francis Cajetan Spataro, 1983. 28 leaves.

12.121. —— *The Lion of God: The Death of Charles Mason Remey.* Bellerose, N.Y.: Remey Society, 1981. [24] leaves.

12.122. —— *The Remeum: Place of Commemoration and Sepulchre of the Family of Rear Admiral George Collier Remey.* n.p. [Bellerose, N.Y.]: F.C. Spataro, 1980. [20] leaves.

12.123. —— *Seder, Eucharist, and Nineteen Day Feast.* Jamaica, N.Y.: Charles Mason Remey Society, 1984. 8 p. [Bjorling 1057]

12.124. *A Statement to All Baha'is on the Living Hereditary Guardianship.* Santa Fe, N.M.: The Baha'is of Santa Fe, n.d. [1964?] [2] p.

12.125. Stenstrand, August J. *A Call of Attention to the Behaists or Babists of America.* Napierville,

Ill.: Stenstrand, 1907 (Downers Grove, Ill.: Kelmscott). 36 p. LC card 8–4261.

12.126. ——— *The Fifth Call of Attention to the Behaists or Babists of America.* Chicago: Stenstrand, 1917. 2 p.

12.127. ——— *Key to the Heaven of the Beyan, or A Third Call of Attention to the Behaists or Babists of America.* Chicago: Stenstrand, 1913. 34 p. Includes: *An Open Letter to the Babi World, or, A Second Call of Attention to the Behaists or Babists of America,* dated 1911.

12.127a. ——— *The Sixth Call of Attention to the Behaists or Babists of America.* Chicago: Stenstrand, 1924. [2] p.

12.127b. *This Stone with Seven Eyes.* Deer Lodge, Mont.: Baha'i, n.d. [197–?] [3] leaves.

12.128. *Torchbearers.* New York: New History Foundation, 1931. 32 p.

12.129. *The Voice of Youth.* New York: New History Society, n.d. [1939] [4] p.

12.130. White, Ruth. *Abdul Baha and the Promised Age.* New York: Ruth White, 1927 (New York: J.J. Little and Ives). xv, 224 p. LC card 27–23781.

12.131. ——— *Abdul Baha's Alleged Will Is Fraudulent: An Appendix to The Bahai Religion and Its Enemy, the Bahai Organization.* Rutland, Vt.: The Tuttle Company, 1930. 21 p. LC card 30–25730.

12.132. ——— *Abdul Baha's Questioned Will and Testament.* Beverly Hills: White, 1946. 129 p. LC card 46–16939.
Review:
Wilson, J. Christy, *The Moslem World* (Hartford, Conn.), v.37 no.2 (Apr. 1947), p. 159.

The major document setting out White's contention that the Will and Testament of 'Abdu'l-Bahá was forged.

12.133. ——— *Bahai Leads Out of the Labyrinth.* New York: Universal Pub. Co., 1944. 259 p. LC card 44–31025.
Reviews:
Christian Century (Chicago), v.61 (July 26, 1944), pp. 878–9.
Wilson, J. Christy, *The Moslem World* (Hartford, Conn.), v.37 no.2 (Apr. 1947), p. 159.

A personal narrative of Ruth White's conversion to the Bahá'í Faith. Also included are selected passages of Bahá'í writings and the author's negative view of the administration of the Faith following the passing of 'Abdu'l-Bahá.

12.134. ——— *The Bahai Religion and Its Enemy, the Bahai Organization.* Rutland, Vt.: Tuttle, 1929. 233 p. LC card 29–24652.

Ruth White's attachment to 'Abdu'l-Bahá's general principles and her opposition to all 'organization' of the Bahá'í Faith.

12.135. ——— *Correspondence Between the High Commissioner of Palestine and Ruth White, Regarding the Alleged Will and Testament of Sir Abdul Baha Abbas.* Los Angeles, Calif.: White, 1932. 11 p.

Letters and documents which Ruth White reproduced in a limited number of copies for libraries and interested individuals in her struggle to have 'Abdu'l-Bahá's Will declared a forgery.

12.136. ——— *Is the Bahai Organization the Enemy of the Bahai Religion?: An Appendix to Abdul Baha and the Promised Age.* New York: White, 1929. 22 p. LC card 58–54460.

12.138. Wilkin, Mary Magdalene. *God's Promised Word and Plan, or the Baha'i Succession and Its Impact Upon the Safety and Peace of All Mankind.* n.p., 1962. 17 p.

12.139. ——— *Support for the Covenant.* Las Vegas, N.M.: Orthodox Baha'i Faith, 1964. 14 p. [Bjorling 1019]

12.140. ——— *This World Has a Guardian: A Documentary Letter.* New York, 1960. 18 leaves.

12.141. Wittman, Robert W. *Close of the Age: The Seven Thunders.* Missoula, Mont.: Wittman, 1980. 104 p.

12.142. Zimmer, Hermann. *A Fraudulent Testament Devalues the Bahai Religion Into Political Shoghism.* English by Jeanine Blackwell; rev. by Karen Gasser and Gordon Campbell. Waiblingen-Stuttgart: World Union for Universal Religion and Universal Peace, 1973. 132 p. LC card 75–509175.

An unscrupulous defamation of the character of the Guardian of the Bahá'í Faith. Zimmer alleges that 'Abdu'l-Bahá's grandson, Shoghi Effendi, emended the Will and Testament of 'Abdu'l-Bahá so as to become 'Abdu'l-Bahá's successor and to gain control of the worldwide Bahá'í community.

Covenant-breaker Periodicals:

12.142a. *The Baha'i News Letter.* no.1 (Aug. 1964)– . Rawalpindi: National Spiritual Assembly of the Baha'is of Pakistan Under the Hereditary Guardianship.

12.143. *Baha'i Newsletter.* v.1 no.1 ([1984?])– . Missoula, Mont.: Baha'is Under the Provisions of the Covenant.

12.143a. *The Baha'i Reporter.* v.1 no.1 ([1973]) – . Las Vegas, N.M.: Orthodox Baha'i Faith.

12.144. *Baha'i Youth Round Robin.* v.1 no.1 ([1963?])– ?. Santa Fe, N.M.

12.145. *Behai Quarterly.* v.1 no.1 (Spring 1934)–v.4 no.1/2 (Spring/Summer 1937). Kenosha, Wis.: Shua Ullah Behai. LC card 39–16010.

Put out by partisans of Muḥammad-'Alí, 'Abdu'l-Bahá's half brother, with support from American 'Behaists', followers of Ibrahim Kheiralla.

12.146. *The Caravan.* v.1 no.1 (Jan. 1935)– ?. New York: New History Foundation. Title varies: *The Children's Caravan,* v.1 no.1 (Jan. 1935)–v.12 no. 4 (Oct. 1945). Absorbed *New History,* (Jan. 1946).

12.147. *The Glad Tidings: A Bulletin of the Baha'is Under the Hereditary Guardianship.* v.1 (1960)– . Santa Fe, N.M.: Spiritual Assembly of the Baha'is Under the Hereditary Guardianship.

12.148. *Green International Bulletin.* ed. Mirza Ahmad Sohrab, no.1 (Dec. 1932)– ?. New York: Green International.

12.149. *Herald of the Covenant.* no.1 (1974?)– . New Mexico: Orthodox Bahá'í Faith.

12.149a. *Herald of the Covenant.* v.1 no.1 ([Jan. 1984?])– . Australia: Orthodox Bahá'ís of Australia.

12.150. *New History.* v.1 no.1 (Oct. 1931)–v.15 no.16 (Jan. 1946). New York: New History Foundation. LC card 37–17877 rev. Absorbed by *The Caravan* (Jan. 1946).

12.151. *Orthodox Baha'i Faith Newsletter.* ? – . Roswell, N.M.

12.152. *Reality.* [v. 1 no. 1] ([Apr.?] 1919)–v.17 no.4 (Apr. 1929). New York: Reality Publishing Corp. LC card 31–908.

While this began as a publication supported by loyal Bahá'ís, it became increasingly the voice for opinions and movements antagonistic to the essential tenets of the Bahá'í Faith and a forum for Covenant-breakers to attack the Guardian and the administrative order. *See* Smith, Peter. '*Reality* Magazine: Editorship and Ownership of an American Bahá'í Periodical', *From Iran East and West.* ed. Juan R. Cole and Moojan Momen (Los Angeles: Kalimát Press, 1984), pp. 134–55.

12.153. Remey, Charles Mason. *The Guardian's Letter.* v.1 no.1 (Nov. 1966)– ? . Florence, Italy: Charles Mason Remey, the Second Guardian of the Abha World Faith – the Orthodox World Faith of Bahá'u'lláh.

12.154. *The Remey Letter.* v.1 no.1 ([Jan. 1980?]–). Bellerose, L.I.: Charles Mason Remey Society. Place of publication changes to Jamaica, N.Y. between v.3 and v.6.

12.155. *The Star of the West.* ? – . Las Vegas, N.M.: Orthodox Baha'i Faith, National House of Justice of the United States and Canada.

XIII
Theses

INCLUDED here are all theses and dissertations in English relating to the Bahá'í Faith which have been required for the obtaining of university degrees, whether Bachelor's, Master's or Doctoral, including theses which have passing reference to the Bahá'í Faith.

13.1. Abadi, Behnaz. (1981). *The World Into One Nation: World Peace and the Baha'i Faith.* M.A., Kyung Hee University. 160 p.

Introduction to Bahá'í peace concepts.

13.2. Adamson, Hugh. (1974). *The Concept of Revelation as Found in Islam and Baha'i.* M.A., Concordia University, Montreal. vii, 191 p.

'Some attempt is made to explore the claims of both Muhammad and Baha'u'llah that their respective Revelations come from a single Source and are, therefore, a progressive continuation of previous Revelations.' Discusses also the 'crisis of continuation' that arises after the death of the Messenger of God.

13.2a. Adlparvar, Kamran. (1967). *Bahá'í Tempes* [sic]. B.A., University of Newcastle upon Tyne. [3], 36 leaves.

Brief study of the architectural interest of Bahá'í temples.

13.3. Alter, S. Neale. (1923). *Studies in Bahaism.* Ph.D., University of Edinburgh. 72 p.

'The purpose of this treatise on Bahaism is to present a brief yet comprehensive discussion of the main tenets of Bahaism, to serve as a handbook on this religion . . . There is no attempt to make an apology for Christianity, except so far as Bahaism and Christianity are contrasted in the chapter on the Philosophy of Bahaism.' [Preface]

13.4. Amanat, Abbas. (1981). *The Early Years of the Babi Movement: Background and Development.* Ph.D., Oxford University. vi, 472 p.

'The purpose of this study is to examine the rise of the Babi movement as the final result of a long millenarian process . . . The main emphasis . . . is to illustrate the way in which a millenarian movement comes into existence, the nature of its claims, the background of the persons involved, and the circumstances under which messianic claims turn into a millenarian movement.' [Introduction]

13.5. Andre, Richard Eugene. (1971). *Responsi-*

tivity, the Evolution of Creative Synthesis. Ph.D., University of Massachusetts. xi, 180 p.

Responsivity is a process to develop the capacity for people to become responsive, sensitive and creative beings. The purpose of the thesis is 'to advance, develop and describe the holistic conceptualization and framework of responsivity as a generally applicable training change model.'

13.6. Archer, Mary Elizabeth. (1977). *Global Community: Case Study of the Houston Bahá'ís.* M.A., University of Houston. xxiii, 279 p.

'The Houston Bahá'í community . . . depends on noncoercive methods . . . The Bahá'í religion . . . offers a new vision of the communal effort. Intellectual and sacred rewards motivate members, who do not withdraw from worldly endeavors but are committed to educational attainment and careers. Members do, however, withdraw from public affairs that do not support the universalistic goals of the faith . . . Commitment mechanisms that support individuals who want instrumental rewards will be needed to build a world community.' [Abstract]

13.7. Banani, Amin. (1959). *Impact of the West on Iran, 1921–1941: A Study in Modernization of Social Institutions.* Ph.D., Stanford University. pp. 39–43.

The Bahá'í Faith's liberal principles prepared some Iranians to accept ideas from the West.

13.8. Bartlett, Jean Eleanor. (1984). *Baha'i World Faith: A Case Study in Adult Socialization.* Ph.D., University of California, Riverside. x, 173 p.

'This study of adult conversion to the Baha'i Faith was undertaken in order to empirically verify two theoretical models that seek to explain religious conversion [Lofland & Stark; Snow, Zucker & Ekland-Olson]. The findings indicate that neither model is adequate to account for conversion in this group.' [Abstract]

13.8a. Bastani Hesari, Hormoz. (1969). *Shrine of Bahaullah in the Bay of Haif* [sic] *Israel.* Bachelor of Architecture, Iowa State University of Science and Technology. ii, 58, 8 leaves.

Proposal that the completed Shrine of Bahá'u'lláh be built in Haifa Bay.

13.9. Bayat Philipp, Mangol. (1971). *Mírzá Áqá*

Khān Kirmānī: 19thC Persian Revolutionary Thinker. Ph.D., University of California at Los Angeles. x, 336 p.

Kirmání, an Azalí Bábí, was prominent in reform and pan-Islamic movements in the 19th century and a close associate of Malkam Khan and Afghani.

13.10. Beckwith, Francis J. (1984). *Baha'ism: A Presentation and Critique of Its Theological Tenets and Apologetic Use of the Christian Scriptures.* M.A., Simon Greenleaf School of Law. vii, 126 p.

The intent is to critique Bahá'í missionary efforts among Christians from an evangelical viewpoint. The conclusions are based on *a priori* theological assumptions that the Bahá'í religion is inferior.

13.11. Behroozi, Shahla B. (1971). *The Role of Baha'i Faith in the Social Development of Baha'i Youth in Los Baños Laguna.* Master of Social Work, University of the Philippines. xiii, 124 p.

'This study sought to determine the impact of Baha'i teaching, through Baha'i administration, on its young members in a Baha'i community in Barrio Batong Malake, Los Baños, Laguna. Specifically it attempted to find out: (1) The participation of the youth in the . . . implementation of the tenets of the Baha'i Faith; (2) The role of Baha'i Faith in facilitating the development of a sense of belonging and self-awareness among Baha'i youth; and (3) The possible areas of conflict [for the youth, upon] accepting the Baha'i Faith . . .' [Abstract]

13.12. Berger, Peter L. (1954). *From Sect to Church: A Sociological Interpretation of the Baha'i Movement.* Ph.D., New School of Social Research. 194 p.

Berger is one of the foremost mid-twentieth century sociologists. His was the first sociological analysis of the Bahá'í religion. Berger sought to describe two fundamental transformations of the Bahá'í Faith: (1) the transformation from a millenarian movement within Shí'í Islam into an independent religion with a worldwide following; (2) the 'routinization of charismatic leadership' into largely rational-legal forms. He uses the concept of 'motif' to study fundamental concerns of the religion and defines two major Bahá'í motifs: the gnostic and the millenarian.

13.13. Bethel, Fereshteh Taheri. (1984). *A Psychological Theory of Martyrdom: A Content Analysis of Personal Documents of Baha'i Martyrs of Iran Written Between 1979 and 1982.* Ph.D., United States International University, San Diego. viii, 262 p.

'The purpose of this study was the formulation of a psychological theory of martyrdom based upon a content analysis of the last per-

sonal documents of Bahá'í martyrs in Iran. This investigation and proposed theory tested the premise that the response of Bahá'í martyrs to severe social stressors (persecution and execution between 1979 and 1982) differed from the typical psychological explanations of response to high stressors.' [Abstract] Curiously, comparison is made with works dealing largely with Christian views of martyrdom rather than with Shí'í and Islamic views.

13.14. Bill, James Alban. (1968). *The Iranian Intelligentsia: Class and Change.* Ph.D., Princeton University. p. 154.

Mentions members of the intelligentsia who embraced the Bahá'í teachings as a source of commitment coupled with liberal and progressive principles.

13.15. Bishop, Helen Pilkington. (1933). *A Study of the Rise and Diffusion of the Bahá'í Religion.* B.A., Reed College. 149 p.

Introductory text on the Bahá'í Faith.

13.16. Bramson, Loni. (1980). *The Baha'i Faith and Its Evolution in the United States and Canada from 1922 to 1936.* Ph.D., Université Catholique de Louvain. v, 430 p.

'. . . The state of the pre-Guardian American community will be briefly sketched, as well as Shoghi Effendi's establishment as Guardian and his acceptance by the Baha'i community. This will be followed by a discussion of the major points of doctrine synthesized by Shoghi Effendi that played a role in the evolution of the Baha'i community during the period under consideration.' [Introduction]

13.17. Bujold, Paul M. (1983). *The Development of Community through the Religious Covenant: A Bahá'í Case History.* M.A., University of Alberta. xii, 189 p.

'This thesis is an examination of religious covenants as community development tools. It proposes that, because religions have covenants that have been given to the community by its God, it has a greater likelihood of being successful in the development of a community than a secular development plan would have.' [Abstract]

13.18. Christensen, Philip Roland. (1969). *The Unity-Diversity Principle and Its Effect on Creative Group Problem Solving: An Experimental Investigation.* B.A., Dept. of Social Relations, Harvard University, vi, 102 p.

'In many problem solving groups an aggressive mode of interaction leads to extreme self-orientation and a reluctance to offer unusual suggestions. An alternative, the unity-diversity principle, was proposed and the consultation technique for increasing group creativity and productivity was derived from it . . . It was . . . hypothesized that groups trained in consultation would produce higher quality solutions than would untrained groups.' [Abstract]

13.19. Deuschle, Hedwig. (1976). *The Secular Gospel in Literature and in the Science of Man According to Thoreau, Whitman, and Fromm*. B.A., College of the Virgin Islands. pp. 36–40.

Shows that Bahá'u'lláh's thought 'parallels' that of Thoreau, Whitman and Fromm on many issues relating to the nature of man and spiritual ideals.

13.20. Faghfoory, Mohammed Hassan. (1978). *The Role of the Ulama in Twentieth Century Iran with Particular Reference to Ayatullah Haj Sayyid Abul-Qasim Kashani*. Ph.D., University of Wisconsin – Madison. p. 112.

Destruction of a dictatorial government in 1941 opened the way for Bahá'ís and other minority religions to attempt to resume their religious practices.

13.21. Filson, Gerald Wesley. (1982). *A Case Study of the Role of Media in an Educational Campaign in the Canadian Baha'i Community*. M.A., Concordia University. vi, 120 p.

An education campaign in the Canadian Bahá'í community is described. Evaluation showed that all main information sources except the audio cassette contributed to information gains. TV programmes were found to contribute to information gains for all participants but especially for the less educated; printed sources contributed to gains for all participants but especially for the more educated.

13.22. Fischer, Michael M.J. (1973). *Zoroastrian Iran Between Myth and Praxis*. Ph.D., University of Chicago. pp. iii, viii, xi, xiii, xvii, 5, 68, 159, 245, 321, 325, 335–9, 408, 409–18, 428, 429, 433, 436, 441–5, 449.

Includes explanatory material on Bahá'í beliefs and discusses conversion of Zoroastrians to the Bahá'í Faith, as well as the massacre of Bahá'ís in 1903 in Yazd.

13.23. Garlington, William N. (1975). *The Baha'i Faith in Malwa: A Study of a Contemporary Religious Movement*. Ph.D., Australian National University. 345 p.

'The main purpose . . . is to examine the various doctrines, teachings and institutions of the Baha'i Faith, both in theory and as they are being implemented in a specific cultural environment.' Both historical and sociological perspectives are used.

13.24. Garrigues, Steve L. (1976), *The Baha'is of Malwa: Identity and Change Among the Urban Baha'is of Malwa*. Ph.D., Lucknow University. 346 p.

An historical overview of the introduction and development of the Bahá'í community in India. The major portion is an ethnographic study of the Bahá'ís of Malwa.

13.25. Gemmell, Jennifer Kay. (1985). *Pure Souls in the Siyah Chal*. M.A., University of Tulsa. 3 p., 10 slides.

Art thesis consisting of paintings (of which slides were made) and a brief written explanation.

13.25a. Goldstein, Judith. (1978). *Interwoven Identities: Religious Communities in Yazd, Iran*. Ph.D., Princeton University.

13.26. Gottlieb, Randie Shevin. (1982). *Needs Assessment Survey to Determine the Training Requirements of International Baha'i Traveling Teachers*. Ed.D., Boston University. xvi, 288 p.

'The purpose of this investigation was to determine selection criteria and training needs for international Bahá'í traveling teachers . . . A questionnaire was developed, tested and mailed to 200 returned teachers and to Bahá'í institutions in the 81 countries they had visited.' [Abstract]

13.27. Hampson, Arthur. (1980). *The Growth and Spread of the Baha'i Faith*. Ph.D., University of Hawaii. xvii, 524 p.

'The objective of this research has been to describe and account for the growth and spread of the Bahá'í Faith. The religion has been considered as an innovation, and its dissemination has been viewed as a consequence of its internal structure and decision-making patterns. It was found that a strong centralized leadership has facilitated diffusion, that religious beliefs have favored dissemination efforts, and that policy and planning have successfully directed Bahá'í expansion. At the same time, the staging and direction of Bahá'í expansion frequently have been influenced by attitudes, conditions and events lying outside the direct control of the Bahá'í movement.' [Abstract]

13.28. Hassall, Graham H. (1984). *The History of the Baha'i Faith in Australia, 1920–1963*. B.A., University of Sydney. iii, 121 p.

Bahá'í historical development in Australia, with brief examination of the influence of the Australian social environment, its reception in a largely Christian environment, and the social strata it attracts.

13.29. Hein, Kurt. (1985). *Community Participation in Radio for Rural Development: Radio Baha'i, Otavalo, Ecuador*. Ph.D., Northwestern University. xii, 424 p.

Study of Radio Bahá'í in Ecuador as an example of two trends in thinking on social and economic development: (1) use of media to promote and support development projects; (2) participation of rural people in the development process.

13.30. Hoffman, Frederic Gordon. (1977). *The Art and Life of Mark Tobey: A Contribution Towards an Understanding of a Psychology of Consciousness.* Ph.D., University of California, Los Angeles. xix, 528 p.

'Little information has yet come to light on the psychological and spiritual motivations, sources and interests which underlay the American artist's move towards a new pictorial language. Newly-discovered paintings and documents, including a significant body of manuscripts written by Mark Tobey, reveal a wealth of insight into the relationship between his search for inner illumination and his creative activity.' [Abstract]

13.31. Jensen, Mehri Samandari. (1981). *The Impact of Religion, Socioeconomic Status, and Degree of Religiosity in Family Planning Among Moslems and Baha'is in Iran: A Pilot Survey Research.* Ed.D., University of Northern Colorado. x, 97 p.

'The purpose of this investigation was to point out two methodological deficiencies in the area of differential fertility research in the Middle East and to propose possible refinements . . . to correct the deficiencies . . . The following hypothesis was formulated and tested: Baha'is and Moslems differ in family planning because specific religious factors present in Islam tend to impede its practice.' [Abstract]

13.32. Johnson,. Vernon Elvin. (1974). *An Historical Analysis of Critical Transformations in the Evolution of the Baha'i World Faith.* Ph.D., Baylor University. x, 444 p.

The thesis focuses on 'the major transformations which have occurred in the religion . . . giving particular attention to the opposition each transformation aroused, the tensions in the faith it produced, and the adjustments it necessitated . . . Each transformation was of a criticial nature, producing a majority who accepted and a minority who rejected each transformation.' [Abstract]

13.33. Kahn, Sandra Santolucito. (1977). *Encounter of Two Myths: Baha'i and Christian in the Rural American South – A Study in Transmythicization.* Ph.D., University of California at Santa Barbara. 465 p.

The problem addressed is that of ' "transmythicization", Pannikar's term referring to the meeting of two "myths", resulting in a third, new myth. The two myths in this case are the Baha'i and Southern Christian myths'. [Abstract]

13.34. Kelley, Edward Rulief. (1983). *Mark Tobey and the Baha'i Faith: New Perspectives on the Artist and His Paintings.* Ph.D., University of Texas at Austin. xiv, 234 p.

An examination of the impact of Mark Tobey's adherence to the Bahá'í religion upon the content of his paintings.

13.35. Lerche, Charles. (1973). *A Religious Movement for World Order: The Baha'i Faith.* M.A., American University. ii, 47 p.

The Bahá'í Faith is studied from the perspective of international relations as an element in the transition to global awareness of interdependence. The thesis is that the Bahá'í Faith 'has succeeded in impressing on a wider and larger selection of humanity the need for world order than any other organization . . .' [Introduction]

13.36. MacEoin, Denis. (1977). *A Revised Survey of the Sources for Early Babi Doctrine and History.* Fellowship Dissertation, King's College Cambridge. 316, [7] p.

An annotated catalogue of the works of the Báb, with location and variations in manuscripts, and a historical context provided for each work; and a critical review of sources for Bábí history, especially the *Kitáb-i-Nuqtatu'l-Kaf* and the *Táríkh-i-Jadíd*.

13.37. MacEoin, Denis. (1979). *From Shaykhism to Babism: A Study in Charismatic Renewal in Shí'í Islam.* Ph.D., Cambridge University. v, 240 p.

A study of the roles of charisma and authority within Shí'ísm in shaping the transformation of Shaykhism to Bábism.

13.37a. Mahmoudi, Hoda. (1979). *The Structure of Organizations in Iran: A Comparative Analysis.* Ph.D. University of Utah. p. 45.

13.38. Mahmoudi, Jalil. (1966). *A Sociological Analysis of the Baha'i Movement.* Ph.D., University of Utah. vii, 147 p.

Not so much a sociological analysis as it is an introductory examination of Bahá'í belief and organization.

13.39. Martin, James Douglas. (1967). *The Life and Work of Sarah Jane Farmer, 1847–1916.* M.A., University of Waterloo. 261 p.

Sarah Jane Farmer undertook a series of educational projects during the 1880–1900 period: the Eliot Public Library, the Greenacre Institute and the Monsalvat School for the Comparative Study of Religion. Two circumstances added considerable importance to her work: (1) her pioneering contributions to the adult education movement; (2) timing of her programmes, occurring as they did during a 'watershed' period in which many American thinkers tried to draw their countrymen into the process of social change.

13.40. Mash, S. David (1985). *An Examination of Baha'i Christology.* M.Th., Dallas Theological Seminary. 100 p.

'Examines the teachings of the Baha'i religion with respect to the person and work of Jesus Christ for the purpose of appraising Baha'i Christology according to the criteria of biblical revelation.' [Introduction]

13.41. Milani, Rahim Baradaran. (1981). *Frontenac United Methodist Campus, Frontenac, Minnesota.* Master of Architecture, University of Minnesota. pp. 1–8.

Bahá'í Faith mentioned in context of the spiritual retreats undertaken by the great Founders of religions. The Greatest Name ring-stone symbol is explained.

13.42. Miloff, Maury. (1978). *A Sociological Study of the Bahá'í Faith.* B.A., Concordia University. 113 p.

'A sociological interpretation of the religion has been made using the theories of Max Weber and Saint-Simon . . .' [Introduction]

13.43. Murthi, R. Ganesa. (1969). *The Growth of the Bahá'í Faith in Malaysia.* University of Malaya. 43 p.

Three main developments in the Malaysian community are described: (1) growth and expansion from obscure beginnings in Singapore to its spread to most of Malaya in 15 years; (2) development of administrative institutions and the acquisition of legal status; (3) the community's attainment of international recognition and international participation.

13.44. Oldziey, Peter. (1985). *Spiritual Ideals in Non-Formal Rural Development: Rationale and Strategies for the Development and Use of Analogical Pictographs.* Ed.D., University of Massachusetts. ix, 304 p.

'The purpose of this dissertation is twofold. First, it seeks to substantiate the inclusion of spiritual ideals within the planning and development of non-formal education programs . . . The second purpose . . . is the development of some initial educational materials and strategies that could symbolize spiritual concepts in a way [that] would permit dialogue with a non-literate population.' [Abstract]

13.45. O'Neil, Linda. (1975). *A Short History of the Baha'i Faith in Canada, 1898–1975.* B.A., Carleton University. 44 p.

Canadian Bahá'í history centering on selected short biographies of several key individuals.

13.46. Ong, Henry. (1978). *Yan Kee Leong: A Biography of a Malaysian Cartoonist.* M.S., Iowa State University. iv, 176 p.

Biography of Yan Kee Leong, a cartoonist by profession, who became in late life a member of the Continental Board of Counsellors in Asia.

13.47. Parnian, Shahnaz. (1974). *A Study of the Methods of Communication Used by Baha'is in Educating Persons to Adopt Baha'i Faith.* B.A., University of Rajasthan. 89, 6 p.

Most people had read pamphlets or literature 'but individual persons play the most important role in the process of communication'.

13.48. Pope, Liston. (1932). *The Humanitarian Ideals of Bahaism: A Study of Bahai History and Doctrine.* B.D., Duke University School of Religion. 132 p.

The thesis treats 'the humanitarian ideals of the faith by tracing the historical development of the ideals of its leaders . . . Of all the fantastical dreams of man Bahaism is perhaps the most ambitious, and its claims for itself the most tremendous.' [Introduction]

13.49. Pruski, Thomas Robert. (1974). *A Symphonic Poem for the People of Baha.* Masters of Music, Northeastern Louisiana University.

Orchestral composition in the form of a symphonic poem, with two movements: one on the life of the Báb and the second on the life of Bahá'u'lláh.

13.50. Rafati, Vahid. (1979). *The Development of Shaykhī Thought in Shī'ī Islam.* Ph.D., University of California at Los Angeles. x, 231 p.

'The Shaykhī school was [a] branch of the Imāmī Shī'a, an intellectual link between Islam and the Bābī movement, and a point of departure for a series of religious and social developments in later periods which had a great impact upon the intellectual life of the Persians.' [Abstract]

13.51. Razi, Gholam Hossein. (1957). *Religion and Politics in Iran: A Study of Social Dynamics.* Ph.D., University of California – Berkeley. pp. 213–15.

'The importance of [the] Bab's religious movement . . . is in its social and economic position which best reflects an urban middle class point of view and is closely related to the aspiration of this class and to the West.'

13.52. Ross, Margaret J. (1979). *Some Aspects of the Bahá'í Faith in New Zealand.* M.A., University of Auckland. ix, 181, [7] p.

History of the Bahá'í community in New Zealand and a sociological analysis of its current condition.

13.53. Rost, Harry. (1969). *The Possible Nature and Establishment of Bahá'í Universities and Col-*

leges Based Upon a Study of Bahá'í Literature. Ph.D., University of South Dakota. 423 p.

'The basic purpose of this study was to attempt to clarify, within the limitations of the Bahá'í literature available, the possible nature of Bahá'í colleges and universities and the means by which such institutions would be established . . .' [Abstract]

13.54. Samimi, Enayat B. (1977). *A Baha'i House of Worship.* B.S., Saint Louis University. 67, 17 p.

Architectural proposals for a temple in the Philippines.

13.55. Schmiedeskamp, Karl W. (1982). *How I Learned to Stop Worrying and Love the Bomb: An Ethnography of Speaking of a Millenarian Movement.* M.A., University of Montana. vii, 245 p.

Description of the 'Joshuans', followers of Leland Jensen, a former Bahá'í who broke the Covenant and then created his own following based on apocalyptic prophecies.

13.56. Scholl, Steven D. (1980). *Imāmī Shī'ism and the Bahā'ī Faith: A Preliminary Study.* B.A., University of Oregon. 76, 25 p.

The author suggests that Bahá'ís uncritically accept the theological and historical assertions of Shí'ism with regard to the twelve Imams, whereas the Bahá'í writings may suggest a more critical stance.

13.56a. Seale, Thomas Scott. (1980). *An Examination of the Science Curriculum as It Reflects Social/Industrial Change: A Proposal for Curriculum Involving Social Interactions and Utilitarian Outcomes.* M.A., University of Georgia, pp. iv, 1, 4, 94–5, 97, 98, 100, 122.

Examination of the changes inaugurated by the industrial and scientific revolutions, the transition in general schooling that accompanied them, and the role of evolving science curricula in this transition. Proposals are then presented, based upon Bahá'í writings, that may be useful in the development of a science curriculum that aids more students to become active in the study and transmission of the practice of science in schools.

13.57. Shaoul, Eshagh Emran. (1971). *Cultural Values and Foreign Policy Decision-Making in Iran: The Case of Iran's Recognition of Israel.* Ph.D., George Washington University. pp. 72–4.

The Bahá'í movement as a precedent for reform within Iran.

13.58. Skelton, T. Lane. (1955). *A Sociological Analysis of the Baha'i Movement.* M.A., University of California at Berkeley.

13.59. Smith, Peter. (1982). *A Sociological Study*

of the Babi and Baha'i Religions. Ph.D., University of Lancaster. xiv, 549 p.

Examination of the changing social and historical context of the Bábí and Bahá'í religions. The author uses the concept of 'motif' – fundamental patterns of religious experience – to describe the various dominant religious concerns which have characterized the two movements. He identifies 'three theoretical frameworks which . . . provide a basis for the analysis of religious movements: a psychologically based theory of differently experienced levels of crisis; a broad consideration of the social location and material and ideal interests of movement participants; and what has come to be termed the "resource mobilization" approach.' [Abstract]

13.60. Staley, William Converse. (1966). *The Intellectual Development of Ahmad Kasravi.* Ph.D., Princeton University. pp. 141–3, 149–62.

Study of one of modern Iran's most celebrated intellectual and literary figures. A full chapter is devoted to his conversations with Bahá'ís. While Kasravi felt that the Shí'ís were not clear in their understanding of the modern world and intellectual thought, he felt that the Bahá'ís were no clearer.

13.61. Stiles, Susan. (1983). *Zoroastrian Conversions to the Bahá'í Faith in Yazd, Írán.* M.A., University of Arizona. vii, 107 p.

Examines the conversion of Zoroastrians to the Bahá'í Faith in Yazd, Iran, in the period from the 1880s to the early 20th century. A new mercantile elite emerged within the Zoroastrian community after the Parsis of India sent emissaries to their oppressed co-religionists in Iran. When religious reform failed to keep pace with social change, an ideational vacuum was created among this educated class which the Bahá'í Faith succeeded in filling.

13.62. Szepesi, Angela. (1968). *A Proposed World Order: Baha'i Teachings and Institutions.* M.A., Laval University. x, 124 p.

A political science thesis focusing on Bahá'í institutions.

13.63. Tamas, Andras Akos. (1978). *Need Identification and Proctor Selection for Distance Education on Isolated Reserves.* Masters in Continuing Education, University of Saskatchewan. pp. 77, 156.

Author mentions his membership in the Bahá'í Faith as affecting his choice of topic and conclusions.

13.64. Ullman, Chana. (1979). *Change of Mind or Heart?: Some Cognitive and Emotional Characteristics of Religious Conversions.* Ph.D., Boston

University Graduate School. pp. v, 34, 36, 37, 39, 67, 70, 72, 95, 96, 97, 117, 118.

'This study focused on the relative predominance of cognitive and emotional factors in precipitating religious conversions. Three hypotheses derived from cognitive theories of behavior were examined . . . Converts and non-converts differed markedly on all the variables that measured emotional dynamics and well-being. Converts reported a more stressful and traumatic childhood and a more stressful adolescence as compared to non-converts. The incidence of father-absence and of conflictual relationships with the father were particularly high in the converts' sample . . . Antecedents to the conversion indicated a high frequency of stress and emotional turmoil prior to the conversion and a low frequency of cognitive search.' [Abstract]

13.65. Vader, John Paul. (1981). *'For the Good of Mankind': August Forel and the Bahá'í Faith.* M.D., Université de Lausanne. 107 p.

Examination of the relationship of August Forel to the Bahá'í Faith.

See 7.2644.

13.66. Vahdat, Nusheen. (1984). *A Comparison of Muslim and Baha'i Persian Women Living in Australia.* B.A., Murdoch University. vi, 157 p.

'Comparative study of Persian Muslim and Baha'i women who live in Australia. The goal of the study was to determine the level of these women's consciousness and practice of equality in their lives . . . In most areas . . . the majority of both Muslim and Baha'i women think and act in a traditional way . . . In the area of divorce and religion . . . there are some structural differences between the two religions which led to a much greater equality among the Baha'is compared with the Muslims.' [Abstract]

13.67. Vaughn, Sharron Lee. (1980). *A Comparative Study of a Conversion and Commitment Process in Three Religious Groups.* M.A., University of Houston. ix, 175 p.

Examination of conversion and commitment processes in religious groups, specifically Catholic charismatics, Bahá'ís and Christian Scientists. Interviews were conducted and tested against the Lofland model of conversion and the Snow/Phillips critique of that model. In general, the data support the Snow/Phillips critique. However, their case study considered only converts to the religions and they overlooked the issue of group differences affecting the conversion process.

13.67a. Walline, David L. (1974). *A History of the Baha'i National Spiritual Assembly of the United States and Canada from Its Origins to 1937.* B.A., Yale University, 53, [15] leaves.

13.68. Ward, Allan Lucius. (1960). *An Historical Study of the North American Speaking Tour of 'Abdu'l-Baha and a Rhetorical Analysis of His Addresses.* Ph.D., Ohio University. ix, 261 p.

Study of 'Abdu'l-Bahá's talks delivered during his 1912 North American tour. 'It was the purpose of this investigation . . . (1) to recreate the historic setting in which the addresses took place; (2) to analyze the content of the addresses and the method of presentation; and (3) to estimate the nature and extent of the influence of these addresses . . .' [Abstract]

13.69. Waterman, Stanley. (1969). *Some Aspects of the Urban Geography of Acre, Israel.* Ph.D., Trinity College – Dublin. pp. 26, 103, figure 2.2., 2.9.

Brief mention of Bahá'ís and Bahá'í properties.

13.69a. Williams, Pontheolla Taylor. (1978). *A Critical Analysis of the Poetry of Robert Hayden Through His Middle Years.* Ed.D., Columbia University Teachers College. pp. 47–50, 52–3, 56, 57, 113, 114, 138, 183, 202, 208.

Includes analysis of the Bahá'í inspiration for a number of Hayden's works.

13.70. Wise, Anny. (1985). *Joseph and His Multi-coloured Story: (The Story of Joseph and His Brothers).* M.A., Faculty of Comparative Religions, Antwerp. pp. 31–8.

Investigation of the changing pattern of use of the Joseph story in Judaism, Islam, Christianity and Babism, especially in its growing allegorical meaning.

13.71. Wyman, June R. (1985). *Becoming a Baha'i: Discourse and Social Networks in an American Religious Movement.* Ph.D., Catholic University of America. 205 p.

'The aim of the study was to examine how American Baha'is interpret their religion and how those understandings shape their social interaction . . . A cultural analysis of these materials showed that American Baha'is interpret the Baha'i religion primarily as a narrative for culturally constituting the individual . . .' [Abstract]

13.72. Yeo Hock Choon. (1980–81). *The Bahá'í Community: A Study of Identity Consolidation, with Special Focus on Witnessing.* B.A., University of Singapore. iii, 75 p.

The main focus is to show how 'witnessing can serve as an instrument of boundary maintenance' between groups. The final analysis studies the structure of the Bahá'í community through Wilson's typology of sectarian movements.

13.73. Zaerpoor, Mahyad. (1981). *Educational Implications of Baha'i Philosophy with a Special*

Consideration of the Concept of Unity. Ph.D., University of Southern California. v, 261 p.

'The purpose of this study was to derive educational implications from Baha'i philosophy with a special consideration of the concept of unity as an underlying structure of both Baha'i philosophy and education.' [Abstract]

STANDARD ABBREVIATIONS FOR MAJOR ENGLISH-LANGUAGE BAHÁ'Í WORKS

THERE is as yet no standard method or scheme for referencing Bahá'í texts. Particularly important are the constantly-quoted works of Bahá'í sacred scripture. The Bahá'í encyclopaedia in preparation by the Bahá'í Publishing Trust of the United States has brought about the development of a list of proposed abbreviations for important Bahá'í texts to ease the burden of citation, and users are referred to that work for a full set of abbreviations for titles in English, Persian and Arabic. Any writer using these abbreviations should bear in mind that there are a number of editions and that it is essential in some instances for clarification to give, in addition to the abbreviation, the date(s), countries and volume numbers. Suggested format is Abbreviation(Date:Country)Volume:Pages, with unnecessary elements omitted as the case may require, e.g. PDIC(1942:India):115 or TAB1:27. *The Hidden Words* (HW) is an exception; see explanation in the list below. Bahá'í World Centre compilations have been published in multiple editions under several titles. The compiler has felt that standard abbreviations for these should not be added to this list until agreement is reached on how to cite them.

AB	*'Abdu'l-Bahá: The Centre of the Covenant of Bahá'u'lláh* / by H.M. Balyuzi.
ABC	*'Abdu'l-Bahá in Canada.*
ABDP	*Abdul Baha on Divine Philosophy.*
ABL	*'Abdu'l-Bahá in London.*
ADJ	*The Advent of Divine Justice* / by Shoghi Effendi.
AFYP	*Analysis of the Five Year International Teaching Plan* / Universal House of Justice.
ALSE	*Arohanui: Letters from Shoghi Effendi to New Zealand.*
ANYP	*Analysis of the Nine Year International Teaching Plan* / Universal House of Justice.
BA	*Bahá'í Administration* / by Shoghi Effendi.
BFI944	*The Bahá'í Faith, 1844–1944* / by Shoghi Effendi.
BFI950	*The Bahá'í Faith, 1844–1950* / by Shoghi Effendi.
BFI952	*The Bahá'í Faith, 1844–1952* / by Shoghi Effendi.
BFI968	*The Bahá'í Faith, Statistical Information, 1844–1968* / Universal House of Justice.
BHDD	*The Báb: The Herald of the Day of Days* / by H.M. Balyuzi.
BHP	*Bahá'í Holy Places at the World Centre.*
BKG	*Bahá'u'lláh: The King of Glory* / by H.M. Balyuzi.
BNE	*Bahá'u'lláh and the New Era* / by J.E. Esslemont.
BP	*Bahá'í Prayers.*
BPTY	*Bahá'í Prayers and Tablets for the Young.*
BR	*The Bahá'í Revelation* (compilation of selections from works by Bahá'u'lláh and 'Abdu'l-Bahá).
BS	*Bahá'í Scriptures* (compilation of selections from works by Baha'u'lláh and 'Abdu'l-Bahá).
BW	*The Bahá'í World* [cite using volume and page only, e.g. BW18:10 is *The Bahá'í World*, volume 18, page 10].
BWF	*Bahá'í World Faith* (compilation of selections from works by Bahá'u'lláh and 'Abdu'l-Bahá).
CF	*Citadel of Faith* / by Shoghi Effendi.
CH	*The Chosen Highway* / Lady Blomfield.
CN	*Call to the Nations* / by Shoghi Effendi.
CUHJ	*Constitution of the Universal House of Justice.*
DB	*The Dawn-Breakers* / Nabíl-i-A'ẓam.

DG	*Directives from the Guardian.*
DND	*Dawn of a New Day* / Shoghi Effendi.
DT	*Declaration of Trust. By-Laws of a Local Spiritual Assembly.*
ESW	*Epistle to the Son of the Wolf* / by Bahá'u'lláh.
FB	*The Faith of Bahá'u'lláh: A World Religion* / by Shoghi Effendi.
FV	*The Four Valleys* / by Bahá'u'lláh (in *The Seven Valleys and the Four Valleys*).
GPB	*God Passes By* / by Shoghi Effendi.
GWB	*Gleanings from the Writings of Bahá'u'lláh.*
HE	*High Endeavours* / by Shoghi Effendi.
HW	*The Hidden Words* / by Bahá'u'lláh. [cite by number, in the form A14 (number 14 from the Arabic), P10 (number 10 from the Persian); e.g. HW:A14].
IQ	*An Index of Quotations from the Bahá'í Sacred Writings* / compiled by James Heggie.
JWTA	*Japan Will Turn Ablaze.*
KA	*Kitáb-i-Aqdas* / by Bahá'u'lláh.
KI	*Kitáb-i-Íqán* / by Bahá'u'lláh.
LDG	*Light of Divine Guidance* / by Shoghi Effendi.
LGANZ	*Letters from the Guardian to Australia and New Zealand.*
MA	*Messages to America* / by Shoghi Effendi.
MBW	*Messages to the Bahá'í World* / by Shoghi Effendi.
MC	*Messages to Canada* / by Shoghi Effendi.
MF	*Memorials of the Faithful* / by 'Abdu'l-Bahá.
MUHJ	*Messages of the Universal House of Justice, 1968–1973.*
PAB	*The Passing of 'Abdu'l-Bahá* / by Shoghi Effendi and Lady Blomfield.
PB	*The Proclamation of Bahá'u'lláh to the Kings and Leaders of the World.*
PBA	*Principles of Bahá'í Administration.*
PDIC	*The Promised Day Is Come* / by Shoghi Effendi.
PM	*Prayers and Meditations by Bahá'u'lláh.*
PP	*The Priceless Pearl* / Rúḥíyyih Rabbani.
PT	*Paris Talks* / 'Abdu'l-Bahá.
PUP	*The Promulgation of Universal Peace* / by 'Abdu'l-Bahá.
PWP	*The Promise of World Peace* / by the Universal House of Justice.
RB	*The Revelation of Bahá'u'lláh* / by Adib Taherzadeh.
SAQ	*Some Answered Questions* / by 'Abdu'l-Bahá.
SCKA	*A Synopsis and Codification of the Laws and Ordinances of the Kitáb-i-Aqdas.*
SDC	*The Secret of Divine Civilization* / by 'Abdu'l-Bahá.
SV	*The Seven Valleys* / by Bahá'u'lláh (in *The Seven Valleys and the Four Valleys*).
SWA	*Selections from the Writings of 'Abdu'l-Bahá.*
SWB	*Selections from the Writings of the Báb.*
TAB	*Tablets of Abdul Baha Abbas.*
TB	*Tablets of Bahá'u'lláh Revealed after the Kitáb-i-Aqdas.*
TDP	*Tablets of the Divine Plan* / by 'Abdu'l-Bahá.
TN	*A Traveller's Narrative* / by 'Abdu'l-Bahá.
TP	*Táhirih the Pure* / by Martha Root.
UD	*The Unfolding Destiny of the British Bahá'í Community* / by Shoghi Effendi.
WG	*Wellspring of Guidance* / by the Universal House of Justice.
WOB	*The World Order of Bahá'u'lláh: Selected Letters* / by Shoghi Effendi.
WR	*The World Religion* / by Shoghi Effendi.
WT	*The Will and Testament of 'Abdu'l-Bahá.*

DIRECTORY OF BAHÁ'Í PUBLISHERS

BAHÁ'Í WORLD CENTRE
World Centre Publications
46 High Street
Kidlington, Oxford OX5 2DN
England

ARGENTINA
Editorial Bahá'í Indo Latino Americana
(E.B.I.L.A.)
Av. Santa Fé 5085
1425 Buenos Aires
Argentina

AUSTRALIA
Bahá'í Publications Australia
P.O. Box 285
Mona Vale, N.S.W. 2103
Australia

BELGIUM
Maison d'Éditions Bahá'íes
205 rue de Trône
1050 Brussels
Belgium

BRAZIL
Editora Bahá'í – Brasil
Rua Enge-heiro Gama Lobo 267
Vila Isabel
20551 Rio de Janeiro RJ
Brazil

FIJI ISLANDS
Bahá'í Publishing Trust
P.O. Box 2007
Government Buildings
Suva
Fiji Islands

GERMANY
Bahá'í-Verlag GMBH
Limesstrasse 2
D-6238 Hofheim 6
Germany

INDIA
Bahá'í Publishing Trust
6 Canning Road
Post Box 19
New Delhi 110001
India

IRAN[1]

ITALY
Casa Editrice Bahá'í
Circonvallazione Nomentana 484-A/1
00162 Rome
Italy

IVORY COAST
Maison d'Éditions Bahá'íes
04 B.P. 770
Abidjan 04
Ivory Coast

JAPAN
Bahá'í Publishing Trust
Shinjuku 7–2–13
Shinjuku-Kul
Tokyo 160
Japan

KENYA
Bahá'í Publishing Agency
P.O. Box 47562
Nairobi
Kenya

KOREA
Bahá'í Publishing Trust
249–36 Huam-dong
Yongsan-ku
Seoul 140
Korea

LEBANON[2]

MALAYSIA
Bahá'í Publishing Trust
32 Jalan Angsana, Setapak
Kuala Lumpur 14–11
Malaysia

NETHERLANDS
Stichting Bahá'í Literatuur
Riouwstraat 27
2585 GR The Hague
Netherlands

1. For addresses write to: Bahá'í World Centre, P.O. Box 155,
   31 001 Haifa, Israel. Not operating at present.
2. For addresses write to: Bahá'í World Centre, P.O. Box 155,
   31 001 Haifa, Israel.

NORWAY
Bahá'í Forlag
Drammensvn 110A
Oslo 2
Norway

PHILIPPINES
Bahá'í Publishing Trust
P.O. Box 4323
Manila
Philippines

PAKISTAN
Bahá'í Publishing Trust
P.O. Box 7420
Karachi 3
Pakistan

SPAIN
Editorial Bahá'í de España
c/o Bonaventura
Castellet 17
Tarrasa, Barcelona
Spain

SWEDEN
Bahá'í-Förlaget
Alströmeragatan 9
12447 Stockholm
Sweden

TAIWAN
Bahá'í Publishing Trust
149–13 Hsin Sheng Nan Lu, sec. 1
Taipei 106
Taiwan

UGANDA
Bahá'í Publishing Trust
Mr. John Tushemereirwe, Sec.
P.O. Box 2662
Kampala
Uganda

UNITED KINGDOM
Bahá'í Publishing Trust
6 Mount Pleasant
Oakham, Rutland, Leics. LE15 6HU
England

UNITED STATES
Bahá'í Publishing Trust
415 Linden Ave.
Wilmette, IL 60091
U.S.A.

NATIONAL SPIRITUAL ASSEMBLIES/
PUBLISHING COMMITTEES[3]

BAHÁ'Í STUDIES ASSOCIATIONS
Association for Bahá'í Studies
34 Copernicus St.
Ottawa, Ont. K1N 7K4
Canada

INDEPENDENT BAHÁ'Í PUBLISHERS

George Ronald, Publisher
46 High Street
Kidlington, Oxford OX5 2DN
England

Kalimát Press
1600 Sawtelle Blvd., Suite 34
Los Angeles, California 90025
U.S.A.

Naturegraph
P.O. Box 1075
Happy Camp, California 96039
U.S.A.

Oneworld Publications (New Era Press)
185 Banbury Road
Oxford OX2 7AR
England

Horizonte Verlag GmbH
Leitzachstrasse 20a
D-8200 Rosenheim
Germany

Tacor International
23 Ave de l'Abreuvoir
78170 La Celle Saint-Cloud
Paris,
France

GEI spl
Via Loreto 58
20035 Lisone (Mi)
Italy

3. For addresses write to: Bahá'í World Centre, P.O. Box 155, 31 001 Haifa, Israel.

NAME INDEX

Included in this index are all names – personal, corporate and conference – which are associated in any way with the published works included in this bibliography. Abbreviations are included for the following functions: au = author; mus = music/ composer; rev = reviewer; tr = translator; comp = compiler; ed = editor; il = illustrator or photographer; int = writer of introduction; rec = recipient; tn = transcriber; ts = transmitter; su = subject. Where no abbreviation is included, the name is mentioned in some other connection with the work, for example, as the person in whose home a talk was given. With the exception of individuals who are extremely well known under a specific name, names are entered under the form(s) of name used in the publication. Varying forms and pseudonyms are connected by 'SEARCH ALSO UNDER' cross references.

Abadi, Behnaz
  au: 13.1
Abasi, M.U.
  au: 7.2
Abbott, Evelyn
  au: 10.1
Abdel Karim Effendi
  SEARCH UNDER 'Abdu'l-Karím Tihrání
'Abdu'l-Bahá
  au: 3.1–3.213, 4.1–4.311, 7.513, 7.1327, 7.2684, 8.1–8.13, 8.46–8.70, 10.758, 10.879, 11.2–11.20, 11.829
  su: 7.3–7.9, 7.519, 7.537–7.538, 7.590, 7.699, 7.720, 7.830, 7.982–7.983, 7.985–7.988, 7.1031–7.1033, 7.1073–7.1074, 7.1094, 1.099–7.1100, 7.1132, 7.1151, 7.1180–7.1183, 7.1220, 7.1313–7.1320, 7.1361, 7.1383, 7.1388–7.1392, 7.1400, 7.1411, 7.1429–7.1430, 7.1472, 7.1498, 7.1535, 7.1541, 7.1543, 7.1551, 7.2097, 7.2104, 7.2118–7.2120, 7.2286, 7.2345, 7.2402, 7.2428–7.2430, 7.2432, 7.2480, 7.2551–7.2553, 7.2570, 7.2658, 7.2668, 7.2673, 7.2676, 7.2735, 7.2751, 7.2760, 7.2800a, 8.14, 8.71, 8.93, 8.103, 8.108, 10.454, 10.484, 10.596, 10.639a, 10.720, 10.816, 10.1097, 10.1172, 10.1372, 10.1455, 11.21–11.25, 11.67, 11.236, 11.242, 11.318, 11.322–11.323, 11.353, 11.406, 11.416–11.417, 11.484, 11.492, 11.494, 11.498, 11.507, 11.518, 11.531, 11.573, 11.618–11.619, 11.677, 11.704, 11.718, 11.734, 11.759, 11.775, 11.796–11.798, 11.814–11.815, 11.830, 11.862, 11.896, 11.898, 11.926, 11.956, 11.961–11.962, 11.1012, 11.1030, 11.1052, 11.1070, 11.1110, 12.103, 12.118–12.119, 12.130, 12.142, 13.68
  Ascension 5.12, 5.106, 5.108, 7.1259, 11.933
  Palms of 7.641, 10.329, 11.367
'Abdu'l-Ḥamíd II
  su: 11.595
Abdul Hussein, Mirza
  au: 7.10

'Abdu'l-Karím Tihrání
  au: 7.11, 7.2278
  ts: 4.428
Abdul Rahman ben Hammad al Omar
  au: 10.3
Abel, Armand
  au: 10.1477
Aberly, John
  au: 10.4
Abimbola, Wande
  au: 10.5
Aboudi, Salman Hougi
  su: 10.676
Abrahamian, Ervand
  au: 10.7
Abrams, Elliott
  au: 11.26
Abu'l-Faḍl Gulpáygání, Mírzá
  au: 7.12–7.22
  su: 10.484
Accouche, Calneh
  au: 7.24
Ackerman, Phyllis
  ed: 10.1403b–10.1403e
Adams, Charles Joseph
  au: 10.6, 10.483
  ed: 10.779
Adams, Eric R.
  au: 11.29
Adams, Isaac
  au: 10.9–10.10
Adams, James N.
  comp: 11.516
Adamson, Hugh
  au: 13.2
Adamson, Jessie
  comp: 10.1389
Addison, James Thayer
  au: 10.11–10.12
Adíb Ṭáliqání
  su: 10.484
Adkins, Eudora
  tn: 8.58
Adler, Alfred
  su: 10.27
Adlparvar, Kamran
  au: 13.2a
al-Afgḥání, Jamálu'd-Dín
  su: 10.838, 10.841, 10.871, 10.1015, 11.591, 11.595, 11.597
Afhkami, Gholam R.
  au: 10.21a
Afnán, Abbás
  comp: 7.62
Afnán, Muhammad
  au: 11.30
Afnan, Ruhi Muhsen
  au: 7.33, 7.386–7.387, 10.1221–10.1222, 12.1–12.2
  su: 12.104
Afrukhtih, Yúnis-Kḥán
  tr: 7.2760

Ayers, John
  au: 10.718
Ayman, Iraj
  au: 7.88
Azari, Farah
  ed: 10.1591

Baal-Teshuva, Jacob
  ed: 10.1014
The Báb
  au: 2.1–2.9, 7.2320, 8.15, 8.16, 8.67–8.70
  su: 3.64, 3.181–3.184, 5.68, 7.92–7.97, 7.520, 7.969,
      7.1177, 7.1515, 7.1517, 7.2360, 7.2369–7.2371,
      8.110, 10.77–10.79, 10.1245, 10.1627–10.1628,
      11.53, 11.57, 11.61–11.62, 11.204, 11.209,
      11.687, 11.766–11.767, 11.822, 11.839–11.840,
      11.917, 11.1093–11.1094, 11.1127
  Declaration of 7.2409
Babcock, Eugene
  mus: 7.668
Bach, Ira J.
  au: 10.100
Bach, Marcus
  au: 7.98–7.100, 10.101–10.105, 11.67–11.72
Bacharach, Jere L.
  au: 10.106–10.106a
Backwell, Richard
  au: 7.101–7.103
Badí'
  su: 7.104, 7.1473
Badi'i, Hooshmand
  au: 7.105
Badi'Ullah, Mirza
  au: 7.106
Baedeker, Karl
  au: 10.107
Baer, Gabriel
  au: 10.109
Bagdadi, Zia M.
  au: 10.110
Bagley, F.R.C.
  au: 11.73
Bagley, Florence
  au: 7.107
Bahá'í Academy (Panchgani, India)
  au: 7.118–7.124
Bahá'í Administrative Committee for Thailand
  au: 9.26
Bahá'í Centenary (1944: Chicago)
  au: 7.144
Bahá'í Centenary (1944: London)
  au: 7.145
Bahá'í Centenary (1953: Chicago)
  au: 7.146
Bahá'í Children's Fair (3rd: 1985: Uttar Pradesh)
  au: 7.149
Bahai Committee of Investigation
  au: 7.152–7.153
Bahá'í Committee on Music
  SEARCH UNDER National Spiritual Assembly of the Bahá'ís
  of the United States. Committee on Music.
Bahá'í Computer User's Association
  au: 9.45
Bahai Conference and Congress, Western States Region
  (2nd: 1924: San Francisco)
  au: 7.156.

Bahá'í European Teaching Conference (1st: 1948:
  Geneva)
  au: 7.165
Bahá'í Intercontinental Conference (1953: Chicago;
  Wilmette, Ill.)
  au: 7.268
  su: 7.1861
Bahá'í Intercontinental Conference (1953: Kampala,
  Uganda)
  au: 7.269
Bahá'í Intercontinental Conference (1953: New Delhi)
  au: 7.270–7.271
  su: 7.814
Bahá'í Intercontinental Conference (1953: Stockholm)
  au: 7.272
Bahá'í Intercontinental Conference (1958: Chicago;
  Wilmette, Ill.)
  au: 7.273–7.274
Bahá'í Intercontinental Conference (1958: Kampala,
  Uganda)
  au: 2.275
  su: 7.1699
Bahá'í Intercontinental Conference (1967: Chicago;
  Wilmette, Ill.)
  au: 7.276a
Bahá'í Intercontinental Conference (1967: Kampala,
  Uganda)
  au: 7.277
Bahá'í Intercontinental Conference (1967: New Delhi)
  au: 7.278–7.279
Bahá'í Intercontinental Conference (1967: Panama)
  au: 7.280
Bahá'í International Community
  au: 7.281–7.321a, 11.108
  comp: 7.2051
  su: 9.57, 11.109, 11.524, 11.711, 11.996
Bahá'í International Conference (1976: Helsinki)
  au: 7.322
Bahá'í International Conference (1977: Bahia, Brazil)
  au: 7.323
Bahá'í International Conference (1982: Canberra, A.C.T.)
  au: 7.323a
Bahá'í International Conference (1982: Lagos, Nigeria)
  au: 7.324
Bahá'í International Conference (1982: Montreal)
  au: 7.325–7.326
Bahá'í International Health Agency
  au: 9.58
Bahá'í International Youth Conference (1974: Hilo,
  Hawaii)
  au: 7.327
Bahai-Kongress (3rd: 1924: Stuttgart)
  au: 7.330a
Bahai Lending Library (London)
  7.334a
Bahá'í National Center (Wilmette, Ill.)
  su: 9.199
Bahá'í Oceanic Conference (1968: Palermo, Sicily)
  su: 7.2567
Bahá'í Oceanic Conference (1970: Mauritius)
  au: 7.364–7.365
Bahá'í Oceanic Conference (1971: Sapporo, Japan)
  au: 7.366
Bahá'í Oceanic Conference (1971: Singapore)
  rec: 7.1771
Bahá'í Public Conference (1928: Chicago)
  au: 7.375a

Enright, Robert
  au: 11.372
Enroth, Ronald
  au: 10.627
Entwisle, Frank
  au: 10.496b
Entzminger, Albert P.
  au: 7.847–7.850
Erlandson, Seth
  au: 11.373
Erskine, Beatrice
  au: 10.496c
Ertugrul, Irene
  au: 11.374
Eskelund, Karl
  au: 10.497
Esphahani, Ahmad
  SEARCH ALSO UNDER Sohrab, Ahmad
  tr: 3.144, 3.147–3.148, 3.157
Esposito, John L.
  au: 10.498
  ed: 10.793
Esslemont, John Ebenezer
  au: 7.854–7.886, 8.79–8.81, 11.375–11.376
  su: 7.158
Esslemont, Peter
  au: 7.887, 10.499, 11.377
Estes, Joseph
  au: 10.500
Esty, Frances
  comp: 4.135
European Bahá'í Youth Conference (1983: Innsbruck, Austria)
  au: 7.890
European Teaching Conference (1st: 1948: Geneva, Switzerland)
  au: 7.891
European Teaching Conference (2nd: 1949: Brussels, Belgium)
  au: 7.892
European Teaching Conference (3rd: 1950: Copenhagen)
  au: 7.893–7.894
European Teaching Summer School (1st: 1950: Copenhagen)
  au: 7.895
Evans, E.P.
  au: 11.379–11.380
Evans, Winston
  au: 7.896–7.897a
Ewart, Gavin
  rev: 7.2731
Ewing, Galen W.
  au: 12.27a

Fádil-i-Mázandarání
  SEARCH UNDER Fazel, Mirza Jenabe
Faghfoory, Mohammed Hassan
  au: 13.20
Faizi, Abu'l-Qásim
  au: 7.910–7.923, 7.2477, 8.83–8.85
  tr: 8.95
Faizi, Gloria
  au: 7.650, 7.924–7.935a, 8.86
  ed: 7.2480
Falk, Richard
  au: 10.507

Farah, Caesar E.
  au: 10.508
Fareed, Ameen U./Ameen 'Ullah
  su: 11.1049
  tr: 1.3, 3.69, 3.138, 7.10, 7.71, 7.74, 7.106
Farhang, Mansour
  au: 11.384–11.385
Farley, Robert Kim-
  SEARCH UNDER Kim-Farley, Robert
Farman, Hafez F.
  au: 10.509
Farmer, Sarah Jane
  su: 11.698, 13.39
Farnsworth, G.
  au: 11.174
Fasá'í, Hasan
  SEARCH UNDER Hasan-i-Fasa'i
Fathe-Aazam, Shidan
  comp: 4.161
Fathea'zam, Hushmand
  au: 7.940–7.948, 8.87
Fathi, Asghar
  ed: 10.1588
Fawcett, Millicent
  au: 10.510–10.511
Fazel, Mirza Jenabe
  au: 7.949
  su: 7.1328, 11.573a
Featherstone, H. Collis
  su: 7.1422
Fennessy, Mark
  il: 1.8
Fentress, David Wendell
  au: 11.387
Ferdowsi, Faran
  au: 11.388
Ferguson, Barbara R.
  il: 7.1593
Ferguson, Charles W.
  au: 10.512–10.513
Ferguson, John
  au: 10.514
Ferguson, Robert L.
  comp: 7.1593
Ferm, Vergilius
  au: 10.515
  ed: 10.494b, 10.1220
Fernea, Elizabeth Warnock
  ed: 10.1586
Ferraby, John
  au: 7.951–7.959. 8.88
Ferré, Nels F.S.
  au: 10.516–10.520
Ferrier, R.W.
  ed: 10.1457
Fertow, Fred M.
  au: 10.520a
Festival of Faith (1955: San Francisco)
  au: 10.521
Fifield, A.C.
  tr: 10.1441
Filmer, Henry
  au: 10.522
Filson, Bruce K.
  au: 11.390–11.392
Filson, Gerald Wesley
  au: 13.21

Gafni, Shlomo S.
  au: 10.567a
Gail, Marzieh
  au: 7.1022–7.1035, 8.92, 8.93, 10.568–10.570
  ed: 7.2120
  int: 7.2309
  su: 7.1030
  tr: 1.47, 1.115–1.117, 3.75, 3.107–3.110,
    3.114–3.115, 7.2337
Gairdner, W.H.T.
  au: 10.571
'Galactic Spiritual Assembly of Bahais'
  su: 10.451
Galvin, Kathleen M.
  au: 10.572
Gammon, Roland
  au: 10.542
Gan-Or, Malkah
  au: 11.422
Gandhi, Mohandas Karamchand
  rec: 7.1542
Gapp, Paul
  au: 11.423
Garcia, David
  au: 7.1036
Gardet, Louis
  au: 10.573
Gardner, Aurora W.
  au: 7.1224
Garis, M.R.
  au: 7.1037
Garlington, William N.
  au: 7.1038, 10.1218, 13.23
Garrida, Gertrude
  comp: 5.43–5.45, 7.2161
Garrigues, Steve L.
  au: 10.765a, 13.24
Garrison, W.E.
  rev: 7.1567
Garrison, Winifred E.
  au: 10.574–10.575
Gartler, Marion
  au: 10.576
Garvey, Eileen
  au: 11.638
Gash, Andrew
  au: 7.1039
Gastil, Raymond D.
  ed: 10.549
Gaudefroy-Demombynes, Maurice
  au: 10.576a
Gaver, Jessyca Russell
  au: 7.1040–7.1041, 8.94
Gaythorpe, Elizabeth
  ed: 10.1167
Gazvini, M.J.
  au: 12.29
Gcinaphi Lindiwe Dlamini (Princess of Swaziland)
  su: 11.430, 11.702
Geden, A.S.
  au: 10.577
Gedern, Alfred S.
  au: 10.578
Geijbels, M.
  rev: 7.1566
Geisendorfer, James V.
  au: 10.579

Gelhorn, Eleanor Cowles
  au: 10.580
Gellner, Ernest
  ed: 10.799
Gemmell, Jennifer Kay
  au: 13.25
Geraci, Francine
  au: 11.425
Germanus, Julius
  au: 10.581–10.581a, 11.426
Gerstner, John H.
  au: 10.582–10.583
Getsinger, Lua
  rec: 11.12
  su: 7.2379
Geyserville Bahá'í School (Geyserville, Calif.)
  au: 7.1043–7.1044
Ghadirian, Abdu'l-Missagh
  au: 7.1045
Ghobadian, A.
  au: 11.427
Ghosh, A.
  au: 10.584
Ghosh, Tirthankar
  au: 11.428
Ghulamali, Ismail Naji
  au: 10.584a
Ghulam Ahmad Qadiani
  su: 10.31, 10.1156a
Giachery, Angeline
  su: 7.1508
Giachery, Ugo
  au: 7.1046–7.1047
Gibb, H.A.R.
  ed: 10.1331a–c, 10.1559
Gibb, Hamilton A.R.
  au: 10.585–10.586
Gibbon, David
  au: 10.587–10.588
Gibbons, Herbert Adams
  au: 10.589
Gibbons, John
  au: 10.590
Gibran, Jean
  au: 10.591–10.592
Gibran, Kahlil [Lebanese author and artist]
  au: 10.593
  su: 10.591–10.592, 10.670, 10.1624
Gibran, Kahlil [son of the Lebanese author]
  au: 10.591–10.592
Gibson, Amoz
  su: 7.351
Gidden, Helen M.
  comp: 4.223, 7.2144
Gift, Maye Harvey
  au: 7.1048
  comp: 7.2196
Gilbar, Gad G.
  ed. 10.1402
Giles, Diane
  au: 11.429
Giles, Herbert
  au: 10.614–10.615
Gill, Sylvia
  au: 11.430

Lee, Anthony A.
  au: 7.1388–7.1392
  ed: 7.690–7.692
Lee, James
  au: 10.899
Lee, Jeremy
  au: 11.626
Leete, Frederick De Land
  au: 10.900–10.901
Legum, Colin
  ed: 10.1001–10.1003
Lehmann, Rosamond
  au: 10.1173
  rec: 10.1167
Leiden, Carl
  au: 10.200–10.201
Leiendecker, Harold
  au: 11.627
Lemesurier, Peter
  au: 10.903
Lenczowski, George
  au: 10.904–10.905
Lengyel, Emil
  au: 10.906
Leonard, Arthur Glyn
  au: 11.628
Leong, Marietta
  comp: 7.2381
Leong, Yan Kee
  su: 7.2073
Lerche, Charles
  au: 13.35
Leslie
  au: 11.629
Levey, Judith S.
  ed: 10.379a, 10.1065
Levi, Avraham
  au: 10.154a, 10.908
Levin, Gail
  au: 11.630
Levine, Evyatar
  ed: 10.1174
Levy, Reuben
  au: 10.909–10.910
Lewensohn, Avraham
  au: 10.911
Lewis, Bernard
  au: 10.91
  ed: 10.289
Lewis, John
  au: 10.92
Lewis, Sinclair
  au: 10.913a–10.913b
Lewis, William
  au: 10.898
Lewis, William H.
  ed: 10.795
Leymarie, Jean
  au: 10.914
Library of Congress. Subject Cataloging Division
  au: 10.915
Lieber, Joel
  au: 7.1398, 11.631
Liggitt, Joyce
  au: 7.1401–7.1403
Limelighters (Singing Group)
  su: 11.190

Lincoln, C. Eric
  au: 10.916
Lincoln, Joany Millar
  au: 11.633
Lindsay, Kate M.
  ed: 10.1240
Lindstrom, Janet
  au: 7.1405–7.1406
Ling, Trevor
  au: 10.917–10.918
Lings, Martin
  comp: 10.252–10.253
Linklater, Eric
  au: 10.919
Linnemann, Russell J.
  ed: 10.21
Linton, J.H.
  au: 10.920
Lipnack, Jessica
  au: 10.921
Lippel, Israel
  au: 10.922
Lippitt, Marian Crist
  au: 7.1407–7.1410
Littell, Franklin
  au: 10.923
Littlefield, David W.
  rev: 7.1240, 7.2347
Littman, David
  au: 11.634
Littrell, Eileen
  au: 7.1410a, 7.1411
Local Spiritual Assembly of the Bahá'ís of Belgaum
  (India)
  comp: 7.547
Local Spiritual Assembly of the Bahá'ís of Bombay
  (India)
  au: 7.1421–7.1424
Local Spiritual Assembly of the Bahá'ís of Brighton
  (England)
  au: 7.1425
Local Spiritual Assembly of the Bahá'ís of Calabar
  (Nigeria)
  au: 7.1426
Local Spiritual Assembly of the Bahá'ís of Cork
  (Ireland)
  au: 7.1426a
Local Spiritual Assembly of the Bahá'ís of Denison
  (Tex.)
  au: 7.1427
Local Spiritual Assembly of the Bahá'ís of Hong Kong
  au: 7.1427a
Local Spiritual Assembly of the Bahá'ís of Lucknow
  (India)
  au: 7.1428
Local Spiritual Assembly of the Bahá'ís of Manchester
  (U.K.)
  au: 7.1428a
Local Spiritual Assembly of the Bahá'ís of New York
  (N.Y.)
  au: 7.1429
Local Spiritual Assembly of the Bahá'ís of Niagara Falls
  (N.Y.)
  au: 7.1430
Local Spiritual Assembly of the Bahá'ís of Peterborough
  (England)
  au: 7.1431

McKenty, Beth
  au: 11.655
McKibbin-Harper, Mary
  au: 10.947
Mackwelung, Rose
  su: 11.723
McLaughlin, Robert W.
  au: 7.1483
McLaurin, R.D.
  ed: 10.1175
Macleod, Donald
  ed: 10.601
Macmunn, George
  au: 10.949–10.950
McNamara, Patrick H.
  ed: 10.1220a
MacNeice, Jill
  au: 11.656
MacNeil-Lehrer Report
  au: 10.951
McNelly, Willis E.
  comp: 10.451
MacNutt, Howard
  au: 7.1484–7.1485, 12.45–12.46
  tr: 1.10–1.14
  comp: 3.98–3.101
McWilliams, Carey
  au: 11.657
Maghzi, Charleen R.
  comp: 7.9
Maguire, John
  au: 10.952
Maharashtra State Bahá'í Annual Planning Conference
  (1984: Bombay)
  au: 7.1486
Mahdavi, Shireen
  au: 11.658
Mahmoudi, Hoda
  au: 10.1588, 13.37a
Mahmoudi, Jalil
  au: 7.1487–7.1489, 13.38
Mahmud, Sayyid Fayyaz
  au: 10.954
Mahmudnizhad, Mona
  su: 7.2485
Mahran, Mirza
  au: 11.661
Main, Katy
  au: 7.1411
  il: 7.1411
Maine, G.F.
  comp: 10.224
Malcolm, Napier
  au: 10.995–10.956
Malkam Khan, Mirza
  su: 10.28
Maloney, Lawrence D.
  au: 11.663
Man, The
  au: 12.59–12.62
  su: 12.19a
Manji, H.M.
  au: 11.664
Mann, Fritz A.
  au: 7.1498
Mann, James
  au: 10.42, 11.665

Mann, Mahnaz
  su: 11.635–11.636
Mann, Sylvia
  au: 10.960
Manocha, Kishan
  au: 7.1499, 11.666
Manuchehri, Rokhsan
  au: 11.667
Marangella, Joel B.
  au: 12.63–12.66
Marangella, Philip A.
  au: 7.1503
Margoliouth, David S.
  au: 10.962
Marie of Romania
  au: 7.1504–7.1505
  su: 7.2059, 10.221–10.222, 10.1118
Markham, Clements R.
  au: 10.963–10.964
Marlowe, John
  au: 10.965
Marnham, Patrick
  au: 10.965a
Marr, Warren
  rev: 10.1533
Marrella, Giustino
  au: 7.1508
Marsella, Elena Maria
  au: 7.1510
Marshall, Edward A.
  au: 10.967
Martin, Alfred W.
  au: 10.968
Martin, Douglas (J. Douglas, James Douglas)
  au: 7.1143, 7.1512–7.1513, 7.1566, 10.292, 10.378,
    10.382, 11.669–11.670a, 13.39
Martin, J. Douglas
  SEARCH UNDER Martin, Douglas
Martin, James
  au: 10.969
Martin, Owen
  au: 11.671
Martin, Walter R.
  au: 7.1514, 10.970–10.972
  ed: 10.195
Marty, Martin E.
  au: 10.973, 10.973a
Marx, Gary
  ed: 10.907
Mary Magdalen
  su: 7.2554
Masefield, Morley
  au: 11.672
Mash, S. David
  au: 13.40
Masih Farhangi Academy (Karachi, Pakistan)
  au: 7.1518–7.1519
Masliyah, Sadok
  au: 11.673
Mason, Barbara
  comp: 4.163
Massé, Henri
  au: 10.975
Masson, Jean
  au: 7.1520–7.1522, 11.674–11.675
Master, Mahvash
  su: 11.913

Masujima, Rokuichiro
  au: 11.676
Mataragnon, Rita H.
  ed: 10.960a
Mathews, Loulie A.
  au: 7.1524–7.1527
  su: 7.1524
Mathews, Shailer
  ed: 10.430–10.431
Mathisen, Nina B.
  mus: 7.1528–7.1529
Mathison, Richard R.
  au: 10.977
Matson, G. Olaf
  au: 10.977a
Matthias, Louise B.
  7.1007
Maud, Constance E.
  au: 10.978, 11.677–11.678
Maung Sein
  au: 7.1530
Maxwell, Mary Elizabeth
  au: 10.980
Maxwell, May
  au: 7.1531–7.1534
Maxwell, William
  au: 10.979–10.980
Maxwell, William Sutherland
  su: 11.392
Mayberry, Florence V.
  au: 10.976
Mayer, Alan James
  au: 11.680
Mázandarání, Jináb-i-Fádil-i
  SEARCH UNDER Fazel, Mirza Jenabe
Mayer, F.E.
  au: 10.981
Mazlish, Bruce
  au: 11.681
Mazzaoui, Michel M.
  rev: 7.2317, 7.2337, 7.2491
Mbiti, John S.
  au: 10.982
Mbuy, Tatah H.
  au: 10.982a
Mc
  All names beginning Mc and Mac are alphabetized as
  though beginning Mac
Mead, Frank S.
  au: 10.983–10.986
Meade, F.H.M.
  au: 10.986a
Meagher, Paul Kevin
  ed: 10.495b
Means, Pat
  au: 10.986b
Mears, I.
  au: 10.987
Mears, L.E.
  au: 10.987
Meghnot, Jamshid
  au: 12.67–12.67a
Mehdevi, Anne Sinclair
  au: 10.988
Meher Baba
  su: 10.1188

Mehrabi, Jackie
  au: 7.1536
Mehrabi, Jacqueline
  au: 7.650, 7.1537–7.1541, 8.109
Mehta, Mani H.
  au: 7.1542, 11.682a
Meisler, Benjamin
  au: 10.989
Meister, Charles W.
  au: 10.990
Meistermann, Barnabas
  au: 10.990a–b
Meljon, Zeev
  ed: 10.1444
Mellgren, Doug-Harald
  au: 11.683
Melton, J. Gordon
  au: 10.991–10.992
Meluch, R.M.
  au: 10.992a
Men of the Trees
  su: 10.1452
Menon, Shashi
  au: 11.684–11.685
Mensching, Gustav
  au: 10.993
Meredith-Owens, G.M.
  au: 10.994
Merritt-Hawkes, O.A.
  au: 10.995, 11.686
Mertens, A.
  au: 10.995a
Mesbáh, K.
  tr: 7.2335
Metta, Vasudeo B.
  au: 11.688–11.689
Meyer, Glenn A.
  au: 11.690
Meyer, Hermann M.Z.
  comp: 10.804
Meyer, Marilyn
  au: 12.68
Meyer, Ray
  au: 7.1559–7.1562
Meyer, Zoe
  ay: 7.1563–7.1564
Meysels, Theodore F.
  au: 10.995b, 10.996
Michener, James
  au: 10.997–10.998
Middlebury College
  su: 11.280
Milani, Rahim Baradaran
  au: 13.41
Mill, George Oxford
  au: 10.1005
Miller, Grant Hindin
  au: 7.1565
Miller, Henry
  au: 10.1007
Miller, Herbert A.
  au: 10.1008
Miller, Janet
  au: 10.1009
Miller, Karen Gray
  au: 11.692

Miller, Milton G.
  au: 10.1010
Miller, William McElwee
  au: 7.1566–7.1568a, 10.1011, 11.693–11.696
  rev: 7.2746
  su: 7.2559
  tr: 1.75
Mills, Dorothy
  au: 10.1012
Mills, Mountfort J.
  au: 7.2751, 10.1221–10.1222
  comp: 4.229
Miloff, Maury
  au: 13.42
Minorsky, V.
  au: 10.1013, 11.697
  su: 10.773
  tr: 10.731
Mírzá Áqá Khán Kirmání
  SEARCH UNDER Kirmani, Mirza Aqa Khan
Mitchell, Bahia Deloomy
  au: 7.1572
Mitchell, Glenford E.
  au: 7.1573, 11.700
Mitchell, J. Murray
  au: 11.701
Mitchum, Robert
  su: 10.469
Mkhize, Nhlumba Bertha
  su: 7.2021
Moazzam, Anwar
  au: 10.1015
Moffett, Ruth J.
  au: 7.1574–7.1580
Molinard, Patrice
  il: 10.286
Momen, Moojan
  au: 7.1581–7.1582, 10.484, 10.1019–10.1019a,
    11.705–11.706
  ed: 7.1010, 7.2491
  tr: 7.1379
Momen, Wendi
  au: 7.1583
Momeni, Jamshid A.
  ed: 10.1176
Moncrieff, A.R. Hope
  au: 10.1020
Moneer, Mirza
  tr: 3.137
Moneereh Khanum
  SEARCH UNDER Munírih Khánum
Monever Khanum
  tr: 3.54
Moneypenny, Leslie
  au: 7.1583a
Monsalvat School for the Comprehensive Study of
  Religion (Eliot, Me.)
  au: 10.1020a
Montagu, Edwin S.
  au: 10.1021
Montagu, Venetia
  ed: 10.1021
Moore, Arthur
  au: 11.707
Moore, George Foot
  au: 10.1022
  rev: 7.2757

Moore, James
  au: 11.708–11.709
Moore, Peter
  au: 7.1584
Moppett, George
  au: 10.1023
Moqtada'i, Mr
  su: 11.710
More, Thomas (Saint)
  su: 11.326
Morey, Frederick
  au: 11.712
Morgan, Dewi
  rev: 7.519
Morgan, Edward P.
  ed: 10.1423
Moribame, Samuel
  au: 11.713
Morris, James Winston
  au: 10.1024
Morrison, Gary L.
  comp: 7.2161
Morrison, Gayle
  au: 7.1585
Morrison, J.A.
  au: 10.1025
Mortimer, Edward
  au: 10.1026–10.1026a
Mortimer, K.J.
  au: 11.717
Mosak, Harold H.
  ed: 10.27
Moses, David
  au: 7.1586–7.1587
Moshiri, Farrokh
  au: 10.1027
Moshrefzadeh, M.
  au: 7.1588
Moslem Student's Association in the U.S. & Canada.
  Persian Speaking Group
  au: 7.1589
Mother, The
  SEARCH UNDER Richard, Mira
Mother Baha'i Council of the United States
  au: 12.69–12.71
Motlagh, Hushidar
  au: 7.1592
  comp: 4.86, 4.291
Mott, Francis John
  au: 10.1029
Mott, John R.
  ed: 10.1028
Mottahedeh, Mildred
  au: 11.719
  su: 11.199–11.200, 11.585a
Mottahedeh, Roy P.
  au: 10.1030
Moulvi, A.M.
  au: 10.1031
Mounsey, Augustus H.
  au: 10.1032
Movius, Mary Rumsey
  comp: 4.164
Moyal, Munir Abdallah
  au: 11.720
Muhajer, Iran F.
  comp: 3.81–3.82

National Spiritual Assembly of the Bahá'ís of Australia.
Public Information Office
au: 7.1647

National Spiritual Assembly of the Bahá'ís of Australia
and New Zealand
au: 7.1648

National Spiritual Assembly of the Bahá'ís of Australia
and New Zealand. Child Education Committee
comp: 3.19

National Spiritual Assembly of the Bahá'ís of the
Bahamas. National Teaching Committee
au: 7.1649

National Spiritual Assembly of the Bahá'ís of Bangladesh
au: 7.1650

National Spiritual Assembly of the Bahá'ís of Barbados
au: 9.316

National Spiritual Assembly of the Bahá'ís of Belize.
National Children and Family Life Committee
au: 7.1651

National Spiritual Assembly of the Bahá'ís of Bermuda
au: 7.1652

National Spiritual Assembly of the Bahá'ís of the British
Isles
SEARCH ALSO UNDER National Spiritual Assembly of the
Bahá'ís of the United Kingdom
au: 7.1653–7.1657, 9.317–9.318
comp: 3.2

National Spiritual Assembly of the Bahá'ís of the British
Isles. National Teaching Committee
au: 7.1658–7.1659

National Spiritual Assembly of the Bahá'ís of the British
Isles. Public Relations Committee
au: 7.1660

National Spiritual Assembly of the Bahá'ís of Burma
au: 7.1661, 9.319

National Spiritual Assembly of the Bahá'ís of Cameroon
au: 7.1662–7.1669, 9.320

National Spiritual Assembly of the Bahá'ís of Cameroon.
Consolidation Committee
au: 7.1670

National Spiritual Assembly of the Bahá'ís of Cameroon.
National Teaching Committee
au: 7.1671–7.1672

National Spiritual Assembly of the Bahá'ís of Canada
au: 7.1673–7.1686
comp: 3.1
su: 11.882

National Spiritual Assembly of the Bahá'ís of Canada.
Bahá'í Education Resource Committee
au: 9.321

National Spiritual Assembly of the Bahá'ís of Canada.
National Indian Reserves Teaching Committee
au: 7.1687

National Spiritual Assembly of the Bahá'ís of Canada.
National Pioneer Committee
au: 7.1688–7.1690

National Spiritual Assembly of the Bahá'ís of Canada.
National Teaching Committee
au: 7.1691–7.1692

National Spiritual Assembly of the Bahá'ís of Canada.
National Treasury
au: 7.1693–7.1696

National Spiritual Assembly of the Bahá'ís of Canada.
Saskatchewan Bahá'í Schools Committee
au: 7.1697

National Spiritual Assembly of the Bahá'ís of the
Caroline Islands
au: 7.1698, 9.322

National Spiritual Assembly of the Bahá'ís of Central and
East Africa
au: 7.1699, 9.323

National Spiritual Assembly of the Bahá'ís of Ceylon
SEARCH ALSO UNDER National Spiritual Assembly of the
Bahá'ís of Sri Lanka
au: 7.1699a–7.1700

National Spiritual Assembly of the Bahá'ís of Colombia
au: 7.1701

National Spiritual Assembly of the Bahá'ís of Cyprus
au: 9.324

National Spiritual Assembly of the Bahá'ís of Denmark
au: 7.1702–7.1703

National Spiritual Assembly of the Bahá'ís of Ethiopia
au: 7.1704

National Spiritual Assembly of the Bahá'ís of the Fiji
Islands
au: 7.1705–7.1708

National Spiritual Assembly of the Bahá'ís of the Fiji
Islands. National Teaching Committee
au: 7.1709

National Spiritual Assembly of the Bahá'ís of the Fiji
Islands. Peace/Proclamation Committee
au: 7.1710

National Spiritual Assembly of the Bahá'ís of Ghana
au 9.325

National Spiritual Assembly of the Bahá'ís of the Gilbert
Islands and Tuvalu
au: 7.1711

National Spiritual Assembly of the Bahá'ís of Grenada
au: 9.326

National Spiritual Assembly of the Bahá'ís of Guyana
au: 7.1712

National Spiritual Assembly of the Bahá'ís of the
Hawaiian Islands
au: 7.1713–7.1714

National Spiritual Assembly of the Bahá'ís of the
Hawaiian Islands. Child Education Committee
comp: 4.63–4.64

National Spiritual Assembly of the Bahá'ís of Hong
Kong
au: 7.1715–7.1716

National Spiritual Assembly of the Bahá'ís of Iceland
au: 7.1717, 9.327

National Spiritual Assembly of the Bahá'ís of India
au: 7.1717a–7.1718

National Spiritual Assembly of the Bahá'ís of India.
National Teaching Committee
au: 7.1719–7.1720

National Spiritual Assembly of the Bahá'ís of India.
National Youth Committee
au: 7.1721–7.1724

National Spiritual Assembly of the Bahá'ís of India and
Burma
au: 7.1725–7.1727

National Spiritual Assembly of the Bahá'ís of India,
Pakistan and Burma
au: 7.1728–7.1729
rec: 11.526a

National Spiritual Assembly of the Bahá'ís of Iran
au: 7.1730–7.1733

National Spiritual Assembly of the Bahá'ís of the
Republic of Ireland
au: 7.1734–7.1738, 9.329

National Spiritual Assembly of the Bahá'ís of Jamaica
au: 7.1739–7.1740
su: 7.1740
National Spiritual Assembly of the Bahá'ís of Kenya
au: 7.1741, 9.330
National Spiritual Assembly of the Bahá'ís of Kenya.
National Education Committee
au: 7.1742
National Spiritual Assembly of the Bahá'ís of Kenya.
National Teaching Committee
au: 7.1743
National Spiritual Assembly of the Bahá'ís of Kenya.
National Youth Committee
au: 7.1744–7.1746
National Spiritual Assembly of the Bahá'ís of the
Leeward Islands
au: 7.1746a
National Spiritual Assembly of the Bahá'ís of Liberia
au: 7.1747
National Spiritual Assembly of the Bahá'ís of Liberia and
Guinea
au: 7.1748
National Spiritual Assembly of the Bahá'ís of
Luxembourg
au: 7.1749
National Spiritual Assembly of the Bahá'ís of Malawi
au: 7.1750–7.1751
National Spiritual Assembly of the Bahá'ís of Malawi.
Women and Children Committee
au: 7.1752
National Spiritual Assembly of the Bahá'ís of Malaysia
au: 7.1753–7.1761
comp: 7.1260
National Spiritual Assembly of the Bahá'ís of Malaysia.
Child Education Committee
au: 7.1762–7.1763, 9.331
National Spiritual Assembly of the Bahá'ís of Malaysia.
Child Education Committee of East Malaysia
au: 7.1764–7.1766
National Spiritual Assembly of the Bahá'ís of Malaysia.
Community Development Committee
au: 7.1767
National Spiritual Assembly of the Bahá'ís of Malaysia.
National Teaching Committee
au: 9.332
National Spiritual Assembly of the Bahá'ís of Malaysia.
National Youth Committee of Peninsular Malaysia
au: 7.1768
National Spiritual Assembly of the Bahá'ís of Malaysia.
National Youth Coordinating Unit
au: 7.1769
National Spiritual Assembly of the Bahá'ís of Malaysia.
National Youth Council
au: 7.1770–7.1771
National Spiritual Assembly of the Bahá'ís of Malaysia.
Secretariat
au: 7.1772
National Spiritual Assembly of the Bahá'ís of the
Mariana Islands
au: 9.333
National Spiritual Assembly of the Bahá'ís of Mauritius
au: 7.1733a
National Spiritual Assembly of the Bahá'ís of the
Netherlands
au: 9.334

National Spiritual Assembly of the Bahá'ís of the New
Hebrides
au: 7.1774–7.1776
National Spiritual Assembly of the Bahá'ís of New
Zealand
au: 7.1777–7.1780
National Spiritual Assembly of the Bahá'ís of New
Zealand. Community Development Committee
au: 7.1781–7.1786
National Spiritual Assembly of the Bahá'ís of New
Zealand. National Child Education Committee
au: 7.1787–7.1788
National Spiritual Assembly of the Bahá'ís of Nigeria
au: 7.1789–7.1790, 9.335
National Spiritual Assembly of the Bahá'ís of Norway.
National Pioneer Committee
au: 7.1791
National Spiritual Assembly of the Bahá'ís of Norway.
National Teaching Committee
au: 7.1792
National Spiritual Assembly of the Bahá'ís of Pakistan
au: 7.1792a
National Spiritual Assembly of the Bahá'ís of Papua New
Guinea
au: 7.1793–7.1796
National Spiritual Assembly of the Bahá'ís of the
Philippines
au: 7.1797–7.1799
National Spiritual Assembly of the Bahá'ís of Puerto
Rico. Teaching Committee
au: 7.1800
National Spiritual Assembly of the Bahá'ís of Rhodesia
au: 7.1801
National Spiritual Assembly of the Bahá'ís of Rhodesia.
National Women's Committee
au: 7.1802
National Spiritual Assembly of the Bahá'ís of Saint Lucia
au: 7.1803
National Spiritual Assembly of the Bahá'ís of Samoa
au: 7.1804–7.1807
National Spiritual Assembly of the Bahá'ís of Sierra
Leone. Children's Education Committee
au: 7.1808
National Spiritual Assembly of the Bahá'ís of Sierra
Leone. National Children's Committee
au: 7.1809
National Spiritual Assembly of the Bahá'ís of Singapore
au: 7.1810–7.1811
National Spiritual Assembly of the Bahá'ís of Singapore.
National Youth Committee
au: 7.1812
National Spiritual Assembly of the Bahá'ís of South and
West Africa
au: 7.1813–7.1816a
National Spiritual Assembly of the Bahá'ís of South and
West Africa. Creative Planning Committee
au: 7.1817
National Spiritual Assembly of the Bahá'ís of South and
West Africa. National Music Committee
comp: 7.413
National Spiritual Assembly of the Bahá'ís of South
Central Africa
au: 7.1818
National Spiritual Assembly of the Bahá'ís of South West
Africa/Namibia
tr: 7.1816a

National Spiritual Assembly of the Bahá'ís of the South
West Pacific Ocean
au: 9.336
National Spiritual Assembly of the Bahá'ís of Sri Lanka
SEARCH ALSO UNDER National Spiritual Assembly of the
Bahá'ís of Ceylon
au: 7.1819, 9.337
National Spiritual Assembly of the Bahá'ís of Sudan.
National Teaching and Deepening Committee
au: 9.338
National Spiritual Assembly of the Bahá'ís of Swaziland,
Lesotho and Mozambique
au: 7.1820
National Spiritual Assembly of the Bahá'ís of Thailand
au: 9.339
National Spiritual Assembly of the Bahá'ís of Tonga
au: 7.1821-7.1822
National Spiritual Assembly of the Bahá'ís of Tonga and
the Cook Islands
au: 7.1823-7.1824
National Spiritual Assembly of the Bahá'ís of Transkei
au: 7.1825
National Spiritual Assembly of the Bahá'ís of Trinidad
and Tobago
au: 7.1826
National Spiritual Assembly of the Bahá'ís of Uganda
au: 7.1827
National Spiritual Assembly of the Bahá'ís of the United
Kingdom
SEARCH ALSO UNDER National Spiritual Assembly of the
Bahá'ís of the British Isles
au: 7.1828-7.1841
comp: 5.70
National Spiritual Assembly of the Bahá'ís of the United
Kingdom. Child Education Committee
comp: 4.170
National Spiritual Assembly of the Bahá'ís of the United
Kingdom. National Consolidation Committee
au: 7.1842
National Spiritual Assembly of the Bahá'ís of the United
Kingdom. National Proclamation Committee
au: 7.1843
National Spiritual Assembly of the Bahá'ís of the United
Kingdom. National Teaching Committee
au: 9.340
National Spiritual Assembly of the Bahá'ís of the United
Kingdom. National Teaching Committee. Travel
Teaching Department
au: 7.1844
National Spiritual Assembly of the Bahá'ís of the United
Kingdom. National Youth Committee
au: 7.1845
National Spiritual Assembly of the Bahá'ís of the United
Kingdom. Service for the Blind Committee
au: 9.341
National Spiritual Assembly of the Bahá'ís of the United
States
au: 7.1846-7.1875, 8.111, 11.629a
comp: 5.27
su: 7.1864, 11.161a
National Spiritual Assembly of the Bahá'ís of the United
States. Advisory Committee on Education
comp: 4.67, 7.248, 7.391, 7.393-7.401, 7.535
ed: 7.2493
National Spiritual Assembly of the Bahá'ís of the United
States. African Teaching Committee
au: 7.1876

National Spiritual Assembly of the Bahá'ís of the United
States. American Indian Service Committee
au: 7.1877
National Spiritual Assembly of the Bahá'ís of the United
States. Area Teaching Committee of the Western
States
au: 1877a
National Spiritual Assembly of the Bahá'ís of the United
States. Bahá'í Committee for the United Nations
au: 7.1878
National Spiritual Assembly of the Bahá'ís of the United
States. Bahá'í House of Worship Activities Committee
au: 7.1879, 7.2606
National Spiritual Assembly of the Bahá'ís of the United
States. Child Education Committee
au: 7.1880
comp: 7.775
National Spiritual Assembly of the Bahá'ís of the United
States. Committee for the United Nations.
au: 7.1881
National Spiritual Assembly of the Bahá'ís of the United
States. Committee on Music
comp: 7.797, 7.2416
National Spiritual Assembly of the Bahá'ís of the United
States. Community Development Committee
au: 7.1882
National Spiritual Assembly of the Bahá'ís of the United
States. Interracial Teaching Committee
au: 7.1883-7.1884
National Spiritual Assembly of the Bahá'ís of the United
States. National Archives Committee
au: 7.1885-7.1886
National Spiritual Assembly of the Bahá'ís of the United
States. National Bahá'í Schools Committee
au: 7.1887
National Spiritual Assembly of the Bahá'ís of the United
States. National Education Committee
au: 7.1888-7.1894
comp: 7.594-7.595
National Spiritual Assembly of the Bahá'ís of the United
States. National Programming Committee
au: 7.1895, 9.342
National Spiritual Assembly of the Bahá'ís of the United
States. National Projects Committee
au: 7.1896
National Spiritual Assembly of the Bahá'ís of the United
States. National Public Information Office
au: 7.1897
National Spiritual Assembly of the Bahá'ís of the United
States. National Reference Library Committee
au: 7.1898-7.1902
National Spiritual Assembly of the Bahá'ís of the United
States. National Teaching Committee
au: 7.1903-7.1918, 9.343
National Spiritual Assembly of the Bahá'ís of the United
States. National Youth Committee
au: 7.1919-7.1920
National Spiritual Assembly of the Bahá'ís of the United
States. Office of Public Affairs
comp: 4.223a
National Spiritual Assembly of the Bahá'ís of the United
States. Office of the Treasurer
au: 7.1921-7.1940, 9.344
National Spiritual Assembly of the Bahá'ís of the United
States. Projects Development Committee
au: 7.1941

Taafaki, Irene
  au: 7.2522
Ṭabáṭaba'í, Muḥammad Ḥusayn
  au: 10.1418
Taeed, Dr.
  su: 10.439–10.440
Tagungszentrum Landegg
  su: 9.283
Taheri, Amir
  au: 11.980
Taherzadeh, Adib
  au: 7.2523–7.2525, 8.137a–8.140
Taherzadeh, Ḥabíb
  au: 7.2526
  tr: 1.134–1.135, 2.7–2.8
Ṭáhirih
  au: 10.1166, 10.1588
  su 7.60, 7.811, 7.1342–7.1343, 7.1516,
    7.2307–7.2309, 7.2527, 10.486, 10.584a, 10.599,
    10.660a, 10.790–10.791, 10.1349a, 10.1588,
    11.189, 11.413, 11.560, 11.678, 11.688, 11.879,
    11.925, 11.1070
Takieddine, Randa
  au: 11.981
Taleghani, Ayatullah Sayyid Mahmud
  au: 10.1419
Tamadun ul Molk
  au: 7.2527a
Tamas, Andras Akos
  au: 13.63
Tammik, Heidi
  au: 11.983
Tatsuro, Yamamoto
  ed: 10.762
Tavris, Carol
  au: 11.984
Taylor, David L.
  au: 11.985
Taylor, Jennie Coe
  su: 11.1069
Tchertkoff, V.
  tr: 10.1441
Teherani, Abdel Karim
  SEARCH UNDER 'Abdu'l-Karím Tihrání
Tehrani, Noreen
  au: 7.2536a–7.2536g
Teinonen, Seppo A.
  rev: 1.75
Temple, Bernard
  au: 11.989
  su: 11.843
Terry, Quinlan
  su: 10.1194
Thielmann, Max von
  au: 10.1422
Thomas, Lewis V.
  au: 10.1424
Thompson, Juliet
  au: 7.2551–7.2554, 11.1002
  su: 7.2553
Thompson, Kenneth W.
  au: 11.1003
Thompson, Robert Farris
  su: 11.559
Thomsen, Harry
  au: 10.1425

Thornburgh-Cropper, Mrs
  au: 3.162
Thorne, J.O.
  ed: 10.321a
Thrower, James
  au: 10.1426
Tierney, Martin
  au: 10.1427
Tihrání, 'Abdu'l-Karím
  SEARCH UNDER 'Abdu'l-Karím Tihrání
Tillich, Paul
  au: 10.1428
  su: 11.245
Tillotson, Peter
  au: 11.1004–11.1005
Tillyard, Aelfrida
  au: 10.1429–10.1430
Tinney, James S.
  au: 11.1007
Tippett, Maria
  au: 10.1431
Tisdall, W. St Clair
  rev: 7.2119, 11.1008
Titus, Murray T.
  au: 10.1432
Tobey, Mark
  au: 10.1433–10.1436
  su: 7.1507, 10.40, 10.249, 10.381, 10.410, 10.422a,
    10.548, 10.914, 10.961, 10.1152, 10.1208,
    10.1270, 10.1293, 10.1314–10.1315, 10.1431,
    10.1433–10.1436, 11.250, 11.368, 11.582, 11.888,
    13.30, 13.34
Tobler, Emile
  au: 11.1010
Toeg, Daood
  su: 7.1547
Tolley, William Pearson
  comp: 10.1181
Tolstoy, Alexandra
  au: 10.1437–10.1438
Tolstoy, Leo
  au: 10.1439–10.1441
  su: 7.2473, 10.1437–10.1438
Tomlin, Viva B.M.
  au: 7.2566, 11.1011
Tony Lease Tours (Laguna Beach, Calif.)
  au: 7.2567
Toronto (Ont.). Board of Education
  au: 10.1442
Toumanski, A.G.
  su: 11.239
Towfiq, Miriam G.
  au: 7.1996
Townsend, Meredith
  au: 10.1445
Townshend, George
  au: 7.2570–7.2601, 11.1013
  comp: 4.137–4.138
  su: 7.1184
Toy, Crawford Howell
  au: 10.1446–10.1447
Toynbee, Arnold J.
  au: 10.1449–10.1451
  su: 11.1068
Treadwell, Dorothy
  au: 7.2604

University of London. School of Oriental and African
Studies
au: 10.566
University of Pennsylvania. Middle East Research
Institute
au: 10.1481
University of the South Pacific
au: 7.384
Upton, Joseph M.
au: 10.1482
Uris, Leon
au: 10.1483
Ussher, John
au: 10.1484

Vader, John Paul
au: 7.2644, 11.1035, 13.65
Vahdat, Nusheen
au: 13.66
Vahid Choral Society (Chicago)
su: 7.67
Vail, Albert R.
au: 7.2645, 10.1485, 11.1036–11.1039a
rev: 7.1567, 7.1612
Vail, Emily McClellan
au: 10.1485
Vail, Virgie V.
au: 7.2646
Vajdi, K.H.
au: 7.2642–7.2648
Vakil, N.R.
au: 11.1040
Vambery, Arminius
au: 3.181, 10.1486
su: 10.24, 11.956a
Van Baalen, Jan Karel
au: 10.1487–10.1490
Van den Hoonaard, Will C.
au: 11.1041
Van Hoof, Mary Ann
au: 10.1491
Van Paassen, Pierre
au: 10.1492
Van Sommers, Tess
au: 10.1493
Vander Werff, Lyle L.
au: 10.1490a
Vanderbilt, Cornelius, Jr.
au: 10.1494–10.1495
Varqa School (Ahmednagar, India)
au: 7.2649
Vashist, D.F.
au: 11.1042
Vashitz, Joseph
au: 11.1043
Vasudev, R.B.
ed: 10.755
Vaswani, T.L.
au: 7.2650, 10.1496
Vatralsky, Stoyan Krstoff
au: 11.1044
Vaughan, George
au: 10.1497
Vaughan, John Gaines
au: 10.1498

Vaughn, Sharron Lee
au: 11.359–11.360, 13.67
Vaupel, Ouise
au: 11.1045–11.1046
Vea, J.
au: 7.2651
Venable, Charles Leslie
au: 11.1047
Verma, Prakash
au: 11.1048
Viator
au: 10.1498a
Vicedom, Georg F.
au: 10.1499
Victory Foundation
au: 10.1500
Vidal, Gore
au: 10.1501
Villard, Henry S.
au: 11.1050
Vilnay, Zev
au: 10.1503–10.1509
Visser't Hooft, W.A.
au: 10.1511
Vizetelly, Henry E.
ed: 10.561
Voliva, Wilbur Glenn
au: 11.1053
Voll, John Obert
au: 10.1517
Voss, Carl
au: 10.732
Voss, Carl Hermann
au: 10.1518–10.1521
Vreeland, Herbert H.
ed: 10.772
Vucinich, Wayne S.
ed: 10.1363

Waamani, Israel T.
au: 10.1522
Wach, Joachim
au: 10.1523
Wade, John
au: 7.2662
Wade, John T.
au: 11.1055
Wadia, Ardaser Sorabjee N.
au: 10.1524
Wafford, Chester
au: 11.42
Wagar, W. Warren
au: 10.1525–10.1526
Wagner, Cosima Liszt
au: 10.1527
Wagner, Richard
su: 10.1527
Waite, Louise R.
au: 7.2663–7.2668, 11.1056
su: 11.122
Waite, Stephen
au: 7.2669
Walcott, Cynthia K.
au: 7.2670

TITLE INDEX

In this index are all titles of books, pamphlets, articles, series and periodicals, including cover titles, alternate titles, spine titles and subtitles where such titles are likely to be remembered by researchers. Initial articles 'a', 'an' and 'the' are ignored at the beginning of a title for purposes of alphabetization. Roman and Arabic numerals in titles come before the letter 'a'.

II Himalayan Baha'i Teaching Conference, 19th, 20th, and 21st Oct. 1983
7.1124
2nd Year, 7 Year Plan
7.1758
3 Simple Steps Why Bahai Philosophy Is Not the Answer
7.2558
3rd Baha'i Children's Fair, 1985
7.149
'4th Humanitarian Awards of the Baha'i'
11.408
4th Inter-Continental Baha'i Conference, New Delhi, India, October 7–15, 1953
7.814
4th Inter-Continental Bahá'í Conference, October 7 to 15, New Delhi, India, 1953
7.271
4th List of Gardens of Abdu'l Baha
7.993a
5 Month Plan, Nov. 21 1976 to Apr. 21 1977
7.1755
5 News 19
9.392
5 Year Global Plan
7.1767
A 6-Year Campaign to Eliminate a Religious Minority
7.306
7-Year Plan
7.1650
7 Year Plan Final Phase: Blue-Print for Individual and Community Life
7.1759
7 Year Plan in Devon and Cornwall
7.2396
7 Year Plan of the Universal House of Justice for Malaysia: 2nd Phase, April 1981 – April 1983
7.1760
11th Annual Oneida Pow-Wow, Festival of Performing Arts, July 1, 2, 3, 4, 1983: Souvenir Program
10.1104
12. Landsthing Bahá'ía, 27., 28. og 29. Mai, 1983, Reykjavík
7.745
14. Landsthing Bahá'ía, 26., 27. og 28. April, 1985, Kópavogur
7.746
14th National Convention B.E. 142 (Singapore, 26–28 April 1985)
7.747
14th National Convention of the Bahá'ís of Iceland
7.746

'16th Annual Report of Higginson Press, the Literary Life, Yokes and Goals'
11.712
19 Baha'i Lessons for Children
7.842
19 Bahá'í News
9.392
19 Dagsfest Barnens Tidning
9.284
19 Day Feast Letter
9.383, 9.385, 9.463
19 Day Feast Letter of the French Antilles
9.388
19 Day Feast Message
9.394
19 Day Feast News Letter
9.389–9.390
19 Day Feast Newsletter
9.94, 9.392, 9.396–9.398, 9.457–9.458
19 Day Feast Newsletter Supplement
9.399
19 Day Star
9.400
19 Days Newsletter for Bahá'ís Only
9.402
19 News Letter
9.394
19 Newsletter
9.394
19 Themes on the 'Dispensation'
7.2028
20/20
10.2
'20 International Conferences in 1963'
11.1020
'21 Ways to Find God'
11.510
24 Picture-Lessons
7.935a
25th Annual Silver Anvil Awards
10.1187
'30 Years of Pioneering on Tyendinaga Honoured'
11.1001a
35th Anniversary Souvenir Brochure
7.2005
50, Baha'i Faith in Ethiopia: A Time to Remember, 1933–1983
7.1704
50th Anniversary Abdu'l-Baha's Visit to the 'Mighty Waters of the Niagara', September 1912–1962
7.1430
50th Anniversary of the Passing of the Greatest Holy Leaf
7.964
52 Bahá'í Talks for All Occasions
7.827–7.828
52 Ways to Raise the IQ of a Child
10.980
75th Anniversary Banquet of the Bahá'í Faith in Hawaii
7.1714
101 Teaching Ideas: 'Bahá'í, a Way of Life'
7.2059

'A Challenge to the Bahais'
11.259
The Challenging Requirements of the Present Hour
5.34
Chambers Biographical Dictionary
10.321a
Chamber's Encyclopedia: A Dictionary of Universal
     Knowledge
10.322–10.323
Champaign-Urbana Guide
11.1008a
'A Champion of Women's Rights'
11.440
Change and the Muslim World
10.325
Change of Mind or Heart?
13.64
'Change Comes to Bible Lands'
11.903
'Changing a World'
11.1045
The Changing Face of Acco
10.1503
The Chaos of Cults
10.1487
The Chaos of Cults: A Study of Present-Day Isms
10.1488
Character: A Sequence in Spiritual Psychology
10.353
Charles Mason Remey: Taken from Who's Who in America
     (with a Few Added Explanations)
12.26
Charter and By-Laws of Green Acre Fellowship
7.1085a
Charter of a Divine Civilization: A Compilation
5.35
'Chasing Technology: Editorial'
11.264
Chicago
10.669
Chicago, 1910–1929: Building, Planning and Urban
     Technology
10.380
Chicago: A Picture Book to Remember Her By
10.587
'Chicago Beautiful'
11.266a
Chicago, an Extraordinary Guide
10.609
Chicago: Calendar
11.132
Chicago Daily Tribune
7.1583a
Chicago Sunday Tribune
7.718, 7.1600, 7.2487–7.2488
Chicago Sunday Tribune Magazine
11.266a
Chicago Sunday Tribune Grafic Magazine
11.278
Chicago Tribune Magazine
11.423
Chicago the Pagan
10.1178
The Chicago World Flower and Garden Show, March
     20–28, 1965
10.328

Chicago's America
7.2697
The Chief Shepherd
7.967
Child Education Teacher Training Handbook
7.1890
Child Education Training Manual
7.642
A Child of the Kingdom: Baha'i Lessons for Children's
     Classes
7.643–7.644
Childcraft: The How and Why Library
10.330
'Childish Barbarism'
11.725
Children Class Teachers' Training Course
7.645–7.646
Children Must Be Taught How to See: A Practical Guide
     for Parents and Teachers
10.729
Children of the Green Earth (Umpqua, Ore.)
11.629
The Children of the Kingdom: The Bahai Junior Movement
7.2295
Children's 19 Day Feast Newsletter
9.205, 9.284
The Children's Caravan
12.146
Children's Chapter: Supplement to New Zealand Bahá'í
     Newsletter
9.200
Children's Classes: Crafts, Games, Songs
7.647
Children's Colouring & Study Book
7.57
Children's Feastletter
9.201
Children's Glad Tidings
9.202
The Children's Hour: A Bahai Leaflet for Children and
     Their Friends
7.648
Children's Journal
9.203
[Children's Lessons]
7.649
Children's Materials: A Compilation
7.650
Children's New Dawn
9.209
Children's Programs for Bahá'í Schools: Director's Resource
     Guide
7.1891
Children's Stories from the Dawn-Breakers
7.1563
Children's Study Course
7.1651
Children's Teaching: A Compilation of Quotes Pertaining to
     the Education of Children
4.87
Children's Prayer Book
4.146
A Child's Prayer Book
4.88
Child's Way
9.207

SUBJECT INDEX

Subject terms cover the broad subject content under which a given publication falls, as well as the specific topic of the Bahá'í reference which occurs in a larger context. It does not cover the micro-contents of the items listed in the bibliography. Terms have been chosen to be reasonably consistent, but some entries were included on the basis of key words used in the title of the publication. Works included in the bibliography may appear under more than one subject entry. Names which are the subject of a publication are in the names index.

1844 (the year)
  7.1596, 10.990
acquiescence
  7.2287–7.2288
actors
  10.469, 11.517, 11.623, 11.813, 11.846, 11.1086
Administrative Order
  SEARCH ALSO UNDER Assistants to Auxiliary Board Members; Auxiliary Boards; Continental Boards of Counsellors; Local Spiritual Assemblies; National Spiritual Assemblies
  4.252, 5.13–5.20, 5.74, 5.115–5.119, 7.28, 7.30–7.31, 7.527, 7.582, 7.725, 7.758–7.759, 7.1221, 7.1817, 7.1823, 7.1847, 7.1941, 7.1944, 7.1950–7.1951, 7.1955–7.1956, 7.1975, 7.1986, 7.1990, 7.2047, 7.2083, 7.2091, 7.2166, 7.2503, 8.111, 8.125, 12.130, 12.133–12.134, 12.136
Adrianople
  11.209
advertising
  11.76, 11.99
Afghanistan
  10.1636
Afnán Family
  10.484
Africa
  7.34, 7.736, 7.738–7.739, 7.908, 7.1239, 7.1876, 7.2361–7.2363, 7.2458–7.2459, 9.3–9.5, 9.27, 9.47, 9.54, 9.86, 9.103, 9.126, 9.215–9.216, 9.315, 9.323, 9.345, 9.352, 9.382, 9.407, 9.471a, 9.487, 9.497–9.498, 10.13, 10.383, 10.795, 10.982, 10.1096, 10.1177, 10.1257, 10.1344, 11.700, 11.761, 11.765
agriculture
  7.937–7.938
Ahmadiyya movement
  SEARCH ALSO UNDER Islam
  7.2022–7.2023, 10.32, 10.1156a, 10.1633, 11.34, 11.701, 11.1118
'Akká (Acre), Israel
  10.18–10.19, 10.343, 10.423, 10.1196, 10.1259, 10.1503, 11.193, 11.275, 13.69
Alaska
  5.72–5.73, 7.41, 7.1634, 9.6–9.10, 9.191, 9.500
alcoholic beverages
  SEARCH UNDER intoxicating drinks

alcoholism
  7.1572
algebra
  10.664
America
  SEARCH ALSO UNDER Canada; United States
  3.92, 3.94, 4.2, 5.1–5.10, 5.36–5.37, 5.41–5.42, 7.52a, 7.142, 7.547a, 7.694, 7.1923–7.1924, 8.124, 8.126, 10.362, 10.620, 10.1331d, 11.7
American Indians
  SEARCH UNDER Native Americans
Amharic language
  7.1111
ancestor worship
  7.995
Anchorage (Alaska)
  11.45
Andaman and Nicobar Islands
  9.398
anthropology
  13.31, 13.33
anti-Bahá'í works
  7.45–7.47, 7.59, 7.61, 7.112, 7.246, 7.363, 7.484, 7.490–7.491, 7.542, 7.573, 7.589a, 7.599–7.600, 7.782–7.783, 7.790, 7.846, 7.1248, 7.1306, 7.1325, 7.1437, 7.1475, 7.1482, 7.1514, 7.1566–7.1568a, 7.1589, 7.1599, 7.2022–7.2023, 7.2034, 7.2045–7.2046, 7.2079–7.2080, 7.2099, 7.2121–7.2122, 7.2290–7.2291, 7.2382–7.2383, 7.2435, 7.2470, 7.2505, 7.2548–7.2550, 7.2558, 7.2607, 7.2651, 7.2700, 7.2716, 7.2757–7.2758, 10.3, 10.16, 10.35, 10.59, 10.87, 10.98, 10.133, 10.135, 10.184, 10.195, 10.242, 10.247, 10.385, 10.399–10.399a, 10.414, 10.416, 10.434, 10.448, 10.582–10.583, 10.611–10.612, 10.624–10.625, 10.627, 10.679, 10.828, 10.850–10.852, 10.858, 10.890, 10.970–10.972, 10.1093–10.1095, 10.1113, 10.1124, 10.1139a, 10.1149–10.1150a, 10.1156a, 10.1247–10.1248, 10.1258, 10.1269, 10.1316–10.1317, 10.1348, 10.1367–10.1370, 10.1375–10.1376, 10.1387, 10.1393, 10.1456, 10.1487–10.1491, 10.1511, 10.1579–10.1581, 10.1633, 10.1639–10.1646, 11.33, 11.55–11.56, 11.81–11.82, 11.101, 11.113, 11.147, 11.164a–11.166, 11.220, 11.259, 11.271, 11.305, 11.311, 11.315, 11.337, 11.357–11.358, 11.363, 11.369, 11.373, 11.404, 11.439, 11.446, 11.462, 11.468, 11.491, 11.574–11.575, 11.606, 11.615–11.616, 11.626, 11.646, 11.657, 11.693–11.696, 11.708–11.709, 11.728, 11.731, 11.771, 11.797, 11.806, 11.827, 11.836, 11.861–11.864, 11.873, 11.892, 11.907, 11.915–11.916a, 11.976, 11.1044, 11.1053, 11.1075, 11.1118–11.1119, 11.1124, 11.1127–11.1128
apologetics
  7.12–7.18, 7.1260, 11.606, 11.612, 11.731, 11.1010
apostasy
  10.1643
appreciations by non-Bahá'ís
  7.63–7.64, 7.2142, 7.2544, 7.2728
Arab-Israeli conflict
  10.37

catalogues
  10.566, 10.1243
catastrophe
  11.854, 11.966, 12.39, 12.91
Catholicism
  SEARCH ALSO UNDER Christianity
  7.2690, 10.399, 10.414, 10.974, 10.1063, 10.1491,
    11.289, 11.717, 11.1072–11.1073
Caucasus
  10.1032, 10.1422, 10.1484
Cayman Islands
  11.98
cement
  10.220, 10.634, 10.1480, 10.1583
Centenary 1944
  11.155
Centenary 1953
  11.97a, 11.159
Central African Republic
  11.633
Central America
  7.2682, 9.408, 10.965a
Ceylon
  SEARCH ALSO UNDER Sri Lanka
  7.1700, 9.85, 9.377
chairman
  7.1636, 7.1825
character
  SEARCH UNDER living the Bahá'í life
Charter of the United Nations
  SEARCH UNDER United Nations Charter
Chicago (Ill.)
  10.100, 10.380, 10.587, 10.609, 10.669, 10.709,
    10.1178
children
  SEARCH ALSO UNDER teachers/teaching of Bahá'í classes
  3.73, 4.87, 4.140, 4.157, 4.284, 7.158, 7.335–7.344,
    7.375, 7.391–7.401, 7.556, 7.642–7.650,
    7.656–7.665, 7.715, 7.731, 7.764–7.768, 7.775,
    7.819, 7.842, 7.920, 7.993a, 7.1011–7.1012, 7.1016,
    7.1126, 7.1501, 7.1610, 7.1622, 7.1651, 7.1752,
    7.1762–7.1766, 7.1787–7.1788, 7.1798,
    7.1808–7.1809, 7.1842, 7.1880, 7.1890–7.1892,
    7.1970–7.1971, 7.2048, 7.2082, 7.2145, 7.2295,
    7.2300, 7.2315, 7.2318, 7.2329, 7.2604, 7.2629,
    7.2819, 8.90, 9.189, 9.234, 9.255a, 9.401, 9.431,
    9.450, 10.729, 10.979–10.980, 12.146
Children of God
  SEARCH ALSO UNDER Christianity
  7.112
children's literature
  1.7–1.9, 3.19, 4.55–4.61, 4.88, 4.113, 4.146, 4.162,
    4.170, 4.177, 4.180, 4.183–4.184, 4.207, 4.214,
    4.226, 4.262, 4.287, 7.37–7.39, 7.56–7.58, 7.62,
    7.147–7.150, 7.248, 7.335–7.344, 7.391–7.401,
    7.583, 7.648, 7.650–7.655, 7.666–7.668, 7.713,
    7.810, 7.822, 7.923, 7.935a, 7.989, 7.1005, 7.1039,
    7.1130, 7.1137, 7.1162, 7.1164–7.1165,
    7.1185–7.1186, 7.1252, 7.1266, 7.1388–7.1392,
    7.1411, 7.1473, 7.1536–7.1541, 7.1563–7.1564,
    7.1583, 7.1584, 7.1602, 7.1607, 7.1992,
    7.2018–7.2019, 7.2053, 7.2081, 7.2197–7.2201,
    7.2211, 7.2281–7.2285, 7.2335, 7.2350, 7.2416,
    7.2477, 7.2480–7.2481, 7.2522, 7.2670,
    7.2761–7.2764, 8.56, 8.109, 10.325a, 10.330,
    10.829, 10.1584

periodicals 9.11a, 9.43, 9.188, 9.200–9.207, 9.282,
    9.285, 9.293–9.295, 9.298, 9.443, 9.492
China
  7.2306, 11.1017
Chinese
  7.1290, 9.489
Christian Science
  SEARCH ALSO UNDER Christianity
  7.2106
Christianity
  SEARCH ALSO UNDER Bible
  3.24–3.27, 3.150, 7.51, 7.59, 7.61, 7.72–7.73,
    7.101–7.103, 7.112, 7.198, 7.363, 7.484, 7.490,
    7.498, 7.542, 7.570, 7.573, 7.586, 7.589a, 7.599,
    7.600, 7.609–7.610, 7.631–7.633, 7.637–7.639,
    7.779–7.780, 7.782–7.783, 7.790, 7.821,
    7.838–7.839, 7.897a, 7.967, 7.980, 7.1124, 7.1145,
    7.1248, 7.1397, 7.1437, 7.1475, 7.1482, 7.1514,
    7.1599, 7.1646, 7.1850, 7.1853, 7.1987, 7.2034,
    7.2050, 7.2099, 7.2105, 7.2121–7.2122, 7.2128,
    7.2136, 7.2158–7.2159, 7.2277, 7.2280,
    7.2290–7.2291, 7.2293, 7.2370–7.2376, 7.2333,
    7.2347, 7.2470, 7.2475, 7.2526, 7.2558,
    7.2571–7.2577, 7.2579–7.2585, 7.2591–7.2599,
    7.2607, 7.2646, 7.2651, 7.2690, 7.2716,
    7.2744–7.2745, 7.2747, 7.2752, 7.2757–7.2758, 8.1,
    8.76, 8.121–8.123, 10.4, 10.11–10.12, 10.35, 10.52,
    10.59, 10.96, 10.103, 10.115, 10.133–10.134,
    10.137, 10.141, 10.147, 10.182, 10.184–10.186,
    10.195, 10.232, 10.257, 10.275, 10.278,
    10.308–10.309, 10.333, 10.337–10.338, 10.379b,
    10.383a–10.383c, 10.416, 10.462, 10.500,
    10.516–10.520, 10.627, 10.650, 10.685, 10.686a,
    10.710, 10.822, 10.824–10.825, 10.858, 10.924,
    10.967, 10.970–10.972, 10.1011, 10.1029, 10.1068,
    10.1092–10.1095, 10.1233, 10.1242a, 10.1269,
    10.1348, 10.1366–10.1370, 10.1375–10.1376,
    10.1393, 10.1395, 10.1427, 10.1428,
    10.1448–10.1449, 10.1463, 10.1487–10.1490a,
    10.1511–10.1512, 10.1528, 10.1535, 10.1543a,
    10.1577, 10.1601, 10.1621a, 10.1622, 11.56,
    11.167, 11.296, 11.311, 11.319, 11.346,
    11.357–11.358, 11.439, 11.626, 11.708–11.709,
    11.771, 11.806, 11.873, 11.915–11.917, 11.964,
    11.1044, 11.1053, 11.1058–11.1059, 11.1061,
    11.1095–11.1104, 11.1107, 12.41–12.44, 12.53,
    13.10, 13.33, 13.40
Christmas
  11.417
civilization
  3.43, 3.79–3.80, 4.108–4.109, 5.35, 5.110–5.113,
    5.139–5.141, 7.1632, 8.3, 11.13, 11.297, 11.1017a
classification of books
  10.915
clubs, college
  SEARCH UNDER college clubs
collective security
  5.142
college clubs
  7.415, 7.1919, 7.2426–7.2427, 9.170, 9.444–9.445
colour
  10.789
colouring books
  7.56–7.57, 7.147, 7.713, 7.1005, 7.1252, 7.1266,
    7.1602, 7.1607, 7.2053, 7.2761–7.2764

family planning
  13.31
Far East
  10.293
fast/fasting
  4.132a, 7.236, 7.603, 7.939, 7.1785
Feast, Nineteen Day
  SEARCH UNDER Nineteen Day Feast
Fiji Islands
  7.1708–7.1709, 9.219, 9.232, 9.397, 10.1184–10.1185,
    10.1319
films
  SEARCH ALSO UNDER audio-visual materials
  7.689, 7.2013
financial planning
  7.1104
Finland
  9.148–9.149, 9.455
firesides
  SEARCH ALSO UNDER teaching the Bahá'í Faith
  7.1946, 7.2536
Five Year Plan, 1974–1979
  6.1, 6.7, 6.10–6.13, 6.19, 7.966, 7.1641, 7.1676,
    7.1691, 7.1767, 7.1800, 7.1839, 7.1904, 7.2384,
    7.2469
flight
  10.1039–10.1040
flowers
  10.327–10.328
Fort Lauderdale (Fla.)
  7.207
Franklin (Canada: District)
  SEARCH ALSO UNDER Canada
  7.2411
freedom of religion
  SEARCH UNDER religious liberty
freemasonry
  10.372
French Antilles
  9.39, 9.388
French Guiana
  9.117, 9.391, 9.432
Fresno (Calif.)
  7.1008
funds
  SEARCH ALSO UNDER Ḥuqúqu'lláh
  4.3, 5.25, 5.52, 5.83–5.84, 7.105, 7.239–7.245, 7.845,
    7.1098, 7.1104–7.1110, 7.1272, 7.1693–7.1695,
    7.1865, 7.1921–7.1922, 7.1925–7.1940, 7.2510,
    7.2556a, 8.133, 9.171, 9.237, 9.248, 9.344,
    9.348–9.350, 9.480
  audit 7.1931
funeral
  SEARCH UNDER burial/funeral
future
  SEARCH ALSO UNDER prophecy, Bahá'í
  7.1135, 7.1510, 7.1626, 7.2351, 11.1068

Gambia
  9.87, 9.238, 9.508
games
  7.382–7.383, 7.530, 7.976, 10.240
gardens
  7.2410, 10.327–10.328, 11.310, 11.585

genocide
  10.873
geography
  10.525–10.526, 10.731, 10.833, 10.1106–10.1107,
    10.1177, 13.69
Germany
  7.330a, 10.1095a, 11.351, 11.755
  Nazi period 11.1001
Ghana
  9.15, 9.128, 9.240, 9.307, 9.325
Gilbert Islands
  9.466
Gilbert and Ellice Islands
  9.98
God
  7.19, 7.1366, 7.826a, 7.2202–7.2203, 10.461, 10.544,
    11.337
  assistance of 4.201–4.204, 4.288, 4.290, 8.68
good and evil
  7.632a, 7.2691, 11.471
government
  loyalty to/duty toward 4.97–4.98, 5.114,
    7.1457–7.1471, 7.1664, 7.2165
Great Schism 1378–1417
  10.569
Greater Antilles
  9.106
Greatest Name
  3.90, 7.911–7.913, 7.2162
Greece
  9.255
Greenland
  7.1703
Grenada
  9.78, 9.326
group
  7.1849
Guam
  11.914
Guardianship
  4.274, 7.2194
  claimants 12.6, 12.30–12.31, 12.63–12.66,
    12.81–12.89, 12.92–12.101, 12.124, 12.138–12.140
Guyana
  7.211, 7.1712, 9.79, 9.117, 9.135, 9.359, 9.380, 9.391,
    9.432

Haifa
  9.115, 10.635–10.637, 10.1098–10.1101, 10.1278,
    10.1357, 10.1552, 10.1626, 10.1630, 11.44,
    11.178a, 11.366, 11.437, 11.454, 11.490, 11.829,
    11.894a, 11.948a, 11.977, 11.1043
Haiti
  9.477
Hands of the Cause of God
  4.156a, 7.40, 7.1127, 7.1582, 7.1815, 7.1826, 8.83,
    11.523, 11.746
happiness
  7.2647, 11.875
Hawaiian Islands
  7.43–7.44, 7.481a, 7.841, 9.56, 9.254a, 9.281, 9.291,
    9.311, 9.348, 10.1033, 10.1089, 10.1516
health/healing
  4.260, 4.282, 7.660–7.661, 9.58, 10.1283, 10.1409,
    10.1417a, 11.188, 11.513, 11.638, 11.815

heaven and hell
  7.2692
hell
  SEARCH UNDER heaven and hell
Hinduism
  SEARCH ALSO UNDER karma
  7.497, 7.935, 7.994, 7.2148, 7.2205–7.2205a, 11.718,
    11.784
history
  SEARCH ALSO UNDER biography
  5.62–5.65, 7.42–7.44, 7.91, 7.142, 7.152–7.153,
    7.247, 7.342, 7.553–7.555, 7.579–7.580, 7.584,
    7.590, 7.592, 7.622–7.623, 7.793, 7.841, 7.930,
    7.1010, 7.1121–7.1122, 7.1175, 7.1236, 7.1321,
    7.1439–7.1440, 7.1563–7.1564, 7.1581,
    7.1612–7.1616, 7.1644, 7.1704, 7.1792a, 7.1827,
    7.2084–7.2091, 7.2317, 7.2364, 7.2370–7.2371,
    7.2449–7.2450, 7.2479, 7.2489, 7.2506,
    7.2516–7.2517, 7.2524, 7.2559, 7.2561, 7.2682,
    7.2741, 7.2801, 8.75, 8.110, 8.131, 8.137a–8.139,
    10.255–10.256, 10.261–10.263, 10.344–10.345,
    10.461, 10.495, 10.597a–b, 10.675–10.676,
    10.692–10.693, 10.744, 10.867–10.868, 10.888a,
    10.948, 10.963–10.964, 10.1042–10.1043, 10.1552a,
    10.1101a, 10.1143, 10.1158, 10.1186, 10.1217,
    10.1371, 10.1411–10.1415, 10.1446–10.1447,
    10.1450–10.1451, 10.1492, 11.58, 11.94, 11.185,
    11.297, 11.586, 11.669–11.670, 11.679, 11.697,
    11.705–11.706, 11.731, 11.824, 11.863, 11.904,
    11.939, 11.1068, 11.1125, 13.16, 13.27–13.28,
    13.32, 13.36, 13.45, 13.48, 13.67a, 13.68
holy days
  7.248, 7.578, 7.652, 7.1536, 7.1897, 7.2081, 7.2485,
    8.109, 10.922, 11.309, 11.487
holy places
  6.6, 7.572, 7.577, 7.655, 7.1602, 7.2317, 7.2410,
    7.2656–7.2657, 11.128, 11.392, 11.422, 11.437,
    11.585, 11.734a, 11.812, 11.923, 11.948, 11.993,
    13.8a
holy war
  11.650
Hong Kong
  9.262–9.263, 9.296, 9.392
hospitality
  7.2457
Houses of Worship (all religions)
  SEARCH ALSO UNDER Mashriqu'l-Adhkár FOR THE BAHÁ'Í
    HOUSE OF WORSHIP
  10.704, 10.1164
human relations
  7.907, 7.1243
human rights
  SEARCH ALSO UNDER persecution
  7.292, 7.321, 7.1117, 7.1244–7.1245, 7.1499, 7.1630,
    7.1680, 7.1848, 7.1878, 7.1952–7.1953, 7.1973a,
    7.2035–7.2036, 7.2212–7.2214, 7.2639, 9.311,
    10.46–10.51, 10.382, 10.496a, 10.507, 10.549,
    10.734–10.735, 10.776–10.777, 10.1090,
    10.1469–10.1475, 11.27, 11.48–11.50,
    11.511–11.512, 11.532–11.535, 11.541, 11.545,
    11.555–11.555a, 11.613, 11.773, 11.856–11.857,
    11.924, 11.952, 11.973, 11.980, 11.987
humanism
  10.626
Hungary
  7.2521

Huntsville (Ala.)
  7.447
Ḥuqúqu'lláh
  SEARCH ALSO UNDER funds
  4.145, 4.145a
Hurufis
  11.237

Iceland
  7.744–7.746, 9.80, 9.83, 9.145, 9.236, 9.327, 9.347,
    9.386
Illinois
  SEARCH ALSO UNDER United States
  10.866, 11.215, 11.515–11.516
immortality
  SEARCH ALSO UNDER death
  4.4–4.5, 4.86, 4.163–4.164, 4.291, 7.1014–7.1015,
    7.1399, 7.1544, 7.2074–7.2077, 7.2125–7.2127,
    7.2325, 7.2693, 8.113, 11.17, 11.608, 12.49–12.50,
    12.54
imperialism
  10.836, 10.838
income
  7.1110
indexes
  7.1155–7.1159, 7.1267–7.1269, 7.1899–7.1900,
    7.2499–7.2501
India
  7.577, 7.623, 7.1486, 7.1542, 7.1623–7.1624, 7.1718,
    7.2001–7.2005, 7.2305, 7.2467, 9.19, 9.25, 9.53,
    9.61, 9.91, 9.116, 9.130, 9.137, 9.154, 9.158,
    9.248, 9.257, 9.269, 9.276, 9.288, 9.328, 9.383,
    9.390, 9.400, 9.424, 9.463, 9.468, 9.490–9.491,
    9.493, 10.126a–b, 10.702, 10.755, 10.796, 10.856,
    10.949–10.950, 10.1021, 10.1218, 10.1292,
    10.1365, 11.121b, 11.268–11.269, 11.411, 11.682a,
    11.701, 11.912, 13.24–13.25
Indians, American
  SEARCH UNDER Native Americans
indigenous peoples
  5.75
Indonesia
  7.2509, 11.1066
initiation rites
  10.756
institutes
  4.17, 7.1279–7.1281, 7.2816, 9.437, 9.481
intellect
  SEARCH ALSO UNDER scholarship
  4.275, 8.104
intelligence quotient (I.Q.)
  10.980
International Bahá'í Archives Building
  11.121
International Human Rights Year, 1968
  7.2036
international organizations
  10.1557
intoxicating drinks
  4.224–4.225, 7.1045
investments
  7.1107
Iran
  3.159, 3.197, 5.101, 7.79, 7.85–7.86, 7.219,
    7.281–7.283, 7.285–7.287, 7.291, 7.298–7.299,

proclamation
  4.223a, 7.1757, 7.1843, 8.117, 11.655
progressive revelation
  SEARCH UNDER revelation, progressive
property
  7.1106
prophecies
  7.1596, 10.903, 11.174
prophecy, Bahá'í
  SEARCH ALSO UNDER future
  7.1510
prophecy, Christian
  SEARCH UNDER Christianity; Bible
protection of the Bahá'í Faith
  7.2161
psychic phenomena
  4.17
psychology
  7.788–7.789, 10.27, 10.848, 10.1298,
    10.1428–10.1429, 10.1463, 10.1541, 11.600,
    11.1022
psychotherapy
  10.1147–10.1148
public information officer
  7.1637
public speaking
  7.1982
publicity/public information
  7.376–7.377, 7.1434, 7.1491, 7.1637, 7.1660, 7.1897,
    7.1974, 7.2020, 7.2141–7.2142, 9.131, 9.271, 9.355,
    9.425–9.426
publishing
  7.378–7.381, 7.1968–7.1969, 7.2006, 9.132–9.134,
    9.177, 9.427
Puerto Rico
  7.1800, 9.296

Qadianis
  SEARCH UNDER Ahmadiyya movement
quotations
  10.617
Qur'án
  SEARCH ALSO UNDER Islam
  7.1160–7.1160a, 7.1299, 7.1303, 7.2435, 7.2440,
    11.468, 13.70

race unity/racism
  SEARCH ALSO UNDER prejudice, elimination of
  3.62–3.63, 4.229, 4.231, 4.295, 7.53, 7.314, 7.321a,
    7.727–7.729, 7.741–7.743, 7.1095, 7.1573, 7.1585,
    7.1590, 7.1883–7.1884, 7.2196, 7.2797–7.2799c,
    10.1044, 10.1110–10.1112, 11.10, 11.96, 11.499,
    11.616–11.616a, 11.887, 11.939a, 11.1031, 11.1039
radio
  SEARCH ALSO UNDER media; television
  7.87, 7.541, 7.618, 7.625, 7.1069, 7.1075, 7.2037,
    7.2197, 7.2377, 7.2401, 7.2724, 9.187, 9.429–9.430,
    10.688, 11.476–11.479, 11.835, 13.29
recantation
  SEARCH UNDER conversion/deconversion/recantation
reconstruction (post-World War I)
  7.2236

refugees
  10.254, 10.602, 10.781, 10.825, 10.1605, 11.144,
    11.642, 11.959
reincarnation
  SEARCH ALSO UNDER immortality
  3.139, 3.150, 4.17, 7.753, 7.996, 7.1001, 11.2, 12.80
religion
  3.97, 3.103, 4.294, 5.126, 7.32, 7.318, 7.662–7.663,
    7.821, 7.1056, 7.2060, 7.2082a, 10.6, 10.13a,
    10.14–10.15, 10.23, 10.34, 10.52, 10.60,
    10.92–10.93, 10.99, 10.101, 10.104–10.105,
    10.111–10.112, 10.124, 10.131, 10.136,
    10.139–10.140, 10.178, 10.187–10.189, 10.192,
    10.210, 10.212–10.214, 10.227–10.229,
    10.235–10.239, 10.245–10.246, 10.276–10.277,
    10.281, 10.294–10.296, 10.299–10.303, 10.306a,
    10.313–10.316, 10.324, 10.341–10.342,
    10.346–10.347, 10.351–10.352, 10.365–10.366,
    10.378, 10.383a, 10.408, 10.411, 10.421, 10.426,
    10.432, 10.446, 10.467, 10.792, 10.470, 10.473,
    10.474, 10.494b, 10.495b, 10.512–10.517,
    10.540–10.542, 10.545–10.546, 10.567,
    10.574–10.575, 10.577–10.579, 10.603, 10.607,
    10.614–10.615, 10.627, 10.629, 10.645, 10.648a,
    10.654–10.656, 10.658, 10.678, 10.684, 10.699,
    10.705, 10.710–10.715, 10.721, 10.730,
    10.736–10.737, 10.741, 10.745–10.746, 10.752,
    10.763, 10.814–10.815, 10.820, 10.834a,–10.835,
    10.837, 10.842–10.843, 10.845–10.847, 10.857,
    10.859, 10.869–10.869a, 10.883–10.884, 10.913,
    10.917–10.918, 10.939, 10.946, 10.949–10.950,
    10.957–10.957a, 10.960a, 10.967–10.968, 10.977,
    10.981–10.986a, 10.991–10.992, 10.993, 10.1010,
    10.1020a, 10.1022, 10.1025, 10.1030, 10.1033,
    10.1060, 10.1069, 10.1076, 10.1078a, 10.1081,
    10.1083–10.1085, 10.1087–10.1088, 10.1095a,
    10.1101a, 10.1103, 10.1127–10.1131, 10.1140a,
    10.1151, 10.1153–10.1154, 10.1157,
    10.1159–10.1162, 10.1180, 10.1186,
    10.1197–10.1200, 10.1206, 10.1211,
    10.1212–10.1213, 10.1214a, 10.1215–10.1230,
    10.1238–10.1239, 10.1244, 10.1253, 10.1258,
    10.1282, 10.1290–10.1291, 10.1292a,
    10.1294–10.1295, 10.1307, 10.1324, 10.1331a,
    10.1337–10.1339, 10.1343, 10.1345–10.1347,
    10.1349, 10.1358–10.1360, 10.1367, 10.1373,
    10.1382, 10.1385a, 10.1386, 10.1393,
    10.1405–10.1406, 10.1425, 10.1426,
    10.1429–10.1431, 10.1439–10.1441,
    10.1446–10.1447, 10.1462–10.1463, 10.1493,
    10.1496–10.1499, 10.1518–10.1519, 10.1521,
    10.1523, 10.1528–10.1529, 10.1541, 10.1543,
    10.1544–10.1545, 10.1546, 10.1549–10.1550,
    10.1553–10.1555, 10.1561, 10.1566, 10.1577,
    10.1584, 10.1601, 10.1603, 10.1606–10.1615,
    10.1626–10.1629, 11.38, 11.45, 11.72, 11.183,
    11.249, 11.277, 11.298, 11.378, 11.431, 11.510,
    11.559, 11.584, 11.594–11.596, 11.637, 11.663,
    11.667–11.668, 11.692, 11.720, 11.850–11.851,
    11.893, 13.51
religion in schools
  7.2408, 10.1442, 10.1606–10.1607, 11.67, 11.837
religious liberty
  7.1871, 11.186, 11.351, 11.432, 11.526a, 11.527,
    11.852, 11.1108a

THE AUTHOR

William P. Collins was the Library Director at the Bahá'í World Centre in Haifa, Israel, from 1977 to 1990. He was born in 1950 in upstate New York, received his B.A. in French and Russian from Middlebury College and his M.S. in Library Science from Syracuse University. He has also studied at the Pontificia Universidad Javeriana in Bogota, Colombia, the Gosudarstvennyĭ Leningradskiĭ Universitet in Leningrad and the College of Librarianship in Aberystwyth, Wales. Since taking his degree in librarianship, he has held positions at Middlebury College Library and the Library of the State Historical Society of Wisconsin. He has published articles on library professional topics, on Bahá'í history and doctrine, Mormonism and Sherlock Holmes. Mr Collins is married and has two children.

ACR-7754

1/24/95
57-

BP
365
A1
C64
1990

Middlebury College

0 00 02 0613906 5